CW00979808

History, Gazetteer, and Directory of Nottinghamshire, and the Town and County of the Town of Nottingham

HISTORY,

GAZETTEER, AND DIRECTORY

OF

NOTTINGHAMSHIRE,

AND THE

TOWN AND COUNTY OF THE TOWN OF

Nottingham,

COMPRISING, UNDER A LUCID ARRANGEMENT OF SUBJECTS,
A GENERAL SURVEY OF THE COUNTY,

AND SEPARATE

HISTORICAL, STATISTICAL, & TOPOGRAPHICAL

DESCRIPTIONS OF

SHERWOOD FOREST,

AND EVERY

TOWN, PARISH, TOWNSHIP, VILLAGE, HAMLET, AND MANOR,

IN THE

SIX HUNDREDS OF THE SHIRE:

WITH A VARIETY OF

Commercial, Agricultural, and Biographical Information;

The Seats of the Nobility and Gentry; the Lords of the Manors; the Owners of
the Soil; the Names and Addresses of the principal Inhabitants; the
Public Charities and Institutions; the Rise and Progress of Trade and
Manufactures; the Mediums of Public Conveyance by Land and Water; the
Civil and Ecclesiastical Jurisdictions, &c. &c.

IN ONE VOL., WITH A LARGE MAP OF THE COUNTY.

BY WILLIAM WHITE,

Author of similar Works for the Northern Counties of England.

SHEFFIELD :

PRINTED FOR THE AUTHOR

BY ROBERT LEADER, INDEPENDENT OFFICE, ANGEL-STREET,

AND SOLD BY WILLIAM WHITE,

At the WICKER LIBRARY, Sheffield; by his Agents, and by the Booksellers.

Price of the Volume and Map, to Subscribers, 10s. 6d. in Boards,

or 12s. in Calf Binding.—To Non-Subscribers, 3s. extra.

1832.

9676
.02

THE LIBRARY
OF CONGRESS

DA670
.N9W5

PREFACE.

In this first attempt to present to the public a popular History and Topography of Nottinghamshire, with a Directory of its Inhabitants, the Author has to acknowledge his unbounded gratitude to the literary and official gentlemen of the county, for the valuable and interesting communications with which they have furnished him, in answer to his multifarious enquiries;—and also to the numerous Subscribers who have favoured him with their support to such a liberal extent that their orders amount to upwards of 300 copies more than the number printed.

This prompt and munificent patronage shews clearly (what has been universally acknowledged in other counties) that works of this description are highly interesting and useful, both in the office and the library,—not only to the man of business, but also to the nobility, gentry, clergy, professional men, and public officers. As authenticity is the grand requisite of topography, all possible care has been taken to avoid errors; every parish, and almost every house in the county has been visited, and the information either collected or verified on the spot; it is therefore hoped that this elaborate work will be found as complete and satisfactory to its numerous patrons as the vast body of information, and the great variety of subjects compressed within its pages, would allow.

The *Plan of the Work* embraces a General History and Description of Nottinghamshire, and of the Town and County of the Town of Nottingham; containing the spirit of all that has previously been written on the subject, extracted from the works of ancient and modern Authors, and from the voluminous Parliamentary Reports of Public Charities, Population, &c. &c.; together with a variety of Statististical, Geological, Agricultural, Commercial, and Biographical Information, elicited by personal enquiry, and comprehending a Survey of Antiquities, Roads, Rivers, Canals, Minerals, Rocks, Caves, Forest and other Liberties; Public Buildings, Institutions, and Charities; Civil and Ecclesiastical Courts, &c. &c.; together with a Chronology of all remarkable Events, from the earliest period to the present time, and a full and comprehensive view of the rise and progress of those varied and beautiful *Manufactures* of which Nottingham is the great emporium, and to which both it and the county at large owe much of their present wealth and importance.

Lists of Magistrates and Public Officers, and of the *Seats* of Nobility and Gentry, are appended to the general Survey of the County. (See p. 67 to 71.) The History of Nottingham, (p. 73 to 215,) like that of all the other places, is followed by a copious *Directory* of its Inhabitants, classed according to Trade or Profession, and accompanied by an alphabetical *Index of Persons*, so that the address and occupation of any individual or firm may be instantly referred to.

The Topography of Nottinghamshire commences at page 299, under an alphabetical arrangement of *Parishes* under their respective Hundreds, and of *Towns, Townships, Villages, &c.* under their respective Parishes; but as in many cases, the Hundred or Parish in which any Town or Village is situated may not be known, a copious *Index of Places* is inserted, which points out the page at which each place in the county is to be found; thus giving to the volume all the advantages of an alphabetical *Gazetteer*, in conjunction with those afforded by connected Histories of the various Civil and Ecclesiastical Jurisdictions. The *Parochial Histories* shew the Situation, Extent, and Population of each village and township, the ancient and present Owners of the Soil and Lords of the Manors; the nature of the Church Livings, with their Patrons and Incumbents; the Places of Worship, Public Charities, and Institutions; Local Occurrences; Trade and Commerce; Objects of Interest and Curiosity; Eminent Men, &c. &c.; and are each followed by a digest of the names and addresses of the Gentry, Tradesmen, Farmers, and other principal Residents; with Lists of Coaches and Carriers, and a variety of other useful and interesting Information;—the whole illustrated by a large coloured Map of the County.

W. WHITE.

SHEFFIELD, *August* 1st, 1832.

INDEX OF PLACES,

CONTAINING IN ONE ALPHABETICAL SERIES, THE NAMES OF ALL THE
HUNDREDS, PARISHES, TOWNS, TOWNSHIPS, HAMLETS AND MANORS,
IN NOTTINGHAMSHIRE.

INDEX OF SUBJECTS.

NOTTINGHAM INDEX OF SUBJECTS.

REFORM BILL.—Under this Act, which passed in June, 1832, Nottinghamshire will send *four* Representatives to Parliament,— viz. two for the *North Division*, which comprises the hundreds of Bassetlaw and Broxtow, and two for the *South Division*, which includes the Hundreds of Bingham, Newark, Rushcliffe, and Thurgarton. The places of election will be at Mansfield and Newark; but the poll will also be taken at Nottingham, East Retford, Newark, Bingham, and Southwell. Under the provisions of this Act, the resident freemen of Nottingham, Newark, and Retford, still retain their elective franchise, in conjunction with all the occupiers of houses, &c. of the annual value of £10 and upwards. The borough of Retford, is still to comprehend Bassetlaw. For further particulars, see the Act, which has already been honoured with great rejoicings at Nottingham and other places, and which will be brought into operation during the autumn or winter of the present year, 1832.

GENERAL HISTORY

AND

DESCRIPTION

OF

NOTTINGHAMSHIRE.

———◆———

NOTTINGHAMSHIRE has long been famed for the number and splendour of the seats of its nobility and gentry, for the diversity of its soil, and the variety and exellence of its agricultural productions; for its immense forest trees, and curious rock-houses and caves; for its profusion of wood, water, and game, and for the extent and importance of its lace and hosiery manufactures. It is an inland county, of an oval figure, 50 miles in length from north to south, and 25 miles in breadth from east to west, and lies betwixt 52 deg. 50 min. and 53 deg. 33 min. *North latitude,* and 43 min. and one deg. 33 min. *West longitude* from the meridian of Greenwich. It is bounded by Yorkshire on the north, by Lincolnshire on the east, by Leicestershire on the south, and by Derbyshire on the west. Its circumference is estimated at upwards of 140 miles, and its *solid contents* at 837 square miles, equal to 535,680 statute acres. Its *population* has encreased since the year 1801, from 140,350 to upwards of 200,000 souls, as will be seen in a subsequent page. Its *climate* is dry and salubrious, the average scale of mortality being only about one in 58, which is nearly the average ratio of the mortality of the whole kingdom. The amount of its *poor-rates* collected in 1815 was £121,461, and in 1823, £81,321; of which latter, £57,613 was levied on lands; £20,215 on dwelling-houses; £2,863 on mills and factories, and £630 on manorial profits, &c. The sum paid out of the

parochial rates in the same year to the *County Rate*, was £9042.
(See p. 128.) The *annual rental* of the land in this county was
assessed for the Property Tax, in 1811, at £534,992 ; and the
amount of real property in 1815, was assessed for the same tax
at £737,922. The county sends eight *members to Parliament*,
viz. two for the county at large,—two for Nottingham,—two
for Newark, and two for Retford, and the rest of the Hundred
of Bassetlaw—which, from its containing the seats of three
Dukes, (Newcastle, Norfolk, and Portland) and several other
noble mansions and parks, has been called " *The Dukery.*"

Under the ancient Britons, Nottinghamshire formed part of
the province inhabited by the *Coritani*, who stood next in rank
and strength to their neighbours, the *Brigantes*, who occupied
all the counties in the Northern Circuit of England, and were
the most numerous and powerful of all the British tribes that
possessed the Island before the invasion of the Romans, by
whom this county was comprised in the consular province of
Maxima Cæsariensis, and in the præsidial district called
Flavia Cæsariensis. During the Saxon Heptarchy, it formed
part of the *kingdom of Mercia ;* but since the union of the seven
Anglo-Saxon States under one monarch, it has been included in
the *Province of York*, and in the *Midland Circuit of England*,
and now forms, in ecclesiastical matters, an ARCHDEACONRY in
the *Diocese of York*, (see p. 144,) subdivided into the four
DEANERIES of Nottingham, Bingham, Newark, and Retford,
and the *peculiar* jurisdiction attached to Southwell Collegiate
Church ; which contain collectively about 180 parishes, 50
chapelries, and 500 villages and hamlets, with nine *market
towns*, (viz. Bingham, Blyth, Mansfield, Newark, Ollerton,
Retford, Southwell, Tuxford, and Worksop,) exclusive of
Bawtry, which is mostly in Yorkshire; and Nottingham,
which, though it is considered the capital of the shire, forms a
distinct town and county of itself, (see p. 73,) except the site
occupied by the County-hall and gaol. In civil government
Nottinghamshire is divided into six HUNDREDS, viz. Bassetlaw,
Bingham, Broxtow, Newark, Rushcliffe, and Thurgarton, each
of which has two chief Constables, except Bassetlaw, which has
three, and is divided into three large *divisions*, distinguished by
the names of *North Clay*, *South Clay*, and *Hatfield*, and containing more than two-fifths of the county, but only about one
fifth of its population, the greater portion of which is in the
southern divisions of the shire, in and near Nottingham. (See
p. 76.) There were anciently two *hundreds or wapentakes**

* *Wapentakes* as the Hundreds of Yorkshire and some other counties are called,
derived their name from an ancient ceremony, in which the governor of every
Hundred, on being appointed to the office, met all the elder men of his district,
and holding up his spear they all touched it with theirs, and from this touch of
weapons they were confirmed in one common interest, and their district was called
a *Weapontouch*.

in the county, called *Lyda* and *Oswardebec*, but the former is now merged in the Hundred of Thurgarton, and the latter forms the North Clay Division of Bassetlaw. According to Judge Blackstone, England was first divided into counties, hundreds, and tithings, by Alfred the Great, to prevent the rapines and disordeis which formerly prevailed in the realm, by making the inhabitants of each district responsible for the damage which might be committed by lawless mobs. *Tithings* were so called because ten freeholders with their families composed one. A number (perhaps 100) of these tithings, towns, or vills, originally composed a superior division called a Hundred, in each of which a court was annually held for the trial of causes. An indefinite number of these hundreds, which now vary both in size and population, form a county, or shire, the civil government of which is confined to the shire-reeve or sheriff, who is elected annually. Soon after the introduction of Christianity, the kingdom was divided into parishes, and afterwards into bishoprics.

ANCIENT BRITONS.—For nearly four thousand years of the world's existence the history of Britain is almost a blank, except so far as it may be read in its geological phenomena; and previous to the invasion of Julius Cæsar, 55 years before the birth of Christ, scarcely any thing is known of its inhabitants, though two zealous antiquarians have assigned dates much earlier than that period to the two Universities of Oxford and Cambridge, the birth of the former of which they have carried as far back as the fall of Troy; and that of the latter to the days of Cantabar, 394 years before the Christian era! We may no doubt find the prototype of these modern antiquaries in the old monkish historians, who inform us that the British King, Ebranc, founded York in the year of the world 2983, and Nottingham about forty years afterwards. (See p. 78.) Historians all agree that the *Aborigines* of Britain were a tribe of Gallic Celts, who emigrated from the Continent and settled here, probably about a thousand years prior to the Christian era.† Previous to the Roman conquest, the ancient Britons in the southern parts of the island, had made some progress towards civilization; but those in the north were as wild and uncultivated as their native hills, and subsisted chiefly by hunting, and the spontaneous fruits of the earth; wearing for their clothing, (when the inclemency of the season compelled them to such incumbrances,) the skins of animals, and dwelling in habitations formed by the "pillars of the forest rooted in the earth, and enclosed by interwoven branches." Their *religion*, which formed one part of their free monarchial *government*, was *Druidical*; but its origin is not certainly known, though some affirm that the Druids accompanied the Celts in early ages.

† Richard de Cir. B. I. c. II. S. 4, and Carte Vol. I. p. 21

from the east; and others, that Druidism was introduced into England by the Phœnicians of Cadiz, who were the first merchants who discovered and traded to this island, and, for a considerable time, monopolized its commerce, by carefully concealing their traffic from other nations; but the lucrative trade in tin, and other useful metals with which Britain abounds, was ultimately traced to its source, and soon brought the Roman and other merchants to our shores.

The civil jurisdiction and religion of the DRUIDS prevailed in every part of the island. They dispensed justice; not under any written code of laws, but on what they professed to be equitable principles—all their verdicts being determined by such sense as the assembled delegates entertained of impartial justice, and on discordance of opinion in the congress, appeal was made to the Arch-Druid, whose sentence was decisive. Their religious ceremonies were few, and nearly in unison with those of the ancient Hebrews; they worshipped on high places and in deep groves; and were not addicted to idolatry, as some authors have asserted, but adored the God of Nature, and rendered him praise on the yearly succession of seasons, which they kept as solemn festivals. Though they dealt largely in allegory, and symbolical representations, they practised but little priestcraft, and held not the ignorance of their votaries in the bonds of superstition, for they clearly explained the mysteries and symbols used in their ceremonies to the initiated, but to none else. To remove from the people all possibility of sophistry and innovation, their maxims of justice were taught orally; the sons of chief pesonages were disciples in their ethic schools, where the rules of moral life were inculcated as the foundation of human wisdom. They studied medicine, and the virtues of plants, of which the *Misletoe* was their chief specific, and they held nothing so sacred as the misletoe of the oak, which, being very scarce, they gathered with great pomp and ceremony on a certain day appointed for their greatest festival. In their civil government, capital offenders were sentenced to death, and publicly sacrificed on the altars of their temples, in the most awful and solemn manner, whilst those convicted for minor crimes were excluded from public worship, and excommunicated from all civil and religious benefits, till they had washed away, with the tears of repentance, the stains with which their guilt had branded them. Julius Cæsar, in his "Commentarii de Bello Gallico," says the Druids, (as the Gauls call call their magicians or wisemen) inculcated the immortality and transmigration of the soul, and discoursed "with youth much about the heavenly bodies and their motion, the size of the heaven and the earth, the nature of things, and the influence and power of the immortal gods." The British Druids exercised their utmost authority in opposing the usurpation of the Roman invaders, who, fired with equal resentment, determined to secure themselves by exterminating the Druidic order, consequently its priests were sacrificed to this inhuman policy; those who fled to the Isle of Anglesea perished in the flames, by the orders of Suetonius, and subsequently, great numbers of them were massacred in the unsuccessful revolt of the Britons under Queen Boadicea. From this period, the power and splendour of the Druids rapidly disappeared.

ROMANS.—Julius Cæsar having overrun Gaul, invaded Britain 55 years before the birth of Christ, and, after a sanguinary struggle renewed in the following year, succeeded in establishing a Roman government, unsettled in its nature, and transient in its duration, for, being distracted by domestic war, the conquerors were obliged to return home, in order to preserve the seat of their empire; consequently, the Britons remained unmolested till the year A.D. 43, when the Emperor Claudius sent over an army under the command of Plautius, who was succeeded by Ostorius Scapula, and he by Suetonius Paulinus, who completed the conquest of a great part of Britain. and, after exterminating many thousands of the Druids, abolished their rites and ceremonies. But the dominion of the Romans in Britain, was not finally established until they were placed under the command of *Agricola,* who did not venture to penetrate into the north of England till A.D. 80, when he marched his legions from *Mancunium* (Manchester,) along the western coast to Scotland, where he endeavoured to secure his conquests by erecting a *chain of forts* across the isthmus between the Friths of Forth and Clyde. He then marched his troops back, through the conquered tribes, and in the year 84, he extended from Solway Frith to Tynemouth, a *chain of stations,* which, in 124, were connected by an earthen rampart raised by the Emperor Adrian, as an obstruction to the Caledonians, who, proudly refusing to crouch to the imperial eagle, frequently descended in rage from their mountains, and penetrating into the Roman territories, committed in them dreadful ravages. This earthen barrier was afterwards strengthened by the *great wall* of stone which the Emperor Severus built across the island, from Solway Frith to the mouth of the river Tyne, in A.D. 208. After this, York (were Severus died,) was made the capital of *Maxima Cæsariensis,* the great Roman province in which Nottinghamshire was comprised. The presence of numerous Roman legions, restrained the warlike spirit of the Britons during the third century, and towards its close, they enjoyed some semblance of independence under Caurausius; but his assassination enabled Constantine again to subject them to the Roman arms, and he soon afterwards took with him to his wars in Gaul, the flower of the British youth; leaving the country again open to the devastating incursions of the Pits and the Scots. Dissensions within, and assaults from without, were now fast hastening the destruction of the overgrown empire of Rome, and in A.D. 446, the Romans finally relinquished all possession, power, and authority in Britain.

Roman Antiquities.—During their residence in Britain the Romans accomplished many great public works. In Lincolnshire they cut several large drains, and raised a stupendous embankment to guard the marshes and fens against the encroachments of the sea. Several of their roads and camps may still be traced in Nottinghamshire. The great *Camp on Holly-hill,* near Arnold, is supposed to have been the central depôt of the Roman forces in this district, as, from its great elevation, all the exploratory camps are easily distinguished, and its vicinity to Nottingham gives great weight to the opinion of Dr. Gale, that the Roman Station *Causennis,* occupied the site of that town (See p. 80.) Near Mansfield, the late Major Rooke discovered extensive remains of a curious *Roman Villa,* which will be described in its proper place. *Spears, fibulæ,* and *keys of brass,* evidently of Roman workmanship, have been found in various parts of the county, especially about Newstead, and between Mansfield and Harlow Wood; many brass *celts* have been found betwixt Hexgrave and Rainworth water, but these are generally considered to be of British origin. Many *Roman roads* have intersected the county in various directions; near Willoughby-on-the-Wolds, the ancient *Fosseway* enters from Leicesterthire, and, passing on to Newark, crosses the *Ermin-street* from London to York; in its course to Lincoln and the coast. This road may be easily traced for many miles along the Wolds, and is literally a *fosse,* dug so deep that an army might march along it even now, without being seen except by those on the very brink of the bank. Several of the roads through the Wolds cross it in different places, particularly about Owthorpe; and in many parts the remains of the old pitching with stones set on edge may be found by clearing away the grass and weeds. The remains of exploratory camps, and of military ways, leading invariably in a north-west direction, may be traced through the Forest tracts. One of them passes from Newark, between Norwood Park and Kirklington, to Southwell and Mansfield; but part of it on the Forest, near Rainworth water has been destroyed, though it was for many centuries after the Norman Conquest, the common high road from Newark to Mansfield, and was called the *Street.*

Of British Antiquities, Nottinghamshire boast but few, except we agree with Dr. Stukely and some other antiquaries, who place many of the rocky cavities about Nottingham in this class, (see pages 79 and 120) *Brent's-hill,* near Barton, four miles S.W. of Nottingham, is generally believed to be the site of a *British camp,* and though the fortifications which once crowned its summit have long been levelled, there are still vestiges enough on its sides to show that it has been a place capable of an obstinate defence, for there have been originally

15 earthen banks, each about half a mile in extent, which must have been successively forced before an enemy could attack the citadel. That it has been a place of importance, is still farther evinced by the number of coins which have been found in its ruins. At *Oxton* there are three large *tumuli*, the largest of which is 53 feet in diameter, and was opened by the late Major Rooke, who found in it an *urn*, made of iron, and filled with ashes and burnt bones; lying near it he also found a large sword in a wooden scabbard, broken into several pieces, two daggars, and 15 glass beads, blue, yellow, and green, which he considers to have been worn by some ancient British warrior. On the western limits of *Worksop Park*, there are also several ancient tumuli, and they have now growing upon them some very old oaks, which add much to their air of antiquity. *Robin Hood's-hill*, on the western verge of the forest, behind New-stead Abbey, form a curious kind of amphitheatre at the end of a little valley, and have, at a distance, the appearance of tumuli, but on a near inspection, they are found too large to have been the work of art, which may, however, have had some hand in producing the regularity of their appearance. On the summit of the highest, there was formerly a seat cut out of the solid rock, with a canopy over it, called *Robin Hood's chair*, though it was probably of much higher antiquity than that legendary freebooter of Sherwood forest.

The SAXONS, who, after the departure of the Romans, were invited over to assist the Britons against the Picts and Scots, had no sooner subdued these enemies, than in their greedy concupiscence to possess the fertile country for which they had been fighting, they turned their weapons upon the Britons, who made an obstinate resistance, which ended in their final over-throw. During this fatal contest, the Britons fought twelve battles under their renowned King Arthur, and several others under Vortigern. In 518, Arthur expelled the Saxons from this and the adjacent counties, and almost from the island; but after the death of that monarch, they again prevailed, and soon gained an entire conquest over the whole country, which they ultimately divided into seven kingdoms, and included Notting-hamshire in that of *Mercia*, of which Lincoln was the capital. The religion of the Druids now gave way to the more barbarous superstitions of the Saxons, who worshipped the sun and the moon, adored the god of thunder, had images in their temples, practised sacrifices, and believed firmly in spells and incanta-tions. Happily this idolatry did not long exist in Britain, for Pope Gregory I. in 590, despatched Augustine, a Roman monk, with forty associates to preach *christianity* to the Anglo-Saxons and the conquered Britons, most of whom became converts to the Christian faith, and Augustine was consequently created *Archbishop of Canterbury*. In 628, *Paulinus*, another Roman Missionary, was created *Archbishop of York*, and was the first

who preached christianity in Mercia, where he followed the victorious arms of Edwin, King of Northumbria, when that newly
converted monarch made Penda, the wicked and hoary-headed
King of Mercia, his vassal. Paulinus baptized many thousands
in the Trent, near Torksey Ferry. The kingdom of Mercia
continued upwards of two centuries, during which, there
reigned in it eighteen kings, and Nottingham is supposed to
have been sometimes the seat of government. The present
name of this county is softened from the Saxon appellation,
Snottingham-scyre. (See p. 80.) The Saxon invaders were
confederated tribes, consisting of the *Angles*, (hence the term
Anglo-Saxons,) the *Jutes*, and the genuine Saxons, who had
long been settled on the shores of the German Ocean, and extended from the Eyder to the Rhyne.

The DANES, who had long envied the Saxons whilst they
possessed the largest and richest island in Europe, fitted out a
mighty fleet, and entered the Humber in 867, from which time
till 940, they frequently penetrated into the interior of the
country, and several times took possession of Nottingham. (See
p. 82.) In their plundering inroads here and in other parts of
the island, these pagans burnt and destroyed villages, monasteries, &c. and spared neither sex nor age. Their repeated incursions compelled the Anglo-Saxon monarchs to lay aside their
own differences, and confederate for mutual defence ; and by
the skill of Alfred the Great, King of Wessex, the invaders
were at length subdued. The sovereignty of Mercia fell into
the hands of Alfred, who stripped it of its regal honours, though
some places were still retained by the Danes, amongst which
were Lincoln, Stamford, and Nottingham. The Saxons, who
had on a certain night massacred all the Danes that lived pro-
miscuously amongst them, brought upon their own heads a just
retribution ; for Sweyn, King of Denmark, to revenge this
cruelty, soon afterwards invaded the kingdom, and in 1013,
brought his fleet up the Trent to Gainsborough, and landing
his forces, created such terror, that the whole country soon
submitted to his yoke. Sweyn, however, did not long enjoy
his success, for he died at Gainsborough in the following year,
and was succeeded by his son Canute, the most powerful monarch of his time, betwixt whom and Edmund Ironside, (the
Saxon heir to the throne,) after several sanguinary struggles,
the kingdom was for a short time divided. Canute was succeeded in 1036 by his son Harold, who died in 1039, when
Hardicanute ascended the throne, but this licentious tyrant
died two years afterwards, when Edward the Confessor (a Saxon)
was raised to the throne by the voice of the people, to the exclusion of Sweyn, the Danish claimant. Edward died in 1066,
and with him ended both the Saxon and the Danish rule in
Britain.

NORMAN CONQUEST.

After the death of Edward, Harold, the son of Godwin, ascended the throne, but was opposed by his brother Tosti, at whose instance, Harfrager, King of Norway, entered the Humber with a mighty armament, embarked on board a kind of Norwegian armada, and landed his forces in Yorkshire, where they were completely overthrown by Harold, who left his brother and his royal confederate dead on the field. Harold's triumph was, however, of short duration, for, whilst rejoicing over his victory at York, he received information that *William Duke of Normandy*, (whom it was said, Edward with his dying breath nominated as his successor,) had landed at Pavensey, in Sussex, with a numerous and well-disciplined army. To meet this foe, Harold marched his forces to Hastings, where, in a sanguinary battle, he lost both his life and his kingdom. No sooner was William the Conqueror seated on the English throne, than he showed that his policy was to root out the ancient nobility, and to degrade the native inhabitants of the humbler classes to the rank of miserable slaves, though in this work he was obstinately but unsuccessfully opposed in the north of England, where he burnt York and many other places to the ground, and swore " by the splendour of God," (his favourite oath,) that he would not leave a soul of his enemies alive.— Conscious of the detestation in which he was held, he entertained a perpetual jealousy of the English. He built aud garrisoned strong castles to keep them in awe, and in the wantonness of his power he obliged them to extinguish their fires and candles every evening at the ring of a bell called " the Curfew." He also caused a survey to be made of all the lands in the kingdom, the register of which is called the DOMESDAY BOOK, and was finished in 1081, after a labour of six years, on the model of the Book of Winchester, compiled by the order of Alfred the Great. Through all time, this " Book of Judicial Verdict" will be held in estimation, not merely for its antiquity, but also for its intrinsic value. It afforded the Conqueror an exact knowledge of his own land and revenue, while the rights of his subjects, in disputed cases, were settled by it; and to this day it serves to show what manor is, and what is not, ancient demesne. It specifies the extent of the land in each district; the state it was in. whether meadow, pasture, wood, or arable; the name of the proprietor; the tenure by which it was held, and the value at which it was estimated. That nothing might be wanting to render this document complete, and its authority perpetual, commissioners were appointed to superintend the survey, and the returns were made under the sanction of juries of all orders of freemen in each district, empanelled for the purpose. This best monument to the memory of the Conqueror, written in Roman, with a mixture of Saxon, is still preserved in the

chapterhouse, at Westminster, amongst the national archives.
This valuable manuscript, which had for so many centuries remained unpublished, was printed in the 40th of George III.
for the use of the Members of both Houses of Parliament, and
the public libraries of the kingdom. As we shall give in the
parish histories in this volume, a translated copy from this
ancient document of all that is important relative to the manors
and estates of Nottinghamshire, it may be necessary to explain
the land measures, and several obsolete feudal terms, used at
the time to which it refers.

MEASUREMENT, &c. IN DOMESDAY BOOK.—A *Perch*, 20
feet. An *Acre*, 40 perches in length and four in breadth. An
Oxgang or *Bovate*, as much as a pair of oxen can keep in husbandry, usually 15 acres. A *Virgate* or *Yard Land*, 40 acres.
A *Carucate*, *Carve* or *Plough Land*, generally 100 acres, or
eight oxgangs. A *Hide*, an uncertain quantity, generally about
120 acres. A *Knight's Fee*, five hides. *Berewicks* are manors
within manors. *Merchet*, or Maiden's rent, was a payment to
the lord of the manor, in commutation of his *right* with the virgin
bride on the marriage of a vassal's daughter. *Heriot*, a tribute
to the lord for his better maintenance in war. *Tol*, *Theam*,
Infangentheof, and *Thelonia*, are described at page 130. *Socmen*,
tenants holding land under a socage tenure. *Bordars*, cottagers.
Villanes, husbandmen in a state of villanage or vassalage.

The Conqueror, in parceling out the lands of the kingdom
amongst his followers, gave in fee to ROGER DE BUSLI no fewer
than 174 manors in Nottinghamshire, being, as Thoroton says,
"the best part of ninety townships, besides very many other
towns, which were partly or wholly in *soc* to some of them."
This Roger, was one of the greatest barons of his time,
and had large estates in other counties, especially in Yorkshire, where he erected a castle at Tickhill, but resided
occasionally at Blyth, in this county. To his natural son,
WILLIAM DE PEVERIL, (whose mother was a tanner's daughter of Normandy, and married to Ralph de Peveril,) he
gave in this county 55 manors, and 48 tradesmen's houses in
Nottingham, besides many other estates in Derbyshire, Leicestershire, and Yorkshire, which together formed the *Honour of
Peveril*, of which *Nottingham castle*, built by the said William,
under the directions of his reputed father, was the baronial residence, (see p. 115,) its first occupant, William de Peveril,
being distinguished by the title of *Earl of Nottingham*, and
having an *Honour Court*, (which still exists,) for the recovery
of debts and damages within his extensive jurisdiction. (See p.
138.) Of the other manors in Nottinghamshire, the Norman
Conqueror gave to Walter de Eincourt, 34; to Ralph Fitz
Hubert, 10; to Hugh de Abrincis, Earl of Chester, 4; to
Alan, Earl of Richmond, 7; to Robert, Earl of Morteign and
Cornwall, 6; to William Mallet, Baron of Eye, 2; to Henry

Ferrers, Earl of Derby, 3; to Ralph de Limesi, 8; to Hugh de Grentsmesni, 1; to Goisfred de Hanselin, 18; to Hugh de Say, of Ricard's Castle, 6; to Ralph de Burun, 8; to Tosti, Earl of Northumberland, 1; to Godiva, Countess of Mercia, 4; and to Algar, Earl of Mercia, 1. The last five were Saxons, and had, before the Conqueror dispossessed them, very extensive estates in this county, where, according to Domesday Book, the following persons were also landholders, viz. " the Archbishop of York, Bishop of Lincoln, Bishop of Bayeux, Abbot of Burgh, Roger Pictavensis, Gilbert de Gand, Gilbert de Tison, Ilbert de Laci, Berenger de Todeni, Hugh Fitz Baldric, Osborne Fitz Richard, Robert Fitz William, and Willam Hostiarus, or the Usher." After the conquest, much of the land in Nottinghamshire passed to the church and the religious fraternities, but at the reformation most of it reverted to the crown, and was subsequently granted to such persons as were then in royal favour. (See p. 145.)

The MONASTIC INSTITUTIONS in this county were no fewer than forty in number, and several of them were richly endowed. At *Lenton*, there were a Cluniac priory, a cell of White Friars, and an hospital of St. Anthony; at *Newstead*, an abbey of Austin canons; at Bauvalle, a Carthusian priory; at *Bingham*, a college; at *Blyth*, a Benedictine priory and an hospital of St. John the Evangelist; at *Bradelusk*, near Gonalston, an hospital; at *Broadholm*, a Proemonstratensian nunnery; at *Clifton*, a college; at *Felley*, an Austin priory; at *Fiskerton*, an Austin cell; at *Marshe*, a Benedictine cell; at *Mattersey*, a Gilbertine priory; at *Newark*, an Austin and an Observant friary, and two hospitals, one for templars and the other for poor; at *Rufford*, a Cistercian abbey; at *Radford*, (in Worksop,) an Austin abbey; at *Shelford*, an Austin priory; at *Southwell*, an extensive college and an hospital; at *Stoke*, an hospital; at *Thurgarton*, an Austin priory; at *Wallingwells*, a Benedictine nunnery; at *Welbeck*, a Proemonstratensian abbey; at *Ruddinton*, *Sibthorp*, and *Tuxford*, each a college; and at Nottingham there were eight establishments, consisting of Friars, Lepers, Knights of St. John, &c. (see p. 145.) The various grants of the lands, &c. belonging to these foundations, which took place at the dissolution of the monasteries, will be recorded in the histories of the parishes where each institution was situated.

Until the 10th of Elizabeth, Nottinghamshire and Derbyshire had but one High Sheriff, and they appear to have been subdivided in eighteen Hundreds, for it is written in Domesday Book that " in *Snottinghamscyre* and *Derbiscyre*, the King's peace, given with his hand, or with his seal, if it be broken shall be amended by the eighteen Hundreds, every Hundred eight Pounds; of this Amends the King hath two parts, the Earl the third;—that is, twelve Hundreds the King, and six the Earl." In the same record it is also written, " If any *man*, according to

law, shall be banished for any guilt, none but the King can re-
store Peace to him. A *Thane* having more than six manors,
doth not give Relief of his Land, except to the King only eight
Pounds. If he have only six, or less, to the Sheriff he giveth
Relief three Marks of Silver, wheresoever he remaineth, in a
Borough or out. If a Thane, having Soc and Sac, forfeit his
Land between the King and the Earl, they have the Moiety of
his Land and Money; and his lawful wife, with his legitimate
Heirs, if there be any, have the other Moiety." The Earl here
alluded to was the Conqueror's illegitimate son, Wm. Peveril,
Earl of Nottingham, who was governor of Nottingham castle,
and Lord of the extensive Honour of Peveril, as has already
been seen.

An ancient manuscript in the British Museum, (Har. MSS.
2041) gives the following "Catalogue of the Earls of Nottingham, with a brief historical collection of their loyalty, arms,
wives, and deaths," down to the year 1624:—

EARLS OF NOTTINGHAM.

"WILLIAM PEVERELL a natural Sonne of William the Conqueror, begotten in Normandy; which William came with his
father to this his conquest; who having been brought up in
military profession, and one that the Conqueror could confide
in, he advanced him to honour, and gave him his new built
castle of Nottingham, with severall lordships within this county.* This William with his Nottinghamsh: forces was one of
the chief Commanders in the third of King Stephen against
those *perfidious* Scots, who had invaded England, so farr as
North Allerton, in the county of Yorke; where theye received
their reward, being totally overthrown: and with king Stephen
in the battle of Lincolne, where he was taken prisoner, so that
Maude the Empress, had seized on his castle of Notingham, and
given it to one William Painell: but it was recovered again by
a stratagem. He married Aveline.

"WILLIAM PEVERELL his sonne and heire, with others, contrived which way to take away the life of Ranulphe Earl of
Chester, which by poison was done.† After hearing of Henry

---

* These amounted to forty-eight tradesmen's houses in the town, and fifty-five
manors in the Shire.

† The circumstances connected with this event, strongly mark the ignorant
superstition of those times, when the simplest and plainest processes were referred
to magic; for the monkish writer who relates the story tells us, that a quarrel having arisen between this *Peverel* and *Ranulph de Mæcenis* Earl of Chester, the
former contrived with many others, by *sorcery and witchcraft,* to kill him; which
he accordingly effected *by poisoning him;* a mode so certain, as surely not to have
required the aid either of sorcery or witchcraft! The perpetrator of this horrible
deed, fled first into a monastery of his own foundation at *Lenton,* had his head
shorn like a Monk, and appeared to have taken the vows; but he soon found that
the power of the Church was not sufficient to protect him against a justly incensed
Monarch.

the 2ds fewry, he fled the Realme, leaving all his castles and lordshipps to the King's dispossal. He left a daughter and heire, Margaret, who married about 1141.

"WILLIAM (EARL of NOTTINGHAM in her right) and Earle of Ferrers and Derby, of whose antiquity and family you may see more in the earldome of Derby, *for Robert his father stiled himselfe Earle junior de Nottingham.*[*] This title came next to

"JOHN, who was sirnamed Sanz-terre, sixt sonne of Henry the Second; which John he made Earl of Moreton (or Martayne) and gave him this castle and honour of Notingham, whom had before a castle seated upon an hill near to *Marl*, in the county of Wiltsh : (now called Marleburgh) and lastly was King of this realm.[†] After this it was granted to the ancient family of the Mowbrays; first to

"JOHN MOUBRAY,[‡] 27th of Edward the 3d, who was slaine in the Holy Land by the Turks, anno. XLII of Edward III. He married Elizabeth daughter and heire of John Lord Segrave who assumed the surname of Segrave, from a lordship in Leicestersh : their son

"JOHN MOWBRAY, created Earle at the coronation of king Richard the Second, and II. of his reign.[§] He was one that entered Scotland, with his joint forces, and died the sixst of Richard the 2d at London, without issue and was buried there.

"THOMAS MOWBRAY his brother, succeeded, being next heire, and was created Earle of Notingham by Richard the second, the VII of the said King's reigne. Hee with other Barons entered Scotland with an army of Spearmen and Archers; and in the IX of his reign, he constituted the said Thomas Earle Marshal of England, for term of life; whose loyalty and great service for his King and countrey, the French and Spaniards both knew; also he attended king Richard into Ireland, the XVIII of his reigne. He was the first that was ever honoured by charter with the office of Earle Marshall.— His first wife was Elizabeth daughter and heire to John Lo: Strange of Blackmere; she died XXIII of August VII of Richard II. without issue. His second wife, viz. Elizabeth

[*] We are told that he was a very pious and devout man, "according to the manners of those times," which may have been one of the reasons that induced King Richard Cœur de Lion to take his castle and honours from him, and bestow them on his brother John.

[†] On the return of Richard from the Holy Land, John refused to resign it, and kept it in his own hands until he came to the Crown, in which it was merged for some time.

[‡] This Earl is not mentioned in the general lists. His creation, if it really took place, must have been in 1352.

[§] With this special clause, that he should hold, *sub honore Comitali*, or as parcel of this Earldom, all his other lands and possessions. He must have entered early on the theatre of public life, as he died under age, and his brother was only seventeen years of age when created Earl in his room.

D

one of the daughters of Richard Fitzalan, Earle of Arundelle. And the XXIX of Septem: Anno M. CCCXCVII. he was created Duke of Norfolke; but suddenly after the scales turned, by subtile and pernicious counsell, for ambition and striving for worldly honours and promotion is a very miserable thing, short of continuance and hastneth a dangrous end; for in the XXI of Richard II. he had an irrecoverable fall, being banished out of this realm never to return into England. He died at Venice in Septem. the I. of Hen. IV.*

"THOMAS MOWBRAY EARLE MARSHALL of ENGLAND (his Son)† who meeting with discontented persons, soon laid hold of that opportunity; for rebellion doth allwaies begin upon revenge, or ambition, and sinister respect. Such was his desperate conspiracy against his lawfull king, for the whiche he had the stroke of the axe at Yorke, anno MCCCCV. He married Constance daughter of John Holland, Earle of Huntingdon and Duke of Exeter.

"JOHN MOWBRAY EARLE MARSHALL and EARLE of NOTINGHAM (his Son‡) hee was a most active and faithful subject to king Henry V. in his warrs in France with horse and foot; allso an eminent commander in his service in Normandy; and I Henry VI. retained by him in those warrs, with one Baneret, IV Knights, one CXIV military men armed a cap-a-pee, and CCC and LX archers. For this his faithfull loyalty he was restored and dignified with that princely title of Duke of Norfolke. He, on the XX of May, VII of Hen. VI bequeathed his body to be buryed within the Isle of Axholme; but died not till Oct XI Henry V. He married Katherine daughter to Ralph Nevile Earl of Westmoreland.

"JOHN LORD MOWBRAY succeeded and enjoyed his father's titles of Honour, and in the XVII of King Henry the VI reign, hee was sent Ambassadour to treat of peace betwixt our King and the French King, and died MCCCCLXI and buried at Thetford in Norfolke.§ He married Eleanor daughter to William Lord Bourchier.

"JOHN LORD MOWBRAY (his Son) was by Henry the VI. the XXIV March created Earle Warrenne and Surrey; a person of good prudence, and put on the belt of military honour, engaging to serve his King in the warres of France, for one

* Various historians give him but an indifferent character, and accuse him of a series of political infamy, which seems to have been punished even by the man for whom he committed some of his worst deeds.

† He was Earl of Nottingam, but is said not to have been Duke of Norfolk.— He was very young, but on coming to the title, and was prevailed on to join in the conspiracy of Scrope, Archbishop of York.

‡ He is by some generally called brother to the preceding Earl.

§ He was also Justice Itinerant of the King's forests south of Trent : and according to the piety of those days, made several pilgrimages to Rome, the Holy Land, &c. and had even vowed to take several more ; but in this he was frustrated by the arrest of death.

whole year. He died at *Framington* Castle (query Framlingham)
in Norfolke, and was enterred at Thetford anno MCCCCLXXV.
He married Elizabeth daughter of John Talbot, first Earle of
Shrewsbury of that name, by whom he had Anne sole daughter
and heire, but she died without issue.*

"Isabel one of the daughters of Thomas Mowbray Duke of
Norfolke by his II wife, married James Lo: Berkley who died
at Berkley Castle in Gloucestersh: anno MCCCCLXIII and
lyeth buried in Berkley Church; to whom she had issue,

"WILLIAM BERKLEY;† who received the order of Knighthood at Calais; he was by King Edw: IV advanced a viscount,
and by King Richard created EARLE of NOTINGHAM. But
after, adhering to Henry Duke of Buckingham, against King
Richard, he fled unto Henry Earle of Richmond, who was
after King, and constituted Earle Marshall of England, and
after advanced to that princely honour of a Marquesse. He
died without issue XIV of Feb: VII Hen. VII. He married
three wives; Elizebeth daughter of Reginald West Lord La
Warre; Jane daughter of Sir Thomas Strangways, Knight;
she died I Richard 3; Anne daughter of John Fiennes, Lord
Dacres of the South, but dyed without issue X Septr: XIII
Hen. VII.‡

"HENRY FITZROY, a natural son to King Henry the Eight,
begotten on the Lady Talboys, widdow, but daughter of Sir
John Blound, Knight; who was by his father the XVIII of June
in the XVII yere of his Raign, made Knight of that noble order
of the Garter, and the same day advanced unto that honourable
title of Earle of Notingham &c; who with the rest of his honours and dignitys dyed without issue the XXIV of July anno
MDXXXVI.

"WILLIAM HOWARD, a collateral branche of the Duke of
Norfolke was by Queen Mary advanced to a Baron by the title
of Lord Howard of Effingham in the hundred of Copthorne in
the Com: of Surrey. He married Catherine daughter and co-
heir to Sir John Broughton of Tuddington in Com: Bedf: Knt.
but had no issue male; secondly Margaret daughter of Sir
Thomas Gamage, Knt. who had issue male.§

* It appears, however, that this Lady having married Richard Duke of York,
second son of Edward the Fourth, he was thereby entitled to possess the Earldom.
His murder in the Tower at an early age, prevented any issue; nor does he appear
in *all* the general lists.

† He is sometimes said to have been her grandson.

‡ Having no issue, he was prevailed on by the politic Henry VII. to make over
his honours and estates to the crown; by which means his brother Maurice, against
whom he is said to have been much enraged, for marrying some person below him
in station, was completely disinherited. Maurice, however, was enabled to
recover some manors which the Crown could not lay hold of, but the earldom of
Nottingham was lost to the family, and lay dormant for some years.

§ It does not appear, however, from other sources, that this William Howard
ever bore the title of Nottingham.

" CHARLES HOWARD, succeeded to the honour, who was (in his father's life time) one of those noble persons, by Queen Elizabeth made choice on for the conducting the Lady Anne of Austria, daughter to Maximilian the Emperor, from Zeland into Spain: and XXIV April the XVI of Eliz: he was made one of the most noble order of the Garter, being then Lord Chamberlayne to the Queen.[*] Hee was made Lord High Admirall of England anno MDLXXXVIII; he was constituted Lieutenant General of the Queen's whole fleet at Sea, against the Spaniards Armado; also in the XXXIX of her raigne he was dignified with the title of *Earle of Notingham,* and at the coronation of King James, he was Lord Great Steward of England and dyed at Havling in Kent, anno MDCXXIV. He married Katherine daughter to Henry Lord Hunsdon (first wife) and his second, but oldest surviving Son by her.

" CHARLES HOWARD succeeded."———

Thus far says the MSS.—to which we have to add that he married three wives, but had issue only by the last of them, Margaret daughter of James the Scottish Earl of Murray. His eldest son James, died unmarried in his father's life time, and his youngest,

Charles Howard succeeded as Earl of Nottingham, but dying without issue, the Earldom became extinct, though the Barony of Effingham went to the ancestor of the present Earl of that title.

Heneage Finch, Baron Finch of Daventry, was created Earl of Nottingham in the reign of Charles the Second. He was son and heir of Heneage Finch, fourth son of Sir Moyle Finch, the twenty-fifth baronet created by King James. Sir Moyle had married Elizabeth, only daughter of Sir Thomas Heneage, Knt. treasurer of the chamber, vice chamberlain of the household, and chancellor of the Duchy of Lancaster, in the reign of Elizabeth, also a member of her Privy Council, and who would have received higher honours, had not his death prevented it. Sir Moyle Finch was also considered as having further claims upon his Sovereign; accordingly soon after his death his widow was raised by James the First to the Peerage, by the title of Viscountess Maidstone; and a short time after, in 1628, Charles the First, gave her the higher dignity of Countess of Winchelsea, in which she was succeeded by her eldest son.

Being highly esteemed for his great knowledge of the laws of England, he was on the restoration of Charles the Second, first appointed solicitor-general, then attorney-general, and soon after, in 1660, a Baronet. In 1673, he rose to the dignity of lord keeper of the Great Seal, was created Baron Finch, and in 1675, Earl of Nottingham. He married the daughter of

---

[*] He was Earl twenty-seven years, and Knight of the Garter during a period of fifty-two.

Daniel Harvey, Esq. a merchant in London, and had a numerous family. His eldest son
Daniel second Earl of Nottingham of that family succeeded,
but shortly after, the earldom of Winchelsea coming to him as
heir to his great grandmother, the first Countess, though descended from her fourth Son, the title of Nottingham became
merged in the older creation of Winchelsea, and is now enjoyed
by the present *Earl of Winchelsea and Nottingham*, whose
other titles are Viscount Maidstone, Baron Fitzherbert of
Eastwell, Baron Finch of Daventry, and a Baronet. His principal *seats* are at Barley in Rutlandshire; at Raunston in
Buckinghamshire, and at Eastwell in Kent.

TITLES.—Though so many noble and wealthy familes reside
in Nottinghamshire, there are, exclusive of Nottingham, but
four places in the county which have afforded titles in the
peerage, viz.—*Mansfield*, that of Earl to the Murray family;
Newark, that of Viscount to the Meadows, now the Pierrepont
family; *Lexington* (now called *Laxton*) that of Baron to the
Suttons of Kelham (now extinct;) and *Granby* that of Marquis
to the Manners family, but the latter is only the secondary title
of the Duke of Rutland. *Langar* in the S.E. part of the
county does not properly come into this class, though it was
intimately connected with the title of the late Lord Howe, who
was styled in the patent " Viscount Howe of Langar; but was
afterwards created Earl Howe." The *Baronetcies* in the
county have been more numerous; these commenced with Sir
Gervase Clifton of Clifton, the 13th Baronet created by King
James the first; Sir John Molyneax of Teversal and Wellow;
Sir Hardolph Wastneys of Heaton, now extinct; Sir Thomas
Williamson of East Markham, extinct; Sir Edward Golding
of Colston-Basset, extinct; Sir William Willoughby of Wil-
loughby, extinct; Sir Francis Leeke of Newark upon Trent,
extinct; Sir Edward Neville of Grove, extinct; Sir Francis
Willoughby of Wollaton, now merged in the peerage; Sir
Thomas Parkins of Bunney, extinct; Sir George Smith of
Nottingham and East Stoke, now Smith Bromley; Sir Samuel
Gordon of Newark upon Trent, extinct; Sir Richard Sutton
of Norwood Park; Sir Richard Heron of Newark; and Sir
John Borlase Warren of Stapleford Hall.

When the order of the *Knights of the Royal Oak* was in
contemplation after the restoration of Charles the Second, the
names of the following gentlemen were on the list for that
honour; Cecil Cooper of Thurgarton, John Palmer, John
Whaley, John Eyre of Mansfield Woodhouse, and John Middleton, Esqrs, and Sir John Curson, Knt. ancestor of the present Scarsdale family.

EMINENT MEN.

The Nottinghamshire temple of fame records a numerous list of worthies, eminent in literature, the arts and sciences, in arms, and in charity, as will be seen in the histories of the parishes where they were born, or resided. Its most distinguished literary luminary of modern times is the late *Lord Byron* (see Newstead Abbey); and next to him in poetic genius stands the late *Henry Kirk White*. (Vide page 179.) Amongst its departed warriors, Earl Howe,* (who in 1792 succeeded the brave Lord Rodney, as Vice Admiral of England,) and *Admiral Sir J. B. Warren†* stand pre-eminent. The county claims several worthies, whose specific birth places are unknown, these will, therefore be noticed here, and the others will be found under their proper heads :—

SIR JOHN FENTON KNT. was born in this county, and was for twenty-seven years a privy counsellor in Ireland to Queen Elizabeth and King James. He translated the history of Guicciardini out of the original Italian into English, and dedicated it to Queen Elizabeth. He died at Dublin in 1603.

EDWARD FENTON, his brother, was also born in this county. He in very early life displayed an inclination for nautical affairs, and was very active in the various attempts at discovery about Hudson's Bay, Greenland, and the other northern parts of the American continent, so fashionable at that period. Much respecting him may be found both in Hackluyt, and in Purchas.

THOMAS HORNE another Nottinghamshire man, became a student at Magdalen Hall, Oxford, in 1624, and was soon admitted to the degree of M.A. He seems to have distinguished himself much by his abilities as a pedagogue ; for soon after taking his degree he was appointed master of a private school in London, was shortly after chosen master of the free-school at Leicester, where he remained only two years, and was thence translated to that of Tunbridge in Kent. His merits did not long remain unnoticed ; for after a residence of about ten years at the latter place, he was preferred to the head mastership at Eton, where he remained during the residue of his life. If we may judge of his practical abilities by several works which he has left behind him introductory to, and illustrative of, classical education, it must be confessed that he was highly deserving of the promotions and encouragement he met with.

RICHARD STERNE, D.D. ARCHBISHOP OF YORK, was the son of Simon Sterne of Mansfield, but the place of his nativity is unknown. His early years were spent at the Nottingham Grammar School; and he afterwards went to Christ Church

---

* See Langer Hall † and Stapelfold Hall.

college, Oxford, where he graduated with much credit to himself, and was soon after admitted to holy orders. He soon attracted the notice of Archbishop Laud, who appointed him one of his chaplains; and his character was now so well established that he was immediately afterwards elected master of Jesus College, by the unanimous vote of the fellows. It does not appear that he took any active part in the affairs which brought his patron to the scaffold; however, when the charges were brought forward against the Archbishop, and he was in consequence committed a prisoner to the Tower, his enemies had sufficient influence to cause Dr. Sterne to be sent thither also. They were unable, indeed, to prove any thing against him, and were obliged, though unwillingly, to permit him to be set at liberty, after the public execution of the Archbishop. During the civil wars, and protectorate, he retired into a safe obscurity; but was called from it on the Restoration, and immediately afterwards appointed bishop of Carlisle. In 1664, he was promoted to the archbishopric of York, which he enjoyed for twenty years, and died in 1684. The Archbishop's third son, Simon, was grandfather of the well-known LAWRENCE STERNE, who was born in Ireland, and held several church livings in Yorkshire, where he became one of the finest writers in the English language; though much indebted to Rabelais, yet no author of the present age can lay claim to so many unborrowed excellencies; and in none, have wit, humour, fancy, pathos, an unbounded knowledge of mankind, and a correct and elegant style, been so happily blended. His " Tristram Shandy" and " Sentimental Journey," have raised him to the rank of a classic, and will long continue to amuse and instruct succeeding generations.

ROBIN HOOD.

Amongst the distinguished characters of the twelfth and thirteenth centuries who flourished in Nottinghamshire, was Robin Hood, alias Robert Head, or Robert Fitz Ooth, the famous archer and freebooter, of Sherwood Forest, of whose popular and interesting story, but little is authentically known, though his exploits have been celebrated in ballad, in every succeeding age. Throsby says, the songs in the " Garland" which bears his name, are simply and historically poetized, and have been the favourites of the lower classes, perhaps ever since his time. They have evidently been written by various persons, and at different periods. As early as 1594, his story seems to have become a favourite subject for the drama; for in that year was printed, " A pastoral comedy of Robin Hood and Little John." Again in 1624 we meet with " Robin Hood's pastoral May Games;" and in 1730 Robin Hood was performed as an opera at Bartholomew Fair. Shortly after came out " Robin Hood

and his Crew of Soldiers,", and in 1751 a musical entertainment under the name of ".Robin Hood" came out at Drury-
lane; besides which we have had " Robin Hood, of Sherwood
Forest" of a recent date; all founded on the original *Garland.*
This collection of ballads, in the events which it relates, differs
considerably from what is considered as the real historical
biography of this extraordinary character. Indeed, his legendary biography seems made up of a tissue of exaggerations.
It tells us that his father was a forester, and could send an
arrow to a distance of two north country miles; and by a strange
anachronism, it describes his mother as niece to the famous
Guy, the Saxon Earl of Warwick. She is stated to have had
a brother "a notable Squire," who lived at Gamewell-hill in
this county, and who was anxious that Robin, when a youth,
should live with him. But Robin's fondness for field sports and
a rambling life, led him to Tutbury, not far from his "birth-
place of Loxley,* in Staffordshire, where he married a shep-
herdess under the poetical name of *Clorinda,* having been
charmed by her dexterous manner of killing a buck in the
forest. Soon after this, he is said to have killed fifteen foresters, who were buried in a row in one of the church yards
at Nottingham. "His fame was now so great that he had
raised a force of nearly one hundred followers; and in a short
time his robberies and frolics, his kindness and charity to the
poor, became the general theme of conversation, and produced
a kind of friendly feeling towards him, although an outlaw."

He appears by the Garland to have made his business his
amusement, and to have been a merry thief, for he sports most
jocularly with the characters and persons of a bishop, and the
sheriff of the county, after robbing them of their purses.
Yet he was not always victorious; but seems to have been
roughly handled at different times, by a tinker, a shepherd, and
a friar, and several others. He is next described as going to
London, and being received at court, where he appeared in a
scarlet dress, whilst his men were clad in *Lincoln green;* all of
them wearing black hats and white feathers: a species of
costume, by the bye, unknown in the reign of Richard the first,
or of John, at which time he lived. Soon after this, he is
stated to have fought a desperate battle with *Little John,* or
John Little, who was *seven* feet high, in which however he was
worsted; but Little John notwithstanding joined the troop, and

---

* Sir Walter Scott in his popular romance of " *Ivanhoe*;" makes Robin Hood,
under the assumed name of *Loxley,* perform some wonderful exploits; in one of
which he has a grand rencounter with Richard I., which secures him the favour of
that romantic and chivalrous monarch.

† There is a loose paper in *Ashmole's* hand writing in the Oxford museum, which
says " the famous Little John (Robin Hood's companion) lies buried in Hethersedge
church-yard, in the peak of Derbyshire; one stone at his head; another at his
feet; and part of his bow hangs up in the church. A.D. 1612.

became his faithful friend. After this the Garland states that a monk whom he sent for to let him blood, was the cause of his death, when all his bowmen fled to different countries to escape that justice which they could not otherwise avoid, now that their chief was gone. Thus far the *Garland;* but the author of the "Anecdotes of Archery," who seems to have paid considerable attention in his research after the real events of this outlaw's life, gives us some other particulars which have a great semblance of authenticity. He describes him as at the head of two hundred strong, resolute men, and expert archers, ranging the forest of Sherwood, but not remaining there always.

Fuller says that his principal residence was in Sherwood forest,* though he had another haunt nearer the sea, in the north riding of Yorkshire, where *Robin Hood's bay* still bears his name : and Charlton, in his " History of Whitby," observes that Robin, when closely pursued by the civil or military power, found it necessary to leave his usual haunts, retreated across the moors to Whitby in Yorkshire, where he always had in readiness some small fishing vessels, and in those putting off to sea, he looked upon himself as quite secure, and held the whole power of the English nation at defiance. The "Anecdotes of Archery" add, that the principal place of his resort at these times, and where his boats were generally laid up, was about six miles from Whily, still known as Robin Hood's bay. In one of these peregrinations, tradition says, he went to dine with the Abbot of Whitby, accompanied by his friend Little John ; when the abbot, who had often heard with wonder of their great skill in shooting with the long bow, requested after dinner that he might have a specimen of their dexterity. The two friends, in order to oblige their courteous entertainer, accompanied the abbot to the top of the abbey tower ; from this elevation each of them shot an arrow which fell close by Whitby Laiths. To preserve the memory of this transaction, and to mark the distance, the abbot set up a pillar on the spot where each arrow fell; the distance being more than a measured mile. That there were two pillars standing at Whitby a few years ago, is beyond a doubt, and that they were called after these two friends is equally certain ; but that there is any real foundation for the story, we will not pretend to say.

The " Anecdotes" then proceed to state that he was outlawed, and a price set upon his head ; and detail several stratagems which were ineffectually put in practice to entrap him ; for, force he repelled by force, and stratagem by more skilful wiles than those of his enemies. But at length the force sent against him was so powerful, that many of his followers fell, and the rest deserted him. Being now worn out with age and care,

* Ritson, who certainly has shewn indefatigable research in his " Robin Hood" in two volumes, says that Barnsdale forest in Yorkshire, and Plompton park in Cumberland, where also two of his favourite haunts.

he sought shelter in Kirklees priory in Yorkshire, the prioress of which was his kinswoman. Here he was seized with a disease which required venesection, and the nun who was called to perform the operation, either intentionally or accidentally, cut an artery, and he bled to death. His mortal remains were interred near the precincts of the nunnery, in Kirklees park, where an ancient cross still marks his grave, and his said to have formerly born the following inscription :—

> " Hear, undernead dis latil steam,
> Laiz Robert Earl of Huntingdon;
> Nea arcir vir as him sa geud,
> An pipl kauld him Robin Heud;
> Sick outauz az hi an iz men,
> Vil Inglande nivr si agen;
> *Obit* 24, *Kal. Dekembris,* 1247."

-. That such a character as Robin Hood existed the testimony of several ancient documents appears to decide, but whether he was, as this epitaph imports, of noble parentage, or an outlaw of humbler birth, is not equally clear, though Stukely in his Palæographia Britannia, vol. 2. p. 115, conjectures that his true name was *Fitz Ooth,* or *Fitz Oeth;*—that he was descended from a Norman Chief of that name, who was lord of Kyme in Lincolnshire; that his mother was daughter of Payne Beauchamp and Roïsia de Vere, and that, by his grandmother, he could prove his descent from Waltheof the first earl of Northumberland, Northampton, and Huntingdon, who was beheaded in 1073. Under these circumstances the title of Earl of Huntingdon might have been claimed by Robert Fitz Ooth, who perhaps was driven to his predatory course of life, in consequence of the troubled state of Henry 2nd's reign, and of a refusal of his claims. That he was something more than a mere robber is evident from the considerable force which he was able to raise, and to keep together, and which must have been much greater than is mentioned in the legendary ballads; as he was able to resist during so many years, all the attempts of the royal army, and of the sheriff, to arrest or even to dislodge him. He was no doubt one of those youths who in the reign of Richard I., resented the enclosing of the forests, and being prosecuted by the officers of the crown, he raised a band of archers, who infested all the towns within the forest and in its vicinity, robbing all the rich travellers, but never proceeding to bloodshed, except in self-defence. It has been said too, that he was a great favourite in many parts of the country, in consequence of his hoarding up the different articles which he obtained in his course of robbery, until they amounted to a considerable stock, when he exposed them for sale at a particular place on the borders of the forest, where his sales were as regularly attended as a fair; and there is no doubt that his customers got their purchases pretty cheap, from whence arose the proverb of selling " *Robin Hood's penny worths.*"

Camden calls him the gentlest thief that ever was, and Major says of him,—

> " From wealthy abbots' chests, and churles abundant store,
> What often times he tooke, he shared amongst the poor !
> No lordly Bishop came in Robin's way,
> To him, before he went, but for his pass must pay :
> The widow in distress, he graciously relieved,
> And remedied the wrongs of many a virgin grieved "

SHERWOOD FOREST.

This once thickly wooded tract, of which upwards of two-thirds is now enclosed and cultivated, comprises nearly one-fifth of the county, being nearly 20 miles in length and from 5 to 7 in breadth, extending southward from Worksop Manor to Nottingham, and occupying part of the three Hundreds of Bassetlaw, Broxtow, and Thurgarton. This favourite haunt of Robin Hood and his daring band of freebooters, was well suited to the wandering and dangerous life of a brigand, as it afforded many secret and almost impenetrable recesses, having numerous rocky caves, and being, as Camden says " anciently thick set with trees, whose entangled branches were so twisted together, that they hardly left room for a single person to pass." In the reign of Elizabeth, when Camden wrote it was much thinner of wood, but it still bred " an infinite number of deer and stags, with lofty antlers." That our woods were often cut down merely for the sake of tillage and pasturage, without any respect to the uses of timber, seems to be evident from the great quantities of *subterranean trees* dug up in various parts of England. These are chiefly found in marshy grounds, which abounded every where before the arts of draining were in use ; and nothing was necessary in such places to produce the future phenomenon of subterranean timber, but to carry the trees, when cut down, upon the surface of some bog, which might easily be done in dry summers. Dr. Plot and some other local historians are of this opinion, and adduce several reasons for supposing that trees might have been buried in this way, to make room for the plough; and they also imagine that the English might begin to clear their lands for tillage as early as the reign of Alfred the Great.

Leland does not seem to have paid much attention to " the wooddy Forest of Sherwood ;" but Thoroton, nearly a century afterwards, tells us that " the pleasant and glorious condition of this noble forest, is now wonderfully declined ; and he adds, there is at present (A. D. 1675,) and long hath been a justice seat held under my Lord's Grace the Duke of Newcastle, Justice in Eyre of all his Majesty's forests north of Trent, wherein it seems his deputies or lieutenants have allowed such and so many claims, that there will not shortly be wood enough left to cover the *bilberries*, which every summer were wont to be an extraordinary great profit and pleasure to the poor people who gathered them, and carried them all about the country to sell." Notwithstanding this early devastation, there is still sufficient woodland scenery in some parts of the forest, to convey a tolerably accurate idea of what was once a forest life. Gilpin in his "Forest Scenery," says that Sherwood was the frequent scene of royal amusement; and as early as the reign of Henry II., Mansfield was the general residence of the court upon these occasions, and it was near that town where Henry became acquainted with the miller of famous memory, Sir John Cockle; as is recorded in an uncouth rhyming tale preserved in "Percie's Reliques," and in Dodsley's dramatic entertainment entitled the *King and Miller of Mansfield*," both of which are generally considered as fabulous legends.

This forest possesses every variety of sylvan scenery; consisting of pasture and woody tracts, intermixed with cultivated enclosures and wild heaths, which are some times bounded by a naked line of horizon, and at others skirted with towering woods, scattered oaks, and young plantations. The open heath with its accompaniments may be traced through the broad tracts which lie been Beskwood and Mansfield, skirting Newstead Abbey, and extending eastward to Oxton and Farnsfield. The wild expanse overgrown with gorse and fern, and skirted with woodland scenery, may be traversed between Mansfield and Ollerton, round Edwinstow and Rufford, and including the pastural scenery of Clipstone park. But the most varied scenery of this extensive forest, consisting of thickening foliage intermixed with open lawns and breaks of cultivation, is to be found round Warsop and Carburton, skirting the four noble and extensive parks of Welbeck, Worksop, Clumber, and Thoresby, and extending to the northern limits of the forest, betwixt Worksop and Retford. The wild scenes in this part of the forest, are finely contrasted on their eastern limits by the richly cultivated country, extending from Haughton park to Southwell, where the ground is sufficiently broken to add the picturesque to the beautiful.

LARGE OAKS.—Among the many large and venerable trees, which are objects of curiosity to the botanical tourist, the most remarkable are, the *Greendale Oak*, (which is 700 years old and has a coach road cut through it,) the *Duke's Walking Stick*, (111 feet high, and 11 tons in weight,) the *Two Porters*, (38 and 34 feet in circumference) and the *Seven Sisters*, all of which are situated in Welbeck park, and will be described with that beautiful seat of the Duke of Portland. *Parliament Oak* on the west side of Clipstone park, is so called from a tradition of a Parliament having been held under it by Edward I., but this is

m error which arose from Edward holding a Parliament in
Clipston palace, the ruins of which are distant 1¼ mile from
his aged oak, of which nothing but the hollow trunk now remains. Near the north end of Clipston park is *Broad Oak,*
which measures 27½ feet in circumference; and near Blidworth
s an ancient *Elm* called *Langton Arbour,* and which, some
centuries ago, was sufficiently remarkable to give name to one
of the forest walks. In cutting down some of the timber in
Birkland and Bilhagh, at the close of the last century, *letters*
were found cut or stamped in the body of the trees, denoting
the King's reign in which they were thus marked. This is
supposed to have been done by the bark being cut off, and the
letters cut in, after which the next year's wood grew over the
inscription without adhering where the bark had been removed.
The cyphers thus found were of James I., of William and Mary,
and one of King John. The latter was eighteen inches within
the tree, and more than a foot from the centre, so that the tree
must have been planted above a hundred years before John's
reign, and when it was cut down in 1791, must have been about
706 years old!!!

ANCIENT WOODS.—The present state of the woodlands of
this forest, and of its modern plantations, is a subject of national
importance, especially when we consider that no timber is so
suitable for naval purposes as English Oak. That Britain, by
proper care and attention, might in fifty years be able to supply
her own wants in this article, is a truth which we believe will
not be denied, and that without interfering with land fit for agricultural purposes; at least whoever traverses this district must
confess that much of it which is unfit for tillage, might be very
beneficially planted with forest trees; and indeed much of this
has already been done, as will be seen by the following survey
of the old woods and modern plantations. The late Major
Rooke tells us, that until the beginning of the last century,
Sherwood was full of trees, and was then one continued wood
from Mansfield to Nottingham; but this tract is now cleared,
and the only remains of ancient woodland are principally in
the *hays of Birkland and Bilhagh,* which form an open wood
of large and venerable oaks, free from underwood, (except in
one part where some natural birch is growing,) and most of
them in a state of decay. Part of these hays are in Thoresby
park, whence they extend westward to Warsop and Clipston,
being about 3¼ miles in length by 1½ in breadth, or about 15,000
acres. In 1790, they contained only 10,117 trees, valued at
about £17,000; and since then, the axe of the woodman and
the scythe of time have stripped them of many of their sylvan
ornaments. Clumber park contains the remains of two ancient
woods, which were called *Clumber and Hardwick Woods;* and
there are some other old woodland districts of small extent, consisting of *Harlow Wood, Thieves Wood,* and some scattered

E

portions of the *Mansfield woods*, which, however, can boast of
very little valuable timber.

The enclosed Parks of Worksop Manor, Welbeck, Clumber, Thoresby, Rufford, Clipston, and Newstead, still retain
many august specimens of the ancient forest oaks, which in
many places are beautifully diversified by the slender and pend-
ant branches of the silver-coated birch. *Thorney Wood Chase,*
which occupies the southern division of the forest, is now nearly
all enclosed. It was well stocked with *fallow deer*, as the other
parts of the forest were with *red deer*, but these are now only to
be found in the enclosed parks of the nobility and gentry, who,
during the late war, made many extensive plantations, some of
which they honoured with the names of our naval heroes.

PLANTATIONS.—The Duke of Portland's extensive plantations in the neighbourhood of Welbeck, are in a flourishing
state, and may be seen at a great distance; whilst the scraggy
oaks in Thieves Wood, betwixt Mansfield and Newstead, have
been filled up with young plants, which are now springing up
to form an union with several other of the *Portland plantations.*
On the highest part of the forest, called *Cock's Moor*, a plantation of 40 acres was made about twenty years ago; and 45 acres
in *Norton forest*, were, about the same time, sown with acorns
and chesnuts, which are now in a thriving state, as also are
two large lumps of evergreens, (one circular and the other
square) planted by the second Duke of Kingston, at the west end
of Birkland. Earl Manvers and his family have made many
plantations about *Thoresby* since it came into their possession.
One of these, partly forest trees, and party firs, is called *Howe
Grove*, in honour of " The glorious First of June ;" another at
the eastern extremity of the assarts, adjoining Thoresby park,
is named after *Earl St. Vincent;* and there is another on the
boundary of Budby forest, called *Duncan Wood*, which, with
some steeps on the forest side of the park, called *Portland Grove*
and *Bentinck Border*, form the whole of the Thoresby plantations on that side. The extensive plantations at *Rufford*, bordering on the forest, were begun by the late patriotic Sir George
Saville, and have been greatly encreased and improved by the
present possessor. The Right Hon. Frederic Montague also
made several plantations on his part of the forest near Newstead,
chiefly of oak ; the first of these, on the west side of the road
leading to Nottingham, is called the *Howe plantation*, and five
others are distinguished by the honourable names of *Spencer,
Nelson, St. Vincent, Warren*, and *Duncan plantations*. South
of these, Henry Cope, Esq. about 25 years ago erected a good
house, and formed several extensive plantations, which are now
highly ornamental. On the eastern limits of Sherwood, near
Farnsfield, Sir Richard Sutton, Bart. made several large plantations about the same time, and in one of them which encir-
cles a hill, he erected an elegant building in the *Turkish* style,

which commands a most extensive prospect. Some large clumps of firs and larches near *Kirkby*, were planted by the late Sir Richard Kay, Bart. Near the northern extremity of Sherwood are several large plantations formed by Earl Bathurst, also about 50 acres of oak and other forest trees planted by Robert Ramsden, Esq. of *Carlton*, and others of a still greater extent round *Osberton*, planted F. Foljambe, Esq.; so that from the laudable exertions of the principal landowners, there is reason to hope that nearly all the unenclosed parts of this extensive forest will again be embowered, and that succeeding generations will long have occasion and opportunity to venerate the majestic oaks planted by their ancestors as monuments of British valour; for many of the plantations, bearing the names of departed heroes, have handsome stone PILLARS, with suitable inscriptions, erected on the most elevated spots.

ENCLOSURES:—According to a SURVEY OF SHERWOOD FOREST, made in the year 1609 it contains 95,115 *acres*, of which 44,839 acres were then *inclosed*; 9486 in *woods*; 35,080 in *wastes*; 1583 in Clipston park; 3672 in Beskwood park; 326 in Bulwell park, and 129, in Nottingham park. From 1799 to 1796 the following *inclosures* took place, viz. 2280 acres in Arnold parish; 1158 in Basford; 2608 in Sutton-in-Ashfield; 1941 in Kirkby. and 261 in Lenton and Radford. Since then, many large portions of the forest in Lambly, Gedling, and other parishes, have been enclosed, so that out of the 95,115 acres, contained within the ancient limits of the forest, upwards of 60,000 acres are now cultivated, and the remainder is partly in woods, plantations, and wastes.

ANCIENT DIVISIONS, &c.—*Sherwood*, or as it was formerly called *Shirewood*, from its being the great woody forest of the shire, was anciently divided or rather known by the names of *Thorney Wood*, and the *High Forest*, which were afterwards subdivided into three *walks*. According to the survey of 1609, the NORTH WALK includes Carburton, Gleadthorpe, Warsop, Nettleworth, Mansfield-Woodhouse, Clipston, Rufford, Edwinstowe, Budby, Thoresby, Palethorpe, and Ollerton, with the hays of Birkland and Bilhagh; the MIDDLE WALK,—Mansfield, Pleasley-hill, Skegby, Sutton, Hucknall, Fulwood, Blidworth, Papplewick, Newstead, and parts of Kirkby; Linby and Annesley; and the SOUTH WALK,—Nottingham, Radford, Sneinton, Colwick, Gedling, Stoke, Carlton, Burton, Bulcote, Gunthorpe, Caythorpe, Lowdham, Lambley, Arnold, Basford, Bulwell, Beskwood, Woodborough, Calverton, Sauntesford Manor, and part of Wilford.

Though Sherwood is not mentioned by name earlier than the time of Henry II., Thoroton says it must have been known as a forest long before A.D. 1155, when William Peveril was called upon to answer "*De Placitis Forestæ*" in this county. At that period he had the whole profit and command of this forest; but it must have soon after passed to the crown, for in 1561 the sheriff of the county prayed to be discharged of £4 *in vasto forestæ;* and two years afterwards he solicited the king for the same discharge, also for "£6. 5s. 0d. paid to the constable, eight foresters, and a warrener; and £40 to the canons of Sherwood for alms." King John, before he ascended the throne, granted to *Matilda de Caux,* and *Ralph Fitz stephen,* her husband, and to their heirs, " all the liberties and free customs which any of the ancestors of the said Maude (Lords of Laxton) held at any time in Nottinghamshire and Derbyshire, that is all the forest of Nottinghamshire and Derbyshire, as their ancesters ever held the same." It afterwards passed to John Birking as heir general of Mitilda de Caux, and in 1226, was in the possession of his son; but this line failing, it descended to the Everingham family, who, by heirship claimed " *Custodiam Forestarum Regis*" in both Nottinghamshire and Derbyshire; but Thoreton is of opinion that this right extended no farther than the limits of Sherwood, as Henry had disafforested all the other parts of those counties, five years before this claim was made. The Everingham family having lost their rights by forfeiture in the reign of Edward I., Sherwood reverted to the crown, and its forest juris-diction has since been granted to various individuals among the nobility and gentry, as special marks of royal favour, but its civil jurisdiction, like the rest of the county, belongs to the Sheriff.

By an inquisition in the reign of Edward I. taken before Geoffrey de Langley, the King's Justice in Eyre north of the Trent, it appears the *chief keeper* of Sherwood had three *deputy keepers* over three districts, whose duty it was to attach all trespassers, and present them at the "attachment before the verdurers." In the *first keeping,* which lay between the rivers Leen and Doverbeck, and contained the hays of Beskwood, Linby, and Willay, the keeper had "one forester riding, with a page and two foresters on foot; two verdurers, and two agisters." The *second keeping,* which comprised Clipston park, the hays of Birkland and Bilhagh, and the rest of the high forest, had two foresters riding, with two on foot, also two pages, two verdurers, and two agisters. The *third keeping,* which included Rumwood, had one forester on foot, and two woodwards, one at Budby and the other at Carburton, also two verdurers and two agisters. It was likewise found in the same inquisition, that the head keeper had "a page bearing his bow through all the forest, to gather *chiminage,*"—a fee for the formation and reparation of roads.

The BOUNDARY of the FOREST, according to a perambula-tion in 1231, passed from "Coningswithford, by the highway towards Nottingham, on to Blackstone-Haugh, and thence fol-lowing the course of the Doverbeck into the Trent. Westerly, it

went from Coningswith, by Mayden Water to the town of Worksop, following the course of the river to Pleasley, so up to Otter
Brigges, then, keeping the great highway to the Mill-ford,
thence to Mayneshead, by Hardwick and Kirkby, to Nun
Carre, on towards Annesley, keeping the high road to Linby,
through the midst of that town, to Lene Water, on to Lenton,
and from thence by the said water, as it was wont of old time
to run into the water of Trent, to the fall of Doverbeck."

FOREST OFFICERS.—Sherwood is the only forest north of
the Trent which now belongs to the crown, from which the
LORD WARDEN (at present the Duke of Newcastle) holds his
office by letters patent, during the royal pleasure. A *bow
bearer and ranger* is appointed by the Lord Warden; and the
freeholders elect four *verdurers*, who hold their office during
their lives, and have each two guineas at the enclosure of a
break, and each a tree out of the King's hays of Birkland and
Bilhagh yearly. They have also the appointment of *nine keepers*,
who have each separate walks, and a salary of £20 paid by the
Lord Warden out of the fee farm rent of Nottingham castle.—
There is also a *steward* of the whole forest, and two sworn
woodwards for Sutton and Carleton. THORNEY WOOD CHACE,
being a branch of the forest, was granted by Queen Elizabeth,
in 1559, to John Stanhope, Esq. as *hereditary keeper*, which
office is now enjoyed by the Earl of Chesterfield. The King's
surveyor-general of the woods, has also a jurisdiction over this
forest, as far as regards the wood and timber of the crown; he
has a deputy in the forest, who has a tree yearly, and a salary
of £20, paid out of the sales of wood. The SOIL of the FOREST
is understood to have been granted by the crown to different
lords of manors, reserving only " the *vert and venison*," or trees
and deer; but the latter are now to be found only in the enclosed parks, though within the memory of persons living thirty
years ago, herds of a hundred or more might be seen together
in the open woodlands and heaths.

HOLYROOD FEAST.—On the north side of Harlow hill, between Mansfield and Newstead, is a large square *pillar*, on
which was formerly a brass plate, with an inscription. Tradition says that this pillar, which is evidently the remains of an
ancient cross, marks the place where the forest officers of the
crown assembled annually on Holyrood-day, early in the morning, to receive the charge of the Lord Chief Justice in Eyre, to
view fences, and take an account of the deer, in order to make
their presentments at the SWAINMOTE COURT, which was held
on that day at Mansfield; but all that now remains of this custom
is an annual *dinner* at the Eclipse inn, Mansfield, to which the
verdurers invite all the principal inhabitants of that town and
its vicinity.

* This office was held by the late Lord Byron.

p 2

We have now completed our delineation of this great forest, except what properly belongs to the following general survey of the climate, soil, surface, produce, rivers, canals, &c. of the county at large.

The CLIMATE of Nottinghamshire is by all writers, even of the earliest date, considered as much drier than that of most other counties in the kingdom. By a comparison of different years and different places, this opinion has met with a considerable degree of confirmation, sufficient to establish it as a general meteorological fact. In the year 1794, the quantity of rain which fell at West Bridgford was only 26¼ inches; in 1795, it was 24¾; and in 1796, only 18 inches; whilst in Lancashire it amounted to 96¼ inches. In 1825, the quantity of rain which fell at Retford was 28.31 inches; but at Kendal, in Westmorland, during the same year, it amounted to 59.973 inches. Mr. Lowe, in his agricultural survey, has accounted for this difference upon very rational grounds, conceiving that although the greatest rains come with the easterly winds from the German Ocean, yet the surcharged clouds, being powerfully attracted by the mountains of Derbyshire, pass over this county too quickly to deposit much of their moisture; whilst on the other hand, the clouds from the Western Ocean and Irish Channel, are attracted and broken by the Yorkshire and Derbyshire hills, before they arrive at Nottinghamshire. This general dryness is considered as favourable to the temperature of the county, and brings it nearly upon a par with the more southern counties, in respect to seed time and harvest.

SOIL and SURFACE.—Nottinghamshire is partly a champaign country, but has a general inequality of surface, seldom rising to any considerable altitude, yet sufficiently broken to avoid the sameness resulting from a dead flat, and having in some parts a beautiful diversity of hill and dale, and swelling undulations, presenting almost every variety of surface. The soil may be divided into three great divisions, first, *sand and gravel;* second, *clay;* and third, *limestone and coal land.*— The first of these occupies more than half the county, and has been subdivided into the *"forest country and borders,"* extending about thirty miles in length, and from seven to ten in breadth; the *Trent bank district;* and the *strip of land* lying east of the Trent, and running into Lincolnshire.

The *Trent bank district* accompanies the river through its whole course in the county, as far as Sutton-upon-Trent, and is in some places only a mile in breadth, and never more than five; it is in general a mellow vegetable mould on a stratum of sand or gravel, which sometimes shows itself on the surface.— The soil in the south-western part of the county, on the banks of the Soar, is of the same description, but the small district on the east side of the Trent, below Sutton, is generally poor land, and much subject to floods, though it is now greatly improved by draining. Most of the *forest district* has a deep red sandy soil, well suited for the growth of turnips, potatoes, &c.

The *clay district* comprises the north and south clay divisions of Bassetlaw, and a great part of the hundreds of Thurgarton, Bingham, and Rushcliffe. The NORTH CLAY division is extremely fertile, arising from a considerable mixture of sand, that renders the soil more friable, and consequently more easily susceptible of agricultural labour than cold clay lands in general. At its northern extremity, it has a level swampy *car*, extending from Misson to Misterton, but this bog has lately been drained and enclosed. A long range of bold promontaries rises on the south side of Misson car, and extends into Lincolnshire, having the appearance of being at some remote period the boundary of an ocean; indeed it is impossible for any person to contemplate the view from Gringley-on-the-Hill, across the car, without drawing this conclusion, and it appears even more evident when these hills are viewed from below, particularly on the road from Bawtry towards Retford, where they have the semblance of islands rising from the bosom of an ocean; their abrupt cliffs being to the northward, whilst on the south they sink gradually into the general line of the county. The SOUTH CLAY has, like the north, generally a reddish clayey soil, in some places stiff and heavy, and in others light and friable, from an admixture of sand; but it has many small patches of black loamy land, and some of a light gravel. The same variety of soil prevails in the hundred of Thurgarton, and also upon the *Wolds*, in the hundred of Rushcliffe, south of Nottingham. The district round Bingham, lying betwixt the Nottinghamshire Wolds and Newark, is generally considered as part of the fertile *Vale of Belvoir*, which extends from Leicestershire, into this county and Lincolnshire, and presents an extensive scene of cultivation, equal in fertility to any other in the kingdom, having generally a rich clay or loamy soil.

The *coal and limestone district* lies on the western verge of the county, adjoining Derbyshire, beginning about Shireoaks, and stretching southward to the Trent. It has generally a sandy soil, resting on limestone and red freestone, and in some places on a blue or yellow clay.

CULTIVATION and PRODUCE.—On the *sandy soils*, before the introduction of turnips and artificial grasses, it was usual to get five crops in succession; viz. oats or pease, barley, rye, oats, and lastly skegs; after which the land was left to recover itself as it could by rest. The introduction of turnips, to be eat off by sheep, was a great improvement, by ensuring a good succeeding crop of barley or other grain. At present, the culture of a "break" in the forest may be stated to be—"1st. Turnips, laying ten quarters of lime an acre; 2d. Barley; 3d. Rye, sometimes wheat; and 4th. Oats, with seeds, *i. e.* wheat, clover,

and rye-grass, which are mown for hay and then thrown open."
But the greatest improvement has been made in the forest lands
permanently inclosed. Amongst these is *Clumber park*, which
contains about 4000 acres, and was, little more than 70 years
ago, merely a black heath, full of rabbits, having a narrow
river running through it, with a small boggy close or two; but
it is now a fertile Paradise, having a magnificent mansion, a
noble lake and river, extensive plantations, and about 2000
acres of excellent arable land, besides extensive pasturage for
sheep, cattle, and deer. Potatoes are grown on the sandy land
with great advantage, and of excellent quality, and large crops
of every sort of grain are produced in many parts, under an
improved system of cultivation. *Liquorice* was formerly much
grown about Worksop, but it was given up many years ago,
the soil not being so deep as that about Pontefract in Yorkshire,
where this juicy root grows in great perfection. The *Trent
bank land* is generally rich either in pasturage or tillage. The
arable is mostly kept under such courses of turnip husbandry as
produce excellent crops of barley and oats, amounting to eight
and sometimes ten quarters per acre. *Winter tares* are sown
by many farmers, to cut for green fodder, as also are *skegs,*
which yield double the quantity of any other kind of oats, in
bulk, but only about the same quantity in weight. The *grass
lands* are employed more for feeding than the dairy, though
almost every farmer keeps a few milch cows, and makes his own
cheese and butter, of which latter, some of them send large
quantities to market; and there are in the southern part of the
county a few large dairies chiefly employed in making cheese.

The *Clay district*, yields fine crops of wheat, barley, beans,
peas, hay, &c. The arable land is generally fallowed once in
three years, and is next sown with wheat or barley, and in the
following year with beans, peas, or both mixed. The latter
crop is very common, owing, it is said, to its smothering the
weeds. But some of the farmers now sow broad or red clover
with their wheat or barley, and mow it in the following year,
instead of their usual crop of beans or pease. Much of the
arable land in "the clays" is in large COMMON FIELDS, most of
which were first cultivated under an act passed in 1773, and the
different occupants distinguish their respective plots by land-
marks. Hops are a considerable article of produce in this district, particularly about Ollerton and Retford, at which latter
town there is a great *hop fair* on the 2nd of October. The hops
grown here are known by the appellation of the " *North Clays,*"
and though they are stronger than the Kent and Sussex hops,

* SKEGS, a species of oats, are the '*Avena stipiformis*' of Linnæus. They grow
where nothing else will, and as they yield a sweet nourishing food, the farmers,
though they seldom bring them to market, raise them in considerable quantities,
particularly in the north-western parts of the county, for their own use, giving
them to their horses in the straw.

in the proportion of nearly two to one, their flavour is not so mild and agreeable, which of course operates against them in the market.

It is thought that this county is favourably situated for the cultivation of ORCHARDS, as much of the soil is a red marly loam with blue veins, similar to the orchard districts of Worcester and Herefordshire. There are indeed in the North and South Clay divisions, and in some other parts of the county, many orchards of apples and pears, but not in sufficient quantities to render the making of cider and perry an object of agricultural attention, particularly as the markets of Nottingham, Sheffield, and the mountainous districts of Derbyshire, are sufficient to carry off any quantity of the fruit that may be raised. *Woad* or *Weld* sometimes called the dyer's weed, is an article of cultivation about Scrooby, and, as it is sown with other crops, either barley or clover, it does not occupy much room. It is a yellow plant used by the dyers for the foundation of many colours, but, though it sometimes yields nearly half a ton per acre, its price is too variable for the farmer to depend upon its culture, being sometimes as low £6 and at others rising to £24 per ton. The county possessing such a diversity of soil, affords its farmers an opportunity of producing every species of grain and grass, and most kind of plants and roots, with as much advantage as is afforded in any county in the kingdom, the most improved systems of culture being here in use.

RABBIT WARRENS were formerly very numerous in the forest and other sandy districts; but those at Farnsfield, Clumber, Beskwood, Sansom-wood, and Haywood-Oaks, were destroyed many years ago; and those at Clipston, Peasefield, Inkersall, Oxton, Blidworth, Calverton, and Newstead, have been greatly reduced, though conies are there by no means scarce, and their burrows may be seen in many other parts of the forest. PIGEONS are still very plentiful, especially in the North and South Clays, though, during the last twenty years, many of the farmsteads have been rebuilt, and the old *Dove-cotes* destroyed, without being replaced, which some farmers consider as a great loss to themselves, but a benefit to the Lord of the Manor, whose *hares, pheasants*, and *partridges*, which abound in most parts of Nottinghamshire, now find a redundancy of food where it was formerly picked up by numerous flocks of pigeons. About thirty years ago, it is said no fewer than 8400 pigeons were sold on one market day at Tuxford for £63. In Zoology, Nottinghamshire has no particular genus except the *old forest breed of sheep*, which is now nearly worn out by various crosses with the Lincolnshire, Leicestershire, Dishley, and Bakewell breeds.

In *Falconry* a curious fact is recorded by Fuller, who says, "We must not forget how two Ayres of Lannards were lately found in Sherwood Forest. These Hawkes are natives of

Saxony, and it seems being old and past flying at the game, were let or set themselves loose, when meeting with lanerets enlarged on the same terms, they did breed together, and proved as excellent in their kind, when managed, as any which were brought from Germany."

FARMS.—It may be observed with propriety, that notwithstanding all that has been said in favour of *large farms*, the system of occupation in this county, is a proof that they are far from being absolutely necessary, at least beyond a certain extent. It may be true indeed, that if very large farms had never existed, many of our present improvements would never have been thought of; but even granting this, it is still pleasant to see a whole county, populous in proportion to the extent and nature of its soil, in a high state of cultivation, intersected by good roads, and inhabited by a respectable yeomanry and leasehold farmers, well lodged and comfortably situated; and all this, where very few farms exceeded £300 per annum; where more farms are below than above £100; and many, in the clay district, as low as twenty. By this equal division, it is easy to conceive how many families are living in honest respectability; and though they may be considered as in a state of poverty on the smallest farms, yet it is not a state of poverty which will send their occupants to the workhouse for relief, as would infalliably have been the case had twenty or thirty of these little spots been consolidated into one, and their hapless tenants obliged to perform as servile drudgery, that which now forms the cheerful labour of themselves and families.

FARM HOUSES AND COTTAGES.—A considerable number of the FARM HOUSES and COTTAGES have lately been rebuilt of brick and tile, but many of the old " stud and mud" buildings still remain, covered with thatch, as indeed are some of the more modern erections. The ground floors of the houses are generally of brick, and the upper floors of plaster, of which latter the barn floors are also constructed. There is generally a good fold-yard to each farm, and the corn is mostly piled in ricks upon stone staddles or brick pillars, three or four feet high, and sometimes upon brick hovels which method keeps the grain sweet and free from vermin. Many of the *cottages* have small plots of garden and potato ground attached to them; and agricultural labourers are as comfortable here as in any other county, though their wages seldom exceed 2s. per day, except in harvest time, and though that injurious system of sending able bodied paupers round amongst the farmers by " house row" to work for a bare parochial pittance is practised in some parishes.

The TENURES are in all the variety of freehold, copyhold, and leasehold; and there is also a considerable quantity of church and collegiate lands ; the church of Southwell, and the archbishopric of York, being still, as formerly, considerable landholders, whilst some of the ancient priory lands are now in possession of the universities. The freeholds are more extensive than numerous; and with respect to the copyholds, a great proportion of the smallest ones are "Borough English,"* and descend to the youngest son. The immediate occupants of the soil, however, are mostly tenants at will, and as their farms in many instances have thus gone through several generations, they feel a kind of hereditary security that prompts them to the same course of improvement as if they were secured by leases. A great part of the land having anciently belonged to the church, is tithe free; and on the other estates the tithes are generally paid by moderate compositions.

The RENTS were (as in other counties) considerably advanced during the late war, about twenty years ago; many of them in the proportion of three to one!—and under circumstances which left the farmer no choice between acceptance and dismission. This great advance was owing to the extraordinary rise which had previously taken place in the price of provisions and other agricultural produce, which however has since been greatly reduced, so that the landlords have been obliged to allow large discounts off their half-yearly demands; but these remissons are generally made with such a sparing hand, and subjected to such nice calculations, that the difference betwixt a good and a bad harvest has but little effect on the real profits of the farmer. However, rents are as reasonable here as in most other counties, and many small parcels of forest land have lately been enclosed by the poor about Mansfield and other places, and are now held at as low a rate as from 2s. to 4s. per acre, though they yield good crops of potatoes and other vegetables; but from £1 to £2 per acre is paid for good land in the old inclosures, and in the common fields which have been long in tillage.

In MINERALOGY Nottinghamshire possesses nothing worthy of notice but coal, lime, and stone. The coal and limestone district lies in the western side of the county, betwixt Derbyshire and a line draw southward from Shireoaks to the river Leen, near Wollaton and Radford. The limestone which is of a hungry nature, and rises up to the vegetable mould, commences at Shireoaks, and begins to abut on the coal near Teversall, and afterwards runs between it and the sand. The line of coal begins a little north of Teversall, and extends south by west to Brook-hill, then south to Eastwood, whence it runs in a south-easterly direction to Bilborough, Wollaton, and the Leen. This field of coal is not more than a mile broad in this

*The origin of this part of our common law is completely involved in mystery, but is supposed to have arisen from the ancient system of vassalage, which gave the Lord certain rights over his vassal's bride, thus rendering the ligitimacy of the eldest born uncertain.

county, and has above it a cold blue or yellow clay, betwixt which and the sand of the forest is the strip of limestone already mentioned. There are only a very few coalpits in this district, most of the coal used in the county being brought from Pinxton and other parts of Derbyshire, by the Railway to Mansfield, and by the canals and rivers to Nottingham; a good deal is also brought up the Trent from Yorkshire. The county contains in several places an abundance of STONE of various descriptions. Very extensive quarries of *red and white freestone* are now in full work round Mansfield, for the purposes of building and paving, and a coarser kind for making troughs, cisterns, &c. At Mansfield Woodhouse is an extensive quarry of *limestone*, which is of such a beautiful light cream colour, and so close in grain, that it would be highly valuable for ornamental building, were it not that its extreme hardness would raise its price far beyond that of Portland stone. At Mapplebeck is a bluish building stone, of which Newark bridge is constructed, and which bleaches with the air to a tolerable white. At Linby is a coarse paving stone much used at Nottingham, where there is also plenty of soft red sand stone, but it is unfit for building purposes. At Gotham, Beacon-hill, North and South Wheatley, and in several other parts of the county, are prolific beds of *gypsum* or *alabaster*,—a bluish stone approaching to marble, which is used for hearths and chimney-pieces, and also burnt for plaster. It is supposed that *marle* might be found here in considerable quantities for agricultural purposes, if that mode of dressing land was once introduced; such veins of it as have been opened by chance, are found to be highly calcareous, and might, under judicious management, be rendered very beneficial to the soil.

The Botanist may find near Mansfield and in some other parts of the county the *deadly-night-shade* and many other rare plants, which will be noticed in the topographical portion of this work.

The MANUFACTURES of the county consist chiefly of *lace* and *hosiery*, which give employment to thousands of the inhabitants in Nottingham, Mansfield, and the surrounding villages. Stocking and other hosiery is the most ancient manufacture of the county, but of late years such great improvements have been made in *bobbin net machines*, that lace may now be considered as the leading article, and as the chief cause of the great increase in houses, shops, and factories, which has taken place in all the manufacturing towns and villages in the county during the last twenty years.—(See page 193 to 206.) There are in the county several *silk and worsted mills*, and upwards of 30 *cotton mills;* the latter are mostly situated in and near Nottingham and Mansfield, and the remainder at Pappelwick, Linby, Newark, Southwell, &c. &c. There are also several *sail-cloth* manufactories, a *paper mill,*[*] and a few *potteries*[†] of coarse red earthenware in the county. *Malting* is a lucrative branch of trade at Nottingham, Newark, Mansfield, and Worksop, and the two former places are famous for the brewing of *ale*. (See p. 206.) The lace and hosiery manufactures give employment to many iron and brass founders, smiths, machine makers, dyers, bleachers, &c. &c.

Of the COMMERCE of the county some idea may be formed by the following enumeration of the various articles of export and import on the numerous lines of water-carriage. The *exports* which pass either from or through the county, are lead, copper, coals, and salt from Derbyshire and Cheshire; Staffordshire ware in considerable quantities; lime and limestone, for building and for agricultural purposes; chirt stone for the glass manufacturers; pig iron and cast metal goods; oak timber and bark, &c. &c. The *imports* for the consumption of the county and the neighbouring districts are timber, hemp, flax, and iron, from the north of Europe; corn, flour, groceries, wine, spirits, cotton wool, &c.; large quantities of flints from Northfleet and the various chalk pits near the Thames, for the Staffordshire potteries; and all kinds of raw materials for inland manufactures.

RIVERS AND CANALS.

The commerce and agriculture of Nottinghamshire are greatly facilitated by the *navigable streams* of the Trent, the Soar, the Erwash, and the Idle; by the *canals* extending from Cromford to Nottingham, from Nottingham to Bingham and Grantham, and from Chesterfield to Worksop, Retford, and the Trent, and by the *railway* from Pinxton to Mansfield. The principal rivers of the county are the Trent, the Soar, the Erwash, the Leen, the Idle, the Maun, the Meden, the Wollen, the Royton, and the Rainworth, which, with their numerous tributary streams, intersect the county in every direction.

The TRENT, which is the noblest stream in the county, ranks in importance as the fourth river in England, being only surpassed by the Thames, the Severn, and the Humber; but though it is not the *largest*, it may be said to run the *longest* course of any, from its rising nearer to the western side of the kingdom than any of the others. It has its source near Biddulph, in the Moorlands of Staffordshire, and receives from Cheshire and Lancashire, even whilst near its head, a number of small rivulets, which have been said to amount to *thirty*, from which a fanciful monkish etymologist has supposed it derived the name of *Triginta*, which he says was afterwards changed into *Trente* in Norman French, but this idea is futile,

---

* At Retford.   † At Sutton-in-Ashfield, and Mansfield.

for it received the Saxon name of *Treonta*, long before the introduction of that language into this country. That a river of
such magnitude should not have received a name from the
Romans is incredible, and it is natural to suppose that whatever
that appellation was, some remains of it should be found in the
present name. The happiest *guess* of this kind may be seen in
the thirtieth volume of the Gentleman's Magazine, page 65,
where a very ingenious writer observes, that we find in a note
of the Grammarian *Servius* upon *Virgil*, that the Tiber in one
part of the city of Rome had the name of " Terentum" in consequence of wearing its banks from the rapidity of its course—
"eo quod ripas terat."–Now supposing this to be true, and that the
Romans might probably enough have given the name of their
favourite river, (as our modern discoverers have done in several
instances) to this one, whose beauty they could not fail to be struck
with, for it is not likely they would have left it without a name,
then the etymology of its present appellation would be simple,
and unforced. Another idea has also been started on the
ground of looking for its etymology in the ancient Roman
name, for there is another word in the Latin language, which is
as good a word for conjecture, and comes even nearer to it in
sound; this is *Tridentum*, or *Tridenta*, from which Trent, or
Treont as in the Saxon, might easily be deduced. These indeed
are only conjectures; but its real Roman name, which however
has no similarity whatever with its present appellation, may
perhaps be traced by the consideration, that although it had
been the general supposition of antiquaries that the Roman
name of the *Humber* was *Abus*, yet Doctor Gale seems to have
been rather fortunate in his conjecture, that its real name was
Urus, of which there are still some vestiges in the names of
Isurium, and *Eboracum* the modern York: the question then
naturally arises, to what river did they give the name of *Abus* ?
why to the *Trent*, says our etymologist, and even of this there
is a vestige in Appisthorpe, or Abusthorpe, the town on the
Abus near Littleborough, the *Agelocum* of the Romans. The
Trent was evidently considered of high importance as early as
the conquest, for it is recorded in Domesday Book, that " in
Snottingham, the water of Trent, and the fosse and the way
towards York, were kept so, that if any should hinder the passage of boats, and if any should plough or make a ditch on the
king's way, within two perches, he should make amends by
eight pounds."

Within a few miles of its source, its stream begins to expand
and assumes the consequence of a large river, coming down
from the hills with a very rapid current, and being augmented
in the more level parts of Staffordshire, by the accession of other
rivers, it flows past Trentham, to which it gives name, and from
thence to Burton; up to which town it is navigable for small
craft. After crossing the south end of Derbyshire it enters

Nottinghamshire near Thrumpton, and receives the Erwash and the Soar. It then rolls in a broad and clear stream past the groves of Clifton and the meadows of Nottingham, in a south-easterly direction, but by many winding reaches, to Holme Pierrepoint, Gunthorpe, Bridgford, East Stoke, Farndon, and Kelham, to within a mile of Newark, whence it takes a more northerly course to Dunham, and from thence forms the boundary of the county as far as Laneham, Torksey, Littleborough, West Burton, Bole, Gainsborough, and West Stockwith, where it enters Lincolnshire, and then flows through that county, by Burton Stather, to the Humber, after a serpentine course of near 200 miles. In its passage through Nottinghamshire it occasionally floods and fertilizes an immense range of meadows, passing frequently over richly cultivated plains, and sometimes betwixt high swelling knolls and green feathered cliffs, that add greatly to the sublimity of the scenery, which, about Nottingham, Holme Pierrepoint, and Ratcliffe, is pleasing in the extreme, being interpersed with handsome villas, neat villages, and scattered farm-houses and cottages.

The *tide* rises up the Trent to a little above Gainsborough, and its close confinement between the banks of the river produces that grand phenomenon, called the *Eagre* or *Hygre*, particularly at spring tides, when the water rises on the surface of the river to the height of six or eight feet, and rolls on in a large mass, from the estuary of the Humber to a considerable distance above Gainsbro' bridge, up to which the river is navigable for vessels of 200 tons burthen, and both above and below great numbers of small craft are employed in the trade to Hull, Nottingham, Leicestershire, Derbyshire, Staffordshire, &c. At " *Trent-falls*" the river forms a confluence with the Humber and Ouse. The Keadby canal joins it with the Don navigation; the Chesterfield canal falls into it at Stockwith; and at Torksey the Fosse-Dyke opens a water communication with the interior of Lincolnshire. At Nottingham a canal branches in a south-easterly direction to Grantham and Bingham, and another extends north-west to join the Cromford canal. The Erwash falls into the Trent from the north, and the Soar from the south, near the junction of this county with Derbyshire and Leicestershire, about eight miles above Nottingham.

The *Trent Navigation* is of such importance to the country at large, in consequence of the numerous communications which it forms with other rivers and canals, that every means have been taken to afford it all the facilities possible. For this purpose a side cut of ten miles in length was made under an act passed in 1784, in order to avoid twenty-one shoals which occur in little more than thirteen miles of its course between the bridge at Nottingham and Sawley-ferry, at the commencement of the Trent and Mersey canal. This side cut, which is sometimes called the *Trent canal*, has a rise of 28 feet, and

crosses the Erwash Navigation near Attenborough. It formerly terminated in the Trent at Beeston, but in 1794, an act
of Parliament was obtained to extend it as far as Lenton, where
it joins the Nottingham canal. (See page 188 to 190)

The ERWASH is only a small river which rises near Kirkby
in-Ashfield, and flows southward to the Trent, near Attenborough, forming in its course the boundary of this county and
Derbyshire. Under an act passed in 1777, it was made navigable by the aid of several side cuts from the Trent to Langley
bridge, in Derbyshire, near which it forms a junction with the
Cromford and Nottingham canals.

The SOAR runs northward to the Trent near Thrumpton.
It is a small river, which has its source in Leicestershire, and
for about ten miles forms the boundary of Nottinghamshire,
flowing by Stanford, Normanton, and Ratcliffe, under the hills
called the Wolds. By an act passed in 1776, it was made
navigable to Loughborough, where it opens a communication
with the Leicester-Union and other canals which intersect the
south of England.

The LEEN, which rises near Newstead Abbey and flows
southward, by Papplewick, Bulwell, Basford, Radford, and
Lenton, to the Trent near Nottingham, is described at page 189.

The DOVER or DARE-BECK rises near Blidworth, and
passing by Oxton, Woodborough, and Lowdham, falls into the
Trent near Caythorpe and Hoveringham. The GREET another
small river rises near Farnsfield, and flows by Southwell and
Fiskerton to the Trent, which likewise receives several other
rivulets that intersect the hundreds of Thurgarton and
Bassetlaw, as well as the following from the southern parts
of the county, viz.—the *Smite,* which rises near Over-
Broughton, and, after receiving the *Wapling* and several
smaller streams, forms the RIVER DEAN, which flows by
Cotham and Hawton, and after being augmented the *Car-
Dyke* from Car-Colston, pursues its course by Newark to the
Trent.

Five fine streams called the Rainworth-Water, the Maun, the
Meden, the Wollen, and the Royton cross Sherwood forest
from east to west, almost parallel to each other, and after-
wards turn to the north and from the river Idle. RAINWORTH
WATER rises a little north of Newstead, and runs through
Inkersall dam and Rufford park, to the Maun at Ollerton. The
MAUN or MAN rises near Kirkby-in-Ashfield, and flows by
Mansfield, and Clipston, to Ollerton. The MEDEN or *Mayden
Water,* has its source near Skegby, and runs by Pleasley and
Warsop, through Thoresby park, and joins the Maun near
Palethorpe, where the united streams take the name of Idle.
The WOLLEN, which rises on the borders of Derbyshire, runs
through Welbeck and Clumber parks where it forms two spa-
cious lakes, and flows to the Idle, near Elkesley. A little below

Welbeck it receives the *Poulter* from Langwith and Cuckney
The ROYTON RIVER rises near Shireoaks, and passes by
Worksop, Scofton, Bilby, Blythe, and Scrooby to Bawtry, where
it enters the Idle.

The IDLE RIVER, formed by the five streams just described,
runs northward, by Haughton park, through Retford, towards
Mattersey, where it turns north-west to Bawtry, and thence
takes an easterly course, across Misson car, to the Trent near
Stockwith and the junction of the Chesterfield canal. That
part of it extending from Bawtry to the Trent was made navigable many years ago, and is called the *Idle River Canal*, except in part of its course betwixt Misson car and Stockwith,
where it has the name of *Bycar-dyke*, owing to its having
been diverted from its original channel, which ran more to the
northward.

The NOTTINGHAM CANAL commences in the river Trent,
and proceeds to the Cromford canal near Langley bridge, very
near to the termination of the Erwash canal; and it is also
connected with the side cut from the Trent and Mersey navigation, generally called the Trent canal. Its bed is not greatly
elevated, and its supply is principally from the river; however,
to guard against deficiencies of water in dry seasons, a
reservoir has been made near Arnswirch, with a self-regulating
sluice, which lets off above 3000 cubic feet of water per hour,
for the use of some mills in its neighbourhood, and also for
the Erwash canal. This navigation was finished in 1802; and
the principal objects of its undertakers were the export of agricultural produce, and of coals from the various mines in its vicinity, together with the importation of lime, timber, and other
heavy articles.

The GRANTHAM CANAL is also connected with the Trent,
commencing near Nottingham, and having a branch upwards
of three miles in length, leading to the town of Bingham. The
system of lockage on that part of the line which is in this
county is very extensive; for on the rise of the wolds from the
Trent to Cromwell Bishop, in a line of only six miles and a
half, there is a gradual elevation of eighty-two feet; but from
Cropwell to Stainwith-closes, there is a dead level of twenty
miles. The proprietors of the Trent river navigation having
been at a considerable expense in deepening the river near
to the entrance of this canal, are entitled to take certain
tolls on all goods passing from this to the Nottingham canal;
which have of late years risen to a considerable amount. In
1793, it was in contemplation to have formed a junction between this and the Newark and Bottesford canal near Stainwith,
which would have made a complete line of water communication between the south-eastern part of Nottinghamshire and the
adjoining country.

The CHESTERFIELD CANAL commences in Derbyshire, close

F 2

to the town from which it has its name, and enters Nottinghamshire near Shireoaks, thence it passes by Worksop through the
northern limits of Sherwood forest, in a circuitous direction by
Babworth to Retford, where it changes its course to the north,
passing through Welham, Hayton, Clarborough, and Clayworth, by Wiseton Hall, Everton, and Drakelow, where it
runs through a _tunnel_ of two hundred and fifty yards, and
thence round Gringley-on-the-Hill, in a north-east direction
through Misson car to Misterton, across Walkeringham moor,
and thence into the Trent at Stockwith. The advantages which
have already resulted from this line of communication are sensibly felt throughout the whole of its course, which is about
forty miles in length. From Chesterfield to Norwood it rises
about forty-five feet, and from the latter place to the Trent it
has a regular fall of 335 feet.

The ROADS of Nottinghamshire have been greatly improved
during the last ten years, under the admirable system which
has been promulgated by Mr. M'Adam in all parts of the kingdom; but in some of the lanes and bye-roads, the traveller has
still to contend with a deep sand, and in some places with an
adhesive clay, which latter he finds as fatiguing in wet weather,
as the former is in dry. That part of the _Great North Road_
which passes through this county from Newark to Bawtry, was
amended under an Act of Parliament passed in 1766, and diverted from its ancient course across the forest,* so as to pass
through Retford. The road from Nottingham to Loughborough was almost impassable till 1738, when an act was obtained to put it in repair. In 1758, acts were passed for making
turnpike roads from Nottingham to Derby, Alfreton, and
Grantham. The road from Nottingham to Mansfield, through
which a great number of coaches and other carriages are constantly travelling betwixt Leeds and London, is now in excellent
condition, having been greatly improved of late years. The
road from Retford to Worksop, has now a good " Macadamized"
bottom, though a few years ago it was the heaviest sandy road
in the county, except that from Worksop to Warsop, in which
Laird says he was three hours in travelling eight miles in a
post chaise; but this has also been amended since he wrote, as
also have the roads from Retford to Gainsbro' and Littleborough.
Though these improvements have caused an advance of perhaps
35 per cent on the tolls taken on some of the forest roads, they
are 75 per cent better, which is freely acknowledged by those
who were in the habit of ploughing the roads with their vehicles
in their original sandy state.

The RAIL-ROAD from Mansfield to Pinxton, in Derbyshire,
opens a communication with the Cromford canal, and the nu-

* The North Road formerly left the present line at Markham moor, near Tuxford, and joined it again at Barnby moor.

merous branches of inland navigation to which that canal has access. It is seven miles and three quarters in length, and was commenced under the powers of an Act of Parliament passed in 1817, but was not completed till 1819. At its western extremity it joins the Pinxton canal-basin, and is terminated at Mansfield by an extensive store-yard and warehouses, which are surrounded by a stone wall, and bear the name of *Portland Wharf*. It is of great advantage to the inhabitants in the central part of the county, for it affords a cheap and expeditious transit for the coal of Derbyshire, which is brought in large quantities to Mansfield, for supplying both the town and a large district extending many miles to the eastward, where the farmers and other inhabitants have frequently to send their waggons or carts to Mansfield for coal, stone, and lime. Before the formation of this rail or tram road, the price of coal at Mansfield was generally from 10s. to 13s. per ton, but it is now seldom higher than 8s. or 8s. 6d. per ton. About a mile south-west of Mansfield, the railway crosses a deep glen, near the King's mill, by a stupendous bridge of five arches, and though the undertaking cost an immense sum of money, it now pays $4\frac{1}{4}$ per cent to the shareholders. One horse will draw upon it as much as would require five horses upon a common road, so that it is of considerable service to the quarry owners of Mansfield, by opening an easy and cheap communication with the inland navigation, for the immense blocks of stone which are sent hence to the western and southern counties. *Steam carriages* have not yet been introduced in Nottinghamshire, though they have long been used on some of the colliery railways in the north of England, and may now be seen propelling both heavily laden waggons and coaches on the Manchester and Liverpool railway, at the amazing speed of from fifteen to twenty miles per hour.— But, should the *projected railways* ever be formed from London to Edinburgh, and across the island from sea to sea, *loco-motive engines* will be as common in Nottinghamshire as draught horses, and *Retford* will become a place of great importance; for, according to a plan proposed, that town will be the centre from which four great rail communications will diverge, viz. one through Lincoln and Cambridge to London; another through Doncaster, and nearly in a line with the Great North Road, to Edinburgh; a third through Sheffield to Manchester and Liverpool; and a fourth through Gainsbro' to to Grimsby, near the mouth of the Humber. Whether these roads will ever be formed or not, remains to be seen, but we think if any railways are likely to succeed, after the example already set in Lancashire, it will be those which connect the two metropolises of England and Scotland, and traverse the island from the eastern to the western oceans.

STATE OF THE POOR, ENCLOSURE OF THE COMMONS, &c.

On this subject, *Mr. Laird*, in the Nottinghamshire portion of the " Beauties of England and Wales," is very explicit, and embodies with his own remarks, the judicious observations and opinions of two former writers, viz. *Eden* on the Poor Laws, and *Lowe* on Agriculture ;—we shall therefore quote his treatise, noting, however, such changes as have taken place since 1811, when it was written.

"Eden, in his very useful work on the state of the poor throughout the kingdom, speaking of a parish in a neighbouring county, but bordering close upon Nottinghamshire, says, that many people of this parish attribute the rise in the poor's rates to the enclosure of the common fields ; because, say they, before the enclosure took place, farms were then from ten to forty pounds per annum, and any person could then rent a small tenement ; but now the parish being mostly thrown into large farms, it requires a very considerable capital to stock one.—This circumstance reduces, therefore, numbers to the necessity of living in a state of servile dependence on the large farmers ; and as they have no prospect to which their hopes can reasonably look forward, their industry is checked, economy is deprived of its greatest stimulant, and their only thought is how to enjoy the present moment!.

" Let us now look at the state of the poor in Nottinghamshire, where large farms are fortunately, as yet, almost unknown.—A very faithful picture of them has been drawn by Mr. Lowe, who tells us, 'that there are few counties in England where the poor will be found better lodged, clothed, or fed, or better provided with fuel. Most cottages have a garden and potatoe garth, and few of them are without a web of cloth of their own spinning ;* many of them, particularly in the clays, have a few acres of land attached to their cottages, and are thereby enabled to keep a cow in addition their pigs ; and here too the poor may be actually said to be industrious, for here they are often seen themselves, as well as their children, employed at their leisure hours in collecting the horse dung from the public roads, either for the use of their own gardens or to sell.' But, adds Mr. Lowe, at the same time, it is a matter of concern to observe, that the manufactures, whilst they increase the popu-

---

* This is not the case now, for during the last twenty years, almost every domestic *spinning-wheel* has been laid aside, and the *village weaver* driven from the agricultural to the manufacturing districts, which, by the aid of modern machinery, now supply the farmers and others with every description of cloth at a less cost than they would incur by making it in their own families, and also of a much more beautiful texture, though perhaps not quite so durable as the *linsey-woolsey* in which every good housewife formerly clothed her family.

lation, increase at the same time the burthen of the poor's rate on the occupiers of land; which may be ascribed to the small manufacturers too frequently spending all their earnings, without looking forward to a time of old age and infirmity.

"As a remedy for this evil in the *manufacturing* part of the county, Mr. Lowe very properly recommends the extension of friendly societies, or the making some more competent provision by the legislature on the same principle; but we fear that until the nature of mankind is altered, no radical cure will ever be found for the evil amongst the *manufacturing poor*, though much may certainly be done in the way of regulation; perhaps by premiums to those who have brought up the largest families without parochial assistance; by *Tontines* on the principles of collection established in Friendly Societies; and even by encouraging those clubs where money is collected for the purchase of various useful but expensive articles of furniture, and where each member's chance of possessing the monthly prize is determined by what is generally termed a *raffle*. All these will tend to produce a spirit of economy; and some of them may in the end be highly beneficial and lucrative to individuals; but perhaps the speediest and most useful reform, both as a temporary and as a lasting expedient, would be the removal of the manufacturers' *pay tables* from the public houses.

"The agricultural will always indeed have advantages over the manufacturing poor; but much will depend on the difference of habits, for the advantage of wages is always on the side of the latter. The farming labourer has seldom in this county been in the receipt of more than eighteen-pence or two shillings per day. The hours of labour for this, are the common ones in general use; but if the labourer undertakes task work, he may increase his gains by a little industry without injuring or over fatiguing himself. His provisions are rather moderate than otherwise; and his fuel may always be had reasonable since the extension of water carriage. Upon the whole we may consider the poor of this county as comparatively comfortable, though much yet remains to be done, both by themselves, and by those of the higher orders who may think it a more charitable act to *prevent* poverty by encouraging economy and industry, than to *relieve* it even with larger sums, where it might have been avoided, by a little prudent circumspection. Much of the comfort of the agricultural Poor must depend, as has been before observed, upon the division of land; and even their number must be much smaller where the farms are small, than where those who would have been farmers, have no other mode of support than becoming the labourers of the rich overgrown capitalist, who regards them no longer than they are useful to him. We mean not this, however as a general argument against large farms; *they* have their advantages, and it must even be confessed that in many parts of the kingdom, small farms would be infinitely less productive, acre for acre, than large ones. What we wish to enter a caveat against is merely that system of uniting many farms into one, which in many places has swept away whole hamlets, nay villages, where the residences of honest cheerful industry have actually been levelled with the dust, and nothing been left, but the solitary church, to mark that here had been the habitation of men; whilst the few unfortunate villagers that are unable to emigate, or not old and helpless enough to gain admission into the workhouse, are crowded into rows of improved cottages, as they are called, and ranged like cattle in a stall without even a slip of garden ground to solace a summer's evening. But even *where* large farms are necessary, this evil might be partially avoided, in regulating the new INCLOSURES, as by a due attention to the probable number of labouring poor in each parish, a sufficient number of small slips of one or two acres each might be enclosed for the purpose of raising cottages and forming garden ground for the agricultural poor, an arrangement tending not only to their benefit, but also to the advantage of the farmers themselves, as it would be an additional stimulus to industry, would excite an emulation amongst the labourers to become possessed of these small advantages, and would soon be sensibly felt in the diminution of poor's rates. It has indeed been objected that small portions of ground given to the poor will make them too independent, and render them unwilling to work for the farmer; but the man who can thus coolly object to the comfort of his fellow creatures, from an idea, and we believe a mistaken one too, of his own interest, deserves not an answer!

" The Nottinghamshire inclosures are now, (1811,) and have been for sometime, going on with great rapidity; the applications to Parliament, every sessions, are numerous, and they have had the effect of raising the value of land very considerably wherever they have taken place. In fact there is now very little left to inclose, except some tracts on the western side, and about the middle of the forest. These are at present mostly rabbit warrens, and seem fit for very little else; indeed we understand that portions of these tracts have been taken into cultivation, but suffered again to run waste from their being totally unproductive.

" That this county has for some years been in a progressive state of improvement is evident even to the passing stranger; but there are some facts recorded by Mr. Lowe in his survey, which prove it indubitably. One instance in particular is conclusive. He tells us that about thirty years ago, the sand lands in Gressthorp, Cromwell, and Muskham fields, all on the great north road between Newark and Retford, were not worth more than two shillings and sixpence per acre, covered with wild

sorrel, and lea lay for six or seven years. Now they produce
from eight to ten quarters of remarkably fine oats per acre ; and
this entirely effected by turnips and clover. Much improvement may also be expected in future from the attention now
paid to *draining*. In the *new inclosure bills*, drains are ordered
by the commissioners, and provision made for their being properly kept up, which has already been found to be more effectual than the old laws of Sewers, of the neglect in the execution
of which there have been great complaints in Nottinghamshire,
as well as in the neighbouring counties."*

THE ARCHITECTURE of the county will be best described under the various heads, and there is perhaps no county
in the kingdom that displays a greater variety, principally
modern ; indeed we may assert that Nottinghamshire contains
the residences of more of the nobility and gentry than any
other county of the same size. The farm-houses and cottages
have already been noticed at page 46. The most common
building materials are bricks and tiles, for making which, the
county possesses an abundance of excellent clay, but many *new
villages* which have sprung up in the manufacturing district
around Nottingham within the last ten years, are roofed with
blue slate, as also are the villas of the gentry and manufacturers. In ECCLESIASTICAL ARCHITECTURE, there are many
elegant specimens of the *antique*, particularly in St. Mary's
church in Nottingham, the collegiate church at Southwell,
Newark church, the church of Radford, with the abbey gate
near Worksop, and several others which will be noticed in
their proper places. Of ANCIENT SEPULCHRAL MONUMENTS,
however, the number is but limited ; for, with the exception of
the Furnival and Lovetot monuments at Radford, near Worksop, there are none older than the 14th century, of which
period, Mr. Gough even with his accurate research could discover but six cross-legged figures of crusaders : one of which
is at Flintham, and belongs to the Husseys, but who were not
in possession of that manor before the eighth of Edward the
the third, so that its date cannot be anterior to 1333.

CHARITIES.

One of the greatest causes which tend to keep the poor-rates
of Nottinghamshire lower than those of most other counties,
is the amplitude of its charity funds and estates, which have
been bequeathed at different periods by numerous benevolent
individuals, for the education and relief of the indigent of
almost every parish within its limits, and which produce collectively upwards of £13,000 per annum, besides affording comfortable dwellings for several hundred alms people. In addi-

* Lowe's Agricultural Survey, p. 96.

tion to this mass of posthumous charity, nearly an equal amount, is subscribed annually by the benevolent inhabitants for the support of various *Charitable Institutions,* among which are Free Schools; Societies for relieving the poor, and promoting the dissemination of religion; the County Hospital, and Lunatic Asylum at Nottingham, and several Medical Dispensaries, and other benevolent institutions which will be noticed in the histories of the towns and parishes to which they belong. The towns richest in bequeathed charities are *Nottingham,* where they produce upwards of £3,700; *Newark* were they yield annually more than £3,600, and *Retford* where their yearly proceeds amount to about £1,800. We trust that our parochial accounts of the posthumous charities of this county, will be found authentic, and sufficiently explicit, as their substance is extracted from the recently published voluminous *Reports of the Commissioners deputed by Parliament to enquire into the state and appropriation of Public Charities in England.* This commission, necessary as it was to correct the numerous abuses of public trust which had long existed in this and in other parts of the kingdom, was justly censured "as being tardy and expensive in its operations," which commenced in 1817, and were not finished till 1830, though up to the year 1827 no less than £138,850 had been paid by the nation to the Commissioners for salaries and other extravagant charges. This commission owed its existence principally to the patriotic exertions of that able and indefatigable senator and lawyer, Henry Brougham, Esq. now Baron Brougham and Vaux, Lord High Chancellor of England, who no doubt intended it to have been conducted in a more effective and less costly manner, similar to those which were instituted for the same purpose in several previous reigns.

PROVIDENT INSTITUTIONS. —Another great relief to the poor-rates, is that laudable desire which prevails amongst the industrious labourers and mechanics to render themselves, as far as possible, independent of the workhouse, by providing funds for their mutual relief in case of sickness and old age; for which object there are now in the county upwards of 300 FRIENDLY SOCIETIES, consisting collectively of about 15,000 members who pay small monthly contributions to their respective funds. Several *Annuitant Societies* are supported by those of the middle class, and there are in the county many *Money* and *Building Clubs.*

SAVINGS' BANKS have also a beneficial effect on the industrious and provident habits of the working classes, by affording them a safe and profitable investment for what they are enabled by economy to lay by in their health and prosperity, against a time of need. Though many of the lower orders of society are so reckless of to-morrow, as to make no provision against need and poverty, it is pleasing to observe, that there are now upwards of 7,500 individuals, whose deposits in the six Savings' Banks of Nottinghamshire, amount to above £240,000, exclusive of about £20,000 deposited by 251 Friendly Societies, and 15 Charitable Institutions. The state of these Savings' Banks, on the 20th of Nov. 1829, was as follows:—

SAVINGS' BANKS.	INDIVIDUAL DEPOSITORS.	FRIENDLY AND CHR. SOCIETIES.	AMOUNNT OF DEPOSITS ON NOV. 20TH, 1829.
Nottingham	3772	169	£101,040 16 1
Southwell	369	3	10,595 14 7¼
Worksop	529	22	29,498 16 9
Mansfield	814	47	32,039 5 10
Newark	1228	9	45,306 4 5½
Retford.........	743	16	27,167 7 9
Total	7455	266	£245,648 5

☞ The Banks at Newark and Worksop were established in 1817, and the other in 1818.

The POPULATION of Nottingham and Nottinghamshire has encreased since the year 1801, from 142,829 to 226,440 souls, as will be seen in the following table, which shows the number of persons in each division, according to the returns made to Parliament in the years 1801, 1821, and 1831.

POPULATION SUMMARY
OF NOTTINGHAMSHIRE & THE TOWN AND COUNTY OF THE TOWN OF NOTTINGHAM.

HUNDREDS, &c.	1801. PERSONS	1821. PERSONS	IN 1831. MALES.	FEMALES	PERSONS
Nottingham Town & Castle Liberties	28,861	40,505	23,636	27,091	50,727
Bassetlaw Hundred*	31,433	37,448	20,402	20,652	41,054
Bingham Hundred	9,055	11,876	6,246	6,196	12,442
Broxtow Hundred	34,847	48,079	32,534	32,765	65,299
Newark Hundred	12,505	15,556	8,394	9,034	17,428
Rushcliffe Hundred	8,163	10,207	6,019	5,990	12,009
Thurgarton Hundred	17,965	23,092	13,714	13,767	27,481
Total	142,829	186,763	110,945	115,495	226,440

* The Bassetlaw and Thurgarton returns include the Liberty of Southwell and Scrooby.
† The population of each parish in the county, will be shewn in separate tables, with the topographical and statistical description of the SIX HUNDREDS or WAPENTAKES.

The total POPULATION OF ENGLAND & WALES in 1831, was 13,894,574; of SCOTLAND, 2,365,807; and of the ARMY and NAVY, 277,017, swelling the aggregate number of souls in GREAT BRITAIN, to 16,537,398; consisting of 8,161,618

males, and 8,375,780 *females,* and being an encrease since
1801, of no fewer than 5,594,752 souls!

COURTS OF LAW.

The ASSIZES are held twice a year, generally in the last weeks
of February and July, at the County-Hall and Town-Hall, in
Nottingham, where commissions of " Oyer and Terminer," and
general Gaol Delivery," are opened, both for the " Town and
County of the Town," and for Nottinghamshire. The QUARTER
SESSIONS are held at Nottingham, Newark, Southwell, and
Retford. PETTY SESSIONS are held weekly, before the county
magistrates, in all the market towns, and in a few of the villages. The Corporate Magistrates of Nottingham, Retford,
and Newark, hold separate Sessions for their respective
boroughs. The *County Court* is held monthly at Nottingham,
and the *Court of the Honour of Peverel,* weekly, at Lenton.—
(See page 138.)

The increase of population, and the influence of feudal lords,
gave rise to MANORIAL COURTS, which were granted to obviate
the necessity of the tenants of a particular class being obliged
to attend the Sheriff's Torn, or general Court Leet of the Hundred. Courts Leet and Baron are now held twice a year, for
many of the manors in the county, before the stewards of their
respective lords; and by custom the leets of several manors
may be held at once, in some certain place within one of the
manors.

The number of *committals for crime,* in the county, in 1810,
amounted to 67, and in 1819, to 196; but it does not appear
that vice is more prevalent here than in other districts of a
similar description. The *County Gaol is at Nottingham,* (see
page 158,) and the *House of Correction* at Southwell. (See *list
of* EXECUTIONS at page 141; LUDDISM, page 102, and REFORM
RIOTS p. 109 to 115.)

The ECCLESIASTICAL COURTS, which exercise jurisdiction
here, are the *Prerogative Court of York,* within the Diocese
and Province of which the whole county is included; and the
Spiritual Court of the Archdeaconry of Nottingham. Probates
of wills and letters of administration of persons dying within
this archdeaconry, which is coextensive with the county, are
granted at the ARCHDEACONRY OFFICE, in Nottingham, except
for the rectorial manor of Mansfield, in which the Dean of Lincoln holds a Peculiar Court, and has a registrar; but the
original wills of the whole county are deposited in the Register,
Office, in York. The Venerable Geo. Wilking, D.D.* is the
Archdeacon of Nottingham, and the Rev. John Staunton, L.L.D.
is his *official.* C. G. Balguy, Esq. of Nottingham, is the *registrar,* and Mr. Wm. Pearson, of East Redford, the *apparitor.*
The Archdeacon holds his visitations yearly in the parish

*Dr. Wilkins, vicar of Nottingham, was elected Archdeacon in 1832.

churches of Nottingham, Newark, Retford, and Bingham, where the clergy, churchwardens, &c. of the four DEANERIES, bearing the names of those towns, are required to attend. (See page 145.) The Chapter of Southwell Collegiate Church have a *peculiar jurisdiction* over 28 parishes in the hundreds of Bassetlaw and Thurgarton, forming the *Liberty of Southwell and Scrooby.* (Vide p. 301 and 661.)

The venerable MINSTER OF SOUTHWELL is the mother church of Nottinghamshire, and in it are held two annual Synods, as has been seen at page 692. It has sixteen prebendaries, of whom the following is a list, shewing the years in which they were inducted, and the names and annual value of their respective prebends in the King's books.

CHAPTER OF SOUTHWELL.

PREBENDARIES.	PREBENDS.	VAL.			INDUC.
William Dealtry, D.D.	Norwell Tertia	5	2	0	1785
Henry Smith, M.A.	North Leverton	5	0	0	1807
Wm. Barrow, D.C.L.	Eaton	2	11	3	1815
J. T. Becher, M.A. Vicar-General	South Muskham	13	4	7	1818
Jas. Jarvis Cleaver, M.A.	Oxton 1st. med.	22	19	7	1820
E. G. Marsh, M.A.	Woodborough	9	17	11	1821
Rt. Chaplin, B.C.L.	Norwell Pallishall	27	19	7	1823
Ven. Geo. Wilkins, D.D. Archdeacon	Normanton	26	6	0	1823
Chas. Nixon, M.A.	Segeston	1	2	6	1825
Frederick Anson, M.A.	Oxton Secunda	24	10	0	1827
John Rudd, M.A.	Halloughton	8	17	6	1827
C. Boothby, M.A.	North Muskham	32	5	3	1829
T. Percival, M.A.	Dunham	23	11	4	1829
Fitzjerald Wintour, M.A.	Rampton	15	17	11	1829
Thos. H. Shepherd, MA.	Beckingham	16	15	10	1830
C. Vernon Harcourt, M.A.	Norwell Overall	48	1	3	1830

VICARS CHORAL.

Rd. Barrow B.D.	T. S. Basnet, M.A.
C. Fowler, M.A.	R. H. Fowler, M.A.
Jas. Foottit, B.A.	Jas. Foottit, jun.

*** Of the 16 prebends, ten were established *before* and the following *six,* after the conquest, viz—Beckingham, Leverton, Dunham, Hallougton, Rampton, and Eaton.

‖‖ Except those of Woodborough and Segeston, the Prebendaries have the patronage of the parish churches which give name to their respective prebends.—The Chapter at large have the patronage of Aslacton, Barnby-in-the-Willows, Bleasby, Edingley, Farnsfield, Halam, Kirklington, Kneesall, Rolleston, S. Wheatley, and Upton, in *Notts.*; Barnoldby-le-Beck, Beelsby, Brigsby, Hatcliffe, Howerby, Beesby-in-the-Marsh, and Waltham, in Lincolnshire, and Barlborough, in *Yorkshire.*

PUBLIC OFFICERS
OF THE COUNTY.

☞ *The figures denote the time of election or appointment.*

LORD LIEUTENANT OF THE COUNTY, and *Steward of the Forest of Sherwood** and *Park of Folewood*—His Grace the Duke of Newcastle.

MEMBERS OF PARLIAMENT, (for the County) John Savile Lumley, Esq. (1826) and John Evelyn Denison, Esq. (1831).

HIGH SHERIFF, (for 1832) Henry Machon, Esq. Gateford Hill

Under Sheriff, George Freeth, Esq. Nottingham

CLERK OF THE PEACE, E. S. Godfrey, Esq. Newark

Clerk of the General Meetings of Lieutenancy, W. E. Tallents, Esq. Newark; also Clerk of Sewers for the whole county

COUNTY TREASURERS, Mr. W. Sculthorpe, Nottingham, (1815) for the South Division, and Mr. John Mee, Retford, (1826) for the North Division

CORONERS, P. R. Falkner, Newark, (1825) and Cphr. Swann, Nottingham, (1828) for the county. W. E. Tallents, for the borough of Newark; John Mee, for East Retford; G. H. & W. H. Barrow, for the Liberty of Southwell and Scrooby; and H. Enfield and J. Dunn, Esqrs. for the Town and County of the Town of Nottingham

STAMP DISTRIBUTOR, George Smith, Esq. Nottingham. The *Sub-Distributors* are Thomas Beckett, Newark; Robert Collinson, Mansfield; Fras. Sissons, Worksop; John Bradwell, Southwell; and George Thornton, Retford

SURVEYORS OF TAXES, Mr. John Jackson Nottingham, and Mr. S. Sketchley, Newark

COUNTY GAOL, at Nottingham, Mr. R. B. Brierley, *gaoler* (1830); Mrs. Mary Cross, *matron* (1823); Rev. Robert Wood, D. D. *chaplain*; Mr. H. Oldknow, surgeon (1831)

HOUSE OF CORRECTION, at Southwell, Mr. Matthew Mole, *governor* (1822); Mrs. Louisa Lee, *matron* (1822); Rev. Thomas Still Basnett, *chaplain*

PEVEREL COURT AND PRISON at Lenton.—(See p. 138)

ARCHDEACONRY OFFICE, &c.—(See page 62)

CHIEF CONSTABLES
AND SURVEYORS OF COUNTY BRIDGES,

Bassetlaw Hundred, for the *North Clay*, Job Conworth, of Worksop; *South Clay*, Joseph Whitake, of Morton; *Hatfield Division*, George Cresswell, of Retford,

Bingham Hundred, North Division, John Pilgrim, of Shelford; *South Division*, Samuel White, of Bingham

* VERDERERS, &c. OF SHERWOOD FOREST.—(See page 41.)—There are now only two surviving *verderers*, viz. John Musters and William Wylde, Esqs., and it is expected that after their death the office will cease, in consequence of the crown having granted in 1818, the hays of *Birkland and Bilhagh* to the Duke of Portland, in exchange for the patronage of the church of Mary-le-Bonne, in London. In lieu of the Tree which each verderer used to receive annually out of these ancient woods, they have now £10 per annum each.—(Vide p. 416.)

Broxtow Hundred, North Division, William Cook, of Mansfield; *South Division,* John Wright, of Beeston.
Newark Hundred, North Division, Edward Neale, *South Division,* Joseph Adams, both of Newark
Rushcliffe Hundred, North Division, John Woodroffe, of East Stoke; *South Division,* John Berridge, of Sutton Bonnington
Thurgarton Hundred, North Division, Richard Esam, of Carlton-on-Trent; *South Division,* Thomas Hind, of Bleasby

SHERIFF'S OFFICERS.

William Archer and Daniel Ward, Nottingham; Richard Bell and Edward Daniels, Newark; Joseph Platts, Mansfield; William Pearson, Retford.—(See also page 254.)

MAGISTRATES.

Launcelot Rolleston, Esq. of Watnall, *Chairman.*

Beaumont Rev. T. East Bridge-ford
Becher, Rev. J. T. *chairman* of Newark and Southwell Sessions
Bristowe S. E. Esq. Beesthorpe
Bromley Sir Rt. Howe, Bart. Stoke Hall
Claye Rev. Wm. Westhorpe
Clay W. W. P. Esq. Southwell
Clifton Sir Rt. Bt. Clifton (1821)
Coape Henry, Esq. Sherwood Lodge (1818)
Coke John, Esq. Debdale House
Denison J. E. Esq. M. P. Ossington
Dickonson Peter, Esq. W. Retford
Edge T. W. Esq. Strelley (1821)
Fullerton John, Esq. Forest Hill
Gardiner J. G. C. Esq. Thurgarton
Godfrey T. S. Esq. Beaconfield
Hall Francis, Esq. Park Hall
Handley W. F. Esq. M.P. Newark
Heron Sir Robert, Bart, Stubton, Lincolnshire
Holcombe Rev. George, D.D. West Leake
Holden Rt. Esq. Nuthall Temple
Kelham R. K. Esq. Bleasby
Kirke Wm. Esq. Retford, (1827)
Knight Henry Galley Esq. M.P. Langolds, near Worksop Yorks
Lee James, Esq. West Retford
Lowe Rev. Robert, Bingham
Martin H. Esq. Colston Basset
Mason Rev. Geo. Cuckney, 1820

Middleton Lord, Wollaton
Miles William, Esq. M. P. (1830)
Musters John, Esq. Colwick
Musters J. G. C. Wiverton
Need John Esq. Mansfield Woodh
Neville Christphr, Esq. Thorney
Nixon Thomas Esq. Papplewick
Norton W. F. N. Esq. Elton
Padley Rt. Esq. Burton Joyce
Pocklington Joseph, Esq. Carlton on-Trent
Portland Duke of, Welbeck
Rudd Rev. John, Blyth, *Chairman* of Retford Sessions
Sherwin J. S. Esq. Bramcote, 1830
Simpson H. B. Esq. Babworth
Simpson John, Esq. Babworth
Sotheron Vice-Admiral, F., Kirklington
Staunton Rev. Dr. Staunton
Steade E. V. Winkbourne
Storer Rev. John, Hawkesworth
Surrey Earl of, Worksop Manor
Taylor Wm. Esq. Ratcliffe, (1826)
Tiffin Rev. Wm. Mattersey
Vernon G. H. Esq. M. P. Grove (1826)
Walker Henry, Esq. Blyth
Wescomb J. E. Esq. Thrumpton, (1828)
Wildman T. Esq. Newstead, (1828
Wright J. S. Esq. Upton
Wright Thomas, Esq. Rempston
Wylde William, Esq. Southwell
Youle Rev. Abrm. East Retford

PEERS OF PARLIAMENT,

WHO HAVE SEATS IN THE COUNTY OF NOTTINGHAM,

WITH THE DATE OF THEIR CREATION.—(SEE P. 29.)

1483. DUKE OF NORFOLK, &c. the Most Noble Bernard Edward Howard, Worksop Manor
1716. DUKE OF PORTLAND, the Most Noble William Henry Cavendish Scott-Bentinck, Welbeck Abbey
1756. DUKE OF NEWCASTLE, &c. the Most Noble Henry Pelham Fiennes Pelham Clinton, Clumber House
1690. EARL OF SCARBOROUGH; the Right Hon. and Rev. John Lumley Savile (Saunderson) succeeded to this title in June, 1832, since nearly all the following sheets were printed.— He and his son have cut off the entail of the Rufford Estate, and annexed it to that of the late Earl of Scarborough.— (See p. 439.) His seats are at Sandbeck, Yorkshire, and Edwinstow and Rufford, Nottinghamshire
1806. EARL MANVERS, the Right Hon. Charles Herbert Pierrepont, Thoresby Hall
1712. LORD MIDDLETON, the Right Hon. Henry Willoughby, Wollaton Hall

PEERS NOT OF PARLIAMENT.

1727. VISCOUNT GALWAY, (of Scotland,) Right Hon. Wm. George Monkton Arundel, Serlby Hall
1795. LORD RANCLIFFE, (of Ireland,) Right Hon. Augustus Henry Anne Parkyns, Bunny Park

ELDEST SONS OF PEERS.

Marquis of Titchfield, (son of the Duke of Portland,) Welbeck
Earl of Surrey, (son of the Duke of Norfolk,) Worksop Manor
Earl of Lincoln, (son of the Duke of Newcastle,) Clumber
Viscount Newark, (son of Earl Manvers,) Thoresby
Viscount Althorp, (son of Earl Spencer,) Wiseton Hall

HONOURABLES.

Hon. Geo. Cavendish Scott-Bentinck, Welbeck Abbey
Hon. John Bridgeman Simpson, (brother of the Earl of Bradford,) Babworth Hall
Hon. Granville Harcourt Vernon, M. P. Grove Hall; and the Hon. and Rev. J. Venables Vernon, Kirkby Rectory; are sons of the Archbishop of York
Hon. Bridget Monkton, *Dowager Countess Galway*, Bawtry Hall
Hon. Capt. Arthur Duncombe, (son of Lord Feversham,) Bishopfield
Hon. Anna Maria, *Dowager Duchess of Newcastle*, Ranby Hall
Hon. Ann Pierrepont, *Dowager Countess Manvers*, Holm Pierrepont
Lady Jane Parkyns, Ruddington | Lady C. Warren, Stapleford Hall
Lady Elizabeth White, Tuxford | Lady C. Sherbrooke, Calverton

BARONETS.

Sir Robert Clifton, Bart. Clifton, near Nottingham
Sir Robert Howe Bromley, Bart. Stoke Hall
Sir Robert Heron, Bart. Stubton, near Newark, Lincolnshire
Sir Thomas Woolaston White, Bart. Wallingwells
Sir Richard Sutton, Bart. Norwood Park

SEATS

NOBILITY, GENTRY, AND CLERGY

IN

NOTTINGHAMSHIRE.

☞ To avoid swelling this List, Gentlemen's Villas in the suburbs
of Market Towns are not inserted here, but will be found subjoined to the Names of their Occupiers, in the Directories of
the respective Towns and Parishes.

Annesley Hall, 6 m. S.S.W. of Mansfield, J. Musters, Esq
Averham, 3 m. N.W. of Newark, Rev. Robert Chaplin, B.C.L.
Arnot Hill, 3 m. N. of Nottingham, Thomas Panton, Esq
Arnot Vale, near ditto, Mrs. Elizabeth Bigsby
Aspley Hall, 2 m. N.W. of Nottingham, W. S. Burnside, Esq
Balderton, 2 m. S.E. of Newark, G. Marriott, Esq
Babworth Hall, 2 m. W. of Retford, Hon. J. B. Simpson
Barnby Moor, 3 m. N.W. of Retford, Samuel Barker, Esq. and
　　Michael Wynne Thorold and John Darcy Clark, Gents
Bawtry Hall, 9 m. N. by W. of Retford, Dowager Countess Galway
Beaconfield, 2 m. E. of Newark, T. S. Godfrey, Esq
Beckingham, 3 m. W. of Gainsbro', Robert Cross, and Thomas
　　Massingberd, Esqrs
Beesthorpe, 6½ m. N.W. of Newark, Wm. Miles, Esq. M.P.
Besthorpe, 8 m. N.N.E. of Newark, Mrs. Naylor
Berry Hill, 1½ m. S.S.E. of Mansfield, Mrs. Walker, gent
Beskwood Hall, 5 m. N. of Nottingham, Thomas Redgate, Esq
Biggins House, 1 m. N. of Retford, George Kippax, Esq
Bilsthorpe, 5 m. S. of Ollerton, Rev. Henry Gordon, M.A.
Bishopfield, 2 m. S. of Bawtry, Hon. Arthur Duncombe
Bleasby, 4 m. S. of Southwell, Rt. K. Kelham, Esq
Blyth Hall, 3 m. S.S.W. Bawtry, Major Gen. Sir H. Bouverie
Blyth Spittal, 3¼ m. S.S.W. of Bawtry, John Bradley, Esq
Brackenhurst, 1¼ m. S.S.W. of Southwell, Rev. Thos. C. Cane.
Bramcote, 5 m. W. by S. of Nottingham, H. Mundy, and C. Wright,
　　Esqrs. and Mrs. C. Longden
Bramcote Hills, near ditto, John S. Sherwin, Esq
Bridgeford, (East,) 3 m. N. of Bingham, P. Brooke and P. Palmer,
　　Esqrs. Rev. Thomas Beaumont, and Rev. Rd. W. Hutchins
Bridgeford (West,) Hall, 2. m. S. of Nottingham, Mrs. Smith
Brook Hill, 7 m. S.W. of Mansfield, Rev. D'Ewes Coke
Broughton Cottage, 10 m. S.S.W. of Bingham, Colonel Wright
Bulcote Lodge, 7 m. N.E. of Nottingham, Robert W. Padley, Gent
Bulwell Hall, 4½ m. N.N.W. of Nottingham, Rev. A. Padley
Bunney Park, 7¼ m. S. of Nottingham, Lord Rancliffe
Burton Joyce, 6¼ m. N.E. of Nottingham, Rt. Padley, Esq. and
　　Misses Jamson

Carcolston, 2 m. N. N. E. of Bingham, Rev. Rt. Ffarmerie
Calverton, 7 m. N. N. E. of Nottingham, Lady Sherbrooke, and
    Capt. E. A. Cotton
Carlton Hall, 3½ m. N. of Worksop, Robert Ramsden, Esq
Carlton, 3½ m. N. of Worksop, Rev. C. W. Eyre, M. A.
Carlton-on-Trent, 7 m. N. of Newark, Roger Pocklington, Esq. and
    George W. Hutton, Esq
Caunton Manor, 6 m. N.W. of Newark, Samuel Hole, Esq
Chilwell Hall, 5 m. W.S.W. Nottingham, Owen Davies, M.D.
Clayworth, 6 m. S.E. of Bawtry, Frederick Davenport, Esq. Thomas
    Colton, Esq. and Rev. Thomas Henry Shepherd, M. A.
Clifton Hall, 4 m. S.W. of Nottingham, Sir Robert Clifton, Bart
Clumber House, 3½ m. S.E. of Worksop, Duke of Newcastle, and
    his son the Earl of Lincoln, M.P.
Cock Glode, 1 m. W. of Ollerton, Col. Henry Lumley Saville
Colston Hall, 5 m. S. of Bingham, Henry Martin, Esq
Colwick Hall, 1½ m. E. of Nottingham, John Musters, Esq
Costock, 9½ m. S. of Nottm., S. B. Wild, Esq. & Rev. W. Beetham
Cotgrave Place, 6 m. S. E. of Nottingham, Rt. Burgess, gent
Cromwell, 5 m. N. of Newark, Rev. C. J. F. Clinton
Cuckney, 5 m. S. S. W. of Worksop, Revs. G. Mason & E. Palling
Daybrook House, 3 m. N. of Nottm. Mark Dennison, Esq
Debdale House, 1½ m. S. E. of Mansfield, J. Coke, Esq
Eakring, 4 m. S. E. of Ollerton, Rev. Theops. Sampson
Easthorpe, ½ m. E. of Southwell, Capt. Trebeck & W. C. May, Esq
Eaton Hall, 2 m. S. of Retford, H. B. Simpson, Esq
Edwinstow, 2 m. W. of Ollerton, Earl of Scarborough, and Rev.
    John Cleaver, L. L. B.
Elksley, 4 m. S. by W. of Retford, Robert Sharpe, Esq
Elms, (The) ¾ m. S. of Retford, John Kippax, Esq
Elston Hall, 5 m. S. S. W. of Newark, W. B. Darwin, Esq
Elton Manor, 4 m. E. by S. of Bingham, W. F. N. Norton, Esq
Everton, 3 m. E. by S. of Bawtry, Rt. D. Otter, Esq. and Rev. R.
    Evans
Farndon Hall, 2 m. S. W. of Newark, Edw. Buck, & W. Brockton,
Farnsfield, 4 m. N. W. of Southwell, E. Howit, and W. Houlds-
    worth, Esqrs.
Finningley, 3 m. N. by E. of Bawtry, Rev. J. Harvey, L. L. B.
Finningley Park, 3 m. N. of Bawtry, Edward B. Beaumont, Esq
Forest Hill, 2 m. N. of Worksop, J. Fullerton, and H. W. Pickard,
Flintham Hall, 7 m. S. W. of Newark, Mrs. Hildyard
Fountaindale, 3½ m. S. E. of Mansfield, General Samuel Need
Gamston, 3 m. S. of Retford, Rev. Joshua Brooke, B. D.
Fiskerton, 3 m. S. E. of Southwell, Thomas Bolger, Esq.
Gateford Hill, 2 m. N. W. of Worksop, Henry Machon, Esq.
Gedling House, 4 m. N. E. of Nottingham, W. E. Elliott, Esq.
Gedling, 3½ m. N. E. of Nottingham, George Walker, Esq. and the
    Rev. Charles Williams.
Hawkesworth, 4 m. N. E. of Bingham, Rev. J. Storer
Gourton, 4½ m. S. of Southwell, Thomas Hind, gent
Grove Hall, 3 m. S. E. of Retford, Anthony Hardolph Eyre, Esq.
    and the Hon. Granville Harcourt Vernon.
Hemshill, 4 m. N. W. by N. of Nottm. Samuel Bolton, Esq.

Hesley Hall, 2 m. N. W. of Bawtry, H. Marwood Greaves, Esq.
Hexgrave Park, 5 m. N. N. W. of Southwell, Edward Werg, and
    Richard Milward, Esqrs.
Hodsock Priory, 2 m. S. by W. of Blyth, Mrs. Ann Chambers
Hodsock Park, 2 m. W. of Blyth, John Shuttleworth, Esq
Holme, 3½ m. N. of Newark, Thos. Adwick, gent
Holme-Pierrepont, 5 m. E. by S. of Nottingham, Dowager Countess
    Manvers, and the Rev. J. C. Cleaver
Hoveringham Hall, 5 m. S. by W. of Southwell, Col. Huthwaite
Kelham Hall, 2 m. N. W. of Newark, Mrs. & J. M. Sutton, Esq
Kirkby Hardwick, 5 m. S. W. of Mansfield, T. Clarke, Esq
Kirkby Rectory, near ditto, Hon. & Rev. J. V. Vernon
Kirklington Hall, 2¾ m. N. W. of Southwell, Vice Adml. Sotheron
Kirton, 3 m. S. W. of Tuxford, Rev. Joseph Blandford
Lamb-close House, 8 m. N. W. of Nottm., T. F. P. H. Barber, Esq
Lambley Hall, 7 m. N. E. of Nottingham, Rev. A. D. Flamstead
Lamcote, 5½ m. E. by S. of Nottingham, J. Wright, Esq
Langar Hall, 4 m. S. of Bingham, (unoccupied)
Langford House, 4 m. N. N. E. of Newark, S. Duncombe, Esq
Langold, near Worksop, H. G. Knight, Esq. M. P.
Langwith Hall, 8 m. N. of Mansfield, R. N. Sutton, Esq
Leake, (East) 10 m. S. by W. of Nottingham, J. Woodroffe, gent
Leake, (West) 10 m. S. S. W. of Nottm., Rev. G. Holcombe, D. D.
Lenton Hall, 2 m. W. S. W. of Nottingham, J. Wright, Esq.; Len-
    ton Grove, Mrs. Dorothy Evans; Lenton Fields, M. Needham,
    Esq.; Lenton Firs, Dr. Storer; Lenton Priory, Thos. Jerram
Linby, 8 m. N. by W. of Nottingham, Richard Hopper, Esq
Lound, 3 m. N. N. W. of Retford, Henry Bagshaw, Esq
Mansfield Woodhouse, Edmund Sykes Esq. and Col. Need
Mantles, 1 m. E. of Blythe, Thomas Crofts, Esq
Mapperley, 1¾ m. N. of Nottingham, Ichabod Wright, Esq
Markham, (East) 1 m. N. of Tuxford, John Rose, Esq
Markham, (West) 2 m. N. W. of Tuxford, Rev. E. H. Dawkens
Mattersey, 4 m. S. E. of Bawtry, Rev. Wm. Tiffin, and Benjamin
    Fearnly, Esq.; Mrs. Honor Graham and Mrs. Eliz. Clarke
Mirfield Hall, 1 m. N. of Tuxford, Mrs. Frances Cartwright
Misterton, 5 m. N. W. of Gainsborough, Robert Corringham, Esq
Muskham House, (unoccupied)
Muskham, 4 m. N. of Newark, Capt. Worsley, and J. Handley, Esq
Nethergreen, 8 m. N.W. of Nottingham, G. Walker, Esq
Nettleworth Hall, 3½ m. N. by E. of Mansfield. Major Bielbie
Newark, E. S. Godfrey, and W. F. Handley, Esqrs
Newstead Abbey, 5 m. S. of Mansfield, Colonel Wildman
Niagara Cottage, 6 m. W. by S. of Nottingham, Capt. Sleigh
Normanton Hills, 12 m. S. by W. of Nottm. J. Buckley, Esq
Norwood Park, 1 m. N.W. of Southwell, Sir Rd. Sutton, Bart
Normanton-on-Trent, 4 m. S.E. of Tuxford, Rev. W. Doncaster
Nottingham.—See Miscellaneous List, (p. 261 to 272,) Ven. Arch-
    deacon Wilkins, D.D.
Nuthall Temple, 4½ m. N.N.W. of Nottingham, Rt. Holden, Esq
Orston Hall, 6 m. E. by N. of Newark, Mrs. Middlemore
Osberton Hall, 3 m. N.E. of Worksop, G. S. Foljambe, Esq
Ossington Hall, 4 m. S. by E. of Tuxford, J. E. Denison, Esq. M.P.

Oxton Hall, 5 m. S.W. of Southwell, Mrs. Sherbrooke
Papplewick Hall, 6 m. S. of Mansfield, Thomas Nixon, Esq
Park Hall, 3 m. N. of Mansfield, Francis Hall, Esq
Pleasley Hill, 3 m. N.N.W. of Mansfield, S. Siddon, Esq
Plumptre, 6 m. S. of Nottingham, Rev. J. Burnside
Ranby Hall, 4 m. N.W. of Retford, Dwgr. Duchess of Newcastle
Ranby House, 3 m. W. by N. of Retford, John Rogers, Esq
Ratcliffe-on-Trent, 6 m. E. by S. of Nottingham, Rev. Henry Bolton,
　　and Wm. Taylor, Esq
Redhill, 9 m. S.W. of Nottingham, Israel Chamberlin, Esq
Rempston Hall, 11 m. S. of Nottingham, J. Smith Wright, Esq;
　　and Rempston Cottage, J. Hunter, Esq
Retford (East,) W. Kirke, John Parker, John Holmes, F. A. S.;
　　Rd. Hutchinson, Frans. T. Foljambe, and Geo. Creswell, Esqrs
Retford (West,) 7¾ m. E. by N. of Worksop, Peter Dickonson, Esq.
　　James Lee, Esq. and the Rev. Abraham Youle
Ruddington, 5 m. S. of Nottingham, Lieut.-Genl. John Grey, Lady
　　Jane Parkyns; Thomas Moore, and Chas. Paget, Esqrs
Rufford Abbey, 2 m. S. of Ollerton, Earl of Scarborough
Scarrington, 2¼ m. E.N.E. of Bingham, H. Flower, Esq
Serlby Hall, 3 m. S. by W. of Bawtry, Viscount Galway
Shelton Hall, 7 m. S. of Newark, Major Hall
Sherwood Hall, (Racing) near Mansfield, T. Houldsworth, Esq. M.P.
Sherwood Lodge, 7 m. N. of Nottingham, Col. S. Coape
Skegby Hall, 3 m. W. of Mansfield, J. Dodsley, Esq
Southwell, William Wylde, Esq. W. W. P. Clay, Esq. and the Rev.
　　J. T. Becher
Standard Hill, near Notm. Danl. Freeth, Esq. & Rev. John Kirkby
Stanford Hall, 11½ m. S. of Nottingham, Rev. Samuel Dashwood
Stapleford Hall, 6 m. W. by S. of Nottingham, Lady Warren
Staunton Hall, 7 m. S. of Newark, Rev. J. Staunton, LL.D.
Stockwith, 4 m. N.W. of Gainsborough, Wm. Walton, Esq
Stoke Hall, 4 m. S.W. of Newark, Sir Rt. H. Bromley, Bart
Strelley Hall, 5 m. W. by N. of Nottingham, T. W. Edge, Esq
Strelley Rectory, near do. Rev. John Webb Edge
Sutton Hall, 3 m. S.W. of Mansfield, S. Woolley, Esq.
Sutton Manor, 11 m. S.S.W. of Nottingham, Geo. Paget, Esq
Syerston Hall, 7 m. S.W. of Newark, G. Fillingham, Esq
Thoresby Hall, 3 m. N. by W. of Ollerton, Earl Manvers, and Vis.
　　Newark, M.P.
Thorney Hall, 8 miles E. of Tuxford, Capt. Nevill.
Thrumpton Hall, 8 miles, S.W. of Nottm. J. E. Westcomb, Esq
Thurgarton Priory, 3 m. S. by W. of Newark, Wm. Martin, Esq
Tollerton Hall, 4¼ m. S.S.E. of Nottingham, P. Barry, Esq
Tuxford, Lady Eliz. White; and Rev. Edw. B. Elliott, A.M.
Upton Hall, 2¼ m. E. by S. of Southwell, Thomas Wright, Esq
Walkeringham, 4 m. N.W. of Gainsbro'; Rev. J. K. Miller
Wallingwells, 4 m. N. by W. of Worksop, Sir T. W. White, Bart
Watnall 6 m. N.W. of Nottingham, C. and L. Rolleston, Esqrs
Warsop 5 m. N. by E. of Mansfield, Rev. S. Marten
Welbeck Abbey, 3¼ m. S. of Worksop, Duke of Portland, and his
　　son, the Marquis of Titchfield.
Welham Hall, 1¼ m. E. by N. of Retford, H. C. Hutchinson, Esq

Welham House, 1¼ m. E. of Retford, Geo. Mower, Esq
Wellow Bar, 1 m. S.E. of Ollerton, Richard Parkinson, Esq
Westhorpe, 1 m. W. of Southwell, Rev. Wm. Claye
White Moor, 2 m. N. of Ollerton, Wm. John Pickin, Esq
Widmerpool, 9 miles S.S.E. of Nottingham, Rev. J. Robinson
Wigthorpe, 3 m. N. of Worksop, John Manwaring, Esq
Wilford, 2 m. S. of Nottingham, Henry Smith, Esq.; Rt. Leeson, Esq. and Rev. Thomas Thorpe
Winkbourne, 3 m. N. by E. of Southwell, P. P. Burnell, and E. V. Steade, Esqrs
Winthorpe Hall, 3 m. N. of Newark, (unoccupied)
Wiseton Hall, 5 m. S.S.E. of Bawtry, Hon. Viscount Althorp
Wiverton Hall, 2¼ m. S. of Bingham, J. G. C. Musters, Esq
Wollaton Hall, 3 m. W. of Nottingham, Lord Middleton
Wollaton House, 3 m. W. of Nottingham, Col. Hancock
Woodhouse Place, ½ m. E. of Mansfield, W. A. Smith, Esq
Worksop, 8 m. W. by S. of Retford, Francis Roe, Esq
Woodborough Hall, 8 m. S.W. of Southwell, Wm. Worth, Esq
Worksop Manor, 1 m. S. of Worksop, Duke of Norfolk and Earl Surrey

---

APPENDIX TO THE NOTTINGHAM DIRECTORY,

Consisting of changes which have taken place since the names were first collected.

Asylum, Carlton rd. Mr. Thos. Powell, director, Andw. Blake, physician
Barber Richard Gresham, coal merchant, Irongate wharf
Barker Geo. vict. Carrington st
Barrett W. plasterer, Glasshouse st
Barwick Samuel, chair maker, Middle Sneinton
Beardsall John, Huntsman's Tavern, Broad st
Beighton William & Co. tatting manufacturers, Castlegate
Bell Jas. grocer, Hollow stone
Bonsor Alex. carver, Park st
Booth Jas. & W. Raworth, jun. coal mercht. Bridge st
Bosworth G. & C. hosiery mfr. Clinton st
Boulougne & Co. lace merchants, Church st
Brewster Geo. draper, Long row
Bullock Horatio Nelson, bookseller, &c. Parliament st
Burrows Thos. straw hat maker, hosier & glover, Carlton st

Burton J. shoemaker, Pelham st
Carver & Son, hosiers, Market st
Carver Wm. bksmith, Vassal st
Chandler Wm. confec. Pilchergt
Chimley Ed. miller, Canal st. & baker, Derby road
Clarke John, vict Artichoke, Highcross st
Clarke Thos. solr. Broadmarsh
Cockayne John, butcher, & beerhouse. Parliament st
Cole Geo. schoolmr. Parlmt st
Colton Jph. small ware dealer, Parliament st
Coope Jas. solicitor, Castlegate
Coupland G. lace mfr. Mount st
Cox J. watch mkr. New Lenton
Cox Gorge, Horse & Trumpet, Trumpet st
Crisp Danl. shoemkr. Carlton st
Crofts W. bobbin net mkr. b. Geo. st. New Radford
Dale Rd. ale and porter mercht. Swann's yard, Long row
Daniel Thos. auctioneer, china and glass dlr. Bridlesmithgate

Darby Augustus, surgeon, Toll st
Dawson Hy. grocer, Carrington st
Deakin Jonathan, hosiery manfr. Swann's yard, Long row
Dean Thos. turner, Talbot yard
Etches John, watch maker, Carrington st
Felkin & Vickers, general agents, Clinton st
Fisher & Co. bobbin net makers, George st. New Radford
Fletcher Jph. grocer, Beck st
Fowler Geo. packing case maker, Point ct. Park st
Frearson and Vickers, lace mfrs. Clinton st
Freeman and Co. lace mfrs. Pilchergate
Gadsby Jas. vict. Hyson green
Gillham & Co. hatters, High st
Gimson Thos. F. lace mfr. Bridlesmithgate
Golling T. baker, Carrington st
Hamerton Wm. vict. East st
Heathcoat & Co. lace mfrs. Clinton st
Hind T. and Co. lace mfrs. Stoney street
Hodgkinson Jno. vict. Count st
Horne Wm. vict. Broadmarsh
Hunt Thos. glover, Carlton st
Husband Rd. confr. Warsergate
Hutchinson T. dentist, Goosegt
Huthersall J. schoolr. Houndsgt
James Rt. painter, Broad st
Jerram Saml. draper, South prd
Jones & Dent, lace mfrs. Warsergt
Kendall & Shenk, lace manufacturers, Churchgate
Kirk John, lace mfr. Castlegate
Kitelee T. surgeon, Haughton st
Lambert Rd. net mfr. Hollow stone
Langham Geo. beer hs. Derby rd
Levers John machine mkr. New Lenton
Levick G. & R. lace mfrs. High Pavement
Lewis Rd. S. lace mfr. Castlegt
Lowe C. & J. lace mfrs. Mount st
Massey Isaac, surgeon, dispensary, Goosegate
Morley John, lace mfr. Castlegt

Nottingham News Room, Pelham street, estab. June 18, 1832
Onn John, painter, Castlegate
Page Jph. Jas. & Jas. lace mfrs. Standard hill
Palmer Geo. hair cutter & cutler, Pelham st
Payne & Daft, solrs. Poultry
Preston ——, lace mfr. Stoney st
Reinbeck Fk. lace mfr. Kendal st
Renshaw Rupert, vict. Albion Hotel, New Lenton
Rigley and Johnson, solrs. Long row
Roberts T. jun. & Co. lace mfrs. Plumptre place
Sanderson Thos. lace thread agt. Stoney st
Sheldon John, silver plate manfr. and hardware dlr. Carlton st
Shelton Jas. grocer and chandler, Middle Sneinton
Shipham Jno. grocer, Parliament street, E
Simpson Ed. wheelt. Derby road
Skinder Jas. vict. Market st
Slater Sl. lace mfr. Stretton's yd
Smith Stephen, rope mfr. Parlt st
Smith J. & W. cabinet makers, South parade
Southam Jno. agent, Spaniel row
Stagg & Ward livery stable and coach proprietors, Castlegate
Staveley Ed. gl. agt. Stoney st
Steegman Hy. lace mfr. Halifax place
Sutton Jas. & Co. carriers, (late Rt. Marshall,) and salt merts. London rd. & Commerce st
Thorp Hy. lace mfr. Market st
Wagg Thos. beerhs. Goosegate
Waine Avery, brushmkr. Goosegt
Ward John, vict. Warsergate
Warner Saml. register office, and library, Houndagate
Waton Wm. baker, Wheelergate
Webster Ralph, saddler, Bridlesmithgate
Wells John, draper, Cheapside
Wheatley Jas. agent, Granby st
Whitworth, J. joiner, Canal st
Windley Thos. dyer, Mortimer st
Woodhouse John, vict. York st

HISTORY

OF THE

TOWN AND COUNTY OF THE TOWN

OF

NOTTINGHAM.

———◆———

NOTTINGHAM, the principal seat and emporium of the lace
and hosiery manufactures, is an ancient, populous, and well-
built market and borough town, forming with its precincts a
county of itself, as well as being the capital of the shire and
archdeaconry to which it gives name, in the diocese of York,
and in the midland circuit of England. It occupies a picturesque
situation, on the rocky eminence which rises in broken declivities, and in some places in cragged precipices, above the
north bank of the small river called the Leen, which, at a short
distance to the south-east, falls into the more magnificent stream
of the Trent, near the opposite locks of the Grantham and
Nottingham canals, and a little below that venerable and noble
structure the Trent bridge, which is connected with Nottingham
by a flood road, raised at an immense expense above the intervening meadows, which in rainy seasons are subject to inundation. It holds a central situation between Newcastle-upon-
Tyne and Portsmouth to the north and south, and betwixt
Newcastle-under-Lyme and Boston to the east and west; being
in the south-western division of Nottinghamshire, at the
junction of the hundreds of Broxtow, Thurgarton, and Rushcliffe; distant 125 miles N. by W. of London, 80 miles S. of
York, 20 miles S. W. by W. of Newark, 14 miles S. of Mansfield, 15 miles E. by N. of Derby, 27 miles N. of Leicester,
and 38 miles S. by E. of Sheffield; and is in 53 degrees north
latitude, and in 1 deg. 13 min. west longitude from the meridian
of Greenwich.

The approach to the town, on any side, is particularly striking
to the traveller, and it may be justly said that there is perhaps
no town in the kingdom which appears under such a variety of
aspects, as this does, from its different points of view. The
tourist, who arrives by the London road, is delighted, on descending Ruddington hill, with a view of the fertile vale of the
Trent, bounded on the north by the august rock on which the
town stands, with the castle on a lofty precipitous hill to the
left, the long range of buildings gradually sinking into the plain
to the right, and the whole, crowned by the graceful tower of
St. Mary's, and terminated, on the west, by the lofty receding
hills of Sneinton and Mapperley,* and on the east by the recently formed semicircular terrace-road of the castle park, now
lined with elegant mansions, gardens, and pleasure-grounds,
which add greatly to the beauty of the scene,—the foreground
of which consists of luxuriant pastures, skirted by the Trent
and the canal, and by numerous wharfs, warehouses, and manufactories. If the traveller comes by the eastern side, from
the Newark road, the whole mass of building is then foreshort-
ened, the tower of St. Mary's and the castle appearing nearly
as one edifice, whilst in the vale below he has a full view of the
long extended line of the Trent and flood bridges, and on his
right is seen the perpendicular rocks and caves of Sneinton, in
which are many grotesque dwellings, occupied by industrious
families, and enlivened in front by shady arbours and hanging
gardens. If he enters from the north, by the Mansfield road,
after rising the hill above the race-ground, the whole view
bursts upon his astonished sight as if by enchantment;—he
finds himself in a long and spacious road, lined with handsome
and newly-built houses, descending to the town, beyond which
he sees the vale of the Trent as if on a map, and still further in
the distance, the extensive vale of Belvoir, skirted by the Leicestershire hills. The western approach, by the Derby road,
is completely different from the others. On passing Wollaton
park, (the delightful seat of Lord Middleton,) the castle, with
its commanding cliffs boldly starting from the verdant swells of
the park, is a near and prominent object; and extending from
it are seen the handsome villas and gardens which line the terrace walk of the Park, and appear to have recently arisen on
the site of the ancient ramparts that once circumambulated the
town. On the opposite side of the park are seen the barracks,
which appear to form a town of themselves, and to the north-
west lies the Forest, having its higher verge studded with a
long line of windmills, and in its centre the race-course and

* ALTITUDE of the PRINCIPAL HILLS, &c. (in and near Nottingham,) above
the level of the river Leen:—Castle yard, 110 feet; Castle parapets, 171; St. Mary's
church steeple parapets, 182; Park hill and Bowling-alley hill, 188; Gallows hill,
top of Mansfield road, 166; top of Derby road, 168; Sneinton hill, on foot road to
Gedling, 266; Mapperley hills, Beskwood park, and Red hill, 340 feet.

cricket-ground; and near its southern and western limits, the populous new villages which have arisen during the last ten years in the parishes of Radford and Basford, as others have done in the parishes of Sneinton and Lenton, adjoining the opposite limits of the pasture and meadow lands which nearly surround Nottingham, and cannot be built upon, owing to their being subject, by ancient grant, to the depasturage of the burgesses. In most of the houses, both in the adjacent villages and in the town, are heard the busy sounds of industry —the noise of the stocking frames and lace machines; except in the principal streets, which contain many good houses, handsome public buildings, and well-stocked shops, with a commodious Market-place, that in extent, beauty, and convenience, has not its equal in the kingdom.

Nottingham, according to Deering, can claim as a town of note, the age of 920 years; as a considerable borough, 780; as a Mayor's town, 537, (being only a century posterior to the metropolis;) as a Parliamentary borough, during which it has constantly sent two representatives, 540; and as a county of itself, a period of 382 years, up to the year 1832.

Its POPULATION, which is the best criterion of its growing prosperity as a manufacturing and commercial town, has, during the last thirty years, nearly doubled itself, and the increase would have been much greater, if the 12,000 acres of burgess pasture lands, which nearly encompass the town, could have been sold or leased for building purposes. Within the last ten years, almost every vacant piece of ground in the town, that was suitable and available for the erection of houses and manufactories, has been built upon;—no fewer than 3617 houses having been erected during that period, and the number of inhabitants swelled from 40,505, to 50,727. The free pastures, which prevent the further extension of the town itself, have driven the insatiable spirit of commercial speculation into the neighbouring parishes, in several of which population and buildings have increased more than fourfold since the year 1801, so that now, within a circuit of four miles round the Market-place, we can number upwards of 80,000 souls, of whom upwards of 64,000 live in Nottingham, Radford, and Sneinton parishes, the buildings in which are so closely connected by modern erections on the Derby and Southwell roads, as to form but one town, though in separate jurisdictions.

About the year 1041, in the reign of Edward the Confessor, Nottingham had only 192 men, who, in the ravages of William the Conqueror, were reduced to 136, though there were then in the town 217 houses. In 1377, when the poll tax was levied, there were in the town 1447 lay persons, of fourteen years of age and upwards; of whom fourpence per head was collected in support of that odious impost, which caused the rebellion of *Wat Tyler*. As one-third of the people were supposed to consist of clergy, mendicants, and children under fourteen years of age, the total population at that period was about 2170.— The registering of burials at the three parish churches of Nottingham, commenced at St. Mary's in 1567, at St. Peter's in 1572, and at St. Nicholas's in 1562; and the total number of funerals annually at these churches was then only about 70; but we find no certain *data* whereby to estimate the number of inhabitants, till 1739, when they were found to amount to 9990. In 1779, according to Lowe's Agricultural Survey, there were 17,711 persons, 3556 families, and 3191 houses in the town; and the number of burials at that time averaged upwards of 650 annually. In 1793, Sir Richard Sutton surveyed the town, and found it to contain 25,000 souls. The great increase which has taken place during the last thirty years, in the three parishes of St. Mary, St. Nicholas, and St. Peter, and in the extraparochial districts called Brewhouse Yard, Standard Hill, the Park, and the Castle, will be clearly seen in the following table, together with the population of Radford and Sneinton, the two parishes which, though in the hundreds of Broxtow and Thurgarton, may be considered as suburbs of Nottingham.

POPULATION OF NOTTINGHAM AND ITS SUBURBS,

According to the Parliamentary Returns, made in the years 1801, 1811, 1821, and 1831. The three parishes form the town and county of the town, and the extra parochial places the liberties of the Castle.

NOTTINGHAM.	1801.	1811.	1821.	In July, 1831.		
	Pers.	Pers.	Pers.	Hous.	Fams.	Pers.
St. Mary's parish	22654	27371	32712	8637	8543	39539
St. Nicholas's parish	3415	3823	4117	1152	1142	5447
St. Peter's parish	2732	2839	3361	1097	1132	5220
Brewhouse Yard, (extra par.)		107	90	21	20	80
Standard Hill, the Park, and the Castle, (extra par.)	60	223	225	86	80	441
Total of Town & Castle Lib.	28861	34363	40505	10992	10917	50727
Radford par. (Broxtow hund.)	2269	3446	4806	2073	2034	9806
Sneinton par. (Thurgarton hund.)	558	967	1212	812	800	3567
Grand total of Town & Subs.	30688	38777	46523	13878	13751	64100*

The males above 20 years of age, in the parishes of St. Mary, St. Nicholas, and St. Peter, amount to 12,524, of whom 4740 are employed in manufactures, and in making machinery; 4545 in retail trade and handicraft; 720 in mercantile or professional pursuits; 1606 as porters, boatmen, and labourers; 61 occupiers of land; 172 agricultural labourers; 407 superannuated,

*. Of the 64,100 persons, 30,088 are males, and 34,112 females.

retired, or infirm; and 98 household servants. The number
of female servants amounted to 1361.

In *Radford parish*, which includes the populous villages of
New Radford, Bloomsgrove, Hyson Green, Kensington, Bobber's Mill, Aspley, and Old Radford, the number of families
is 2034, of whom 1486 are employed in trade and manufactures,
37 in agriculture, and 528 otherwise engaged or unemployed.
The household servants amount to 15 males and 210 females.

Sneinton parish includes Old Sneinton, New Sneinton, Middle Sneinton, and the Hermitage, and has 900 males upwards
of 20 years of age.

Within four miles of the town are the following populous
parishes, viz. Basford, containing 6341 inhabitants; Lenton,
3077; Gedling, 2500; Beeston, 2468; and Arnold, 4054;
swelling the total population within that circuit to upwards of
80,000 souls.

Much of this increase has arisen from the introduction, improvement and great extension of the lace manufacture, which
has lately outsripped in importance the ancient staple trade of
the town. Some portion of it, however, must be attributed to
the healthy situation, and to the general salubrity of the air,
which is less contaminated with smoke and other offensive
vapours, than that of any large manufacturing town in the
kingdom, owing to there being in the neighbourhood but few
mills and factories where machinery is propelled by the agency
of *steam*,—most of the cotton and silk used here being spun in distant parts of the county, and in Lancashire;—and all the stocking frames and twist-net machines, being worked by manual labour, and generally in the dwellings of the operatives, which are
provided with large upper rooms for that purpose. The aggregate power of all the steam engines used within two miles of
the town, only amounts to the strength of about 700 horses,
nearly one-half of which is employed in the town water-works
and in the few collieries of the neighbouring parishes. A large
portion of the increase which has taken place in the population
of this and other parts of the kingdom, during the present century has resulted from the introduction of *vaccine innoculation*,
for the discovery of which, Dr. Jenner, in 1802, received a
Parliamentary grant of £10,000.

Amongst the numerous instances of LONGEVITY which have
occurred in Nottingham, we may enumerate the following, viz.:
Henry Ward, who died in 1736, at the advanced age of 109
years, and Mary Ryley, Mrs. Freeland, Mr. Crampton, George
Tacy, and Goody Gedling, who died during the succeeding
five years, each aged one hundred. During says "Goody
Ryley, was, during the last years of her life, a pauper in St.
Mary's workhouse, and when she was not pleased with her
usage there, she would every now and then, ramble on foot to
London, where she had some children; and if they gave her

the least offence, she would as readily trot back again to Nottingham.

ANCIENT HISTORY.

Nottingham, is certainly one of the most ancient towns in
England, but its origin, which has given rise to a great variety
of conjectures, is hid in the impenetrable gloom, which is cast
over the early ages of the aborigines of Britain. Its name is
evidently softened from the Saxon appellation *Snottengham*,
which was given to it on account of its early inhabitants, dwelling in caves and subterraneous passages, cut in the yielding
rock on which the present town is built. Stukely, in his Itinerary, says, " one may easily guess Nottingham to have been an
ancient town of the Britons. As soon as they had proper tools,
they fell to work upon the rocks, which every where offer themselves so commodious to make houses in," and he doubts not
that there were a considerable number of these excavated dwellings. John Rouse, a monk of Warwick, and canon of Osney,
in his history addressed to King Henry VII., relates a long
and doubtful story of the antiquity of Nottingham, 980 years
before the Christian era; at which time he says, *King Ebranc*[*]
built a town upon "Dolorus hill," so called from the extreme grief of the Britons, in consequence of a great slaughter
of them by King Humber, in the reign of King Albanact.
Leland, in his *Collectanea, vol.* 3, *p.* 43, quotes a monkish
Chronicle, which, after telling the same tale about King
Ebranc, states in another page, that Lucius, son of Helena,
caused four cities to be founded, one of which was Nottingham. This contradictory evidence caused Mr. Laird, the editor
of the Nottinghamshire portion of the Beauties of England and
Wales, to remark that " the Monkish writers were ignorant
of, or inattentive to the wholesome adage, that people of a *certain
habit* ought to have good memories."

Dr. Deering, who published his " *Nottinhamia vestus et
nova*," in 1751, indulges himself in several plausible conjectures respecting the origin of the town, of which the following is the substance. He conceives that the most which can be
supposed with a due regard to probability is, considering the
convenient situation of that part of *Sherwood Forest*, in the
immediate vicinity of the site of the present town, that several
colonies of Britons " planted themselves hereabouts, where
they were sheltered from the inclemency of the most prevalent

---

[*] *Ebranc or Ebraucus*, the son of Mempricuis, a British king, the third from
Brute, reigned about the time when David held the sceptre of Judea, and Gad,
Nathan and Asaph, prophecied in Israel. He is said to have built *Eboracum*, now
the city of York, in the year of the world, 2983, which is only about 40 years earlier
than the period at which the monk above-named states Nottingham to have been
founded by the same king.

winds of the winter season, and accommodated with the convenience of a southern aspect, and with plenty of water." Like
Dr. Stukely, he imagines, that a considerable population dwelt
here in the *rock apartments*, long before the Romans visited
the neighbourhood. He seems to lay the greater stress upon
this conjecture, in consequence of the discovery made by some
workmen employed by Lord Middleton, in 1740, to level a deep
and narrow way between the two hills called the Sand-hills
on the Derby road approaching to Chapel Bar; for when these
workmen had removed a good deal of the sandy part of the
hills, they met here and there with excavations which (upon
clearing away the sand from them,) appeared to form the
partition walls of several rooms, of different altitudes, cut out
of the solid rock. These, the Doctor thought, had no marks of
being of Roman workmanship, and he therefore considers them
as British. These remains he even considers as of higher antiquity than the excavations in the rocks on which Nottingham
stands; and having roundly asserted, (which may indeed be
true,) that the whole rock on which the town is built, is so un-
dermined and hollowed out, that it is almost a question, whether the solid contents of what is erected on the top would fill
up the cavities under ground, he comes to the conclusion, that
the sand of the place in question was brought from the Nottingham excavations, and that it would not have been lodged
upon the site of these chambers, if they had not been in a ruinous state, and therefore of considerable antiquity. He adds,
that there are other sand-hills about the town, where the same dis-
coveries have been made, which have given rise to a tradition that
the ancient town of Nottingham stood further to the northward;
and is of opinion that these straggling habitations formed no
part of the town in the Saxon times, being considerably without that wall which Edward the elder constructed for the defence of Nottingham.

The Doctor then adverts to a story of *Coilus*, a British king,
having been buried here in the year of the world, 3832, a period which in ancient chronology falls in between the destruction of Sodom and Gomorrah, and the destruction of Troy: but
though possessed of all the prejudices natural to a local historian, he acknowledges that even this is no more a proof, if
true, of the antiquity of Nottingham, than that the certainty of
some Indian huts having stood a thousand years ago on the present sites of New York and Philadelphia, would carry their antiquity back beyond the days William Penn. After all these
conjectures, we can only say, that the only thing certain is,
that the caverns of our ancient *Troglodytes*, were formed anterior to all authentic history, and of course, before the time of
the Romans, but how long they existed before that epoch, will
for ever remain a mystery.

The Roman emperor, *Antoninus*, in drawing up his Itine-

rary, through the island of Britain, seems to have been anxious
to settle both the names of places, and their distances, with
great precision; but not being gifted with prophetic powers, he has not told us, what these places would be called
in succeeding ages by the Saxons and the Normans; consequently many disputes have arisen respecting both the
stations and the roads of the Romans, and it has not been settled, whether Nottingham was, or was not occupied by the
" Lords of the Universe" as the Roman soldiers vainly designated themselves. Two learned antiquaries, Dr. Gale and Mr.
Baxter, differ materially on the subject,—the former placing
Causennis at Nottingham, and the latter asserting that Grantham is the site of that station. Mr. Baxter and his supporters
say, that there have never been any Roman coins, or urns, discovered at Nottingham, as is invariably the case at all their acknowledged stations; yet as there is sufficient proof, that there
were Roman stations within sight of the rock on which Nottingham stands, it is not likely that a place whose situation was
so commanding, and so capable of defence, would have escaped
their notice. But Dr. Gale brings further proof in support of
his opinion, that *Causennis* was our modern Nottingham; for
he shews clearly, that Causennis, or Caufennis, where the Roman changes of the word *Ceven*, from whence, in various
places, were the names of " Gofennis," " Gobannium," &c.—
Ceven being the ancient British for a cluster of rocks, and
Kaff, or *Kaou*, in the same language, signifying a cavern.
    Dr. Gale, indeed, perhaps goes too far, in supposing that
the excavations are Roman; if they had been so, it is not probable that they would have had a name latinized from the British; for there is no instance whatever, on record, in which the
Romans had adopted British words for the names of places of
their own erection. That the caverns existed, therefore, before
the Roman settlement seems beyond a doubt; it is still probable, however, that the Romans may have availed themselves of
the then existing caves, and may even have added others.
    A period of greater certainty begins in the seventh cen-
tury, at which time it is allowed by all historians, that
Nottingham was a considerable place, and had a strong
tower, for its defence, and it is certain, that, during the
Saxon heptarchy, it had the name of Snottingham, from
Snottinga, signifying caves, and *Ham*, a home or dwelling
place, or perhaps used with a plural signification. It is Dr.
Deering's opinion, that this Saxon name was doubtless given to
it, by that people, from the condition they found the neighbourhood in, before they themselves made improvements by
building. It then belonged to the kingdom of Mercia, and a
part of that kingdom took afterwards, in king Alfred's reign,
its name from this town—*Snottingham Scyre.*
    Laird says it is rather curious, that all the learned investiga-

tors of the origin of Nottingham should have overlooked a particular circumstance, which seems to throw a new light upon its state, in the Saxon times, and perhaps, for some ages previous to them. If the Saxon origin, of the name of Nottingham, is correct, may we not suppose also, that *Snottenga*, or *Snottengaton*, may have been corrupted into *Sneuton*, or *Sneinton*. If, then, there were two places existing in the Saxon times, by the names of Snottinga*ham*, and Snottenga*ton*, it is a very probable conjecture, that the spot designated by the appellative of *ton*, was more considerable than that which had only the adjunct of *ham*, inasmuch as a town is larger than a village, or hamlet. That such was the origin of the name of *Sneinton*, now a village adjoining to Nottingham, seems almost beyond a doubt, when we consider it possesses extensive caverns of an antiquity equal to those of the latter place.

From the period of the Saxon heptarchy, Nottingham seems to have increased in consequence. In Edward the Confessor's reign, immediately preceding the Norman conquest, there were 173 burgesses, and nineteen villeins, in this borough; and Earl Tosti had lands and houses here.

But, perhaps, the proper era from whence we should commence our view of the rise and progress of this place, is that period when the kingdom was settled, after the Norman accession, and the survey of *Domesday-book*, was made. From this register it appears that Hugh, the sheriff, found here 120 dwelling houses, of which the Sheriff himself possessed thirteen; Roger de Builly had eleven; William Peverel the Earl, son of Ralph Peverel, who came in with the Norman, had forty-eight tradesmen's houses, which brought thirty-six shillings per annum rent,* seven knights', and thirteen gentlemen's houses, besides eight bordars, forming, in the whole, his honour of Peverell, in the town; Ralph de Burun had twelve gentlemen's houses, and one merchant's house; one Guilbert, had four houses; Ralph Fitzherbert, eleven houses; Goisfrid de Alselyn, twenty-one houses; Acadus the priest, two houses; in the croft of the priest there were sixty houses; Richard Fresle had four houses; and in the borough ditch were twenty-three houses. At this time " the church, with all things belonging to it, was of 100 shillings annual value." The burgesses had twenty carucates of land,† and twenty bordars, and they " were

---

* It is curious to contrast this sum with the value of land in Nottingham, at the present century. In 1811, the ground for some new buildings, in a street, at the end of Smithy Row, was sold at the rate of £9 per square yard; so that three square yards, without buildings, in the year 1811, would yield as much in interest of money, as forty-eight houses, in rent, in the year 1086 !!

† These *twenty carucates* would be equal to about 1,200 acres, and may perhaps be comprised in the present *burgess lands*, which are of a similar extent. A *hide* contained about 120 acres, but the *bovate* and the *oxgang* were as much as an *ox* and a plough could cultivate, and varied from 10 to 20 acres, according to the nature of the soil.

wont to fish in the Trent, but complained that they were then prohibited." The annual rental of "Nottingham was £18 in the reign of Edward the Confessor, and £30 with £10 *de moneta* at the time of Domesday survey, which was commenced in 1080 and finished in 1086, by order of William the Conqueror. In the reign of the former king the town had 173 burgesses, nineteen *villeins*, (husbandmen) but in that of the latter, the two classes were reduced to 120.

The state of the country under the ancient Britons and under the successive dynasties of the Romans, the Saxons, the Danes, and the Normans, has already been shewn in the general survey of Nottinghamshire, therefore it is only necessary, in this portion of the work to present a faithful chronological view of the local history of the town, shewing the momentous events of which it has been the scene, and its rise and progress in the national scale of civilization and commercial importance.

The first great historical event, we find connected with it, was in the year A. D. 868, when the Danes, in the course of their frequent ravages, came to the town, in which they were immediately afterwards besieged by Buthred, the Mercian king; but, with so little prospect of success, (as the Danes had possessed themselves of a strong tower on the scite of the present castle) that he was obliged to send for assistance to Ethelred, king of the West Saxons, and Alured his brother, who, having collected a large army, proceeded towards Nottingham, and offered the invaders battle. This, however, they thought proper to decline, when the Saxon chiefs attempted to batter down the walls, but even this, they were unable to perform; and at length the Danes, starved out perhaps, agreed to conclude a peace, and return home under their leaders *Hinguar* and *Hubba*. From this time, until 940, the Danes were very troublesome to Nottingham, and the surrounding parts of Mercia; for having landed with a large army, and got military possession of all the northern parts of Britain, they left a large force there, and proceeded to Nottingham, which they took with facility, and fixed their winter quarters there. From this they were again driven by the Saxons; but again returned; and remained until the middle of the tenth century, when king Edmund made a final reconquest of the town, which in 910 had been encircled with a strong *wall* by Edward the elder.

William, the Norman Conqueror, (whom Edward the Confessor, had with his dying breath, nominated as his successor to the crown) drove Harold from the throne and subjugated the kingdom in 1066, two years after which he visited Nottingham, and built a castle on the site of an aged and ruinous tower. In parcelling out the estates of the realm amongst his followers, the Conqueror gave to his natural son, William Peverel, his castle of Nottingham, and 103 lordships in this and the adjacent counties, forming the *Honor of Peverel.* He also conferred

upon him the title of *Earl of Nottingham*,—the Saxon name of
the town, being now rendered more agreeable to the Norman
ear, by the removal of its initial (S.).

In the troublesome times of Stephen's reign, Ralph Paynell,
who was governor of the castle, and in the interest of Prince
Henry, afterwards Henry the II., invited the Earl of Gloucester
in 1140, to take possession of the town. It is recorded that
the town being thus easily taken, was plundered, and the inhabitants killed, or burnt in the churches, to which they had fled
for safety. It is also stated by Stow that one of the richest of
the inhabitants was forced by a party of the robbers to shew
them where his treasure lay; he, acccordingly, took them into
a low celler, from whence he escaped, whilst they were intent
on plunder; and, having shut the doors, set fire to his house, in
consequence of which, not only they were burnt, but the whole
town was set in flames. Nottingham met with the same misfortunes only thirteen years afterwards; for being taken by
Henry, in 1153, we are told by Leland, that the garrison retir-
ing from the city to the castle set fire to the town on their
evacuating it. It has, however, been otherwise asserted, that
this conflagration was caused by the Earl of Ferrers, in the
contests between Henry the II. and his son Henry, who came
suddenly, with a good number of horsemen to Nottingham,
which Reginald de Lucy had then in keeping for the king;
and, having taken it, burnt the town, slew the inhabitants, and
divided their goods amongst his soldiers.

After this, from whatever cause it may have proceeded, the
town of Nottingham appears to have lain in ruins, until the
kingdom became quiet by the death of Prince Henry, whom his
father had been so imprudent as to cause to be crowned during
his own life time: the inhabitants then, having some prospect
of protection for their lives and property, began to make great
exertions to restore it to its former consequence, and the king,
in order to make them amends for what they had suffered from
their loyalty, not only gave them every encouragement, and assistance, in the rebuilding of it, but also granted them a new
charter, in which he confirmed all those free customs which
they had enjoyed in the reign of Henry the I. This is a convincing proof, that Nottingham had been a corporation, for a
considerable time, before the grant of this new charter; and it
is, with great probability, supposed, that they enjoyed a market,
and paid a farm rent to the crown, some time previous. John
Earl of Morteyn, Henry's younger son, afterwards king, procured them some further privileges on being made Earl of
Nottingham; and by a new charter, which he confirmed on
coming to throne, granted all the advantages, which his father
and great-grandfather had bestowed upon them, together with
a merchant's guild.

During the contest between Richard I. and his brother John, Nottingham changed hands several times; and, on the king's return from his captivity, this castle held out a siege of several days, though the king himself besieged it in person.

Soon after, Richard called a parliament here, in which he demanded judgment against John and his accomplices; and the parliament immediately issued summonses for John, and the Barons, his friends, to appear in forty days, to answer all complaints, under pain of forfeiture on the part of John, and for the others, to stand such censure, as might be awarded against them, by the parliament. In consequence of non-compliance, Earl John incurred the forfeiture, but was soon restored by his brother; however, after coming to the crown, we find that, in his contest with the Barons, an attempt was made to deprive him of this place, by the "army of God, and the holy church," as it was then called, but without success. In 1199 he granted a charter to Nottingham.

On a subsequent occasion in 1212, John was so pressed, that, having received repeated intelligence of a plot against him, he distrusted even the officers about his person, and relying solely on the loyalty of this town, and of some foreign archers, disbanded his army, and retired here to shut himself up in the castle, where (according to Rapin) he cruelly ordered twenty-eight Welch hostages to be hanged.

In 1330 a parliament was held here, and the young king Edward passed in the night by the guidance of Sir William Eland, the governor, through a secret passage into the castle, and there apprehended in the apartment of his Queen mother, her favourite nobleman, Mortimer Earl of March, whom he brought out through the same intricate passage cut in the rock, which still bears the name of MORTIMER'S HOLE. Notwithstanding the Queen's cries to spare the gallant Mortimer, or as she is said to have exclaimed "*Bel Fitz, Bel Fitz, ayes pitie du gentill Mortimer*,"—the king sent him direct to London, where he was soon afterwards drawn and hanged on the common gallows at Tyburn as a traitor, without being heard in his defence; an unjust irregularity which brought much censure on the king, but which afterwards proved of considerable advantage to the unfortunate Earl's grandson, Roger, who obtained an act which declared this sentence to be erroneous; and his descendants, in the female line, subsequently ascended the throne of England;—Edward the fourth being the son of Anne Mortimer, Duchess of York, and Heiress of Edmund her brother, the last Earl of March.

Seven years afterwards a parliament was called together for very important purposes, and Nottingham has the honour of being the spot, from whence emanated laws that were the first foundation of England's greatness, as a manufacturing country; for here it was enacted, that whatsoever *cloth-workers of Flan-*

ders, or of other countries, would dwell, and inhabit in England, should come quietly, and peaceably, and the most convenient places should be assigned to them, with great liberties and privileges, and the king would become surety for them, until they should be able to support themselves by their several occupations. The same Parliament also passed that patriotic law, that no person should wear any foreign made cloths, with the exception of the royal family : they also prohibited the exportation of English wool.

1357. " There is a curious record of pardon in the Tower of London, granted to *Cecily Ridgeway*, who, refusing to plead guilty of murdering her husband, at Nottingham assize, A. D. 1357, was remanded back to prison, and remained *forty days without sustenance*, for which miraculous preservation she obtained this pardon under the great seal of England." Whilst the impostor, Anne Moore, so long deceived the superstitious of the enlightened age in which we write, we need not wonder that the credulity of those who legislated for our forefathers nearly five centuries ago, should have been occasionally abused by the artful and the designing.

In 1376, *Sir Peter de la Mare*, speaker of the House of Commons, was committed prisoner to Nottingham castle, by Edward III., for having made Alice Pierce, the king's mistress, the object of his reproach, for her overbearing and abandoned conduct. He remained here till after Edward's death in the following year.

A curious attempt to infringe on the *liberty of election* took place here, in the reign of Richard II., which is well worthy of notice. In 1386, the Marquis of Dublin, the royal favourite, having been dismissed in consequence of the remonstrances of Parliament, he, and some of his adherents, soon after procured access to the king, and was, in a few weeks, accompanied by the misguided monarch into Wales; where it was privately settled, that a plan for the assumption of arbitrary power should be put in force, and that the patriotic Barons, the Duke of Gloucester, the Earls of Arundel, Derby, Warwick, and Nottingham, should be the first victims, not only for the purpose of revenge, but of security. In order to insure the success of their plan, it was determined that the king should raise an army to keep those Barons in check, and that he should then call a Parliament, the elections for which should be so managed as to have none but the friends of the favourites summoned or elected, so that there would be no difficulty in passing any law which might be proposed. No sooner was every thing prepared, than Richard, with his favourites and their friends, proceeded to Nottingham, where all the sheriffs and all the judges were sent for, together with many of the principal citizens of London ; to these, when assembled, the monarch communicated his design of proceeding with an army to

I

chastise the noblemen already mentioned, and demanded of
the sheriffs, what number of troops they could raise immediately.
He then told them to permit no representatives to be chosen
for the new Parliament, that were not in the list which he
should deliver to them himself; but the sheriffs immediately
answered, that it was not possible to execute his orders; for the
people were in general so partial to those noblemen, that it
would be difficult to levy an army against them; and they con-
cluded by stating, that it would be still more difficult to deprive
the people of their right of *freely electing their representatives*
in Parliament.

The judges, however, were neither so scrupulous nor so
patriotic as the sheriffs; for they answered to the queries put to
them, " that the king was above the law;" yet, when required
to sign this opinion, they endeavoured to evade it, until forced
by the menaces of the court party. Notwithstanding this forced
submission of the judges, Richard found it impossible to do
any thing at Nottingham, and therefore returned to London.
'Tis almost unnecessary to state to those acquainted with English history, that the judges were Sir Robert Tresilian, Lord
Chief Justice of the King's Bench, who was afterwards hanged
at Tyburn; Sir Robert Belknap, Chief Justice of the Common Pleas; Sir John Holt; Sir Roger Fulthorp; Sir William
de Burgh; and John Lockton, Sergeant at Law.

In 1392, the same thrifty monarch (Richard II.) sent Sir W.
Standon, Mayor of London, and William Mansfield, and Thos.
Newington, Sheriffs of London, prisoners to Nottingham, because the city had refused to lend him £1000. He also removed the *Court of Chancery* to Nottingham, and the *Court of
King's Bench* to York, where they remained until the Lon-
doners regained their charter by satisfying the cupidity of the
royal spendthrift, who, in 1397, summoned the Peers of the
realm to meet at Nottingham, and two years afterwards was
murdered at Pontefract Castle, and his throne ascended by
Henry IV.; thus ended the reign of the Plantagenets, which
was speedily followed by the wars of the houses of York and
Lancaster, which so long deluged the kingdom in blood. In
1403, Henry IV. was at Nottingham to witness a combat. In
1429, Henry VI. constituted the town a *county of itself*, a
privilege which it had virtually enjoyed from the year 1422,
when Henry V. ordered the Nottinghamshire magistrates,
" who had heretofore acted in the town, to discontinue that
usage."

Nottingham was afterwards, in 1461, the rendezvous of Edward IV., where he collected his troops, aud caused himself to
be proclaimed king, immediately after landing at Ravenspur in
Yorkshire. Hence he marched to Newark, to attack the Duke
of Exeter, who retired on his approach. His majesty then
marched his army to Towton, in Yorkshire, where in a fatal

battle he overthrew the hopes of the house of Lancaster. In 1470, Edward issued a proclamation from his court at Nottingham, denouncing the Duke of Clarence, his brother, and the Earl of Warwick, as traitors and rebels; though he had been raised to the throne by the influence of the latter nobleman, who was commonly called the "King-maker," and who in his revenge forced Edward to fly from Nottingham, and for a time from the kingdom.

In 1485, Richard III. marched from Nottingham towards Bosworth-field, in order to decide the fate of England in his fatal contest with Henry VII.; and Henry VII. two years afterwards, (in 1487) held his council of war at Nottingham previous to the battle of Stoke.

Before the year 1503, there was not a house in Nottingham but what was *thatched* with straw or reeds, and built of wood and plaster, but in that year the Unicorn Inn, at the end of the Long-row, was tiled, "which circumstance is expressed in the writings of that house." In 1513, *Agnes Mellor* founded the Grammar School, but we shall reserve the description of this and the numerous other charities of the town for a subsequent chapter. That lascivious monarch, Henry VIII., was in the town about the year 1430, on an affair of gallantry, and obtained £147. 13s. 4d. from the corporation in aid of the war against France and Scotland.

A violent tempest, which happened here in 1558, is described by Thoroton as follows:—"All the houses of the little hamlet of Sneinton, and those of Gedling, with both their churches, were blown down; and the water and mud from the Trent was carried a quarter of a mile and cast against some trees with such amazing force that they were torn up by the roots. A child and five or six men were killed, and the hailstones which fell measured fifteen inches round." This year Richard Barnes, the last suffragan bishop of Nottingham, was installed; the bishopric having then existed twenty-four years. Many suffragan bishops were consecrated after the dissolution of the larger monasteries by Henry VIII., about A. D. 1534, but they were nearly all discontinued in the reign of Mary, who again established the Roman Catholic religion, which, on the accession of her sister Elizabeth, again gave place to the Protestant faith, not however till many sacrifices had been made, and much blood spilled on both sides.

In 1589, the *Stocking frame*, to which Nottingham owes the greater part of its wealth and consequence, was invented by the Rev. William Lee, M.A, a native of Woodborough in Nottinghamshire. It afterwards received many improvements, as will be shewn in the history of the hosiery and lace trades in this volume.

1591 was remarkable for an uncommon drought, which continued till the summer of the following year, when the Trent and other rivers were almost without water. An act passed in 1595 for erecting *workhouses* for the poor, and another, passed in 1691, provided for the *relief of the poor*, and the appointment of *overeeers*.

In 1607, a dispute arose about the disposal of the town's money. The aldermen contending that they had a right to sit in council and vote at the disposal of the bridge money, school lands, &c. The council opposed them, and referred the matter to the judges, who determined that the aldermen had no right to vote on such occasions; but they have since continued to do so. At this time the *council* was reduced to 24, of whom six were to be elected by the burgesses at large, and called junior councilmen. King James was several times in Nottingham about the year 1615. The County Hall was built in 1648.

CIVIL WARS.—In the fatal contentions between the prerogatives of the crown and the privileges of Parliament, in the reign of Charles I., Nottingham was the place were the royal standard was first unfurled, though the town was soon afterwards garrisoned by the Parliamentarians, who retained possession of it during the whole of this intestine war, which so long deluged the kingdom in the blood of its inhabitants. The principal causes which led to this distraction of the country, were the levying of ship money and the duty of tonnage and poundage, without the sanction of Parliament; and the cruel proceedings of that secret and inquisitorial court, called the *Star Chamber*. There also prevailed in the nation a disposition and a strong leaning to republican, in preference to kingly government; and religion was too often made the stalking-horse to avarice and ambition. From these combined causes the elements of government were thrown into disorder, and they never perfectly reassumed their proper station till the glorious revolution of 1688, although many patriotic addresses were sent by the people of this and other counties to the Parliament and to the king, praying for an amicable adjustment of their differences.

In 1642, Clarendon says, the King "published a proclamation, by which he required all men who could bear arms to repair to him at Nottingham, by the 25th of August, on which day he would set up his royal standard there, which all good subjects were obliged to attend." Previous to this, his Majesty left London while the Parliament was sitting, and went to York, where he issued his famous commission of array to the respective counties, appointing Lord-Lieutenants and persons of distinction in each, to array, train, and muster the people. Some of his advisers proposed York or Warrington, in preference to Nottingham, for the erection of the royal standard; but the King chose the latter place, where he thought he would be nearer to some friends, who were stirring in his favour in the south and west. He accordingly came to Nottingham, a few days previous to the 25th, and having gone towards Coventry with a few troops, the gates were shut against him, and he found it necessary, in consequence of the appearance of some of the Parliamentarian forces, to return to Nottingham on the 24th. "According to proclamation, on the 25th August, the standard was erected about six o'clock in the evening of a very tempestu- ous day. The King himself, with a small train, rode to the top of the Castle-hill; Varney, the Knight-Marshal, who was standard-bearer, carrying the standard, which was then erected on that place, with little other ceremony than the sound of drums and trumpets,—melancholy men observed many ill pre- sages at the time. The standard was blown down the same night it had been set up, by a very strong and unruly wind, and could not be fixed again for a day or two." The flag used on this occasion was inscribed "Give Cæsar his due," and a herald proclaimed that his Majesty sought only to suppress the rebel- lion raised against him; "that his military arms were blest; that he would govern according to the known laws of the land; and if he failed in these things, he would expect no relief from man, nor protection from heaven." Charles, however, soon found that the standard, when formally erected on the ground now called Standard-hill, possessed no more charms than it had done on the three preceding days, during which it had waved over the old tower of the castle; for at a general muster, about the middle of the following month, his force only amounted to near 1200 men, the greater part of whom had accompanied him from the north; he consequently left Nottingham, which was speedily garrisoned by the Parliament, who entrusted its go- vernment to Colonel JOHN HUTCHINSON, whose memoirs, written by his widow, were published about thirty years ago, by one of his descendants. The Colonel, in spite of all the royal offers of wealth and distinction, remained a firm and pa- triotic friend of the people; and though he was so unfortunate as to be chosen one of the judges who tried and signed the death- warrant of Charles I., he deserved not the odium of those who maintain in practice, as the English constitution asserts in theory, that "Kings can do no wrong," though the persecution which he experienced after the restoration, was no greater than might be expected at the hands of a son standing in power over those whom he considered as the instigators of his father's mar- tyrdom. It is not the business of this history to take a political view of these calamitous times, we shall, therefore, confine ourselves to a brief narration of those events which are con nected with Nottingham and its neighbourhood, as recorded by Rushworth, Whitlock, and Deering.

In 1643, Captain Hotham, son of the celebrated Sir John Hotham, governor of Hull, was brought prisoner to Notting- ham, charged with carrying on a correspondence with the roy- alists, for which offence both he and his father were tried by a

court-martial, and executed at Hull, in 1645, "The same
year, (1643,) about Christmas, Colonel Hutchinson, governor
of Nottingham, acquainted the Parliament with an offer of the
Earl of Newcastle, to pay him £10,000, and to make him a
Lord and governor of the castle, to him and his heirs, if he
would deliver it to him for the King; which Hutchinson refused." During the following year, a paltry kind of warfare
was carried on against this incorruptible governor, by the royal
garrison of Newark, at the commencement of which he took 70
prisoners, and slew Captain Thimbleby, the leader of the New-
arkers. Shortly after, a detachment of the Newark garrison,
having come rather too near Nottingham, to levy contributions,
they were pursued by a party of the Nottingham troops, who
took several prisoners, but in their turn were routed by a rein-
forcement of the enemy, and escaped with the loss of twenty-
eight horsemen and two officers.

In 1645, such serious disputes took place between the garrison
and the town committee, that Parliament was obliged to refer
them to a committee of both houses, a measure evidently necessary, as during these intestine broils in the town, a party of
horse had stormed a fort upon Trent bridge, and put forty men
to the sword. From this fort, however, they were soon afterwards driven by two detachments from Nottingham and Leicester. In the same year, the Scotch army was at Nottingham,
whence it was ordered to the siege of Newark, where the unfortunate King placed himself under its protection, and was
afterwards conveyed to Newcastle-upon-Tyne, where he was
delivered to his merciless enemies, in consideration of the sum
of £200,000, paid to the crafty Scotchmen by the English Parliament, and a promise of £200,000 more, to be paid in two
moieties. On June 30th, Colonel Hutchinson took sixty horse
and forty-eight prisoners; and on October 4th, £1000 was paid
to the Nottingham cavalry, for fighting so gallantly at the battle
of Chester.

In 1647, February 13th, Charles I. was brought through
Nottingham, on his way to London. General Sir Thomas
Fairfax stopped the King's horse near the town, and having
alighted he kissed his Majesty's hand, "and afterwards mounted
and discoursed with the King as they passed to Nottingham;—
for, though the General was one of the most active enemies of
the royalists, he had more honour and sympathy than to wound
the feelings of fallen Majesty with taunts and rebukes." In July,
the Nottingham troops and the forces in the north, published
a declaration of their adherence to the army of General
Fairfax.

In January, 1648, the garrison of Nottingham consisted only
of 100 men, commanded by Captain Poulton, who surprised
and took prisoners in the town several disguised royalists,

amongst whom was Sir Marmaduke Langdale, and ten other gentlemen.

In 1649, after Cromwell had secretly solicited and contrived the King's death, the garrison of Nottingham was disbanded, and *Lawrence Collin,* who had long been a gunner at the castle, commenced the business of a woolcomber in the town, but not being a freeman, he was greatly annoyed by the corporation, till Cromwell wrote a letter in his favour, and ordered that, as he had faithfully served the Commonwealth, he should be allowed to follow his calling in the town,' for the maintenance of himself and family. After this, Collin lived in quiet, and laid the foundation of a thriving family, which intermarried with the family of George Langford, an eminent surgeon, who held a commission in the Parliament army, and was Mayor of Nottingham in 1688. Betwixt the years 1648 and 1672, money was so scarce that many of the tradesmen in the town issued copper halfpennies, and other local coins.

In 1650, General Fairfax's regiment and train of artillery marched through the town to the north.

In 1655, the framework knitters petitioned Cromwell to incorporate them by charter, but the Protector did not answer their prayer.

In 1656, Colonel Hacker apprehended several conspirators, in Nottinghamshire and Leicestershire, who declared themselves to be "in arms against the *tyrant Cromwell.*" The death of Cromwell, and the abdication of his son Richard, were followed in 1661 by the restoration of Charles II., who soon raised monarchy and episcopacy to the greatest splendour. The bishops were allowed to resume their seats in the House of Peers, and an Act of Uniformity was passed, requiring of all clergymen, episcopal ordination, canonical obedience, and a general assent to every thing contained in the Book of Common Prayer. For not conforming to this act, more than 2000 clergymen were deprived of their preferments in the church; thus originated nonconformity, or protestant dissent; for prior to this time, the Puritans had remained members of the establishment, though labouring to promote a further reformation. The ejected ministers suffered much under the operation of several severe laws, amongst which were the Conventicle, the Oxford, the Corporation, and the Test Acts, all of which are happily now abolished,—the two former being annulled by the Toleration Act, passed in 1689, but the two latter were not repealed till 1828, a few months before the passing of the Catholic Emancipation Bill.

In 1662, the three nonconformist ministers of Nottingham, viz. Whitlock, Reynolds, and Barret, were ejected for not reading the Common Prayer in the church. In 1665, they were seized in a meeting-house at Colwick, and suffered a long imprisonment. They settled at Nottingham in 1651, in consequence of an invitation from the churchwardens and principal inhabitants. Dr. Calamy says, while living "they studied together, lived together, and preached together!"

During the year 1667, Nottingham was visited by the *plague,* which made much greater ravages in the higher than in the lower part of the town, owing it is said to the effluvia arising from the tan-yards, of which there were then no fewer than 47 on the banks of the Leen.

In 1681, the *Corporation charter* was surrendered to the Ministers of Charles II., by the Mayor "and his party," which caused great dissatisfaction amongst the rest of the burgesses; though a new charter was received in its place. At the next election for a Mayor, a riotous contest arose, in which "the *new chartermen* elected William Toplady, and the *old,* Wm. Greaves,"—the former, however, prevailed, after much tumult.

In 1687, James II. attempted to new model the corporation, and to reserve to himself the power of electing and removing the members of that body; six of whom he displaced by a writ of *quo warranto.* In the succeeding reign, which commenced in the following year, the town received a full confirmation of all its rights, privileges, and immunities.

James II. was strongly attached to the Catholic faith, and soon discovered his intention to complete the fabric of despotism begun by his predecessor. The nation taking the alarm, called in the Prince of Orange, and brought about the glorious revolution of 1688, in which Nottingham took an active part; for, Deering, who wrote in 1751, says "There are men now living who well remember that the Duke of Devonshire,* the Earl of Stamford, Lord Howe, and other noblemen, and abundance of gentry of the county of Nottingham, coming to the town and going to meet one another at their respective inns, daily increasing in numbers, till the arrival of Lord Delamere with about 500 horse at the Feather's Inn, whither all the rest of the noblemen and gentlemen went to meet him: the people of the town were unacquainted with the result of all these consultations, till Lord Delamere having a mind to try the disposition of the populace, on a sudden ordered the trumpets to sound to arms, giving out that the King's forces were within four miles of Nottingham, whereupon the whole town was in alarm, multitudes who had horses mounted and accoutred themselves with such arms as they had, whilst others in vast numbers on foot appeared; some with firelocks, some with swords, some with other weapons, even pitchforks not excepted;—and being told of the necessity of securing the passage over the Trent, they immediately drew all the boats that were then at hand, to the north side of the river, and with them, and some timber and barrels on the wharf, and all the frames of the market-stalls,

* He was then only *Earl* of Devonshire, but was created a Duke in 1694.

raised a strong barricado. Lord Delamere, well pleased with the readiness of the people, sent his men and some officers to the Prince of Orange, but himself with a few officers staid till next day, being Saturday, (the principal market) when he, the Duke of Devonshire, Lord Howe, &c. appeared at the Malt Cross, and in face of a full market, declared to the people, the danger their religion and liberty were in, under the arbitrary proceedings of the King, and that providence had sent his highness the Prince of Orange, under God, to deliver them from popery and slavery, and give them a free Parliament! Their speeches were followed by the shouts of the multitude who cried out *a free Parliament! a free Parliament!* This done, Lord Delamere departed to follow his troops, whilst the Duke and Lord Howe made it known that they were for raising horse in defence of their liberty, and would enlist such as were willing to serve in the glorious cause; whereupon upwards of one hundred entered the same day." The Princess Anne, the King's favourite daughter, having resolved to leave her father and take part with the prevailing side, departed privately from court, and went direct to Nottingham, accompanied by several ladies of distinction, and the Bishop of London, the Earl of Dorset, and a guard of 40 horsemen, which, on their arrival was strengthened with 200 of the Duke of Devonshire's troops. Hence she went to Oxford where she was met by Prince George of Denmark, at the head of a detachment of the Prince of Orange's forces. James soon afterwards left the kingdom, and William III. was placed on the throne, to which, Anne succeeded in 1702, to the general satisfaction of all parties. In 1707, Queen Anne granted the stewardship of the Peverel Court to Sir Thomas Willoughby, Bart., and his heirs.

In 1715, when that fruitless rebellion broke out, which had for its object the reinstatement of the Stuart family, there were but few partisans of that dynasty left in Nottingham, though Thomas Hawksley, the mayor, was committed to the house of correction, by one of the aldermen, " for having drank success to the Pretender, on his bare knees in his own house." This jacobite mayor kept the house then called the Eagle and Child Inn, at the north-west corner of Chapel Bar. He afterwards instituted three suits against the alderman who signed his commitment, with the hope of recovering damages for false imprisonment; "but the only recompence he got was that of having to pocket the disgrace, and to pay costs, which amounted to more than £2000."

In 1720, whilst the Duke of Newcastle "kept openhouse at the castle," John Chambers, a gingerbread baker, in a fit of inebriation, rambled from the paved yard upon the verge of the rocky precipice, down which he fell, above 110 feet, into a garden near the river Leen, without receiving much injury!

In 1724, the *town-clerk's office* took fire, and many of the Corporation records were destroyed. In 1736, during a great *flood*, the houses near the Leen were two feet deep in water; in the month of May, 104 persons who had died of the *small pox* were buried in St. Mary's church-yard, and so fatal was that malady during the year, that the burials exceeded the births by 380.

1731, the mayor, Thomas Trigge, placed a woman in the CUCKSTOOL for prostitution, and left her to the mercy of a foolish mob, who ducked her so severely that she died soon after, in consequence of which, the mayor was prosecuted and the ancient instrument of punishment destroyed.

During the rebellion of 1745, when a second unsuccessful attempt was made by the House of Stuart to regain the throne lost by the bigotry and tyranny of its ancestors, Thoroton says " but little occurred at Nottingham more than at other places, near which the forces of Prince Charles approached. Some, however, were panic struck at their so extraordinarily advancing into the heart of the country, and others friendly to the cause, shewed signs of friendly intentions, but very few of them indications of courage ; very few joined the daring little host of Scotchmen." However, the town supplied many recruits for the *Duke of Kingston's Light Horse*, which did so much execution at the battle of Culloden, where it is said three butchers of Nottingham killed fourteen rebels. This regiment was raised by a subscription amounting to £8526. 10s. 6d., of which sum the Dukes of Kingston and Newcastle contributed £1000 each, and the Duke of Norfolk, and Lords Byron, Middleton, Sutton, Cavendish, and Howe, with other persons of distinction in the country, about £200 each. *Wade's regiment* consisting of 500 Dutch, and 200 English infantry, with sixteen pieces of cannon, two mortars, and 200 artillerymen, arrived at Nottingham on the 13th of October, and proceeded next day to meet the rebels, who were completely overthrown in the early part of the following year.

During a remarkable storm in May, 1749, hailstones fell, measuring four inches in circumference. In 1755, the northern lights, or *Aurora Borealis*, were frequently seen in this neighbourhood, as they were afterwards at the commencement of the American war, when the superstitious believed them to be the forerunners of disastrous events. In 1758, acts were obtained for making turnpike roads from Nottingham to Derby, Grantham and Alfreton. The Nottingham and Loughborough road was repaired under an act passed in 1738.

On September 22d, 1761, in honour of the *Coronation of George III. and Queen Charlotte*, Nottingham joined in the national festivity. The morning was ushered in by the ringing of bells, and after divine service, a large and splendid procession paraded the streets, headed by the Corporation in their robes of office, and followed by the company of *woolcombers*, dressed in Holland shirts, black breeches, white stockings, and wool wigs, with sashes and cockades also of wool, and having one of their order mounted on horseback, and attired so as to represent the famous *Bishop Blaize*, the patron saint Armenia, who is said to have first discovered the art of woolcombing. There were public dinners at all the inns, and the indigent were plentifully regaled in large booths erected in the streets. At night the town was brilliantly illuminated, and there was a grand display of fireworks in the market place.

THE BITER BIT.—In 1762, a framework-knitter, residing near Nottingham, fell into the fatal snare which he had laid for his unoffending wife. Having taken home a piece of veal, he ordered his wife to roast it for dinner by twelve o'clock; but he not coming home at the time, she set it by untouched. At four o'clock he came home, and brought a beef steak, which he ordered to be dressed for his dinner, saying he should prefer it to the veal. It was accordingly cooked by the wife, and when he had eaten part of it, feeling himself unwell, he anxiously enquired what she had fried it in? to which she answered "the *veal dripping:*" "Then," said he, "I am a dead man; for having a mind to poison you, I rubbed the veal over with arsenic." He expired shortly after; and the surgeon who examined the veal declared that it retained as much poison as would destroy a hundred persons.

At the Goose Fair, in 1764, there was a tumultuous riot, on account of the high price of cheese, which was selling at from 28s. to 30s. per cwt. The violence of the people burst forth like a torrent, in the open fair;—cheeses were rolled down Wheeler-gate and Peck-lane in abundance, and the Mayor, in his attempt to restore the peace, was knocked down with one in the Market-place. The riot act was read; a detachment of the 15th Dragoons was called in, many of the rioters were taken prisoners, and one innocent man was shot by the military.

In 1770, there was great rejoicing here, on account of the liberation of John Wilkes, Esq. the champion of the people's liberties. In June this year, Dominick Lazarus walked twenty-five times round the race-course (upwards of fifty miles) in 10¾ hours. The grand stand was built in 1777; and during the same year, some workmen, whilst digging on Standard-hill, found a number of human bones, along with a dagger, and a copper token dated 1669. The *Nottinghamshire militia* were embodied in 1775, and first marched out of the county in 1778, when they went to Hull. On February 12th, 1780, was laid the first stone of that house of mercy, the Nottingham General Hospital. On July 30th, 1784, the Wilford ferry-boat was upset, and six persons were drowned. In August, 1785, the large mace was stolen out of the Mayor's house by two thieves,

who were detected in consequence of their not knowing how to
separate the gold from the silver, after they had melted it down.

WATER SPOUT.—A most extraordinary natural phenomenon
took place here in 1785, which has been considered as perhaps
one of the largest water spouts ever seen in this country. It
happened on the first of November, at four o'clock in the afternoon, when it was first seen proceeding from a dense cloud,
apparently about a quarter of a mile to the southward of the
Trent, and moving slowly towards it; and it was remarked,
that the branches of the trees, over which it passed, were bent
downwards to the ground. As the cloud came nearer to the
river, it appeared to be strongly attracted by it, and when it
crossed did not seem more than thirty or forty feet from the
surface of the water, which was violently agitated, and flew
upwards to a great height in every direction. Some persons
who saw it from the Trent bridge, then only about 300 yards
distant, mistook it at first for a column of thick smoke rising
from a warehouse by the Trent side, which they supposed to
be on fire; but they were soon undeceived, and now beheld
with astonishment a large black inverted cone, terminating
nearly in a point, and in which they perceived very plainly, as
they afterwards said, a whirling spiral motion, whilst a rumbling noise like thunder was heard at a distance. By the description which those people gave of it, (and indeed they may
be supposed to have examined it coolly, whilst they supposed it
to be only a column of smoke,) the middle of the cone appeared
nearly twenty feet in diameter. After passing the river, it ascended slowly and majestically in a north-east direction; and
nothing coming within the limits of its electric powers, until it
came over Sneinton, it there first began its devastation, taking
the thatch from several barns and cottages, and tearing up some
apple trees by the roots, one of which was four feet in circumference, yet was broken short off near the ground, and the
trunk and branches carried several yards. A barn, nearly thirty
yards long, was levelled with the ground; the adjoining house
was unroofed, and otherwise much shattered; a sycamore in
the yard, which measured nearly two yards in circumference,
was torn up; in short, nothing could resist the impetuosity of
its action; and the rain falling heavily at the time, joined to the
roaring noise of the spout, and aided by the *novelty* of the phenomenon, produced among the spectators a scene of terror and
confusion which, they acknowledged, was not easy to be described. It was stated, also, that in a tavern in the outskirts
of the village, it tore off part of the roof, whilst the people
within were almost all of them seized with a painful sensation
in the head, which lasted some hours; and the spout, in passing
over the adjoining close, where a number of people were collected, it being the usual statute for hiring servants, afforded
rather a ludicrous scene, wherein hucksters, stalls, baskets,

&c. were all thrown into confusion, and some of the people hurled with great violence against the hedge, but happily without any serious accident. One boy, indeed, about fourteen years of age, is said to have been actually carried over the hedge into an adjoining field, but without being injured. Some flashes of light were observed in its passing the fields; and as the cloud passed over the hill, opposite to the tavern, the spout was observed to contract and expand alternately, as if it had been attracted and repelled by some extraneous force. It continued about twenty minutes, and was accurately described in the Gentleman's Magazine of 1785, from which we quote.

On May 12, 1788, a serious riot took place, in consequence of the high price of meat; the doors and shutters in the shambles were taken into the Market-place and burnt, along with many of the butchers' books, and much meat was carried away; but the conciliatory interference of the magistrates happily quelled the tumult without any lives being lost. On June 7th, *Lieutenant Bright*, of the Nottinghamshire Militia, was burnt to death in his bed-room. It is said that he first introduced into the town " the fashion of wearing *braces* to the breeches."

In 1789, Richard Butler was chosen mayor, agreeable to a writ of *mandamus* issued from the Court of King's Bench.— The burgesses insisted upon their right to vote, but were overruled by reading the charter of Henry VIII.

A great *cricket match* was played on Nottingham forest in 1791, betwixt eleven of the Nottingham club, backed by Colonel Churchill, and eleven noblemen and gentlemen of the Mary-lebonne club, headed by the Earl of Winchilsea. Though the playing of the former excited the admiration of their opponents, they had no chance of success. The late Earl of Winchilsea, the late Duke of Dorset, and the late Sir Horace Man, were members of the famous Hambledon club, and about this time assembled at the Star and Garter, London, for the express purpose of settling a new code of laws, by which the game of cricket has since been regulated. The Town-Hall was rebuilt this year, during which a riot was created by the "two-needle stocking makers," in opposition to some new regulations adopted by their employers; but it was quelled without much mischief, by the Oxford Blues, who, in return for their services, gained the hatred and contempt of the workmen, and on leaving the town soon afterwards, were rewarded, whilst passing the deepcut road at Hollowstone, with showers of odoriferous perfumes brought from the neighbouring privies, and poured upon their heads by the insulting people, planted upon the rock above them.

On March 2d, 1792, an alarming shock of an earthquake was felt in the midland counties, but was most severe at Nottingham, where many of the inhabitants fled from their houses, which they expected would fall upon them. The shock, which

K

happened about nine o'clock in the evening, was preceded by a "rumbling noise like the rolling of a cannon ball on a boarded floor." Happily no mischief was done. In May, an act was obtained for cutting a *canal* from Nottingham to Cromford; and four years afterwards, another act was passed for improving the Trent navigation.

In 1793, whilst the workmen were digging the foundation of a cotton-mill, near Poplar-place, a great quantity of hazel nuts were found, in a perfect state, two feet below the surface.

During the American and the French revolutionary wars, Nottingham, like many other manufacturing towns, was much agitated by political animosities; but to record the ebullitions and outrages of party spirit is an unpleasant task; we shall, therefore, confine ourselves to historical fact, without animadversion. Throsby, the most moderate of all the local historians that have noticed these unhappy disturbances, says "the year 1794 was marked by the loyalty of the inhabitants of the town and county, in support of that constitution which Englishmen so much admire. Four troops of Yeomanry Cavalry were raised out of the most respectable inhabitants, similar to what was done at other places; their clothing scarlet and buff; their commander Anthony Hardolph Eyre, Esq., of Grove, near Retford. None showed more loyalty on this occasion, by way of subscription, than a club in Nottingham, called the Loyal society." A liberal subscription was raised here during the same year, for the purpose of providing extra warm clothing for the British troops on the continent. A few of the *democrats*, in opposition to the loyalists, who had joined the Volunteer corps for the defence of their country, repaired early every morning for some time to Sneinton plain, where they received instructions in the military exercise from a discarded drill-sergeant, using, for want of muskets, sticks, which were sarcastically called "*wooden guns*." On July 2d, 1794, a serious disturbance was occasioned in the town, by a party of democrats showing signs of pleasure on the arrival of some disagreeable news from the continent, which so enraged the loyalists, that they ducked several of them in the river Leen, and committed other violent outrages on the persons and property of those whom, in their mistaken zeal, they considered as jacobinical enemies of their country. During the night, they set fire to some outworks of Mr. Dennison's cotton-mill, in which some of the opposite party had taken shelter, and in their defence, it is said, had fired upon the mob. The vigilance of the magistrates and their friends, however, assisted by the light horse from the barracks, prevented further mischief—except the burning of some premises not of any great value; but a scene of ducking and disorder appeared again on the following day, and was continued until the popular ebullition subsided.

In February, 1795, a frost of seven weeks was succeeded by

a rapid thaw, which occasioned the greatest flood in the Trent ever remembered by the oldest persons then living. The damage done on the banks of the Trent and its tributary streams was estimated at £1,000,000. All the inhabitants of the low grounds near the river suffered greatly in this overwhelming inundation, which swept away cattle, sheep, carts, waggons, furniture, &c. and did much damage to the bridges at Nottingham and other places, owing partly to the immense bodies of ice which were carried down the raging torrent. So high was the water at Nottingham, that it was three feet deep in many of the houses in Narrow-marsh and the Meadow-platts, where some of the inhabitants were kept prisoners in their upper rooms during two days and nights. The losses of many of the sufferers were afterwards alleviated by the subscriptions of their more fortunate neighbours. In February, 1809, there was another great flood, during which the water again entered the houses in Narrow-marsh, but the damage was trifling compared with that of 1795.

On April 18th, 1795, there was a riot at Nottingham, in consequence of the high price of provisions; but the Yeomanry and a troop of heavy Dragoons soon restored order, by seizing thirteen of the most active disturbers of the peace.

In January, 1796, wheat sold for 12s. or 13s. per bushel, and, during the succeeding fifteen years, it was several times as high as 20s. and 21s. per bushel. The first house in New Radford was built in 1796, by Benjamin Darker, a needle maker of Nottingham.

In February, 1797, the suspension of cash payments at the Bank of England, produced serious consequences in all the manufacturing districts; a great many of the workmen of this town and neighbourhood were thrown out of employment, and the ordinary business of the town could not be carried on until the banks issued a quantity of *seven-shillings tickets*. In the following month, numerously signed petitions were sent from the town, praying his Majesty to discharge his Ministers, whom the people considered as the authors of the national distress, by plunging the country in an unnecessary and expensive war.— The canal from the Trent to Grantham was opened this year, during which there died in St. Mary's workhouse, a *woman* who had many years lived as one of the masculine gender, had been groom to Sir Harry Harper, and had figured on the turf under the name of *Jockey John*; the deception was only discovered by a *post-mortem* examination. The Nottingham Volunteer Infantry was raised this year, consisting of three companies, under the command of Lieut.-Colonel Elliott, Major Hooley, and Captain Statham. The Burton and Clifton Volunteer companies acted in concert with those of Nottingham, under Lieut.-Col. Smith. Their uniform was a dark blue jacket, turned up with scarlet, and trimmed with gold lace;

L. of C.

white pantaloons, short gaiters, and a light horseman's helmet with white feathers. They were disembodied in 1802, in consequence of the peace of Amiens.

In 1799, during the race week, the Earl of Strafford died at the White Lion Inn, where he had arrived on the evening before, for the purpose of attending the races ; he was found dead in bed at eight o'clock in the morning.

1800.—In April, there was another riot about the high price of provisions, but it was suppressed before much damage was done. In August, George Caunt, a reputable hair-dresser who had been charged with stealing a set of window curtains from the house of a dancing-master, shot George Ball, the constable, whilst attempting to apprehend him. The unfortunate officer died on the spot, and the murderer was taken next day at Alfreton, but being determined not to survive his fame, he poisoned himself two days afterwards, in the town gaol; and, pursuant to the coroner's inquest, was buried on the Sand-hills near the Derby road, but his body was removed in the night by his friends, to the Baptist burial-ground. A handsome subscription was raised for the family of the murdered constable. The enormous high price of bread created a serious riot, which commenced on Sunday night, August 31st, and was continued during the two succeeding days; the houses of many of the bakers were attacked, and several granaries were broken open ;. "and it was really distressing to see with what famine-impelled eagerness many a mother bore off the corn in her apron to feed her famished children." On the Tuesday, a most awful storm of thunder and lightning finally dispersed the riotous mobs, who previously had no sooner been driven from one place by the military, than they assembled in another. In October, owing to the avarice of the great land owners and the monopolising corn factors, bread rose to a higher price than it had ever been known during the worst times of England's sufferings, and many persons died from absolute want. To alleviate the distress of the poor, subscriptions were raised by the benevolent, and a soup-house was opened in Goose-gate. Amongst the most generous friends of the indigent, at this alarming crisis, were Messrs. Davison and Hawksley, of Arnold, who purchased an immense quantity of corn, and not only sold it to the poor at less than prime cost, but ground it gratis at their own worsted-mill, in which they erected stones, &c. for the purpose —there being at the time a lack both of wind and water at the corn-mills in the neighbourhood. They also ground the corn purchased by the charitable subscribers of Nottingham, and carried it in their own waggons to the Market-place, free of expense. For these benevolent acts, they received the blessings of thousands ; and Mr. Hawksley was presented with the freedom of the town, as also was Mr. Towle, of Broxtow, who regularly brought corn to market, and sold it at a moderate price, during this distressful period.

In 1801, the parishioners of St. Mary's revived their long-dormant right of chusing a churchwarden alternately with the vicar. On November 29th, Mr. Dennison's cotton-mill, at Penny-foot-stile was burnt down.

On May 7th, 1803, the *bill* which authorises the magistrates of Nottinghamshire to interfere with the police of the " Town and county of the town of Nottingham," received the royal assent. It originated in a petition sent to the House of Commons in the preceding year, by D. C. Coke, Esq., against the return of Joseph Birch, Esq.,—the former complaining that he had been disappointed of his election at the late contest, by the corporate magistrates not doing their duty, in suppressing the riotous behaviour of the people. In consequence of this act, which is entitled the " NOTTINGHAM ELECTION AND POLICE BILL," Mr. Birch was expelled the House, and in the following year, he lost his election in a contest with Mr. Coke, which cost the town £1406. 17s. This was the first time that the merits of any election petition from Nottingham had been tried in the House of Commons since the year 1701, when the House determined that George Gregory, Esq. had been returned by corrupt and illegal means, and that Robert Sacheverill, Esq. was duly elected. The House at the same time declared that the right of election was vested in the burgesses, and the freeholders of 40s. per annum. In 1803, the first house at *New Sneinton* was erected; and a new regiment of Volunteer Infantry was raised in Nottingham.

In 1806, the mayor and town-clerk were deputed to attend the funeral of the *Right Hon. Charles James Fox*, who was interred on the 11th of October. This year Lieut. Brown, of the 83d regiment, a youth of seventeen, in the recruiting service, was killed in a *duel* with Ensign Butler, of the 36th, then quartered in the town. The coroner's jury returned a verdict of " wilful murder," in consequence of which, Butler and the two seconds absconded and were never brought to justice.

In 1807, a party of the parishioners of St. Mary and St. Nicholas parishes, applied to Parliament for a Bill to erect an *Incorporated House of Industry* for the reception of all the paupers in the district, extending 12 miles round Nottingham. The public at large were not acquainted with the existence of this " hole and corner job" till the Bill was on the eve of being read a second time;—previous to which, however, Parliament was dissolved, and such detestation was expressed againt the Bill by the great body of the parishioners, that its authors never again brought it forward. In November, the corporation presented *Lord Holland* (the son of the late Right Hon. C. J. Fox,) with the freedom of the town, and in 1809, he was elected to the office of *Recorder.*

. In 1808.—On February 11th, the roads about the town were from six to twelve feet deep in snow. On the 6th of April, Robert Calvin, a Scotchman, was exposed one hour in the PILLORY for assaulting two female children. An exhibition of this kind had not taken place for seventy years before, and its novelty consequently attracted many spectators. The pillory was made for the purpose and erected in the Market-place. In November, the Nottingham Volunteers were disbanded, but upwards of 500 of them, including all the officers, transferred their services to the Local Militia.

In 1810, a *Reform Petition* was sent to the House of Commons, and also a congratulatory Address to Sir Francis Burdett, Bart., who had just been sent to the Tower. In May, the fellmongers' vats on the Leen side were destroyed as a nuisance. During the year, the *Police Office* was built on the site of an old public-house; and the south-east corner of Bridlesmithgate was taken down, and "the road widened the breadth of a carriage." In October, the new church at Sneinton was opened, and in November, the Lancasterian School was rendered a permanent charity, at a public meeting, which was addressed by Mr. Lancaster, who pointed out in an animated speech, the benefits that would be derived from his system of education.

LUDDISM.—In February, 1811, such was the depressed state of the hosiery trade, that large numbers of half-famished workmen were reduced to pauperism, and obliged to sweep the streets for a paltry support. On the 11th of March, some hundreds of the country framework knitters assembled in the Market-place, and expressed a determination to take vengeance upon some of the hosiery manufacturers, who had reduced the prices paid for making stockings. The appearance of the military prevented any violence being committed in the town, but at night the men retired to the village of Arnold, and broke 63 frames, chiefly belonging to Mr. Broksop. Owing to the general depressed state of the trade, and the consequent abatement of wages, the mischief caught fire, and spread itself many miles round the neighbourhood, with such rapidity and success, that during the succeeding three weeks, upwards of 200 stocking frames were broken to pieces, by midnight bands of distressed and deluded workmen, who were so closely bound together by illegal oaths, and so disguised, and organized for their work of destruction, that but very few of them could be brought to justice, though they frequently renewed their nefarious practices during the succeeding five years, under the assumed name of LUDDITES,—an appellation which well suited their character, as it is said to have been derived from one *Ludlam*, an ignorant youth of Leicestershire, who, when ordered by his father, (a framework knitter) to "square his needles," took his hammer and beat them into a heap. During the reign of this system of "*Luddism*," upwards of one thousand stocking

.frames and a number of lace machines were completely destroyed in the county of Nottingham, and the alarming evil extended
itself into the counties of Leicester, Derby, Lancaster, and
York, in the two latter of which counties, the object of the
workmen was to destroy those machines which had been introduced for the purpose of superseding manual labour, but the
frame breakers in the hosiery and lace trades had not this griev-
ance to complain of; no, their sole object was an advance of
wages, and this, they blindly imagined, would be effected by
destroying the very tools which enabled them to follow their
occupations. The plan adopted by these midnight prowlers,
was to assemble in parties of from six to sixty, according as
circumstances required, under a supposed leader styled *General
Ludd*, and sometimes *Ned Ludd*. Whoever took upon him-
this title, had the absolute command of his party, some of whom,
armed with swords, pistols, firelocks, &c., were placed as guards,
whilst those armed with hammers, axes, &c., entered the houses
and demolished the frames, after which they re-assembled at a
short distance from the scene of destruction, where their leader
called over his men, who answered to certain numbers, and if
all were there, and their work finished for the night, he
signified the same by firing a pistol; after which they
immediately departed to their respective homes, removing
on the way, the black handkerchiefs which had covered
their features. In consequence of these daring outrages
being continued, a large military force was brought into the
neighbourhood, and two of the London police magistrates, with
several other officers, came down to Nottingham to assist the
civil power in attempting to discover the ringleaders;—a *secret
committee* was also formed and supplied with a large sum of
money for the purpose of obtaining private information, but in
spite of all this vigilance, and in contempt of a Royal Proclamation, the offenders continued their course of devastation,
with redoubled violence, as will be seen by the following brief
notice of the leading features of these unhappy disturbances,
abridged from the newspapers of 1811–12–14–and–16.

On Sunday night, November 10th, a party of Luddites proceeded to the village of *Bulwell*, to destroy the frames of Mr.
Hollingworth, who, in anticipation of their visit, had procured
the assistance of three or four friends, who with fire arms resolved to protect the threatened property. Many shots were
fired on both sides, and one of the assailants, John Westby, of
Arnold, was mortally wounded, which so enraged the mob, that
they soon forced an entrance, and the little garrison was obliged
to make a precipitate retreat, when the rioters not only destroyed the frames, but also every article of furniture in the
house. On the succeeding day, they seized and broke a waggon load of frames near Arnold, and on the Wednesday following, proceeded to *Sutton-in-Ashfield*, where they destroyed

37 frames; after which, they were dispersed by the military, who, took a number of prisoners, of whom four were fully committed for trial, viz.: John Bradbury, Gervas Marshall, George Green, and John Clarke. During the following week, only one frame was broken, but several *stacks were burnt* at Sneinton, Mansfield, and Hucknal Torkard, as was supposed by the frame breakers, in revenge against the owners, who, as members of the Yeomanry Cavalry, had been active in suppressing the riots. On Sunday night, November 24th, 34 frames were demolished in *Basford*, and 11 more were added to the same wreck on the following day. On December 6th, the magistrates published an edict, which ordered all persons in the disturbed districts to remain in their houses after ten o'clock at night, and all victuallers to close at the same hour. Notwithstanding this proclamation, and a great civil and military force, 36 frames were broken in the villages around Nottingham during the six following days. This bold defiance called forth the following MAGISTRATES' LETTER :—" There has now existed in the neighbourhood of Nottingham for a considerable time, a most outrageous spirit of *riot and tumult :* Houses have been feloniously broken into, and a great number of stocking frames have been broken and destroyed by an armed multitude, accompanied with menaces to the lives of those who should endeavour to interfere in preventing the mischief; various threatening letters have been sent; arms have been feloniously demanded and seized ; stacks have been fired, and private property destroyed ; and contributions have been levied under the pretence of applications for charitable relief, but under the real influence of terror. These are acts of so flagrant a nature, and leading to insurrection and such fatal consequences, that the magistrates, as legal guardians of the public peace, have the duty incumbent upon them of suppressing the evil, by the *civil and military force*, and by putting the laws in execution on the offenders, many of whom have committed crimes for which the law demands the forfeiture of their lives." The hosiery and lace manufacturers, finding the above letter had no effect, tried conciliatory measures, and at a general meeting, offered, as soon as peace could be restored, to consider proposals from their workmen, and to remove any grievances that might be found to exist; but even this failed, and the stupid, misguided men, as if bent on their own ruin as well as that of their employers, destroyed during the same week nearly 20 frames in the town and neighbourhood. After this a Royal Proclamation was issued, offering £50 reward for the apprehension of any of the offenders, but this only tended to inflame the frenzy of the men, who now began to plunder the farm houses both of money and provisions, declaring " they would not starve whilst there was plenty in the land." The number of unemployed families who were relieved out of the Poor Rates in the three

parishes of Nottingham, on the 30th of January, 1812, amounted 4248; consisting of no fewer than 15,350 individuals, or nearly one-half of the population.

1812.—No fewer than 41 frames were broken in the first week of this year, viz.: 15 at Radford, nine at Basford, nine at Hucknal-Torkard, five at Nottingham, and three at Bulwell and Arnold. On the Sunday night following, eight more were destroyed in Nottingham. For the purpose of affording more liberal rewards for informations against the perpetrators of these alarming outrages, a large subscription was raised, towards which the Duke of Newcastle, Lord Middleton, the Duke of Portland, and Earl Manvers, each contributed 500 pounds; and William Sherbrook, Esq., J. Manners Sutton, Esq., and many other gentlemen, one hundred pounds each. At the March Assize, *Judge Bailey* sentenced seven frame breakers to transportation, viz.—four for fourteen, and there for seven years. And on leaving the town his lordship left open the commission of Assize, so that in case of any further disturbances he might return immediately, and administer summary justice on the delinquents. At the July Assize two others were convicted, and one transported for fourteen years, and the other imprisoned for three years. In March, an act of Parliament was passed, making it *death to break a stocking or lace frame*. In April, Mr. Trentham, a considerable manufacturer, was shot by two ruffians while standing at his own door, but happily the wound did not prove mortal; the offenders were not discovered, though a reward of £600 was offered for their apprehension. In the gloomy month of November, the evil spirit of luddism again broke loose, and as before, generally selected the Sabbath evenings as the most favourable periods for performing its wicked deeds. After paying several destructive visits in Sneinton, on Sunday night, December 6th, an armed band of Luddites, with their faces covered with black handkerchiefs, entered the house of Mr. Black, who, on hearing them ascending, suddenly appeared at the head of the stairs with a poker, and boldly exclaimed, "you have my life to take first." Upon which they became panic struck, and made a precipitate retreat.

1813, November 1st, Mr. Sadler, senior, ascended in his balloon, from the Canal Company's Wharf, and after an aerial voyage of fifty-nine minutes descended near Stamford. This was the first time that any æronaut had ascended from Nottingham.—In July 1785, a Mr. Cracknall advertised that he would ascend from the forest, but to the great disappointment of the people he sent off his balloon to the ærial regions, and remained himself on *terra firma*. On November 30th, 1813, there were great *rejoicings* at Nottingham, on account of several victories gained by the allied forces over the French army; two bullocks and twenty sheep were roasted, and in the evening there was a partial illumination and a display of fireworks.

1814, June 6th, there was a general illumination and much rejoicing in the town, in consequence of the French armies being again defeated, but trade still being in a depressed state, these scenes of public joy were soon interrupted by the outrages of the *Luddites*, who, in this county, had slumbered during the preceeding year, but they now awoke, and blackened their former crimes with that of murder. On October 14, a party of them proceeded to Basford, and attacked the house of Mr. Thomas Garton, who had been the means of apprehending one of their sworn brethren. Mr. Garton being apprized of this visit, had obtained the assistance of several constables, who, after the assailants had broken into the house, and discharged several shots, returned their fire; when one of the Luddites fell, and the rest retreated, and in their flight, shot dead at his own door, *Mr. William Kilby,* who lived in a neighbouring house, and had been drawn to his threshold on hearing the report of fire arms.

1815, March 22d, peace with America was proclaimed; Aug. 6th, the Baptist Chapel, in George-street, was opened; and during the year the Lancasterian School was completed, and several petitions were singned against the corn laws.

1816, on the 17th of March, a slight shock of an earthquake was felt in the town and neighbourhood, and on the night of the 8th of June, the Luddites broke nineteen lace frames in the houses of William Wright and Thomas Mullen, for which offence two men were tried at the July Assize, but acquitted for want of evidence. This is the last act of "Luddism" which we have to record; for its mistaken votaries, consisting chiefly of youths from 22 to 18 years of age, had now discovered that their destructive practices were in the end more injurious to themselves than their employers, whose losses had of course to be borne by the county rate. *Napoleon Bonaparte,* after his final defeat, was sent by the allied powers to the Island of St. Helena, were he arrived October 15, 1816, and died on May 5, 1821.

In 1817, the general *peace* not having brought with it its expected concomitant *plenty,* numerous political meetings were held; and loud and imperative cries were raised for Parliamentary Reform. In this state of public distress and excitement several Government spies were sent out to gain information from the disturbed districts, and one of these emissaries, a Mr. Oliver, visited the reformers of Nottinghamshire, Warwickshire, Lancashire, and Yorkshire, but the principal scene of his pestiferous mission was in the latter county, where, after exciting numbers of distressed workmen to assemble for illegal purposes, he caused them to be seized by the military and arraigned for high treason, but none of them were convicted.

GUNPOWDER EXPLOSION.—A calamity of the most dreadful description occurred at the warehouse of the Nottingham Canal

Company, on Monday, Sept. 28, 1818, about three o'clock in the afternoon, by the accidental explosion of a large quantity of gunpowder, contained in twenty-one barrels, each weighing about 100lbs. The powder had been received in the morning by a boat from Gainsborough, and had just been deposited in the warehouse, previous to its being forwarded by another boat to Cromford, when the heedless conduct of one of the boatmen in applying a hot cinder to a train of loose powder, which had fallen from one of the casks during the removal, caused the whole to blow up. The report was so tremendous as to be heard at Bingham, a distance of ten miles, Castle Donington, Risely, and at other places even more distant. Every house in the town was shaken as if by an earthquake, and the inhabitants were thrown into the utmost consternation and dismay. The company's warehouse, a very spacious building, which at the time contained about 4,000 quarters of corn, besides cheese, groceries, paper, &c. was completely lifted into the air and scattered in heaps of ruins; not one stone being left standing upon another. The explosion was followed by a cloud of smoke which completely darkened the atmosphere, and on its clearing away, such a scene of devastation presented itself, as it is scarcely possible to describe. The roofs of most of the buildings in the immediate neighbourhood appeared to be torn off or rent assunder, and windows innumerable shattered and broken, or wholly forced out of the frames, while the yard and wharf were strewed with the wrecks of the building and merchandize. But the most lamentable part of the story remains to be told, no less than ten human beings lost their lives by the dreadful effects of the explosion, viz. eight men and two boys, most of whose bodies were bruised and mangled in a shocking manner; one had his head blown entirely off—others were found with their limbs severed from their bodies—others with the tops of their skulls carried away, and otherwise torn and disfigured; and the unfortunate author of the mischief was thrown a great distance into the meadows, where his remains were found rent asunder and scattered in several parts. The names of the sufferer were Joseph Musson, William Norman, John Seals, Benjamin Wheatley, George Hayes, William Parker, Thomas Baker, John Howell, William Stevenson, and Job Barnes.— At the Coroner's inquest, Joseph Champion deposed that Joseph Musson came on board his boat, then lying about thirty yards from the canal warehouse, and asked for a light, saying, " Lads I'm going to have a flush," and that he went to the fire and took away a live coke between two pieces of stick, and that almost immediately afterwards the warehouse was blown up, and the deponent and his companions were knocked down in their boat. A subscription, which did honour to the benevolent feelings of the inhabitants of Nottingham, was opened for the relief of the families of the poor sufferers. The disaster proved extremely detrimental to many traders who had goods in the warehouse, and the loss sustained by the Canal Company was immense.

1819 was a year of great national distress and disaffection. *Reform Meetings* were held in all the principal towns; and in Lancashire "Female Reform Societies" were formed. Contrary to law, Birmingham elected a person to represent it in Parliament, and Manchester and Leeds intended to have followed the example, but the capture of Mr. Hunt and some other travelling agitators of the public mind at the "Manchester Massacre," on the 16th of August, gave another bias to the aggravated feelings of the people.

1820, *George III.* died January 29th, in the 82d year of his age, and the 60th year of his reign. His eldest son, *George IV.* was proclaimed during the following month, amidst some marks of disapprobation, and was crowned July 19th, 1821, when the exclusion of the Queen from the regal ceremony gave great dissatisfaction.

1825.—This year *weights and measures* were equallised by an act of Parliament. In December the failure of many country banking houses caused a great stagnation in trade.

1827.—His Royal Highness Duke of York died January 5th, and the Right Honourable George Canning on the 8th of August.

1828.—No fewer than 154 corps of Yeomanry Cavalry were disbanded this year, by which the country saved £200,000 per annum.

1829.—This year was the *centenary of Methodism*, which was founded by the Rev. John Wesley, M.A., at Oxford, in 1729. As Nottingham is in the diocese of York we may notice that on the 2d of February, Jonathan Martin, a wandering fanatic, set *fire to York Minster*, by which the interior of the choir and chancel, with the roof of that extensive and beautiful edifice was reduced to a heap of ruins. For the restoration of this "chief of houses as the rose of flowers," large sums of money were subscribed ; and the *organ* was replaced by the Hon. and Rev. John Lumley Saville, M.A. at the cost of about £8000. This year there were 6680 English mechanics France.

The year 1830 was big with the fate of kings and nations. *George IV.* died July 26th, in the 68th year of his age, and the 11th of his reign. The second French Revolution was effected during the "glorious three days" of July 28th, 29th, and 30th, and Charles X. was driven from the throne which both he and his ancestors had so often abused. During the succeeding month, the spirit of liberty broke loose in Belgium and Brunswick, and soon afterwards in Saxony and Poland, but England was fortunately saved from the continental infection by the ascension of his present patriotic majesty William IV., whose throne is enshrined in the hearts of his people. *Five thousand francs* were subscribed at Nottingham, in aid of the families of those who suffered at Paris in the cause of liberty. This sum, and a congratulatory address, were conveyed to Paris, by Messrs. Richard Booker and William Taylor, who, for the faithful discharge of their mission, were each rewarded with a silver snuff box, bearing an appropriate inscription. That great and useful statesman, *Mr. Huskisson*, was unfortunately killed this year, on September 15th, at the opening of the Liverpool and Manchester Railway. The *New Beer Act* came into operation on the 11th of October, and under it, upwards of sixty houses for the sale of beer, were opened during the year in Nottingham and its suburbs.

1831, the year in which we write, stands conspicuous in the political annals of the kingdom, for in it the long-cherished hopes of the people, after being raised to the highest pinnacle of popular excitement by the patriotic and equitable conduct of the King and his Ministers, and by a consequent triumphant majority in the House of Commons, in favour of Lord John Russell's REFORM BILL, were dashed to the earth in the House of Lords, by an overwhelming majority of Bishops and junior Peers, the latter of whom, being mostly hatched in the Pitt and Castlereagh administrations, have always been in the ranks of the boroughmongers, and opposed to popular representation. This oligarchical majority, which had the temerity to beard both the King and the people, and to give "the lie direct" to that branch of the Legislature which had declared its own corruption, brought the nation to the verge of a baneful revolution, which was only averted by the prompt exertions of the influential members of the community, who, in animated speeches at the great public meetings simultaneously assembled in almost every town in the kingdom, on this mournful occasion, succeeded in restoring the confidence of the people in favour of the King and his present Ministers, who pledged themselves to bring forward in the course of the year another bill for the Reform of the Commons House of Parliament, "as full and efficient" as that which was lost by a majority of forty-one in the House of Lords, at a quarter past six o'clock on the morning of Saturday, October 8th, when 158 voted for, and 199 against Lord John Russell's bill. The news of this lamentable defeat reached Nottingham at seven o'clock the same evening. The unwelcome intelligence was no sooner read in the news-room at Bromley-house, than a respectably signed *requisition* was sent to the mayor, calling upon him to convene, without delay, a *public meeting*, to be held on the Monday morning following, to address the King, praying that he would continue his Ministers, and that such measures might be adopted "as would ensure the carrying of Earl Grey's measure of Reform, and preserve the peace and happiness of this kingdom." In the course of the evening, nine other requisitions were presented to the mayor,

L

after he had acted upon the first. The spirit of excitement
throughout the town was so great, that from an early hour on
Sunday morning the inhabitants began to assemble in the principal streets, to talk over the doleful news, and wait the arrival
of the mails and coaches, which brought certain intelligence
that very considerable disturbances had taken place at Derby,
and also false rumours that similar commotions had taken place
at London, Birmingham, and other places. This so encouraged the ignorant part of the mob, that the windows of many
persons, said to have signed an anti-reform petition, were
broken during the evening, and the town thrown into such an
alarming state of confusion, that the mayor found it necessary
to read the riot act, and call in the only remaining troop of the
15th Hussars then at the barracks. The shop of Mr. Wright,
bookseller, on the Long-row, was broken into by a gang of
mischievous youths, who seized parts of the market stalls and
used them as battering-rams in breaking in the shutters and
window frames. A provision shop at the corner of Charlotte-
street and York-street, was also broken open, and its contents
strewed about the street. The troops and constables continued
patrolling the streets till a late hour, without coming in contact
with the mobs of idle youths, by whom the greatest part of the
mischief was committed.

On the following morning, Monday, October 10th, the people began to assemble at an early hour in the Market-place,
where the various stall keepers and proprietors of exhibitions
intending to stay through the last days of the fair, soon perceived that it was not safe for them to remain longer, and they
consequently commenced packing up, with such dispatch, that
before twelve o'clock there was not one vestige of the fair to be
seen. The public meeting took place as appointed, and was
attended by upwards of 20,000 people, who, after hearing the
conciliatory speeches of Thomas Wakefield, Esq., Lord Rancliffe, W. F. N. Norton, Esq., Alderman Oldknow, Colonel
Wildman, Mr. Thomas Bailey, and Mr. Charles Wilkins,
voted a loyal address to his Majesty, praying him to retain his
Ministers and stand firm in the cause of Reform. They separated quietly about two o'clock, but such sullen looks of dis-
content were noticed amongst the multitude, that many close
observers feared something serious would occur before next day.
In the course of the afternoon, crowds of people began to collect in different parts of the town, and most of the respectable
housekeepers were summoned to the Police-office, and after
being sworn in as special constables, they were ordered to assemble whenever the great bell of the Exchange should ring.—
Meanwhile, the magistrates, the police, and the military were
on the alert. The first breach of the peace was in Hockley,
where a mob consisting principally of disorderly youths from
the country, broke the windows of Mr. Smith and Mr. Prickard,

though both of them were zealous friends of Reform. They were, however, soon dispersed by the military, who captured a crape flag, inscribed "*the Bill and no Lords.*" The mob next attacked Mr. Sharp's wind-mill, on the forest, and before the Hussars could gallop thither, had cut the sails, injured the wheel work, and thrown about the corn and flour. The windows of many persons in various parts of the town were afterwards demolished.

A little before dusk, a body of sturdy youths passed up the Sneinton road, and at Nottintone-place, tore down a long range of *iron* pallisades, with which they armed themselves. They then proceeded to COLWICK HALL, reinforced by continual arrivals of people from the lower parts of the town. Having arrived at this beautiful seat, they broke all the windows, and after splitting the furniture in pieces, piled it in heaps and set fire to it. All the family, except *Mr. Musters,* were at home, and the ladies had only just time to hide themselves in a secret room, where they remained concealed from the search of the mob, who carried off every thing that was valuable. The servants succeeded in extinguishing the fires, after the departure of the rioters, who on their return tore up a number of rails, with which many hundreds, marching eight or ten abreast, entered the town, where they separated into divisions, moving in different directions, so that the magistrates could not discover where the next attack would be made.

Soon after seven o'clock, information was received at the Police-office, that the Castle was the object of attack, and one of the Aldermen, with a party of military, set out to defend it, but they were met on the road with intelligence that a vast multitude were breaking open the *House of Correction ;* upon which the magistrates deemed it more advisable to march their forces for the defence of their own prison, where they arrived in time to prevent the entrance of the misguided mob, but were obliged to remain, and leave the empty Castle to its fate.

THE CASTLE DESTROYED BY FIRE.—That splendid but unoccupied mansion, Nottingham Castle, being the property of the Duke of Newcastle, was, on account of his Grace's unqualified opposition to the Reform Bill, marked out for destruction by the infuriated mob, part of whom, in order to divert the attention of the magistrates and the civil and military forces, marched from the Market-place to the House of Correction, whilst the main body, consisting principally of the rioters who had returned from Colwick Hall, proceeded by different routes to the Castle lodge, where they arrived soon after seven o'clock in the evening, and commenced a battering attack upon the lodge gates, whilst others scaled the walls of the Castle yard, opposite to the flight of steps leading to Standard-hill, where a breach was soon made, so that by the stones pulled down into the road, entrance into the yard was easily effected. The

assailants then rushed up to the Castle, mounted the great flight
of stairs, broke in the windows, and collecting the materials
best suited for burning, they piled them in different heaps and
set fire to them, so that in a short time this proud ornament
of the town was on fire in so many parts, that all hope of extinction was vain;—the great height and distance to which
water would have to be carried, aided by the dryness of the
timber, would have made it impossible for the whole population
of Nottingham to have subdued the conflagration, which by
half-past nine o'clock had reached its height. At this time the
atmosphere was filled with a lurid glare, vast volumes of flame
issued from every window, and rolled forth masses of smoke,
which gradually spread and mounted aloft, till it formed a
gigantic bulk, to which even the stupendous building, and the
great rock on which it stands, were diminutive. A man with
a large crow-bar commenced the destruction of the beautiful
equestrian statue, placed in a niche in the centre of the east
front, and very speedily left the horse and the rider headless
and limbless trunks;—the parts broken off were carried away
as trophies! The circumstance of the Castle being without the
limits of the town magistracy, and the disturbances in the populous parts of the town keeping the few military busily engaged, gave the assailants of the Castle almost unbounded
license, and as the flames burst forth in each new direction,
they were hailed with loud and exulting shouts! At the commencement, many persons were seen carrying fire from room
to room, and stripping the antique and beautiful tapestry from
the walls. About eleven o'clock, the conflagration began to
subside, and heavy showers of rain acted as a check in preventing further outrage, by causing a great part of the mob to retire
to their respective homes. But on the following morning, the
mob again assembled at an early hour, about the Castle-yard,
and soon made their entrance into it. For some time they
wandered amongst the still burning ruins, in search of
relics. Two boys were crushed and scorched to death, in their
attempt to secure some of the large masses of lead, glass, and
calcined stone and marble, which were found completely fused
together. Three men, who ventured upon the stone steps of
the geometrical staircase at the north end, were precipitated a
depth of seven or eight feet, amongst the smoking ruins, and
with great difficulty extricated themselves.

During the forenoon of Tuesday, a large body of men and
boys, chiefly from the neighbouring villages, collected in the
Market-place, whence they marched out of the town, after refusing to believe any thing that was told them about the peace-
able state of the metropolis. It was soon ascertained that they
had set fire to the large SILK MILL at Beeston, belonging to
Mr. William Lowe, of Nottingham, and the flames and smoke
were in a little time distinctly seen from the skirts of the town,

By three o'clock the mill was reduced to a heap of ruins, and its 200 workmen thrown out of employment. The loss of property was estimated at near £12,000. On leaving the town in the morning, the rioters called at the Greyhound and the Durham Ox, where they ate and drank all that the houses contained, without paying the landlords for their entertainment. On their return from the burning mill, they called at the house of Matthew Needham, Esq., where all the wine and eatables speedily disappeared, together with silver plate of the value of about £40. They also asked for food at the house of John Wright, Esq., but went away on that gentleman giving them two sovereigns. They next commenced an attack on the gate of WOOLLATON PARK, the seat of Lord Middleton, and soon obtained an entrance, but being immediately charged by a troop of Yeomanry Cavalry, they made a precipitate retreat, in which sixteen of them were taken prisoners, and escorted by a party of the 15th Hussars to the county gaol. To prevent an attempt at rescue, the soldiers, in passing through the town with their prisoners, were obliged to have their swords drawn and pistols presented, —so closely were they followed up by the mob, who on arriving in the Poultry, threw several stones, which so exasperated the officer who brought up the rear of the soldiers, that he fired his pistol down High-street, and severely wounded two individuals, one of whom was an old pensioner, acting as a special constable. This was about five o'clock, and as evening approached, the soldiers began to charge upon the crowds in and near the Market-place, and soon dispersed them, by galloping along the pavements and striking with the flat of the sword those who did not move onward. To prevent them returning again to the Market-place, all the narrow passages leading to the Long-row were barricaded, and orders were issued for all houses of public resort to be closed, and for all housekeepers to retain their families within doors. On Wednesday, the alarm appeared to have subsided, the market was supplied as usual, and all the shops were re-opened. At night, the smaller thoroughfares into the Market-place were again closed, and by vigilant patrols the streets were kept clear of crowds during the night, in which, however, two *stacks* were destroyed by fire in the village of Plumptre, as is supposed by two incendiaries, who just before had obtained relief at the house of Mr. Cole, with which they expressed themselves highly dissatisfied, and went away grumbling. Owing to the indefatigable exertions of the magistrates, the police, the special constables, and the military, the tranquillity of the town was not again disturbed.

Though the whole country was in mourning on account of the rejection of the Reform Bill, peace was happily preserved in almost all the populous districts, except at Nottingham, Derby, Mansfield, Loughborough, and a few smaller places, where the hosiery and lace trades are carried on, in which occupations, the real manufacturers have lost their due influence over the workmen, by the introduction of a sort of "*middle-men*," through whose medium nearly all the work now passes betwixt the employer and the operative. At no place was the destruction of property so great as at Nottingham and its vicinity;* it is however due to the great body of the inhabitants to remark, that the wanton mischief was mostly committed by disorderly youths, incited and assisted by ignorant and depraved adults, of whom numbers are to be found in all large towns, ready to take advantage of popular clamour, for the purpose of plunder, and to whom no "Reform" would be acceptable, but that which would give them idleness and plenty. We cannot better close this brief detail of the last scene of popular outrage in Nottingham, than by quoting the following passage from a lengthy and truly patriotic *address*, published during the week by Mr. Thomas Bailey, who, after condemning his townsmen for madly attempting to "ruin the best cause in the world, by the adoption of the worst possible means for its alleged support;" says, "My dear fellow countrymen, I entreat you to avoid every one who would lead you into acts of violence and outrage, as you would avoid a wild beast, or a pest-house; for be assured, they seek generally, by such a course, but to make you instruments for the gratification of their private malice, or tools for the establishment of a system of lawless domination, in the furtherance of which they would in turn trample contemptuously upon your blood, should it serve their purpose, or remorselessly wring the solitary crust of bread from the hands of your helpless children, should the gain be necessary, to feed their own greedy concupiscence. Abstain then, I again entreat you, as you love yourselves—as you love your wives and children—as you love your parents and kindred—as you venerate our beloved country—as you respect the talented, virtuous, patriotic band of men who are pledged to accomplish the great measure of Parliamentary Reform, from any acts of violence against the person or property of any individual, however opposed to this grand scheme of our social amelioration. What is done, I am

* BRISTOL RIOTS.—Since writing the above, the devastation in Nottingham has been greatly surpassed by the most brutal scene of wanton outrage and plunder that ever disgraced the kingdom. This blot in our national history was caused by the obstinacy of Sir Charles Wetherell, who, after rendering himself highly unpopular by his inveterate opposition to the *Reform Bill*, persisted in his determination to enter the city of Bristol (of which he is Recorder,) and open the Court of Quarter Session, though strenuously advised to the contrary. He accordingly entered on Saturday, October 30th, and created such a storm of popular fury, that, during the two following days, the city was given up to the plunder and devastation of dissolute bands of rioters; who *burnt to the ground* the Mansion-house, the Bishop's palace, the three Prisons, the four Toll-houses, the Custom-house, the Excise-office, and forty-two dwelling-houses and warehouses. Many lives were lost in the flames and by the sword, and the loss of property amounted to upwards of £500,000.

aware cannot now be undone; but it can be repented of—the repetition of it can be avoided. The stain cast by the hand of violence upon the page of our local history, I know cannot be effaced, but unfortunately will endure when the present generation has ceased to exist; do not, then, I entreat you, deepen these frightful characters, nor add to the shame and embarrassment of your friends, by lengthening the catalogue of burnings and spoliation of property which have marked the transactions of the passing week." The *damage* at Nottingham Castle, Beeston Silk Mill, and Colwick Hall, amounted to upwards of £50,000, exclusive of the loss in broken windows, &c. which was very considerable. The damage at Mansfield amounted to £137.

Having given a rapid, but we hope faithful and comprehensive sketch of all that is interesting in the general history of this important town, our next task is to present separate historical and descriptive views of its ancient and modern buildings and institutions; its civil and ecclesiastical jurisdictions,—manufactures, trade and commerce,—its rivers, canals, and public works,—its objects of interest and curiosity, &c. &c.; together with biographical sketches of its eminent men, list of streets, squares, courts, &c. and a variety of other interesting matter detailed under a lucid arrangement of subjects, to which we hasten to introduce the reader.

NOTTINGHAM CASTLE.

This once majestic ornament of the town, as has just been seen, now stands in smoky ruin, a sable monument of the evil effects of popular frenzy; and whether it will ever be again restored to its pristine state is doubtful, as it long since ceased to be the occasional residence of its owner, the Duke of Newcastle. The historical events connected with it have already been inserted in the preceding annals of the town, therefore, the following recapitulation will suffice :—In 868, before the union of the heptarchy under one sovereign, the Danes having come up the Trent, established themselves in a fortress built on the rock, and were there besieged by Buthred, King of Mercia, and Prince, afterwards King Alfred; a treaty of peace was afterwards made between the Saxons and Danes, without taking the fortress. Immediately after the conquest, William de Peverel, natural son of the conqueror, in the year 1068, built a castle at the summit of the rock; this was always possessed as a royal castle. In the reign of Henry II. it was besieged and held out against his rebellious son, Henry; in the time of Richard Cœur de Lion, and during that monarch's captivity on the continent, it was seized by Earl, afterwards King John, as one of the strongest holds in the kingdom, in his project to make himself king; Richard, after a long siege, got possession of the place, and afterwards held a Parliament in the castle, for the trial of his brother and his accomplices, but they did not appear. Here Mortimer, paramour of Queen Isabella, and governor of the kingdom, during the minority of Edward III., held his court, and it was here that he was surprised by the young king in 1330. King Edward IV. very much enlarged the castle, by various towers extending to the brow of the hill on the north, and covering what is now the Castle-green. Richard III. held his court, and mustered his forces here before he marched to Bosworth Field. During the reigns of the Tudors, the place fell into a dilapidated state, but still it was sufficiently strong to be an important place in the wars between Charles I. and his Parliament; for that Prince erected his standard in the castle, on the 22d of August, 1642, and on the hill north of it, three days after. It was for some time in the possession of the Parliamentary forces, and had the celebrated Colonel Hutchinson for its governor; after standing nearly 600 years, it was destroyed during the protectorate of Cromwell. Previous to this, however, it had been granted by James I. to the Earl of Rutland, and descended to his heir, Villiers, Duke of Buckingham. After the restoration, it was claimed by his heirs, and sold by them to William Cavendish, Marquis, and afterwards Duke of Newcastle, who in 1674, commenced the building of the present edifice; it was completed in the year 1683, by his son, Henry. The equestrian statue in front, is that of the founder, and was cut by Wilson, out of one single block of stone, brought from Donington, in Leicestershire. The entire cost of the building is stated by Deering to have been £14,002. 17s. 11d., and the name of the architect March. The second Duke of Newcastle dying without male issue, his property descended to the Earl of Clare, who had married his third daughter, and was created Duke of Newcastle by William III. This nobleman also died without issue, and the property went to his nephew, Lord Pelham, who in 1718, was created Duke of Newcastle by George I. The castle has not in the memory of man been the residence of the family to whom it belongs, but has generally been inhabited by private families. It was many years occupied as two separate mansions by Mrs. Plumbe and Miss Kirkby; after their death, it was occupied by the late W. B. Rawson, Esq., by Miss Greaves, and the Rev. Joseph Gilbert. It has now been untenanted for about two years. The great dining-room was hung with a splendid piece of tapestry, which tradition says was the work of Queen Anne, who was here in 1688, before her accession to the throne. A vast quantity of cedar was used in its erection, and the perfume which was occasioned by its burning, was distinctly perceptible during the night at a considerable distance.

The *Castle*, though now reduced to a mere roofless shell, still appears to the distant observer as it did before the late con-

flagration, the exterior walls being all left standing ; it rests
on a rustic basement, and its principal front is highly ornamented in the Corinthian, order ;   with a handsome double
flight of steps, above which (over the door which led to the entrance hall) is the now mutilated equestrian statue of the founder.   The whole is surrounded by a beautiful terrace, with an
arcade on the south side.   It is 72 yards long, and 30 yards
broad, and was terminated by a flat monotonous roof, without
any towers, turrets, or embattlements, in remembrance of the
formidable fortress which once occupied its site, or in unison
with the bold features of the lofty frowning rock on which it
stands.

The CASTLE LODGE, which escaped. the late fire, consists of
a venerable gothic- gateway, flanked by two bastions, which
formed part of the outworks, by which the ancient castle was
surrounded. One of the bastions has been long occupied by a
porter, who, for a trifling fee, admits visitors into the castle-
yard, which, commands a delightful. and extensive prospect,
being on the summit of the bold rock, which on the south and
west rises nearly perpendicularly, 133 feet above the river Leen.
The deep *ditch* which passed in front of the lodge and along
the north side of the castle wall, was filled up in 1807, when.
the new road from Houndsgate to the park was made.

MORTIMER'S HOLE is a subterraneous passage, 107 yards in
length, seven feet high, and six feet wide, leading from the
court of the old castle to the brewhouse yard, at the foot of the
rock, and formerly having six gates, distant about 17 yards
from each other.   All the way down, till within 15 yards of.
the bottom, are openings in the side of the rock, intended to.
light the passage, and for the soldiers to shoot their arrows
through upon the enemy ; in the upper part are cut out several
large port holes, which show, that during the civil wars cannon
were planted there, so as to command the road from Trent
bridge ; for near them are several excavations, evidently intended for the reception of balls and powder.   This " wonderful passage was cut during the Danish invasion, by some of
the Saxon kings, for the better security in case of siege ;" and
indeed in times of peace it was useful, for it afforded a direct
communication with the corn-mill, malt-kiln, and brewhouse of
the garrison, in the Rock-yard, now called Brewhouse-yard.
About 17 yards above the lower entrance to this spacious vault,
which is ascended by nearly worn out steps of living rock, is
the entrance to a dark and narrow passage, which branches off
to the right, and formerly led by sercet doors into the keep of
the old castle, in which were the state apartments.   This was.
that secret passage through which Sir William Eland, in 1330,
conducted king Edward, when he seized Lord Mortimer in the
apartment of his royal mother and brought him out of the castle
through the same passage, which in memory of the fate of that

unfortunate nobleman, was ever after called *Mortimer's hole*, (see p. 84) a name which has been erroneously given to the principal vault. All the entrances to these passages are now walled up, to prevent boys passing that way into the castle gardens.

The ANCIENT WALLS AND GATES, which formerly encompassed the town, are now scarcely to be traced, though *Leland* says "The town hath been meetly welle wallid with stone, and hath had dyvers gates; much of the walle is now downe, and the gates savinge 2 or 3." This wall, of which a considerable portion seems to have been standing in Leland's time, was built by Edward the Elder, about 910, when the country was troubled with the incursions of the Danes. After building the Castle, William Peverel, the natural son of the Conqueror, made considerable additions to the wall and gates, and in 1259, Henry III., commanded the burgesses " without delay to make a *postern* in the wall, near the Castle towards Lenton, of such a breadth and height that two armed horsemen carrying two lances on their shoulders, might go in and out, where William, Archbishop of York had appointed it." This postern is supposed to have stood where the reservoir now is, behind the Infirmary, and Deering says a bridge in front of it, crossed the town-ditch at the place still called *Boston-bridge*, a corruption of *Postern-bridge*. In Deering's time, the ditch extending to Chapel-bar, was converted into kitchen gardens and called " *Butt-dyke*, from some neighbouring butts, where the townsmen used to exercise themselves in shooting at a mark with bows and arrows." About the year 1800, Butt-dyke, now the site of *Park-row*, was let as building land by the Corporation, on perpetual leases, and in digging the foundation of the houses, several fragments of the old wall were discovered. The Town-wall passed from the north-west corner of the Castle-wall, along the site of Park-row to Chapel-bar, and thence across Parliament-street, and through Roper's-close and Pannier's-close, to St. John's-street, Coalpit-lane, Cartergate, Fishergate, Hollow stone, Short-hill, and the High, Middle, and Low Pavements, to the end of Listergate; whence it passed up the south side of Castlegate, and below St. Nicholas' Church-yard to the Brewhouse-yard, where it joined the Castle-rock. In consequence of part of this wall being destroyed in the wars between King Stephen and the Empress Matilda, Henry II. repaired it by erecting a wall, which extended from Chapel-bar, down Parliament-street, to Coalpit-lane. In 1740, one of the old posterns was standing at the top of Drury-hill, facing Bridle-smithgate. A little above this is *Postern-place*, in which Blackner says, there is standing " a part of the old town wall, the dimensions of which are as follows :—in height 102 inches; thickness 38 inches; and six yards in length," with the arch of a *Sally-port*, 92 inches in height and 62 in width. Tradition says, there were two posterns at the top of Listergate and Clumber-street, but the principal entrance gates were those at Chapel-bar and Hollow-stone.

HOLLOW-STONE, though much altered of late years, may still be considered as the remains of one of the ancient entrances to the town. About 90 years ago, it was a very narrow passage, having been secured by a strong *portcullis*, of which at that time there were some evident, traces to be seen. Each side of the gateway was formed of living stone, and above it on the western side, was a large cavity cut in the rock, capable of holding twenty men, with a fire place and benches, evidently designed for a guardhouse, and having a staircase cut from the top of the rock to communicate with the centinels. This cavity gave the name of Hollow-stone to the street which was widened by the Corporation in 1740, and by the Commissioners of the Food-road in 1800, when the road from thence to the Leen bridge was raised so much that the chambers of some of the old houses in Bridge-street were converted into the first floors. Much of the perpendicular rock on each side of the deep cut road called Hollow-stone, is now hid behind many good houses which have lately been erected against it.

CHAPEL-BAR, was a strong gateway tower, having on each side an arched room of a pentagonal figure, one of which was used as the guardhouse, and the other as a chapel. The top of the arch was well earthed and cultivated as a pleasure garden, in which grew a large sycamore tree. The whole was taken down in 1743, and, during the present year, (1831) most of the houses in the south side[*] of the street called Chapel-bar, were taken down, for the purpose of widening that previously contracted entrance into the Market-place. Long before the gate was taken down, the old chapel was converted into a brewhouse, as an appendage to the Inn which stood at the corner; the mash tubs being placed on the altars, without regard to their former sanctity, caused a facetious layman to write the following epigram:—

> " Here priests of old, turned wafers into God,
> And gave poor laymen bread for flesh and blood,
> But now a liquid myst'ry's here set up,
> Where priest and layman both, partook the cup' "

The FORT which stood near the north end of Trent bridge, was a bone of great contention betwixt the Royalists and the Parliamentarians in the civil wars, (see p. 90.) but every vestige of it has long since disappeared; though the lines of the trenches raised by Colonel Hutchinson, when he forced the " Newark-ers" to make a precipitate retreat from the fort, might be traced a few years ago, on the *Rye-hills*, in the higher part of the meadows.

[*] The other houses on the south side of Chapel-bar were taken down in 1811.

On *Nottingham-hill*, about a mile from the town, are " some lines of fortification, and several *Barrows*, in one of which, Deering says, great quantities of human bones have been found, supposed to be the remains of some Saxon soldiers, for it was their custom to cover the graves of their slain with mounds of earth, now called Barrows.

The BARRACKS, pleasantly situated at the western corner of the Park, form the only military depôt now possessed by the town, and they are of modern erection; being built in 1792, on ground given by the Duke of Newcastle. They contain convenient apartments for the officers; a Sutling-house; barrack rooms and stabling for three troops of horse; an hospital, &c. &c., —with an extensive yard, enclosed by a strong wall of brick. The garrison is supplied with water by a well, from which the water is raised by a horse into a large cistern.—William Hanmer, Esq., is the *Barrack-Master*.

CAVES.—Of the numerous caves, caverns, and rock-houses, we have already given a brief historical view at pages 78 to 81, showing that many of them were excavated and inhabited by the ancient Britons, and afterwards enlarged and converted into store-houses by the Saxons; since whose time, many modern excavations have been made, and many of the old ones, either wasted by the corroding tooth of time, or hid from public view, for the improvement and extension of the town, under which some of them now form deep and capacious cellars. In digging the foundations of the houses on the north and south sides of the Market-place, many very extensive vaults with arches supported by pillars, with carved capitals were discovered; and Deering says, a bricklayer informed him, that whilst digging in the Week-day cross, he got into a spacious subterraneous passage, supported by ornamented pillars, and extending to the upper end of Pilchergate, under which he found " a wooden cup and a wooden can, which seemed to be sound and whole, but on being taken hold of, mouldered into dust." The most interesting caverns, now accessible are the Papist or Druids' Holes, in the Park; and the Rock-houses at Sneinton Hermitage.

The PAPIST HOLES, as they are vulgarly called, are a curious range of excavations in the perpendicular rock, which rises above the river Leen, at the south-east corner of the *Park*, a little to the west of the Castle. In the early part of the last century, when Stukely visited them, they were more perfect than at present: he says, " what is visible at present is not of so old a date as the time of the Britons, yet I see no doubt that it is founded upon theirs. This is a ledge of perpendicular rock hewn out into a church, houses, chambers, dove house, &c. The church is like those in the rocks at Bethlehem, and other places in the Holy Land. The altar is natural rock, and there has been painting upon the wall: a steeple, I suppose where a bell hung, and regular pillars. The river here winding about makes a fortification to it, for it comes to both ends of the cliff, leaving a plain before the middle. The way to it was by gates cut out of the rock, and with oblique entrance for more safety. Without is a plain with three niches, which I fancy their place of judicature, or the like: between this and the Castle, is a hermitage of like workmanship." To this description, it is scarcely possible to add any thing that will give a better idea of the place. We can only say, that it has suffered considerably from the effects of time and weather since Stukely wrote; but enough still remains to gratify, and, at the same time, to excite curiosity. The outer part has fallen down in several places, evidently from the effects of damp and frost; but the church and altar, and even some vestiges of the ancient paintings may be easily traced;[*] many of the pillars are ornamented with capitals, &c. and the spandrilled *Gothic arch* is very well imitated in several places; a fact indeed which militates against their very early antiquity. It is much to be regretted that no care whatever is taken to preserve this venerable specimen; the floor of it is broken into holes, where the water lodges, and much of it is disfigured with the grossest filthiness. In the summer, these excavations have become haunts of the very lowest of society, who there take up their nocturnal abode; and if not a den of thieves, it may be considered as something worse.

On a careful examination, it is evident that the whole line of excavation has been the work of different periods. The Dove-cote, for instance, is but of modern date; and close by it, where there are chimnies cut through the rock, the marks of the smoke still remain. Deering says that, in his time, some old people remembered them much more extensive; and he adds from tradition, " that in the time of the civil war, the Roundheads had demolished a part of them under the pretence of their abhorrence to Popery," which may perhaps be the sole origin of their receiving the name of Papist holes. We will not follow the various authors through their wide range of conjectures; but must confess that there seems most probability in that which supposes them to have been the residence of some order of anchorets or hermits, not endowed, though perhaps dependent upon some religious house, and, therefore, not recorded in any list of religious foundations. To which we must add, that it is extremely probable that, when more entire, their entrance was more easily concealed; and, therefore, that in the early days of the reformation, they may have been occupied at times for religious purposes, by those who were averse from the new order of things, and wished to enjoy the exercise of

[*] Some *ingenious* artist has added a number of paintings, such as elephants, soldiers in full accoutrements, &c. not inelegantly done, but which must be classed amongst " modern antiques."—*Laird*, 1811.

M

their ritual in secret. The place designated by Stukely, as an hermitage, has nothing remarkable; and we were not fortunate to find out the spot mentioned by Deering as affording the most clear and perfect echo he had ever met with.

SNEINTON HERMITAGE on the east side of the town, in the parish of Sneinton, consists of a long range of perpendicular rock, overlooking the vale of the Trent, and having within its craggy front many grotesque habitations and curious caves; some of which are of great antiquity.—(See p. 81.) Many of the houses have staircases leading up to the gardens on the top, and on the shelves of the rock, in the rugged front of which the stranger is struck with the romantic appearance of doors and windows ranged in irregular tiers, and shaded in many places with ivy and other umbrageous foliage. A few brick buildings have been erected in front of some of the old rock houses which still serve as kitchens and lumber rooms to the modern erections. Two of these are *public-houses* much resorted to in summer, and one of them is not only extremely pleasant from its garden plats and arbours in front, but also very curious from its great extent into the body of the rock, where visitors may almost choose their degree of temperature on the hotest day in summer. About three o'clock in the morning of May 10, 1829, a lofty overhanging part of the rock above the White Swan public-house fell with a dreadful crash, and knocked down part of that building and an adjoining rock house; giving the inhabitants only just sufficient warning to hurry from their beds and escape to a place of safety. Several large portions of rock fell in other parts of the neighbourhood during the same year; and on a Sunday night, about eleven o'clock, in March, 1830, a high perpendicular rock, which stood behind the Lancasterian school, in Derby road, fell and knocked down the roof and side wall of that building.

Many ROCK HOUSES are still inhabited within the limits of the town of Nottingham, though a considerable number have of late years been destroyed by the corporation, and the sites let on building leases. A long range of these singular dwellings are now in ruins on the east side of *Mansfield-road*, where they were broken up a few years ago by the corporate body, who are prevented from building a projected row of handsome brick houses upon them, to correspond with those on the opposite side of the road, by the cupidity of the sturdy *troglodyte,** who inhabits the uppermost house in the rock, opposite to which he has erected a blacksmith's shop;—and having many years occupied the place without paying any acknowledgment, he now claims it as his own freehold property, and consequently refused to *budge* when the corporate officers ejected his neighbours. The rock on the opposite side of the road and on the,

* Samuel Caulton, a superannuated smith.

south side of the Derby road, though now built upon, has been perforated in many places by persons who obtained a living by getting the sand-stone for the purpose of selling it to the good housewives to sprinkle their floors with. One of these excavations under the Dog kennel hill formed the largest cave in the town, being the work of the late industrious sand-man James Ross, who worked in it thirty years; but it is now broken up and a large manufactory built on its site. Many of the caves and scattered fragments of rock near Gallows hill, were levelled in 1811, by the distressed workmen who were in that year reduced to pauperism.

EXTRA-PAROCHIAL PLACES

Are found generally to have been the sites of ancient castles or religious houses, the owners of which were privileged with an independent jurisdiction, and did not permit any interference with their authority within their own limits. Hence they enjoy a virtual exemption from maintaining the poor, because they have no overseer on whom a magistrates' order may be served; from the militia laws, because they have no constable to make returns; and from repairing the highways, because they have no surveyor. In the language of the ancient Law of England, such places were not " *Geldable* nor *Shireground*," and as the sheriff was the receiver-general in his county till about the time of the Revolution of 1688, extra-parochial districts were neither taxable nor within the ordinary pale of civil jurisdiction; they are still virtually exempt from many civil duties, and the inhabitants are not called upon to serve many public offices to which others are liable. These exclusive privileges are enjoyed by all the *castle-ground* at Nottingham, viz. the *Castle-enclosure,* the *Park, Standard-hill,* and *Brewhouse-yard;* which, though they contain upwards of 100 houses, (see p. 76,) at the west end of Nottingham, are not within the jurisdiction of the " Town and County of the Town," but included in the county at large. If these four extra-parochial districts could be united by an act of Parliament, and made responsible for the maintenance of their own poor, it would be of considerable advantage to the three parishes of Nottingham; for here it is that many of the principal merchants, manufacturers, &c., build their handsome mansions, and whilst Nottingham is their principal source of wealth, they thus avoid paying their just share of the parochial burthens of that town.

BREWHOUSE-YARD is a small district under the south-east side of the Castle-rock, and on the north bank of the Leen, where the Old Water-works' Company have lately built a new engine-house. As has already been seen, it was formerly within the jurisdiction of the castle, and contained a malt-kiln and brewhouse for the use of the garrison, but in 1621, James I., constituted it a separate *Constablery*, and granted it to Francis Philips, gent., and Edward Ferres, mercer, both of London. It has now 80 inhabitants, several dye-houses, and two public-houses, one of which has a room cut in the rock, with "a hole at the top for the admission of light, on which account it has obtained the name of the *Star Parlour.*" The other tavern has two large chambers and other conveniences cut in the rock, near the entrance to *Mortimer's Hole*, which is now built up. (See p. 84.) Thoroton says this place was once an asylum for a fraternity of fanatics called *Philidelphians* or the *Family of Love*, "from the love they professed to bear to all men, though never so wicked, and their obedience to all magistrates, though never so tyrannical, be they Jews, Gentiles, or Turks." Their founder was one David George, an Anabaptist of Holland, who propagated his new doctrine in Switzerland, where he died in 1556, after which his tenets were declared to be impious, and his body and books sentenced to be burnt by the common hangman.

Since King James' reign, Brewhouse yard has had a *constable and overseer*, and the united office is now held by Mr. Joseph Yates.

STANDARD HILL comprises about five acres, nearly one-half of which is occupied by St. James' Church and the gardens, &c., of the General Infirmary :—the north end of which charitable institution is within the limits of the county of the town, in the parish of St. Nicholas, which bounds Standard hill on the east, as the Park does on the north and west, and the outward wall of the Castle on the south. This portion of the ancient Castle Land, perhaps originally part of the Park, derives its name from the Royal Standard which Charles I. erected here in August 1642.—(Vide p. 89.) In 1807, the Duke of Newcastle divided nearly all that part of it, which is not occupied by the Infirmary, into 32 building lots, containing together about 9000 square yards, which he sold for nearly £7010, and which now form four handsome STREETS, viz. Hill street, Charles street, Standard street, and King street. Each purchaser at the time of the sale covenanted, "to pave and keep in repair one half of the streets, so far as they respectively extend in front, or by the side of his lot; to make foot pavements four feet broad; and not to build any house upon the premises of less value than £25 per annum, nor erect any manufactory, nor suffer any obnoxious trade whatever to be carried on upon the premises. Since this sale, St. James' Church, and upwards of 60 large and handsome houses have been erected, so that every building site is now occupied. In 1814, the parishioners of Nottingham complained that the wealthy inhabitants who had built houses on Standard hill, were not only exempt from the heavy poor rates of the town, but refused to relieve those paupers who by servitude were considered to have gained a settlement in that extra-parochial district. In consequence of these grievances, the magistrates appointed two of the inhabitants to act as *overseers*, and afterwards gave orders for the removal of a pregnant servant girl from St. Mary's parish to the house of one of the said overseers, where she was refused admittance. After an expensive legal contest, in which the three parishes of Nottingham made common cause against the inhabitants of this extra-parochial district, it was finally determined by the Court of King's Bench, " that Standard hill, not having been proved to be an ancient *ville* or a *ville by reputation*, is not subject to the jurisdiction of magistrates in the appointment of overseers," consequently, according to this decision, no settlement can be made within its boundaries, either by servitude, by the occupation of property, or by any other means.

The CASTLE ENCLOSURE is bounded on the north by Standard-hill, on the east by Gilliflower-hill, on the south by Brewhouse-yard, and on the west by the Park. It contains about nine acres, including the abrupt declivities of the rock on the south and west sides, where many trees have been planted, and where one or two modern Gothic dwellings may be seen peeping through the sylvan recess. The RIDING SCHOOL stands within its limits, a little below the castle lodge, where some part of the old castle wall was removed in 1798, to make room for that building, which was erected by the Nottingham troop of Yeomanry Cavalry, and is occasionally fitted up for equestrian exhibitions, for which it is well adapted.

The PARK, which contains 129 acres, 3 roods, and 9 perches, is bounded on the south by the Leen, on the east by the Castle-rock and Standard-hill, and on the north and west by the parishes of Radford and Lenton. It is now an open pasture, except a bowling-green and garden plot at its south-east corner, the site of the barracks at its north-west corner, and its eastern and northern boundaries, which have lately been lined with large and beautiful houses, with hanging gardens in front, descending by an abrupt but picturesque semicircular sweep to the green pasture of the park, which extends by irregular undulations to the verge of the parish of Lenton, and to the north bank of the Leen, where are situated those curious caves called the *Papist Holes*, (see p. 120.) The park forms a pleasant summer promenade, and is much frequented, from different roads leading through it to Wilford, Lenton, Wollaton, &c. Until 1720, it was well stocked with deer, and had many large trees, but both have now disappeared, except a cluster of sycamores, which form a pleasant alcove a little below the barracks. There was formerly a FISH POND in the lower angle of the park, facing the Castle-rock, but about the year 1700, it was converted into a reservoir by the Waterworks Company, who so neglected it, that it became a filthy bog, and in 1795, was divided by the Duke of Newcastle's steward into GARDEN PLOTS, and let to the inhabitants of the town;—as also was, in 1809, the picturesque acclivity of the park hill, which rises to a considerable altitude above it, and the river Leen, and had been unproductive for ages. The numerous occupants of this once steril spot, have by great labour and horticultural skill, converted it into a fertile and delightful paradise, producing almost every variety of flowers, fruits, and shrubs, and tastefully decorated with pleasure houses, arbours, &c. One portion of it has been converted into an excellent *bowling green,* and on the north side of the park is the appearance of an embankment enclosing an oblong area, to which tradition has given the name of the *Queen's garden,* being, it is supposed, cultivated betwixt the years 1327 and 1330, when the castle was the amorous retreat of Queen Isabella and Mortimer, Earl of March. Thoroton is of opinion that about fifty acres of the Park was an enclosed orchard during several ages after the conquest; as William Peveril had a license from the Conqueror for that purpose. Deering says the gardeners of Nottingham were not very skilful until after the arrival of Marshal Tallard and the other *French officers* taken at Blenheim, who " resided at Mrs. Newdigate's house in Castlegate, and made very fine gardens there."

PARISHES

IN THE TOWN AND COUNTY OF THE TOWN.

(See population, &c. at page 76.)

St. Mary's Parish is the largest of the three parochial divisions of the Town and County of the Town of Nottingham, as it contains four-fifths of the buildings and population, and the whole of the forest and burgess lands. It includes all the buildings and land on the south side of the Leen, betwixt the Trent and the parishes of Sneinton and Lenton, and all that part of the town on the north side of the Leen lying east of Sussex-street, Middle-hill, Market-street, and Fletcher-gate, whence its boundary turns westward, and includes all the buildings north of Bottle-lane, Poultry, Timber-hill, Beast-market-hill, Chapel-bar, and the Park, until it joins the parish of Radford. Its *principal streets* are the High Pavement, St. Mary's-gate, Stoney-street, Carlton-street, George-street, Pelham-street, Clumber-street, Smithy-row, Long-row, Parliament-street, Derby-road, and Mansfield-road. Its most important *public buildings* consist of the Exchange, the Town-Hall, the churches of St. Mary and St. Paul, the Catholic chapel, many large dissenting meeting-houses, the Grammar, National, and Lancasterian Schools, the Theatre, the Town Gaol and House of Correction, &c. &c. Though the County-Hall and Prison are within its boundaries, the ground on which they stand is excepted from the jurisdiction of the town by a charter of Henry VI.

The WORKHOUSE consists of several large buildings, enclosed by a high wall, which extends from Mansfield-road to York-street, and gives this gigantic establishment more the appearance of a prison than that of a house of industry, for the reception of the friendless poor. It was built in 1729, on ground granted by the Corporation, on a lease of 999 years, at the annual rent of one shilling. But since the year 1808, owing to the rapid increase of population, it has been greatly enlarged at the cost of upwards of £5000. A *dispensary* and a surgeon are attached to the workhouse, for the purpose of giving advice and medicine to the lame and sick poor. The poor rates of this parish have augmented faster than the population; in the year 1764, they amounted to £380; in 1768, to £513; in 1792, to £3657; in 1797, to £5457; in 1802, to £11,050; in 1804, to £15,382; in 1808, to £18,499; in 1812, to £24,763; and in 1831, to £21,493; but of the latter sum only £15,206 was collected during the year ending March 25th. Until 1808, only *two overseers* were appointed annually, but since that year *four* have been chosen, as well as *two churchwardens*. The *Parish Office* is in Pilchergate, and the following is a list of the

PARISH OFFICERS, (ST. MARY'S.)

☞ The sums attached to their names show the amount of their yearly salaries.

	£		£
Absalom Barnett, asst. overseer,	200	Wm. Valentine, surgeon,	150
Peter Black, bastardy dep	90	John Spurr, dispenser,	52
Benj. Barnes, governor,	75	Rev. S. M'Lund, chaplain,	30
Rt. Cartwright, collector,	80	Jph. Parnham, vestry clerk,	10
James Sugden, office clerk,	50	GRATUITOUS.	
Wm. Lineker and Thomas Moody,		G. Howitt, physician,	
assistants,	85	Henry Oldknow, surgeon,	

The *Vagrant Office*, in Chandler's-lane, is supported by the three parishes,—three-fourths of the expense being paid by St. Mary's, and the remainder, in equal portions, by St. Nicholas's and St. Peter's. The yearly expenditure is about £200. Mr. Charles George is the superintendent.

ST. NICHOLAS'S PARISH averages about 500 yards in length, and 250 in breadth. It is bounded on the west by Brewhouse-yard, the Castle-wall, Standard-hill, the General Infirmary, and Park-row; and on the north by Chapel-bar, Angel-row, and Beast-market-hill, whence its boundary (including the greater part of Friar-lane) passes in an irregular line, behind the Friends' Meeting-house and the Sandemanian and Independent Chapels, across Castlegate, to Greyfriargate; down which it passes to the Leen, which forms the southern limit of the parish. Its *principal streets* are Castlegate, Houndsgate, Park-street, Rutland-street, St. James's-street, Mount-street, and Park-row. It has its parish church, several chapels, and other public buildings, one of which is Bromley-house, which contains the large Subscription Library and News-room. The *workhouse* stands at the northern corner of the parish, at the foot of Park-row, and was purchased by the parish in 1813; the old one, which had stood at the bottom of Gilliflower-hill since 1729, being then too small for the accommodation of the paupers. The poor rates for the year ending March, 1831, amounted to £2365. 6s. 3d. Mr John Cheetham is the governor.

ST. PETER'S PARISH, the smallest of the three, is encompassed by St. Mary's and St. Nicholas's parishes, and averages about 450 yards in length, and 200 in breadth. It extends from Timber-hill, the Poultry, and Bottle-lane, to the north bank of the Leen; and is bounded on the east by Sussex-street, Middle-hill, Middle Pavement, and the buildings behind Market-street and Fletchergate; and on the west by Greyfriargate, the Independent, Sandemanian, and Quakers' Chapels, and the north end of Friar-lane. Its *principal streets* are Bridlesmith-gate, Low Pavement, Listergate, St. Peter's-square, Wheeler-gate, Timber-hill, and the Poultry. Its public edifices are the Parish Church, the Police-office, and the Assembly-rooms.— Its *workhouse*, in Broad-marsh, was built in 1788, in lieu of the old Gregory almshouse, which stood at the east end of Houndsgate, and was used as the workhouse till the present fabric was erected. The poor rates here are not so high as in St. Mary's, but in the year ending March, 1831, five rates of two shillings in the pound were collected on the assessed rental, which latter, however, amounts only to about half the rack rental. Mr. John Hudson is the governor of the workhouse.

The COUNTY RATES of the "*Town and County of the Town of Nottingham*" are, as in other places, paid out of the poor rates. Two-thirds of their amount are paid by St. Mary's parish, and the remainder in equal moieties by the parishes of St. Nicholas and St. Peter. These rates usually consume about one-fourth of the poor rates, so that the privilege of Nottingham being a *county of itself* is a very expensive burthen to the inhabitants; for if they had remained in the county at large, their quota of the general expenses of the shire would not have amounted to more than one-third of its present amount, as may be seen by a comparison of the expenses in the year 1823, when the county rate for *Nottingham* amounted to £6150, whilst that for the whole of *Nottinghamshire* was only £9042. Of the former sum, £193 was paid for repairing bridges; £234 to the clerk of the peace; £112 to the coroners; £941 for expenses of the Town Gaol; £1847 for House of Correction; £360 for the Town Hall (or Police Office); £71 for Militia expenses;

£688 for the conveyance of offenders; £1153 for the prosecution of felons; £7 for conveyance of vagrants; £444 for incidental expenses; and £26 for treasurer's salary. These items include the following yearly salaries, viz.—Town Prison, gaoler, £185; turnkey, £50; chaplain, £60; apothecary, £42; and matron, £10:—House of Correction, governor, (including fees,) £175; turnkey and overlooker of tread mill, £114; chaplain, £60; apothecary, £42; and matron, £30. A very large portion of those items entered in the treasurer's account as incidental and other expenses, consists of salaries and fees paid to the constables and police officers, several of whom find "good picking" in their occupation, though they have no stated salary, except the high constable, who has eight guineas per annum. Whether any expense has latterly been thrown upon the town, which ought to be borne by the corporation funds, we have not been able to ascertain, but it certainly appears from the following statement of the sums collected in the years specified, that since 1799, the "town rates" have increased to an extent which has far out stripped the growth of the town :— In 1799, the sum collected was £269; in 1800, £902; in 1801, £1368; in 1802, £1338; in 1803, £2982; in 1804, 1661l.; in 1805, 1322l.; in 1806, 3013l.; in 1807, 2901l.; in 1812, 2808l.; and in 1830, 6020l.! Mr. H. Enfield is the treasurer, as well as town clerk, and clerk of the peace.

THE COUNTY OF THE TOWN includes the Forest, Mapperley Hills, Hunger-hill gardens, St. Anne's, the Sand and Clay Fields, and the Meadows, which are subject to the depasturage of the burgesses. Measuring the indentations of its boundary line, it is about ten miles in circuit, and is bounded on the south by the Trent, on the west by the Castle Liberties and the parishes of Lenton and Radford, on the north by Basford parish, and on the east by the parishes of Gedling and Sneinton. Its boundaries are perambulated twice a year by the " middle-ton jury," with the coroner at their head. This jury consists of a number of the respectable burgesses appointed for the same purpose as leet juries, its duty being not only to walk the boundaries, but to remove all nuisances, and prevent any encroachments on the high roads, &c. &c. It is supposed to have been called the middle town jury, because it commences its survey in the centre of the town, whence it proceeds through all the streets, and afterwards over every part of the extreme boundaries.

CORPORATION, CHARTERS, PRIVILEGES, &c.

It has been seen in the preceding annals of the town that Nottingham is an ancient borough by prescription, for at the time of the Domesday survey it had 123 burgesses, and nineteen villeins, (see p. 82,) and had evidently enjoyed the privileges of a borough long before that period, and prior to the date of any of its charters or records now extant. The Normans, soon after the conquest, divided it into two districts, one called the *English borough* and the other the *French borough*. The division line extended southward, across the Forest, down Mansfield-road, Milton-street, Clumber-street, Bridlesmith-gate, Drury-hill, Middle Marsh, Sussex-street, and over the Meadows to the Trent-road, separating what now forms the "Town and county of the Town" into two nearly equal portions,—the eastern one being the French and the other the English borough. If blood was shed by violence in the latter, the offender was only fined 6s. 4d.; but if in the former 18s. Till 1714, separate juries were empannelled; and there were two *Town-halls;* that belonging to the French borough stood at the north-west corner of Wheelergate. The charter granted by Henry II. in 1155 confirmed to the burgesses all those "free customs" which they had in the time of Henry I., namely, *Tol, Theam, Infangentheof,* and *Thelonia,* from Thrumpton to Newark, and from Rempston to Retford, &c. *Tol* and *Theolonia* imply a power to take, and a right to be free from toll, and the burgesses are still exempt from the market and fair tolls of Nottingham, and all cities and boroughs in the kingdom, except Beverley and Gainsborough. *Theam* gave them a manorial jurisdiction, and *Infangentheof* or *Infangthefe,* conferred on them the power of passing judgment on any theft committed within their liberties. The charter of King John, dated Clipston, 1199, exempted the burgesses from toll at all the fairs and marts in the kingdom, gave them a *guild of merchants,* and expressly declared that " If any person in time of peace, whencesoever he comes, shall abide in this borough a year and a day, without being claimed by his lord, no one shall afterwards have legal claim of him, except the king himself." Henry III., by his charter in 1229, confirmed their former privileges and gave them power to choose coroners from amongst themselves. Edward I., in 1283, granted them power to elect a *mayor* and *two bailiffs,* previous to which they had been governed by a *borough-reeve.* In this charter the ancient yearly *ferme* paid to the crown is stated to be £52. Henry V. by his charter in 1414, gave them a *recorder,* and power to nominate a mayor and four others to act as justices of the peace in the town, without the interference of the county magistrates. The *charter of Henry VI.,* in 1449, not only confirmed all the former immunities and privileges of the borough, but made it a *county of itself,* (except the castle and the shire hall) and gave the burgesses power to elect seven aldermen out of their own body, to be justices of the peace, and wear scarlet gowns of the same fashion as those worn by the mayor and aldermen of London; and one of them to be yearly chosen mayor, and be the king's escheator. It also empowered them to elect two sheriffs in stead of the two bailiffs, to hold a county court every fourth Wednesday, a petty session every day, and a court of all manner of pleas, &c. "The burgesses to have the chattels of all convicted of felony, murder, &c. all amerciaments, post fines, issues of pledges, and bails." James I., in 1623, and William and Mary, in 1692, renewed the town's charters, and Queen Anne granted the burgesses two new fairs, each to continue nine days, beginning on the Thursday before Easter, and on the Friday before the first Tuesday after Epiphany. Charles II. and James II. also granted new charters to the corporation, who, in the 17th century, had several riotous contests with the burgesses. (See pages 88 & 92.)

The CORPORATION now consists of seven aldermen, (one of whom is annually chosen mayor) 18 senior and six junior councilmen, a recorder, two sheriffs, two chamberlains, two coroners, and a town clerk, with the following officers, viz.:—two bridge masters, two school wardens, a sheriffs' clerk, a surveyor, two bailiffs, a mayor's sergeant, a common sergeant, who is also called the mayoress's sergeant; a gaoler, a keeper of the house of correction, a town cryer, a field pounder, a meadow pounder, and a keeper of the fields and woods. There are also about 38 *livery men*, who, having served the office of chamberlain, form the body from which the senior council is filled up. Formerly there was a *scavenger* and a *purveyor*; but the duty of the former is now performed by the chamberlains, and the latter has ceased to be necessary since hot entertainments went out of fashion. There was also a bill-bearer, but the office has long been obsolete.

The MAYOR is nominated out of the body of aldermen, on the 14th of August, and succeeds to office on the 29th of September. The last elected alderman is generally chosen mayor during the succeeding year, otherwise the office goes by rotation, except some particular cause connected with the alderman next in succession be assigned for deviating from the usual practice, as was the case during the year 1831. The ALDERMEN are chosen by the common hall out of the senior council, but there have been a few deviations from this rule, for in 1733, Mr. Thomas Langford "went into the church sheriff and came out mayor;" and in 1810, Mr. John Bates was elected alderman, though he had never been a member of the council. The COMMON COUNCIL consists of eighteen senior and six junior councilmen, the latter of whom are chosen from the burgesses at large, and the former from the livery. To constitute a hall for the transaction of business, the mayor, three aldermen, and nine senior councilmen must be present. The junior councilmen are summoned as well as the other members of the hall, and they have now the privilege of voting on all questions. The council does not appear to be a chartered branch of the corporation, for it is not mentioned in any of the royal grants with which the town has been favoured; but from time immemorial

an indefinite number of councilmen were elected by the burgesses to watch over and defend their interest and privileges in
the borough, till the year 1607, when their number and distinction were fixed as they now remain. (See p. 88.) The *chamberlains* have a right to vote on all questions which relate to the
chamber estates. Both them and the sheriffs are elected
annually, being nominated by the new mayor immediately after
the inauguration ceremony at St. Mary's church, and voted in
by the clothing.

The SEVEN WARDS into which the borough is divided for
municipal purposes, have each their own alderman, and are
named as follows :—Chapel-ward, Castle-ward, Market-ward,
North-ward, Bridge-ward, Middle-ward, and Mont-hall-ward.
The aldermen are not obliged to live in their respective wards;
nor is their authority as magistrates confined to these petty
divisions, but extends alike to the whole town.

The MAYOR'S FEAST, which used to be held at his own
house on the 29th of September, is now laid aside, with the
exception of his friends being invited to breakfast with him
before he goes to church for inauguration. It is customary, however, for the mayor to give four *session dinners*, to two of
which it is usual for him to invite all the resident " clothing".
of the body corporate. The *salary* usually allowed to the
mayor to meet these and other expenses, was formerly only
£150; but in 1804 it was advanced to £200, and is now more
than twice that sum, besides which he and the aldermen derive
considerable yearly dividends from the surplus corporation
funds. There is likewise an annual meeting in the Exchange
hall on the King's birthday, to drink his majesty's health, the
expenses of which are defrayed out of the chamber purse. To
this meeting the mayor has the exclusive privilege of issuing
invitations, which generally extend to all the gentlemen and
respectable tradesmen in the town.

The CORPORATION SEAL is generally allowed to be cœval
with the charter of King John, and presents a very handsome
pictorial representation of an ancient Norman castle, enclosed
within a circular wall, and having four circular towers, above
which are portrayed a crescent and star. The TOWN ARMS
are a *Gules shield* bearing three crowns *Or*, with a cross
raguled, and resting on a trunked *vert*,—evidently alluding to
Nottingham being once a forest town, and to its former connection with royalty.

BURGESS LAND, &c.—Thoroton, who wrote in 1677, says the
town (with the land in the county of the town) is " within the
Metes and Bounds of Shirewood forest, but not within View
and Regard. The town hath long made that claim of discharge,
and it hath been allowed them in Eyre. There are very fair
possessions belonging to the corporation, some in general and
some for particular uses; as for the maintenance of their Free

school, and their costly Trent bridges, called Heathbet bridges."
There is no document or tradition to show how the burgesses
became possessed of the pasture, meadow, and forest lands,
which contain nearly 12,000 acres, and are comprised within
the liberties of the town. It is very probable that in Saxon times
they held part of the lands which surround the town, in consideration of their rendering military service at the castle, which
was always a fee of the crown; and that after the accession of
the Normans they were allowed by the feudal lord of Shirewood,
to cut wood, get stone, and depasture their cattle on that portion of the extensive forest which was afterwards separated
from the Swainmote-court and annexed to the borough as a
separate jurisdiction. About one half of this land, now called
the Sand and Clay Fields, has long been enjoyed by a number of
private owners as freehold property, except during three months
in the year, when it is subject to the depasturage of the burgesses at large. It is not unlikely that this land, being reduced
to a steril condition for want of proper culture, was at an early
period sold under the above conditions, the purchasers stipulat-
ing to fertilize the soil and keep it in a good state of cultivation,
so that the burgesses would in three months derive more benefit
from it than they had previously done in twelve. Blackner,
the last historian of the town, whose quarto is fraught with
wild opinions and rhapsodical digressions, ventures some very
strange conjectures, to fill up the vacuum in the archives of
the corporation. He supposes that King John, when he instituted the merchants' guild, gave the land in question to that
company, and that they held it to themselves till Henry VI.
empowered the burgesses to elect seven aldermen out of their
own body; but which election Blackner surmises was given up
to the said fraternity of merchants, on condition of their allow-
ing the burgesses at large to participate with them in the enjoyment of the said land. If such an important compact as
this had taken place less than four centuries ago, it would certainly have been mentioned by Deering, and some record of it
preserved by the corporation, whose archives are, however,
carefully hid from public inspection, and whose yearly accounts
of receipts and disbursements are not published to the burgesses
at large, as is the practice at some other places where much
property is vested in corporate bodies for the general benefit of
their fellow burgesses, and for particular charitable uses. Leaving the origin of the "burgess grounds" still a mystery, we
will proceed to a description of their several divisions, which
consist of the Meadows, the Sand and Clay Fields, the Forest,
Mapperley-hills, Hunger-hill, and the Coppices.

The MEADOWS, which lie on the south side of the town, betwixt the Leen and the Trent, consist of the East and West
Crofts divided by the Flood-road and the Canal, and containing
334 acres of fertile grass land. The West-croft, comprising

283 acres, is divided into 16 *burgess parts ;* but from the 6th. of July to Old Candlemas-day it is commonable to the burgesses at large, who during that period have each a right to the pasturage of three head of cattle, or 45 sheep ; except from the 13th of August to the 3d of October, when the stock is turned out for the purpose of letting the herbage grow. The *Eastcroft* contains 51 acres, 2 roods, 31 perches, divided into 35 *burgess parts,* except 3 acres and 1 rood, which form the *Pinder's fee.* From the 19th of September to Old Martinmas-day, each burgess has a right of pasturage for three head of cattle, by paying 2s. 6d. for each cow, and 3s. for each horse ; out of which yearly payments the pounder of the meadows has one penny for every head of cattle. The herbage of the 51 *burgess parts* in the East and West Crofts, during that part of the year when it is not commonable to the burgesses at large, belongs to as many poor and aged burgesses or their widows. On the south side of the Trent, and adjoining the bridge, is OVER-TRENT-CLOSE, which is divided amongst the *aldermen,* each having his own *part* allotted to him at the time of his election. If an alderman become reduced in circumstances and resign his gown, it is usual for him to have a pension granted by the corporation, who continue the stipend to his consort if she be the latter liver. A piece of land bounded by the Whey-house farm, the Boat-close, and the Meadows, is also the sole property of the corporation.

The SAND and CLAY FIELDS, which lie on the north and north-west sides of the town, contain 654 acres, and are, as has just been seen, the private property of a number of individuals, subject only to the general depasturage of the burgesses from the 12th of August to the 12th of November. About 150 years ago these fields were entirely open, and were cultivated two years by their respective owners, and on every third year they were enjoyed exclusively by the burgesses. But as this plan was found inconvenient to both parties, it was agreed that each proprietor should fence his own lot, that the land should be laid down for mowing and pasturage, and that two *gaps* should be made in each fence on the 12th of August, so as to admit the free range of the burgesses' cattle till the 12th of November. A number of non-burgess housekeepers, who occupy those ancient freeholds called *Toftsteads* have the same privilege of common right on these fields as the burgesses, though the latter unsuccessfully disputed their claim so lately as 1808. The owners having erected several houses and barns upon these fields, the burgesses, in 1791, instituted an action against them, and obtained a verdict " that the buildings then standing should remain ; but none other should henceforth be erected under any pretence whatsoever." Notwithstanding this legal decision, several other encroachments were subsequently made, and at the Midsummer assize, in 1805, the burgesses obtained another verdict, and an order from the judge " that all buildings which had been erected since 1791 should be taken down, and that the burgesses should have the power at every Lammas of destroying or removing every new encroachment upon the fields." About 200 burgesses avail themselves of their common right in these fields and in the meadows, and they may at any time of the year send their cattle upon the *forest* and *waste lands*, which are however too poor and at too great a distance from the town to be of much benefit to many of them.

The FOREST lies in the north side of the Sand and Clay Fields, betwixt them and the parishes of Radford and Basford. It contains about 124 acres, and falls from the higher verge of the fields, by a steep and rugged declivity, on the summit of which is a long line of wind-mills and several pleasant dwellings, and in the vale below is the Race-course and Cricket-ground; to the east of which, on the opposite side of the Mansfield-road, is the long tract of high waste land called MAPPERLEY HILLS, where there are inexhaustible beds of excellent *clay*, from which most of the bricks of which the town is built have been made; hence originated the old saying, " *Nottingham once stood on Mapperley-hills.*" These hills comprise about 57 acres, and properly form part of the forest, as also did HUNGER-HILLS, which adjoin them on the east, and now form about 400 highly cultivated *gardens*, each let for about £1 per annum. These gardens are divided into about 40 burgess parts, which are given to as many aged burgesses or their widows, who let them to the inhabitants of the town, and each derive from them about £10 yearly. The rents of the land which has lately been built upon on both sides of the Mansfield-road, and on the southern verge of the forest are, or ought to be divided into burgess shares for the relief of indigent freemen or their widows, as well as some other rents arising from building sites which belong to the burgesses, but which have been let on leases by the corporation.

The COPPICES which covered the hill extending from Hunger-hills to St. Anne's Well, were cut down many years ago, and the land now forms a fertile farm of 190 acres; out of the rents of which the corporation pay "30 burgesses 30s. a year each." In 1809 the corporation advertised a part of the coppice lands for sale towards discharging a debt of £5000, which had been contracted partly for repairing the town prisons previously to the collection of the Town and County Rate, and partly in defending themselves " in certain law suits commenced against them by individual burgesses from captious and political motives." This intended sale was however prevented by the burgesses, though the town-clerk* asserted at a public meeting held on the occasion, that there were no burgess-parts upon the

* The late Mr. Coldham.

Coppice-lands, and that they were formerly part of the Royal
chase, and were given to the corporation by King James, as a
mark of respect for the handsome manner in which he was
treated when enjoying his carousal at St. ANNE's in 1615,
when the sportive monarch, with a number of his toping cour-
tiers, and the corporation " *drank the Wood-ward and his
barrels dry.*" The house called St. Anne's stands at the foot
of the Coppice-lands, on the site of an ancient chapel, and was
formerly the residence of the mayor's wood-ward. Till lately
it had a victualler's license, and is still a place of considerable
resort in the summer season, having in front a neat pleasure
garden, in which is a WELL of cold spring water, with a bath
and dressing room formed in the solid rock. On the green in
the garden, a maze or *labyrinth* has been cut, as a miniature
resemblance of the SHEPHERD'S RACE, which occupied an
elevated spot on the opposite side of the valley, and was supposed to be of Roman origin, but was ploughed up in 1797, on the
enclosure of Sneinton Lordship.

ANCIENT CUSTOMS.—Formerly the mayor and corporation,
dressed in their robes, and followed by all their officers and
most of the burgesses, used to go in procession to Southwell
on Whit-Monday, and to St. Anne's Well on Easter Monday,
with the town waits playing before them. A *general watch*
used to be held every Midsummer-eve at night, to which every
respectable inhabitant sent forth a man or went himself, each
wearing garlands on their heads, fashioned like a crown imperial, and bearing in their hands such arms as the town afforded,
viz. pikes, swords, halberts, calivers, &c., whilst some few were
cased in complete suits of armour. This gay corps of nocturnal guardians assembled on the Long-row, and, after receiving
an oath from the mayor's sergeant, patrolled the town during
one of the shortest nights in the year, after which their duty
was ended till that day twelve month, except on the occurrence
of any sudden alarm, when they were liable to be called
out at a moment's notice, for the purpose of defending the town
against any danger which might approach.

PARLIAMENTARY RIGHTS, &c.—Nottingham has continued
to send two representatives to Parliament since the reign of
Edward I.; and three Parliaments were held in the town in the
years 1330, 1335, and 1337.—(See p. 84.). In 1701, it was
decided by the House of Commons, that the right of election at
Nottingham was in the mayor, freemen, and freeholders of
40s. per annum, and that the eldest sons of freemen by birth,
and the younger sons of freemen who have served seven years'
apprenticeship (any where,) and persons who have served seven
years to a freeman, are entitled to the *freedom of the town* on paying the *admission fees*, which amount to £1. 6s. 6d. to those admitted by birthright, and £1. 13s. 2d. to those admitted by servitude. The elective franchise was anciently in those paying

scot and lot; but Oldfield, in his history of boroughs, complains
that the decision of the House of Commons in 1701 has rendered the right of voting so complicated and open to fraud, that
every freeman may qualify as many as he pleases by surreptiti-
ous indentures of apprenticeship. He adds, however, that
Nottingham is under no immediate influence, owing to the great
number of electors, (now about 3000,) yet complains that the
leading men of each party have formed a coalition to return one
member each. This, he asserts, neutralizes the *two* votes, and
he recommends that *three* should be allowed to prevent it; but,
however plausible this may look in theory, it is extremely probable, that those who have been witnesses to popular contests
in large towns are very glad to secure peace and quiet, by any
arrangement which will put a stopt to scenes where every thing
is considered but *liberty and property,* both of these being
very apt to suffer during the concussions of Whigs and Tories.
The necessity of something of this kind at Nottingham, or
some other powerful palliative, seems acknowledged by the act
of Parliament which was passed in 1803, in consequence of the
tumultuous riots at the prceeding contested election. This
act gives a concurrent jurisdiction in this borough, to the magistrates of the county at large—(See p. 101,) and was much
complained of as an infringement on the town's charters.
About 20 years ago, the asperities of party feeling in Nottingham assumed such a forbidding character, that a news-room
was established, which admitted none but the journals which
advocated the side espoused by the subscribers; but since then,
the "high and low parties" have become more friendly, and
established another news-room on a true liberal plan, without
reference to party politics or local prejudices. The *general
spirit* of the town is liberal and patriotic, but bribery and corruption sometimes rear their sordid heads both at the Parliamentary and civic elections, as was the case in 1831, when one of
the two candidates for a vacant seat in the *senior council* of the
corporation publicly offered, through the medium of his friends,
half-a-crown to every poor burgess who would give him his
vote;—though at a similar election in 1797, the corporation and
candidates had agreed, " that a final stop should be put to the old
abuse of giving money, &c., as practiced on former occasions."

COURTS OF LAW.

The COUNTY COURT OF THE TOWN is held at the Guildhall
on every fourth Wednesday, before the Sheriffs of the Town
and County of the Town, for the recovery of debts and damages
under 40s.; but by virtue of a special writ called a *justicies,* this
court " may hold plea of many real actions, and of all personal
actions to any amount;" though it is not a court of record;
and proceedings may be removed from it to the King's superior

N 2

courts, by writ of *pone* or *recordare*. In 1785, the inhabitants applied to Parliament for a Bill to establish a *Court of Conscience*, whereby they might recover small debts at a less expense than in this court, but their prayer was refused.

The MAYOR AND SHERIFFS' COURT, sometimes called the *King's Court of Record*, is held at the Guildhall, on every alternate Wednesday, before the mayor and sheriffs, who are its judges. It holds pleas of all actions, whether real, personal, or mixt, to any amount, arising within the county of the town of Nottingham. It is of infinite service in the easy recovery of small debts, and, in the recovery of possessions when withheld from the owners, who otherwise could have no redress, except at the expense of nearly one-fifth of the value of the property withheld. The judges depute a steward for the purpose of issuing writs of *capias ad respondendum*, and *ad satisfaciendum*; the first of which makes the defendant answerable to the plaintiff, and the second is a writ of execution after judgment, empowering the officer to take and detain the body of the defendant until satisfaction be made to the plaintiff. The *steward* is the under-sheriff of the town, and the *officers* are the two sergeants at mace.

The QUARTER SESSIONS for Nottingham are held in the Guildhall on the first Wednesday in January and February; on the last Wednesday in June, and on the second Wednesday in October. Those for Nottinghamshire are held in the county hall on the preceding Mondays. The recorder presides at the former, and one of the county magistrates at the latter. The ASSIZES are held twice a year, generally in the last weeks of February and July. By virtue of the act passed in 1803, the county magistrates sit in the town courts on the left, and the mayor and aldermen on the right hand of the judges. PETTY SESSIONS are held every Tueday and Friday at the Police office for the town; and every Wednesday and Saturday at the county-hall for Nottinghamshire.—Mr. H. Enfield is *clerk* to the town, and Mr. William Sculthorpe to the county *magistrates*. Mr. George Freeth is the under-sheriff.

The PEVERIL COURT, which was anciently held in Nottingham, is now held at *Lenton* every Tuesday, for the recovery of small debts and for damages in case of trespass. Twice a year, viz. October 25th and May 14th, it sits to try causes as high as £50. It is a court of pleas, and extends its jurisdiction over the whole of the *Honour of Peveril*, which comprises 170 towns and villages in Nottinghamshire, 120 in Derbyshire, and several in Leicestershire and Yorkshire. The hundreds of Thurgarton and Broxtow, and the towns of Sheffield and Rotherham, were added to its jurisdiction by Charles II., but persons living in those places, which are at a considerable distance from Lenton, seldom sue in this feudal court, they having generally better and cheaper justice at home. Till

1316, this court was held in St. James's Chapel, in Nottingham, but in that year it was removed to the County-hall, and the town was exonerated from its jurisdiction. In 1368, it was removed to Basford, the Honour of Peveril being in that year granted by Edward III. to William de Eland, who, as high-steward, had a right to hold it at any place within its jurisdiction. Queen Anne, in 1707, granted the Honour of Peveril to Sir Thomas Willoughby, from whom it descended to the present Lord Middleton. In 1791, Mr. John Sands, the gaoler, set all the prisoners at liberty, " because there was no food allowed for their support, and because he had been *legally* informed, that if any of them died of want, he would be liable to take his trial as a murderer." The court was then removed to *Lenton*, and the prisoners placed under the care of Mr. Wombwell, who in 1804 built the *White Hart Inn*, and the apartments behind it, which have since been used as the *prison*, and which are enclosed by the walls of the pleasure gardens and bowling-green ; so that the poor debtor may see through his grated window, the merry throngs who resort thither in the summer season. The gaoler, who is also the innkeeper, sometimes permits his prisoners to wait upon the company on the green ; and those whom he can trust have occasionally been allowed to pay a nocturnal visit to Nottingham, under a promise to return early next morning, and perhaps in consideration of a fee. Lord Middleton is *high-steward* of the court, which is held before John Balguy, Esq., the *deputy-steward*, and Mr. Samuel Sanders, the *prothonotary*. Mr. Thomas Wright is the *gaoler*, and Mr. John Wheatley the *bailiff.*— The *office* is in Wheelergate.

The " Market Place Association" for the PROSECUTION OF FELONS, was instituted in 1787, and Mr. George Hopkinson, jun., is now its solicitor.

COURT HOUSES AND PRISONS.

The COUNTY HALL and GAOL of Nottinghamshire, which stand on the south side of the High Pavement, were built in 1770, partly on the site of the old ones, which had stood since 1618. The HALL which fronts the street, is a heavy looking stone building, defended by a range of iron railing, and approached by a flight of steps leading to the grand entrance, over which is a pediment supported by four massive pillars, and ornamented with the *Fasces* and *Pileus*—emblematic of its being a place for the administration of justice. The entrance hall is lighted by a circular window in the roof; on the right is the nisi-prius court, and on the left the crown court, both of which are small, but very conveniently fitted up, having lately undergone considerable alteration in their internal arrangements.— The petty sessions are held in the grand jury room, in which are full-length portraits of George III. and Queen Charlotte. There are in the building all the necessary apartments for the accommodation of the judges, juries, &c.; and at the entrance to the council chamber are some old standards and a kettle drum, which belonged to the Duke of Kingston's light horse, in the rebellion of 1745. The PRISON is behind the hall, on a slope of the rock which rises to the height of seventy feet above Narrow Marsh, and commands an extensive view of the country south of the Trent. It has a good house for the gaoler, Mr. R. B. Brierley; and a convenient chapel, in which the Rev. Robert Wood, D. D. officiates. The cells and courts are clean and airy, and very secure, though a female prisoner in 1831 escaped by throwing herself over the prison wall into the Narrow Marsh, where she was taken up by some of the inhabitants, who concealed her till she regained the use of her limbs, and then so disguised her that she left the town, and escaped the vigilance of her pursuers. The elections of knights of the shire, of the county coroners, and of the verderers of Sherwood forest, and also the county court, are held in the hall, which, as well as the prison, is not within the jurisdiction of the town.

The TOWN-HALL and GAOL form a good brick building, faced with stucco, and fronting the Weekday-cross, at the foot of the High Pavement. In 1741, the Town or Guild-Hall was an ancient tiled building of wood and plaster, presenting four irregular gables to the principal front, and supposed to have then stood nearly 700 years. It was rebuilt soon after 1741; as also was the prison in 1791, since which many alterations have been made. The front is projected over ten wooden pillars, forming a piazza, under which is the entrance to the prison and the gaoler's house. The hall where the town assizes, sessions, courts, and corporation elections are held, is approached by a flight of steps at the west end. It is 39 feet long and 32 broad, and on the east side of it is a handsome council chamber, which serves also as the grand jury room, and is adorned with portraits of Sir Thomas White, George Coldham, Esq. (late town clerk,) and other distinguished characters. The length of the building is only 104 feet, so that it is much too small for the numerously attended festive meetings of the corporation, which are now held in the EXCHANGE, a large and elegant edifice, stuccoed in imitation of stone, and presenting a noble front at the east end of the Market-place, having its pediment richly ornamented, and surmounted in the centre by a large statue of Justice, below which is an excellent clock. The whole of the *Exchange buildings* form a square pile, about 130 feet in length and breadth, but the ground floor is formed into a convenient shambles, except round the exterior parts of the wings, which are divided into good shops and dwellings, with several apartments on the north side used as

the Police-office, and one occupied by the Artisans' Library.—
There is also a good inn, which communicates with the hall or
long room, which is 123 feet in length, 30 feet in breadth,
and 30 feet in height, and is lighted at that end next the Market
place with a large and elegant Venetian window, ornamented
with two Ionic columns. Here public meetings, and the election of the Members of Parliament for the town are held, and
sometimes balls and assemblies, as well as the corporation
feasts. This room, on ordinary occasions, is divided into three
apartments, by large folding doors. The west front was begun
to be built in 1724, and cost the corporation £2400, but it
subsequently underwent considerable alteration. The shambles
and all the other parts of the building were commenced in 1814,
and finished in the course of two years, at considerable expense.

The HOUSE OF CORRECTION for the Town and County of
the Town of Nottingham, stands in St. John-street, at the
corner of Glasshouse-street, on the site which was formerly
occupied by a convent of hospitallers of *St. John of Jerusalem*;
hence it is sometimes called *St. John's prison.* These hospitallers possessed considerable estates in the town, of which
they were deprived by Henry VIII., who gave them to the
corporation, by whom the convent was converted into a bridewell, to which from time to time great additions have been
made. A new wing was added in 1806, and in 1826 a *tread
mill* was erected, the labour of which raises water from a spring,
not only for the use of the prison, but also for the supply of a
public tap, placed on the outside of the high wall which surrounds the prison.

EXECUTIONS.—In the south east angle of the prison wall,
which commands a view of a great part of Parliament-street,
Broad-street, and St. John-street, a NEW DROP was erected in
August 1831, and the first victims who suffered on this appaling
engine of justice, were two young men (Reynolds and Marshall)
who were executed on the 24th of the same month, for a rape
on the body of Mary Ann Lord. Criminals previously suffered
the extreme penalty of the law upon *Gallows-hill*, on the forest,
near the Mansfield-road, where the following persons were
hanged for the crimes and in the years specified, viz. T. Pem
berton, for housebreaking, in 1727; John Briggs, for murdering his wife, 1728; John Revell, gent. for shooting a man, (he
went to the gallows in his own carriage,) in 1729; W. Pyecroft,
coiner, 1732; Henry Parnell, for murdering his wife, 1735;
James Gibbins, highwayman, 1737; Thomas Hallam, cow
stealing, 1738; Smith and Miller, robbers, 1748; James
Woyden, murderer, (he was the first culprit dissected in Nottingham,) 1752; Roberts and Sandham, for cutting and maim-
ing, 1753; Richard Sturges, for robbing dye-houses, 1757;
Robert Wilson, for robbing a pedlar, 1758; Samuel Ward,
house-breaking, 1759; Wm. Andrew Horne, Esq. of Butterley,

for murdering his illegitimate child, (35 years before,)* 1759 ;
Elizabeth Morton, (only 16 years of age,) for murder, 1763;
Wm. Wainer and J. Bromage,† highwaymen, 1766; R. Downe
and T. Reynolds, burglary and murder, (the body of the latter
was *hung in chains* near Mansfield,) 1767; Wm. Hebb, murder,
1770; R. Wheatley, for returning from transportation, and J.
Shaw, for burglary, 1774; Wm. Voce, for murdering a wash-
erwoman, at Sneinton wakes, 1774; John Spencer, for murdering the keepers of Scrooby toll bar, near which his body
was hung in chains, 1779; G. Brown and A. Bagshaw, for
burglary, 1781; Cooper Hall, for robbing the Newark post
boy, 1782; R. Rushton and Ann Castledine,‡ for murder,
1784; T. Henfrey and W. Rider, highwaymen, 1784; Wm.
Cook, horse stealer, and J. Anderson, J. Pendrill, and J.
Townsend, highwaymen, 1785; Thomas Cobb, for burglary,
1785; W. Hands and J. Lister, horse and sheep stealers, 1786;
S. Martin and A. Farnsworth, burglary, 1790; W. Healey,
horse stealing, 1793; D. Proctor, for a rape, 1795; J. Milner,
cow stealing, 1797; J. Brodie, a *blind man*, for murdering a
boy on the forest, 1799; J. Atkinson, forgery, 1800; M. Denman, W. Sykes, and T. Bakewell, burglary, 1801; Mary
Voce, for murdering her infant, 1802; Ferdinando Davis,
highwayman, 1802; J. Thompson, for robbery, and Wm. Hill,
for a rape, 1803; R. Powell, burglary, 1805; Wm. Davis,
forgery, 1806; T. Lampin, forgery, 1809; B. Renshaw, for
arson, &c. 1812; W. Simpson, burglary, 1813; J. Hemstock,
murderer, 1815; J. Simpson, highwayman, 1816; D. Diggle,
for attempting murder, (executed in front of the county hall,)
1817; C. Rotherham, for murder, 1817; Needham and Man-
derville, burglary, 1818; T. Wilcox, highwayman, 1820;
Bamford, Adie, and Sanderson, murderers, 1822; T. Rowe
and B. Miller, highwaymen, 1823; T. Dewey, murderer,
1825; S. Wood, for murdering his wife, and J. Shepherd and
G. Milnes, for burglary, 1826; W. Wells, for highway robbery, 1827;—since which no execution took place, neither in
the town nor county, till the one already mentioned in 1831,
though many persons were convicted of robbery and other
offences, which are now generally punished with transportation;
and we hope soon to see such a revision of our criminal code as
shall render the punishment of offenders more certain, but more
equitably proportioned to the nature of their crimes than has
hitherto been the case.

* He was driven to the gallows by his own coachman.

† They went to hear their condemned sermon, and after laying down in their
graves, they walked in their shrouds to the place of execution.

‡ She was hanged for destroying her infant as soon as it was born. Her body
was dissected at Derby, where "a strange gentleman took up the heart, kissed it,
shed tears upon it, squeezed a drop of blood out upon a handkerchief, and then
rode away."

The following is a list of the Members of Parliament, the
Corporate Body, and the Municipal Officers of the Town and
County of the Town of Nottingham :—

MEMBERS OF PARLIAMENT.

Thomas Denman, Esq. Attorney-General, Lincoln's Inn, London.
General Sir Ronald Crawford Furguson, G. C. B. 5, Bolton-row,
Piccadilly, London.

CORPORATION—1831–32.

☞ *The figures show the year in which each was appointed.*

MAYOR, John Houseman Barber, Esq. 1831.

RECORDER, Rt. Hon. Henry Rd. Vassal Fox, Lord Holland, 1809.

DEPUTY RECORDER, Wm. Reader, Esq. barrister, 1830.

ALDERMEN.

John Allen, Esq. 1804.	William Soars, Esq. 1817.
William Wilson. Esq. 1810.	Octavius Thos. Oldknow, 1821.
Chas. Lomas Morley, Esq. 1814.	Samuel Deverill, Esq. 1822.
John H. Barber, Esq. 1816.	

CORONERS, Mr. Henry Enfield, 1808; and Mr. Jon. Dunn, 1816.

SHERIFFS, Mr. John Harrison and Mr. F. Leaver, 1831.

UNDER SHERIFF, Mr. Wm. Hurst; office, High Pavement.

CHAMBERLAINS, Messrs. John Rogers and George Harvey, 1831.

TOWN CLERK, *(Clerk of the Peace and Town Treasurer,)* Mr.
H. Enfield, 1815; office, Low Pavement.

LAND AND BUILDING SURVEYOR, Mr. E. Staveley; office, Pelham-st.

SENIOR COUNCILMEN.

Thomas Wyld, 1800.	John S. Howitt, 1821.
Henry Enfield, 1808.	Nathl. Barnsdall, 1821.
Jonathan Dunn, 1809.	James Roger Allen. 1823.
William Morley, 1814.	Alfred T. Fellows, 1823.
Richard Hopper, 1817.	Kirke Swann, 1823.
Thomas Wakefield, 1817.	Henry Leaver, 1825.
Thomas Richards, 1819.	William Roworth, 1830.
William Hurst, 1819.	Thomas Guilford, 1830.
Edward Staveley, 1821.	Henry Homer, 1831.

JUNIOR COUNCILMEN.

John James, 1793.	Lewis Alsopp Lowdham, 1807.
Richard Hooton, 1798.	Martin Roe, 1810.
James Lee, 1799.	James Dale, 1815.

LIVERY, (DATED AS CHAMBERLAINS.)

John Hancock, 1780.
John Need, 1782.
John Heath, 1784.
Thomas Nelson, 1786.
Timothy Fellows, 1787.
Joseph Heath, 1788.
Elihu Samuel Fellows, 1789.
Thomas Pepper, 1791.
Thos. Carpenter Smith, 1792.
John Ashwell, 1794.
Nathaniel Need, 1795.
William Howitt, 1801.
Nathaniel Denison, 1802.
Charles Mellor, 1804.
John Carr, 1807.
Francis Wakefield, 1807.
Charles Wakefield, 1809.
Isaac Woolley, 1810.
Samuel Hall, 1810.
Alfred Lowe, 1811.

John Michael Fellows, 1812.
George Gill, 1815.
Calverley Huish, 1816.
John Theaker, 1817.
Robert Seals, 1819.
John Heard, 1820.
John Wells, 1821.
Francis Hart, 1823.
James Fellows, 1823.
William Walker, 1824.
Samuel H. Swann, 1824.
Wm. Enfield, 1825.
Thomas Shipman, 1825.
Christopher Swann, 1826.
Samuel Hollins, 1826.
Nathaniel Barnsdall, jun. 1827.
Robert Davison, 1828.
Wm. Cartledge, 1828.
Thomas Allen, 1829.
Rd. Gresham Barber, 1829.

MAYOR's SERJEANT and CHIEF CONSTABLE.—Mr. Richard Birch, Police-office, Smithy-row.—(With 23 Police officers.)

COMMON SERJEANT and WOODWARD, and KEEPER of the FIELDS, Woods, and MEADOWS. —Mr. Saml. Kilbourn, Warser-gate.

BAILIFFS and SERJEANTS-AT-MACE. —W. Gibson, Houndsgate, 1828, and Henry Cox, Castlegate, 1829.

TOWN CRIER.—T. Barwick. Greyhound-street, 1814.

PINDARS.—T. Whittle and J. Cox.

RECEIVER OF ASSIZE RETURNS.—J. Ashwell, farmer, Bobber's-mill.

TOWN GAOL:—Mr. George Vason, Gaoler, 1820; Rev. Samuel M'Lund, Chaplain, 1820; Mr. Robt. Davison, Surgeon, 1820.

HOUSE OF CORRECTION:—John Rainbow, Governor, 1814; Mrs. Jarman, Matron, 1821. The Surgeon and Chaplain are the same as at the Gaol.

PARISH OFFICES and WORKHOUSES:—See p. 127.

☞ The Nottinghamshire Magistrates and Public Officers are inserted in the general survey of the county, at a preceding page.

ECCLESIASTICAL GOVERNMENT.

Nottingham, as has already been seen, is in the *Diocese of York*, and is the head of the *Archdeaconry*, which comprises the whole of Nottinghamshire, and of the *Deanery*, which includes most of the parishes in the hundreds of Broxtow and Thurgarton. The See of York was first divided into Archdeaconries by Archbishop Thomas, in 1090. Henry VIII., after dissolving many of the monasteries, instituted twenty-six *Suffragan Bishoprics*, and the See of one of them was at Nottingham ; but they were all discontinued in the reign of Eliza, beth. Richard Barnes, the last *Suffragan Bishop of Notting-.ham*, was consecrated in 1558; and afterwards became Bishop of Durham. Robert Purseglove, who was Archdeacon of Nottingham in 1552, was the last Suffragan Bishop of Hull, and was deprived of both these dignities by Queen Elizabeth, in 1560, for refusing to take the oath of supremacy. In 1662, two thousand clergymen, in different parts of England, were ejected from their livings, for not conforming to the Act of Uniformity, which came into operation on St. Bartholomew's day; many of these were from Nottingham and Nottingham-shire.—(See p. 91.)

The present ARCHDEACON OF NOTTINGHAM is the Venerable John Eyre, M.A. rector of Babworth, and one of the residen-tiaries of York Cathedral, who was inducted to the office in 1810. The archdeaconry is not endowed, so that the dignity is supported solely by the perquisites of the office, which in 1534 were valued at £61. 0s. 10d. Formerly, the archdeacon paid a triennial visit to the town, for the purpose of confirming the children of the neighbourhood, but his visits have of late been uncertain. The archdeacon holds an annual *visitation* in St. Mary's church, at which the churchwardens of the several parishes are sworn into office.

The SPIRITUAL COURT of the archdeaconry has been held for ages in St. Peter's church, but the judicial power is now removed to York. The Rev. Dr. Wilkins is the *official* of the archdeaconry, and surrogate for proving of wills, &c.; and Mr. Charles George Balguy is the registrar, at the archdea-conry office, on Timber-hill. The court meets, as usual, in St. Peter's church, four, five, or six times a-year, but about 1795 it ceased to try causes, and now merely issues citations for the court at York.

The CLERGY CHARITY, which has for its object the relief of the widows, orphans, and necessitous families of the clergy, within the archdeaconry of Nottingham, holds an annual meet-ing in July, at the Clinton Arms, Newark; the Rev. Charles Nixon, of Nuthall, is the treasurer.

MONASTIC INSTITUTIONS.—The ancient religious foundations of Nottingham, which arose in Catholic times, were neither numerous nor splendid, though there were some very rich ones in the county. The rocky cavities commonly called the *Papist holes*, are supposed to have been anciently places of druidical worship, and afterwards occupied by some of the earliest followers of the Christian faith.—(See p. 120.)—In the first centuries of Christianity, many of its persecuted votaries, in order to avoid a cruel death, "and the better to give themselves up to fasting, prayer, and contemplation, re-tired by themselves into desert places," in allusion to which they were called *hermits*. "After the persecutions of the Christians were over, and the church enjoyed peace, these

o

hermits by degrees returned to towns and cities, and associating together; they lived in houses called *monasteries*, and confined themselves to certain rules agreed upon amongst themselves." But it was not till the beginning of the seventh century that Christianity obtained a firm footing in England. *Monachism* first commenced in Asia, and afterwards spread itself all over Europe, and its reign in England was as brilliant as in any other part of the world, till Henry VIII., who was perhaps a necessary scourge for the sins and bigotry of the times in which he lived, swept away nearly all its institutions, and threw their immense wealth into a more corrupt channel than even that which it had previously occupied; for instead of preserving it for the spiritual and bodily support of the poor, as was the intention of the original donors, he sold or granted most of it to private individuals, for the gratification of his own concupiscence, and for the satisfaction of those who connived at his lascivious errors. That the monks had become insolent and corrupt, and that a religious reformation was necessary, all must admit, but this perversion of property intended for charitable uses, all must condemn. But to discuss this subject is the province of our national historians, we shall therefore confine ourselves to a description of the monastic houses which existed in Nottingham, where the white and grey friars, and the knights of St. John of Jerusalem, had each a separate establishment, besides which there were in the town an hospital of lepers, a college of secular priests, and two religious cells.

The GREY FRIARY, which stood at the south-west corner of Broad-marsh, had an enclosed garden which extended to the river Leen. It was founded in 1250, for mendicant friars of the order of St. Francis, of whom there remained only seven in the house at the time when it surrendered to the commissioners of Henry VIII., in 1539. Edward VI., in 1548, granted it to Thomas Henage.

The WHITE FRIARY, which stood in St. Nicholas parish, betwixt St. James's-street and Friar-lane, was founded by Reginald Lord Grey, of Wilton, and Sir John Shirley, Knight, in 1276, for Carmelite friars, who obtained permission from Pope Honorius IV. to exchange their party-coloured mantle, (which they wore in imitation of the prophet Elias,) for a white cloak, from which they obtained the name of white friars; their original cognomen being derived from a set of hermits who dwelt on Mount Carmel, in Palestine. This house surrendered at the same time as the grey friary, and had then a prior and six friars. The site was granted to James Sturley, in the 33d of Henry VIII. *St. James's chapel*, which stood near this monastery, in St. James's-street, was granted to the white friars by Edward II., previous to which it was the place where the Peveril court was held. This chapel is supposed to have been of Saxon origin, but all traces of it have long since disappeared.

St. John's Hospital, which stood without the ancient wall of the town, on the site of the house of correction, belonged to the knights of St. John of Jerusalem, who, after loading themselves with honour in the unsuccessful crusades against the Turks and Saracens, dispersed themselves into different parts of Europe, and a party of them settled at Nottingham, about the year 1215, and obtained there considerable possessions, which at their dissolution in 1539, were valued at £5. 6s. 8d., and were given to the corporation, for the purpose of enabling them to keep the Trent bridge in repair. The establishment consisted of a master, two chaplains, and several brethren, who observed a perfect equality of property, took the vow of chastity, and wore a habit of russet and black cloth.

St. Leonard's Hospital stood at the south-west corner of the Narrow-marsh, and was founded for the reception of *lepers*, who in 1226 " had reasonable estrover of dead wood to be gathered in the forest of Nottingham," and was endowed with half an acre of land in the King's domains, at the hermitage then called *Owswell.* That dreadful disease, *leprosy*, was introduced into Europe by the Moors and Arabs, about the beginning of the eleventh century, and so prevalent was it in England, that several hundred hospitals were founded for the reception of the afflicted, who, being considered as unclean, were compelled to live apart from those who were so fortunate as to escape the ravages of the scrofulous malady.

Thoroton says, in the reign of Henry III. there was a *fraternity of St. Sepulchre*, and a *college of secular priests* in the castle, and likewise a cell for four monks in the *chapel of St. Mary*, in the rock under the castle.

There were several CHANTRIES in the parish churches, which were endowed for the support of priests to sing mass for the souls of the founders; but these, as well as the monasteries, were swept away by the broom of reformation. In St. Mary's church was the *guild of Holy Trinity*, consisting of six priests, (who had a house in the High Pavement,) also two chantries dedicated to St. Mary and St. James, and another called *Amyas chantry*, from a family of that name who lived in the Long-row. In St. Peter's church there were three chantries, two of which were dedicated to St. George and St. Mary. In St. Nicholas's church, there was a guild or chantry dedicated to the Virgin Mary. In monastic times, much of the land and many of the houses in the town belonged to the rich abbeys and priories in Nottinghamshire and the adjacent counties, and the rectory of St. Mary's was appropriated to Lenton priory.

CHURCHES.

There are in the town five episcopal places of worship, three of which are *parochial churches*, and two, *chapels of ease;* be-

sides which it is supposed that one dedicated to St. Michael an
ciently stood betwixt Fox-lane and St. Anne's-street, where
many human bones have been found on the ground still called
St. Michael's church yard. There was also St. James's chapel,
of which no traces now remain.—See p. 146.

St. Mary's, the largest of the three parish churches of Nottingham, is a venerable edifice in the collegiate style, in the
form of a cross with a very august tower, and standing on the
north side of the High Pavement, upon a bold eminence, which
rises nearly 100 feet above the river Leen, so that it presents a
commanding appearance to the spectator in almost every direction. It has evidently been rebuilt in the gothic style, which
prevailed in the reign of Henry VII.; and Leland, who visited
it about 1540, describes it as being "*newe, and uniforme yn
worke.*" Its interior dimensions are, from east to west, 216
feet; from south to north, at the transcepts, 97 feet; in the
nave, 67 feet; and in the chancel, 29 feet. The height of the
roof is 60 feet, and that of the tower 126 feet. In 1726, the
west end was rebuilt in the doric order, and the south wall of
the nave was new faced in 1761, since which many other parts
of the walls have been renewed, and the interior has just been
cleansed and beautified. Much of the stone used in its frequent
repairs is a very soft and perishable freestone, so that many of
the modern parts now present an air of antiquity. The organ,
which stands in front of the glass screen which separates the
chancel from the nave, was built in 1777, by the celebrated
Snetzler. It has two fronts, and, both in tone and elegance, is
a convincing proof of the skill of its maker. In the steeple is
an excellent peal of ten musical bells, all cast betwixt the years
1605 and 1761. Many of the monuments and all the brass
plates in the church were destroyed or defaced by the *liberal
roundheads* in the civil commotions of the seventeenth century.
In the south aisle is "Our Lady's chapel," which contains the
tombs of the first and second Earls of Clare, over which is a
mutilated alabaster figure. On the opposite side is the *chapel
of All-saints,* where many of the ancient family of Plumptre are
interred, and on one of their tombs lies the recumbent figure
of a man dressed in a gown with wide sleeves. The Earl of
Meath and several other distinguished characters lie interred in
the church, as is recorded on many mural monuments, several
of which belong to the family of Wright. In the north window
is a beautiful figure of St. Andrew. The enclosing of the
church-yard with iron railing was commenced in 1792, but was
not completed till 1807. Three other burial grounds have been
purchased and consecrated for the use of St. Mary's parish;
they are at a considerable distance from the church, one being
on the north and another on the south side of Barkergate, and
the other on the west side of Cartergate, which latter was purchased in 1814, at the cost of 8s. per square yard.

· The *Vicarage of St. Mary's* is in the patronage of Earl Manvers, and is now enjoyed by the Rev. George Wilkins, D.D.,
who is also vicar of Lowdham, and prebendary of Normanton in
Southwell Collegiate Church. The Rev. I. C. Colls is the
curate. The vicarage house stands opposite the south-east
corner of the church-yard, and was built on the site of the old
one in 1653. The living is valued in the King's Books* at
£10. 5s. per annum. From a *Terrier* published in 1748, and
containing an account of the *glebe lands, tithes, &c.,* it appears
that there are belonging to the vicarage 27 acres of land, viz.:
six in the Sand-field, 13 in the Clay-field, and eight in or near
the Meadows, the Ryehills and Hooper's Sconce; besides a
garden and close in Cartergate, and the TITHE of all tofts and
crofts, of bread, potatoes, gardens, pigs, sheep, flax, &c. &c.
The tithe of the Leen Mill is stated at 20s. payable at
Easter; the tithe of the bread of every baker in the parish, an
halfpenny loaf every Saturday; the tithe of all gardens, occupied by gardeners, two shillings in the pound rent; the tithe
of all sheep that go in the fields from Michaelmas to Martinmas, fourpence per score; and the Easter-offerings, sixpence-
halfpenny for each house in the parish. The vicar has also 20s.
yearly left by *Alderman Staples* for preaching two sermons
upon Charity, on the Sundays before Whitsuntide and Christmas; and 10s. yearly left by the *Rev. William Thorpe* for a
sermon to be preached on the day of the restoration of Charles
II., besides surplice fees, which in this populous parish, are
very considerable. The temporal affairs of the church are
managed by two *churchwardens,* each assisted by a sidesman
of their own choosing, and remaining two years in office;—only
one being changed annually by the alternate election of the
vicar and housekeepers of the parish. Mr. William Aspull is
the *organist;* Thomas Hardwick Almond is the *clerk;* Mr.
Joseph Parnham, the *deputy clerk;* and William Johnson, the
sexton. For the other officers and a description of the parish,
see page 126.

Blackner says, since the death of the Rev. Dr. Haines in
1806, the vicarial *tithes* of St. Mary's parish have been collected
with considerable severity, and that two *customs* which are
still continued, originated with *King John,* who in one of his
visits to the town, called at the houses of the *mayor* and the
vicar, and finding neither *ale* in the cellar of the one, nor
bread in the cupboard of the other, his Majesty ordered that
every publican in the town should contribute sixpenny worth
of ale to the mayor yearly; and that every baker in St. Mary's
parish should give a halfpenny loaf weekly to the vicar.

St. PETER's CHURCH stands upon the declivity which falls

* KING's BOOKS.—In 1535, a valuation was taken of all the church livings in the
kingdom, by order of Henry VIII., from whom the records obtained the name
of the King's Books.

westward from Bridlesmithgate to the foot of Wheelergate, Houndsgate, and the Low Pavement. It is a Gothic structure with a tower at the west end, supporting the only *spire* in the town, and containing a peal of eight bells, cast in 1771, and said to be the best attuned and the most melodious of any within many miles. The fabric is supposed to have been built in the early part of the 15th century. It was greatly damaged in the civil wars, when the garrison threw several bombs into it to dislodge a party of royalists who had taken possesion of it. Since then it has been frequently repaired; and in 1789, a mason of the name of Wooton,* took down and rebuilt four yards of the spire, without the aid of scaffolding. In 1800, the south side of the church was rebuilt, and in 1807 the north side was stuccoed and the portico taken down. In 1814, the chancel was repaired. The interior is peculiarly neat and has a good organ, which was purchased by subscription in 1812. A large square window at the east end, which contained a variety of coats of arms in stained glass, was built up in 1720, when an altar piece was placed against it, representing the Last Supper, but which has since been removed to make room for a beautiful painting by Mr. Barber, of Christ's agony in the garden. The chancel is graced with several mural monuments, and in the church-yard, which was enclosed in 1804, there was a *serio-comic epitaph* to the memory of " *Vin Eyre*," a needle maker, who had much influence with his brother burgesses, and was a " great stickler for the *high, or blue party* in this town, at elections;" but every letter is now worn out of the stone, which covers the remains of this poor but incorruptible burgess, who died in the street in 1727, after the fatigues of a contested election, in which he had over exerted himself for the successful candidate. Upward of 700 free seats for the use of the poor were erected in the church a few years ago. In 1831, a new *burial ground* containing 16,000 square yards, near the Workhouse in the Broad Marsh, was opened for the use of St. Peter's parish. The benefice is a RECTORY valued in the King's books at £8. 7s. 6d. ; in the patronage of the King, and now in the incumbency of the Rev. Robert White Almond, M.A. The Rev. S. M'Lund is the *curate*; Mr. Woolley is the *organist;* Mr. W. M. Kidd, the *clerk ;* and Mr. Martin, the *sexton ;* The Rector receives 20s. a year for preaching two *sermons* on Easter and Whit-Monday, from the bequest of *John Burrows,* left in 1659. He also possesses an acre of land in the Meadows, left in 1730, by *John Paramour,* for sermons on Ash Wednesday and Ascension Day.

* STEEPLE CLIMBERS.—*Mr. Philip Wooton,* a descendant of the abovenamed " steeple climber" performed a similar feat at *Manchester,* where, in 1823, he took down and re-fixed the ball and cross, which surmount the lofty spire of St. Anne's. He ascended solely by the means of ladders, which he contrived to fasten to the spire, one above another from the bottom to the top.

, ST. NICHOLAS' CHURCH is a neat brick edifice ornamented with stone, and like St. Peter's, shaded by a number of trees. It occupies a pleasant situation on the south side of Castlegate, whence its large burial ground extends to Chesterfield-street and Rosemary-lane. The building was commenced in 1671, and finished in 1678, on the site of an ancient fabric which was destroyed in 1647, when a party of royalists took possession of it, and from, the steeple so annoyed the parliamentarians in the castle, that they could not "play the ordnance without ,woolsacks before them," and the bullets from the church " played so thick into the outward castle-yard, that they could not pass from one gate to another, nor relieve the guards, without very great hazzard."[*] The church, however, was soon set on fire, and the royalists obliged to fly from its falling ruins. The present edifice has a light and airy appearance, and has a tower with one *bell* at the west end. It has a spacious nave and two side aisles, the southermost of which was much enlarged by subscription in 1756; and a similar extension of the north aisle took place in 1733, when £500 was raised for the purpose. It has since been new paved and ornamented with a handsome pulpit and a reading desk, and also with a new gallery on the north side. The organ was erected in 1811; on each side of the communion table are elegant paintings representing the good Samaritan and the Prodigal Son; and the walls are decorated with many neat monumental tablets, and four hatchments belonging to the families of Newdigate, Smith, Bromley, and Cooper. Amongst the numerous *epitaphs* in the church-yard is a facetious one to the memory of " *Old Tom Booth*," a noted deer stealer, who died in 1752; and another of a very pathetic character, in remembrance of William John Gill, an exemplary youth who was drowned in the Trent in 1802. The living is a RECTORY valued in the King's Books at £2. 1s. 8d. It is, like St. Peter's, nominally in the patronage of the King, but virtually in the gift of the Lord Chancellor. The Rev. William Joseph Butler, M.A., is the incumbent; Mrs. Cooper is the *organist;* Mr. William Archer the *clerk;* and Mr. Robert Allen the *sexton.*

Tithes.—There is no farm land in the parishes of St. Nicholas and St. Peter, both of which are circumscribed within the skirts of the town, consequently the rectors have no *great tithes.* And as to the *small tithes,* Blackner could not discover that any attempt had been made to collect them, except in 1793, when the rector of St. Nicholas, said to one of his officers, " if you will inform me of any person who keeps breeding sows in the parish, I will make it worth your while." The officer replied, that he knew of but one, whom he named, and in a day or two he told him that his sty would shortly be ha-

* Memoirs of Colonel Hutchinson.

noured with a *tithe-pig visit*, which the owner determined to
prevent, by carrying to the parson's door a young pig, and contriving to make it move the knocker, by which it soon gained
a welcome reception; but the rector was afterwards so severely
assailed with the jeers of the parishioners, that he lost all relish for
tithe-pig, and never made any further inquiries on the subject.

ST. PAUL'S CHURCH is a *Chapel of Ease* to St. Mary's parish. It is a handsome stone fronted building, erected in 1822,
and is situated in George-street, opposite the Catholic Chapel.
It has a portico with four large fluted columns supporting an
elegant cupola, in which there is but one bell. The interior
is light and neatly pewed, and has spacious free-galleries for the
use of strangers and the poor; the seats on the ground floor
being the only ones which are let for the benefit of the minister;
the Rev. A. Sadler, is the incumbent, and Mr. Joseph Aldridge the *clerk*.

ST. JAMES'S CHURCH or *Extra-Parochial Chapel* is pleasantly situated on Standard-hill, opposite the top of Rutland-
street, without the boundaries of the " county of the town." It
was built by subscription in 1808, at the cost of nearly £13,000,
including the expense of an act of Parliament, which the subscribers were obliged to obtain for its erection in consequence
of their being strenuously opposed by the vicar and two rectors
of Nottingham, who have no control over this place of worship,
which stands on the extra-parochial ground that once belonged
to the castle.—(See p. 124.) It is a neat brick structure cased
with stone, and the doors and windows are in the gothic style.
The tower, which is low, contains but one bell; the interior is
neatly fitted up, and has commodious galleries over the side
aisles. The present *minister*, the Rev. John Burnett Stuart,
M.A., " is one of the evangelical clergy, and the congregation
is very wealthy and respectable." The first three presentations
are in the three largest subscribers to the building, viz. the
present incumbent, Edmund Wright, Esq., and Thomas Walker, Esq.; after which, the benefice will be in the patronage of
the Crown. The Rev. Samuel Rogers is the assistant *curate ;*
Mr. Henry Bond the *organist ;* Mr. William Glover, the *clerk ;*
and Mr. George Fogg the *sexton*.

The ROMAN CATHOLIC CHAPEL, in George-street,
was erected in 1827, and will seat about 600 persons, being 84
feet in length, 41 feet in breadth, and 31 feet in height. It is a
substantial and well finished edifice, with a handsome stone
front in the Doric order; and is dedicated to St. John the Evangelist. The organ which was built by Parsons of London, is
considered a very fine instrument. The Rev. Robert William
Willson is the PRIEST; and Mr. Woolley the *organist*. The
congregation had previously a small chapel in an obscure situation in King's-place, but it is now converted into a school-
room.

DISSENTING CHAPELS.

In most large towns Dissenters are numerous and influential; and so great is their preponderance in Nottingham, that out of the 30 places of worship in the town, no fewer than 25 belong to congregations not connected with the Protestant established church. Of these chapels, many of which are large and numerously attended, five belong to the *Baptists*, seven to the *Independent Calvinists*, five to the *Methodists*, and one each to the *Unitarians*, *Sandemanians*, *Huntingtonians*, *Quakers*, *Swedenborgians*, *Southcotarians*, and *Jews*.

The UNITARIAN CHAPEL, which stands in a court behind the High-pavement, was erected about the close of the 17th century, soon after the passing of the Toleration Act; previous to which its congregation suffered much persecution, and was obliged to assemble secretly in a vault under a house at the top of Drury-hill. They were anciently called *Socinians* from their founder, *Faustus Socinus*, who died in Poland in 1604. The chapel was new roofed, the floor flued, the walls stuccoed, and otherwise repaired in 1805. It will seat about 800 hearers, and has a Free-school attached to it. The late George Walker, a celebrated philosopher and politician, was some years minister of this chapel, which is now under the pastoral care of the Rev. Benjamin Carpenter.

INDEPENDENT CHAPELS.—The *Castle Meeting-house* stands next in seniority to that in the High-pavement, being built in 1689, when its founders adhering to the doctrine of John Calvin, separated from the Socinians, and formed themselves into an independent church of "*Congregationalists*." The chapel which stands near the bottom of Castlegate has been several times altered and enlarged, so that it will now seat 1200 people, and is generally well filled, having about 320 communicants. In 1826 it was thoroughly repaired and enriched with a good organ. The building stands in the parish of St. Nicholas, but the large *Burial Ground* in front is in the parish of St. Peter. The congregation, which is wealthy and respectable, supports a large Sabbath school, and subscribes to a benevolent fund for the relief of the poor: and since the year 1795, it has been under the ministry of the Rev. Richard Alliott, who is now assisted by his son, of the same name. The *Independent Chapel*, in FRIAR-LANE, was erected in 1828, for the congregation under the pastoral care of the Rev. Joseph Gilbert. It is a large brick edifice, stuccoed in the gothic style, and ornamented with two towers. Exclusive of the upper galleries for the use of its three Sunday-schools, it will seat 750 hearers. SALEM CHAPEL, in BARKERGATE, built in 1817, at the cost of £2000, is a square brick structure, adjoining one of St. Mary's Burial-grounds. It was erected by the Rev. W. Butcher and a number of his followers, who originally separated from St.

James's Church, but are now under the ministry of the Rev. James Orange. Near the chapel the congregation have just built a large Free-school, which will be described with the other charities of the town. SION CHAPEL, in Fletchergate, was built in 1819, for a sect of Independents attached to the high Calvinistic sentiments, under the ministry of the late Rev. James Jack, but it is at present without a regular pastor. St. MARYGATE CHAPEL was erected in 1801, by an Independent congregation, known by the name of *Inghamites*, who profess sentiments nearly allied to the *Sabellians*, and are under the pastoral care of two *elders*, Mr. J. Bailey and Mr. J. Churchill St. JAMES'-STREET CHAPEL was built in 1823, for the Rev. Richard Cicil's congregation, which is now without a regular minister, as also is EBENEZER CHAPEL, a small Independent place of worship in Robin-Hood-yard, Coalpit-lane. SION CHAPEL, in HALIFAX-PLACE, was built in 1761, and was successively occupied by the Unitarians, the Independents, and the followers of the doctrine of George Whitfield, but is now used only as a day and Sunday-school, being rented for that purpose by the Methodists. *Hephzibah Chapel*, now the National-school, was built in 1804 by a party of Independents, attached to the Rev. Mr. Crockford, who sold it to the *Universalists*— now extinct.

BAPTIST CHAPELS.—The *Scotch Baptist Chapel*, in Park-street, is supposed to have been the third dissenting place of worship erected in the town, being built about 1724, for the use of a Baptist congregation, which existed as early as the 17th century, but which afterwards separated into two sects, viz. *Particular* and *Scotch Baptists*, both of which embrace the Calvinistic tenets, and differ in nothing but their church government. It measure 65 feet by 27, and has lately been repaired. Mr. Samuel Ward and two other elders officiate as pastors. The PARTICULAR BAPTIST CHAPEL, in George-street, is a neat brick edifice, erected in 1815, by the congregation which previously occupied the Park-street Chapel. It cost about £6000, including the purchase of the site, and the erection of the large Sabbath-school which adjoins it. The interior is neatly pewed, and will seat 1000 people. The burial ground is at a considerable distance, being at the west side of Mount-street. The late Rev. John Jarman was pastor of this congregation from 1803 till 1830, when he was succeeded by the Rev. James Edwards. The GENERAL BAPTIST CHAPEL, in Plumtre-place, is a large, square brick fabric, adjoining one of St. Mary's Burial-grounds It was built in 1799, and has near it a large Sunday-school, erected in 1811. The Rev. William Pickering is the minister, and is assisted by the Rev. Henry Hunter. The *General or Arminian Baptists* have also a large chapel in BROAD-STREET, erected in 1818, by a number of members, who, with their pastor, the late Rev. Robert Smith at their head, separated from the congregation in Plumptre-place, in consequence of some disagreement in their church government. Its present minister is the Rev. Adam Smith. There is likewise a Baptist chapel, in Paradise-place, Barkergate, but it is a very small building without any regular minister.

METHODIST CHAPELS.—The *Wesleyan* or *Armenian Methodists* in Nottigham, are, as in most other places, numerous and popular, and date their orgin from the days of their founders, John, and Charles Wesley, who commenced their pious labours at Oxford about the year 1730, and during the remainder of their lives travelled into all parts of the kingdom, preaching to the poor and the ignorant, inculcating the general part of the doctrine taught by *Arminus*, a native of Holland, who defended the religious principles of *Beza* in opposition to those of *John Calvin*. After meeting some time in a house in Pelham-street, they erected the " *Tabernacle*" in 1762, but in 1782 they sold it to the General Baptists, soon after which it was taken down; and the site is now occupied by domestic buildings, betwixt Mount-East street and Milton-street, They went from the Tabernacle to HOCKLEY CHAPEL, a large and handsome brick building, which they erected in 1782, at the foot of Goosegate. Their numbers being greatly increased in 1798, they erected HALIFAX CHAPEL, which stands in Halifax place, and is the largest dissenting place of worship in the town, being 84½ feet long, and 53 feet broad, exclusive of the vestry and other conveniences. This chapel will seat about 1600 persons; and that at Hockley 1300. St. ANN'S CHAPEL, in St. Ann's-street, was built in 1824, and is occupied six days in the week as an Infant-school; and every Sabbath morning as a Sunday-school. The *New Connexion* or *Kilhamite Methodists* separated from the Wesleyans in 1797, and were in possession of Hockley chapel till 1816, when they built their present large and handsome CHAPEL in PARLIAMENT-STREET, in which is an inscription to the memory of their founder, the Rev. Alexander Kilham, who died in 1798, after fighting hard against the "priestly domination" of the Wesleyan conference. The PRIMITIVE METHODISTS have a large chapel in Canaan-street, erected in 1823, with a Sunday-school attached.

The *Wesleyan ministers* in the Nottingham station are, the Revs. Robert Pilter, Thomas Harris, W. H. Clarkson, and Edward Batty. The *ministers of the New Connexion* are, the Revs. John Wilson, J. Hillock, and S. Hulme. The *Primitive Methodist ministers* are, the Revs. J. Garner, W. Martin, and A. F. Beckerleg.

The FRIENDS' MEETING HOUSE is a plain unobtrusive edifice, standing in a small paved yard in Spaniel-row. It was built in 1737, at the cost of only £337, but it has since been considerably improved by its congregation, which, though not very numerous, is highly respectable. The Quakers formerly had a burial-ground in Walnut-tree-lane, but it being full, another piece of ground, on the north side of Park-street, opposite the end of Spaniel-row, has been devoted to that purpose. George Fox, the founder of this "Society of Friends," was born at Fenny-Drayton, in Leicestershire, about 1624, and was imprisoned at Nottingham in 1649, "for setting the *inward* influence of the spirit, and the plain testimony of the Scriptures, in opposition to the *outward* forms and explanatory ceremonies of the other preachers. He had not, however, been fourteen days in confinement, before he had made a confirmed proselyte of one of the sheriffs, John Reckless, who preached Quakerism in the Market-place." George Fox who it is said was either a shoemaker or a breeches-maker, afterwards wandered all over England, and suffered persecution in every town till at last he ingratiated himself under the wings of Judge Fell, of Swart-moor-hall, near Ulverstone, whose widow he afterwards married.

The SANDEMANIAN CHAPEL, in Houndsgate, was built in 1778, by the Glassites or Sandemanians, who profess the doctrine of John Glass and Robert Sandeman, the former of whom was expelled in 1728 from the church of Scotland, for maintaining "that the kingdom of Christ is not of this world;" and the latter in 1775, contended in a series of letters, "that faith was a mere simple assent to the testimony of Christ." The peculiarities of this sect are, that they administer the Lord's supper weekly, dine together every Sabbath-day, use the kiss of charity, wash each others' feet, abstain from blood and things strangled, and hold the community of goods, so far that every one is to consider all that he posseses liable to the calls of the poor of the church. Mr. Lewis Rigby is their present elder.

The HUNTINGTONIANS occupy Providence chapel, a small building in Plumptre-street, which was first converted into a place of worship in 1806, by the Universalists, now extinct.— The present congregation are adherents to the tenets of the late William Huntington. They have no regular minister, but are occasionally visited by one from Leiceister, and read prayers, &c. every Sunday.

The NEW JERUSALEM CHAPEL is a small building in Sheep-lane, occupied by a few of the followers of Emanuel Swedenborg, a Swedish nobleman, who died in London in 1772.— J. W. Hancock is the leader. The *Israelites*, or Southcotarians, worship in a small room in King's Arms Buildings, behind Woolpack-lane and Barkergate.

The JEWS' SYNAGOGUE is at the house of one of their brethren, in Glasshouse-street, and they have a burying-ground near the forest, at the top of Sherwood-street, which, according to an inscription, was enclosed in the year "A. M. 5583," when the ground was given to them by the corporation.

RELIGIOUS INSTITUTIONS.

The institutions which have for their object the promotion of Christian knowledge, are as numerous and as liberally supported in Nottingham as in any other place of the same importance;—the members of the church, and the various sectarian communities, each subscribe to their respective Bible, Missionary, and Tract Societies. The depository of the Nottingham and Nottinghamshire BIBLE SOCIETY is in Park-street, at the house of Mr. T. W. WINTERTON, and is open every Wednesday, from ten till two o'clock. The Independent congregations of the town and county, have an *Auxiliary London Missionary Society*, of which R. Morley, Esq. is treasurer, and the Revs. J. Gilbert and R. Alliott, jun. are secretaries. In this class stand the SUNDAY SCHOOLS, of which useful institutions, Nottingham availed itself as early as the year 1804, when the New Connection of Methodists erected the large school-room at the corner of East-street, about thirteen years after the first Sabbath school had been established in London. There are now in the town and suburbs upwards of thirty-five Sabbath schools, which, under the superintendence of several hundred gratuitous teachers, afford instruction in the humbler branches of learning, to thousands of poor children, many of whom, from the abject poverty of their parents, are obliged to labour at an early age during six days in the week, and have consequently no opportunity but on the Sabbath to attend to civil or religious tuition.

The Nottingham SUNDAY SCHOOL UNION was established in 1810, and has now connected with it no fewer than one hundred and eight Sunday-schools, belonging to the Methodists, the Independents, and the Baptists, and attended by upwards of 14,000 children, who receive instruction from nearly 1000 gratuitous teachers. Of these schools, twenty are in the town, and the remainder in the parishes within a circuit of ten miles round Nottingham. The affairs of the Union are managed by a committee of forty subscribers, four secretaries, a treasurer, and a depositary, which latter office is now filled by Mr. R. Preston, of the Long-row, Nottingham.

The late Mr. Raikes, a respectable printer of Gloucester, is generally considered as the founder of Sabbath schools, which Blackner says were first introduced about the year 1778, by John Moore, a framework knitter of Leicester, and Wm. Hallam, a native of Kirton, in Nottinghamshire, but then a schoolmaster, at Moneyash, in the Peak of Derbyshire;—both of whom taught gratis on the Sabbath, at least two years before Mr. Raikes commenced his labours for the promotion of these useful institutions, of which, though not the original inventor, he was the earliest and most active patron.

P

CHARITY SCHOOLS.

Besides the numerous Sunday schools, ample provision is made by the benevolent inhabitants of Nottingham, for the education of those poor children who can attend during six days in the week, for out of the 7276 children now receiving instruction in the town, either gratuitously or for very trivial payments, nearly 2000 are *day scholars,* as will be seen by the following

LIST OF DAY AND SUNDAY SCHOOLS IN NOTTINGHAM.

Date.	Day Schools.	No. schlrs.	Sunday Schools in Union.	No. schlrs.
1811	National (boys)	560	St. Ann's-street, Wes. Meth.	195
1810	Lancasterian (boys)	220	Halifax-place, ditto	444
1820	Lancasterian (girls)	100	Hockley, ditto	243
1831	Barkergate Free, (170 b. 80 g.)	250	Parliament-street, New Meth.	312
1808	School of Industry (girls)	150	Mansfield-road, ditto	150
1706	Blue Coat (60 boys, 20 girls)	80	Woodland-place, ditto	150
1513	Free Grammar (boys)	90	Canaan-street, Prim. Meth.	180
1789	Unitarian (40 boys, 24 girls)	64	Kingston-place, ditto	47
1827	*Infant Schools,* St. Anne's,	120	Cross-lane, ditto	188
1827	Ditto, Rutland-street,	120	Castlegate, Independent	380
1829	Ditto, Canaan-street,	100	Friar-lane, ditto	305
1829	Ditto, Independent-hill,	140	St. James's-street, ditto	231
			Fletchergate, ditto	180
	Total	1994	Barkergate, ditto	165
			Broad-street, General Baptist	146
	Sunday Schools,		Fishergate, ditto	57
1810	Three parish churches	500	Stoney-street, ditto	437
1824	St. James's, Rutland-street	200	George-street, Particular Baptist	260
1831	St. Paul's, George-street	100	Independent-hill, ditto	162
	Catholic chapel, ditto	170	Park-street, Scotch Baptist	80
	Total	970	Total	4312

GRAND TOTAL of day and Sunday scholars, 7276. Perhaps a few hundreds of these may be reckoned twice, owing to their attending both day and Sunday schools.

The FREE GRAMMAR SCHOOL, in Stoney-street, is now a handsome building, having lately been enlarged, and ornamented with a beautiful stone front, in the gothic order, though it had been repaired in the years 1689, 1708, and 1792. It was founded in 1513, by *Agnes Mellers,* widow of Richard Mellers, bell founder, and was by her endowed with lands and tenements in the town and neighbourhood, left in trust to the corporation, for the maintenance of a master and usher. Robert Mellers, the son of the foundress, bequeathed to it, in 1515, a close in Basford, and a house in Bridlesmith-gate, betwixt Petergate and Pepper-street. His brother, Thomas Mellers, who died in 1535, endowed it with " all his lands, tenements, and hereditaments in the town and fields of Basford;" but all the property in Basford parish left by these brothers, was sold by the corporation sometime betwixt the years 1702 and 1720, (together with three tenements in London, left by John Wast,) to defray the expenses of a law suit which they had instituted against Richard Johnson, who was then master of this school. *John Hesky*, alderman, in 1558, left to this school the tithes of the Nottingham fields and meadows, and also a house in Carlton-street, except 10s. to be paid yearly out of the rent to the poor. *John Parker*, alderman, in 1693, left £160, with which a rent charge of £13. 10s. per annum was purchased at Harby, in Leicestershire, for the purpose of founding and supporting a library in the school, and for furnishing £3 *apprentice fees* for poor boys, and £3 gifts to assist them after they have served their apprenticeships in setting up in their respective trades. In 1828, £72 was received as arrears of this rent charge. Four small closes, betwixt Trough-close and Free-school-lane, belong to the Grammar school, as also do all the houses in Broad-street, from Agnes-yard to Goosegate, and several others in St. Petergate and St. Peter's-square, most of which were left by the foundress. The gross yearly income of this excellent charity, arising from rents and tithes, amounted in 1728, to £93; in 1750, to £132; in 1770, to £200; in 1790, to £264; in 1800, to £336; in 1810, to £592; in 1820, to £619; and in 1828, to nearly £700, out of which are paid *yearly salaries and gratuities*, amounting to £150 to the master, £110 to the usher, £50 to the writing master, and £20 to the surveyor of the school estates. This institution, like many other Grammar schools, was during a long period of no service to the poor, for extravagant charges were made by the teachers for every branch of learning except the dead languages, until 1807, when the corporation, being the trustees, established new ordinances for its future regulation, by which the school was declared to be free both for the English grammar and the classics, and that no school fees should be charged, except 10s. a-year to be paid by each boy to the writing master, whilst learning writing and accounts. It is open to all the boys of the town, but the number admitted at one time is limited to about 90. The Rev. Robert Wood, D. D. is the present master, and has a good house adjoining the school, but is not allowed to take boarders. The Rev. Samuel M'Lund is the usher; and Mr. Richard Dudley, the writing master.

The BLUE COAT SCHOOL was founded in 1706, but the present building, which stands at the foot of the High Pavement, was erected in 1723, on ground given by Mr. Wm. Thorpe, a benevolent attorney. It contains a large school room, and a suit of apartments for the residence of the master. Two statues, in niches at the front of the building, represent a boy and a girl in their school costume. This charity educates and clothes sixty boys and twenty girls, till they arrive at fourteen years of age, when the former are put out apprentice, with a premium of five guineas each, and the latter have each two guineas, for the purpose of clothing them for servitude. Mr. and Mrs. Cokayne are the teachers, and attend as well to the religious as the moral instruction of the scholars. The charity, which is supported partly by annual subscriptions and collections at the parish churches, is endowed with property which produces upwards of £380 per annum, of which £139 arises from rents, £2. 5s. from annuities, £8. 17s. 9d. from turnpike securities, £210 from the dividends on £7000 reduced three per cent. annuities, and £16 from £400 exchequer bills. The annual subscriptions and church collections amount to about £150. The expenditure for the year 1827, was £412. 10s. 10d., of which £176 was for clothing the children, and £131 for five quarters' salary to the master. The benefactions left to this excellent institution are as follow :—£2 yearly, out of two houses in Pilchergate, bequeathed by Thomas Sanderson, in 1711; two houses in Houndsgate, by Charles Harvey, in 1711; a house and garden near St. Peter's church, by Jonathan Labray, in 1718; a yearly rent charge of 5s. by Thomas Roberts, in 1729; a close of 1a. 3r. in the Clay-field, by Gilbert Beresford, in 1747; £177. 15s. vested in the Nottingham and Grantham turnpike, by John Kay, in 1774; and the following pecuniary donations, amounting to £2507, but now laid out in land and buildings, viz. in 1715, Wm. Trigge, £100; and Wm. Rippin £100; 1760, Mary Holden, £600; 1764, Wm. Caunt, £50; 1765, Richard Purcell, £65; 1770, Sir George Smith, Bart. £100; 1770, Mary Key, £115; 1777, Rev. Thomas Lovatt, £100; 1782, Mrs. Key, £100; 1785, Susannah Lovatt, £100; 1796, Wm. Lovatt, £100; 1796, Wm. Elliott, £50; 1798, John Morris, £200; 1818, Samuel Unwin, £50; and in 1825, John Elliott, £50; besides which several smaller donations have been paid to the school trustees, who are about twenty in number, and have for their treasurer Henry Smith, Esq. banker.

The UNITARIAN FREE SCHOOL, behind the chapel in the High Pavement, was founded in consequence of a division which took place in 1788, amongst the subscribers to the Blue Coat school. It is supported by annual contributions, for the education of forty boys and twenty girls of any religious denomination. Ten of the girls are also clothed. Mr. John Taylor and Miss Charlotte Sansom are the teachers.

The SCHOOL OF INDUSTRY, which was founded by subscription in 1808, for the instruction of 150 poor girls in reading, writing, and plain needlework, now occupies part of St. James's church Sunday school, which was erected in Rutland-street, in 1824, and has another room occupied as an infant school, with 120 pupils.

The BOYS' LANCASTERIAN SCHOOL is a spacious building of one story, on the Derby road, erected in 1815, previous to which the charity had existed in a rented room since its foundation in 1810. It is supported principally by the contributions of Dissenters, but the ground on which the school stands was given by the corporation. The roof and back wall were destroyed by the falling of a rock in 1830.—(See p. 122.) Mr. Samuel Langworth is the master, and has now under tuition on the Lancasterian System of mutual instruction, 220 boys.

The GIRLS' LANCASTERIAN SCHOOL in Houndsgate, was built in 1820, and is supported by annual subscriptions, for the education of 100 poor girls, who are now taught by Miss Emma Longden. The building also serves as a Sabbath school, to the Castlegate Independent chapel.

The NATIONAL SCHOOL in High Cross-street, is a gigantic seminary where no fewer than 560 boys are educated on Dr. Bell's plan, at the cost of little more than £100 per annum, the master's salary being only £80. The yearly subscriptions amount to about £90, and the annual collection at St. Mary's church in aid of this charity averages about £25. The building which was formerly a chapel, was purchased in 1811, when the school was commenced. The principal donations received by the charity are £200 from the National Society in 1815, and 1817; and £200 given by J. S. Wright, Esq., in 1815, besides a piece of land for the enlargement of the school room. The Duke of Newcastle subscribes ten guineas, and the Dowager Duchess of Newcastle five guineas annually. Mr. Joseph Aldridge is the *master*, the Vicar is the *secretary*, and Mr. T. Tollington the *treasurer*.

The NEW CHARITY SCHOOL, in Barkergate was established in 1831, in the large Sunday school-room attached to the Salem Independent Chapel. This valuable institution which is supported by the contributions of the benevolent, arose principally from the pious exertions of the Rev. J. Orange, and William Wilson, Esq., the late mayor, who (observing that there were in the town several hundred children of the poorest parents, who refused to attend the Sabbath schools from the want of decent clothing, and who were running about the streets through the week, imbibing the germs of idleness and sin,) made a successful appeal to the respectable inhabitants, for their support in the establishment of this school, for the moral and religious instruction of the children of the destitute poor; of whom no fewer than 170 boys and 80 girls are now under the tuition of two masters and a governess, who teach them reading, writing, arithmetic and the English grammar.

The four INFANT SCHOOLS enumerated at page 158, are conducted on the ingenious system introduced by Messrs. Wilderspin and Wilson, by which, infants betwixt the ages of two and six years, under a pleasing interchange of exercise, amusement, and instruction, experience a gradual development of their bodily and mental powers; and are also kept during the

day from that danger and neglect, to which so many of the
young children of the poor are exposed whilst their parents are
engaged in their respective avocations. The schools are supported partly by subscription, but small weekly payments are
properly required from those parents whose circumstances are
sufficient to bear the demand.

AMOUNT OF CHARITABLE FUNDS.—The stream
which flows from the Nottingham fountain of charity for the
education of poor children, is not more copious than that which
issues for the solace of age, poverty, and sickness. Fifteen
HOSPITALS in the town, *endowed* with property which produces upwards of £2100 per annum, afford comfortable asy-
lums for 155 poor aged *alms-people*, besides relieving 32 out-
pensioners. Many indigent families receive pecuniary and other
relief from the periodical distribution of the funds arising from
the BENEFACTIONS of deceased friends of the poor, and now
producing collectively about £550 per annum, which with the
£1080 per annum belonging to the Grammar and Blue Coat
schools, swells the total yearly amount of posthumous charity
to £3730, exclusive of numerous bequests to the *General Hospital* and the *General Lunatic Asglum*, whose yearly incomes
arising from donations, legacies, and subscriptions amount collectively to about £3000. Upwards of £500 is subscribed annually for the support of the recently established *Dispensary*,
and £1000 is dispensed annually by the various BENEVOLENT
SOCIETIES in the town, which seek out the abodes of the wretched;—provide warm clothing for the indigent in winter;—supply the friendless poor, whether natives or strangers, with temporary relief;—furnish poor married lying-in-women with necessary comforts, and distribute Bibles, Prayer Books, and Religious Tracts amongst the ignorant and the depraved. To this
mass of benevolence, we may add about £800, subscribed annually in aid of the Public Schools, which swells the TOTAL
AMOUNT OF CHARITY, dispensed in and near Nottingham to
upwards of £8000 per annum. Notwithstanding the amplitude of these charitable funds, and the great benefits derived by
the freemen of the town from the burgess lands and "burgess
parts,"—(See p. 133,) no less than £24,000 per annum has of
late years been levied as *poor rates* in the three parishes of
Nottingham.—(See pages 127 and 128)

ALMS-HOUSES.

The PLUMPTRE HOSPITAL in Plumptre-square, is the most ancient charitable institution in the town, being founded in 1392,
by John de Plumptre, for the maintenance of two chaplains and
thirteen poor widows "broken with old age and depressed with
poverty." The founder directed that one of the chaplains
should be master or warden of the hospital, which, after the

dissolution of the religious houses, was untenanted till 1582, when Nicholas Plumptre, of Nottingham, became the master under a patent granted by Queen Elizabeth, and repaired the building with the fines which he received from the tenants of the land and tenements with which it is endowed. In 1650, and 1751, it received considerable repairs from two descendants of the founder, whose present representive, *John Plumptre, Esq.,* of Fredville, in the county of Kent, erected in 1824, a *new hospital* on the site of the old one;—having in the preceding year obtained an act of Parliament to sell a piece of the hospital land, to defray the expense. He is now the sole master of the hospital which is endowed with land and buildings let for about £680 per annum, out of which he allows £1. 2s. 6d. every calendar month, to each of the thirteen almswomen, with a ton of coals, and a gown yearly, besides a yearly stipend to the man who reads prayers in the chapel. *Thirty out-pensioners* receive each £10 per annum, but these are, we consider, improperly selected near the master's own residence in the county of Kent, for if it pleased him to remove from the seat of his ancestor, we see no right that can justify him in transplanting to a distant soil, one-half of that ancestor's ancient charity which was bequeathed to the poor of Nottingham. The present hospital, is substantially built of brick in the ancient style, and covered with stucco in imitation of stone. The widows are admitted at the age of 70, and have each comfortable apartments. Henry Percy, Esq. is the *steward.*

COLLIN'S HOSPITAL at the corner of Park-street and Spaniel-row, is a large quadrangular building, with a paved yard in the centre, and two detached buildings at the entrance from Houndsgate, called the Lower Hospital. The whole contains 24 dwellings for the same number of poor widows and widowers, who each receive 4s. per week and 2¼ tons of coals yearly. *Abel Collin,* by his will dated 1704, left a large property to his nephew, Mr. Thomas Smith, for building and endowing this hospital, which was erected in 1709. In 1804, the Rev. *Abel Collin Launder* bequeathed 20-27th parts of an original share in the Nottingham Waterworks, to Samuel and Thomas Smith, Esqrs. in trust, to pay the yearly dividends (which in 1827, amounted to £25. 18s. 7d.) in equal portions to the 24 poor alms-people in Collin's Hospital. The original endowment produced in 1829, no less than £759 per annum, of which, £450 arises from an estate at Burrough in Leicestershire; £105 from land and buildings in Nottingham; and £204 from £6800 consolidated 3 per cent. stock, a part of which has lately been sold by Henry Smith, Esq. and the other *trustees,* for the purpose of extending the founder's charity, by the erection of a NEW HOSPITAL in *Carrington-street,* which was completed in 1831, and is now occupied by 12 alms-people who have the same allowance as the 24, in the old hospital. This new erection forms the handsomest alms-house in Nottingham, and stands in a modern part of the town, upon a large grass-plot, enclosed with neat iron palisades. The new street in front (which with all the land in its vicinity, belongs to this extensive charity) has its name from *Lord Carrington*, who is a collateral descendant of the founder, and the head of the family of Smith.

LAMBLEY HOSPITAL pleasantly situated on the Derby road, forms three sides of a square, with a grass-plot enclosed with iron palisades in front. It has 22 dwellings for as many poor burgesses or their widows, who have each a ton of coals yearly; and it is expected that in a few years they will have small weekly stipends, for the debt incurred by the erection of the building must be now nearly, if not wholly liquidated. It was built in 1812, at the cost of £2700, by the corporation as trustees of an ESTATE AT LAMBLEY, which consists of 104A. 3R. 26P. let for £160 per annum, and was purchased by them in 1654, with money left for charitable uses, of which £200 was bequeathed by *Lady Grantham*, who directed the yearly proceeds thereof to be expended in giving *apprentice fees* with poor children.

WILLOUGHBY'S HOSPITAL stands in Fishergate, near Pennyfoot-stile, where it was erected in 1780; in lieu of the old hospital which stood on Malin-Hill, and was founded in 1524, by Thomas Willoughby, who in that year, endowed it with landand buildings in Friar-lane, Cartergate, and Malin-hill, which now let for £180 per annum. In 1810, two additional dwellings were built, making in the whole 14, for as many poor aged men or women, who each receive £10 a year and an allowance of coals from the churchwardens of St. Mary's, who are trustees of this, as well as of Woolley's and Warsergate alms-houses, to which it was determined at a vestry meeting in 1828, that none should be admitted under the age of 60 years, and none but such as are legally settled in the parish of St. Mary's, and have not received parochial relief for ten years previous to their application.

LABRAY'S HOSPITAL, on the Derby road, consists of a row of six dwellings for six poor *frame-work knitters* of the age of 70 and upwards, who have each 4s. per week and 2½ tons of coal yearly. It was founded by *Jonathan Labray*, a manufacturer of hosiery in Nottingham, but a native of Calverton, where in his youth he had worked as a frame-work knitter. He died a batchelor in 1718; and left his property for the foundation of this charity, in trust to Thomas Smith, Esq., and the other trustees of Collin's hospital, whose successors, Henry Smith, Esq. and others, are still governors and treasurers of both institutions. The endowment consists of a farm of 129A. 2R. 22P. in Calverton parish, now let for £110 per annum; and £1100 consolidated 3 per cents, making the total yearly income about

£150, out of which six pounds is paid annually to Calverton School agreeable to the will of the founder. This income is nearly twice as much as the present expenditure, it is proper therefore that the benefits of the charity should be extended, either by the erection of a new hospital, or the admission of a number of out-pensioners.

WOOLLEY'S BEAD HOUSES, in Beck-lane, were founded in 1647, by Thomas Woolley, gentleman, for *three* poor persons with a rent charge of 40s. per annum; but in 1809 they were repaired and enlarged for the accommodation of *six* poor widows, by the Churchwardens of St. Mary's, who, with the vicar and overseers, are the trustees. In 1818, *Samuel Unwin,* shoemaker, bequeathed £1000, and directed the interest to be divided equally amongst the 12 almspeople, in Woolley's Bead-houses and Warsergate hospital. This sum was vested in £986. 16s. four per cent stock, yielding £39. 9s. 4d. per annum, from which each of the said almspeople receive £2. 5s. and a ton of coal yearly, besides which Woolley's *"bead folk"* receive 2s. per week, arising from the above named rent charge, from a part of the hospital garden let on a lease, and from the sacrament-money collected in St. Mary's church.

WARSERGATE HOSPITAL is of unknown origin, but was re-built in 1775, with rooms for six poor women, who have each 2s. per week from the rent of three small pieces of land; and £2. 5s. and a ton of coal yearly from the above named bequest of Samuel Unwin. Immediately behind this hospital four new dwellings were erected in 1823, in lieu of PILCHERGATE HOSPITAL, which, together with the site was sold for £180, of which £143 was expended in the new building, which has no endowment but the small balance of £37, kept for future re-pairs; consequently the inmates have no allowance except from the poor rates. The churchwardens of St. Mary's are trustees of both hospitals, the founders of which are unknown.

HANDLEY'S ALMSHOUSES, in Stoney-street, consist of a row of 12 small ancient habitations only one story high, with gar-dens behind them, for the 12 aged almspeople, who each receive 16s. 8d. per quarter, arising from a rent charge of £40, left in 1650 by the founder, *Henry Handley, Esq.* to be paid yearly out of his estate at Bramcote, together with £60 for other *charitable uses,* viz. £20 for a weekly lecture in St. Mary's church; £20 for the officiating minister at Bramcote; £5 for the poor of Bramcote; £4 to the poor prisoners in the *gaols* of the county of Nottingham; £5 to the poor of Wilford; and £1 each to Beeston, Chilwell, Attenborough, Trowell, Stapleford and Wollaton, for the poor of those parishes. The *estate* on which this £100 per annum is charged now belongs to John Sherwin Sherwin, Esq. of Bramcote, who has the presentation of the four centre alms-houses, but the four at the north end are in the gift of the mayor, and the other four in the gift of Earl Manvers.

WARTNABY'S ALMHOUSES, at the corner of Fletchergate and Pilchergate, form an aged brick building consisting of three lower and three upper rooms; the former of which are occupied by three women, and the latter by three men. They were built in 1665, by Barnaby Wartnaby, an industrious blacksmith, who by his will, dated 1672, endowed them with two houses in Fletchergate, adjoining the almshouses, and a house in Woolpack-lane; the rents of which now amount to £39 per annum. Each of the six almspeople receive 6s. per month; 6s. at the goose fair; 10s. 6d. yearly in lieu of clothing; and a ton of coals every six months. The *trustees* are Messrs. F. Hardwick, Thomas Hall, John Stirland, William Jamson, Thomas Evison, and Thomas Dufty.

BILBY'S HOSPITAL, in St. John's-street, was founded in 1709 by the excentric but philanthropic *William Bilby*, who, though once a shoemaker, long practiced the following learned sciences in the town, viz. surgery, chemistry, physic, astronomy, and astrology, as was recorded by himself in a rhyming inscription in front of the hospital, now obliterated. The building which contains eight apartments for eight poor burgesses or their widows was repaired and stuccoed a few years ago. Each inmate has a sixpenny loaf weekly; 3s. on St. Thomas'-day, and one and a half ton of coals yearly, with the use of a small garden. The endowment consists of the Black Swan public house, in Goosegate, and the ten adjoining dwellings, all of which were imprudently let by the corporation (who are the trustees) in 1794, on a lease for 70 years, at the small annual rent of £16, on condition that the lessee should lay out £400 in rebuilding some of the premises. The property now lets for about £80 per annum, consequently the lessee is reaping a lucrative harvest at the expense of the charity.

GREGORY'S "WHITE RENTS" derived their name perhaps from their being the last tenements that paid a *quite or white rent* to the Peveril family. They consisted originally of eleven tenements in *Houndsgate*, bequeathed in 1613, by William Gregory, town clerk of Nottingham, for the use of the poor, with a rent charge of 40s. a year out of Baycroft-close, to keep them in repair. But in 1788 these ancient buildings were sold with the ground on which they stood, and the money divided amongst the three parishes, and expended in the erection of twelve rooms in York-street for as many poor of St. Mary's; eight rooms on the north bank of the Leen, betwixt Finkle-street and Greyfriargate, for eight poor of St. Nicholas's; and a building in Broad-Marsh, used as the workhouse of St. Peter's parish.

PATTEN'S ALMSHOUSES, in Maiden-lane, consist of only two humble dwellings for two poor women, one of whom is admitted by the owner of two houses in the same lane, and the other by the owner of the adjoining public-house in Barkergate. They were founded in 1651 by *John Patten*, a brickmaker, who endowed them with the rents of two houses then occupied by two of his workmen, whose successors afterwards sold the property which has been rebuilt, and now consists of the above mentioned houses, the owners of which have long since ceased to contribute anything towards the support of the two aged women whom they place in the almshouses.

GELLESTROPE'S HOSPITAL, which stood in Barkergate, consisted of five miserable huts with a large garden, but the site and ground belonging to it is now occupied by St. Mary's Burial-ground, (No. 2) and by Salem chapel and the Barkergate Free-school. The almshouses were taken down in 1812, by the corporation, who are the trustees; though the presentation was confined to two of their body, serving the office of Bridgemasters, from whom, the now obsolete almshouses were called "*Bridgemasters Hospital*," owing perhaps to the foundress having left part of her property for the repairs of the Trent-bridge. MARGERY MELLOR'S HOSPITAL, founded in 1539, consisted of four cottages and a garden, in the Low-pavement, left in trust to the corporation for the residence of six poor women for ever; but they disappeared many generations ago, and the site is now occupied by the Assembly-rooms, without any other building being provided for the almswomen. The foundress also left some property for keeping the Trent-bridge in repair, and we trust that the corporation will, e'er long, atone for the errors of themselves and their predecessors, by erecting 10 or 12 almshouses on some part of their grounds, to supply the place of Gellestrope's and Mellor's hospitals, which they first suffered to decay, and then sold the sites and the materials for their own emolument.

BENEFACTIONS

LEFT FOR DISTRIBUTION IN NOTTINGHAM.

Sir Thomas White's Loan Money, which has raised many of the industrious inhabitants of Nottingham, from the rank of journeymen to that of masters, now amounts to upwards of £12,000 which is lent *free of interest* for nine years, in £50 shares, to the burgesses "of good name and thrift," who choose to claim the use of it, and can find sureties for its re-payment. This lending fund arose and still continues to be augmented from the proceeds of the bequest of *Sir Thomas White*, who, in 1552, placed in the hands of the corporation of Coventry £1300 to be laid out in land and buidings ; and directed the rents thereof to be employed solely for the benefit of that city till 31 years after his death, (which happened in 1566,) and afterwards to be given yearly to the five following places in rotation, viz. Coventry, Northampton, Leicester, Nottingham, and Warwick, to be lent by the corporations of each place to young burgesses as stated above, to enable them to begin business. The annual rent of the charity estate is now about £1600, but the sum received for Nottingham every 5th year is only about £1100, owing to large deductions being claimed for alms at Coventry, and for the Merchant Tailor's Company of London, of which latter the founder was a member, and seems to have appointed them as special trustees to prevent the corporation with whom the property is vested, from misapplying the charity, as they did for many years, till 1712, when a sequestration was issued out of chancery against them for £2241, which they had embezzled by concealing the encreased value of the land and buildings, which they commonly let on leases at very small rents, in consideration of *large fines*, which they never carried to the account of the charity. A *Mr. Perks*, in 1620, gave £30, and *Robert Staples*, in 1631, left £40, to be lent to poor burgesses, but these sums are either lost or have been indiscriminately added to Sir Thomas White's charity.

Anthony Acham, in 1638, left £5 yearly out of lands, at Asterly, in Lincolnshire, to the corporation to be distributed in *bread* amongst the poor of Nottingham.

Lady Grantham, in 1658, left £200 for apprenticing poor children. It is now vested in the Lambly charity estate.— See page 164.

Henry Martin, in 1689, left 20s. yearly to each of the parishes of Nottingham, out of a house in St. James's-street, for apprenticing poor children.

Abel Collin, the benevolent founder of the hospital in Friar-lane, left £20 to St. Mary's, £20 to St. Nicholas', and £15 to St. Peter's parish, for the purpose of buying coals in summer to sell to the poor in winter at prime cost, but these sums have been absorbed in the general expenses of the parishes.

William Willoughby, in 1587, bequeathed £8. 6s. 8d. per annum, now paid by Mr. Plumptre's agent, to the churchwardens of St. Mary's, and four other parishes in rotation. Of this sum £6 is given to poor tradesmen; £2 to purchase frize gowns for four poor women, and 6s. 8d. for a sermon on Whit-Monday.

Roger Manners, Esq. left in 1598, a yearly rent charge of £5 out of two closes in Wilford. Half of this is given to the poor of St. Mary's, and the remainder to those of St. Nicholas' and St. Peter's parishes. The churchwardens are the trustees, and receive the money from Mr. Cox, of Wilford.

Robert Sherwin, in 1638, left half the rent of the Bell Inn, to be divided equally amongst the three parishes of Nottingham for the poor. This charity now produces £22. 10s. per annum; and the churchwardens and overseers are the trustees.

John Parker's charity for the library and apprentice fees now amounts to £13. 10s. yearly.—See Grammar-school, page 159.

William Robinson, in 1703, gave £100 to the corporation, in trust that they should pay yearly to the vicar of St. Mary's £3, and to the rectors of St. Nicholas' and St. Peter's, £1. 10s. each, to be distributed in bread amongst the poor of their res-. pective parishes.

Thomas Saunders, in 1711, left two houses and a garden in Pilshergate, (now let for £32 a year) to the poor of the three parishes of Nottingham, except £2 a year to the Blue Coat-school. Mr. George Bunting and others are trustees.

Joseph James, in 1715, left land and buildings at Basford and Ashover, now let for £20 per annum, of which £3 is given to two dissenting ministers, and the remainder divided (in sums varying from £2 to 10s.) amongst about 15 indigent town's people. Henry Enfield, T. Fellowes, A. Lowe, J. Stubbins, and T. C. Smith, Esqrs. are trustees.

Mary Holden, in 1760, left £400 in three per cent stock, and directed the yearly dividends, amounting to £12, to be paid as follows, viz.—£6 to the vicar of St. Mary's, and £3 each to the two rectors of Nottingham, to be by them distributed amongst such poor of their own parishes as have not received parochial relief. This charity is received yearly at Messrs. Smith and Co.'s bank. The same benevolent lady left £600 to the Blue Coat school.

William and *John Gregory,* in 1654, gave a yearly rent charge of £5. 4s. out of four houses in Barkergate, to provide two shillings worth of bread every Sunday for the poor of St. Mary's. The houses were rebuilt in 1792, by George de Ligne Gregory, Esq., and they now belong to Gregory Gregory, Esq. of Rempston.

Hannah and *Eliz. Metham,* in 1687 and 1695, left 50s. yearly out of a house and bakehouse in the Spread Eagle yard, to provide 300 twopenny loaves, to be given to as many poor people of St. Mary's parish by the churchwardens, on the 11th of November.

William Burton, in 1726, left £100 to St. Mary's poor, in consideration of which £5 is paid yearly out of the poor's-rate, and distributed in coals.

Thomas Roberts, in 1729, bequeathed 10s. yearly out of a house in Narrow-marsh, to be distributed in bread.

William Frost, in 1781, left £500, and *Henry Lockett,* in 1790, £55, to the poor of St. Mary's, who do not receive parochial alms. These sums were laid out in 1793, in the purchase of £700. 15s. 10d. consolidated three per cents, producing £21. 0s. 4d. per annum. The vicar and churchwardens are the trustees. In 1828, a committee of the inhabitants recommended that Manners', Staples', Roberts', Frost's, and Lockett's charities, should be given towards the support of the

Q

inmates of Woolley's and Warsergate almshouses, who also receive from the churchwardens the interest of £118, which arose from small donations, and from the sale of several old butchers' shops which stood on the church land. In 1647, *Mary Wilson* left 30s. yearly out of *Trough-close*, near Mapperley-hills, to the poor, but it has not been paid for many years.

BENEFACTIONS TO ST. NICHOLAS' PARISH.

Eliz. Bilby, in 1697, left the interest of £20, vested in the corporation, for 20 poor widows.

Dr. Robert Gray, in 1705, left £20, since encreased by other gifts to £50, three per cent consols, standing in the names of William Chamberlain, Thomas Marriott, John Wild, and Samuel Hollins, in trust for the poor.

Jacob Tibson, in 1729, bequeathed several tenements in Greyfriargate, to the rector and churchwardens in trust, to divide the rents amongst " the better sort of poor at 5s. each." These buildings were sold in 1801, for as much money as purchased £215. 18s. 10d. consolidated three per cents, yielding £6. 9s. 2d. per annum. The same donor gave during his life, £40 to the same trustees for the use of the poor.

Anthony Walker, a traveller, by his will, in 1714, left two cottages and 12 acres of land, at Matlock, " to the poor of that parish where he might chance to breathe his last." He died in St. Nicholas', and the rent of the property, which is now let for £13 a year, is distributed in bread, in weekly portions every Sunday, at the parish church, together with those moieties of Robinson's, Acham's, Manners', and Serwood's charities, which are allotted to this parish.

BENEFACTIONS TO ST. PETER'S PARISH.

Luke Jackson, in 1630, left two-thirds of the tithes of Horsepool, and directed 40s. thereof to be paid yearly to the rector for preaching two sermons on July 28th, and November 5th, " to return thanks for the deliverance of this land and people from the ' Invincible Armada' in 1588, and from the gunpowder plot in 1605;" and the residue to be given to the poor on the same days. By the Stanton and Charnwood Forest Inclosure Act, these tithes were commuted for 62A. 3R. 37P. of land, on which a good homestead was built, and the whole is now let for £74. 16s. per annum, besides a yearly composition of £9. 2s. 5d. making the total annual income £83. 18s. 5d. Henry Smith, Esq. and others are trustees, and distribute the charity at the workhouse.

Francis Skeffington, in 1633, left a yearly rent charge of 20s. out of the house, No. 1, in Bridlesmithgate, which has long been occupied by Mr. Sutton, publisher of the Nottingham Review, who pays the money to the churchwardens for the use of the poor.

Thomas Trigge, in 1703, left £50, with which was purchased the Duck-meadow, in Sneinton, now let for £10 a year, which, except 12s. for the land-tax, is distributed in bread on Good-Friday and Christmas-day, by the churchwardens and overseers.

William Drury, in 1676, left 20s. yearly out of two leys of land on the Rye-hills, to be given to six poor widows. The land thus charged now belongs to Mr. Low, of Locko, Derbyshire.

Robert Sherwin, in 1660, left 26s. yearly out of his estates, to be divided amongst six poor widows. His father's charity, from which this parish receives £7. 10s. yearly, is noticed at page 168.

Amongst the LOST CHARITIES recorded on the benefaction tables of Nottingham, we find the following, viz. £100 left in 1635, by *Sir George Peckham*, to the town at large; £1. 10s. yearly by *Mrs. Lawton* in 1632 ; £1 yearly by *William Greaves* in 1639; and a legacy of £50 by *John Barker* in 1732, to the poor of St. Peter's parish; and £20 left in 1784 by *Timothy Pym*, to the poor of St. Nicholas' parish.

GENERAL HOSPITAL.

The Nottingham General Hospital, pleasantly situated on Standard-hill, is " *open to the sick and lame poor of any county or nation,*" and ranks as the largest and most useful charitable institution in the town. The building, which is large, elegant, and convenient, was erected by subscription in 1781, and is surrounded by an extensive lawn and garden, comprising about two acres of land, which was given by the Duke of Newcastle and the corporation. Several additions have been made to the infirmary, and near the east end of it a commodious *fever house* has lately been erected, for the reception of persons affected with contagious diseases, so that this Samaritan institution is now as complete and as liberal in its benefits as any other in the kingdom. All proper objects for the fever-ward, and persons injured by serious accidents, are admitted on the first application, at any hour of the day or night, without any recommendation whatever ; and in other cases a subscriber's recommendatory letter opens to the bearer the doors of this house of mercy, either as an *in* or *out*-patient. Since its commencement, upwards of 68,000 patients have partaken of its healing benefits, and the average number on the list at one time is generally about 70 *in* and 600 *out*-patients. The *annual expenditure* of this gigantic establishment is generally about £2000. Since its commencement it has received *benefaction* and *legacies* to the amont of £23,334, of which £6337. 2s. 10d. was given by an unknown* benefactor; £1000 by Mrs. Eliz. Bainbridge, of Woodborough; £400 by "a friend;" £300 by John Morris, Esq. of Nottingham; £300 by the Duke of Newcastle; £305 by the Duke of Portland; £1000 left by Mr. and Mrs. Kay, of Fulford; £500 by James Chadwick, Esq. of Mansfield; £300 by Mrs. Jerrom, of Nottingham; £1000 by the Rev. J. B. Copestake, of Kettleby, and many other sums of from £100 to £200 by other charitable individuals. The following *contingent legacies* have also been bequeathed in favour of this infirmary, viz. £1000 in the 4 per cents left by *Edward Bennett, Esq.* sugar-baker, of Sheffield, to be paid at the decease of his widow, who is still alive; and £1400 left by the *Reverend Creed Turner*, of Treeton, in Yorkshire, payable at the decease of his sister, the widow of the late Dr. Storer. The *annual sub-scriptions* amount to upwards of £1000, besides which the in-stitution receives £952 *yearly interest*, arising from £19,000, 3½ per cent stock; £7900, 3 per cent stock; and from £1000, secured on the Nottingham *town rate*. The *physicians* and *surgeons* of the town lend their assistance gratuitously. Mr. Eddison is the resident surgeon and apothecary; Lord George Bentinck is the *president;* the bankers of Nottingham are the treasurers, and Mr. Richard Dale is the secretary and deputy receiver. In the minutes of the hospital is recorded the most extraordinary case of *Kitty Hudson*, who in 1783, voided from different parts of her body a great number of *pins* and *needles*, which she had swallowed at various times, owing to her long continued practice of eating, drinking, and sleeping with them in her mouth! After remaining some time in the hospital she re-covered her health, and subsequently became a wife and a mother.

The DISPENSARY AT ST. MARY'S WORKHOUSE is supported at the cost of about £350 per annum, paid out of the poor rates of St. Mary's parish. (See p. 127.) It was established in 1813, and has for its object the gratuitous administration of medical and surgical aid, to all the poor parishioners. In the following year a *fever house* was built in the workhouse yard, towards erecting which the late *Francis Wakefield, Esq.* paid to the overseers £326. 17s. 8d. as part of a subscription raised in 1802, after the peace of Amiens for the purpose of erecting an institution for the reception of poor persons afflicted with febrile deseases, instead of having an illumination. The ba-lance of this subscription, £149. 13s. was paid in 1829, towards the erection of the fever house attached to the generel hospital, by the executors of the late Francis Wakefield, Esq. who during a great part of his life was a liberal benefactor to the

---

* This "unknown" benefactor also left two sums of the same amount to the Infirmaries of Sheffield and Derby. The money was paid by Messrs. Coutts and Co., bankers, London, and the donor is generally believed to have been that great philosopher and chemist, the HONOURABLE HENRY CAVENDISH, who died at Clapham, in 1811.

town. The number of patients relieved at St. Mary's Dispensary during the year ending March 1831, was 2612, exclusive of *Vaccine inoculation*, which was first propagated in the town (gratis to the poor,) by Mr. John Attenburrow, in the year 1800.

The "NOTTINGHAM DISPENSARY for the relief of the sick poor resident in the county and town of Nottingham," was established in 1831. It occupies a large and commodious house, betwixt Hockley and Woolpack-lane. It has already received donations amounting to upwards of £650, and annual subscriptions amounting to nearly £550. Its affairs are managed by a president, six vice-presidents, a committee of twelve subscribers, two honorary consulting physicians, (Drs. Howitt and Cursham;) four honorary acting surgeons, (Drs. Williams; White, Greaves, and Davison;) a resident surgeon, (Mr. Robert Garner;) and an honorary secretary, (Mr. Thomas Wakefield.) Those patients who cannot attend the dispensary, are visited at their own dwellings, and though the charity does not practice midwifery, it relieves poor married women after childbirth, provided they need medical assistance, and are recommended by a subscriber.

The GENERAL LUNATIC ASYLUM for *Nottingham* and *Nottinghamshire*, is a large and handsome building, pleasantly situated on the declivity of a hill, in the parish of Sneinton, on the Carlton road, about a mile from the Market-place. The foundation stone was laid May 31, 1810, and the building was opened for the reception of patients on the 15th February, 1812; since which several additions have been made to the fabric, and in 1829, the want of room was so great, that two new wards, for the reception of 20 male and 20 female incurable patients, were erected during that and the following year, at the expense of £2074. 16s. 3d., swelling the total cost of the buildings, furniture, land, planting, &c. to upwards of £31,000, of which seven-twelfths was raised by voluntary subscription, and the remainder paid out of the county rates, viz. four-twelfths by Nottinghamshire, and one-twelfth by Nottingham. The establishment is well adapted for the comfort and recovery of those afflicted with that most distressing of all human maladies—insanity; being provided with commodious and well ventilated apartments, separated into distinct wards for the classification of the patients, who have the best medical assistance, and are provided with an excellent suit of baths; and with extensive courts and gardens for their recreation. It contains accommodation for about 120 patients, and its wards are generally all occupied. Pursuant to an Act of Parliament passed in the 48th of George III. all pauper lunatics or dangerous idiots, must be placed in some asylum sanctioned by the magistrates; and those belonging to Nottingham or Nottinghamshire are sent to this institution;—their respective parishes paying small yearly stipends for their support. Some of the apart-

Q 2

ments are appropriately fitted. up for those patients. who can afford to pay for superior accommodation ; and the paupers and other poor, unfortunate inmates are assisted by a charitable fund, arising from benefactions, legacies, and annual subscriptions. Lord George Bentinck is the president; Colonel Wildman the vice-president; the magistrates and principal voluntary subscribers are the visiting governors; Henry Smith and E. S. Godfrey, Esqrs. are the treasurers; Alexander Munson, M. D., F. R. S. E. the physician; Mr. Henry Oldknow the surgeon; Mr. Thomas Morris the director; Mrs. Morris the matron; and Mr. Richard Dale the deputy-receiver.

The PUBLIC BATHS may also be classed amongst the medical institutions, though in Nottingham they are neither supported by charity, nor remarkable for their accommodation,—the cold water bathers being mostly obliged to avail themselves of that salubrious exercise by immersion in the open river or canal, where many scores may often be seen laving themselves, in the summer-season, at very improper hours, (even on the Sunday afternoon,) to the great annoyance of the fair sex, who may wish to enjoy a walk across the meadows.— At the house of Mr. Flewitt, in Parliament-street, there is an excellent suit of " *Whitlaw's patent vegetable medicated vapour baths*," established in 1830 ; and Mr. Raynor, in Bellargate, has had a suit of *fumigating baths* since 1829. Of cold water baths, there are but three small ones in the neighbourhood, viz. two on the Leen, and one at St. Ann's, (see p. 136;) but the latter is at too great a distance from the town to be of much benefit to the inhabitants.

PROVIDENT SOCIETIES.—Belonging to this class there are in the town a considerable number of *Benefit Societies*, the members of which pay small monthly contributions to their respective funds, from which they are relieved in case of sickness, infirmity, and superannuation, and from which the friends of deceased members receive sums of £8 or £10, to provide for their decent interment, &c. &c. Amongst these fraternities are several secret orders, viz. *Lodges of Freemasons, Ancient Druids*, and *Odd Fellows*, whose splendid "regalia" gives an imposing effect to all public processions. The Druids and Odd Fellows are very numerous, both in Nottingham and the neighbouring villages. Here are also a *Trades Union*, a *Political Union*, and a *Co-operative Society*, but they are neither conspicuous for numbers nor wealth; the first is a branch of the National association of workmen for the protection of labour; the second has for its grand object the promotion of Parliamentary Reform; and the third consists of about 64 members, with a small trading fund, and a store of provisions, &c. in Milton-street, from which they purchase what they consume in their families, and divide their profits quarterly.

The SAVINGS BANK, in Smithy-row, is a provident institution, which affords a safe and beneficial investment for the savings of the humbler classes. It was established in April, 1818; and is open every Monday, and on the last Saturday in every month, from eleven till two o'clock. It is under the management of thirty-six directors, and the Duke of Newcastle, the patron; Sir Robert Clifton, Bart. the president; C. J. Wright, Esq. the treasurer; Wm. Jarman, the secretary; and John Patterson, the clerk. On November 20th, 1830, the deposits amounted to £105,492. 2s., belonging to 4322 depositors, who receive £3. 8s. 5¼d. per cent. interest per annum. Of this sum, upwards of £8000 is the property of 168 benefit or friendly societies, and the rest belongs to individual depositors.

LITERARY INSTITUTIONS, &c.

The SUBSCRIPTION LIBRARY and NEWS ROOM, founded in 1816, occupy *Bromley House*, in the Market-place, one of the largest and best built mansions in the town, being erected by Sir George Smith, Bart. whose son afterwards took the name of Bromley, and removed to Stoke; though this house long continued to be used as the occasional residence of himself and his descendants. After being untenanted for some time, it was purchased and repaired for the Subscription Library, which now contains upwards of 7000 volumes, amongst which are many scarce and valuable works, in every branch of literature and the arts and sciences, and most of the Parliamentary records of public charities, &c. &c. Adjoining the large library room, is a smaller apartment in which is deposited the STANDFAST LIBRARY, a collection of about 2000 ancient volumes, on theology, law, history, &c. most of which were given in 1774, by the Rev. Wm. Standfast, D. D. as the foundation of a public library, and for that purpose placed in the Blue Coat charity school, whence they were removed to their present situation in 1816, on the proprietors of the subscription library agreeing to pay five guineas yearly to the trustees, to be employed in repairing the said books, and in adding other works to their catalogue. In the library rooms is a cabinet of mineralogy, and also many antiquities, curiosities, and excellent paintings, two of which latter bear honourable testimony of the talents of two native artists, viz. a full length portrait of Dr. Storer, by Mr. Barber; and a view of Clifton Grove, by Mr. J. R. Walker. The building and the library, &c. belong to 250 shareholders, who each pay an annual subscription of two guineas. The *News Room*, which occupies the ground floor, is under the management of the library committee, and is well supplied with London and provincial papers; each subscriber paying 25s. per annum. Connected with it is an excellent billiard table. The present officers of the institution are the Rev.

R. W. Almond, president; J. Wright, Esq. treasurer; Thomas Wakefield, Esq. sub-treasurer; Saml. Newham, Esq. secretary; and Mr. James Archer, librarian.

The ARTISANS' LIBRARY, in Smithy-row, was established in 1824, and now consists of nearly 2400 volumes, belonging to forty-two shareholders, and 380 subscribers;—the former of whom gave £5 each towards the foundation, but most of them have relinquished all interest in the library, except that of promoting its welfare, for the general benefit of the subscribers, who each pay 1s. 6d. per quarter. It is open every evening except Sunday, from seven till nine o'clock. Thomas Wakefield, Esq. is the president; Francis Hart, Esq. the treasurer; and Mr. V. Kirk, the librarian.

The YOUNG WOMEN'S LIBRARY, at Mrs. Carbet's, in Houndsgate, was established in 1825, and is open every Wednesday, from twelve till two o'clock. It was founded by a number of benevolent ladies, but is partly supported by the readers, who each pay one shilling per quarter.

At the shops of the booksellers are several extensive CIRCULATING LIBRARIES, as will be seen in the subjoined Directory.

The Nottingham FLORIST and HORTICULTURAL SOCIETY has several exhibitions yearly at Bromley House. Lord Middleton is the patron; Rt. Padley, Esq. the president; J. J. W. Rigley, the treasurer; and R. Johnson, the secretary.

The MUSEUM, in Petergate, belongs to Mr. Richard Knight, and consists of fine specimens of the crocodile and gauana, stuffed birds, marine and other shells, the skins of boa constrictors, Indian arrows, clubs and canoes, old paintings, and a great variety of other curiosities, all of which may be seen for an admission-fee of sixpence.

NEWSPAPERS.—The periodical press of Nottingham is confined to three weekly newspapers, viz: the *Journal*, commenced in 1769, and now published every Friday morning, by Mr. George Stretton, at No. 64, Long-row; the *Review*, established in 1808, by Mr. Charles Sutton, and now issued by his son, Mr. Robert Sutton, at No. 1, Bridlesmith-gate, every Friday morning; and the *Mercury*, commenced a few years ago, by Mr. Jonathan Dunn, and now published at his shop on the South Parade, every Saturday morning. Mr. Wm. Ayscough, who died in 1719, established the first printing-office in the town; and about six years afterwards, Mr. John Collyer commenced printing a weekly newspaper called the "*Nottingham Post*," but it was discontinued in 1732, when Mr. George Ayscough began the "*Nottingham Courant*," which in 1769 was sold to Mr. Samuel Cresswell, who converted it into the "*Nottingham Journal*," he having previously been a joint proprietor of a paper published from 1757 till 1769, at Leicester, under the name of the *Leicester and Nottingham Journal*. In

1772, Mr. George Burbage began the *Nottingham Chronicle*, but in 1775, he discontinued it, and joined the proprietor of the Journal. In 1780, Mr. George Cox commenced the *Nottingham Gazette*, which died before it was a year old; another paper was established under the same title by Mr. William Topham, in 1813, but it had little better success than its deceased namesake, for after lingering two years, it ceased to live for want of necessary support.

EMINENT MEN.

Though Nottingham is not very conspicuous in our National Biography, for the number and brilliance of its literary characters, it is inferior to no town in the empire, in manufacturing and commercial genius, and in mechanical inventions; and it yields the palm but to few, in its progress in the fine arts. Amongst the most distinguished worthies who were born, or have flourished in the town, we find the following :—

William de Nottingham, an Augustine friar, who wrote a Concordance of the Evangelists, and died in 1336.

John Plough, rector of St. Peter's, who wrote against clerical celibacy, for which, after the accession of Queen Mary, he was obliged to fly to Bazil in Switzerland, where he wrote an " Apology for the Protestants," a " Treatise against the Mitred Man in the Popish Kingdom," and " The Sound of the doleful Trumpet." He died in 1550.

Colonel Hutchinson, the patriotic and gallant governor of the castle in the civil wars of Charles I., is already noticed at pages 89 and 90.

Gilbert Millington, of Felly Priory, was M. P. for Nottingham, when he sat as one of the judges who tried and signed the death warrant of Charles I.

The Rev. William Brightmore, who died in 1710, was a native of the town, and long held the benefice at Hawnes in Bedfordshire, where he " made many *prophecies*," which he published under the title of Illustrations of the Book of Revelations.

William Holder, D. D., a native of the county, received the rudiments of his education at Nottingham Grammar school, in the reign James I., and was afterwards ejected from a small living in Oxfordshire for nonconformity. He is said to have been the inventor of the *art of teaching the deaf and dumb to speak*. He also wrote " A Treatise on Music," both theoretical and practical, and was esteemed a great virtuoso and natural philosopher. He died about 1675.

Charles Deering, M. D., was a native of Germany, and took up his degrees as a Doctor of Medicine at Leyden in Holland; after which he went to London, and was appointed secretary to the British embassy to the court of Russia. Shortly after his return, he married in London, and came to Nottingham, where

he settled during the rest of his life; which it is said was ended
in poverty and severe affliction, in 1749, before he had finished
his elaborate *History of Nottingham*, which was published in
1751 by Mr. George Ayscough, a printer, and Mr. Thomas
Willington, a druggist, then resident in the town. In 1738, he
published a " Botanical Catalogue of Plants growing about
Nottingham."

Thomas Peet, an eminent mathematician, astronomer, and
schoolmaster, was the son of a poor farmer at Ashley-Hay in
Derbyshire, but came to Nottingham at the age of 14, and died
there in 1780, aged 72 years. He was the oldest almanac writer in England " having wrote the Gentleman's Diary, and Poor
Robin, upwards of forty years ;"—the latter of which was afterwards written by *John Pearson*, who died 1791, and the former
by *Charles Wildbore*, who died in 1802, both of whom were natives of this town, and distinguished mathematicians.

The Rev. Andrew Kippis, D. D., was born at Nottingham
in 1725; under the tuition of the celebrated Dr. Doddridge, he
became an eminent dissenting minister, and afterwards published many excellent works on divinity, and edited the greater
portion of a new edition of the *Biographia Britannica*. He
died in 1795 in London, where he was 42 years minister of
Prince's-street chapel in Westminster.

Walter Merrey was a native of York, but was apprenticed
and ended his days in Nottingham, where in 1794 he published
a treatise on the Coinage of England, and died in 1799.

Thomas Sandby was born at Nottingham in 1721, and died
in 1798, after being many years professor of architecture in the
Royal Academy. His brother, *Paul Sandby*, was considered
the best draughtsman, and water-coloured landscape painter in
the kingdom. He was chosen royal academician of the Royal
Society of Arts, on the foundation of that institution in 1768,
and was afterwards appointed drawing master of the Royal
Academy at Woolwich, which offices he held till his death in
1809.

Amongst the eminent oil painters who have flourished in
the town were the late *Mr. Bonnington* and *Mr. Tomson ;*
and to these we may add *Mr. Barber*, and some others now
living.

Gilbert Wakefield, B. A. was born in 1756, at the rectory-
house of St. Nicholas, and received the rudiments of his education at the Nottingham Grammar school, but in 1767, he removed with his father to the vicarage of Kingston-upon-Thames.
He was afterwards a fellow of Jesus College, Cambridge, where
he published a collection of Latin Poems. He subsequently became classical teacher of an academy at Warrington, in Lancashire, where he published *new translations* of the first epistle of
St. Paul to the Thessalonians, and of St. Matthew's Gospel;
besides many other controversial works on theological subjects.

In 1790, he was chosen classical tutor of the new college at Hackney, but he soon afterwards left that institution and devoted the rest of his life to literary pursuits. He published many excellent works both theological and political; one of which was written in such a bold republican spirit, against a pamphlet published by Dr. Watson, bishop of Llandaff, in defence of the French war, that he was prosecuted for a libel on the Ministers, and suffered two years' imprisonment in Dorchester gaol. Such was the opinion which the public held of his distinguished merit, and of the severity of his sentence, that, during his confinement £5000 was subscribed and settled on him as an annuity; and Michael Dodson, nephew to the great Judge Foster, bequeathed him £500. He was released from prison in June, 1801, but only survived his liberty about three months. It has been justly said of him, that " his talents were rare, his morals pure, his virtues exalted, his courage invincible, and his integrity spotless." His brother, the late *Francis Wakefield, Esq.* who died a few years ago, was a liberal benefactor of Nottingham, and an extensive manufacturer, and is now ably succeeded by his sons.

Samuel Ayscough, son of George Ayscough, the printer, was born in Bridlesmithgate, and is remarkable for having arranged and published a catalogue of the numerous collections of manuscripts belonging to the British Museum. He was also employed to arrange the papers, &c. in the tower; and wrote an index to the works of Shakspeare, by the aid of which, every sentiment in that extraordinary author, may be traced to its source. He took orders in 1790, and obtained the curacy of St. Giles-in-the-Fields, which he held till his death in 1805.

Henry Kirk White, whose memory will long remain as a proof that genius and talents will always burst through the thickest veil of obscurity, was born at Nottingham in 1785. The spirit and perseverance with which he adhered to, and at last accomplished his youthful wishes, as related by Mr. Southey, are almost incredible, yet strictly true; and ought to be a convincing proof to parents that the early inclinations of their children should not be thwarted under the name of obstinacy, where they may be the result of conscious genius. He was the second son of John White, a respectable butcher; and his mother having discovered that he possessed strong mental powers, determined to foster them as far as her limited means would admit. After receiving a suitable education, he was apprenticed to Messrs. Coldham and Enfield, attorneys; and at the age of seventeen, he published a small volume of poems, dedicated to the Duchess of Devonshire. Two years afterwards, being seized with an unconquerable deafness, which would have disqualified him for the profession of an attorney, he obtained a release from his masters; and, by the assistance of his friends, he was placed in St. John's College, Cambridge,

where he soon became a brilliant luminary,—being acknowledged victor at the two first college examinations after his arrival; but a wasting consumption, aided by his incessant application to study, extinguished his vital flame in 1806, before he had finished his second year within the walls of the
University, and a few months after he had passed the 21st
year of his age. The sisters of this lamented youth now
conduct a respectable seminary in Nottingham. A monumental tablet, with a medallion by Chantrey, has been erected to
his memory in All-Saints' church, Cambridge, at the expense
of Francis Boott, Esq., of Boston in America. It bears the
following beautiful *inscription* from the pen of William Smyth,
Esq. :—

> " Warm with fond hope, and learning's sacred flame,
> To Granta's bowers the youthful Poet came;
> Unconquer'd powers, th' immortal mind display'd,
> But worn with anxious thought the frame decay'd:
> Pale o'er his lamp and in his cell retired,
> The martyr Student faded and expired.
> O Genius, Taste, and Piety sincere
> Too early lost, midst duties too severe!
> Foremost to mourn was generous SOUTHEY seen,
> He told the tale and show'd what WHITE had been,
> Nor told in vain—far o'er th' Atlantic wave,
> A wanderer came and sought the Poet's grave;
> On yon low stone he saw his lonely name,
> And raised this fond memorial to his fame."

Henry Shipley, another worthy native, was born in 1763, and
died in 1808. He was the son of a poor gardener emplyed
by the late John Sherwin, Esq., but he raised himself from
his poverty to the rank of an eminent schoolmaster, and long
shone as a political writer on the side of the Whigs, after the
French revolution had set all Europe in a ferment.

Gravener Henson, an humble but ingenious workman (a " twist
hand") now living in the town, deserves notice in this list of
worthies, he having lately published a complete " History of
the Lace Trade," which displays much talent, great depth of
research, and sound reasoning. This self-taught author has
been of considerable service to the manufacturing and commercial interests of the town, by the prompt and able manner in
which he generally combats, either in person or through the
medium of the press, all abuses either of masters or workmen,
and all local or national regulations which he considers injurious to the lace and hosiery manufactures of Britain;—in the
defence of which he has frequently given satisfactory and influential evidence before the Board of Trade, and Committees
of the House of Commons.

The town now possesses several other men distinguished for
learning, philanthropy, charity, and ingenuity ; but to speak of
the living is an invidious task, we shall therefore leave them for
the pen of some future biographer.

WITCHCRAFT.—Having extracted the gold, we will now examine the dross. Among those who have raised themselves in the town to a "*bad eminence*," we find WILLIAM SOMERS and the Rev. JAMES DARREL, two impostors, who, at the close of the 16th century, came to Nottingham, and practised their vile frauds upon the credulity of the inhabitants, under the delusion of witchcraft and demonology, of which so many instances were exhibited during many ages after the reformation. Somers in his boyhood had lived servant at Ashby-de-la-Zouch, in the house where Darrel lodged, and where that wily priest (who had entered the church from lazy and selfish motives,) first instructed him in the art of contorting his body so as to exhibit what were called " the fourteen signs of demoniac possession." Somers having come to live at Nottingham, repeatedly threw himself into these violent paroxysms, in which he declared he was bewitched, and that no person could relieve him but the "*pious Mr. Darrel*," who was then living at Mansfield, but was sent for to " cast the devils out" of the supposed sufferer. Having arrived, he declared that the impostor was " suffering for all the sins of Nottingham," and that there must be a *fast* in the town, held especially for the youth's recovery. This fast afforded Darrel an opportunity of performing a grand exorcism in the face of a crowded congregation in St. Mary's church, where the youth, after feigning much agony during the imposing ceremony, as ingeniously feigned a recovery, and declared the pious man had " dispossessed" him. After this happy conclusion, the duped auditors made a large collection for the performers, and Mr. Darrel was chosen curate of the church, where he afterwards gave out in his sermons, that Somers was still in great danger as well as the rest of his family; for, said he, the devil often repeats his visits to the same house, coming sometimes " in the shape of a cock, a crane, a snake, a toad, a newt, a set of dancers, or an angel." To verify the prophecies of this reverend cheat, Somers again showed signs of " possession," and added to them the discrimination of pointing out WITCHES, under which name, he caused 13 poor aged women to be committed to the town gaol. Soon after this, Mary Cooper, the " half-sister" of Somers, commenced the lucrative profession of " witch finder," and pointed out Alice Freeman as her bewitching tormentor; but this lady being sister to alderman Freeman, (who was mayor in 1606 and 1613,) caused Somers to be apprehended and examined by the corporate magistrates, to whom he confessed the whole to be an imposition, in which he had been instructed by the Rev. James Darrel, who was afterwards conveyed to London and tried before the Archbishop of Canterbury, the Bishop of London, and the two Lord Chief Justices, who convicted him of contriving the whole imposture, for which he was ejected from his living, and committed to prison.

Amongst the ECCENTRIC CHARACTERS who have enlivened

n.

the town of Nottingham, were *James O'Burns* a celebrated ventriloquist, commonly called "Shelford Tommy," who died in 1796.;—*Charles Oldham*, a deformed mendicant, who died in 1802, having, during the preceeding, fifty years paraded the streets in a fantastic dress, playing upon a whistle, which gave him the name of *Whistling Charley*; and *Benjamin Mayo*, a silly pauper, who died a few years ago in St. Peter's Workhouse, and was long honoured with the title of *General Monk*, from the pride which he took in heading all processions, even those of funerals, and from his annual custom on "Middleton Monday," of collecting all the scholars from the common day schools, and parading the streets at their head, exhibiting in his course, all the pranks of a mountebank, to the great amusement of his juvenile followers. To this list we may add, the late *Mr. Rouse*, a man of some property, but a little deranged in his intellects. He once offered himself as a candidate to represent the town in Parliament, and in order to purchase the lower orders of electors in his favour, he treated many of them with ale, purl, and sometimes with rhubarb, which he strongly recommended to all as an excellent thing for the human constitution; and no doubt would have proposed measures of a similar tendency for the political constitution, had his ambition been gratified. He resided in the street then called the *Backside*, but, considering the residence of an aspiring man, should bear some reference to his ambition, he caused a number of boards to be nailed up at the most conspicuous corners and passages, by which those who could read, were informed that they were in "*Parliament-street*,"—a name which is still retained.

PLACES OF AMUSEMENT.

The ASSEMBLY ROOM, in the Low Pavement, possesses no external beauties, though its interior is spacious, and handsomely fitted up;—being repaired and beautified in 1807, at the cost of £1545, raised by subscription. It is not now so much used as formerly; the large superb room at the *Exchange*, being now often used for balls and concerts.—(See p. 140.)

The THEATRE, in Stoney-street, is a gloomy barn-looking edifice, built about 1760, by the late Mr. Whitely, whose company of comedians visited it several years. The interior is well arranged and neatly fitted up, but, though it is small compared with the size of the town, it is seldom filled above two or three times in a season, owing to the greater part of the middle class being now dissenters, and averse to theatrical performances. Messrs. Robertson and Manley occupied it many years, and it is still held on a lease by the latter gentleman, who has long been celebrated as a powerful veteran of the *buskin*; as his late partner "*Jemmy Robertson*" was of the *sock*,—from which he retired and settled in Nottingham, where he died on the 1st of January, 1831;—but where his widow is still living, and is indulged with an annual benefit at the theatre.

RACE COURSE, &c.—Nottingham is one of those towns which has the King's plate. The present course is of an oval figure, being altered from its original form in 1813. It occupies a part of the forest on the west side of the Mansfield road, and has on its south side a long range of high ground, from which thousands of spectators may have as good a view of the sport as those who ascend the *Grand Stand*, a large and handsome brick building, which was erected in 1777, under the patronage of Sir C. Sedley. Till lately, the *Races* were held in July or August, and were well attended; but they are now held in October, after the Goose fair, and though the course is never out of order owing to its having a sandy soil, the races are not now so numerously attended, nor so well supported by the sporting gentry as formerly.

The CRICKET GROUND adjoing the Race Stand, is an open verdant plain, on which many matches have been played. In this healthy exercise, the Nottingham "*Cricketers*" have long been in great celebrity, and, considering their advantages, they are now second to none in England. (See p. 97.) The RIDING SCHOOL, at Castle-place, is noticed at page 125; and the Subscription BOWLING GREEN in the Park, at page 126.

The PUBLIC WALKS AND GARDENS about Nottingham, are numerous, and picturesque. The castle, the park, the burgess lands, the rock houses, and the caves have been already described, (vide p. 115 to p. 136,) as also have the views commanded by the different heights in the various approaches to the town.—(See p. 74.) The favourite walks in summer are to Wilford, Clifton Grove, Colwick Hall, St. Anne's Well; (See p. 136,) Radford Grove, Wollaton Park, and Lenton, (See p. 139,) at most of which are large public gardens, with good houses of entertainment. RADFORD GROVE situated about a mile W.N.W. of the town, is a delightful place of public resort, being originally planned and laid out at great expense in 1780, by the late William Elliott, Esq. The mansion now forms a commodious Inn; and in the beautiful garden are numerous bowers and seats, and a large lake, in the centre of which is a small island and summer house, approached by an elegant Chinese bridge.

PUBLIC ACCOMMODATION, &c.

The Inns, the Stage, and Hackney Coaches,* the means of

---

* *Hackney Coaches* were first established in the town on new-year-day, 1825, by Mr. John King. They are here called "FLYS," and are tolerably well employed; owing to many of the merchants and manufacturers being now resident in the skirts of the town, and in the surrounding parishes.

conveyance for the transit of goods both by land and water, the Banks, the Bridges, the Market-place, the principal streets, and foot-paths, the Gas-works, and the Water-works, are all on a scale suited to the magnitude and wealth of the town; though the Post Office, in High-street, has long been too small and inconvenient for the extent of its business; but a new and more appropriate building is now erecting on the opposite side of the street, by the Duke of Newcastle, for the use of this branch of the public revenue. The *Excise-office* is at the George IV. Inn, but the *Permit-office* is in Peck-lane. The *Stamp-office* is in St. Peter's-gate, and George Smith, Esq. is the distributor. The *Hawker's License Office* is at the Post Office, and Mr. G. Neilson is the clerk. The *Tax Office* is in Park-row, and Mr. John Jackson is the surveyor.

MARKETS AND FAIRS,—The regular market days are Wednesday and Saturday, but the latter is the principal one, and is abundantly supplied with meat, fish, poultry, butter, eggs, vegetables, corn, cattle, sheep, swine, &c. &c. The fairs for horses, horned cattle, &c., are on the Friday after January 13th; on the 7th, 8th, and 9th of March; on the Thursday before Easter; and on the 2nd, 3rd, and 4th of October; the latter of which is called the *Goose Fair*, from the plenitude of roast geese, and goose-pies, with which many of the inhabitants treat their visiting friends. The March and October fairs, are also great marts for cheese, woollen cloth, and other merchandize. The fairs at Lenton, near Nottingham, are held on the Wednesday after Whit-Sunday, and on November 11th, for horses, horned cattle, and hogs.

The MARKET-PLACE, which was newly paved in 1827, occupies a triangular area of about five and a half acres, and has long been admired; for Leland, who wrote in the reign of Henry VIII., says, "both for the buildings on the side of it, for the very great wideness of the streete, and the cleane paving of it, it is the fairest without exception of all England." It is now lined with lofty and well built houses, the fronts of which are nearly all projected over the basement story, and supported by massive pillars, forming long piazzas, under which are retail shops, many of which are elegant, and richly stocked.—The range of buildings on the north side is upwards of 400 yards in length, and is called the Long-row. The houses and shops on the south side bear the names of Angel-row, Beast-market-hill, the Poultry, and Timber-hill, but the latter is now generally called South Parade. At the east end, betwixt the Long-row and the Poultry, is a centre pile of building, the west end of which presents to the Market-place the spacious and elegant front of the Exchange, which is described at page 140. Behind the Exchange are the Shambles and the Police Office, and two rows of shops and houses called Cheapside and Smithy-row, in front of the latter of which there is on Saturdays

a.long range of stalls occupied by butchers, chiefly from the
the country. The cattle and sheep pens are moveable, and
are set up in the Market-place on Wednesdays, and in a broad
part of Parliament-street on Saturdays, when the whole extensive area of the Market-place is occupied with stalls of provisions, shoes, clothes, hardware, baskets, coopers' ware, furniture, earthenware, glass, books, &c. &c. Anciently, the
Market-place was divided lengthwise by a wall breast high, but
it was taken down in 1711, together with the *Butter-cross*,
which stood facing the Exchange, and the *Malt-cross*, which
stood opposite the end of St. James's-street; but the latter was
rebuilt on a larger scale, and was not finally removed till 1804.
The *Hen-cross*, at the top of the Poultry, and the *Weekday-
cross*, at the south end of Market-street, opposite the Guildhall, were built in 1712, but the former was taken down in
1801, and the latter in 1804—being great obstructions in two
public thoroughfares. A market was held on Wednesdays at
the Weekday-cross till the year 1800, and in 1750, an unsuccessful attempt was made to establish a Monday market, in St.
Peter's-square, where a cross was erected, but it was taken
down in 1787, when the *obelisk*, which is now surmounted by
a large gas lamp, was erected on its site, over the pit where
several channels and soughs empty themselves into a large
common sewer. Mr. John Ashwell is inspector of the corn returns, and has his office in Exchange-alley.

TOLLS.—Much disquietude and litigation has lately been occasioned by the corporation having considerably advanced their
ancient customary tolls of the market, which for every stall set
up by a non-burgess, amounted only to one penny, without
reference to its size; but they now demand one penny *per foot*,
according to the length of each stall. A considerable increase
has also been made in the tolls of baskets, carts, &c.; and also
in the cattle tolls, for which latter there may be some justifiable
plea, as the corporation are at some expense in providing and
in setting up and removing the pens every market day; but in
the open market, where the venders provide their own stalls,
or expose their articles in baskets or on the pavement, the
ancient customary tolls were amply sufficient for the satisfaction
of any just claim which the municipal body may have for their
own emolument, or for the remuneration of the officers whom
they appoint to regulate the markets, and for the expense which
they incur in paving the Market-place. In resisting these additional imposts, the non-burgesses who have stalls in the
market, and many of the country farmers, have made common
cause, and opened a subscription for the support of *Mr. John
Gainsley*, a baker and confectioner, who lately filed two actions
in the Court of King's Bench against the corporation, for
seizing part of his goods as payment of the toll which he had
R 2

disputed. In the first of these actions, the corporation petitioned the Court to stay proceedings, and convict them in costs, which was done; and thus, by the " glorious uncertainty of the law," the plaintiff and his supporters were obliged to wait for another assault, on which to ground a second action, which is now pending, but which it is hoped will speedily be decided to the satisfaction of the injured party, and to the final annihilation of these exorbitant claims, which if continued would be highly detrimental to the busy market of Nottingham, and consequently injurious to the inhabitants at large, who would eventually feel the evil effects of these unnecessary imposts, in the shape of a scanty supply and dearness of provisions; for many of the growers, instead of incurring a heavy toll, and the trouble of retailing their produce in the market, would prefer selling it to the hucksters or shopkeepers.

The GAS WORKS, in Butcher-street, were built under the authority of an Act of Parliament passed in 1818, and were finished on the 13th of April, in 1819, when the town was first lighted with their luminous vapours. They are arranged on a judicious plan, and have four gasometers, which will hold together about 60,000 cubic feet of gas. The capital expended by the company in this useful and profitable establishment, was £16,000, raised in 320 shares of £50 each. Mr. Reuben Young is the engineer and clerk. Gas was first used in the town in 1814, by Mr. Tatham, a brass-founder of Bridlesmith-gate, who erected a small apparatus to light his own premises. It is now used in most of the manufactories, shops, and public-houses, and in the lamps of the principal streets.

LAMPS and WATCH.—In 1762, an act was obtained for *lighting the town*, and for levying a rate of sixpence in the pound on the assessed rental of all houses and buildings above a certain value, to defray the expense. The aldermen and others are the commissioners of this act, which is now too limited in its powers for the present increased state of the town, and ought to be abrogated by another, to provide both for the better lighting and watching of the town and suburbs, which, though they now contain upwards of 64,000 souls, are still left, even during the gloomy nights of winter, to the inefficient care of a very few undisciplined watchmen, who are maintained by the voluntary subscriptions of the inhabitants of the principal streets. Out of the vast sums which are exacted annually in Nottingham, under the name of *county or town rates*, (see p. 128,) more money is expended in detecting, supporting, and prosecuting delinquents, and supposed delinquents, than, if partially employed in maintaining an organised and efficient body of nocturnal guardians, would prevent the greater part of the robberies and other crimes from being committed, so that under such a salutary regulation, the town would derive both a pecuniary and a moral advantage.

WATERWORKS.—Until a few years ago, the town had but a very scanty and indifferent supply of soft water, but it now possesses two new establishments for supplying it with that pure beverage of nature, in addition to the old works, which have lately been much extended and improved.

The OLD WATERWORKS COMPANY obtained their original lease (of which 60 years are unexpired) of the corporation, in 1696, and erected an engine-house on the south bank of the Leen, near the bottom of Finkhill-street, whence they forced the water into a large reservoir behind the General Hospital.— In consequence of long-continued complaints against the quality and scarcity of the water raised from the river Leen, the company, in 1827, obtained an Act of Parliament to make new works at Scottom, in the parish of Basford, where a reservoir covering one acre of ground now receives the water of the Leen and some of its tributary streams, before it is contaminated by the filth and sewers in the town and its vicinity.— They also discontinued the old engine-house, and erected a new one in Brewhouse-yard, to which the water is conveyed by pipes, and then forced by a steam-engine and water wheel at the rate of five hogsheads per minute, into the old reservoir behind the General Hospital, whence it passes through various lines of piping to the houses of many of the inhabitants. Mr. John Hallam is the engineer, and Mr. James Hewitt the collector.

The NORTHERN WATERWORKS, at the top of Sherwood-street, near the forest, were formed in 1826, and are supplied with excellent water, pumped by a steam-engine from a copious spring into a large cistern, which will hold 2000 hogsheads.— These works supply the north-eastern portion of the town, and feed a small cistern in York-street, at which the water-carters are supplied. Mr. James Slark is the engineer.

The TRENT WATERWORKS, near the Trent bridge, about a mile and a half south of the Market-place, were finished in August, 1831. They consist of one engine-house, with a large reservoir, fifty yards from the bank of the Trent, covered with sand and gravel, through which the river water is filtered, and then pumped by a steam-engine of forty horses' power, at the rate of 10 hogsheads per minute, along the main pipe, which is two miles long, to an elevation of 130 feet, where it falls into a capacious reservoir at the top of Park-row, from which upwards of twelve miles of piping is extended through different parts of the town. The company was established by Act of Parliament, in 1825, but, owing to a great panic in trade, occasioned by the failure of many country banking-houses, a sufficient number of shareholders could not be procured till 1830, when the great increase made in the rates charged by the old company, after they had enlarged their works, caused the project of the Trent company to be revived and carried into effect. Mr. Thomas Hawksley is the engineer.

SPRINGS AND PUBLIC PUMPS.—Spring water at Nottingham is very plentiful, and may be obtained by means of wells and pumps in almost every part of the town, but it is generally of a hard and curdling quality, which renders it both unwholesome and unfit for the purposes of washing. About forty years ago, the corporation erected eight public pumps, in the following situations, viz. one at the west end of Chapel-bar, two in Parliament-street, one at the top of Charlotte-street, one at Weekday-cross, one in the Shambles, and two in the Market-place, opposite the Exchange and Beastmarket-hill; and to these we may add the public tap at the House of Correction, which is supplied with water by the treadmill. *Beycroft spring* and *Rag spring* are famed for curing sore eyes, and are situated near the town, on the road leading to St. Anne's well. The *Spaw*, in Spaw-close, opposite the castle, was of a strong chalybeate quality, but in 1811, the spring head was removed out of the close, to the bank of the Leen, where it has ceased to flow in dry weather. *Trough-close spring*, near Mapperley hills, is also of some note amongst the inhabitants, and is within the liberties of the town.

RIVERS, CANALS, and BRIDGES :—No manufacturing town possesses a more extensive and direct communication with the Inland Navigation of England, than Nottingham. The TRENT, which is the longest river in the kingdom, passes within a mile south of the town, and rolls its expansive waters to the Humber, opening a navigable intercourse with the German Ocean, and with the rivers and and canals of Yorkshire and Lincolnshire. The *Nottingham Canal*, which falls into the Trent, a little below the bridge, and nearly opposite the lock of the *Grantham Canal*, passes close to the lower part of the town, and at Langley Mill, about eight miles to the north-west, forms a junction with the Cromford Canal, down which immense quantities of the rich produce of the mines and mountains of Derbyshire are brought. The Trent is navigable to Burton, in Staffordshire, but has in the passage from thence to Nottingham, several shoals and circuitous reaches, which are avoided by a side cut called the *Trent Canal*, which extends from the Nottingham Canal, at Lenton, to the Trent and Mersey Canal, which opens the passage to the Grand Trunk Canal, and all the navigable rivers and canals of Staffordshire, Lancashire, Cheshire, and the western parts of the island. Near Sawley Ferry, about eight miles S. W. of Nottingham, the Trent Navigation is joined by the Derby and the Erewash Canals, and the River Soar, which latter, with the Leicester Union, the Grand Union, the Grand Junction, the Paddington and the Regent Canals, forms a direct line of navigation betwixt the Trent and the Thames, and thus opens a communication with all the canals in the south of England. The rivers and canals of Nottinghamshire are already described at a preceding page, in the general survey of the county, therefore it is only necessary here to notice those parts of the Trent and the Leen, which are locally connected with the town.

The River Leen, which passes through the lower part of Nottingham, in a line nearly parallel with, and about 200 feet north of the canal, is a small stream contaminated with the filth of many common sewers, dye-houses, &c.; but a great part of it is now arched over for the improvement of the town. It rises near Newstead Abbey and flows southward to Lenton; whence, previous to Norman conquest, it ran direct to the Trent, but William de Peveril turned it into a new cut for the use and better defence of his castle of Nottingham, on the south side of which it now runs to Sneinton Meadows, where it forms the boundary of the liberties of the town, and falls into the Trent a little below the bridge. The Tinker's Leen is a small rivulet which arises from several springs in the Meadows and flows eastward under the Flood-road to the Leen.

Flood Road.—The Trent and Leen Bridges, which are distant nearly a mile from each other, are connected by a broad and level road, raised across the intervening low and swampy meadows, and having under it a long range of arches and culverts, for the purpose of affording a free passage for the water during the floods, which so frequently inundate the meadows on both sides of the Trent. The old road from the town to the Trent was intercepted by two large pools, over which were two wooden bridges; which in 1766 were rebuilt by the corporation, who afterwards removed them, and erected in their place a stone bridge of ten arches, which was so shattered in the great flood of 1795, (see p. 99) that it had to be entirely taken down. In the following year an act of Parliament was obtained for making the present *Flood-road*, &c. entitled "An act for raising, maintaining, and keeping in repair the road from the north end of the old Trent Bridge to the west end of St. Mary's churchyard, by way of Hollow-stone; and for erecting and maintaining so many flood bridges upon the said road, as may be necessary to carry off the flood water." This act empowers the 25 commissioners to take tolls on the road, and secures to them £100 a-year, to be paid by the corporation out of the bridge estates. The *Seven Arch Bridge*, which forms 120 yards of the road, was finished in 1796, and the *Nine Culverts* and the *Chainy Pool Arch* in 1809. These as well as the walls and abutments on both sides of the road are all of stone, and present a noble appearance. The road is from 15 to 20 yards broad, and has a good foot path; and on each side a well constructed parapet, composed of huge blocks of stone nearly as hard as granite. The arches which cross the canal and the Leen are at the north end of this costly road, which is

now so secure as to bid defiance to every thing but the silent
attacks of time.

The TRENT BRIDGE, at the south end of the Flood-road,
crosses the river and its sloping banks by seventeen venerable
arches, some of which are elliptical and the rest semi-circular.
It was built by the corporation, after the old one had been destroyed by the ice in the great flood of 1683. The original
bridge, said to have been built by Edward the Elder, consisted
of stone piers supporting a platform of wood. The present
bridge was so narrow at the south end that two carriages could
scarcely pass each other, till the corporation in 1806, ordered
the eastern parapet to be rebuilt, and the arches lengthened.
In 1810, the north end was widened, and a range of buildings
that stood on the east side was removed. In 1826, it was again
repaired, and so altered that the water which before only ran
through three of the arches (except in time of flood) now runs
through six. It was anciently called *Heathbeth-brig*, which
Deering supposes to be a corruption of *Highbath-bridge*, an appellation said to have originated from a number of wooden
baths which formerly stood upon piles in the river. At the north
end of the bridge was *St. Mary's chapel*, founded in the reign
of Edward I. for a priest to celebrate divine offices for the
souls of John de Paumer and Alice his wife. "For the amend-
ing, supporting, and repairing their bridges upon the water of
Trent," Edward VI. granted to the mayor and burgesses of
Nottingham, all the possessions of the dissolved chantry of St.
Mary, and the hospital of St. John, and they have since received
several bequests of lands and buildings for the same purpose, so
that the "*bridge estate*" is now of considerable value. Within
a short distance from the north end of the Trent is a dead
water crossed by a small bridge of one arch, and called the *Old
Trent*, from its being as is supposed the ancient channel of the
river.

FISHERY.—The Trent has long been famous for the plenitude and variety of its fish, amongst which are "barbel, bream,
bulhead, burbot, carp, chub, crayfish, dace, eel, flounder, gray-
ling, gudgeon, lampery, loach, minnow, muscle, perch, pike,
roach, rud, ruff, salmon, salmon-trout, salmon-pink, sand-eel,
shad, smelt, strickleback, sturgeon, stream-pink, tench, trout,
and whiting." All the burgesses have by prescription, the
right of fishing in that part of the river within the liberties of
the county of the town, though for some time after the conquest
they were deprived of it by William de Peveril, who granted
the tithe of the fishery to the monks of Lenton. All the
anglers of the town, whether denizens or not, now exercise
the privilege of fishing in the Trent, and in their thirst for
sport as well as profit do not always confine themselves to their
own liberties, but traverse the river for miles both above and

below the town, and often return heavily laden with pike, salmon, trout, &c.

The TRENT NAVIGATION COMPANY'S OFFICES are near the junction of the canal and the Trent, in Sneinton parish; Mr. Samuel Brummit is the *agent*, and Mr. John Hopkin the *surveyor*. As the passage across the Trent from the Nottingham to the Grantham Canals is very difficult, the company employ a pilot to conduct the vessels from one lock to the other.

IMPROVEMENTS, &c.—In 1536 nearly all the houses and other buildings of Nottingham were constructed of wood and plaster, and mostly thatched with straw or reeds, and many of them had then been so long in a state of decay and ruin, that Henry VIII. caused a statute to be enacted for the re-edification of "*Nottingham*" and several other places, under the following forfeitures for neglect, viz.—" That if the owners of the decayed houses did not re-edify them within three years, they should become the property of the lord of the manor; if he neglected the same length of time, they should be seized by the corporate body, where such bodies existed; and if they should be equally neglectful for the same period, the houses should revert to their original owners." This injunction appears to have been promptly attended to, for Leland, who visited Nottingham a few years afterwards, says, " it is both a large towne and welle builded for tymbre and plaister, and standeth stately upon a clyning hille." In 1641, Deering informs us that the *Trent-lanes* were very dirty, and that the traveller found the entrance to the town at Hollowstone deep and miry, and was there assailed (if the wind was northerly) with a volley of suffocating smoke, caused by the burning of gorse and tanners knobs in the adjacent rock houses. At this time (1641) Bridlesmithgate was lined with the roughest kind of blacksmiths; the Market-place, though spacious, was paved only on one side, and on the other, called the sands, it was very miry: St. Peter's-square was so boggy that a bridge of planks was laid across it with a single rail, and all the ground from thence through Listergate to the Leen was one continued swamp. Tiles were first introduced in 1503, (see p. 87) and the first brick house in the town was built in the Long-row in 1615, on the site now occupied by the Derby Arms public-house. Some slight improvement took place during the civil wars; but it was not till after the restoration that the increase of manufactures produced any considerable melioration in the style of building. The town is now as clean, and as well paved and built, as any other manufacturing town in the kingdom.

Its great increase in buildings and population during the last 30 years is noticed at page 75, and the removal of its ancient walls and gates, at page 118. In its suburbs, as well as in its principal streets are many large and beautiful *mansions*, some of which possess all the advantages of country villas, as well as those of town residences. Amongst the *noblemen and gentle-men of rank and fortune*, who have resided here are the following, viz.—" Lord Edward Earl of Rutland, Sir Thomas Manners, Sir William Courtney, Sir Thomas Stanhope Sir Thomas Willoughbie, Anthony Strelley, Sir Edmund Stanhope, Lord Scroope, Sir Henry Pierrepont, Sir John Byron, Sir John Zouch, Sir Philip Strelley, Sir Henry Cavendish, Lord Stanhope, Sir Edward Osborne, Sir Thomas Peckham, Sir Thomas Hunt, the Earl of Clare, Lord Houghton, Sir Thomas Hutchinson, and Sir Thomas Walmsley."

THURLAND HALL, the largest and most ancient mansion in Nottingham, was taken down in 1831, for the improvement of Pelham-street, on the north side of which it stood, nearly opposite the Black's Head Inn, which was pulled down in 1830. It was sometimes called *Clare Hall*, from its former owners, the Earls of Clare, one of whom married the heiress of the third Duke of Newcastle, and had the latter title conferred upon him in 1694, together with that of Marquis of Clare. It was originally built by Thomas Thurland, who was mayor of Nottingham in 1449 and 1468, and was probably rebuilt and much enlarged by the Hollis's, Earls of Clare, and afterwards Dukes of Newcastle, whose estates and titles passed to the Pelhams and the Clintons, by the latter of whom they are now held.— The hall was a long, lofty, and gloomy building, with massive walls, and extended backward to within a few yards of Lincoln-street. It was principally of brick, except the end fronting Pelham-street, which was ornamented with a double row of pilasters and window frames of heavy stone work, with an antique entrance door, approached by a flight of steps, and semi-circular zigzag pointed fronts to the roof. It was many years occupied by two or three families, and part of it was occasionally used for assemblies, &c. The Duke of Newcastle has now occupied its site, and also that of the Black's Head Inn, on the opposite side of the street, with good houses and shops. He has also formed several new streets, betwixt Pelham-street and Parliament-street, where many good houses have been erected.

BUGGE HALL, now the Old Angel public-house, in the High Pavement, at the corner of St. Mary-gate, is an aged structure, without any architectural beauties. It was long occupied by the family of Bugge, from whom descended the Bugges of West Leak, the Biggs, of Stamford, and the Willoughbys of Wollaton.

BROMLEY HOUSE, in the Market-place is already noticed at page 175.

PLUMPTRE HOUSE, on the north side of St. Mary's church-yard, stands conspicuous for age as well as beauty. It was built in the early part of the last century, by the wealthy and charitable family whose name it bears, and it is now occupied by Alderman Wilson. The High, Middle, and Low Pavements, contain many spacious and elegant mansions, and one of them, occupied by James Fellows, Esq., has in front of it a rural vista, extending to Narrow-marsh, and affording an extensive view of the country south of the Trent. St. Mary's-gate, Castlegate, and Stoney-street, contain several large and well built houses, and others of a modern date are to be found on Standard-hill, in the Park, and in several other parts of the town and suburbs, which have long been admired, as may be seen by the following descriptive poem transcribed from Deering :—

> " Fair Nottingham, with brilliant beauty graced,
> In ancient Shirewood's south-west angle placed;
> Where northern hills her tender neck protect,
> With dainty flocks of golden fleeces deckt;
> No roaring tempests discompose her mein ;
> Her canopy of state's a sky serene.
> She, on her left Belvoir's rich vale descries,
> On th' other, Clifton hill regales her eyes ;
> If from her lofty seat she bows her head,
> There's at her feet a flowery carpet spread.
> Britain's *third stream*, which runs with rapid force,
> No sooner spies her, but retards his course ;
> He turns, he winds, he cares not to be gone,
> Until to her he first has homage done;
> He carefully his wat'ry tribute pays,
> And at her footstool foreign dainties lays,
> With assiduity her favours courts,
> And richest merchandise from sea imports ;
> *Ceres* her gift with lavish hand bestows,
> And *Bacchus* o'er his butt of *English nectar* glows.
> Thy sons, O! Nottingham, with fervour pray,
> May no intestine feuds thy bliss betray ;
> Health, plenty, pleasure, then will ne'er decay."

TRADE AND MANUFACTURES.

The two great staple trades which have raised Nottingham to its present wealth and magnitude, and which employ many thousands of its inhabitants of both sexes, are the *hosiery and lace manufactures*, the former of which, (though the stocking-frame was invented in 1589,) was not of much importance till the middle of the eighteenth century, nor the latter till 1778, when the point-net machine was invented and appended to a stocking-frame, but has lately been superseded by warp and bobbin net machines, working on various new and improved principles. The BONE or CUSHION LACE was, from an early period, a source of profitable industry to a considerable number of females in this town, till they found a more constant and perhaps a more lucrative employment, in *chevining** hosiery

*Ornamenting stockings with clocks, &c.

S

and in embroidering machine-wrought lace net. But the first manufacture by which Nottingham enriched itself, and which it has long since lost, was that of WOOLLEN CLOTH; for we find that as early as 1199, King John founded in the town a merchants' guild, and granted a charter to the burgesses; forbidding all persons within ten miles round Nottingham to work *dyed cloth*, except in the borough. This branch of business was the immediate rise to opulence of several great families in the town, (merchants of Calais,) amongst whom may be enumerated the Willoughbys, Binghams, Tannesleys, Plumptres, Thurlands, Mapperleys, Amyases, Allestrees, Salmons, and the Hunts. But no cloth appears to have been made for exportation till after 1331, when Edward III., by an Act passed at Nottingham, (see p. 84,) induced many of the *Flemish and Brabant manufacturers* to come and settle in England, where one of them, called *Hanks*, gave his name to the skein of worsted, as *Thomas Blanket*, a weaver of Bristol, did to the woollen sheets which cover us in bed. But at the close of the sixteenth century, the cloth trade in Nottingham gave place to the hosiery manufacture, which soon afforded ample employment for the worsted mills, the weavers, the dyers, and the *smiths* of the town, the latter of whom were very numerous, and had previously occupied the whole of Bridlesmith-gate, Girdlergate, (now Pelham-street,) and Smithy-row, where they had long manufactured bits, snaffles, buckles, and other articles for bridles, girdles, &c ; but they now discarded their ancient occupation, and began to make *Stocking frames*, many of which consist of 6000 parts, principally of iron. Deering says Nottingham was anciently famous for the production of the most curious articles in iron, and hence, he says, arose the following proverb, recorded by Fuller,—

> " The little smith of Nottingham,
> Who doth the work that no man can."

But we opine that the lines may rather be considered as an enigma than a proverb; that the "little smith" *was a lady;* and that the whole is merely a humorous allusion to her skill and her sex;—for even in the present age, we have seen many a lusty dame wielding the hammer of a Cyclopian forge.

Many hundreds of smiths, and workers in iron and brass, are now employed in the town, in making and repairing Stocking-frames, and the various newly improved BOBBIN NET MACHINES, which latter vary in width from five to twenty quarters, and are worked on the different principles distinguished by the names of *Levers', Rotary, Circular-bolt, Straight-bolt, Pusher, Traverse Warp*, and *Loughbro' machines*, each containing from 1000 to 4000 BOBBINS and CARRIAGES—the merit of inventing which was claimed by Robert Brown and George

Whitmore, of Nottingham, and by John Lindley, of Loughbro', about the year 1799; but they were greatly improved in 1807 by Edward Whitaker, of Nottingham, who made them traverse at every motion of the machine from one bar to the other.— But none of these ingenious machinists derived any benefit from their inventions, for bobbins and carriages of the same construction were included in the specifications of the Loughbro' machine, for which Mr. John Heathcoat* obtained a fourteen years' patent in 1809, during the existence of which, he and his partner, Charles Lacy, Esq † of Nottingham, levied a heavy tax upon all persons using the said bobbins and carriages, amounting on some machines to upwards of £30 per annum.— After the expiration of this patent, in 1823, a ruinous speculation prevailed in Nottingham for more than two years, during which, almost every capitalist was anxious to embark his money in bobbin net machines, to assist in the construction of which, hundreds of mechanics, tempted by extravagant wages, poured into the town from Sheffield, Birmingham, Manchester, and other places; machines and houses "sprung up like mushrooms," money circulated freely, and the town was intoxicated with an unstable prosperity, which was suddenly dispelled by a consequent glut in the home and foreign markets, and by the failure of many of the London and country banks and great commercial houses, in December 1825, and the following year. Since then, machines which cost from £400 to £500, have been sold for less than £100, and they are now made on the best principles for less than half the amount that was charged for those which were hurried together in the bustling years of 1824 and 1825. Numerous improved bobbin net machines have been introduced during the last twenty years, the principal of which are the Traverse Warp, invented by John Brown and George Freeman, Esqrs. in 1810; the Straight-bolt, by William Morley, in 1812; the Pusher, by James Clark and Joshua Roper; the Levers', by three John Levers, (father, son, and nephew,) in 1814; the Rotary, by John Lindley, in 1816; the Circular-bolt, by the before-mentioned William Morley, in 1817; and the Rotary Levers' Traverse Warp, by William Barnes, in 1827. To enumerate all the inventions of the various kinds of machinery used in the manufacture of hosiery, lace, &c. would greatly exceed our limits, and be uninteresting to the general reader; we shall therefore

* Mr. John Heathcoat has amassed considerable wealth, and now lives at Tiverton, in Devonshire. He was many years a working *setter-up* of machinery in Nottingham, and introduced several improvements, besides the Loughbro' machine, which is now nearly disused, being too slow for the other improved principles.

† Mr. Lacy was a large manufacturer in Nottingham, and was uncle to John Lindley, one of the persons who claimed the invention of bobbins and carriages.

conclude with the following notice of the founder of frame-work knitting:—*

The *Rev. William Lee, M. A., who invented the first* STOCKING FRAME in 1589, was a native of either Calverton or Woodborough, in Nottinghamshire. Deering says, that he was heir to a pretty freehold estate, and being deeply in love with a young person to whom he paid his addresses, but whom he always found more intent upon her knitting than to his vows and protestations, he was induced to contrive a machine which should render the mode of knitting by hand entirely useless. We have, however, seen it stated differently; that Mr. Lee was a poor curate, and married; and his wife being obliged to occupy herself industriously with knitting, which interfered very much with the attention necessary to her family, he was prompted to attempt the invention of the present complex, yet simple machinery. It is certain that he or his brother exhibited the loom before Queen Elizabeth; but his invention being despised in his native country, he went to France, with several English workmen, where he was patronised by Henry IV.— The murder of that monarch overturned all his hopes of success; he died of grief and chagrin at Paris, and his few surviving workmen returned to England. After some time, a company of frame-work knitters was established in London; but no trade of this kind, where *small* capitals are sufficient, can possibly flourish under a monopoly; of course, even the London dealers in hosiery found it more profitable to purchase their goods in the country, than from the manufacturers of the metropolis; and the trade has since spread itself over a great part of Nottinghamshire, Leicestershire, and Derbyshire, and a few frames are at work in almost every large town in the kingdom. By an enumeration in 1812, there were found to be 2600 STOCKING FRAMES in Nottingham,† 900 in Old and New Radford, 400 in Mansfield, 1700 in Leicester, 1500 at Hinckley, and 400 in and near Derby. The total number in Nottinghamshire, was 9285; in Leicestershire, 11,183; in Derbyshire, 4700; in Gloucestershire, 970; in the other counties of England, 980; in Scotland, 1419; in Ireland, 976; in France, 6855; in the Netherlands, 520; in Spain and Portugal, 1955; in Italy, 985; in Germany, 2340; in America, 260; in St. Petersburg, &c.

* The first Stocking-frame produced only *plain* work. The *Derby-rib* machine was invented in 1758, by Jebediah Strutt, of Derby; the *Knotting* machine, in 1776, by Mr. Horton; and the Warp machine, (which united the stitch of the stocking-frame with the warp of the weaver's loom,) in 1775, by Mr. Crane, of Edmonton. The last was superseded in 1782, James Tarrant's *Warp-frame*, which makes an inferior kind of shapeless stockings called *cut-ups*, and is also used in making warp lace. The *Point-net* machine, (appended to a stocking-frame,) was invented in 1778, by Messrs. Lindley, Taylor, and Flint, of Nottingham.

† In 1641, there were only two stocking-frames in Nottingham, and in 1739 they had only increased to sixty.

200; and at Stockholm and Copenhagen, 65; making the grand total, 42,768! Many of the frames in Nottinghamshire and the adjoining counties were destroyed by the Luddites, betwixt the years 1812 and 1816, (see p. 102 to 106,) and some of them were perhaps never replaced, owing to their owners embarking in the *lace trade*, in which there are now employed in England upwards of 4500 Bobbin Net Machines, belonging to about 1380 owners, of whom nearly 1000 work in their own machines, and enter both into the class of journeymen and masters, and thus, in all depressions of trade, operate injuriously on the wages of the one and the profits of the other. More than half of these machines are in Nottingham, Mansfield, and the surrounding villages, and the remainder are mostly in Leicestershire. About 1000 of them, (principally in Leicestershire,) are worked by the agency of steam, but those in the towns of Nottingham and Mansfield are nearly all worked by hand, the broad machines having generally two men each, who work them "in four hour shifts."

In the "*Calculations illustrative of the present state of the Bobbin Net Trade*" published in August 1831, by a gentleman of Nottingham, who is extensively connected with that important manufacture, we find the following conclusions, viz. that 25,000 lb. of raw silk, and 1,600,000 lb. of Sea-Island cotton, worth £150,000, is manufactured annually into 23,400,000 square yards of bobbin net, worth £1,891,875; of which net, 3-8ths is sold unembroidered at home; and 4-8ths is exported in the same state, and most of it embroidered on the continent: The remaining 1-8th is embroidered in this country, (principally in the midland counties,) at the cost, in wages, &c., of £1,525,825, making its total ultimate value £3,417,700!!! He also estimates the total *capital employed* at £2,310,000, of which £935,000, is sunk or employed in 35 Cotton Mills, (principally in Manchester,) engaged in spinning and doubling lace thread; and £1,020,000 in machines.

The following COMPARATIVE VIEW OF THE British AND French Lace Trades, *containing a description of the* Queen's Dress, *made at Nottingham in* 1831, *is extracted from the Nottingham Review of June 3rd in that year, and is, we presume, from the pen of Mr. Gravener Henson.*

" The *dress worn by Queen Adelaide* at the Juvenile Ball given by their Majesties on the 24th of May, 1831, in honour of the Princess Victoria of Kent, the heiress presumptive of the Crown, and mentioned in the *Court Circular* as being made of white lace and silver, was made of Nottingham machine wrought bobbin net silk lace, in imitation of the French chantilly blond, and tulle, so extensively made at Lyons, Nismes, Troyes, and Barcelona, and so largely imported into this country.

" The circumstances under which her Majesty was induced to

order this British silk blond dress were of the most extraordinary nature, and important to the manufacturing and commercial interests of the country,—deeply involving the question as to the policy and wholesome practicability of the free trade system adopted by the British Legislature, erroneously termed the "reciprocity sytem," as the reciprocity on the part of France and Spain is entirely on one side, they absolutely prohibiting as contraband almost every article of British manufacture.

"This blond dress was made to compete with the article called by the French, TULLE, and also with the beautiful fabrics imported from the continent termed CHANTILLY BLOND, the former of which is made from a machine, the latter from the cushion by the hand. The French tulle is made in the exact manner termed by the workman single press point net, against which the Luddites, from 1812 to 1816, directed so much of their vengeance, when made of cotton, as being a fraudulent article. The first lace made by machinery in England was formed by removing the loops of the plain stocking fabric to form the mesh; this was made for a period of from ten to twelve years, but the mesh was very imperfect; at length, about the year 1778, the thread which conjoins the loops was placed round two loops alternately, keeping the stocking loop unremoved; this method formed a complete sexangular mesh, but had little or no sale, the article being loose, and only retained its form by stiffening, which was very imperfectly done. This effect was produced by an instrument exactly resembling a barleycorn, called a *point*, for which a patent was obtained, which fell into the hands of *Messrs. William Hayne and Co.*, who instituted a great number of actions for infringement. A person of the name of Harvey, to evade this patent, invented (in London,) an instrument to make the same net, by using a bent thin pin, by which he placed conjoint thread on the loops by a different mode from the patentee, who agreed to give him an annuity of £60 a year not to use the machine. The French, who are ever on the alert to pirate British inventions, deputed the Duke du Liancourt to London, to obtain the numerous new inventions which had been introduced to the stocking frame; he was accompanied by a workman of the name of Rhambolt, who wrought in the frame as a journeyman, and obtained a knowledge of this machine, and introduced it into France, (the barley corn point not then being known in London) for which service the committee of public safety, in 1793-4, awarded him the sum of 11,000 francs (bout £450.) The English, in 1786, had effected a method of making *point net* by improved machinery, and re-looping the conjoined thread, made a fast mesh, so as to require little or no care in stiffening. From this period, lace made by machinery began to be in considerable demand; the English making their lace from the barley corn point, a fast-wrought net—the French from the pin, a loose-

wrought, net, or single press. At this period commenced the
revolutionary war, which obstructed all communicaton between
the two countries, each state proceeding with its own machinery. At the conclusion of the war by the treaty of Amiens, in
1802-3, England had made nearly 1200 frames, all employed
upon silk fast net. The French had increased their machinery
at Lyons and Nismes to near 2000, all employed on single press
net, and in order to protect it against the superior quality of
English net, the French Republic had prohibited the latter so
early as 1794-5; at that period, when Mr. John Morris, of Nottingham, was at Lyons and Nismes, they had made some progress in improving their machinery and in stiffening the lace,
though not so as to come in competition with English net; so
decided was the superiority of fast net considered, and so strict
the prohibitory laws, that Mr. George Armitage was induced
to remove from London to Paris, to introduce the English method. The war again commencing, separated the two countries; the French machines were found totally incompetent to
make fast net. Mr. William Hayne, the original patentee,
was in Paris, and was detained by Bonaparte at the commencement of the war; his object was to smuggle British net into
France, which he continued to do with varied success until
1809, when, his agents having betrayed him, no less than
£25,000 worth was seized in one week, which together with
the fines, amounted to £40,000; he had before sustained great
losses from seizures in this contraband trade, and succeeded by
almost a miracle in making his escape to England. In Nottingham, the capital of Mr. Hayne was supposed to be almost
inexhaustible, as he had carried on a flourishing business for
twenty years, and had commenced with a freehold estate worth
£7000 a year, yet his French speculations in smuggling had so
deranged his concerns, that in 1811, he was found completely
insolvent, and died in a state of childish inanity, though a man
of strong mind, completely exhausted by his misfortunes.

  "At the conclusion of the war, in 1813-14, by the peace of
Paris, the speculations in Nottingham were ruinously extensive; lace machines rose in value from £25 to £130, under the
impression that British lace would have the same demand as in
1802-3. Mr. Morris, however, who had been at Lyons and Nismes, knew better, and a little before he died, sent a long memorial
written with his own hand to Lord Sidmouth, pointing out the
danger from French competition in the silk lace manufacture,
and predicted its total extinction in England. That minister
was too much elated by his unexpected success to listen to any
warning, and the admonition was thrown by as ill-timed and
useless. So great were the speculations that premiums were
actually given by the masters to the work-people, to obtain each
others' nets surreptitiously; but when their nets were conveyed to the great markets in Spain, Sicily, and South America,

they were met by the French single press net, stiffened and dressed in such a superior manner as to wholly supersede British nets in those markets; many thousand pounds worth of British lace is now lying at Palermo, Cadiz, Rio, and Buenos Ayres, unsold to this day, which has led to the failure of most of the old established houses. But however strange it may appear, these circumstances were not known to the working classes in Nottingham, until the year 1819-20. By the large importations of French wrought nets into this country, the workmen had been deprived of employment, their frames either palmed upon them for wages, or sold for a mere trifle to make slop stockings, to the utter injury and disgrace of the regular hosiery manufacture. The duty charged upon the importation was 40 per cent. on the declared value, which duty was much evaded by the importers. A memorial upon this subject was presented to Mr. Robinson (Lord Goderich) by Mr. Birch, which was treated with great coolness and neglect; another was presented by Mr. Denman, who made such strong remonstrances, aided by Mr. Birch, that the duty was altered to 2s. per square yard, or more than 75 per cent.—This continued until Mr. Huskisson, by his celebrated measure in 1824, altered the whole scale of duties, which took place in 1826, and lowered the tariff to 30 per cent.; since which period the point net frames, from 1500, in 1808, have gradually disappeared, until John Martin is now the last solitary point net hand! The extent of the importation of a manufacture in which the English conceived they should ever have remained unrivalled from their superior skill, may be estimated by a return made to the Lords of Trade, 5th Nov. 1830, by which it appeared, that in one year nearly 200,000 square yards were imported, but so slovenly is the business carried on at the Custom House, that the French import their ells of 45 inches, which are passed as yards, making the total more than 240,000 yards, exclusive of the system of which the merchants of Deal and Dover know so much—smuggling!

"While the English were thus totally losing the silk lace trade, the French were rapidly gaining the cotton lace trade, though they affected to prohibit both; the former being really and rigidly prohibited, the latter only speciously, in order to encourage English workmen to establish machines in France, and to make one piece and smuggle another, thus completely outwitting us, in which the original patentee unfortunately took the lead. The British Government, instead of checking this ruinous system, which will ultimately be found so dreadful in its consequences, winked at the subject as unworthy their notice, under the infatuation that the skill of the English workmen had nothing to fear from competition.

"The workmen (principally inventors of machinery) conceiving themselves in the most imminent jeopardy, as the bobbin net machines were extending at the rate of more than twenty per month in France, came to the resolution of presenting a memorial to the board of trade upon these important subjects, urging a careful inquiry into the state of the hosiery and lace trades, which was presented to Mr. Herries by Mr. Legh Keck, M.P. for the county of Leicester, and Mr. Birch, M.P. for Nottingham, who promised a careful investigation.

"On the meeting of Parliament, Mr. Herries determined to redeem his pledge to those gentlemen, directed his secretary to require the attendance of *Gravener Henson*, whose mission was interrupted by the dissolution of the Wellington administration. Before the new minister, Lord Auckland, had taken the oaths and entered upon office, Sir R. C. Ferguson, M.P. for Nottingham, had urged the matter upon his Lordship, and requested him to permit Henson to wait upon him. The result of this interview was, that his lordship expressed considerable doubts as to the propriety of interference; and that Mr. P. Thompson, the vice president of the Board of Trade, treated the matter as frivolous and unworthy his attention.

"But their majesties, soon afterwards, with a praiseworthy attention to the distresses of the country, gave the most positive directions that no person should appear at court dressed in any but British manufactures. This order was nearly tantamount in its consequences to directing that no lady should appear in white silk lace.

"Silk lace had begun to be made from the *bobbin-net machines* which had increased since 1813, from little more than 200, to more than 4500, at an expense of nearly a million and a half of capital. A species of white silk lace had been made from the warp frame, another distinct mode of making machine lace. Several abortive attempts had been made, for a long period, to stiffen the lace after the French method, and persons had gone to Lyons, for the express purpose of learning their method, who had all lamentably failed. *Mr. Joseph Crowder*, of Nottingham, who had made considerable improvements in the lace machinery, had (induced by some of the manufacturers who imported the French lace, and employed their work-people in Nottingham, to ornament net made at Lyons,) directed his attention to the subject, and as he was said to have obtained some hints from the continent, he, by dint of great perseverance, was enabled to produce an article fully equal in appearance to the French tulle, from the bobbin net, but decidedly superior in its stamina. The French tulle made, single prest, is nothing more than a series of stocking warpings, owing the whole of its stamina to the glutinous stiffening, which wet or damp will cause the web to lose every appearance of a fabric of lace. The bobbin net lace is made exactly in the same manner by the machine, as the cushion lace in Buckinghamshire, and as the blond lace imported from France; but infinitely superior in the regular for-

mation of the meshes. The infinite difficulty was to stiffen an
article of so gossamer an appearance; perfectly pliable, as lace
made from a single thread of Italian silk; but this, Mr. Crowder had fully accomplished, with this drawback, that the cost
was materially greater than the ordinary method, which it appears, upon inquiry, is the case with the French dressed lace,
five persons being enabled even in their improved state, to dress
only about seventy or eighty yards per day.

" It was conceived, that if her majesty would order a dress of
this net, and thus, from such a distinguished patronage, introduce it to the notice of the nobility and gentry, their patriotism
might induce them to use a British in preference to a foreign
article; and G. Henson was advised to apply to the principal
manufacturers upon his return, and present a petition to her
Majesty for that purpose. This petition was proposed, and
signed by Mr. Samuel Hall, Mr. John Kendall, Messrs. Train
and Wesson, and by J. Crowder and G. Henson, and presented
to her Majesty by Sir Herbert Taylor. Her Majesty, with a
condescension and attention which ought to endear her to
every considerate person, not only gave the order, but directed
Messrs. Train and Wesson, who undertook in the handsomest
manner to complete it, to apply to her milliner, through whom
she gave directions as to the manner in which the dress, when
made, was most likely to meet the public approbation, leaving
the exact pattern to the discretion of the manufacturer. G.
Henson, during the completion of the dress, was induced to
proceed to town upon the question of the Truck Bill, and presented to her Majesty's milliner, for her inspection, specimens
of the English and French lace, and explained the nature of
the fabrics, and the test of placing each of them in water, for
the information of her Majesty and her court.

" This dress, when completed by Messrs. Train and Wesson,
was sent, by direction of Sir H. Taylor, direct to her Majesty,
at St. James's Palace. The pattern was made in stripes of
nine inches, and consisted of an elegant star, having a large
open work in the middle, beautifully worked with the needle,
encircled with a series of roses; the whole appearance of the
dress was of the most brilliant description imaginable, and absolutely dazzled the eye. The appearance was that of flowers
of brilliant shining silk, worked upon a gossamer light fabric,
having more the appearance of net made of mother-of-pearl,
than of any other substance. A most material improvement
had been made in preparing the ornamental silk, by the sugges-
tion of Mrs. Bitton's, her Majesty's milliner, which heightened
the effect, by preserving the gloss of the ornamental silk. Her
Majesty, with that attention and politeness which confers the
greatest lustre upon her character, took the earliest and most
effectual method of introducing the article to the notice of her
court, by wearing it, ornamented with silver, over a white satin

dress, and that too at a juvenile ball, principally composed of young ladies of her court, in honour of her niece, the heiress presumptive; thus displaying the new article to a body of influential young ladies, most likely to patronize white ornamental dresses, the characteristic and proper dress for their rank and age.

"Thus has her Majesty, in the noblest manner, done her duty, in introducing the article in the most effectual way to her court, to become the prevailing fashion. It now remains to be seen whether Nottingham or Lyons shall have the silk net trade. If the English nobility patronize this article, which is of superior quality to French tulle, the consumption must necessarily increase in this country, and wherever English fashions or influence predominates. The beauty and stamina of bobbin net is so decided, above single press, that it will bear no comparison, where the articles are known and appreciated. France employs more than 3000 frames, making more than 3,000,000 yards of silk lace annually; Spain from 500 to 700, making more than 600,000 yards yearly; whilst in Italy, Germany, and the whole amount manufactured upon the continent, cannot be estimated at less than 4,000,000 square yards annually, or near a million in value. But when it is considered that an immense number of persons are employed to ornament it, the subject increases to immense importance, and is probably to the extent of £10,000,000 annually, as in Catalona alone, the ornamenters of lace are computed by the Spaniards at 5000 persons. Thus has the last effort been made on the part of the English workmen, to meet the French by a fair competition; the result will be seen, and posterity and Europe will judge whether the English mechanic has had fair play—as whilst French silk net is allowed to be imported upon a light duty, not rigidly levied, British lace is rigorously and sternly seized, whilst the most influential and spirited of her manufacturers have been ruined and undone by confiscations. But it is hoped that a reformed Parliament will very early devote their attention to the employment of the population of this kingdom, and adopt a firm line of conduct with foreign states, respecting reciprocal duties and prohibitions, and make them *really reciprocal*."

The abolition of the *East India Company* would be an inestimable benefit to the trade of Nottingham, for, in the absence of that great chartered monopoly, *British lace* would find an extensive market in the countries eastward of the Cape of Good Hope, where it is now almost unknown, though it is so suitable and desirable an article of dress for the inhabitants of warm climates. The present *exports of bobbin net* are principally to Holland and Belgium; to France by contraband; to Italy; and to North and South America. A durable and elegant article in bobbin net, suitable for curtains, &c. is now exported at the low price of fourpence per square yard, and another article used for many

purposes of female dress at sixpence per square yard. The
hosiery manufactured here, consists chiefly of the finer sorts of
silk, cotton, and worsted stockings, gloves, &c.

COTTON MILLS, &c.—" *The first cotton mill erected in the
world*" was built at Nottingham, on a piece of ground betwixt
Hockley and Woolpack-lane, in 1769, by the celebrated Richard
Arkwright. It was burnt down a few years afterwards, but
was rebuilt by its founder, and now bears the name of *Hockley
Mill*, and is occupied by Mr. Benjamin Moore. The machinery
which was here introduced for the spinning of cotton, was invented in Lancashire, and the principal cause which gave
Nottingham the honour of first applying it, was the determination of the Lancashire workmen to resist all improvements
which had a tendency to supersede manual labour. Until the
latter part of the 18th century, the warp of cotton goods was of
linen yarn, principally imported from Germany or Ireland; and
the weft was of cotton which was carded by hand, and spun in
the weaver's own family by the *distaff* and *spindle*, which (after
England began to export cotton goods) were soon found greatly
insufficient to supply the encreasing demands of the loom;
though upwards of 50,000 spindles were daily in motion in
Lancashire, turned by as many individuals. At this juncture,
Thomas Highs, a reed-maker, of Leigh, assisted by John Kay,
a clock-maker, invented a machine which gave motion to six
spindles, and which he named after his own daughter, *Jenny*.
In 1767, *James Hargrave*, of Blackburn, constructed a spinning jenny, that would spin 20 or 30 threads into yarn, but it
was destroyed by a mob, in consequence of which he left
Lancashire and came to Nottingham, where he set several
similar machines to work, but his patent was invaded, and he
died in obscurity and distress, having no just claim to the invention, which belonged to the before named *Thomas Highs*,
who also (in 1767) invented the *Throstle*, for the spinning of
twist by rollers, but of this he was also robbed, but by a more
successful adventurer, ycleped Richard, afterwards *Sir Richard
Arkwright*, who was a barber at Preston, where he had the address to possess himself of a model of High's machine. This
was the germ of Mr. Arkwright's future prosperity, and of the
extension of the cotton trade. To supply his lack of pecuniary
means he effected a partnership with Mr. Smalley, of Preston,
in Lancashire, and in 1768, he removed to Nottingham, where
he built Hockley Mill, and obtained a patent for the exclusive
benefit of spinning cotton by the new process, which privilege
he enjoyed till 1785, when his patent-right was destroyed by a
decision of the Court of King's Bench, after a long protracted
litigation. Though Sir Richard has been deprived of the
honour of the original invention, and subjected to a charge of a
want of fair dealing towards Highs, he possessed the merit of
having perfected that which before had attained only an embryo

tate, and of having surmounted difficulties by the force of his own mind which hardly any other man in the same situation could have triumphed over. His capacity of combination, if not of invention, was of the highest order, and his manufactories in Nottinghamshire and in Derbyshire, in the infancy of the cotton trade, manifested the intelligence of a presiding genius. He became one of the richest commoners of England, and died at his works at Cromford, in 1792, in the sixtieth year of his age. In 1791, Mr. Robert Denison built a large cotton mill at Nottingham, near Poplar-place, but it was burnt down in 1802, and was never rebuilt. There are now in the town and neighbourhood several *silk, cotton, and worsted mills* for supplying the lace and hosiery manufactures, but the greater part of the cotton lace thread used here is spun at Manchester.

It is estimated that the cotton twist and weft spun in Great Britain amounts to 110,000,000 lbs per annum, of which nearly one-tenth is used in the lace, thread, and hosiery manufactures; two-tenths is exported to the continent of Europe in twist, and the remainder manufactured at home into calicoes, muslins, fustians, &c.

The *annual value of the cotton manufactures* of this kingdom is now estimated at from 30 to 40 millions sterling, though in the early part of the reign of George III. it did not exceed £200,000. The growth of this manufacture, now the first in the world, has been greatly facilitated by the introduction of Boltain and Watts' *rotative steam engine;* by the spinning *mule* invented in 1775, by Samuel Crompton, of Bolton-le-Moors, and by the *power-loom,* invented by the Rev. — Cartwright of Kent, in 1785, but not brought into extensive use till about 1820. In 1815, Mr. George Oldfield Needham, of Nottingham, obtained a gold medal and sixty guineas from the Society of Arts, for improving the machinery used in carding, roving, and spinning cotton wool. *Mr. Samuel Cartledge,* of Nottingham, was the first who brought to perfection the spinning of the fine cotton twist used in making British lace, for which he received the thanks of the Buckinghamshire manufacturers of bone or cushion lace, in 1815.

Besides the numerous machine works, there are in the town several iron and brass *founderies,* a steam engine manufactory, and an extensive *white lead works.* There were formerly two *glass-houses* and two *potteries* in the town, but they have long since disappeared. The *Tanners* here once formed a numerous and respectable company, with a master and two wardens chosen annually. In 1664, here were 47 tan-yards, but in 1750 they were reduced to three, of which only two now remain, besides four *felmongers'* yards; though there are in the town thirteen *curriers.* In the vicinity there are no fewer than thirty *wind mills,* which supply the town and the surrounding villages with flour. Most of the inhabitants purchase their bread of the

T

numerous common *bakers,* one of whom, Mr. Edwin Clayton, has lately obtained a patent for a *bread-making machine,* which works on the principle of a barrel-churn, and enables the baker to convert one or two sacks of flour into fine light *dough* in the space of a few minutes. The MALTING business has, ever since the period of the Norman conquest, been a source of profit to the town and suburbs, where there are now upwards of fifty master maltsters. The goodness of the barley grown in some parts of Nottinghamshire, and in the vale of Belvoir; the excellent quality of the coal used in the malt kilns; and the deep and cool rock cellars, possessed by almost every house in the town, have long since established the fame of Nottingham Ale, which Stukely notices as being "highly valued for softness and pleasant taste." There is however but one *common brewery* in the town, as many of the private families and nearly all the publicans brew their own beer, and the latter are many of them wholesale as well as retail dealers. From 1800 to 1804, the Newark brewers attempted to force their liquor upon the town by purchasing all the public-houses they could obtain, but the great aversion of the inhabitants to what is termed "brewery ale," and the determination of the magistrates to withhold the licences of all such houses, destroyed the monoply in the latter year; so that the traveller may still regale himself, in almost any inn or tavern in the town, with a "*can*" (a plated gill) of that excellent and wholesome beverage, which many years ago inspired Mr. Gunthorpe, a naval officer, but a native of Nottingham, with a popular bacchanalian song, of which the following is the last verse and chorus:—

> "Ye poets, who brag of the Helicon brook,
> The nectar of gods, and the juice of the vine;
> You say none can write well, except they invoke
> The friendly assistance of one of the *nine*—
> Here's liquor surpasses the streams of Parnassus,
> The nectar ambrosia, on which gods regale;
> Experience will show it, nought makes a good poet,
> Like quantum suffivit of Nottingham ale!
>
> Nottingham ale, boys, Nottingham ale;
> No liquor on earth like Nottingham ale!"

NUMBERING OF THE HOUSES.—Before dismissing this succinct (but we hope comprehensive,) historical, statistical, and descriptive view of Nottingham, we, with much deference, offer the following remarks for the consideration of the authorities of the town, both corporate and parochial. We have not found in any other large town in the kingdom so great a want of that necessary facility to the every-day transactions of residents and strangers which is afforded by the proper numbering of the houses. Each street, square, court, and alley in the town ought to have a separate set of numbers affixed or painted upon its doors, but the greater part of them are yet without such distinction, even in many of the longest streets, where the postman, the porter, and other inquirers often incur much trouble before they can find the object of their search. And in those streets which partially enjoy this facility, the numbers are placed in such irregular order as to be of but little service; many of them beginning at wrong ends of the streets, progressing from right to left, and very often having duplicates on opposite sides of the same street. Cast iron plates, bearing the names of the streets, were put up in 1831, and we trust the authorities will, ere long, order and superintend the numbering of all the houses in the town and suburbs, on the plan suggested above.

LIST OF STREETS IN NOTTINGHAM

As they appear on Spede's plan of the town, published in 1610

☞ The names printed in *Italics* show the present appellations of those which have been changed.

Barker lane (*gate*)
Bearward lane (*Mount street*)
Bellargate
Bridlesmith gate
Broad marsh
Castle lane
Cartergate
Chaler's lane (*Chandler's lane*)
Cow lane (*Clumber street*)
Fishergate
Fleshergate (*Fletchergate*)
Gossegate (*Goosegate*)
Gridlesmith gate (*Pelham street*)
Halifax lane
High pavement
Hungate
Low pavement

Lymby lane (*Bottle lane*)
Malin hill
Middle pavement
Narrow marsh
Newark lane (*Woolpack lane*)
Pepper street
Pilshergate
St. James' lane
St. Mary's gate
Stoney street
Swine green (*Carlton street*)
Vault lane (*Drury hill*)
Wheelwright lane (*Wheelergate*)
White Friars' lane
Wooller lane (*Byard lane*)
Worser lane (*Warsergate*)

* A *Plan of Nottingham* was published in 1820, by T. H. Smith and H. Wild, (engraved by J. Carr, of Houndsgate.) Two other plans of the town, one on a large and the other on a small scale, have lately been published by Mr. E. Staveley

ALPHABETICAL LIST

OF

STREETS, SQUARES, GATES, LANES, COURTS,
AND ALLEYS,

IN NOTTINGHAM AND ITS VICINITY, IN 1832,

WITH REFERENCES TO THEIR RESPECTIVE SITUATIONS.

☞ The CONTRACTIONS used in the following list and in the subjoined Directory of Nottingham, will, it is hoped, be easily understood; those most frequently used are, bdgs. for buildings; bookr. bookeeper; coml. commercial; coms. commission; fkr. framework-knitter; gt. gate; h. house; L. Lenton; lgs. lodgings; Msfd. rd. Mansfield road; Mkp. Market-place; mfr. manufacturer; N. R. New Radford; O. R. Old Radford; Parlt. st. Parliament street; pl. place; pvt. pavement; rd. road; rtl. retail; spr. spinner or doubler,; S. Sneinton; solr. solicitor; sq. square; St. Saint; st. street; ter. terrace; tvr. traveller; vict. victualler; whl. wholesale; and whsm. warehouseman.   Many of these abbreviations are likewise used in the other Town Directories in this Volume, as also are the common contractions of christian names.

Agnes yard, Broad st
Albion court, Kingston st
Albion place, Albion st
Albion st, Grey friars' gate
Alfreton road, Sion Hill, N. R.
Andrew court, York st
Angel alley, Woolpack ln
Angel row, Market place
Angler's yd, Plumptre st
Ant-Hill, Cur lane
Apple row, Milk st
Armfield's yard, Mount st
Arrow yard, Fishergate
Ashton's yard, Bridlesmithgate
Aspley terrace, New Radford
Augean place, Maiden ln.
Babhington st, Mansfield rd
Back Common, Mansfield rd.
Back lane, Parliament st
Bail row, York st
Ball lane, Coalpit lane
Ball yard, Broad marsh
Balloon ct, Mount East st
Barkergate, Stoney st
Barker's yard, St. Ann's st
Barlow's ct, Sneinton rd
Baron row, Earl st

Barrow's yd, High Pavement
Bat lane, York st
Bath row wharf, Canal st
Bath place, Canal st
Beans yard, Eyre st, S.
Bear ct, Mansfield rd
Bear yard, Long row
Beast market hill, Market pl
Beck barn, *now* Beck street
Beck court, Beck st
Beck square, Coalpit lane
Beck street, John st
Beehive yard, Beck st
Bedford row, Tyler st
Bedford street, Tyler st
Bellargate, Barkergate
Bell founder's yard, Long row
Birch Row, New Radford
Bilbie's yard, Mansfield rd
Bishop row, Sussex st
Black Lion yd, Coalpit lane
Black yard, Narrow marsh
Black Boy yard, Long row
Black Horse yard, Woolpack ln
Blewitt's yard, Beck st
Bloomsbury pl, Millstone ln
Bloomsgrove, New Radford

Blucher row, Butcher st
Bond st, York st
Bond st, New Sneinton
Bost ct, Milton st
Boot ln, *now* Milton st
Booth's bdgs, St. Ann's st
Bottle alley, Bottle ln
Bottle ln, 1, Bridlesmithgate
Bran ct, Mansfield rd
Brewer street, Mill st
Brewery st, Old Glass house ln
Brewhouse yd, Castle rd
Brewitt's pl, 8, George st
Bridge st, Plumtre sq
Bridlesmithgate, Poultry
Bright Alley, Cartergate
Britannia yd, Mount st
Broad Marsh, Listergate
Broad st, Parliament st, to Carleton street
Bromley house, Angel row
Brook alley, Coalpit ln
Brook st, Beck st
Brunswick pl, Kingston st
Budge row, Mount st
Bull court, Red Lion st
Bull yard, Long row
Bunhill row, Poplar pl
Bunker's hill, Parliament st
Bussey's yd, 46, Bridlesmithgate
Burdett's ct, Old Glass house ln
Burial ground yd, Mount st
Burrow's yd, Bedford row
Butcher st, Plumtre sq
Butcher's row, Coalpit ln
Butler's ct, Narrow Marsh
Bunker's Hill, Parliament st
Butcher's ct, Beck st
Buttery's yd, Long row
Byard ln, 19, Bridlesmithgate
Byron st, *Middle Sneinton*
Cabbage ct, Charlotte st
Canaan st, New Bridge st
Cannon yard, Long row
Canal st, Bridge st
Capon ct, Charlotte st
Carey's yd, Coalpit ln
Carlisle pl, Cur ln
Carlton hill, Sneinton
Carlton road, Sneinton
Carlton st, Pelham st
Carrington st, Listergate
Cartergate, Sneinton st

Carter row, Cartergate
Castle ct, Millstone ln
Castlegate, Low Pavement
Castle pl, head of Park st
Castle road, Brewhouse yd
Castle street, New Bridge st
Castle terrace, Castle rd
Castle wharf, Brewhouse yd
Caunt st, Barkergate
Cavendish street, Red st
Chancery ct, Broad marsh
Chandler's ln, 1, Bridlesmithgate
Chapel Bar, Long row
Chapel st, Alfreton rd, N. R.
Charles street, Plat st
Charlotte street, Milton st
Charlotte sq, Milton st
Chatham st, Mansfield rd
Cheapside, Market place
Cherry place, Coalpit lane
Chesterfield st, Grey Friargate
Churchgate, Peters' Church side
Clare court, Clare st
Clare street, Parliament st
Clark's square, Glasshouse st
Clayton's yd, 34, Bridlesmithgate
Click ln, Parliament st
Clifton st, New Bridge st
Clinton st, Lincoln st
Clinton street, Nile st
Close alley, Fishergate
Clumber st, E. end of Long row
Coach and Horses' yd, Mansfield road
Coal court, Parliament st
Coalpit lane, St John's st
Cock court, Old street
Cockayne's yd, Pierrepont st
Collin st, Carrington st
Colwick st, Middle Sneinton
Commerce ct, 20, Barkergate
Commerce row, Beck st
Convent st, St. John's st
Cork alley, Parliament st
Commercial st, London rd
Corn street, Brook st
Cottage place, Sneinton
Cousin's yd, Pierrepont st
Cow court, Cartergate
Cow yard, Cartergate
Cowslip ct, Hockley
Crank ct, Glasshouse st
Cricket ct, 51, Barkergate

Cross ct, Glasshouse st
Cross street, Mount East st
Cross street, Beck st
Crossland yd, Narrow marsh
Crosland st, Narrow marsh
Croshaw's yd, Pierrepont st
Crow court, Park st
Crown court, Millstone ln
Crown yd, Long row
Crown and Anchor yd, Bridge st
Cullen's ct, Parliament st
Cur lane, St. John's st
Cumberland pl, Park row
Currant street, Sussex st
Curtis's yd, Parliament st
Cyprus-street, Beck st
Darker's ct, Broad marsh
Darker's ln, Broad marsh
Daykin's ct, 58, Barkergate
Daykin's yd, West st
Dean street, Bellargate
De Ligne st, Wood st, N. R.
Denman st, George st, N. R.
Derby Arms' yd, Long row
Derby road, Tollhouse hill
Derby st, Derby rd
Derby terrace, Derby rd, Park
Devonshire pl, Sherwood st
Dickenson's yd, 7, Bridlesmithgt
Dobb's court, Orchard st
Dodsley's ct, Parliament st
Dot yard, Listergate
Dove yard, Parliament st
Drake street, Plat st
Drury hill, Middle Pavement
Duke's yard, Long row
Duke's pl, 27, Barkergate
Dutch alley, Narrow marsh
Dutton's yd, Newcastle st
Earl street, Water st
Earl st, New Radford
East st, St. John's st
East street, Plat st
Edward st, Castle st
Eland st, Mortimer st
Element hill, Carlton rd, S.
Elliott's yd, Mount st
Elliott st, New Radford
Ely court, Chesterfield st
Eyre street, Sneinton
Exchange, Market place
Exchange ct, Mount st
Exchange alley, Exchange

Exchange row, Exchange
Eyre st, Pierrepont, *partly in Sneinton*
Felix place, 37, Barkergate
Fen yard, Barkergate
Fine street, Nile st
Finkhill st, Grey Friargate
Fish court, Fishergate
Fishergate, Plumptre sq.
Fletchergate, Bottle ln
Flint ct, Garner's hill
Flint's yd, Chandler's ln
Flood road, Bridge st
Forest side, Mansfield rd, to Radford
Foster's place, Rick st
Eoundry yard, Narrow marsh
Fountain place, Goosegate and Woolpack ln
Fowler's yard, Long row
Fox lane, Mansfield road
Frame court, Parliament st
Frame yard, Parliament st
Fredville st, Cartergate
Freeman's ct, Glasshouse st
Freeman's st, Nile st
Friar lane, Beast market hill
Friary yard, Friar lane
Frog alley, Milk st
Galloway's yard, Milton st
Garden court, Mansfield rd
Garner's hill, High Pavement
Garter court, Old street
Gedling street, Hockley
George & Dragon yd, Long row
George st, Carlton st
George st, New Radford
Gibraltar Straits, Bellargate
Gilliflower hill, *now* Castle rd
Glass court, York st
Glasshouse st, Parliament st
Glue court, Narrow marsh
Goodall's yard, Canal st
Goodall's yard, North st
Goodhead's yard, Listergate
Goodhead's court, Derby rd
Goosegate, Carlton st
Granby st, St. James's st
Greek st, Montford st, N. R.
Green's yard, Angel row
Gregory st, Sion hill, N. R.
Grenville place, Corrington st
Grey Friargate, Listergate

Greyhound yd (or st.) Long row
Groom ct, St. Peter's Church side
Grosvenor pl, Parliament st
Grove st, New Bridge st
Halifax place, Pilchergate
Hare yard, Mount st
Harley place, Carrington st
Harrington st, Sussex st
Harris's pl, Lincoln st
Harrison's ct, Lincoln st
Harrison's yard, Houndsgate
Hart's place, Goosegate
Harvey's row, Buck ln
Haughton pl, Lincoln st
Haughton st, Lincoln st
Hayhurst st, Denman st, N. R.
Haywood st, N. Sneinton
Hazard's yd. Long row
Heath st, Alfreton rd, N. R.
Herbert st, Pierrepont st
Hermitage, (Sneinton) Pennyfoot stile
Hickling's bdgs, St. Ann's st
High Cross st, Broad st
High Pavement, Weekday cross
High st, Smithy row
High st, New Radford
Hill's ct, Millstone lane
Hind's yard, Angel row
Hockley, Goosegate
Holland street, Goosegate
Hockley place, Goosegate
Hollows, now St. James's terrace
Hollowstone, High Pavement
Hoop Alley, Cartergate
Hopkinson's ct, Park st
Houndsgate, St. Peter's sq
Hornbuckle's yd, Narrow marsh
Howard st, Glasshouse st
Hulse's yard, Long row
Hunt's yd, 14, Woolpack ln
Hyson green, New Radford
Ice court, Petergate
Ilkeston rd, Sion hill, N. R.
Independent hill, Nile row
Iron yard, Narrow marsh
Irongate wharf, Bridge st
Isabella st, Castle road
Islington, Denman st, N. R.
James's yard, Milton st
James's yard, West st
Jason pl, Penny foot lane
Jew lane, now Nicholas st

Jerrom's yard, Park st
John's ct, Glasshouse st
Kelk's yard, Caunt ct
Kendall street, Mount st
Kennel hill, Mansfield road
Kenton's square, Edward st
Kenyon square, Mortimer st
Keyworth's yd, Glasshouse st
Kid street, Plat street
King st, Old Glasshouse ln
King's Arms bdgs, Woolpack ln
King's Arms yd, Woolpack ln
King's ct, King's square
King's place, Stoney st
King's square, King street
King's st, 5, Woolpack lane
Kingston ct, Parliament st
Kingston place, Kingston st
Kingston street, Water st
Knight's yard, Long row
Knotted alley, Narrow marsh
Lamb lane, Charlotte st
Lammas place, Back lane
Lane's buildings, St. Ann's st
Latimer alley, Lamb lane
Leather alley, Narrow marsh
Leaver's yd, Spaniel row
Leen court, Canal st
Leen row, Canal st
Leen side, Canal st
Lees' court, Newcastle st
Lees' yard, Rutland st
Lees' yard, Canal st
Lemon court, Hockley
Lenton street, George st
Lewis street, Rancliffe st
Lewis's place, Kingston st
Lincoln court, Millstone lane
Lincoln street, Clumber st
Line alley, Fishergate
Lion st, Sion hill, N. R.
Lison's row, Canal st
Listergate, Low Pavement
Little Butt dike, Tollhouse hill
Lock court, Narrow marsh
Lodge yard, Parliament st
Lomas's yard, 17, Bellargate
London road, Bridge st
Long row, Market place
Long stairs, 21, High Pavement
Loop alley, Water st
Low Cross st, East st
Low Pavement, Bridlesmithgate

Lowe's yard, Canal street
Lynedock row, Poplar place
Maiden lane, 18, Woolpack ln
Mail ct, Mansfield rd
Malin hill, Plumptre sqr
Malt court, Charlotte st
Maltmill lane, Red Lion st
Mansfield road, Milton st
Mansfield terrace, Mansfield rd
Manver's sqr, Manver's st, S.
Manver's st, Old Glasshouse ln
Manver's yd, Manver's st, S.
March st, Walnut tree ln
Mark lane, Back lane
Market place, Exchange
Market street, Weekday cross
Marsden's court, Sussex st
Martin's yard, Red Lion st
Matthew's court, Back lane
Maypole yard, Long row
Meadow street, Canal st
Meal ct & yd, St. James's st
Melsonby pl, Narrow marsh
Meynell ct & row, Plat st
Meynell street, South st
Middle hill, Weekday cross
Middle marsh, Broad marsh
Middle street, Gedling st
Middle Pavement, Bridlesmithgt
Middle row, Exchange
Middleton pl, New Lenton
Milk square, Milk st
Milk street, Glasshouse st
Mill alley, Hockley
Mill street, Butcher st
Mill yd, Narrow marsh
Mill street, Back lane
Mill's yard, Long row
Millstone lane, Beck st
Milton st, Clumber st
Minnitt's yard, Parliament st
Mirror alley, Caunt st
Mitchell's terrace, Mortimer st
Mole court, Milton st
Monk court, St. Ann's st
Montford st, George st, N. R.
Moor's yard, 25, Barkergate
Mortimer st, Finkhill st
Mount court, Mount st
Mount street, Chapel bar
Mount East ct, Mount East st
Mount East st, Parliament st
Mount Hooton, Forest side

Mount Pleasant, Mount st
Mount Vernon, Forest side
Nameless alley, Parliament st
Narrow marsh, Plumptre sq
Navigation row, Canal st
Needle place, Back lane
Needle row, Milk st
Nelson street, Gedling st
Nelson's yard, Rutland st
Neptune place, Albion st
New Bridge st, Canal st
New street, Parliament st
New street, Fishergate
Newark lane, Sneinton st
Newcastle ct, Newcastle st
Newcastle st, Parliament st
New Charles st, Gedling st
New Radford. Derby road
Nicholas place, Houndsgate
Nicholas street, Houndsgate
Nile row, Cross street
Nile street, Cross street
Nob alley, Narrow marsh
North street, Clumber st
North street, N. Sneinton
Norton's yard, Castlegate
Nottingham terrace, *Park*
Nottington place, *Mid. Sneinton*
Octagon yd, Lamb lane
Old street, Milk street
Old Glasshouse lane, Sneinton st
Oldknow's yd, Long row
Old Pottery, Beck st
Old Rose yd, Bellargate
Olive row, Mount st
Olive yd, 3, Barkergate
Orange's yd, 9, Woolpack ln
Orchard pl, Orchard st
Orchard square, Orchard st
Orchard st, Greyfriargate
Orchard yd, Butcher st
Owen's ct, Newark lane
Pack place, Maiden lane
Paddock ct, Paddock st
Paddock st, Greyfriargate
Palace yard, Clare street
Pannier row, Mount East st
Paradise place, 22, Barkergate
Paradise row, Coalpit lane
Park (The), Park row
Park hill, Sion hill, & Park
Park row, Chapel bar, to Postern street

Park terrace. Park
Park street, Friar lane
Park wharf, at the head of Canal street
Parker's yd, Coalpit lane
Parkinson's yd, Parliament st
Parley's yd, 31, Fletchergate
Parliament row, Parliament st
Parliament st, Chapel bar, to St. John's street
Parrott's place, Corn st
Patriot st, Old Glasshouse st
Paul yard, St. Peter's gate
Peach street, Sussex st
Pear street, Sussex st
Peck lane, Poultry
Pelham court, Pelham st
Pelham street, Smithy row
Pelican st, Alfreton rd, N. R.
Pelt alley, Narrow marsh
Pennell's yard, Long row
Penny foot lane, Water st
Penny foot stile, Penny foot ln
Pepper alley, Narrow marsh
Pepper st, 38, Bridlesmithgate
Pepper's yd, 34, Bridlesmithgate
Perch court, Fishergate
Pheasant square, Lamb lane
Pierrepont street, Water st
Pilchergate, Fletchergate
Pin alley, Fishergate
Pipe street, Gedling st
Pitt yard, Coalpit lane
Plat court, Gedling street
Plat street, Hockley
Platoff row, Gedling st
Pleasant place, Mount st
Pleasant place, 7, Pilchergate
Pleasant row, Gedling st
Plum street, Sussex st
Plough & Harrow yd, Milton st
Plumptre place, Stoney st
Plumptre square, Hollow stone
Plumptre street, St. Mary's gate
Point court, Park street
Pomfret court, Cartergate
Poplar place, Butcher st
Poplar square, Poplar place
Portland place, Coalpit lane
Portland street, Coalpit lane
Postern place, Mid Pavement
Postern street, head of Park row
Pottery place, Beck street

Potter's yard, Warsergate
Pott's square, Pierrepont st
Pott's yard, Hockley
Poultry, Timber hill, to Bridlesmithgate
Poynton st, Tollhouse hill
Prickard's yard, Hockley
Princes st, Millstone lane
Princes st, Gedling street
Prior court, Spaniel row
Province court, Millstone lane
Pump street, Plat street
Queen street, Warsergate
Rabbit court, Parliament st
Radford terrace, Wood st, N. R.
Radford's yd, 2, Woolpack ln
Ram yard, Long row
Rancliffe street, Sussex st
Ratcliffe row, Coalpit lane
Raven court, Old street
Red street, Plat st
Red Lion street is now Narrow marsh, the original name
Renshaw's yd, 22, St. Mary's gt
Rice pl, 37, Barkergate
Rice row, Barkergate
Richmond st, Charles st
Rick st, Glasshouse st
Ridsdale's yd, Houndsgate
Rigley's yard, Long row
Robin Hood pl, Coalpit lane
Rookery, Howard st
Rosemary lane, Greyfriargate
Rose row, King's square
Rose yard, 9, Bridlesmithgate
Rumford place, Beck st
Rushton's court, Bellargate
Russell street, Postern st
Rutland place, Granby st
Rutland street, Granby st
Salisbury square, Cur lane
Salmon court, Charlotte st
Shakspeare yard, Milton st
Shambles, behind the Exchange
Sharpe's yard, Mount st
Sharpe's Bdgs, Rick st
Shaw lane, Parliament st
Sheep lane, Long row
Sheridan street, Gedling st
Sherwin's ct, Coalpit lane
Sherwin st, Old Glasshouse ln
Sherwood lane, Charlotte st
Sherwood place, Broad marsh

Sherwood place, Sherwood st
Sherwood st, behind Mansfield rd
Shore yard, Greyfriargate
Short hill, High Pavement
Short stairs, Short hill
Silk mill yard, Sussex st
Silverwood place, Bellargate
Simpson's ct, 11, Lenton st
Simpson's pl, Sherwood st
Sinker alley, Mansfield rd
Sion hill, Derby rd, N. R.
Sion place, Holland place
Skinner st. Mill st
Slop court, Milk st
Smalley's yd. Beck st
Smith's sq, Pierrepont st
Smith's yd, Glasshouse st
Smithy row, from N. end the Exchange to High st
Snail alley, Barkergate
Sneinton (New), begins with Manver's street
Sneinton pl, N. Sneinton rd
Sneinton rd, Old Glasshouse ln
Sneinton street, Hockley
Snow hill, Meynell st
Sollory's yd, Pilchergate
South parade, (was Timber hill,) Market place
South st, Coalpit lane
South st, New Radford
South st, New Sneinton
Southampton st, Millstone ln
Spaniel row, Friar lane
Spaw meadow, Park
Spencer's yd. Fishergate
Spurr's yd, Derby road
Spread Eagle yd, Long row
Stag court. Lamb lane
Standard hill, St. James's terrace
Stanhope st, Water st
Star ct, St. James's st
St. Ann's st, York st
St. James's pl, Granby st
St. James's sq. St. James's st
St. James's st, Beast market hill
St. James's terrace, Postern st
St. John's st, Parliament st
St. Mary's gt, 6, Warsergate
St. Mary's pl, 41, St. Mary's gt
St. Michael row, Mansfield rd
Stone ct, Parliament st
Stoney street, Carlton st

Storey's yard, Holland st
St. Peter's church side, St. Peter's square
St. Peter's gate, St. Peter's sq
St. Peter's sq, Wheelergate
Stretton's yard, Long row
Stubb's yd, Fletchergate
Sun Hill, Drake street
Sussex sq, Harrington st
Sussex st, Middle marsh
Sydney street, Red st
Taft's yard, Carrington st
Talbot yard, Long row
Tanner's hall ct, Narrow marsh
Taylor's ct, Milton st
Taylor's ct, New Bridge st
Ten bells yd, Red Lion st
Theaker's yd. Chesterfield st
Theobald's bdgs, Earl st
Thompson's yd, Castlegate
Thread yd, Mount st
Thurman's yd, Castlegate
Thurman's yd. Orchard st
Tilley's yard, Drury hill
Timber hill, or South parade, Market place
Toll st, Toll house hill
Tollinton's yard, Long row
Toll house hill, Chapel bar
Tomlin's yd, Parliament st
Tradesman's mart, Parliament st
Tree yard. Plumptre st
Trent bridge, Flood road
Trent row, Canal st
Trim court, Parliament st
Trumpet street, Beck st
Truswell's yard, Castlegate
Turncalf alley, now Sussex st
Tuff court, Middle marsh
Twigg alley, Goosegate
Tyler street, Plat st
Union place, Glasshouse st
Union street, Plat st
Valentine place, Broad marsh
Vassal st, Old Glasshouse ln
Vat yard, Narrow marsh
Vernon street, Derby road
Vine court, Glasshouse st
Virginia street, Meynel st
Walker street. Cartergate
Walker's yard, Houndsgate
Walnut tree lane, Castlegate
Warren court, York st

Warsergate, Bottle lane
Washington st, Meynell st
Water street, Carter row
Waterloo court, Newcastle st
Watts' yard, Chesterfield st
Web court, North st
Weekday cross, Mid. Pavement
Wellington-ct, Mount East st
Wellington st, Water st
Welsh's bdgs, Pierrepont st
West-st, High Cross st
West st, Sneinton place, S.
Wharf street, Mill st
Wheat Sheaf yard, Long row
Wheat Sheaf yard, Sneinton rd
Wheelergate, Beastmarket hill
White street, Cartergate
Wild's yard, Houndsgate
Willoughby st, Middleton pl, L.

Willowby row, Fishergate
Wilson's yard, Milk street
Wing alley, Woolpack lane
Wood court, Mansfield rd
Woodhouse's yard, 43, Barkergt
Woodland pl. Parliament st
Wood street, Gedling street
Wood street, George st, N. R.
Woodland pl, Parliament st
Wool alley, Woolpack lane
Woolley's yard, Sussex st
Woolpack lane, 5, Stoney st
Wright's yard, Charlotte st
Wright's yard, Wood street
Yates' yd, Middle Pavement
York court, Millstone lane
York court, St. Ann's street
York street, Glasshouse street

THE POST OFFICE,

Situated in High street, Nottingham, closes at 10 at night, and opens every morning at 7, from April to October, and at 8 during the rest of the year.

Mr. GEORGE KEPPLE WHITE, POST-MASTER.

Mr. W. G. Neilson is the OFFICE CLERK, and the following are the LETTER CARRIERS, viz. John Simpson, of Byard lane, William Brown, of Coalpit lane, and Joseph Fetcher, of Parliament street. They are sent out on delivery three times a day, viz. at half-past 8; at 11; and at half-past 2 o'clock.

The letter bags for LONDON and all parts of the *South*, are made up at 3 afternoon, and are received from thence at half-past 10 morning. No mail bags are sent to London on Saturday, nor received from thence on Monday.

The bags for LEEDS and all parts of the *North* are made up at half-past 9 morning, and are received at half-past 5 morning.

The bags for DERBY (*mail gig*) and the *West* are closed at half-past 6 morning, and received at half-past 1 afternoon.

The bags for NEWARK and LINCOLN, (*mail gig*) and all parts of Lincolnshire and the *East*, leave at 5 morning and arrive at 2 afternoon.

The bags for LOUGHBRO' and STAMFORD (*mail gig*) leave at half-past 3 afternoon, and are received at half-past 10 morning.

☞ *The Country Carriers take letters to their respective villages.*
(See list of mails, coaches, and carriers.)

CLASSIFICATION

OF THE

PROFESSIONS, MANUFACTURES, & TRADES,

IN THE

𝕮𝖔𝖜𝖓 𝖆𝖓𝖉 𝕮𝖔𝖚𝖓𝖙𝖞 𝖔𝖋 𝖙𝖍𝖊 𝕮𝖔𝖜𝖓

OF

NOTTINGHAM.

₊ This portion of the Nottingham Directory, contains a *classification* of the names and addresses of all the professional gentlemen, merchants, manufacturers, traders, and other inhabitants carrying on business on their own account; and is followed by an ALPHABETICAL LIST of the names and residences of the clergy, gentry, partners in firms, persons out of business, travellers, bookkeepers, and others, who are not arranged under any of the following trades and professions, to which an INDEX of the names of persons is subjoined, so that if the occupation of any person sought for is not known, it may be instantly referred to; and thus the whole will be found to possess all the advantages of an *Alphabetical* as well as a *Commercial Directory.*

☞ Though RADFORD and SNEINTON join the town of Nottingham, it has been deemed advisable to give separate directories of these populous parishes, as well as of BASFORD and LENTON, which are also in contiguity with the liberties of the town.

(1) ACADEMIES.
See also Professors.
Baker W. H. High Pavement
Barker James, 15, Sheep lane, h. Mansfield road
Biddulph Sampson, Halifax pl, h Fountain pl
Barkergate Charity School, W. K. Herrick and William Taylor, masters; Mrs. Taylor, governess
Bluecoat Charity School, Thos. Cokayne. High Pavement
Blackwell. Eliz. *Poplar Cottage, Hyson Green*
Brice Wm. St. James' st

Carpenter Rev. B. Castlegate
Carver John, Maling hill
Chambers Mary, Mount plt.
Clayton Ann, Boot ct
Clayton Eliz. Castlegate
Cole Geo, (writing) Mansfield rd
Cowley Ann, Castlegate
Drewry Mrs, 17, Plumptre st
Farnsworth Eliza, Pelham st
Featherstone Jane E, Middle hill
Fell Ann, Canal street
Fisher Mary, Parliament st
Free Grammar School, 16, Stoney st, Rev. Rt. Wood, master, Rev. Sam. M'Lund, usher, and Rd. Dudley, writing master

Gilbert and Nelson, Parliament st
Gregory Frans. Hill, Malt mill ln
Grisenthwaite Wm. St. James' st
Harmston Mary, Rick st
Hemment Eliza, Derby rd
Holt Sarah, St. Ann's st
Hoone Samuel, St. John's st
Horner Mary, Mount st
Hutchason Wm. St. Ann's st
Infant School, Canaan st. Miss
  Mary Prior, h. Woolpack ln
Infant School, Rutland st. Mrs.
  Ann Dean, h. Mansfield road
Infant School, (P. Baptist,) Inde-
  pendent hill, Samuel Rushton
Infant School, St. Ann's st. Wm.
  and Harriet Teesdale
Jacks Jemima, Crown yard
Jarman Eliz. and Eliza, 30, St.
  Marygate
Joynes Lucy, Castlegate
Kelk Sarah & Eliz. 2, Plumptre st
Lancasterian School, Derby rd.
  Samuel Langworth, master.
Lancasterian (Girls) Houndgate,
  Emma Longden, h. Middle pt
Lee Sarah, 12, Haughton st
Lowe Samuel, 1, Pilshergate
Lee John, (writing) Mount East st
Martin Martha, Mansfield road
Maudley Jthn. Newcastle st
Milligan Alex. Kingston ct
National School, Jph. Aldridge,
  h. 5, East street
Newbold Mary Ann, Sherwood st
Newton Isaac, Bottle ln. h. Short
  hill.
North John, King's place
Oliver Anthony, St. James' st
Page Ann, Albion st
Palfreman Ann & Har. Sussex st
Pearson Ann, Stoney st
Pettinger, Barb & Mart. Hounds-
  gate
Place Richard, Glasshouse st
Pugh Eliz. 32, Warsergate
Roe William, Woodland pl
Rogers Jer. D. Nottingham ter.
Roper John Anthony, Toll st
Sailbury William, Finkhill st
School of Industry, Rutland st.
  Ellen Green and Rose Ann
  Bishop

Selby Isaac. Mole ct. h. Lenton
Shepherd James, Herbert st
Sleath Thomas, Short hill
Smith Ann, Houndsgate
Smith Misses, E. B. & M. B. 6,
  Haughton st
Sparey Isaac, Wheelergate, h. 10,
  Haughton st
Sollory Mrs Ann. Market st
Stenson Sarah, Parliament st
Tatham William, Peter's Church
  side
Taylor Mary and Ann, Derby rd
Truman Ann, 16, Parliament st
Turner Catharine, Park row
Turner Sarah, Parliament row
Unitarian Charity, High Pave-
  ment, John Taylor & Charlotte
  Sansom
Ward Francis Milner, Clare st
Ward Samuel, Park st
Warner Sarah, 19, Stoney st
Warsop Sarah Richards, Pepper
  street
Wells Charles, Lenton st
Wheatley Robert, Mortimer st.
  h. Castle road
White Sarah & Ann, 7, St. Mary-
  gate
Whitehead George, 10, St. Mary-
  gate
Wilson Hannah and Eliz. Park st
Wortley Jph. St. Peter's Church
  side
(2.) AGENTS—(LACE, &c.)
Those marked are general agents,
  the rest sell Bobbin net on com-
  mission.
Adderton Thomas, Woodland pl
*Allen Jas. Roger, St. James's st
Ashwell J. Heard, St. James's st
*Attenborough, Rt. 7, Clumber st
Beecroft Jacob, 7, Pilshergate
Bestow William, Clayton's yard
Bingham James, Orchard street
Booker Alfred, Mount East st
*Booker Richard, Buttery's yard
Booker Rd. Peter's Church side
Broadhead William, Postern pl
Brown George, 8, Lenton st
Cartwright Ed. Parliament st
Cartwright Wm. Grosvenor pl
*Crowther Thos. St. Marygate

U

Dickisson James, Houndsgate
Dobson John, Sherwood st
*Etherington & Duplex, Byard ln
Ferguson John, 9, Woolpack ln
*Garton Thomas, 36, Broad st
Gee William, 4, Cannon yd
Gibson Thomas, 29, H. Cross st
*Gill Geo. and Son, Houndsgate, h. Park
*Gill Robert Mount st
Goddard Edward, Portland pl
*Grundy Sam. Low Pavement
Hall Samuel March st
Hallam Wm. Apple row
Harper Joseph, Derby rd
Haskard Thos. Low Cross st
Haythorn Fdk. 16, Rigley's yd
*Haythorn Jonth. Wright, ct. 33, Long row
Hearson Thomas, 28, George st
Herrap James, 13, Broad st
Hickling, William Toll st
Holmes Jonth. Spaniel row, h. Radford
Hooley Thomas, 34, Barkergate
*Hutchinson John, 24, Carlton st
Letherland John, Mansfield rd
Maples Rd. (Lace Broker,) Rose yard, h. St. Petersgate
Marriott Jph. Wild's yd. Houndsgate
Morris John, Clayton's yd
Nixon John, Friar ln. h. Houndsgate
*Parker and Kirk, Maypole yd
Reckless, Joseph, Castle terrace
*Rogerson Wm. ct. 9, Poultry
Rushton James, 4, King's place
Samuels Lewis, Castle terrace
*Sanderson Edgar, 26, Carlton st
Sanderson George, Houndsgate
Sanderson Thomas, 19, Stoney st
Shipman Wm. Clayton's yd
Shipman Wm. 3, Lincoln st
Smith Peter Stanley, Carrington street
*Stenson John, 29, Parliament st
Stenson Wm. Mortimer st
Sturt James, Crosland's yard
Sulley Richard, 9, Stoney st
*Taylor Isaac, (Law, Money, and House,) Parliament st
Taylor John, 3, Haughton st

Taylor Wm. (Law, Money and House,) Derby road
Walker George, 2, Rigley's yd
*Walsh Geo. Nelson, Park st
Webster David, 33, St. Marygate
*Wells Wm. 9, Clumber st
Wentworth Henry, Castle road
Westmoreland John, Galloway's yard, Milton street
*Wetzlar & Sarazin, Woodland pl
Wheatley Arthur, Canal st
Wheatley James, 3, Rigley's yd
Whitby John, Air yd. Mount st
Whitchurch Richard 8, East st
Whitfield William, Leen row

(3.) ARCHITECTS.

Staveley Edward, Pelham street, h. Park
Surplice William, 2, Clumber st
Wood Henry Moses, Park st

(4)—ARTISTS & DRAWING MASTERS.

Barber Thos, (portrait) Park hill
Clubley Samuel, (portrait) Mansfield road
Huskinson Henry, (portrait) Castlegate
Johnson William, (portrait) Hyson green
Lees Henry, (portrait) Mansfield road
Parker Alexander, Castlegate
Shaw William Drury, (portrait and animal painter) Market st

(5.) ATTORNIES.

Andrew Joseph 16, Grehound yd
Bowley John, Wheelergate
Bradshaw Job, Wheelergate
Brewster John, Castlegate
Buttery John, 29, Long row
Clarke and Wells, George st
Clarke Thomas, 12, Lenton st
Coope James, 4, Haughton st
Coope Jesse, Rutland street and Radford
Chursham Wm. St. Petersgate, h. Derby terrace
Enfield Henry and Wm. (Town-clerks,) Low Pavement
Fearnhead & Campbell, Fletchergate
Fox John, ct. 39, Long row, h. Neville Cottage, Park

Foxcroft Alexander and Son, Low Pavement
Foxcroft John, (Clerk to Sub-Division-Meetings and to Comss. of Land and Assessed Taxes, for S. Div. of Notts.) Low Pavement
Greasley Thomas Tait, Beast Market hill
Hague John, St. James's st
Hardwick Alfred, Churchgate
Hopkinson George, 30, Long row
Hopkinson George, jun. 19, Bridlesmithgate
Hurst Nicholas Charles, Weekday cross, h. Beck lane
Hurst William, (Under Sheriff and Steward of the Mayor and Sheriff's Court,) Weekday cross
Inkersley Thos. ct. 33, Long row
Jackson Thomas, Wheelergate
Leeson and Gell, Pelham st.
Lowdham and Freeth, Low Pavement and London
Nuttall John, Beastmarket hill
Parsons Saml. & Son, St. James's street
Payne and Daft, Low Pavement
Percy and Smith, Wheelergate
Redgate Thomas Blatherwick, ct. 66, Long row, h. Calverton
Renshaw Rd. St. Petersgate
Rigley Joseph James Ward, ct. 39, Long row
Sanders Samuel, (Prothonotary of the Peveril Court,) Wheelergate, h. Basford
Sculthorpe William and Robert, St. Petersgate, (Wm. is Magistrates' Clerk and Treasurer of the S. Divison of Notts.)
Shilton Caractacus D'Abigney, 74 Long row and Sneinton
Swann and Browne, Churchgate,
Swann Chpr. (Coroner for the County) Churchgate
Turner Wm. Hy. 6, Warsergate
Wadsworth Jno. 25, Fletchergate
Ward Joseph Septimus, ct. 66, Long row, h. Aspley terrace
Williams William, Maypole yard, h. Basford
Wise & Eddowes, 8, Clumber st

Wood John, ct. 39, Long row
(6.) AUCTIONEERS AND APPRAISERS.
Barton Chas. Bond st. N. S.
Blackwell W. sen. 75, Long row
Blackwell W. jun. 34, Long row
Clark Thomas, Milton street
Duckworth George, Pelham st
Eyre Wm. St. James's street
Hayes John, 24, H. Pavement
Hickling Geo. 3, Clumber street
Maples Rt. S. Bridlesmithgate
Morley Edward, St. Petersgate
Parker Wm. 4, Carlton street
Peet John, 36, Long row
Robinson E. B. 61, Long row
Wild Wm. (comssr. for taking special bail) Weekday cross
Wright C. N. 50, Long row
Wright Wm. Milton street
(7.) BAKERS & FLOUR DLRS.
Adamson George, East street
Annibal Rd. Derby road
Attenborough Thos. Hockley
Baker Wm. Mid. Pavement
Barnes John, Cavendish street
Barnes Thomas, King street
Beadles John, Narrow marsh
Beardmore John, St. Peter's sq
Bennett Edward, Edward street
Bennett John, Houndsgate
Bissil Thomas, 10, Chapel bar
Carnall Isaac, Goosegate
Chamberlin Wm. 17, East st
Chester John, Parliament st
Clarke John, 29, Clumber st
Clayton Benj. Glasshouse st
Clayton Edwin, (patentee of the machine for making dough,) ct. 35, Bridlesmithgate
Cooper Edward, Milton st
Copley John, 13, Parliament st.
Crafts Rd. Charlotte st
Dickenson Wm. Goosegate
Dore Thomas, Milk st
Doxey Thos. Parliament st
Emmerson P. Mansfield road
Fletcher George, Beck st
Flewitt Saml. Bridlesmithgate
Flewitt Wm. 37, Barkergate
Foulkes Thos. 12, Charlotte st
France Henry & Co. Hockley and Narrow marsh

Gadsby Saml. Walnut tree ln
Gainsley John, 11, Lenton st
Greenfield Sarah, Richmond st
Greenfield Wm. 16, Broad st
Guy Wright. York st
Hall John; Listergate
Hammond Thos. Brook st
Harpham David, Mansfield rd
Harrison Clifford, Pierrepont st
Haywood Robert, Nile st
Hedderley J. 31, Bridlesmithgt
Hickling Wm. Old Glasshouse ln
Hogg John, Goosegate
Holmes Jas. Pierrepont st
Hutchinson John, Mount st
Innocent Ann, Meynel row
Ireland Rt. (and horse corn dlr.)
Bridge street
James Henry, Star court
James John, Canal st.
Kidd Wm. Mansfield road
Marshall Geo. Narrow marsh
Marshall Wm. Spread Eagle yd
Marvin Chas. 7, Bridlesmithgate
Minta Thos. Virginia st
Moore Jas. New Bridge st
Moore Edward, Cherry street
Morley Mark, Mill street
Morley William, Mount st
Needham John, 23, Barkergate
Oliver Wm. Parliament row
Orchard John, Pierrepont st
Orchard Saml. Butcher st
Palethorpe Wm. 25, Woolpack ln
Parkin George, Hockley
Patchet John, Listergate
Pyatt John, Orchard st
Reddish Saml. 15, Parliament st
Reddish Wm. Sussex st
Reed Jph. Patriot street
Ridsdale Wm. Houndsgate
Robinson John, Caunt st
Sanders John, Millstone ln
Smith Edw. Sneinton st
Smith Robt. 6, Parliament st
Spencer Benj. Fishergate
Stretton Ann, 22, Warsergate
Sylvester Wm. St. Ann's st
Taylor Jph. Narrow marsh
Thorpe John, Pelham st
Tinker Rd. Mansfield rd
Tipler. James B. Narrow marsh
Townroe Rd. St. Peter's sq

Travis Barnabas, Mt. East st
Turner Thos. 24, Long row
Voce Wm. Clare st
Warsop Wm. Cartergate
Watson Eliz. (dlr.) Bottle ln
Watton Wm. 5, Bridlesmithgate
Whitlock Natl. Cartergate
Woffit Rd. Narrow marsh
Wright Francis. Narrow marsh
Wood James, Bellargate

(8.) BANKERS.
Hart, Fellows, & Co. 38, Bridlesmithgate (draw on Hanburys
and Co.)
Moore & Robinson, Beastmarket
hill (draw on Sir Rd. C. Glyn
and Co.)
Smith Saml. Esq. & Co. Timber
hill (draw on Smith, Payne, &
Smiths)
Wright I. & I. C. & Co. 1, Carlton st (draw on Robarts, Curtis, & Co.)
Savings' Bank, Smithy row, open
every Monday, and on last Saturday in every month, from
eleven till two o'clock ; Wm.
Jarman, secretary, and John
Paterson, clerk.

(9.) BASKET MAKERS.
Barker John, 29, Greyhound yd
Clayton James, 6, Sheep lane
Clayton John, Derby road
Clayton Jph. 22, Greyhound yd
Merrin Eliz. 2, Hollow stone
Smith Henry, Fishergate
Watts Hy. & Sons, Bromley house

(10.) BILLIARD TABLES.
Pride Jph. Maypole yard, h. 8,
Haughton st
Subscription Table, Bromley hse

(11.) BLACKING MFRS.
Those marked * make composi-
tion for cleaning stove grates,
&c.
Allsop Geo. Parliament st
*Radnell Chas. 2, Greyhound yd
Selby Wm. Trent bridge
Skelton Wm. Pierrepont st
*Soar Rd. St. James's st
*Wright Wm. & Gervase, (& ink)
Canal street

(12.) BLACKSMITHS.

Caborn George; Minnett's yd
Carver Wm. Hockley
Chamberlain Wm. Cartergate
Clay John, Butcher street
Copeland Jerh. Tollhouse hill
Cooper Emanl. Cartergate
Dalby Wm. Paddock st
Drabble Francis, Derby rd
Fisher George, Canal st
Gadd Wm. (& farrier) Fishergt
Graham Geo. Vassal st
Greenbury Jph. St. Mary's pl
Grocott John, North st
Kent Wm. Shaw lane
Lord Thos. Derby Arms yd
Lovatt Gervase, Bottle lane
Richardson Thos. Mansfield rd
Stapleton James, Toll st
Starr Saml. Canal st
Strangeway James, Canal st
Walker Jph. London road

(13.) BLEACHERS.

Allcock Charles, Bulwell
Bostock Edw. sen. Lovett mills
Bostock Edward, jun. Bobber's
mill
Brown Geo. Whitemoor spring
Brown John, Basford
Diggle James, Whitemoor
Diggle John, Whitemoor
Garton & Woodward, Stump cross,
Basford
Hall Saml. & Co. (& patent gas-
ers) Two-mile house, Basford
Hill Thomas, Arnold
Jennison & Robinson. Bulwell
Milnes John, Hall mill
Milnes Thos. B. Lenton works
Mitchell Wm. Bobber's mill
Pearson Joseph, Basford, b. 27,
High Pavement
Stanford John Fry, Bulwell
BLEACHING POWDER, &c.
MANUFACTURERS
Tennant Chas. & Co. Glasgow;
T. Garton, agent, 36, Broad
street

(14.) BOAT BUILDERS.

Marshall Wm. Poplar place
Roberts Benj. Lenton, h. Canal
street
Simpson John, Park wharf

(15.) BOBBIN & CARRIAGE
MAKERS.

*See also Circular Comb and Bolt
makers, and Watchmakers.*
Aulton Wm. Plumptre square
Beha Thaddeus, 1, Woodland pl
Boyes Rt. Minnitt's yard
Bullock Elijah, 12, Charlotte st
Hall Wm. Smithy row and Grey-
hound yard
Hett & Bostock, Granby st
Kirk Wm. Agnes yd, Broad st
Lees Charles, Kingston court
Mather Wm. Parliament row
Marshall John, Houndsgate
Milner James, Goosegate
Milner Wm. ct. 31, Fletchergate
Mortimer Thos. Mount East st
Mosley John, Lowe's yard
Ordoyno George, Castle terrace
Pindar George, Holland st
Rudd James, Canal street
Rutland Thos. Mansfield rd
Smith Edward, Burton st
Stokes Geo. (and all interior work
for bobbin-net machines)
Duke's place
Thornton Chas. Castle terrace
Turner Saml. 12, Beck lane
Walker Geo. Kingston st
Whitaker Thos. Holland st

(16.) BOBBIN NET MKRS.

*These are Lace-net makers, who
employ machines and sell their
net in the brown state to the
merchants and manufacturers,
who finish it for the home and
foreign markets.*
Alldred Jph. Mansfield rd
Allister Wm. Mansfield rd
Anderson Wm. East st
Anderson Robert, Sherwood st
Anderson John, Sherwood st
Arnold Jph. Mount East st
Arnold Wm. Hind, Broad marsh
Ashton John, 13, Bridlesmithgt
Ashworth Robt. Mount East st
Ashmore Jph. Glasshouse st
Aulton, Ashmore, and Mosley,
Sherwood place
Barker Thomas, Sherwood st
Barnes Wm. Sherwood st
Barnett Hy. Rose, Bedford row

Baxter Charles, Back lane
Beadles Eliz. King street
Beardsall Rt. Wellington st
Bell John, Glasshouse street
Bell Joseph, York street
Belshaw Wm. Wellington st
Billiard Thos. 22, Rice place
Bilbie Walter, Mansfield rd
Birkin Geo. Glasshouse st
Birkin Thos. Babbington pl
Bonsor Stephen, Mt. East st
Booker Alfred, Mt. East st
Booth James, Newcastle st
Bowmer John, Back lane
Bradley Wm. Tollhouse hill
Brazier Wm. Sherwood st
Brookes Thos. Plumptre sq
Brookes Thomas, Toll street
Brotherton Benj. Postern pl
Brown Thomas, Mansfield road
Brown John, Hollow stone
Brown William, Nile street
Burgoin James, Cartergate
Burley Thos. 12, St. Mary's pl
Burton Samuel, Grove street
Burton Thos. 35, York street
Bushby John, Hollow stone
Caunt John, Newcastle street
Chand William. Kingston court
Cheshire Wm. Ten Bells yard
Clark Samuel, Butcher street
Clarkstone Joseph, Mansfield rd
Clayton John, Wool alley
Collishaw John. (tatting) East st
Colson James, Mount court
Cooper Thos. S. Trent bdg
Cooke Robert, Goosegate
Creswell Cph. jun. Babbington st
Creswell Cphr. Mansfield rd
Coxon Peter, Navigation row
Corah Samuel, Sherwood st
Cowley George, Rose yd
Crofts Jas. Freeman st
Cropper Jas. Bridge st
Cummins John, 5, Mansfield ter
Curtis William, Canal st
Daft Wm. Mount pleasant
Dann Wm. Navigation row
Davis Wm. Babbington st
Davis Wm. Mortimer st
Daykin John, Glasshouse s
Day John, Mount st
Dent Jas. Castle terrace

Derrick John, 9, Plumptre st
Derry Samuel, 13, Mansfield ter
Dufty Rd. Castle road
Dyer John, Greyfriargate
Earp Thos. Derby rd
Ellis Wm. 4, Rice place
Evans Wm. Broad marsh
Flather Jas. Poplar square
Flather John, Poplar sq
Fletcher Wm. Mortimer st
Fletcher Samuel, Mansfield rd
Fox Charles, North st
Freeman & Co. Houndsgate
Freeman Wm. Sherwood st
Gadd John, Penneyfoot lane
Galloway Robt. Milton st
Gamble Jph. Newcastle st
Garner Jas. Cross street
Gilderthorp Jph. Watt's yd
Gisborn John, Pleasant row
Godber Samuel, King st
Goodhead Elijah, 27, Woolpack ln
Goodhead Luke, Beck st
Goodall Rd. Back lane
Goode Thomas, Parliament st
Gothard Wm. Sherwood st
Green Alfred, Castlegate
Green Jthn. Verginia st
Greensmith Rd. 17, Milton st
Greenwood John, Parliament st
Hall S. & T. E. (by power) Mount
  street
Hampson Wm. 20, New st
Hardwick Jph. Forest side
Harper Jph. Derby road
Harrison John, Cross st
Hebb Fras. Wright's yd. Wood st
Hebb Wm. 22, Parliament st
Henson Gravener, Sherwood ln
Henson John, 30, Broad st
Heron Thos. Wellington st
Hibbert Robt. Cross st
Hickling Wm. Toll st
Hill John, Brook alley
Hill John, Chapel st
Hill Wm. Charlotte street
Hill Thos. Sherwood street
Holland John, Mansfield rd
Holland John, Glasshouse st
Holland Thos. 12, Mansfield ter
Holland Rd. Knotted place
Hollis Wm. Bellargate
Holmes Geo. 10, Mansfield ter

Holmes Samuel, Pleasant row
Hood Robert, Milton street
Hoyles John, Mansfield road
Humphreys John, Sherwood st
Jackson James, Kingston ct
Jarman Henry, 25, H. Cross st
James Edw. Mount East st
Jarvis Samuel, Malt court
Jeffries Rt. 26, Broad st
Kendall John, (by power) Canal st
Killingley Edward, York st
Kirk Thomas, (Caps) Nile st
Lamb Jph. Mansfield rd
Lamb John, Martin's alley
Lambert Thos. Walnuttree ln
Langham Jph. Mansfield rd
Langham Thos. 42, Barkergate
Leavers Elias, Mill st
Leavers Jph. Derby road
Lee Jph. Raven ct. Old st
Letherland John, Mansfield rd
Lewis Jph. Midle pavement
Longmire Edwin, 49, Barkergate
Marriott John, Independent hill
Machin Wm. Finkhill st
Macklerith Adam, Glasshouse st
Maloney Cor. Freeman st
Marshall Thos. Mansfield road
Maddack Rt. Castle Terrace
Mason Samuel Bonnell, Hollow
　stone
Marson Thos. Castle terrace
Massey Wm. Chesterfield st
Massey John, East street
Meats Isaac, Nob yard
Middleton John, Walker st
Miller George, Fishergate
Middleton Thos. 48, Barkergate
Milner Wm. Glasshouse ln
Morley Samuel, Mount st
Morris Jph. 2, Beck ln
Newton Geo. Mansfield rd
Newton Jph. Mansfield rd
North Samuel, Pleasant row
Oldham Thos. Castle road
Packer Isaac, Beck st
Parker Isaac, Mansfield rd
Parker Thos. Sherwood st
Pass Wm. Hornbuckle's yd
Pass Wm. Commerce row
Pearson Wm. Parliament st
Pegg Carter, Mansfield road
Pole Wm. Bedford row

Poole George, Bilbie's yard
Porter James, 4, Broad st
Price Thomas, Canal st
Raynor Samuel, Mount East st
Rawson Samuel, Canal st
Read William, Poynton st
Reckless Richard, Castle terrace
Renshaw Henry, Sneinton st
Revill Erasmus, Sherwood st
Richardson Wm. Mount court
Robinson Thomas, Kingston ct
Rudd James, Canal st
Rutland John, Mansfield rd
Sands Thomas, Castle terrace
Saunders Thomas, York st
Sansom Samuel, 8, Kings pl
Scott Richard, Mansfield rd
Selby Thomas, Cross st
Selby Wm. Trent bridge
Sewell Thos. R. 3, Canal st
Seymour Richard, Olive row
Shaw John, Babbington st
Shaw Robert, Derby rd
Shepherd Wm. Knotted pl
Shipham John, Coalpit ln
Shipman Charles, Freeman st
Shorrock Edward, Mansfield rd
Simmons Thos. Houndsgate
Simpson Wm. Glasshouse st
Skelton Wm. Toll street
Smith John, Nile street
Smith Joseph, Bedford Row
Smith William, Paddock st
Smith Wm. Pleasant row
Smith John, St. Michael row
Spencer Thos. Castle terrace
Squires John, Mansfield rd
Stanfield Samuel, 1, York st
Stanton Eliz. 39, York st
Street Wm. Houndsgate
Stubbins John, Poynton st
Sturtivant Chpr. Castle terrace
Sumner George, Cartergate
Sutton John, Sherwood st
Swanwick Geo. Beck square
Sylvester John, Clare st
Tew William, Mill st
Thornton Chas. Castle terrace
Thorpe Geo. Trumpet st
Throne Thos. Pleasant row
Timm George, Milk st
Timm Charles, Sherwood st
Tome Wm. St. Peter's Churchside

Topham John, Sherwood st
Townsend James, Castle terrace
Trusswell John, Listergate
Turner Wm. Beck square
Unwin Samuel, Derby st
Ward Peter, Independent hill
Ward Samuel, St. Petersgate
Walker Fras. Mansfield rd
Warsop Emanuel, Cross st
Warsop Samuel, Tomlin's yard, Parliament street
Watts George, Finkhill street
Whiles James, Mansfield rd
Whiles John, York st
Webster David, 33, St. Marygate
Whitchurch Wm. Penny foot ln
White Robert, Greyfriargate
White Thomas, Mansfield rd
Whitehead Jph. Mount East st
Whittaker John, Castle terrace
Whittle James, York st
Widdowson Wm. Navigation row
Wills Benj. Houndsgate
Wood Wm. Coal court
Wood Henry, Serwood st
Witham Wm. Castle terrace
Woodhouse Jacob, 32, Woolpk. ln
Woolley John, Beck ln
Woodward John, Penny foot ln
Wright Edward, Newcastle st
Wright Nathl. 6, East st
Wright Wm. Gedling st
Yates Jph. Brewhouse yd
Yates Thos. 11, York street

(17.) BONE MERCHANTS.
Fothergill Jas. & John, Canal st
Shelton & Harvey, Canal st

(18.) BOOK BINDERS.
Bayne Charles, Bottle ln. H. Park square
Bull John, Newcastle st
Bull Robert, 19, Fetchergate
Jones Thos. Backlane
Leighton John, (wholesale stationer) Lincoln street
Rothera John, Clare st
Whittingham John, Parliament row

(19.) BOOKSELLERS, PRINTERS, BINDERS, & STATIONERS.
See also Periodical Publishers
Barber Alfred, Angel row

Bennett Samuel, 57, Long row
Deardon Wm. 3, Carlton st
Duckworth Geo. Pelham st
Dunn Jonathan, South parade
Kirk Thomas, St Peter'sgate
Maples Rt. Sewel, 16, Bridlesmithgate
Mercer Richard, 3, Chapel bar
Robinson Edw. Briggs, 61, Long row
Simons George, 13, Long row
Staveley John, 1, High street
Stretton George, 64, Long row
Sutton Richard, 1, Bridlesmithgate, h. 14, Bottle lane
Wells Wm. 9, Clumber st
Wright Clipr. Norton, 50, Long row

(20.) BOOT & SHOE MAKERS
Abbott David, 6, Pennell's yard
Astle Edward, Pelham street
Baker Wm. Mount East st.
Baker John, 15, Long row, h. Derby road
Bannister Chas. Hockley
Barlow Wm. Cartergate
Beck George, Cross st
Bestow Luke, Charles st
Bishop Wm. Goosegate
Bishop Wm. Spaniel row
Booth Chas. 6, Lenton st
Boyington Rd. Garner's hill
Bown Thos. Glasshouse st
Bradfield Thos. York st
Braley Wm. Cheapside
Briggs Wm. Cross st
Brown Hy. Milton st
Brunt John, Hollowstone
Burton Thos. Mill st.
Camm Richd. Hockley
Clark Joseph, Bottle ln
Clayton Hphy. Mansfield rd
Clover Thos. Sherwin st
Collyer John & Son, 26, St. Marygate
Crisp Danl. Goosegate
Cumberland Jas. Freeman st
Daft Wm. Nelson st
Davis John, Goosegate
Dobson Thos. Brewhouse yd
Dorrard Fras. Sherwood st
Edwards George, Mount st
Edwards James, Angel row

Fearn Michl. Coalpit ln
Fearn Wm. 4, Stoney st
Flinn Cphr. Drury hill
Foster Noah, Gedling st
Foulkes Geo. Glasshouse st
Fox Hy. 2, Angel yard
Getley Geo. Patriot st
Gray Arthur, Plat st
Green Joseph, Mount st
Gregg Jas. Carter gate
Hanley Robert, 14, Sheep lane
Hawksley Mary. Charlotte st
Heaton Saml. Beck st
Heazell Arthur, 40, Woolpack ln
Heazell Robt. 2. Smithy row
Hickling Wm. 19, Low Cross st
Hobb John, Fletchergt
Hockney Thos. Sussex st
Hogg Jas. Middle Marsh
Holmes Wm. Listergate
Hopkins John, Newcastle st
Howett Wm. Simpson's pl
Howett John, Pierrepont st
Hurst Danl. Mount East st
Jaquiss Issachar, 27, Broad st
Jaquiss Issachar, jun. St. Ann's st
Jeffs Edw. (shoe whs.) St. Peter's square
Jeffery Samuel (ointment mfr.) Goosegate.
Kenton Rd. Virginia st
Kerry Thos. Plat st
Kirkby Wm. Peck lane
Knight John & Sarah, 10, Clumber st
Kynnersley Edw. Pipe st
Lacey Henry, Houndsgate
Lee John, Narrow Marsh
Lawson Edw. Perliament row
Lindley Leonard, Fishergate
Lownds Robert, Exchange alley
Maltby John, Albion st
Marriott Geo. St. James's st
Mann John, Beck st
Martin Jas. Back ln
Maxfield Mtw. Newcastle st
Massey Peter, Pump st
Meeson & Sons, 46, Bridlesmith gate and Stafford
Meldram Jas. Glasshouse st
Merrin Frdk. Derby road
Merrin Saml. Hockley
Metheringham John, Mt East st

Mitchell Geo. Middle hill
Mitchell Hy. Sussex st
Moody Jasper, Clare st
Needham Geo. Broad Marsh
North Henry, Tree yard
Oxley Walter, Houndsgate
Parkinson Jas. New Bridge st
Parnham Thos. & Co. 76, Long row
Pickard Geo. Parliament st
Pickard Jph. High pavmt.
Pollard Thos. ct. 8, Bridlesmith gate
Poole Wm. Parliament st
Popple John, Rancliffe st
Porter Thos. Charlotte st
Raynor Jph. High Cross st
Raynor Wm. Cur lane
Richards Wm. Wellington st
Read Edw. Drake st
Roberts Thos. Finkhill st
Rockley Geo. York st
Rose John, 37, Broad st
Salsbury Josiah, Charlotte st
Saunders Hy. Newcastle st
Scarles Jas. Broad Marsh
Sharp John, Fishergate
Shaw Chas. Listergate
Shipley Joseph, Wheelergate
Slater Chas. Mount East st
Snelson Frederick, Nicholas st
Sotheran John, Barkergate
Steel Aaron, Cavendish st
Steel Reuben, 9, Broad st
Stenson Robert, Mount st
Starling Wm. 1, Barkergate
Storer Geo. Sherwood st
Sweet Thos. 2, Queen st
Swindal Thos. Pierrepont st
Taylor John, 10, York st
Taylor John, 5, Clumber st
Taylor Thomas, Hockley
Thatcher Benj. 2, York st
Thompson Thos. Old Glasshouse lane
Tyas Moses, Houndsgate
Turner John. West st
Vansor Wm. 3, Mansfield terrace
Waite Robert, Derby rd
Walker Wm. 14, Carlton st
Ward Rt. 28, Bridlesmith gt
Webster Wm. York st
Webster Wm. Mid. Pavement

White Hiram, St. Petersgate
Woolley Wm. York st
Wood Geo. Bellargate
Whiteley John, Newcastle st
Widdowson Matthew, Kingston st
Wildig Ann, Bottle lane
Williamson Fras. York st
Winfield Rt. 7, Milton st
Wilks Elias, St. James's st
Wright John, Sydney st
Wright Wm. 14, Lenton st

(21.) BRACE MAKERS.
See Smallware Dealers.
Ash Saml. sen.(and fancy articles)
  4, Castle terrace
Ash Saml. jun.(and fancy articles)
  Poplar place

(22.) BRASS FOUNDERS AND
  GAS FITTERS.
See also Iron Founders.
Cooper Jas. Harrington st
Coulby Wm. 12, Greyhound yd
Pegg Samuel, Park row
Tatham Robert, S. 49, Bridle-
  smithgate

(23) BRAZIERS & TIN-PLATE
  WORKERS.
Beard Henry, St. Peter's square
Cooke Thos. Martin, Bridge st
Farnsworth Daniel, Sussex st
Fidler John, Milton st
Gillett Jph. Plat st
Goodbid John, Narrow marsh
Harrison Nettleship, Hockley
Higginbottom John, Broad marsh
Holmes Jph. Old Glasshouse ln
Jones Danl. York st
Knight Thos. Sneinton st
Lewis Wm. 53, Bridlesmithgate
  and Peck lane
Milford Wm. Derby rd
Morley James, Cheapside
Nash Wm. Broad st
Pearce Anthony, Derby rd
Riddell Thos. Tradesmen's mart
Robinson Cpr. St. John st
Wapplinton Wm. Plat st
Whyatt John, Pelham st
Woodward Wm. Angel row
  BREWERS.
See Porter Dealers.
(24.) BRICK MAKERS.
*Marked thus * have Brickyards*

*at Mapperley hills, and † at
  Sneinton.*
*Bean Saml. Lincoln st
†Bradshaw John & Sons, Canal
  street
Clay James, Coalpit ln
*Clay Wm. York st
*† Daykin John, West Bridgford
†Hooton Rd. Fishergate
*James Thos. Mansfield rd
James Saml. Carlton hill
*Neep Thos. Wm. Apple row
*North Thos. London rd.
*Pritchard Jas. St. Ann's st
*Robinson Danl. Cartergate
*Robinson Jas. Wharf st
*Smith John, 21, Mansfield ter
Smith Martha & Sons, Carlton
Surplice Wm. 2, Clumber st. and
  Forest
Taylor John, Carlton rd. and
  Radford
†Wood Moses, Sneinton
  (25.) BRICKLAYERS.
See also Stone Masons.
Anderson Michl. Parliament row
Astick John, Mount st
Bradbury Wm. 6, Broad st
Butler Rd. Castlegate
Dale Thos. 39, Woolpack ln
Elliott Fdk. 20, Warsergate
Hardwick Saml. 43, Barkergate
Hare J. Wild's yard, Houndsgt
Hawley John, Fishergate
Jackson Saml. Washington st
James Wm. Coalpit ln
Lane Samuel, 56, Barkergt
Lucas Thos. 1, Fountain pl
May Jas. Beck street
Ostick Thos. 1, Beck lane
Overend Geo. Mount East st
Parker Wm. New Charles st
Perceival Geo. Carter row
Smith Wm. 9, West st
Spurr Rd. 36, Warsergate
Spurr Thos. Water street
Stephenson Wm. Rose yard
Taft John, Carrington st
Ward Joshua, Derby rd
Wootton Pp. (steeple bldr.) Pier-
  repont st
Wootton Wm. Castlegate

(26.) BUILDERS.

Drewry W. & B. 17, Plumptre st
Inger Wm. Glasshouse st
Kenton Rt. Glasshouse st
Parrott John & Sons, 22, George st
Patterson Wm. St. James's st. h.
  Park terrace
Soar Jph. 27, George st
Surplice Wm. 2, Clumber st
Tomlinson Jas. Listergate
Walker John & Saml. Derby rd
Weston, Field and Son, 23, St.
  Mary's gate
Winter Thos. Nottingham ter

(27.) BRUSH MAKERS.

Savage Geo. Coalpit lane
Waine Avery, Pelham st
Wallace & Keiling. Parliament st

(28.) BUTCHERS.

*Those marked 1 have Shops in the
Cheapside Passage. 2 Dark
Shambles. 3 New Shambles. 4
Old Shambles. 5 Police Passage. 6 Smithy Row Passage,
and 7 in Cross Shambles.*

3 Abbott John. Smalley
1 Allen Silas, 55, Barkergate
Appleby Thos. Sneinton st
4 Archer Thos. Keyworth
3 Armitage John, Houndsgt
6 Armitage Saml. Newcastle st
Armitage Saml. Chatham st
2 Armitage Wm. Trent bridge
5 Attenborough Geo. Ruddington
Attenburrow Wm. Change alley
  and Parliament st
7 Ayre Rd. Broad marsh
4 Ayre Thos. Basford
1 Bailey Anthy. Castlegate
4 Bagaley John, Cotgrave
4 Barber Geo. Chandler's ln
2 Baudon Rt. Parliament row
Bee Thos. Old Glasshouse ln
2 Borrows Thos. Coalpit ln
Bramley Fras. Narrow marsh
Brazier Jas. Albion place
4 Brewin Wm. Lenton
4 Briddon Rt. Parliament row
Briddon Thos. Derby rd
Briddon Wm. Milton st
7 Brown Jph. Goosegate
3 Buttery Rd. Ratcliffe
Cartledge Benj. Goosegate

Clay John, Plat st
Clayworth Wm. New Clare st
Cliff Thos. Albion place
5 Cockayne John, Parliament st
1 Cockayne John, Sherwood
4 Cockayne Thos. Grey Friargt
1 Cockayne Wm. 2, Mansfield ter
3 Collins Jph. Bunney
3 Cooke John, Bingham
Curtis Rt. Narrow marsh
Dakeyne John, 15, Bellargate
3 Day Wm. Beeston
Deeker John, Wheat Sheaf yd
3 Dixon John, Cotgrave
2 Dixon John, Mount st
4 Drake Thos. Newcastle st
4 Draper Geo. Gotham
6 Dutton Silas. Newcastle st
Eite Henry, Millstone lane
Eite James. Mortimer st
Eite John, Sussex street
Farrands John, Cartergate
Farrands Thos. Plumptre sq
Fisher Micha, Penny foot stile
6 Fletcher Wm. Tollhouse hill
4 Foster Richard, Ratcliffe
3 Foster William, Ratcliffe
Gadd Thomas, Malt court
3 Glover Jph. Wymeswould
4 Glover Thomas, Plumptre
6 Goodall Chas. 13, Bottle lane
Goodall John, Chapel bar
4 Goodall T. Old Glasshouse ln
Goodburn John, 53, Barkergate
3 Goode John, Mount East st
5 Greensmith Joseph, Boot lane
4 Hall Chas. Houndsgate
2 Hall John, Houndsgate
Hall Samuel, Houndsgate
Handley Wm. Glasshouse st
3 Hardy Rd. Hickling
Hardy Thomas, Narrow marsh
3 Harpham George, Wilford
3 Hart John, Rancliffe street
1 Harvey Jas. Weekday cross, h.
  Middle hill
3 Helmesley Rd. Bunney
4 Hickling James, Angel row
1 Hickman John, Change alley &
  Mansfield road
Hind Benj. 15, Mansfield terrace
Hobson John, Washington st
3 Hodgkin John, Ruddington

Holland Thos. Mount court
4 Hooper Wm. Whatton
4 Houghton Henry, Nuttal
Inocent Francis, Cur lane
Jerrom Frederick, Friar lane
Kelsall Edmund, Cartergate
3 Lacy James, Caunt street
4 Lawrence Hastings, Rempston
4 Lineker Siddons, Greyhound yd
6 Lloyd Robert, 3, St Marygate
3 Machin Richard, Papplewick
Maidens George, Talbot yd
Malthy Jph. (pork) 6, Chapel bar
Martin Gervase, Charlotte st
4 Mee John, Broad marsh
Millar Samuel, Narrow marsh
1 Moody Charles, Glasshouse st
2 Morley Ann, Broad st
4 Morley John, Beck st.
3 Neep Thomas, Houndsgate
Neep Wm. Finkhill st
3, Newton John, Cropwell Bishop
Nix Thomas, St. Ann's st
Norton John, Exchange & Mansfield road
4 Ogle George, Ratcliffe
Osborn Samuel, Pierrepont st
3 Page Wm. Ruddington
3 Palethorpe Thomas, Shelford
2 Palmer David, Coalpit lane
Parker Wm. Gedling st
Parlby Thos. Canal street
5 Pearson John, Charlotte st
Pearson Wm. (& bacon factor) 8, Smithy row
4 Pearson Wm. Glasshouse ln
3 Pearson Wm. jun. Newcatle st
3 Peet Edward, Edwalton
Perkins Mary, Tradesmen's mart
Pettinger Thos. Pelham st
4 Plackett John, Breaston
4 Plackett Rd. Breaston
2 Plowright Henry, Mount st
2 Plowright Wm. Parliament st
Pollard John, 38, Warsergate & St. James' st
5 Prew John, Paliament st
3 Prew Wm. 8, Bell founders yd
Prew John, Mansfield rd
3 Price Wm. Clifton
3 Richmond John, Carlton
3 Richmond Samuel, Ratcliffe
Rowbotham Rd. Narrow marsh

3 Russell Thos. Ockbrook
3 Salt Richard, Sandyacre
Sanders Charles, Houndsgate
2 Seals Robt. 17, Stoney st
3 Shuter John, Bridgford
4 Simkin John, Carrington st
2 Simkins Chas. Houndsgate
2 Simkins Daniel, Narrow marsh
Simkins Eliz. Listergate
4 Simkins James Sneinton
2 Simkins John, Mansfield rd
3 Simpson Mrs. Car Corston
2 Smith John Abm. Mount East street
Smith John, Narrow marsh
3 Southgate Wm. Newcastle st
3 Spearing Benj. Woolpack ln
3 Stevens John, Draycott
7 Street Geo. Chandler's ln
2 Strelley Richard, Pepper st
4 Tebbutt John, Hockley
4 Thornton Hy. Parliament st
Thraves Wm. 26, Barkergate
4 Tipping Wm. Chilwell
Tomlinson Thos. Canal st
Topley Wm, Cross st
Torr George, Drury hill
Torr James, Derby rd
4 Turner George, Clayton's yd
7 Turner James, ct. 36, Bridle-smithgate
4 Turton George, 18, Stoney st
Tutin George, Hockley
3 Vessey Joseph, Scarrington
Walker John, Plat st
Watson Samuel, St. Peter's sq
1 Watts Richard, 13, Warsergate
4 Wells Andrew, Hazard's yd
4 Wheatley John, Whatton
Wheeldon John, Back ln
3 Whittaker Ed. Parliament st
Whitby Edward, Geo. & Drag. yd
White Robert, Narrow marsh
2 Whitfield John, Newcastle st
Whitworth John, York st
Widdowson Reuben, Exchange alley
Wigley Henry, St. Peter's sq
4 Wilford Thomas, Newcastle st
3 Williamson Luke, Bridgford
4 Wilson Carn, Cartergate
4 Wood George, Virginia st
4 Wood John, Castle rd

5 Wood Thomas, Pilchergate
Woodward James, 20, Long row
1 Wright Hy. New Sneinton
Wright John, Exchange and N.
  Radford
2 Wright John, 11, Broad st

(29.) CABINET MAKERS.
*Those marked * are Upholsterers.*
See also Joiners and Furniture
       Brokers.
Allen Silas, Rosemary lane
Breckels Thos. Listergate
*Brothers Benj. ct. 65, Long row
Cope James, Milton st
Goodrich Wm. Milton st
*Green Joseph, Angel row
Harrison Wm. Tradesmen's mart
*Jones Edw. Beastmarket hill
*Lakin Thos. Angel row
Lock Wm. Cook, Angel row
*Stoney & Clarke, High pave-
  ment
*Thurman Thos. Finkhill st
Wilson Joseph, 8, Pennell's yd

(30.) CALICO GLAZERS.
Bignall Robt. 15, Stoney st
Peach Cath. 3, Queen st

(31.) CARPET WAREHSES.
Blackwell Wm. sen. 75, Long row
Brothers Benj. 65, Long row
Leake Thos. Milton st

(32.) CARVERS & GILDERS.
*Thus * are also Thermometer,*
Barometer, and Looking Glass
Manufacturers.
*Bregazzi Peter, High payement
Cooper John, 19, Broad st
Everitt John, Bridlesmithgate
Fitzwalter Fras. Toll st
Fitzwalter Thos. 29, Bridlesmith-
  gate
*Guggiari Domenico, Pelham st
Leader Geo. (carver, and mould
  and block cutter,) Bridge st
Tiddiman Geo. Union place
Wright Rt. Newcastle st

(33.) CATTLE DEALERS.
Barrow Joseph, Darker's yd
Brown Wm. 7, George st
Hakes Thos. Darker's yd
Milner David, Carrington st
Marshall Jph. (pigs) Narrow
  marsh

(34.) CHAIR MAKERS.
Adderton John, 24, Greyhound
  yard
Allen Wm. West st, h. Pine st
Barwick Jas. Goosegate
Halfpenny Jph. Canal st
Lawson Eliz. Listergate
Meadows Samuel, Mount st
Smart Thos. Fishergate
Wilkinson Rd. Broad marsh

(35.) CHEESE AND BACON
      FACTORS.
   See also Shopkeepers.
Child Frances, Pelham st
Fisher Chas. (and flour) Bridge st
Flint Thos. Sneinton st
Goodliffe Arnold, 33, Bridlesmith
  gate
Greaney Walter, Tradesmen's mt
Hall Thos. 6, Carlton st
Kennedy Bridget, Drury hill
Midlam Jph. 1, Charlotte st
North Wm. Charlotte st
Parr Samuel, Pelham st
Smith and Newton, 65, Long row
Taylor Robert, St. Peter's square
White Jas. York st

(36.) CHIMNEY SWPRS., &c.
Baxter J. Twigg alley
Hickling Mary, Queen st
Henis Wm. 5, Charlotte st
Lowe Wm. St. Peter's church
Turner John, York st

(37.) CHINA, GLASS AND
EARTHENWARE DEALERS.
Marked 1 are Earthenware Dea-
  lers, and 2 Glass Dealers only.
Bradbury John, Goosegate
Dutton Jph. (glass cutter) 4, Bridlesmithgate
Gray Rt. (crown glass) Canal st
2 Haywood Wm. & Son, (bottle,
  phial, and vitriol merts.) Middle hill
Inger George, 46, Long row
Inger Wm. Chapel bar
2 Jackson Henry, (cut glass mfr.)
  4, Bridlesmithgate and Tutbury. J. Dutton, agent
1 Leeming Thos. 14, Riley's yd
1 Loach Fras. Coalpit lane
1 Pinder Wm. Mansfield road
1 Smith Thos. Green's yard

X

Stenson Wm. Listergate
1 Towle John, 26, York st
1 Vaughan Rt. 3, Charlotte st
Wass Geo. Parliament st
(38.) CHEMISTS AND DRUG-
    GISTS.
*Marked thus † are only Drug-
    gists and Grocers.*
Bassett Jph. Oldknow, 1, Clum-
    ber street
Beardsley Jas. Sneinton st
†Bell Wm. 1, Mansfield terrace
Brothers and Williams, 60, Long
    row
Buttery Chas. & Fredk. 14, Long
    row
Cheetham Henry, 63, Long row
    and Drury hill
Clarke John, 17. Beck lane
Cooke Hy. 9. Mansfield terrace
Cox Edw. jun. Fishergate
Cullen Samuel, Cheapside
Dale Jas. & Sons, Weekday cross,
    Exchange row, & High st
†Felkin Thos. 20, Charlotte st
Harrison John, 46, Bridlesmith-
    gate
Harrison Thos. St. Peter's sqr
Hart Edmund, 11, Narrow marsh
Hedderley John, 14, Clumber st
Howitt Rd. Parliament st
Howitt Wm. South parade
Humphreys John. Sussex st
Marlow John. High street
Need and Coltman, 39. Long row
Nunn John, 36, Bridlesmithgate
Potts Rd. Smith, Hockley
Sanderson A. R. 10. Carlton st
Southam Geo. Glasshouse st
Spencer Jph. Gedling st
†Taylor Wm. 42. Warsergate
Towne Leonard, 43, Bridlesmgte
Underwood Rd. Beastmarket hill
Ward Hy. Pilkington, 41, Bridle-
    smithgate
Warren John, Cartergate
Waterall Geo. 5, Chapel bar
†Whitchurch Saml. Cross st
Wilcockson Chas. Vigani, Lister-
    gate
Wilcockson John, 7, Carlton st
†Wood Thos. Carlisle place
Yates & Guilford, 53, Long row

†Yeomans Wm. Charles st
(39.) CIRCULAR COMB AND
    BOLT MAKERS.
Beck Chas. St. James's st
Greensmith Saml. (bolt) Mount
    East street
Mortimer Geo. Mount East st
Marriott Hy. Rutland st
Stokes Geo. Dukes place
Wardle Wm. 2, Barkergate
(40.) CLOTHES DEALERS.
    See also Pawnbrokers.
Bush Lydia, Glasshouse st
Forgie John, King st
Forgie Andw. Goosegate
Gee Josiah, 6. Greyhound yard
Habbijam Jas. Coalpit lane
Hallam Chas. 10. Queen st
Hardy Thos. 26, Greyhound yrd
Hardy Thos. Old Glasshouse lane
Hartley Jonas, 9, Charlotte st
Kelland John, Pelham st
Leet Wm. Glasshouse st
Martin John. Drury hill
Newbolt Gervase, Charlotte st
Robinson Martha. Milton st
Simmons Chas. Narrow marsh
Smith Wm. Plat street
Theobald Wm. Pierrepont st
Wallace Saml. Bridlesmithgate
Watson George, Cross st
Willimott John, Sussex st
(41.) COACH BUILDERS &
    HARNESS MAKERS.
Butler Sarah & Son, Bottle lane
Hunt Wm. 29. George st
Ragg Saml. Glasshouse st
Rutland Thos. High Pavement
Stones John & Co. Lincoln st. &
    Parliament st. h. Park
COACHES (HACKNEY.)
    See Livery Stables.
(42.) COAL DEALERS.
Bradshaw John & Sons, Canal st
Brough John, Canal st
Cooper T. S. Trent bridge
Derry Saml. London road, h.
    Canal street
Dobb Samuel, Canal st
Fothergill Jas. & John, Canal st
Hilton Fras. & Son, Castle Wharf
Lewis Jph. & Rd. Bath row wharf
Marriott John, Castle wharf

Marshall Rt. London road
Mitchell John & Wm. Canal st
North Thos. Babbington Colliery
  h. London road
Pyatt John, Walnut tree lane
Pyatt Wm. Canal st
Richards Saml. Mill st
Robinson Jas. Wharf st
Robinson John, Brewery st. h.
  Sneinton
Ramsey Thos. London road, h.
  20, St. Marygate
Shelton and Harvey, Canal st
Swanwick Geo. Trent row
Swanwick John, Canal st
Swanwick Jph. Canal st
Thorpe Saml. Canal Co.'s Wharf,
  Canal street.

(43.) COLLECTORS OF RENTS.

Fann John, 57, Coalpit lane
Holland Jph. 29, Barkergate
Machin Joseph, Derby road
Tipler Jas. Parliament row
Wheatley John, (bailiff of the
  Peveril Court) 2, Lincoln st
Wheatcroft Thos. 43, Stoney st

(44.) CONFECTIONERS.

Beardall Fred. 35, Long row
Beardmore John, St. Peter's sqr
Benton Jas. (dlr.) Bridge st
Brampton Jas. Old Glasshouse
  lane
Carnall Isaac, Goosegate
Clarkson Allred, Derby road
Clarkson Matw. Mount East st
Coulton Owen, Goosegate
Croshaw John, 55, Long row, and
  Pelham st
Cumberland George, 39, Bridle-
  smithgate
Derrick Geo. Sneinton st
Fox Thomas, 62, Long row
Fox Wm. Pelham st
Glover Philip, 6, Carlton st
Gainsley J. 11, Lenton st
Husband Rd. Goosegate
Lambert Thos. Hewitt, Beck st
Metheringham Dennis, Derby rd
Needham and Green, 6, Bridle-
  smithgate
Parker Thos. Derby road

Taylor Rd. Listergate
Towers Rd. Listergate
Wood John, Hockley

(45.) COOPERS.

Dickisson James, Mount st
Evans Thos. Independent hill
Halford John, Listergate
Halford Wm. Cartergate
Ley Wm. Brewhouse yard
Lowe Chas. Goosegate
Morris Thos. Houndsgate
Petty Saml. Houndsgate
Roome Wm. Coalpit lane
Savage Geo. Drury hill
Whittington Wm. Frame yard
Yates Hy. Maypole yard

(46.) CORK CUTTERS AND FLEECY SOCK MANFRS.

Bussey Wm. 47, Bridlesmithgt
Gamble Rt. 10. High Pavement
Gamble Wm. Sneinton st
Lewis Walter, 25, Bridlesmithgt

(47.) CORN MERCHANTS.

Marked 1 are Corn and Flour
Dealers.

1 Curtis Wm. Canal street and
  Bridge st
1 Fisher Chas. Bridge st
Fox Thos. Long row
1 Hodgkinson Thos. Parliament
  street
Roworth Wm. London road
Sims John, Canal st. and Middle
  Pavement
1 Smith Jph. & Co. Canal st. and
  Weekday cross
1 Spencer John, Cheapside
1 Taylor Jas. Sneinton st

(48.) CORN MILLERS.

*Marked * have Windmills on the*
Forest side.

Barradell John, Canal st
Bennett John, Sneinton
*Bissill Thomas, 10, Chapel Bar
Bostock Ed. sen. Lovett Mills
Chimley Edward, Derby road
Cooper Edward, Basford
*Fletcher George, Beck st
*Hall John, Listergate
*Hickling W. Old Glasshouse In
Hodkinson James, Parliament st.
  and Newstead

Innocent Ann, Meynel row and Sneinton
*Johnson John Forest side
Leavers and Smith, Canal st
*Morley Abraham, Forest side
Morley William, Sneinton
Oliver Wm. Parliament row and Basford
*Ossinbrook John, Forest side
Reddish William, Basford
Robinson William, Mill st. h. 28, Stoney st
*Rowland Wm. York st
*Sharp Wm. 19, Mansfield ter
Simpson Joseph, Bobber's mill
Stapleton John. Beck ln.
Thorpe John and Thomas, Pelham street and Basford
Tinker Rd. Sand hill, h. Mansfield road
*Toyne Wm. Derby road
*Toyne Samuel, Radford
Wagstaff Wm. Sneinton
*Wright Francis, Narrow marsh
*Walker John, Old Radford

(49.) COTTON SPINNERS AND LACE THREAD MANUFACTURERS AND DEALERS.

*Those marked † are Cotton Spinners, * Lace Thread Manufacturers, and the rest are dealers only.*

Allen Jas. Rogers, St. James's street
†Arkwright Peter, Esq. Park row and Cromford. Wm. and David Melville, agents
*Ashwell John Heard, (and silk) St. Jame's st
Attenborough Rt. 7, Clumber st
Bishop James and Thomas, St. Peter's square
Booker Richard, Buttery's yard, Long row
*Bradley and Harvey, Park st
*Cartledge Samuel and Son, Postern street
Chambers John, 27, St. Mary's gate and Manchester
Crowther Thos. 25, St. Mary's gt
*Earp Edwin, Hockley Mill
Etherington and Duplex, Byard lane

Gill George and Son, Houndsgate, h. Park terrace
Gill Robert, Mount st
Gray B. 24, Carlton street and Manchester. John Hutchinson, agent
Haythorn Fdk. 16, Ridley's yd
Haythorn Jonathan Wright, ct. 33, Long row
*Heywood and Jones, ct. 33, Long row
Hodson Wm. and Co. Spaniel row and Mansfield. John Leavers, agent
†Hollins H. and C. and Co. Angel row and Langwith
†Hollins, Siddons, and Co. Angel row and Pleasley. Wm. Woodward, jun. agent
Hughes John & Co. St. James's st
†Livingston and Cheetham, Parliament st. and Manchester
†Manlove S. and Co. 16, St. Mary's gate
*Melville William and David, Park row
*Mills and Elliott, 45, Long row and Commercial street
†Mills George and John (and Merino yarn) Long row
*Milnes Thomas Brown, Lenton works
†Murray A. and G. 36, Broad st. and Manchester. Thos. Garton, agent
*Moore Benjamin, Hockley mill
Moore Samuel and Son, Friar ln. and Manchester. Jph. White, agent
Parker and Kirk, Maypole yd
Rideout Henry George, Rutland st. h. Mansfield road
Rushton James, 4, King's place
Russell William, Pawlet's yard, Long row
†Rutt and Williams, 26, Carlton st. and Manchester. —Edgar Sanderson, agent
Sanderson George, Houndsgate
*Sanderson Thos. 19, Stoney st
*Sneath William and Co. 44, Bridlesmithgate & Mansfield
Stenson John, 29, Parliament st

Sulley Richard, 9, Stoney st
*Thackeray, John, St. James's st
*Towle Thomas, John, and Benj.
Angel row. John Cooper, agt
Trueman David and Co. 74, Long
row
†Wakefield Francis and Thomas
Churchgate and Mansfield
Walsh George Nelson, Park st
Wells William, 9, Clumber st
†Wilson Wm. & Samuel (and Me-
rino Yarn) Radford

(50.) CURRIERS AND LEA-
THER CUTTERS.
Hood Wm. 11, Bridlesmithgate,
h. Park hill
Hopkinson William, Mount st
Hopkinson Charl. Chandler's ln
Lowe Wm. Fletchergate
Page Samuel, Wheelergate
Pearson George, 26, Clumber st
Philbrick Thomas, Fletchergate
Shipley Francis Edward, 21, Bri-
dlesmithgate
Smart Wm. 46, Bridlesmithgate
Smith Wm. 2, St. Mary's gate
Thorpe Joseph, St. Peter's sq,
Willy David, Beck lane
Wilson Wm. 34, Bridlesmithgate

(51.) CUTLERS AND HARD-
WARE DEALERS.
Bartlett Thomas, (file cutter)
Narrow marsh
Greaves, Fras. Narrow march
Hardy George, Derby road
Hattersley Joseph Plat st
Hattersley John, Derby rd
Micklewait John, Listergate
Simpson Jph. 10, Bridlesmithgt
Townsend Robt. St. Peter's gate
Townsend Septimus , 12, Bridle-
smithgate

(52.) DENTISTS.
Clare Isaiah William 32, Bridle-
smithgate
Forbes John Luke (bleeder) 10,
Olive yard
Hutchinson Thos (cupper, &c.)
11, Broad street
Thompson Wm. Low Pavement

(53.) DRAPERS AND TEA
DEALERS.—(Travelling.)
Brown James, Mount st

Carson Wm. Tree yard
Davidson Thos Sherwood st
Graham George, 7, Lincoln st
Grierson Wm. Mansfield road
Henry Samuel, 31, Parliament st
M'Call John, 11, George st
M'Quhae Thomas, Carrington st
M'Monies James, Derby road
Murdock Nath. Plumptre sqr
Saulsbury And. Mansfield rd

DRYSALTER, &c.
Fry William, Lincoln st. h. Parliament st.

Druggists, see Chemists, &c.

(54.) DYERS.
Armfield Joseph, Mount st
Atherstone Hugh, Brewhouse yd
Bagnall James Fred. Finkhill st
Bartley Sam. (job) Knotted alley
Broughton Mary, Canal st
Bullivant John, Canal st
Chamberlain Wm. Pomfret st
Chawner Thomas Ealand st
Damant Edward, Brewhouse yd
Doncaster Wm. Rutland st
Fellows and Crosby (silk) High
Pavement
Garrick Thomas 13, Sheep ln
Haslam Samuel, Salmon yd
Keeley John and Son, Walnut
tree ln
Manners John, Goosegate
Marshall George, Queen st
Marshall Thomas, Wheelergate
Musham William, Hockley
Shakespear Han. St. Peter's sq
Shelton Wm. Castlegate
Smith Samuel, Robin Hood yd
Spooner George, Tilley's yd

(55.) EATING HOUSES.
Ashton John, 13, Bridlesmithgt
Brightmore Hannah, 18, Parlia-
ment st
Hardy Joseph, Mansfield rd
Marvin Chas. 7, Bridlesmithgate
Reddish James, Goosegate
Shipley James, 18, Clumber st
Weatherall George, Drury hill
Wainwright Ann, Goosegate

(56.) ENGRAVERS & COP-
PERPLATE PRINTERS.
Carr Joseph, Houndsgate
Lees John, Bottle lane

x 2

Palethorpe Job, St. James's st
Wilkins John, Greyhound yd
Wild Ebenezer, (Wood and Lithographic) Harley pl. Carrington street

(57.) FELLMONGERS AND LEATHER DRESSERS.
Armitage Jph. jun. Trent bridge
Bayley Isaac, Lenton
Mitchell John & Wm, Finkhill st
Parr Thomas, Narrow marsh
Roberts Sam. Plumptre sq

(58) FIRE AND LIFE OFFICE AGENTS.
(Six Fire Engines are supported by the Corporation; J. C. Griffin, of Broad street, is the Engineer.)
Alliance, British, & Foreign, J. W. Haythorn, ct. 33, Long row
Birmingham, Leavers & Smith, Canal st
Clerical and Medical, Thomas Crowther, 25, St. Mary's gt
Crown Life and Protector Fire, John Stenson. 29, Parliament st
County Fire and Provident Life, Thos. Crowther, 25, St. Mary's gate
Globe, James Coope, 4, Haughton st
Guardian, John Watson, 1, Carlton st
Norwich Union, William Morland, Wheat Sheaf yard
Palladium, William Wild, Weekday cross
Phœnix, John Parker, 16, Carlton st
Protector, Christopher Norton Wright, 50, Long row
Promoter Life Ass. and Annuity, S. Payne, Low Pavement
Royal Exchange, Edward Staveley, Pelham st
Suffolk, S. Turner, 20, Warsergt
Sun, Jph. Jas. Ward, Rigley's ct. 39, Long row
West of England, Thomas Alex. Campbell. ct. 39, Long row

(59.) FISHING TACKLE MAKERS.
Eaglesfield Charles, Coalpit ln

Etches Jeffrey, Hockley
Lees Edward, Sussex st
Wells John, Sussex st
Wetherbed Charles, Cartergate
Young John, Bridge st

(60.) FISHMONGERS.
Baggarley Thomas, Crown yard
Broadburrey Wm. Crown yd
Ford Moses, 10, Pennells yd
Gear Saml, Timber hill
Gilbert Richard, Vernon st
Hickling Thomas, Plat st
Hodgson Hy. 19, Greyhound yd
Stevenson Edward, Park st
Trueman David, Change alley
Weightman Wm. 7, Pennell's yd

(61.) FRAME SMITHS.
See also Machine Makers and Whitesmiths.
Bates Wm. Caunt st
Bishop John, Washington st
Burton Thomas, 46, Barkergate
Corah Thomas, Mansfield rd
Davis George, Robin Hood yd
Fox Thomas, Holland st
Harvey Henry, Dove yd
Hind Wm. 22, Beck lane
Hopcraft Wm. & John, Sneinton
Kerry, James, Hockley
Mortimer James, (frame broker) Pleasant row
Oldham Robert, Castle road
Pineger Edward, Derby road
Robinson George, Wool alley
Rogers Joseph, Mansfield rd
Stone John, Granby st. h. Brewhouse yd
Straw Edward, Parliament st
Turner Thomas, Toll st
Ward Joseph, 21, Rice pl
Wilcocks George, Sneinton st
Woodhouse David, 42, Barker gt
Yeomans John, Duke's pl
Young Wm. Manver's st,

(62.) FRAMEWORK-KNITTERS.
(Owners and Employers of Stocking Frames.)
See also Hosiery Manufacturers.
Billiard Thos. sen. 22, Rice pl
Blower Thos. 11, Olive yard
Brailsford Wm. 14, Bellargate
Brown Saml. Beck lane

Burnham John, Independent hill
Chambers John, Wellington st
Cheetham Geo. Newark lane
Dobbs John, Sinker alley
Elliott Thos. 21, York st
Guest Wm. 38, York st
Guest Thos. Glasshouse st
Hayes Jph. Old Pottery
Hogg Rt. Portland place
Hollis John, King st
Hulland John, Back lane
Hutchinson Wm. Bran court
Kent Jph. 25, Rice place
Kirkman Jas. Nile st
Lacy Jas. Maiden lane
Lamb Chas. 23, Broad st
McCalaum Wm. King's square
Miller John, Cur lane
Pepper Saml. Nile st.
Phipps Saml. Newcastle st
Pole John, St. Ann's st.
Poyzer Geo. Back lane
Sands John. Mansfield road
Scattergood John, Sinker alley
Spray John, 23, Rice place
Swain Jph. Woolpack lane
Thompson Edw. Nile street
Towers Thos. Mansfield road
Turton Wm. Trumpet st
Varney John, Newark lane
Wainman John, Nile street
Wainwright John, Mansfield rd
Webster Gervase, 12, Woolpk ln
White Eliz. Richmond st
Winterton Wm. King sq
Wood John, 13. York st

(63.) FURNITURE BROKERS.
*Marked • are Cabinet Makers
also.*

*Bailey Gilbert, Goosegate
Barwick Jas. Goosegate
*Binkley Geo. 28 & 30, Clumber st
Blackwell Wm. sen. 75, Long row
Brittan Fras. Narrow marsh
Chapman John, 31, Greyhound yard
Clark Thos. Milton st
Goodwin Thos. Goosegate h. New Sneinton
Hather Wm. Milton st.
Knight John, St. Peter's gate
Newell Jas. Millstone In

Parsons Thos. Hulse's yd
Porter John, Sheridan st
Richards Eliz. Drury hill
Wells Wm. Gedling st
Wain Jph. Parliament st
Wild Wm. Weekday cross
Wright Wm. Milton st

(64.) FURRIERS.
Cooke & Farmer, 56, Long row
Else Fras. Parliament st
Harrison & Brockmer, High st
Wayre Chas. 16, Exchange row

GLASS CUTTERS & DLRS.
See China & Glass Dealers.

(65.) GLOVERS & BREECHES MAKERS.
Hunt Thos. Parliament st
Lakin John, St. Peter's gate
Marlow Wm. ct 7, Bridlesmithgt
Watson Susan. 9, East street

(66.) GREEN GROCERS.
Marked thus • are Gardeners.
Booth Wm. 9, Sheep lane
*Bussey Wm. 47, Bridlesmithgt
*Barton Saml. 5, Beck lane
*Bramley Chas. Beck st
Cheshire John, Broad marsh
Curzon John. Caunt st
Elliott Wm. 1, Warsergate
*Gresham Rd.(seedsmn.)Hockley
*Hawksley John, Coalpit ln
*Hillery John, Parliament st
Hind Abm. Bellargate
Johnson John, 8, Charlotte st
*Kirk Saml. Chesterfield st
*Lowater Jph. Water street
*Lowater Saml. Fishergate
Mason Sylvester, Pomfret st
Roberts —, Coppice house
Slater John (& egg mert.) 2, Cannon yard
*Straw John, Parliament st
Trueman Chas. Tradesmen's mt
Wilson Wm. (herbalist) Goosegt

(67.) GROCERS AND TEA DEALERS.
(See also Shopkeepers)
Marked thus ‡ are Tea & Coffee dealers only.
Ash Robert, Howard street
Attenborough Hy. South parade
Baines Thomas, Listergate
Baldock William, Hockley

Barber John Houseman, Hollow-
stone
Beardsall Edw. 3, Woolpack ln
Bell Jph. Hollowstone
Bell Wm. 1, Mansfeld terrace
Bennett Wm. Wheelergate
Bowman Thos. Narrow marsh
Bradley. Thos. Lowe, 3, Smithy
row
‡ Bradley Thos. and Joshua, 7,
Smithy row
Bunting Geo. & Co. 67, Long r
Chalenor Wm. 21, Parliament st
Cheetham Isaac, Water street
Clark Jph. & Co. 3, Bridlesmith-
gate
Cole Eliz. 8, Poultry
Cooke & Barnsdall, 4, Chapel br
Copley Wm. 1, Parliament row
Cox Edward, Cartergate
Dean Chas. Parliament row .
Elliott Elias, 20, Bridlesmithgate
Elliott John Jeffery, Bridge st
Felkin Thos. 20, Charlotte st
Ford William, Houndsgate‡
‡ Fowler Smith, 23, Long row
Fox Samuel, High street
Fry Wm. (& drysalter) Lincoln st.
h. Parliament st
Gill William, Derby road
Goodacre Rd. & John, Pelham
street & Carlton street
Hall Thos. 14, Carlton st
Harrison Wm. Derby road
Hemsley Thos. 77, Long row &
Clumber st
Henson Thomas, 3, Poultry
‡ Hopkins Thos. & Co. 66, Long
row
Hucknall Jph. Hockley
Hudson William, Castlegate
Keep John & Co. Smithy row
Leake Thos. Goosegate
Lightfoot Thomas, Mount st
Lomax Jas. & Son, South parade
Midlam Jph. 1, Charlotte st
Milward Lucy, Carrington st
Mitchell Henry, Sussex st.
Parker Wm. Plat street
Pawlett Daniel, 74, Long row
Potter Thos. 7, Broad st
‡ Preston Rd. 47, Long row
Prickard Jas. Wm. Hockley

Pye Thomas, 4, Poultry
Quinton Hezekiah & John, 37,
Long row
Sargent Thos. Toll house hill
Sheldon John & Rt. Broad marsh
‡ Shuttleworth Jph. & Co. Beast-
market hill
Spencer Jph. Gedling st
Spencer Saml. Chesterfield st
‡ Swann Saml. Hy. ct. 66, Long
row
Tatham Thos. (& oil mert.) Mid-
dle pavement
Taylor Wm. 42, Warsergate
Tollington Thos. 32, Long row
Torr Lot, Milton street
Towers Wm. 1, Timber hill
Urry Geo. Plumptre sq
Walker Mtw. Woolpack ln
Wass Wm. Mount street
Webster Eliz. Ann. 10. Poultry
Webster Jas Mansfield rd
Whitchurch Saml. Cross street
Wood Thos. Carlisle place
Wortley Eliz. 37, Bridlesmithgt
Yeomans Wm. Charles st

(68.) GUN MAKERS.
Hetherington John, 56, Bridle-
smithgate
Jackson John, Churchgate
(69.) HAIR DRESSERS.
(See also Perfumers.)
Ashley Rd. Narrow marsh
Bailey John. Sussex st
Banks Jas. Glasshouse st
Bartle Thos. Millstone ln
Beastall Thomas, Rutland st
Blackwell Ebzr. Tradesmen's mt.
Bloom Thomas, 10, Milton st
Boot John, Cartergate
Bottom Jabez, Canal st. h. 24,
St. Mary's gate
Bowler Fras. Listergate
Bowler James, Wheelergate
Bowler Jph. Derby road
Brown Wm. Millstone ln
Clark John, Brook st.
Clayton Thos. Sneinton st
Cohorn Jas. Peter's church side
Coope Samuel, 15, Sheep lane
Corder Thos. Walnut tree lane
Daft Jph. St. Ann's st
Eaglesfield Chas. Coalpit lane

Etches Jeffry, Hockley
Etches George, Plat st
Fletcher Daniel, Parliament st
Fox Jas. Middle pavement
Gadsby Wm. jun. Water st
Green Henry, Mount st
Hibdis Thos. Sneinton st
Hardy Geo. Derby road
Hardy Mary, Parliament st
Hawksley John, 14, Mansfield ter
Hebb Wm. 24, Warsergate
Hindley John, 2, Maypole yard
Holland Jph. St. Jame's st
Holmes Edward, Listergate
Holmes Wm. Hy. Narrow marsh
Hind Jas. C. Milton st
Mason Joseph, 20, Clumber st
Mellow James, Fishergate
McCreery Jas. Mansfield road
Moore Wm. Charlotte st
Moreton Edw. 14, Bridlesmithgt
Mottrom Thos. 1, Goosegate
Peach David, Howard st
Randall John, Middle marsh
Richmond Thos. Spaniel row
Sansom James, 27, Clumber st
Starr Abm. Coalpit ln
Sweet Jas. (& books) Goosegate
Sumner John, 43, Barkergate
Worthington John, Cross st
Wright Chas. Coalpit lane, and
  Cross st
Wright Rt. Old Glasshouse ln
Wright John, Bridge st
Young John, Bridge st

(70.) HARDWARE DEALERS.
  See Cutlers & Ironmongers.
Cox Wm. 17, Rigley's yd
Mordan Saml. Truswell's yd

(71.) HATTERS, HOSIERS,
  AND GLOVERS.
Marked thus ‡ are Hat Manu-
  facturers.
Blackwell John, 23, Bridlesmith-
  gate
‡ Bodell Rd. 25, Greyhound yd
Carey Geo. & Son, 15, Clumber st
Carver Edward, Pelham st
Darkins John, 13, Exchange
Harrison & Brockmer, High st
Harison Rd. (dresser) Drury hill
Lacy Robert, 13, Rigley's yard
Lamb Rd. & Co. South parade

Lowe Wm. (dresser) 3, Warsergt
Roe Jas. 42, Bridlesmithgate
Spyvey Geo. Newcastle st
‡ Taylor George, Green's yard,
  Angel row
Thurman Samuel, 4, Smithy row
‡ Walker Daniel, 9, Poultry
Wayre Chas. 16, Exchange row

(72.) HOP MERCHANTS.
Attenborough Hy. South parade
Dabell Wm. 19, Long row
Fox Saml. (& seed) High st
Maltby Samuel, Beastmarket hill
Pawlett Daniel, 74, Long row
Small Ann, 1, Poultry
Swann Saml. Hy. (& Seed) Long
  row

(73.) HOSIERY MANUFAC-
  TURERS.
Allen John & Sons, St. James's st
Barker & Adams, Greyhound yd
Barrowcliff Samuel, & Son, 19,
  George street
Beckwith Wm. 7, Short hill
Berridge, and James, and Son,
  Houndsgate
Berridge John, Houndsgate
Bond Abijah & Son, 1, Bond st. S
Braithwaite Fras. & Jph. Peck ln
Brocksopp Thos. Park st. (& 10,
  Wood street, London)
Carrier Henry, ct. 33, Long row
Cheetham Wm. & Saml. Pepper
  street
Churchill, Daft, Smith, & Co. 25,
  High pavement
Corah John, ct. 44, Long row
Deakin Jonathan, Rigley's yard
Dodd Geo. (silk) Convent st
Farthing James, Clinton st
Galloway, Taite, & Son, (silk)
  George street
Gascoigne Thos. Parliament st
Gibson Geo. & Sons, Park row
Gibson John, Freeman st
Glover & Furley, Carrington st
Godber John, Peck lane
Greensmith Thos. Parliament st
Hadden Alexander & John & Co.
  Castlegate, (& 2, King street,
  London)
Hallam Saml. Tollhouse hill
Hardwick Fras. & Co. Pepper st

Heard & Hurst, Houndsgate
Henson Thos. & John, Bottle ln
Hewitt Fras. Pike, & Co. Rutland street
Hollins and Marshall, Houndsgt
Horner Robert, (silk) Mount st
Jackson Thomas, Castlegate
Jarratt Thos. Nile street
Jenkins Charles Watson & Co. Park hill road, & Milk street, London
Keely Thos. Friar ln. h. Walnut-tree ln
Kewney, Richardson, & Kewney, Wheelergate
Lart John, Halifax pl. & London
Leeson Saml. Weekday cross
Lowater John, Fishergate
Lowe & Smith, 23, Pilchergate
Lupton Wm. (fancy) Listergate
Mills Geo. & John, 45, Long row
Morley John & Rd. Fletchergt
Mortimer Jas. (drawers, &c.) Pleasant row
Mullen Jonathan, Mount st
Nelson Thos. Low pavement
Nixon John, 32, H. pavement
Oldham Thos. (& silk gloves) Tollhouse hill
Page Thos. Watts' yd. Chester-field street
Parker John, 6, St. Mary's gate
Pope & Co. 25, St. Mary's gate, and London
Rawson Wm. 8, Short hill
Ray Geo. & Co. (silk) Park st. & 41, Gutter ln. London
Renshaw, Shelton, & Co. 11, H. pavement
Renshaw Chpr. Park street
Renshaw Samuel, (silk & cotton) Rose yd. h. Park row
Roe Jas. 42, Bridlesmithgate
Rogers & Carver, 42, Warsergt
Scorer & Acomb, Mount st
Shaw Richard, St. James's st
Stanley John, (silk gloves) Peach street
Starr George, 11, Seeep lane
Tomkin Wm. Mount pleasant
Turner Thos. Standard hill
Warner Thos. ct. 33, Long row
Wells Rd. 47, Barkergate

Wilson Jph. John, and Isaac, Angel row
Wilson Js. & Son, (fleecy hosiery) East st. St. John's
Woodhouse Samuel, Park st
Yates Joseph, Brewhouse yd

(74.) HOSIERS, (Dealers).
See also Hatters and Linen and Woollen Drapers.

Mills Geo. & John, 45, Long row
Morris & Pickering, 44, Long row
Newbery Thos. St. Peter's church side
Timms Thos. (& lace dlr.) Beast market hill

(75.) HOTELS, INNS, AND TAVERNS.

Alderman Wood, Thos. Barker, Charlotte st
Anchor, Jph. Kendall, Walnut-tree lane
Ancient Druid, Thomas Hardy, Newcastle st
Apollo. Wm. Alvey, 41, Bar-kergate
Artichoke, Thomas Pilkington, High Cross st
Ball, James Clay, Coalpit ln
Balloon, Jph. Doer, Mount East street
Barley Mow, Eliz. Goodrich, Weekday cross
Bee Hive, Isaac Parker, Beck st
Bell, Hannah Bennett, ct 56, Long row
Bird-in-Hand, Jph. Marriott, 17, Sheep lane
Black Boy Inn, Rd. Hall, 69, Long row
Black Bull Inn, Jas. Horrocks, 11, Chapel bar
Black Horse, Rd. Coppock, 8, Stoney st
Black Lion, Mary Ann Harvey, Coalpit lane
Black Lion, Geo. Mann, Castlegt
Black's Head, Wm. Pick, Broad marsh
Black Swan, Harriet Buller, Goosegate
Blue Ball, Jph. Barker, Broad marsh

Blue Bell Inn, Wm. Clark, Angel row
Blue Bell, Jph Perry, Peck ln
Blue Bell, John Wood, Parliament street
Bowling Green, Thos. Palethorpe, Canal street
Britannia, John Day, Mount st
Bugle Horn, Wm. Pass, Commercial row
Bull's Head, Wm. Flinders, Fishergate
Bunkers Hill, Sarah Holmes, Parliament st
Butchers' Arms, John Dutch, Newcastle st
Canal Inn, Jas. Hickling, London road
Carpenters' Arms, John Hickman, Mansfield rd
Castle & Falcon, Jas. Bedles, Goosegate
Coach & Horses, Wm. Jackson, Mansfield rd
Coopers' Arms, Geo. Tootey, Plat street
Cricket Players, Mary Inglesant, 51, Barkergate
Cross Keys, Hy. Millington, Byard lane
Crown Inn, Mary Roberts, ct 57, Long row
Crown & Anchor, Geo. Handley, Bridge st
Crown & Anchor, John Harrison, Sneinton st
Crown & Cushion, Thos. Flower, Market st
Derby Arms, Hy. Cross, 21, Long row
Dog & Bear, John Pratt, 54, Bridlesmithgate
Dog & Gun, Hy. Blundell, Low Pavement
Dog & Pheasant, Charlotte Ireland, Castlegate
Dolphin, John Hoyles, without Chapel bar
Dove & Rainbow, Jph. Oakland, Parliament st
Druid's Tavern, John Cox, 31, Warsergate

Duke of York, Wm. Clarkson, 14, York st
Durham Ox Inn, John Farrands, 1, Pelham st
Eclipse, John Pidcock, Chapel bar
Eight Bells, John Everall, Peck ln
Elephant & Castle, Thos. Haywood, Houndsgate
Feathers, Sl. Bestow, Exchange
Filho-da-Puta, Robert Anncliffe, Mansfield rd
Flaming Sword, Thomas Stayner, Drake st
Flying Horse Inn, Jane Clark, 11, Poultry
Forest Tavern, John Taylor, Mansfield rd
Fox & Grapes, Fras. Parker, Old Glasshouse ln
Fox & Hounds, Dymock Hustwayte, Cartergate
Gate, Geo. Boggis, Brewhse. yd
General Ferguson, Rd. Smeeton, 28, Barkergate
George IV. Inn, Eliz. Ward, Carlton st
George & Dragon, Jas. Worth, 16, Long row
George & Dragon, Jph. Ingham, North st
Globe, Thos. Dutton, Poynton st
Goat's Head, Jph. Norman, Pump street
Golden Ball, Fras. Talbot, 25, Long row
Golden Fleece, Wm. Baldwin, Water st
Green Dragon, John Redfern, Park st
Greyhound, Rt. Burgess, Greyhound yard
Half Moon, John Cragg, Cartergate
Hare & Hounds, Thos. Taylor, Meynel row
Hearty Good Fellow, Edw. Thurman, Mount st
Highland Laddie, Saml. Stanfield, 1, York st
Hope & Anchor, Saml. Vincent, Parliament st
Horse & Groom, John Bower, 31, Clumber st

Horse & Groom, Wm. Porter, St. Peter's sq

Horse & Trumpet, Jph. Gelsthorp, Trumpet st

Hotel, Lewis Wilson, 7, Poultry

Huntsman, Rt. Moore, Old st

Jolly Angler, Benj. Hamtson, 9, Plumptre st

King George on Horseback, John Franks, 1, King st

King's Arms, Patrick Potts, Woolpack ln

King's Head, Wm. Hill, Charlotte st

King's Head, John & Rt. Green, Narrow marsh

King William IV. Wm. Dabell, 19, Long row

Kingston Arms, Thos. Ely, Parliament st

Leather Bottle, Wm. Laughton, Hockley

Leg of Mutton, Dd. Watts, Millstone lane

Leopard, Saml. White, Derby rd

Lion Hotel, (& postg. house) Wm. Smith, 17, Clumber st

Loggerheads, Saml. Godkin, Narrow marsh

Lord Byron, Wm. Lehy, Narrow marsh

Lord John Russell, Wm. Hague, Houndsgate

Lord Nelson, Wm. Hart, 20, Carlton street

Malt Cross, Jph. Mart, St. James's st

Marquis of Granby, John Hedderley, Drury hill

Masons' Arms, John Dutton, Glasshouse st

Maypole Inn, John Hardy, et 71, Long row

Milton's Head Inn, Thos. Pitchfork, Milton st

Milton's Head, Thos. Rowell, Derby road

Nag's Head, Wm. Barwick, 1, Stoney st

Nag's Head, John Smith, 21, Mansfield terrace

Navigation Inn, John Mawby, Canal street

Neptune, Jno. Hampson, Beck st

New George, Wm. Pilkington, 10, Warsergate

News House, Thos. Johnson, St. James's street

Nottingham Arms, Benj. Richards, Trent bridge

Nottingham Castle, Wm. Halford, Cartergate

Old Admiral Duncan, Thos. Potts, 25, Clumber street

Old Angel, John Billings, 12, High Pavement

Old Angel, Saml. Varney, 5, Stoney street

Old Cross Keys, Isaac Willatt, 46, St. Mary's gate

Old King's Head, Saml. Barton, Chapel bar

Old Peacock, John Cressey, St. Peter's gate

Old Plough, John Woolley, 25, Beck lane

Old Punch Bowl, Alex. Tomlinson, Garner's hill

Old Rose, Thos Waldram, Bellargate

Old Royal Oak, Edw. Nix, Broad marsh

Old Shoulder of Mutton, George Turner, 3, Barkergate

Peach Tree, Wm. Hilditch, Parliament street

Peacock, Wm. Gell, Pelham st

Peahen, Thos. Scotney, Peter's church side

Pheasant, Jno. Grant, Charlotte st

Plough and Harrow, Nathaniel Adgo, Milton st

Plough & Sickle, Ann Collishaw, 20, Broad st

Poplar Tree, Thos. Hart, Poplar place

Postern Gate, Charles Johnson, Weekday cross

Prince Blucher, Wm. Dabell, Chandler's lane

Punch Bowl, Thos. Stubbs, Peck lane

Queen Caroline, John Guyler, 15, Charlotte st

Queen's Head, Gervase Lovatt, Bottle lane

Ragged Staff, William Millar, Plumptre square

Ram Inn, Wm. Swanwick, 52, Long row

Rancliffe Arms, John Lee, Sussex street

Rancliffe Tavern, Jph. Simpson, Gedling street

Red Lion, Geo. Dann, Narrow marsh

Red Lion Inn, Ann Ward, Plumptre square

Rein Deer, Wm. Chester, Wheelergate

Robin Hood, Jph. Foster, Coalpit lane

Robin Hood & Little John, Gervase Thorp, Milton st

Rose, John Knowles, Mount st

Rose, Dorothy Potts, 10, Bridlesmithgate

Royal Children, Josiah Burrows, Nicholas st

Royal Arch Druid, Wm. Swindell, Listergate

Royal Oak, Wm. Cooper, 1, Chapel bar

Salutation, Wm. Bagshaw, Nicholas street

Sawyers Arms, William Wildgust. Listergate

Shakspeare, Rt. Shelton, Milton street

Ship, Nathl. Warren, Pelham st

Shoulder of Mutton, Samuel Hooper, 5, Smithy row

Shoulder of Mutton, John Rushton, High st

Sinker Maker's Arms, Charles Potts, Cartergate

Sir Francis Burdett, Rd. Kendall, Mount st

Sir Isaac Newton, John Beardshall, Howard st

Sir J. B. Warren, Edw. Henson, Old street

Sir Thomas White, Geo. Roberts, Cartergate

Spread Eagle Inn, Rt. Chapman, 35, Long row

Stag and Hounds, Eliz. Howitt, Caunt st

Stag and Pheasant, Geo. Harrison, Butcher st

Star, Jas. Gibson, St. Peter's sq

Star & Garter, John Woodhouse, Narrow marsh

Strugglers, Joseph Woodhouse, Tollhouse hill

Talbot, Wm. Hopkin, 35, Long row

Ten Bells, John Bennett, Narrow marsh

Three Crowns, Edw. Daniels, 23, Parliament st

Three Horse Shoes, John Orme, Tollhouse hill

Three Tuns, William Bailey, 26, Warsergate

Trent Bridge Inn, Mary Chapman, Trent bridge

Tiger's Head, Wm. Leeson, Narrow marsh

Trip to Jerusalem, J. F. Bagnall, Brewhouse yard

Unicorn, Wm. Pailthorpe, Milton street

Union, Thomas Simons Cooper, Trent bridge

Wheat Sheaf, Luke Davies, ct. 60, Long row

White Hart, Jph. Robinson, 22, Parliament st

White Hart, William Bailey, 42, York st

White Lion, Carver Savidge, Hollow stone

White Swan, Wm. Ogle, Beastmarket hill

Windmill, Rd. Summerfield, Market street

Woolpack, Benj. Mayo, Sussex st

(76.) BEERHOUSES.

Under the New Beer Act.

Board, Wm. Leby, Mortimer st

Bricklayer's Arms, Wm. Barker, New Charles st

Broom Girl, Benj. Moore, jun. Hockley

Castle Tavern, Wm. Pickering, Cross st

Colwick Lodge, Jph. Perkins, Water st

Cottage Tavern, Isaac Sampson, Poplar place

Y

Forest Miller, Rt. Greaves, Forest
Fox and Goose, Mary Moore, Mansfield road
Garden Gate, Samuel Jackson, Hunger lane
Grey Horse, John Read, Herbert street
Greyhound, Rt. Burgess, Greyhound yard
Greyhound, John Newton, Castlegate
Greyhound, Wm. Topley, Cross st.
Harp and Crown, Isaac Cowen, Cherry street
Hedge Hog, Fras. Hallam, Canal street
Highland Laddie, John Bishop, Washington st
Hon. Geo. Canning, Hy. Sprigg, Glasshouse st
Hop Pole, Wm. Wright, Woolpack lane
Hunger Hill Tavern, John Cleaver, Beck st
Huntsman's Tav. Thos. Hutchinson, Broad st
Jolly Britton, Wm. Horne, St. Ann's street
Jolly Colliers, Thomas & George Brown, Mansfield road
Lord Rancliffe, Wm. Longland, Howard street
Louis Philip I., Wm. North, King street
Marquis of Anglesea, Jas. Turner, St. James's street
Mortimer's Hole, Jas. Mortimer, Pleasant row
Mulberry Tree, Wm. Wilkinson, Narrow marsh
News House, Robert Cartwright, Canal street
Nottingham Arms, Jph. Whitehead, Derby road
Old Bob Hudson, Jas. Turner, Glasshouse street
Oyster Girl, Hy. Johnson, Plat st
Porcupine & Dogs, Wm. Stokes, East street
Plough & Farmer, Geo. Skidmore, Houndsgate
Queen Adelaide, Wm. Rollett, Mansfield road

Reformer, William James, New Bridge street
Robinson Crusoe, William Whitchurch, Mansfield road
Rose and Crown, Wm. Burbage, Spaniel row
Samaritan, Emanl. Lindsey, Clare street
Sir Thos. Denman, Wm. Daniels, Orchard street
Sun, Joshua Wardle, Sherwin st
Sun hill Brewery, Saml. James, Sun hill
Turk's Head, Lewis Woolley, Crossland street
Twist Machine, Geo. Watson, Caunt street
Walnut Tree, Jas. Gilberthorpe, Walnut tree lane
William IV., Saml. Scroop, Cavendish street
Woodman, Thos. Bartlett, Narrow march

(77.) IRON FOUNDERS, &c.
See also Brass Founders and Gas Fitters.
Aston Samuel & Co. Britannia Foundry, Canal st
Boothby Benj. & Co. (and stovegrate mfrs.) Rutland Foundry, Granby street
Cowen Robt. and Co. (and fender mfrs.) Beck st
Lingford John, 9, Parliament st
Redgate Henry, (and stovegrate mfr.) Houndsgate

(78.) IRON, &c. MERCHANTS
Cowen Rt. & Co. Beck st
Leavers Chas. Canal st. h. Park
Wood Edw. Canal st

(79.) IRONMONGERS.
See also Cutlers, &c.
Bell Wm. 28, Long row
Britton Thos. Goosegate
Carr Jas. (and saw maker) 23, Clumber st
Danks Isaiah & Thos. Beastmarket hill
Leavers Charles, Canal street
Lingford John, (wholesale) 9, Parliament st
Sherwood John, 12, Clumber st
Stanley John, Pelham st

Tatham Robert Serjeantson, 49, Bridlesmithgate
Wright James, South parade
(80.) JEWELLERS (WORKING.)
Band Robt. 7. Sheep lane
Doleman John, Middle pavmt
Rose Thos. (lipidary) ct. 21, St Mary's gate
Woodborough Thos. Peach st

(81.) JOINERS.
Marked 1 are Cabinet Makers. See also Builders.
1 Ashby Wm. Peach st
Atkin Thos. Sheridan st
Attenborough Geo. Trim ct
1 Atterbury Job, Rutland st
1 Bagshaw John, 7, Parliamnt. st
1 Barnsdall Edward, (and paper hanger) 39, Warsergate
Barnsdall Jph. 19, Warsergate
Bartram Saml. Coalpit lane
Bee Robt. Cherry st
Bell Thos. 18, Duke's place
Black & Lees, Houndsgate
Black John, 5, Broad st
Blatherwick Geo. Mansfield rd
Bott Saml. Brewhouse yd
Bull Geo. Mount East st
Burgess Geo. 19, Woolpack ln
1 Butler Rt. Derby road
1 Chiswell John, Drury hill
Collyer Saml. Coal court
Cooper J. Woolpack lane
Cox Rd. Old Glasshouse ln
1 Cullen Thos. 4, Parliament st
Dams John, Friar lane
1 Dennis Wm. 14, Fletchergt
1 Dennis Jas. Sneinton st
1 Drewry William and Benj. 17, Plumptre street
1 Eden Wm. Derby road
Elliott Thos. St. James's st
Ellis Wm. Goosegt. h. Pott's yd
England Geo. Coal court
Fann Wm. Byard lane
Fish & Stead, 33, Barkergate
Fish Thos. 33, Barkergate
Fisher Han. Parliament st
Flamson Thos. & Henry Walnuttree lane
Foster Thos. 5, Lincoln st
Gee Edw. Mount East st

Gelsthorpe Geo. Park row
Gelsthorpe Jph. Trumpet st
Glover Wm. Wheelergate
Goodson John, Wood's row, Canal street
Gould Thos. Nile row
Green & West, Derby road
Greenshield Dd. 29, York st
1 Greenwood Thos. Derby rd
Grundy Mary, Parliament st
1 Hallam John, Jph. & Thos. St. Peter's gate
Harmston John, Rick st
Hawley Hy. Martin's alley
Hickling Geo. 3, Clumber st
Holbrook Wm. Leenside, h. Grey Friar's gate
1 Hunter & Wyles, Bellargate
Lakin Thos. Angel row & Mount street
Lees Philip, Leenside
Lees Thos. Air yd. Mount st
1 Lees John, Newcastle st.
Littlewood Wm Carrington st
Marr Wm. High pavement
Millington Mattw. Broad st. h. Parliament street
Mosley Hy. 10, Woolpack ln
1 Newton Wm. Mount st
Nicholson Jas. Coalpit lane, h. East street
1 Nightingale Wm. Glasshouse st. h. Goosegate
Norton John, Broad marsh and Houndsgate
Pinder Wm. Mansfield road
Porter Hy. Crosland's yd. Canal street
1 Saxton Joshua, Listergate
1 Saxton Thos. Chesterfield st. h. Middle Pavement
Sharp Thos. Toll street
Shaw Wm. Hollowstone
Sheldon Wm. Mortimer st
1 Sheraton Ralph, Derby rd
Skerritt Francis, Pepper st. h. Chancery court
1 Smith Jas. 45, St. Marygate
Sparrow Jas. Mount street and Grosvenor place
1 Stainrod & Byfield, Derby rd
1 Stevens Isaac, Houndsgate
Stokes Geo. 22, Parliament st

Stoney and Clarke, H. Pavement
Swann Geo. Poplar place
Taylor John, Parliament row
1. Thornhill Wm. Kid street
Thurman John, Finkhill st
1 Toyne John, Milton st
1 Truswell Joseph, Mount st
Turner Edw. 18, East st
Walton John, Brook st
Ward & Allen, Star ct. St. James's
　street
Webster John, Derby rd
1 Wells Joseph, Plat st
1 Woodall John, Goosegate
Woodford David, 31, Broad st. h.
　20, Beck lane
Woolley Jas. 16, Beck lane
Wratt Geo. Pear st
Wratt Geo. Patriot st
1 Wright John, 3, George st
Wright Wm. Black Bull yd. and
　Woolpack lane

(82.) LACE DRESSERS.

Bacon & Elliott, Sherwood st
Baker Geo. Eyre street
Bentley Robt. ct 4, Parliament st
Birkhead John, Durham Ox yd
　and Houndsgate
Boot Gervase, Point court
Brown John, Mansfield road and
　Basford
Brown Wm. Commercial st
Crowder Jph. (silk lace dresser
　after the French manner) Mount
　Hooton
Hill Jane, Isabella st
Hill Robert, Mount st
Hudson & Bottom, Herbert st
Jacklin Thos. New Lenton
Lambert John, ct 9, Parliament st
Morris Ann, New Bridge st
Oastler Matthew, Melsonby pl
Parker Saml. Beck lane
Spencer, Harrison, & Co. Car-
　rington, and Finkhill st
Spittlehouse Wm. 7, Fletchergate
Taylor Benj. Sussex street
Taylor John, New Bridge st
Taylor Wm. Haughton st
Wain & Blackner, Canal st
Webster John, New Sneinton

(83.) LACE MFRS.

*Marked thus * make Purl and*

*Tatting, and thus † are Fancy
Warp Lace mfrs.
See also Bobbin Net mfrs.*

Adams & Morley, 9, Stoney st
Allcock Geo. 22, High Pavement,
　h. Short hill
Allen John & Sons, St. James's st
Ashwin James, Mount st
Astill Wm. Carrington
Aveson Stockdale, Mount street,
　h. Hyson green
Bacon Edw. & Son, Park row
*Baggaley Wm. Wheelergate
*Balm & Rothwell, (Mecklin and
　Tatting) Wheelergate. John
　Perry, agent
Banks Wm. 45, Stoney st
Barnett Lazarus C. Parliament st
Bees Bennet, 56, Coalpit lane
Berrey Geo. & Co. 13, St. Ma-
　ry's gate
Bingham Archelaus & James, St.
　James's street
Blatherwick John, (caps) Car-
　rington street
Boden James, Houndsgate
Boden & Morley, Houndsgate
Boot Cyrus G. 3, Plumptre st
Boot Francis, St. James's street
　and Beeston
Bowley Wm. & Son, Standard hill
Bradley Geo. & Son, Park st
Bramley Thos. Rutland st
Broadhurst John, Castlegate
Brothwell Wm. H. Mount st
Brough Edw. Pelham st
Burge James, Derby road
Burton John C. 16, Pilchergate
Burton Saml. New Bridge st
Butt Thos. Mount street
Callow Chas. (& quilling) St.
　James's street
Campbell James, Fletchergate
Campbell M. 26, Fletchergate
Carey Geo. 12, St. Mary's gate
　and Pelham st
Carrier Henry, ct 33, Long row
Carter & Cheetham, 22, High
　Pavement
*Carter Wm. Brown (and fast
　purled gimp thread edging)
　Rutland street
Castle Cath. Middle hill

Chambers Benj. (caps) Newcastle street
Chamberlain Mallet & Co. 9, Stoney street
Chambers John, 27, St. Mary's gt
Christie Hector, Cumberland pl
Clark John, 8, Warsergate
Clark Thos. 9, Warsergate, h. Broughton Lodge
Cooper Thos. 18, Broad st
Copestake Marcus, 5, Plumptre st, h. Mount Hooton
Cox Chas. 29, High Pavement, h. Wilford
Cullen Thos. & Jas. 21, Pilchergate, h. 2, Parliament st
Curtiss Thos. 26, High Pavement
Dakeyne Jph. Park st. & Lenton
Desmed John & Co. St. Petergt
Dodson Nathaniel, Park st
Doubleday Thos. St. James's st
Duclos & Caron, Potter's yard, Warsergate
Dunnington Hy. 25, Parliament street
Edensor Wm. et 24, H. Pavement
Elvidge Agnes, Castlegate
Etherington & Duplex, Byard ln
Fishers & Robinson, 11, Short hill
Flewitt Wm. Parliament st
Foote Robt & Co. 20, Stoney st, h. Scotholm Lodge
Frearson & Hovey, 32, St. Mary's gate
Frearson & Vickers, Castlegate
Frost Rt. & Thos. & Co. Wheelergate
Galloway Wm. & Co. Houndsgt
Gedling Micah & Son, Mount st
Gilbert James, Parliament st
Gimson Thos. F. Parliament st
Gray Rd. St. James's st
Green Wm. (caps) Clare st
Gregory Thos. St. James's st
Haimes Thos. & Co. Mount st
Hall Henry, Houndsgate
Hall James, Castlegate
Hardwick Fras. & Co. Pepper st
Hart Newcomb, 14, George st
Heathfield & Cartledge, 20, Stoney street
Heathcoat & Co. 46, Bridlesmith-

gate & Tiverton. Wm. Felkin, agent
Henson John, Babbington st
* †Herbert Wm. (purl & tatting) St. Mary's pl, h. Park
* †Herberts & Sneath, 17, Greyhound yd
Hind John, Standard hill
Hind Thos. & Co. 17, St. Marygt
Holbrook Jas. N. Houndsgate
Hollins Saml. Houndsgate
Hopkins John, 19, Pilchergate
Howitt John, Houndsgate
Hubbart Hy. 26, George st
Hughes Jno. & Co. St. James's st
Hurst Saml. 35, St. Mary's gt
Jerram Jas. St. James's st
Jerram John T. Halifax pl
Johnson Rt. 11, Warsergate
Johnson Geo. 25, Stoney st
Jones & Dent, 27, Pilchergate
Kaye Thos. 18, Bridlesmithgate
Kelk Jas. Burrows, Houndsgate
Kendall Geo. Kendal street, h. Walnut tree lane
Kendall John, Postern st
Kimber Jas. & Co. H. Pavement
Kulp H. N. & Son, Houndsgate
* Lamb Jph. 45, Stoney st
Leaver Hy. 37, Stoney street, h. St. Mary's gate
Leevers Wm. Rutland st
Lightfoot Rt. Mount st, h. Derby terrace
Lowe Chas. & John, Houndsgt
M'Coul David, Toll st, h. 38, Stoney street
M'Donald John, Tollhouse hill
Manlove Thos. & Son, 16, St. Mary's gate
* Middleton Saml. 7, Plumptre st
†Morrison Jthn. Fell, (caps) Newcastle street
†Morrison Geo. & Co. 5, St. Mary's gate, h. White moor
Morrison & Jenks, 27, Warsergt
Mullen Jthn. & Co. Mount st
Needham Matthew, 14, Sheep-ln
Newball & Copeland, Mount st
Nichols Edwin, 39, St. Mary's gt
Oram John & Wm. 3, King's pl. & Chard, Somersetshire
Page Joh. & Sons, Standard hill

Pearson Jas. Rutland st
Peat Edw. Granby street
Peet & Co. Houndsgate
Perry Joshua B. 14, H. Pavement
Pogson Geo. Owen, St. James's st
Polak D. M. & Co. Granby st
Ragg Thos. 17, Woolpack ln
Rawlinson G. & Co. 31, H. Pavement & Taunton
Reinbeck Frederick, Castlegate
Renshaw, Shelton, & Co. 11, High Pavement
Rideout Hy. Geo. Rutland st
Roberts Thos. & Co. 18, Plumptre street
Robinson Saml. 16, Clumber st
Robinson Saml. 15, Plumptre st
Roe Thos. & Co. Rutland st
Rogers Stephen Stevenson, Houndsgate
Saalfeld A. J. Parliament street and *Hambro'*
Sands Robert, Houndsgate
Sansom Saml. 8, King's pl
Seals John, 4, Plumptre st
Seals Robt. Plumptre st, h. 5, King's place
Selby Wm. Houndsgate
Shaw Thos. 39, Stoney st
Shipman Thos. 9, Chapel bar
Skipwith & Atherstone, 1, Bell founder's yd
Slater Thos. St. Peter's gate
Smedley Thos. & Jph. Rutland st
Smith Job, St. James's st
Spears John, Houndsgate
Spencer Chas. 2, Fletchergate
Stevenson John, Cheapside
Stevenson Moses, 10, Parliament street
Swanwick John, Houndsgate
Taylor Mary, Buttery's yd, Long row
Theaker & Birkhead, Rutland st
Train & Wesson, (tulle, &c.) Mount street
Trueman Dd. & Co, 74, Long row
Turner Jas. (tatting) Glasshouse street
Turner Geo. J. 3, Stoney st
Turner Saml. 20, Warsergate
Wakefield & Smith, Halifax pl
Walker Joseph, Houndsgate

Walker Wm. 38, St. Mary's gate
Wardle & Brown, 18, Pilchergt
Wardle Isaac & Co. 18, Pilchergate, h. 37, St. Mary's gate
Watson Wm. Pennell's yard, h. Daybrook
Watts Edw. Castle road
Waynman & Nunn, Bottle ln
Webster Hammond, 6, Plumptre street
Wesson John, 12, Plumptre st
Wesson Thos. Rutland st
Wheatley & Riste, South parade & Leicester. J. S. Whitlark, agent
Whitchurch John & Co. St. James's street
White Joseph, Castlegate
Whitfield Geo. Castlegate
Whitlock Matthew & Co. Park st
Whitt John, St. James's st
Widdowson & Robinson, Standard hill
Wild John, (tulle) Houndsgate
Wildsmith Joseph, Houndsgate
Wilmott John, 8, Plumptre st
Wolff Wm. & Co. Chandler's ln
Wood Wm. Wheelergate corner
Woodhouse Thos. & Co. 13, Fletchergate
Woolley Isaac, Castlegate
*Woolley John, 21, Beck lane
Wright & Trivett, 27, St. Mary's gate
Yates Geo. 36, St. Mary's gate

LACE THREAD DLRS.
See Cotton Spinners, p. 232.

(84.) LACE SINGERS.
Cook John, 6, Woolpack lane
Hallam Jph. Woolpack lane
Hickling John, Crosland st
Newell Wm. 42, Barkergate

(85.) LACE PATTERN DE-SIGNERS & STAMPERS.
Conduit Wm. Tree yard
Dutton Thos. Bedford st
Fitzwalter Joseph, Houndsgate
Holmes Thos. Mount East st
Jephson Henry, Houndsgate
Lightfoot John, Mount st
Mather John, Holland st
Tomlinson Jno. Dot yd, Listergt

(86.) LAND & BUILDING SURVEYORS.

Barnsdall Jph. 19, Warsergate
Campbell Thos. Alex. ct. 39, ↑ Long row
Dudley Wm. Pelham st
Elliott Fdk, 29, Warsergate
Hickling Geo. 3, Clumber st
Lees James, Rutland st
Surplice Sam. Herrick, Parliament st
Surplice Wm. 2, Clumber st
Walker Geo. Fdk. Derby rd
Warsop Thomas, Pepper st
Wood Hy. Moses, Park st

(87.) LAW STATIONERS.

Goodall Isaac, Castlegate
Roe, Thos. 2, Beck lane

(88.) LEAD MERCHANTS.

Cox, Poyser, and Co. (and Patent Shot) Butcher st. and Derby
Gray Robt. (and Glass) Canal st

(89.) LIBRARIES—(CIRCULATING.)

Artizan's—Smity row, open from 7 to 9 evening. V. Kirk, Librarian
Beastall, Thos. Rutland st
Belfit Hannah, Drury hill
Britton Eliz. Portland pl
Clerical & Medical.—John Staveley, 1, Smithy row
Dearden Wm. 3, Carlton st
Duckworth George, Pelham st
Fisher Mary, Parliament st
Kirk Thomas, St. Peter's gate
Morrison Mary Ann, Narrow marsh
Robertson James, 7, East st
Smith and Haslam, Greyhound yd
Subscription.—Bromley House, Angel row.—Mr. Jas. Archer, Librarian
Wright Chpr: Norton, 50, Long row

(90.) LINEN AND WOOLLEN DRAPERS.

*Those marked * are Silk Mercers, and † are Linen Drapers only.*
Alliott and Pepper, South parade
Atkin James (wholesale) South street
Bailey Thomas, South Parade

Brewster George, High street
Brewster, Wm. South parade
Cave Thomas, Hockley
Chatterton John Hocker, 11, Clumber st
Churchill Charles 41, Long Row
*Cooke & Farmer, 56, Long row
Corner Robert Cur lane
*Cullen Henry, 38, Long row
Cullen Samuel, 49, Long row
Dickinson Mary, Long row
Doubleday Josha. (smock frocks) Bottle lane
Edwards Thomas. 3, Timber hill
Fowler Geo. & Co. 14, Exchange
Hazard Geo. 42, Long row
Helmsley and Pick, 6, Poultry
Hepworth Frdck. South Parade
Hoe Thomas, Hockley
Hubbert Thos. Pelham st
†Hudson Wm. Castlegate
Jardin Andrew. Houndsgate
†Jennings Geo. 58, Bridlesmithgate and Pelham st
Knight Thos. 33, Long row
Ledlie John, (Irish Linen Whs.) Broad march
Levick Robert, South parade
*Manlove Ebz. 59, Long row
Marriott and Munk (wholesale Manchester and Scotch whs.) St. James's st
Musson Thomas, 72, Long row
Need Nath. Peniston, 51, Long r
*Oldershaw John. 52, Long row
Oldknow and Wilson, Beastmarket hill
Preston Richard, 47, Long row
Pyatt Abraham, South parade
Reynolds and Woodhouse (woollen) 13, Clumber st
†Rogers Abraham Isaac, South parade
Smith Wm. Jas. Mansfield rd
Swann and Son, 43, Long row
Thorpe William, 31, Long row
Toplis Thomas, Pelham st
Toplis Wm. 2, Timber hall
*Townsend & Daft, 69, Long row
Wells and Burkitt, Cheapside
Wilson and Cutts, South parade
Wright and Harriman, 5, Poultry

(91.) LIVERY STABLE KEEP-
ERS, &c.

*Thus * are also Horse' Dealers,
and thus † have Hackney Coaches.*

Chester John, 6, Friar lane, Castle place

*Chester Wm. St. Peter's sq
†Glew John, Goosegate
†King John, Castlegate
†Ouseley Thos. John, Castlegate
*Spink Mark, Wheelergate
Wigginton Jph. Friar lane

(92.) MACHINE MAKERS.

*See also Bobbin & Carriage, and
Circular Comb & Bolt Makers,
and Frame smiths.*

Abbott John, Newcastle st
Booth John, 7, Rigley's yd
Corah Thos. Mansfield rd
Creswell Chpr. Mansfield rd
Creswick John, (dealer, springer
and repairer) 15, Sheep lane
Fletcher Saml. (dealer, repairer,
&c.) Mansfield rd
Hall Wm. 15, Pennell's yd
Higgins & Wharton, (and Steam
Engine bldrs. and Mill smiths)
Canal st
Holland Saml. Chandler's lane
Kidger & Topham, Sherwood st
Lingford John, 9, Parliament st
Nelson Abm. B. Holland st
Nutt James, Broad st
Price Thomas, Canal st
Pritchard Thomas, Castle terrace
Rawson and Barraclough, Wool-
pack ln
Watts Geo. Finkhill st
Whitehall Thos. Batkin, (Drum
and Engine) 10, Grey Hound
yard
Woodhouse Dd. 42, Barkergate
Wyre Isaac, Howard st
Yeomans John, Duke pl
Young Saml. Mansfield rd

(93.) MALTSTERS.

Allcock John, 4, Bond street,
Sneinton
Anncliff Rd. Mansfield rd
Barker Jas. Taft's yard
Beadles John, Narrow marsh
Carver Thomas and Son, South
street, N. S.

Clay James, Coalpit lane
Clay Wm. York street
Cox John, 31, Warsergate
Cross Henry, Long row
Dennis Jph. Mansfield rd
Dann Geo. Narrow marsh
Deverill and Co. Pelham st
Dennis Jph. Mansfield rd
Ely Thomas, Parliament st
Farrand John, Listergate
Flinders Wm. Fishergate
Galloway Thos. 16, Milton st
Hall and Harrison, Canal st
Hamtson Ben. 9, Plumptre st
Harrison John, Sneinton st
Harvey Geo. Canal street and
Sneinton
Hewitt James, Park row
Hooton Richard, Fishergate
Hopkinson Richd. Castlegate, h.
Park st
Hoyles John, Chapel bar
Hustwayte Dymock, Cartergate
James Samuel, Sunhill
Johnson Charles, Postern place
Kendall Rd. and Co. St. James's
street
Langford Thomas, Grey Friarsgt
Leavers and Smith, Canal st
Lowe John, Angel row
Mackley and Maltby, Poplar pl
Oakland Jph. Parliament st
Pailthorp Wm. Milton st
Perry Jph. Peck lane
Pilkington Thos. H. Cross st
Pratt John, 54, Bridlesmithgate
Rollett Joshua, Mansfield rd
Rowarth Wm. London rd
Seals Robert, Plumptre st
Shelton Robert, Milton st
Smith George, 23, George st
Stubbs Thomas, Peck lane
Tallant Jane, Crown and Anchor
yard, Bridge st
Thorpe John, Pelham st
Tomlin Edmund, Dean street, h.
Carrington
Turner Geo. 3, Barkergate
Tyers John, 5, Bell Founder's
yard and Newcastle st

(94.) MATTING MANUFRS.

Smith James, St. Peter's gate
Smith Wm. Manver's st.

(95.) MATTRESS AND BED
MAKERS.
Detheick John, Sussex st
Odam Hannah, Talbot yd
Stone Thomas, Gedling st
(96.) MERCHANTS.
† See Lace and Hosiery Mfrs.
Antonin Dinoyel, High Pavement
Bishop James and Thomas, St.
Peter's sq
Bishop Thos. jun. St. Peter's sq
Fishers and Robinson, 11 Short
hill
Fry Wm. (fruit, &c.) Lincoln st
Kulp, H. N. & Son, (lace) Hounds
gate
Parker and Kirk, Maypole yd
Renshaw, Shelton, and Co. 11,
High Pavement
Wilson W. & S. Plumptre house
(97.) MILLINERS & DRESS
MAKERS.
Allen Mary Ann, Brewhouse yd
Almond Eliz. St. Peter's Church-
side
Anderson Eliz. Glasshouse st
Ashley Eliz. Mount st
Baldock Mary Ann, 6, Cannon
yard
Barber Mary Ann, Newcastle st
Beastall and Fryer, Pleasant pl
Binkley Emma, Parliament st
Black, Elizabeth, Castlegate
Blatherwick Ann, ct. 26, Clum-
ber st
Borrows Eliz. Coalpit ln
Bradbury Hh. 13, Lenton st
Broomhead and Kelsall, Angel yd
Bordicot Mary, Collin st
Brough Mrs, (upholsterer) Flet-
chergate
Brown A. & J. ct. 39, Long row
Brown Hanh. and Eliz. Catlegate
Burton Mary, Goosegate
Byrne Mary, Angel row
Carter Henriette, Clinton st
Cropper Hanh. Chandler's ln
Charge Thos. (child bed linen,)
23, Carlton st
Cartwright Eliz. St. Jame's st
Crisp Sarah and Mary, Listergt
Chatterton Ruth, 11, Clumber st
Crowther Mary W. Houndsgate

Davison Mary Ann, Park st
Doubleday Jane, Carrington st
Drage Mary, Pelham st
Ellis Mary, Clare st
Evans Sarah, 9, Bridlesmithgate
Foster Eliz. Postern place
Garratt S. 10, Plumptree st
Green Mary Ann, Buttery's yd
Henson C. Babbington st
Hall Sarah, Castlegate
Harvey Ann, Parliament row
Hayes Maria, Grosvenor pl
Hickling Eliz. Mansfield rd.
Holland Mary, Castlegate,
Hovey Harriet, Derby rd
Holmes Sarah, Friar lane
Hunt and Parsons, St. Peter's sq
Hodges Mary Ann, Carrington st
Hodges Mary, Houndsgate
Howard Mary, Spaniel row
Jardine H. 6, Haughton pl
Kirby Mary, 30, Greyhound yd
Kirk Jane, 20, Barkergate
Lane S. and M. 56, Barkergate
Linecar Sarah, 14, Greyhound yd
Lindley Martha, Wheelergate
Lloyd Ann, 32, Warsergate
Lomas Jane, 16, Mansfield ter
Marple Sarah, 24, Clumber st
Milner Ann, Glasshouse st
Morley Mary and Hannah, Lis-
tergate
Morris A. and E. Beck lane
Morrison Eliz. 27, Bridlesmithgt
Myres M. and A. Chesterfield st
Newton Mary Ann, Mount st
Ordoyno Eliz. Castle terrace
Parsons Mary, Line alley
Pattenden Eliz. St. James's st
Peet Mary Ann, Rutland st
Peet Mary Woolpack lane
Place Mary, Beastmarket hill
Porter Rebecca, Brook street
Pratt Mary, 40, Stoney st
Redgate Ann, Mount st
Ramshaw Emma, Sneinton st
Rigby M. & S. Beck lane
Roberts Mary Ann, Canal st
Robinson Eliza, Park st
Robertson M. High pavement
Savidge Eliz. Derby road
Saunders Cath. Cheapside and
Houndsgate

Scott Emery &. Mary,. Castlegate
Sharpin Elizabeth,. Mount st
Shaw Eliz. 37, Warsergate
Shore Cath. 2, Parliament st
Skidmore J. & H, Castlegate
Smart Catherine, Broad marsh
Smith Frances, Bridge st
Smith Martha, Grosvenor pl
Stretton Sarah,. Spaniel row
Teale M. 12, Bridlesmithgate
Thompson & Wilkinson, Park st.
Thornton Eliz. Mount East st
Tinkler Ann, 32, Warsergate
Tow & Wootton, Castlegate
Urry & Fry. 24, Parliament st
Wain Harriet, Castle terrace
Waite Jane, Holland st
Walker Mary, Derby road
Ward Sarah, St. Peter's gate
Wass Mary, Parliament st
Watson Mrs. Rt. Clinton st
Webb & Palmer, ct. 47, Bridle-
. smithgate
Wheeldon Eliz. 13, George st
White Mary, Houndsgate
Whittle & Butler, 22, Carlton st
Wilkinson Eliza, Derby road
Woolley Mary, Sussex st
Wright Eliz. 8. Greyhound yd

(98.) MILLWRIGHTS.

Constable Wm. New Radford
Howard Saml. Derby road
Reddish Samuel, Beck st

(99.) MUSIC SELLERS.

See also Professors.

Allsop John & William, Peter's
Church side
Garland Wm. (& tuner) I' Clum-
ber street
Owencroft Jph. (& tuner) 26,
Long row
Woolley Thomas, Wheelergate

(100.) NAIL MAKERS.

Aston Elias, 33, Greyhound yd
Bennett John, Wheat Sheaf yd
Copeland Jeremiah, (cut) Toll
house hill
Jackson John, Narrow marsh
Sidney John (& screw) Pelham st
Starr Samuel, Canal st
Taylor John, Toll house hill
Wood Edward, Canal st
Wood Samuel, Canal st

(101.) NEEDLE MAKERS.

Marked thus . also make Points,
Guides, &c.*

Arnes Robert, Sinker alley
Battersley Samuel, 52, Barkergt
Berwick John, Salmon yd
Bradfield John, Bond st
Brooks Wm. Long stairs
Burrows Josiah, Nicholas st
* Chadwick J. L. Talbot yd
Church Benj, Ten Bells yard
Clark Richard, Beck st
Dickisson George, South st
Fowkes John, 5, Greyhound yd
Gibbons Wm. Union place
Gibson Fredk. Cross st
Goodhead Geo. Horse Shoe yard,
Toll House Hill
Goodwin Frances, Wright's yard,
Gedling st
Hall Clay, Cross st
Hefford Wm. East street
Hickton Wm. Robin Hood yard
Hammonds Jph. Chesterfield st
* Hopewell Thos. 20, Beck lane
James John, Cartergate
Lorriman Geo. Pomfret st
Maxfield Jph. Charlotte st
Milner Frdk. Glass house st
Milner Jas. Goosegate
Mortimer Jph. Mount East st
Newton Isaac, Cross st
Randall Thos. Coalpit lane
Rayner George, 7, Greyhound yd
Roper Wm. 9, Mansfield terrace
Saxby Jas. Mansfield road
Sewell Samuel, Marsden's court,
Sussex st
Sheldon Wm. Broad marsh
Shipman John, Derby road
Smith Hy. 4, Charlotte st
Stanley Wm. Mansfield road
*Stevenson John, Commerce row
Stokes George, Duke's place
Tomlinson John, Howard st
Tomlinson Wm. 19, Lenton st
Truman Sarah, Derby road
Ward Saml. 12, West st
Wheatley Wm. Carter row
*Whittington Robt. Hockley
Whitworth Benj. King st
Wild Wm. Broad marsh
Wood Wm. Beck st

Yeomans Saml. Cherry place

(102) NEWSPAPERS.

Journal, (Friday mg.) Geo. Streton, 64, Long row

Mercury, (Saturday mg.) Jonth. Dunn, South Parade

Review, (Friday mg) Rd. Sutton, Bridlesmithgate

(103.) NURSERY & SEEDSMEN.

Daft Rd. Beskwood park

Lee Wm. (Florist) Lenton

Pearson John, 15, Exchange row, and Chilwell (attds. Wed.& Sat)

(104.) OPTICIANS & MATHL. INSTRUMENT MAKERS.

Myers Philip, Pelham street

Pagani Anthy. 15, Greyhound yd

(105.) PAINTERS—HOUSE, SIGN, &c.

Allen John, Narrow marsh

Armston Danl. St. Michael's row

Armston Thomas, 7, Hazard's yd

Austin Danl. King street

Barnsdall John Spensley, 44, Bridlesmgt. h. Mount Vernon

Barratt John, High pavement

Bretland Peter & Thos. (& gilders) Chandler's lane

Cubley Saml. Parliament st

Dikes Geo. (& glazier) Tradesmen's mart

Dodsley Wm. Parliament st

Elliott John Jeffery, Bridge st

Fox James, Glass house street

Gell Wm. Coalpit ln

Hague James, St. Jame's st

Hague Wm. Houndsgate

Hamerton Wm. Narrow marsh

Holland Saml. Vernon st

Jennings Thos. 41, Warsergate

Kirby Thos. 30, Greyhound yard

Lacy Jas. Parliament street

Lees Hy. 3, Clumber street, and Mansfield road

Lloyd Thos. 33, Warsergate

Marshall Geo. 7, Stoney st

Marshall Wm. Goosegate

Neaves Geo. Needle place

Oxley Sus. Maria & Co. Houndsgate

Pegg Jas. Mount East st

Perkins Edward, (Bronzer) Derby road

Pocklington Wm. Coalpit lane

Read Wm. 24, Broad st

Scrimshaw Joseph, Parliament st

Shepperd Wm. Houndsgate

Shipham Benj. ct. 33, Long row

Sissling Jph. Drury hill

Sparrow Jas. & Son, 17, Long row

Steele Wm (& gilder) 48, Clare street

Stretton Saml. Milton street

Walker Isaac, (job) Paradise st

Walls Geo. Chesterfield st

Whitmore Thos. Cartergate

Wood Math. Mount st. & Angel row

(106.) PAPER WAREHOUSES.

Allen Jas. Roger, St. Jame's st

Dowson Ralph, St. Peter's gate

Leighton John, Lincoln st

Hockney John, (paper hangings) 7, Haughton st

Nelson Thos. (Wm. Robinson agent) 9, Poultry

Wells Wm. 9, Clumber st

(107.) PATTEN AND CLOG MAKERS.

Alvey Wm. Drury hill

Barwick Jas. Goosegate

Holmes Wm. Listergate

Goodwin Thos. Goosegate

Thornton Joseph, (& ring) 26, Bridlesmithgate

Thorpe Jph. (& ring) St. Peter's square

(108.) PAVERS.

Fido, Tetley, & Taylor, Holland street

Squires John, Holland st

(109.) PAWNBROKERS.

Marked thus 1 *are Dealers in Silver Plate*

Cooke Hannah, Goosegate

1 Denner John, 73, Long row

1 Eames Fras. Goosegate

Gresham Wm. Middle pavement

Hartwell Robert, 71, Long row

Lock and Gresham, Angel row

Reynolds and Woodhouse, 13, Clumber street

Sibley Wm. Beck street

Travel George, 22, Long row

Wallace Saml. 30, Bridlesmithgt
Wickham Jph. & Wm. Goosegt

(110.) PERFUMERS, &c.
See also Hair Dressers.

Allen Thos. Peck lane
Bombroff Thos. Houndsgate
Bunting Adam, Chapel bar
Clarke Richard, 20, Long row
Corbett & Warner, 2, High st
Crofts John, 70, Long row
Drover Joshua, 58, Long row
Emblow Chas. 36, Long row
McArthur Thos. Bridlesmithgt
Wragg Charles, Pelham st

(111.) PERIODICAL PUB-
LISHERS.

Brown Geo. Mansfield road
Clarkson Geo. Pennyfoot lane
Goldsmith Jacob, Rutland st
Mercer Rd. Chapel bar
Pacey Wm. Bellargate
Robinson Jas. 18, Barkergate

(112.) PHYSICIANS.

Blake Andrew, Parliament st
Davidson John Mitchell, Wheel-
ergate
Howitt Godfrey, High pavement
Hutchinson Rd. Scholes, Friar ln
Manson Alex. 24, Stoney st
Marsden William, Wheelergate
Payne Henry, Castlegate
Pigot John, M. B. St. James's st
Williams J. Calthrop, Rose place

(113.) PIPE MAKERS.

Derbyshire Jas. 12, East st
Derbyshire James jun. 7, St.
Mary's gate
Edwards Thos. Old Glasshouse
lane
Henson Lucy, High Cross st
Langford John Wyer, Boot ct

(114.) PLANE MAKER.

Hields Wm. Parliament street

(115.) PLASTER MANUFAC-
TURERS.

Fothergill Jas. & John, Canal st
Leavers & Smith, Canal st
Lewis Jph. & Rd. Canal st

(116.) PLASTERERS AND
STAINERS.

Elliott Fdk. 29, Warsergate
Hames Joseph, Pepper st
Ingram Valentine, 6, Pilchergate

Spurr Rd. 36, Warsergate
Surplice Wm. Clumber st
Martin Geo. Roe, St. Peter's sq
Walker John & Saml. Derby rd

(117.) PORK BUTCHERS.

Haines Wm. 51, Bridlesmithgate
Hukman J. Middle hill
Tansley Ann, Coalpit lane
Maltby Joseph, 6, Chapel bar
Marchington John, Carrington st
Pearson Charles, Hockley

(118.) PLUMBERS AND
GLAZIERS.

Addicott Rd. Old Glass house ln
Askew Wm. Milton st
Attenborough Rd. Pepper st
Bilbie John, York st
Briggs John Boyd, Castlegate
Cook Samuel, Market street
Crackle Wm. 10, Parliament st
Cullen Richard, Clare st
Dickinson Thos. Beck st
Dunnicliff Atton, Houndsgate &
Parliament street
Flewitt Saml. Bridlesmithgate
Gell Saml. Middle marsh
Goodson Jas. 10, Broad st
Gunn Saml. Derby road
Hirst John, Dot yd. Listergate
Jackson John, Goosegate
Langton John, Butler's ct. Nar-
row marsh
Maidens Wm. Fishergate
Nix Thomas, Mount st
Parley Daniel, Fletchergate
Rawson Thos. 19, Carlton st
Roberts Rd. Crown ct. Long row
Smith Wm. New Bridge st
Sollory James, 22, Bridlesmithgt
Sollory Henry, Postern place
Stephenson Geo. Sneinton st
Stevenson & Rhodes, Wheelergt
Towle Mark, St. James's st
Walker Wm. 29, Carlton street
Whitworth Richard, Clare st
Whitworth Thos. Surplice (and
painter) Hollow stone

(119.) PORTER, &c MER-
CHANTS.

Attenborough Hy. South parade
Cutts Hanb. Canal st
Deverill and Co. (brewers of ale
and porter,) Pelham st

Lewis, Jph. and Rd. Canal st
Perry John, Wheelergate
(120.) PRESERVERS OF BIRDS
 AND BEASTS.
Jones Thomas, Beck lane
Mellow James, Fishergate
Roberts Thomas, Finkhill st
Yates Geo. Holland st
 (121.) POULTERERS.
 See Fishmongers.
Parr Samuel, Pelham st
(122.) PRINTERS(*Letter Press*)
 See also Booksellers, &c.
Dawson Ralph, Chandler's lane
Hopkinson Rt. Mount East st
Ordoyno Wm. Cross st. Mount
 East street
Shaw Jph. St Mary's place
Waterson John, Rose yard
Westwick Rt. Back lane
Wheelhouse Thos. Newcastle st
Wild Henry, Rutland st
 (123.) PROFESSORS AND
 TEACHERS.
Aspul W.(Organist of St Mary's,
 & professor of singing, & piano
 forte) High pavement
Allsop John & Wm. (music) St.
 Peter's Church side
Alliott Wm. (languages) Castle
 gate
Bond Hy. (organist) 1, Bond st
De Lasalle Henry Pole (French)
 Park street
Fryett Mrs. William, (dancing)
 Castlegate
Garland Wm. (music) 1, Clum-
 ber street
McNamara Michl. (music) Castle
 terrace
Owencroft John, (dancing) Park
 hill
Owencroft Jph. (music) 25, Long
 row
Quick Edw. (dancing & painting)
 Park street
Thirlwall John (music) Park st
Wilkinson Mary Ann (piano) 44,
 Stoney st
Woolley Thos. (music) Wheeler-
 gate
 (124.) RAG MERCHANTS.
Ashling Jane, Glasshouse st

Dodd David, (& bone) Narrow
 marsh
James Rt. Gedling street
Leighton John, Lincoln street
Smalley John & Son, Beck st
Walker Mtw. Woolpack lane
(125a.) REGISTER OFFICES.
Africanus Geo. Chandler's ln
Chester Wm. St. Peter's square
Fletcher Wm. Tollhouse hill
Husband Rd. Goosegate
 (125.) ROPE AND TWINE
 MAKERS.
Allen Hugh, Milton st
Brookhouse Jph. Needle place
Godber Esther, Parliament st
Haynes Geo. 17, York st
Simpson Wm. Parliament st
Taylor Barnabas, Parliament st
Taylor John, Mansfield road
(126.) SADDLERS & HAR-
 NESS MAKERS.
Andrew John, Listergate
Betts Thos. Low Pavement
Bradwell Thos. Canal st
Caddick John, 14, Milton st
Creeke Wm. Woollard, 14, Pel-
 ham st
Hardy & Mallett, 68, Long row
Hogg Robert, Canal st
Holmes Wm. Cartergate
Nelson Thos. Milton st
Place John, sen. Cheapside
Place John, jun. Beast market
 hill
Radnall Chas. 8. Sheep lane
Ward Eliz. Hockley
(127.) SAIL CLOTH & SACK-
 ING MANUFACTURERS.
Millington Thos. & Co. (& sail)
 Canal st
Tomlinson Thos. Portland place
(128.) SCALE-BEAM & STEEL
 MILL MFR.
Leake Wm. 42. Woolpack lane
(129.) SEDAN CHAIRMEN.
Bamford Wm. Middle hill
Doubleday John, 21. Mary's gt
 (130.) SEED CRUSHER.
Barnsdall Nathl. Canal st
(131.) SETTERS UP OF MA-
 CHINERY.
Barraclough Thos. Broad st
 z

Dowker Richard, Narrow marsh
Elliott Leond, York st
Fletcher Saml. Mansfield road
Gildin Hy. 38, Woolpack lane
Goodburn Thos. Nob yard
Jefford John Parliament st
Notman John, Cross st
Notman Wm. Woolpack ln
(132.) SHERIFF'S OFFICERS.
*Marked * are for the Town, and
thus ‡ for the County.*
‡ Archer Wm. Castle terrace
* Cox Henry, Castlegate
* Gibson Wm. Houndsgate
‡ Ward Daniel, Parliament st
Wheatley John, (bailiff of the
Peveril court) 2, Lincoln st
(133.) SHOPKEEPERS.
*See also Cheese and Bacon Factors
and Bakers & Flour Dealers.*
Allen Ann, Crosland st
Allen John, St. James's st
Alvey Ann, Goosegate
Alvey Thos. Mansfield road
Asling John, St. Ann's st
Atkinson Mtw. Mount East st
Baines Thomas, Parliament st
Bartram Thos. St. Ann's st
Beck Charles, St. James's st
Bell John, Orchard st
Benson John, Bellargate
Bingham John, 37. York st
Blythe Saml. Newcastle st
Boldock Wm. Snienton st
Bradbury Matw. Mortimer st
Brammer John, Poplar place
Brookes John, (butter dlr.) 4,
Greyhound yard
Brown Samuel Gedling st
Burnham John, 44, Barkergate
Burrows Fras. Coalpit lane
Butterworth Saml. Glasshouse st
Campion John, Commercial st
Campion Robert, York st
Carver Fredk. Narrow marsh
Chester William, St. Peter's sq
Cholerton Ann, Parliament st
Clark Thos. Albion st
Clarke Hy. South st
Clark Roderic, Gedling st
Cliss Eliz. Milk st
Co-Operative Society, Thomas
Haddon, agent, Milton st

Cope Benj. Chandler's lane
Corner Rt. Cur lane
Culley Wm. New bridge st
Daft Emery, 20, Fletchergate
Dawson Henry, Sussex st
Dawson Thos. Newcastle st
Dexter Ann, Castlegate
Dodd David, Narrow marsh
Drayton Benj. Bellargate
Dutton Thos. Bedford st
Elliott Thos. St. James's st
Eve Thos. Herbert st
Farnworth Rt. Narrow marsh
Fell Thos. Grey Friar's gate
Fletcher John Bailey, Milk st
Forbes John, Water st
Gell Saml. Hollowstone
Gell Wm. Coalpit lane
Goodhead John, Trumpet st
Greaves Jas. Newcastle st
Green Ann, Glasshouse st
Gunn Mary, Isabella st
Greensmith Saml. Mount East st
Guest Bartholemew, Canal st
Harris Jph. Millstone ln
Hart Mary Ann, Old Glasshouse
lane
Hawthorne Wm. Finkhill st
Hawley Fras. Millstone lane
Hextall Sarah, Cross st
Higton Eliz. Parliament st
Hill Thomas, Parliament st
Hinks Wm. Narrow marsh
Hodgkinson John, Babbington st
Holland John, Middle marsh
Holroyd John, Newcastle st
Hopkinson John, Cross st
Hopkinson Thos. Derby road
Humphrey Thos. Beck st
King Wm. Parrott's place
Kirkby Thos. Finkhill st
Kitchen John, Sherwood st
Kitchen Rebecca, Parliament row
Kitchinman Eliza, St. John's st
Knight Rd. Cherry place
Latham Thos. (& corn roaster)
Middle marsh
Leavers Edward, Paul court
Leeson Wm. 3, Charlotte st
Lewis Thos. 28, Broad st
Loseby Wm. Simpson's pl
Lovitt Peter, 6, York st
Lowater Wm. Millstone lane

Mann Edwin, Eyre st
Marshall John, Edward st
Marshall Jph. Narrow marsh
Marshall Wm. Trent row
Mason Jas. Cartergate
Meadows Eliz. Broad marsh
Morley Robert, Paradise st
Morris Geo. Parliament st
Newbold Gervase. Charlotte st
Norman John, Derby rd
Nunnalee Wm. Pipe st
Palethorpe Mtw. 13, Plumptre st
Paulson Chas. Bellargate
Peet Edwin, Rutland st
Peet Ann, Sussex st
Pick Saml. Castle court
Pickard Jph. St. Ann's st
Pinder Eliz. Coalpit lane
Popple Benj. New bridge st
Porter Wm. 40, York st
Potts Benj. Pierrepont st
Poulter Rd. Narrow marsh
Price Jas. Parliament st
Prior John, 34, Woolpack lane
Raworth John, York st
Read Sarah, Beck st
Reavill Sarah, Parliament st
Reavill Fras. Water st.
Reckless Jonathan, Derby road
Riddell Melicent, Friar lane
Robinson Jas. 18, Barkergate
Robinson Jas. Cartergate
Rogers Saml. White st
Rowbottom John, Beck st
Seaton John, Narrow marsh
Sheldon Wm. Mortimer st
Shipham John, Coalpit lane
Simmons Eliz. Narrow marsh
Sims John, Mill st
Slack Mary, Beck st
Smith Abhm. Beck st
Snowden Hy. Gedling st
Snowden Thos. Rumford place
Spearing Ann, Maiden lane
Sprigg Benj. Snow hill
Squire Ann, Plat st.
Stanley Jas. 24, Barkergate
Stevenson Jas. Sussex st
Sulley Richard, Parliament st
Sutton Mary Ann, Rancliffe st
Taylor John, Broad marsh
Tebbutt Robt. Glasshouse st
horpe Geo. Trumpet st

Titterton Thos. 36, Barkergate
Walstow Jas. Millstone lane
Wells Thomas, Mount st
White Jas. 41, York st
Wilby David, Beck lane
Wildsmith Saml. Albion st
Wilkinson Eliz. Plat st
Williamson Wm. Canal st
Wills Benj. Houndsgate
Wilson John, Cartergate
Withers Frances, Mount st
Walden John, 9, George st
Wood Benj. Plat st
Wood Mary, Clare st
Woodhead John, Nile row

(134.) SILK THROWSTERS AND MERCHANTS.

Ashwell John Heard, (dlr.) St. James's st
Baker Wm. (dlr.) 6, King's place
Bean & Johnson, Clinton st
Fellows & Crosby, High Pavmnt
Lowe & Smith, (merts,) 23, Pilchergate
Rogers Jonthn. Pierrepont st S
Truswell & Heap, 7, Fletchergt

(135.) SILVERSMITHS AND JEWELLERS.

Marked thus † are Plated Measure, &c. Manufacturers.

Danks Isaiah & Thomas, Beastmarket hill
Driver Joshua, 58, Long row
Gresham William, Exchange
† Kitchen Thos. Derby road
Lazarus Isaac, Pelham st
† Powell Chas. Glasshouse st.
† Sheldon John, (& hardware) Parliament st
Sollory Jas. 22, Bridlesmithgate

(136.) SINKER MAKERS.

See also Framesmiths and Machine Makers.

Birkins John, Stone court
Bradbury John, Parliamet st
Elnor John, Parliament st
Howett Geo. 22, Parliament st
James Robt. Hart's pl
Johnson John, Vernon st
Leavers Everard, Earl st
Lenton Hy. Coalpit ln
Milnes John, 11, West st
Moore Wm. Derby road

Potter Samuel, Mount st
Smith Wm. Robin Hood's yd
Turner Wm. Toll st
Wells Jph. 17, New st
Woodward Saml. 24, Rice pl
(137.) SLATERS AND SLATE
MERCHANTS.
Fothergill Jas. and John, Canal st
Lewis Jph & Rd. Bath row wharf
Walker John and Sam. Derby rd
(138.) SMALLWARE DLRS.
Clarke Mary S. 32, Bridlesgt
Colton Jph. Mount East st
James Rt Gedling st.
Lamb Rd. South parade
Leighton John, Lincoln st
Page James & Sons, (cotton ball
&c. mfrs.) Maypole yard and
Drury hill
Watts Henry. 12, Chapel bar
(139.) STARCH MANUFAC-
TURER.
Hall Lawrence, Wheelergate and
Stanton-by-Dale
(140.) STAY MAKERS.
Alvey, Thos. Mansfield rd
Atkinson Geo. 28, Pilchergate
Clark Ann, Goosegt
Cockram John Wm. St. James's
street
Croley John. 2, Warsergate
Flether Wm. Tollhouse hill
Machin Eliz. 1, Greyhound yd
Mercer Richard (London whs.) 3.
Chapel bar
Pacey Thos. 50, Bridlesmithgate
Robinson Maria, Kingstone st
Slater James, Bridlesmithgate
Stafford Sarah, Mount ct
Vernham Ann, Coalpit ln
Wallis James, Peck lane
(141.) STOCKING PRINTERS.
M'Callum John, Canal st
(142.) STONE AND MARBLE
MASONS.
*Those marked * are Marble Ma-
sons.—See also Builders.*
Allen Thomas, Castle terrace
Booth John, Broad st. h. New
Sneinton
Brassington John, Mansfield rd
Clayson John. Carrington st
*Earnshaw Thos. Grey Friarsgate

Granger John, Tollhouse hill
Hall Jas. Ebrank, Hockley
Hastie Geo. Glasshouse st
Hawley and Cox, New st
Palethorpe Geo. Canal st
Peacock Thos. 14, Broad marsh
*Pratt Brothers, (& sculptures)
Leen bridge
Walker John & Saml. (& statu-
aries) Derby road
(143.) STRAW HAT MKRS.
Barnsdall M. 39, Warsergate
Belk Elizabeth, Cross st
Bigg Edw. (presser) 3, Lenton st
Cooke Eliz. Coalpit lane
Darkins Jno. (whs.) 13, Exchange
Deverill Mary, Hockley
Dick Mary, 31, York st
Dunnicliff Ann. 7, Parliament st
Else Eliz. 17, Bottle lane
Evans Sarah, 9, Bridlesmithgate
Fisher Ann. Pepper st
Fletcher Sarah, 59, Barkergate
Greensmith Mary, Back ln
Gregory Mary, Peter's church side
Harwood Isabella, Sneinton st
Hawkins Martha, Parliament st
Headley Louisa, Friar lane
Hodges Eliz. Houndsgate
Holburd Mary, 6, Lincoln st
Kemp Eliz. Sneinton st
Kennedy Cath. Drury hill
Marriott Eliz. Peter's church side
Mercer Rd. (plat whs.) 3, Chapel
bar
Meredith Thos. Angel row
Merrin Maria, Derby road
Nash Mary, 8, Mansfield terrace
Newton Eliz. Mount st
Parsons Wm. Cur lane
Pierce & Sanson, 9, Milton st
Richards Ann, Cartergate
Sands M. Drury hill
Simpson Sarah, Goosegate
Smedley C. 21, Carlton st
Teale Mary, 12, Bridlesmithgate
Waddington & Wilson, Narrow
marsh
Waite Eliz. Queen st
Walker Wm. 14, Carlton st
Ward Eliz. Water street
Wheatley Frances, Pleasant pl
Whittle Eliz. 18, Warsergate

(144.) SURGEONS.

Allen Thos. Listergate
Attenburrow Jno. Beastmkt. hill
Beveridge Thos. Market st
Butlin Jas. Low Pavement
Caunt John, ct. 66, Long row
Darby Augustus, Clinton st
Davison Rt. Peter's church side
Eddison Booth, (General Hospital) Postern st
Garner Rt. Dispensary, Goosegt
Greeves Augustus Fdk. Adolphus, Angel row
Higginbottom John, H. Pavement
Jarman John, Mdle. Pavement
Jowett Thos. Mdle. Pavement
Mann Stph. John, Derby rd
Oldknow & White, St. James's st
Sanderson Aymor Richard, 10, Carlton street
Truman Beckit, Plumptre sq
Valentine Wm. (St. Mary's workhouse) Mansfield rd
Walker Fdk. 38, St. Mary's gate
Watts Wm. 11, Smithy row
White Jph. 23, Warsergate
Wright John, 21, H. Pavement
Wright Wm. Pelham st

(145.) TAILORS AND HABIT MAKERS.

*Marked * are also Woollen Dprs. and † are Slopsellers – the rest are Tailors only.*

Addicott Thos. 7, Woolpack ln
Bailey Jas. Cartergate
*Baldwin Geo. Hollow stone
Ball Geo. 16, Sheep lane
Ball James, Poynton st
Barnett Wm. Miles Douthwaite, 42, Queen street
Bayley Wm. New Charles st
Bell Geo. 5, Hazard's yd
Bennett John, 5. Parliament st
*Beresford Rd. 2, Bridlesmithgt. h. Carrington
Berkins Mtw. Conven st
Berridge Fras. 14, Plumptre st
*Bradbury Thos. Wheelergate
*Burton Jph. 7, Chapel bar
*Bywater John & Jas. Carlton st
†Cantrell Thos. 5, Clumber st
Cheetham Geo. Grey Friar gate
Clarke John, 4, Parliament st

Codling Wm. Virginia st
Dawson Edw. Sussex st
Dooley Geo. ct. 39, Bridlesmith-gate
Edson Hy. Low Pavement
*Fearn John, Market st
*Finn David Bennett & Co. 74, Long row
*Finn Thos. 5, Clumber st
Fitzhugh John, Low Pavement
*Fleming Geo. 27, Carlton st
Foulkes John, Carter row
Gibbons Benj. Coalpit lane
Goldsmith Edw. Rutland st
Goodwin Wm. Hockley
Gore Arthur, Rice place
Gorse Wm. Ram yard
Greenberry John, Broad marsh
Grundy John, Beck st
Hall Edw. Rawson, Park st
Hardy John, 3, Huzard's yard
Harpham Wm. Toll street
Harrison Saml. 1, Lincoln st
Harvey Edw. Fountain pl
Harvey Thos. Parliament row
Hatton Wm. Buttery's yd. Long row
Holland Jas. Angel yard
Howard John, 2, Haughton st.
Howell Rd. Parliament st
Hutchinson John, Broad st
King Wm. 41, Woolpack lane
*Lacey Alex. St. James's st
Lamb John, Glasshouse st
Langstaff Thos. 4, Lincoln st
Lees John, Houndsgate
Lewis Thomas, Rutland ct
*Liverseege John, 13, Carlton st
Manderfield Jas. Carrington st
Manfull John, Mount East st
*Marple Jacob, 24, Clumber st
Mycroft Wm. ct 26, Clumber st
Newbold Chas. St. Peter's church yard & Peck lane
Newton Mark, Mount st
*Nightingale Rd. 9, High st
Norman Wm. Harris place
*Owen Samuel, Cheapside
Palmer Wm. Cross st
*Parker John, 16, Carlton st
Peach Hy. Newcastle st
*Philps Geo. 15, Bridlesmithgate
Pigott John, Parliament st

z 2.

Press Thos. Mansfield road
Ragsdale Rd. Listergate
Richards Abm. Parliament st
Roper John Narrow marsh
Rouse John, Derby road
Scrimshaw Saml. Sussex st
Scott Matthew, Convent st
*Sharp John, Wheelergate
Sharp Geo. Chapel bar
*Slater Jas. 40, Bridlesmithgate
*Stagg Wm. 24, Bridlesmithgate
Stubbins Chas. & Co. Mount
   East street
Taylor Geo. 18, Low Cross st
Taylor Jas. Glasshouse st
Timms Thos. Beastmarket hill
Wadsworth Wm. 21, George st
†Walker Jph. Fishergate
*Wallis Jas. Peck lane, h. Not-
   tingham terrace, Park
Warburton & Astle, 30, War-
   sergate
Ward Isaac, Goosegate
*Ward John & Rd. Angel row
Whait John. Exchange court
Whait John, jun. Mount ct
White Wm. Portland place
Window Rt. Mount East st
Wolden John, 9, George st

(146.) TALLOW CHNDLRS.
Baldock Wm. Hockley
Barber J. H. Hollow stone
Beardmore Josa. Sion Hill, N.R.
Felkin Thos. 20, Charlotte st
Ford Wm. Houndsgate
Henson Thos. 3, Poultry
Keep John & Co. Smithy row
Millward Lucy, Carrington st
Minnett John, ct 24, Long row
Powlett Daniel, 74, Long row
Sheldon John & Rt. Broad marsh
Urry Geo. Plumptre square

(147.) TANNERS.
Alton Elias, Basford
Cox, Poyser, & Co. Butcher st
Parr Thos. Narrow marsh

(148.) TIMBER MRCHTS.
Marked 1 *are English wood dlrs.*
1 Allen Wm. Tollhouse hill, h.
   Mount Vernon
Barnsdall Nathl. Canal st. h.
   Middle Pavement

Chiswell John, (mahogany) Tollhouse hill
1 Ellis Wm. Goosegate
1 Harrison John, Rick street
1 Hawkins Wm. Hockley, h. New
   Sneinton
Knight Rt. Grey Friar gate, h.
   Paddock street
1 Martin Saml. Shaw lane
1 Oldham John, Canal st
Youle John & Henry, Castle
   wharf, and *Hull*

TINNERS—See Braziers, &c.

(149.) TOBACCO & SNUFF
   MANUFACTURERS.
*Thus * are only Dealers.*
Bradley Thos L. 3, Smithy row
*Nelson Rd. High street
*Peet Thos. 5, Carlton st
Soars Wm. Pelham street
Wright John, Middle marsh

(150.) TOY DEALERS.
Corbett Josiah, (cutlery, &c.) 2,
   High street
Crofts John, 70, Long row
Driver Joshua, 28, Long row
Hebb Wm. 24, Warsergate
Sweet Jas. Goosegate
Wright Jas. South Parade

(151.) TRIMMERS & PRESS-
   ERS OF HOSIERY.
Christian Thos. Byard lane
Davis Hy. Page's bldgs
Davis Ann, Nicholas street
Davis Wm. Mount East st
Dunbar Sarah, 29, St. Mary's gt
Metheringham Cath. Brewhouse
   yard
Kirk Thos. (silk hose) Maiden ln
Rooke Mary. Chandler's ln

(152.) TRUNK AND PAPER
   BOX MAKERS.
Shepherd Eliz. Listergate
Shipman Chas. Darker's ln
Simpson Thos. Narrow marsh
Swinney Saml. Millstone ln
Wrigley Saml. Sion hill

(153.) TURNERS IN WOOD,
   See also Chair Makers.
Bamford John, Narrow marsh
Brown Thos. Back lane
Foster Fras. 31, Parliament st
Fowke John, Earl street

Hall Wm. 15, Pennell's yd
Hutchinson John, 19, Parliament street
Hutchinson Thos. Frame court
Kershaw Thos. ct. 10, Parliament street
Kirk Saml. Mount East ct
Langham John (& coach axletree) 7, Pilchergate
Longman Saml. 19, New st
Loversuch Wm. Mansfield rd
Myers P. (lathe & tool mfr.) Pelham street
Parker John, (& winding mchns.) 50, Barkergate
Sheraton Ralph, Derby road
Skelton Wm. (& spring maker) Toll street
Soar John, Wm. IV.'s yard, Parliament street
Stretch Jas. Broad street
Taylor Dd. (wood bobbins) Hockley mill, h. Sneinton
Thompson John, (& lathe maker) Clare street
Walker Thos. (& ivory) Glasshouse street
Woodford Dd. 31, Broad st
(154.) UMBRELLA MKRS.
Morris & Pickering, 44, Long row
Scorrer Jph. 16, Bottle lane
Theaker John, Plum st
(155.) UPHOLSTERERS.
See also Cabinet Makers.
Blackwell Wm. jun. 34, Long row
Dean Wm. Broad marsh
Dixon Moses, (wkg.) Carey's yd
Lackenby Wm. (wkg.) Granby st
Smith Job, St. James's st
Stone Thos. Gedling street
Wild Wm. Weekday cross
(156.) VETERINARY SURGEONS.
Kewney Jonas, St. James's st
Rowland Thos. 4, Clumber st
Taylor Chas. 21, Clumber st
(157.) WATCH AND CLOCK MAKERS.
Those marked * are Jewellers, &
† Bobbin and Carriage Makers.
Barber John, Newcastle st
Behrens Jacob, Goosegate

Brownsword John, (and dealer in German Clocks) 8, Chapel bar
*Cox & Adams, Goosegate
Drury Wm. Sneinton st
Etches John, Listergate
Goodwin Wm. Narrow marsh
*Hallam Thos. 48, Bridlesmithgt
Harper Jas. Parliament st
Harper Richard, North st
Hopkin Wm. Mansfield road
*Kelvey Ebenezer, Pelham st
Lees Chas. Kingston court
†Mather Wm. 11, Milton st
Pratt John, 54, Bridlesmithgate
*Shepperley & Pearce, 27, Long row
Stevenson Wm. 2, Poultry
Sulley Rd. Hollow stone
Webster George, Derby road
Whitehall Thos. Caunt st
*Yeomans Henry, 19, Clumber st
(158.) WHARFINGERS.
Barnsdall Nathaniel, Canal st
Bradshaw John and Sons, Leen row wharf, Canal st
Cutts Hannah, Bath row
Marshall Rt. London road
Pickford & Co., Leen bridge
Richards Saml. Mill st
Robinson Jas. Wharf st
Roworth Wm. London road
Simpson John, Park wharf, h. Castle road
Thorpe Saml. Canal Company's wharf, Canal street
Wheatcroft G. & Son, Commercial street
(159.) WHEELWRIGHTS.
Cross Henry, Shaw lane
Fairholme Geo. Water street
Haddon Wm. Butcher st
Quinton John, Sherwin st
(160.) WHIP MAKERS, &c.
Clarke Roderick (thong) Gedling street
Edwards Jph. Sneinton st
Lowe Jas. (hand whip) Wheat Sheaf yard
Place John, jun. Beastmarket hill
Wapplinton Thos. (thong) Red st
White Jervas, (cord) Mount st
Whittle John, (thong) North st

(161.) WHITE LEAD MRFS.
Cox, Poyser & Co. Butcher st
(162.) WHITESMITHS AND
    BELLHANGERS.
Abbott John, Bellfounder's yard
Barker Thos. Wheelergate
Booth John, 7, Rigley's yard
Brentnall George, 6, Bellfounder's
    yard
Cowen Rt. & Co. Beck Works,
    Beck street
Drabble Fras. Derby road
Hackett Wm. Broad st
Hawksworth Wm. (and elastic
    spring mkr.) 9, Greyhound yd
Holland Saml. Chandler's lane
Hood Edw. Narrow marsh
Hood Rd. Garner's hill
Leak Robert, Pennell's yard
Miller John, Canal st.
Millington David, Broad marsh
Needham Geo. Oldfield, (mecha-
    nist) Sussex street
Nelson A. B. Holland st
Orme John, 13, Pennell's yard
Philips Geo. Narrow marsh
Sanders John, Newcastle st
Selby Jph. Goosegate
Sims Geo. 22, Barkergate
Smedley Richard, Houndsgate
Stanley John, Pelham st
Stephenson Wm. Houndsgate
Taylor John, Nottingham house
    yard
Taylor Wm. Beck street, h. Inde-
    pendent hill
Topping Joseph, Stretton's yd
Walker Wm. 29, Carlton st
Yates Thos. (lock) Middle hill
(163.) WINE AND SPIRIT
    MERCHANTS.
Marked thus . are only Retailers.*
Bailey Thos. Wheelergate
Bason Henry, Sion hill, h. Ashby
    terrace
*Cooper Wm. 1, Chapel bar
Cox Edw. & Fredk. Parliament st
*Cross Hy. 21, Long row
*Dabell Wm. 19, Long row

Deverill Wm. Pelham st
Homer, Watson, and Crossland,
    Pennell's yard
*Hopkin Wm. 35, Long row
Jalland Eliz. Goosegate
*Killingley Melicent, 9, Smithy
    row
Maltby Saml. Beastmarket hill
Parker Wm. 4, Carlton st
Perry John, Wheelergate
Severn Jas. Middle Pavement
*Skipwith Mary, 54, Long row
*Slater. Thos. Beck lane
Small Ann, 1, Poultry
Smith William, Bromley house
    Angel row
*Talbott Fras. 25, Long row
*Wilson Lewis, 7, Poultry
Wright Chpr. Norton, (wine) 50,
    Long row
(164.) WIRE WORKERS.
Marked . are Wire Drawers.*
Ashforth Henry, (springs) Broad
    marsh, and Sheffield, Rebecca
    Crisp, agent
Cottrell James, (and pin maker)
    Broad marsh
Cowen Rt. & Co. Beck st
Massey John, 17, Broad st
Raynor Rd. (spring) Bellargate
*Redgate Hy. (& fender makers),
    Houndsgate
*Taylor John, Broad marsh
Wood Saml. Canal street
(165.) WOOLLEN CLOTH
    MANUFACTURER.
Hobson Wm. Parliament st
    (166.) WOOLSTAPLERS.
Bakewell John, Friar lane
Hodgson Saml. & Jph. Houndsgt
Phipps Geo. Poplar sq. & Arnold
    (167.) WORSTED YARN
    SPINNERS.
Mills Geo. & John, (merino) 45,
    Long row
Raynor Wm. Beck st. and Wake-
    field; Geo. Wilson, agent
Wilson Wm. & Saml. (merino),
    Radford

MISCELLANEOUS LIST

OF

GENTRY, CLERGY, PARTNERS IN FIRMS, AND OTHERS,

NOT

Arranged in the Lists of Trades and Professions.

Ackroyd Thos. carter Toll st
Acott Mrs. Eliz. Park row
Acton Jas. joiner, 9, Lincoln st
Acton Mrs. Mary, Canal st
Adams Saml. mfr. 20, High Pavement
-Adams Thos. mfr. 9, Stoney st
Aldred Mrs. Ann, Toll st
Allcock Wm. hosier, Portland pl
Allen Jno. sexton of St. Nicholas', Brewhouse yard
Allen John Roger, hosier, h. Derby road
Allen Rd. lace mfr. h. Granby st
Allin Wm. Hardstaff, traveller, Tree yard
Alliott Rev. Rd. (Ind.) Castlegt
Alliott Rev. Rd. jun. (Ind.) Middle hill
Almond Rev. Rt. White, M.A. Rector of St. Peter's, Russell st
Alvey Sarah, cowkeeper. Fishergt
Archer Fanny & Eliz. Low Pavmt
Archer Jas. librarian, Bromley h
Archer Wm. St. Nicholas's Parish Clerk, Castle terrace
Armitage Jph. gent. Trent bridge
Andrew Thos. list shoe maker, Mount East st
Ash Jas. whsman. Poplar place
Astill Mrs. Ann, 4, Lenton st
Astle John, shopman, Derby rd
Attenborough Thos. bookkeeper, Spread Eagle yard
Aulton Chas. net mkr. Sherwood place
Bacon Geo. mfr. Park row
Bagshaw Wm. shopman, Mill st
Baguley Mrs. F. Low Pavement
Baker Wm. 10, St. Mary's place

Baker Wm. cowkpr, 18, Woolpack lane
Baker Wm. cowkpr. Independent hill
Balguy Charles Geo. Esq. Registrar of the Archdeaconry of Nottingham, Timber hill and Colwick
Barber Mrs. Isbl. 3, Hollowstone
Barber Mr. John, 1, Lenton st
Barker Misses Ann & Mary, Castlegate
Barker Mattw. Hy. editor of the *Mercury*, h. Clayton's yd
Barker Sarah, lodgings, Bottle ln
Barnes Benj. governor St. Mary's workhouse
Barnes Wm. clerk, 12, York st
Barney Mrs. Ann, Houndsgate
Barnett Absalom, assistant overseer of St. Mary's, Pilchergate
Barney Rd. bookpr. Castle st
Barratt Wm. plasterer, Mansfield road
Barrows Rd. carrier, 26, Stoney street
Barrows Rd. gent. 24, H. Pavement
Bartle Mrs. midwife, ct. 15, Bridlesmithgate
Barton Fras. 47, St. Mary's gate
Bartram Mrs. Hockley
Barwick Thos. town-crier, Greyhound street
Basnett Misses, 24, Fletchergate
Bates Mr. Thos. Ranchffe st
Batty Rev. Edw. (Wes.) Fountain place
Beale Mrs. Ann, Mortimer st
Bean Saml. mert. Lincoln st

Beardmore Mrs. Hannah, Mansfield road
Beardsley Mrs. Sarah, Castlegate
Beeby Mrs. Mary, Derby road
Beighton John, hay, &c. dealer, Tollhouse hill
Bell Mr. Chas. Forest side
Berridge Jas. hosier, Park st
Best Wm. whsman. Back lane
Bestall Saml. gent. Mid. Pavemt
Betts Edw. coachman, Chesterfield street
Biddle Rd. net mfr. Park row
Bilbie Mrs. Ann, Mansfield road
Bingham Mrs. Lydia, Canal st
Birch Rd. Mayor's serjeant, Police-office
Birkhead John, lace mfr. Hollows
Bishop John Fillingham, bookpr. Mount East st
Bishop Mrs. 11, Parliament st
Bishop Thos. jun. mert. Standard hill
Black John, joiner, Spaniel row
Black Peter, assistant overseer, Mansfield road
Bakey Mgt. feather dresser, 27, Parliament street
Blatherwick Hermon, gent. 6, Short hill
Blatherwick John, warehouseman, Mount East street
Boden Wm. mfr. Houndsgate
Bonsor Hy. Assembly rooms
Bonsor Hy. upholsterer, Castlegt
Booker Wm. surveyor, Carrington street
Boot Miss Frances, Castlegate
Booth Mr. Rt. 20, Plumptre st
Boothby Benj. sen. and jun. iron founders, Park terrace
Bosworth Geo. agt. Aspley ter
Bottom John Fras. lace dresser, h. Pierrepont st
Bower Benj. coach proprietor, Parliament st
Bower Jas. Lincoln Postman, 15, Charlotte st
Bowler Mr Saml. Mount-hooton
Bowley John, warper, Portland st
Bradbury Rd. gent. Derby rd
Bradfield Jas. warper, Portland pl

Bradford John, porter, Boot ct
Bradley Jas. coll. of Grantham canal tonage, Canal lock
Braithwaite Fras. hosier, 13, Poultry
Braithwaite Jph. hosier, Park ter
Braley Mr. Peter, Mansfield rd
Bramley Geo. warper, Manfield road
Bretland Thos. painter, Nottington pl. S.
Bridger Geo. Mansfield rd
Brierley Thos. warper, Mansfield road
Brierly Rd. Butler, Governor of County gaol
Briggs Wm. 6, St. Mary's gt
Broadhurst Miss Eliz. Wheelergt
Brockmer John, hatter, Cheapside
Broksopp Mrs Sarah, Standard hill
Brothers Rt. Allen, druggist, Mount Vernon
Brown John, sexton, Duke's pl
Browne Mich. solicitor, 34, Pelham street
Brown W. letter carier, 56, Coalpit lane
Brown Wm. lace dresser, Mansfield road
Brownell John, bookr. Derby rd
Broxholme Nathl. clothier, 19, Plumptre st
Bryon, Mrs. Sarah, 18, H. Pavement
Bullock Mrs. Sarah, Bellargate
Bullivant Mr. Wm. Canal st
Burkitt Rd. Scott, draper, Cheaside
Burley Chas. tripe dresser, Maiden ln
Burrows Mrs. Mary, St. John's st
Burton Mrs. Ann, Spaniel row
Burton Mrs. Eliz. 17, Charlotte street
Burton Jas. hawker, Kingston ct
Burton Jonth. lace mfr. Park row
Butler Saml. cowkpr. Kingston street
Butler Rev. Wm. Jph. M.A. rector of St. Nicholas, Castlegate
Butler Thomas, 19, Woolpk. ln
Buxton Andw. pilot, Canal st

Campbell Hugh Bruce, solr. Park
Campbell Mrs. Sophia, Notting-
ham terrace
Campbell Thos. Alex. surveyor,
h. Park
Campbell ——, coach proprietor,
9, Haughton st
Carpenter Rev. Benj. Unitarian,
High Pavement
Carter Alfred, warper, St. Ann's
street
Carter Mr. John, Clinton st
Cartlidge Saml. mfr. 16, High
Pavement
Cartwright George, book-keeper,
Pierrepont st
Cartwright Robert, collector of St.
Mary's poor rates. Canal st
Carver Thomas, hosier, 11, Carl-
ton st
Caunt Mary, Eliz. and Ann, gen-
tlewomen, Mid. Pavement
Chadburn Mrs. Har. 5, Lenton st
Chamberlin W. gent. Houndsgt
Chambers John, 6, Broad st
Chapman Geo. cowkpr. Convent
street
Chapman Mrs. Elouisa Ann,
Shore's lane
Chapman John, cowkpr. North
street
Chapman Rev. Leonard, vicar of
Wysall, Angel row
Chapman W. excise officer, Wa-
ter street
Chatteries Mrs. Eliz. H. Pavemt
Cheetham Thos. gent. Lincoln st
Cheetham S. hosier, Clumber st
Cheetham John, Governor of St.
Nicholas's Poorhouse, Park row
Cheetham Wm. hosier, 26, Pil-
chergate
Cheetham Wm. mfr. h. Mansfield
road
Church Hy. gent. Park hill
Churchill Han. draper, St. James'
row
Churchill Jph. gent. H. Pavemt
Clark Mrs. Ann, 25, Carlton st
Clark Charles, 2. Woolpack ln
Clark Jph. gent. Park row
Clark Saml. gent. Park terrace
Clark Wm. cart owner, Vassal st

Clarke Charles Harrison, solici-
tor, George st
Clarke Harriet, midwife, Narrow
marsh
Clarke Rt. builder, H. Pavement
Clarkson Rev. W. H. Wesleyan
Min. Sneinton
Clifford Richard, coachman, 4,
Haughton pl
Clifton Capt. Joseph, N. L. M.
Mansfield rd
Cloak Hugh, wool sorter, Park st
Close Thos. Esq. St. James's st
Cokayne Thomas, stenographer,
Blue Coat School
Coltman Mrs. Susanna, Park st
Colton Sarah, Chandler's ln
Cooke Marshall, Forest side
Cooley David, lodgings, 44, St.
Mary's gate
Cooper Jane and Mary, Glass-
house st
Cooper John, clerk, Parliament st
Copeland Geo. lace mfr. 1, Not-
tingham terrace
Copestake Mary, lace dlr. 5,
Haughton st
Copeleston Wm. Postern place
Cotton Saml. modeller, 36, Sto-
ney st
Cotton Wm. gent. 2, King's pl
Cowley Geo. Molona, attorney's
clerk, Castle st
Cox Alfred, mason, Trent Bridge
Cox Humphrey, gent. Parliament
street
Crabtree Eliz. bone button mfr.
Woolpack ln
Crisp Wm. Fletchergate
Crosby John, silk mert. High
Pavement
Crossland Edw. wine merchant,
Park hill
Cross Mrs. Mary, 23, High Pave-
ment
Curtis Jas. gent. Parliament st
Curtis Joseph, Sheep ln
Dabell Thos. warper. 30, York st
Daft John, sol. Low Pavement
Daft Sarah, midwife, Mid. marsh
Dakeyne Ralph, saddler, Lincoln
street

Dale Ricd. Meadows, druggist High st
Danks Isaiah, ironmonger, Forest hill
Darker Mr. Geo. Derby st
Darker John Lomas, gent. Broad marsh
Davis Mr. Tho. 18, Mansfield ter
Dawson Mrs. Bridge st
Day Edw. herbalist, St. Michael's row
Daykin. Mrs Milicent, 27, Stoney street
Deacon, Harrison and Co. carriers, Milton st
Dean John, bookpr. Mansfield rd
Dear Preston, herb distiller, Lamb lane
Dearman Nat, agent, St. James's street
Dethick John, mattress maker, Sussex st
Deverill Thos. bookpr, 17, Mansfield terrace
Dickenson Rt. draper, 41, Long row
Dobeler Rev. Clement, 8, King's place
Dobson John, gardener, Carter r
Dodd Mrs. Mary, Postern st
Dodd Mrs. Jane, Babbington st
Donaldson Mrs. Sophia, Derby rd
Drewry Benj. joiner, h. Commercial st
Duclos Gabriel, mfr. h. St. Mary's place
Dudgeon Steph. clerk, Rutland st
Dudley Rd. writing master, Castlegate
Dumelow Mrs. Hanh. Vernon st.
Dutton Geo. farmer, Newcastle st
Dutton Mr. Samuel, Hockley
Earp Saml. gent. Park hill
Eastwood Thos. 30, Woolpk. ln
Eato Jph. White Lion Stables
Eddowes Geo. solr. 7, Warsergt
Eden Wm. joiner, Back lane
Edinborough Hugh, gent. Nottingham terrace
Edwards Rev. Jas. (bapt.) Mansfield road
Eley Isaac, tripe dresser, Finkhill street

Elliott Geo. 11, St. Mary's gate
Elliott W. lace thread mfr. Commercial st
Elliott T. bookpr. Hollowstone
Elliott Joshua, silk knitter, King's Arms yard
Elliott John. dresser, Shaw ln
Elsom Jno. boot closer, 8, George street
Ely Thos. farmer, Paradise pl
Etherington John, mfr. h. Nottingham terrace
Evers Wm. coachman, Lincoln st
Everson Miss Mary, Castle st
Favance Miss Harriet, Castle pl
Fearnhead Peter, solr. Fletchergt
Featherstone John, Middle hill
Felkin Wm. agent, Clinton st
Fellows Alfred Tho. Esq. banker, High Pavement
Fido Wm. paver, Holland st
Fitzwalter John, stamper, Coal court
Flintoff Jas. bookpr, Warsergate
Fox Saml. grocer, h. Houndsgate
Franks Jas. Dean street
Frearson Hy. mfr. Mansfield rd
Frearson Jph. mfr. Mansfield rd.
Freeman Geo. mfr. St. James's terrace
Freeman Thomas, laceman, St. James's terrace
Freeth Danl. Esq. Standard hill
Freeth Geo. solr. Low Pavement
Frost John, farmer, 10, Sherwood street
Frost Thos. bookpr. Wheelergt
Frost Thos. lace mfr. South parade
Frost Mr. Wm. 3, Cannon yard
Frost Wm. gent. Mansfield road
Fryett Wm. riding-master, Castle gate
Gamble Geo. cowkpr. Sherwood lane
Gedling Micah. sen. mfr. Park row
Gedling Micah. jun. mfr. h. Mount Vernon
Gell John, Sherbrooke, sol. Standard hill
Gelsthorp Jph. (ldgs.) Park st
George Chas. vagrant office kpr. Chandler's lane

German Mr. Anty. 25, Geo. st
Gibson John, hosier. Park row
Gibson Mrs. Mary, Parliament st
Gibson Wm. hosier, Park row
Gilbert Wm. ostler, Haughton st
Gilbert Rev. Jph. (Ind.) Castlegate
Gill John, gent. Postern st
Gill John, banker's clerk, Goose gate
Gilliver Eliz. cowkpr. Poynton st
Gilson Thos. trvlr. Mount st
Glover Wm. bookbinder, Clare st
Godber Mary, ldgs. Rutland st
Gordan Rt. cowkeeper, Mill st
Goodacre Rt. jun. editor of the Nottingham *Review*, Castlegt
Goodall Mrs. Eliz. 16, Fletchergt
Goody Mrs. Eliz. Sneinton st
Gordon Mrs. Susanna, Standard hill
Gough John, clerk, Park st
Greasley Chas. bookpr. ct. 19, Stoney street
Greaves Mrs. Wheelergate
Greaves Miss Frances. Castlegt
Green Mrs. Ann, St. James's st
Green John, gent. Castlegate
Green Saml. confectioner, Basford lane
Green Mr. Thos. Pleasant place
Griffin John Cooper, fire engineer, Broad st
Guilford Thomas, Druggist, 53, Long row
Gunn James, Packet Master, Severn's yard, Mid. Pavt
Haddin Mrs. Violet, Castle place
Hall Mrs. Eliz. Standard hill
Hall John Edm. mfr. Park ter.
Hall Samuel, net mfr. Mount Pleasant
Hall Thos. Esq. Angel row
Hall Thos. bookkpr. Postern pl
Hallam John, engineer, Old Waterworks, Brewhouse yard
Hallam John, joiner, Pepper st
Hallam Jph. joiner, Grosvenor pl
Hallam Wm. turnkey, Albion st
Hampson Jas. hawker, Kingston court
Hancock John, Esq., 14, St. Mary's gate

Handley Eliz. Mansfield rd
Hardwick Fras. hosier, Low Pavement
Hardy Rd. cowkpr, Chandler's ln
Harriman John, draper, Poultry
Harris John, gent. 17, Parliament street
Harris Rev. Thomas Hockley Chapel
Harrison Geo. brewer, Rice pl
Harrison Edw. lace dresser, b. Carrington street
Harrison John, carter, Jason pl
Harrison Noah, hatter, St. James's terrace
Harrison John, bookpr. Hollowstone
Harrison Thos. brazier, Mansfield road
Haseldine Jas. gent. Holland st
Hart Miss Eliz. midwife, 11, Narrow marsh
Hart Fras. Esq. banker, Pepper street
Hart Jph. warper, Rancliffe st
Harvey Geo. coal mert. Canal st
Harvey Mrs. Sarah, Derby rd
Harvey Wm. coach maker, 6, Beck lane
Hawkins Jacob, sawyer. East st
Hawkins Mich. sawyer, King st
Hawley Wm. mason, Butcher st
Haywood Wm. and Son, glass and vitriol mercts. Middle hill
Haywood Jph. porter, 25, Broad street
Heap Geo. silk throwster, Fletchergate
Heard John, hosier, Castlegate
Heath, Mr. Jph. Park st
Heath John, bookpr. Pleasant pl
Hemsley Stph. draper, Poultry
Henshaw Mrs. Ann, 17, Carlton street
Herbert Thos. mfr. Mansfield rd
Herbert Wm. mfr. Parliament st
Hett Chas. bobbin, &c. mfr. Back lane
Hewitt F. P. hosier, Park
Hewitt Jas. col. of Old Waterworks rates, Park row
Hickling Mrs. Susanna, Mansfield road

2 A

Higgs Mrs. Ann, H. Pavement
Higgins Thos. machine maker, Greyfriargate
Hill Thos. carter, St. Ann's st
Hilton, Rt. Auld. coal dlr. Neptune place
Hind Benj. Watt's yard
Hind Jas. hay dlr. Goosegate
Hine Jthn. lace mfr. Mount st
Hinton Wm. 34, Warsergate
Hitchcock Simeon, excise officer, Harley place
Hodges Wm. paver, Cross st
Holbrook W. bailiff, Rutland ct
Holbrook Rt. Gregory. warper, St. Ann's st
Holbrook Geo. weighing machine, Derby road
Holland John, mfr. Mansfield rd
Hollinshead Edw. clerk, Walnut-tree lane
Hollingworth W. 7, Charlotte st
Homer Hy. wine mert. Park hill
Hook John, gunsmith, 2, Lenton street
Hosley John, carter, Warren st
Hope Wm. clerk, Grosvenor pl
Hopin Wm. bookpr. Ealand st
Horsfall John, gent. Standard hill
Horsfall Mrs. Mary, Standard hill
Hovey Thos. mfr. 32, St. Mary's gate
Howe Dixon, permit writer, Peck lane, h. Old Sneinton
Howell Hy. agent to the Canal Com. Canal street
Howett John, gent. 42, Stoney st
Hubbert Mrs. 4, George st
Hudson, Maria, lace dresser, h, Herbert street
Hudson John, governor of St. Peter's Workhouse, Brd. mar
Huff Mrs. Jemima, Castle ter
Hughes Jas. Lyster, clerk, Cumberland place
Hull Wm. hawker, Exchange ct
Humpreys John, East st
Hunt Mr. John, 14, Woolpack ln
Hurst Nathan, hosier, Houndsgt
Hutchinson Mrs. Eliz. Parliament street
Hutchinson, W. coachman, Postern place

Huthwaite Hy. sol. Park ter
Huthwaite, Miss Mary, Park ter
Ibberson Rd. gent. Postern st
Inglesant Thos. 6, George st
Inman John, warper, Stanhope st
Jackson John, surveyor of taxes, Park row
James Mrs. Hanh. 31, Warsergt
James John, gent. Houndsgate
James Rt. hosier, Park st
Jarman Mr. Wm. Castlegate
Jeffery Tho. wool sorter, Houndsgate
Jeffries John, constable, Plumptre square
Jenks John, mfr. 27, Warser st
Jerram Jas. lace mfr. Derby rd
Johnson Saml. gent. Park st
Johnson W. sexton of St. Mary's, 25, Pilchergate
Jones Alex. traveller, York st
Jones Thos. com. trvlr. Friar ln
Jordan, Mrs. Eliz. Castle rd
Jubb Mrs. Sarah, Parliament st
Kain Ambrose, barrack sergeant,
Kain Geo. Cowkpr. Mark ln
Kean Frans. 15, York st
Kelham Mr. Hy. Mount street
Kelsall Edm. drug dlr. Cyprus st
Kewney Chas. Ginnever, hosier, St. Peter's square
Kidd Wm. Moses, clerk of St. Peter's, Byard lane
Kidger Wm. Forest side
Kilbourn Saml. common sergeant, woodward, &c. 25, Warsergate
King Mrs. Cath. Glasshouse st
King Mrs. Sarah, Mount st
Kirk Edw. Bellargate
Kirk John, agent, Red hill
Kirk Samuel cotton preparer, Mount Pleasant
Kirk Valentine, stamp office clerk, Carrington st
Kirkby Rev. John, M. A. Rector of Gotham, Standard hill
Kitchen Thomas, toll collector, Forestgate
Knight John, agent, Cartergate
Kyte Jph. gent. Park st
Lavender John, gent. Parliament street

Lawton Edward, banker's clerk, Forest side

Lawson James, police officer, Bridge street

Leavers Jno. mfr. h. Spaniel row

Lee Rt. clerk, Carrington st

Lees Geo. joiner, Houndsgate

Lees Mr. John, Glasshouse st

Lees Philip, gent. Canal st

Leeson Robt. solr. h. Wilford

Lewin Geo. mfr. Goosegate

Lightfoot John, warehouseman, Castle terrace

Limbert Wm. clerk, Carrington place

Linecar Rt. constable, 14. Greyhound yard

Linecar Wm. col. of St. Mary's poor-rates, Greyhound street

Lloyd Mrs. Sarah, Bottle alley

Lock Wm. Cook, cabinet maker, Forest side

Lomax Edw. grocer, Nottingham terrace

Long Jas. bookpr. Lee's yard

Lord John, plasterer, Malt ct

Lowdham Lewis Alsopp, solr. h. Low Pavement

Low Wm. mfr. 23, Pilchergate

Lownds Wm. turnkey, County Gaol

Lucas Thomas, jun. Paradise pl

Lyle Joseph, coachman, Grosvenor place

M'Lund, Rev. Saml. Bridgeford

Machin Mrs. Sarah, Back lane

Machin Wm. bookpr. Castlegate

Mallet Henry, saddler, 68, Long row

Mallet Hy. mfr. 10, Stoney st

Manlove Thomas, jun. 40, St. Mary's gate

Marriott Jas. carter, Pomfret st

Marriott John, porter, Castle

Marriott Thos. draper, St. James's street

Marsh Jas. lace mfr. h. Park sq

Marshall Thos. Jas. hosier, Castlegate

Martin Abm. cow keeper, Finkhill street

Martin Miss Ann, 12, Poultry

Martin Mr. John, Mansfield rd

Massey Danl. excise officer, Mansfield road

Mather Anthony, millwright, Beck lane

Mather Rt. 19, Barkergate

Matthewson Rev. Geo. (P. Baptist) Castle terrace

Medlam Thos. D. warehouseman, Carrington street

Mee John, waiter, ct. 32, Long row

Mee Josiah, carter, Sneinton st

Melets Mrs. Eliz. Parliament st

Melville Wm. mfr. Standard hill,

Mettam Misses Margt. & Frances, Castlegate

Miller Mr. Hy. Derby rd

Millington Jas. bookkeeper, 17, Rice place

Mills Miss Eliz. Castle place

Mills Geo. hosier, 45, Long row

Mills John, hosier, Castlegate

Millward Wm. foreman, Harrington street

Mitchell John, leather dresser, Canal street

Mitchell Wm. leather dresser, h. Finkhill street

Mitchell Rt. fiddler, Old Rose yd

Moody Thos. clerk, Glasshouse st

Moody Thos. constable, Glasshouse street

Moore Saml. Weston, cotton doubler, h. Mansfield rd

Moore Thos. Esq. banker, Ruddington

Morley Chas. Lomas, alderman, Beck lane

Morley John, mfr. h. Sneinton

Morris Mrs. Anna Maria, Castle terrace

Morris Mr. John, 1, Woolpack ln

Morton Mrs. Flora, Poynton st

Moss Mrs. Mary, Forest side

Mugleston Mr. Rt. Mark lane

Mugleston Mr. Saml. Mark lane

Munk Edw. draper, St. James's street

Need Miss Eliz. 40, Long row

Needham Miss Priscilla, Castlegt

Neilson Wm. Geo. hawkers' license office, High st

Nelson Mrs. Ann, St. James's st

Nelson Geo. overlooker, Plum st

Nelson Isaiah, machinist, Sneinton street

Neuberg Jph. merct. Houndsgt

Nevill Jthn. mfr. H. Pavement

Newball Thos. mfr. Sherwood hill

Newbery Mr. Rt. sen. Glasshouse street

Newham Saml. gent. Mt. Vernon

Newham Wm. carter, Fishergate

Newton John, cheesefactor, 65, Long row

Newton Jph. schoolmr. Bottle ln

Nightingale Hy. Mt. Hooton

Nix Mr. Saml. 23, York st

Norris Thos. secretary to the Lunatic Asylum & the Dispensary, Castle terrace

North Wm. High Cross st

Norton Mrs. Ann, Mansfield rd

Norton Miss. Market street

Norton Wm. Fletcher Norton, Esq. Castlegate

Nunn Saml. Beeton, lace mfr. 30 Fletchergate

Oakland Mrs. Hannah, St. Michael's row

Odam Hannah, bed mfr. Talbot yard

Oliver Mrs. Eliz. Forest Cottage

Oldknow Mrs. Cath. Mansfield rd

Oldknow Miss Hannah, Meadow street

Oldknow Henry, surgeon, St. James's street

Oldknow Octavius Thos. draper, Beastmarket hill

Orange Jph. 9, Woolpack lane

Orange Rev. John, (Ind.) Carlton grove

Osborne Henry, fendersmith, 5, Woodland place

Outram John, guard, Parliament street

Owen Edw. cowkeeper, 14, Parliament street

Owen Wm. lodgings, 20, George street

Page Hy. carter, York ct

Page Jph. jun. lace mfr. Mount street

Palethorpe Mr. Jph. York st

Parker Mrs. N. Postern st

Parker Rt. agent, 17, Bridle-smithgate

Parnham Jph. dep. clerk of St. Mary's, 6, Hollowstone

Parr John, tax collector, 35, Warsergate

Parr Misses Ann & Hannah, Castle place

Parr Wm. carter, Tollhouse hill

Parrey Geo. coachman, 5, Haughton place

Parsons Saml. solicitor, Nottingham terrace

Parsons Wm. solr. St. James's st

Patterson John, clerk to savings bank, Castlegate

Patterson Wm. builder, h. Park

Patterson Mr. Wm. 19, East st

Payne Mrs. Derby terrace

Payne Saml. solr. Park cottage

Peake Mr. John, Coalpit lane

Pearce Jas. bookkpr. Fletchergt

Pearson Mrs. Ann, 41, Stoney st

Pearson Mr. John. Derby rd

Pell Jph. Plough & Harrow yd

Peet Mrs. Mary, Castlegate

Peet Thos. lace mfr. Castlegate

Penticost Jas. bookkeeper, Postern place

Pettinger Wm. cowkeeper, Wellington street

Percy Hy. solicitor, Wheelergate

Perry John & Jph. Mt. Hooton

Pettifor Wm. carrier, Park st

Pettinger Wm. supervisor, 28, Fletchergate

Pick Wm. draper, Park st

Petty Jas. chapel keeper, 43, St. Mary's gate

Pickard Hy. whsman. Gedling st

Pickard Susan, farmer, St. Ann's Well

Pickard Wm. cotton preparer, Burdett's court

Pickering Urban, hosier, Grosvenor place

Pierce Thos. manager. Mills's yd

Pilter Rev. Rt. Hockley chapel

Place John, whsman. Vernon st

Pollicott Thos. hosier, Exchange court

Potter Wm. gent. 13, Warsergate

Pratt Mrs. Eliz. Bridge st
Pratt Wm. mason, Bridge st
Pratt Jonn, mason, Plumptre pl
Pratt Saml. sculptor, 40, Stoney street
Price Rt. gent. Park st
Pritchard Thos. farmer, Coppice
Probett Stphn. Thos. medicine vender, Park st
Radford Thos. gent. 42, Barkergate
Rainbow John, governor, House of Correction
Rather Mr. Wm. Forest side
Rayner Mrs. Eliz. 1, St. Marygt
Raynor Wm. gent. Mill st
Reek Mrs. Eliz. 20, Mansfield terrace
Renshaw Mrs. Low Pavement
Reynolds Stpn. pawnbroker, Lincoln street
Rich Thos. traveller, 29, Stoney street
Richards Mrs. Sarah, Mansfield road
Richards John, York st
Richardson Wm. Geo. hosier, 19, St. Mary's gate
Rigby Lewis, Sandemanian elder, 18, Beck lane
Rippon John, cowkeeper, Vernon street
Rippon John, cowkeeper, Plough & Harrow yard
Rivington John, coachman, 15, Broad street
Robinson Fredk. Esq. banker, Beastmarket hill
Robinson Mr. Thos. Park st
Robinson Wm. hosier, Park st
Roe Miss, Parliament st
Roe Mr. Rd. Narrow marsh
Rogers John, hosier, 8, St. Mary's gate, & Carrington
Roper John, Independent hill
Rothera Jas. bkbndr. Wild's yd
Roulston Jph. cowkpr, Canal st
Rowbotham Wm. cowkeeper, Woolpack lane
Rowe Rd. whsman. Back lane
Rushton Saml. hay & straw dlr. 4, Hazard's yd
Salt Benj. pig dlr. Rick st

Salthouse Thos. gent. Market st
Sanders Misses Hannah & Charlotte, 7, Rigley's yd
Sanderson Mrs. Ann, 4, Warsergate
Sanderson Jph. porter, ct. 21, St. Mary's gate
Sansom Charlotte, tea dlr. Lincoln street
Sansom Mr. John, Glasshouse st
Sarazin Aime, agent, Castlegate
Scattergood Saml. cowkpr. Bran court
Scorer Hy. hosier, Forest house
Scottorn Saml. miller, Sherwood street
Sculthorpe Rt. solr. Standard hill
Sculthorpe Wm. solr. St. Petergt
Seaton Jph. guard, Parliament st
Senior Jerh. gent. Wheelergate
Severn John, High Pavement
Sharp Freeman, cowkpr. Rick st
Shaw John, hay, &c. dlr. weighing machine, Tollhouse hill
Shaw Rt. cart owner, Toll st
Sheldon Miss Mary, Cumberland place
Shelton Mrs. Park row
Shelton John, coal mrcht. Meadow street
Shelton Jph. mattress maker, Sneinton street
Shipley Hy. Wm. whsman. Park street
Shipley Miss Sarah, Nicholas st
Shore Thos. bookpr. Back lane
Simes Wm. gent. 31, George st
Simons Mr. John, Pilchergate
Simpkin Wm. overlooker, Coppice
Simpson Mrs. Ann, Granby st
Simpson Geo. periodical agent, Parliament street
Simpson John, coach proprietor, Fletchergate
Simpson Thos. coach proprietor, 2, Carlton street
Simpson John, letter carrier, Byard lane
Simpson Thomas, excise officer, Parliament street
Singlehurst Martha, cowkeeper, Narrow marsh

Sisson Hy. Mount Hooton
Skipwith Mrs. Isabella, Woodland place
Skipwith Rd. mfr. 55, Long row
Stark Jas. Northern Water Works Forest side
Slide John, fwk. Warren court
Smart Mr. Robt. Mount Hooton
Smedley Danl. trvlr. Bottle ln
Smith Mrs. Peggy, 9, Short hill
Smith Geo. Esq. stamp distributor, St. Petergate, h. Stoney st
Smith Jas. gent. Tollhouse hill
Smith Henry, Esq. banker, Wilford
Smith John, lace mfr. Toll st
Smith John, solr. Castlegate
Smith John, whsman. Mill's yd
Smith Mrs. Sarah, Castlegate
Smith Thos. Hollins, corn miller, Canal st
Smith Wm. wine mert. Park
Smith Thos. carter, Millstone ln
Smith Wm. hosier, St. James's sq
Smith Wm. boatowner, Mill st
Smith John, Derby post man, Crown & Anchor, yd. Bridge st
Smoke Mr. Jph. Harvey, Chesterfield st
Sneath Chas. mfr. h. Mansfield rd
Sollory John, accountant, Market street
Solomon Dd. hawker, 8, Broad st
Sowter Jph. van office, Maypole yard
Sparks Wm. York st
Sparrow James, painter, Park row
Speed Mrs. Hannah, Glasshouse street
Spencer John, lace dresser, Carrington st
Spencer Saml. lace dresser, Castle terrace
Spurr John, bricklayer, 3, Broad street
Spurr John, druggist, 37, Warsergate
Stainrod Saml. joiner, Derby rd
Staples Wm. bookpr. 8, Lincoln street
Stevenson John, gent. Grosvenor place

Stevenson Thomas, coachman, Parliament street
Stones Mrs. Ellen, High Pavmt
Starr Mrs. Deborah, Derby rd
Strahan Mrs. Mary, Castlegate
Stuart Rev. John Burnett, M.A. Incumbent of St. James's, Standard hill
Styring Geo. bkpr. Newcastle st
Sugden James, tax collector, 14, Broad street
Sulley Mrs. Ann, 18, George st
Summers Mr. Jph. 9, Broad st
Summer Thos. cowkeeper, Barkergate
Swainscow Hy. whsman. Park st
Swann Chpr. Esq. solr. & coroner for the county, Castlegate
Swann Chpr. draper, Derby rd
Swann John, draper, 43, Long row
Swann Kirk, gent. St. James's terrace
Swann Saml. spring truss mkr. 31, Woolpack lane
Taylor Mrs. Eliz. 33, H. Pavmt
Taylor Isaac, paver, Pierrepont street
Taylor John, lace mfr. Park hill
Taylor Saml. gent. Cur lane
Taylor Wm. gent. Park row
Taylor Wm. whsman. Glasshouse street
Tetley Edw. paver, Gedling st
Thackeray John, mfr. Forest side
Theaker John, mfr. Park st
Thornton Mrs. Eliz. 5, George st
Thornton Mr. Hy. Mount East st
Thorp Wm. carter, Warren ct
Thraves Saml. cowkpr. Union pl
Throop Geo. coachman, 5, Lincoln street
Thurman Mr. Jas. Pepper st
Tomlinson Miss F. Forest side
Tomlinson Mr. Wm. 17, High Pavement
Topham Jph. machine mkr. h Babbington st
Train Rt. lace mfr. h. Derby rd
Trentham Wm. gent. Derby ter
Trivett Ephraim, lace manufacturer, Silverwood place
Trosha Mrs. R. Postern st

Truman Mr. Robert, North st
Truswell John. Geo. silk throwster, Carrington st
Truswell Rd. cowpr. 18, Carlton street
Turner John, carter, Line alley
Upton John, mfr. 24, George st
Upton Saml. cowkeeper, Millstone lane
Vason Geo. governor of Town Jail Weekday cross
Vaughan James, Mole court
Vaughan Ann, doctress, 6, Stoney street
Veni Mark, plaster figure maker, Drake st
Vickers Wm. lace mfr. Park
Wade Rd. carrier, 8, Milton st
Wakefield Mrs. Mary, Low Pavt
Wakefield Thos. cotton spinner, &c. Low Pavement
Wakefield Chas. gent. Low pvt
Walker John, thread preparer, 20, East st
Walker Mrs. Dorothy, St. James's street
Walker Jph. traveller, North st
Walker Miss Sarah, Tollhouse hill
Wallis Thos. shopman, Peck lane
Walters Jph. cowkeeper, Derby street
Wand Wm. cowkpr. Woolpack ln
Ward Geo. bookpr. 41, St. Mary's gate
Ward John, joiner, Mount st
Ward Hanh. farmer, Coppice
Ward Mrs. Martha, 9, Parliament st
Ward Rd. tailor, h. Mansfield rd
Wardle Chas. foreman, 4, Bottle lane
Waring Mr. Thos. 19, H. Pavmt
Warren Anna, midwife, Cartergt
Waters John, warper, Cross st
Watson Mr. Rt. Clinton st
Watson Thos. cowkpr. Hockley
Watson Thos. trvr. Houndsgate
Watts Mr. Edw. Chesterfield st
Wattshurst Miss Sarah, Houndsgate
Waynmann Wm. mfr. Beeston
Wells Henry, solr. Castlegate
Wells John, draper, Forest side

Wells George Navy surgeon, 17, Bottle lane
Wells Mr. Jonathan, Milton st
Werford Fras. gent. Nottingham terrace
Wesson John, lace mfr. Mount st
Wetzlar Gustavus, agent, Castlegate
Wharton Rph. machine maker, Canal street
Wheatcroft Alex. carrier, London road
Wheatcroft Wm. warper, Willoughby row
Whitchurch Mr. Rd. Caunt st
Whitchurch Rd. Bedford row
White Alfred, shopman, Mount street
White Geo. Mills, surgeon, St. James's street
White Geo. Kepple, post master, High street
White Saml, police officer, Mansfield road
Whitlark Jno. Start, agent, Sherwood hill
Whittle Edw. clerk, Carrington street
Whyatt Rev. William, curate of Sneinton, 31, St. Mary's gate
Widdowson Wm. mfr. Standard. hill
Wilkins Rev. Geo. D.D. vicar of St. Mary's, High Pavement
Wilkins Mr. James, Granby st
Wilkinson Mark, High Pavmt
Wilkinson John, wharehouseman, St. Peter's square
Williams Wm. supervisor, Milton street
Williams Wm. joiner, Parlt. st
Willson Rev. Robert William, Catholic priest, George st
Wilmot John, coach proptr. St. James's street
Wilson Geo. bookpr. Finkhill st
Wilson Isaac, hosier, Park ter
Wilson John, hosier, Angel row
Wilson Rev. John, Park row
Wilson Jph. hosier, Long row
Wilson Robert, draper, Park ter
Wilson William Esq. Plumptre house

Winterton Thomas Wm, Bible Society Depository, Park st
Wise Wm. solr. h. 8, Clumber st
Wolfe Fras. cowkpr. Boot ct
Wolfe Wm. carter, Parliament st
Wood Mrs. Eliz. Park st
Wood Mrs. Mary, 18, Warsergt
Wood Rev. Robert, D.D. gram. school, Stoney st
Wood Wm. whsman. Cross Beck street
Woodcock Joseph, bookkeeper, Paddock st
Woodhouse Mrs. Eliz. Chapel bar
Woodhouse James, coachman, 2, Haughton place
Woodward Sarah, medicine vender, Cross st.

Worsdall Mrs. Ann, Castlegate
Wright Ichabod, Esq. banker, Mapperley
Wright Ichabod Chs. Esq. banker Bramcote
Wright Mrs. Eliz. 28, H. Pavmt
Wright Fras. clerk, Mid. Pavmt
Wright John, warehouseman, Paddock street
Wright Mrs. Mary, St. Peter'sgt
Wright Stephen, mfr. 28, St. Mary's gate
Wright Thos. draper, Standard hill
Wyer Mr. S. John, Milton st
Wylde Mrs. Esther, 12, Short hill
Youle Hy. timber mert. Melville. Cottage, Park.

INDEX OF PERSONS,

ARRANGED IN THE

NOTTINGHAM TRADES' DIRECTORY.

☞ To facilitate the finding of any Name, when the trade of the person sought for is not known, the following Alphabetical Index is given, pointing out the corresponding *Number of the Trade or Profession* under which that name stands in the Commercial Directory, in which all the Lists are arranged in numerical order, so that a reference may be instantly made to any of them; The names in the preceding *Miscellaneous* part of the Nottingham Directory being already in alphabetical order, are not inserted in this Index.

2 B

Loach Francis, 37
Lock W. C. 29
Lock & Gresham, 109
Lomas Jane, 97 ; J. & Son, 67
Longman Samuel, 153
Longden Emma, 1
Longmire Edwin, 16
Lord Thomas, 12
Longland William, 76
Larriman George, 101
Loseby William, 133
Lovatt Gervase, 12, 75
Loversuch William, 153
Lovitt Peter, 133
Lowater Jno. 73 ; Jph. 66 ; Saml.
66 ; William, 133
Lowdham & Freeth, 5
Lowe Chas. 45 ; C. & J. 83 ; Jas.
160 ; Jno. 93 ; Saml. 1 ; Wm.
36, 50, 71
Lowe & Smith, 73, 134
Lownds Robert, 20
Lucas Thomas, 25
Lupton William, 73
M'Arthur T. 110
M'Callum Wm. 62 ; John, 141
M'Call John, 53
M'Creery James, 69
M'Coul David, 83
M'Donald John, 83
M'Monies James, 53
M'Qubal Thomas, 53
M'Namara M. 123
Machin Jph. 43 ; Eliz. 140 ; Rd.
28 ; William 16
Macklerith A. 16.
Mackley & Maltby, 93
Maddock Robert, 16
Maidens Geo. 28 ; W. 118
Maloney Cor. 16
Maltby John, 20 ; Jph. 28, 117 ;
Samuel, 72, 163.
Manderfield James, 145
Manfull I. 145
Manlove Edward, 90 ; Thos. &
Son, 83 ; S. & Co. 49
Mann Geo. 75 ; Edw. 133 ; John,
20 ; S. J. 144
Manners John, 54
Manson Alexander, 112
Maples Richard, 2 ; Rt. S. 6, 19
Marchipton John, 117
Marlow J. 38 ; Wm. 65

Marple J. 145 ; S. 97
Marr William, 81
Marriott Eliz. 143 ; Geo. 20 ;
John, 16, 42 ; Jph. 2, 75
Marriott & Munk, 90
Marsden William, 112
Marshall Geo. 7, 54, 105 ; John,
15, 133 ; Jph. 33, 133 ; Rt.
42, 158 ; Wm. 7, 14, 105, 133 ;
Thos. 16, 54
Marson Thomas, 16
Mart Joseph, 75
Martin Geo. R. 116 ; John, 40 ;
Gervase, 28 ; Martha, 1 ; Sa-
muel, 148
Marvin Charles, 7, 55
Mason Jas. 133 ; Jph. 69 ; Saml.
B. 16 ; Svr. 66
Massey John, 16, 164 ; Peter,
20 ; Wm. 16
Mather John, 85 ; Wm. 15, 157
Maudsley Jonathan, 1
Mawby J. 75
Maxfield Jph. 101 ; Mtw. 20
May James, 204
Mayo Benjamin, 75
Meadows Eliz. 133 ; Saml. 34.
Meats Isaac, 16
Mee John, 28
Meeson & Sons, 20
Meldram James, 20
Mellow James, 69, 120
Melville Wm. & David, 49
Mercer Richard, 19, 111
Meredith Thomas, 143
Merrin Eliz. 9 ; Fdk. & Saml. 20 ;
Maria, 143
Methringham Cath. 151 ; J. 20 ;
Dennis, 44
Micklewait John, 51
Middleton John, 16 ; Thos. 16 ;
Samuel, 83
Midlam Joseph, 35, 67
Milford William, 23
Miller Geo. 16 ; John, 62, 162 ;
Saml. 28 ; Wm. 75
Milligan Alex. 1 ; Mtw. 81
Millington Thos. & Co. 127 ;
Hy. 75 ; David, 162
Mills & Elliott, 49
Mills Geo. & John, 49, 73
Milner Dd. 33 ; A. 97 ; Jas. 15,
101 ; Wm. 15, 16 ; Fdk. 10

Staveley Edwad, 3 ; J. 19
Steel A. & R. 20, Wm. 105
Stenson Jno. 2, 49 ; Robert, 20 ;
 Sarah. 1 ; Wm. 2, 37
Stephenson Wm. 25, 162 ; Geo.
 118
Sterling William, 20
Stevens John, 28 ; Isaac, 8
Stevenson Edw. 60 ; Jas. 133 ;
 John, 83, 101 ; Moses, 83 ; Wm.
 157
Stevenson & Rhodes, 118
Stokes Geo. 15, 39, 81, 101 ; Wm.
 76
Stone John, 61 ; Thos. 155
Stones John & Co. 41 ; Thos. 95
Stoney & Clarke, 29, 81
Storer George, 20
Storr Geo. 73 ; Saml. 12. 100 ;
 Abm. 69
Strangeway James, 12
Straw Edward, 61 ; J. 66
Street George, 28 ; Wm. 16
Strelley Richard, 28
Stretch James, 153
Stretton Ann, 7 ; Geo. 19 ; Sml.
 97, 105
Stubbins C. and Co. 145
Stubbins John, 16
Stubbs Thomas, 75, 93
Sturt James, 2
Sturtivant Cphr. 16
Sulley Richard, 2, 49, 133, 157
Summerfield Richard, 75
Sumner Geo. 16 ; John, 69
Surplice Saml. 86 ; Wm. 3, 24,
 26, 86. 116
Sutton John. 16 ; M. A. 133 ;
 Richard, 19
Swain Joseph, 62
Swann and Son. 90
Swann and Browne, 5
Swann Chpr. 5 ; Geo. 81 ; S. H.
 67, 72
Swanwick Geo. 16, 42 ; John, 42,
 83 ; Jph. 42 ; Wm. 75
Sweet J. 69 ; T. 20
Swindall Thomas, 20
Swindell William, 75
Swinney Samuel, 152
Sylvester Wm. 7 ; Jno. 16
Taft John, 25
Talbot Fras. 75, 163 ; John 28

Tallant Jane, 93
Tatham Rt. S. 22, 79 ; Thos. 67 ;
 Wm. 1
Taylor Bbs. 125a ; Benj. 82 ;
 Chas. 156 ; Dd. 153 ; Geo. 71 ;
 145 ; Is. 2 ; Jas. 47, 145 ; Jno.
 1, 2, 20, 24, 75, 81, 82, 100,
 125a ; 133, 162, 164 ; Jph. 7 ;
 Mary, 83 ; M. and A. 1 ; Rt.
 35 ; Rd. 44 ; Thos. 20, 75 ;
 Wm. 1, 2, 38, 67, 82, 83, 162
Teale M. 97
Tebbutt J. 28 ; Rt. 133
Teesdale William, 1
Tennant Charles and Co. 13
Tew William, 16
Thackeray John, 49
Thatcher Benjamin, 20
Theaker and Birkhead, 83
Theaker John, 154
Thompson & Wilkinson 97
Thompson Wm. 52 ; Jno. 153 ;
 Thos. 20 ; Edw. 62
Theabald William, 40
Thirlwall John, 123
Thornhill William, 81
Thornton Chas. 15, 16 ; Eliz. 97 ;
 Hy. 28 ; Jph. 107
Thorpe Gervase, 75 ; Geo. 16,
 133 ; John. 7, 93 ; J. & T. 48 ;
 Jph. 50, 107 ; Saml. 42, 158 ;
 Thos. 16 ; Wm. 90
Thraves William, 28
Throne Thomas, 16
Thurman Edward, 75 ; John, 81 ;
 Saml. 71 ; Thos. 29
Tiddiman George, 32
Timm Chas. & Geo. 16
Timms Thos. 74, 145
Tinker Rd. 7, 48 ; Ann, 97
Tipler Jas. B. 7 ; James, 43
Tipping Wm. 28
Titterton Thos. 133
Tollington Thos. 67
Tome Wm. 16
Tomkin Wm. 73
Tomlin Edmund, 93
Tomlinson Alex. 75 ; James, 26 ;
 John, 85, 101 ; Thos. 28, 127 ;
 Wm. 101
Tootey George, 75
Topham John, 16
Topley Wm. 28, 76

Toplis Thos. 90 ; Wm. 90
Topping Joseph, 162
Torr Geo. 28 ; Jas. 28 ; Lot. 67
Tow and Wootton, 97
Towers Rd. 44 ; Ts. 62 ; Wm. 67
Towle John, 37 ; M. 118 ; T. J.
  and B. 49
Towne Leonard, 38
Townroe Richard, 7
Townsend and Daft, 90
Townsend Jas. 16 ; Robert, 51 ;
  Septimus, 51
Toyne J. 81 ; Saml. 48 ; Wm. 48
Train and Wesson. 83
Travell George, 109
Travis Barnabas, 7
Truman Ann, 1 ; Becket, 144 ;
  Dd. & Co. 49, 83 ; Dd. 60 ;
  William, 66
Truswell and Heap, 134
Trusswell J. 16, 81
Turner Cath. 1 ; Edw. 81 ; Geo.
  28, 75, 93 ; G. J. 83 ; Jas. 28,
  76, 83 ; John, 20, 36 ; Saml.
  15, 83 ; Sarah, 1 ; Thos. 7, 61,
  73 ; Wm. H. 5 ; Wm. 16, 136
Turton Geo. 28 ; W. 62
Tutil George, 28
Tyas Moses. 20
Tyers John, 93
Underwood Richard, 38
Unwin Samuel, 16
Urry George, 67, 146
Urry and Fry, 97
Valentine William, 144
Varney John, 62 ; Saml. 75
Vaughan George, 37
Vausor William, 20
Vernham Ann, 140
Vessey Joseph, 28
Vincent Samuel, 75
Voce William, 7
Waddington and Wilson, 143
Wadsworth John, 5 ; Wm. 145
Wagstaff William, 48
Wain and Blackner, 82
Wain Av. 27 ; Jph. 63 ; Har. 97
Wainman J. 62
Wainwright Ann, 55 ; John, 62
Waite Robt. 20 ; Jane, 97 ; Eli-
  zabeth, 143
Wakefield F. & T. 49
Wakefield & Smith, 83

Waldram J. 75
Walker D. 71 ; Fras. 16 ; Fdk.
  144 ; Geo. 2, 15 ; Geo. Fdk.
  86 ; Isaac, 105 ; John & Saml.
  26, 116, 137, 142 ; John, 28,
  48 ; Jph. 12, 83, 145 ; Mary,
  97 ; Matt. 67, 124 ; Thos. 153 ;
  Wm. 20, 83, 118, 143
Wallace Samuel, 40
Wallace and Keiling, 27
Wallis James, 140, 145
Walls George, 105
Walsh George N. 2, 49
Walstow James, 133
Walton John, 81
Wapplinton Wm. 23 ; Thos. 160
Warburton and Astle, 145
Ward and Allen, 81
Ward Ann, 75 ; Eliz. 75, 126,
  143 ; F. M. 1 ; Hy. P. 38 ;
  Isaac, 145 ; John & Rd. 145 ;
  Jph. 61 ; Jsh. 25 ; Jph. S. 5 ;
  Peter, 16 ; Rt. 20 ; Saml. 1,
  16, 101 ; S. & M. 97
Wardle and Brown, 83
Wardle Isaac & Co. 83 ; Jos. 76 ;
  William, 39
Warner Sarah, 1 ; Thos. 73
Warren John, 38 ; Natl. 75
Warsop Eman. 16 ; S. R. 1 ;
  Saml. 16 ; Thos. 86 ; Wm. 7
Waterson John, 122
Wass George, 37 ; Wm. 67
Waterall George, 38
Watson Eliz. 7 ; George, 40, 76 ;
  Sush. 65 ; Saml. 28 ; Mrs. R.
  97 ; Wm. 7, 83
Watts David, 75 ; Edw. 83 ; Geo.
  16, 92 ; Hy. 138 ; Hy. & Sons,
  9 ; Rd. 28 ; Wm. 144
Waynman & Nunn, 83
Wayre Chas. 64, 71
Weatherall Geo. 55
Webb & Palmer, 97
Webster E. A. 67 ; David, 16 ;
  Geo. 157 ; Hamd. 83 ; Dd. 2 ;
  Gv. 62 ; Jas. 67 ; Jno. 81, 82 ;
  William, 20
Weightman Wm. 60
Wells Andrew, 28 ; Benj. 16 ;
  Chas. 1 ; John, 59 ; Jph. 81,
  136 ; Rd. 73 ; Thos. 133 ; Wm.
  2, 19, 49, 63, 106

2 c

Wells & Burkitt, 90
Wentworth Henry, 2
Wesson John, 83 ; Thos. 83
Westmoreland J. 2
Weston, Field, & Son, 26
Westwick Robert, 122.
Wetherbed E. 59
Wetzlar & Sarrazin, 2
Whait John, 145
Wheatcroft G. & Son, 158 ; Fras.
    143 ; Thos. 43
Wheatley Arthur, 2; James, 2;
    Robt. 1 ; Wm. 101 ; John, 28,
    43, 132
Wheatley & Riste, 83
Wheeldon Eliz. 97 ; John, 28
Wheelhouse Thos. 122
Whiles John & Jas. 16
Whitaker Thos. 15 ; Edw. 28
Whitby John, 2 ; Ed. 28
Whitchurch J. & Co. 83 ; Rd. 2 ;
    Saml. 38, 67 ; Wm. 16, 76
White Eliz. 62 ; Hiram, 20 ; Jer.
    160 ; Jas. 35, 133; Jph. 83,
    144 ; Mary, 97 ; Robt. 16, 28 ;
    S. & A. 1.; Saml. 75; Thos.
    16 ; Wm. 145
Whitfield John, 28 ; George, 83 ;
    Wm. 2
Whitehall Thos. 92, 157
Whitehead Geo. 1 ; Jph. 16, 76
Whiteley John, 20
Whitlock M. & Co. 83
Whitlock Nathl. 7
Whitmore Thomas, 105
Whitt John, 83
Whittaker John, 16
Whittingham John, 18
Whittington Robert, 101
Whittington William, 45
Whittle Jas. 16 ; Eliz. 143 ; John
    160
Whittle & Butler, 97
Whitworth John, 28 ; Benj. 101 ;
    R. & T. 118
Whyatt John, 23
Wirkham Jph. & Wm. 109
Widdowson Wm. 16 ; Matthew,
    20 ; Reuben, 28
Widdowson & Robinson, 83
Wigginton Joseph, 91
Wigley Henry, 28
Wilby David, 50, 133

Wilcocks George, 61
Wilcockson C. V. 38 ; John, 38
Wild Eb. 56 ; Hy. 122 ; John 83 ;
    Wm. 6, 63, 101
Wildgust William, 75
Wildig Ann, 20
Wildsmith Jph. 83 ; Saml. 133
Wilford Thomas, 28
Wilkins John, 56
Wilkinson Eliz. 97, 133 ; M. A.
    123 ; Rd. 34; Wm. 76
Wilks Elias, 20
Willatt Isaac, 75
Williams John C. 112
Williams William, 5
Williamson Fras. 20 ; Luke, 28 ;
    Wm. 133
Wills Benjamin, 16, 133
Willimot John, 40
Wilmott John, 83
Wilson Carn, 28
Wilson & Cutts, 90
Wilson H. & E. 1 ; Jas. & Son,
    73 ; J. J. & I. 73 ; Jno. 133 ;
    Jph. 29 ; Lewis, 75, 163 ; Wm.
    & S. 49, 96 ; Wm. 50
Window Robert, 145
Wingfield Robert, 20
Winter Thomas, 26
Winterton William, 62
Wise and Eddowes, 5
Witham William, 16
Withers Francis, 133
Wolden John, 133, 145
Wolff William, and Co. 83
Wood Benjamin, 133
Wood Edw. 42, 78, 100; Geo.
    20, 28 ; Hy. 16 ; Hy. M. 3,
    86 ; Jas. 7 ; Jno. 5. 28, 44, 62,
    75 ; Mary, 133 ; Matt. 105 ;
    Moses, 24 ; Rev. Rt. 1 ; Saml.
    100, 164 ; Thos. 28, 38, 67 ;
    Wm. 16, 83, 101
Woodall John, 81
Woodborough Thomas, 80
Woodford David, 81, 153
Woodhead John, 133
Woodhouse Dd. 61, 92 ; Jacob.
    16 ; Jno. and Jph. 75 ; Saml.
    73 ; Thos. and Co. 83
Woodward Jas. 28 ; John, 16 ;
    Saml. 136 ; Wm. 23
Woofit Richard, 7,

Woolley Isaac, 83; James, 81; John 16, 75, 83; Lewis, 7; Mary, 97; Thomas 99, 123; Wm. 20
Wootton P. and W. 25
Worth James, 75
Worthington J. 69
Wortley Eliz. 67; Jph. 1
Wragg Charles, 110
Wratt George, 81
Wright Chas. 69; C. N. 6, 19, 163; Ed. 16; Eliz. 97; Fras. 7, 48; Hy. 28; Jas. 79, 150; Jno. 20, 28, 69, 144; I. & I. C. & Co. 8; Jno. 148; Nath.

16; Rt. 32, 69; Wm. 6, 16. 20, 81, 144; W. & G. 11; W 63, 76
Wright and Harriman, 90
Wright. Trivett, and Co. 83.
Wrigley Samuel, 152
Wyer Isaac, 92
Yates Geo. 83, 120; Hy. 45; Jph. 16, 73 ; Thos. 16, 162
Yates and Guilford, 38
Yeomans Hy. 157; Jno. 61, 92 ; Saml. 101; Wm. 38, 67
Youle John and Hy. 148
Young Jno. 59, 69; Saml. 92; Wm. 61

MAILS, POST COACHES, &c.

(The Post-Office Regulations are inserted at page 199.)

FROM THE LION HOTEL.

(THOMAS AND JOHN SIMPSON AND CO.)

London Times day Coach (alternately from the Milton's Head) daily, at six in the morning; returns at ten in the evening.

London Mail, through Melton, Bedford, &c. every morning at half-past five.

Leeds, Carlisle, and *Glasgow* Mail, every morning at ten.

London Express, every evening, at seven

Leeds Express, every morning, at eight.

Manchester and *Liverpool* Lord Nelson, through Matlock Bath, every morning, at a quarter before six; returns every evening, at four.

Birmingham Dart, through Castle Donington, Ashby-de-la-Zouch, and Tamworth, every morning, (except Sunday) at eight o'clock; returns at four in the afternoon.

Lincoln, Barton, and *Hull* Imperial, through Bingham and Newark, with branches to Horncastles, Louth, and Boston, daily, (except Sunday) at a quarter before nine; returns at eight in the evening.

Doncaster Royal Forester, through Mansfield and Worksop, every Monday, Wednesday, and Friday mornings, at half-past ten; returns the following days, at half-past two.

Derby Royal Sovereign, every morning at a quarter to seven; returns at five in the evening.

Derby Times, daily at eleven in the morning; returns at nine the next morning.

Newark Wonder, daily at four in the afternoon; returns at eleven in the morning

Leicester Pilot, every morning, at a quarter before seven, through Loughborough; returns at seven in the evening.

FROM THE MILTON'S HEAD INN.

(BENJAMIN BOWER AND CO.)

London Times day Coach, every morning (alternately from the Lion Hotel,) at six o'clock; returns in the evening at a quarter before ten.

London Royal Hope Coach, every afternoon, at half-past two o'clock.

Sheffield Royal Hope, every morning, at half-past ten o'clock.

Manchester and *Liverpool* Champion, every morning at half-past seven, by way of Mansfield, Chesterfield, Stony Middleton, Chapel-en-le-Frith, &c.; returns every evening at six o'clock.

Leicester, Coventry, Warwick, and Birmingham Royal Pilot, every morning at a quarter before seven o'clock; returns at half-past six in the evening.

Newark and Southwell Accommodation, every day at half-past three; returns every morning at eleven.

Mansfield Robin Hood, daily (except Sunday) at five in the evening; returns at ten in the morning.

To *Boston, Hull, and Lincoln*, the Royal Pilot, every morning at half-past five, and returns the same evening at seven.

To *Doncaster and York*, the Union, every morning at half-past six (Sunday excepted); returns at eight o'clock in the evening.

FROM THE BLACK BOY INN.

London Courier, every evening at seven; through Leicester, Harborough, Northampton, Newport Pagnell, Woburn, Dunstable, and St. Albans.

Leeds Courier, every morning at a quarter before six; through Mansfield, Chesterfield, Sheffield, Barnsley, and Wakefield.

Manchester Champion, every morning at half-past six; through Derby, Ashbourne, Leek, and Macclesfield.

Derby Tally-ho, every afternoon, at three.

Derby, Burton-on-Trent, Litchfield, &c. the Champion, every morning at half-past six.

Birmingham, Warwick, Coventry, &c. the Harkforward, every morning at a quarter before seven,

Leicester Harkforward, every morning at a quarter before seven.

Leicester Lark, every afternoon at two.

Newark, Lincoln, &c. Perseverance, every morning at half-past five.

Grantham and Stamford, through Bingham, the Tally-ho, daily at twelve noon.

FROM THE MAYPOLE INN.

Derby Royal Defiance, every afternoon at half-past three.

Derby Times, every morning at eleven.

Grantham, Dunnington, Holbeach, Lynn, &c. every morning, (Sunday excepted) at half-past five.
Leicester Accommodation, every afternoon at a quarter before three.
Stamford Queen Adelaide, every morning at half-past five.

MARKET COACHES AND CARS.

Belper, Wm. Winson & Co.'s *Omnibus,* from the Blue Bell Inn, every Saturday, arrives 9 mg. departs 3 afternoon.
Castle Donnington, Wm. Oliver's *Van;* every Wed. & Sat. from the Derby Arms, Chapel Bar. arr. 10 mg. dep. ½ past 4 aft.
Heanor and Eastwood, George Wysall's *Car,* from the George and Dragon, Long Row, Wed. and Sat. arr. 10 mg. dep. 5 evening.
Ilkeston, Hives Jackson & Co.'s *Car,* from the Derby Arms, Chapel Bar, Mon. Wed. and Sat. arr. 10 mg. dep. 5 evening.
Ilkeston and West Hallam, Hune, Rollinson, & Co.'s *Coach,* from the Black Bull Inn, Chapel Bar, every Saturday, arrives 10 mg. departs 4 afternoon.
Loughborough, the Tradesman, from the Windmill, Market-street, every Tue. Wed. Fri. and Sat. at 5 evening.
Stapleford and Sandiacre, Matthew Bramley's *Reform* Coach, every Wed. and Sat. from the Malt Cross; Edward Brown's *Omnibus,* every Sat. from the Blue Bell Inn; and Thos. Greasley's *Car,* every Sat. from the Derby Arms;—arrive 9 mg. dep. 3 aft.
Kegworth, Robert Mee's *Car,* from the Horse and Groom, St. Peter's-square, Wed. and Sat. at 3 afternoon.
Melton, John Helmsley's *Car,* from the Black Boy, Mon. Wed. and Sat. at 3 afternoon.

MAIL GIGS.

☞ *They take parcels, but* NO *passengers.*

To *Derby,* from the Crown and Anchor, Bridge-street, every morning, at half-past 6.
To *Loughborough,* from the Durham Ox, Pelham-street, every afternoon, at half-past 3.
To *Newark and Lincoln,* from the Durham Ox, every morning, at half-past 4. ☞ Parcels for the north arrive one day sooner in the north by this conveyance than by any other which leaves Nottingham.

HACKNEY COACHES.

Stand at the Lion Hotel, at George IV. Inn, at Castle Place, in Castlegate, and in the Market place.—*(See Livery Stables, &c. page* 248.)

CARRIERS BY LAND.

DEACON, HARRISON, & Co. Milton-street, *(Fly Waggons,)* to London, every night at 10; to Sheffield, Leeds, York, Manchester, Liverpool, &c. every evening at 6; to Birmingham, every Monday,

Wednesday, and Friday afternoon, at 4; and to Melton, Stamford, Peterborough, Cambridge, and Norwich, every Monday, Wednesday, and Friday night, at 7.

PICKFORD & Co. from their *Van Office*, Maypole-yard, and their *Waggon Warehouses*, at Leen bridge and Clumber-street, to London, Sheffield, Manchester, and all parts of the kingdom, daily.

GERMAN WHEATCROFT & SONS, Three Cranes Wharf, Commercial-street, *Fly Waggons*, to and from Bristol and Leeds, in three days, through Birmingham and Sheffield, daily; also to Leicester, London, Newark, Gainsbro', Hull, Cromford, &c.

WM. & JPH. PETTIFOR, Houndsgate, *Waggons* to London, Bath, Bristol, Birmingham, Liverpool, Manchester, Newark, Lincoln, Hull, and all parts of the south, every Monday, Wednesday, Friday, and Saturday evening.

WATER CONVEYANCE.

To *London*, Liverpool, Manchester, Derby, Bath, Bristol, Hull, Birmingham, and nearly all parts of England, by *Fly Boats* daily from *Thos. Pickford & Co.'s*, Leen Bridge Wharf, and from *Robert Marshall's*, London-road.

To Derby, Liverpool, Grantham, and all intermediate places, *Samuel Thorpe's Fly Boats*, from the Canal Co.'s Wharf, Leen side.

To Liverpool, Manchester, Newark, Gainsbro', and all parts of the West of England, and Cheshire, *Richard Barrows' Boats*, from Canal-street, every Tuesday and Friday night, and *German Wheatcroft and Sons' Boats*, from London-road, several times a-week.

To Gainsbro', Hull, Cromford, Mansfield, High Peak Railway, Retford, Liverpool, and all parts of Scotland and the West of England, *John Simpson's Boats*, from the Park Wharf.

To London, *Deacon, Harrison, & Co.'s Fly Boats*, every Monday and Friday, from Mrs. Cutts's Wharf, Leen side.

CARRIERS FROM THE INNS.

☞ The letters W. F. S. &c. signify the *days*, and the figures after them, the *hours*, when each carrier departs. Most of them arrive on Wednesday and Saturday mornings about nine o'clock, and leave at three or four, afternoon.

Alfreton. J. Nicholson, Derby Arms, S.; Thos. Topham, Blue Bell. S.; Wm. Wheatley, George and Dragon, Long row, W. and S.; John Hardstaff, Bull, S.; Martin Durham, Spread Eagle, W. and S. 3.

Annesley, John Lee, Wheat Sheaf, W. and S. 2.

Arnold, Edw. Seagrave, George and Dragon, North street, S. 4.

Arnold, Robt. Denison, Admiral Duncan, M. W. F. and S. 5.

Arnold Post, John Hutchinson, Admiral Duncan, daily at 5.

Aslackton, Mr. Greaves, White Swan, S.; Rd. Sanderson, Blue Bell, S.; H. Potter, Rein Deer, W. and S.

Bagthorp, John Farnsworth, King William IV., W. and S.

Barkstone, John Cant, Crown Inn. S. 4.

Barton, John Woodland, Star, S. 4.

Beeston, Thomas Stone, Derby Arms, S. 4; W. Martin, Blue Bell,

S. 5; Joseph Oldham, Colonel Wardle, every day at 3; Rd. White, White Swan, W. and S.

Belper, Horsley Woodhouse, and West Hallam, Samuel Saxton.

Belper and Derby, William Winson, Blue Bell, S.

Bingham, Robert Green, Rein Deer; J. Jones, Wheat Sheaf; John Sills, Horse and Groom, Peter's square; and Ann Moult, Wheat Sheaf, W. and S. 3.

Bleasby, Wm. Wilson, Durham Ox; Rt. Pacey, Spread Eagle; and Wm. Mountney, News house, St. James's street, S. 4.

Blidworth, John Barrowcliff, Kingston's Arms; Thos. Frost, News house, James's street; and Geo. Wheeldon, Milton's Head, S. 3.

Bottesford, George Wilson, King William IV., W. and S.; John Wilson, George and Dragon, S.; Wm. Jackson, Bell, S.

Bradmore, Wm. Marriott, Rein Deer. S. 3.

Bramcote, George Hardstaff, King William IV., W. and S..

Breason, Robert Plackett, White Swan, Beastmarket hill, S.

Breason, Thomas Eden, Derby Arms, S. 3.

Bridgeford, (East,) John Brown, Durham Ox, S. 5.

Bridgeford, (East,) Wm. Upton, Horse and Groom, W. and S. 4..

Brinsley, George Moss, Bull, W. and S. 3.

Brinsley, Matthew Cooper, Talbot Inn, S. 3.

Brinsley, Thomas Trueman, Swan, W. and S. 3.

Broughton Sulney, John Hemsley, Black Boy. M. W. and S. 3.

Broughton, (Nether) and Melton, Rt. Taylor, Geo. and Drag. S..

Broughton, (Over) Joseph Brown, Rein Deer, W. and S. 3.

Broughton, John Holmes, Talbot, S. 3.

Broughton, (Over) John Hopkins, Talbot, S. 3.

Bulwell, John Gent, Old Admiral Duncan, *daily.*

Bulwell, Joseph Walker, White Hart, Sheep lane, W. and S. 3;.

Bunney, Wm. Hart, News house, James's street, W. and S. 3.

Bunney, Wm. Henson, Horse and Groom, Peter's square, S. 3.

Burton Joyce, John Swinscoe, Lord Nelson, S. 4.

Calverton, Rt. Watson, Robin Hood, Milton street, S. 3.; Robert Watson, jun., Black Boy, S. 4.; Simeon Cundy, Bell, Parliament street, W. and S..4.

Car Colston, T. Asher, Black Boy, Tu. and S. 3.; John Baker,. Horse and Groom, S. 3.; Thomas Cragg, Swan, S. 3.; and John. Simpson, Wheat Sheaf, S. 3.

Castle Donington, Chas. Greaves, Wheat Sheaf; Isaac Hodson,. Black Boy; and Wm. Oliver, Derby Arms, W and S. 4.

Claythorpe, John Bailey, Nag's Head. Stoney street, W. and S. 5.

Chesterfield, John Townsend, Black Boy, S. 12.

Chilwell, John Lee, Swan, Angel row, S. 5.

Clawson Long, J. Wilkinson, Milton's Head, S. 3.

Clawson Long, Joseph Scarborough, George and Dragon, S. 4.

Clawson Long, John Marriott, Maypole, S. 4.

Clifton, Henry Allen, Star. S. 3.

Colston Bassett, Thos. Hicks, Swan, S. 3.; Wm. Herrick, Black. Boy, S. 4.; and Thos. Newton, Rein Deer, W. and S. 4.

Cotgrave. Wm. Archer, Star, Wheelergate, W. and S. 4.; and Saml. Upton and James Sharp, Horse and Groom, Peter's sq. S. 3

Cotmanhay, Saml. Booth, Golden Ball, Long row, W. and S. 3.

Cropwell Bishop, John Abbott, Black Boy; Wm. Clark, Horse and Groom; and Saml. Swinscoe, Star, S. 4.

Cropwell Butler, Thos. Beecroft, Black Boy, S. 4.

Cropwell Butler, Richard Marriott, Horse and Groom, S. 4.

Derby, Birmingham, and the Potteries, Wm. Barnes, Black Boy, Tu. Th. and S. 5

Derby, Nottingham, and Loughborough, A. Smith, Ball, S. 4

Draycot, Edward Smith, News House, James's-street, S. 4

Draycot, Edward Astle, Blue Bell, S. 3

Eastwood, William Bentley, Blue Bell, W. and S. 3

Eastwood, George Meakin, Ball, Long Row, S. 3

Epperstone, James Taylor, Crown, W.; J. Smith, Black Boy, and George Harrison, New George, S. 4

Farnsfield, Edward Hodgson, Milton's Head, W. and S. 3

Fiskerton, J. Walker, Queen's Head, S. 3

Flintham, Thomas Cupit, Abbott's, Belfounder's-yard, S. 2

Gainsborough, Grantham, and parts of Lincolnshire, Messrs. Wheatcroft and Sons, Bridge foot

Gotham, Thos. Maltby, Red Lion; Mr. Hemsley, Rein Deer; Rd. Hallam, Bell Inn; and Wm. Dutton, New George street, S.

Goverton, Robert Pacy, Spread Eagle, S. 3.

Granby, Mr. Pritchard, Milton's Head, S.

Grantham, Mr. Gibson, Milton's Head, S.

Gunthorpe, Jarvis Mayfield, Durham Ox, S. 4.; Wm. Allwood, Lord Nelson; John Brittle, Old Angel, S. 3.

Hallam Little, Wm, Strelley, Horse and Groom, Peter's sq., S.

Hallam West, John Lee, King William IV., W. S. 5.

Harby (Notts.) Thomas Kemp, White Swan, S. 3.

Harby (Leicestershire) Richard Knapp, White Swan, S. 3.

Hathern, Thomas Storer, Talbot, W. and S.

Hathern, Samuel Braley, Horse and Groom, Peter square, F. 4.

Heanor, James Nelson and George Wysall, George and Dragon, W. and S.; and Samuel Searson, Black Bull, S.

Hickling, Richard Copley, Rein Deer, S. 3.

Hickling, Samuel Mann, Wheat Sheaf, S. 3.

Hockbrook, Mr. Bradley, Black Bull, S. 2.

Holme Pierrepont, Samuel Wheatley, Eight Bells, Peck lane, S. 3.

Horseley Woodhouse, Samuel Saxton, Spread Eagle, S. 3.

Hose, Thomas Corner, Milton's Head; and H. Morrison, Black Boy, S. 4.

Hoveringham, Cphr. Armstrong, Lord Nelson; John Pride, Nag's Head, Stoney street; and Wm. Morris, Black Boy, S. 4.

Hucknall Torkard, Wm Thums, White Hart, W. and S. 3.

Hucknall, Thomas Hanson, Robin Hood, S. 3.

Hucknall Torkard, Thos. Wilmott, News house, S. 3.

Ilkestone, Robert Burrows; Hives Jackson & Co.; and Thomas Curtis, Derby Arms; Charles Chadwick, George and Dragon; and Joseph Holmes, Blue Bell, W. & S. 4

Kegworth, Robert Mee, Horse and Groom, W. and S. 3

Kegworth, Robert Smith, White Swan, S. 3

Keyworth, T. Eggleston & Walker, Horse and Groom, S. 4

Kimberley, C. Leavers, George and Dragon, M. W. and S

Kimberley, Michael Leavers, William 4th. W. and S. 3

Kinoulton, Samuel Pollard, Elephant and Castle, S. 3

Kinoulton, John Peet, Horse and Groom, Peter's-square, S. 3.

Kirkby, Samuel Wilmott, News House, James's-street, S. 3
Kirkby Woodhouse, John Morris, Elephant & Castle, W. & S. 3
Lambley, Wm. Watson, New George, W. and S. 4
Lambley, John Selby, Nag's Head, and W. Watson, New George, S
Langley, Samuel Searson, Black Bull, S. 2
Leake Thomas Gunn, Rein Deer, Wheeler-gate, S. 3
Long Eaton, James Huss, Derby Arms, W. and S. 3
Loughborough, William Potter, Black Boy, Tue. W. and S. 4
Loughborough Mail Gig, Durham Ox, daily, half-past 3
Loughborough, John Fisher, White Swan, W. and S. 5
Loscoe and Codnor, T. Fetcher, Black Bull, S. 2
Lowdham, John Archer, & J. Garrat, New George, Warsergate;
    and J. Reddish, Nag's Head, S. 3
Mansfield, William Jackson, Black Boy; John Oldfield, Unicorn;
    and Henry Blackwell, Horse and Groom, W. & S. 3
Melbourne, Thos. Pass, and Fras. Dallman, Derby Arms, W. & S. 4
Melton, John Hemsley, Black Boy, M. W. & S. 3
Morton, Thomas Hainsworth, News house, S. 3
Newark, G. Skidmore, Newcastle street, W. & S.
Newark, J. Wilcock, Houndsgate, S. 4 morning
Newark, Palmer, Maypole yard, M. W. and F. 6 morning
New Brinsley, Thos. Truman, White Swan, W. & S.
Newthorp and Moorgreen, George Meakin, Ball, Long row, S. 3
Normanton, Derbyshire, George Slater, Derby Arms, S. 2
Normanton, Nottinghamshire, —— Wass, Old Bear, S. 3
Nuttall, Moses Plant, William the Fourth, S. 4
Ollerton, Thos. Rushby, Milton's Head, W. and S. 2
Orston, John Fryer, Horse and Groom, and J. Henson, Swan, S. 3
Overingham Cphr. Armstrong, Lord Nelson, S
Oxton, Elizabeth Thorpe, Maypole; John Palethorpe, Milton's
    Head; and Thomas Dalton, Maypole, S. 3
Pentridge D. Moore, Old King's Head, S.
Plumptre, Wm. Astill, Wheat Sheaf, S. 3
Plungar, Thos. Worthington, Bird-in-Hand, S. 4
Ratcliffe, Wm. Morley, Eight Bells; Thos. Walker, Swan Inn, W.
    and S. 3; George Duke, Black Boy, S. 3
Ratcliffe-upon-Soar, —— Morris, Horse and Groom, S. 2
Redmile, Robert Patchet, Crown, S. 3
Redmile, John Rick, Wheat Sheaf, S. 3
Retford, John Rushby, Milton's Head, W. and S. 1
Ripley, George Savidge, Swan, W. and S. 2
Ripley, Edward White, Derby Arms, S. 3
Ripley and Codnor, Thomas Duncan, Swan, S. 3.
Risley, Edward Mears, Bell Inn, S. 3
Ruddington, John Dennis, Star, S. 4
Ruddington, Edward Smith, Peacock, S. 5
Sawley, William Wright, Bell, W. and S. 4
Sawley, Joseph Meads, Swan, and C. Wright, Bell, W. & S. 3
Scarrington, William Hitchcock, Queen's Head, S. 3
Screveton, John Padgett, Horse and Groom, S. 4
Screveton, Joseph Hallam, Crown, S. 3
Selston, John Lee, Wheat Sheaf, W. and S. 2
Sheepshead, Robert Martin, Talbot, W. and S. 3

Sheepshead, Joseph Allsopp, Star, Peter's square, S. 3
Shelford, John Holland, New George, Warsergate, W. and S. 3
Shelford, William Watson, Lord Nelson, Carlton street, S. 3
Sibthorpe, Thomas Richman, Black Boy, S. 3
Skegby and Sutton-in-Ashfield Accommodation, Thomas Ward
    Milton's Head, S. 4
Southwell, Wm. Revill, Crown, Long row, Tu. and S.
Southwell and Newark, Joseph Pilgrim, Maypole, S. 3
Southwell, John Fryer, Black Boy, Tu. and S. 4
Sproxton, Richard Brown, Maypole, S. 3
Stanton-by-Dale, Matthew Hancock, George and Dragon, S. 3
Stanton-by-Dale, Matthew Stevens, Derby Arms, S. 3
Stapleford, Matthew Bramley, Malt Cross, W. and S. 4; Thomas
    Greasley, Derby Arms, S.; John Doar, Bell, Angel row, W. and
    S. 3; Jacob Barroclough, Three Horse Shoes, S. 4; George
    Brown, Bell, S. 4; Geo. Attenborough, Swan, W. and S. 3
Stathern, William Gratton, Rein Deer, S. 3
Stathern, John Hebb, Maypole, S. 2
Strelley, John Martin, King's Head, W. and S. 3
Summercotes, Samuel Thornley, George and Dragon, W. and S. 3
Summercotes, Benjamin Bailey, Black Bull, S. 3
Sutton-in-Ashfield, Thos. Wilson, Milton's Head, W. and S. 4
Sutton-in-Ashfield and Mansfield Accommodation, Thomas Wilson,
    Black Boy, W. and S. 4
Sutton-in-Ashfield, Wm. Wilson, Milton's Head, S. 3
Sutton-in-Ashfield, Thomas Bullock, Black Boy, W. and S. 4
Sutton Bonington, Wm. Marshall, Star, S. 3; G. & T. Dutton,
    Swan, W. and S. 3; Edward Whitby, Rein Deer, S. 4.
Waltham, John Osborn, George and Dragon, S. 3.
Whatton, Henry Parnham, Black Boy, W. and S. 3
Whatton, W. Tutbery, White Swan, S. 3
Whatton-in-the-Vale, George Moss, Golden Ball, W. and S. 4
Whitwich, Jph. Ball, Milton's Head, W.
Willoughby, Jthn. Goodacre, Peacock, S. 5; Thos. Charles, Red
    Lion; and Wm. Wheatley, Rein Deer, S. 4
Wimeswould, Robert Mee, Horse and Groom, S. 4
Woodborough, John Lee, Bell, S. 4; William Pool, Swan, S. 3;
    John Bish, Swan, W. and S. 3; Wm. Pool, Bell, Parliament street,
    S. 3
Wysall, John Blood, Peacock, Petergate, S. 3

BASSETLAW HUNDRED.

This great northern division of Nottinghamshire is, like the county, of an irregular oval shape, and is bounded on the north-ast by Lincolnshire, on the north-west by Yorkshire, on the outh-east by the Hundred of Thurgarton, and on the south-west y Broxtow Hundred and a small part of Derbyshire. It comprises nore than two-fifths of the county, being about 25 miles in length, 7 in breadth, and 80 in circumference. It contains about 80,000 acres of land, 56 *parishes,* four *extra parochial places,* nd nine *chapelries ;* divided into 88 *Townships,* in which are early 200 *villages* and *hamlets,* and four MARKET TOWNS, viz. Retford, Worksop, Tuxford, and Ollerton, with part of Bawtry. From Fledborough to the Heck dyke, below Stockwith, a dis-ance of about 14 miles, it is bounded on the east by the noble tream of the Trent, except in two instances, at Laneham and Littleborough, where it takes a few short strides across the iver.* The greater portion of it is watered by the river Idle, and its numerous tributary streams; and the Chesterfield canal vinds through it by a circuitous route from Stockwith-on-the-Trent, to Retford, Worksop, and Shireoaks, which latter place s at the junction of the three counties of York, Derby, and Nottingham.

This large hundred is subdivided into THREE DIVISIONS, viz. *North Clay, South Clay,* and *Hatfield,* the last of which is the argest, and includes all that portion of Sherwood forest (see 3. 35) lying on the west side of the Idle, where are situated .he beautiful parks of Clumber, Thoresby, Worksop, Welbeck, and Rufford. The North and South Clay, include the district between the Idle and the Trent, which, from the nature of the soil, is highly fertile, both as arable and pasture land. (Vide p. 42 to 45.)

Bassetlaw, from its containing the seats of the Dukes of Norfolk, Newcastle, and Portland, has been called the DUKERY, an appellation with which it was frequently honoured during the contentious discussions in Parliament, (A.D. 1827 to 1830,) which terminated in declaring the corruption of East Retford, and in extending the elective franchise of that borough to all the freeholders of this hundred, who now vote both for the county and the borough representatives ; but, should the Reform Bill which now (Feb. 1832) lies before Parliament, pass into a law, the elective franchise of the whole kingdom will be changed, and those alterations which refer to Nottinghamshire, will be noticed in the appendix to this volume.

* Owing to the Trent having changed its ancient course from two circuitous reaches at West Burton and Bole, there are now two slips of land, containing about 210 acres, on the west side of the river, belonging to Lincolnshire.

In Domesday Book, this hundred or "*wapentak*" is variously called *Bassetlaw, Bernedeslawe, Bernedsetlawe,* and *Bersetlaw;* and in the Nomina Villarum, which was compiled in 1315, when the King was lord of it, we find it written *Bersetelowe;* indeed none of our ancient writers seem to have paid much attention to orthography.* Soon after the Norman conquest, there was in the county a distinguished family of the name of Basset, for in the year 1121, we find "Ralph Basset, Justice of England," and in 1390, died "Ralph, the last *Lord Basset of Draiton,*" whose large estates in this and the adjacent counties passed to his heirs, Thomas Earl of Stafford, and Alice wife of. Sir Wm. Chaworth. Whether this family gave its name to some *lowe* or *barrow*† from which this hundred has its present appellation, has not been clearly ascertained, but it certainly had much property here and in other parts of the county, and from it Colston-Basset, in Bingham Hundred, and Drayton-Basset in Staffordshire, derived the distinctive portion of their names. *Oswardebec* or *Oswaldbec Soc,* was anciently a separate wapentake or hundred, but it now forms the North Clay Division of Bassetlaw. Part of the three divisions of this hundred are comprised in the *Archiepiscopal Liberty of Southwell and Scrooby,* the greater part of which is in the hundred of Thurgarton as will be seen in a subsequent page.

Though Bassetlaw comprises more than two-fifths of the surface of the county, it has only about one-fifth of its *population,* being entirely an agricultural district, free from the noise and bustle created by the lace and hosiery manufactures in and about Nottingham and Mansfield, except at Cuckney and Langwith, where there are two cotton mills. There is, however, a paper mill at Retford, and another at Ordsall, also several large *Hop-yards* in the North and South Clay Divisions, and many malt kilns at Worksop and other places.

POPULATION OF BASSETLAW HUNDRED.

The following table shows the number of *Inhabitants* in each Parish and Township in the years 1821 and 1831, and also the number of *Houses* at the latter period, as they appear in the Parliamentary Census :—

---

* As if intent on still further confusing the orthography of Bassetlaw, Thoroton calls it in one place *Berteselowe,* aud Throsby *Bassinglaw.*

† *Lowe,* from the Saxon *hleaw,* signifies a hill or barrow.

HATFIELD DIVISION.

Names of Places.	1821. Ints.	Hses.	1831. Ints.
Aukley	297	74	362
Babworth	416	76	449
Barnby Moor with Bilby	182	39	205
Blythe	801	168	811
Bothamsall	310	69	326
Boughton	289	75	295
Budby	140	19	139
Carburton	154	28	143
Carlton-in-Linderick	838	189	974
Clipstone	142	49	223
Cuckney	427	93	633
Edwinstow	648	166	740
Elksley	347	73	377
Finningley	368	80	424
Harworth	395	90	526
Hodsack	224	22	228
Holbeck	230	46	244
Houghton	40	8	55
Langwith	378	66	437
Mattersey	426	97	455
Misson	720	184	841
Norton	391	62	334
Ollerton	576	130	658
Ordsall	632	205	809
Palethorpe	93	14	89
Retford (West)	571	152	593
Rufford (ex. par.)	323	64	322
Sookholme	69	11	68
Styrrup	447	105	510
Thorworth	219	42	205
Walesby	308	68	340
Warsop	1072	254	1213
Wallingwells (ex. par.)	7	2	21
Welbeck (ex. par.)	64	7	63
Woodhouse Hall (ex. par.)	5	1	11
Worksop	4567	1170	5566
Total	17,175	4003	19,626

LIBERTY OF SOUTHWELL AND SCROOBY,

WITHIN THE HUNDRED.

Names of Places.	1821. Ints.	Hses.	1831. Ints.
Askham	270	79	329
Beckingham	515	102	481
Everton	611	157	708
Hayton-cum-Tilne	244	52	256
Laneham	347	77	347
Lound	370	91	382
Ranskill	317	66	347
Scaftworth	100	19	84
Scrooby	269	65	281
Sutton	347	91	419
Total	3480	799	3624

NORTH CLAY DIVISION.

Names of Places.	1821. Ints.	Hses.	1831. Ints.
Bole	193	35	144
Burton (West)	37	6	40
Clareborough	1929	507	2106
Clayworth	431	105	459
Cottam	74	17	77
Gringley-on-the-Hill	647	168	737
Habblesthorpe	103	22	95
Leverton (North)	300	74	303
———— (South)	300	71	323
Littleborough	64	15	82
Misterton	811	205	944
Retford (East)	2465	546	2491
Saundby	101	15	104
Stockwith (West)	618	165	635
Sturton	605	118	638
Walkeringham	513	116	529
Wheatley (North)	441	87	435
———— (South)	47	6	25
Wiseton	126	23	118
Total	9810	2301	10,295

SOUTH CLAY DIVISION.

Names of Places.	1821. Ints.	Hses.	1831. Ints.
Bevercotes	48	8	51
Bilsthorpe	252	43	217
Darlton	153	28	162
Drayton (East)	266	55	256
———— (West)	117	23	107
Dunham	269	77	389
Eakring	564	128	595
Eaton	225	48	238
Egmanton	320	67	341
Gamston	385	64	306
Grove	106	20	121
Headon-cum-Upton	241	56	248
Kirton	200	45	247
Laxton	615	120	659
Markham (East)	756	188	805
———— (West)	209	44	197
Ompton	106	20	120
Ragnall	146	36	168
Rampton	391	67	411
Stokeham	45	8	48
Treswell	216	49	224
Tuxford	979	232	1113
Wellow	444	110	473
Total	7043	1542	7499

	Houses.	Inhabits.
Grand Total in 1831	8,645	41,054
in 1821	7,615	37,448
Increase	1,030	3,606

2 D

Of the Liberty of Southwell and Scrooby, Askham and
Laneham are in the *South Clay*, Beckingham, Everton, Hay-
ton-cum-Tilne, and Scaftworth in the *North Clay*, and Lound,
Ranskill, Scrooby, and Sutton in the Hatfield Division.

THE NORTH CLAY DIVISION.

IN which we shall commence our topographical description of
Bassetlaw, extends southward from West Stockwith and Misson Car, to East Retford, South Leverton, and Cottam, and is
bounded on the east by the Trent, and on the west by the
river Idle.

HISTORY OF RETFORD.

EAST RETFORD, the capital of the hundred of Bassetlaw, is
an ancient borough by prescription, and a well-built, populous,
and busy market town, pleasantly situated on the Great North
Road, upon the river Idle and the Chesterfield canal, which
skirt it on three sides. It is in 53 deg. 19 min. 46 sec. north
latitude, and 51 min. 49 sec. west longitude; being distant 144
miles N.N.W. of London, 32 miles N.N.E. of Nottingham,
23 miles W. by N. of Lincoln, 18 miles S.E. by S. of Doncaster,
9 miles E. of Worksop, and 27 miles E. of Sheffield. The *borough* is co-extensive with the *parish* to which it gives name,
and is all comprised in the town and the " cars and commons,"
which altogether only occupy a surface of about 120 acres; but
the suburbs of the town include West Retford, on the opposite
side of the Idle, the hamlets of Moorgate and Spittal hill, in
Clareborough parish, and the lordship of Thrumpton, in Ordsall
parish, so that what may properly be called the *Town of Retford*, extends into two of the three great divisions of Bassetlaw;
the spacious Market-place, and the rest of the borough of East
Retford, with its extensive suburbs in the parish of Clareborough,
being in the *North Clay*, and the parishes of West Retford and
Ordsall in the *Hatfield* division. At the last Parliamentary census, in 1831, the borough contained 2491 inhabitants,* West Retford 593, Clareborough 2106, and Ordsall parish 809, making
the total *population* of the town and suburbs nearly 6000 souls.
The approach to the town from every side is by a beautiful and
gradual descent, and its open airy Market-place, surrounded
by good regular buildings, and having several commodious

---

* Of the 2491 inhabitants of East Retford, 1137 are males and 1354 females, consisting of 525 families, of whom 256 are employed in trade, manufactures, or handicraft, and the remainder are either unemployed or engaged in professional
pursuits.

streets of neat houses branching from it, gives the whole such an air of importance, comfort, and wealth, as is possessed but by few country towns of the same size ; whilst the surrounding district, being in a high state of cultivation, fills its weekly market and annual fairs with an abundance of agricultural produce ; and the *Chesterfield canal*,* which crosses the *river Idle*, and winds round the south and east sides of the borough, gives it a tolerable share of inland traffic, supplies it with coal and lime from the mines and quarries 'of Derbyshire, and opens a water communication with the Trent, the Humber, and other navigable rivers and canals. The *Great North Road*, (see p. 54,) and the roads which diverge from the town to Gainsbro' and Lincoln, and to Worksop and Sheffield, also impart to it a considerable degree of gaiety and bustle, by bringing to it daily great numbers of coaches and travellers of every grade.

ANCIENT HISTORY.—Though the borough certainly existed and was of some importance before the Norman conquest, the name of *Redeford* does not occur in any known document of an earlier date than Domesday Book, (see p. 21.) and even that record does not make the distinction of East and West Retford, but merely implies that in *Redforde* there was one mill belonging to *Sudton* (Sutton) of the fee of the Archbishop of York, and that in *Odesthorpe* (now unknown) and *Redforde*, there was one bovate and three quarters of land to be taxed, besides waste land, four acres of meadow, and one villain ; but it has not been definitely ascertained whether the latter of these, and some other entries in Domesday Book, refer to East or West Retford, or to either of the two Radfords near Worksop and Nottingham. In the writings of the early part of the 13th century, the borough is distinguished by the name of *Este Reddfurthe*, which in the subsequent century was written *Est Redeforde*, afterwards *East Redforde*, and up to the middle of the last century, *East Redford*, which latter is more correct in orthography than the present appellation, as it is evident that the two Retfords were named after the ancient *ford* that crossed the Idle a little below the bridge which now unites them, and was called the *red ford*, from its stratum of red clay being so frequently disturbed by the passage of cattle, &c. as to tinge the water with its colour.

East Retford being allowed to be a borough by prescription, it is scarcely necessary to observe, that the name of its founder is unknown, though Piercy† conjectures that its incorporation must have taken place between the years 1185 and 1200, and

* The Chesterfield canal, which was commenced under an act of Parliament in 1771, and opened throughout the whole line on September 12th, 1777, is already described, together with the river Idle, at pages 53 and 54. From Retford to the Trent the canal locks are double the width of those betwixt Retford and Chesterfield.

† History of Retford, by John S. Piercy, published in 1828.

from the frequent mention of Richard I. in many ancient documents which he perused, he is of opinion that the warlike
monarch, Richard Cœur de Lion, was the original benefactor
of this ancient borough, which afterwards received many royal
charters, confirming former privileges and granting new ones,
but several of them are now lost, and some of the others have
become illegible.

CHARTERS.—In 1246, Henry III. granted the burgesses an
annual *fair*, to continue eight days from the eve of Holy Trinity, and released them from the payment of *toll, pannage*, and
murrage, in all parts of the kingdom. He likewise granted to
them and their successors in fee farm for the yearly rent of 20
marks of silver, " the *tolls* of the bridge of Kelim (Kelham) and
all along to Dourbeck, (Doverbeck,) where it falls into the
Trent, and of Eperstone, and the bridge of Mirald and of
Retford, and of all other places where the burgesses of Nottingham were wont to take toll." On November 27th, 1279,
Edward I. granted the *town* in fee farm to the burgesses, for
the annual rent of £10, and gave them a *market* to be held
every Saturday, with tollage and other immunities. He also
gave them a *court* " to plead the writ of a certain patent of the
common law," and to have the amendment of the assize of
bread and beer, the use of the *pillory* and *ducking-stool*, and
power to claim wrecks and waifes, and to elect a bailiff for the
government of the town. Edward III. confirmed all their
former privileges, and exempted them from all tolls and foreign
services, from serving as jurymen at the assizes, and from the
cognizance of any matters with foreigners, on occasion of lands
and tenements, either without or within the borough. Soon
after this, the burgesses of Nottingham brought an action
against those of Retford, for having taken toll at Mattersey,
which the bailiffs did not deny, but pleaded their right to the
same by the power of a former charter. The King, however,
in order to satisfy both parties, and to enable the burgesses of
Retford to pay to those of Nottingham the yearly fee farm of
£10, and the 20 marks of silver before-mentioned, granted
them " the return of all manner of writs, precepts, attachments,
bills, mandates, &c.; also all manner of goods and chattels belonging to felons, fugitives, and suicides, and all fines, ran-
soms, and amerciaments whatsover;" together with a *fair*, to
be held on the eve, day, and morrow of St. Gregory the Bishop,
and the five following days, in lieu of the fair granted by Henry
III. Another annual fair was also granted to the borough by
the same monarch, (Edward III.) in 1373, to commence four
days before, and continue till the day after the feast of St.
Margaret.

CORPORATION.—Henry VI. in 1424, confirmed most of the
before-named grants, and gave to the bailiffs and burgesses a
Court of Record, to hold pleas of actions for debts and damages

to any amount. He also gave them power to appoint an escheator, a clerk of the market, and a clerk of assay, and granted them a *fair* to be held yearly on the eve and feast of St. Matthew the Apostle, and the two following days. All these charters and grants were allowed by succeeding Kings, till the reign of James I., who in 1607, not only confirmed their former immunities, but incorporated the burgesses anew by the name of the bailiffs and burgesses of East Retford, with a common council consisting of *two bailiffs* and *twelve aldermen*, who have a common seal, and power to alter the same at pleasure; also a "*learned steward*," or recorder, a *town clerk*, and two *sergeants-at-mace*. The two bailiffs and the recorder are "justices of the peace and quorum within the borough." The senior bailiff is chosen yearly, on the first Monday in August, from amongst the aldermen; and the junior bailiff is elected on the same day, out of the body of freemen—the aldermen having previously named two individuals for the choice of the burgesses at large. The aldermen hold their office during life, unless removed for some serious offence. When a vacancy occurs, the bailiffs and surviving aldermen submit the names of two of the burgesses to the freemen at large, whose choice is determined by a majority of votes. The steward or recorder is appointed by the bailiffs and aldermen, and he has, with their consent or the major part of them, the appointment of the town clerk or deputy steward.

ROBES AND REGALIA.—The bailiffs and aldermen have each a GOWN of purple cloth, edged with fur, in which they usually appear at church, four times a year. Two very elegant MACES of silver, gilt, are borne before the bailiffs, on these and other public occasions; one of them was presented to the corporation in 1679, by Sir Edward Nevile, Bart. of Grove, and the other, which is the oldest and smallest, was given by Sir Gervase Clifton, Bart. together with four silver bowls, two silver salts, and twelve silver spoons, all of which are still possessed by the corporate body, who have also a stately silver cup, presented by the Earl of Lincoln.

The Duke of Newcastle is the LORD HIGH STEWARD of the borough; and the present body corporate, and their officers, are as follows:—

Mr. George Thornton, SENIOR BAILIFF.
Mr. John Hoult, JUNIOR BAILIFF.

ALDERMEN.

John Parker,	George Thornton
John Thornton,	William Meekley
Darker Parker,	Thomas Appleby,
William Clarke,	Francis Dewick,
Joshua Cottam,	John Dawber,
George Hudson,	William Kirke.

RECORDER, James Clinton Fynnes Clinton, Esq. M. P.

Town Clerk, Mr. John Mee.

Sergeants-at-Mace, Wm. Pearson and Wm. Tootell.

Town Crier, Samuel Tomlinson.

PARLIAMENTARY PRIVILEGES, &c.—East Retford first sent representatives to the national senate in 1315, but in 1330 the burgesses petitioned the King to release them from this privilege, as, " on account of their poverty, they were unable to pay the wages and other expenses of their representatives." Their prayer was granted, and what was afterwards considered as one of the borough's most valuable rights, lay dormant nearly two centuries and a half; for it was not resumed till 1571, since which the town has regularly sent two members to Parliament, except during the Commonwealth. This small borough has like many others of a similar description been the frequent scene of boistrous dissensions, arising from Parliamentary and municipal differences. The interference of the House of Commons, to determine the extent of the rights of the burgesses, and the manner in which their representatives should be chosen, has been often called for; and the Court of King's Bench has been many times occupied, on *mandamus* motions, and *quo warranto* informations, by which the corporation have been compelled to *admit* several to their freedom, whom they had arbitrarily kept out of their right, and to *oust* others whom they had illegally admitted for the purpose of serving their own political party. From 1571 to 1700 three petitions complaining of undue returns from East Retford were laid before the House of Commons, but on two of them no report was made, and the other was reported to be in favour of the sitting Members. Other petitions having the same complaint were presented in 1702, 1705, 1710, 1796, 1802, and 1826. As at all other places wealth and interest will have their influence, and the Newcastle family have long been the principal favourites of the corporation, but in 1797, this influence was successfully opposed by Sir Wharton Amcotts and Wm. Petrie, Esq., and in order to arm themselves against a similar defeat, the corporation, swore in thirty-eight *honorary freemen;* consisting of the most respectable inhabitants of the town. This measure led to a long expensive law suit in which the burgesses were supported by Mr. Bowles, who brought the question respecting the power of the bailiffs and aldermen to make the honorary freemen, by *quo warranto*, into the Court of King's Bench, where they were all declared to be illegal, and judgment of ouster was issued not only against the new created denizens, but also against five of the aldermen. At the next election in 1802, Mr. Bowles who had achieved such a decisive victory for the burgesses, in favour of " birth-right and servitude," came forward, " quite confident of success," and offered himself as a candidate; but both he and his friend Mr. Bonham, where shamefully left at the foot of the poll, for no fewer than 45 of the "lovers of independence" who had promised them their suffrages, actually voted for the other candidates, who were both of them proposed by the individual who had been the chief cause of the initiation of the aforesaid honorary freemen. Soon after the unexpected issue of this contest, the defeated candidates laid a petition before Parliament, complaining that J. Thornton and G. Baker, had usurped the office of bailiffs, and had illegally admitted several to their freedom who had no right, and had rejected several others who had a right, and who had claimed to be admitted; but the chairman of the committee reported in favour of the sitting members.

After 1802, the bribery and corruption which had so long ruled the major part of the burgesses of East Retford, remained free from Parliamentary enquiry till 1827, when Sir Henry W. Wilson, Kt., (the unsuccessful candidate in the election of the preceding year) presented a petition to the House of Commons, against the return of W. B. Wrightson, Esq., and Sir Robert L. Dundas, Kt. The committee appointed to enquire into the merits of this petition; after examining witnesses during eight days, from the 4th to the 12th of April, 1827, declared that the preceding election was illegal, and that they "considered it their duty to direct the serious attention of the House to the *corrupt state of East Retford*, and that it appeared from the evidence of several witnesses, that, at elections of burgesses to serve in Parliament for that borough, it had been a notorious, long-continued, and general practice for the electors who voted for the successful candidates, to receive the sum of *twenty guineas* from each of them; so that those burgesses who have voted for both members have customarily received *forty guineas* for such exercise of their elective franchise!!"* In consequence of this report, the Commons, on June 11th, 1827, resolved, that the corrupt state of this borough required their serious consideration, and Mr. Tennyson, brought in a bill to transfer its elective franchise to Birmingham, which bill was read a second time on the 25th of February, 1828, but in the following month, Mr. Nicholson Calvert, obtained a majority in favour of his motion, that 'the committee sitting on the bill should have power to make provision against the bribery and corruption complained of by *extending* the right of voting for the borough members,

---

* *Rotten Boroughs.*—Retford has not stood alone in bribery and corruption, for several other boroughs have been convicted and punished for these sordid crimes. In 1771, the elective franchise of *Shoreham* was extended to the Hundred of Fishergate; that of *Chrichlade* in 1784, to the Hundreds of Chrichlade, Highworth, Staple, Kingsbridge, and Malmesbury; and that of *Aylesbury* in 1804 to the three Hundreds of Aylesbury. *Grampound* was disfranchised in 1821, and its two members given to Yorkshire; and *Penryn* narrowly escaped a similar fate, at the time when Retford was undergoing the Parliamentary ordeal.

to *all the freeholders of Bassetlaw*, and after much desultory
discussion, and many protracting adjournments, the bill was
finally altered to that effect; but, owing to the intervention of
the great question of Catholic Emancipation, and the removal
of the Civil and Religious disabilities of all classes of his Majesty's subjects, by the repeal of the Test and Corporation
Acts, the Bill for extending the franchise of Retford to the
freeholders of the Hundred of Bassetlaw, did not pass the
House of Commons till the 15th of March 1830. It was read
a third time in the House of Lords, on the 21st of July, and
received the Royal assent on the 23rd of July in the same year.
On the second reading of the bill, (July 19th,) the Lord Chancellor entered into a review of the whole of the evidence which
had proved the existence of bribery at the elections of 1818
and 1820; and he contended that at both these periods a great
majority of the voters had received twenty guineas from Mr.
Evans, and a similar sum from Mr. Crompton, and that
out of 120 voters, which with the 24 out voters, made the
whole number of the burgesses of East Retford, 96 were fully
proved at the bar of the House of Lords to have *sold their
votes!!!* It was also clear that money had been promised at
the election of 1826, and there was little doubt that it would
have been paid to the burgesses, had not the two members been
petitioned against, and ejected. The first Parliamentary representatives of "*East Retford cum Bassetlaw*," were Lord
Newark, eldest son of Earl Manvers, and the Hon. Arthur
Duncombe, second son of Lord Feversham; who were elected
on the 4th of August, 1830, after a feeble opposition from G.
V. Vernon, Esq., the seventh son of the Archbishop of York.
The present members, are the Hon. Charles Evelyn Pierrepont Lord Viscount Newark, of Thoresby Hall, and Granville
Harcourt Vernon, Esq., of Grove Hall, who were elected in
1831. The whole number of burgesses is only about 150, so
that their influence at elections is now completely overbalanced
by the freeholders of the Hundred of Bassetlaw, who are very
numerous, for though there are in that large district many
very extensive landowners, yet there are several hundred small
freehold tenements, which are not much above the yearly value
(40s.) required to bring their respective owners within the
pale of the elective franchise, which was formerly confined
to "such freemen only, as have a right to their freedom of
East Retford by birth, as the eldest sons of freemen, or by
serving seven years apprenticeship to a freeman, or have it by
redemption, whether inhabiting or not inhabiting, in the said
borough, at the time of their being made free."*

The Corporation holds in trust for various charitable uses
much landed and other property, a large portion of the yearly

* Committee of the House of Commons, A. D. 1765.

proceeds of which they have long been in the habit of misapplying, as appears by several parliamentary enquiries, but we hope the commissioners of the last of these national inquisitions have so clearly defined the channels in which the various streams of posthumous charities should run, that the abuses so long practiced by trustees are now annihilated. Throsby says, that the municipal body in Retford had formerly power either to *hang* or *transport* criminals but we do not find any document to prove that they ever possessed more power than that which is vested with magistrates.

The Historical Events of Retford are neither numerous nor momentous. In 1377, John Attie Vykers granted to the bailiffs and burgesses towards the support of the chaplains of the *chantries* of the Holy Trinity and the blessed Virgin Mary in St. Swithin's church, eight tenements in the borough, together with a garden and a croft called Bolton Yherd, on condition that they should pay him £10 a-year for the term of his life. In 1385, Richard II. empowered the priests of East and West Retford, Clarborough, and Tresswell, and some others, to grant to the corporation, nine messuages, five tofts and 8s. rent in the borough, which they had held of the King in free burgage by the service of 1d. per annum, to find two chaplains for the *altars* of St. Trinity and St. Mary in St. Swithin's church. The *Town Hall* was built in 1388. William de Burgh and John de Tyreswell, granted a house in Kyrkgate to Cicilia Mayson, for the term of her life, and at her decease to become the property of the corporation. In 1426, and 1474, the vicar and chaplains obtained the gift of two tenements in " Briggate and the Market-stede." The town seems to have been greatly encreased in wealth, population, and buildings, during the 16th century. In 1518, Thomas Gunthorpe, parson of Babworth, agreed with the corporation and burgesses, that he should at his own cost erect a *school-house* in the town. In 1537, Henry VIII. granted the *Manor and Lordship of East Retford* to George Earl of Shrewsbury and Waterford, but the Duke of Newcastle is now the Lord of the Manor or rather the " *Lord High Steward*," though the land and buildings belong to numerous proprietors. After the suppression of the monasteries by Henry VIII. the people began to thirst after knowledge, and amongst the numerous schools which were then established, was the *Free Grammar School* of East Retford, founded by the letters patent of Edward VI., in 1551. That dreadful malady the *plague* visited the town in 1558, and from July to October, swept away no fewer than 82 persons in West Retford, where 66 others fell victims to the same disease in 1664, from May 20th to October 10th. During the civil wars of the 17th century, Retford was often occupied by the Royal troops, and on the 20th of August, 1645, King Charles passed through the

town on his route from Doncaster to Newmarket.—(See p. 86.)
From this time the town seems to have reposed in quiet till the
rebellion of 1745, when an army of 6000 English and Hessian
troops encamped on Wheatley Hills, and when halting in their
march through Retford, they converted the church into a
stable. On August 23rd, 1750, the inhabitants were alarmed
by the shock of an earthquake. In 1752, the *church* was new
roofed, and the *bridge* over the Idle was laid with new planks.
A *Sheep Market* was established in 1753. The *Town Hall*
was rebuilt in 1755, at the cost of £1773. 19s. 1d. The
whole of the streets were repaired in 1777, and in 1782,
they were first publicly lighted with lamps. In 1798, the
the corporation voted an address of thanks to the Right Hon.
William Pitt for his Parliamentary services. In February,
1795, a sudden thaw after a long frost, caused great *floods* in
all the lower parts of Nottinghamshire, and so swollen was the
Idle at Retford, that the water was three feet deep in the
Market-place, and the torrent was so strong, that it tore up the
pavement in several parts of the town, and washed down a
house and grocer's shop in West Retford. In 1796, the *Stock-
house* or Gaol which stood in the Market-place, was pulled
down by order of the corporation, who, in 1798, voted £100
per annum, to be paid to Government towards supporting the
war. In 1788, the late patriotic *Major Cartwright* established
a *worsted-mill* here, which for some time employed several
hundred people, but the speculation failed and ruined the fortune of its founder; who, however, continued many years afterwards one of the ablest and most active defenders of popular
rights, and Parliamentary Reform. A mill for the manufacture of candlewick flourished here for a short period, but after
the death of its original proprietor (Mr. Brumby,) it fell into
complete decay, as also did the cotton mill established by Mr.
Plant; indeed Retford does not seem to be a soil favourable for
the growth of manufactures, though there are in the town and
neighbourhood two paper mills, and a number of persons employed in making sail-cloth, hats, shoes, &c., as will be seen
in the subjoined directory. In August 1831, Retford like
many other places in the county, was visited by dreadful storms
of thunder and lightning, followed by torrents of rain, accompanied with hailstones which measured half an inch in diameter.
Amongst several persons killed in the county was a poor old
man, Eli Markham, who on his return from shearing at Gamston, had imprudently taken shelter under an oak, where both
himself and his ass fell victims to the electric fluid. On the
same day, (August 17th,) much damage was done to cattle and
property at various places, and the streets in the town were
completely inundated, so that the water flowed into the houses.
The town was first lighted with *gas* on December 22nd, 1831.

The CARS AND COMMONS which comprise only about 50 acres, form the common pasture of those freeholders in the borough, who hold either by heirship or purchase, those tene- to which the 276 " cattle gates" are attached. Formerly they were of little value, but now instead of a swampy bog, they present the cheerful aspect of a luxuriant pasture, in the southern environs of the town. Anciently they were the pro- perty of William de Anne, Lord of Noraisfee, who in 1319, granted them "to all the men of Rettforde," together with the "Dallcroft" where their fair was held. For these grants, however, the men of Retford, gave him a certain sum of money. The Chesterfield Canal now occupies six acres of the Cars and Commons, for which the Canal Company paid £47 7s. 6d. which was expended in draining the rest of the land.

The BRIDGE which crosses the Idle and connects the parishes of East and West Retford, was partly rebuilt and con- siderably widened in 1794, so that is now a substantial fabric, of five good arches.

The MARKET PLACE and SQUARE form a spacious area, which on the market and fair days, is crowded with buyers and sellers of corn, sheep, cattle, provisions, merchandise, &c. The whole is lined with good shops and houses, and on the north side, under the Town Hall, are clean and commodious Shambles. In the centre of the Square, stands the remains of an ancient cross called the *Broad Stone,* round which the corn market is held. Tradition says, that this stone formerly stood on an eminence to the south-east of the town, now called *Domine Cross,* but anciently "*Est-croc-sic.*" Another stone of the same form and dimensions may now be seen in the church-yard wall of West Retford, but its original situation was in West Retford field. The *Bank* is on the south side of the Square, and the *Post-Office,* in Grove-street. The *Market* is held every Saturday, and two FAIRS annually, viz. on March 23rd, for cattle, &c. and on October 2nd for *hops,* cheese, &c. In the surrounding country are many hop-yards, and the growers, in the town and neighbourhood have lately established a great hop market, which is held on the first Saturday in November, and continued for some weeks afterwards. The Corporation have much improved the market, by giving up the *tolls,* which they formerly levied on all corn, fruit, &c. exposed in the market place, and upon all the carriages, horses, &c. which passed over the bridge. A large portion of the fruit, butter, eggs, fowls, &c. which are brought to this market are bought up by the hucksters who attend from Sheffield and and other parts of Yorkshire, which a late historian says, the inhabitants consider as a regrating evil that ought to be de- stroyed by municipal authority, but we consider it rather as a *benefit* than an *injury;* for immense quantities of butter, eggs,

&c. are brought here which the town could not consume, and
which consequently would not be brought to the market at all
if the farmers were not met there by wholesale purchasers
who supply those districts where there is a greater population
and a less fruitful soil; indeed, many of the villages of Nottinghamshire have their own resident hucksters, who weekly carry
the surplus produce of their respective neighbourhoods to the
markets of the adjacent counties.

The Town Hall is a plain, yet handsome and commodious
structure, built in 1755, on the site of the Old Moot Hall. The
Quarter Sessions* for the Borough, and also for the northern
division of the county are held here in the large court room,
which is 70 feet long and 26 broad, and is occasionally used for
the public Assemblies of the gentry of the neighbourhood,
which Piercy says, are like angels' visits—"few and far between." Adjoining to the Sessions' Room is the Council
room (26 feet by 20) which is used by the Grand Jury, and also
by the corporate body who hold in it a Petty Session every
alternate Saturday.

The only building in the town which has amusement for its
especial object is the Theatre, in Carolgate, which was built
in 1789, by the late Mr. Pero, then manager of this circuit,
which has long been visited yearly by Mr. Manley and his
company of comedians. The exterior has not a very imposing
effect, but the interior is handsomely decorated, and the boxes,
pit, and gallery are neatly fitted up, and will hold at the usual
prices from £40 to £50. The News Room in the Market-
place was built several years ago by the corporation, and is
supported by about forty gentlemen, who each pay an annual
subscription of £1 11s. 6d. It is well supplied with London
and country papers, and contains full length portraits of George
II. and his consort Queen Caroline, which were presented to
the institution by Lord Viscount Galway. A Book Club
was established about 12 years ago, and now consists of 21
members, who subscribe £1 11s. 6d. yearly. The Gas-Works
were erected in 1831, by Mr. James Malam, and the town was
first illuminated with their lucid vapour on December 22nd in
the same year. A handsome cast iron *pillar*, 22 feet high,
bearing five lamps has been erected in the square, and the
whole town now presents a cheerful appearance even in the
gloomy nights of winter.

The CHURCH of East Retford, dedicated to St. Swithin,
and commonly called the Corporation Church, to distinguish it
from that in West Retford, is a neat gothic edifice, which has
just been thoroughly cleansed and beautified. It has a very

* *Petty Sessions for the Hundred of Bassetlaw* are held in the Town Hall
every Saturday.

handsome square tower, containing six bells, and its nave, two side aisles, and transept, are on a commodious plan, and well lighted. Its length is nearly 117 feet, and its breadth in the nave and side aisles is 51 feet, and in the transept 85 feet. The height of the tower to the top of the pinnacles is 97 feet. None of the windows at present exhibit any specimens of stained glass, except a few small fragments; though in Thoroton's time (1677) the western window (which is now nearly new) displayed many heraldic and other ornaments. There are now four *galleries*, three of which were built in the years 1740, 1778, and 1820, but the other in the north aisle, is supposed to be as old as the fifteenth century. The first *organ* which the church possessed came from the Theatre at Newark, and was presented by Robert Sutton, Esq. in 1770, but the one now in use was built by Donaldson, in 1797. The *font* is very ancient, as also are several of the sepulchral monuments, but some of the more modern ones are highly ornamental. In 1392, the church contained two altars dedicated to St. Trinity and St. Mary, and endowed with £16. 8s., issuing out of nine messuages and five tofts (see page 111) for the support of two *cantarists*, who were appointed by the bailiffs. These altars stood behind the chancel in a large chapel, which being in a decayed state, was pulled down in 1528, and the materials used in repairing the church, which in 1651, was nearly destroyed by the falling of the tower, which having been some time ruinous, was blown down in that year. The parish appears to have been too poor to repair this demolition by a rate on the inhabitants, for it is said, in an old corporation document, dated 1652, that the parishioners having previously been at much cost in repairing that part which was standing, were unable to rebuild what had fallen down, and that they were consequently obliged to defray the expense, which amounted to £1500, by selling part of the corporation land, and the chantry lands at Kirton, Willoughby, and Walesby, which belonged to the Grammar School, reserving only the ancient yearly fee farm rents for the use of the said school. The living is a VICARAGE, the Rectory being in the Cathedral at York, whose Archbishop, in 1258, allotted for the Vicar's maintenance 100s. of alterage, and the small tithes, with the Easter offerings, the surplice fees, and two gates on the common, also, "all the bread, wine, ale, and beer, which should happen to be brought to the altar," but the tithe of the mills was to be given to the poor. According to a terrier dated in 1687, the glebe and vicarage house consisted of "one dwelling-house, containing three bays of building, one layth containing two bays of building; and one garden, with a yard butting upon ye church-yard. The vicarage is valued in the King's books at £5. 5s., and is in the patronage of Sir Robert Sutton, Bart. and incumbency of the Rev. Thomas F. Beckwith, M. A. Property which produces

2 E

about £16 a-year, has been bequeathed for *afternoon prayers*, and a *Sunday evening lecture* in this church. See *George Wharton* and *Jonathan Minnitt's benefactions*, at page 318.

The DEANERY OF RETFORD, as has been seen at pages 62 and 145, now exists merely in name, the power of the *rural Deans* having, since the days of Otho, the Pope's legate, been concentrated in the Archdeacon, who holds a visitation yearly in East Retford church, where the clergy, churchwardens, &c. of the following places are required to attend, viz. Austerfield, Bawtry, Babworth, Blyth, Boughton, Bothamsall, Bilsthorpe, Carburton, Carlton-in-Linderic, Clareborough, Clayworth, Cottam, Edwinstow, Egmanton, East and West Markham, East and West Retford, Elkesley, Everton, Finningley, Gamston, Gringley-on-the-Hill, Grove, Hayton, Harworth, Headon, Kirton, Littleborough, Mattersea, Misson, Norton Cuckney, North Wheatley, Ollerton, Ordsall, Palethorpe, Rossington, Saundby, Scrooby, South Leverton, Sturton, Sutton-cum-Lound, Tresswell, Tuxford, Wellow, Walesby, Warsop, West Burton, West Drayton, Walkeringham, and Worksop.

ST. SAVIOUR'S CHAPEL OF EASE, on Moorgate Hill, though in Clareborough parish, was erected for the use of a populous suburb of East Retford. It is a handsome edifice of white brick, in the gothic style, with a nave, chancel, and two side aisles; a beautiful window of stained-glass at the east end, and two octagonal towers at the west end. The first stone was laid on June 2d, 1828, by H. C. Hutchinson, Esq. of Welham, who gave the site and burial-ground. It contains 1040 sittings, of which 600 are free, and was opened September 27th, 1830.— The whole cost of the building, &c. was £4145. 3s. 8d.; of which £800 was given by the incorporated society for promoting the building of new churches, and the remainder was raised by voluntary subscription.

The *Dissenting Places of Worship* in East Retford are, an INDEPENDENT CHAPEL in Chapelgate, erected upwards of 30 years ago, by a Mrs. Bond, of Morton, near Gainsbro', for the use of the followers of Lady Huntingdon's tenets, but afterwards purchased by Wm. Brownlow, Esq. of London, and presented to its present congregation, which is now under the pastoral care of the Rev. Benjamin Ash;—and a large METHODIST CHAPEL in Grove-street, erected in 1823, at the cost of £2000, in lieu of the old Wesleyan chapel in Meetinghouse-lane, which had become too small for its increasing congregation, and is now disused.

The WORKHOUSE, in Grove-street, was erected by the corporation in 1818, at the cost of £1000, for which they receive 5 per cent. interest from the parish, which was previously without a house for the residence of its destitute poor. Twenty-six other parishes and townships pay £3 each per annum, towards supporting the institution, and three shillings per week for the maintenance of every pauper they send into the house. The *poor rates* of East Retford, for the year ending March, 1831, amounted to £1133. 0s. 11d. collected by an assessment of 2s. 3d. in the pound on the rack rental; but out of this sum, £67. 7s. 6d. was paid to the county rate. Mr. Joseph Cheater is the governor.

As Retford possesses CHARITABLE FUNDS amounting to upwards of £1800* per annum, and has several *Friendly Societies,* a *Savings' Bank,* and some other provident institutions, we expected to have found its poor rates much lower than they are, but they are no doubt considerably augmented by the great number of vagrants who pass through the town from the four points of the compass.

The SAVINGS' BANK, at the house of the secretary, Alderman George Thornton, bookseller, in the Square, was established in 1818. On the 20th of November, 1829, its deposits amounted to £27,167. 7s. 9d.; and at the same date in 1830, to £26,129. 19s. 11d.; besides a balance of profit in favour of the institution amounting to £350. The number of individual depositors at the latter date was 758, whose collective deposits amounted to £25,381. 7s. 7d.; and of the remainder, £332. 14s. 3d. belonged to six charitable societies, and £415. 8s. 1d. to seven friendly societies.

The GRAMMAR SCHOOL, with a house adjoining it for the master, and another on the opposite side of the street for the usher, is in Chapelgate, near the church, and is as it ought to be, plain and spacious. It was founded by the letters patent of Edward VI. in the fifth year of his reign, by the name of "*The Free Grammar School of King Edward VI.*" for the instruction of boys and youths in grammar. For its support, his Majesty granted in trust to the bailiffs and burgesses, all the lands, tenements, &c. of the dissolved chantries of Sutton-in-Lound, Tuxford, and Annesley, with power for the trustees to receive and purchase other property for the use of the said school. As has already been seen, that portion of the school property which had belonged to the chantry at Tuxford, was sold in 1652, to defray the expense of rebuilding the parish church. Sir John Hercy, in 1554, granted to the corporation, for the use of the grammar school, a messuage in Briggate, and two tofts in Chapelgate, together with certain lands at Little Gringley. In 1763, the Rev. Wm. Haughton bequeathed to it an estate at Ordsall, now let for about £28 per annum, of which, according to the testator's will, £4 should be paid yearly to the master, and the remainder to the usher. For more than two centuries the school funds have been shamefully misapplied by the trustees, who have at various times, in consideration of large fines, let several of the school estates on long leases, at

* This sum includes the Hospital and other charities at West Retford.

trifling yearly rents; and have so exchanged and mixed up some of the others with land, which they claim as their own property, that much litigation has existed betwixt them and the master, and the Parliamentary Commissioners and the Court of Equity have several times been obliged to interfere between them. Since the last parliamentary enquiry, in 1819, the corporation have given up to the Court of Equity property granted by Edward VI., which produces upwards of £300 per annum, arising from 120 acres of land at Bleasby, 15 acres at Moreton, and 84 acres at Sutton and Lound. By an issue directed by the Court of Chancery, and tried at the Nottingham assizes on July 23, 1831, they were obliged to restore other property left to the school by the before named Sir John Hercy, and which they had, ever since it came into their possession, applied to other uses; so that it is expected that when the Court of Equity has decided between them and the master, the yearly revenue of the school will be upwards of £600; though never more than £80 a-year has been paid to the master, and £40 to the usher; and from 1763 to 1801, the salary of the former was only £53, and that of the latter £21. But nothing has been paid to the present master (the Rev. William Mold) since 1821, for from that year till 1831 he left the school almost entirely to the care of the ushers, and employed himself in fighting the battles of the charity against the trustees,—considering that his salary was too small, and that the rents of the estates had been unjustly applied. We hope, however, their differences are now at an end, and that the school, instead of being confined to 17 or 20 free scholars, will be thrown open for the gratuitous instruction of all the poor boys of the parish, as was undoubtedly the intention of its donors. Amongst the items of expenditure in the school account, we find in 1779, £290 for rebuilding the school-house; in 1797 £360 for erecting a new house for the master, and in 1810, £556. 16s. 8d. for erecting a new house for the usher, upon the site of the old houses formerly occupied by him and the master. A large NATIONAL SCHOOL for the reception of 160 scholars was erected in 1813, and was for some years well supported under the patronage of the Duke of Newcastle and many other yearly contributors; but from deaths and other causes, it has been suffered to decay, and it is now without a master, and almost without a whole pane of glass in its windows.

The DORCAS SOCIETY, established in 1823 for the purpose of furnishing the poor with cheap clothing, and the LYING-IN-CHARITY, for the relief of poor married lying-in women, are supported by the yearly contributions of the benevolent, as also are the Bible, Missionary, and several other *religious societies.* Besides the St. George's Independent Lodge of ODD FELLOWS, there are in the town five Friendly Societies or SICK CLUBS held at different public houses.

SLOSWICK'S HOSPITAL in Churchgate, or as an inscription in front of the building calls it, the "*Mease de Dieu,*" was founded by Richard Sloswicke, in 1657, and endowed with land and buildings in East and West Retford, (now worth upwards of £80 per annum) "for the maintenance of six poor old men of good carriage and behaviour." It was vested with five trustees, but in 1681 they were all dead but Francis Stringer, and the neglected state of the charity became the subject of a chancery suit, which ended in the trust being transfered to the corporation, who in 1806, pulled down the old hospital and built a new one, consisting of four small houses, to which they added two more dwellings in 1819. The cost of these erections was £710. The six imates each receive £2: 12s. 6d. quarterly, and two tons of coal yearly; besides which one guinea is paid annually to the person who takes care of the grass plot and garden attached to the hospital.

The Corporation ALMSHOUSES formerly stood in Carolgate, but in 1823, being very old and dilapidated, they were taken down, and the site of them and of the ancient premises annexed to them was sold for £1,370. 18s. 0d., being at the rate of one guinea per square yard. Out of this money the corporation erected the present almhouses, which contain apartments for eighteen poor women, and form part of the west side of an intended new street. The buildings cost £750, and the land (1,158¼ square yards) £289. 12s. 6d. In 1824, after the completion of the new hospital, there was a balance of £266. 10s. 11d. in favour of the charity, for which the corporation pay £12. 10s. 0d. yearly interest, which with £6, the rent of a close in Clareborough, is distributed in coals amongst the 18 almswomen, who have no other allowance. The documents relating to this ancient charity are all lost; its date, and the name of its founder are both unknown; and if it ever was endowed with any estates, they have either been sold, or are so mixed up with the other possessions of the corporation, as to be undistinguishable.

The BENEFACTIONS which belong to the poor of East Retford are as follows: In 1621, *William Clark* left £3 a-year to be paid out of an estate at Walkrith, in Lincolnshire, (now belonging to Richard Atkinson, Esq.) to three aged poor. *William Wharton,* at some date unknown, gave to the corporation £40 in trust, to distribute 40s. yearly. *Barbara Moody,* in 1726, gave £24, and *Mr. Sharpe,* £20, for which the corporation distribute interest at the rate of 5 per cent. *George Wharton,* in 1727, charged his estate at Little Gringley, (now belonging to —— Wilson, Esq.) with the following yearly payments, viz. £5 for teaching poor boys not sons of freemen; 15s. for bread for the poor, and 5s. to the vicar, for giving notice every Easter Sunday of William Wharton's legacy. He also gave a close at Domine Cross, now worth £10 per annum, to

the head master of the grammar school, on condition that he
reads the *Common Prayer* every Sunday afternoon in the parish church. *Hannah Saltmarsh* left £100 to repair the
church; £50 for teaching poor children, and £20 to the poor.
The corporation pay 20s. yearly for the latter sum, but of the
others we find no account. In 1776, *Robert Sutton,* Esq., of,
Kelham, gave to the vicar and churchwardens, a share in the
Chesterfield Canal, worth about £8 per annum, in trust, that
they distribute the yearly proceeds amongst the needy parishioners. During his life, he was a great benefactor to the town
and neighbourhood, for it is recorded on his monument in the
church, that he gave £100 towards rebuilding the Town-Hall,
£100 towards Barnby Common Road,—built Pelham Bridge,
paid the assessement of the poor on new roofing the church,—
gave an organ and a bell to the church, and £200 towards pro-
curing *Queen Anne's Bounty*. In 1784, *Ald. George Popplewell* gave the corporation £50 to distribute interest amongst
the poor. In 1795, *Mrs. Sarah Brown*, of Sheffield, left £21,
for which the corporation, pursuant to her will, pay 21s. yearly,
to a schoolmistress for teaching *two poor girls* reading and knitting. *Ann Woolby*, in 1812, left to the corporation a yearly,
rent charge of £10, out of Longholme Closes, in Clareborough
parish, in trust, that they distribute two-thirds of it amongst 20
of the oldest and poorest women in East Retford, at Christmas, and pay the remainder to the Rector of West Retford for
distribution amongst 10 of the poorest and oldest women of
that parish. In 1815, *Jonathan Minnitt*, by his will, directed
his sole executor, Mr. Francis White, to pay to the vicar and
churchwardens, £150, to be invested for the use of a lecturer to
preach a *sermon every Sunday evening* in the parish church.
This legacy was not paid till 1827, when it was received with
£60, the amount of eight years' interest. Of the arrears
£22. 10. was paid to the vicar for having preached the lecture
during the preceding three years, and the residue was given to
the poor. The capital (£150) is vested in Government security. In 1818, *Thomas Welsh* left £100, for which the corporation distribute £5 yearly amongst 10 poor widows. *William Coleby* gave 5s. yearly for the poor, and 5s. yearly for the
use of the church, out of a house on the south side of the church,
now belonging to William Clark. *John Smith* gave to the
corporation £4, in consideration that they should pay 8s. yearly
to the impotent poor. In 1826, *Beaumont Marshall* left £100
to the corporation in trust, that they distribute the interest
yearly amongst ten poor families in equal shares. An annuity
of £10 is yearly distributed amongst ten of the most poor and
aged parishioners of East Retford, from *Lady Frances Pierrepont's Charity*, of which the chapter of Southwell are trustees,
as will be seen in the history of that town.

WEST RETFORD PARISH.

WEST RETFORD, in the Hatfield Divison of Bassetlaw, is a pleasant village and parish on the western bank of the Idle, opposite to East Retford, with which it is connected by a good stone bridge. It has no dependent townships, and contains only 593 inhabitants, 152 houses, and 950 acres of land, of which 450 acres belong to the hospital in the village, and 173 acres and 1 rood to the rector, who received the greatest part of it in an allotment made as a commutation of all the tithes of the parish, in 1774, when the common was enclosed. A large portion of the remaining 327 acres, belongs to Peter Dickonson, Esq., of *West Retford Hall*, a picturesque mansion standing on the brow of an eminence, the declivity of which is covered with shrubs and evergreens, " whilst the dark Idle sullenly flows at its base." But Henry Hardolph Eyre, Esq., is Lord of the *Manor*, which comprises the whole parish, and is intersected by the great North Road, and skirted by the river, Idle, the Chesterfield Canal, and a brook which flows by Babworth under the canal and the turnpike to the Idle, within 1½ mile S. E. of Barnby Moor. Near the bridge is an extensive paper mill, and on the opposite side of the river is a large corn mill. "A dash of rural beauty" pervades a large portion of the village, and many of the houses bear the stamp of antiquity. Near its north-west end is *West Retford House*, the delightful seat of James Lee, Esq., once the property of the Emerson family. Laird says, it is a matter of great boast here, that his late Majesty George IV., when Prince of Wales, spoke highly of its situation in one of his journies from the north.

In *Doomsday Book*, this manor as well as East Retford, is joined to Odesthorpe, (now unknown,) and appears to have been (like a number of the surrounding parishes) of the fee of Roger de Busli, and part of it was *soc* to Clumber and Weston. It afterwards belonged to the Hercy family, proprietors of Grove and Weston, with whom it remained till 1570, when John Hercy, Kt., died without issue, and settled this manor on one of his eight sisters, who was married to Nicholas Denman, Esq.,* and with whose descendants it continued, until Barbara, daughter and co-heiress of Francis Denman, Esq., carried it in marriage to Edward Darrel, Esq., the last of whose descendants, John Darrel, M. D., died in 1665, and bequeathed the manor house to be converted into a hospital, and the family estate for the endowment thereof; but as before stated, Anthony Har-

* The mother of *Queen Anne* was a collaterial descendant of the *Denmans*, of West Retford. One branch of this family is now settled at Bevercotes, and another resides in Derbyshire, of which latter is Thomas Denman, Esq., the eminent barrister.

dolph Eyre, Esq., of Grove, is now Lord of the Manor, though most of the soil belongs to the hospital, the church, and the poor.

The parish CHURCH (dedicated to St. Michael,) is a small ancient fabric, standing upon an eminence, and having a handsome octagonal spire, resting upon a lofty square tower, in which are three bells. The body of the church is low, and though the exterior is in excellent repair, the pewing and most of the interior work is in a very decayed and neglected state. The living is a *Rectory*, valued in the King's Books at £9. 13s. 4d., but now worth nearly £300, having, as has just been seen, received a large allotment of land in lieu of tithes. The advowson was from the 13th to the 16th century, possessed by the Hercy family, from whom it passed to the Denmans, and from them to the Darrels, whose trustees sold it in 1668, to the corporation of East Retford, in whose possession it still remains. The Rev. Abraham Youle, M. A., the present rector, has held the living since 1787, and one of his predecessors, the Rev. Thomas Gylby, held it upwards of 82 years, viz. from 1678 to 1760.

The GENERAL BAPTIST CHAPEL was built in 1815, near the old meeting house, which is now used as a sunday school, and was bequeathed for the use of a Baptist Congregation in 1691, by Richard Brownlow, of London, who endowed it with " one acre of land, two beast-gates, and five lands ends," situated in West Retford parish.

TRINITY HOSPITAL was founded in 1665, by John Darrel, Esq., whose " capital messuage" it was, and who endowed it with all his heriditary estate in West Retford and Ordsall, for the maintenance of 16 poor impotent men, with the sub-dean of Lincoln as their master and governor. He also directed by his will, that the said sub-dean and his successors, upon the death of any of the brethren, should admit others in their place, preferring, if any should apply, those of the blood and kindred of the testator, and after them, those of the neighbourhood; and that he should have for his pains as governor of the hospital, £20 per annum, and each of the brethren £10 per annum. After the testator's death, it was discovered that his brother Thomas had some years before made some secret or other conveyance of that portion of the hospital lands, situated at the Biggins, in Ordsall parish, to Lady Diana Cranborne, whose heir, Richard Cooke, Esq., recovered for himself and his heirs, an annuity of £40 to be paid for ever out of the rents of the said lands. For many years after the endowment, only 10 brethren were admitted; but in 1796, when land had encreased in value, and when that eminent divine Dr. William Paley became master of the hospital, he appointed six additional brethren, and erected for them six new dwellings at the cost of £609. 18s. 7d., of which expense £230 was paid by the executors of the preceding master, Dr. Dowbiggin, who, in 1777, had received £300 for part of the hospital land which had been sold to the Chesterfield Canal Company. The hospital property was augmented with several allotments in 1774, at the enclosure of West Retford Common, and it now produces upwards of £1040 per annum, so that, the master receives yearly £100, and each of the brethren, £50, and the surplus revenue is appropriated for necessary repairs, for paying the annuity of £40 before named, and also £2 yearly to Gainsbro' School. The hospital contains a small chapel, and besides 16 dwellings for the brethren, it has apartments for a resident nurse, whose duty it is to take care of the sick brethren. A great part of the houses are old and decayed, and those which were erected in Dr. Paley's mastership are not very substantial; it has therefore been determined to take them all down, and erect a *new hospital* near the same site, upon a more elegant and commodious plan, for which purpose a "fabric fund" has been some years accumulating out of the surplus revenue, and it now amounts to upwards of £1000, so that we expect the design will be carried into execution during the present year, 1832.

DARREL'S SCHOLARSHIP.—John Darrel, Esq. the founder of Trinity Hospital, bequeathed "those lands and tenements which he himself had purchased in West Redford," for the maintenance of some ingenious scholar, whose father has not above £30 per annum in lands or estate, to be chosen out of Nottinghamshire and Lincolnshire alternately, by the archdeacon of Nottingham and the sub-dean of Lincoln, and to be educated at Exeter College, Oxford, where the testator directs that the scholar so elected shall receive the rents and profits of the said lands and buildings until five years after he has taken the degree of master of arts, or until he has obtained a benefice; after which another is to be chosen and maintained in the same manner. The property now produces £52 per annum.

FREE SCHOOL.—Stephen Johnson, by will, dated 1723, and codicil dated 1725, bequeathed a cottage with its appurtenances, (22 perches of land) near Northfieldgate, for the use of a school, and £10 a year out of his estate at Tilne, in the parish of Hayton, to be paid to the schoolmaster for teaching all the poor children of West Retford, betwixt the ages of five and thirteen, to read and write. His will states that this bequest was made in consideration of the non-fulfilment of the benevolent intention of his kinsman, Richard Brownlow, of London, who in 1691 bequeathed £500 for the foundation of a school on certain conditions, which the churchwardens and overseers of West Retford did not comply with. The incumbents of West Retford, Grove, Ordsall, and Babworth, are the trustees.

The CHURCH and POOR LAND, &c. consists of 27A. 1R. 39P. of land in West Retford field, and four tenements, a barn, and a stable in the village, which are vested in twelve trustees, and are now let for £80 per annum, half of which is appropriated for repairing the church, and the remainder for the relief of the poor, according to an agreement made at the enclosure of common land. The church also possesses other land in the parish, viz. a *garden* containing one rood, and let in 1803, on a 99 years' lease, to Martin Bower, at the yearly rent of 2s. 6d., in consideration of a fine of £105; and a *garden and orchard*, containing 1A. 3R. 22P., let at the same time and for the same term, to Thomas Beardsall, for the yearly rent of 2s. 6d., and a fine of £155. Part of the sums received as fines was expended in ceiling the church, and the rest was lost by the failure of the bank of Messrs. Pocklington & Co.

The BULL MEADOW, left by some person unknown, consists of 3A. 0R. 30P., and is occupied by a person, in consideration of his keeping a *bull* for the use of the parish, which possesses several other small parcels of land, the rents of which are carried to the overseers' accounts.

The other BENEFACTIONS belonging to West Retford are—3s. 4d. yearly out of a house now occupied by Miss Bonsor, left in 1558, by John Backhouse, to be divided equally between the surveyors of the highways, and the overseers of the poor; 3s. 4d. yearly out of a house in Chapelgate, East Retford, (now belonging to the corporation) left in 1613, by John Coleby, to be divided in the same manner; 40s. yearly out of a house in West Retford, now belonging to P. Dickonson, Esq. left in 1725, by Stephen Johnson, to be distributed yearly, on the 8th of November, amongst the most needy poor; and £3. 6s. 8d. from the bequest of Mrs. Ann Woolby, already noticed at page 318.

LIST OF STREETS, &c. IN RETFORD AND ITS SUBURBS.

☞ *Those marked * are in Clareborough parish, and † in Thrumpton lordship, in the parish of Ordsall.*

†Appleby's Bldgs. South road
Beardsall's court, Grove street
Beardsall's row, Grove street
*Beck close or Factory row, Spittal hill
Bettison's yard, Bridgegate
Bridgegate, Market street
Canal row, near south end of Carolgate
Carolgate, south side Mkt. place
Carr lane, the Square
Chapelgate, Market place
Churchgate, Market place
Clark's yard, Chapelgate
Cooke's yard, Bridgegate

Colton's yard, West Retford
Cotterill's yard, Churchgate
Grove street, Market place
*Little lane, Moorgate
Littlewood's yard, Churchgate
Market place, from Churchgate to Carolgate
Market street, the Square
Mermaid yard, West Retford
*Moorgate, Churchgate
Newgate, now Grove street
New row, Carolgate
New street, Carolgate
Old Sun yard, Chapelgate
*Old Tan yard, Moorgate

Ridgway's buildings, Carolgate
†Russell place, South road
South road, Carolgate
Spa lane, Carolgate
*Spittal hill, Chapelgate
†Storcroft terrace, South road
The Square, Market street
Theatre or Fox's yard, Carolgate
†Thrumpton, Russell-place

Travis's buildings, Carolgate
Turk's Head yard, Grove street
Turn lane, Chapelgate
West Retford, Bridgegt.
†White houses, one mile south
*Wellington place, Spittal-hill
†Wright Wilson place, South rd
†Wright Wilson street, South rd

DIRECTORY OF RETFORD AND ITS SUBURBS,

COMPRISING

East and West Retford, the lordship of *Thrumpton* in Ordsall parish, and the hamlets of *Moorgate* and *Spittal hill*, in Clareborough parish. The streets, &c. in these parochial divisions are distinguished in the foregoing list.

POST OFFICE, Grove-street, Mrs. Elizabeth Taylor, Post Mistress. Letters from London and the South arrive daily at 12 morning, and are despatched at one afternoon; to York, Glasgow, &c they are despatched at twelve, and arrive at one aft. A Mail Gig arrives from Worksop every morning at a quarter past eleven, and departs at two afternoon.

Allcock Mr. Wm. West Retford
Allen Mary, clothes dlr. Moorgt
Allison Wm. M. R. C. S. Bridge gate
Ash Rev. Benj. (Indt:) Moorgate
Bannister Jas. net mfr. Wright Wilson street
Barker Wm. gent. Moorgate hill
Baxter W. excise officer, Moorgt
Beardsall Mrs. Charlotte, Carolgate
Beckwith Rev. T. F. (M. A.) vicar of East Retford, Chapelgate
Benson Miss Letitia & Sisters, Carolgate
Bigsby Thos. solr. Churchgate
Billyard Wm. cabt. mkr. Beardsall's row
Bonsor Miss Jane & Sisters, West Retford
Bower Mrs. Eliz. West Retford
Bower William, gent. Moorgate house

Brooks Rev. Joshua, Wm. Vicar of Clareborough, Moorgate
Brown Edw. Cromwell, sol. Storcroft terrace
Brown Miss Mary & Eliza, Wright Wilson street
Brown Wm. sweep, Grove st
Bullivant Mrs. Martha, Moorgate
Burden Mr. Jas. Churchgate
Burton Eliz. mattress maker. Moorgate
Burrows Thos. parish clerk, West Retford
Carter Mrs. Eliz. Spittal hill
Chapman Mrs. Mary, Tilne road
Chappell Mrs. Esther, West Retford
Cheatter Jph. gov. Workhouse
Cheavin Jas. boat owner, New row
Clark Chas. dyer, Little lane
Clark John, boat owner, Canal row

Clark Mary, grocer, Moorgate
Clarke Miss Mary, Market place
Clarke Wm. gent. Chapelgate
Clayton Mrs. Mary, Beardsall's row
Clayton Wm. cowkeeper, Moorgate
Colton Wm. gent. Moorgate
Cook John, tea dealer, Wright Wilson street
Cook Richard, hawker, Moorgate
Cooke Dawber, gent. Russell pl
Cowlishaw Mrs. Eliz. Churchgt
Cresey Wm. gent. Spittle hill
Creswell Geo. Esq. Square
Cusa Chas. hawker, Wellington place
Dickonson Peter, Esq. Retford hall
Donson John, carter, New st
Eyre Wm. gent. Appleton's bdgs
Fisher Wm. grocer, Grove street
Flower Jph. draper, Grove street
Foljambe Fras. Thornhough, Esq, banker, The square
Fox Jtn. bank cashier, Carrolgt
Fullard John, farmer, Moorgate
Ginever Mrs. Eliz. Terrace house
Gould George, gent. Appleton's Bdgs
Goodger Jph. hawker, New row
Gray Mr. Chas. Wright Wilson place
Gylby John, gent. Moorgate
Hackett Wm. boat owner. Canal row
Hall Quibel, gent. Spittal hill
Hartshorne Mrs. Cath. Grove st
Hill John, laceman &c. Factory row
Heane Mrs. Ann, Grove street
Hickson Mrs. Mary, Grove street
Hindley Pearce, boatowner, Canal row
Hinds Wm. carter, West Retford
Hodgkinson Edw. grocer Grove street
Holmes Jervas King, solr. Square
Hodgkinson Mrs. Ruth. Moorgt
Holmes John, Esq. F. A. S Carol gate
Hutchinson Rd. gent. New street house

Jackson Miss Mary & Sisters, Star croft, terrace
Jackson Wm. gent. Appleton's Bdgs
Johnson Hy. gent. Wellington pl
Johnson Mr. Saml. Spa lane
Johnson Thomas, carter, Wright Wilson place
Kippax John, Esq. The Elms
Kippax Mrs. Sarah, Churchgate
Kirke Mrs. Maria, Carolgate
Kirke Wm. Esq. Carolgate
Lambert Cornls. cab. mkr. Carol gate
Lee James, Esq. West-Retford House
Makepeace Rt. gent. Moorgate
Markham Jude, beesom maker, Canal row
Mason Mrs. Eliza, Carolgate
Mee Wm. surgeon, b. Bridgegt
Meekley Wm. net maker, Travis's Bdgs
Merrill Mrs. Eliz. Grove street
Mold Rev. Wm. Chapelgate
Moor Munton, bleacher, Thrumpton
Moss James, farmer, West Ret.
Moss Thomas, gent. Appleton's Bdgs
Mudford John, fishing net mfr. Spa lane
Nettleship Mrs. Susanna, Churchgate
Oldham Mrs. Frances, Grove st
Oldham John, governor of Clareborough Workhouse, Moorgt
Olpherts Robert, gent. Wright Wilson place
Parker Darker, gent. Churchgt
Parker John, Esq. The Square
Pearson W. sheriff's officer and apparitor, Market place
Peck Richard, clerk, Spital hill
Piercy John Shadrack, parish clerk, Beardsall's row
Richardson Mrs. Ann, Moorgate
Richardson Mrs. Mary, Whitehouses
Ridley Miss Mary, Grove st
Riley Mrs. Eliz. Grove st
Rimington Mr. Mark, Turk's head yard

Roberts John, gent. The Grove
Rogers Jerh. farmer, Whitehs
Rushton Mr. Jph. Spittal hill
Scales Mrs. Mary, West Retford
Scott John, sweep, Moorgate hill
Slaney Broxholm, Sexton, Chapelgate
Smith John, gent. The Square
Snow Mrs. Ann, Theatre yard
Stenson Mrs. Sarah, W. Retford
Stocks Mary, boat-owner, Canal row
Stocks Thomas, carter, Moorgate
Sugden Mr. Wm. New st
Taylor Mrs. Jane, stay maker, h. Carolgate
Taylor Mrs. Sarah, Market pl
Thorold Mrs. C. Moorgate
Tomlinson Samuel, town crier, Turn lane
Tootell Wm. sergeant at mace, Beardsall court
Undy Rd. farmer, West Retford
Walker Faith, farmer, West Retford
Walker Fras. cowkpr. Whitehs
Wharburton Jph. Lock house
Ward Edw. sweep, Moorgate hill
Wigfall Mr. Jph. Grove street
Whitaker Miss Ann, Carolgate
White Chas. gent. The Square
Williams Jph. gent. Thrumpton
Wilkinson John, grocer, Carolgt
Wilkinson John, excise officer, Moorgate
Wilson Rev. Geo. (Meth) Grove street
Wilson Rev. John, (Meth) Grove street
Wilson Wm. supervisor, Moorgt
Woolfitt Mrs. Mary, Beardsall's row
Worsley Geo. chairman, Theatre yard
Wright Thos. farmer, West Retford
Youle Rev. Abraham, M. A. rector of West Retford

ACADEMIES.
*Those marked * are Boarding Schools.*
Allen Jane, Beardsall's row

*Allen Wm. Carolgate
*Ash, Rev. Benj. Moorgate
Bower George, Wellington pl
Beardman John, Moorgate
*Cass Susanna, Grove street
Free Grammar School, Chapelgate; Rev. W. Mold, master; James Holderness, usher
Free School, West Retford; George Harpham, master
Harpham Hannah, Wright Wilson place
Piercy John Shadrach, Grove st. h. Beardsall's row
*Rawlinson Ann, (Ladies) The Square
Waddington Eliz. Carr lane
*Whalley Henry, Churchgate

ARCHITECT & SURVEYOR.
Weightman John Gray, Market place

ATTORNIES.
Hannam Richard and Son, clerks to magistrates, Carolgate
Holmes and Brown, The Square
Marshall George, Chapelgate
Mee and Bigsby, Churchgate
Mee John, (town clerk, clerk to the Deputy Lieutenancy, and County treasurer,) Castlegate

AUCTIONEERS.
Becket Samuel, Carolgate
Hodson Francis, Carolgate
Hopkinson Fran. (and Bdg. surveyor) Grove street
White Francis, (and land valuer) New street

BAKERS & FLOUR DLRS.
Barton John, Churchgate
Bingham Thomas, Bridgegate
Burton Thomas, Carolgate
Denham John, Wellington place
Hindley John West Retford
Holberry Jph. West Retford
Levick John, Wellington place
Nicholson Chpr. Carolgate
Small George, Carolgate
Taylor Thephilus, Moorgate

BANKERS.
Cook (Sir Wm. Bryan) Foljambe Parker, and Walker, The Square; drawn on Coutts & Co.

Savings Bank, The Square ; open Monday morning, from 10 to 12 o'clock ; George Thornton, secretary.

BASKET MAKERS.
Bettison William, Bridgegate
Holliday John, Spa lane

BLACKSMITHS.
Banks John, Carolgate
Banks Jonathan Bridgegate
Burrows Thomas, West Retford
Clayton William, Moorgate
Hudson T. Twelve, Travis's Bdgs
Hudson W. Jas. Beardsall's row
Littlewood Jas. Churchgate, h. West Retford
Scott Benjamin, Carolgate
Siddans William, Carolgate

BOAT BUILDER.
Woodruff William, New street

BOOKSLRS. STATIONERS, & PRINTERS, & BINDERS.
Clayton John (and paper hanging whs.) Carolgate
Dewhirst Benj. (and carpet whs.) Market place
Hodson Fras. (and carpet, and paper hang. whs.) Carolgate
Holderness Margt. Bridgegate
Thornton Geo. (stationer) The Square
Turvey Thos. (and paper hang. whs.) The Square
Whiteside Jph. (binder) Grove st

BOOT & SHOE MAKERS.
Atkinson James, Spittal hill
Baker John, Spa lane
Baker Valentine, Turn lane
Baker William, Carolgate
Bowmer George, Moorgate
Brown John, Spittal hill
Burton Richard, Little lane
Dernie James, Churchgate
Dernie Thomas, Moorgate
Elvidge William, Market street
Footitt James, Theatre yard
Frost William, Spittal hill
Gace John, Moorgate
Harrison John, Canal row
Hindley Samuel, Grove street
Hodson Thomas, Beardsall's row
Hodson William, Carr lane
Hoult John, Grove street

Hoyland Thomas, Turn lane
Hunt John, Moorgate
Jubb Uriah, Chapelgate
Lawrence Ellen, Bridgegate
Lawrence Stephen, Turn lane
Nance Thomas, Moorgate
Payne John, Travis's Bdgs
Richardson John, sen. New st
Richardson John, jun. New st.
Slaney Thomas, Carolgate
Slaney William, Carolgate
Snowden James, Moorgate
Tomlinson Wm. Cotterill's yard
Walker Thomas, Moorgate
Wash Robert, Carr lane
Whittam George, Moorgate
Wood William, New street

BRAZIERS & TINNERS.
Atkinson Robert, Factory row
Clark William, Bridgegate
Ledger George, Churchgate
Reddish John, Carolgate
Watson Gervas, Market place

BREWERS.
Burton John, Spittal hill
Littlewood George, Moorgate

BRICK & TILE MAKERS.
Hudson Robert, The Square
Justice John, Spittal hill
Littlewood Jph. Clarborough
Martin William, Raskill
Ogle George, Moorgate
Waite Robert, Hayton

BRICKLAYERS AND PLAS- TERERS.
Beardsall Wm. Beardsall's ct
Freeman Jas. Wellington place
Hind Wm. Moorgate
Ledger John, Spittal hill
Lowe Wm. Grove street
Small George, Carolgate
Watson Joseph, Factory row
Wilson John, Turk's Head yard
Woolstenholme Jph. Car lane

BRUSH HEAD MAKERS.
Burton John, New row
Hawksley Richard, Turn lane
Hawksley Wm. Turn lane
Shaw John, Canal row

BUTCHERS.
. *Those who live in the country have stalls in the Shambles.*
Ashmore John, Thrumpton

Bailey George, Carolgate
Bailey Joseph, Moorgate
Clark Saml. East Markham
Clough Henry, Moorgate
Cottam Joshua, Carolgate
Dean George, Mattersey
Dean Isaac, Turk's Head yard
Flower John, Spittal hill
Fowe Thomas, Bolham
Golland Wm. West Retford
Gyles Nathan, Spittal hill
Gyles William, Chapelgate
Hawksley Henry, Chapelgate
Hudson Charles, Blyth
Jackson Swinscho, Whitehouses
Littlewood George, Moorgate
Littlewood Jph. Churchgate
Loughton William, Everton
Marsh Denis, South Leverton
Needham James, Spittal hill
Needham James, New row
Nicholson Robert, Sturton
Pearce George, Carolgate
Rushby Richard, Grove street
Saldin Thomas, New street
Spray John, Grove street
Taylor William, Carolgate
Theaker Thomas, Scrooby
Turner Samuel, North Leverton
Walthead Richard, Carolgate
Wright John, Moorgate
Wright Thomas, West Retford
Wright William, Moorgate

CABINET MAKERS, &c.
Marked * are Joiners also.
Lambert Henry, Moorgate
Leadbeater Wm. Chapelgate
*Liller John, Churchgate
Richardson John, Spa lane
Saunders John, (case mkr.) Spa
 lane
*Scorah Wm. West Retford
Shaw Thomas, Carolgate
Stocks Thomas, Moorgate
Tomlinson Thomas, Market pl
Whitlam Benjamin, Churchgate

CARVER & GILDER.
Kippax George, Carolgate

CHAIR MKRS. & TURNERS.
Saunderson James, Turn lane
Stocks Wm. Old Tan yard
Standage Peter, Old Sun yard
Stubbings Thomas, Moorgate

CHINA, GLASS, &c. DLRS.
Burley Mary, Old Sun yard
Buxton Thomas, New row
Moor George, Turk's Head yd

CHEMISTS & DRUGGISTS.
Clater John, Market street
Fleck Wm. Henry, Bridgegate
Hudson George, Market place
Rawson Wm. Carolgate
Towler James, Bridgegate

COAL DEALERS.
Burton Wm. Spittal hill
Dixon Bilby, West Retford
Jackson Robert, Carolgate
Jackson William, New street
Hoyland Thomas, Turn lane
Ogle George, Moorgate
Parker Edw. (& lime and stone)
 Carolgate
Pashley Geo. Wright Wilson pl
Rushby Joseph, Carolgate

COACH BUILDER.
Hodgson Edward, Russell place

CONFECTIONERS, &c.
Clarke Fdk. (& British wine dlr.)
 Market street
Levick John, Wellington place
Littlewood Ed. (fruiterer) Moor-
 gate
Ridgway Thos. (fruiterer) Bridge-
 gate
Tattersall Thos. Chapelgate
Watson Gervas, Market place

COOPERS.
Bettison Wm. Bridgegate
Brown Geo. Beardsall's row
Sprentall Wm. West Retford
Warburton Wm. Spittal hill

CORN MERCHANTS.
Foster Thomas, Bridgegate
Hodgkinson Thos. Chapelgate
Holmes John, Moorgate
Ridgway Thomas, Bridgegate
Smith John, Moorgate

CORN MILLERS, &c.
Marked * are Flour Dlrs. only.
Appleby Thomas, Grove st
*Bailey Charles, Moorgate
Clixby Benjamin, Churchgate
Foster Thos. Bridgegate
*Oldham John, Carolgate
Subscription Mill, Geo. Brown,
 Thrumpton

Swinburne Thomas, Thrumpton
Tudsbury Fras. Tipping's mill,
CURRIERS & LEATHER CUTTERS.
Kippax William, Spittal hill
Spencer Wm. Moorgate
Travis Thos. Travis's bdgs
Whitlam Rt. & Son, Churchgate
CUTLER.
Barraclough Jph. Carolgate
DYERS.
Clark Hezekiah, Moorgate
Cooper Charles, Moorgate
FELLMONGER.
Wright Charles, Old Tan yard
FIRE & LIFE OFFICES.
County, Geo. Thornton, Square
Hope. Rt. Hudson, Square
Norwich Union, J. Fox, Carolgt
Sun, Wm. Fisher, Grove street
FISHMONGERS.
Graves Robert, Market place
Graves Thomas, Carolgate
Swales Wm. Spittal hill
GLOVER.
Leadbeater Westby, Spa lane
GROCERS & TEA DLRS.
Beeley Edw. (& cheese) Grove st
Bingham Thomas, Bridgegate
Clarke & Wilkinson, Carolgate
Clarke Wm. Bridgegate
Cook Wm. Market place
Cottam John, Market place
Dean Catherine, Carolgate
Denman Philip, Square
Dewick Francis, Square
Fisher & Hodgkinson, Grove st
Padley Geo. Market place
Padley Joseph, Moorgate
Parnham Thos. Carolgate
Woolstenholme Thos. Carolgate
GUN MAKERS.
Butler James, Carr lane
Slingsby Thos. Carolgate
HAIR DRESSERS, &c.
Bomforth Rd. Carolgate
Hall Edward, Moorgate
Hall Wm. Market place
Hodson Wm. Spital hill
Hudson Rt. & Son, (toy dealers)
* Square and Carolgate
Penington Wm. West Retford
Wilson Thomas, Bridgegate

HAT MFRS. & DLRS.
*Marked * are Dealers only.*
*Golland Charles, Bridgegate
*Holderness Mgt. Bridgegate
Mawer Wm. Beardsall's row
*Merryweather John, Bridgegate
Plant Thos. Chapelgate & *Workshop*
Thornton Geo. (stamp dis.) Sq
Turner Saml. Carolgate
HOP GROWERS
In the surrounding Villages.— See also Ollerton and Tuxford Directories.
Camm John, Bothamsall
Cocking James, Lower Headon
Dewick Ann, Bothamsall
Fisher William, Grove street
Fox Richard, Elksley
Hill Matthew, Elksley
Hill George, Upton
Hill William, Upton
Hudson Rt. & Son, Square
Hutchinson Rd. New St. House
Ibberson John, Upton
Ibberson Wm. Upton
Jackson Swinscho, Whitehouses
Johnson Thomas, Elksley
Ridgway Thos. Bridgegate
Moss John, Bothamsall
Taylor Eliz. Elksley
Taylor Thomas, Elksley
Ward William, Lower Headon
Weightman John, Elksley
Wheelwright Thomas, Welham
HOSIERS.
Cutts Wm. (mfr.) Wellington pl
Fearnside David, Churchgate
Golland Chas. Cottam h. Bridgegate
Nelson Danl. Moorgate
HOTELS, INNS, & TAVERNS.
Anchor, Jasper Manwell, Carolgt
Angel, Wm. Walker, Bridgegate
Black Bull, Geo. Ibberson, Moorgate
Black Head, Ann Green, Chapelgate
Black's Head, Wm. Hawkins, Moorgate
Boat, Bilby Dixon, West Retford
Brick & Tile, Rd. Cobb, Moorgt

Butchers' Arms, Wm. Bonsor,
Carolgate
Crown, John Howe, Chapelgate
George Inn, Ann Sheppard,
Moorgate
Granby, Mary Barlow, Carolgate
Half Moon, Saml. Cuckson, Sq.
Horse & Jockey, Jas. Webster,
Carolgate
Mermaid, Francis Coup Lamb,
West Retford
Newcastle Arms, Robert Hardy,
West Retford
Odd Fellows Arms, Wm. Taylor,
Russell place
Old Sun, Wm. Eyre, Chapelgate
Pheasant, Geo. Heane, Carolgt
Red Lion, Edward Hopkinson,
Carolgate
Sun, Sarah Walker, Spittal hill
Turk's Head, Ann Clarke, Grove
street
Vine, Geo. Clark, Churchgate
Waggon & Horses, Jas. Rayner,
West Retford
White Hart Inn, (& *Excise Office*)
Wm. Dennett, Bridgegate
White House Inn, Geo. Laughton, Whitehouses
White Lion, Ralph Moody,
Churchgate
White Swan, Timothy Ogle, Carolgate

BEER HOUSES.

Board, Geo. Hurst, Chapelgate
Board, John Shaw, Canal row
Board, Geo. Milnes, Moorgate
Board, Jnath. Holmes, Moorgt
Board, Wm. Shatliff, Whitehs.
Butchers' Arms, John Ashmore,
Thrumpton lane
Boat House, Edward White,
Thrumpton lane
King's Arms, John Richardson,
New street
King William IV., John Burton,
Spittal hill
Packet Inn, Wm. Pinder, Grove
street
Robin Hood & Little John, Geo.
Pearce, Carolgate
IRON & BRASS FOUNDERS.
Ledger and Holliday, Churchgt

IRONMONGERS.

Clark Wm. Bridgegate
Hewitt Robert Lightfoot, (& iron
mert.) Market place
Oats Richard, Square
JOINERS & BUILDERS.
See also Cabinet Makers.
Antcliff Robert, Russell place
Beardsall Henry, Grove street
Beardsall Seth, Carolgate, h.
Beardsall's row
Hill Benjamin, West Retford
Hooson Thos. Churchgate
Kirkby Eliz. Carolgate
Morton James, Churchgate
Shaw Thomas, Carolgate
Tomlinson Wm. (and dealer in
paviers for tessellated pavements) Grove street
LINEN MANUFACTURER.
Allesbrook John, Grove street
LINEN & WOOLLEN DRPRS.
Beardsall John, Churchgate
Bullivant Job, Carolgate
Cockill Jph. (woollen) Carolgate
Cottam Thos. Market place
Flower & Newboult, Carolgate
Golland Wm. Bridgegate
Roberts John, jun. Market street
Whittington Jane, (and carpet
warehouse) Bridgegate
MALTSTERS.
Foster Thos. Bridgegate
Holmes John, Moorgate
Littlewood George, Moorgate
Ogle Jacob, Moorgate
Oldham Fras. West Retford
Ridgway Thos. Bridgegate
Smith John, Moorgate
MILLINERS & DRESS MKRS.
Ashton Ellenor, Bridgegate
Denman Jane, Wellington place
Flower Rebecca, Churchgate
Hawksley Caroline, Chapelgate
Kirkby Mary, West Retford
Lee Ann, Travis's buildings
Ogle Abigail, Beardsalls' court
Roper Mary, Wright Wilson st
Sherratt Harriet, West Retford
Theaker Elizabeth, Moorgate
Wager & Sprentall, Carolgate
Watson Maria, Beardsall's row
Wilkinson Cath. Market place

2 F 2.

MILLWRIGHTS & MACHINE MAKERS.
Hooson Thos. Churchgate
Martin James, Moorgate
Pinder John, Moorgate

NAIL MAKERS.
Smedley Joseph, Canal row
Sutton Edward, Moorgate
Sutton Fras. (and pipe) Carolgt
Sutton Charles, Factory row

NURSERY, SEEDSMEN, &c.
Anderson John, Carolgate
Bowman Richard, Market place
Bowmer Isaac, Moorgate
Clark Thos. Bridgegate
Edeson Jph. Wright Wilson st
Garratt Jph. Factory row
Ghest Jph. Moorgate
Hampston Wm. Moorgate hill
Hudson Charles, Carr lane
Penington Frdk. Carolgate
Penington Thos. Cooke's yard
Penington Wm. West Retford
Read Jas. Wellington place

PAINTERS.
Best William, Grove street
Bingham Chas. Beardsall's row
Crawshaw Jas. Chapelgate
Foster Jonas, Moorgate
Uttley John, Churchgate
Winks John, Carr lane

PAPER MAKERS.
Nelson Horatio, West Retford
Nelson Thos. Ordsall & Notm

PHYSICIAN.
Bigsby John, Grove street

PLUMBERS & GLAZIERS.
Batty Thos. New street
Dawber John, Carolgate
Hawksley John, Spa lane
Hudson Robert, Grove street
Pashley Richard. Churchgate
Twelves Wm. Factory row

PROFESSORS OF MUSIC.
Bugg Henry Thos. (org.) Beardsall's row
Saxby Edw. Spa lane
Turvey Thos. (and dlr.) Square
Wakeley Chas. (and dlr.) New st

ROPE & TWINE MAKERS.
Burton Geo. West Retford
Colton Reb. (& flax dsr.) West Retford

Davison Rt. West Retford
Dent Wm. Spittal hill

SADDLERS, &c.
Hadwick Wm. Market place
Bailey Thos. Bridgegate
Cutts Joseph, West Retford
Swinburn Wm. Carolgate

SAILCLOTH AND SACKING MANUFACTURERS.
Bailey Joseph, Moorgate
Beardsall Adam, West Retford
Haxby Edw. Cookes' yd. Bridge gate
Parker Jas. Bridgegate
Skidmore Samuel, West Retford

SHOPKEEPERS.
Banks John, Bridgegate
Bannister Geo. Russell place
Burton Ann, Factory row
Chester Mary, West Retford
Dernie John, Moorgate
Gace John, Moorgate
Greenan John, Spittal hill
Hurst George, Carolgate
Merryweather Rd. Carolgate
Peck Richard, Spittal hill
Read Geo. Carolgate
Small Geo. Carolgate
Smith Wm. Spittal hill
Walker Jane, West Retford
Walker Wm. Moorgate

SILVERSMITHS, &c.
Hewitt Robert L. Market place
Parker Jas. Bridgegate

STAY MAKERS.
Holliday Frances, Churchgate
Hopkinson & Bonington, Carolgt
Slaney Susanna, Carolgate
Taylor & Son, Grove street
Wilkinson Eliz. Chapelgate

STONE MASONS.
Bailey John, Moorgate
Campsell Wm. New street
Sharpe Gervas, Wright Wilson st

STRAW HAT MAKERS.
Appleby Ann, Market place
Ashmore M. & S. Carolgate
Colbeck Ann, Moorgate
Graves Sarah. Carolgate
Penington Mary. Carolgate
Penington Sus. West Retford

SURGEONS.
Flower Saml. Fras. Carolgate

Gylby Worthington Thos., M.R.
C.S. Churchgate
Mee & Allison, Bridgegate
Smalley Jno. Frdk. Wellington pl
TAILORS.
Beardsall Nathan, West Retford
Dunk Benj. Moorgate
Ellis Edw. Chapelgate
Gantly John, Moorgate
Handley John, Little lane
Hopkinson Edw. sen. Carolgate
Hopkinson Edw. jun. Carolgate
Hopkinson Thos. Moorgate
Keetley Jas. Grove street
Kirk John, Turn lane
Lawrence Thos. Spittal hill
Mallender Geo. Churchgate
Merryweather Saml. Carolgate
Smedley Thos. West Retford
Smith Wm. Spittal hill
Tissington Henry, Thrumpton
Ward ——, Carolgate
Woolfitt Wm. Grove street
TALLOW CHANDLERS
Cook Wm. Market place
Cottam John Market place
Dewick Fras. Square
Fisher Wm. Grove street
Littlewood Geo. Moorgate
Padley Geo. Market place
TANNERS.
Rose & Wardell, Moorgate
Spencer Wm. Moorgate
Suter Geo. Peter, Bridgegate
TIMBER MERCHANTS.
Scorah Wm. West Retford
Sharp Wm. & Geo. Corporation
Wharf & Gainsbro'
TOBACCO PIPE MAKER.
Sutton Fras, Carolgate
UPHOLSTERER.
See Cabinet Makers.
Hodgkinson Rd. Grove street

VETERINARY SURGEONS.
Hudson John, Moorgate
Hudson Thos. Twelves, Travis's
buildings
Hudson Wm. James, Beardsall's
row
Taylor John & Geo. Carolgate
WATCH & CLOCK MAKERS.
Chumbley Wm. Bridgegate
Fletcher Charles, Bridgegate
Levick Wm. Carolgate
Parker James, Bridgegate
Sharp Wm. Carolgate
WHARFINGERS.
Elliott Thos. (and agent to the
Canal Co.) Corporation wharf
White Fras. New wharf, New st
WHEELWRIGHTS.
Cobb Wm. West Retford
Holliday George, Churchgate
Holliday John, West Retford
Holliday Thos. West Retford
Swinden Jph, West Retford
Ward Thomas, New row
WHITESMITHS, &c.
Bailey James, Churchgate
Palfreman Robert, Grove street
Palfreman Wm. jun. Cooke's yd
Taylor George, Bridgegate
Wolton John, Carolgate
WINE & SPIRIT MERCHTS.
Marked ‡ are Spirit Merchants
only.
‡Allen Peter, Churchgate
‡Becket Samuel, Carolgate
‡Cook William, Market place
‡Denman Philip, Square
Dewick Fras. Square
Hudson Rt. & Son, Square
Hutchinson Jph. Market place
Williams Wm. Rowland, New st
WOOL MERCHANTS.
Cockill Jph. Carolgate
Fearnside David, Churchgate

COACHES.

FROM THE WHITE HART INN.

The Royal Mail, to *London, &c.* every afternoon at 1; and to *Edinburgh, &c.* at 12 noon.

The "Rockingham," to *London* daily, at half-past 2 afternoon; and to *Leeds* at half-past 8 morning.

The " Express," to *London*, at 4 afternoon ; and to *York* at 1 morning.

The " Union," to *London*, at half-past 7 evening ; and to *Leeds* at half-past 2 morning.

The " Highflyer," to *London*, at half-past 11 night ; and to *Edinburgh* at half-past 2 morning.

The " Wellington," to *London*, at half-past 2 morning ; and to *Newcastle-upon-Tyne* at 11 morning.

The " Amity," to *Doncaster*, every afternoon at half-past 4 ; and to *Stamford* at 10 morning.

FROM THE VINE INN.

The " Industry," to *Nottingham*, every morning at 6, except Sunday ; and to *Sheffield* every Monday, Tuesday, Thursday, and Saturday morning at 6.

A Car to *Gainsborough* every morning at 6, to meet the Hull Steam Packets and the Lincolnshire Coaches.

CARRIERS.

To London, Deacon, Harrison, and Co. from the Newcastle Arms every night, at 10 ; and James Jackson, from the Half Moon, daily, at 5 afternoon.

To Bawtry, Thomas Stansfield & Thomas Tattersall, from Chapelgate, every Thursday, at 9 morning.

To Gainsboroub, Thomas Stansfield & Thomas Tattersall, from Chapelgate, every Tuesday at a quarter before 6 morning.

To Leeds, Deacon, Harrison and Co. from the Newcastle Arms, every morning at 4 ; and James Jackson, from the Half Moon, daily, at 9 morning.

To Lincoln, William Morton, from the Half Moon, every Wed.

To Nottingham, Edward Hudson, from the White Swan ; and John Rishby, from Moorgate, ever Tuesday and Friday ; depart 6 morning.

To Ollerton, Thomas Stansfield, from Chapelgate, every Friday ; departs 7 morning.

To Sheffield, George & Wm. Smith, through Blyth & Maltby, from Wright Wilson place, every Monday ; depart 3 afternoon ; and from the Half Moon, George Malkin, Thursday & Saturday, and Wm. Morton, Friday.

To Tuxford, Thos. Stansfield & Thos. Tattersall, from Chapelgate, every Monday ; depart 9 morning.

To Worksop, Thos. Stansfield & Thos. Tattersall, from Chapelgate every Wednesday ; depart 9 morning.

MARKET CARRIERS.

If not otherwise expressed they arrive on Sat. mg. about 10, and depart 4 afternoon.
Marked ‡ put up at the Half Moon
Blyth, White Lion, M. Kirky
‡ Chesterfield, Wm. Warner
‡ Dunham, Richard Tomlinson
‡ Gainsbro', Thomas Cuckson ; John Taylor, (Crown) Tues. & Saturday

Gringley, &c. Vine, M. Kirkby
Laneham, Pheasant, G. Bolton
Leverton, Black's Head, Robert Wilkinson
Normanton-on-Trent, Butcher's Arms, Thomas Waller
Tuxford & Newark. Vine, Benj. Godfrey ; Granby, John Briggs ‡ Worksop, Wm. Godfrey and Mr. Wilmot

CONVEYANCE BY WATER.

FROM THE CORPORATION WHARF.

Two Packets for goods and passengers arrive from Stockwith and Gainsbro' every Wednesday and Saturday, at 11 morning, and dep. at 3 afternoon.

Boats to Chesterfield, Worksop, and adjacent places, and to Lincoln, Sleaford, Horncastle and Boston, daily.—Thomas Elliott, *Wharfinger.*

FROM THE NEW WHARF NEW STREET.

Boats regularly to Stockwith and Gainsbro', from whence goods are forwarded to all parts.—Fras. White, *Wharfinger.*

BECKINGHAM PARISH.

BECKINGHAM, in the liberty of Southwell and Scrooby, is a well built village, occupying a circular area, and pleasantly situated on the turnpike road, 9 miles E. by S. of Bawtry, and 3 miles W. of Gainsborough. The parish, which extends eastward to the Trent, contains 2400 acres of land, the annual rental of which was valued at £2646. 8s. 5¾d. at the enclosure of the commons in 1779. It contains 102 houses and 481 inhabitants, and its poor rates in 1831 amounted to £396. 19s. 3¾d. of which £71 was paid to the county rate. At the time of the Domesday survey, "Bechingham was a *Beru* of Lancham, the Archbishop of York's Soc;" and in the 9th of Edward II. the King and the chapter of Southwell were its joint lords ; but the Duke of Newcastle is now *lord of the manor ;* and the chapter of Southwell received for their manorial rights an allotment of 198A. 1R. 21P. at the enclosure in 1779, when 194A. 3R. 7P. of land was allotted to the *prebendary of Beckingham,* in Southwell collegiate church, and 58A. 3R. 38P. to the vicar, in lieu of the tithes of the parish. The other principal land owners are Robert Cross, Thomas Massingberd, and Robert Duckle, Esqrs. A large inn at *Trent Port wharf,* (see Saundby,) and two large farms, called the *Pear Tree Hill* and the *Woods,* distant about one mile from the village, are within the parish.

The *Church* is a large ancient fabric, dedicated to All Saints, and has a nave, side aisles, and tower. The prebendary of Beckingham is patron of the vicarage, which is valued in the King's books at £6 15s. 3d., and is discharged from the payment of first fruits. The Rev. Henry Watkins, M.A. is the incumbent, but the Rev. J. K. Miller officiates. In the village is a *Methodist Chapel,* which was built in 1807, and enlarged in 1821.

The parish *School* is endowed with one eighth part of the

rents of 33 acres of land in Beckingham, and 28¼ acres in
Saundby, which were bequeathed in 1731, by James Wharton,
Esq. who directed that the remaining seven-eighths of the rents
should be paid to Gainsbro' grammar school. This land is
now let for £120 per annum, so that the yearly sum received
by this school is £15, for which the master teaches ten free
scholars; and four others are educated for the interest of £100
left in 1825 by Miss Sarah Richardson, whose father was nearly
50 years vicar of this parish. Two others are also taught for
£1. 12s. paid out of two acres of meadow land, which was given
at the enclosure in exchange for the POOR'S LAND, and is now
let for £4. 15s. per annum; of which, the remaining £3. 3s. is
given at Easter to the poor of the parish, to whom the following
CHARITIES belong, viz. 40s. yearly, left in 1621, by William
Clark, out of Land at Walkrith, to two indigent parishioners;
the interest of £20 left in 1753, by John Burton, to be distributed on the day of of St. John the Evangelist; £1 yearly out
of lands in Beckingham, now belonging to T. Massingberd,
Esq., left in 1729, to be given in bread; and the interest
of £34, left by William Jackson in 1772, and now in the
hands of Mr. Robert Cross.

For Trent Port Wharf, see Saundby.

Andrew Hy. shoemaker
Beaumont Jph. shoemkr. Toll bar
Burkinsheare Jph. shoemaker
Buttery John, tailor
Byron Thos. weaver
Casson Geo. butcher
Cobb John, joiner
Cobb Wm. joiner
Cottingham John, bricklayer
Cross Robert, esq.
Curtis Sus. vict. Hare & Hounds
Eyre Thos. cheese dealer
Farr Thos. corn & seed mercht.
Gray John, shoe maker
Hankin Fras. corn miller
Hemingway Geo. blacksmith
Jenour Capt. Matthew
Jubb Mary, blacksmith
Maltby John, butcher
Martin Mrs. Elizabeth
Martin Miss Mary
Massingberd Thos. Esq.
Moody Mrs. Elizabeth
Parkin Geo. weaver
Parkin Barzilla, parish clerk
Robinson Wm. wheelwright
Robinson Samuel, wheelwright
Smith James, bricklayer

Smith Thos. nail maker
Stovin Edw. schoolr., shopkpr.,
 and post-office
Wagstaff Geo. tailor
Wagstaff Matthew, swine jobber

FARMERS.
*Thus * are Yeomen.*
*Best John, *The* Harwood Geo.
 Woods　　　　Hurt Seth
Broomhead Seth Nicholson John
Cliff Charles　　Otter Wm.
Cooke John　　Trimingham W.
*Cottam Rt.　　Walker John
*Cross William, *Watson Henry
 Peartree hill Webster John
*Gamson Jervs. Wiswould Sml.

COACHES.
The *Mail* to Sheffield, at 11 mg.
 and to Louth, at 3 aft. —Mr. E.
 Stovin keeps the Post-office
 for Beckingham, Walkeringham and Saundby
The *Hope* to Gainsbro' at 8 mg.
 and to Sheffield in the aft.
A Coach to Doncaster at 9 mg.
 and to Lincoln at 6 evening.

BOLE PARISH.

Bole is a small village and parish on the west bank of the Trent, 2 miles S. S. W. of Gainsborough, containing 35 houses nd 144 inhabitants. The soil is a strong clay, except on the Trent bank, where there is a rich loamy marsh. Owing to the iver having here changed its ancient course, by avoiding a winding reach, about 110 acres of land which adjoin this pa- ish, are in Lincolnshire. The poor rates in 1831 amounted o £121. 10s, of which £22. 19s. 3d., was paid to the county ate. The *Manor and Rectory* of Bole, form a PREBEND for he maintenance of a Prebendary in York Cathedral, but Lord Venlock is the lessee of the prebendal lands and rectoral ithes. The CHURCH is a small ancient structure, dedicated to it. Martin, and has a handsome pinnacled tower, with three ells. The living is a vicarage, valued in the King's Books t £4. 13s. 4d. It is a peculiar of the dean and chapter of York; the prebendary of Bole is the patron, and the Rev. John Singleton is the incumbent, but the officiating curate is the Rev. James Hawton. In 1394, Richard II. granted leave to William Rothwell, to assign for the support of the vicar and his uccessors, " eight acres of land, and six of pasture," which ands " were held of John Danby, clerk, as of the prebend of Bole, by two appearances at the Court of Bole, and paying 2d."

CHARITIES.—In 1671, a person unknown, left 5s. yearly to he poor, out of a farm at Welham, which now belongs to S. Thorold, Esq. In 1745, George Mower, Esq., paid 68 years' rrears of this annuity, amounting to £17, which with other ifts, was expended in the purchase of a house and rood of and, now let for £4. 4s. per annum, which is distributed yearly y the churchwardens. The following legacies have been be- queathed for the education of the poor, and their yearly, mount of £4. 6s., is paid to a schoolmaster for teaching nine oor children; viz. 40s. yearly, left in 1781, by William Net- leship, out of an estate now belonging to Elizabeth Nettle- hip; £30 left in 1807, by John Nettleship; and £30 be- queathed in 1820 by Robert Wilkinson.

Bingley George. vict. Dog
Boswell John, Beerhouse
Crossby William, shoemaker and parish clerk.
Fenton John, shoemaker
Taylor Wm. shopkeeper

Winks John, schoolmaster

FARMERS.
Atkinson Jas.   Marriott John
Casson Jane   Scott Wm
Fenningley Geo.   Wilkinson John
Jackson Geo.   Winks Wm.

BURTON (WEST) PARISH.

West Burton is a small parish containing only six houses,

40 inhabitants, and 900 acres of rich land, on the west bank of the Trent, lying south of Bole, seven miles N E by E of Retford, and four miles S by W of Gainsbro'. The church, or as it is generally called, the CHAPEL is a small edifice with a turret; in which hangs a bell. The living, which is now enjoyed by the Rev. Wm. Moulds, is a perpetual curacy of the certified value of £12. 13s. 4d. and is in the gift of David Walters, Esq. of Gloucester House, who is also the lay impropriator and owner of all the land in the parish, except the Mill Estate which belongs to Lord Wenlock. Until 1797 the TRENT here took such a circular sweep that a boatman might have thrown his hat on shore, and after sailing two miles have taken it up again, but in that year the stream forced itself through the narrow neck of land in a straight line, in consequence of which the old winding channel was filled up, and divided betwixt the counties of Nottingham and Lincoln, besides which, the latter has now about 100 acres on the west side of the present course of the river. Before the conquest there was a manor here possessed by "Speranoc," and after that epoch, part of the parish was "a Berue of the Archbishop of York's Soc of Laneham." After the dissolution, the rectory which had belonged to Worksop priory was given by Henry 8th. to one Wm. Nevill, gent. and his heirs. The present occupiers are W. Ashton, of *East House*, Francis Bingham, of *Middle House*, and John Cook, of *West House*, farmers; and Benjamin Crosby, corn-miller.

CHARITIES.—Twenty shillings are given yearly to one poor person of West Burton, from the bequest of Wm. Clark, (in 1621) out of an estate at Walkrith, in Lincolnshire, now belonging to Richard Atkinson, Esq. In 1710, George Green left 3 acres of land on the Upper Ing of Sturton, and directed the rent of it to be paid to a schoolmaster for teaching 3 poor children of West Burton. At the Sturton Enclosure, in 1824, the school land was augmented with an allotment of 1A. 0R. 27P. and is now worth £4 per annum.

CLAREBOROUGH PARISH.

This large parish, which extends from Retford to Hayton, and Leverton, is intersected by the Chesterfield Canal, and is skirted on the west by the river Idle. It contains 3,410A. 1R. 18P. of good clay land, which in 1807, was valued for the poor rates, at the annual rent of £4,165 9s.. It is divided into five HAMLETS, viz. :—Clareborough, containing 1223A. 2R. 17P. valued at £994 19s.; Welham 804A. 2R. valued at £688 4s.; Little Gringley 811A. 1R. 10P. valued at £871. 14s.; Moorgate 337A. 1R. 20P. valued at £1287. 2s. 6d.; and Bolham

223A. 2R. 11P. valued at £326. 9s. per annum, including the rents of the buildings. These hamlets repair their own roads separately, but maintain their poor conjointly. The *workhouse* is in the hamlet of Moorgate, which forms a populous suburb of East Retford. The sum collected for poor-rates in 1831, was £356. 4s. 10d., of which £102. 16s. 3d. was paid to the county rate. The parish contains 507 houses, 501 families, and 2106 inhabitants, of whom upwards of 1800 reside in the hamlet of Moorgate, and Spittal Hill. At the *enclosure* of Clareborough and Welham Commons, in 1777, two allotments, consisting of 197A. 2R. 37P. in the former, and 133A. 2R. 13P. in the latter, were awarded to the lay impropriator (now the Duke of Devonshire) in lieu of the *great tithes*, and they have since been sold to various freeholders. At the same time 43A. 2R. 12P. in Clareborough, and 43A. 0R. 25P. in Welham, were allotted to the vicar as a commutation of the *small tithes* of those hamlets. The *impropriation* of Little Gringley was sold about 10 years ago, to A. H. Eyre, Esq. of Grove, and that of Bolham and Moorgate, to the Hon. John Bridgeman Simpson, of Babworth.

The CHARITIES belonging to the parish are,—a yearly rent charge of £3. 6s. 8d. out of the rectory farm to the poor ; £4 per annum, left by *William Broomhead*, to the poor of Moorgate and Spittal Hill, out of a house and land at Moorgate, now belonging to Mr. Joseph Guest ; 9s. yearly to the poor of Clareborough, left by *Mr. Fisher* out of land at Welham ; an annuity of 14s., left by *George Mower*, to the poor of Clareborough out of a house in Welham, which now belongs to Mr. Thorold ; and an annuity of 10s. paid out of the poor-rates as the interest of £12 left by a *Mr. Andrew.*

CLAREBOROUGH is a long straggling village, on the Retford and Gainsbro' road, two and a half miles N.E. by E. of the former town. The parish CHURCH is an ancient fabric, consisting of a nave chancel and side aisles, with a square embattled tower, containing three bells. The interior was, a few years ago, cleansed, beautified, and repewed, and a gallery erected at the west end, where a small organ has been placed by the munificence of H. C. Hutchinson, Esq. It was founded, endowed, and consecrated in 1258, by Sewal, Archbishop of York, who gave it to his newly founded chapel of St. Sepulchre, in York, but reserved for the use of the vicar, a toft and croft lying near the churchyard, the tithes of the enclosed crofts of the town and of the mills at Bollam, and also the altarage, on condition that he should support two chaplains to serve at Gringley, Welham, and Bollam. The *vicarage*, which is discharged from the payment of first fruits, is valued in the King's books at £9. 15s. 4d. and is now in the incumbency of the Rev. Joshua Brooks, and patronage of the Rev. C. Simeon and others. After the dissolution the impropriation was vested in the Crown, until James I.

granted it to Lord Cavendish, whose descendant the Duke of Devonshire sold it as before stated, except the advowson, which was purchased by Richard Woodhouse, Esq. of London, by whose heirs it is now possessed. In 1393, Clareborough had a *prependary* in York Cathedral, but by whom the office was created, or when it was discontinued, is unknown. The vicar now resides in a new house near *St. Saviour's Church*, which, though in the suburbs of Retford, is a chapel of ease to this parish. (See page 314.)

At the Domesday survey, part of *Claverbury* or Clareborough, belonged to the King's great soke of Mansfield, and had then " two socmen, one villain, and one bordar," having six oxen in plough and two mills, the whole valued at 32s. Roger de Busli had lands here, which, previous to the conquest, belonged to " Reginald." In 1537, the Bannister family had ten messuages, four tofts, and 580 acres of land, in Clareborough and else-where. The land now belongs to a number freeholders, and a large portion of it was, till a few years ago, the property of the Duke of Devonshire.

BOLHAM or BOLLAM is a romatic hamlet, one mile N. of Retford, on the east side of the river Idle, where there is a corn mill, a mill for glazing paper, and three *rock houses* formed by excavations in the shelving rocks of red-sand stone, in which are the ruins of eight or nine other troglodyte dwellings. There was anciently a chapel here, and its site is still called the *chapel yard*. Half a mile east of the hamlet are a few cottages called *Bolham Lane Houses*, and a little to the north east is *Bolham Hall*, a neat farm house, with 150 acres of land, now belonging to Mrs. Pearson, of Tickhill; and formerly to the Harrisons; but the principal land owner in this division of the parish is Michael Wynne Thorold, Esq. of Barnby Moor, who is lord of the *manor*, which, together with the mills, was granted by Henry VIII. to Sir Robert Swift, with whose heirs it remained till 1651, when it was conveyed to Francis Wortley, Esq.

LITTLE GRINGLEY or *Greenley*, is a hamlet of scattered houses, generally of an humble description, and occupying a picturesque situation on the declivity of a hill, 1½ mile E. of Retford. A large quantity of *underwood* is grown in the neighbourhood, and is here cut up and used for making gates and fences. A good deal of *plaster* is also got and prepared here for making floors, &c. A. H. Eyre, Esq. is the principal land-owner, and lord of the *manor*, which was anciently possessed by the Norry's family, from whom it passed to the Annes, the Hercys, the Clarkes, and the Sherbrooks. At the Domesday survey it belonged to the soke of Dunham, and some time afterwards it had a *chapel*, of which no traces now remain, though some years ago a stone coffin and several human bones were dug up near its supposed site.

Moorgate hamlet, which includes Spittal Hill, forms a populous and handsome suburb of East Retford, and has lately been ornamented with a beautiful *new church,* or chapel of ease. (See p. 314.) Within the last 50 years, the number of buildings has been greatly encreased, and the land is chiefly in grass or divided into gardens, except the common, which was enclosed in 1799. Neither Moorgate nor Spittal Hill are mentioned before the year 1525, and they owe their present consequence to their participation in the prosperity of Retford.

Welham, or as it was anciently called *Wellome,* is a pleasant village of good houses, one and a half mile E. by N. of Retford, on the Gainsbro' road. It derives its name from *St. John's Well,* which has long been famed for the cure of scorbutic and rheumatic complaints, and is now converted into a commodious *bath,* though it has lost much of its former celebrity. Near the well house is a large *bone mill* and a *hop yard,* on the banks of the Chesterfield Canal. In the village are several gentlemen's villas, one of which is an elegant stone fabric, built in 1831, by H. C. Hutchinson, Esq. A great part of the land here was given by Matilda, the last of the Lovetots, to Radford Abbey, and was afterwards the property of the Duke of Devonshire, who sold it in 1813 to various proprietors.

CLAREBOROUGH PARISH DIRECTORY.

BOLLAM.

Fowe Thomas, butcher
Herring Geo. corn miller
Salmon Wm. farmer, Hall
Wilby Rev. Thomas, Hall

CLAREBOROUGH.

Beard Geo. fruit dealer
Bigsby John, M.D. & Retford
Bingham Mrs. Eliz.
Clark Thomas, shoe maker
Dixon Hanh. School mistress
Golland Rd. butcher & beer hs.
Hempstock Wm. blacksmith
Homer John, nail maker
Justice Eliz. beer house
Littlewood Jph. butcher & brick maker
Milles Jas. joiner & wheelwright
Pettinger Jas. vict. Stag
Sherratt John, vict. & coal dlr Gate, Canal bank
Smedley Jas. nail maker
Smedley Jph. nail maker
Smith Thos. schoolmaster
Strawson Wm. grocer
Swinburn Geo. tailor
Walker Richard, corn miller

Wheat Saml. shoe maker

FARMERS AND YEOMEN.

Bartle Wm,   Parr John
Barton John   Rogers Thos. sen
Bell John   Rogers Thos. jun
Freeman John   Storrs Thos. and
Johnson John   maltster
Melles Thos   White Edward

LITTLE GRINGLEY.

Allen John, plaster preparer
Allen Thos. plaster preparer
Allen Sarah, beer house
Auckland Booker, farmer
Bower John, farmer
Crofts Jas. & G. hedge carpenters
Fletcher Mary, cowkeeper
Freeman Jph. farmer
Jackson Wm. farmer
Skelton John, shoe maker

MOORGATE AND SPITEAL HILL.

☞ *The names are included in the Retford Directory.*

WELHAM.

Fenton Wm. farmer, Wellhouse
Hunt Thos. bone dust maker, Wellhouse
Hutchinson Mrs. Ann

Hutchinson Hy. Clark, Esq. Hall
Mower George, Esq.
Rushby Thos. vict. Hop Pole, &
 coal mert. Canal bdg
Sargeson John, shopkeeper
Sykes Saml. Jas. gent. Cottage

Thorold Samuel, Esq.
Thorold Mrs. Susanna
Walker Rt. bath kpr. Wellhouse
Wells John, farmer, Whinleys
Wheelwright Thomas, gent.

CLAYWORTH PARISH

Comprises the two manors and townships of *Clayworth* and *Wiseton*, which together contain 3116 acres of land, and a population of 577 souls. It is intersected by the Chesterfield canal, and is bounded on the west by the river Idle, and on its other limits by Gringley-on-the-Hill, Beckingham, and North and South Wheatley. The two townships maintain their poor separately, and have both a fertile soil, that of Clayworth being a rich clay, and that of Wiseton a fine red sandy mould.

CLAYWORTH, or *Claworth*, is a good village on the east side of the canal, six miles N. by E. of Retford. The *church* dedicated to St. Peter, is an ancient structure with a tower, and contains many old monumental inscriptions. The living is a rectory valued in the King's books at £26. 10s. 10d.; in the patronage of the Dean of Lincoln, and now enjoyed by the Rev. Thomas Henry Shepherd, M.A. The *manor* of Claworth or "*Clavard*" was at the Domesday survey, of "the King's *Soc* of Mansfield, in his Wapentac of Oswardebec," and had one carucate and six bovates for the geld. It contains 2076 acres, and was enclosed in 1791, when 281A. 1R. 19P. was alloted to the rector in lieu of tithe, and is now called Clayworth-High-Field, or the *Tithe Farm.*. Peter Dickonson, Esq. is lord of the manor, and the principal proprietors of land are the Rev. John Otter, and Thomas Colton, F. Davenport and G. S. Foljambe, Esqrs. In the village is a *Methodist chapel,* which was built about 30 years ago, and a FREE SCHOOL, which was founded in 1702, by the Rev. Wm. Sampson, rector of the parish, who endowed it with 26A. 1R. 6P. of land, now let for £58 per annum. In 1707, Cphr. Johnson left an orchard worth £2 a-year, to be occupied by the schoolmaster, who has also a house and grass plot left in 1813, by Francis Otter, subject to a rent charge of £4, to be paid yearly to two of the best ploughers, and two of the best female shearers of the parish; but the contest for these prizes gave rise to such great dissensions, that the £4 has for some yesrs been carried to the school account. The master now receives £48 yearly, for teaching eleven poor boys of Clayworth, and two of Wiseton; and the remainder of the school income is given by the rector in prizes, to those free-scholars who are most proficient in learning, pursuant to the will of the founder.

The other Charities of Clayworth are six small rent charges, amounting to £5 13s. 4d. yearly, left to the poor by donors unknown, and distributed at Easter and Christmas. The benefactions belong to Wiseton township, are two yearly sums of 18s. and 6s. 8d. paid by Lord Althorp, as the rent of the *Poor's close*, and an annuity left out of his land by an unknown donor; £1 yearly, left to poor out of William Gray's land; and £3 yearly, left in 1751, by Richard Acklom, out of land which now belongs to Lord Althorp.

DRAKEHOLES, or *Drakelow*, is a hamlet four miles E.S.E. of Bawtry, on the Gainsbro' road, partly in Wiseton township and partly in the parish of Everton. This is one of the depôts for the Chesterfield and Trent canal, which passes by here, through a *tunnel* 250 yards in length, and 15 feet in height and width, in cutting which many *coins* of Constantine, and human bones, were found. There is no doubt that this has been a Roman station, for a Roman road, of which some faint traces may still be seen, has passed through it, and connected it with the station of *Agelocum*, or Littleborough. Here is also a good *inn*, and a handsome entrance lodge to Wiseton Hall, built by the late Mr. Acklom, whose long life seems to have been principally occupied in improving the country around him, and his place is well supplied by his successor, Lord Althorp, who in 1829 erected a steam-engine of eight horses' power, for the purpose of pumping off the drainage water from the low lands on both sides of the Idle, in Wiseton and Mattersea.

NEW WISETON is a small hamlet of cottages in Wiseton township, half a mile N.W. of Clayworth, built by the late Mr. Acklom, and now belonging to Lord Althorp, through whose estate the canal pursues a winding course of two miles.

WISETON is a small village in the township to which it gives name, five miles S.E. by E. of Bawtry. The *Lordship* contains 930 acres, all of which, except 48 acres, belongs to the Hon. John Charles Spencer Viscount Althorp, eldest son of Earl Spencer, to whom it passed in marriage with the granddaughter and heiress of the late Jonathan Aclom, Esq. of WISETON HALL, a handsome mansion which was rebuilt by him and his predecessor, but is seldom visited by its present owner. Its situation is highly pleasing, standing on a gentle swell, with a lawn of upwards of thirty acres in front, finely belted by trees and ornamental shrubs, and judiciously broken at intervals by picturesque clumps. The grounds command extensive prospects over the four adjacent shires of York, Lincoln, Nottingham, and Derby. The hall consists of a centre three stories high, with two wings of one lofty story each; the whole light and airy, and accompanied with a commodious range of offices. The interior is elegantly finished, and contains some good paintings by Holbein, Barlow, Caravaggis, and other artists. The *manor* is so well wooded as to appear one

great ornamental plantation, and a well conducted walk round
the home grounds is led for upwards of a mile in a circuitous
route, so as to connect the exterior woods with the domestic
scenery, whilst on the surrounding eminences may be seen the
new farm houses erected by the late Mr. Aclom. The old hall
was originally the residence of the Nelthorpe family, but was
purchased about two centuries ago by one of the *Ackloms* or
Acloms, an ancient Yorkshire family, often honoured with
knighthood in earlier times, when that title was conferred for
important services to the state, and on those whose birth entitled them to it. The branch of this family which was settled
at Wiseton is now extinct, as its last heiress, the late Lady
Althorp, died a few years ago without issue.

CLAYWORTH PARISH DIRECTORY.

CLAYWORTH TOWNSHIP.
Barlow Mrs. Mary
Bennett Saml. vict. White Swan
Bingham Mrs. Ann
Cheetham William, tailor
Clayton Geo. vict. Swan inn
Colton Thomas, Esq.
Davenport Frederick, Esq.
Dixon Wm. butcher & beer house
Gamble Wm. beer house
Gray Mr. Samuel
Gray Miss Sarah
Groves Mrs. Elizabeth
Hindley Thomas, coal dealer.
Hunt William, shopkeeper
Jackson Wm. bricklayer
Lamb George, corn miller
Latham George, boat owner
Ledger Mrs. Sarah
Levick James, wheelwright
Maples Mrs. Mary
Nicholson Wm. shopkeeper.
Otter Henry, gent.
Palmer John, boat owner
Parkinson Thos. parish clerk
Pashley Wm. tailor
Pearson John, blacksmith
Scott Saml. shopkeeper
Shepherd Rev. Thomas Henry,
  M.A. rector
Standfield Mr. John
Stevenson John, boat owner
Stovin George, gent.
Swinden James, wheelwright
Taylor Rt. coal merct. Common
Taylor Wm. boat owner

Teal John, bdg. & day school
Theaker Wm. shoe maker
Tissington John, tailor
          FARMERS.
    *Marked * are Yeomen.*
Borley John   Standfield Seth
Fox John   Waterhouse Dd.
Gamson W. H.   Highfield
  Woodhouse   *Waterhouse So-
Ledger Thos.   lomon
  Field   White George,
*Moss John   Grange
*Nicholson Ed.   Wilkinson Wm.
Pearson Thos.
    WISETON TOWNSHIP.
Bletcher John, farmer
Chowler Wm. gamekeeper
Colton Jas. shpkr. New Wiseton
Duncan George, gardener
Greasby Wm. shoe maker, New
  Wiseton
Hall John, land agent to Lord
  Althorp
Kirkby Edward, joiner
Parkinson Thos. vict. wharfinger,
  and coal dlr. Swan inn, Drake-
  holes
Rollinson John, farmer
White Mary, cowkeeper
          ————
  COACHES, which call at the Swan
inn, Drakeholes:—
  The Royal Mail from Louth to
Sheffield, at 20 min. p. 11 mg.
ret. 2 aft.

The Express from Lincoln to Doncaster, at ¼ p. 9 mg. ret. 5 evening.

The Hope from Sheffield to Gainsbro', at ¼ bef. 7 mg. ret. according to tide.

EVERTON PARISH

Comprises the two townships of *Everton* and *Scaftworth*, the former of which contains about 3500 acres, and the latter 1049A. 3R. 34P. It is skirted on three sides by the river Idle, and extends westward from Misson Car to Bawtry, and southward to the parishes of Clayworth and Mattersea. The eastern part of it has a bed of clay, noted for making excellent bricks and tiles, and the western side, near the river, has a fine tract of rich sandy land. The population of the whole parish, which is included in the *liberty of Southwell and Scrooby*, amounted in 1831, to 792 souls, living in 176 houses. The *common land* in Everton was enclosed in 1760, and in Scaftworth in 1773. The *rectorial tithes* of the new enclosures in Everton township were commuted for an allotment of 225A. 2R. 8P. given to Lord Charles Cavendish, who was then the impropriator. At the same time the *vicarial tithes* of the whole parish were redeemed by two allotments of 90 acres in Everton and 15 acres in Scaftworth, besides ten acres of old glebe. The great tithes are still paid on all the old enclosures in the parish, and also on the new enclosures in Scaftworth. Wm. Walton, Esq. of Stockwith, is now the impropriator.

The CHARITIES belonging to this parish are £1. 6s. 8d. to the poor of Everton, and 13s. 4d. to those of Scaftworth, to be paid yearly out of Stonehills farm, donor unknown; an annuity of 10s. out of an estate belonging to J. Walker, Esq.; and 5s. yearly left by Robert Ducklin, in 1721, out of a house belonging to the vicar, for the poor of Everton; and £100 left in 1800, by Elizabeth Ella, who directed half of the interest to be given to poor married lying-in women, and the remainder to be paid for the education of poor girls of Everton, where a school has been built by subscription.

EVERTON is a good village three miles E.S.E. of Bawtry, on the Gainsbro' road. The *church* is dedicated to the Holy Trinity, in consequence of which the village feast is held on Trinity Sunday. The living is a discharged vicarage, valued in the King's books at £7. 2s. 2d. The Rev. Robert Evans, M.A. is the incumbent, and John Hall, Esq. of Hull, is the patron, having purchased the advowson of the Duke of Devonshire, who has sold all his property in this parish to various proprietors.— The Archbishop of York is lord of the manor, but of the soil no less than 1095A. 3R. 38P. belongs to Magnus's charity, bequeathed for the weal of Newark, and 253A. 3R. 0P. to Clerkson's charity, for schools, &c. at Mansfield and Mansfield Wood-house. The other principal land-owners are Viscount Althorp, Robert Dawson Otter, Esq., and Thomas Jackson, Esq. Car-hill, a small hamlet, and two farms called *Pusty-hill*, are in this township, as is also part of *Drakeholes*. (See Clayworth.)

HARWELL, or *Harewell*, though in Everton township, and within half a mile of the village, is a separate hamlet and *manor*, of which the corporation of Newark, as trustees of Magnus's charity, are lords, and also principal owners of the land, part of which belongs to Viscount Althorp, and to Clerkson's free-schools in Mansfield and Woodhouse. According to Throsby, this manor is within the jurisdiction of the royal Duchy of Lancaster.

SCAFTWORTH is but a small village, one mile E. of Bawtry, near the river Idle. The *manor*, which comprises the whole township, has for its lord, Viscount Althorp, who is also owner of all the land except about 40 acres. His Lordship, however, pays for the manor a quit rent to the See of York, and holds with it free warren in the paramount manor of the archbishop's soke of Southwell and Scrooby. During the enclosure of the common, several specimens of *Roman antiquities* were found here, particularly part of a spear, and some fragments of urns. This discovery seems to have confirmed the opinion that the vestiges of some fortifications near the village are the remains of a Roman fort or station, through which passed the Roman road from the stations at Doncaster and Littleborough.

EVERTON PARISH DIRECTORY.

Barker Mrs. Frances
Blythman Miss Mary
Boswell William, tailor
Brown Edward, cart owner
Buchanan Mrs.
Burkinsheare Wm. tailor
Dickinson John, gardener
Ellis Mrs.
Emson John, blksmth. & beer hs
Evans Miss Mary
Evans Rev. Rt. M.A. vicar
Favell Michael, gardener
Gordon Captain Augustus
Gordon Captain Cyrus
Graham Jph. shopkpr. & vict
Guest Richard, tailor
Kent Jas. tailor & parish clerk
Kitching Valentine. tailor
Loughton Wm. butcher
Lowther Mrs.
Naylor George, nail maker
Neitleship Mr. Benj. Drakeholes

Nettleship Wm. brick maker & coal merct. Drakeholes
Nicholson Geo. joiner & whgt.
Oldfield John, wheelwright
Otter Miss Catherine
Otter Rt. Dawson, Esq. brick & tile maker
Parkin Wm. bricklayer, maltster, and overseer
Pasmore Thomas, gent
Raynes Fras. land surveyor and valuer
Raynes Henry, surgeon
Raynes George, gent
Rhodes Edw. Hy. grocer & dpr
Rhodes Wm. butcher
Ridley Jph. land bailiff
Ridley Wm. vict. & maltster, Sun
Stephenson Geo. bricklayer
Stephenson Geo. shopkeeper
Taylor James, corn miller
Valentine James, tailor

Walker John, blacksmith
Walton Geo. schoolmaster
Webster Godfrey, shopkeeper
Whitesmith Miss
Wilburn Hannah, shopkeeper
Williamson Fras. nail maker
Williamson Mrs. Mary

BOOT & SHOE MKRS.
Burton John   Nicholson Thos
Graham Wm   Spencer Geo
Hague Thos   Spencer Rt
Hirst Wm

FARMERS.
Marked • *are Yeomen, and* † *re-
side at Harwell.*
Bingley Peter, •Mallender Rd.
  Stone hill   Carr hill
•†BrewertonG. Parkin Francis,
Ellis Philip   Carr

†Ellis Thos   †Roberts Thos
Fletcher Thos   Stephenson Jph
•Griffin John   Stephenson Thos
Harrison Saml   •†Taylor Wm
†Hirst Rt   Whaley Wm
Hobson Ezra   Whitaker David
•†Justice Thos   Williamson Thos
•Knowles John

SCAFTWORTH.
Graves Thomas, farmer
Hutchinson James, farmer
Sampson Thomas, farmer
Smith Joshua, vict. King William
Thorn Lieut.-Col. assistant quar-
  ter-master general for the
  northern district

Coaches and Carriers.— See Bawtry and Gainsbro'.

GRINGLEY-ON-THE-HILL

Is a delightful village, forming four streets of detached houses
on the highest part of the road from Bawtry to Gainsborough,
six miles E.S.E. of the former, and the same distance W. by
N. of the latter town. From its situation, on the loftiest of the
loftiest of the bold promontaries which overlook the wide extent
of *Misson* and *Misterton Cars* (see page 43,) it commands
such extensive prospects, that it is said, the Minsters of York,
Lincoln, and Beverley, may be seen from it on a clear day,
across the vales of the Trent and the Idle; whilst the Chesterfield Canal appears in the nearer distance, emerging from the
tunnel at Darkholes, and winding under the long ridge of hills
which extends eastward to the Trent. Near the village are
several swelling mounds, which, were it not for their size,
might be supposed artificficial from their very bases : on them,
however, have been thrown up three others in ancient times; a
a small one to the west of the church, and two large ones on
its eastern side, one of which is called *Beacon Hill*. These
are evidently the remains of Saxon or Danish works, and the
land which is still called " The Parks," is traditionally said to
have belonged to a Saxon Lord. As the sites of several Roman
stations in the adjacent counties may be distinctly seen from
this place, it has no doubt been used as an exploratory camp.
A great annual FAIR is held here on December 13th, for
sheep, cattle, boots, shoes, cloth, blankets, &c.; a *hiring for
servants* on November 1st, and a *feast* on the nearest Sunday
to St. Peter's day.

The *Church* is a neat Gothic structure, with a nave, side aisles and tower, and is dedicated to St. Peter and St. Paul. Near it stands an ancient *cross*, which was repaired about ten years ago, when it narrowly escaped the desecrating intentions of some of the parishioners, who wanted to use its materials for the reparation of the roads. Tradition says, it was built in commemoration of one of the Edwards having passed this way into Lincolnshire. The benefice is a discharged *vicarage* valued in the King's books at £7. 18s. 4d. The Duke of Rutland is the patron, and the Rev. John Holt is the incumbent, but the officiating minister is the Rev. T. Owston.

The Rectory formed part of the possessions of the priory of Worksop, but after the dissolution, Edward VI. granted it to Sir James Foljambe, Knight, and his heirs for the yearly rent of £22. 13s. 4d.

The *Parish* contains 168 houses, 737 inhabitants, and 4139A. 1R. 10P. of land, nearly 2,000 acres of which are comprised in the *Car*, the drainage of which has cost much labour and expense. (See Misterton.) At the inclosure in 1800, when the annual rental of the parish was estimated at £3,192 15s. 10d., about 500 acres were alloted to the Duke of Rutland in lieu of the impropriated tithes, and 179A. 1R. 19P. to the vicar, as a commutation of the vicarial tithes. The Duke of Rutland has since sold his allotment to several purchasers. Two poor parishioners receive yearly 40s. from the bequest of *William Clark*, who, in 1621, charged his estates at Gainsbro', Walkrith, and Morton, with this and some other annuities. An unknown benefactor left to eight poor widows of this parish £1 yearly out of an orchard which now belongs to George Cross.

The *Manor of Gringley*, or as it was anciently called *Greene-lege*, was in the soke of Mansfield, and of the fee of Roger de Busli. It was long held by the Lovetots and the Furnivals, but in the 3rd of Edward III. Simon de Beresford claimed in it "emendation of bread, ale, free warren, park, wreck, and weyf." William de la Pole granted it to Edward III. It was afterwards granted to John of Gaunt, Duke of Lancaster, as part of the honour of Tickhill, in which it continued till it was sold out by King James. It has long been held by the family of the Duke of Portland, who, as well as being lord of the manor, is owner of a great part of the soil, a large portion of which is copyhold. For the Manor of *Gringley-on-the-Hill*, *with its members*, viz., Misterton, Walkeringham, and West Stockwith, his Grace holds, at the White Hart Inn, a *Court Baron* every third Monday for the recovery of debts under 40s., and for proving the wills of the copyholders. He also holds a *Manorial Court* twice a-year, on the day following the Retford May-day and Michaelmas Sessions, for the swearing-in of juries, &c., and for the transfer of copyhold land, which is here-subject to a yearly chief rent of about 6d. per acre, and to a fine amounting generally to about four per cent. on the estimated value, on every change of tenant, whether by death or purchase. Mr. F. H. Cartwright, of Bawtry, is the manor *Steward,* and Mr. Reuben Worley is the *Bailiff.* The district around Gringley is a fine sporting country, and a little to the east of the village is an extensive *fox cover* belonging to the Duke of Portland.

Ancliff Wm. Gringley lock
Ancliff Wm. jun. bricklayer, Lock
Banks Geo. bricklayer
Barrowcliff Chas. jun. brickmkr.
and timber merchant
Barrowcliff Miss Hannah
Barrowcliff Rd. coal merchant & victualler, Canal bridge
Bedford Wm. saddler
Bee Robert, butcher
Bentley Cath. boardg. academy
Burkinsheare Rt. tailor & draper
Crump Wm. shopr. & nail mkr
Cross Jas. corn merchant
Cross Wm. maltster & corn mert
Eggleston John, sen. parish clerk
Eggleston John, joiner
Fretwell Robert, gentleman
Gamson Mrs. Sarah, East house
Gregg Thos. tailor & shopkeeper
Hunt Wm. schoolmaster
Hutchinson John, plumber, &c.
Kirkby John, joiner
Marshall Stph. tailor & draper
Meanwell Hewson, shopkeeper
Moss Robert, gentleman
Newton Elizabeth, shopkeeper
Oliver John, boat owner
Owston Rev. T. curate, Grange
Parkinson John, tallow chandler, grocer and draper
Parsons Elizabeth, schoolrs.
Pilfoot Charles, butcher
Raven Mrs. Dorothy
Smith John, boat owner
Stringer Peter, vict. Cross Keys

Tindall Mrs. Dorothy
Walker James, surgeon
Walker John, wheelwright
Walker John, Gringley lock
Weightman Thos. vict. & baker, Blue Bell
Wilkinson Jabez, corn miller
Worley Rueben, vict. and blacksmith, White Hart
Yates Charles, excise officer

BOOT & SHOE MAKERS.
Brewitt James   Medcalf George
Eversden Wm.   Tindall Joseph
Johnson Wm.   Walker Wm.

FARMERS.
*Marked thus * are Yeomen.*
Barrowcliff C.   Lilliman John
Barrowcliff T.   *Marples Jonas
*Carnell John   Marples Wm.
Davison Thos.   *Newton Geo.
Park Border   *Newton Wm.
*Down Chad.   Nettleship Chas
Simpson   *Scott William
Gamson Edw.   Smith Thomas
Gamson Robert,   Spencer John
Grange   Sykes William
Johnson James   White John
Lilliman Chas.   *Williamson W

COACHES from Doncaster and Sheffield to Gainsborough, call at the White Hart daily.
CARRIER, Michael Kirkby, to Bawtry on Thur. to Gainsbro on Tues. and to Retford, on Sat. dep. 7 mg. ret. evg.

HABLESTHORPE PARISH

Includes the two hamlets of *Hablesthorpe and Coats,* and contains only 22 houses, 95 inhabitants, and 783A. 2R. 10P. of land, extending from North Leverton to the Trent.

HABLESTHORPE, *Apesthorpe* or *Abusthorpe* (see page 50), 5¼ miles E. of Retford, is so closely connected with North Leverton, that a stranger would suppose it to be part of that village and parish, especially as it has *no church* of its own, though it has a desecrated burial ground (which has not been used during the last 70 years) a non-resident *vicar* and a *prebendary* in York Cathedral. The vicarage was certified at £9. 11s. 8d. per annum. The Rev. Edward Youle is the incumbent, the Prebendary of Hablesthorpe is the patron and appropriator. At the enclosure in 1795, an allotment of 293A. 0R. 23P. was awarded to the appropriator in lieu of the great tithes, and 31A. 3R. 31P. (including the old glebe) to the vicar, in lieu of the small tithes. A *Methodist Chapel* was erected in the village in 1806. Though Hablesthorpe is not mentioned in Domesday Book, it is supposed to be of much greater antiquity than the Norman Conquest. In the 9th of Edward II. "*Hablesthorp and Cotes*" answered for one whole villa, and Lodovic de Bellomote and Adam de Everingham were lords of the manor, which now belongs to several proprietors, and B. Walker and R. Woollen, Esqrs. of Wakefield, are lesses of the prebendal land. *Elizabeth Palmer*, in 1726, charged her estate at Coates with the payment of two *annuities*, viz., £20 to the poor widows and orphans of Coates, and £30 to the minister of North Leverton and Hablesthorpe, which the testatrix seems to have considered as one parish, there being no church in the latter, even in her time. The £30 is paid yearly to the vicar of North Leverton, where the parishioners of Hablesthorpe are provided with church room. In 1740, *Penelope Bryan* left £200, and directed 40s. of the yearly interest to be given to the poor of Hablesthorpe, and the residue to be divided amongst the poor relations of her brother Michael Bland, on the feast of St. Michael. The money is now vested on mortgage of a house in East Retford, belonging to Jarvis Watson. She also left a yearly rent, charge of 40s. out of a cottage and 8A. 2R. of land in Coates, (now belonging to Joseph Woodhouse) to be distributed in weekly doles of bread every Sunday at North Leverton Church, amongst the poor of Hablesthorpe. The vicars of North and South Leverton and Sturton are the trustees.

COATES, a small hamlet two miles east of Hablesthope, is all in this parish, except one cottage, which is claimed by North Leverton, and in which that parish places a poor widow, who partakes of Palmer's charity.

Drake Thomas, shoemaker
Olivant Thos. jun. vict. Sheep Shears Inn

Stevenson Geo. schoolmaster and shopkeeper

FARMERS.

Marked thus • *live at Coats.*

Baun John   Gray Robert
•Diggles Geo.   •Jackson Thos.

Needham Jtn. Smith John
Olivant Isaac   •Smith Eliz.
Olivant Thos. White Samuel
Olivant Wm.

HAYTON PARISH,

On the east side of the Idle, in the *Liberty of Southwell and Scrooby*, is intersected by the Chesterfield Canal, and comprises the hamlets of *Hayton and Tilne*, which contain 52 houses, 256 inhabitants, and 2,600 acres of land, of which 600 acres are in Tilne, which is the only part of the parish mentioned in Domesday Book, but the whole belongs to the Archbishop of York's fee of Sutton, commonly called the North Soke of Southwell and Scrooby. The archbishop is lord of the manor, but T. Walker, Esq. is his lessee, and also one of the principal land-owners, amongst whom are the Hon. Bridgeman Simpson, Robert Aston Barber, Esq. and Mr. Benjamin Fearnley.

HAYTON is a straggling village betwixt the Canal and the Gainsbro' road, 3 miles N.N.E. of Retford. The *Church* dedicated to St. Peter is an ancient fabric with a lofty tower, and near it was formerly the mansion of the *De Hayton's.* The living is a discharged vicarage, valued in the King's books at £4. 15s. 5d. The Archbishop of York is the patron, and the Rev. Wm. Tiffin the vicar. At the enclosure of the commons in 1760, land was allotted in lieu of the great tithes to the impropriator Lord George Cavendish, who sold his estate here to R. A. Barber, Esq. and others. In the village is a small *Wesleyan Chapel*, built about 1825.

Charities :—The Poor's land called Little Close, was purchased by the overseers in 1682, for £19. 4s. 4d. and is now let for £2. 12s. 6d. per annum, which, with an annuity of £2. left by an unknown donor out of a farm belonging to R. A. Barber, Esq. is distributed at Easter.

TILNE or *Tylne* on the east bank of the Idle, 1½ miles N. of Retford, is but a small hamlet, consisting of four farms and a few cottages. Here, says Mr. Gough, " was found a *Druid amulet* of an opacous transparent colour with yellow streaks, and many *Roman seals* on Cornelians.

Atkinson Miss Sarah
Bradley George, shoemaker
Bucklow Mrs. Eliz.
Chambers George
Eversden Wm. shoemaker
Hellifield Mr. John
Holbery Mrs. Mary
Moore Thos. wheelwright, blacksmith, & machine maker

Peck Mrs. Ann
Pettinger Geo. shpr. & boat own.
Pettinger John, joiner
Smith Geo. vict. and bricklayer
Smith Luke, vict. Anchor
Spittlehouse Thos. shoemaker
Swinburn John, ass. overseer
Waite Robert, brickmaker

2 H

FARMERS.
*Marked * are Yeomen.*
*Ash Daniel   *Cliff Samuel
Barlow Thos.   Creighton Dvd.
Barrett Wm.   Hayton Castle
*Beeley Ann   Holbery Edw.
*Bingham John Ledger Sarah
*Bingley Jph.   *Palfreman Benjamin
*Cartwright G.

*Smith George   Steedman Thos.
Smith John   *Taylor Edw.
*Smith Thos.

TILNE.
Peck John, farmer
Ramsker James, farmer
Spencer W. farmer, *Broomhouse*
Walker Mary, farmer

NORTH LEVERTON PARISH

Has 74 houses, 303 inhabitants, and 1513A. 1R. 12P. of land, extending from Welham to Hablesthorpe, with which latter parish it is so connected that one church serves for both, and the common land of each was enclosed under one act of Parliament passed in 1795, when an allotment of 149A. 3R. 18P. was awarded to the *prebendary of North Leverton*, in Southwell Collegiate Church, as a commutation of the appropriated tithes, and 79A. 2R. 13P. to the *vicar* in lieu of the small tithes. Wm. Mason, Esq. the lord of the manor, is lessee of the Prebendal land, and owner of a great part of the parish, which in Domesday Book is called *Legreton*, and certified as a " Berue" of the Archbishop of York's " great Soc. of Laneham."

NORTH LEVERTON is a good village 5 miles E. by N. of Retford, but the houses at the east end of it are in Hablesthorpe parish, (see p. 344). The *church* has a nave, side aisles, tower, and three bells. It is a discharged vicarage valued in the King's books at £5. and is in the patronage and appropriation of its own prebendary as stated above. The Rev. John Williams now enjoys the living, which has been augmented with Queen Anne's bounty, with which 14 acres of land was purchased at Skegby. The parish participates in two of the charities noticed with Hablesthorpe at page 344, and the poor receive £2. 10s. yearly from Wm. Mason, Esq. as the interest of £50. left in 1745 by *Abraham Colton*, and they have also divided amongst them yearly £2. arising from the rent of the *Poor's Close*, consisting of 1A. 3P. allotted to them at the enclosure in 1795.

Ashton Wm. shoemaker
Astick James, bricklayer
Blagg Fras. surgeon, M.R.C.S.
Bows Thomas, wheelwright
Brown Wm. wheelwright
Burton Thos. blacksmith
Coup Fras. cooper & grocer
Godfrey Joseph, joiner
Goodyer Joseph, joiner
Harrison Ann, vict. Oak Tree

Hind William, blacksmith
Hird William, gent.
Lumby Thomas, shopkeeper
Major Benjamin, saddler
Roberts Mrs. Hannah
Rogers William, gent.
Staniland George, tailor
Thorsby Chas. corn miller
Turner Samuel, butcher

FARMERS.

Baker Edw.
Cooper John
Cuthbert H.
Ellis Wm. sen.
Ellis Wm. jun.
Godfrey Geo.
Jackson Wm.
Keeton John
Moore Thomas
Motley George
Rogers Thos.
Skelton Reg.
Smith Edward
Smith John
Woodhouse Jph.

SOUTH LEVERTON PARISH

Contains 88 houses, 400 inhabitants, and about 2000 acres of land, of which, by an agreement of the parishioners some years ago, one quarter was formed into the distinct township of Cottam, which maintains its poor separately from the rest of the parish, which lies south of North Leverton, and extends eastward to the Trent.

SOUTH LEVERTON village is pleasantly situated 5 miles E. of Retford, commanding a most extensive prospect, in which Lincoln Minster may be seen at a distance of 20 miles. The church dedicated to all saints, is, by the gift of William Rufus, in the appropriation and patronage of the Dean of Lincoln. The living is a vicarage valued in the King's books at £6. 13s. 4d. and the Rev. John Cleaver, L. L. D. of Edwinstow, is the incumbent, for whom the Rev. John Mickle officiates. At the inclosure in 1795, 381 acres were allotted to the appropriator, and 56A. 3R. 15P. to the vicar, in lieu of the great and small tithes, in addition to 10A. 1R. 17P. of ancient glebe. Lord Middleton, and George Foljambe, Esq. the *lord of the manor*, are the principal owners of the soil, and G. H. Vernon, Esq. s lessee of the great tithe land. J. Parker and Richard Hodgkinson, of Retford, Richard Keyworth, of Laxton, and H. Parnell, of Gainsbro', have also estates in the manor, which was of the King's great soke of Mansfield, and was granted in the 2nd of Henry III. to Henry de Hastings. The parish *feast* is held on the last Sunday in September.

Free School:—In 1691, John Sampson granted to eight trustees, the school buildings, and a yearly rent charge of £20, out of an estate now possessed by Joseph Motley, for the maintenance of a master to teach poor children of South Leverton. The vicars of this parish and those of North Wheatley and Sturton, are appointed visitors to inspect the school and the trustees' accounts.

COTTAM is a hamlet, township, and chapelry, at the east end of the parish, on an eminence overlooking the vale of the Trent, 7 miles E. by S. of Retford, and 2¼ from South Leverton. It contains 17 houses and 77 inhabitants, and has a small chapel dedicated to the Holy Trinity, in which service is performed only once a month.

SOUTH LEVERTON,

Barton Theopls. blacksmith and shopkeeper
Fisher John, shoemaker
Hastings John, tailor
Hindley Thomas, shoemaker
Markham Wm. tailor & shopkr.
Mickle Rev. John, curate
Milns Geo. vict. Plough
Risdall Wm. wheelwright
Roberts John, schoolmaster
Smith Thomas, shoemaker
Tagg Wm. corn miller
Undy Rd. parish clerk.

FARMERS.

Bacon Thos.   Oxley John
Bacon Wm.   Richards Wm.
Bailey Wm.   Spittlehouse A.
Fletcher John   Taylor George
Flint Samuel   Walker Jtn.
Moody John   Walker Thos.
Motley Jph.   White Samuel

COTTAM.   (FARMERS.)

*Marked thus * are Yeomen.*

*Brandon John   Hall John
Fairbanks Sam.   *Thomas Geo.
Futtil C. shoem. Webster Thos.
*Futtil John

LITTLEBOROUGH PARISH.

LITTLEBOROUGH is but a small village and parish on the west bank of the Trent, 5 miles S. of Gainsborough, and 8¾ miles E. by N. of Retford, containing only 15 houses, 85 inhabitants, and about 900 acres of land, belonging chiefly to G. S. Foljambe, Esq. the lord of the manor and patron of the benefice, which is a perpetual curacy, certified at £4. 3s. 4d. and now in the incumbency of the Rev. Francis Hewgill. The *church*, which is a Norman structure, underwent such a thorough repair in 1831-2, that it has now a modern appearance. Mr. Foljambe was at the expense of renovating the chancel, and the other repairs were at the cost of the parishioners, except the new vestry and Sunday school room, which were built by the incumbent. In the old walls are many Roman bricks, and the stones are laid in that angular manner which is distinguished by antiquaries as the herring bone style of masonry. The *manor* was of the King's soke of Mansfield, and the church was given by King John to the monks of Welbeck abbey. The parish has generally a rich soil, and was enclosed in 1825, when the Act was obtained for making a new turnpike from Retford to *Littleborough Ferry*, which crosses the river Trent close to the village, near the site of a *Roman Ford*, which consisted of a stone pavement protected by piles of oak, but the latter were removed some years ago by the Trent Navigation Company, so that the stones are nearly all displaced.

Littleborough, though now only a small place, has employed the pens of most of our antiquaries, and is generally believed to have been that important *Roman station* which in the Itinerary of Antoninus is called AGELOCUM or SEGELOCUM, and is placed on the military way betwixt Lincoln and Doncaster. Great numbers of *Roman coins* were found here in Camden's time, and were then called swine pennies, from their being so near the surface as to be rooted up by those animals. Stukely, in his description of Littleborough, at the early part of the last century, says, it is a small village just upon the edge of the river, and in an angle (" *Agel-Auk*,"—hence its Roman name), and that it appeared to have been encompassed by a single ditch of a square form, with water running quite round it, so that it was a station of considerable strength. He also observes that the Trent had washed away part of the eastern side of the town, and that foundations and pavements were then visible in the bank of the river. In 1684, when some of the old enclosures on the west side of the village were ploughed up, many coins of Nerva, Trajan, Hadrian, Constantine, &c. were found, together with *Intaglios* of Agate and Cornelian, the finest coloured urns and pateræ, some wrought in basso relievo with the workman's name impressed on the inside of the bottom; also a *Discus* or Quoit, with an emperor's head embossed on it. Again in 1718, two very handsomely moulded *altars* were dug up, and fixed as piers in a wall on the side of the steps that lead from the ferry to the Inn. Stukely adds, that near Whites-bridge he had seen extensive foundations of ancient buildings, and that in dry seasons and when the tide was low, coins were then often found at low water mark. Dr. Gale saw an urn here, which, besides ashes and bones, contained a coin of Domitian. It would be an useless task to examine all the various antiquarian conjectures with which this place has been honoured, we shall therefore conclude by observing, that, though the tourist will not find here anything to gratify his curiosity, he may still tread with reverential awe, that ground which is hallowed by the remembrance of past ages, and contemplate the striking changes of political power, and of the exertions of man, and the instability of a fancied immortality—the names and actions of its once proud possessors having mouldered into oblivion like their decayed sepulchral dust.

Barlow Wm. farmer
Harrison John, yeoman
Lister Samuel, farmer
Parker David, coal merchant

Smith John, farmer
Warburton Geo. yeoman
Wilkinson Wm. Ferry Boat Inn

MISTERTON PARISH

Is situated in the north-east angle of the county, where the river Idle and the Chesterfield canal terminate in the Trent. It contains 1579 inhabitants, and upwards of 4709 acres of land, of which about 600 acres form the township and chapelry of *West Stockwith*, which maintains its poor separately from that of Misterton. A great part of it was formerly a swampy bog, but it is now drained and improved. In the higher parts of the parish are found both *foliated* and *fibrous gypsum* or plaster, used both for floors and ornamental work.

MISTERTON is a large village on the north side of the Chesterfield canal, where there are several wharfs, within one mile of the Trent, 5 miles N. N. W. of Gainsborough, and 9 miles E. of Bawtry. Its township, in which are the farms of *Cornley, Fountain-Hill, Grove,* and *Haxey Gate,* (a public-house), contains 205 houses, 944 inhabitants, and 4109A. 3R. of land, estimated in 1826, at the annual rent of £4630. 7s. 6d. on which the assessment for the poor rates in 1831 amounted to £483. 6s. 9d. including £3. 6s. 10½d. paid to the county rate. The *church* is a large ancient structure dedicated to All Saints, and has evidently been re-constructed from the ruins of a former edifice. In March, 1824, a tremendous hurricane blew from the roof about two tons of lead, which in its fall broke down the south-east corner of the building. This damage was repaired at the cost of about £300. raised by a parochial rate, except £50. given by the Dean and Chapter of York, who are the appropriators and patrons of the benefice, which is a discharged *vicarage* valued in the King's books at £10. 5s. and is now enjoyed by the Rev. Wm. Mould, of Retford, for whom the Rev. Philip Grisdale, of Haxey, officiates. At the enclosure, the appropriators had allotted to them in lieu of the rectorial tithes, 797A. 2R. 23P. in Misterton, and 102A. 1R. 8P. in West Stockwith. At the same time 34A. 23P. were allotted to the vicar as a commutation of the small tithes, so that the living is now worth upwards of £100. a year, as the incumbent has exclusive of this allotment, a house and 17A. 2R. 23P. of old glebe, £12. a year from the appropriators, and the rents of the following lands purchased with Queen Anne's bounty and several benefactions, viz. 12A. 36P. in Haxey, 4A. 2R. in Clareborough, and 14A. 15P. in Misson. The earliest baptismal register in the church is dated 1540. Wm. de Lovetot gave the church to Worksop monastery.

The parish forms one of the members of the *manor* of Gringley-on-the Hill, of which the Duke of Portland is lord paramount. In Domesday Book, it is called " *Munstreton,* of the King's *Soc* of *Maunsfield,*" and in the 9th of Edward II. it " answered for an entire villa, and the King, the prior of Newstead, and Thomas de Hayton were returned lords of it," but its present lords are the Dukes of Portland and Newcastle, except the right of fishing and fowling in the Idle, which is enjoyed by Lady Galway. The soil belongs to various proprietors, the principal of whom are the Dean and Chapter of York, R. and J. Corringham, J. Wilson, W. Carter, W. and C. A. Walton, and the executors of the late Adam Bird. Near the village is an extensive bone mill and a ropery.

Misterton, though its church is large and commodious, has

both a *Methodist* and a *Baptist Chapel,* the latter of which was built in 1761, for the use of the General or Calvinistic Baptists, by Samuel Richardson, who endowed it with a house and 8A. 0R. 36P. of land. The congregation have a burial ground in another part of the village, and the Rev. S. Skidmore is their present minister. The Wesleyan Chapel was built at the cost of £700, on the site of an old meeting-house in 1826, and has a handsome light Gothic front. The village *School* was built in 1805, and the master receives for teaching 12 poor children an annuity of £12. arising from property belonging to the township, which has also the benefit of the following *charities,* viz. 3A. 1R. 32P. let for £10 a year, and bequeathed in 1706, by *Gregory Standering,* to provide clothing for the poor,—20s. yearly from *Wm. Clark's* benefactions (see West Burton), for one poor aged person; and 12s. yearly out of an estate at Laceby, in Lincolnshire, now belonging to Thomas Johnson, left in 1729 by *Thomas Edlington* to be distributed in 12 penny loaves on the first Sunday in every month, amongst 12 poor people. The two last mentioned donors also made similar bequests to the poor of West Stockwith.

WEST STOCKWITH village, the south end of which is in Misterton township, forms a long line of buildings on the west bank of the Trent, at the point where the Idle and the Chesterfield canal (vide p. 53.) fall into that river, 4 miles N. N. W. of Gainsborough. It has risen from the rank of a small hamlet to that of a flourishing river port or creek (under Hull), since the Idle was made navigable to Bawtry, and since the formation of the Chesterfield canal, which has at the South end of the village a commodious *Basin* that covers 1A. 2R. 7P. of land, and is entered from the Trent by a lock 18½ feet. wide. It has a "Principal Coast Officer," and during 1831 its *number of vessels* with cargoes was 112 inward and 70 outward. :

The *township* contains 165 houses, 635 inhabitants, and about 600 acres of land, bounded on the south by the Idle, and on the north by the *Heck Dike,* a small beck which divides it from Lincolnshire, and gives name to three of its farms. The Duke of Portland is lord of the manor, but the land belongs to various owners, and is tithe free. The Chapel of Ease was built in 1722, pursuant to the will of *Wm. Huntington,* who in 1715 bequeathed £740. for the erection of a CHAPEL and ten ALMSHOUSES in his ship yard. The chapel he endowed with a house and 6 acres of land now occupied by the incumbent, and a farm at Gunhouse consisting of 76A. 2R. 27P. and now let for £180. per annum. The benefice is a donative in the gift of the trustees, and is now enjoyed by the Rev. William Adamthwaite. The almshouses, for the reception of the poor widows of mariners and ship carpenters, were endowed by the benevolent founder with the rents of land and buildings in West Stockwith and Misterton (now let for £110. per annum), subject to the following charitable payments, viz. an *annuity* of £10. for a schoolmaster to teach the poor children of seamen and shipwrights to read; and 3s. 6d. *weekly* to be distributed every Sunday at the chapel, in penny and twopenny loaves, amongst the poor of the township, who also partake of *Clarke's and Edlington's Charities*, as is already noticed with Misterton. In 1788, £34. was received as the arrears of Edlington's charity, and it is now vested with Mrs. Pearson, who pays for it 34s. yearly, which, with the rent of part of Crabtree Close held by Huntington's trustees, and purchased with £100, left in 1777 by *Wm. Hall*, is included in the weekly distribution of bread at the chapel. The almshouses, which consist of five rooms on the first, and five on the second floor, are now only occupied by six pensioners, who have each £12. per annum. A small *Methodist Chapel* was built here in 1803. A Fair for horses and cattle is held in the village annually on September 4th.; but in the 9th of Henry III. it is noticed as having both a market and a fair.

DRAINAGE OF THE CARS.

The CARS belonging to the townships of *Misterton, Everton, Scaftworth, Gringley-on-the-Hill, and Walkeringham,* form an extensive tract of low marshy land, which some years ago was a swampy unproductive bog, but is now drained and cultivated under acts of parliament passed in 1796, 1801, and 1813, at an immense expense to the proprietors, who have, however, been amply remunerated by the improved value of the soil. After having undergone a 30 years' drainage, the surface became so consolidated and so wasted by repeated burnings and parings, that it sunk 18 inches lower than its original level, and in 1828 it was found necessary to erect a forty horse power *steam engine* at Misterton *soss* or *lock,* for the purpose of pumping the water out of the main drain into the river Idle, when the tide is too high in the Trent to admit of a fall from the *drain,* which terminates in that river betwixt and near the confluence of the Idle and the Canal, which latter is, like the drain, protected by flood gates from the influx of the tide, which flows up the Idle about three quarters of a mile, as far as the lock called the *Soss.* The cost of the steam engine and the new works constructed in 1829, was upwards of £5,000. The annual expenditure incurred by keeping these drainage works in constant operation is very considerable, as will be seen in the following table, which shows the quantity of land in each township, the *improved annual value,* and the amount of the *assessment* paid to the Drainage Commissioners, both for the *Old* and the *New Works.*

DRAINAGE LAND	UNDER THE OLD WORKS.			UNDER THE NEW WORKS.		
IN	ACRES.	IMP. VAL.	CESS.	ACRES.	IMP. VAL.	CESS.
Everton	1637	£503	£168	1037	£279	£70
Scaftworth*	294	£94	£32	—	—	—
Gringley	1760	£640	£213	1616	£862	£215
Misterton........	1848	£610	£203	1377	£764	£191
Walkeringham ··	132	£37	£12	40	£22	£5
Total····	5662	£1,886	£628	4080	£1,927	£481

This tract of low land, which has been changed from a morass to a fruitful plain, extends from Misson to Misterton, and is nearly 5 miles in length and 2 in breadth, bounded on the north by the Idle, and having on its south side a long range of bold promontaries, which appear to have been at some distant period the bounds of an ocean (see p. 43). It formed the southern part of the " *Level of Hatfield Chase*," which extended from the vicinity of Hatfield and Thorne, in Yorkshire, and comprised upwards of 65,000 acres of low and monotonous land, most of which is now enclosed and preserved from inundations by the high banks and flood gates that enclose the rivers. *Sir Cornelius Vermuiden* and his Dutch and Flemish settlers drained the northern portion of this extensive chase, about the year 1650, by raising strong embankments on the Ouse, Trent, and other rivers, and by cutting the canal called the *Dutch River*, into which they diverted the river Don, that used to flow more to the eastward by Crowle to Trent falls, instead of falling into the Ouse at Goole, as it does at present. They also diverted the course of the Idle, by cutting *Bycar Dyke*, through which the water of that river now runs along the margin of the Cars, eastward from Misson to the Trent at West Stockwith, as has been seen at page 53.

MISTERTON.

Berry Geo. shopkeeper
Berry John, gardener
Bingham Coulson, schoolmaster
Borley Wm. shoemaker
Clifton John, grocer & draper
Colton Wm. blacksmith
Cooper Thos. shoemaker
Corringham John, sen. gent.
Corringham Robert, Esq.
Crackles Mr. John
Draper Wm. wheelwright
Gladson Thos. grocer & draper

Hakes Jas. O. plumber & glazier
Hallifield Wm. cattle dealer
Hill Mr. Thomas
Hindley Thomas, tailor
Horey Wm. saddler
Holmes Jas. vict. Haxeygate
Hurst Wm. tailor
Jackson John, maltster and coal merchant
Lyon Ann, vict. Wind Mill
Moate Mr. John
Moate Samuel, joiner

* Scaftworth and some other portions of the Cars being higher than the rest, are sufficiently drained by the Old Works, and are consequently not assessed for the New Works.

Moate Richard, vict. Packet Inn, Canal side
Moate Wm. maltster & coal mer.
Otter Wm. vict. Blue Bell
Roberts Mrs. Elizabeth
Rookes Charles, baker
Rookes Wm. corn miller
Rose Mr. Samuel
Rusling John, bricklayer, brickmaker, and parish clerk
Saul Mrs. Ann
Smith Wm. wheelwright & blacksmith
Sutton John, shoemaker & shopr.
Taylor Thos. butcher

BOAT OWNERS.

Bingham John
Clifton John
Dewick John
Hunt John
Lee George
Redfern Wm.
Richardson W.
Teal Emanuel
Teal John, sen.
Teal John, jun.
Thompson Jph.

FARMERS.

Thus * *are Yeomen.*

Bingham Benj.
Bingley T. Soss
*Cooper John
*Carringham R.
Draper John
Faram James
Fritchley John,
  North Carr
*Gagg John
Gagg Thos.
*Gamson Jas.
*Grundy Eliz.
Hill William
Makins Roger
Milner George
Moat Robert
*Morley Wm.
Parkinson Wm.
Grove
Pickering Edw.
*Richardson C.
Cornley
Roberts Wm.
Seels Geo. Fountain Hill
*Stothard Jas.
Satton Wm.
*Tompkinson J.
Wheelwright W.
*Wilson John,
Cornley

STOCKWITH (WEST).

Marked † are in Misterton Township.

Adamthwaite Rev. Wm. curate
Aldam Wm. millwright & joiner
Bradbury John, blacksmith
Belshaw Wm. joiner
Bird John, surgeon
Bird Mrs. Pœbe
Briggs John, bricklayer
Broomhead Samuel, farmer
†Brown Geo. foreman, Ropery
Brown Mr. John.

†Cartwright Wm. clerk to the Canal Company
Casey John. bricklayer
Clarke Geo. farmer
Clarke Geo. schoolmaster and accountant
Coates Edward, principal coast officer
†Cooke James, shoemaker
Cooke James, tailor
†Cooke John, tailor
†Cooper Fras. vict. Vine
Cooper Robert, tailor
Crosby John, butcher
Cross W. maltster, h Gringley
Curtis Wm. vict. beerhouse
Dunston Wm. victualler, Newcastle Arms, & Shipping Agent
Easton Jackson, cooper
Elvidge Thos. shipwright
Farr John, chapel clerk
Farr Wm. blacksmith
Fish John, corn miller
Flower Robert, butcher
†Foster Rd. ship & whitesmith
Graham George, grocer
Gray John, fishmonger
Gray Taylor Sthn. fishmonger
Green Jas. yeoman
Hewitt Jph. gent.
Hoodless John, corn miller
Hughes John & Co. bone crushers
Isle Wm. blacksmith
Johnson Mr. John
Johnson Jph. vict. Brancaster Arms
Lord Jph. mattress maker
Newton Jas. bricklayer
Pagdin Wm. maltster, h Worksop
Palmer Geo. farmer
Petrie Hy. mast & block maker
Pinchon Mary, schoolmistress
Pycock Rt. gardner & shop kpr.
Pycroft Wm. yeoman, Heckdyke
Rawling Geo. vict. Ship
†Raynes Jerh. agent to Canal Co.
†Robinson Sampson, hair dsr.
Robinson John, weaver
Rusling Edward, farrier
Russell Wm. excise officer
Sefton Thos. joiner & cabt. mkr.
Skidmore John, shoemaker
†Sleight Wm. hair dresser

Smith Rt. grocer, draper, & drug.
Smith Mrs. Susanna
†Smith Henry, rope maker, and
  Gainsbro'
†Stowe John, cowkeeper
Strawson Edw. beerhouse
Thornhill Fras. shoemaker
Tonge Rd. baker
Wallhead Thos. baker
Walton Chas. Allenby, gent
Walton William, Esq.
Watkin Rd. shoemaker
Wells Michael, gent
Whyers Wm. surgeon
†Wilson & Marriott, bone crush-
  ers, and Hull
Windle Fras. vict. Black Swan
Wright Samuel, hair dresser and
  button mould maker

BOAT OWNERS.
Allison Wm.   Farr William

Brown Robert Fish Thos.
Collingham M. Grime George
Curtis Wm.   Newton Wm.
Ellis John   Nicholson Wm.
Farr George Redfern John
  WATER CONVEYANCE.
Wm. Curtis's packet to Retford.
  every Wed., & Sat. at 5 mg.
  ret. half-past 8 evng. and to
✠ Gainsbro' Tue. & Thur. at 8
  mg. ret. 6 evg.
Goods are conveyed by the Canal
  Company to Retford, Worksop,
  Chesterfield, and Hull daily.
  Mr. J. Raynes, Wharfinger
Steam Packets to Hull & Gains-
  brough daily
  CARRIER & POSTMAN.
James Tonge, to Gainsborough,
  Mon. Tue. Thu. & Sat. at 12
  noon, returns seven evening

SAUNDBY PARISH.

SAUNDBY is but a small village, pleasantly situated on an eminence overlooking the Trent, 3 miles S. W. by W. of Gainsborough, and 7½ miles N.E. of Retford. The parish, which extends
to the Trent, contains 15 houses, 104 inhabitants, and about
1300 acres of rich enclosed land, all of which belongs to Lord
Middleton, the lord of the manor, except a small quantity of
glebe, and 28 acres belonging to the poor of Gainsborough.
At the Domesday survey, the whole was of the Archbishop of
York's soke of Laneham, except one garden, which a villain
held of the soke of Mansfield by the service of finding " salt
for the King's fish in *Bigredic.*" The CHURCH, which has
evidently been a much larger edifice, is dedicated to St. Martin,
and contains some ancient monumental inscriptions, one of
which is to the memory of *William de Saundby*, who died in
1418. The living is a rectory, valued in the King's books at
£14. 8s. 6d., and is in the gift of Lord Middleton, and incumbency of the Rev. Francis Hewgill, M. A. The Rectory house
is a handsome mansion built in 1831.

TRENT PORT, on the west bank of the Trent, opposite to
Gainsborough, is partly in this parish, and partly in that of
Beckingham, and contains a good inn, two large ship yards,
an oil mill, and several wharfs, warehouses, &c.

₊ *Those marked * are at Trent Port in Saundby, and † at Trent
Port in Beckingham Parish.*

Billiald Henry, yeoman
*Capes John, sen. wharfinger and
ship builder
*Capes John jun. rope maker,
*Capes Wm. vict. Trent Port
Inn
*Cross Henry, ship bldr. Trent
Port House
Draper Robert, farmer

†Furley, Brothers, and Cross,
ship builders
Hewgill Rev. Fras, M. A. rector
†Metcalf Mary & George, seed
crushers
Rayner John, farmer
White Joseph, farmer
Wiles Robert, shoemaker
†Wilkin Abraham, shipwright

STURTON PARISH

Comprises the village, of *Sturton-in-the-Clay* and the hamlet of
Fenton, and contains 118 houses, 638 inhabitants, and about 4000
acres of land, of which, at the enclosure in 1823, an allotment of
727A. 1R. 4P. was awarded to the Dean and Chapter of York,
in lieu of the rectorial tithes, and 127A. 3R. 8P. to the vicar in
lieu of the small tithes.

STURTON-IN-THE-CLAY is a good village, consisting of four
streets, in which are nearly 100 houses, on the Littleborough
road, 6 miles E. by N. of Retford. It was anciently called
Streton, from the Roman road which passed through it to Doncaster. The *church* dedicated to St. Peter, is a large ancient
structure with a lofty tower, handsomely pinnacled. It is inferior to none in this part of the country, and contains some
neat monuments of the Thornhaughs of Fenton Hall, one of
which has a handsome white marble effigy of a female as large
as life, but the inscription has long been illegible. The *benefice* is a vicarage valued in the King's books at £5. 7s. 3¼d.
The Dean and Chapter of York are the patrons; the Rev.
Francis Hewgill, M. A., the incumbent, and the Rev. H. V.
Hodge, the curate.   G. S. Foljambe, Esq., is lord of the
manor, and owner of a great part of the soil, as well as lessee,
of the Chapter land. His ancestor obtained the manor in marriage with one of the Hewitts of Shireoaks, who descended
from the *Thornhaughs, of Fenton*. It was of the King's
soke of Mansfield, and was held by the Darcys from the reign
of Edward III., till the attainder of Lord Darcy, whose estates,
&c. were granted by Henry VIII. to George Lascells, Esq.
whose heiress married Sir Fras. Rodes. John Serjeant, Esq.
owns several farms in the parish, which lately belonged to the
Ramsdens. The annual *feast* is on the last Sunday in September.

FENTON hamlet is distant three-quarters of a mile S.E. of

Sturton. It was formerly the seat of the Fenton family, the first of whom was Sir Richard Fenton, and the last, Katherine, wife of Sir Richard Boyle, Earl of Cork, in Ireland. In 1614, t belonged to the Thornhaughs, who resided here till one of them took the name of Hewitt, and removed to Shireoaks.

CHARITIES.—In 1725, *Francis Hopkinson* left £24, and all his lands in Sturton, to the overseers in trust, that they distribute the interest and rents yearly, in clothing to the poor of the parish. At the enclosure, an *allotment* of 5A. 2R. 16P. now let for £7 a-year, was given in exchange for part of this charity estate; the rest of which consists of the *Poor's close*, 3A. 0R. 18P. (also let for £7 a-year,) and four gardens and cottages, occupied rent-free by four poor people. In 1710, *George Green* left Goodsmore close, (3A. 3R. 34P.) now let for £6. 14s. per annum, for a *schoolmaster* to teach eight poor children to read. This close is exonerated from tithe, and John Walkinson is the trustee. In 1800, *William Connell* left the interest of £100 (now vested with Mrs. Stancer) to be divided amongst the poor parishioners on St. Thomas' day.

Those marked * reside at Fenton, and the rest at Sturton.

*Ashton Mrs Ann
Bell Joseph, shopkeeper
Bingham Mr. John
*Bingham Wm. shoemaker
Briggs Wm. shoemaker
Dawson Edward, schoolmaster
Downs Joseph, shopkeeper
Drayton Ann, shopkeeper
Drayton Geo. blksmith & shpkpr
Hallifax James, wheelwright
Hill William, shoemaker
Hind George, joiner
Hodge Rev. Hy. Vere, curate
Illingworth Wm. shoemaker
Johnson David, blacksmith
Justice Mrs. Elizabeth
Levick Wm. corn miller
Lister Thos. vict. Stag
Otter Jas. tailor & parish clerk
Pearce John, joiner
Pearce William, joiner
Staniland John, sen. tailor
Staniland John, jun. shoemaker
Warburton Mary, vict. Crown
Welton Chas. shoemaker
FARMERS.
Marked † are Yeomen.
†Ashton Benj.   †Ashton John

Barlow Wm.
Bingham Fras.
Bingham Jas.
Bingham John,
Field house
Bingham John
Bingham Mary
Booth Jas.
Brown John
Burwell Wm.
Carver Wm.
Chambers Wm.
Clayton Geo.
Clayton John
Cobb James
Downs Mary
Drayton Ann
Fenton Jph
†Fletcher Wm.
†Gauntley T.
Gray Jph
Hiley Jph
Hill Geo.
Hind Geo.
Jackson John
Johnson Fras.
†Johnson Geo.
& Newark

†Johnson Wm.
Justice John
Keyworth John
Keyworth T.
Merrills Wm.
& overseer.
†Motley Geo.
Ollivant John
†Parkinson J.
Quible Thos.
Rouse John
Seels Thos.
†Smith John
Spencer Wm.
Stancer Hanh.
†Stancer John
Stancer Wm.
†Temporal Jno.
Watkin Thos.
Welton Geo.
†Watkinson E.
†Wilkinson J.
High house
Wilkinson My.
Wright Wm.

2 i

WALKERINGHAM PARISH

EXTENDS from Gringley-on-the-Hill to *Walkrith Ferry*, on the Trent, and contains 116 houses, 529 inhabitants, and 2861A. 3R. 3P. of land, of which, at the enclosure in 1802, an allotment of 349A. 1R. 25P. was awarded to Trinity college, as a commutation of the rectorial tithes, and 157A. 2R. 11P. to the vicar in lieu of the small tithes. The Duke of Newcastle is lord of the manor, and owner of a great part of the soil; but Earl Manvers and Gervas Woodhouse, Esq. have estates here, and Christopher Neville, Esq. is lessee of the College land. Part of the *Cars* already described with Misterton, are in this parish.

WALKERINGHAM is a straggling village, nearly a mile in length, four miles N.W. of Gainsborough, and nine miles E. by S. of Bawtry, on the road and about one mile from the Ferry which crosses the Trent to Walkrith, in Lincolnshire. The *church* is a large ancient pile, dedicated to St. Mary Magdalen, and was given to Worksop priory by Wm. de Lovetot, in the reign of Henry I.; but it is now in the appropriation and patronage of Trinity College, Cambridge. The vicarage, which is now enjoyed by the Rev. J. K. Miller, is valued in the King's books at £7. 11s. 5d. A *Methodist Chapel* was built here in 1796, and has since been enlarged. Near the church is the base of an ancient *cross*, and an old *hall*, which, with the ancient demesne belonging to the King's soke of Mansfield, was given by Henry II. to Newstead Abbey, and afterwards belonged to the Byron family. The *Grange* which had been given to Roche Abbey, in Yorkshire, was granted by Henry VIII. to Sir Richard Lee, but now belongs to Earl Manvers. The capital messuage and all the lands in Walkeringham, which had belonged to Worksop priory, were granted by the same Monarch to Lawrence Harwood and Stephen Termpte.

CHARITIES:—In 1621, *William Clarke* left to five aged poor of this parish £10 a-year out of his estate at Walkrith. In 1719, *Robert Woodhouse* charged his lands in Misterton and Walkeringham with the following annuities, viz. :—£15 for a schoolmaster to teach the poor children of Walkeringham, reading, writing, and arithmetic; 20s. to buy books for the said free scholars, and £4. to be divided yearly in clothing and victuals amongst eight poor people not receiving parochial relief. The donor was buried in his own yard, and the lands on which he settled these rent charges, now belong to G. Woodhouse, Esq. The *Poor's Meadow* let for £3. 13s. was allotted at the enclosure, in exchange for land purchased many years before, with £45 left by two persons named *Porge and Barrell.* An annuity of 10s. is given to the poor in bread, out of an estate in Walkeringham, now belonging to Mary Lister, of

Pontefract. It is called the *Marmy Dole*, and is supposed to have been left by one Marmaduke Aukland.

Armitage Wm. boat owner, Canal bridge
Baines Mrs. Susanna
Barthrup John, joiner
Belton John, maltster
Butler Wm. grocer &, draper
Cartwright Thomas, butcher
Cave. Henry, shoemaker
Clark John, shoemaker
Cousins Robert, shoemaker
Fenton John, vict. & blksmith
Harris Seth, jun. blacksmith
Hibbart Wm. wheelwright
Jackson Gervas, tailor
Markham Wm. tailor & draper
Miller Rev. Jph. Kirkman, vicar
Morris Wm. schoolmaster
Newton William, joiner
Parkin Benj. bricklayer
Renshaw Thos. vict. & whlwrgt
Slater Miss Catherine
Taylor Jph. corn miller

Taylor Thomas, shoemaker
White John, swine jobber
Woodhouse Gvs. Esq. & Owston

FARMERS.
Thus * *are. Yeomen.*

*Belton Fras.
Berry John
Berry Rd.
Bettison Wm.
Brett Wm.
Catley Sarah
Draper John
Elwick Wm.
Graves John
Grime Geo.
Harris Seth
Henderson J.
*Horberry Jas.
Keeley John
Kirtland Sarah
*Parker John

Pyecroft John
*Pyecroft Ths.
Raddish John
*Saundby John
Smith Wm.
Spencer Geo.
Grange Lodge
Spencer Jas.
Spencer John
Sutton John
Tagg John
Taylor David
Tomlinson J.
*Webster Geo.
West Martha
*Williamson T.

WHEATLEY (NORTH) PARISH.

NORTH WHEATLEY is a considerable village, built upon a steep declivity on the south side of the Gainsborough road, five miles N.E. of Retford. The parish, which is partly open field land, contains 87 houses, 435 inhabitants, and about 2,000 acres, most of which belongs to Lord Middleton; but Lord Wenlock is lord of the manor, which is mostly held on copyhold tenure, paying a fine on the death or change of tenant, equal to one and a half year's rent. Mr. Heaton, of Gainsbro', is steward of the *Copyhold Court*. At the Domesday survey, part of " *Wateleg*" was a *Berue* of the Archbishop of York's soke of Laneham, and the rest belonged to the King's soke of Mansfield, and was of the fee of Roger de Busli. The *church* dedicated to St. Peter, appears to have been erected in the 16th century, but the chancel was rebuilt in 1824. Lord Middleton is the patron, and has also the impropriation of two-thirds of the great tithes; but the other third belongs to the vicarage, which was valued in the King's books at £3. 18s. 10½d., and is now enjoyed by the Rev. Fras. Hewgill, who in 1826, erected a *National School* for the use of the parish. The Methodists have a small *Chapel* here, which was built about 40 years ago, by Mr. John Pagden. A *feast*, and a *hiring for servants*, are held on the first Thursday in November, when the green round the lofty *Maypole* is crowded with merry throngs, dressed in their holyday garbs.

CHARITIES.—In 1719, *William Spencer* left a house, barn, garden, and an orchard, in the village, and 1A. 2R. 39P. of arable land in the open fields, to the poor of North and South Wheatley. They are now let for £3. 10s. per annum, subject to a chief rent of 2s. 3d. Two-thirds are distributed here, and the rest in South Wheatley; but the following belong solely to this parish, viz. :—£2. yearly out of Lord Middleton's estate, for the poor, pursuant to the will of the *Earl of Kingston ;* 20s. yearly to four poor widows out of Thomas Wells' estate, as left in 1721, by *Katherine Porter ;* 10s. yearly to the school, left by *Thomas James,* and now paid by Mr. F. Richardson, of Horncastle; and £50 bequeathed in 1813, by *Job Serratt,* but not yet paid by his executor, Mr. Flower, surgeon, of East Retford, who enjoys the testator's *real* estate, worth £50. a-year, and in 1816, paid the duty on this legacy, but has since declared that the *personal* property out of which it was to be paid, was not sufficient to pay the testator's debts.—*Comss. Rep.*

Blythman John, shoemaker
Borley Wm. vict. Sun
Branford Edward, schoolmaster
Crosland John, maltster
Elston William, saddler
Freeman Geo. corn miller, East Field
Green Rev. Wm. curate
Hallifax Wm. wheelwright
Kidney John, maltster
Kidney Sarah, vict. Red Lion
Kidney Wm. butcher
Kirk Jerh. & Thos. tailors
Lane Wm. shoemaker
Newton Absalom, joiner
Newton Joseph, joiner
Ostick James, bricklayer
Padley Rt. corn miller & baker
Pagden Mr. John
Sherratt Ann, shopkeeper
Sherratt Mr. Thomas
Sherratt Mr. William
Sibsaph John, road surveyor
Smith John, blksmith & par. clk.
Smith Saml. gardener & seedsman
Stevenson John, shoemaker

Taylor John, vict. Sherwood Ranger
Wilson Thomas. stay maker

FARMERS.

Marked ‡ are Yeomen.

Barker Wm.
Bingham Geo.
Bingham Geo.
‡Bingham Ob.
Bingley John
Black John
Black Wm.
‡Boswell Geo.
‡Boswell Wm.
Brown John
‡Camb John
Cartledge Wm.
Chambers —
Clayton Rd.
‡Clayton Thos.
Cocking Rt.
Cole Isaac
‡Cook Wm.
‡Crowder Jas.
Gilstrap Geo.
‡Goodger John
Goodger Jph.

‡Hancock T.
Hanson Sarah
Harrison Wm.
Hempseed J.
Hill Henry
‡Holmes Thos.
‡Leadworth J.
‡Lilliman John
‡Lilliman Wm.
Moore Jph.
Naylor Geo.
Newbould Geo.
‡Newton Ann
Porter Fras.
Sherratt Sarah
Sherratt Wm.
‡Smith Eliz.
‡Smith John
Taylor John
Ward Wm.
Whitlam Wm.
‡Wilson Wm.

WHEATLEY (SOUTH) PARISH.

SOUTH WHEATLEY is a parish of small extent, containing only three farm houses, three cottages, 35 inhabitants, and about 700 acres of land, nearly all belonging to William Mason, Esq. the lord of the manor. It is five miles and a half N.E. of Retford, and is separated from North Wheatley by a rivulet or beck, which runs through a deep and narrow valley. The *church* is a small structure on an eminence near the houses. The living is a rectory, valued in the King's books at £6. 14s. 2d., and is discharged from the payment of first fruits. It was anciently of the fee of Roger de Busli, and "formed part of the chapelry of *Tykhill*," but it is now in the patronage of the Chapter of Southwell, and the Rev. Richard Barrow is the rector, for whom the Rev. John Mickle officiates. The farms in this and the adjacent parishes are chiefly occupied by *dairies*, from which great quantities of butter are sent to Retford and other markets.

Bullivant Job, farmer
Bullivant Mr. Samuel
Hardy Henry, farmer
Radford William, farmer
Smith Joseph, cattle dealer

SOUTH CLAY DIVISION.

THIS division of the Hundred of Bassetlaw is bounded on the north by Retford, South Leverton, and Cottam; on the east by the Trent, which divides it from Lincolnshire; on the south by the Hundred of Thurgarton, and on the west by the Idle, and Lound, Walesby, Boughton, Ollerton, Rufford, and the Rainworth Water. It is of about the same extent as the North Clay, and a large portion of the arable land is in nine open-field lordships. Its soil, as has been seen at page 43, is generally fertile, and its surface is in many places beautifully diversified with hill and dale, and wood and water. It contains 15 parishes and townships, 1,698 houses, and 8,175 inhabitants, as enumerated at page 301. Its only *market town* is Tuxford; but Retford and Ollerton are on its borders, and much of its produce is carried to the markets of Mansfield and Newark.

ASKHAM PARISH.

ASKHAM village, in the liberty of Southwell and Scrooby, stands on a pleasant declivity, three miles N. of Tuxford. Its parish, which extends westward to the Idle, includes the new hamlet of *Rockley*, and contains 79 houses, 329 inhabitants,

and 1400 acres of good clay land, 48 acres of which are in hop-
yards, and nearly all the rest in large open fields. It is noted
in Domesday Book, as a Berue of Laneham, consequently the
Archbishop of York is lord of the *manor*, which is partly
copyhold, and partly held on lease for the term of three lives.
The archbishop holds a court once a year. The *church*, which
has lately been repaired, is a gothic fabric, and the living, which
is a perpetual curacy, not in charge, is a member of the vicarage
of East Drayton, being in the patronage and enjoyment of the
incumbent of that benefice; but the great tithes are in the appropriation of the Dean and Chapter of York, who have let
them on a long lease to Samuel Crawley, Esq. An *hospital*
in the village, founded about 1658, is the asylum of six poor
widows, who each receive an allowance of coals, and 10s.
yearly out of an annual rent charge of £21 from lands at South
Wheatley. The surplus of this charity is carried to the
overseer's accounts. The indigent parishioners have also 10s.
yearly, out of a meadow in Beastwood, left by Elizabeth
Dickenson.

ROCKLEY, a small newly built village, one mile west of
Askham, contains several neat cottages, and *Rockley-house*,
the mansion of Mr. William Calvert. Near it, upon the Idle,
is *Jacket Mill*, and the farms of *Brotherwoods* and *Gameston-
wood*, all within the parish.

Appleby Rt. corn miller, Jacket
  Mill
Atkinson William, gent.
Bailey Mr. James
Bettison Mrs. Elizabeth
Booth Jonas, millwright
Calvert Wm. land surveyor and
  valuer, Rockley House
Charlesworth Isaac, shoemaker
Clark Jonth. vict. & wheelwright,
  Nag's Head
Cooling Abm. shoemaker
Crookes Charles, shoemaker
Crookes Geo. schoolmaster
Crookes Wm. shoemaker & shpkr
Gascoyne George, shoemaker
Knight Geo. pig jobber, Rockley
Nicholson Geo. chair maker

Pearce Mr. Richard
Pearson George, tailor
Pearson Thomas, blacksmith
Walker Fdk. joiner & chair mkr
Warrener Richard. shopkeeper
FARMERS.
Bullivant Wm. Padley John
Clark Allison Pearce John
Diggles Wm. Scrimshaw Eliz.
Harvey Wm. Jacket Mill
Hodscroft Jno. Scrimshaw Ts.
  Brotherwood Smith Benj. h.
Ketton W. jun. Cromwell
Ketton Wm. (& Smith John
  parish clerk) Tomlinson Jph.
Laughton John, Wyre John,
  Gamston Wd. Old Town

BEVERCOTES PARISH.

THIS churchless parish contains only eight dwellings, 51
inhabitants, and about 800 acres of fertile land, divided into
four farms, except 50 acres, on which grow the finest hops in
he county. It has had neither church nor pastor during the

last 150 years, so that its inhabitants are obliged to use the church at West Markham, were they pay a modus of 1s. 11d. to the archbishop at his visitations, and are provided with seat room, &c. in consideration of an annuity paid by the Duke of Newcastle, to whom the whole parish belongs. The manor was held of the Honour of Tickhill, during many generations, by a family of its own name, whose heiress, in the reign of Henry VI., carried it in marriage to Rutland Mollyneux, Esq. who sold it to the Earl of Clare, from whom it has descended to the Duke of Newcastle. The four *farms* are occupied by four *Johns*, bearing the surnames of Bellamy, Denman, Field, and White.

BILSTHORPE PARISH.

BILSTHORPE is a tolerable village, about one mile east of Rainworth-water, and five miles S. of Ollerton. The parish comprises 43 houses, 217 inhabitants, 1420 acres of arable and pasture land, and 60 acres of plantations, all belonging to the Hon. and Rev. J. L. Saville, who is lord of the manor, and patron of the rectory, which is valued in the King's books at £5. 1s. 8d., and is now enjoyed by the Rev. Henry Gordon, M.A. The church stands on an eminence above the village, and is dedicated to St. Margaret. The tower, which has two bells, appears to have been built in 1663. In the chancel, amongst several ancient monuments, is one to bishop Chappell, who is noticed with Laxton and Mansfield. Before the Conquest, *Bildesthorpe* or *Byllesthorp* was the property of Ulph, the Saxon, but was given by William the Conqueror, to Gilbert de Gand, being at that time *soc* to Rufford. From him it passed to the Tregoz, Lowdham, Broughton, and other families, till it came to that of its present possessor. An ancient house near the church is said to have been one of the many hiding places of King Charles I.; but there is perhaps as little truth in this tradition as in that mentioned by Throsby, of a large hollow rock near the village, having served the humble purpose of a nocturnal utensil to the redoubtable Robin Hood! The *church land* left in 1662, consists of 1½ acres at Eakring, but the yearly rent 21s. is now paid to the schoolmaster. The overseers distribute 5s. yearly as the interest of £5 left to the poor in 1732, by James Lynam.

Bucklow John, shopkeeper	Holmes John, shoe maker
Butler Edw. blacksmith	Hopkinson Wm. shopkeeper
Dixon Rev. Matthew	Outram Isaac, land bailiff
Gordon Rev. Henry, M. A. rector, Rectory House	Smith John, shoe maker
	Tesh Mary, wheelwright
Herod Fras. parish clerk	Ward Luke, tailor

FARMERS.
Bucklow Edward
Bucklow John
Flint Elizabeth
Flint Joseph
Flower David, Clifton Lodge
Hage John

Harvey Edward, Bellow Park
Jackson Samuel, Wicketleys
Wright William

Carrier to Mansfield, John Bucklow, Thu. dep. 6 mg. ar. 8 ev.

DARLTON PAROCHIAL CHAPELRY.

DARLTON is a small village, township, and parochial chapelry, annexed to the vicarage of Dunham, and situated on the road to Dunham Bridge, three miles N. E. by E. of Tuxford. It contains 28 houses, 162 inhabitants, and about 1360 acres of land, which was enclosed about 1765, and formerly belonged to the Cartwrights, of Marnham, who sold it to J. Walker, Esq. of Rotherham, by whom it was resold, in 1793, to Wm. Calvert, Esq. who, soon afterwards, sold it out in small lots, reserving only 200 acres for himself, together with the manorial rights. The *church* is a small ancient fabric, dedicated to St. Giles. The living is a perpetual curacy, of which the vicar of Dunham is patron and incumbent. The great tithes are appropriated to Southwell Collegiate Church, and are let to W. Crawley, Esq. A *Methodist Chapel* was built here about 20 years ago. In the parish are the scattered farm-houses of *Honey-well, Outgang*, and KINGSHAUGH HOUSE, the latter of which is an ancient moated building, erected by King John, who converted the King's *hay* or *wood* into a park, "and made war in this place" against his brother Richard I.

Barrowcliff Wm. shoe maker.
Fisher, William, joiner
Markham Wm. beer house
Penny Edw. stay maker & beer house
Stockdale John, blacksmith
Walker William, joiner
FARMERS.
Marked ‡ are Yeomen.
Barr John, Gap ‡Black Thos.

‡Byron Thos. Pearce Joseph,
‡Cullen Wm. Honeywell
‡Gray Rt. Out- Short Stpn. C.
gang Kingshaugh-
Kidney Geo. house
Markham Jno. Waltis John.
‡Moor Wm.
‡Palfreyman W.
Outgang

DRAYTON (EAST) PARISH.

EAST DRAYTON is a large but indifferently built village, four mile N. E. by E. of Tuxford. The parish contains 55 houses, 256 inhabitants, and 1520 acres of land, which was enclosed in 1819. The *church*, dedicated to St. Peter, is a large gothic edifice, with a lofty tower. The living is a vicarage, valued in the King's books at £9. 3s. 4d. and has annexed to it those of Askham and Stokeham. The Rev. Chas. J. Sympson, of Teversall, is the vicar, and the Rev. Archibald Galland, the curate. The Dean and Chapter of York are the patrons, appropriators, and lords of the manor, which was a " Berue" of the King's manor of Dunham, and is now held on lease by the devisees of the late Lord Howard, to whom nearly half the land in the parish belongs. The village has a small Methodist Chapel, and an annual *feast* on the Sunday after the nearest Sunday to Old Michaelmas Day.

Those marked ‡ are Hop Growers, and § Yeomen.

Chatterton John, shoe maker
Elliott Wm. vict. Harrow
Galland Rev. Archibald, curate
Harpham Rd. vict. & blacksmith
  Blue Bell
Harpham Wm. grocer
Hempstock Thos. vict. & shoe
  maker
‡Rawson Robert, wheelwright
Salmon Mr. —
Skelton Francis, corn miller
Slingsby Thomas, shoe maker

FARMERS.
§Anderson Wm
Bell Jph
§Byron Faith
‡§Byron Wm.
  & Geo.
East Robt.
Kelton Geo.
§Milns Wm.
§Newbould J.
‡Norfolk T.
Norfolk Wm.

Parnham Edw.
‡Parnham Geo.
‡Parnham Wm.
Salmon Geo.
Salmon John
§Scott John
§Swinburn Rd.
§Whitlam Ann.
Whitlam Wm.
  & shopr.

DRAYTON (WEST) PAROCHIAL CHAPELRY.

WEST DRAYTON is a small village, township, and parochial chapelry, containing only 23 houses, 107 inhabitants, and about 600 acres of land near the confluence of the rivers Maun, Wollen, and Idle, on the Worksop and Tuxford road, 2¼ miles N. N. W. of the latter town. The Duke of Newcastle is the proprietor, and lord of the manor, which was of the fee of Roger de Busli. The church or *chapel* is a small edifice, with a turret and one bell. The living is a perpetual curacy annexed to the vicarage of East Markham.

Walter's Charity:—In 1688, Henry Walter bequeathed out of his lands in Yorkshire, £25 per annum towards the maintenance of a school at West Drayton; £20 a-year for four poor widows of ministers, to be elected by the ministers of East and West Markham and Kirton; and £3 a-year to the trustees for their trouble in executing his will. The master is appointed by the Duke of Newcastle, and the before-named ministers are visitors of the school, which is open to the poor of West Drayton, Bothamsall, Houghton, Elksley, Gamston, Milton, and Bevercotes.

Black Thomas, farmer
Blenkhorn John, schoolmaster,
  Haughton Park
Hubbard John, farmer & p. clerk
Marshall John, joiner

Rawson John, farmer
Stockdale John, maltster, h.
  Elksley
White James, weaver
Withley Richard, farmer

DUNHAM PARISH.

DUNHAM, 6 miles E.N.E. of Tuxford, is a large and pleasant village, seated on a gentle eminence on the west bank of the river Trent, where a broad and shallow ferry has just been superseded by a handsome cast IRON BRIDGE of four arches, resting upon stone piers, and each 118 feet in span. The cost of this noble structure was about £17,000, which was sub- scribed by the proprietors in £50 shares. The first stone was laid March 3, 1831, and the whole was completed in May, 1832. The iron work, which weighs 900 tons, was cast by Messrs. Booth and Co., of Sheffield Park; Messrs. Harmer and Pratt were the contractors, and Mr. George Leather, of Leeds, the engineer. According to the Act of Parliament under which the bridge has been erected, the proprietors are to purchase the ferry at a fair valuation. The spring tides rise here about four feet, but the common tides seldom flow much higher than Gainsbro,' which is 12 miles below Dunham. The weekly *Market*, and the annual *Fair* which was held here on August 12th, have been some time obsolete; but it is ex- pected that the bridge will in a little time so increase the pros- perity of the place, that the fair will be re-established, together with a Thursday market; indeed large quantities of butter, &c. are now taken up here every Friday by the hucksters, who pass through the village from Lincoln to Sheffield, &c. The annual *feast* is on the Sunday after August 12th. A fine old *cross* which stood in the village, was taken down by order of William Crawley, Esq., who lately sold the *manor* and fishery to John Angersteen, Esq., who is also owner of a great part of the soil. The other principal landowners are William Mason, Esq., Thomas Newstead, and Christopher Alderson, besides whom, there are several smaller freeholders. The *Parish* con- tains 77 houses, 389 inhabitants, and about 900 acres of land, most of which, as well as much of the land of the adjacent parishes, is subject to inundations from the Trent, to prevent which, an act is about to be obtained for raising an embankment nine feet high upon the river. Thoroton says, " the men of *Dunham Soc and Manor*, being tenants of ancient demesne, ought to be quit of murder, pontage, and all other fines with the com- monalty of the county."

The CHURCH is a small fabric dedicated to St. Oswald, and was rebuilt in 1805, except the tower, which is ancient and lofty. Previous to this reparation, the nave and chancel had been many years in ruins. Henry I. gave it to Thurston, Arch- bishop of York, " that he might make a PREBEND of it in the church of Southwell." The living is a discharged vicarage, valued in the King's books at £4. 13s. 4d., and has attached to it the parochial chapels of Ragnall and Darlton. The Rev. John Sedley Venables Vernon is the incumbent, and the Rev. Edward Younghusband the curate. The *Prebendary of Dunham*, in Southwell Collegiate Church, is the patron and appropriator. At the *enclosure* of Dunham and Ragnall, in 1803, the *tithes* of those parishes were commuted for the following allotments, viz. in Dunham 211A. 1R. 36P. to the prebendary, and 23A. 0R. 3P. to the vicar; and in Ragnall, 29A. 1R. 13P. to the prebendary, and 91A. 3R. 31P. to the vicar. There is in the village a *Methodist Chapel.*

CHARITIES.—In 1658, *John Addy* left land which, at the enclosure, was augmented with 3R. 27P. and is now let for £3. 12s. a-year, which is carried to the poor rates. In 1763, *Mrs. Hainsworth* left £50, which, with an arrear of £10, is now in the hands of Thomas Newstead at 5 per cent. *Leonard and John Hainsworth*, in 1728, left £50 to the poor of Dunham, but it is lost together with £50 left to those of Ragnall, by one of the Mellish family. The *church land* consists of 2A. 2R. 7P. allotted at the enclosure.

Baxter Thos. clog & patten mkr
Bayes Thos. vict. Bridge Inn
Bellamy Fras. shoe maker
Bennett Geo. butcher
Bingham Jane, grocer & draper
Bingham Wm. wheelwright, &c.
Birkitt Mrs. Sarah
Bycroft James, fisherman
Clark John. boat owner
Clark Jph. boat owner
Clifton John, fisherman
Cobb John, watch maker
Cook Geo. boat owner
Dixon Mr. Septimus
Fox Mr. Thomas
Hempstock John, blacksmith
Hempstock Jph. tailor
Johnson Edw. grocer & draper
Marshall Geo. shopr. schoolr. & parish clerk
Mason Eleanor, vict. Rein Deer
Miles Thos. tailor
Newstead Thos. maltster, & Retford and Laneham
Nicholson Mary, vict. Swan
Oliver Geo. surgeon, and Newton
Roberts Thos. schoolmaster
Rose Mrs. Hannah
Stokes Wm. shoemaker
Taylor Chas. gardener
Taylor Mr. John
Teft Thomas, tailor
Tomlinson Richard, shoemaker
Whate John, jun. shoe maker
Whate John, sen. bricklayer
Wilson Geo. wheelgt. & joiner
Woolhouse Wm. keel owner
Younghusband Rev. Edw. curate

FARMERS.
Thus † *are Yeomen.*
†Bacon Thos.   †Newstead Thos
†Eyre Geo.   Nicholson Chas.
†Hempstock J.   Nicholson Thos
†Houghton Jno. Wigfall Joseph
†Millns Rt.

Carrier, Rd. Tomlinson, to Retford, Sat. dep. 7 mg. arr. evg.

EAKRING PARISH.

EAKRING, or ECHERING, is a considerable village and parish 4 miles S. by E. of Ollerton, containing 128 houses, 591 inhabitants, and 2045 acres of land, of which 500 acres are in large open fields, and 70 acres in common. Earl Manvers owns 1040 acres; the Hon. and Rev. J. L. Saville, 700 acres, and Henry Machon, Esq., 200 acres; and the rest belongs to smaller freeholders, except 40 acres of glebe. The *church*, which stands pleasantly on an eminence, has a tower and three bells. The living is a rectory valued in the King's books at £9. 16s. 0¼d, and is now enjoyed by the Rev. Theophilus Sampson, who in 1830, succeeded the Rev. J. H. Browne, who had held the benefice 38 years. It is in the alternate patronage of Earl Manvers and the Hon. and Rev. J. L. Saville, who are Lords of the Manor;—the former being possesed of that part of the ancient demesne which was retained by the heirs of Gilbert de Gaunt, and the latter having that portion which the said Gilbert gave to the monks of Rufford. A great part of the parish was of the King's soke of Mansfield, and a small portion of it was " *Soc* to Laxton of Goisford de Alselia's fee." An annual festival called "EAKRING BALL PLAY," is held on Easter Tuesday, and has no doubt derived its name from its being anciently a great meeting for a trial of skill in the game of *foot ball*, which was formerly such a favourite amusement in this county, that the lusty peasantry often kicked the ball to and from the church on a Sunday; indeed we ourselves have witnessed this polution of the Sabbath, and have some times seen the kicking of balls changed on the same day to the kicking of shins,—another sport in which this county has long excelled, and has perhaps never been surpassed, not even by the famous *wrestlers* of the southern counties. A *Mr. Forster*, in 1770, left £17 to the poor, for which the overseers distribute 17s. yearly out of the poor rates.

Booth Richard, tailor
Browne Miss Mary Ann
Buckels Hy. painter and shopr.
Bull George, corn miller
Carlisle Robert, wheelwright
Cooper Richard, parish clerk
Doncaster Wm. solicitor
Haywood John, shoemaker
Johnson John, wheelwright
Lacy John, butcher
Machon Hy. Esq. & Gateford hill
Manners John, bricklayer
Osbourn Wm. shopkeeper
Randall John, shoemaker
Roberts J. vict. Horse & Trumpet
Rose John, schoolmaster
Rose Wm. shoemaker
Roworth Geo. blacksmith
Salmon Wm. shopkeeper

Sampson Rev, Theophilus, rector
Shircliff Thos. butcher
Stanley Wm. shoemaker
Story Robert, butcher
Tarr Thos. joiner
Tilley Mr. Joseph
Tilley Wm. shoemaker
Ward Samuel, tailor
Waters Thos. shoemaker
Weightman Ellen, blacksmith
Williamson Hy. vict. Ostrich
Wood Wm. joiner

FARMERS.

Thus are † Yeomen, and ‡ Hop Growers.

††Barker John   Cooper Geo.
Bowman Jph.   †Cooper Thos.
‡Bunby Thos. Dobb Wm.
(& vict.)

Hallam David,	Kay Richard	Tomlinson Geo.	Waters John
Lady Park	Peck Richard		& shopkeeper. Wilson Richard,
Hunt John	Pinder Jane	Ward Richard	Coulters
Hurt George	Rose Geo. T.		
Hurt George	Rose George	Carrier, Samuel Wibberley, to
Hurt John	‡Ryal John	Newark, Wed.; to Mansfield,
‡Hurt Wm.	Tilley Abel	Thu.; and to Ollerton, Friday.
Johnson John		

EATON PARISH.

EATON or IDLETON is a small village on both sides of the Idle, connected by a brick bridge, 2 miles S. of Retford. Though now only remarkable for being a *prebend* of Southwell, it was a place of some consequence before the Norman Conquest; "for here were ten manors, and ten thanes, each thane having a Hall:"—at the survey, however, they were reduced to one *manor*, of which the Hon. John Bridgeman Simpson is now lord, and owner of a great part of the soil which he purchased about 1785, of Earl Fitzwilliam; but the Duke of Newcastle and the Hon. J. L. Saville have each estates in the parish, which contains 48 houses, 238 inhabitants, and about 1400 acres of land, part of which was not enclosed till 1810. The *church* is a small edifice with a turret and a bell. The living is a vicarage valued in the King's books at £4. 13s. 4d. The Rev. Charles Fowler is the incumbent, and the Prebendary of Eaton in Southwell Collegiate Church is the patron and appropriator. *Eaton Hall*, now occupied by H. B. Simpson, Esq., is a neat and pleasant villa, which was thoroughly repaired and greatly enlarged in 1831.

Simpson Henry Bridgeman, Esq.	FARMERS.
Eaton Hall	Denham Reb. Starkey Thos.
Booth George, shoemaker	Knight John Walker Wm.
Swallow Martha, shopkeeper	Marriott Fras. Warrick Jonas
Wilson Mr. Abraham	

EGMANTON PARISH.

EGMANTON or AGEMANTON, 1¼ mile S. of Tuxford, is a village and parish, containing 67 houses, 341 inhabitants, and 2159A. 1R. 31P. of rich land, most of which was in a large open arable field till 1821, when an act was obtained to enclose it, and when the tithes were commuted for an allotment of 200 acres to the impropriator, and 36A. 0R. 36P. to the vicar, exclusive of 63A. 2R. 17P. of ancient glebe. Before the Conquest, it formed two manors belonging to " Turchetell and Ulmer." Henry I. bestowed Egmanton with its parks,

2 K

and appertenances upon his bow-bearer, *Nigellus de Albanei*, brother to the Earls of Clare and Arundel, who soon afterwards gave it to his bosom friend *Robert de Aiville*, and told his sovereign that " he had now got two honest knights instead of one." Nigellus was the founder of the Mowbray family, of whom the descendants of D'Aiville held this manor till the reign of Edward I., when Joan de Aiville carried it in marriage to the Everinghams of Laxton, one of whom sold the *East Park* to Henry Deyvill. In the reign of Henry VI. one moiety of the manor belonged to Sir Richard Stanhope, of Kampton. The *Park* was afterwards purchased by Nicholas Poutrell, who built upon it Egmanton Hall, which stood on or near *Gaddick Hill*, a large conical mound with a trench or moat cut round it. The manor is still in two moieties, and the Duke of Newcastle and the Hon. J. L. Saville are the lords.

The CHURCH is a small structure with a short thick tower, and is dedicated to St. Mary. In the 37th of Henry VIII. John Bellowe had license to alienate the rectory and church, (which had belonged to Newstead priory) to Robert Thornehill, Esq. The impropriation and advowson now belong to Pendock Barry, Esq. but he has sold their reversion to the Duke of Newcastle. The vicarage is valued in the King's Books at £4. 6s. 0½d.; and the Rev. Edward Smith is now the incumbent. The annual *Feast* commences on the nearest Sunday to Old Michaelmas-day. The *Methodist Chapel* here, was erected in 1804, on land given by Robert Price.

CHARITIES.—In 1616, *John Sudbury* left to the poor of Egmanton and Mapplebeck, an acre of land in Tuxford Southfield. At the enclosure, the Duke of Newcastle gave in exchange for this land, Outgangbridge and Beetoning Closes, containing 2A. 3R. 15P. in Egmanton, and now let for £6. per annum, which is divided equally amongst the poor of Egmanton and Mapplebeck. In 1666, *Francis Oldham* left a rent charge of 6s. and *Christopher Sudbury* in 1678, two lands in Egmanton Field, to the poor of this parish, but these benefactions were exchanged at the enclosure for an acre of the common field, now divided into six gardens let for 6s. each. The *Church land* consists of 6A. 1R. 29P., let for £5. 11s. per annum, and was also allotted in exchange at the enclosure.

Ashmore Geo. tailor
Cook Mary, vict. New Plough
East James, corn miller
Hallam James, shoemaker
Jackson Sandys, vict. Old Plough and blacksmith
Rose Mr. George
Sprowell Jas. baker & shopkpr

Stoakes John, bricklayer, victualler and shopkeeper
Tinker Richard, wheelwright
Tissington Robert, shoemaker
Truswell Richard, tanner
      FARMERS.
    Thus † are Yeomen.
†Bills Rt. Villa Bingham John

Booth George   Hill John
Burton Richard   Johnson Rd.
Gale John   Lee Edward
Gray John   †Maples John
†Hempsall Thos †Oldham Fras.
   (hop grower)   Price Robert

Priest Thomas   †Sudbury Saml.
Ramsden Fras.   Thompson Wm
Ramsden Wm.   †Wardell George
Rose William   (hop grower)
Sprowell James Wilson William

GAMSTON PARISH.

GAMSTON or GAMELSTON, three miles and an half S. of Retford, is a good village on the east bank of the Idle, where there is a corn mill and a candlewick manufactory. The parish, which has only about 1,100 acres of rich land, contains 64 houses, and a population of 306 souls. The Duke of Newcastle is sole proprietor and lord of the manor, which was enclosed in 1809, when the tithes were commuted for an allotment of land. Before the conquest there were two mills here, and two manors held by "Gamel and Swain," but the whole was afterwards possessed by the Materseys, from whom it passed to the Thurlands, who sold it to the Markhams, of whom it was purchased, together with Thurland Hall, in Nottingham, by the Earl of Clare, an ancestor of the Duke of Newcastle. The *Church* dedicated to St. Peter, "has *once* been antique," but its brasses have been all destroyed or stolen, and its sculptured ornaments are hid behind many coats of whitewash. The benefice is a rectory in the patronage of the King, and valued in the King's Books at £11. 16s. 5¼d. The Rev. Joshua Brooke, B.D. is the rector. Here is an ancient *Baptist Chapel* with a burial ground. LOUND HALL FARM, though two miles and a half south of Gamston, and surrounded by Bothamsall, Bevercotes, and Haughton, is attached to this parish, and this unnatural connection is accounted for by a traditional tale, which says, it was occasioned by Bothamsall chapelry refusing to bury a corpse found at Lound Hall, and which was consequently brought to Gamston, where it was interred. In 1740, *John Holt* and *William Ibberson* left £2. each to the poor of Gamston, for which the overseers distribute 4s. yearly in bread. JOOKEY HOUSE, now a farm-house, one mile west of Gamston, on the opposite side of the Idle is in this parish, and was formerly a noted Inn, being near the junction of several old roads.

Brooke Rev. Joshua, B.D. rector
Buckle Marmaduke, manufactr.
Dixon John, corn miller
Flintham Isaac, wheelwright
Freeborough Wm. vict. Newcastle Arms

Haworth & Buckle, linen & cotton candlewick manufacturers
Haworth Stph. Rose, manufactr
Laughton Sarah & Eliz. shopkrs
Parkinson Miss Sarah & Sisters
Salmon Ann, grocer and draper

Shipston Samuel, shopkeeper
Shipston Mr. William
Tattersall George, tailor
Theaker Geo. shoemaker
Wait Wm. blacksmith
Whitworth John, wheelwright

FARMERS.
Bailey Eleanor   Baker William

Batty William   Salmon Joseph
Hopkinson Jon.   Shaw Thomas
Lound Joseph,   Shipston Thos.
    Jockey-house Simpson Wm.
Redgate John,   Swallow Wm.
    Lound Hall   Walker George

GROVE PARISH.

GROVE is a small but pleasant village and parish, 3 miles E.S.E. of Retford, containing 20 houses, 121 inhabitants, and about 900 acres of land, the higher parts of which are planted with oak, ash, and other trees, now in a thriving state, and the rest is either in pasturage or tillage. Being so near the line of the Roman road which passed by Littleborough to Lincoln, the bold and commanding situation of Grove could not escape the notice of the Roman legions, as fit for an exploratory station, and we may therefore conclude, that the double-trenched mount in *Castle Hill Wood*, a little to the north of the village, was occupied by them for military purposes, though it may originally have been a British work. The *lordship* of Grove was partly ancient demesne of the soke of Dunham, but after the Conquest, it was of the fee of Roger de Busli, and in the reign of Henry II. was held by Gilbert de Arches *Baron de Grove*, whose heiress carried it in marriage to the *Hercy family*, with whom it continued till Sir John de Hercy bequeathed it to his sister, who was married to George Neville, Esq., of Ragnall, with whose descendants it remained till the latter part of the 17th century, when Sir Edward Neville sold it to Sir Creswell Levinz. In 1762, William Levinz sold it to Anthony Eyre, Esq., of Rampton and Adwick,—the father of its present possessor, *Anthony Hardolph Eyre, Esq.*, of Grove Hall, who was a Lieut-Colonel in the 1st Regiment of Foot Guards, in which, his only son was unfortunately killed at the victory of Barrosa, in Spain, March 7th, 1811. He has three daughters, all married; the eldest to Earl Manvers, the second to Granville Venables Vernon, nephew to the Archbishop of York, and the third to Henry Gally Knight, Esq. His brother John, is now Archdeacon of Nottingham, and his brother George, was knighted for his gallantry in taking the Island of Santa Maria, and afterwards became an Admiral, and was distinguished with the honour of K. C. B. The family of Eyre came over with William the Conqueror, and settled at Hope, in Derbyshire, and Kiveton, in Yorkshire. They have now large estates in Nottinghamshire.

GROVE HALL, the beautiful seat of A. H. Eyre, Esq., who

has represented the county in Parliament; in conjunction with his son-in-law Lord Newark, has a commanding appearance when seen from the north road, being situated on a considerable elevation in the midst of a well wooded park. Of the ancient mansion built here by the Hercy family, nothing has been removed except the front, which is modern, and in a pleasing style of architecture; the other part of the house is certainly as old as Henry VIII.'s reign, and has been an edifice of great elegance according to the style of that period.

The CHURCH, a small gothic edifice dedicated to St. Helen, is seated on an eminence and surrounded by aged trees. It has a tower and two bells, and contains some curious antique monumental stones of the Hercy family. The living is a rectory valued in the King's books at £11. 14s. 2d. The lord of the manor, A. H. Eyre, Esq., is the patron, and the Rev. Abraham Youle, of West Retford is the incumbent. The Rectory house is a pleasing habitation with about 30 acres of glebe, and was liberally improved by the late rector, the Rev. Charles Eyre, who died in 1799, and was brother to the patron. Adjoining the churchyard are two ALMSHOUSES with each a garden, which were endowed in 1696 by Sir Christopher Levinz, with £10. 8s. per annum, for two poor people, who now receive 2s. each weekly, from the trustee, A. H. Eyre, Esq.

Eyre, Anthony Hardolph, Esq., Grove Hall	Freeman Joseph, farmer
Vernon Granville Harcourt, Esq , M. P., Grove Hall	Hill John, farmer
	Park William, gardener
Barlow George, parish clerk	Thompson John, farmer, Moor-house
Brown Edward, joiner	
Cocking Thomas, farmer	Unsworth Thomas, farmer

HEADON-CUM-UPTON PARISH

Comprises the hamlets of Upper and Nether Headon, Thorpe, and Upton, lying south of Grove, and mostly belonging to the same proprietor, A. H. Eyre, Esq., who is lord of the manor, part of which is the property of William Mason, Esq., and Mr. William Hill. The parish contains 56 houses, 248 inhabitants, and about 2000 acres of land. The *commons* were enclosed in 1817, when 184 acres were allotted to the impropriator, and 164 acres to the vicar, in lieu of tithes. The parish *feast* is on the Sunday before St. Peter's day, or on that day when it falls on a Sunday.

HEADON (NETHER AND UPPER,) are two hamlets distant a quarter of a mile from each other, and 4 miles S.W: by S. of Retford. HEADON HALL was built in 1710, by *Sir Hardolph Wastneys*, the last Baronet of his family, whose heiress carried it in marriage to Anthony Eyre, Esq., of Grove, father of the

2 K 2

present lord of the manor, who pulled down the hall in 1796, so that nothing now remains of the ancient seat of the Wastneys but the park. The *church* which stands at Upper Headon, is a large gothic structure dedicated to St. Peter, and contains some monuments of the Wastneys family. It is a curious fact, that the impropriate rector must be a clergyman, although he has no cure of souls in the parish, that duty being performed by the vicar, or his curate. The *sinecure rectory* is valued in the King's books at £15. 12s. 6d., and is now enjoyed by the Rev. Charles Harcourt Vernon. The *vicarage* is valued at £4. 3s. 4d., and the Rev. George Wastneys Eyre is the incumbent, for whom the Rev. George Gould officiates. A. H. Eyre, Esq., has the advowson of both livings, and has lately erected a *school* in the park, where about 20 poor children are educated at the expense of G. H. Vernon, Esq., and other members of his family.

THORPE is a hamlet and three farms, a little to the south of Upper Headon.

UPTON is a small village occupying the highest part of the parish, where there are 18 acres of hop plantations, 4¾ miles S.S.E. of Retford.

In the following Directory of Headon parish, those marked 1, live in Lower Headon; 2, in Upper Headon; 3, in Thorpe; 4, in Upton; ‡ are hop growers.

4Bamforth John, shoemaker
4Bellamy William, vict. White Horse
2Brown Edward, blacksmith
4Brown Robert, joiner
2Gould Rev. George, curate
1Pettinger George, joiner
1Rushby George, schoolmaster and parish clerk
4Smissons John, shoemaker
2Wilkinson Eliz. free school
4Wilkinson James, shoemaker
4Wilkinson Robert, shopkeeper

FARMERS.
3Brown Wm.
‡1Cocking J.
3Harpham Rd.
‡4Hill Geo.
‡4Hill Wm.
2Hilton John
4Houlton Wm.
‡4Ibberson J.
‡4Ibberson W.
4Lees John
4Lees T. & W.
4Nettleship S.
2Parkinson J.
‡1Ward William
3Whelpdale W.
4Wilkinson Wm. and maltster

KIRTON PARISH.

KIRTON or KIRKTON, is but a small parish, having only about 900 acres of land, 247 inhabitants, and 45 houses, forming a pleasant village at the foot of a steep and well wooded declivity, 3 miles E.N.E. of Ollerton. In 1612, the principal owners were the Earl of Shrewsbury, William Clarkson, the Corporation of East Retford, William and Robert Ingham, Henry Wright, and John Eastwood; but most of it now belongs to Henry Gally Knight, Esq., and the Hon. and Rev. J. L. Saville, the latter of whom is lord of the manor, which in Domesday book is called *Schidrington*, and was " of diverse fees." The *church* which has a lofty tower, is dedicated to the Holy Trinity. The living is a rectory, valued in the King's books at £7. 14s. 9½d. but is now endowed with 50 acres of old glebe, and 130 acres allotted at the enclosure in 1822, in lieu of all tithes. The Duke of Newcastle is the patron, and the Rev. Joseph Blandford, the incumbent. There are several *hop yards* in the parish, and many of the growers here have yards at Bevercotes. The *feast* is on the Sunday after Whitsuntide.

CHARITIES.—The Rev. J. Sykes, in 1622, left £10.; Lady Anne South, in 1659, £2.; and John Ambler, in 1692, £20. These sums were laid out in land, which, at the enclosure received an allotment, so that it now consists of more than three acres, let for £8. per annum, of which, 25s. is paid to a school-mistress, 11s. distributed at Christmas, and the rest is carried to the poor rates.

Those marked ‡ are Hop Growers.

Blandford Rev. Jph. rector	FARMERS.
Gilbert Wm. shoemaker	‡Camm Jthn. Lee Wm.
Hurt John, vict. & shoemaker	Chambers Isaac ‡Manuel Jasper
Roberts Thos. vict. Fox&Hounds	Dean Wm. Priest James
‡Rollitt John, wheelwright	‡Frogson Wm. ‡Wass Fras.
Stanfield Rt. corn miller	‡Gilbert John ‡Wass Mattw.
Wass Geo. vict. & blacksmith	‡Harvey John Watkinson John
Young John, shopr. & parish ck.	‡Jackson Geo. ‡WeightmanRd.
	‡Jepson Hy. ‡Woolhouse Chr

LANEHAM PARISH.

Is on the west side of the Trent, north of Dunham, 8 miles E. S. E. of Retford, and 7 miles N. E. by E. of Tuxford; containing about 1700 acres of land, and the hamlets of *HighTown* and *Low Town*, in which are 77 houses, occupied by 347 persons. The whole is in the liberty of Southwell and Scrooby, and with its *Berues* of Askham, Beckingham, Saundby, Bolham, West Burton, Wheatley, and Leverton, forms the Archbishop of York's *Manor and Soke of Laneham*, but the land is held by a number of freeholders and copyholders, the latter of whom, on the death or change of tenant pay a fine certain. The parish was enclosed about 50 years ago, and exonerated from tithe, except an estate belonging to Mrs. Minnitt, of Ollerton, who has the FERRY across the Trent—from which the largest assemblage of houses, called the High Town, is distant about half a mile. The Low Town is on the bank of the river, near the *church*, a small ancient fabric dedicated to St. Peter. The living, valued in the King's books at £5. 13s. 4d. has 28 acres of glebe, besides 4 acres purchased about thirty years ago, with a portion of Queen Anne's bounty. The Dean and Chapter of

York are the patrons, and the Rev. Edmund Wallas is the incumbent. The principal landholders are J. Beely, T. Newstead, J. Draper, Mrs. Minnitt, G. Cole, G. Goodger, and R. and T. Newboult. The *feast* is on the Sunday before Old Lammas.

Charities.—The poor of this parish have given to them 2s. worth of bread every Sunday, and a supply of coals in winter, from the rent of the *Poor's land*, (2 acres let for £11. 6s. !) and the following benefactions, viz. the interest of £10. left by W. Shelton; 20s. yearly, left in 1821, by Sarah Fillingham out of Clay-half close; and 13s. 4d. yearly out of three closes belonging to the vicar of Hablesthorp, left by an unknown donor.

Those marked † reside at Low Town.

Anderson Wm. blacksmith
†Atkinson Jonth. ferryman
Bagshaw Thos. corn miller
Blyth Mrs. Winnifred
Bonington Wm. tailor
Cobb George, joiner
Cooling W. vict. Butcher's Arms
†Cooper John, jun. wheelwright
Darley John, bricklayer
Darwin Wm. joiner
Draper Robert, gent.
Fletcher Thos. boat owner
Ginever Wm. boat owner
Hill James, shoemaker
Hill Wm. parish clerk
Keyworth John, vict. & maltster
Mason Geo. boat owner
Metham Rd. shopkeeper
Milner Geo. butcher
†Newstead Thomas, maltster, h. Dunham
Ostick John, maltster
Pettener Samuel, baker
Ruston Thos. boat owner

Scott Michael, shoemaker
Shuttleworth Hy. vict. Ring of Bells
Sims Mr. Wm.
Wallas Joseph, cooper
Warriner John, grocer & draper
Wheat Geo. shoemaker
Wheat John, tailor
Wildman Thos. schoolmaster

FARMERS.

Atkinson Jonth.
†Beeley John,(& maltster)
Binge Wm.
Bolton Geo.
Cartwright Tho.
†Cooper John
Darwin John
Goodger John
Ledger Thos.

Marshall Geo.
Marshall John
Newboult Rt.
Newboult Thos.
Nicholson Caleb
†Rawson Wm.
Smith Ed. John
†Tompkin Frs.
Walker Benj.
Walker John

Carrier, Geo. Bolton, to Retford, Sat. dep. 8 mg. ret. 8 evg.

LAXTON OR LEXINGTON PARISH.

This large parish which extends eastward from the lofty summit of Cockin Hill, to Ossington in Thurgarton Hundred, contains 3,955 acres of Land, of which 1245 acres are in open fields and commons, and 118 in woods and plantations. It comprises the long village of *Laxton*, the humble hamlet and chapelry of *Moorhouse* at its eastern extremity, and 10 scattered farmsteads called *Brecks, Brockilow, Cockin-Moor, Copthorne, Hartshorn, Knapeney, Laxton Lodge, Primrose-hill, Saywood,* and *Straw-Hall,* all within one mile and a half of the village. Its population amounts to 659 souls living in 120 houses, and its soil is generally a strong fertile clay, except about Moorhouse where there is a low swampy common, and some enclosed patches of black vegetable mould, abounding in shell-snails and ant-hills. More than two-thirds of the land belongs to Earl Manvers, who is lord of the manor; and the remainder, except a few small freeholds, is the property of the Hon. and Rev. J. L. Saville.

LAXTON or LEXINGTON, 3 miles S. by W. of Tuxford, and 5 miles E. of Ollerton, is a considerable village on a pleasant declivity, celebrated for having given the title of *Baron* to a family of its own name, and afterwards to the Suttons of Averham. Before the Norman invasion it belonged to *Tochi*, and was afterwards part of the fee of Goisfred de Alselin, which was in the reign of Henry I. divided into two great baronies possessed by Ralph de Alselin, of Shelford, and *Robert de Caux*, of *Lexington* or *Lessinton*. In the reign of John, *Richard de Lexington*, who had his name from the residence of his ancestors, held lands here of the de Caux family, and having purchased large estates at other places, was summoned to parliament under the title of *Baron Lexington*. Henry de Lexington, the fourth Baron Lexington died in 1257, when the title became extinct, and his property was divided betwixt his nephews and heirs, Richard de Marcham, and Wm. de Sutton, from the latter of whom descended *Robert Sutton*, who in 1645 was created *Baron Lexington of Averham*, but at the death of his successor of the same name, in 1723, the title again became extinct, and has not since been revived, though sometime ago, it was expected to have been conferred on that branch of the Sutton family now resident at Kelham, one of whom, Charles Manners Sutton, was Archbishop of Canterbury, from 1792 till his death in 1805; and his son of the same name, has long held the office of Speaker in the House of Commons, but none of them have now any property in this parish. Laxton is also remarkable as the birth place of *Wm. Chappell*, Bishop of Cork and Rosse, in Ireland, who died in 1649, and was eminent in learning, piety, and charity, and as Fuller says, " he parted his estates equally betwixt his own kindred and distressed ministers." The parish has also produced an instance of great herculean strength, in the person of the late *John White*, of Copthorne, who died January 6th, 1782, in his 70th year, and had long been famed as the heaviest and strongest man in the county, being in weight 33 stone, and having on many occasions displayed an equal preponderance of power, in the exercise of which he once took up a sack of wheat in his hands and threw it from him over a waggon which his servants were loading.

Laxton CHURCH, which stands on an eminence on the south west side of the village, is a large ancient structure, consisting of a spacious nave and chancel, with two side aisles, and a lofty tower in which are five musical bells. It is dedicated to St. Michael, and had once many beautiful monuments and armorial carvings and paintings of the ancient families of Roos, Evering-ham, Hastings, Gray, Longvillers, &c. but these are now either mutilated or totally gone, partly through the irresistible decay of time, but principally owing, according to Mr. Throsby's observations in 1795, to the unpardonable neglect of those who ought to have preserved them from wanton destruction. Throsby gives in particular a most horrid description of the accumula-tion of filth and broken tombs which he found in the north cemetry or chapel, but it is pleasing to observe that a change for the better has lately taken place. The *chapel* which has long been used as the parish school has been cleansed, and three effigies of *Crusaders* in full armour, have been removed from the mischievous company of the scholars into the chancel, where there are three other recumbent figures on a tomb nearly six feet high, representing another crusading knight and his two wives. At the south east corner of the nave is a curious square pew, on which is carved a shield with five weeping eyes upon it, and this inscription—" *Robert Trafford, Vic. de Laxton, hoc fieri fecit, Anno Domini*, 1532." There was anciently a *chantry* in the church, endowed with land in the parish. The rectory was appropriated to Jesus' college, in Rotherham, which was found-ed by Thomas Rotherham, Archbishop of York, in 1500, but the patronage and impropriation now belong to Earl Manvers. The benefice is a *vicarage* now enjoyed by the Rev: Richard Procter, and is valued in the King's books at £11. and by Bacon at £38. 10s. 6d. A little north of the church is a coni-cal hill which has had a deep *moat* round it, and is supposed to be the site of an exploratory tower erected by one of the early lords of the manor, to communicate with another raised by his kinsman at Egmanton. The annual FEAST is on the nearest Sunday to Old Michaelmas Day.

MOORHOUSE, 1½ mile E. of Laxton, and 3 miles S. by E. of Tuxford, is a small hamlet and chapelry, consisting of eleven small farms, and about 20 humble dwellings, dispersed round an extensive quagmire green or common, from which it has ob-tained the distinctive name of *Moorhouse-in-the-Bogs.* It has a constable, and repairs its own roads, but maintains its poor conjointly with Laxton. The *chapel* is a very small ancient building, which has lately been cleansed and repaired, previous to which its clumsy and decayed oaken benches were so worn by the tooth of time as to tremble under the monthly pressure of its slender congregation. It had formerly a *guild* or *chantry*, endowed with land in the hamlet. The *curacy* is annexed to the vicarage of Laxton, and is endowed with the rectorial tithes of the chapelry, all the land in which belongs to Earl Manvers, except two small farms belonging to J. E. Dennison, Esq. and

Mr. Francis White; the latter of whom, found in 1831, three human *skeletons* buried in a close, where tradition says there were formerly several houses, the inhabitants of which are said all to have died of the plague. Some years before, the head and part of a human body was found in the field called *Esther King's*. The *sand* which is washed from the higher grounds into the drains that intersect the quagmire, is, by the petrifying quality of the peat water, transformed into a hard porous substance resembling pumice stone.

The CHARITIES belonging to Laxton parish are as follows. The *schoolmaster* teaches ten poor children, for the use of the school in the church, and 40s. yearly paid by Samuel Wheatcroft, of Norwell, as the interest of £40. left many years ago, by an unknown donor. *John White*, merchant, of Sheffield, but a native of this parish, by will dated Septr. 26th, 1806, left £40. to the poor, to be distributed in bread. He was son of the before named John White, of herculean memory, and great uncle to the author of this work. His legacy is now in the hands of his nephew, Wm. White, of Copthorne, who pays 40s. yearly interest. *John Hunt*, in 1818, left £100. and *George Lee*, in 1822, a yearly rent charge of 20s. for the same charitable purpose. The £100. is now lent on mortgage of a close belonging to William Stanfield. These doles of bread, amounting to £9. per annum, are distributed by the overseers and churchwardens on Christmas and New Year's Day. The CHURCH-LAND, appropriated for the repairs of the church, consists of 13A. 3R. 6P. situated in the *West-field*, the *Southfield*, the *Millfield*, and the *Inclosure*, as described minutely upon a tablet in the church. No deeds can be found relating to it, but the yearly rents amounting to £28. 3s. 6d. are always carried to the churchwardens' general account. The homestead with all the land is occupied by John Cook, except a rood, rented by Wm. Pinder, jun. and 35 perches in *Saville's Tenter-close*, held by Mr. Thomas Newstead.

LAXTON DIRECTORY.

Bowman John, wheelwright
Clarborough Jph. shoemaker
Clover Jph. shoemaker
Dewick Thos. tailor
Dewick Wm. parish clerk
Gabbitas John, shoemaker
Giles John, blacksmith
Hurt Thos. vict. Volunteer and blacksmith
Johnson Rd. blacksmith
Lacey Wm. shopkeeper
Newboult John, shopkeeper
Pearse John, woodman, *Saywood*
Pinder Geo. vict. Sun
Pinder Saml. butcher
Procter Rev. Rd. vicar, *Vicarage house*
Rose John, bricklayer
Rushby Wm. shopkeeper
Twibell Jas. gent.
Twibell John, gamekeeper
Truswell John, schoolmaster
White John, corn miller
Woodward Ann, shoemaker
Wright John, tailor
Wright Sarah, vict. Dove Cote
Wright Wm. tailor & draper

FARMERS.
Marked * *are Yeomen.*

Bartram Wm. *Keyworth Rd.
Burkitt John Lambert Thos.
Brownlow Robt. Straw Hall
Knapeney *Lee Mary
Cook John Lee Rt.
Doncaster Mr. Lee Wm.
Middlethorp MerryweatherG.
Eyre Robert. Newstead Thos.
Breck-wong Nicholson Wm.
*Glazebrook W. Cockin Moor
Hopkin Wm. Pearse Edmund,
Johnson Wm. Saywood
Keyworth John Peatfield Wm.

Peck George, *Taylor George
Brockilow Weatherall Rt.
Pickin John White William,
Pinder Wm. Copthorne
*Pinder Wm. Whittington W.
Pinder Wm. Woombill John,
Quibell Wm. Laxton Lodge
Swinman Ann Wright Mary
(MOORHOUSE.) FARMERS.
Bartle Geo. Jepson John
Bartle Jthn. Palian Martin
Clarke John vict. Ship
Greasby Wm. White Edw.
Harpham Robt. White Fras.
Harpham Wm. White Wm.

MARKHAM (EAST) PARISH.

Includes *Markham Moor*, on the great north road, and extends
about two miles eastward from the river Idle. It has 2,700
acres of land, 188 houses, and 805 inhabitants. The moor was
enclosed in 1810 and 1811, when land was allotted as a commutation of all the tithes of the parish, which since then, has
been greatly improved by many new buildings, and carriage and
foot roads, all upon a liberal scale. The soil is generally a fertile clay, and some of it is planted with hops. The greater
part of it belongs to the Duke of Newcastle, who is also impropriator and lord of the manor, but Mrs. Frances Cartwright,
Wm. Kirk, John and Thomas Rose, and some others, have
small estates here.

EAST MARKHAM, on the road to Dunham Bridge, 1¼ miles
N. of Tuxford, is a large and handsome village, seated on a
pleasant declivity. It has a fine large gothic *church*, with a
lofty embattled tower and four bells, dedicated to St. John the
Baptist, and still retaining several ancient monuments and armorial paintings of the Markhams, Cressys, Merrings, and
others. The living, which is in the patronage of the Duke of
Newcastle, is a vicarage valued in the King's books at £11, 8s.
11¼d. and has annexed to it that of West Drayton. The Rev.
Sherarad Becher, is the incumbent. Before the conquest there
was here a church and a priest, and the parish was divided into
several manors and was partly " *Soc* to Dunham," but all of it
was afterwards of the fee of Roger de Busli, and was held successively by the Thurold, Cressy, Chevercourt, Lynham,
Marcham, Bosevill, Topcliffe, Williamson, Hewett, and other
families. *Avicia*, wife of Jordan de Chevercourt, gave to the
monks of Blyth one bovate of land here, " for a refection of
the monks on the day of her anniversary, that by their inter-

cession, her soul in heaven might have a refection with celestial meat and drink." *Richard de Marcham* granted to the said monks 20s. yearly, for the moiety of the mill at *Murihield Bridge*, which is now unknown, except it refers to the *Mirfield Hall Estate*, now the property and residence of Mrs. Cartwright. The church, like that at West Markham, was anciently annexed to the King's chapel, at Tickhill, and was granted by Philip and Mary, to the Abbey of St. Peter's, in Westminster.

SIR JOHN MARKHAM, who was knighted by Edward IV., and made Lord Chief Justice of the King's Bench, " in room of Sir John Fortescue," was a native of this parish, and lies interred in the chancel under a tomb which bears the date 1409. He was as learned and as upright a judge as ever sat on the bench, and Fuller calls him and his predecessor " the two Chief Justices of the Chief Justices, for their singular integrity; for though one of them favoured the House of Lancaster, the other of York, in the titles to the crown, both of them favoured the *house of justice*, in matters betwixt party and party." When Sir Thomas Cook, Lord Mayor of London, was arraigned for high treason on a charge of having supplied Margaret of Anjou with money during the wars of the roses, his life and lands were saved, by Judge Markham directing the jury to find it only misprision of treason. This so offended Edward IV., that the honest Chief Justice was ousted from office, and lived privately during the rest of his life.

MARKHAM-MOOR, at the west end of the parish, on the great north road, 2 miles N.N.W. of Tuxford, is celebrated for a comfortable inn, used as a posting stage by the various public conveyances. Since the inclosure in 1810, several good houses have been built here on CLEVELAND-HILL and SIBCOCK-HILL, near which is *Priestgate*, the road that leads to East or Great Markham, which is distant 1½ mile to the east.

The SCHOOL at East Markham is endowed with two yearly rent charges of £5 each, one left in 1706 by *James Gunthorpe*, and now paid out of 36 acres of land at Markham-moor, belonging to the Jackson family; and the other bequeathed in 1713 by *William Dunstan*, out of Southunderwood close, which is now the property of William Kirk, Esq. For these sums the master teaches 20 poor children, who are provided with shoes or other articles of clothing, purchased with four guineas paid as the interest of £105, which is lent to William Kirk, Esq., and arose from £50 left to the poor in 1725, by *Jeremiah Elliot*, and from several balances saved by the former trustees of the school, for which the vicar is receiver.

BREAD MONEY, &c.—*John Atkinson*, in 1753, left a house and 16A. 0R. 36P. of land at East Markham, in trust, to distribute the yearly rent (now £21) to the poor in weekly doles of bread every Sunday, at the church. William Mason, Esq.,

2 L

is the only surviving trustee. In 1772, *Ellen Cosen* left £50, and directed the interest to be given to the poor at Christmas, by the vicar. An unknown donor left £22, for which Joseph Tomlinson gives a ton of coal yearly to the poor of the parish.

*Those marked ‡ are Hop Growers, and * Yeomen, thus † live at Markham-moor, and § Cleveland-hill.*

Appleby Thomas, weaver
Atkinson Richard, baker & shopkeeper
Becher Rev. Sherarad, vicar
Bingham Wm. joiner
†Blenkhorn Mrs. Ann
Booth John, vict. schoolmaster, & parish clerk
‡Bowman John, butcher
†Bradley Jonth. victualler, Black Horse
†Brown Saml. road surveyor & shopkeeper
Burrows Wm. shoemaker
Cartwright Mrs. Fras. gentlewoman, Mirfield Hall
Cooper Edward, farrier
Dixon Thomas, horse dealer
Fox Thos. grocer & draper
Freeman Wm. corn miller
Gabbitas Wm. gardener, Kingshaugh Common
Gregg Wm. shoemaker
Hall Jas. vict. Crown Inn, Sibcock Hill
Harrison John, shoemaker
Hempsall Mark, weaver
Hempsall Rt. joiner & shopkpr
Hodgkinson George, saddler
†Hunt Geo. blacksmith
Hurst Saml. beer house
Hutchinson Wm. brick & tile maker, h. Sutton
†Jackson Mrs. Mary Ann
Leach John, tailor
Leach Wm. tailor
Lightfoot Thomas, corn miller, Priestgate
Littlewood John, tailor
Littlewood Samuel, tailor
Moss Wm. tailor
Moss Wm. wheelwright
Otter Mr. Hollis
Parker Frank, vict. & shoemkr. Old England

Parker Geo. shoemaker & shopkeeper
Richards Geo. vict. Greyhound
‡Richards Wm. vict. Bottle and Glass
Rose Mrs. Ann
‡Rose John, Esq
§Scott Wm. vict. White Hart
§Sculthorp Mrs. Eliz
Staniland Chpr. shoemaker
Stockdale John, blacksmith
Stockdale Jph. nerseryman, Sibcock hill
†Sunderland Squire, bar-keeper
Swinglehurst John, beerhouse
Thompson Saml. bricklayer
Thompson Wm. vict. bricklayer
White John, blacksmith
Willies Matthew, bricklayer
Willies Thos. bricklayer
Wilson John, joiner

FARMERS.

Betts George
Billiald Sus.
*Billiald Thos.
*Billiald Wm.
Booth Geo.
*Butler Geo.
Clark John
‡Clark Samuel
*Cobb Richard
Cook Geo.
Dixon Ann, Priestgate
*Harrison, Wm.
Hempsall Geo.
Hempsall Jas.
†Jackson Eliz.
Jackson Jerb.
*Jackson Gerv.
‡*Lees Rd. and maltster
†Long Wm.
*Maples Job.

Marriott Wm.
Brecks
Moss Benj.
Quibell Benj.
Quibell William, Brecks
Bayner Jas.
‡*Rose Thos.
‡*Simpson Wm.
Smith Chas.
Smith Geo.
§Spencer Thos.
brick maker, Hill
Spencer Wm. & maltster
Stockdale Wm.
‡Swinglehurst J. & maltster
†Taylor Wm.
*Walters Jas.
Walters John
‡Walters Wm.

MARKHAM (WEST) PARISH

Occupies a picturesque situation betwixt the north road and the river Idle, south of Markham-moor. It contains about 1000 acres of land, and the two small villages of *West Markham and Milton*, in which are only 44 houses and 197 inhabitants.

WEST MARKHAM, or, as it is sometimes called, *Little Markham*, stands on a pleasant declivity above the vale of the Idle, and a little to the west of the north road, 1¼ mile N.W. of Tuxford. The ancient church, dedicated to All Saints, is a small edifice at the foot of the village, but it is now superseded by a beautiful NEW CHURCH, erected in 1831-2, upon a commanding eminence, by his Grace the Duke of Newcastle, who has formed two splendid chapels in the transept, with spacious vaults under them, intended as the future place of sepulchre for his family. It is in the Grecian Doric order, with a portico at the east end, and a handsome octagonal tower rising from the centre, and crowned by a handsome dome. The length of the fabric from east to west is 105 feet, its width in the chancel 32 feet, and in the transept 57 feet. The whole was constructed from a plan by Robert Smirke, Esq., the celebrated architect of London. Adjoining the churchyard, is the vicarage-house, an elegant Swiss building, also erected at the expense of the Duke of Newcastle, who is lord of the manor, owner of the greater portion of the land, and lessee of the remainder under the Masters and Fellows of St. John's College, Cambridge. His Grace is also lay-rector, and patron of the vicarage, which is valued in the King's books at £7. 12s. 1d., and has attached to the cure of Bevercotes, which adjoins this parish on the west, and has been many years without a church. The Rev. E. H. Dawkins now enjoys the living, which was anciently appropriated to Westminster Abbey. The manor was of the fee of Roger de Busli, and had *soc* in Grove, Drayton, and Tuxford; and the church had tithes and offerings in the latter parish, as appears by a composition dated 1179.

MILTON, or *Milneton*, half a mile N.W. of West Markham, stands on an eminence on the east bank of the Idle, and derives its name from an ancient mill, of which every vestage has long since disappeared.

CHARITIES.—The yearly rents of the following lands, amounting to £8. 11s., are distributed amongst the poor of the parish, on the Friday before Whitsuntide, and on St. Thomas' day, viz. 3A. 2R. in Nether Westwood; 1A. 15P. in Millfield; and 1A. 39P. at Mill-hill, in Tuxford; all allotted at the enclosure; when £20 left by John Minnett, in 1758, and some other benefactions were called in and expended in fencing and cultivating the said poors' land. In 1721, *Richard Miller* left £200, now secured on an estate at East Markham, belonging to William Kirke, Esq., who pays the interest, £8, to a schoolmaster for the education of 15 poor children.

WEST MARKHAM.

Bell Leonard, farmer
Booth Benj. farmer
Booth Benj. jun. farmer
Booth Wm. tailor & shopkpr.
Dawkins Rev. E. H. vicar
Denman Jph. farmer
Hempsall Thos. farmer & parish clerk
Johnson Thos. farmer
Tindall Thos. farmer

MILTON.

Bailey Eliz. farmer
Billyard Rd. farmer
Clayton John, joiner
Gabbitas Geo. shomaker
Gilbert John, farmer
Manuel Edward, farmer & hop grower.
Pierrepoint Jph. Downing, farmer
Pierrepoint Wm. farmer
Wood Wm. farmer

OMPTON TOWNSHIP.

Ompton, or Almpton, is a small village and township in *Knecsall parish,* the rest of which is in the Hundred of Thurgarton, and will be there described. It is 3 miles S.E. by E. of Ollerton, on the Newark road, and contains 20 houses, 120 inhabitants, and about 600 acres of land, all belonging to the Hon. and Rev. J. L. Saville. In Domesday Book it is called *Almentune,* and represented as *soc* to several manors, but most of it was subsequently given to the monasteries of Rufford and Lenton. The great tithes belong to the Chapter of Southwell, but Earl Manvers is the lessee.

Marked thus ‡ are Hop Growers, and the rest Farmers.

Bennet Wm. shopkeeper
‡Harvey John
Saxelby Michael
Scratchard Jtn.
Ward William
‡Wombwell John
Wombwell Wm.

RAGNALL PAROCHIAL CHAPELRY,

Is, like its neighbour Darlton, a member of the vicarage of Dunham, and contains about 1000 acres, 36 houses, and 168 inhabitants. Its small village is near the Dunham road, 5 miles E.N.E. of Tuxford. The church or chapel is a small ancient fabric, which has been repaired with £150, obtained by selling the poor's land allotted at the enclosure of Dunham and Ragnall. John Angersteen, Esq., is lord of the manor, and owner of nearly all the land, 100 acres of which is extra-parochial; perhaps from its being the ancient demesne attached to Kingshaugh House.—(See Darlton, p. 364, and Dunham, p. 366.)—The *Hall,* now a farm house, was occupied by Charles Mellish, Esq., who died in 1781, when £50, vested with him, and left to the poor of Ragnall by one of his family, was lost.

Barthorp Edwin, farmer, Hall
Hempstock, Samuel, shoemaker
Hempstock, Wm. blacksmith
Horner, James, brickmaker
Markham Mary, schoolrs.
Quibell John, shoemaker

Redgate Geo. farmer. Wimpens
Roberts Wm. farmer and chapel
  clerk
Walker Benjamin, victualler and
  joiner
Wilson George, farmer

RAMPTON PARISH.

RAMPTON is a good village, six miles E.S.E. of Retford, and about one mile from the Trent, to which its parish extends opposite to Torksey Ferry, where there are in Lincolnshire, the ruins of an ancient castle. It contains 67 houses, 411 inhabitants, and about 2000 acres of land, mostly belonging to Anthony Hardolph Eyre, Esq., the lord of the manor, to whom it has descended in regular succession from a period soon after the conquest, when it was of the fee of Roger de Busli. *Rampton Hall* which was built in the reign of Henry VIII. was pulled down about 120 years ago, except a very curious *gateway* which still remains, and is highly ornamented with the armorial bearings of the Stanhope, Babyngton, and Eyre families, of whom there are many sepulchral memorials in the church. This manor descended by marriage from the knightly family of *Stanhope* to that of *Babyngton*, and from the latter to the *Eyres* of Grove, one of whose maternal ancestors was *Lady Pakynton*, of Westwood House, Worcestershire, the pious authoress of the original " *Whole Duty of Man*," which was written partly for the purpose of correcting the vices which prevailed during the civil wars of Charles I., in whose defence Colonel Sir Gervase Eyre, who espoused the heiress of the Babyngtons, lost his life at the seige of Newark:

The CHURCH, dedicated to All Saints, is large and handsome, with a lofty tower. It is in the patronage and appropriation of its own *prebendary* in Southwell Collegiate Church. The vicarage is valued in the King's books at £10, and is now enjoyed by the Rev. Richard Barrow. It has been augmented with Queen Anne's Bounty, with which land was purchased in the Isle of Axholme, and it has about 30 acres of old glebe. A. H. Eyre, Esq. is lessee of the prebendal tithes. About one half the parish is enclosed, and has a rich clay soil, but the rest consists of a common and a large open fertile marsh, divided by land marks, and protected from inundation by a strong embankment on the Trent.

CHARITIES.—In 1703, *Gervas Cole* left two closes (now let for £3. 18s.) and directed the rents to be distributed in weekly portions of bread every Sunday. In 1734, four acres of land in Treswell was purchased with £110. 5s. bequeathed by several of the Eyre family, and is now let for £8, which is paid yearly to the trustee, A. H. Eyre, Esq. who transmits it to the vicar, together with £2, as the interest of £50, left by *Diana Egre* in 1763. This £10 is distributed amongst the poor on St. Thomas's day. The SCHOOL is endowed with 3½ acres of Rampton Marsh, and three cow gates on the common, worth together about £4 per annum, for which the master teaches 13 poor children. The founder is unknown. The profit of the *first grass* of an acre of the Marsh belongs to the poor. The Marsh, after being mown, is thrown open as a common.

Bingham Rt. grocer & draper
Brown Rt. parish clerk
Brown Thos. joiner
Butler Geo. vict. Swan
Chambers Thos. corn miller
Flower Isaac, vict. Nag's Head
Gunthorpe Geo. shoemaker
Hill Thos. tailor
Hurst John, vict. Wheat Sheaf
Milner Geo. butcher
Otter Chas. tailor
Otter Thos. tailor
Richmond Chpr. whgt. & smith
Scott John & Wm. shoemakers
Spencer Geo. shoemaker
Twedell Jph. schoolmaster
Wallas Rev. Edmund, curate

Wheat Wm. tailor
Wright Geo. blacksmith

FARMERS.

Bacon John
Binge John
Bingham Rd.
Bingham Wm.
Binney John
Butler Geo.
Butler Wm.
Chambers Thos.
Cocking Rt.
Coulson Wm.
Douglas Wm.
Draper Jonth.
Elsom John
Fisher Saml.
Freeman Nichls.
Key Henry
Ledger Thos.
Levick Saml.
Marshall Geo.
Pigott Geo.
Priest Jonth.
Scott Jph.
Simpson Thos.
Turner Wm. and maltster
Ward John
Wells Thos.

STOKEHAM PARISH.

STOKEHAM is but a small hamlet and parish, five miles N.E. of Tuxford, containing only 8 houses, 48 inhabitants, and about 600 acres of land, nearly all of which is the freehold property of five of the inhabitants; but Earl Manvers is lord of the manor, which in Domesday Book is called *Estoches*, and was *soc* to Fledborough, of the fee of the Bishop of Lincoln. It was successively held by the families of Lysure, Bassett, Swift, and Amstrudders.

The CHURCH is a small fabric, annexed to the *vicarage of East Drayton*, which has all the tithes of the parish. (See page 364.) The Rev. Charles J. Sympson is the incumbent, and the Rev. A. Galland, the curate. Of the following inhabitants all are yeomen except the two last:—

Keeton Thomas
Lynn William
Otter John & William
Quibell Joseph
Ward George
Williamson Mrs. D.

TRESWELL PARISH.

TRESWELL, or TIRESWELLE, four and a half miles E. by S. of Retford, is a tolerable village and parish, having 49 houses, 224 inhabitants, and about 1,700 acres of land, all of which is a fertile clay, except the east end, which is sandy, and adjoins the Trent marsh. A. H. Eyre, Esq. is lord of the manor, but the land belongs to several proprietors, amongst whom are, William Wells, Henry Parnell, John Holmes, and William Hutchinson, Esqrs. It was anciently in two manors, called the *East and West Hold*, the latter of which was long the property and residence of the Mustera family, who held it of the Richmond fee; and the other, which was held of the Tickhill fee, passed from Roger, the tenant of Roger de Busli, to William de Lovetot, who gave his portion of the church here to Worksop priory. These manors were afterwards united in the Hercy family, and from them passed to the Roos's and the Broughton's. The *Church* is an ancient structure, with a lofty embattled tower, and is dedicated to St. John the Baptist. The *Rectory* was, like the manor, in two medieties valued in the King's books, one at £9. 15s. 8d. and the other at £8. 1s. 4d., but it was consolidated in 1764, and is now in the alternate patronage of the Dean and Chapter of York, and the heirs of the Stephenson family. The Rev. Robert Affleck, of Silkstone, Yorkshire, is the rector, and the Rev. John Mickle, the curate. A small *Methodist Chapel* was built here in 1825. The *Feast* is held on Old Midsummer Day.

Briggs John, bricklayer
Gyles Mrs. Catherine
Norman John, vict. Red Lion
Radford Wm. grocer
Temporal John, shoemaker
Whitehead John, shoemaker
Young Jas. shoemaker

FARMERS.
Marked § are Yeomen.
§Cocking John §Hewitt John

Levick Samuel,Taylor Jph.
Foreward   §Temporal Ann
Levick John   §Turner Jonth.
Linley Richard,§Wells John,
  Woodhouse   Quibell
§Lumby Wm.,   §White Thos.
Popple John   §Whitehead Jno.
Skelton Jph.   §Whitehead W.
§Smith William,
  Floss house

TUXFORD PARISH

Is about two miles and three furlongs in length, and is intersected by the Great North road, and nearly eight miles of bye roads. It contains 232 houses, 1,113 inhabitants, and 2913A. 1R. 21P. of good clay land, which was enclosed in 1799, when the tithes were commuted for two allotments, viz. 326A. 2R. 39P. to the appropriators, and 103A. 3R. 27P. to the vicar, in

addition to 8A. 2R. 11P. of old glebe. In Saxon times, Tuxford or *Tuxfarn* formed two manors, but after the Conquest it
was part of the fee of Roger de Busli, and had *soc* in 'Schi-
drinton* and *Walesby.* It was afterwards held by the Lexing-
tons, the Longvillers, the Suttons, and the Markhams, from the
latter of whom it passed to three co-heiresses, and has since
undergone a further sub-division, so that it now belongs to several
proprietors;—the farms at *Merrifields, Scarthing Moor Bridge,*
and *Tuxford Lodge,* are the property of the Duke of Newcastle, and those at *Westwood* and *Cock Park* belong to the Hon.
and Rev. J. L. Saville, and to Trinity and St. John's Colleges,
in Cambridge. *Mill Hill,* where there are two wind-mills,
and *Holywell* a spring of cold water, noted for curing rheu-
matism and scurvy, are both in this parish.

  TUXFORD, which stands on the North road, in the centre
of the parish, and contains most of its population, is a small
market town, seven miles S. by E. of Retford, 28 miles N.N.E.
of Nottingham, and 137 miles N. by W. of London. It has a
good weekly *market* on Monday, and two annual *fairs,* viz. on
May 12th for cattle, sheep, millinery, &c., and September 25th
for *hops,* of which considerable quantities are raised in the
vicinity. A great part of the town was burnt down on September 8th, 1702, and afterwards rebuilt, so that it has now a
modern appearance. It has no manufactures, but being a great
thoroughfare, and the centre of a very productive agricultural
district, its market and fairs are well supported, and its inns
and taverns derive much of their prosperity from the numerous
travellers constantly passing to the north and south. It is a
well-known posting stage, and is often called *Tuxford-in-the-
Clay.* The CHURCH, which stands opposite to the principal
inn, is dedicated to St. Nicholas, consists of a nave and side
aisle, and has a spire with five good bells. All the ancient
monuments mentioned by Thoroton, as well as the armorial
glass, are in a state of decay; there is, however, still in existence a representation of *St. Lawrence roasting on a grid-
iron;* one man is employed in blowing the fire, another turning him with a pair of tongs, and a third looking on; also some
specimens in the north porch of a priest in the attitude of
prayer. This latter is on a stone of a coffin shape; the figure
is only a bust, with his head shaven, and a cushion under it,
accompanied by a quatrefoil, rondeau, chalice, and paten, the
emblems of the sacerdotal office. In the north wall also is a
very ancient figure of a lady in a square head dress, strait sur-
coat, and long sleeves, and a hound at her feet; opposite to her
is an altar tomb with the mutilated trunk of an armed knight;
but the armorial bearings are too obscure to be ascertained. Of
its former history, we find recorded in Tanner, that here was
a college founded by John de Longvillers, who obtained leave
to place in the parsonage house here a *college* of five chaplains,

one of whom to be warden; but that not taking effect, he got leave from Edward III. to give this advowson to Newstead priory, that they might find five chaunting priests, viz. three at Tuxford, and two at their own conventual church, whose duty should be to pray for his soul, &c.

In 1545, Henry VIII. gave the *patronage* and *appropriation* to Trinity college, Cambridge, to which institution they still belong. The *vicarage* is valued in the King's books at £4. 14s. 7d. and the Rev. Edward Bishop Elliott is the incumbent. The church was repaired and its pews renewed in 1811, at the cost of £1400, and in 1812, a small organ was purchased by subscription, for £100. The vicarage house is a handsome mansion surrounded by tasteful shrubberies, &c. About 35 years ago, Mr. Samuel Waddington, brother of the late vicar of Tuxford, was prosecuted and heavily fined, for monopolising hops. On his trial, he said "the *hop grounds* were the *gold mines of England.*" Since then the hop yards in this neighbourhood have been greatly reduced. The *Methodist chapel*, in Eldon-street, was built in 1809. The *workhouse* was erected in 1828, in lieu of the old one, which stood in Newcastle-street. The *prison* or lock-up, with the *pinfold* behind it, was constructed in 1823. The parish enjoys three public schools, and several benefactions.

The *Grammar School*, which is held in a well-built house, and has long been in considerable repute, was founded in 1669, by Mr. Charles Read, who gave £200 towards building the school-house, and endowed it with lands at Falkingham, in Lincolnshire, which appear to have been exchanged for a yearly rent charge of £48. 15s. 5d. paid by Sir Gilbert Heathcote, Bart. Of the rents he directed £20 to be paid to the master, and £5 each yearly to four of the scholars, who must be sons of poor widows of ministers, or of decayed gentry, and be admitted at the age of seven or upwards, and remain till they arrive at sixteen, when their places are to be supplied by others. The master has the free use of a house and garden, and is allowed to take boarders. The founder made a similar bequest to Corby, in Lincolnshire, and appointed six trustees at each place, and the mayor and aldermen of Grantham to be visitors.

The *Girls' National* and the *Infant Schools* form one building, with two dwellings in the centre for the teachers, and were built in 1830, on the vicarage land, at the cost of about £400, by the present vicar, aided by individual subscriptions, a grant of £40 from the National Society, and £30 from Trinity College. There are now upwards of 50 girls and 50 infants in these seminaries, which are supported by the vicar and voluntary contributions.

BENEFACTIONS.—Lady White left to the poor a close of 12 acres adjoining Westwood common. At the enclosure it received an allotment, and is now let for £21 per annum. In

1750, the sum of £50, left by Wm. Railton, and fifteen smaller donations, amounting collectively to £171. 10s., were laid out in the purchase of the *poors' land*, consisting of 9¾ acres, in three closes, at Tuxford and Normanton, now let for £17. 6s. 7d. yearly, which is distributed at Whitsuntide and on St. Thomas' day, except 10s. to the vicar for a sermon on Good Friday.— These closes are exonerated from tithe. The *church land*, consisting of Scarthingmoor close, 5A. 2R., and an allotment made at the enclosure, called Long-lands, and containing 2A. 3R., was let on a lease for 21 years in 1813, at the trifling yearly rent of one shilling, in consideration of a fine of £416, which was expended in repairing the church, for which purpose the land was bequeathed, but by whom is now unknown.

The POST OFFICE is in the Market-place, at Mrs. Mary Scott's. Letters are despatched to London and the South at half-past two afternoon, and to Edinbro' and the North at half-past eleven morning.

TUXFORD DIRECTORY.

Marked 1 *are Farmers.*

Appleby Mrs. Mary, Manvers st
Barker Mr. Thos. Newcastle st
1 Beedham Saml. Lincoln st
Bennett Mrs. Sarah, Manvers st
1 Blagg Ann, Lodge
1 Bowman Thos. Merrifields
1 Bowman John, Eldon st
1 Briggs George, Lincoln st
Briggs Mr. Joseph, Chandos st
Briggs Robt. sen. gent. Eldon st
1 Briggs Robt. jun. Newcastle st
Brooke Mrs. Mgt. Newcastle st
Brown Wm. letter carrier, Eldon street
1 Brumby Geo. Newcastle st
Cocking Mrs. Ann, Lincoln st
Clark Mr. Jas. Church yard
Creed Dorothy, baker, Eldon st
Curtis Sarah, matron. poorhouse
Cotton Geo. turner & spinning-wheel mfr. Eldon st
Cotton Saml. cooper, Mill hill
1 Daft Saml. Newcastle st
Day Mrs. Maria, Eldon st
1 Denby Rd. Scarthing moor bdg
Elliott Rev. Ed. Bishop, vicar
Ellis Geo. toy dlr. Newcastle st
Ellis Mark, toy dlr. Newcastle st
1 Glossop Saml. Westwood

Hall Thos. coachman, Newcastle street
1 Jackson Jph. Eldon st
Jameson Jno. veterinary surgeon, Newcastle street
Keyworth Mrs. Jane, Manvers st
Ludlam Isaac, solicitor, & agent to the Yorkshire Fire and Life office, Newcastle street
Ludlam Wm. gent. Newcastle st,
Marshall Wm. hair dresser & patten mkr. Market place
Mason Rev. John, curate of Bothamsall, Market place
1 Metheringham John, Westwood
1 Newcombe John, Eldon st
Pratt Geo. hosier, Newcastle st
1 Read John, Newcastle st
Shacklock John, hat mfr. Newcastle street
Shelton Mrs. Sarah, Manvers st
Storey Benj. watch mkr. Eldon st
Taylor Thos. town crier, Lincoln street
Turner Wm. gent. Eldon st
1 Tustin Ann, Lincoln st
1 Unwin Mark, Lincoln st
Warriner Jph. fellmonger, Newcastle street

1 Watmough Edw. Newcastle st
1 Weightman John, Newcastle st
White Lady Eliz. Lincoln st
ACADEMIES.
Grammar School, Lincoln street,
  Martin Bower
Girls' National & Infant, South
  broad, Susanna Hopper & Fanny
  Easterfield
Holmes Margt. (ladies' bdg. &
  -day) Eldon street
Thornton Ann, Eldon st
BAKERS & FLOUR DLRS.
Scott Mary, Market place
Wilson Matthias & Co. Eldon st
BLACKSMITHS.
Taylor Wm. Newcastle st
White Wm. Eldon street
BOOT & SHOE MKRS.
Browne William, Eldon st
Daft John, Chapel yard
Gascoyne Edw. Newcastle st
Johnson William, Eldon st
Savage Jonathan, Manvers st
Scarliff John, Eldon st
Scarliff Wm. Newcastle st
Smith Robert, Eldon st
Tunnard John, Eldon st
Whitworth Thos. Newcastle st
BRAZIERS & TINMEN.
Clark Mary, Eldon st
Rates Thos. Newcastle st
BRICKLAYERS.
Richardson John, Eldon st
Stoakes John, Newcastle st
Thompson John, Newcastle st
BRICK MAKERS.
Moss John, Mill hill
Salmon Wm. Clark's lane
BUTCHERS.
Crome Wm. Chandos court
Flower Wm. Chapel yd
Spurr Fras. Market place
Watmough John, Mill hill
CORN MILLERS.
Birkett Thos. Newcastle st
Leonard Wm. Mill hill
CURRIERS, &c.
Buxton Robt. Eldon st
Story John, Market place
DRUGGISTS.
Appleby Wm. Eldon st
Cowlishaw Rd. Hy. Eldon st

Hemsworth Wm. Newcastle st
Naylor Thos. Market place
EARTHENWARE DLRS.
Bacon Saml. (dlr.) Newcastle st
Moss John, (mfr.) Mill hill
GROCERS & TEA DLRS.
Clark Mary, Eldon st
Keyworth John, (& tallow chand-
  ler & wine & spirit mert.) El-
  don street
Naylor Wm. Market place
Wilson Matthias & Co. Eldon st
HOP GROWERS
IN THE PARISH AND NEIGHBOUR-
  HOOD.
  See also Ollerton & Retford.
Bellamy Geo. Bevercotes
Blagg Thos. Market place
Briggs John, Eldon st
Briggs Rt. jun. Newcastle st
Bullivant Wm. Askham
Buxton Robert. Eldon st
Byron Wm. & Geo. East Drayton
Camm Jonth. Kirton
Camm Jph. Willoughby
Clark Bryan. Eldon st
Clark Fras. Walesby
Clark John, East Markham
Clark Saml. East Markham
Daft Wm. Eldon street
Dean Hannah, Walesby
Denman John, Bevercotes
Field John, Bevercotes
Frogson Wm. Kirton
Gilbert John, Kirton
Gilbert Wm. Walesby
Haywood Alex. Walesby
Hempsall Thos. Egmanton
Jackson Jeremiah, East Markham
Justice Wm. Walesby
Ketton Wm. Askham
Lees Rd. East Markham
Manuell Edw. Milton
Manuell Jasper, Kirton
Norfolk Thos. East Drayton
Parnham Edw. Geo. & Wm. East
  Drayton
Quibell Benj. East Markham
Ratcliff Rd. Walesby
Rawson Rd. Walesby
Rawson Rt. East Drayton
Read Saml. Newcastle st
Richards Wm. East Markham

Robinson Wm. Market place
Rollitt John, Kirton
Rose John, East Markham
Scrimshaw Thos. Askham
Short Stephen C. Kingshaugh
Sudbury Saml. Egmanton
Swinglehurst Jno. East Markham
Walters Wm. East Markham
Wardell Geo. Egmanton
Wass Fras. Kirton
Wass Matthew, Kirton
Weightman John. Newcastle st
Weightman Rd. Kirton
White John, Bevercotes
Willmer Jas. Market place
Woolhouse Chpr. Kirton
Wombill John, Walesby
Wyre John, Askham

HOTELS, INNS, & TAVERNS.
Black Horse, Wm. Robinson, Market place
Blue Bell, John Woolfit, Eldon st
Coach & Horses, Wm. Wand, Eldon street
Fox, Ann Girton, Eldon st
King William IV. John Moss, Mill hill
Newcastle Arms, (inn & posting house) Jas. Willmer, Market place
Rein Deer, Chas. Laughton, Eldon street
Sun, Thos. Blagg, (& wool dlr.) Market place
Beerhouse, James, Blenkhorne, Eldon street

IRONMONGERS.
Clark Mary. Eldon st
Keyworth John, Eldon st

JOINERS & CAB. MKRS.
Blenkhorne Jas. Eldon st
Hannah John, Eldon st
Marples Wm. Chapel yard
Shaw Wm. (& looking glass dlr.) Manvers street

LINEN DRAPERS.
Dexter Geo. Eldon st
Ellis James, Newcastle st
Hewitt Thos. Newcastle st

MALTSTERS.
Beedham John, Newcastle st
Bennett & Bowman, Chapel yd
Daft Wm. Eldon street

MILLINERS AND DRESS MAKERS.
Atherton Mary, Chapel yard
Boyd Mary, Scotland bank
Briggs Ann, Eldon street
Crome Eliz. Chandos court
Maples Eliz. Eldon st
Storey Mary, Chandos court
Tustin Sarah, Lincoln st

NAIL MAKERS.
Butler Jph. Chandos st
Naylor Ann, Eldon st

NURSERY & SEEDSMEN.
Clark Geo. Eldon street
Taylor Jph. Lincoln st

PAINTERS, PLUMBERS, & GLAZIERS.
Langstaff Robert, Manvers-st
Pearson Henry, Eldon st
Sharman Abel, (& gilder) Ntle. st

ROPE & TWINE MAKERS.
Beedham Thos. Scotland bank
Briggs John, Eldon st
Johnson John, Eldon st

SADDLERS.
Beedham Gabriel, Eldon st
Hodgson Thos. Chapel yd.

SHOPKEEPERS.
Atkinson John, Newcastle st
Briggs Mary, Chandos court
Buttery Sarah, Eldon st
Godfry Benj. Newcastle st
Leak Richard, Eldon st
Scarliff Wm. Newcastle st
White Thomas, Lincoln st

STAY MAKERS.
Atkinson Mary, Newcastle st
Taylor Francis, Manvers st

SURGEONS.
Cooper Wm. J. Eldon st
Hornby Thos. Chantry house
Sorby Wm. Newcastle st

TAILORS.
Slingsby Geo. Eldon st
Whitworth Geo. Newcastle st
Wright Jph. Manvers st

WHEELWRIGHTS.
Bowman John, Newcastle st
Cocking Robert, Eldon st

COACHES.
The *Royal Mail*, to London at half-past 2 aft. and to Edinbro'

at half-past 11 mg. Also mails to London & Glasgow at half-past 2 afternoon

The *Express* to London, at 6 evg. and to York at 12 night

The *Rockingham* to London at 4 evg. and to Leeds at 8 mg

The *Highflyer* to London at 1 mg. & to York half-past 1 mg

The *Union* to London at half-past 8 evg. and to Leeds at 2 mg

The *Wellington* to London 3 mg. and to Newcastle-upon-Tyne, at 10 morning

The *Amity* to Stamford at 11 mg. and to Doncaster at 4 evg.

CARRIERS.

To London & Leeds, Deacon, Harrison & Co.'s vans from the Blue Bell, and Jackson & Co. from the Fox daily

To Newark, Benj. Godfrey, from Newcastle st. every Wednesday, dep. 6 mg. ar. 9 evg.

To Nottingham, John Bish and J. Taylor, from the Sun, every Mon. arrives 8 mg. dep. 2 aft.

To Retford, Thos. Stanfield and Wm. Cook, from the Blue Bell every Monday, arrives at 9 mg. departs 4 afternoon. And Benj. Godfrey, from Newcastle st. every Sat. dep. 8 mg. ar. 8 evening

---

WELLOW PARISH.

WELLOW, on the Worksop and Newark road, one mile E.S.E. of Ollerton, is a large village and a small parish, containing 110 houses, 473 inhabitants, and 956A. 0R. 5P. of land, of which more than 254 acres are in *Wellow park*, a thickly wooded eminence, which rises to a considerable altitude on the north side of the village, to *Cockin hill*, near Boughton.— Within a mile west of the village is the park and lake of Rufford. Some of the villagers are employed in turning wood and making chairs, and others are engaged in cultivating hops in the adjacent parish of Boughton. The *church*, dedicated to St. Swithen, was partly rebuilt and thoroughly repaired about 20 years ago, principally of brick, roofed with blue slate. It was anciently appropriated to Rufford abbey, and is now in the patronage of the Hon. and Rev. J. L. Saville, and appropriation of the Dean and Chapter of Lincoln, who have let the tithes on lease to the Duke of Newcastle, who owns part of the land, most of which belongs to the patron, who is also lord of the manor. The living is a perpetual curacy, worth only about £70 a-year, and now enjoyed by the Rev. Joseph Blandford, of Kirton. Wellow is not mentioned in Domesday Book, but is supposed to be included under the names of *Cratela* and *Grymston*, places which were partly in the soke of Mansfield, but are now unknown; though the superstitious wives here often frighten their children with a traditional tale of " *Grymston Ghost*," said to haunt the site of a village of that name, which was swallowed up by an earthquake. *Jordan Foliot*, in the 36th of Henry III. had free warren here, and obtained leave to

2 M

embattle his manor house of *Grimston*, which occupied the elevated site of a farm house now called *Jordan castle*. The estates here held by the Foliots, passed in marriage to the Hastings, and from them through various families to their present possessors. *Wellow hall*, now a farm house, was occupied about 35 years ago by the late Sir Fras. Molyneux, Bart.

*Those marked ‡ are Hop Growers, and * Yeomen.*

Allwood Paul, shopkeeper
Camm Jph. shopkeeper
Clark Jonth. shoemaker
Cutts Jph. shopkeeper
Duckmanton Thos. shoemaker
Goodwin John, chair manfr.
Hart John, saddler
‡Hill Eliz. shopkeeper
Hind Rd. shoemaker and parish clerk
Housley John, butcher
‡Kitchen Wm. vict. Black Horse
Newton Abm. joiner
Outram Jph. shoemaker
Pottinger Jph. blacksmith
Ralphs John, vict. &chairmaker, Red Lion

Walker Wm. wheelwright
Woolridge Edw. bricklayer
Woombell Geo. tailor
Woombell Henry, tailor
Woombell Rt. vict. Durham Ox

FARMERS.

Ashmore Wm.
Brett Chas.
Cartledge John
*Cougill John
Cougill Wm.
Day Wm.
Gadsby John
Hind Edw. & John
Marshall Rt.
*Moor Jph.
Moor Rd.
Parkinson Rt.
Peatfield John
‡Walker John
Walker John,
  Jordan castle
Weston Geo.
*Woolhouse Ts.

HATFIELD DIVISION.

This large division comprises all the Western side of Bassetlaw, (see p. 299,) and is more extensive than both the other two divisions of that hundred,—having 4316 houses, 21055 inhabitants, 4 extra-parochial places, 21 parishes, and 11 chapelries, divided into 36 townships, in which are a considerable number of villages and hamlets. It contains the four noble *parks* and *mansions* of Clumber, Thoresby, Welbeck, Worksop manor, and Rufford, and the *market towns* of Ollerton and Worksop, with part of Bawtry; and also the towns of Blyth and Warsop, which had formerly markets. It is bounded on the west by Yorkshire, and is watered by many small *rivers*, the principal of which are the Ryton, the Wollen, the Medin, the Maun, the Raiworth-water, and the Idle, the two latter of which bound it on the east, and separate it from the North and South Clay divisions. It has generally a deep sandy soil, and was formerly all included in the great *forest of Sherwood*, (see p. 35;) most of it is now enclosed and cultivated, but it has several extensive tracts of open forest land, and many large *plantations*. It had formerly nearly as many monasteries as all the rest of the county, for the *abbeys* of Rufford and Welbeck,

and the *priories* of Worksop, Blyth, Mattersey, and Wallingwells, were all within its limits. Its name is no doubt derived
from its being anciently considered as part of *Hatfield Chace.*—
See p. 353.

BABWORTH PARISH.

Contains the hamlets of *Babworth, Morton,* and *Ranby,* and
several scattered dwellings. It lies betwixt the Ryton rivulet
and the great north road, and is crossed by the Chesterfield
Canal. It extends northward from Ordsall to Barnby-moor,
and contains 76 houses, 449 inhabitants, and 6020A. 3R. 20P.
of excellent forest land, all enclosed and tithable, and belonging
to several freeholders, who have each the manorial rights of
their own property. *Babworth lordship* contains 1184A. 1R.
and is all in the occupancy of the owner, the Hon. J. B. Simpson; *Morton* has 3614A. 9R. 22P., mostly belonging to the
Duke of Newcastle, the Hon. and Rev. J. L. Saville, and Wm.
Mason and George and John Kippax, Esqrs.; and *Ranby* has
1222A. 2R., of which the Duchess Dowager of Newcastle, and
John Rogers, Esq. are the resident proprietors.

BABWORTH is a small but pleasant village, on the Worksop
road, 1¼ mile W. of Retford. Its vicinity contains some of the
finest scenery in this part of the county, and its beauty has
been greatly enhanced by its present possessor, the Hon. John
Bridgman Simpson, Esq. (brother to the Earl of Bradford,) of
BABWORTH HALL, a handsome mansion, situate on a gentle
declivity, in the midst of tasteful pleasure grounds and thriving
plantations, near which are a fine sheet of water, a Swiss cottage, and other picturesque objects. The CHURCH, dedicated
to All Saints, stands on an eminence near the hall, and is a
small neat gothic edifice, with a tower, three bells, and several
marble monuments of a modern date. Near it is the charming
little sequestered *rectory house*, in which comfort and elegance
are happily blended. It is now occupied by the curate, but was
lately the residence of the rector, the Ven. John Eyre, M.A.
Archdeacon of Nottingham, to whom, and the Simpson family,
the parish is much indebted for its internal prosperity. The
rectory is valued in the King's books at £14. 19s. 2d., and is
in the patronage of the Hon. J. B. Simpson, the lord of the
manor, which has passed by purchase to various families, and
was before the Conquest the property of Earl Tosti, but soon
afterwards it was given to Roger de Busli.

MORTON or *Moreton* hamlet and lordship occupies the
southern portion of the parish, about two miles S.W. of Retford, and includes the estates and scattered houses of *Great,*

Little, and *Upper Morton, Morton-on-the-Hill,* and *Morton Granges.* In Domesday Book it is called Northern Morton, and before the Conquest was held by two Saxons, named Alfrid and Lufchell.

RANBY hamlet is the north-west division of the parish, extending from 2 miles W. to 3½ miles W.N.W. of Retford. In the Conqueror's time it was mostly waste, and of the King's manor of Bothamsall, except a small part, which was *soc* to Grove. *Ranby Hall* is now the seat of the Duchess Dowager of Newcastle, who purchased it some years ago of H. Blaydes, Esq., by whom the mansion was new fronted. Her Grace has since made considerable improvement in the walks and pleasure grounds; which are agreeably romantic, and command a fine view of the woody scenery round Osberton. *Great* and *Little Ranby,* in this division, are two small villages, one on the Worksop road and the other on the canal, and near them is the mansion and extensive farm of John Rogers, Esq.; and *Rushy inn,* now divided into cottages, but formerly a noted posting-house on the great north-road, which in 1766 was diverted so as to pass through Retford.—Vide p. 54.

Ranby lordship is included in the *constablewick* of Barnby Moor, with which it contributes for the reparation of roads, and to the county rate, but maintains its poor conjointly with Babworth and Morton.

In 1802, there were found on Mr. Mason's estate, in Morton, 62 copper and 29 silver *Roman coins,* and a square stone has been set up on the spot, to commemorate the circumstance.

CHARITIES.—*Lindley Simpson,* in 1781, left a share in the canal, now worth £8 per annum, for the instruction of poor children and a yearly distribution of Old and New Testaments. The school at Lane houses was rebuilt in 1771, with £15 left in 1702 and 1746, by Wm. and Mrs. Simpson; and the mistress is remunerated partly by subscription. *Clerk's field,* at Lane houses, belongs to the parish clerk, but the donor is unknown.

Marked I *live at Great, and* 2 *at Little Ranby.*

Duchess Dowager of Newcastle, the Right Hon. Anna Maria, Ranby Hall
Simpson Hon. John Bridgeman, Babworth Hall
2 Barker Geo. vict. & blacksmith
1 Bentley Rt. maltster, & Rotherham
Caley Martha, schoolmrs. Babworth
1 Foster John, corn miller
2 Gilling John, beer house
2 Glossop John, maltster, and Harthill
Jackson Mr. Thos. Ranby cottage

Jackson Wm. blacksmith, Rushy inn
Johnson Geo. overseer, Great Morton
2 Marriott Thomas & Co. bone crushers, and Eaton
1 Pigott Geo. malting agent
Rogers John, Esq. Ranby
2 Shipston Wm. malting agent
Twells Rev. John, B.A. curate
Whitaker Jph. chief constable of South Clay div. Morton

FARMERS.
Brownlow Eliz. Upper Morton
Brownlow Geo. Little Morton

Fluring William, Ranby | Jackson John, Ranby cottage
Hawson John, Ranby | Johnson Wm. Great Morton
Hawson Thomas, Ranby ·. | Lister John, Morton Grange west
Hodgkinson Rd. Morton Grange | Turner Thos. (& coal merchant,)
Holmes Jno. Morton-on-the-Hill | Ranby wharf

BLYTH PARISH.

This extensive parish, which is partly in Yorkshire, is nearly eight miles in length, stretching from Barnby-moor, northward to Finningley park. It is intersected by the river Idle, the great north road, and the turnpikes leading from Tickhill to Worksop and Gainsbro'. It contains the two *chaperies* of Bawtry and Austerfield and six other townships, in which are 693 houses, 3735 inhabitants, and 15,477A. 0R. 11P. of fertile land, as will be seen in the following enumeration, which shows the contents and population of each parochial division.

TOWNSHIPS.	A.	R.	P.	HS.	POP.	TOWNSHIPS.	A.	R.	P.	HS.	POP.
Austerfield ·····	2612	0	24	54	280	Hodsock with					
Barnby Moor with						Goldthorpe····	4092	2	32	22	228
Bilby···· ········	1721	0	31	39	205	Ranskill ·······	1265	2	13	66	347
Bawtry* ········	205	0	14	200	1149	Styrrup with ⎫	2019	1	34	105	510
Blyth··· ········	1257	2	22	168	811	Oldcoates†· ⎭	940	1	19		
						Torworth···· ··	1362	3	32	42	205

* *Bawtry* and *Austerfield* are wholly in Yorkshire, except a small part of the former town.

† *Styrrup* township includes Oldcoates, and more than two-thirds of it is in *Harworth parish*, which see.

BLYTH, 4 miles S. by W. of Bawtry, and 7 miles from Worksop and Retford, is a large and well built village on the east bank of the Ryton, seated on a gentle ascent, which gives it a prepossessing appearance at a distance. It had formerly a weekly *market* on Wednesday, but it has long been obsolete, so that the inhabitants now use those of Bawtry and Tickhill, which are distant only about four miles. Here are, however, two annual *fairs*, one on Holy Thursday, for horses and cattle, and the other on the 20th of October, for sheep and swine. After the Norman Conquest, *Roger de Busli* had a CASTLE here, and procured for it the title of an *Honour;* but his chief residence being at Tickhill, in Yorkshire, the honour of Blyth was dependent on that manor. We are told that afterwards, this Roger " being of a pious and grateful disposition, with the consent of his wife Muriel, did for the stability of William then King of England, (who had given him a full fourth part of this county, if not more; besides what he had given him in

others) and of his successors, as also for the health of the soul
of Queen Maud, and their own, by the advice of their friends,
erect a PRIORY in this town, and by way of endowment, gave
and granted to God, St. Mary, and the *monks* there serving
God, the church of Blyth, and the whole town entirely, with
all the privileges and customs thereunto belonging." This
grant is said to have been confirmed by the first two Henries;
and yet Maddox asserts, that an ancient feoffment had been
made of the honour of Blyth; and also that in the reign of
Henry the First, that honour was in the King's hand either by
escheat or wardship, for the profits of it were accounted for
to him; which position he proves by reference to the rolls of
the honour. Tanner, however, makes no mention of this in the
Monasticon, but merely says that here was a priory of Benedictine monks, built by Roger de Busli and Muriel his wife,
about 1068, to the honour of the blessed Virgin. It was in
some respects subordinate to the abbey of the Holy Trinity of
Mount St. Catherine at Rouen, in Normandy, and was at the
dissolution worth £126 per annum. In the 35th of Henry
VIII, "the site of the priory, and the demesnes" were granted
to William Ramsden and Richard Andrews, who had license
to alineate them to Richard Stansfield and his heirs, from whom
they passed to the Saunderson, Cook, Clifton, and other families. As to the origin of the name of *Blyth* or *Blythe*, Fuller
says, "John Norden will have it from *jocundidate*, from the
mirth and good fellowship of the inhabitants therein. If so,
(says our quaint author,) I desire that both the name and the
thing may be extended all over the shire; being confident that
an ounce of *mirth* with the same degree of grace, will serve God
more, and more acceptably than a pound of *sorrow*."

The CHURCH, dedicated to St. Martin, is a spacious and
elegant Gothic structure, with a very ancient tower; and at its
east end, an elegant arch is inserted in the wall, which must
have led to a former chancel, or else to some other religious
building which has been attached to the church. The interior
presents a noble nave with arches supported by lofty pillars,
and interspersed with some splendid monuments of the Mellish
family. It has evidently been the priory church, as the few
remains of that ancient edifice are adjoining to it. The *rectory*
was granted by Henry VIII., to Trinity College, Cambridge, to
which it still belongs, together with the advowson of the *vicarage*,
which is valued in the King's books, at £4. 9s. 4½d. The Society of Friends have had a *Meeting House* in the village more
than a century and a half.

BLYTH HALL, a handsome mansion of considerable magnitude, stands near the church, upon an eminence surrounded
by beautiful pleasure grounds, and commanding an extensive
prospect of the surrounding country, which seems one con-

tinued garden; interspersed with lawns and shady groves, and traversed by winding walks; indeed,. the whole district as far as eye can reach, presents such a scene of ornamented cultiva-tion, as is rarely beheld. The hall is an elegant brick build-ing, decorated with stone, and having turrets at the corners. It was long the seat of the Mellish family, to whom it is in-debted for all its modern improvements. The additions and alterations have been so considerable, that we may say it has been re-built on the site of the old one. It is now the property of Henry Walker, Esq., but is occupied by Major General Sir Henry Bouverie. About 35 years ago, the town of Blyth and the country around it for several miles, belonged to *William Mellish, Esq.*, who cut "a river four miles long and ten yards wide, as a drainage to a large extent of low land in the centre of his estate, capable of being made as fine meadow as any in England." He also made at his own expense, ten miles of road, and built several farm houses and above 30 cottages, all in the most substantial manner, of brick and tile. Besides beautify-ing and enlarging the hall, he erected an extensive pile of stabling, and ornamented his estate with upwards of 200 acres of plantations, which are now in a thriving state. He also built on the high road, in front of the hall, a superb bridge of Roch Abbey stone, for the convenience of crossing the extensive piece of water which is formed on a most magnificent scale, by damming up the river Ryton and a small brook which falls into it a little below the town.. Little did this spirited gentleman imagine, whilst making these costly improvements, that his ex-tensive estate was so soon to pass from his family by the improvidence of his son, the late *Charles Mellish, Esq.*, *F. R. S.*, who, though "of a literary turn," became at length so enamoured of the company of royalty, and so addicted to the vices of the turf and the fashionable gaming table, that in 1805, he was obliged to sell the Blyth Hall estate, which was pur-chased by the late *Joshua Walker, Esq.*, the founder of the Masbro' Iron Works, where by great skill and industry, he amassed an immense fortune. In the church is an elegant re-cumbent figure of *Edward Mellish, Esq.*, who, after being twenty years a merchant in Portugal, retired to this place, where he died in 1703. His son, Joseph, married the sister of Mr. Gore, governor of the Hamburgh Company, and died in 1733, when his estate passed to his son, the before-named William Mellish, Esq., who was a commissioner of excise in 1751, and married the widow of Villa Real, Esq. From him the estate passed to its last possessor of the Mellish family; who, in the early part of his life, was long occupied in col-lecting genealogical additions to Thoroton's History of Not-tinghamshire, but his manuscripts were never published; for before their completion, he devoted his time to fashionable follies, and became the intimate friend of his Royal Highness George Prince of Wales, afterwards George IV.

BEETLES.—Those most destructive insects, *May-bugs*, or *Dorr-beetles*, here called *Cockchafers*, and in some places *Brown-clocks*, were formerly so numerous in Blyth and Hodsock, that the inhabitants employed people to kill them at the rate of 3d. per peck. In 1788, no fewer than 3743 pecks were destroyed at the cost of £47. 1s. 2d., of which one-third was paid by William Mellish, Esq. Nearly the same quantity were killed in 1792; yet still the vegetation here is often greatly injured by these insects, which live four years as worms in the bowels of the earth, before they join the winged tribes.

CHARITIES.—The ancient SCHOOL in Blyth, is supposed to have been formerly a chapel, and is endowed with 6A. 2R. 26P. of land, called Drawbridge-moor Fields, worth £18 per ann., and received in exchange at the enclosure in 1814, in lieu of land in Blyth Marsh, left by an unknown donor. The master also receives a yearly gift of £5 from the churchwardens' fund. The "SPITAL HOUSES," are six dwellings for as many poor people of Blyth township, with an endowment of £3 per annum, paid by the owner of Blyth Hall estate. The present dwellings were built a few years ago by Mr. Charles Champion, within 109 yards of the site of the old ones, which were supposed to have been the remains of an ancient HOSPITAL founded by William de Cressy, lord of Hodsock, in the reign John, for a warden, three chaplains, and several leprous persons;—dedicated to St. John the Evangelist, and valued in the 26th of Henry VIII., at £8. 14s. per annum. Two ALMS-HOUSES adjoining the Quakers' Chapel, were built in 1700, by John Seaton, and endowed with £10 a-year, for two inmates, one of whom is to be of the poor of Blyth, and the other of the Society of Friends, of which, the trustees, Joshua Armitage, John Bakewell, and Francis Hart, of Nottingham, are all members. The annuity is charged on the estate of Henry Walker, Esq. Two houses in the village, occupied by paupers, were built with £65, left in 1703, 1720, and 1759, by the Rev. William Smith, James Ryals, and Thomas Greaves, but the overseers distributed £2. 18s. yearly, as the interest thereof. *Edward Farfoot*, left to the poor of Blyth, a house and land at Scaftworth, which the trustees sold in 1807, for £320, now vested in £347. 5s. 5d., new 4 per cent. Stock, standing in the names of Henry Walker and Charles Champion, Esqrs. *Dorothy Barlow*, sister of Edward Farfoot, left £20 to the poor, with which the overseers built a cottage, but distribute the interest on St. Thomas' Day. The interest of £40 left by *John Crofts*, is distributed on St. John's Day. There are also some other small houses, a croft of 1½ acres, and part of a field of 1¼ acre, which belong to the poor; but the rents are now carried to the overseers' accounts. The *Church land* consists of Drawbridge-moor Closes, 5A. 5R. 47P. let for £11; and an allotment made at the Styrrup enclosure in 1802, and now let for £9. The first was received at the Blyth enclosure in 1814, in exchange for land on Cunscar and Rails Commons, and on the Long Brecks.

BLYTH NORNAY is a small hamlet, only a quarter of a mile N. of Blyth, though in Styrrup township.

BLYTH SPITTAL is a hamlet at the southern extremity of Blyth, and is partly in Hodsock township.

AUSTERFIELD, though in this parish, is a village, township, and chapelry, in the Wapentake of Strafford and Tickhill, and West-Riding of *Yorkshire*, 1 mile N. of Bawtry. It is said to have its name from the Roman general *Ostorius*, being defeated here by the [Britons. The Dowager Countess Galway is lady of the manor, and owner of most of the land. The *chapel* is a small edifice with two bells, and is a curacy in the gift of the vicar of Blyth. The Rev. William Snowden, B. D. is the incumbent. The township extends two miles N. of the village, and includes FINNINGLEY PARK, the handsome seat of John Hervey, Esq., occupied by E. B. Beaumont. Esq.; the hamlet of BRANCROFT, and the scattered farmsteads called *Hirst House, Partridge Hill*, and *Woodhouse*, all in Yorkshire, but on the borders of Nottinghamshire.

BARNBY-MOOR, a neat hamlet with a good inn and posting-house on the North road, 3 miles N.W. of Retford, forms a joint township with BILBY,—a district of scattered houses on the banks of the Ryton, 2 miles west of the inn. Henry Walker, Esq. is lord of the manor of Barnby, and G. S. Foljambe, Esq. is lord of Bilby, and owner of the *hall* there, which is now unoccupied. Both were of the fee of Roger de Busli; the latter was long held by the Chaworth family, and part of the former was given by *Adam de Barnely* to the monks of Blyth. In 1790, Anthony Barker left £20 to the poor of this township, and the interest is now paid yearly by Mr. Samuel Barker.

BAWTRY

Is a small, handsome, well-built *market town*, and being situated on the Great North Road, at the junction of the turnpikes from Sheffield, Gainsbro', and Thorne, it is a busy thoroughfare, and has a large and commodious Inn and Posting-house, besides several other public-houses, which afford comfortable accommodation for travellers. It is distant 9 miles from Doncaster and Retford, 4 miles E. of Tickhill, 12 miles W. by N. of Gainsbro', and 4 miles N. by E. of Blyth. Though nearly surrounded by Nottinghamshire, it is all in the Wapentake of Strafford and Tickhill, and the West-Riding of Yorkshire,

except a small suburb which forms the south side of Top-
street, and is in the parish of Harworth. It is situated on the
site of the Roman road which passed from Littleborough to
Doncaster. A fair of four days in the year was procured from
King John, by Robert de Vipount, lord of the manor, for a
present of four palfreys. The *market*, which was formerly on
Wednesday, is now on Thursday, and is principally for corn
sold by sample. It has now two fairs for cattle and horses, on
Whit-Thursday and November 22nd. The town has no trade
except the traffic on the river Idle, which is navigable from
hence to the Trent for small craft, principally employed in im-
porting coal, groceries, &c. The object most worthy of attention here, is BAWTRY HALL, the elegant seat of the Dowager
Viscountess Galway, which is situated at the southern extremity of the town, in the midst of extensive pleasure grounds,
all in excellent condition, agreeably interspersed with shrubberies and plantations, and containing a beautiful *aviary*, well
stocked with Chinese pheasants and other rare birds. The
township forms a chapelry, and has a small CHAPEL OF EASE
annexed to the vicarage of Blyth. The Rev. Wm. Snowden,
B.D. is the curate. In the town are also a *Methodist Chapel*,
built in 1827, and an *Independent Chapel* built in 1826, on land
given by Mr. James Dobson. The Rev. Robert Kirkus is
minister of the latter, which has attached to it a large school
with eight free scholars. In 1691, *Barbara Lister* left £200,
and directed the interest to be paid yearly to the curate of
Bawtry, "if placed there by the consent of her executor or his
heirs, if not, to the poor of Bawtry." The Earl of Rosslyn
now pays this annuity. In 1780, *Elizabeth Foster* bequeathed
the *Bell Houses* with a garden, for the residence of two poor
women, and endowed them with a yearly rent charge of £1 out
of a close at Misson, called the Paddock.

HODSOCK with GOLDTHORP form a large township of scattered houses, extending westward from Blyth more than two
miles to the borders of Yorkshire, across the Worksop and
Tickhill road, betwixt Oldcoates and Carlton in Lindrick.
They were anciently called *Ordesache* and *Cossardthorpe*, and
belonged to the families of *Cossard*, *Hoddisac*, and *Cressy*, who
gave part of the land to the priory at Blyth. They afterwards passed to the Markhams and Cliftons, with whom they
remained till the middle of the last century, when they became the property of the Mellish family, but are now divided
amongst several owners. *Hodsock Hall*, which was defended
by a moat and tower gateway, has been partly rebuilt, and new
fronted in the monastic style, from which it is now called HOD-
SOCK PRIORY. It is the seat of Mrs. Ann Chambers, and
stands in a beautiful valley 1¼ miles S.W. of Blyth. HODSOCK
PARK, 2 miles W. of Blyth, belongs to Mr. John Shuttleworth,
and the two farms called *Fleecetrep* (Flyrthorp) and *Millhouse*,

are the property of G. S. Foljambe, Esq. *Goldthorpe* forms the N. W. part of the township, and Henry Gally Knight, Esq. is its principal owner.

RANSKILL is a pleasant village and township in the *liberty of Southwell and Scrooby*, on the great North road, 2 miles E. of Blyth, and 6 miles N.W. by N. of Retford, where there is a good inn, a boarding academy, and a neat Independent Chapel. Samuel Barker, Esq. and Mr. John Crofts are the principal owners, but the Archbishop of York is lord of the manor, and has here some copyhold tenants. *Quarter sessions* are held here at Easter and Michaelmas, and *petty sessions* once a fortnight, for the *North Soke* of the liberty of Southwell and Scrooby. The *feast* is on the Sunday after Old Michaelmas-day. The *common* was enclosed in 1805.

STYRRUP AND OLDCOATS.—See *Harworth parish.*

TORWORTH is another pleasant village on the North road, lying a little south of Ranskill, 5¼ N. W. by N. of Retford. Viscount Galway is lord of the manor, and owner of most of the soil, and Mrs. Chambers is lessee of the great tithes both here and at Ranskill. A *Methodist Chapel* was built in the village in 1826. On the highest part of the township stands MANTLES HOUSE, the seat of Thomas Crofts, Esq. In excavating the foundation of this mansion in 1820, a *Roman urn* ten inches in diameter, was found covered with a globular vessel, supposed to have contained a human heart. The common land was enclosed in 1800 and 1807, by a mutual agreement of the proprietors. An *annuity* of 10s. is paid to the poor of this township out of Viscount Galway's estate.

BLYTH DIRECTORY.

LETTERS are despatched by a foot Post every morning at 10 to Bawtry, and arrive at half-past three in the afternoon.

Ambler Robert, painter
Bouverie Major Gen. Sir Henry, Blyth Hall
Booth Mrs. Dorothy
Booth Joseph, woodman
Bradley John, Esq., Spittal
Butler Wm. constable
Dickinson George, farmer
Downs Geo. plumber & glazier
Foster Joseph, maltster
Fowler Richard, gent.
Giles Wm. earthenware dealer
Green Barth. saddler
Hodgson Geo. earthenware dlr.
Jones William, land surveyor and English timber dealer
Manwaring John, gent.

Mills Chas. nurseryman
Morrison Thos. cooper
Nettleship Edw. farmer, Blyth Nornay
Parkin Thos. corn miller
Pigott Mrs. Ann
Pritchard Mrs. Ann
Quibell John, veterinary surgeon
Radley Wm. grocer & druggist
Rogers Thos. farmer
Rogers John, maltster, Blyth Nornay
Rudd Rev. John, M.A. vicar
Russell Samuel, surgeon
Stacey Mrs. Lydia
Taylor William, maltster, Blyth Nornay

Taylor Robert, weaver & parish clerk
Thornton Hy. grocer & druggist
Thorpe Mrs. Hannah
Torr Edw. postman and sexton
Widdowson Thos. grocer
Wilson Benj. brush mfr., grocer, and draper
Winter Mrs. Hannah
Woolley Jph. fellmonger, Blyth Nornay
Wright Hugh, sawyer

INNS AND TAVERNS.
The last three are Beerhouses.
Angel, George Creassey
Red Hart, Joseph Foster
Rose & Crown, John Swindin
White Horse, John Marsh
Blacksmith's Arms, John Hoggard
Red Lion, George Moore
White Swan, Richard Turner

Academies. Marrison Wm.
Free school, Jno. Rowland Geo. Woodcock
Pattison Ellen
*Winter Hannah
Bakers, &c.
Garthsides Jas.
Taylor Geo.
Blacksmiths.
Hoggard John
Hill John
Kelk John, (and gun smith)
Boot & Shoemkrs.
Apley Emanuel
Bell Jonathan
Crumpton John
Hancock Wm.
Swinburn John
Turner Rd.
Bricklayers.
Blackburn Saml.
Marrison Edw.

Butchers.
Gabbitas John
Hudson Charles
Newstead Geo.
Joiners.
Hardy Wm.
Rich Joseph
Milliners, &c.
Ambler Sarah
Beighton Jane
Blake Matilda
Tailors.
Apley Wm.
Colgreaves Jthn.
Hopkin John
Moore George
Walker Wm.
Wheelwrights.
Swinden John
Watson Wm.
Wilkinson John

Carrier, Martin Kirkby to Bawtry, Thurs.; Retford, Sat.; Sheffield, Monday, & Worksop, Wednesday.

AUSTERFIELD, (Yorkshire.)
Batty Rd. vict. White Hart
Beaumont Edw. Blackett, Esq. Finningley Park
Cappiter Wm. wheelwright
Dyon Mr. John
Green John, blacksmith
Milner John, shoemkr. & chapel clerk
Parker Wm. shopkeeper
Radley Wm. Esq. Brancroft
Woodhouse Wm. shoemaker

FARMERS.
Birks Richard, Woodhouse
Brogden James
Dickinson John, Brancroft
Dickinson John, Pattridge Hill
Fox William
Jackson George
Jennings Thomas
Long Samuel Maw
Ramsey William, Hird House
Spencer George
Tomlinson John, Finningley Cottage
Wood Wm. Finningley Park

BARNBY MOOR with BILBY
*Marked * are in Bilby.*
*Allinson Joseph, farmer
Barker Saml, Esq. Barnby Hall
Clark George, vict. Bell Inn and posting house
Clark John Darcy, gent.
Habbijam Benjamin, farmer
Kitchin George, shoemaker
Kitchin John, blacksmith
Pagdin George, shoemaker
Pagdin Thos. shopkeeper
Scott Joseph, vict. White Horse
Scott Wm. farmer
Thorold Michael Wynne, gent.
*Wagstaff James, farmer
*Whale William, farmer

HODSOCK WITH GOLDTHORPE.
Marked † are Farmers.
†Ashton Wm., Lodge
Bradley John, Esq. Blyth Spittal
†Cartledge Samuel, Goldthorpe
Chambers Mrs. Ann, Hodsock Priory

†Coupe John, Fleecetrep
†Cross George. Priory Farm
†Gibbs Thos. Hodsock Cottage
Mower C. C. surgeon, Woodhouse
†Musgrove ——, Forest Farm
Peniston Wm. corn miller, Gold-
 thorpe
†Radley Wm. Hodsock
Shuttleworth John, gent. Hod-
 sock Park
†Taylor John, Goldthorpe
†Wood John, Hodsock Mill Hs.

RANSKILL.
Dawson John, gent
Dean John C., vict. Blue Bell Inn
Denmar Mr. William
Foulds Samuel, blacksmith
Jackson Thomas, blacksmith
Kirk Robert, tailor
Martin Wm. boarding academy
Millns John, shoemaker
Morley George, shoemaker
Norton Wm. shoemaker
Parkinson Wm. grocer & draper
Reddish Robert, tailor
Shillito George, wheelwright
Teale Thos. grocer & draper

Weightman Rt. jun. maltster and
 seed merchant
FARMERS.
*Those marked * are Yeomen.*
*Chester Fras.   *Matthews Wm.
Chester Richard Pinning Thos.
*Crofts John   *Welsh Thos.
*Curtis Sarah

STYRRUP.
See Harworth Parish.

TORWORTH.
Close John, excise officer
Crofts Thos. & Wm. gents. Man-
 tles House
Crookes John, blacksmith
Hopkin Thos. wheelwright
Newcombe Wm. shoemaker
Selby Joseph, vict. Northampton
 House
Weightman Rt. land agent
FARMERS.
Bingham Wm. Maples Thos.
Chambers John, Maples Wm.
Grange   Scott John
Hodgkinson W. Skidmore Geo.

BAWTRY DIRECTORY.

Post-Office, Crown Inn Yard, David Adams, Post-Master. *Let-*
ters from all parts are received at 12 noon, and are despatched at a
quarter-past one afternoon:

Baines John, clerk to Magis-
 trates, High street
Baines Matt. hair drssr. High st
Barrowcliff John, timber mer-
 chant, Church street
Bellamy Robert, boat owner
Benson John, boat owner and
 coal merchant, Wharf street
Binney Benj. farmer, Church st
Brooke Jnth. clothier, Church st
Coldwell Joshua, coal dlr. Church
 street
Cutts Thos. nail mkr. North End
Dobson Jas. currier. Church st
Dyon Mrs. Betty, High street
Fisher Mrs. Mary, Church st
Galway Lady Bridget, Dowager
 Viscountess, Bawtry Hall
Garner Jno. nurseryman, Church
 street
Gooddy Mrs. Eliz. High street
Hargrave Mr. Jas. Top street
Hett Jas. farmer, High street
Hopkinson Mrs. Eliz. Church st
Hume Mrs. Eliz. High street
Kirkus Rev. Rt. (Ind.) Scott ln
Marrison Mrs. Ann, High st
Mitchell John, wine mer. High st
Nettleship Thos. gent. High st
Pratt Jas. Daubney, veterinary
 surgeon, Church street
Roberts Bnj. excise-off. Church st
Sandys Mrs. Sally, Top street
Shirtcliff Eliz. dressmkr. Scott ln
Smith Timothy, blacking mfr. &c
 High street

2 N

Soer John, sawer, Church street
Speller Mrs. Caroline, High st
Spilsbury Mrs. Eliz.Char. High st
Stephenson Wm. saddler, High st
Swallow Wm. staymaker, Swan ln
Taylor Thos. hat mfr. & furrier, High street
Taylor & Williams, dressmakers, Swan lane
Unwin Jno. stone mason, Church street
Wade Mrs. Ann, Wharf street
Wakefield Thos. glass, china, &c. dlr. High street
Walker Mrs. Mary, High street
Webster Thos. horse breaker, Cht
Whaley Mr. John, High street
Winter Mr. Thos. Top street
Winterburn Jas. matron, Work-house
Wood Michael, Esq. Brigade-Major, High street
Wood James, farmer, Top st

ACADEMIES.
Everard Miss Ann, Wharf st
Holland James, Church street
Snowden Rev. Wm. B.D., (pre-paratory for Holy Orders,) Church street
Wood James, North End

ATTORNIES.
Broughton Wm. High street
Cartwright F. Hawksley, High st
McKenzie George, High street
Raynes Fras. High street

AUCTIONEERS.
Grasby Joseph, High street
Watts Jonathan, High street

BAKERS & FLOUR DLRS.
Thickitt Joseph, Church street
Womack Mary. Scott lane

BLACKSMITHS & FARRIERS
Towler Samuel, North End
Windle Thomas, (& bell hanger) High street

BOOKSELLERS, STATION-ERS, &c.
Grasby Jph.(stamp office) High st
Tailor Joseph, High street
Wilson Jph. (printer & cir. li-brary) High street

BOOT & SHOEMAKERS.
Fillingham Wm. High street

Freeman Wm. Scott lane
Hackford Joseph, Church street
Hawson George, High street
Jenkinson Thos. Swan lane
Wilson John, Church street
Winter Benjamin, High street

BRICKLAYERS.
Marrison Jonathan, High street
Marrison Wm. Scott lane

BUTCHERS.
Dowson John, Church street
Tow Edward, Swan lane
Sissons John, High street
Thickitt John, Swan lane

CABINET MAKERS, &c.
Swift Joseph, Swan lane
Wilson & Bedford, High street
Winter Richard, Top street

COOPERS.
Eaton Benjamin, Church street
Oldfield John, Church street

DRUGGISTS.
Barber Thomas, High street
Nettleship Thos. jun. High st

FIRE & LIFE OFFICES.
County Fire and Provident Life, Joseph Grassby, High street
Sheffield, Joseph Tailor, High st

GROCERS & FLOUR DLRS.
Birley Jno. (& seedsman) High st
Herring Wm. High street
Rhodes Thos. High street
Soer John, Swan lane
Williams Elizabeth, Swan lane

INNS & TAVERNS.
Angel, Jph. Taylor, High st
Black Bull, John Stockdale
Black's Head; (excise off.) Jonth. Watts
Blue Bell, Eliz. Wilson, Church street
Crown Inn (& postg.) Dd. Adams, High street
Marquis of Granby, Saml. Briggs, North End
Ship, Wm. Beck, Church st
White Hart, Geo. Hibbert, Swan lane

BEERHOUSES.
Red Lion, William Hy. Lambert, North End
Travellers, Mary Malthouse, North End

IRONMONGERS.
Heath John, (& brazier) Swan ln
Whittington Hy. Swan lane

JOINERS.
Carr Richard, North End
Drabwell Paul, (& wheelwright)
  High street
Hackford John, Church street
Howard Charles, Scott lane
Lambert Wm. Hy. North End

LINEN & WOLN. DRAPERS.
Herring Wm. High street
Hill Thomas, Swan lane
Kidson Wm. High street

MALTSTERS.
Couch John, Church street
Jackson John, North End
Johnson Thos. Church street
Nicholson Mary, Wharf street

PAINTERS.
Bailey Geo. (& gilder) High st
Fisher Thos. (hs. & coach) High st

PLUMBERS & GLAZIERS.
Credland Jonathan, High street
Marrison Wm. Church street
Wakefield George, High street

ROPE & TWINE MANUFRS.
Blythman Joseph, (& sheep net)
  High street
Hall Wm. Church street
Haxby Robert, Gainsborough rd

SADDLERS.
Stephenson Wm. High street
Woodcock Isaac, North end

STRAW HAT MAKERS.
Bennett Mary, North end
Hunt Mary, High street
Jenkinson Sarah, Swan lane
Moore Elizabeth, High street

SURGEONS.
Cocking John, High street
Nicholson John, M.D. Ivyhouse
Wright Wm. Top street

TAILORS.
Bennett James, North end
Goodlad John, High street
Moorhouse James, Church st
Wakefield Thomas, High street

TALLOW CHANDLERS.
Herring Wm. High street
Rhodes Thomas, (& soap boiler)
  High street

WATCH & CLOCK MAKERS.
Bell James, High street
Jenkinson Edward, High street
Lowe Joseph, High street
Whittington Henry, Swan lane

WINE & SPIRIT MERTS.
Nicholson Mary, Wharf street
Weightman & Mitchell, High st.

MAILS & COACHES.
From the Crown Inn.
Royal Mails, to London at 12
  noon; to Edinbro' and Glasgow,
  at 1 aft.; & to Louth & Shef-
  field, at a ¼ past 1 aft.
The *Rockingham* to London at
  ½ past 2 aft., and to Leeds at
  ½ past 9 morning.
The *Wellington* to London at 10
  evg., and to York at 12 noon.
The *Amity* to Doncaster at 6
  mg. & to Stamford, 9 morning.
From the Marquis of Granby.
The *Highflyer* to London at 1
  mg., and to York ½ past 3 mg.
The *Express* to Lincoln at 4 aft.
  & to Wakefield at 10 morning.
The *Union* to Leeds ½ p. 3 mg.
From the Angel Inn.
The *Express* to London at ½ p.
  2 aft., & to York, ½ bef. 3 mg.
The *Hope* to Doncaster & Gainsbro' daily, (except Sunday) to
  meet the *Hull Packets.*

CARRIERS.
To London, Deacon, Harrison, &
  Co.'s Van, from the Angel every
  morning at 1; and their Wag-
  gon every morning at 8. Also,
  Jackson & Co.'s every day at
  12 noon, from the Marquis of
  Granby.
Barnsley & Leeds, Chpr. Embley
  from Wharf-st. every Friday
  night.
Doncaster, Geo. Moore, High-st.
  Sat.; Rd. Shillito, Church-st.,
  Mon. Thur. and Sat.; Chpr.
  Embley, Wharf-street. Mon.;
  and Peacock & Ashmore, every
  Saturday morning.
Gainsborough, John Gee, every

Mon.; and Hibberson & Co., (from Sheffield) Wed. & Thurs. from the Black Bull; and Rd. Shillito, from Church-st. Tues. dep. 4 morning.

Gringley-on -the - Hill, Michael Kirkby, Black Bull, Thur. 4 af.

Leeds, Jackson & Co. Marquis of Granby, daily, at 10 mg.

Retford, Thos. Stanfield, Black Bull, Thursday, 4 afternoon

Sheffield, John Gee, Wed., and Hibberson & Co. Wed. & Fri. from the Black Bull

Tickhill, Robert Booth, Angel, Thursday, 4 afternoon

Wakefield, Deacon, Harrison, & Co. from the Marquis of Granby daily, at 7 evening

Worksop, John Wilmott, from the Marquis of Granby, Thurs. 4 afternoon

CONVEYANCE BY WATER.

To Gainsborough, Christopher Embley's Packet Boat every Monday morning; returns on Wednesday

BOTHAMSALL PARISH

Lies east of Clumber park, betwixt and near the confluence of the rivers Wollen and Idle. It contains 59 houses, 326 inhabitants, and about 1700 acres of land, which was enclosed about 60 years ago, and belongs solely to the Duke of Newcastle, who is lord of the manor and impropriator of the tithes. About seven acres are in hop yards.

BOTHAMSALL is a pleasant village near the Retford and Ollerton road, 4¼ miles N. by E. of the latter town. The *church* is an ancient edifice, which, with the predial tithes and the glebe of the rectory, was granted by Queen Elizabeth in 1578, to the Earl of Lincoln, an ancestor of the Duke of Newcastle, whose domestic chaplain, the Rev. John Mason, now enjoys the perpetual curacy, which was certified at £21. 6s. 8d. The manor before the Conquest was held by Earl Tosti, and afterwards by the Furnivals, the St. George's, the Boselingthorps, &c. The *feast* is on the nearest Sunday to St. Peter's day.

HOUGHTON PARK, mostly in this parish, and partly on the south side of the river in Houghton parish, was enclosed about 30 years ago. Here are situated the Duke's *kennels,* with a house occupied by his gamekeeper. The poor of the parish enjoy the interest of £48, left in 1799, by Joseph Holliday, and now in the Retford savings' bank.

Baines Mary, wheelwright
Ball Wm. shoemaker
Cowley Samuel, wheelwright
Hind John, blacksmith
Mansell John, gamekpr. Houghton Park
Marshall Geo. vict. Fox
Nutt John, shoemaker

Olivant Thos. butcher & shopkpr
Padley Mark, cooper
Pickering Geo. shoemaker
Spencer Geo. shopkeeper
Stubbings John, shoemaker
Turner Wm. English timber dlr
Walker Christopher, stone mason, Houghton Park

FARMERS.
Thus ‡ are Hop Growers.
‡Camm John   Hempseed Wm.
‡Dewick Ann   Johnson John

‡Moss John   Padley Wm.
Padley Thos.   Peck Wm.
Padley Jenny,   Stacy Robert
Haughton Park

BOUGHTON PAROCHIAL CHAPELRY,

Though in the Hatfield division, is annexed to the parish of Kneesall, in the hundred of Thurgarton. It includes the steep acclivity of *Cockin Hill*, (under which are several hop yards,) and extends westward over a wild tract of *forest land*, which is noted as a *fox cover*, adjoins Thoresby park, and is intersected by the river Maun, over which a bridge was erected by subscription in 1812, the ford being often very dangerous. On the bank of the river is a deep cavity in the rock of red sandstone, called *Robin Hood's cave*. The forest has a deep light sandy soil, well riddled with the burrows of rabbitts and foxes; about 50 acres of it were enclosed a few years ago, by the lord of the manor, and is now called *New England*. The parish contains 75 houses and 295 inhabitants.

BOUGHTON, 1¼ mile N.E. of Ollerton, is a small village near the hop yards, at the east end of the parish, which is enclosed and sheltered from the westerly winds by the abrupt acclivity that extends northward from Wellow to Kirton and Walesby. It was anciently called *Bucheton*, and was of the fee of Roger de Busli, of whom it was held by a family of its own name, one of whom, *Aeliz de Bucton*, gave part of the land and the advowson of the church to the priory at Blyth. It afterwards passed to the Markhams, but most of it now belongs to the Hon. and Rev. J. L. Saville, who is lord of the manor, and lessee of the great tithes, which are appropriated to the Dean and Chapter of Southwell. The *church* is a humble building, with a turret belfry, and is a curacy annexed to Kneesall vicarage. The *General Baptists* have a neat chapel here, which they built in 1826. The only benefaction belonging to the parish, is £12. 10s. left in 1791, by *Squire Markham*, and now vested in the Retford savings' bank.

Arnold Geo. joiner
Bennett John, tailor
Gray Samuel, bricklayer
Markham Leond. butcher & vict
Moss Joshua, wheelwright, shopr. and parish clerk
Otter John, shoemaker
Ratcliff Wm. tailor
Robshaw Wm. vict. Plough
Taylor John, blacksmith
Wells Wm. vict. Harrow

Woodhead Geo. shoemaker
FARMERS.
Thus † are Yeoman and § Hop Growers.
§†Alvy Chpr.   §Lawrence Chas.
§Alvey John, & § †   Methering
   maltster   ham Geo.
§Flower Wm.   Newbart Wm.
§†Frogson Hy.   §Squires John
§Gibson Wm.   Wilson Richard,
Hage John   Cockin hill

2 N 2

CARLTON-in-LINDRICK PARISH

Comprises the two contiguous hamlets and constablewicks of *Carlton-in-Lindrick* and *Kingston-in-Carlton*, pleasantly situated near Walling-wells, on the road betwixt Tickhill and Worksop, 3½ miles N. of the latter. It was of sufficient consequence in Saxon times to have six resident Thanes, each having a hall or manor, but these were all swallowed up by that leviathan, Roger de Busli, at the Norman Conquest. The family of Chevercourt held it under him, but their heirs failing, it was divided between the Latimers and Fitzhughs, from whom it passed to the Dacres, Molyneuxs, Taylors, and Cliftons, the latter of whom built a fine seat here. It contains 189 houses, 974 inhabitants, and 4073A. 0R. 15P. of land, of which about 1518 acres now belong to the lord of the manor, Robert Ramsden, Esq. of Carlton Hall; 600 acres to H. Gally Knight, Esq.; 463 acres to Sir Thomas White, Bart.; and 558 acres to the rector, the latter of whom received his portion at the enclosure in 1767, as a commutation of all the tithes of the parish. The *church*, dedicated to St. John, is now a handsome gothic edifice, having lately received considerable repairs, and a new south aisle, erected in 1831, in unison with the rest of the building, which is in the style that prevailed in the reign of Henry VI. Under the new aisle, Sir Thomas White has formed a spacious vault for the interment of himself and family. The living is a rectory, valued in the King's books at £15. 13s. 4d. The Archbishop of York is the patron, and the Rev. Charles Wastneys Eyre, M.A. is the incumbent. Kingston-in-Carlton, which is commonly called NORTH CARLTON, was anciently so called from its being the King's manor; and Carlton-in-Lindrick, often called SOUTH CARLTON, may be supposed to have had the distinctive part of its name from the Saxon *Lind* or *Linden*—here being probably in monastic times several shady avenues of lime trees,—under which the monks of Wallingwells used to promenade. The *South Common Field*, 2A. 3R. 36P., let for £6, belongs to the church. A house and two small fields in the valley betwixt North and South Carlton, formerly belonged to the parish schoolmaster, until they were sold to the Ramsden family, more than 20 years ago; but in 1831, Robert Ramsden, Esq. repaired the loss of the poor by erecting a new *school*, near the same site, and he now allows a salary to a master and mistress, who have under their care nearly 200 children and infants. He has also furnished a library of 200 volumes for the use of the parishioners. The western side of the parish adjoins Yorkshire, and has a rich limestone soil, but the eastern side is sandy, and rises to a considerable altitude.

WIGTHORPE is a pleasant little hamlet, 3 miles N. of Worksop, in the constablewick of South Carlton, which repairs its roads separately, but maintains its poor conjointly with North Carlton.

CARLTON NORTH.

Anderson Thos. vict. Blue Bell
Anderson W. sen. vict. New Bell
Brammer Geo. shoemaker
Brown Mary, schoolmistress
Cattam A. vict. Butchers' Arms
Cowley Wm. butcher
Dean George, butcher
Drabble Jas. cabinet maker and joiner
Fletcher Mrs. Hannah
Glossop Robert, butcher
Haigh Wm. grocer and draper
Harrison Mrs. Sarah
Henson John, schoolmaster
Hepper Rev. Geo. curate
Lindley Wm. shopkeeper
Marsden Joseph, tailor
Rich Geo. joiner & wheelwright.
Ryalls John, shoemaker
Scorah John, blacksmith
Scott Wm. shopkeeper
Swanwick Thos. shoemaker
Tinker John, shoemaker
Tinsley Wm. excise officer
Travis Wm. shoemaker
Turner John vict. Blacksmiths' Arms
Ward Wm. gardener
Worsley Mrs. Lydia
Yates Mrs. Ann

FARMERS.

Bowmer Wm. Eyre Robert
Cowleshaw Wm. Field Joseph, &
Duckmanton J. maltster
Duckmanton Sl. Hides Geo.

Ingall Anthy.   Traves John
Mellors John   Turner John
Pigott Thos.

CARLTON SOUTH.

Ramsden Rt. Esq. Carlton hall
Cowlishaw Jph. gent
Dawson Sarah, schoolmistress
Foster Richard, joiner
Jarvis Wm. parish clerk
Liversidge Rich. shoemaker
Manwaring John, Esq. Wigthorpe
Pearson Geo. blacksmith
Ranson Wm. grocer & draper
Rawson Fras. gamekeeper
Shillitoe Robert, tailor
Spencer Wm. vict. Red Lion
Staneland Jph. vict. Grey Horses
Townrow Fras. corn miller
Whitehead Mrs. Eliz.

FARMERS.

Brooks Geo. Holme House
Johnson William
Levick Saml. Broom House
Otter George
Palmer Geo. Pen cottage
Spencer Wm. yeoman
Spurr Wm. & maltster, Wigthorpe
Ward Thos. Wigthorpe

COACHES ;—The Forrester and Royal Union, from Nottingham to Doncaster- call at the Grey Horses

CUCKNEY PARISH

Extends eastward from the vicinity of *Creswell Crags*, in Derbyshire, to near Thoresby park, and is bounded on the north by Welbeck, and on the south by Church Warsop. It is watered by the river Poulter, on which are two large *cotton mills*, and contains 267 houses, 1648 inhabitants, and 5284A. 3R. 21P. of good forest land, all enclosed, but partly in plantations and extensive pastures. It is divided into four townships, of which the following is an enumeration, with the population and extent of each :—

Townships	Houses.	Persons.	Acres.	Townships.	Houses.	Persons.	Acres.
Cuckney,	93	633	1095	Langwith,	66	437	1295
Holbeck,	46	244	1718	Norton,	62	334	1297

CUCKNEY is a considerable village on the small river called the Poulter, 5 miles S. by W. of Worksop. Here are two large mills for spinning cotton and grinding corn, and also the ruins of a cotton mill which was burnt down in 1792. Throsby, who wrote in 1796, says, " here are children from the foundling hospital, London, who are employed at the cotton and worsted mills, and live in cottages built for the purpose, under the care of superintendents ; boys under one roof and girls under another ;" but this is not the case now, the poor parishioners having a sufficient number of children to watch the mill machinery. The *church*, which is a large ancient structure with a handsome tower, was re-pewed, new-roofed, and thoroughly repaired in 1831, when a number of free seats were provided. Towards this necessary reparation, the Duke of Portland and Earl Bathurst, each gave £100, and the Society for building Churches, £50. The vicarage is valued in the King's books at £9. 8s. 6½d. The Rev. Edward Palling, B.A. is the incumbent, and Earl Manvers the patron, but Earl Bathurst is owner of the soil, and lord of the manor of Cuckney, which was held by Sweyn the Saxon, and after the Conquest, given in fee to Hugh Fitz-Baldric and Joceus de Flemaugh, except two carucates, which Gamelbere, an old Saxon Knight, was allowed to retain for the service of shoeing the King's palfrey, " as oft as he should lie at his manor of Mansfield." A great part of this parish was given by Sir Henry de Fawkenburg and others, to the monks of Welbeck. In *Cuckney* township are the extensive farms called *Mount Pleasant, Park House*, and *Shireoak Hill*. The great tithes of the whole parish belong to the owners of the different manors, and are included in the rents of the farms, but the vicarial tithes are paid by the tenants in money.

HOLBECK, or *Howbeck* township, is the largest and most thinly populated division of the parish. It contains five small hamlets, called HOLBECK, BONBUSK, WOODHOUSE, WOODEND, and a few scattered farmsteads lying at the west end of the parish, from 4 to 5 miles S.S.W. of Worksop, one of which is *Collingthwaite*, where there is a corn mill. It is all the property of the Duke of Portland, who in 1810, obtained it from Earl Manvers in exchange for that part of the forest land called Bilhagh. At Woodhouse, is a small *Catholic chapel*, established by the Rev. John Tristram, and now visited monthly by a priest from Spink-hill, near Eckington.

LANGWITH is a romantic village and township, on the verge
of the county, near the source of the Poulter, where there is
a large cotton mill, and several fine woody acclivities, 2 miles
W. of Cuckney, and 7 miles S.S.W. of Worksop. The village is called *Nether Langwith*, and near it, in a delightful
situation, is LANGWITH HALL, now occupied by R. N. Sutton,
Esq., but once the occasional seat of Earl Bathurst, to whom
it still belongs, together with the rest of the township and
manor, of which he is lord and impropriator. His Lord
ship's seats are now at Oakley Grove, near Cirencester, Glou
cestershire, and at Fairy Hill, in Kent.

NORTON, sometimes called *Norton Cuckney*, is a pleasant
village and township lying in a delightful vale near the confluence of the Poulter, with the extensive lake of Welbeck
park, 1 mile N.E. of Cuckney, and 4½ miles S. of Worksop.
It all belongs to his Grace the Duke of Portland, the lord of the
manor, whose benevolent Duchess supports a *school* here for
the education of 35 poor girls, whom she also provides with
frocks, cloaks, and bonnets.

MILNTHORPE is a hamlet in Norton township, distant a quarter of a mile from the village; and near it is *Hatfield Grange*, the
only place in the county which bears the name of this great
division of Bassetlaw.

CRESWELL CRAGS, about half a mile north of Holbeck, and
3 miles S.W. of Worksop, are in Derbyshire, but so adjacent
to Nottinghamshire as to be often considered a part of that
county. Lying out of the usual track of good roads, and being
almost inaccessible for carriages, they are not often visited by
tourists, though they are remarkably curious;—consisting of
lofty precipitous rocks, torn by some convulsion of nature into
a thousand romantic shapes, and presenting a miniature resemblance of the more majestic scenery on the Derwent, near
Matlock.

Cuckney parish participates in *Dame Frances Pierrepont's
Charity*, of which the Chapter of Southwell are trustees. The
Parish FEAST is on the nearest Sunday to Old Michaelmas Day.

CUCKNEY.

Allen Thos. shopkeeper
Bird John, tailor and draper
Bowles Benj. bookkeeper
Chadwick John, wheelwright
Cocking Wm. butcher
Day Henry, butcher
Frost John, shoemaker
Goucher Rd. stone mason
Harland Wm. shoemaker
Haskins John, Esq. land agent
Hollins Henry & Charles, & Co. cotton spinners.
Holt Mrs. Elizabeth
Johnson John, schoolmaster and parish clerk
Keeton John, joiner & cabt. mkr
Mason Rev. Geo. M.A. vicar of Whitwell
Needham Geo. shoemaker and shopkeeper
Palling Rev. Edw. B.A. vicar
Parker John, baker
Parker Robert, shopkeeper
Pearce Jas. vict. & maltster, Green Dale Oak

Shaw Wm. blacksmith
Teather Rd. shoemaker.
Thirkhill Benj. vict. & shoemakr.
Red Lion
Webster Jph. tailor
Wallas Miss Sarah
Worsley Geo. shoemaker

FARMERS.

Armstrong Samuel, Park House
Davy Saml. Shire Oak Hill
Miller Thomas
Pressley Wm. Mount Pleasant
Turner Wm.
Wright Willows

HOLBECK.

*Marked 1 reside at Bonbusk, 2
at Holbeck, 3 at Holbeck-
Woodhouse, & 5 at Woodend.*

5 Beeley Josiah, vict. Blue Bell
Bouler Geo. corn miller, Collingthwaite
2 Booth Wm. blacksmith
Castledine Jas. shopkeeper
Castledine Jas. jun. shoemaker
3 Drabble Rt. shoemaker
3 Eyre Geo. shopkeeper
2 Eyre John, Nurseryman
3 Frost Sarah, vict. Fox
2 Highfield John, tailor
3 Taylor Jas. vict. Gate
Windle Jas. shopkeeper

FARMERS.

5 Beeley John   Presley Ralph,
  Hilltop   Hursecroft
3 Bell John   Presley William,
1 Coupe John   Norwood
1 Hurst Geo. . 3 Revill Edw.
5 Johnson John 2 Skinner John
        1 Skinner Wm.

LANGWITH.

Booth John, blacksmith.
Chapman Geo. tailor
Coupe Wm. wheelwright & tim-
ber dealer
Cox George, maltster
Fox Thos. shoemaker

Hollins Hy. & Chas. & Co. cot-
ton spinners
Johnson Wm. Gooddy, grocer &
bookkeeper
Naylor Jph. vict. & maltster,
Jug and Glass
Pickard Geo. shoemaker
Slack Isaac, shopkeeper
Stanley John, stone sawyer
Sutton Peter Nassau, Esq. Lang-
with Hall

FARMERS.

Bagshaw Fras. Jackson Joseph,
Flint John   Boon Hill
Flint Saml.   Pigott Eliz. Pas-
Fox Thos. jun.   ture Hill
Goucher Mary

NORTON.

Marked † reside at Milnthorpe

†Ashbery George, wheelwright
Beeley Jonth. butcher
Boaler Mr. Joseph
Downs Geo. corn miller & baker
Evans Richard, tailor
Flower Williamson, butcher
†Gibbens Charles, baker
Green John, vict. Packhorse
†Helt John bricklayer
Hodgkinson Rt. shopkeeper
Marlow Chpr. valet
Marlow John, blacksmith
Marshall Wm. butcher
Miller Edw. excise officer
†Oldham John, farmer
Parkin John, vict. & maltster,
White Hart
Roper Timothy, brewer & cooper
Russell Ann, schoolmistress
Smith Benj. vict. & horse dealer
Storey Geo. farmer, Hatfield
Swift Thos. woodman
Taylor Thos. farmer, South Car
Waller John, blacksmith
Webster Hanh. vict. Plough
Wild Geo. shoemaker
Woodhead Wm. joiner

EDWINSTOW PARISH.

This very extensive parish is situated in the heart of Sherwood Forest, (see p. 35.) and contains some fine old woodland
scenery, many modern plantations, and several open tracts of

forest land, which afford good pasturage for sheep. A large
portion of it was not enclosed till 1818, and about 2000 acres of
it form the beautiful park and pleasure grounds of *Thoresby
Hall*, from which it stretches northward to Carburton, near
Clumber and Welbeck,—southward to the *market town* of Ollerton,—and westward to *Clipstone Park*, which now forms a
highly cultivated farm, within 3 miles of Mansfield. The rivers
Medin and Maun traverse it from west to east, as also does the
Duke of Portland's FLOOD DIKE, which commences near
Sutton in Ashfield, and passes nearly parallel with the Maun,
to the village of Edwinstow, and is provided with numerous
flood gates and sluices, by means of which the sloping and once
barren meadows on each side of it are so regularly irrigated in
the dry seasons, and so preserved from inundation when there
is a redundancy of rain, that they now produce several plentiful
crops of grass, clover, &c., every year. Besides the *church* at
Edwinstow, the parish has three *Chapels of Ease*, and contains
upwards of 16,000 acres divided into six townships, of which
the following is an enumeration, with the population and super-
ficial contents of each.

Townships.	Houses.	Persons.	Acres.	Townships.	Houses.	Persons.	Acres.
Edwinstow,	166	740	5815	Clipstone,	49	223	1648
Budby,	19	139	1300	Ollerton,	130	658	2400
Carburton,	28	143	1500	Palethorpe	14	89	4000

EDWINSTOW, or *Edenstowe*, is a large village, pleasantly situated on a gentle declivity, 2 miles W. of Ollerton. It is extremely rural, and its venerable *church* has a lofty spire, highly
ornamented with "turret looking Gothic niches." It was originally a "*berue*" of the King's great manor of Mansfield, and
the inhabitants had the right of pasturage in the King's hays of
Bilhagh and Birkland. Henry LV. granted them a FAIR for
two days, but it is now held only one day, viz. on October 24th
for cattle, sheep, and swine; and the parish *feast* is on the Sunday
following. In the 3d of Edward III., the Dean and Chapter
of Lincoln pleaded that they were rectors of "*Edenestow* and
Orston," and that they had possessed from time immemorial in
the former place, view of frank-pledge, assize of bread and
ale, and had several tenants there. Thoroton says, "the
royalties and wastes of Edwinstow and Carburton, are the in-
heritance of the Duke of Newcastle by agreement," but these
manors both belonged to the Duke of Porland, till about twenty
years ago, when his Grace gave that of Edwinstow to Earl
Manvers, in exchange for the manor of Holbeck, except the hay
of Birkland, which he still retains. The CHURCH is dedicated
to St. Mary, and its lofty spire which was repaired in 1816,
may be seen at a considerable distance. It has annexed to it
the chapels of Ollerton, Palethorpe, and Carburton, and is in
the appropriation of the Dean and Chapter of Lincoln, under

whom the Duke of Portland and Earl Manvers are lessees of the
great tithes. The *vicarage*, valued in the King's books at
£14, is in the gift of the Dean of Lincoln, and is now enjoyed
by the Rev. John Cleaver, LL. D. The Hon. and Rev. J. L.
Savile has a seat in the village, and Col. H. L. Savile, resides
at COCKGLODE,* a beautiful mansion embowered in wood, and
distant 1 mile W. by N. of Ollerton. This seat belongs to Sir
R. S. Milnes, Bart., but after his death it will become the
property of Earl Manvers.

Poor's Land, &c.—In 1627, Ann and Wm. Monday granted
their homestead and 16A. 3R. 22P. of land in Edwinstow to the
churchwardens, for the use of the poor of Edwinstow, Clipstone, and Budby. At the enclosure in 1818, this charity received an allotment of 132 acres, of which the trustees sold 40
acres for £375, which they expended in enclosing and fencing
the remainder, except £97. 14s. 6d., which is now in the Retford Savings' Bank. The whole property produces £60 per
annum, half of which is given to the poor of Edwinstow, two-
thirds of the remainder to those of Clipstone, and the rest to
those of Budby.

Edwinstow FREE SCHOOL, which is open to all the poor boys
of the parish, on the National system, was founded in 1719, by
John Bellamy, who endowed it with 5A. 2R. 39P. of land, which
in 1828, was exchanged by Earl Manvers for Parkinson Close,
(5A. 2R. 18P.) and the Manor-house garden (21 perches). The
school-house was rebuilt in 1824 by Earl Manvers, who subscribes with the vicar and inhabitants towards the master's
salary, which is about £40 per annum. The founder also left
two houses adjoining the school for *poor widows*, but they were
pulled down about 30 years ago, and four cottages built on the
site for the reception of as many pauper widows. The whole
parish participates in the charity called the *Lincoln Dole*, of
which the Dean and Chapter of Lincoln are trustees.

BIRKLAND and BILHAGH are two ancient woods of Sherwood
Forest, and though they have long been cleared of underwood,
they still contain many large and venerable oaks, in every stage
of perfection and decay. They form a wild and open forest
tract, 3½ miles in length, extending westward from Thoresby
Park to the liberties of Warsop and Clipstone. Birkland,
which contains 947A. 2R., is the property of the Duke of Portland; and Bilhagh, which extends eastward from Birkland,
now belongs to Earl Manvers, and comprises 540A. 2R. 37P.
At the east end of Bilhagh is an extensive FOX COVER, called
Ollerton Corner. (See page 37, where the contents of these
wastes should be stated 1500 acres, and not 15,000.). They are
in Edwinstow township, as also is the newly enclosed district

---

* *Cockglode* was built in 1778, by the late George Aldridge, M. D., who had
the estate on a lease from the Duke of Portland.

called the SOUTH FOREST, which lies betwixt Rufford and the river Maun, and has a small new hamlet bearing the name of KING'S STAND, and distant 2 miles W.S.W. of Ollerton. VILLA-REAL, a large farm, half a mile W. of Edwinstow, is so named from the family who, about 50 years ago, held a great portion of the copyhold lands in this manor.

BUDBY township, on the Worksop road, 3 miles N.W. of Ollerton, has a handsome rural village of *Gothic cottages*, at the south-west corner of Thoresby park, under a thickly wooded acclevity, and on the south side of the river Medin, which is here crossed by a neat bridge. In Domesday survey, it is called *Buteby*, and was *soc* of the King's great manor of Mansfield, of which it is now held in fee by Earl Manvers, whose Countess pays for the education and clothing of 18 poor girls, in the school which was built by his late mother in 1807. *Budby North and South Forest*, are unenclosed, but form excellent sheep walks.

CARBURTON, or *Carberton*, is a small village on the west side of Clumber, upon the small river called the Wollen, near the Ollerton road, 4 miles S. by E. of Worksop. Its township and chapelry includes *Carburton Forge*, a small hamlet one mile W. of the village, where there was formerly an iron forge. The Duke of Portland is owner,* and lord of the manor, which is all enclosed; and in the reign of Edward II., was partly claimed by the abbot of Welbeck, who enclosed "*Carberton Storth*," lying near the gate of his abbey," though the inhabitants pleaded that it was part of their ancient demesne. The *chapel* has a small burial ground, and is annexed to Edwinstow vicarage. The *turnpike* from hence to Worksop and Newark, was formed under acts passed in the 10th and 31st of Geo. III.

CLIPSTONE, once the seat of Royalty, is now one of the poorest and most decayed villages in Bassetlaw, though seated in the most picturesque part of the vale of the Maun, 5 miles E.N.E. of Mansfield, and nearly 2 miles S.W. of Edwinstow. Of the 1648 acres in this township, nearly 900 form one of the wildest wastes of the forest, and a large portion of the remainder has been enclosed, and brought into a rich state of cultivation by the present owner and lord of the manor, the Duke of Portland, who formed, at an immense expense, the *flood dike* and sluices already noted at page 415. Amongst the numerous farms which his Grace retains in his owns hands, that of *Clipston Park* is now perhaps the most productive; though it was lately only a wild tract of cleared woodland, once famous for its large oaks, most of which were cut down during the civil wars, and the commonwealth. This park was nearly 8 miles in circumference, and at its south-east corner, upon a commanding eminence, stood CLIPSTONE PALACE, of which

* Except about 40 acres belonging to the Duke of Newcastle, and enclosed in Clumber park.

2 o

some venerable ruins still remain, consisting of several fragments of massive walls, formed of small rough stones embedded
in mortar, which is as hard as the stones themselves. It is
said to have been built and occupied by one of the King's of
Northumberland. Throsby, says it was a palace for the King's
of England, so early as the reign of Henry II. It was such
a favourite residence of King John, both before and after his
accession to the throne, that it obtained the name of " KING
JOHN'S PALACE," and several of his grants to Nottingham and
other places are dated from it. A Parliament was held here by
Edward I. in 1290, but it is " uncertain whether they met
in the palace, or under an oak on the edge of the park, to
which tradition has given the name of *Parliament Oak*.—
(See page 37.) One story, however, says, that this aged
oak (of which the hollow trunk still remains,) obtained its
name as early as 1212, when King John, whilst hunting with his
Barons in the park, received intelligence of a second revolt of
the Welch, and hastily assembled his followers under the
branches of this oak, where, after a brief consultation, it was determined that the 28 Welch hostages then at Nottingham Castle
should be hanged.—(See p. 84.) The only part of the palace
now remaining, stands in a large field close to the village,
and seems to have been the hall. The foundations have
formerly been very extensive, with several large vaults, but
in 1810, a great part of these were dug up to be employed
in a system of drainage, which the Duke of Portland then commenced upon his estate here; but we understand that his Grace
gave strict orders, that the venerable walls of this once royal
pile should not be touched, yet in opposition to this edict, much
demolition has taken place; and on our visit we observed under
the ruins large heaps of stones which some churlish surveyor
appeared to have broken for the purpose of repairing the roads,
and which would have been so appropriated, had not his Grace
on hearing of the dilapidation, forbidden their removal. The
manor of Clipstone, was given by Henry VIII. to the Duke of
Norfolk. It afterwards passed to the Earl of Warwick and
Henry Sidney, who forfeited it to the crown, with which it remained till James I. granted it to the Earl of Shrewsbury's
feoffees, from whom it was passed to the Newcastle family, and
from them to that of Portland. *Clipston Feast* is on the first
Sunday in November.

OLLERTON, is a small market town, pleasantly situated
near the confluence of the Maun and the Rainworth-water, upon
the high road betwixt Worksop and Newark, 9 miles S.S.E. of
the former, 13 miles N.W. of the latter, and 6 miles W.S.W.
of Tuxford. It has a weekly *market* on Friday, and two *fairs*
annually, viz. May 1st, for cattle, sheep, and pedlery, and the
nearest Friday to October 18th, for *hops*,—of which considerable quantities are grown in Boughton and other adjacent

parishes, but nearly all the hop-yards in this township have been subjected to the plough. At the Conquest, Ollerton, or *Allerton*, formed two manors, one of the fee of Roger de Busli, and the other of the fee of Gilbert de Gand. In the 4th of Edward III., the Earl of Kent "held the manor of *Ollerton* of the honour of Donnington, which belonged to the King as Earl of Chester." It afterwards passed to the Suttons and Markhams, and the lands now belong principally to Earl Manvers and the Hon. and Rev. J. L. Saville, the latter of whom is lord of the manor, and holds a *Court* yearly on the 24th of October. The township contains 130 houses and 658 inhabitants, and has a neat CHAPEL OF EASE, which is annexed to the vicarge of Edwinstow, and was rebuilt about 55 years ago, when money was raised for that purpose by mortgaging the "*Town Lands,*" which comprise 58A. 2R. 33P., let for £50 per annum, and have belonged to the chapelry from time immemorial. The rents are received by the constable, and out of them he pays the county rate. In 1739, *Francis Thompson*, left £24, and in 1743, Thomas Markham, left £5 to the poor; the interest of these sums is paid out of the poor rates and distributed in bread. The *Methodists* have a small chapel here, and near the town is a large *paper mill*, which has long been unoccupied. The *bridge* here, like many others, was thrown down in the *flood* of 1795.—(See p. 99.) *Colonel Thomas Markham*, of Ollerton, was a distinguished soldier in the royal cause during the civil wars, and was drowned in the Trent in 1643, after engaging the Parliament forces near Gainsborough.

PALETHORPE, or *Peverelthorpe,* is a small village on the east side of *Thoresby Park,* within which most of its township and chapelry is enclosed. It is 3 miles N. of Ollerton, and is the property of Earl Manvers, but has passed through many families since William I. granted it to Roger de Busli. All the land is in the occupancy of the noble owner, and consequently the inhabitants are all in his employ. The CHAPEL, which has an entrance from the park, is an elegant stone fabric, with some beautiful stained glass in the windows. In niches at the west end are figures of Hope and Meekness, and at the east end is a neat monument in memory of Charles Alphonso Pierrepont, who lost his life after evincing much bravery at the storming of an outwork, near Bruges, on Sept. 19th, 1812. The curacy is annexed to the vicarage of Edwinstow. *Whitemoor* is a large farm near the confluence of the Maun and the Medin, occupied by the Earl's land agent.

THORESBY HALL, the seat of Earl Manvers, is a large and elegant mansion, in an open but rather a low situation, at the east end of a spacious lake formed by the river Medin, and is enclosed within a beautiful *park*, which is well stocked with deer, and no less than ten miles in circuit, extending northward to that of Clumber, and westward to the picturesque hamlet of Budby. The hall is distant 3 miles N. by W. of Ollerton, and was built on the site of the old house which was burnt down on the 4th of March, 1745, when nothing was saved but the family writings, the plate, and a small portion of the best furniture. It consists of a rustic stone basement, with two stories of brick-work, and the principal front is ornamented with a tetrastyle portico, of the Ionic order, of a beautiful stone. The window frames are richly gilt, and the principal entrance is in the basement, opening into the hall, in which are some good paintings and engravings, and a Chiaro Scuro of the Trojan horse, &c. There are also many fine paintings, &c. in the Earl's dressing room, and the drawing and dining rooms. The ascent to the principal story is by a double stair-case, which opens into the *dome*, a circular apartment of facti-tious marble, supported by 14 pillars, alternately round and square, on which rests a gallery ballustraded, and opening into the upper chambers. The light is admitted by a handsome cir-cular skylight, and the walls have a correct resemblance of yellow variegated marble, beautifully contrasting with the white pillars and pillasters, and others resembling the · *verd. antique ;* the floor is laid with the same substance tessellated. All the prin-cipal rooms are superbly furnished, and the dining room has a recess at one end formed of curious twisted pillars. A well moulded bust in the octagonal drawing room, represents *Pascal Paoli*, who, after fighting gallantly, first against the Genoese and then against the French, was obliged to fly from a long and unequal contest, and leave Louis the 15th in the posses-sion of his once free and independent country, from which he retired, and at length found an hospitable asylum at Thoresby. The present mansion was built by the last Duke of Kingston, and the *gardens*, which are very fine, were part of them con-structed by his Duchess, in the German style with arbours, and treillagated. In the Shrubbery a fine cascade falls into the river Medin, which, a little below the house, is crossed by a light and elegant bridge, and for more than a mile above forms a broad and spacious *lake*, on which are several handsome vessels, one of which is a full rigged *ship*, built near Gainsbro', and brought here upon a carriage made for the purpose, and supposed by the ignorant believers of Mother Shipton, to be the identical vessel which she prophecied would " sail over Nottingham Forest."

The PIERREPONT FAMILY, of whom Earl Manvers is now the head, descended from *Robert de Perpoint*, who, was of French extraction, and came first to England with the Norman Conqueror. His progeny soon acquired both fame and property, and in the reign of Edward IV. Henry Perpoint was distin-guished for his services against the Lancasterians. His son George purchased large estates after the dissolution of the reli-gious houses, and was knighted in the 1st of Edward VI.

Henry, his son and heir, married the daughter of Sir William
Cavendish, and left issue Robert, who, in 1627, was created
Baron Pierrepont of Holm-Pierrepont, and *Viscount Newark;*
and in the following year was raised to the dignity of *Earl of
Kingston*. In the civil wars of Charles I. he was a Lieutenant
General, and raised 1200 men for the king's service. He was
succeeded by his son Henry, who also distinguished himself in
the cause of royalty, and was created *Marquis of Dorchester*,
in 1644. He died in 1680, without issue, when the Marquisate
became extinct, but the Earldom devolved on his grand-nephew,
Robert Pierrepont, who in 1682 was succeded by his brother
William, who died in 1690, leaving his honours and estates to
his brother Evelyn, who was created Marquis of Dorchester in
1706, and *Duke of Kingston-upon-Hull*, in 1715. He was
succeeded by his grandson, Evelyn, the last Duke of Kingston,
who died without issue, in 1773, when his titles became extinct.
Three years after his death, his Duchess was tried for bigamy,
she having married him during the life of her first husband,
Augustus John Hervey, Esq. All the Peers found her guilty
except the Duke of Newcastle, who said, *"erroneously but not
intentionally guilty upon my honour,"*—upon which she was
discharged "on paying her fees of office." The Duke's
estates devolved upon his sister's son, *Charles Meadows,* who
assumed the name of Pierrepont, and was created *Baron
Pierrepont,* and *Viscount Newark,* in 1796, and *Earl Manvers,*
in 1806. He died in 1816, and was succeeded by his son, the
Right Honourable Charles Herbert Pierrepont, the present
Earl Manvers, Viscount Newark, and Baron Pierrepont, who
has large estates around Thoresby Hall, and in other parts of
the county. The *family name* in old writings is variously spelt,
Pyrpount, Peerpont, Poripont, Perpoynt, Perpont, Pourpont,
Perinpont, and Pierrepont—the present orthography.

The walk from Thoresby to Clumber, across the parks, presents such a beautiful succession of sylvan scenery, that the
tourist may almost conceive himself rambling amidst transat--
lantic forests.

"Majestic woods, of every vigorous green,
Stage above stage, high waving o'er the hills;
Or to the far horizon wide diffused,
A boundless deep immensity of shade."

EDWINSTOW PARISH DIRECTORY.

BUDBY.
Allen John, corn miller, Pale-
    thorpe mill
Bawdwen Wm. asst. clk. of wks.
Burks Eliz. schoolmistress
Carter Wm. bricklayer
Gottam Wm. stone mason

Hill John, joiner & cab. maker
Oldham Thos. farmer
Schneider Mr. Peter Alex.
Sidda Edw. farmer
Taylor Wm. shopkeeper
Wagstaff John, blacksmith
Walter Jas. clerk of works

2 o 2

CARBURTON.

Bradley Hanh. vict. Old Sun
Brett David, shoemaker
Burchby Thos. cab. mkr. Clumber park
Candlin Rt. lodge keeper
Cutts Henry, hind
Eardley Jph. wood turner
Greenwood Rd. farmer
Tidswell Jas. shopkeeper
Vickers Edw. farmer
Widdowson John, shopkeeper

CLIPSTONE.

Amos Cornl. vict. & joiner, Fox and Hounds
Hatton Rd. gamekeeper
Jepson John, shopkeeper
Paulson George, keeper
Staniland Abm. vict. Dog & Duck
Whitworth Saml. shopkeeper

FARMERS.

Amos Thos.   Sabine Wm.
Amos Wm.   Broom-hill
Dunstan Thos.   Grange
Gilbert Thos.   Wood John,
Lindley John   bailiff, Park
Millns Wm.   Farm

EDWINSTOW.

Savile, the Hon. & Rev. John Lumley, (& Rufford)
Savile, Col. Hy. Lumley, Esq. Cock Glode
Bowring John, tailor
Brett Wm. tailor, King's stand
Bullivant Thos. butcher
Bullivant Wm. vict. Black Swan
Butler Wm. shoemaker
Cleaver Rev. John, LL.B. vicar
Day John, shoemaker
Dickinson John, M.D. and M.R.C.S. & L.S.A.
Doncaster Geo. gent
Fanniwell John, butcher
Fieldsend Marfleet, miller & bkr.
Fletcher Geo. wheelwright
Foster Wm. shoemaker
Freeman James, shoemaker
Freeman John, shoemaker
Godson Decimus, land surveyor, King's stand, and Ollerton
Hanson Waddington, butcher
Hawksley Mrs. Ann
Hinds Wm. shoemaker

Hoggard Saml. blacksmith
Hufton Wm. woodman
Hurst Fras. vict. Royal Oak
Hurst Geo. grocer & draper
Johnson Jph. joiner
Mitchell Wm. weaver
Morley John, shoemaker
Morley Thos. blacksmith
Parnhill Abm. shoemaker
Peatfield John, maltster, h. Wellow
Pocklington Rev. Roger, curate
Robinson Hy. sawyer
Russell Hy. schoolr. & clerk
Slingsby Wm. tailor
Smith Mary, shopkeeper
Stocks Hy. bricklayer
Trueman Rueben, shoemaker
Tudsbury Chas. vict. Robin Hood, King's stand
Tudsbury Rd. joiner
Tudsbury Wm. joiner
Wadsworth Jph. wheelwright
Ward Wm. nursery man, South Forest
Webster Miles, grocer, dpr. &c.
Webster Saml. vict. jug & glass
Widdowson Rt. stone mason
Woodhead Edw., John, & Rd., wheelwrights

FARMERS.

1 live at South Forest, and 2 at Mount Pleasant.

1 Argyle John   2 Jackson John
Ashline John   Lee Saml.
Brett Wm.   Peatfield Jph.
Bullivant John, 1 Smith Wm.
  Villa Real   1 Stubbins Chs.
Fowe Edward,   Stubbins Jthn.
  Black hills   Webster Php.
Hewgill Jas.   Weightman Hu.
Hodgkinson J.

PALETHORPE & THORESBY.

Earl Manvers, the Rt. Hon. Chas. Herbert Pierrepont, Thoresby Hall
Viscount Newark, the Hon. Chas. Evelyn Pierrepont, M. P. Thoresby Hall
Barrer Mr. house steward
Bennett Selby, gardener
Brown Titus, sailor

Budd Mrs. Mary, Buckgates lodge

Hartley Rt. joiner, &c.

Hufton Stpn. woodman, Budby lodge

Hutchinson Hy. clerk, Ivy cottage

Kemp Rt. poulterer

Manall Thos. whitesmith

Mansell Hy. gamekeeper, Kennels

Paschoud Chas. park keeper, Proteus lodge

Pickin Wm. John, Esq. land agent, Whitemoor

Shaw John, groom

Upton John, land bailiff

Snowden Samuel, tailor

Witham Samuel, shepherd

OLLERTON.

Post Office, Hop Pole Inn, Jph. Lister, post master. Letters are despatched by a mail gig to Newark at ¼ past 7 mg. and arrive at 1 noon.

Becket Thos. cht. & druggist

Bennitt Charles, gent

Bolton Wm. farmer

Botham Mrs. Elizabeth

Butt John, draper

Dawson Jane, confectioner

Doncaster John, gent

Eyre Charles, farmer

Godson Decimus, land surveyor

Gravenor Rt. tanner and bone crusher

Graves Rd. cart owner

Gregory Wm. Johnson, wine, spirit, & seed merchant

Hawkins Wm. Hy. excise officer

Justice John, road surveyor

Lesiter John, farmer

Osborne Samuel, cooper

Patterson Thos. gent. Ashen-Oak cottage

Pepper Thos. baker & flour dlr.

Pinder Geo. corn miller

Scatchard Mrs. Ann

Scatchard Wm. gardener

Turner Miss Elizabeth

Turner Samuel, farmer

White Mr. Sampson

Wood Saml. parish clerk, town crier, & sexton

Woodruff Wm. braizier, &c.

HOP GROWERS

In the Neighbourhood.— See also Tuxford & Retford.

Alvey Chpr. Boughton

Barker John, Eakring

Boot Sarah, Ollerton

Bolton Wm. Ollerton

Brownlow Thos. (hop and corn merchant) Ollerton

Bunby Thomas, Eakring

Cox Edward, Ollerton

Doncaster John, Ollerton

Eaton John, Rufford mill

Flower Wm. Boughton

Frogson Henry, Boughton

Gibson Wm. Boughton

Gravenor Rt. Ollerton

Gregory Wm. Johnson, Ollerton

Harvey John, Ompton

Hill Elizabeth, Wellow

Hurt William, Eakring

Kitchen Wm. Wellow

Lawrence Charles, Boughton

Lesiter John, Ollerton

Lister Joseph. Ollerton

Machon Hy. Gateford hill

Metheringham Geo. Boughton

Parkinson John, Ley fields

Peatfield John, Wellow

Ryals John, Eakring

Squires John, Boughton

Turner Rd. Ollerton

Walker John, Wellow

Walker Wm. Wellow

Williamson Luke, Rufford

Woombill John, Wellow

Woombill John, Ompton

INNS & TAVERNS.

The last three are Beerhouses.

Blue Bell, Thos. Brownlow

Hop Pole Inn, Jph. Lister

White Hart, Sarah Boot

Board Jph. Thompson

King William IV., Rd. Gill

Maltsters' Arms, Wm. Woolley

Academies.

Brockner Geo. (bdg.)

Hibbs Wm.

Blacksmiths.

Horsman Wm.

Teather Geo.

Boot & Shomkrs.
Bull Geo.
Cook John
Harrison Jas.
Johnson Geo,
Mills Geo.
Morley Wm.
Teather Geo.
   Bricklayers.
Brown Geo.
Thompson Geo.
   Butchers.
Bennett Jph.
Turner Rd.
Widdowson W.
   Drapers.
Lilley Sarah
Willey & Co.
   (& Sheffield)
   Grocers, &c.
Doncaster Ann
Ogle Atkin,(hop
  & seed mert.)
Osborne Dd.
Smith Mary
Sterland Wm.
  (chandler &
  ironmonger)

Joiners, &c.
Marshall Wm.
Roades Rd. (&
  broker)
Ward Wm.
   Maltsters.
Lister Jph.
Ogle Atkin,
  (malt, hop, &
  corn factor)
Wright John,
  Ashen Oak
Nurserymen, &c.
Smith Peter
Ward John
   Painters.
Halladay Rt.
Holliday Benj.
  Plumbers. &c.
Walker John,
  (& hosier)
Wilson Wm.
   Saddler.
Ward Jas.
   Surgeons.
Lilly John W.
Ward Rd. Chas.
  & Cox Edw.

Tailors & Dprs.
Collinson John
Ward John
Whitelaw Cpr.
Wood Saml.
Wright John
Wright Wm.
Vetny. Srgns.
Horseman Wm.

Osborne David
  Watch & Clock
   Makers.
Cobb Geo.
Powell Thos.
  Wheelwrights.
Bailey Rt.
Reynolds Geo.

CARRIERS.

To *London*, Rt. Hunt's waggons,
  from the White Hart. every
  Sun. Tu. Wed. and Fri. at 2
  aft., and to *Sheffield* every Mon.
  Wed. Fri. & Sat. aft. at 4, and
  Rt. Fletcher every Thurs.
To *Mansfield*, John Scathard and
  Geo. Taylor, Thu. 7 mg.
To *Newark*, Jno. Scatchard, Wed.
  7 mg.
To *Nottingham*, from the White
  Hart, John Rushby, Tu. & Fri.
  12 noon.
To *Retford*, from the Blue Bell,
  Thos. Johnson. every week, &
  John Rushby, Tu. & Fri. dep.
  11 night, ar. 12 noon.

ELKSLEY PARISH.

Lies on the east side of Clumber Park, and on both sides of the
Wollen, but the village of Elksley, is on the north bank of
that river, near its confluence with the Idle, 4 miles N. N. W.
of Tuxford. It contains 73 houses, 377 inhabitants, and about
2000 acres of land, a large portion of which formed a wild
tract of the forest till 1780, when it was enclosed and exonerated
from tithes, and an allotment of 66 acres awarded to the king as
Duke of Lancaster, under which Duchy the Duke of Newcastle holds this manor of Elksley, or "*Elchesleig;*" but
Robert Sharpe, Esq. and St. John's College, Cambridge, have
estates here. It was partly *soc* to Bothamsall, and of the fee of
Roger de Busli. A great portion of the land was given to the
monasteries of Worksop, Blyth, Rufford, Newark, Mattersea,
and Welbeck, the latter of which had the rectory and church,
which in the 4th of Edward VI. were granted to Richard
Winlove and Richard Field, and afterwards passed to the Earl
of Clare, whose descendant, the Duke of Newcastle, is patron
of the vicarage, which is valued in the king's books at £6. 16s.
and is now enjoyed by the Rev. William Hett, who receives

from the owners, as a commutation of the small tithes of the
old enclosures, about £80.a year; and possesses an allotment
of 83 acres of the new enclosures. 'The *church* is an ancient
edifice, with a nave, chancel, and tower. The *feast* is on the 2nd
Sunday after Old Michaelmas. The parish has about 14 acres
of *hop ground*, and a *benefaction* of £14, left in 1694, by Mary
Pitts, for which the overseers pay 14s. yearly to poor widows.

NORMANTON is a district in this parish, where there is a good
inn on the old Blyth and Ollerton road, 2 miles W. by S. of
Elksley village.

Bell John, bricklayer
Bown John, shoemaker
Colton Thos. vict. & shopkeeper,
  Bricklayer's Arms
Hett Rev. Wm. vicar
Kempshall John, gardener
Needham John, wheelwright
Ostick Wm. shoemaker, Dover
  lodge
Richards John, parish clerk
Richards John, jun. joiner and
  cabinet maker
Salvin Dd. vict. Robin Hood
Salvin David, jun. painter
Salvin James, butcher
Sharpe Robert, Esq.
Shirtliff James, blacksmith
Stockdale Jph. maltster, h. West
  Drayton
Towler George, blacksmith

Twible Rebecca, vict. Newcastle
  Arms, Normanton
Wells Thos. wheelwright and
  shopkeeper
Western Robert, saddler
Woodhead Jph. shoemaker
FARMERS.
Thus † are Hop Growers.
Belk Reginald Johnson Stpn.
Eyre Thos. †Johnson Thos.
†Fox Rd. Forest
Giles John, †Taylor Eliz.
  Normanton †Taylor Thos.
Hancock Rbca. †Weightman J.
†Hill Mtw. White Jph.
Hudson Ann Forest

CARRIER, Edw. Warrington to
  Lincoln, Thu. 9 mg. and to
  Sheffield, Fri. 9 evg.

FINNINGLEY PARISH

Occupies that northern apex of the county which stretches
northward from the Idle, betwixt Lincolnshire and Yorkshire,
within which latter county a large portion of this parish is comprised. It is divided into the three townships of *Finningley,
Auckley,* and *Blaxton,* which contain 184 houses, 962 inhabitants, and about 7000 acres of land; most of which has a good
sandy soil. The waste lands were enclosed by an act passed
in 1774; and in 1778, an allotment of 1156 acres was awarded to
the rector, in lieu of all the tithes, except those paid for 300
acres which had no common right, and which still remain
tithable.

FINNINGLEY is a large village and township, 4 miles N. by
E. of Bawtry, and has 80 houses, 424 inhabitants, and
2391A. 1R. of land, all in Nottinghamshire. The CHURCH is
dedicated to St. Oswald, and has lately been repaired, and

ornamented with a handsome stained glass window. The *rectory* is valued in the king's books at £13. 14s. 9d. The Rev. John Harvey, LL. B. is the incumbent, and John Harvey, Esq. of Finningley Park, is the patron, and also owner of most of the township, and lord of the manor, which was formerly the property of the Forbisher family;—of which was *Admiral Martin Forbisher*, an enterprising navigator, who was sent out by Queen Elizabeth, with three ships in 1567, in hopes of discovering a *north-west passage to India*. Having proceeded as far as Labrador, he was stopped by the approaching winter, but returned with a quantity of gold marcasite, or *pyrites aureus* which tempted the members of the "Society for Promoting Discovery," to send him out again with three ships, in 1577, when he discovered the Strait, now known by his name, but was again stopped by the ice; and having taken on board more of this glittering substance then supposed to be gold, he returned to England. Soon after this, Queen Elizabeth determined to form a settlement in these countries, and Admiral Forbisher was sent out for that purpose with 15 small vessels; but he could not get so far as he had done in his preceding voyages; so that he soon after returned, and gave up all further attempts to discover what has since been often sought for in vain. *Mr. John Bigland*, a venerable worthy, is now living in the village, where he was many years schoolmaster. He is a native of Skirlaugh, in Holderness, and author of the Yorkshire portion of the Beauties of England and Wales, and also of "A View of the World," and some other works.

AUCKLEY, or *Awkley*, 4 miles N. of Bawtry, is a village and township, containing 362 souls, 74 houses, and 2391A. 1R. of land, more than half of which is in Yorkshire within the soke of Doncaster, and belongs to Wm. Childers and John Smilter, Esqrs. Of the Nottinghamshire portion of the manor, John Childers, Esq. of Cantley, is lord and principal owner. Of the inhabitants, 127 are in Notts. and 235 in Yorks.

BLAXTON, or *Blakestone*, though in this parish, is a small village and township, wholly in Yorkshire, in the Wapentake of Strafford and Tickhill, and partly in the soke of Doncaster. It is 5 miles N. of Bawtry, and forms a *manor*, of which John Harvey, Esq. is lord and principal owner.

CHARITIES.—*William Hall*, in 1668, left 10s. yearly out of two acres in Blaxton-fields to the poor of Finningley parish, and it is now paid by Mr. George Wood. In 1672, *Richard Metcalf* gave to the poor of Finningley township, 2 acres, which, at the enclosure in 1774, were exchanged for 1A. 3R. 18P. in the Mill-field, let for £2. In the 28th Charles II. *John Tuke* gave to the poor of Auckley two acres, which, at the enclosure, were exchanged for 1A. 2R. 4P., now let for £1. 10s. *Auckley* has also 6s. 8d. yearly out of land belonging to Wm. Ramsey; the *Poor's-close*, let for £1; and the *Town-close*, containing 7A. 3R. 34P. which was awarded at the enclosure, and is placed to the poor rate account. *Sarah Wood* left 2s. 6d. yearly to Finningly; and the parish receives 10s. yearly from the overseers of Auckley, as interest of £10, left by an unknown donor. There is also about half an acre of land in Blaxton belonging to the poor.

AUCKLEY.

Marked † are in Yorkshire, and ‡ are Yeomen.

Binge Jph. shoemaker
Burkinshaw Geo. bricklayer
Garnett Saml. blacksmith
Gillatt Rd. vict. butcher, and shopr. Eagle & Child
†Gleadhill George, shoemaker
Halifax Wm. shopkeeper
Johnson Wm. bricklayer
†Kitching Thomas, tailor
Laycock Geo. shoemaker
Loftis William, butcher
†Rawson Abm. wheelwright
Shaw Geo. vict. Plough
Tyas William, shoemaker
Ward Chpr. shopkeeper
Woodward Thos. shopkeeper

FARMERS.

Allen Saml.
‡Baxter Rd.
†Brooke John
Gillott Hy.
‡Gleadhill Jph.
Hickson Thos. Highfield
‡Hirst John
Johnson John
Lee Wm.
‡Weld Wm.
Whitaker Geo.
†Younge Thos.

BLAXTON (YORKS.)

Coggan Jph. vict. saddler, and shopkeeper
Hoyle Rd. blacksmith
Richardson Rd. wheelwright
Robinson John, wheelwright

FARMERS.

Allin Isaac
Bradbury Wm.
Hague Rd.
‡Machon Jas.
‡Richardson S.
Senthouse Wm.
Wood Matthias

FINNINGLEY.

Bigland Mr. John
Chester Geo. butcher
Chester Geo. parish clerk
Coulthread Wm. blacksmith
Crookes John, wght. & smith
Cudworth Thos. vict. Harvey's Arms
Fox John, corn miller
Gillatt John, tailor
Godley Thomas, shoemaker
Gregory Hannah, shopkeeper
Gregory Thos. shoemaker
Harvey Rev. John, LL.B. rector
Laister Geo. vict. Horse & Stag
Lister Matthew, shoemaker
Rawlin George, butcher
Robinson Rev. Disney, M.A. curate
Robinson Chas. grocer, druggist, and schoolmaster
Saint Paul Geo. joiner, &c.
Skelton Geo. shopkeeper
Wilson Jph. shoemaker
Wilson Wm. shopkeeper
Woombill W. vict. Horse & Stag

FARMERS.

Cragg Wm.
Fowler Wm.
Gibson Chas.
Jackson Geo.
Lindley John
Machin John
Moulson Jas.
Newsome Rd.
‡Robinson W.
Seaman Wm.
‡Turner Wm.
‡Wood Benj.
‡Wood Geo.
Wood Jph
Wood Rt.

HARWORTH PARISH

Contains upwards 7000 acres, lying in the western verge of the county, betwixt Blyth and Tickhill, and has about 900 inhabitants, but those who live in "*Styrrup and Oldcoates*," are all returned with Blyth parish, in which part of that township is comprehended. The hamlets of *Hesley and Limpool, Martin, and Serlby*, are all in this parish, and maintain their poor conjointly with Harworth, which is the only part of the parish that was exonerated from tithe at the enclosure in 1804, when 108A. 1R. 36P. was awarded to the vicar, and 115A. 3R. 21P. in lieu of the great tithes appropriated to Shrewsbury Hospital, in in Sheffield Park, of which the Duke of Norfolk is trustee.

HARWORTH village is in rather a low situation, with a small stream running through it, 2 miles E.S.E. of Tickhill, and 2½ miles W.S.W. of Blyth. The *church* is dedicated to All Saints, and was built about the 12th century, except the chancel, which was erected in 1672. In repairing the building in 1828, an arched recess was discovered in the wall, with a cupboard containing a *garland*, a *cribbage board*, and several other articles of a more sacred character. At the same time a handsome *cross* was found in the churchyard, and is now placed above the east window. The Duke of Norfolk is patron of the *vicarage*, which is valued in the King's books at £5. 9s. 7d., and is now enjoyed by the Rev. William Downes. "The Church of *Harewode*, with the chapels of *Serleby* and *Morton*, were by King John granted the church of *Roan*, with many others, as part of the chapelry of Blyth, but in the 6th of Edward VI., they were granted to the Earl of Shrewsbury." The *feast* at Harworth, is on the 1st, and that at Styrrup on the 12th of November. The manor of Harworth, of which the Duke of Norfolk is lord, contains 1428A. 3R. 2P. The *School*, where 60 boys and girls are educated, is open to all the children of the parish, and was built in 1700, by Robert Brailsford, who endowed it with land, &c., now worth upwards of £88 a-year.

HESLEY and LIMPOOL, containing 617A. 1R. 35P., form the north-western hamlet of the parish, adjoining Yorkshire, 2 miles N.W. of Bawtry. HESLEY HALL, a neat mansion upon a commanding eminence, is the property of George Bustard Greaves, Esq., but is occupied by H. Marwood Greaves, Esq.

MARTIN, or *Morton*, forms the north-eastern hamlet of the parish, adjoining Bawtry, and comprising 1461A. 2R. 14P. divided into three farms, belonging to the Duke of Newcastle. Here is the site of a ROMAN STATION, where in 1828, three silver coins of *Antonius, Adrianus*, and *Faustina*, were found, together with part of a Roman vase, and many pieces of Roman pottery. The form of the fort or station may still be distinctly traced, and even when the field is covered with full grown wheat, an octagon figure is perceptible, from the stems being shorter and poorer on the site of the buildings, than in other places. Near the town of Bawtry, is the HOSPITAL OF ST. MARY MAGDALEN, founded about the year 1390, by *Robert Morton*, (whose family long held this estate,) "for a priest, there to be resident, and

to keep hospitality for poor people, and to pray for the founders's soul and all christian souls." It is valued in the king's
books at £8, of which £5. 6s. 8d. is still paid out of the possessions of the dissolved priory of St. Oswald, at Nostell, in Yorkshire. The hospital consists of two small dwellings for two poor
widows, and an ancient CHAPEL, in which no duty has been
done during the last seventy years, though the present master,
the Rev. John Rudd, vicar of Blyth, receives the above-named
rent charge, and also the rents of the following lands belonging
to the hospital, viz.—15 acres in Scrooby, two closes in Scaftworth, and 14 acres in this parish, out of which he only pays
40s. yearly to the two almswomen, whom he places in the
hospital.

PLUMBTREE is a farm of 339A. 2R. 24P. belonging to the
Archbishop of York, but held on lease by the Dowager Viscountess Galway, of Bawtry Hall.

SERLBY HALL, now the property and delightful residence of
Lord Vicount Galway, is pleasantly situated in a sylvan park
above the river Ryton, 3 miles S. by W. of Bawtry, and about
1 mile N. by E. of Blyth. In early times *Serleby* was the manor
of Alured the Saxon; but at the Norman Conquest was given
to Roger de Busli, of whom Gislebert his man held it. From
the Busli family it came to that of Mowbray, and in the reign of
king John, Roger de Mowbray, for what reason is not assigned,
gave it to Maud de Moles, who married *Hugh*, a man very likely
without a sirname, as he immediately adopted that of de Serlby.
For many generations it remained in this family, until the last
male, Anthony, in the beginning of the seventeenth century,
being childless, left it to his wife, Gertrude, daughter of Ralph
Leek, of Hasland, Esq. for her own life and twenty-one years
after. During this long interval of expectation, the male heir
of the Serlby family was obliged to sell the reversion to Mr.
Saunderson of Blyth; but the widow marrying Sir George
Chaworth, that family also purchased a part of it; and from
them it has come to the present possessor, to whose family it
belonged as far back as the beginning of the last century, at
which time there was a very old mansion standing on it. The
present building is of brick and stone, consisting of a centre of
very handsome elevation, with two appropriate wings, having
the offices in the underground story, and the stables and out
offices on the eastern side. The situation is extremely agree
able; on the south front is a sapcious lawn, beautifully interspersed with clumps of trees; whilst the north front has a
charming prospect over some very luxuriant meadows, watered
by the little river Ryton. The principal plantations are on the
south west side, with many avenues and shady walks cut
through them, opening to the most striking prospects in the
vicinity. The terrace is a part of the grounds always very
much admired, not only for its own beauty, but for the exquisite

2 P

view which is seen from it.   There are many fine *paintings* in
the various apartments ; amongst which are two undoubted
originals by Hans Holbein ; one of these is in the dining room,
and is a portrait of Henry the Eighth on wood; the other is in
the drawing room, and is a finely executed portrait of *Nicholas
Kreatzer*, astronomer to that monarch. The drawing room
also contains a very large picture, being twelve feet two inches
in height, and fifteen feet four in breadth, from the pencil of
Daniel Myton. Its subject is Charles the First and his queen,
with two horses, on one of which is a side saddle, and some
dogs, all as large as life. It also contains another figure as
large as life, but who, of himself, would not have required such
a breadth of canvas; this is Jeffery Hudson, the famous dwarf,
who is in the act of striving to keep back two small dogs, with
collars on. This picture having come into the possession of
Queen Anne, was by her presented to *Addison*, from whom it
came to the Arundels, of which family is its present noble possessor, the Right Hon. George Monkton, *Viscount Galway and
Baonr of Kildare, in Ireland*, whose ancestor, John Monkton,
was honoured with these titles by George II., and whose grandfather took the sirname of *Arundel*, agreeable to the will of
Lady Frances Arundel. His Lordship however is not a peer
of Parliament. His family was of great repute in Yorkshire,
in the reign of Edward I., when some of them resided at Nun-
Monkton, and "afterwards formed respectable and honourable
matrimonial alliances." The manor or hamlet of Serlby contains 502A. 1R. 22P. and is annexed to the *Constablewick* of
Torworth, though it maintains its poor jointly with Harworth.

STYRRUP and OLDCOATES, or " *Styrup and Ulcotes*," form
a township of 2959A. 2R. 36P., of which 940A. 1R. 22P. are in
the parish of Blyth, (see p. 397,) and the remainder in Harworth parish. OLDCOATES is a consideraale village on the
western verge of the county, 2¼ miles S. of Tickhill, and 7
miles N. of Worksop, and had near it a small lake, called the
White Water, but it is now drained and cultivated. STYRRUP
lies east of Oldcoates, and includes a village of its own name,
and the hamlet of NORNAY, which forms the northern suburb
of Blyth. There is a small *Methodist chapel* both at Styrrup
and Oldcoates. Viscount Galway is lord of the manor, but the
land belongs to a number of small freeholders. The common
land was enclosed in 1802. In Mr. Winter's orchard, at Oldcoates, is a remarkable black heart cherry tree, the bole of
which is 7 feet 10 inches in circumference, with branches extending over a circle of 52 yards. This tree is said to be 300
years old, and about 50 years ago it bore a *ton weight of fruit !*
which was sold for £5 to a Mr. Gleadhill, of Tickhil, who only
cleared 15s. by his bargain, owing to the cherries being cracked
by the rain before they were pulled.

CHARITIES *belonging to Harworth Parish :*—The *hospital*

at Martin, and the *school* at Harworth are already noticed. The school was endowed in 1700, by *Robert Brailsford*, who was cook to the Saundersons, of Serlby Hall, with a farmhouse and 58A. 1R. 12P. of land, in the manor of Hatfield, and parish of Fishlake, in Yorkshire, for clothing and educating the poor boys of Harworth, Serlby, and Styrrup. In 1811, it received an allotment of 2 acres of common land, and the whole is now let for £59 per annum. There is also belonging to the school £253. 13s. stock, in the 3½ per cents., standing in the names of the trustees,—Viscount Galway, Henry Walker, George Greaves, and Wm. Downes, Esqrs. In 1724, *Mary Saunderson* bequeathed out of the Serlby estate a yearly rent charge of £20, to be applied in educating and apprenticing the poor boys and girls of Harworth school. She also gave £20 to the poor, which, with £20 left in 1723, by *Bridget Neville*, is vested in £39 stock, 3½ per cents., the dividends of which are received by the vicar, and distributed at Easter. Out of the school revenue the master has a salary of £35. 15s. and the mistress £26. 6s.; and the remainder is given in clothing to the scholars.

HARWORTH.

Viscount Galway, Serlby Hall
Greaves Henry, Marwood, Esq. Hesley Hall
Bradford Wm. tailor & p. clerk
Brown Wm. vict. Crown
Butler Thos. gamekeeper, Serlby
Clark David, shoemaker
Dickin John, blacksmith
Downes Rev. Wm. vicar
Fulwood Jph. jun. shoemaker
Haslehurst John, shopkeeper
Hickson Mrs. William
Huddleston, Mr. Jno. Hawknest
Jackson Robert, shoemaker
Jackson William, surgeon
Malkin Charles, butcher
Marr John, shoemaker
Marrison John shoemaker
Meek Thomas, schoolmaster
Milner John, shoemaker
Morris James, tailor
Needham Mary, shopkeeper
Parkin Charles, gardener, Serlby
Saxton Joseph, wheelwright
Savidge Sophia, shopkeeper
Sidwell Thomas, butcher
Whitaker Robert, beerhouse

FARMERS.
Cartwright Ann, Fisher John
 Martin Fullwood Jph.

Haslehurst Geo. Smith Ed. Limpool
Job Rt. Martin
Lane Joseph Smith W. Hesley
Pinning Joshua Weatherhog E.
Short T. Martin Wickfield Wm.

OLDCOATES.
Marked † are in Blyth Parish, and ‡ are Yeomen.
Anston Wm. shoemaker
Barlow Thomas, shoemaker
Bell Jane, vict. Spotted Bull
Booth Mary, blacksmith
Bower Henry, wheelwright
†Clark Wm. corn miller
Hiles Jph. tailor
Hopkinson Jph. wheelwright
Hurwood Geo. brick & tile maker
Mitchell Thos. shopkeeper
Newsom Saml. vict. Fox
Richardson Geo. shopkeeper
Smith Wm. vict. William IV.
Stockdale Geo. blacksmith
Taylor Rd. maltster, (and Blyth)
Thorpe J. vict. Coach & Horses
Wilson Wm. lime burner
Wragg Mrs. Elizabeth

FARMERS.
‡Bell George Waterhouse T.
‡Bell John †‡Winter John
‡Bellard Sarah Wright Thos.

NORNAY.—*See Blyth—p.* 403.

STYRRUP.

Marked thus † are in Blyth Parish, and ‡ are Yeomen.

†Lambert Geo. hedge carpenter
Lambert Thomas, shoemaker
†Lambert Wm. vict. & joiner
Liversidge John, shopkeeper
†Thorpe Betty, vict. Wht. Swan
Wasden Wm. blacksmith
†Worstenholm Mr. George

FARMERS.

‡‡Bingham W. †Bletcher Fras.

††Carr Wm.   †‡Parker John
†Cottam Wm.   †‡Sidwell John
Hurwood Sarah   †Sidwell Robt.
†Layland Eliz.   †Sissons Wm.
†Lees Henry   †Woodcock Hy.

The *Coaches* from Nottingham to Doncaster call at the Coach and Horses in Oldcoates, as also does the Tickhill and Worksop *Carrier* every Wednesday.

HOUGHTON PAROCHIAL CHAPELRY.

This decayed parish was once the splended and hospitable seat of the Earls of Clare, and the first Duke of Newcastle, but has now only the ruins of a chapel, a deserted paper mill, a corn mill, and eight scattered houses on the rivers Medin and Idle, 5 miles N. W. of Tuxford, and 7 miles S. S. W. of Retford. It comprises about 900 acres of rich land, with several vigorous plantations, and an excellent *decoy* for wild fowl, consisting of 20 acres of water, and about the same extent of " cover." The venerable ruins of the church or *chapel* are now embowered in a plantation of firs, and appear to be the remains of the nave and north cemetery, in which are several mutilated tombs, and armorial bearings of the Stanhope and Holles families. The inhabitants having no church of their own, now use that at Walesby, and they participate in the benefits of the free school at West Drayton. (See p. 365.) The Duke of Newcastle is owner, impropriator, and lord of the manor, which at the Norman Conquest was given to Roger Pictavensis, but it afterwards passed with his other possessions in this county to the Earl of Lancaster. In the 35th of Edward III., John de Longvillers held here of Nicholas Monboucher, by the service of a rose, two messages, half a carucate of land, ten acres of meadow, and two water-mills. The manor afterwards passed in marriage with the heiress of the Longvillers to Mallovell, lord of Rampton, and from his descendants it went to the Stanhope family, with which it continued till Saunchia Stanhope was married to John Babington, who sold it to Sir Wm. Holles, a great merchant and lord mayor of London; and great-grand-father to John Holles, who in 1624 was created *Baron Houghton and Earl of Clare*, titles which are now merged in the dukedom of Newcastle, as will be seen with *Clumber*, which has been the chief seat of the family since about the year 1770. A tourist, who wrote in 1789, says, Sir Wm. Holles, son of the before-named Sir Wm., possessed an estate of £10,000 a year in

the reign of Henry VIII., and lived at Houghton in great splendour and hospitality. "He began his Christmas at All-hallow-
tide, and continued it till Candlemas, during which any man
was permitted to stay three days, without being asked whence
he came or what he was. The fourth and last Earl of Clare
married the co-heiress of H. Cavendish Duke of Newcastle,
and was himself, after the death of his father-in-law, in 1691,
created duke by that title,—his own estate and the Cavendish
together amounting to £40,000 per annum. Houghton, upon
the acquisition of these estates, was neglected, and the Duke
resided at Welbeck abbey. Afterwards, when the Holles and
the Cavendish estates came to separate again, and the latter
went through the Harleys to the Bentincks, a mansion was
probably wanted for the former, and Clumber park, which
might be the lodge before, was by degrees extended to its present size and importance." Thus the once princely seat of
Houghton was left to ruin and decay; all that is now left of the
mansion is occupied as a farm-house, and the extensive *park*,
which was mostly on the north side of the Medin, in Bothamsall parish, is now divided into meadows and arable fields.

Brooke John, farmer	Padley J. farmer, Warren House
Chappell John, corn miller	Ward J. farmer, Decoy House
Mansell Geo. farmer, Old Hall	

MATTERSEY PARISH.

MATTERSEY, or *Mattersea*, is a genteel and very retired
village, on the western bank of the Idle, 4 miles S.S.E. of
Bawtry, and 6 miles N. by W. of Retford. It stands on a
gentle rise, and has several handsome mansions. Its parish,
which comprises *Blaco-hill, Mattersey abbey*, and the hamlet
of *Mattersey Thorpe*, is about 1½ miles in length, and contains
97 houses, 455 inhabitants, and about 2500 acres of land, which
was enclosed by an Act passed in 1770. Lord Althorp is now
the principal owner and lord of the manor, which was purchased
of Captain Frankland, by his late father-in-law, Jonathan
Acklom, Esq. of Wiseton Hall, for £40,000, to pay which he
re-sold some of the farms to Samuel Barker, Jonathan Nettleship, and John Dickenson, the latter of whom left his portion
to the tenants, and Mr. Nettleship's has been partly sold by his
daughter, who married first H. Wormald, Esq. of Leeds, and
afterwards B. Hughes, Esq., and still holds the abbey farm, 150
acres. Before the Conquest, it was the manor of Earl Tosti,
and afterwards belonged to the family who took the name of
De Mattersey, or *Maresey*, but ended in an heiress Isabel married to Sir Philip Chauncy, who gave the village to the monks.

2 r 2

of the neighbouring GILBERTINE ABBEY, founded by her ancestors, and dedicated to St. Helen. The prior had then free
warren here, and the village had a market and fair. The abbey was founded before 1192, by Roger Fitz Ranulph de
Maresey, for six canons, and was valued at £60 after its dissolution, when this manor was granted to the Neville family,
whose heiress married Sir Wm. Hickman, whose descendants
resided here till the early part of the last century, in a house
which still remains. The abbey stood nearly a mile east of the
village, and its site is now occupied by a farm-house, and the
remains of part of its cloisters and cells are occupied as cart-
houses, and filled with poultry roosts. The *church*, dedicated
to All Saints, is a handsome gothic edifice, in excellent preservation, and is a most pleasing object in the village. It has
some curious carvings, which were discovered about 50 years
ago under the old pavement of the chancel, one of which represents the benevolent action of St. Martin dividing his cloak. It
had a chantry dedicated to St. John the Baptist, and in the
reign of Edward I. was appropriated to Mattersey abbey, to
make amends for some losses the monks had sustained by fire.
The vicarage, valued in the King's books at £6. 8s. 9d., is in
the patronage of the appropriator, the Archbishop of York,
and is now enjoyed by the Rev. Wm. Tiffin. The parish *school*
was endowed by Edward Nettleship, in 1742, with £140, now
increased to £248. 10s. 7d., 3½ per cent. stock, the yearly dividends of which, £8. 13s. 10d., are paid to the master for
teaching seven poor boys, who are admitted by the vicar and
churchwardens. The *Methodist chapel* was built about forty
years ago.

Bailey James, blacksmith
Brett Jonathan, shoemaker
Burkinsheare Wm. shopkeeper
Camm Wm. vict. and maltster
Clarke Mrs. Elizabeth
Fearnley Benjamin, Esq.
Gabbitas John. wheelwright
Graham Mrs. Honor, gent.
Greenwood Mdk. shoemaker
Graham Geo. wheelwright
Hodgkinson Miss Ann
Johnson Thomas, blacksmith
Laycock William, shopkeeper
Marrison Edward, spring truss
    and cork leg maker
Millner Betty, shoemaker
Milner Thomas, schoolmaster and
    parish clerk
Rich Amor, joiner

Sampson Mr. Thomas
Tiffin Rev. William, vicar
Wainwright Elizabeth, victualler,
    Blacksmiths' Arms
Wright John, tailor
Wright William, shoemaker
Wright William, butcher
    FARMERS.
*Thus ‡ are Yeoman, and † live at
    Thorp.*
Andrews John
    Abbey
‡Brownlow Rd.
†Dean Ed.
‡Dean Wm.
†Gabbitas Thos.
†Heane Geo.
Hewson Jas.
†Hich Joseph
Jackson George
Johnson George,
    Blaco-hill
‡‡Talents Wm.
    Jessop
‡Tone Chpr.
‡Tricket Joseph
    Mattersey-hill

MISSON PARISH

Lies south of Finningley, on the north side of the Idle, bounded
on the west by Yorkshire, and on the east by Lincolnshire, and
is partly in the latter county, which is here so intermixed with
Nottinghamshire that the boundaries of the two counties are
almost indefinable, from which circumstance the parish is supposed to have been anciently called *Misne or Myssen*. It contains 184 houses, 841 inhabitants, and about 5700 acres of good
sandy land, which was mostly enclosed in 1760, when 286A. 2P.
was allotted to the vicar, in lieu of the small tithes, but the
great tithes are still paid in kind, except on the old enclosures,
which pay a composition of 2s. 9d. per acre. Lord Althorp is
the impropriator, and Mr. Henry Cooke is his lessee. His
lordship is also principal owner and lord of the manor of the
Nottinghamshire part of the parish; and the Rev. John Otter
is lord of the Lincolnshire part, which pays a modus of £5.
9s. 8d. to the seigniory of Kirton,* and is in the deanery and
hundred of Corringham; but the land belongs to a number of
freeholders, the principal of whom are Joseph Taylor and John
Smilter, Esqrs. and the Hon. J. B. Simpson.

  Misson is a well-built village, on the north side of the Idle,
over which there is a ferry, 3 miles E. by N. of Bawtry, and 7
miles W. of Stockwith-on-the-Trent, from which the Idle is
navigable for small craft up to Bawtry. The *church* is a handsome building, with a nave, chancel, side aisles, and tower.—
The vicarage is valued in the King's books at £6. 4s. 4½d.,
but is now worth upwards of £250 per annum. The King
is the patron, and the Rev. Robert Evans, M. A. is the incumbent.

  Newington is a small village at the west end of the parish,
where there is an extensive brewery and malting establishment,
1 mile E. by N. of Bawtry. Like the rest of the parish, it is
partly in the two counties of Nottingham and Lincoln.

  Misson School stands in the church yard, and at the enclosure in 1762, was endowed with an allotment of 32 acres of
land in Ruffam Car, awarded in lieu of £8 per annum which
had been previously paid out of other lands, pursuant to the
wills of Thomas Mowbray and John Pinder, who built the
school in 1693. This land now lets for £64 a year, besides
which the master has a rent charge of 20s. out of Deep-hole
close, left in 1700 by Wm. Wood, and an annuity of 10s. left
by an unknown donor out of land at Ruffam. For these sums
the master only teaches 9 free scholars, but they certainly
ought to be increased to *thirty*, as is remarked by the late Par-

* The seigniory of Kirton is attached to the King's duchy of Cornwall.

liamentary commissioners. The vicar pays a schoolmistress for teaching six poor girls.

ROADS, &c.—At the enclosure, the Hagg hill, 10A. 3R. 39P. was awarded for the purpose of getting gravel, sand, and other materials for the reparation of the public and private roads of the parish, reserving only the herbage and crops of the said land to be let by the trustees, and the rents to be applied in repairing the school, public bridges, drains, sewers, and other works on the common fields.. The open green at the west end of the village of Misson was allotted for the same purpose.

BENEFACTIONS TO THE POOR.—About 1700, Hill Lee, Thos. Richardson, Robt. Drury, and Wm. Hopperwhit, left several small sums amounting to £18. 13s. 4d., the interest of which is paid out of the poor rates. The poor have also the following yearly rent charges, viz. 10s. left by Wm. Richardson, out of a farm at Everton, now belonging to John Walker, Esq. ; 10s. left by Wm. Hindley, out of a meadow at Misson, now possessed by Wm. Grasby ; and 5s. out of a house and land belonging to Mrs. Jephson.

Marked thus † are in Lincolnshire, and ‡ are Yeoman.

†Atkinson John, blacksmith
Burr Wm. grocer and draper
†Capel William, shoemaker
Cooke Henry, gent.
Dale Mr. John
†Davison Robert, victualler, Old George and Dragon
Dickinson James, butcher
†Francis Edmund, corn miller
Gambles Thomas, tailor
Graham Wm. vict. Ferry Boat
Grant William, blacksmith
Gurnell John, bricklayer
Hatfield Wm. jun. wheelwright
Hatfield William, shopkeeper
Hindley Richard, tailor
Holland William, gent.
†Johnson Mrs. Jane
†Kitchen Valentine, tailor
†Laister Thomas, shopkeeper
†Machin Mrs. Martha
Marrison William, bricklayer
†Marsden Thomas gent.
†Marsden Miss Ann
Mason William, shopkeeper
Moyson Richard, schoolmaster
Moxon Josh. bdg. and day school
Oldfield Robert, wheelwright
Parkin John, victualler & cattle dealer, White Horse

Perkins William, shoemaker
Pinder John, shoemaker
Robinson Martha, vict. Red Lion
†Styring Geo. vict. Globe
†Turner James shoemaker
Wootton Rev. John, curate
†Youdan John, bricklayer
Youdan John, blacksmith
Youdan Miles, bricklayer

FARMERS.

Batty John	†‡Keightley J.
Springs	†Law R. Springs
Batty William	†Machin M.
Nevilles	‡Marsden T.
‡Beale John	Peaker Stph.
‡Beale Nwm.	‡Peaker W.
‡Brown Wm.	Pigot William
Cartwright W.	Vicarage
Childs Thomas,	‡Richardson W.
Nevilles	‡St. Paul Wm.
Emson James	Styring Thos.
‡Fisher Wm.	‡Styring Wm.
†Garner Jas.	Wagstaff W. jun.
Gibson Wm.	Middlewood
†‡Hobson Fs.	†Wells Thos.
‡Horton Jph.	‡Whittaker Fs.
†Hunt John	†‡Wilson Rt.
†Jackson John	‡Worrell John

NEWINGTON.

†Burton William, vict. Ship
†Ellis William, shopkeeper
Peacock Thomas, bricklayer
†Pooley William Thos. managing
brewer

†Soulby William, book-keeper
Taylor Joseph and Co. ale and
porter brewers, maltsters, and
merchants.

ORDSALL PARISH.

LIES south of Retford, and comprises the *Lordship of Ordsall,*
on the west side of the Idle, and the *Lordship of Thrumpton,*
on the east side of that river. These lordships form one
township, and contain 205 houses, 809 inhabitants, and about
200 acres of rich sandy land, part of which was not enclosed
till 1804.

ORDSALL is an old and irregularly built village, on the west
bank of the Idle, where there is a large paper mill, one mile S.
by W. of Retford. In Edward the Confessor's time, "*Ordes-
hale*" contained four manors held by *Osward, Turstaun, Oderic,*
and *Thurstan,* but after the conquest it was all of the fee of
Roger de Busli, and had one bovate which was *soc* to the King's
manor of Dunham, and 1½ bovate which was *soc* to Grove.
Early in the 13th century the greatest portion of it became the
property of the Hereys, of Grove, from whom it passed to the
Mackworths, the Bevercotes, and the Cornwallis's; the latter
of whom sold their portion to the Countess of Devonshire,
who settled it upon her eldest son, Sir Edward Wortley. *Ordsall* is now in the soke of Elksley, and the Duke of Newcastle
is lord of the manor; but the land belongs mostly to the Hon.
J. B. Simpson, of Babworth, who has erected a neat SCHOOL
in the village, and pays for the education of 12 poor children.
Thrumpton Lordship is mostly the property of John Parker,
and John and George Kippax, Esqrs.; but A. H. Eyre, Esq. of
Grove, is lord of the manor, in which are 4½ acres of hop
ground.

The CHURCH is an ancient Gothic edifice, with a lofty tower,
which was greatly injured by lightning in 1823. The interior
has several old monuments, and was in a very decayed state till
1831, when it was re-pewed and thoroughly repaired. The
living is a rectory in the patronage of Lord Wharncliffe, and
is valued in the King's books at £19. 10s. 7¼d. The Rev.
Francis Foxlow is the incumbent, for whom the Rev. William
Bury officiates. The *tithes* are now paid by a modus which
amounts to £450 per annum. The *Rectory House* is a neat
modern mansion, as also is *Biggins House,* the seat of John
Kippax, Esq. The *Rev. William Denman,* in the *popish*
reign of Queen Mary was ejected from this rectory, but was
restored again after Elizabeth ascended the throne. An instance of the practice and principles of *puritanic* times, also

occurred here in 1652, when the Rump Parliament, not only ejected *Dr. Marmaduke Moor* from this rectory, but also sequestrated his paternal estate "for treason, and for the heinous and *damnable* offence of playing at cards, *three several times, with his own wife ! ! !*"

THRUMPTON LORDSHIP includes the neat hamlet called WHITEHOUSES, on the great North road; WHINNEY MOOR-ROW; STORCROFT-TERRACE, and several handsome modern dwellings which form the southern suburbs of East Retford. See pages 302 and 322.

HOPS.—Mr. Young says, some years ago, two spirited agriculturalists of this parish (Mr. Mason and George Brown, Esq.,) drained at a small expense, by open cuts, a deep black *Bog* which had been let for 3s. per acre, and planted it with hops in squares of six feet, and succeeded so well as actually to clear £62 per acre in one year.

CHARITIES.—*Elizabeth Johnson*, in 1717, bequeathed to this parish, the *Poor's Close*, 1A. 8P. now let for £3. 10s. per annum, which is distributed on Good Friday and St. Thomas' day. In 1727, *Jeremiah Halfhide* left 40s. yearly out of an estate, now belonging to J. and G. Kippax, who distribute the money amongst such poor as do not receive parochial relief. The sum of £60 left in 1727, 1764, and 1798 by *Ann Turnell, Robert Palmer*, and *Wm. Ellis*, was lost in 1816, by the bankruptcy of John Stoakes, a large farmer, whose creditors only receive 1½d. in the pound, though shortly before, his father had died and left him £2,000. But in consideration of this loss, the overseers distribute £3 yearly out of the poor rates, viz. 40s. on Candlemas-day, 10s. on St. Thomas' day, and 10s. on Good Friday.

☞ *The names of the Inhabitants of Trumpton are included in the Directory of Retford.*

Batty John, shoemaker
Blagg John, shoemaker
Blagg William, tailor
Bury Rev. William, curate, Rectory House
Cook John, maltster
Dawson Samuel, wheelwright
Fowe Edward, farmer
Gibbs William, foreman
Himsworth Stephen, vict. Gate, and plumber and glazier
Jackson Richard, blacksmith

Kippax John, Esq. Biggins House
Lambert John, corn and flour dealer
Morley William, shopkeeper
Nelson Thomas, paper manufacturer, and Nottingham
Olivant John, farmer
Roberts William, farmer
Rogers Mrs. Mary
White Edward, shopkeeper

RUFFORD (EXTRA PAROCHIAL.)

THIS Extra-Parochial manor extends southward from the vicinity of Ollerton, along the banks of the Rainworth-Water, more than six miles, to the junction of Bassetlaw with the Hundreds of Broxtow and Thurgarton. It contains 64 scattered dwellings, 322 inhabitants, and upwards of 10,000 acres of good forest land, of which 1090 acres were planted with oak and ash by the late Sir George Savile, who also enclosed and brought into cultivation 1960 acres of the open forest, after the year 1776. This fine rural liberty was anciently called *Rugforde* or *Rumford,* and before the conquest was held by *Ulf* the Saxon, but was afterwards of the fee of *Gilbert de Gaunt,* who was nephew to the conqueror, and was succeeded by his son Walter, whose eldest son, Gilbert de Gaunt, married the Countess of Lincoln, and was himself created Earl of Lincoln, after which, in 1148, he founded here a CISTERCIAN ABBEY for a colony of Monks, whom he brought from Rivaulx abbey, in Yorkshire, in honour of the blessed Virgin Mary. He endowed it with the manor of Rufford and several estates. At the dissolution it was found to contain 15 of this holy brotherhood, whose revenues amounted to £254 per annum. Its site and possessions, with many other manors in Nottinghamshire, and the adjacent counties, were granted to George *Earl of Shrewsbury and Waterford,* in exchange for many large estates in Ireland, which he had given up to Henry VIII.[*] The Rufford estate passed in marriage with the heiress and grand-daughter of the said Earl of Shrewsbury to *Sir George Savile,* of Barrowby, in Lincolnshire, whose descendant of the same name was created *Marquis of Halifax,* in 1682, but that title became extinct on the death of his son William, in 1700. The last *Sir George Savile,* who was highly esteemed both as "an upright senator and an honest man," died in 1784, and left his estate to Richard the *second son* of his sister, (the wife of the Right Honourable Richard Lumley Saunderson, *Earl of Scarborough,*) who consequently assumed the sirname of Savile, but on the death of his eldest brother, in 1807, he succeeded to the Scarborough title and estate, and the more valuable estate of Rufford passed to his younger brother, the Honourable and Rev. John Lumley Savile, its present possessor, to a younger branch of whose family it must always belong, agreeable to the will of the late Sir George Savile, during whose life Rufford abbey was in all its splendour, but its present owner resides mostly at Edwinstow.

RUFFORD ABBEY stands in a beautiful and well wooded *Park* of about 1400 acres, within 2 miles S. of Ollerton. It is an immense edifice erected upon and engrafted into, the re-

---

[*] The *manors* in Nottinghamshire, which were included in the above grant to the *Earl of Shrewsbury,* were Rufford, Eakring, Bilsthorp, Warsop, Walesby, Ollerton, Wellow, Nottingham, Ompton, Kneesall, Mapplebeck, Beesthorp, Boughton, Kelham, Codington, Parkelathes, Kirton, Starthorpe, East Retford, Holme, Foxholes, Littleborough, Rohagh, Southwell, and Marton.

mains of the ancient monastic building. Its situation is extremely sequestered, and the entrance front is so completely embowered in a grove of elm and beech, as to preserve much of the original character of the fabric, though it has been so much altered by several of the Savile family. Thoroton speaking of it in his time, says that it had often been the residence of King James I. and his son Charles, who found it very commodious for hunting in Sherwood Forest, and were hospitably entertained there. The entrance front is approached by a flight of steps over an area which surrounds the house, and gives light to the offices in the underground story. The spacious *entrance hall* was altered to its present state in the reign of Queen Elizabeth, and with its lofty ceiling, high raised screen, and brick floor, marks the taste of that period. Here are some ancient portraits; but the most valuable collection of paintings is in the *Long Gallery*, which is 114 feet long, and 36 broad, and contains a rich feast for the connoisseur. An apartment called "the Prince of Wales's bed room," is hung with very handsome tapestry, and has its name from his late majesty, George IV., who slept in it on one of his visits to the North, when Prince of Wales. The attic story has an immense number of rooms, in which there are also many good paintings. There are no less than three-and-twenty *stair cases* in the house, one of which leads to the *great drawing-room*, in which is a fine portrait of the late Sir George Savile, and three views of Roch Abbey, but the greatest curiosities amongst the paintings in this mansion, are two exquisite little pieces which Laird says, (1811) the housekeeper has been directed to lock up in one of her presses below. "One of them is a Dutch painting of a *fiddler and groupe*, and the other an *old woman with flowers*, the painter we believe is unknown, but the execution done in the most exquisite style of high finishing. In short, as pictures they may almost be considered as invaluable, and we could not help expressing our astonishment, that two *cabinet bijoux* of such exquisite taste should be thus suffered to lie unseen amidst table cloths and napkins." Though the noble owner lives chiefly at the neighbouring village of Edwinstow, he has a small establishment of servants here for the culture of his extensive farm, and the preservation of his game, park, woods, gardens, and pleasure grounds, which, with a religious affection for the memory of his ancestors, he keeps in excellent condition; indeed, every thing is so elegant both in and about the mansion, that even a stranger cannot help feeling regret that such a spot should be in a great measure unenjoyed!— but perhaps its present possessor, being a prebendary of York Cathedral, is obliged to live within the pale of Episcopacy, which has no control over this churchless extra-parochial district.

Besides the beautiful LAKE in Rufford Park, the Rainworth

water fills a large *Dam* of 100 acres at INKERSALL, near the south end of the parish, 3 miles S. by W. of the Abbey. At SAVILE ROW cottages, near the north-west corner of the park, the Hon. Mrs. Savile supports a FREE SCHOOL, and gives a gown yearly, and a dinner every Sunday to 24 poor girls. About 400 acres of the forest land is still in open sheep walks; but the farms are all in high cultivation, and their scattered dwellings are distinguished by different names, as will be seen in the following list of the inhabitants.

Savile Hon. and Rev. John Lumley, Rufford Abbey, (and Edwinstow)
Brown Mary, farmer, Hills
Butler George, park and gamekeeper, Rufford Lodge
Cartledge James, farmer Inkersall
Cox Rev. James, domestic chaplain, at Rufford, Crow-lane
Crawford William, farmer, Inkersall
Davies James, huntsman, Savile row
Eaton John, corn miller, Rufford Lake
Frost Mrs. Eliz. housekeeper, Rufford Abbey
Godfrey William, blacksmith, Rufford Inn
Howson John, bailiff, Rufford Farm

Knuttall William, farmer, Labour in Vain
Machon Hy. Esq. North Laiths and Gateford Hill
Parkinson John, land agent, land surveyor, and valuer, Leyfields
Parkinson Richard, land agent, Wellow Bar
Potter Samuel, farmer, Elmsley Lodge
Shooter Crisp, gardener, Rufford Inn
Feather George, woodman, Crow-lane
Vessey Miss Mary, North Laiths
Wadeson John, keeper, Rufford Inn
Whelpdale William, gamekeeper, Savile row
Williamson Luke, gent. Robin Hood's Farm
Wilson Richard, farmer, Primrose Hill

SCROOBY PAROCHIAL CHAPELRY

Is within the North Soke of the archiepiscopal *Liberty of Southwell and Scrooby*, betwixt and near the confluence of the rivers Idle and Ryton. It contains 65 houses, 281 inhabitants, and 1523A. 3R. 36P. of fine sandy land. The common was enclosed in 1775, when 160A. 3P. were allotted to the impropriator, and 34A. 2R. 22P. to the vicar in lieu of all the tithes of the chapelry, except those which are still paid on 310 acres of the old enclosures.

SCROOBY village, on the south bank of the river Ryton, and on the east side of the great North road, about 1 mile S. of Bawtry, now merely contains a few farm-houses and cottages, with a CHURCH dedicated to St. Wilfred, which has once been handsome, but now possesses nothing of its ancient grandeur.

2 Q

except its lofty spire, which was greatly injured by lightning on
Sunday, August 7th, 1831; but has since been substantially
repaired. The former glory of Scrooby was its PALACE, which
was long one of the principal seats of the successive Arch-
bishops of York, but of this ancient abode of splendour and
hospitality nothing now remains except some small fragments
incorporated into a farm-house. Leland describes it as "a
great manor place standinge withyn a mote, and builded yn to
courtes, whereof the first is very ample, and all builded of
tymbre, saving the front of the haule, that is of bricke, to the
wych *ascenditur per gradus lapidis.* The ynner courte building, as far as I marked, was of tymber building, and was not
in compace past the 4 parte of the utter courte." In Domesday
book, Scrooby is only described as a *berue* or hamlet of the
Archbishop's soke of Sutton, now commonly called the *North
Soke* of Southwell and Scrooby. The prelates of York had
free warren here as early as the 17th of Edward II. In the
reign of Henry VII, Scrooby was the favourite hunting seat of
Archbishop Savage. In the next reign it was occasionally the
residence of Cardinal Wolsey; and in Elizabeth's reign, this
palace was not only considered as excellent in itself, and more
capacious than that at Southwell, but "a better seat for provision,"—having a greater jurisdiction and a fairer park attached
to it. Archbishop Sandys appears to have then resided here,
at least occasionally, as one of his daughters is interred in
the church. During his episcopacy he caused this seat to be
demised to his son, Sir Samuel Sandys, and the palace was afterwards so mush neglected that it had almost fallen to the ground
in the early part of last century, soon after which, the large
gateway and the porter's lodge were taken down, and the extensive park converted into a farm, in the garden of which is a
large mulberry tree, that tradition says was planted by the
haughty Wolsey. The Archbishop of York is still lord of the
manor, and owner of 426 acres, but the Dowager Viscountess
Galway is his lessee, and has the impropriation, which was
purchased of the late Lord George Cavendish. But the living
is annexed to the vicarage of Sutton-cum-Lound, and is in the
patronage of the Duke of Portland. Lord Althorp has 456
acres, and the rest of the manor belongs to Vicount Galway,
and to several copyholders, who pay small and certain fines.—
The *Methodists* have a chapel in the village, which was built in
1829. The *charities* belonging to this parochial chapelry are
two annuities left by unknown donors, viz. £1 paid by Viscount
Althorp, and 13s. 4d. by Viscount Galway.

Scrooby Inn, on the high road, about half a mile south of the
village, was formerly a noted posting house, but is now occupied by a farmer, and belongs to Viscount Althorp. Early in
the morning of the 3d of July, 1779, a horrid murder was committed at Scrooby toll-bar, by John Spencer, who, after play-

ing at cards with the keeper, Wm. Headon, and his mother, then on a visit, returned to the house, and after gaining admittance under the pretence that a drove of cattle wanted to pass, killed both his victims with a hedge stake. After having got what money he could find, he was detected in the act of dragging the bar-keeper's body across the road towards a pond, by Mr. Wm. White, of Copthorne, who happened to be passing on horseback at the time, and pursued the murderer, who was soon secured, and afterwards hung in chains on a gibbet which still remains. Bishop-field is a large new house one mile S. of the village, erected by its present occupant, the Hon. Captain Duncombe, son of Lord Feversham.

Camm William, vict. Saracen's-Head
Cobb Richard, blacksmith
Duncombe Hon. Arthur, Bishop-field
Goacher Geo. vict. George and Dragon
Hurt Rev. Thomas, vicar
Richardson John, shoemaker
Ross John, wheelwright
Shepherd Benjamin, parish clerk and tailor
Shillito George, vict. and wheelwright, Galway Arms
Shillito John, shoemaker
Skelton Benj. corn miller
Theaker Thomas, butcher
Walkinson Sarah, shopkeeper
Wilson Joseph, shoemaker

FARMERS.
Those marked ‡ are Yeomen.
Birks Jonathan, Neale Jane
Birks William   Scott J. Scrooby
‡Booth Thos.   House
‡Camm Henry   Smith H. Manor
Eyre John   House
‡Haynes John

SUTTON-CUM-LOUND PARISH

Is also in the north soke of the *liberty of Southwell and Scrooby*, and is divided into the two townships of Sutton and Lound, which are bounded on the east by the Idle river, and on the west by Barnby-moor and Torworth. It contains 182 houses, 801 inhabitants, and about 3000 acres of rich black sandy land, which produces fine crops of wheat and turnips, and is noted for its early peas and potatoes, of which large quantities are sent to Sheffield and other markets. The common land was enclosed in 1777, when 718A. 3R. 26P., now called *Danes-hill farm*, were allotted to the impropriator, the Duke of Portland, and 106A. 22P. to the vicar, in lieu of all the tithes of the parish. The Archbishop of York is lord of the manor of both Sutton and Lound, the former of which is copyhold, subject to small certain fines, and the latter is mostly in small freeholds, occupied by the owners. The principal proprietors are the Duke of Portland, the Hon. J. B. Simpson, Benjamin Fearnley, Esq. and Wm. Markham, Esq. of Becca Lodge, Yorkshire, the latter of whom is owner of *Bell-moor*, a farm of 700 acres, mostly in Lound. About 200 acres, called *Lound field*, belong

to the Crown. At the Domesday survey, the archbishop had
the manor of *Sutton*, but *Lound* was partly *soc* to the King's
manor of Bothamsall, and partly of the fee of Roger de Busli.

SUTTON village stands nearly a mile east of the north road,
3 miles N. N. W. of Retford. The *church*, dedicated to
St. Bartholomew, is a small gothic edifice, with a tower and
three bells. The *vicarage* is valued in the King's books
at £10, and has annexed to it that of Scrooby. The Duke of
Portland is patron and impropriator, and the Rev. Thomas
Hurt is the incumbent, for whom the Rev. Wm. Mould, of
Retford, officiates. The *Independent chapel*, in the village, was
built in 1816.

LOUND is a good village, pleasantly situated about one mile
N.E. of Sutton. Here are the neat mansions of Henry Bagshaw, Esq. and Captain James Barrow.

The parish SOHOOL and master's house stand half way betwixt
the two villages, and were built in 1783, at the cost of £100,
which partly arose from the interest of £70, left in 1742, by Rd.
Taylor, and now vested in £112. 10s. 3¼ per cent. stock, yielding £3. 18s. 8d. yearly. At the enclosure in 1777, two allotments, containing 6A. 22P. now let for £24 per annum, were
awarded to the overseers of the two townships, for the use of
the schoolmaster, for which, and the dividends of the aforesaid
stock, he teaches all the children of the parish, but is allowed
to charge 3d. per week each for those who can afford to pay.

BENEFACTIONS.—The following annuities are received in
equal moieties by the overseers of Sutton and Lound, and distributed amongst the poor at Easter, viz. £2 out of Danes-hill
farm; 10s. out of Chapel-house; 10s. out of the Old Sun inn,
Retford; £2 out of George Johnson's estate, in Lound; and
10s. out of an estate that belongs jointly to the Hon. J. B. Simpson and Benj. Fearnly, Esq.

SUTTON.

Broomhead George grocer and
  draper
Brownlow Miss Ann
Fenton James, vict. Gate
Foster William, shopkeeper
Gandy John, shoemaker
Graves William, flour dealer
Greaves Mrs. Ann
Greaves William, beerhouse
Hollin William, shoemaker and
  parish clerk
Hopkin John, shoemaker
House Thomas, shoemaker
Kay Samuel, butcher
Kemshall Thomas, vict. & wheel-
  wright
Kitchin Jonathan, blacksmith

Matthews Thomas, shoemaker
Renshaw John, wheelwright
Steel John, shopkeeper
Stubbins Mark, tailor
Whitlam Wm. stone mason
Wragg Wm. schoolmaster

FARMERS.

*Those marked * are Yeomen.*

Brownlow Jph.   *Kelk Geo. (and
Cook Jph.   comsr. of
Gravener Wm.   Sewers)
  Bell Moor   *Lee George
Graves Wm.   Otter John
                *Walker Thos.
                  Daneshill

LOUND.

Atkinson George, shoemaker

Bagshaw Henry, Esq.
Barker Thos. shoemaker
Barrow Capt. James, Highfield
Fenton John, shoemaker & shopr
Gilbert John, blacksmith
Harrison, Eliz. shopkeeper
Hewitt Mr. Paul
Hudson John, vict. Blue Bell
Levick Geo. wheelwright
Robinson Rd. joiner & beerhs.
Rollinson Geo. joiner & machine maker
Shaw Mrs.
Smales Wm. corn miller

Walker Geo. vict. & butcher
Warburton Jph. blacksmith
Yates Wm. blacksmith

FARMERS.
*Those marked * are Yeomen.*
*Barker Samuel
Booth Wm.
Clark George, Loundfield
*Cuckson John
*Green Joseph
Hill Thomas
*Johnson Geo. (& Blaco-hill)
*Justice Geo.
*Parkin Samuel
*Raynes George, Lound Lodge
*Taylor Wm.
*Walker John
*Watts John
Whelton John
Whitehead John

WALESBY PARISH

Includes the hamlets of *Walesby* and *Willoughby*, and forms a fine champaign district, extending northward from Kirton to Bevercotes, under an abrupt acclivity, and westward to the river Idle. It contains 68 houses, 340 inhabitants, and 1429A. 1R. 24P. of land, all of which is a fertile sand, except the eastern side about Willoughby, which is a strong clay, mostly in hop-yards. The open fields were enclosed in 1821, when 152A. 3R. 27P. were awarded to the rector, in lieu of the tithes of the whole parish.

WALESBY is a large village, half way betwixt Tuxford and Ollerton, being 3½ miles W. of the former, and the same distance N.E. of the latter. After the Conquest, the parish was of several fees, and Reginald Ursell gave to the monks of Rufford "in pure alms, the service which Robert de Lexington was wont to do him, for one bovate that he held of him in Walesby, viz. a pair of spurs of iron, or 2d. yearly, with all reliefs, wards, escheats, &c." Several other parcels of land were subsequently given to the same monastery; and after the dissolution passed to the Earl of Shrewsbury. The Duke of Newcastle and the Hon. and Rev. J. L. Savile are now the principal land owners, and the latter is lord of the manor and patron of the rectory, which is valued in the King's books at £6. 1s. 2d. and is now enjoyed by the Rev. Theophilus Sampson, M.A., who resides at Eakring. The *church*, as Throsby says, "is set off with a tower," and is dedicated to St. Edmund. The *school* was endowed in 1760 with a rent charge of 40s. by the Rev. Richard Jackson, rector of this parish. This devise was void by the mortmain act, but the donor's niece, Elizabeth Hall, gave in lieu thereof two acres of land in Normanton, which, at the enclosure in 1800, was exchanged for 1A. 19P. now let for £5 a year. The *poor's land* consists of two roods.

2 Q 2

let for 15s., and was received at the enclosure of Walesby, in
exchange for other land, in Yard-ends field and Outgang-side.
The *sheep clipping* or *feast* is on the nearest Wednesday to
June 24th.

WILLOUGHBY is a small village distant only a quarter of a
mile N.E. of Walesby, and has in its vicinity several fruitful
hop yards.

Those marked thus ‡ are Hop Growers, thus § Yeomen, and thus †
live at Willoughby.

Ashmore Mr. William
†Dale Cornls. wheelwright
Ellis Wm. vict. & wheelwright
Gabbitas Hanh. vict. New Inn
Hoggard John, blacksmith
Hollis Wm. shoemaker
‡§Justice Wm. butcher
Ratcliff John, schoolmaster
‡Ratcliff Rd. vict. Red Lion
Robbins Rd. shoemaker & shopr
Smith Charity, shopkeeper
Snowden Thos. blacksmith

Tissington John, tailor
Wesley Wm. schoolmr. & clerk
Woodward James, shoemaker
      FARMERS.
‡†Camm Jph.   Ryals Wm.
‡Clark Fras.   Sarginson Thos.
‡†Clark Saml.   ‡Smith Jph.
‡§Dean Hanh.   Smith Thomas
†Gilbert Wm.   Ulyeat Thomas
‡Haywood Alex. ‡§Woombill Jn.
Rawson Fras.   §Woombill Wm.
‡Rawson Rd.

WALLINGWELLS (EXTRA PAROCL.)

WALLINGWELLS, 4 miles N. by W. of Worksop, is the beautiful mansion and park of Sir T. W. White, Bart., and is an
extra parochial district, partly in Yorkshire. It appears to
have been anciently a parcel of the manor and parish of Carlton-
in-Lindrick, until Ralph de Cheurolcourt, in the reign of Stephen, granted " to Almighty God and the Virgin St. Mary, a
place in his park of *Carletun*, by the wells and stream of the
wells, whose name should be called *St. Mary of the Park*, to make
and build there an habitation for holy religion, so free that this
place shall not depend on or belong to any other place." The
priory which he built here was a BENEDICTINE NUNNERY, dedicated to the blessed Virgin St. Mary, and afterwards called
St. Mary's of " *Wallondewelles*," from its situation amongst
wells, fountains, and streams. At its dissolution it was valued
at £59, and was granted by Queen Elizabeth to Richard Pype
and Francis Bowyer, but is now the property and seat of Sir
Thomas Wollaston White, who was created a baronet in 1802.
The house, which was originally built out of the ruins of the
priory, is now a handsome structure, having been improved
by many modern additions. It stands on the Nottinghamshire
side of the well wooded park, in which is a long line of trees
marking the boundary between the two counties. In excavating

near the house in 1829, several stone coffins were found, and one of them contained the remains of *Dame Margery Dourant*, the *second prioress*, who died in the reign of Richard I. On opening the coffin the body appeared entire, but it was soon reduced by the air to a shapeless mass of dust. The shoes and a silver chalice were quite perfect, but were re-interred with the ashes of the holy abbess, who nearly seven centuries ago presided over the sisterhood of this convent. Mr. John Fisher, land agent, resides at *Mills house,* so called from the abbey corn mills, which formerly stood near it.

WARSOP PARISH

Lies in the south-west corner of Bassetlaw, and is bounded on the west by Derbyshire, on the north by Cuckney, on the east by Budby, and on the south by the parishes of Edwinstow and Mansfield. It is divided into the two *townships of. Warsop and Sookholme,* which contain together 265 houses, 1286 inhabitants, and 6953A. 3R. 10P. of land, of which 200 acres are in woods and plantations. The forest land was partly enclosed in 1775, and the remainder by an act passed in 1818, but the award was not signed till 1824, when 713A. 3R. 13P. were allotted to the rector, in lieu of all the tithes of the parish.

WARSOP township contains more than six-sevenths of the parish, having 5971A. 1R. 8P. of land, and 1213 inhabitants, mostly living in the two villages of CHURCH WARSOP and MARKET WARSOP, which are distant nearly half a mile from each other, and are situated on the opposite banks of the river Medin, 5 miles N.N.E. of Mansfield, and 7 miles S. by W. of Worksop. The market here has long been obsolete, but three FAIRS are still held annually, viz. on the Monday after Whit-Monday, for cattle, sheep, &c.; September 29th, for sheep; and November 17th, for cattle. After the Conquest, the *manor of Warresoppe* was mostly of the fee of Roger de Busli, but a small part of it was of the King's soke of Mansfield. It was successively held by the Arches, the Suttons, and the Willoughbys, but Henry Gally Knight, Esq. is now the principal owner, lord of the manor, and patron of the rectory, which is valued in the king's books at £22. 15s. 2d., and is now in the incumbency of the Rev. Samuel Martin, B. A. The CHURCH, dedicated to St. Peter and St. Paul, is a neat gothic edifice, standing near the antique rectory-house at Church Warsop, on the north side of the Medin, and was thorougly repaired in 1831, at the cost of £600.

GLEDTHORPE, an estate of 714A. 3R. 29P., is in the township of Warsop, and was part of that manor, until it was granted by Gilbert de Arches to the monks of Welbeck since which it has been tithe-free, and now belongs to the Duke of Portland.

NETTLEWORTH is a manor, in the township of Warsop and Sookholme, and partly in the hundred of Broxtow, and parish of Mansfield Woodhouse. It has lately been purchased by Henry Gally Knight, Esq., of William Wylde, Esq. of Southwell, except PARK HALL, which is the seat of Francis Hall, Esq. and is distant 2½ miles N. N. E. of Mansfield. NETTLEWORTH HALL is occupied by Major Beilby, and is a handsome mansion, erected in 1785, on the site of the old one, at the head of a delightful valley, embosomed in woods, and having several fine pieces of water in front, formed by the union of 2 streams. This hall was built by the Wylde family, who long held the manor, and of whom was *Gervas Wylde*, who, after being some years a factor in Andalusia, returned, and was made captain of a ship in 1558, against the Spanish Armada, in defeating which, " he made use of arrows with long steel heads, shot out of muskets, some of which he left at Nettleworth," where he died at the advanced age of 93 years.

SOOKHOLME or SULKHOLME is a small village, township, and chapelry, at the western extremity of the parish, 3½ miles N. of Mansfield. It has only 11 houses, 68 inhabitants, and 983A. 3R. 2P. of land, abounding in excellent *limestone*. Henry Gally Knight, Esq. is owner and lord of the *manor*, which anciently belonged to Nostel Priory, in Yorkshire. The *chapel* is a small ancient building, in which the rector of Warsop occasionally performs divine service. A small stream runs through the village, and joins the Medin from Pleasley.

The Parish SCHOOL is situated betwixt the two Warsops, and is endowed with 15 guineas a-year, for which the master teaches 20 poor children. This endowment arises from £393. 15s. new four per cent. stock, purchased with £400, left by Thomas Whiteman, in 1818. Mr. Parsons, of Mansfield, is the trustee.

BENEFACTIONS.—*John Hall*, in 1697, left £61. 10s. to be bestowed in lands, for the use of the poor of the Church Town and Market Town of Warsop, together with all his lands at Warsop, and at Newton, in Lincolnshire. The property now belonging to this charity produces £109 per annum, and consists of a farm at Newton, let for £90; land at Willoughby and Walesby, let for £15. 10s., and land in Warsop and the forest, let for £3. 10s. Mr. Nathan Jackson, one of the trustees, receives the rents, and sends forty shilling-loaves to the church every Sunday, for distribution to as many poor parishioners. In 1763, *Francis Peacock* left a cottage and garden at Shirebrook, in Pleasley parish, and directed the rents (now £3) to be given half yearly, on February 2nd and August 8th, to the poor of Warsop. *Sarah Whiteman*, widow of the founder of the school, bequeathed in 1818, a copyhold house and garden, in Warsop, and directed the rent to be divided twice a year amongst eight poor widows and widowers. They are let for £7, and at the enclosure received an allotment, which is let for

£3 per annum. The same benefactress also left £50, and ordered the interest to be given in *bread*, on St. Thomas Day, and August 18th. This legacy is now in the hands of Henry Reynolds. Nathan Jackson, and others are the trustees. *Ann Wylde* gave the interest of £20, now in the Mansfield Savings' Bank, to six single women. Mrs. Richardson gave the interest of £9, also in the Savings' Bank, to be distributed in bread on Good Friday.

WARSOP DIRECTORY.—*Marked thus ‡ live at Church Warsop, and the rest at Market Warsop, or where specified.*

Allcroft Jas. vict. & tailor
Amcoats Thos. tailor & draper
Armitage Thos. stone mason
Bartram John, shoemaker
Beeston John, grocer
Beilby Major, Nettleworth Hall
Blythman John, plumber, &c.
Bowler Rt. schoolmaster
Brothwell Thos. baker
Brummett Wm. gun smith
‡Burrows & Shippam, corn mlrs.
‡Burrows Emanuel, miller
Burton Wm. blacksmith
Butterworth Benj. shopkeeper
Clayton Wm. shoemaker
Cowlishaw Wm. saddler
Crooks John, butcher
Crooks Fras. tailor & draper
‡Davy Mr. Henry
‡Downs Wm. stone mason
Duckmanton John, vict. Swan
Hall Fras. Esq. Park Hall
Hallam Edw. joiner & cabt. mkr
Hallifax Geo. shopkeeper
Hallifax Wm. basket maker
Hamilton Miss
Hinchcliffe John, wood steward
Hind James, fellmonger
Hind Thos. shopkeeper
Ilett Chas. bricklayer
Jackson Nathan, gent.
Kerchevall Robert, gent.
Lee Charles, vict. Gate
‡Martin Rev. Saml. B.A. rector
Moody Thos. shoemaker
Needham James, tailor & draper
Newton Miss Ann
Norman Matthew, shoemaker
Parkin Joseph, bricklayer
Pearce John, butcher
Radford Wm. miller & baker

Reavell Matthew, stone mason
Reynolds Hy. vict. & butcher,
‡Reynolds Mrs. Ann
Robinson John, surgeon
Robinson Wm. butcher
Sansom Wm. chairmaker
Shippam Samuel, miller
Short Saml. vict. Hare & Hounds
‡Singleton Geo. shoemkr. & shopr
Smith Jacob, wheelwright
Smith Thos. vict. Old White Lion
Turner Samuel, weaver
‡Unwin Samuel, blacksmith
Webster Wm. joiner
Wilkinson Valentine, vict. Dog
  & Rabit, & rope manufacturer
Woodhead Wm. wheelwright
Woodhouse Sarah, matron at the
  workhouse
Woodward John, gent.
  FARMERS.
Beard Jno. *Net-*‡Hodgson Val.
  tleworth Jackson Charles,
Beeston Fras. *Eastland*
Beeston Wm. ‡Jackson Rt.
  Williams'. Lee Charles
  Wood Robinson John,
Bowitt John *Burns*
‡Davy Hy. jun. Short —; *War-*
Davy Sm. *West- sop Lodge*
  field House Turner James
Duckmanton J. Turner John,
Duckmanton R. *Gledthorpe*
Featherstone Sl. Turner John
Hallifax Thos.

SOOKHOLME (FARMERS.)
Boaler Wm. Herinshaw Elea-
Chapman Wm. nor, corn mlr.
Eyre George Wilson John
  Wood William

WELBECK (EXTRA PAROCHIAL.)

WELBECK ABBEY, the beautiful sylvan seat of his Grace the
Duke of Portland, stands in a sequestered situation on the margin of a spacious lake, 3½ miles S. by W. of Worksop, embosomed in an extensive woody park, which, with the demesne
and adjacent plantations, forms an Extra Parochial district, containing 2283A. 3R. 5P. of land, which anciently formed part of
the manor and parish of Cuckney, (see p. 412) till Thomas,
Lord of Cuckney, grandson of Joceus de Flemangh, built a
castle at Cuckney, and founded here an ABBEY for Præmonstratensian canons from Newsome, in Leicestershire; begining
the monastic edifice in the reign of Stephen, and completing
it in that of Henry II. He dedicated it to St. James, and gave
it and the adjacent lands to the monks, in free and perpetual
alms, for his own, father's, mother's, and ancestors' souls, "and
theirs from whom he had unjustly taken any goods."   After
this, many troubled consciences bestowed numerous gifts on
this abbey, and it at length became one of the richest monasteries in the county. In 1329, John Hotham, Bishop of Ely,
bought the manor of Cuckney and settled it upon the monks,
on condition of their finding eight canons who should enjoy the
" good things," and pray for Edward III. and his queen, their
children and ancestors, &c.; also for the bishop's father and
mother, brother, &c., "but especially for the health of the said
Lord Bishop whilst he lived, and after his death for his soul,
and for all theirs that had faithfully served him, or done him
any good," to which was added this extraordinay injunction,
that they should observe his *anniversary*, and on their days of
commemorating the dead, "should absolve his soul *by name* ! !"
At its dissolution, in the 13th of Henry VIII., its yearly
revenues were valued at £249. 6s. 3d., and it was granted (by
purchase) to Richard Whalley, from whom it passed to Sir
Charles Cavendish, youngest son of the celebrated Countess of
Shrewsbury, by her marriage with Sir William. He marrying
the heiress of Lord Ogle, his son succeeded to that barony, and
became afterwards Duke of Newcastle; this was the noble
duke the author of the famous Treatise on Horsemanship, and
the builder of the large *riding-house* here. Though the duke
was very active during the civil wars on the side of Charles,
yet this seat and park escaped the fury of the Parliamentarians;
in other respects, however, he suffered to the amount of nearly
one million sterling. His grandaughter and heiress, Mur-
garet, married John Holles, 4th Earl of Clare, afterwards
created Duke of Newcastle; but she left only a daughter, who
inherited the estates, and marrying the Earl of Oxford, another
heiress, the only issue of this union, carried it to the ancestor of
the present noble proprietor, the most noble William Henry

Cavendish, Scott-Bentinck, *Duke of Portland,*[*] *Marquis of Titchfield, Viscount Woodstock, Baron Cirincester, Lord Lieu-tenant of Middlesex, and D. C. L.,* who resides chiefly at Wel-beck Abbey, and occasionally at his other seats, viz.—Bolsover Castle, in Derbyshire, and Fullarton House and Dean Castle, in Ayrshire. His town residence is in Cavendish-square.

The *Bentinck family* is descended from the noble family of that name, who were of the province of *Overyssel,* in the republic of the United Provinces of the Netherlands, where they flour-ished for many generations. The Westons were *Earls of Portland,* from 1633, till 1665, when the title became extinct, by the death of Thomas Weston, without issue, but was revived again in 1689, in the person of William Bentinck, who was page to William, Prince of Orange, and was in the suit of that monarch when he came over to take possession of the English throne. His lordship had previously visited England in 1677, when he successfully solicited for his royal master the hand of the Princess Mary, daughter of James Duke of York, afterwards James II. He served under William and Mary with great re-putation, both in Ireland and the Netherlands, and was sent ambassador extraordinary to the court of France. "His in-tegrity was proved relative to certain transactions about passing an act for insupporting the East India Company, when he dis-dainfully refused a bribe of £50,000." The House of Com-mons, however, was not always partial to him, for in 1696 they opposed a grant which King William wished to bestow on him, of some lordships in Wales, and in 1701 they impeached him with the Earl of Oxford, Lord Halifax, and Lord Somers, for advising and negociating "a treaty of partitions." He had two wives of the families of Villiers and Temple, and died in 1709, when he was succeeded by his son Henry, who in 1716, was created *Marquis of Titchfield* and *Duke of Portland,* and was governor of the island of Jamacia, where he died in 1726. His son William, the second Duke of Portland, married Lady Margaret Cavendish Harley, daughter of Edward Harley, *Earl of Oxford,* the founder of the celebrated *Harleian Library,* with whom he obtained Welbeck and the rest of the Cavendish estates, as has already been seen. (Vide also p. 433.) He died in 1762, when his estates and titles devolved on his son, *William Henry Cavendish Bentinck,* the late duke, who was High Steward of the City of Bristol, Recorder of Nottingham, Lord Lieutenant of Ireland, from April 8th to Sept. 15th, in 1782, and First Lord of the Treasury from April to December, in 1783. He died in 1809, and was succeeded by his son, the present duke, who assumed the name of Scott-Bentinck, and is now considered the *greatest farmer* in England, as he retains in his own hands and superintends the cultivation of a large por-

* Portland is a small Island on the Dorsetshire coast.

tion of his estate himself. His father held the same rank
amongst the English *planters*, and to them Welbeck and many
of the neighbouring manors are indebted for most of their
sylvan honours and agricultural improvements. (Vide p. 38
and 415.) Besides making about 700 acres of plantations, the
late duke cultivated nearly 2000 acres of waste land, which has
since been greatly enriched by his present representative.

Welbeck Abbey is a large irregularly built mansion, which
has been enlarged at various periods, and appears to retain none
of the ancient monastic walls, except in the interior, where, in
some of the apartments, even the sepulchral monuments fixed
in some of the ancient walls are not destroyed, " but only hid
by the wainscot pannels and other hangings." What is seen,
however, is of comparative modern erection, being begun in
1604, yet it has towers, turrets, some small battlements, and
some ballustrades, which altogether give it an impressive air of
antiquity, though by no means assimulating with our ideas of an
ancient abbey. Those which are called the new apartments
are very spacious, but, with the exception of additions, no great
alteration, has been made in the house since the early part of
the 17th century, though the late duke fitted up all the principal
rooms in their present state. The principal apartments are all
elegantly furnished, and contain an immense collection of family
portraits and other *paintings* by eminent masters. There is
nothing extraordinarily superb, except the *library*, (44 feet by
30) which is in the florid gothic style; yet neatness and elegance pervade the whole mansion, without either gaudiness or
profusion.

The *equestrian* Duke of Newcastle built a most magnificent
riding-house here in 1623, and finished the stables in 1625,
under the direction of John Smithson, an ingenious architect;
it seems, however, that his immediate successor did not keep
up his favourite *hobby*, as it was for some time permitted to go
to decay, but is again restored to its original use; and the great
stable is now one of the finest in the kingdom, (with the exception of the royal establishment at Brighton,) being 130 feet long
by 40 broad, and containing 40 stalls, the outside being finished
in what may be called, not the *modern*, but the *moderate* style
of gothic.

The PARK is about eight miles in circumference, and powerfully excites the attention of the visitor on his approach to the
house, as it contains several noble woods of very ancient *oaks*,
many of which are of an extraordinary size. The largest of
these is the GREENDALE OAK, which is supposed to be upwards
of 700 years old, and measures in circumference 33 feet at the
bottom. Its branches once covered a space equal to 700 square
yards, but it is now in a state of decay, having but one small
branch to crown its venerable trunk, which is now supported
by props, clasped with iron bars, and in some parts capped with

lead to preserve it from the wet. A *coach road* upwards of
10 feet in height, and six feet three inches in width, was cut
through this aged oak in 1724, yet it never contained so much
timber as some other trees in this park, which have been estimated at from 7 to 800 solid feet. The *Duke's walking stick*
is 111 feet 6 inches in height, and 11 tons in weight, having
upwards of 440 solid feet of timber. The *Two Porters* have
received their name from there having been a gate between
them; their respective heights are 98 and 88 feet, and their
circumference 34 and 38. These are in the *Rein Deer Park*,
on the west side of the lake, near Norton Cuckney, where there
are many other trees which are supposed to have braved the
tempests for upwards of six centuries. On the opposite side of
the park, near the gate which goes in from Worksop, is a remarkable tree called the *Seven Sisters*, from its consisting of
seven stems springing from one root in a perpendicular direction, but one of them was unfortunately broken off upwards of
twenty years ago. The circumference of the common trunk,
close to the ground, is 30 feet, and the height of the stems 88
feet. That part of the park which is seen in the vicinity of the
house, and in which the plantations are upon a very large scale,
has been rendered ornamental, and contains a very fine piece of
water, occupying a winding valley, meandering through the dark
foliage of the surrounding wood, and whose bottom being boggy
was dug out by order of the late duke, and being made the receptacle for all the drainage, is now completely floated. This
charming *lake* is a great embellishment to the grounds, being of
a considerable breadth, and more than a mile in length; winding
with the most natural effect in an easy but bold line at the foot
of several small promontories shaded with planting, and presenting the most picturesque prospects at every turn, till it arrives
at the hamlets of Milnthorpe and Carburton-Forge, where it
receives the Poulter, and forms the river Wollen, which flows
eastward through Clumber Park. The late duke made many
considerable alterations and improvements, independent of this
piece of water; but he was rather unlucky in one proposed embellishment, for having erected a most elegant, nay magnificent,
bridge of three arches, the centre one of which was ninety feet
in span, and the side ones seventy-five each, it fell down just as
it was finished.

The sons of his Grace the *Duke of Portland*, who reside with
him at Welbeck Abbey, are the Hon. John Scott-Bentinck,
Marquis of Titchfield, and the *Hon. George Scott-Bentinck*,
M. P.; the following are their upper-servants:—

Atkin David, house steward	Dunn Edward, butler
Boaler Jph, gamekeeper, Kennels	Field Samuel, land bailiff, Grange
Boaler Wm, parkkeeper, Kennels	Farm
Bolton Mrs. Eliz. housekeeper	Thompson Jph. gardener

2 R

WOODHOUSE HALL,

With an estate of 300 acres, forms another EXTRA-PAROCHIAL
district, lying near the west side of. Welbeck Park, adjoining to
Holbeck Woodhouse, 4½ miles S. S. W. of Worksop. It is
the property of the *Duke of Portland*, who occupies 50 acres
himself, and has let the other to John Ludlow, *farmer*, who
resides in the HALL—a large ancient mansion which is still surrounded by a moat. Thoroton says, Robert, the first *Earl of
Kingston*, who died in 1643, "resided in his ancient house of
Woodhouse, the most part of forty years," but his son and heir
dwelt at Holm-Pierrepont. This was anciently part of the
parish of Cuckney, and is no doubt the site of the " Castle of
Cuckney," which was built by the founder of Welbeck Abbey,
and which was afterwards occupied by the descendants of his
brother Ralph, who took the name of *Silvan*, from their residence at this manor in the woods," which they subsequently
gave to the monks of Welbeck.

WORKSOP PARISH.

This is the largest and one of the most interesting parishes in
the county, as it has several objects worthy the attention of the
antiquary, and includes *Worksop Manor* and *Clumber Park*,
the princely seats of the Dukes of Norfolk and Newcastle, and
extends eastward from Shireoaks (at the junction of the three
Counties of York, Derby, and Nottingham,) to Osberton and
Rushey Inn, near Babworth, a distance of seven miles. Its
population, which is thinly scattered, except in the handsome
market town of Worksop, amounts only to 5,566 souls, living in
1170 houses; being an increase of 2303 persons, and 411 houses,
since the year 1801. Its territorial extent amounts to no less
than 17,445A. 1R. 7P. of land, a large portion of which is in
woods and plantations, and in the two noble parks just mentioned,
and the remainder is in a high state of cultivation, the *commons*
and forest wastes being all enclosed by an Act passed in 1803,
but the award was not executed till 1817, when the tithes were
commuted for a yearly corn rent, fixed by the commissioners
according to the average price of good marketable wheat in the
county during the preceding 21 years, but subject to be altered
either by the vicar or the land owners, so as to be on an equitable
scale with the average price of wheat in every succeeding 14
years. This modus is charged on about 9300 acres of arable
land, which has generally a fine deep sandy soil, and like the rest
of the parish, was anciently part of the great *Forest of Sherwood*.
(See p. 35.) The *annual value* of the parish, according to an

assessment made for the poor rates in 1826, was £15,146. 1s. 0d. exclusive of woodlands estimated at £926. 4s. per annum, but not rateable to the poor. The parish is divided into *six constablewicks,* viz.—WORKSOP, RADFORD, GATEFORD, HAGGINFIELD, SHIREOAKS, and OSBERTON-*with*-SCOFTON, all of which maintain their poor conjointly; and also their roads, except Osberton and Scofton, which make and repair their roads separately from the rest of the parish. These divisions comprise several manors and hamlets, belonging mostly to the Dukes of Norfolk and Newcastle, and to G. S. Foljambe, Esq., as will be seen in the following description of each. The Chesterfield and Trent *Canal,* and the small river called the *Ryton,* cross the parish from west to east, close by the town of Worksop, in which, and the neighbourhood, there are about forty *maltsters,* whose MALT DUTY amounted in 1821 to £51,022; in 1825, to £36,639; and in 1831, to £36,596; indeed their yearly payments to the excise are seldom less than £30,000. Excellent *barley* (as well as other grain and roots,) is produced in the parish; but *liquorice,* for which Worksop was once famed, is no longer cultivated here. The *turnpike* from Worksop to Mansfield and Retford was made under an act passed in 1822.

WORKSOP, the capital of the parish, is a clean and plesant market town, with an eastern suburb, called RADFORD, pleasantly situated on the Sheffield and Newark road, 9 miles W. by S. of Retford, 12 miles N. by E. of Mansfield, 26 miles N. of Nottingham, and 146 miles N. by W. of London. On the approach from the east, the appearance of the town, lying in a valley, overtopped by the magnificent towers of the church, and backed by swelling hills finely clothed with wood, is extremely picturesque. Its situation is indeed delightful, and both nature and art have contributed to its beauty, for the houses are in general well built; the two principal streets spacious and well paved, and the inns clean and comfortable; and there are more noblemen's seats in its vicinity than any other spot in the kingdom, so distant from London, can boast of. "Much of the bustle of business enlivens it, from being on the post road to Sheffield, and having the advantage of the Chesterfield Canal, which runs close to the north side of the town, and near to the little river Ryton." Though there are no manufactures here, the condition of the poor is better than in most other places, for many of them find employment either in agricultural pursuits or in the numerous *malt kilns* in the town and neighbourhood, where there are also six extensive corn mills. The germes of abject poverty are promptly stifled by the bounty of the rich. The poor Catholics, who are rather numerous here, are much indebted to the benevolence of the Howards, for though the Duke of Norfolk does not often fix his residence at Worksop Manor, his son, the Earl of Surrey, is its frequent tenant. The MARKET, which is held on Wednesday, is well supplied, as also are the two annual FAIRS, held on March 31st, for cattle, and on October 14th, for horses, cattle, and pedlery. The fair which was held on St. Waldberg's day, June 21st, has long been obsolete. The *Workhouse* for the whole parish is but a small building, in Ward-lane. *Petty Sessions* for the Hatfield Division of Bassetlaw are held at the George Inn, on the last Wednesday, in every month. Besides the Abbey Church, there are three other *places of worship* in the town, viz.—a *Methodist chapel*, in Bridge-street, built in 1813; an *Independent chapel*, in Westgate, erected in 1830, and now under the pastoral care of the Rev Wm. Joseph; and a *Catholic chapel*, at Sandhill, near the Parkgate, on the Barlborough-road, which was built and endowed about fifty years ago by Charles, the Tenth Duke of Norfolk, of the Howard family, who is said to have built it and settled it upon the Catholics, under the impression that after his death, his son, the late Duke, who had then declared himself a Protestant, would expel the Romish rituals from the family chapel in the manor-house. A subscription *News Room and Library* was established in 1831, at Mr. Sissons', in Potter-street, and has now 100 members, who pay 10s. yearly. The *Boys' and Girls' National Schools*, where 250 children are educated, were opened in 1813, and are supported by voluntary contributions. The *Savings' Bank* was commenced in 1817, and had on Dec. 28th, 1831, deposits amounting to £26,804. 14s. 10d., belonging to 491 individuals, and to four *Charitable and* 12 *Friendly Societies*. G. F. Foljambe, Esq. is the treasurer, Mr. P. Sissons, the clerk, and Mr. Henry Owen, the secretary. The posthumous CHARITIES of Worksop parish are but few. In 1716, the sum of £230 left in 1623 and 1628, by James Woodhouse, Wm. Medley, and Mary Sterne, was laid out in the purchase of 17A. 3R. 30P. of land in six fields in the parish of Ecclesfield, let for £30 per annum; which, with the interest of £316. 2s. 6d., accumulated out of the former income, and now in the Savings' Bank, swells the total yearly value of this charity to upwards of £40, out of which 4s. each is given to 20 poor widows; 10s. to the parish clerk; £3 to the vicar for preaching sermons on Good Friday and St. Thomas day; £14 to the master of the National School, at the Abbey-gate; £14 to 60 poor families, and the remainder is expended in repairing the highways, &c. The *trustees*, are Messrs. J. and G. Champion, M. Binney, J. Froggatt, William Grafton, Henry Owen, and the Rev Thomas Stacye, the vicar. In 1581, John Smith left a yearly rent charge of 10s. to be distributed on Good Friday amongst 30 poor persons, out of a house and garden now belonging to Mrs. Dorothy Bates, but anciently the property of the Ellets, from whom this is called " *Ellet's Charity*." The £20 left in 1681, by Rosamond Magson, was lost many years ago.

The MANOR OF WORKSOP forms a separate *Constablewick*

and comprises the greater part of the town, the manor-house
and park, Worksop Lodge, and the scattered dwellings, of
Ratcliffe, Ratcliffe-Grange, Harness-Grove, Darfould, and
Sloswick, on the borders of Derbyshire, 2 miles W. of the town.
The Duke of Norfolk is sole proprietor and lord of this manor;
but RADFORD, the largest township or *constablewick* of the parish, contains several manors and hamlets, belonging to different
lords, viz. *Clumber* and *Hardwick Grange,* the property of the
Duke of Newcastle; *Rayton* or *Ryton,* on the north side of the
rivulet of that name, 2 miles E. by N. of Worksop, belonging to
G. S. Foljambe, Esq.; and *Kilton,* a large manor extending
northward from the canal near Worksop to Carlton and Hodsock, of which the Duke of Norfolk is lord, and also owner of
all the land, except the neat mansions and estates of *Forest Hill*
and *Forest Farm,* which are the property and residence of John
Fullerton and William Champion, Esqrs. and are distant about
2 miles N. of Worksop. His Grace of Norfolk is also lord and
owner of the *manor of Radford* which includes the parish
church, all the eastern part of the town, and the hamlet of *Manton,* distant 1¼ miles to the east.

Before the Norman Conquest, Worksop, or *Wirchesop,* was
the property of *Elsi* a Saxon Nobleman; but he was obliged
to yield it to the Conqueror's favourite *Roger de Bush,* whose
man *Roger* became his feudal tenant, and was succeeded by
William de Lovetot, lord of Sheffield and Hallamshire, who
founded the Abbey in Radford, and built a *Castle* here on the
west side of the town, upon a circular hill which is still called
"CASTLE-HILL," and is enclosed with a trench, except on the
north side, where its precipitous bank is defended by the river
Ryton. Of the castle nothing now remains, but its site is
marked by a small plantation. After many generations, the
estates of the Lovetots, were conveyed in marriage with their
heiress Matilda de Lovetot, to the family of *Furnival,* and
from them they passed to the *Nevills,* and afterwards to the
Talbots, who first became, on that account, *barons* of Furnival,
afterwards earls and dukes of Shrewsbury, though now extinct
as a dukedom; but the earldom in a junior branch. *John, the
first Earl of Shrewsbury,* was a man of great military prowess,
and became such a terror to France, as to be extremely useful
to Henry the Fifth in his wars with that country. He became
so much attached to Worksop, as to build here an immense
mansion house, with a magnificence in full accord with the
splendour of his family: this, however, was unfortunately
burnt down in 1761, as will be seen with the description of the
present manor house; and it is much to be regretted, as there
is reason to believe that it was a complete antique specimen of
old-fashioned elegance. The Talbot estates being divided
amongst coheiresses, this portion came to the Howards; Earls

of Arundel, now Dukes of Norfolk; and is still held by them
as tenants in chief of the crown.

The PRIORY, sometimes called the *Abbey*, was the greatest
ornament of Worksop, and stood in that part of the town
called Radford, adjacent to those fine specimens of gothic architecture, the *Church* and the *Abbey-gate*, near which some
few fragments of the cloisters, &c. still remain, and some parts
of the monastic walls have been converted into small dwelling-
houses. It was founded in the reign of Henry I., by William
de Lovetot, for canons regular of St. Augustine, and dedicated
to St. Mary and St. Cuthbert. The first grant "consisted of
the whole chapelry of his whole house, with the tithes and
oblations; of the church of Worksop in which these canons
were, with the lands and tithes, and all things belonging to the
church, and the fishpond and mill near to the church, and a
meadow adjoining to them; of the tithes of the pence of all his
set rents, as well in Normandy as in England; of a carucate of
land in the field of Worksop, and of a meadow called *Cratela;*
of all the churches of his demesne in the honour of Blyth,
with all the lands, tithes, and other things belonging to these
churches: of the tithes of paunage, honey, venison, fish, fowl,
malt, and mills, and all other things of which tithes were wont
to be given." This grant was confirmed by King Henry the
First, and added to by Richard de Lovetot, who approved of
his father's gifts, granting also his part of the church of Clarborough and two bovates of land. Cecilia de Lovetot gave the
church of Dinesley, in Hertfordshire, also to this Monastery;
but that grant was not valid until confirmed by Pope Alexander
the Third. Gerard de Furnival granted to it "pasture for 40
head of cattle in his park at Worksop, every year from the
close of Easter to the feast of St. Michael." He also gave his
body to be buried in the Monastery,* and with it he gave to the
canons a third of his mills at Bradfield, with the suit of the
men of that soke. His wife, the pious Matilda, also granted
them a mark yearly out of her mills at Worksop, to "celebrate
the anniversary of her husband." Bertha, the widow of Sir
Thomas de Lovetot, afterwards gave them an additional four
pounds of silver, out of the said mills at Bradfield, and they
subsequently received many other benefactions, all of which
were confirmed by the Roman pontiffs, until Henry VIII.,
whether for the good of his own soul or not we will not pretend
to say, thought proper to take them all into his own hands. It
appears from a *bull* of pope Alexander in 1161, that the canons
had a power of appointing the priests for their parish churches,

---

* This was always considered as a bequest of some value, as it brought large
sums in shape of oblations, offerings, masses, requiems, &c. There have been
many instances where the monks of one church have by force taken a rich man's
body from the monks of another, in order to bring all the grist to their own
mill!!!

" who were answerable to the bishop for the *cure* of the people's souls, and to the prior for the *profits* of their livings!" At its dissolution, the yearly revenue of the priory was valued at £239. 15s. 5d.

The CHURCH, which belonged to, and has the same tutelary saints as the priory, has yet an august appearance, and its two lofty towers strike the eye of the beholder with an impression equal to those of Westminster Abbey. The style of architecture was originally Saxon; but on the outside, it is much mixed with the gothic; and the whole is in the form and nearly the size of a cathedral. The west entrance is superb, consisting of a Saxon arch with zigzag ornaments; and the towers over it have " Saxon Anglo-Norman, and gothic windows in different gradations." On the north side of the edifice are some fragments of the priory; and in the meadows below, many traces of foundations have at various times been discovered. But the most splendid specimen of antique architecture is the ruinous *Chapel of St. Mary*, at the south-east corner, the windows of which are still in good preservation, and are perhaps the most perfect model of the lancet shape now remaining in England. On entering the church, the visitor is struck with its spacious and venerable appearance, though it now consists only of a nave and two side aisles, 135 feet in length; the chancel and the centre tower having long since disappeared. The roof of the nave is supported by eight pillars on each side, alternately cylindrical and octangular, joined by Saxon arches, ornamented with quatrefoils. Over these are two alternate rows of windows, one over the arches, the other over the intervals above the respective pillars. The *pulpit* is a curious proof of the ingenuity of ancient workmen, and of the profusion of labour which they bestowed on sacred things. The *monuments* are only remarkable for their antiquity, and are principally in memory of the Furnivals and Lovetots, or, as the *Cicerone* who showed them to Laird designated them, " morals of Antikkity, merable of the Funnyfields and Lovecats." Most of these mutilated tombs have been removed from their original places, and some of them lie in a neglected state, with the effigies " most luxuriantly ornamented with whitewash." Three of these figures, representing two knights and a lady, are now placed upright in the wall at the end of the north aisle. The approach to this venerable pile is through the ABBEY-GATE, a fine specimen of the latest gothic mode of workmanship, with apartments over it covered with a pointed roof, and lighted by florid windows and niches of great beauty. The statues which stood on each side of the gateway are gone, but there are still three over it; the gateway itself has a flat ceiling of oak, with gothic groins and supporters; but this is nothing more than the floor of the room above, which is now used as the National School. The gate

was double, with a wicket; and the whole, even now, is a
pleasing specimen of ancient architecture, especially when
viewed in connection with the venerable Cross that stands in
front, and consists of a lofty conical flight of steps, surmounted
by a slender pillar which has long since lost its transverse capital.

    Henry VIII. in 1542, granted to *Francis Earl of Shrews-
bury,* " the whole site and precinct of the priory of Worksop,
and all messuages and houses, and several closes and fields, and
four acres of arable land in *Manton,* in the parish of Worksop,
to hold to him and his heirs of the King, in capite, by the service of the tenth part of a knight's fee, and also by the *royal
service* of finding the King a right-hand *glove* at his coronation,
and of supporting his right arm that day, as long as he should
hold the sceptre in his hand, paying yearly £23. 8s. Ob. rent."
This grant is said to have been made in exchange for the manor
of Farnham-Royal, in the county of Surrey, which the Furnivals had held for many generations, by the aforesaid *coronation
service,* which was last performed by the present *Duke of Norfolk,* at the coronation of William IV., in 1831.

    Edward VI. granted to Henry Holbeach, *Bishop of Lincoln,*
and his successors in pure and perpetual alms, the reversion of
the RECTORY, and all the tithes of corn, hay, &c., of the parish
of Worksop, and " all that yearly rent of £35, reserved upon
the demise made to William Chastelyn, merchant of London."
This grant was conferred on the said bishop, in consequence of
his having given up to the King many of the ancient possessions
of the See of Lincoln, in which the impropriation of Worksop
still remains, but is leased to the Duke of Norfork, who has
also the advowson of the VICARAGE, which is valued in the
King's books at £12. 4s. 2d., and is now in the incumbency of
the Rev. Thomas Stacye. The yearly sums of £12 on Lady-
Day, and £6. 13s. 4d. on Michaelmas-Day, are paid out of the
great tithes to the vicar, and he also receives £10 annually from
the Duke of Norfolk, for not exercising his right to the patronage of Shireoaks Chapel.

WORKSOP MANOR HOUSE,

The property and occasional seat of his Grace the Duke of Norfolk, stands on the south-west side of the town, in the centre
of an extensive park, which is eight miles in circumference,
and contains 1100 acres of land, with much fine timber, some
of it so ancient as to be falling into decay. The principal
entrance, at the foot of Park-street, consists of a lodge and
gateway, with a pair of iron gates of elegant open work, beyond
which is a long avenue deeply shaded by umbrageous oaks and
other spreading trees ; and at the end of this sylvan walk may
be seen in the distance the *Castle Farm,* an extensive range of
agricultural buildings with a gothic front and embattled para-

pet, surrounded by a large tract of cultivated ground; much of the park being under the farmer's hands, and intersected by enclosure fences, consisting generally of a light railing. The *deer* are now confined in an enclosure of about 70 acres. The park has within its ample limits an extensive range of hills, sufficiently high to bound the view from the house on one side, and magnificently covered with a series of woods, which over-hang the landscape with a most charming effect. On the side next the farm, an abrupt swell rises in the boldest manner, tufted with wood, finely contrasting with the cultivated scene below, and presenting from its summit a most extensive prospect over the western part of the county. The trees in this park, which once formed part of the forest of Sherwood, are in general upon a very large scale; there are some, mentioned nearly a cen-tury ago by *Evelyn* in his "Sylva," which will bear two feet square of timber, at a height of forty feet, so that each will contain more than six solid tons of timber: and one tree in par-ticular was 180 feet from the extreme ends of the opposite branches, covering more than half an acre of ground. The avenue towards its end affords some casual glimpses of the house itself, which, on turning round a wood, bursts at once upon the view. A handsome gate now leads into the yard of offices, separated from the front lawn by an immense screen of light architecture with iron folding gates.

. The HOUSE is not only justly celebrated for its beauty, but for the surprising expedition which was used in its erection: and the visitor is struck with astonishment when told that what he sees is only the fifth part of the original design, so that, as Mr. Young in his tour very fairly observes, it would, if finished, be the largest house in England. It is, indeed, even now a masterpiece in architecture, and may be considered among the noblest mansions in England. Payne was the architect; but we understand that some of the most beautiful parts of the edifice must be attributed to the architectural skill of a former Duchess of Norfolk, who is said to have superintended its erec-tion. The ancient structure, which contained about 500 *rooms*, was *burnt down* in 1761 by an accidental fire, and it was esti-mated that the loss sustained in paintings, furniture, antique statues, (many of which were of the old Arundelian collection, and discovered in digging the foundations of some houses in the Strand in London, on the scite of Arundel house) and in the library, must have amounted to upwards of £100,000.

. The then Duke, on this unfortunate event, began a new house on a most magnificent plan; and now the present building, which is only one side of an intended quadrangle, is not unfit for the residence even of, majesty itself. This quadrangle and two interior courts would have completed the plan; but the execution of it was prevented by the sudden death of the heir! The front which is finished, of a handsome white freestone, is

318 feet in length, presenting a façade of lightness, beauty, elegance, and grandeur: in the centre, a portico makes a light projection, consisting of six very striking Corinthian pillars resting on the rustics, and supporting the tympanum and pediment with all the grace of the *Antinous* added to the apparent vigour of *Hercules*.

Three handsome statues representing Divine Truth, Peace, and Plenty,* are placed upon the points of the pediment; and in its centre is an emblematical carving allusive to the high family alliances. A light and airy ballustrade crowns the edifice from the tympanum to the projecting part at the ends, which mark the terminations in the style of wings, and upon this are a number of elegant vases.

The front entrance is into a vestibule, opposite the principal staircase, which is spacious and handsome; occupying an area 37 feet by 25, and having its walls richly ornamented with paintings in *Chiaro Scuro* by Thomas de Bruyn, a Fleming, who has pourtrayed the figures in such high relief that they actually appear protruding from the canvas, yet they have all the softness of smaller paintings, combined with the strong contrast of light and shade always adopted in fresco and in scene painting. The apartments are numerous, elegantly furnished, and many of them very spacious, but to particularize them and their extensive and valuable collection of paintings, several of which are by Vandyke, would require a volume. The furniture, portraits, and other decorations, are all in the ancient style of magnificence, with hangings and beds of crimson damask and sky blue velvet, with the history of Joseph in Brussels tapestry, Indian scenery, in Gobelin work, and " all the Howards, who frown along the deserted galleries, some in armour, some in whiskers, and those of a still later date in their large wigs and square shoes." In one of the rooms is the bed on which His Majesty George III. was born at Norfolk House, in London; it is a silk damask, and still in good preservation. The *chapel* possesses a gloom suitable to such a holy place, the altar is highly gilt, and has a large crucifix of exquisite workmanship, and a splendid painting of the Resurrection. The *gardens*, as specimens of the antique style of horticulture, are not undeserving of notice, though they have lost many of their beauties since the family ceased to make this their principal residence, and removed many of its best paintings and other ornaments to their favourite seat of Arundel Castle. The *menagerie* which a late Duchess had filled with a numerous collection of birds is gone, as also is much of the beauty of the home grounds, except in the vicinity of the *lake*, an expansive sheet of water, receding with all the boldness of a river betwixt broken rocks and hanging lawns, and under the

* The statues are said to have been executed from drawings by a late Duchess of Norfolk.

arches of an elegant bridge of white freestone, into the bosom
of a deep and dark wood, and having on one side of it a gentle
swell crowned with a Tuscan temple, that forms a fine object
from whatever direction it is seen.

The HOWARD FAMILY, which ranks in the British
peerage next the Blood Royal, has had its share of state sufferings; the block has been several times stained with its blood,
and its dignities and possessions have been often forfeited to the
crown, but as often restored. It has already been seen that the
illustrious Howards obtained Worksop Manor and many other
of the ancient possessions of the Lovetots, Furnivals, and Talbots, by one of the three daughters and coheiresses of Gilbert
Earl of Shrewsbury, who died in 1616. They descended from
the Earl of Passy, in Normandy. *William Howard*, "a learned
judge in the reigns of Edward I. and II. was one of their early
ancestors, and his son John Howard was sheriff of Norfolk and
Suffolk, from the 11th to the 16th of the latter reign, and
served in the wars against the French and Scots." *Sir John
Howard*, the son of the latter, was "a renowned Admiral in
the reign of Edward III. and was succeeded by his son *Sir Robert*, who was committed to the tower, in the 2nd of Richard II.
for detaining Margery de Narford, from her grandmother Aliee
Lady Nevil." His son *Robert* married Margaret, daughter and
coheiress of Thomas de Mowbray, first Duke of Norfolk, and
had issue by that lady (whose ancestors were allied to Edward
I.) *John Howard*, who was commonly called "*Jocky of Norfolk*," and distinguished himself in the wars with France in the
reigns of Henry VI. and Edward IV., in the latter of which
he was "Captain-general of the King's forces at sea, Deputy
Governor of Calais, summoned to parliament among the
barons, and constable of the Tower of London, and obtained a
grant in special tail of divers lands and manors. He had a pension from France, and in addition to it, he received from Louis
XI. in less than two years, in money and plate, "24,000 crowns
by way of direct bribe." (Philip Commines.) He got all the
honours of *Earl Marshal, &c.* from the Mowbray's, Dukes of
Norfolk just then extinct, in return for his favouring the usurpation of that blood-stained monarch, *Richard Crookback*, with
whom he was killed in the battle of Bosworth-field, on the 22nd
of August, 1485, and being attainted, all his honours were forfeited. His son *Thomas* subsequently obtained the favour of
Henry VII. and was restored to the title of *Earl of Surrey*.
He afterwards routed the Scots at Flodden-field, and rendered
such other essential service to Henry VIII. that in 1514, he
was created *Duke of Norfolk*. William, his second son, was
created *Baron Howard of Effingham*; and Thomas, his eldest
son, succeeded him as Duke of Norfolk; but after rendering
great services to Henry VIII. both as a soldier and a plenipo-
tentiary, he was seized and attainted with his son *Henry*, who

lost his head on Tower Hill, in 1547.' He himself, however, lived till the Catholic Mary restored the throne, and restored him to all his honours and estates in 1553, but he died in the following year; when he was succeeded by his grandson *Thomas*, who, in the Protestant reign of Elizabeth, was attainted and beheaded in 1572, for "taking part with Mary Queen of Scots." His son *Philip, Earl of Arundel,* (by Margaret, sole heiress of Henry Fitz Alan, Earl of Arundel,) was found guilty of high treason in the 23d of Elizabeth, and died in the tower six years afterwards. His son, Thomas Earl of Arundel, introduced the "*Arundel Marbles*" into this kingdom as already noticed, and after obtaining the favour of James I. and Charles I. was created *Earl of Norfolk* in 1644, but taking no part in the subsequent troubles, he retired to Italy, where he died in 1646. He left issue by Alethia, daughter of Gilbert Earl of Shrewsbury, *Henry Frederick,* sixth Earl of Norfolk, whose son and successor, *Thomas,* was created *Duke of Norfolk* by Charles II. in 1660; but dying without issue, his honours descended in 1677, to his brother Henry, who had been created *Lord Howard of Castlerising,* by the same monarch. The latter died in 1684, and was succeeded by his son *Henry,* who was a "stanch Protestant." One day, says Burnet, "the King (James II.) gave this Duke of Norfolk the sword of state to carry before him to the popish chapel; and he stood at the door. Upon which the King said unto him, "My lord, your father would have gone further;' to which the Duke answered, " Your Majesty's father was the better man, and he would not have gone so far.'" It was owing to his nephew succeeding him that the title came again into the Roman Catholic line, in which it still remains. This nephew, *Thomas,* Duke of Norfolk, died without issue in 1732, and was succeeded by his brother *Edward,* who also died without issue in 1777, when the titles of Norfolk, Arundel, Surrey, &c. descended to *Charles Howard,* of Greystock, in Cumberland, who, in 1786, was succeeded by his son *Charles,* the late Duke, who likewise died without issue in 1815, when his honours passed to his cousin and heir, the present Most Noble BERNARD EDWARD HOWARD, *Duke of Norfolk, Earl Surrey* and *Arundel, Hereditary Earl Marshal, Premier Peer, Baron Fitz Alan, Clun and Oswaldestre,* and *Maltravers, F.R.S. and F.S.A.* who married Lady Elizabeth Belasyse, by whom he has issue *Henry Charles Howard, Earl of Surrey,* who married in 1814, Lady Charlotte Leveson Gower, by whom he has issue *Henry Lord Fitz Alan* and other children. The late Duke renounced the ancient religion of his ancestors, but his present Grace professes the Roman Catholic Faith, as also does his son and grandchildren, who reside generally at Worksop Manor. His Grace's principal seat is at Arundel Castle in Sussex, and his town residence in St. James's-square. He is the twelfth Duke of Norfolk of the

Howard family, before whom that title was borne by *Richard Duke of York*, the infant son of Edward IV., who was murdered in the tower by order of his uncle, Richard III., who subsequently conferred the dignity upon the Howards. Before Prince Richard, there had been four Mowbrays Dukes of York, the title being first created in 1397; but the Bigod family had been *Earls* of Norfolk from 1135 to 1270, and previous to them there had been *Ralph Waher*, whom William the Conqueror created Earl of Norfolk and Suffolk, titles which he soon afterwards forfeited for treason.

CLUMBER PARK,

The elegant and magnificent residence of his *Grace of Newcastle*, is also within the ample limits of Worksop parish, except about 40 acres belonging to the township of Carberton. It extends from 2 to 5 miles S.E. of Worksop, and comprises 3412 acres of land; all of which is in *Radford Constablewick*—(See p. 457,) except the 40 acres just named. It is about three miles in length and breadth, adjoins Thoresby park on the south, and is crossed by the river Wollen from Welbeck, which forms near the house a beautiful lake of 87 acres. About 80 years ago it was one of the wildest tracts of Sherwood forest, being then " little more than a black heath full of rabbits, having a narrow river running through it, with a small boggy close or two;" but now, besides a princely mansion and a noble lake, it has 1393 acres of plantations, and 1892 acres of richly cultivated land in tillage and pasturage. Within its precincts are the remains of two woods of venerable oaks, viz. *Clumber Wood*, from which it has its name, and *Hardwick Wood*, which gives name to *Hardwick Grange*, his Grace's farming establishment, at the north-east corner of the park. Throsby says, " when I visited Clumber, (1796,) I entered the park two miles S. of Worksop, through an entrance more than two miles from the house, crescent formed, and topped with the arms of the family. Within the park the country opens upon you with splendour, rich in effect, and delightful to the eye. The fir and woody scenery around, in May, were warmed with patches of broom and gorse, then in golden hue, left, it may be presumed, for ornament. The hills, or rather rising grounds, are beautifully clothed with woody scenery; the lawns smooth; the walks every where adorned with rich plantations seated in the happiest succession; and the cross-roads all furnished with excellent direction posts,"—pointing the way to the house, which being in rather a low situation, would not be easily found by a stranger without the aid of these friendly monitors, the want of which, our author sorely lamented in his rambles in the neighbouring parks of Thoresby and Welbeck, in the latter of which he met with one of these stationary " gentlemen," who,

2 s

putting on a forbidding aspect, told him in broad characters that there was " *No road this way.*"

CLUMBER HOUSE, 4 miles S.E. of Worksop, is a spacious and elegant mansion, built since the year 1770, of white free-stone,* and occupying a central situation in the park, on the north side of the serpentine *lake*, which is enlivened [by a great number of swans, and by several handsome vessels, one of which is a *Frigate* called the Lincoln, and another bears the appellation of the *Clumber Yacht.* So much has been said in praise of this mansion, that it is difficult to find novel terms in which to express its elegance. It has been said that it embraces magnificence and comfort more than any other nobleman's seat in England; that, every thing reflects the highest credit on the taste displayed in the accommodations and ornaments found in this delightful retreat; and that in this "princely abode, the writer of romance might enrich his fancy, and the poet imagine himself wandering through an enchanted palace." The house consists of three fronts, and in the centre of that which faces the lake, there is a very light ionic colonade, which has a pleasing effect, especially when viewed in connection with the rest of the edifice, which is best seen from the lofty and elegant *bridge* that crosses the expansive lake, to which the lawn descends by two terraces forming ornamental shrubberies, and having on the lower one, two fountains, and two flights of steps into the lake. The *entrance hall*, which is very lofty, and supported by pillars, contains several good paintings, an elegant marble medallion of Dolphin and Tritons, a marble table inlaid with landscapes; another tesselated, and some fine antique busts. The lofty *Staircase* has a handsome railing, "curiously wrought and gilt in the shape of crowns, with tassils hanging down between them, from cords twisted into knots and festoons." It is adorned with the *Kitcat club*, and Dr. Measuobre giving lectures, by Doddridge; a marble model of the Laocoon groupe, exquisitely finished; a small painting of Apollo and the Hours preceded by Aurora; and in the upper part are some Roman monuments in good preservation. The *Library* is 45 feet by 31, and 21 feet in height, and contains in elegant mahogany cases, a splendid and well-chosen collection of English, foreign, and classical literature. A Corinthian arch, the columns of which are of jasper, opens into the *new reading room*, (30 feet by 27,) which was finished in 1832, and has an octagon front commanding a charming prospect of the lake and pleasure grounds. The *Duke's Study*, has several excellent family portraits, viz. John Holles, first *Earl of Clare*; Edward *Earl of Lincoln*, by Holbein; Thomas *Duke of Newcastle*; Mr. *Henry Pelham*, in his gown as Lord Chancellor of the Exchequer; his daughter *Miss Pelham*, grandmother of the present Duke; *Sir Henry*

* Brought from a quarry on the Duke's estate, about 5 miles from Clumber.

Clinton, Commander-in-Chief of the British army, during part
of the American war; also a very remarkable small original of
Henry VIII.; and two good landscapes by Binge, the young
artist of Tickhill, who was patronized by his Grace about 20
years ago. The principal apartments are superbly furnished,
and contain a great variety, of exquisite paintings, amongst
which are several by Rembrandt, Rubens, Vandyke, Snyders,
Hoare, and Corregio; one by the latter, or, as some say, by Fu-
rino, is the famous piece of *Sigismunda weeping over the heart
of Tancred.* But the greatest glory of Clumber is its STATE
DINING ROOM, a most magnificent apartment, 60 feet in length,
34 in breadth, and 30 in height; it is sufficiently large to ac-
commodate 150 guests at table, independent of a superb recess
or saloon for the sideboard, &c. The ceiling and pannels are
extremely rich in stucco and gilding, yet chaste without glare;
the lustres are of the finest cut glass; and the marble chimney-
piece and steel grate may be seen, but cannot be described;
they are in fact an honour to English taste and execution. On
the walls hang seven beautiful paintings, valued at no less than
£25,000; four of them are market pieces, by the joint pencils
of Snyder and Long John, and consisting of a display of flesh,
fish, fowl, and fruit and vegetables; and the others are dead
game, by Wenix, and two landscapes by Zuccarelli. If Clumber possessed no other paintings than these gems, the time and
attention of the tourist or artist would be amply repaid by
their examination. The *Chapel* is a very pleasing apartment,
admirably fitted for its purpose, and having a very sombre effect
from the four windows of stained glass, in which the family
arms are very handsomely emblazoned. In the *Dressing Room*
up stairs are seven fine paintings in water colours, of ancient
Roman taste, brought from Herculaneum. The *Bed Rooms*
are most superb; the beds are fitted up in imitation of tents
and pavillions, with their curtains even picturesquely arranged;
in short, every thing about the house breathes the essence of
taste and "the very soul of magnificence."

DUKES OF NEWCASTLE.—*Sir William Cavendish,* nephew
of the first Earl of Devonshire, was created Baron Ogle, and
Viscount Mansfield, in 1620; Baron Cavendish, of Bolsover, in
1628; Earl of Newcastle, in 1651; Marquis of Newcastle, in
1643, and *Earl Ogle and Duke of Newcastle-upon-Tyne,* in
1644. This was the famous Equestrian Duke of Newcastle,
who resided at Welbeck, as noted at page 450. He died in
1676; and was succeeded in his honours and estates by his son,
Henry Cavendish, who married the daughter of William Pierrepont, Esq., of Thoresby Hall, and died in 1691, when his titles
became extinct, in consequence of his leaving no male issue.
Margaret, one of his daughters and co-heiresses, married *John
Holles,* fourth Earl of Clare, who in 1694, was created Marquis
of Clare, and Duke of Newcastle-upon-Tyne. Previous to his

marriage he resided at Houghton, (vide p. 432,) but he afterwards removed to Welbeck, where he died in 1711, when, for
want of issue, his titles became extinct ; but he bequeathed his
estates to his sister's son, *Thomas Pelham*, second Baron Pelham, of Laughton, in Sussex, who assumed the name of *Holles*,
and in 1714, was created *Duke of Newcastle-upon-Tyne*, and
in 1715, *Duke of Newcastle-under-Lyme*. At his death in 1768,
all his titles became extinct, except those of Duke of Newcastle-under-Lyme, and Baron Pelham, of Stanemere, which
descended in marriage with his niece Catharine, to *Henry
Fiennes Clinton*, ninth Earl of Lincoln, who assumed the name
of Pelham, and died in 1794.   His son, Thomas Pelham Clinton, the late Duke, died in the following year, and was succeeded by his son, the present most Noble Henry Pelham
Fiennes-Pelham Clinton, *Duke of Newcastle, Earl of Lincoln,
Lord Lieutenant of Nottinghamshire, K. G., &c. &c.* whose son,
the *Right Hon. Henry Pelham Clinton*, bears his father's
secondary title of Earl of Lincoln, and resides with him at
Clumber House.

The *family of Clinton*, who now inherit the Clumber portion
of the Cavendish estates, (vide p. 433,) is of Norman origin,
and settled in England at the Conquest.   They took their name
from the Lordship of *Climpton*, in Oxfordshire.   Roger Climpton or Clinton was *Bishop of Coventry*, from 1228 till 1249.
John de Clinton was summoned to Parliament in the first of
Edward I., by the title of *Baron Clinton, of Maxtoch*.   His
second son, William, was Lord High Admiral of England in
1333, and created *Earl of Huntingdon* in 1337.   The 2nd, 3rd,
4th, and 5th Lords of Clinton distinguished themselves in the
wars of Edward III. and Henry V. and VI.   Edward the
ninth Lord Clinton, Lord High Admiral of England, was
created *Earl of Lincoln* in 1572.   His successor, Henry, second
Earl of Lincoln, was one of the commissioners on the trial of
Mary Queen of Scots.   Henry, the seventh Earl, was Constable
of the Tower, and Paymaster of the forces in the reign of
Queen Anne.   Henry, the ninth Earl, became as has just been
seen, Duke of Newcastle, and was succeeded by his son Thomas,
the late Duke, who married Anna Maria, daughter of William,
second Earl of Harrington.   Before his father's death he was a
major-general in the army, and served in the American war.
After enjoying the dukedom about one year, he died in 1795,
and was succeeded by his son, the present noble Duke, who was
born January 31, 1785.

GATEFORD *constablewick* is a hamlet of its own name, on
the Seffield road, 2 miles N. N. W. of Worksop, and several
scattered houses.   It comprises about 1100 acres, belonging
chiefly to Henry Machon, Esq. of *Gateford Hill*, a handsome
stone mansion, half a mile N. of the village, occupying the site
of the ancient residence of the Lascelles family.   *Raymoth*, a

large farm, belongs to Mr. B. Eddison. The Duke of Norfolk and Sir Thos. W. White have also estates here, and the owners have the manorial rights of their respective property. Mrs. Mary Dunston, who now lives with her daughter at *Claylands*, is 101 years of age, though so lately as 1830 she joined in a country dance.

HAGGINFIELD is but a small hamlet and constablewick, having only 800 acres of land, belonging to the Duke of Norfolk, 2 miles W. N. W. of Worksop. It is crossed by the river Ryton and the canal, and has on its eastern side a fine bed of *clay*, which makes excellent bricks, and on its western verge is plenty of good *limestone*, and also the noted freestone quarry and lime kilns, called *Lady Lee*.

OSBERTON and SCOFTON are two lordships, forming a joint constablewick, and lying on opposite sides of the river Ryton and the canal, from 2 to 5 miles E. of Worksop. They are both the property of George Savile Foljambe, Esq. of OSBERTON HALL, an elegant modern mansion, with a portico of four ionic pillars, supporting a highly ornamented architrave and pediment. The country around is very romantic, and richly clothed with wood, a large portion of which has been planted by the present owner, who charitably supports a *school* at Scofton, on the north side of the Ryton, for the education of 20 poor children. In the hall is a valuable MUSEUM, consisting of a complete collection of British birds, several cases of foreign and geological specimens, &c. &c., also a carving in alabaster representing the *Assassination of Thomas-a-Becket*, and supposed to have been the original altar-piece of Beauchief Abbey, near Sheffield. Another antique relic which the visitor will find here is a *Roman Altar*, that was found some years ago at Littleborough. The east front of the hall opens upon a spacious lawn, shut in on one side by a noble boundary of oak, and on the other by a screen of thriving plantations. The two lordships comprise 3841 acres, of which 1592 are in Osberton. *Chequer House*, at the eastern extremity of the latter, is partly in Babworth parish. Scofton was the property of the late Robert Sutton, Esq., of whom it was purchased about 30 years ago by the late F. F. Foljambe, Esq. who pulled down the hall.

SHIREOAKS, 2½ miles W. N. W. of Worksop, is a manor and chapelry, which had its name from an ancient oak that stood many centuries on the spot where the three counties of Nottingham, York, and Derby converge. A fine thriving young oak occupies the site of the original tree, which is not remembered by any person now living. William de Lovetot gave this lordship to Worksop priory, but at the dissolution of the religious houses, Henry VIII. granted it to Robert and Hugh Thornhill, together with Gateford and Darfould, for the yearly rent of 13s. 4d. From the *Thornhills* it passed to the *Hewitts*, with whom it remained till Sir Thomas Hewitt disinherited his daughter for marrying against his will, and bequeathed this estate to his godson, John Thornhaugh, Esq. for the term of his life ; after which it passed to the Rev. John Hewitt, rector of Harthill, who built and endowed here a *chapel of ease*, in 1809, and in the following year sold the Shireoaks estate to the Duke of Norfolk, who, after the death of Mr. Hewitt, pulled down the ancient mansion house, except a small portion of the walls, which have been fitted up as a dwelling by Mr. Froggatt. Since the Duke purchased the estate, much of its fine timber has fallen a sacrifice to the woodman's axe. The *chapel* is a neat stone edifice, consisting of a nave and chancel, with an octangular tower, surmounted by a cupola. The Rev. George Savile, B. A., the first and present incumbent, was presented to the curacy by the founder, but by the archbishop's license, dated 1810, the future patronage will be in the Duke of Norfolk, in consideration of his paying £10 a-year to the vicar of Worksop. The endowment consists of £90 a-year for the curate, besides a neat parsonage house, adjoining the chapel-yard, and £10 a-year for the clerk. Shireoaks contains about 800 acres, and is crossed by the Chesterfield canal and the Ryton rivulet.

GATEFORD.

Beardshaw John, gent. Baker's Plat

Bingham Wm. blacksmith

Carr Benj. farmer

Carr W. maltster, Ashley cottage

Eddison Mrs. Ann

Eddison Henry, maltster

Fell Samuel, shoemaker

Hodgkinson Jas. maltster, Gateford villa

Machon Henry, Esq. Gateford hill

Rhodes Eliz. farmer

Silvestor George, farmer

Vessey Miss Eliz. Gateford hall

Wright Mary, vict. Plough

Wright Mary, farmer, Claylands

HAGGINFIELD.

Cook George, farmer

Hawson John, maltster

Knight Wm. Rd. lime burner & stone merchant, Lady Lee and Worksop

Lewis Edward, brickmaker

Mosley Wm. maltster, Lady Lee

Pressen Thos. farmer

Smith John, farmer

Storey Wm. farmer

Thornton John, brickmaker and maltster

OSBERTON AND SCOFTON.

Marked ‡ are in Scofton.

Foljambe Geo. Savile, Esq. Osberton hall

‡Athron Wm. woodman

‡Broughton Godfrey, land bailiff

Foster John, corn miller, Diamond nook

Hodgkinson Rd. Grange

‡Hall Wm. gamekeeper

‡Horton John, blacksmith

Marshall Fras. Mill

Mason Mrs. housekeeper

Thorn Leond. house steward

Wagstaff Wm. land agent, Chequer house

‡Wilkinson Ann, school mistress

Wilkinson John, farmer

Wilkinson Wm. farmer

SHIREOAKS.

Challoner Peter, farmer

Durham John, corn miller

Froggatt John, gent. Shireoaks hall

Hatfield Wm. shopkeeper and clerk

Hudson Wm. blacksmith

Metcalf Mr. Joseph
Plant John, miller

Radley Wm. farmer
Savile Rev. Geo. curate

WORKSOP DIRECTORY.

LIST OF STREETS, HAMLETS, &c. IN WORKSOP AND RADFORD CONSTABLEWICKS, *both of which are included in this Directory.*

Those marked † are in Radford. The figures and capital letters show the distance in miles, and the bearings of each hamlet, &c. from the town.

†Abbey St. Potter street
Binney's yard, Bridge street
Blackburn's yard, Bridge street
†Brace Bridge, Potter street
Bridge Place, Bridge street
Bridge street, Market place
Canal side, foot of Bride street
Castle farm, Manor park
†Clumber house, 4 m. S. E.
Coal moor, Bridge place
Coney st. top of Market place
Creswellholm, Bridge place
†Cross bldgs. Potter street
Darfould, 1¼ m. W.
Eastgate. Bridge place
Forest hill, 2 m. N.
Forest road, foot of Newgate st
†Friar Well road, Abbey gate
Hardwick grange, 4 m. E.
Harness grove, 1¼ m. W. by S.
Hetts bldgs. Eastgate
Hodgkinson's yd. Bridge pl
Justice's yard, Bridge street
Kilton, 1 m. N. E.
Lead hill, Westgate

†Low street, Potter street
†Manton, 1½ m. E.
Market place. Bridge street
Marson's yard, Bridge street
†Mayor's croft, Newgate street
Newgate street, Coney street
Nicholson's yard, Market place
Norfolk st. Westgate
Park street, Coney street
Pearce's bldgs. Newgate street
Playhouse yd. Potter street
Potter street, Market place
Radford place, Forest road
Ratcliff, 2 m. S. W.
Sandhill, Westgate
Skinner's row, Bridge place
Sloswick, 2½ m. S.
Sparkenhill, ½ m. S. by E.
St. Mary's grove, Bridge st
Ward lane, Bridge st
Westgate, Market place
Worksop lodge, 1 m. W.
Worksop manor, ¼ m. S. E.
N.B. Eastgate, Newgate st. and Potter st. are partly in Radford

POST OFFICE, Market Place,—Edward Parker, Post Master.

A Mail gig is despatched to Retford at 10 in the Morning, & returns at three in the Afternoon.

Duke of Norfolk, Worksop manor
Duke of Newcastle, Clumber house
Earl of Surry, Worksop manor
Earl of Lincoln, Clumber house
Allan Henry, supervisor, Potter street
Armstrong John, excise officer, Norfolk street
Bates Mrs. Dorothy, Bridge st
Bates Capt. Robert, Bridge st

Baxter Edward, corn merchant, Bridge street
Baxter John, carter, Newgate st
Beachey Mrs. Ann, Newgate st
Beardsall William, toll collector, Moot Hall
Bingley Mrs. Ann, Bridge st
Blackburn Samuel, gent. Lead hill
Booth Mrs. Mary Ann, Gateford road

Brace William, road surveyor, Abbey street
Bradley Wm. woodman, Hardwick
Broome Mrs. Ann, Potter street
Burchby Thos. cabinet maker, Clumber
Burn William, town cryer, Newgate street
Bullivant Thomas, farmer, Sloswick
Candlin Robert, keeper, Carburton lodge, Clumber park
Carter Mr. John, Potter st
Champion William, gent. Bridge house
Clarke, Samuel, farmer, Eastgate
Clayton Richard, gent. Newgate street
Conworth Job, chief constable for N. Clay Divison, Bridge street
Cross Thomas, farmer, Castle farm
Dawson George, coach proprietor and livery stable keeper, Lead hill
Dibble Henry, park and game-keeper, Sparken hill
Dixon William, shepherd, Clumber park
Downs, Mrs. Eliz. Potter street
Dowse John, clerk, Newgate st
Eccles William, farmer, Ratcliffe
Eddison, Benjamin, sen. gent. Bridge street
Ellis Mr. Joseph, Norfolk st
Ellum Charles, groom, Clumber lodge
Ewbank Rev. Wm. Potter st
Eyre John, Mayor croft
Falkner Mrs. Frances, Bridge st
Fletcher Thomas, painter, Newgate street
Fullerton John, jun. Esq. Forest hill house
Girdler Richard, gent. Potter st
Grafton William, timber mercht. Gateford road
Gregory William, gent. Gateford road
Habbijam Robert, horse breaker, Kilton lane

Hall John, carter, Eastgate
Harrison Wm. farmer, Carlton road
Harpham Thomas, fishmonger, Bridge street
Haykin Mrs. Phœbe, Norfolk st
Hicks Mr. James, Mayor croft
Hodgkinson, Mrs. Ann, Potter street
Hodgkinson Saml. farmer, Kilton
Hopkin Thos. maltster, Mayor croft
Horncastle Jno. farmer, Manton
Horrobin Samuel, sweep, Nicholson's yard
Hovenden Thomas, house steward, Clumber house
Hunt Richard, agent, Clumber office
Hutchinson George, bailiff, Ladies' farm, Clumber park
Jackson John, excise officer, Potter street
Johnson William, book-keeper, Bridge place
Jones Rev. Jas. Catholic Priest, Sandhill place
Joseph Rev. Wm. (Ind.) Potter street
Kelp John, farmer, Eastgate
Kemp Samuel. writer, Low st
Kirk Thomas and Wm. stone-masons, Clumber park
Kirkby Mrs. Mary, Newgate st
Knight Wm. Rd. lime and stone merchant, Bridge street
Langley Miss Mary Ann, Mayor croft
Leith Matthias, millwright, Potter street
Leith Thomas, millwright, Playhouse yard
Littlewood Samuel, joiner, Clumber park
Lowley Misses Ann and Sarah, Potter street
Makins Jas. gamekeeper, Hardwick
Marr Mr. James, Bridge street
Marsh John, farmer, Forest farm
Marston Wm. Esq. Bridge st
Mawe Francis, clerk, Potter st

Mosley Wm. maltster, Bridge st
Mellors Jno. keeper. Apley head
  lodge, Clumber park
Moffatt Thomas, gardener, Clum-
  ber park
Newton, Mrs. Sarah, Park st
Nock, Mrs. Ann, Shireoaks road
Offen Robert, sailor, Hardwick
Outram Francis, farmer, Rayton
Oxley Francis, farmer, Creswell
  holm
Parkin Miss Sarah, Newgate st
Parr William, land bailiff, Hard-
  wick
Peacock William, parish clerk,
  Brace bridge
Pearce Misses Betty and Letitia,
  Mayor croft
Pearce Mr. Robert, Newgate st
Pegge Mrs. Eliz. Newgate st
Pickard Henry William, Esq.
  Forest hill
Potter Richard, governor of the
  workhouse, Ward lane
Radley Miss Eliz. Bridge street
Richardson John, gent. Gateford
  road
Roe Curtis, sweep, Nicholson's
  yard
Roe Francis, Esq. Potter street
Sharman Thomas, job gardener,
  Norfolk street
Shaw John, game dealer, Bridge
  street
Shaw Rueben, whitesmith, Bridge
  street
Shipman John, travelling sta-
  tioner, Newgate
Sissons Miss Mary, Newgate
Sissons Peter, gent. Westgate
Slack William, carter, Eastgate
Smith John, gent. Bridge st
Stacye Rev. Thomas, vicar, Pot-
  ter street
Stephenson Henry, (Meth.) St.
  Mary's grove
Temple William, cook, Clumber
  house
Thomas Theop. valet, Clumber
Thompson Miss Hannah, Potter
  street
Thompson Mr. Jonathan, Clum-
  ber cottage

Thompson Joseph, hosier, Pot-
  ter street
Truman Mr. George, Lead hill
Truman Wm. baker, &c. Mayor
  croft
Turner George, cowkeeper, Kil-
  ton lane
Turner Mrs. Samuel, Friar well
  lane
Wake, Mrs. Jane, Potter street
Walkins Samuel, land agent, Park
  street
Waring Thomas, stone mason,
  Potter street
Webb Mrs. Sarah, Newgate st
Webster Thomas, bank agent,
  Potter street
Whitaker Mr. William, Potter
  street
White Joseph, machine maker,
  Newgate street
Wood Thomas, cart owner, New-
  gate street
Worthington, Mr. John, Newgt

ACADEMIES.
Bartlam Edw. Bridge street
Bower Wm. Potter street
Burdon Eliz. Market place
Coates Wm. (bdg. & day) Carl-
  ton road
Day Eliz. Bridge street
Dent Lucy, Newgate st
Huertley Frances, (ladies' bdg.)
  Park street
Huertley Wm. (drawing) Potter
  street
Lockwood Jph. Norfolk st
National, Wm. Haslewood, Ab-
  bey gate
National (Girls), Ann Fitzaker-
  ley, Newgate st
Newbolt Henrietta, Clumber
Tunstall Isaac, Lead hill
Tyzack Jph. Park street
Wilson Sarah, (bdg.) Potter st

ATTORNEYS.
Beardshaw Thos. Bridge st
Owen Henry, (& clerk to the ma-
  gistrates) Bridge st
Wake Henry Stephen, Potter st

AUCTIONEERS.
Broome Thos. Bridge st
Sissons Francis, Potter st

BAKERS & FLOUR DLRS.
Godfrey Edward, Bridge st
Harris Martha, Newgate st
Harrison Fras. Low street
Hewson Robt. Bridge street
Hooson Fras. (& confr.) Potter st
Houghton Wm. Park street
Skelton John (& confr.) Market place
Willmot John, Lead hill

BANKERS.
Cooke, (Sir Wm. B.) Foljambe, Parker, & Walker, Potter st. ; (draw on Coutts & Co. London)
Savings' Bank, George Inn, Bridge st. ; open every Monday, from 10 to 12

BASKET MAKERS.
Flint Wm. Potter street
Parsons John, Market place

BLACKSMITHS.
Ball John, Westgate
Fletcher Geo. Park street
Grayson Geo. Bridge street
Green Wm. Potter street
Stringfellow Saml. Leadhill
Webster Geo. Potter street

BOAT BUILDERS.
Froggatt & Grafton, Bridge pl

BOAT OWNERS.
Beeston Geo. Canal side
Hodgkinson Joshua, Carlton rd
Hurst Jas. Friarwell lane
Marples Geo. Bridge place
Walker Geo. Eastgate
Watson Geo. Friarwell lane

BOOKSELLERS, PRINTERS, LIBRARIES, &c.
Sissons Fras. (& stamp office) Potter street
Whitlam John, (& paper hanger) Coney street

BOOT & SHOEMAKERS.
Barlow Jph. Potter street
Barlow Thos. Leadhill
Bartrop Wm. Park street
Coupe John, Norfolk street
Fricknall Wm. Potter street
Gilling James, Eastgate
Gilling John, Norfolk street
Holbrey Paul, Newgate street
Lilley John, Gateford road
Lockwood John, Potter street

Machon Hy. Newgate street
Newcombe John, Newgate st
Pearce Anthony, Newgate st
Pye John, Newgate street
Richardson Wm. Benj. Coney st
Robbins Thos. Park street
Shirtcliff Geo. (whs.) Bridge st
Smith Geo. Market place
Smith Geo. jun. Bridge place
Twelves Wm. Justice's yard
Wall John Bridge street
Wall John, jun. Eastgate
Whitehead Chas. Newgate st
Whitehead John, Westgate
Whitehead Saml. Low street

BRAZIERS & TINMEN.
Heane Hy. Bridge street
Shayle Thos. Potter street

BRICKLAYERS.
Keeling Wm Market place
Knock Stanley, Mayor croft
Rooke Saml. Common
Waring Thos. (& stone mason) Potter street
Webster John, Lead hill

BRICKMAKERS.
Lewis Edw. Hagginfield
Thornton John, Hagginfield

BUTCHERS.
Ashmore Geo. Bridge street
Ashmore Wm. Newgate street
Bee Jonathan, Bridge street
Bee Wm. Newgate street
Clarke John, Potter street
Clarke Thos. Eastgate
Cowley Geo. Potter street
Eyre Robert, Bridge street
Futtit Hannah, Coney street
Goacher Geo. Bridge street
Greathead Thos. Market pl. and Park street
Greathead Thos. jun. Potter st
Leeson Rd. Mkt. pl. & Coney st
Mayor Jph. Bridge street
Slack John, Eastgate
Wardle Isaac, Bridge street
Watkin Wm. Abbey street
Whitaker John, Potter street

CABINET MAKERS, BUILDERS, &c.
Hyde Rd. (& bdg. surveyor and appraiser) Park street
Miller John, Bridge place

White Wm. Potter street
Wright John, Leadhill
CHAIR MKRS. & TURNERS.
Gabbitas John, Eastgate
Moss & Alsop, Potter street
Sharp Saml. Park street
COAL MERCTS., WHARFIN-
GERS, & CARRIERS.
Canal Company's Wharf, Canal
side, Jas. Bennett, agent
Dethick Saml. jun. & Co. Bridge
place
Mapson Rd. & Co. Bridge st
Pashley & Storey, Bridge st
COOPERS.
Flint William, Potter street
Newton Fras. Bridge street
CORN MILLERS.
Durham John, Worksop Mill
Eddison, Baxter & Co. Bridge st
Gibson Thos. Forest mill
Millns Robert, Eastgate
Skelton Fras. Radford
CURRIERS, &c.
Pattison Jph. Lead hill
Story John, Park street
DRUGGISTS.
Eddison John, Market place
Justice George, Bridge street
Harrison Edward, Westgate
Latham Robert, Market place
FIRE & LIFE OFFICES.
British, Fras. Sissons, Potter st
County, Thos. Broome, Bridge st
Norwich Union, Thos. Webster,
Potter street
Sheffield, John Black, Park st
GLASS, CHINA, &c. DLRS.
Cartwright St. John, Market pl
Read John, Newgate street
GROCERS & TEA DEALERS.
Cartwright St. John, Market pl
Cutts George, Norfolk street
Eddison John, Market place
Hooson Fras. Potter street
Latham Robert, Bridge street
McBurnie Robert, Potter st
Paling Samuel, Potter street
Robbins Samuel, Newgate street
Scott James, Bridge street
Skelton John, Market place
Story John, Low street
Stubbs Randall, Newgate street

West Robert, Park street
Wilson Matthew, (& chandler)
Bridge street
GUN MAKER.
Bonell Wm. Bridge street
HAIR DRESSERS.
Shirtliffe Geo. (perfumer) Bridge
street
Tomlinson Wm. Market place
Vallance Andrew, Market place
HAT MANUFACTURERS.
Cree Wm. Westgate
Plant Thos. Bridge street
Sissons Fras. (London hats) Pot-
ter street
INNS & TAVERNS.
Blue Bell, Stephen Wilson, Park
street
Bull Inn, Sarah Thorpe, Mkp.
Cross Keys, Wm. Wale, Potter st
Crown Inn, (& excise office) Rd.
Beedall, Potter street
French Horn, Wm. Barlow, Pot-
ter street
George Inn, Thomas Broome,
Bridge street
Golden Ball, John Northige,
Bridge place
Golden Lion, Jph. Child, Bridge
street
Grey Hound, W. Benj. Richard-
son, Coney street
Holly Bush, Wm. Keeling, Mkp
Lord Nelson, Jane Marples,
Bridge street
Marquis of Granby, John Butt,
Bridge street
New Ship, John Wallis, Westgt
Norfolk Arms, Wm. Hett, Nor-
folk street
Old Black Bull, John Marsden,
Market place
Old Ship, Mary Sibery, Market
place
Red Lion Inn, (posting) Richard
Gilbert, Market place
Rein Deer, John Salmon, New-
gate street.
Smiths' Arms, John Markham,
Potter street
Sportsman's Inn, Rt. Didsbury,
Bridge street

Wheat Sheaf, Thos. Eyre, Bridge street

White Hart, John Woolhouse, Market place

Yellow Lion, Wm. Cowley, Potter street

BEER HOUSES.

Anchor, John Ellis, Eastgate

Board, Jph. Garside, Potter st

Board, Jas. Tewson, Newgate st

Board, Phineas Smith, Norfolk st

Board. Geo. Froggatt, Norfolk st.

Boat, Wm. Footet, Friar Well ln

Half Moon, Wm. Warner, Newgate street

King William, Thos. Hancock, Abbey street

Pheasant, Robert Arthur, Gateford road

Royal Oak, Robert Drake, Newgate street

White Lion, Thomas Robbins, Park street

IRON & BRASS FOUNDER.

Ellis Thos. Potter street

IRONMONGERS.

Heane Edw. Bridge street

Parker Edw. Market place

Shaw Mary & Son, Bridge st

Shayle Thos. Potter street

JOINERS.

See also Cabinet Makers.

Driver Edw. Potter street

Lees Samuel, Westgate

Mellars John, Mayor croft

Levick Thomas, Bridge street

LAND SURVEYORS.

Black John, Park street

Hickson John, Bridge street

LINEN & WLN. DRAPERS.

Bailey Joshua, (woollen) Potter st

Creswick John & Co. Potter st

Kerr John, Bridge street

McBurnie Rt. Potter street

Morgan Wm. (linen) Market pl

Nicholson Susannah, Market pl

Pearson Isaac & Edw. Bridge st

Smith Thos. Park street

Tewson Jas. (Gingham & check mfr.) Newgate street

MALTSTERS.

Baxter Edward, Bridge street

Carr Wm. Ashley, Cottage

Clark Thomas, Eastgate

Cox George, Carlton road, and Bolsover

Dethick Saml. & Son, Bridge st

Dowland Kaye, Bridge pl. and Brimington

Durham John, Worksop mill

Eddison Benj. jun. Bridge st

Eddison Henry, Gateford

Field Jph. North Carlton

Hawson John, Hagginfiel

Heywood John, Creswellholm & Brimington

Hickson John, Bridge street.

Hodgkinson Jas. Gateford villa

Hopkin Thos. Mayor croft

Hunt Wm. Lead hill.

Mapson Rd. Bridge street.

Marsden John, Market place

Marsh Frances, Low street

Mosley & Traunter, Bridge st

Mycroft Geo. Newgate street

Pagdin John, Low street

Pagdin Wm. Low street

Parkin Mary, Newgate street

Pashley Robert, Bridge street

Paulton Wm. Eastgate

Peck Thomas, Potter street

Skelton Fras. Radford mill

Smith George, Bridge street

Spurr Wm. Wigthorpe

Thornton John, Hagginfield

Turner John, Potter street

Watkins Samuel, Park street

Watson Edward, Newgate st

MILLINERS & DRESS MKRS.

Birch Amelia, Park street

Birkinshaw Eliz. Potter street

Bower Eliz. Bridge street

Downs Eliz. Potter street

Fletcher Mary, Bridge street

Langham Ann, (stay) Bridge st

Martin Eliz. Bridge street

Norkitt Sarah, Westgate

Pegge Anne, Westgate

Townley Rebecca, Mayor croft

Thurston Amelia, Ward lane

Waterass Sarah, Nicholson's yd

White Mary, Bridge street.

Wilson Eliz. Newgate street

MILLWRIGHTS, MACHINE MAKERS, &c.

Darby George, Newgate st

Leiths & White, Potter street
NAIL MAKERS.
Cutts Thos. Norfolk street
Tomlinson John, Potter street
NURSERY & SEEDSMEN.
Madin John, Bridge street
Mellish John, (& fruiterer) Mkp
Saunderson John, Canal side
Stemson Stephen, Abbey street
PAINTERS.
Fletcher & Taylor, Newgate st
Roberts John, Newgate st
Smith Wm. Potter street
Stephenson Joshua, Norfolk st
Watkinson Edward, Bridge st
PLUMBERS & GLAZIERS.
Broome Thomas, Bridge street
Lithgow John, Newgate street
Waddilove John, Park street
Waring Wm. Potter street
ROPE & TWINE MAKER.
Cutts Thos. Bridge street
SADDLERS.
Baxter Wm. Coney street
Belfit Saml. Mkp. h. Park st
Mallender John, Bridge st
Pearce Jph. Mkp. h. Potter st
Preston Thomas, Potter street
SHOPKEEPERS.
Armstrong John, Bridge street
Bargh Wm. Low street
Beardshaw Thos. Mayor croft
Bewton Wm. Canal side
Cuckson Thos. Potter street
Ellis Thos. Norfolk street
Gregory Sarah, Coney street
Hewitt George, Abbey street
Holmes Geo. Friar well lane
Hoggart Wm. Bridge st
Johnson Eliz. Bridge st
Johnson Thos. Abbey street
Layhe Wm. Low street
Lowther Wm. Gateford road
Rhodes Wm. Park street
Simpson Thos. Abbey street
Saxton Thos. Norfork street
Simpson Wm. Grafton's row
Theaker Jph. Norfolk street
Vallance Eliz. Bridge street
Warner Wm. Newgate st
Watkinson Thos. Eastgate
Wilson Matthew, (& chandler) Bridge street

STRAW HAT MAKERS.
Cutts Sarah, Norfolk street
Marsden Eliz. Norfolk street
Newbolt Marg. Market place
Story Ann, Market place
Woodward Charlotte, Norfolk st
SURGEONS.
Beardsall Geo. Potter st
Dethick John, Bridge street
Frith Geo. Bridge place
TAILORS.
Binks Jph. Nichson's yard
Bramer Rt. Bridge st
Brown George, Bridge street
Brown John, Lead hill
Brown Thos. Potter street
Fitzpatrick Jas. Coney street
Grantham Wm. Potter street
Hickling George, Bridge street
Marsden Geo. Park street
Mellins Wm. Low street
Noton Charles, Park street
Peck Henry, Market place
Peck Thos, Newgate st
Quibell Wm. (and stay maker) Potter street
Sissons John, Norfolk street
Unwin James, Market place
Westby John, Westgate
Widdowson Geo. Lead hill
TANNERS.
Binney Mordecai, Gateford road
Pattison Geo. Westgate & Hart-hill
TIMBER MERCHANTS.
Those marked ‡ are English Timber Dealers, Sawyers, and Hedge Carpenters.
‡Ellis John, Eastgate
Froggatt & Grafton, Canal side
‡Garside Benjamin & Jph. Friar Well lane
‡Garside Wm. Friar Well lane
‡Hancock & Son, Mayor croft
‡Hancock Thos. Abbey street
‡Marsden John. Bridge street
‡Mellars & Saunderson, Kilton ln
Miller John, Bridge place
‡Tesh Robert, Eastgate
VETERINARY SURGEONS.
Clark Wm. Bridge street
Naylor Wm. Coney street

2 T

WATCH & CLOCK MKRS.

Binks Jph. Bridge street
Hutchinson John, Potter st
Martin Robert, Bridge street
Mason Robert, Potter street
Stacey Geo. (& jeweller) Bridge st

WHEELWRIGHTS.

See also Millwrights, &c.

Cuckson Thos. Potter street
Grantham Geo. Bridge street
Levick John, Low street
Taylor Wm. Mayor croft
Wale William, Potter street

WHITESMITHS, &c.

Shaw Mary & Son, Bridge st
White Henry, Coney st

WINE & SPIRIT MERCHTS.

Beedle Rd. Potter street
Cartwright St. John, Market pl
Lowther Rt. (wine) Gateford rd
Pashley Robt. (& brewer) Bridge
 street, house Harness grove
Short Eliz. (& retail) Market pl

COACHES,

From the George Inn.

The *Forester* to Doncaster
every Mon. Wed. & Fri. at half-
past 3 aftr. and to Nottingham
every Tue. Thur. & Sat. at half-
past 9 morning

The *Union* to Doncaster daily,
except Sunday, at 4 aftr. and to
Nottingham at 10 morning

To Chesterfield, a *Car*, every
Mon. Tue. Thur. & Sat. at 7 mg.
to meet the Manchester & Liverpool coaches

The *Industry* to Retford, every
Mon. Wed. & Fri. at half-past 3
aft. and to Sheffield every Tues.
Thur. & Sat. at 7 mg. and the
Mail gig from the Red Lion,
to Retford every morning at 10.

CARRIERS BY WATER.

See Coal Merchants, &c.

CARRIERS BY LAND.

To *London*, Robert Hunt's waggons from the White Hart,
every Sun. Tues. Wed. & Fri.
mornings at 9.

Barlbrough & Chesterfield, John
 Salvin, from the White Hart,
 Wed. afternoon at 3.

Blyth, the White Hart, Martin
 Kirkby, Wed. 4 afternoon

Carlton-in-Lindrick, J. Bramer,
 4 afternoon.

Doncaster, through Tickhill,
 R. Wrigglesworth, White Hart,
 Wed. aft. at 4.

Clown and Chesterfield, Black
 Bull, Wed. 3 aft.

Gainsbro' and Retford, Thomas
 Tattershall & Thos. Gleadell,
 Smiths' Arms, Wed. 4 aft. and
 Thos. Stansfield, White Hart,
 Wed. 5 aft.

Lincoln, Edw. Warrington, from
 the Crown inn, Thurs. at 6 mg.
 and Joseph Morton, Smiths'
 Arms, Wed. 5 mg.

Mansfield, John Preston & Geo.
 Roberts, White Hart, Wed.
 Fri. & Sat. 2 aft.

Nottingham, &c. Pettifor's waggons from the White Hart, every
 Wed. & Sun. at 4 mg.

Retford, Edward Godfrey, from
 Bridge st. Sat. mg. at 8.

Sheffield, Jno. Ward, from Bridge
 st. Mon. & Thu. dep. 9 mg. &
 John Thorpe, from Radford pl.
 Tue & Fri. 9 mg.; Edw. War-
 rington, Fri. night, at 11; and
 Joseph Morton, Smiths' Arms,
 Sat. mg. at 2; also Rt. Hunt's
 waggons, from the White Hart,
 Sun. Mon. Wed. and Fri. at
 10 mg.

Wellow, Robt. Jackson, Wheat
 Sheaf, Wed. 4 aft.

York, Pettifor's waggons, from the
 White Hart, every Tu. mg. at
 8, and Sat. mg. at 4.

BINGHAM HUNDRED

Is about 12 miles in length and 8 in breadth, and lies in the southern part of the county, bordering upon Leicestershire, and bounded on three sides by the Hundreds of Thurgarton, Newark, and Rushcliffe, with which latter division it forms the *Deanery of Bingham*, in the Archdeaconry of Nottingham and Diocese of York. (Vide p. 14, 144, and 314.) Thoroton says, its ancient name was "*Binghamshou Wapentac*, so called from the usual place of meeting, viz. a certain Pit on the top of the hill on the *contrary* side of the FOSSE WAY, near the most westerly corner of Bingham Lordship, called *Moot-House Pit*," where the Hundred Court used to be held, though they sometimes "removed to Cropwell Butler as the nearest town for shelter." Its POPULATION amounts but to 12,442 souls, living in 28 parishes and chapelries, of which the following is an enumeration, shewing the number of persons in each in 1801, 1821, and 1831, and the *annual value* of the land and buildings, as assessed for the property tax in 1815;—distinguishing also the two *divisions* into which the hundred is divided betwixt its two Chief Constables.

Ann Val. £.	NORTH DIVISION.	POPULATION IN 1801··1821··1831			Ann Val. £.	SOUTH DIVISION.	POPULATION IN 1801··1821 1831		
3252	Bridgeford East ··	526··	763··	938	7493	Bingham ········	1082··	1574	1738
2365	Car-Colston ······	152··	213··	249	2361	Broughton Sulney	230··	348	344
1006	Elton ··········	90··	93··	91	945	Clipstone (town-			
4157	Flintham ········	459··	546··	545		ship)§ ·········	62··	72	82
3354	Granby-with-Sut-				5341	Cotgrave ········	596··	779	842
	ton ···········	329··	389··	342	2333	Colston Basset····	220··	348	387
995	Hawksworth ····	154··	215··	212	1706	Cropwell Bishop··	307··	392	473
4687	Holme Pierrepont-				2898	Hickling ········	391··	497	529
	with-Adbolton··	171··	205··	205	3101	Kinoulton‖ ······	275··	370	389
1916	Kneeton ········	88··	104··	119	3130	Radcliffe-on Trent	761··	993	1125
4963	Langar-cum-Barn-				975	Owthorpe ········	107··	138	144
	ston ···········	266··	287··	274	2280	Tollerton ········	176··	153	149
2890	Orston* ··········	351··	391··	439	7729	Shelford-with-			
1968	Screveton ········	225··	292··	312		Newton and	486··	671	704
1273	Scarrington†······	152··	171··	188		Saxondale····			
3171	Stoke East ······	203··	424··	320		Tithby with	155··	146	144
1212	Thoroton†········	110··	145··	143	2702	Cropwell			
2916	Whatton ········	308··	390··	388		Butler‡····	362··	489	551
1931	Aslacton Chap.····	171··	273··	289					

* Orston includes part of Flawborough, which is mostly in Staunton parish.—See Newark Hundred.

† Scarrington and Thoroton are Chapelries to Orston parish.

§ Clipstone is in Plumptre parish.—*Vide* Rushcliffe Hundred.

‖ Kinoulton includes *Lodge-on-the-Wolds*.—*(Extra Par.)*

‡ Tithby includes *Wiverton-Hall (Extra Parochial).*

The river *Trent* forms its northern boundary, and the *Grantham Canal* crosses it in a south-easterly direction from Nottingham to Hickling, passing under the *Wolds* on its south western borders, and having a branch extending to Bingham. The principal rivulets that intersect it are the Wipling, the Smite, and the Car-Dyke. It is generally a fertile district, especially near the banks of the Trent, and some of the smaller streams, which frequently flood and enrich the pastures for a considerable extent. Its principal mineral production is a blue slaty stone which is found upon the wolds, and makes excellent lime.

BINGHAM PARISH.

BINGHAM, the capital of the Deanery and Hundred to which it gives name, is pleasantly situated on the Nottingham and Grantham road, 10 miles E. by S. of the former, 11 miles S.W. of Newark, and 123 miles N.N.W. of London. Though once of considerable repute from its religious establishment and collegiate church, of a date nearly as old as the conquest, it is now merely a straggling and inconsiderable market town, having a branch from the Nottingham and Grantham *Canal*, and a few *stocking frames* and *bobbin-net machines* employed in the Nottingham trade, and also a *printing press* manufactory belonging to Mr. Stafford. Its market place is large and open, but is disgraced by some mean looking shops, which are seldom occupied, but it has in the centre a very convenient butter cross. The MARKET, which is only of trifling importance, is held on Thursday; but the FAIRS for cattle, horses, and swine, held on February 10th and 11th, Whit-Thursday, and November 8th and 9th, are tolerably well supplied. *Hirings for servants* are held on Candlemas Thursday, and on the last Thursday in October, and the *feast* is at the November fair. The parish contains 370 houses, 1738 inhabitants, and about 3,000 acres of rich red loamy land, mostly belonging to the Earl of Chesterfield, who is lord of the *manor*, which was enclosed upwards of 150 years ago. After the conquest it was of the fee of Roger de Busli, and had *soc* in *Newton*, which perhaps accounts for a small part of that township being considered as part of this parish. Since the Conqueror's time, Bingham has gone through a variety of possessors, and once belonged to a family of its own name. There are now no remains of its two *Chapels of St. James and St. Helen*, nor of its *Guild or College of St. Mary*, which Speed says, was valued at £40. The buildings and possessions of these monastic institutions were granted by Edward VI. and Queen Elizabeth to various persons.

The Parish Church, dedicated to All Saints, is a fine specimen of the ancient gothic; built in the form of a cross, with a handsome tower and spire, 40 yards in height, and containing a peal of six bells. A great part of the nave was rebuilt in 1584; the chancel, which is spacious and handsomely ceiled, was repaired and beautified in 1773, and the whole has just undergone a complete reparation at the cost of £150. Several of the windows are highly ornamented with stained glass, representing Moses and Aaron, Faith and Hope, and the armorial bearings of two Bishops; and also of the Earl of Chesterfield, who is patron of the rectory, which is valued in the King's books at £44. 7s. 11d., but is now the richest benefice in the county, being worth about £1,100 per annum. The Rev. Robert Lowe, M.A. is the incumbent, and has a handsome Rectory-house with extensive gardens, and about 39 acres of glebe. The Wesleyan and the Primitive Methodists have each a chapel in the town. Petty Sessions are held here every alternate Thursday. In 1784 and 1785, several plays were performed here by amateurs, for the purpose of raising a fund for a School. They produced a profit of £80, to which Messrs. George Baxter and John Foster added £70, and the whole (£150,) was laid out in a share of the Grantham Canal, now worth about £10 a-year, which is paid to the master of the school in Church-street. A few years ago, the Earl of Chesterfield gave nearly one acre of land in the southern suburb of the town called Longacre, for the erection and endowment of a Day and Sunday School, which has been built by subscription.

Charities.—Chapel Close was purchased with £28 poor's money in 1693, and now lets for £8 per annum, which is distributed at Christmas. In 1721, Thomas and Ann Tealby left £110, with which Lowmoore Closes, in Carcolston, were purchased, and now let for £15 a year, half of which is given to the poor, and the rest to the schoolmaster for teaching ten free-scholars. Part of the £10 left by Dr. Burnsell and Thomas Porter, was expended in purchasing the land on which the Workhouse was built in 1769. In 1764 and 1779, George and Elizabeth Bradshaw each left a £50 share in the Bingham Turnpike. These shares now produce upwards of £5. 10s. yearly, which is distributed amongst the poor of the parish.

Events.—The oldest register in Bingham church is dated 1598. The plague raged here in 1646, and many of its victims were buried in a large yard near the west end of the town, where human bones have been frequently found. In 1768, a stone coffin containing the bones of a mother and child, with several trinkets, was found in Chapel-close. In 1710, the town was set on fire in three different places, but it was providentially extinguished before much damage was done. The

2 x 2

incendiary was *Thomas Patefield*, surgeon, who had for some time laboured under a slight mental derangement, and was, after being tried at Nottingham, directed by the judge to be confined during the rest of his life, at Bingham, where a strong building of two rooms was erected for him in the middle of the Market-place, in which he lived nearly 30 years. On September 21st, 1775, the church spire and clock were greatly injured by lightning. The sacrament linen, and the gold lace of the pulpit cloth and cushion, were stolen December 1st, 1776. The *Post-Office* was established in 1790.

Mr. *Robert White*, a celebrated astronomer, who was many years a compiler of almanacks for the Stationers' Company, was a native of Bingham, where he kept a school, and died in 1773, aged 80. He was author of the " *Celestial Atlas*, or *new Ephemeris*," which is still published annually under the name of " *White's Ephemeris*." He was born of humble parents, but being a cripple, he was indulged with a liberal education. After his death, he was ably succeeded both in his school and as a compiler of almanacks, by his pupil, the late Mr. *Stafford*, who died in 1783. Another worthy of this town was *Thomas Grove*, a poor lad, who ran away from his apprenticeship and entered as a private in the Marines, in which he rose to the rank of Colonel, and died in 1790, after 75 years service.

The POST-OFFICE is at Mr. John Strong's, in Church-street. The mail gig passes through the town, to Nottingham at 12 noon, and to Newark at half-past six in the morning.

Baxter Geo. gardener Long acre
Brown John, tinner, &c. Mkp
Brown Wm. butter factor, Fair close
Buck John, gent. Union street
Buxton Mrs. Mary, Market place
Dean. Edward. governor of the workhouse
Denman. Hy. gamekeeper, Chancel row
Essex Thos.. hawker, Union st
Fisher Joseph. Union street
Gelsthorpe John, horse breaker, Needham street
Gilman Thomas, collector
Goodacre Mrs. Sarah, Union st
Grant Mrs. Eliz. Market place
Harrison George and John, hair cutters, market place
Hart John, saddler, Long acre
Heathcote Mr. Ed. Long acre
Hill Rd. hawker, Chancel row
Horsepool Mrs. Long acre
Huckerby Mr. Wm. Market pl

Huckerby William, jun. auctioneer Market place
Jackson Joseph, nail maker and ironmonger, Market place
Lowe Rev. Robert, M.A. rector
Moffatt Wm. tea dealer, Long acre
Oliver Joseph Dodsley, tanner and spirit merchant, Long acre
Parr Richard and Samuel, gardeners, Newgate street
Richards Samuel, hawker, Chancel row
Spoug Thomas, herbalist, &c. Chancel row
Stafford John, gent. East street
Stafford John, jun. improved Stanhope printing press manufacturer, East street
Swanwick Saml. gardener, Long acre
Talbot Fras. veterinary surgeon
White Samuel, chief constable for Bingham S. D. Fisher lane

Wilson Robert, corn miller, Fair close
Widnall W. gardener, Long acre
Wolstenholm Adam, excise officer, Church street
Wood Mr. Thomas, Market pl
Wright Thos. gardener, Fisher ln

Academies.

Hewitt Richard, Long acre
Strong Jane, Church street
Strong John, Church street

Attorney.

Tallents William Edward, (and magitrates clerk)

Bakers and Flour Dealers.

Brice Robert (and confectioner) Newgate street
Challands Charles, Market place
Hemstock Wm. & Son, Church street
Pilgrim Samuel, Union street
Walker Thomas, Church street

Blacksmiths.

Brown Thomas, Long acre
Skellington Richard, Long acre
Stubbs John, Long acre
Widnall Joseph, Long acre

Bobbin Net Makers.

Beckett John, Fisher lane
Clifton and Esdaile, Market pl
Hitchcock William, Cherry st
Hollingworth Thos. Long acre
Oliver Jph. Dodsley, Long acre
Rushton John, Needham street
Wright John, jun. Union street

Boot and Shoe Makers.

Dring Wm. Fisher lane
Newton Isaac, (and leather cutter,) Market place
Slack James, Market place
Ward Robert, Church street

Bricklayers.

Doncaster John, Union street
Doncaster Jph. Union street
Doncaster Rd. Long acre
Stokes Wm. Long acre
Wilson John, Fisher lane

Butchers.

Crook John, Market place
Gilman Wm. Long acre
Horsepool Jas. Church st
Horsepool John, Market pl
Tomkinson Wm. Market st

Coal Dealers.

Beet John, Fair close
Roadley Jph. Newgate st
Wright Thos. Fisher lane

China, Glass, &c. Dealers.

Brown John, Market place
Brown Rd. Market place

Coopers.

Bellamy Thos. Newgate st
Skinner Geo. jun. Long acre

Corn Millers.

Hemstock Wm. & Son, Church street
Walker Thomas, Church st

Druggists.

Buck Edw. Bowker, Market pl
Jones John, (& hatter) Mkp-

Farmers.

Atkin John, Long acre
Barratt John, Market pl
Beet Thos. Newgate st
Bingham Geo. Long acre
Brewster Rt. Holmes
Chettle Wm. Long acre
Chettle Wm. jun. Long acre
Dikes Jane, Long acre
Felton Wm. Long acre
Fisher Thos. Long acre
Foster Saml. Long acre
Gamble Wm. Market place
Goodwin Geo. South road
Greenwood John, Church st
Harris Rt. Brocco
Harrison Geo. South road
Hart Thos. Long acre
Horsepool John, Long acre
Horsepool Stephen, Long acre
Horsepool Stpn. jun. Long acre
Hutchinson Wm. Starn hill
Lee Thos. Newgate street
Pacey Wm. Market place
Roadley Thos. Newgate st
Scott Arthur, Long acre
Skinner Geo. Long acre
Wheatley Wm. East street
White Rt. Long acre
Wickham Ann, Newgate st
Wickham Jph. East st
Wright Wm. East street

Grocers & Tea Dealers.

Baxter Geo. Church street
Doncaster Eliz. (& ironmonger) Market place

Hardstaff Jas. (chandler & iron-monger) Market place
Oliver John, Market place
Ratley Thos. Union st
Skinner Geo. (& draper) Long acre
White Chas. (& tobacconist) Long acre

Inns and Taverns.
Blue Bell, Hy. Crooke, Mkp
Chesterfield's Arms, Wm. Pilgrim, Church st
King's Arms, Wm. Whitworth, Market place
Marquis of Granby, John Tinkler, Long acre
Wheat Sheaf, John Coulishaw, Long acre

Beer Houses.
John Geeson, Long acre
Wm. Horsepool, Market pl
William IV. Jonth. Crook, Long acre
Stingo Tap, John Innocent, Long acre
Windmill, Rt. Wilson, Fair close

Joiners.
*Thus * are also Cabinet Makers.*
*Clifton Thos. Market place
Spencer Wm. & John, Banks
*Stone Rd. Banks
*Whitworth Geo. Market pl
*Widdowson Thos. Church st
Wright John, Union st
Wright Thos. Church st

Linen and Woollen Drapers.
Baxter Geo. (and stamp dis.) Church street
Berry Geo. (woollen) Needham street
Parley Eliz. Church street

Maltsters.
Pilgrim John. Newgate st
Walker Wm. (& hop, seed, & spirit dealer) Market place

Milliners & Dressmakers.
Crook Jane, Needham street
Graves Eliz. Newgate st
Parr Alice, (straw hat) Newgate street
Stubbs Eliz. Needham st

Painters.
Pilgrim Rd. Chancel row

Wood John, (& paper hanger) Market place
Plumbers and Glaziers.
Nowell Wm. Long acre
Strong Wm. Market place
Welch & Bass, Long acre
Shopkeepers.
Padgett Benj. (& pig jobber) Mkp
Palmer Benj. Long acre
Richmond John, Chancel row
Scott Wm. Market street
Smith Rd. Long acre
Wright John, Union street
Surgeons.
Lee Henry, Market place
Rose Jas. Newgate street
Smith Wm. Holroyd, Church st
Tomlinson Panks Wigginton, Union street
Tailors.
Dickman Rt. Union st
Hallam Thos. Needham st
Harvey Jas. Market place
Mann James, Needham st
Richmond John, Chancel row
Richmond Thos. Needham st
Watch and Clock Makers.
Brown Saml. Market st
Esdaile Andw. Market place
Wheelwrights.
Nowell Adam, Banks
Wilson Saml. Langar ln
Wilson Thos. & Wm. Langar ln

COACHES.
To Nottingham at half past 6, & at 7 evening. To Lincoln, at 7, and to Stamford at ½ past 7, morning.

CARRIERS.
To Boston, W. & J. Pettifor, from the Marquis of Granby, Long acre, every Tues. & Sat.
To Newark, John Jackson, from Long acre, every Wednesday, at 5 morning.
To Nottingham, Jph. Jones, from Market place; and John Sills & Rt. Green, from Long acre, every Wed. & Sat. at 5 mg.

BRIDGEFORD (EAST) PARISH.

EAST BRIDGEFORD, or *Bridgeford-on-the-Hill*, is a large and well built village on the summit of a lofty precipitous bank that rises on the south side of the Trent, opposite Gunthorpe Ferry, 10 miles E. by N. of Nottingham, and 3 miles N. by W. of Bingham. The parish contains 938 inhabitants and upwards of 1800 acres of loamy land, which was enclosed in 1798, when 276 acres (now called New Bridgeford) were allotted in lieu of the rectorial tithes. Magdalen College Oxford, belongs to the greater part of the parish. The remainder is the property of Philip Palmer, Esq., and several smaller freeholders, and he and the College have the manorial rights. After the Conquest, the manor was given to Roger de Busli, who gave the tithes of the Hall in *Brugeford* to the priory of Blyth. The manor was successively held by the Carpenters, Bisets, Caltofts, Brabazons, Basingburns, Deyncourts, and Botelars, the latter of whom, in the 8th of Edward Fourth, gave their moiety to William, Bishop of Winchester, who bestowed it on Magdalen College, which he had founded at Oxford. The other moiety afterwards passed from Lord Sheffield to the Hackers, Chaworths, Scroopes, &c. &c. In the parish is found both opaque and transparent *Gypsum*, the latter of which is very beautiful, and during the last seven years has been in great demand amongst the lapidaries of Derby and other places, who turn it into beads and various other ornaments, in which it looks as brilliant and as richly variegated as the Derbyshire spar. There are in the village several neat *mansions*, occupied by Philip Palmer, Esq., Peter Brooke, Esq., the Rev. Thomas Beaumont, and the Rev. R. William Hutchins, M.A., the latter of whom now enjoys the *rectory*, which is valued in the King's books at £19. 8s. 6½d., and is in the alternate patronage of Magdalen College, and John Musters, Esq.

The *Church*, dedicated to St. Mary, is an ancient fabric, and has evidently been much larger than at present. It has much armorial glass of the former lords of the manor, but most of its monuments have been detroyed or defaced, and some of them turned out "into the churchyard to perish through the attacks of the weather." Three mutilated effigies of knights in armour, one of them a crusader, were lying under the eaves of the church roof in Thoresby's time! The church has a square tower and six bells. The *Methodists* have a small chapel in the village, where there are several *Sick Clubs*, and an annual *feast* is held on the last Sunday in June.

CHARITIES.—£290, Three per Cent. Consols were purchased in 1792, with several benefactions left by the Revs. H. Smith, C. Overend, and P. Priaux, John Wilson, Sarah Kirk, and two unknown donors. The yearly dividends. £8. 14s. are given to the poor in February. In 1827, Thomas Holland left £40, for which Mr. John Wilkinson pays £2 yearly to be distributed in bread. In 1828, the Rev. Peter Broughton, who was rector of this parish 44 years, left £50 to the poor. The *National Schools*, where 100 boys and 63 girls are educated by subscription, were built on the glebe land in 1829, at the cost of £300, towards which the present rector, Magdalen College, and the National Society, gave liberally, and the rest was raised by small contributions.

In modern history, Bridgeford is remarkable as being the birth-place of " the regicidal parliamentarian, *Colonel Hacker*, who attended the unfortunate King Charles to his last scene, for which he afterwards suffered as a traitor, and his estates were confiscated; yet his two brothers were active partizans in the royal cause, in which one of them was slain."— But it is in ancient history that this place stands most conspicuous, for Stukely says, it lies within a mile of the ROMAN STATION *Ad pontem*, and adds that there was here in Roman times, a bridge across the Trent, with "great buildings, cellars, and a quay for vessels to unload at." Near the place called *Old-wark Spring*, he found "the Roman foundations of walls, and floors of houses, composed of stones set edgeways into clay, and liquid mortar run upon them." Upon an eminence of the road beyond Bingham lane, he also found a *tumulus*, commanding " a fine prospect of Belvoir," &c. Horseley differs from Stukely, and considers *Old-wark*, near Bridgeford, to be the *Margidunum* of the sixth Iter of Antoninus. The great *Fosse-way* (See p. 18,) passes within a mile west of the village, through which an upper Fosse-way proceeds from the ferry to East Stoke.

Ashwell John, gent.
Ayland Mrs. Elizabeth
Beaumont Rev. Thos. Bridgeford hill
Bonser Wm. tailor and draper
Brooke Peter, Esq. Old Hall
Brown Thos. shoemaker
Challand Jehu, plumber & glazier
Chapman Saml. blacksmith
Clarke Geo. bricklayer
Clough Edw. bdg. & day school
Crofts Thos. bobbin net maker
Freeman Thos. joiner
Gilbert John, bricklayer
Gill Wm. shopkeeper
Green Rd. boat owner
Green Miss ——
Green Wm. baker & shopr.
Hall S. brickmaker, Trent side
Henson John, butcher

Herod Saml. brickmaker and gypsum dealer
Heathcote Rev. Ralph
Hill Benj, baker and shopr
Hole Saml. & Co. maltsters, Trent bank
Holgate Geo. National schoolmr
Huskinson Geo. shoemaker
Huskinson Wm. parish clerk
Huskinson Wm. wheelwright
Huskinson Wm. boat owner
Hutchins Rev. Rd. Wm. M. A. rector
Jalland Sabina and Eliza, victrs. Six Bells
Lockwood Wm. sen. gent.
Mason Edmund, butcher
Mason Geo. tailor
Mason John, shoemaker
Mason Mary, vict. Rein Deer

Millington John, tailor, draper, and shopkeeper
Millington Jonas, joiner
Millington Mw. maltster, coal mert. and wharfinger
Millington Saml. joiner
Newbound Chas. shoemaker
Newton Thos. blacksmith
Palmer Philip, Esq. Bridgeford hill
Parnham Wm. shoemaker
Randall Wm. vict. joiner, & gypsum dlr. Royal Oak
Richardson Rd. blacksmith
Reddish Paul, corn miller
Stokes Hy. corn miller, rope mkr. flax dresser, & shopr
Taylor Jas. bobbin net maker & vict. New Inn
Taylor John, bobbin net maker
Upton Eliz. National school
Upton John, tailor
Walker Mr. Benj.

Walker Hy. blacksmith
Wright Bently Wm. surgeon

FARMERS.

Blagg John
Bradley John
Bradley John
Challand John
Challand Jph
Challand Thos
Eateh Fras
Foster Thos
Freear Fras
Freear John
Green Rd
Huskinson Frs

Huskinson John
Huskinson Thos
Huskinson Wm
Levers John
Levers Mary
Lockwood W. jn.
Speick Courtney
Taylor Wm
Taylor Wm
Towe John
Whitaker Wm
Wilkinson John

The Hope coach to Nottingham, ev. mg. (Sunday excepted) at ½ past 9, and to Newark, at ¼ past 5 evg.
CARRIERS to Nottingham. Wm. Upton, Wed. & Sat. and John Brown, Sat. at 5 mg.

BROUGHTON-SULNEY PARISH.

BROUGHTON-SULNEY, or OVER BROUGHTON, 12 miles S.S.E. of Nottingham, is a pleasant village seated upon a declivity on the Melton Mowbray road, near the Leicestershire border, and at the foot of the Nottinghamshire Wolds, where the Roman *Fosse-way* enters this county.—(See p. 18.) The parish which was enclosed about 70 years ago, contains 57 house, 344 inhabitants, and about 2000 acres of good clay land, of which the lord of the manor, Thomas Hall, Esq. is the principal owner, but part of it belongs to and is occupied by several small freeholders. At the enlosure, 280 acres were allotted to the rector in lieu of tithes. The manor was anciently called *Brockton-Sulney*, from its Norman owners, the family of *de Suleni*, from whom it passed to the Cresseys and the Cliftons. It is sometimes called *Over-Broughton*, to distinguish it from *Nether* Broughton, in Leicestershire. The *Church* has a nave, side aisles, and a low tower with three bells. The rectory, valued in the King's books at £11. 9s. 4½d., is in the patronage of Sir Joseph Radcliffe, of Campsall, in Yorkshire. The Rev. Joseph Burrell is the incumbent, and the Rev. John Wilson the curate. The *General Baptists* have had a chapel in the village since 1795. The parish *feast* is on the second Sunday after Old Michaelmas Day. At the west end of the village stands an ancient *Cross*, and near the rectory-house is "*Woundheal Spring*," so called from its supposed medicinal virtues.

CHARITIES.—In 1727, Mr. Morris and Mrs. Bley left £15, for which 15s. is paid yearly out of a farm in the parish. The yearly sum of 17s. 8d. is paid by John Brett and John Cross, as the interest of £17. 13s. 4d. left by an unknown donor. The *Poor's Close* is let for 8 guineas per annum, out of which 6s. each is paid to the parishes of Ab-Kettleby and Hobb, and the residue is distributed with the above-named charities at Christmas, in coal, amongst the poor of Broughton-Sulney.

Barnett Edw. bobbin net maker
Brett Rt. Wheat Sheaf, beer hs
Brett Mr. Thos
Brown Luke, gent.
Brown Wm. joiner
Clark John, shoemaker
Grice Mr. John, jun.
Grice John, wheelwright
Grice Rd. shoemaker
Harding Jph. grocer
Hemsley John, vict. and carrier, Golden Fleece
Holmes John, parish clerk
Hopkins Fras. brick maker
Julian Edw. tailor
Scott Wm. butcher
Sheffield David, shopkeeper
Skerrit John, castrator
Turner Wm. Greyhound, beer hs
Walker Wm. tailor
Wartnaby Mr. Edward
Wartnaby Edw. baker
Wartnaby Jph. corn miller
White Wm. blacksmith
Wild Jph. butcher, Fox & Hounds, beer house

Wilson Rev. John, curate and bdg. academy, Rectory hs
Wright Col. Saml. Broughton cottage

FARMERS.

Brett John	Cross Thos
Brett Wm	Daykin John
Brett Wm	Daykin John
Brown Wm	Daykin Wm
Clark Wm	Grice Wm
Lodge	Mills Wm
Crafts Wm	Nichols Peter
Lodge	Lodge
Cross John	Stephenson Saml
Cross Thos	

The Mail every morning to London, at ½ past 7, and to Leeds at 9.

CARRIERS.—Jno. Helmsley, Jno. Holmes, and Jph. Brown, to Nottingham, on Wed. & Sat. at 7 mg.; and to Melton Mowbray on Tues. at 7 mg.

CAR-COLSTON PARISH.

CAR-COLSTON is but a small village and parish, situated 2¼ miles N.N.W. of Bingham, and containing 249 inhabitants, and 1500 acres of strong clay land, of which the Rev. Robt. Lowe is principal owner, lord of the manor, and impropriator. At the Conquest, *Coleston* was partly ancient demesne, and partly of the fee of Roger de Busli, and passed successively to the Cheyneys, Lovetots, Vauxes, Colstons, Thorotons, Arnalls, Willoughbys, &c. This village was the residence of *Robert Thoroton*, M.D., the celebrated author of the History and Antiquities of Nottinghamshire, published in 1677, in which he informs us that he had an estate here on which he built a house for himself. The *Church*, dedicated to St. Mary, has a handsome tower and four bells, and was appropriated to

Worksop priory in 1349. In Thoroton's time, the tithes belonged to the Duke of Newcastle, but being charged with £20 yearly to the King, and £4 to the church of Lincoln, they were not then of much value to his Grace. The *vicarage* is valued in the King's books at £6. 1s. 10½d., and the Rev. Robert Ffarmerie is both patron and incumbent. The parish *feast* is on the Sunday after June 15th. In 1616, Gregory Henson bequeathed *Sharpe close*, (let for £2. 10s.) for the reparation of the church, and *Brusmore close*, (let for £14,) for the use of the poor, who have also *Alvey close*, (let for £2,) purchased with the legacy of John Whalley, in 1735, and £10 in the Newark savings' bank, left in 1737, by Margaret Sherrard.

Baker John, shopkeeper & beer-
  house
Clarke John, blacksmith
Clarke Thomas, parish clerk
Cragg Rd. joiner & beerhouse
Cragg Rt. shoemaker
Ffarmerie Rev. Robert, vicar
Goulson Mrs. Grace
Hill Wm. gentleman
Huthwaite Wm. gentleman
Marriott John, bricklayer
Marshall John, shoemaker
Palmer John, Shopkeeper

Sampey Mrs. Mary
Sampey Mrs. Susanna
Simpson Eliz. butcher
    FARMERS.
Barker Richd. Hall Matthew
Blagg Thomas Matthews Thos.
Chittle Ann Wilkinson John
Forrest Thos.

CARRIER TO NOTTINGHAM.—
John Baker, Saturday, and to
Newark, Wednesday, 5 morning.

CLIPSTONE TOWNSHIP

Is in the parish of Plumptre, the rest of which is in the hundred of Rushcliff. It comprises 800 acres of fine clay land, 82 inhabitants, and 14 houses, forming a small village, seated on a declivity of the Wolds, six miles S. E. of Nottingham. Earl Manvers is owner and lord of the manor, and the following are his tenants, viz. Allcock John, Geo. sen. and Geo. jun. *farmers ;* and Burgess John, *gent.*—*See Plumptre Par.*

COLSTON-BASSET PARISH.

This village and parish lies on the river Smite, bordering upon Leicestershire, 5 miles S. of Bingham, and contains 387 inhabitants, and about 2500 acres of land, of which 1800 acres belong to the lord of the manor and impropriator, Henry Martin, Esq. Master in Chancery, who purchased it some years ago of Viscount Wentworth, whose ancestors bought it in 1714, of Sir Edward Godling. The other part belongs to Robert Pigou, Esq. of London, and several smaller freeholders. The manor anciently belonged to the family of Basset, and from them passed to the Staffords, Dukes of Buckingham, from whom it descended

2 U

to various families. The *church* stands half a mile from the village, and is dedicated to St. Mary. It is a vicarage, valued in the King's books at £8. 7s. 6d., but it has now 19A. 32P. of glebe, and its tithes yield about £114 per annum. The King is the patron, and the Rev. Joshua Brooke, of Gamston, is the incumbent. The ancient *cross* in the village was rebuilt in 1831, in commemoration of the coronation of William IV.— The villagers have a tradition, that when the plague raged here in 1604, the inhabitants of Nottingham and Bingham not only refused to permit any articles to be brought from hence to their markets, but "cut off all communication with them whatever." From July to September, the pestilence swept away 83 of the parishioners. The *feast* is on Whit-Sunday. The *hall* is a handsome mansion, seated on a gentle eminence near the church, on the north side of the Smite rivulet, and is the seat of Mr. Martin, who pays for the education of 18 free scholars, and supports a Sunday-school.

Allison Wm. schoolmaster
Bonser John, baker & parish clerk
Boyce John, shoemaker
Buxton Rt. vict. & blacksmith
Collett Wm. butcher & beerhouse
Faulks John, joiner
Herrick Wm. shopkeeper
Levett Joseph, tailor
Marriott George, shoe maker
Marriott John, surgeon
Marriott Mr. Wm.

Martin Henry, Esq. Master in Chancery, Colston Hall, and London
Newton Thos. shopkeeper
Richards John, tailor

FARMERS.
Brown Thos.   Giles Thos.
Buxton Wm.   Hallam Geo.
Crabtree Wm.   Innocent Geo.
  & Thomas   Thompson Jph.
Crabtree W. jun. Thompson John
Franks Thos.

COTGRAVE PARISH.

COTGRAVE, or as it was anciently called, *Godegrave*, is a large pleasant village and parish, under the north side of the Wolds, 6 miles S.E. of Nottingham. It contains 140 houses, 842 inhabitants, and about 4000 acres of land, of which Earl Manvers is sole proprietor and lord of the manor, except 555 acres, which were allotted to the rector in lieu of tithes, at the enclosure about 40 years ago. The high grounds on each side of the village contain an abundance of blue marl, intermixed with layers of red clay. After the Conquest, this manor was given in fee to Roger Pictavensis and Rad. de Burun, whose descendants gave it to the priories at Lenton and Swineshead, with which it remained till Henry VIII. granted it to Harold Rosel and Geo. Pierrepont, Esqs.; to the latter of whom he also gave the advowson of the *rectory*, which was then in two moieties, valued in the King's books at £10. 7s. 3¼d. and £9. 14s. 9½d., but it is now consolidated in the patronage of Earl Manvers, and incumbency of the Rev. John Henry Browne.—

The CHURCH, dedicated to All Saints, has a nave, chancel, side aisles, and a tower containing five bells, and crowned by a handsome octagonal spire. *Agnes Cross*, in 1722, left 50s. yearly to the poor of this parish, out of Brackenhurst farm, near Southwell. The parish *school* and master's house were built in 1752, by subscription, except £60, which was part of a legacy of £120 left by a benevolent lady, and of which £60 still remains as the school fund. The annual *feast* is ruled by All Saints' Day, being held on that day if it falls on a Sunday, but if it falls on a Monday, the feast is kept on the preceding day; and if on any other day, the Sunday following is the festival.

STRAGGLETHORP is a hamlet of four farms, near the Grantham canal, at the east end of the parish, 1¼ mile E. of the village.—COTGRAVE PLACE, 1 mile N. of the village, is the handsome mansion of Robert Burgess, Esq.

Archer Edw. baker & flour dlr.
Archer John, vict. Black Lion
Baguley John, butcher
Baguley Saml. vict. Five Bells
Barlow Rt. veterinary surgeon
Browne Rev. John Henry, rector
Brown Thos. schoolmaster
Burgess Rt. Esq. agent to Earl Manvers, Cotgrave Place
Cooper John, shopkeeper
Cowlishaw John, blacksmith
Davenport John, gardener
Disney John, shopkeeper
Dixon John, butcher
Dixon Mrs. Mary
Hickling Geo. corn miller
Hill Wm. brickmaker
Lewin Wm. joiner
Marriott George, gentleman
Mensing Wm. tailor
Morley John, blacksmith
Ogle Thomas, bricklayer
Parker Wm. bricklayer

Parr George, gamekeeper
Peet Thomas, shoemaker
Richards Samuel, coal merchant, (and Nottingham)
Scottorn Wm. saddler & tawer
Simpson Samuel, tailor
Stafford Joseph, shoemaker
Timm Samuel, wheelwright
Timm Wm. shoemaker
Upton Wm. butcher

FARMERS.

Baguley Chas.
Barlow Robert
Clater Henry
Hoe Thomas
Holmes Wm.
Lewin John
Mann Joshua
Morley John

Morris Cath.
Morris Samuel
Morris Wm.
Parr Jonathan
Rayner Richard
Smith Thomas
Thornton Jane

CARRIER TO NOTTINGHAM.—
Upton Samuel, Sat. dep. 7 mg.

CROPWELL-BISHOP PARISH.

CROPWELL-BISHOP is an indifferently built village, upon a gentle declivity on the east side of the Grantham canal, 1 mile S. of Cropwell Butler, and 4 miles S. E. of Bingham. Its parish contains 473 inhabitants, and about 1500 acres of strong clay land, nearly all of which belongs to the two prebendaries of Oxton, in Southwell collegiate church, who let it on renewable leases for the term of three lives, but the Duke of Newcastle is lord of the manor, though he does not own an inch of the soil. Sir Robert Clifton, John Hamer, Esq., Wm. Marshall, and John Smith, are the principal lessees. It was anciently called *Crophill-Bishop*, from the round hill on the north side of the village, and from its being included in Domesday Book amongst the manors of the Archbishop of York, though it was afterwards given to Southwell church and Lenton priory. Part of the wastes were enclosed in 1788, together with Cropwell-Butler, (each having a right in the *Fern field*,) and the rest in 1803, when allotments were awarded in lieu of all the tithes. The *church* is dedicated to St. Giles, and has a tower with four bells. The living is a vicarage, valued in the King's books at £5. 3s. 4d., but it has now about 80 acres of glebe. The Rev. Robert Wood, D. D. of Nottingham, is the incumbent, and the two prebendaries of Oxton are the patrons and appropriators. A small *Methodist chapel* was built here in 1824. The parish *feast* is on the first Sunday in old September. Gypsum is found on the south side of the parish. The only charity here is £50, left in 1779, by Wm. Fillingham, for the interest to be distributed in bread on New Year's day.

Allcock Mrs. Sarah
Brewin Lank, corn miller
Brown John, wheelwright
Clarke Wm. shopkeeper
Cooper Mary, shopkeeper
Hopewell George, blacksmith
Hopewell Robt. maltster
Leavis John, bricklayer
Mackley Richard, shoemaker
Marshall James, shoemaker
Newton John, butcher
Pilkington Mrs. Mary
Richards Jas. wharfinger & vict
Riddle Gervas, boat owner
Rose Amos, vict. Chequers
Simons Thos. shoemaker
Simpson John, vict. Wheat Sheaf
Smith John, corn miller

Smith Richard, lime burner
Starbuck Wm. boat owner
Thraves Wm. shopkeeper
Wheat Wm. vict. and joiner
White Edw. plumber & glazier
Widdowson John, shoemaker
Wilson James, boat owner
Wilson Wm. boat owner
Woodward Benj. parish clerk
Wragsdale Wm. tailor
Wright Henry, joiner

FARMERS.
Brownhill Geo.   Slater John
Howard Thos.   Smith John
Shelton Wm.   Smith George

CARRIER to Nottingham, Wm. Clark, Saturday 5 morning.

ELTON PARISH

Is but of small extent, consisting only of about 1000 acres, and a small village with 91 inhabitants, on the Grantham road, near the verge of the county, 4 miles E. by S. of Bingham. In Saxon times it was called *Ayleton*, and was afterwards of the fee of Roger de Busli, who gave it to the priory at Blyth, but at the dissolution it was granted to the family of York, from whom it passed to the Lions, Mores, Collins, and Launders, and is now possessed solely by Wm. Fletcher Norton Norton,

Esq., who resides in the MANOR-HOUSE, (a large and handsome mansion,) and is patron of the *rectory*, which is valued in the King's books at £8. 0s. 5d. and is now enjoyed by the Rev. J. Staunton, LL.B. The *church*, dedicated to St. Michael, is a small humble edifice, which Thoresby describes as being " dove-house topped." The parish was enclosed in 1808, when land was allotted in lieu of all the tithes. In 1780, the parish clerk found, whilst digging a grave in the church-yard, upwards of 200 *silver pennies*, of the reign of Henry II., and on taking them to Mrs. Collin, then lady of the manor, his honesty was rewarded with a present of £10. In 1784, a blacksmith in Elton purchased a piece of rusty iron, about 2 feet long and 1½ inches in diameter, apparently solid, and which had beed used as a pestle upwards of 60 years. Having some doubts about its solidity he put it into his fire, when it exploded with great force, and a musket ball from within it grazed his side, and lodged in some coals behind him. This surprising accident led to further examination and enquiry, when it was discovered to have been a *gun barrel*, dug up in the year 1723, but so completely filled with earth and rust, that no cavity had ever, till then, been noticed. The *feast* is on the Sunday after Old Michaelmas day.

	FARMERS.	
Norton W. F. N., Esq. Manor hs		
Branston Rd. vict. Norton's Arms	Burrows John	Marshall Thos.
Clay Rt. parish clerk	Gilding Thos.	Ridge David
Greatrix Abm. brickmaker	Hawkin Jtn.	Watts John

FLINTHAM PARISH.

FLINTHAM is a pleasant and well-built village, 6½ miles S.W. by S. of Newark, including within its parish 545 inhabitants, and 2101 acres of rich loamy land, which was enclosed about the year 1780, when 172 acres were allotted to the vicar, and about 300 acres to Trinity College, in lieu of the tithes, exclusive of 165 acres which had previously belonged to the said College. The rest of the parish belongs mostly to Mrs. Hildyard, whose son and heir, Thomas Hildyard, Esq., is a minor; but the Duke of Newcastle is lord of the manor, which he holds in fee of the King's Duchy of Lancaster, together with several others in this neighbourhood. His Grace has no land here except 6 acres allotted to him at the enclosure. FLINT-HAM HALL, which has been successively the seat of the Husseys, Hackers, Woodhouses, Disneys, Fytches, and Thorotons, is now the residence of Mrs. Hildyard, relict of the late Col. Thomas Blackburn Hildyard, and heiress of the late Colonel Thoroton, who was a descendant of Dr. Thoroton, the topographer. It is a handsome modern edifice, erected on the site of the ancient mansion. It owes many of its present beauties to the late Col. Hildyard, who rebuilt the whole of the *church* except the chancel, in 1827-8, at the cost of £1100, exclusive of the carriage of the materials, for which the farmers made no charge. The chancel would also have been re-edified, had not death put a period to the Colonel's pious intentions on the 30th of July, 1830. It has a tower and four bells, and is dedicated to St. Augustin. The patronage and appropriation belong to Trinity College, Cambridge. The *vicarage,* which is valued in the King's books at £6. 2s. 6d., has had several augmentations from Queen Anne's Bounty, and is now in the incumbency of the Rev. Charles John Myers, M.A. Laird says, (1811,) "A former incumbent of this parish was an odd character, and saved upwards of £1500 by a most beggarly and penurious mode of life; he has been known to serve the thatchers to get a penny, and once went to Newark with a letter for the sum of twopence!" The *Methodist chapel* was built about 30 years ago, and the parish *school* in 1779. The latter is endowed with 12 acres of land at Caythorpe, let for £20 per annum, and left in 1727, by *Robert Hacker,* for the education of 14 free scholars. He also bequeathed 20 acres at Brandon, (let for £30) to the vicar and churchwardens, in trust, that they distribute the rents amongst the poor of the parish at Whitsuntide and Christmas. The poor have also 20s. yearly, left by *John Smith,* out of two house in Stodman-street, Newark, belonging to the Duke of Newcastle. The *feast* is on Whit-Sunday.

Hildyard Mrs. Ann Cath. Flintham Hall
Bettison Mrs. Ann
Bettison Jph. miller & baker
Boyle Richard, wood valuer
Cliffe Thos. miller and flour dlr
Cliffe Thos. & Wm. maltsters
Cuckson Jph. tailor & draper
Cutton Geo. vict. Black Horse
Fletcher Wm. tailor
Fryer Samuel, butcher
Gardiner Edw. shopkeeper
Hand Thos. parish clerk
Harston Richard, gentleman
Harvey John, wheelwright
Jobson Henry, blacksmith
Myers Rev. Chas. John, M.A. vicar
Parnham John, joiner
Pikett John, bricklayer
Radford Wm. shoemaker
Ragsdale Thos. shopkeeper

Rayworth John, blacksmith
Richardson Samuel, joiner
Rimmington Richard, butcher
Smalley Peter, gamekeeper
Talbot Joseph, bricklayer
Waite James, schoolmaster
Webster John, baker & beerhouse
Whyman Richard, tanner
Wood Joseph, shoemaker
Wood Wm. vict. Boot and Shoe

FARMERS.

Cliffe Wm.
Curtis Fras. Cut-hill
Foster William,
Holme
Green John
Harston Thos.
Lings
Harston Wm.
Ragsdale Henry
Smith Thomas
Taylor Frans.

CARRIER, Thomas Cupit to Newark, Wed. 6 mg. and to Nottingham, Saturday 4 morning.

GRANBY PARISH.

GRANBY is a well-built village, overlooking the delightful vale of Belvoir, 4 miles S.E. of Bingham, and near the borders of Leicestershire; remarkable for giving the title of *Marquis* to the *Duke of Rutland*, whose ancestor, Sir John Manners, purchased the estate of Lord Viscount Savage, to whom it had been granted by Henry VII., after the attainder of Henry Lord Lovel, whose unhappy and mysterious fate will be noticed under the head of East Stoke. The parish includes the hamlet of *Sutton*, and contains 320 inhabitants, and 2100 acres of land, which has generally a fertile soil, and is noted for several excellent limestone quarries, and brick and tile yards. The commons were enclosed in 1794, when land was allotted as a commutation of all the tithes of the parish, most of which belongs to the Duke of Rutland, who is lord of the manor, impropriator, and patron of the *vicarage*, which is valued in the King's books at £6. 3s. 6d., and is now enjoyed by the Rev. John Hutton, A.B. The glebe consists of 75 acres. Messrs. Charles Blagden, Matthew Hall, and Thomas Keyworth, have also estates here, and there are in the parish, several small freeholders. The *church*, dedicated to All Saints, has a tower and five bells. In the village is a small *Methodist chapel*, and the parish *school*. The master teaches 24 free scholars for £27 a-year, of which £17. 5s. is given by the Duke of Rutland, and the remainder is raised by subscription. Mr. Matthew Hall pays 20s. yearly, as the interest of £25 left in 1816, 1821, and 1824, by Matthew, William, and Henry Hall, to the poor of Granby and Sutton; and those of the latter hamlet have 8s. yearly as the interest of £10 left in 1767, by William Newberry. In 1776, Thomas Harrison left £100 to the poor of Granby, but it was lost by the insolvency of his namesake. After the Conquest, *Graneby and Sudton* were of the fee of the *Lords D'Ayncourt*, and continued their principal seat till the reign of Henry VI., when their sole heiress married Lord Lovel.

SUTTON hamlet is 1 mile E. of Granby, and those marked * in the following Directory reside in it, and the rest at Granby. The three public-houses are under the New Beer Act.

*Arnold Mrs. Mary
Bateman William, tailor
Bates John, joiner
Bates Wm. butcher
Beeson Wm. tailor
*Burbage John, shopkeeper
Calverley Wm. shoemaker
Copley Thos. blacksmith
Doubleday Benjamin, shoemaker

Hanbery Mrs. Ann
Harby George, joiner
Hart Samuel, vict. Plough
Hickling Ann. vict. Boot & Shoe
Hourd Wm. miller and baker
Hoyter Mordecai, gamekeeper
Hutton Rev. John, A.B. vicar
Newbray Miss Mary
Pritchit Wm. joiner

Roe Wm. gentleman
Slater Wm. shoemaker
Smith Thomas, schoolmaster
*Wakerley John, lime burner, brick and tile maker, and preparer of plaster
Watson Jno. vict. Marq. of Granby
            FARMERS.
Bates Daniel   Bonser John

*Burrows John Keyworth Thos.
Doubleday Rd. *Levers William
Goodacre Wm.   Marriott John
Hall Matthew   Pepper James
*Hall Wm.   *Richards Anty.

CARRIER, William Pritchet, to Nottingham, Saturday, 5 morng.

HAWKSWORTH PARISH.

HAWKSWORTH, anciently called *Hochesword*, is a small village and parish 4 miles N.E. of Bingham, and 8 miles S.S.W. of Newark. It was of the *fee* of Walter D'Ayncourt, and partly *soc* to Aslacton. It now contains 212 inhabitants, and about 800 acres of land, most of which belongs to John Storrer, M.D., who is lord of the manor, and patron of the *rectory*, which is valued in the King's books at £8. 13s. 9d., and is now in the incumbency of the Rev. John Storrer. At the enclosure (in 1761,) 150 acres were allotted in lieu of tithes. The *church*, dedicated to St. Mary, is a small building with a brick tower. Thomas Hall, Esq., has 160 acres in the parish. Of the glebe 3A. 20P. are in Scarrington-lordship.

Askew Wm. tailor.
Brown Thos. gardener & seedsn.
Brown Thos. jun. gardener, &c.
Green John, shoemaker
Marshall Thos. joiner
Mather Thos. blacksmith
Storrer Rev. John, M.A. rector

Sumner Benj. tailor & shopkr
Wade Wm. gardener & par. clerk
            FARMERS.
Baxter Thos.   Marriott Fras.
Clark Edward   Oliver John
Green Eliz.   Walker Wm.

HICKLING PARISH.

HICKLING is a large village on the Grantham canal, at the foot of the Wolds, near the Leicestershire border and the Vale of Belvoir, 12 miles S.E. of Nottingham, and 8 miles S. by W. of Bingham. In 1771, a farmer, whilst ploughing near the village, found an *urn* containing about 200 Roman silver coins and medals, most of them "the age of Vespasian." This discovery seems to confirm the opinion of Camden, that there has been a *Roman station* here. The parish is called in Domesday Book, *Echeling* and *Hegeling*, and was partly *soc* to Cropwell and Granby. It contains 529 inhabitants, and about 3000 acres of strong clay land, which was enclosed in 1777, when 413A. 8P. were allotted in lieu of tithes, in addition to 55A. 12P. of ancient glebe. About one-fourth of the parish belongs to W. F. Norton Norton, Esq., and one-sixteenth to the two pre-

bendaries of Oxton, in Southwell Collegiate Church; the rest
is the property of Messrs. Paul and Robt. Hardy, and other freeholders, but Earl Manvers is the lord paramount. The parish
church is dedicated to St. Luke, and has a fine lofty tower with
four bells: A stone coffin bearing a Runic inscription, was
found some years ago under the chancel. The living is a rectory
valued in the King's books at £18. 8s. 4d., and is in the patronage
of Queen's College, Cambridge, to which it was given in 1676,
by the widow of Dr. Bardsey. The Rev. Edward Anderson,
B.A., is the incumbent. The *Methodists* have a small chapel
here. The *school* has an endowment of 15s. yearly, left by J.
Westby and Robert Mann, to which the parishioners subscribe
for the education of 15 poor children. Five small benefactions
producing 25s. yearly, have been left to the poor of this parish
by Robert and William Mann, Richard Smith, William Marriott, and John Faulkes. The *River Smite* rises on the lofty
hills at the west end of the parish, and flows in a north-
easterly direction through a rich and winding vale to the river
Dean, near Shelton, and is joined here by a smaller stream,
called the Dalby. *Fossils*, chiefly shell fish, are often found here
in the limestone. At the rectory-house is a spring of MINERAL
WATER, each gallon of which contains as follow, viz. Insoluble
matter, 0. 30; Vegetable, 0. 25; Common Salt, 4. 83; Sulph.
Soda, 12. 38; and Carbonic Soda, 7. 65.—Total, 25. 41.

Anderson Rev. Edw. B.A. rector
Bampton Mr. Joseph
Basilico John, corn factor
Chapman Geo. blacksmith
Clay Wm. tailor
Collishaw Dorothy, wharfinger &
  coal dealer
Corner Septimus, tailor
Daft Jph. vict. and wheelwright
Daft Mr. Robert
Dickman Wm. boat owner
Faulks John, joiner
Faulks Michael, joiner
Hardy Robert, butcher
Harvey Wm. tailor
Hives Geo. vict. & corn miller
Holmes John, boat owner and
  shopkeeper
Holmes Thomas, tailor
Hopkinson John, beerhouse
Lovett Henry, tailor
Mann Mrs. Elizabeth
Mann Mrs. Mary
Mann Thos. bobbin net maker &
  shopkeeper

Shipman John, boat owner
Starbuck John, tailor
Sutton Hugh, parish clerk
Wheatley Samuel, boat owner
Wright John, mason & beerhouse
Wright Mr. William

FARMERS.
*Those marked * reside at the
Pastures.*

*Barnett Jph.	*Flewitt Saml.
Bell John	*Flewitt Wm.
Blount Wm.	Hardy Paul
Clay John	Hardy Robert
Collishaw Wm.	Hives John
& John	Hopkinson John
Collishaw Wm.	Maltby Joseph
Cross Samuel,	March George,
Lodge	Folly
Daft George	Mann John
*Davies John	Mann Mary
Davies Richard	Parker John

CARRIER, Rd. Copley, to Nottingham, Sat. 4 mg.; and to
Melton Mowbray, Tues. 7 mg.,

HOLME PIERREPONT PARISH

Comprises the hamlets of *Adbolton, Basingfield, Holme Pierre-*
pont, and *Lamcote,* with part of *Gamston* township, which is
mostly in West Bridgeford Parish. It contains 205 inhabitants, and 2600 acres of land, stretching southward from the
Trent to the Nottingham and Grantham canal. The low
grounds near the river have a rich alluvial soil, and the higher
parts have a good sandy clay. The whole has long been possessed by the *Pierrepont family,* from which it has the latter
part of its name, and is now the property of Earl Manvers, who
inherits the estates of the late Duke of Kingston, whose ancestor, Henry Pierrepont, obtained this parish in the reign of
Edward I. by marrying the heiress of the *Maunvers family,*
(hence the title of Earl Manvers).—See page 420.

HOLME PIERREPONT village, though small, is rich in rural
beauty, occupying a picturesque situation on the south side of
the river Trent, 5 miles E. by S. of Nottingham. The farm-
houses here and in other parts of the parish are mostly new and
handsomely built, and the cottages neat, with small gardens
attached to them. HOLME PIERREPONT HOUSE, now occupied
by the Dowager Countess Manvers, is still a large and ancient
mansion, though much of it has at different periods been taken
down. It stands close to the church, and was thoroughly repaired about 20 years ago, and cased in imitation of stone,
forming a very handsome specimen of the gothic of the latter
ages. The CHURCH, dedicated to St. Edmund, is rich in mural
monuments, in altar tombs, and in ancient armorial brasses.
Its form is gothic, but in the style of the time of Henry VII.,
with large and numerous windows, and consisting of a nave,
side aisles, and a square tower, surmounted by a handsome lofty
spire. The family vault of the late Dukes of Kingston and of
Earl Manvers, is on the north side of the choir, with a lofty
monument over it, supported by corinthian pillars, and most
gloomily ornamented with death's heads, in wreaths, intermixed
with fruit and foliage. Its inscription is rather in a superior
style of sepulchral bombast, for it informs us that "Here lyeth
the *Illustrious Princess Gertrude,* Countess of Kingston,
daughter of Henry Talbot, Esq., son to George, late Earl of
Shrewsbury. She was married to the most noble and excellent
Earl of Kingston," &c. A very fine altar tomb to the memory
of Sir Henry Pierrepont, knt., in 1615, is on the south side ; he
is in armour, and in the usual attitude of prayer. On the sides
of the tomb are a son, four daughters, and an infant in swad-
dling clothes ; and over it an highly ornamented tablet. Near
it is another, who, by his habit of a pilgrim, seems to have been
in the Holy Land ; he has angels playing round his head. Here
too is buried, "young *Oldham,*" considered as a poet of con-

siderable merit, and patronized by William, Earl of Kingston, who also wrote the very elegant latin inscription on his monument. The benefice is a rectory, valued in the King's books at £15. 7s. 6d. Earl Manvers is the patron, and the Rev. James Jarvis Cleaver is the incumbent.

ADBOLTON, 2 miles W. of Holme Pierrepont, and 3 miles S. E. by E. of Nottingham, was once a separate parish, though it now consists only of two farms, with two dwellings near the site of its *church*, which was taken down in 1746, when its materials were sold for £12. 7s. 6d., and its communion plate removed to Holme Pierrepont, to which its *rectory*, valued in the King's books at £2. 13s. 9d., is now annexed. A fine pear tree marks the site of the church, and some of its grave stones form part of the pavement of the adjoining farmstead. The manor of Adbolton was long held of the honour of Peverel, by the Strelley family; but in 1598½,it was granted by Queen Elizabeth to Sir Henry Pierrepont, and now belongs to his descendant, Earl Manvers.

BASINGFIELD is a small village, partly in Gamston township, 4 miles S. E. by E. of Nottingham.

GAMSTON village lies on the canal, nearly one mile W. of Basingfield, and its township extends into the hundred of Rushcliffe, and is partly in the parish of West Bridgeford. It was anciently called *Gamelston*, and was long held by the family of Lutterell, but was granted by Henry II. to Robert Pierrepont, to whose descendant, Earl Manvers, it now belongs.

HOLME-LANE is a hamlet consisting of a good inn and a few dwellings, on the Bingham-road, 4 miles E. S. E. of Nottingham.

LAMCOTE or *Lambecote* is another *manor*, belonging to Earl Manvers, and containing a small part of the village of Radcliffe on Trent, 1 mile E. of Holme Pierrepont.

A *close* at Lambly, now let for £3 a-year, belongs to the poor of Holme Pierrepont parish, as also does £30, left in 1718, by the Rev. Humphrey Perkins, and £10, left in 1730, by John Clayton, to the poor of Basingfield and Gamston. Timber that grew upon it was sold some years ago for £40, now in Smith's bank, at Nottingham.

Those marked 1, reside at Adbolton; 2, Basingfield; 3, Gamston; 4, Holme-grange; 5, Holme-lane; 6, Holme Pierrepont; 7, Lamcote.

6 Manvers Ann, Dowager Countess
  Holme Pierrepont House
Cleaver Rev. Jas. G. rector
5 Burrows J. vict. Fox & Crown
2 Foster Stephen, joiner
7 Gee Jonas, tailor
7 Hallam Rt. vict. Red Lion
5 Smallwood Wm. gardener
1 Spencer Jno. gardener & florist

5 Wheatley John, joiner
5 Wheatley Mary, blacksmith
     FARMERS.
6 Burgess Jph.   2 Morris Hy.
  Stubbins   3 Knight Thos.
2 Franks John   3 Milner Cath.
1 Hilton John   2 Parr Ann
4 Lowe John   5 Sanday Wm.
2 Lowe William 1 Spencer John

KINOULTON PARISH.

KINOULTON is a large village and parish, on the Grantham canal, under the eastern declivity of the Wolds, 10¼ miles S. E. of Nottingham, and 7 miles S. W. by S. of Bingham, containing 389 inhabitants, and 2950 acres of land, mostly belonging to the lord of the manor, Christopher Henry Neville Noel, Esq.; but about 260 acres belong to Thomas Black, William Day, and Henry Martin, Esq.; and 120 acres have been allotted in lieu of the great tithes to the appropriator, the Archbishop of York, who is also patron of the vicarage, which has 14A. 2R. of glebe, and is valued in the King's books at £7. 18s. 11d. The Rev. Thomas Hoe is the incumbent, and collects the small tithes in kind. The village was anciently called NEWBOLD, and was a chapelry to the mother CHURCH, which was dedicated to St. Wilford, and stood on a lofty eminence, more than half a mile west of the village, where it was long in ruins, and was taken down about the year 1793, when the Earl of Gainsborough, then lord of the manor, erected the present church nearly in the centre of the village, on or near the site of " the wretched chapel, mentioned and called by Thoroton *Newbolt chapel.*" It is a neat brick structure, with a lofty tower. In the old church-yard only a very few grave-stones now remain, though about three years ago a Mr. Peet was buried there. A large granite *stone,* which had lain for many ages upon the hill, about half a mile north-east of the old church, was removed about ten years ago into the village. It is supposed to have been part of a *Druidical Temple,* though a traditional fable says the Devil threw it from Lincoln Minster with the intention of knocking down Kinoulton church! The *Wesleyan chapel* in the village was built in 1813. A *Chalybeate Spring,* upon the hill on the west side of the village, is said to possess considerable medicinal virtues. The parish *feast* is on the Sunday after St. Luke's day; and two *sick clubs* in the village hold their festivals on Whit-Wednesday and Thursday. The manors of Kinoulton and Newbold were of the fees of Walter D'Ayncount and William Peverel, and were successively held by the Villers, Foljambes, Plumptons, Cliftons, Bugges, and Noels, from the latter of whom they passed to their present lord, C. H. Neville, Esq. who assumed the name of *Noel,* on succeeding to the estates of Henry Noel, the last Earl of Gainsbrough, who died without issue in 1798.

Bailey Thos. schoolmaster	Hardy William, tailor
Bailey Wm. vict. Volunteer	Harvey Thomas, joiner
Bonser Wm. sen. & jun. joiners	Healey Thomas, parish clerk
Gardner John, blacksmith	Jalland William, weaver
Gillman William, tailor	Nash James, brickmaker
Green Charles, shoemaker	Oxby Miss Sarah, Ladies' school

Pollard Thomas, shoemaker
Pollard Wm. vict. Bull's Head
Simpson John, boat owner and
  coal dealer
Spencer James, tailor
Spenser Joseph, boat owner and
  coal dealer
Street John, shoemaker & shop-
  keeper
      FARMERS.
Abbott Geo.   Baguley Ann

Black Thomas Mountnay John
Bonser John   Oxby Robert
Bonser Saml.   Peet William
Clark T.Grange Peet William
Clarke W. Hall Sharp Thomas
Marsh Richard Shephard Hanh.
Milner Thos. Stokes Robert

CARRIERS to Nottingham, Wm.
Pollard & Jno. Peet, Sat. 5 morning.

KNEETON PARISH.

KNEETON or *Kneveton* is a small village and parish, occupying
a commanding situation, upon a lofty precipitous cliff, on the
south side of the Trent, 8 miles S. W. of Newark. It contains 119 inhabitants, and 800 acres of land, all belonging to
Lord Porchester, except about 140 acres, which are the property of Mrs. Hildyard, to whom they descended from the
Story family. A great part of the manor was given to Welbeck
Abbey, but in the reign of Edward VI. it was held of the King
in capite by Sir Edward Molyneux, whose descendants resided
here during many generations, but their mansion was taken
down in 1781, when their estates passed with their sole heiress,
to the late Lord Howard, whose daughter, the Hon. Henrietta
Howard Molyneux, was married in 1830 to Lord Porchester,
the present lord of the manor, and patron of the *perpetual
curacy*, which is valued in the King's books at £4. 9s. 4d., but
has received three augmentations from Queen Anne's Bounty,
two of which have been laid out in land, and the third (£400) is
still in the augmentation office. The Rev. Philip Palmer is
the incumbent. The *church* is a small fabric with a tower and
three bells, and has some monuments of the Story family. The
views in the vicinity are extensive and beautiful, including a
considerable portion of the picturesque vales of the Trent and
Belvoir.

Fisher Nathaniel, farmer
Foster William, shoemaker
Hall John, shopkeeper

Hill Edward, farmer
Neale Thomas, farmer
Walker George, shopkeeper

LANGAR-CUM-BARNSTON PARISH.

Lies betwixt the Smite rivulet and the Leicestershire border,
and includes the neighbouring villages and lordships of Langar
and Barnston, which form but one manor and township; containing 274 inhabitants, and 3825A. 3R. 5P. of strong fertile

2 x

land, all of which belongs to John Wright, Esq. except three farms in Barnston, and 400 acres allotted to the rector at the enclosure in lieu of 'the tithes.   In the Conqueror's time they were of the fees of William Peverel and Walter D'Ayncourt, and were afterwards held by the familes 'of Rodes, Tibetot, Scrope, and Howe, of the latter of whom they were purchased by their present proprietor in 1818.

LANGAR is a small but pleasant and well built village, 4 miles S. by E. of Bingham.   Thoroton,- in 1677, says *Langar Hall*! and nearly the whole of the parish have lately become the estate of Mr. Howe, who made a convenient park of the closes around the mansion, and stocked it with deer.   The hall was subsequently nearly all rebuilt, and ornamented with a handsome portico and pediment, with six lofty ionic pillars, the height of the house, which is three stories, but is now unoccupied, and a great part of it has been taken down since it was purchased by the present lord of the manor, John Wright, Esq. who bought it in 1818 of the present Earl Howe, and has since divided the park, and cut down all its fine timber.   It was the seat of the late gallant *Admiral Howe*, who, in 1792, succeeded the brave Rodney as Vice-Admiral of England. He (Richard Howe) was the fourth Viscount Howe, in Ireland, and was created Viscount Howe of Langar, in 1782, and Baron Howe of Langar, and Earl Howe, in 1788.   He seldom visited his seat of Langar Hall, for his time was his country's, and during a long course of active service he gained the most illustrious naval honours.   He died universally regretted, in 1799, when his titles became extinct, except the Barony, which devolved on Sophia Charlotte, his eldest daughter and coheiress, who married Pen Asheton Curzon, afterwards created Viscount Curzon, which title descended to their son and heir, the present Richard Wm. Penn Asheton Curzon, who sold this estate in 1818, and was created Earl Howe in 1821. · . . .:

Langar CHURCH stands near the hall, and consists of a nave and two side aisles, with a tower and a ring of five bells. . It is dedicated to St. Andrew, and contains many beautiful monuments of the Lords Scrope, &c., particularly one dated 1609, which is ornamented in the richest sepulchral style. The recumbent figures are all in excellent preservation. Here also are busts of the two Lords Howe, who died in 1712 and 1734. It was anciently appropriated to Lenton and Thurgarton priories, but is now a rectory in the patronage of John Wright, Esq. and valued in the King's books at £10. 7s. 11d., but Thorosby says (1795) its real value is nearly £300 per annum. The Rev. W. Bowerbank purchased the rectory of the late patron, with the intention of inducting his son as soon as he should have passed the University; and until then he gave it to his friend, the Rev. Joseph Rollin Unwin, the present incumbent, who has possitively refused to give it up to the younger

Mr. Bowerbank, in consequence of which a law suit has ensued, which we should think will terminate in his favour, though he may have committed a breach of friendship. The lordship of Langar comprises 2439A. 2R. 25P. The *feast* is held on the second Sunday after Whit-Sunday.

BARNSTON is a hamlet and chapelry, 1 mile E. by N. of Langar, and 4 miles S. S. E. of Bingham. It contains 1386A. 0R. 20P. of fertile land. The houses, which are few in number, occupy an eminence that commands an extensive view of the vale of Belvoir. The chapel is a small building, with a short tower, and is annexed to the rectory of Langar. This we suppose is the remains, or rather, perhaps, the successor of the ancient chapel of St. Atheburga, or St. Aubrey, which Thoroton says stood in the fields of Langar, and was considered as partly belonging to Granby church, with which it was given to Thurgarton priory. The *feast* here is on the Sunday after Whit-Sunday.

LANGAR.
Bates John, vict. Unicorn's Head
Newton Robert, butcher
Stokes Rueben, bobbin net mkr
Swift William, shopkeeper
Unwin Rev. Jph. Rollin, rector
Wright John, joiner
FARMERS.
Goodwin Thos. Hall Isaac
Hall Vincent
Hall Wm.
BARNSTON.—(FARMERS.)
*Marked * are Yeomen,*
Daft Stephen
*Howe Gervas
James John
*James Wm.
Harrison Roger
Newton John
*Pacey J. North-
field house
Smith Saml
Topham Wm.
Whittle ——

LODGE-ON-THE-WOLDS

Is an EXTRA PAROCHIAL liberty, upon the Roman Fosse-way, 8¼ miles S. E. of Nottingham. It contains only one house and 25 acres of land, occupied by Henry Randall, but belonging to Henry Cole Bingham, Esq. Stukely says, that in 1724 there was an *inn* here, "under a great wood, upon the declension of a stiff clayey hill. Here the pavement upon the Roman road is very manifest; of great blue flag stones, laid edgeways very care-fully. The quarries from whence they took them are upon the side of the hill." The pavement is two feet broad, and in some places is so sunk in the *Fosse*, that an army might be marched without observation for many miles. It is said the house here was once a noted *Lying-in-Asylum* for pregnant ladies, who wished to secrete their illegitimate offspring, and afterwards pass themselves upon the fashionable world as "virgins chaste and fair."

ORSTON PARISH

Includes the townships and chapelries of *Scarrington* and

Thoroton, and also part of *Flawborough*, which is mostly in Staunton parish, in the hundred of Newark. It contains 761 inhabitants, and 2150 acres of rich land, in the vale of the Smite river. Orston and the two chapelries maintain their poor separately, and in the population returns are entered as three distinct parishes, though they have long been united under the same pastor.

ORSTON village and township contains about 90 houses, and 1850 acres of land on the south side of the Smite, 5 miles E. of Bingham. It was enclosed in 1796, when 272A. 2R. 31P. were alloted to the appropriators, and 68A. 3R. 20P. to the vicar, as a commutation of all the tithes. Earl Manvers is lord of the manor, and owner of about 200 acres, but the largest proprietor is Henry Cole Bingham, Esq. who has 500 acres. This manor of Orston or *Oschinton* was held by the crown from the reign of Edward the Confessor to that of Richard I.; the latter of whom granted it to William de Albini, Lord of Belvoir, from whose descendants it passed to the families of Roos, Montague, and Bozon, the latter of whom sold it to the Earl of Kingston, an ancestor of the present Earl Manvers. The *church* is dedicated to St. Mary. The body is ancient, but the tower, which has four bells, was rebuilt about the year 1763. Wm. Rufus gave it to Lincoln Cathedral, and the dean and chapter of Lincoln are still the appropriators, and also patrons of the *vicarage*, which is valued in the King's books at £12. 4s. 7d., and is now enjoyed by the Rev. Charles J. Fiennes Clinton, for whom the Rev. Gabriel Valpy, M. A. officiates both here and at Scarrington, and Thoroton. Here is a small *Methodist chapel*, and near the village is a *chalybeate spring* noted for its tonic qualities. The *feast* is on the Sunday after the 19th of September. Mrs. Middlemore, who resides in the *hall*, is lessee of the rectorial land. The *Ladies Dole* is a rent charge of £1. 14s. 6d. paid to poor widows every Christmas out of Mr. Bingham's estate, but the donor is unknown.

SCARRINGTON is a small village, township, and chapelry, 2½ miles E. N. E. of Bingham. It has only 188 inhabitants, and 900 acres of land, belonging to Henry Flower, Esq., and several other resident freeholders, except 115 acres allotted to the appropriators at the enclosure in 1779; but Earl Manvers is lord of the *manor*, which in Domesday-Book is described as a *Berue* of Orston. The *church* is in the same appropriation, patronage, and incumbency, as that at Orston, to which it is a chapel of ease. Being in a ruinous state, it was partly rebuilt, and thoroughly repaired about 30 years ago, at the cost of £300. It has a spire steeple with three bells. A small Methodist chapel was built here in 1818. An *annuity* of 10s. left by an unknown donor, is paid out of Robert Watson's farm to poor widows.

THOROTON, on the north side of the Smite, 1 mile N. of Orston, and 4 miles E.N.E. of Bingham, is a smaller village than Scarrington, but has a larger township and chapelry, containing 143 inhabitants, and 1400 acres of land, which was inclosed in 1796, when 195A. 3R. 1F. were allotted to the dean and chapter of Lincoln, in lieu of the great tithes, and 19A. 1R. 5P. to the vicar of Orston, in lieu of the small tithes. The soil is generally a rich clay, producing fine crops of grass, wheat, and beans. Earl Manvers and Dr. Staunton are joint lords of the manor, which was a berue of Orston, and at the Domesday survey was held by a "sokman," whose posterity took the name of the place, and from whom descended Robert Thoroton, M.D. the first Nottinghamshire topographer, whose ancestors sold their patrimony here in the reign of Henry VIII. and removed to Car-Colston.—(See p. 488.) The principal land owners are now Mrs. Esther Wylde, of Nottingham; Mr. Stuart, and Sir Peter Payne, Bart. The *church* or chapel is annexed to the vicarage of Orston, and is a handsome structure, with a tower containing two bells, and surmounted by a fine spire.

ORSTON.
Beaumont Miss Susanna Maria
Cheetham John, shoemaker
Cheetham Thomas, blacksmith and shopkeeper
Dewey Richard, tailor
Hand Wm. vict. Plough
Hart Richard, saddler and tawer
Harvey Thos. shoemaker and beer house
Henson William, victualler and shopkeeper, Royal Oak
Leake Thomas, miller and baker
Lowe Thomas, schoolmaster
Maltby Thomas, maltster
Marshall William, maltster
Middlemore Mrs. Susanna, gent. Orston Hall
Rippengale John, tailor
Stephens John, joiner
Twintberry Thos. blacksmith
Valpy Rev. Gabriel, M.A. curate
Weghtman Jph. butcher
Wilson George, shoemaker and parish clerk
Wilson John, shoemaker
Wingfield Thomas, wheelwright

FARMERS.
Baguley John
Bean John
Bean Thos.
Hollis John
Marshall Thos.
Marshall Wm.
Morris John
Vincent Robt.
Walker J. Field
Weckham Ann

CARRIERS, John Fryer and W. Greaves, to Newark Wed. 6 mg., and to Nottingham Sat. 4 mg.

SCARRINGTON.
Flower Henry, Esq.
Graves Robert, joiner
Harvey Robert, pig jobber
Hitchcock Thomas, wheelwright
Marsh John, gent.
Mee John, shoemaker
Vessey Joseph, butcher

FARMERS.
Blagg Wm.
Fisher Saml.
Ludlow John
Marsh Thos.
Marshall Wm.
Watson John
Watson Thos.
Watson Robt.

THOROTON.
Branston Thos. shopkeeper
Gibson George, shopkeeper
Moggs Thomas, miller & baker
Smith Thomas, shoemaker

FARMERS.
Chettle Thos.
Massey Fras.
Moggs Jph.
Treece James

2 x 2

OWTHORPE PARISH.

OWTHORPE is a small village and parish upon the Grantham canal, and on the eastern side of the lofty range of hills called the Wolds, 9 miles S.E. by E. of Nottingham, and 6 miles S.S.W. of Bingham. It contains only about 30 humble dwellings, 144 inhabitants, and 1600 acres of cold clay land, of which Sir Robert Howe Bromley, Bart. is lord and principal owner; his father, Sir George Smith Bromley, Bart. having purchased the manor, with 1300 acres of land, in 1773, of the Hutchinson family, who had held it for many generations. For some time after the Conquest it was held by a family of its own name, and was of the fee of Roger de Busli. The *hall* and the *church* were both rebuilt about 1650, by *Colonel John Hutchinson*, who, as has been seen at page 89, was an active Parliamentary partisan during the civil wars of Charles I., in which he was some time governor of Nottingham castle. Though he sat in judgment upon his Sovereign, no very active means were taken to apprehend him at the Restoration, and he seems to have lived secretly in Owthorpe Hall, till 1663, when he was arrested on his road to the church, by a party of horse under the command of Cornet Atkinson, and was conveyed to Deal castle, in Kent, where he died a prisoner, but was interred in Owthorpe church. The HALL was a large square mansion, which was pulled down by the present owner of the estate. The present CHURCH is much smaller than the original fabric, out of the ruins of which it is built. It is dedicated to St. Margaret, and consists of a nave, with a low tower and one bell. It was anciently appropriated to Thurgarton priory, but is now in the impropriation and patronage of Sir R. H. Bromley, Bart. The living is a perpetual curacy, certified at £10, and now in the incumbency of the Rev. Thomas Smith. Two houses on the hill, near *Lodge-on-the-Wolds*, (see p. 503,) are in this parish.

Barlow John, shoemaker
Hanson J. p. clerk & schoolmstr
Lovett Wm. tailor
Wild T. lime burner, Odd house

FARMERS.
Mackley Rd.   Spencer Thos.
Marsden Thos. Wild John
Martin John   Wild William

RADCLIFFE-ON-TRENT PARISH.

RADCLIFFE-ON-TRENT is a large and well-built village, six miles E. by S. of Nottingham, remarkable for its very romantic scenery, being situated upon a lofty cliff on the south bank of the Trent, from which it has its name, and which affords it some extensive and beautiful prospects over the vale watered by that broad and meandering river. It contains 190 houses, 1125 inhabitants, and about 1800 acres of fertile land, which was enclosed in 1788, when the tithes were exonerated by an allotment of 100 acres to the impropriator, and 40 acres to the vicar. Earl Manvers is proprietor of nearly all the land, and lord of the MANOR; also impropriator and patron of the VICARAGE, which is valued in the King's books at £4. 12s. 6d., and has received two augmentations from Queen Anne's Bounty, with which 26 acres of land have been purchased. The CHURCH, which was anciently appropriated to Thurgarton priory, is dedicated to St. Mary, and was thoroughly repaired, with the addition of a gallery and 195 free seats, in 1829, by subscription and a gift from the society for building and enlarging churches. It has a nave and chancel, with a tower and four bells, and has, lying in a niche, "a wooden figure of Stephen Radcliffe, said to be the founder." The Rev. Edward Denison, M.A. is the incumbent, and resides in the vicarage-house, besides which here are several other handsome modern mansions. There are in the village a number of malt-kilns, and some of the inhabitants are employed by the Nottingham lace and hosiery manufacturers. The *feast* is on the Sunday after September 19th.— The Dowager Countess Manvers has many years supported a *school* here, for the education of 21 poor boys and girls. In 1714, the *benefactions* belonging to the poor of this parish amounted to £33, and were laid out in the purchase of 2R. 16P. of land, which was augmented at the enclosure with an allotment of 2A. 3R. 6P., and is now let for £7 per annum, half of which is distributed at Christmas, and the rest is dispensed at various times amongst the sick parishioners. The south-west extremity of the village stands in the manor of LAMCOTE, which is mostly in the parish of Holme Pierrepont.—(See p. 499.) After the Conquest, Radcliffe was held of Wm. Peverel, by Fredgis and Ulviet, except a portion of it which was of the fee of Walter D'Ayncourt. It subsequently passed to the Hotot, Baseley, Hoveringham, Radcliffe, Rosel, and other families.— The Pierreponts had possessions here as early as Edward III., and have since, by purchase, &c. become possessed of the whole manor; some portions of which were granted by its early proprietors to the Knights of St. John of Jerusalem, and others to the abbeys of Newstead, in this county, and Dale, in Derbyshire.

Allsebrook Eliz. shopkeeper
Barker Edward, smith, farrier, and net maker
Barrott William shoemaker
Bates John, shoemaker, Lamcote
Beeson John, boat owner and shopkeeper
Beeson Thomas shopkeeper

Bell Geo. vict. Manvers' Arms, and bricklayer
Blackwell George, shoemaker
Bolton Rev. Edward, Radcliffe Lodge
Brewster Robert, maltster
Brice William, baker and flour dealer

Butler Mary, maltster and vict.
Butler Richard, butcher
Buxton Timothy, miller and baker
Denison Rev. Ed. M.A. vicar
Duke George, parish clerk
Eastwood Wm. stonemason
Foster John, joiner
Foster Richard, butcher
Foster Wm. butcher
Gee Jacob, taylor and draper
Gee Jonas, shoemaker
Glew Samuel, wheelwright
Green John, maltster
Hallam Richard, maltster
Haynes Thos. vict. Royal Oak
Haynes William, joiner
Hemsley Samuel, schoolmaster
Hind John, job gardener
Knight Thomas, gent.
Lockton Ed. vict. Black Lion
Marriott John, tailor
Morley John, maltster
Morley John, shomaker
Morley Sarah, shopkeeper
Morley Wm. overseer & constable
Murden Ann, shopkeeper
Ogle George, butcher
Parr Ed. wharfinger and coal dlr
Parr Henry, baker & flour dealer
Parr Mary, boat owner and shop-keeper
Parr Richard, maltster
Randall William, boat owner, Lamcote

Rayworth Thomas, tailor
Richards George, shoemaker
Richmond Ann, teacher, girls' school
Richmond Samuel, butcher
Richmond William, shoemaker
Rockley William, shoemaker
Saunders Mary, shopkeeper
Scrimshaw John, tailor
Stokes William, shoemaker
Talbot John, joiner
Taylor William, Esq.
Terry Ann, boat owner
Tugman John, joiner
Whitehead Richard, shoemaker
Whitworth Francis, saddler
Whitworth Thomas, baker and flour dealer
Wood Samuel, shopkeeper
Wright Francis, Esq., Lamcote
Wright Elizabeth, shopkeeper

FARMERS.

Bowren Jph.   Parr Samuel
Brewster Edw.   Rose John
Butler Richard   Stone Thomas
Green Robert   Walker William,
Parr Jno. Lam- , Gillmoor, field
   cote

CARRIERS, George Duke and William Morley, to Nottingham, Wed. and Sat. 7 mg.

The *Coaches* to Nottingham, and Newark, call at the Manvers' Arms, daily.

SCREVETON PARISH.

SCREVETON is a small village and parish lying betwixt the Fosse-way and the Car-dike, 4 miles N.E. by N. of Bingham, containing 312 inhabitants, and about 1100 acres of land, which was enclosed in 1706, when 120 acres (since exchanged for 90 acres nearer the church), were allotted to the rector in lieu of his tithes. At the same time, about 50 acres were allotted to the appropriators of Orston and the impropriator of Car-Colston, in lieu of their right to the tithes of those parts of this parish which were *soc* to the said manors and parishes. This parish was anciently of three fees, and was successively held by the Kirketons, the Leeks, the Whalleys, and the Thorotons, who occupied *Kirketon hall*, which was so named from its

standing near the church, "in the very division of the lordships of Car-Colston and Screveton," as we are informed by
our old Nottinghamshire topographer, Dr. Thoroton, who was
born in it, and one of whose family, Thomas Thoroton, Esq.
was living in it in 1796; but none of the name are now left in
the neighbourhood, and their mansion was pulled down about
six years ago by the father of the present owner of the estate,
Thomas Hildyard, Esq. (now a minor,) who has the deputation
of this and several adjacent manors, of which Earl Manvers is
lord paramount, and occasionally holds a manorial court. The
church is dedicated to St. Winifred, and is a neat edifice, with
a nave, two side aisles, three bells, a curious old font, and several antique and highly ornamented monuments of the Whalleys. The living is a rectory, valued in the King's books at
£6. 19s. 2d. Mr. Hildyard is the patron, and the Rev. John
C. Girardot is the incumbent. The *feast* is on the Sunday
after Old Michaelmas-day. A *benefaction* of £5, left to the
poor of this parish by John Parr, in 1748, has been twice lost,
and as often replaced by the parishioners.

Bean Robert, farmer
Branston William, shoemaker
Blagg Wm. farmer, Red Lodge
Cragg William, blacksmith
Flinders Geo. parish clerk
Flinders John, tailor
Fostor John, blacksmith
Foster John, shoemaker
Gibson Henry, shoemaker
Gibson William, shopkeeper
Heathcote Robert, gent.
Houseley Richard, rag merchant

Marsh Thomas, yeomen
Marshall Edw. baker and flour
  dealer
Marshall John, rope maker
Musson John, joiner
Neale John, Barley Mow, beer-
  house
Voce Thomas, farmer

CARRIER, John Patchett, to
Newark, Wed., and Nottingham,
Sat. 5 mg.

SHELFORD PARISH

Consists of two *townships*, viz. Shelford-with-Newton, and
Saxendale, which maintain their poor separately, and contain
together 704 inhabitants, and upwards of 3000 acres of land,
lying on the south side of the Trent, betwixt Radcliffe and East
Bridgeford.

SHELFORD, 6¼ miles E. by N. of Nottingham, is a pleasant
village, seated on a gentle eminence, which in very great
floods is sometimes completely surrounded by the Trent water,
as was the case in 1793, though it is distant half a mile from
the regular channel of the river, and is backed by a lofty ridge
of land to the south. After the Conquest, it was nearly all of
the fee of Goisfred de Halselin, whose descendant, Ralph,
founded an *Austin Priory* here in the reign of Stephen, which,
at its dissolution in the 29th of Henry VIII., was valued at

£116. 1s. 1d. per annum, and was granted to Michael Stanhope, Esq. ancestor of the Earl of Chesterfield, who is now sole
owner (except half an acre) and lord of the manor of Shelford,
which comprises about 2500 acres. The ancient *manor house*,
which was long occupied by the *Stanhope family*, was burnt
down in the civil wars, when the Parliamentarians took it by
storm, after it had long held out for the King, under the command of Colonel Stanhope, (son of the first Earl of Chesterfield,)
who was slain in the conflict. Some years after this, the family
rebuilt it partly out of its ruins, and it is now occupied by John
Hassall, Esq. captain of the Holme troop of Yeomanry. The
church, dedicated to St. Peter and St. Paul, is a respectable
edifice, containing many monuments of the Stanhope family,
one of which is to the memory of the *accomplished Earl of
Chesterfield*, who died in 1752, and whose character and writings
are too well known to require any encomium here. The tower
is massive and lofty, and has a peal of five bells. The living is
a perpetual curacy, certified at £40, and is in the patronage of
the Earl of Chesterfield. The Rev. John Rollestone, of Burton
Joyce, is the incumbent. The ALMSHOUSE, near the village,
was founded in 1694, by Sir. Wm. Stanhope, for *six* poor men
of the parishes of Shelford, Bingham, Carlton-by-Nottingham,
Gedling, Burton Joyce, or Whatton, each having a garden, 2s.
per week, and a yearly allowance of coal and clothing. Only
three almsmen are now admitted, and the rest of the building
is occupied by a schoolmaster, who receives £40 a year from
the Earl of Chesterfield, for teaching 30 poor children. The
parish *feast* is on the first Sunday in July.

NEWTON hamlet is pleasantly situated upon a declivity, 1¼
mile E. by S. of Shelford, and 2 miles W.N.W. of Bingam.
The manor contains 800 acres, and was all of the fee of Goisfred de Halselin, except 50 acres, which were soc to Bingham,
and still belong to that parish. The whole is now the property
of the Earl of Chesterfield, except 25 acres belonging to the poor
of Bunny, and 35 belonging to the Rev. John Popplewell and
Mr. John Allwood.

SAXENDALE hamlet and township has only 118 inhabitants,
and 600 acres of land, and is distant 2½ miles S.E. of Shelford,
and 1¼ mile W. of Bingham, being situated at the junction of
the Nottingham and Grantham road with the Roman Fosse-
way. The whole, except about five acres belonging to Mr. John
Green, is the property of the Earl of Chesterfield. There
was formerly a *church* here, appropriated to Shelford priory,
but after the dissolution, Thoroton says, the family of Stanhope
"swore it was but a Chapel of Ease" and pulled it down to save
the expense of a chaplain. In our author's time, some of the
inhabitants had taken up stone coffins, and converted them into
troughs for swine.

SHELFORD.

Calah John, bricklayer
Fisher John, parish clerk
Foster Edward, shopkeeper
Hassall Capt. John, Manor house
Henton Thomas, schoolmaster, Hospital
Hill Isaac, brickmaker
Howett John, joiner and cabinet maker
Jackson John, overlooker Trent navigation
Julian Willam, tailor
Loach William, shoemaker
Miles Thomas, shoemaker
Newcomb John, corn miller, Newton
Palethorpe Thomas, butcher
Pilgrim John, chief constable for N. Div. of Bingham Hundred
Reason John, Robert, and Wm. joiners
Reason William, blacksmith
Towers Thomas, butcher
Walker George, shoemaker and shopkeeper
Walker Thomas, gardener
Watson William, butter dealer
Widdowson William, gent.
Wood John, overseer and constable
Wood John, shoemaker

Woolley Mr. Joseph

FARMERS.

Bailey Nath.
Binks Fras.
Cook Wm.
Duckinfield Jn.
Ellis Henry
Fisher John
Fox John
Girton John
Jallands John
Julian Eliz.
Marriott Benj
Marshall W.
Palethorpe My
Parks Ann
Raven Saml.
Swanwick Wm.
Tomlin Geo.
Whitaker Mary

CARRIERS, John Holland, and Thomas Walker, to Nottingham, Sat. 6 mg.

NEWTON.

Allwood William, farmer
Greaves John, bobbin net mkr
Jones William, gardener
Martin Thomas, farmer
Palmer Rev. Philip, Newton Hall
Popplewell, Rev. John
Parr William, farmer
Walker Robert, farmer
Wilson Hannah, farmer

SAXONDALE.—(FARMERS)

Foster John
Green John
Hemsall G. mole catcher
Horsepool Wm.
Lamin Wm.
Pilgrim John
Radford Thos. and shopkpr
Upton George

TITHBY PARISH

Consists of the two *townships of Tithby and Cropwell Butler,* the former of which contains 144 inhabitants, and 567A. 1R. 28P. of land, and the latter 555 inhabitants, and about 1800 acres. They maintain their poor separately, but were both enclosed under one act in 1788, when 232 acres were allotted to the impropriator, and 30A. 3R. 32P. to the incumbent curate in lieu of tithes, and 5A. 3R. 34P. to the Duke of Newcastle, as a commutation of his manorial claims in Cropwell Butler.

TITHBY is a small but pleasant village, 2½ miles S. S. W. of Bingham, and after the Conquest was of the fees of W. Peverel, and Walter D'Ayncourt. For many generations it was the property of the Chaworths, of Wiverton, whose late heiress carried it in marriage to John Musters, Esq. the present lord of the manor, impropriator, and patron of the perpetual *curacy,* which is certified at £14. 11s. 1d. and is now in the incumbency of the Rev. Edward Palling, for whom the Rev. P. H. Palmer officiates. The *church*, dedicated to the Holy Trinity, was thoroughly repaired and new pewed in 1824, at the cost of £900. The *feast* is on the Sunday after St. Peter's day.

CROPWELL BUTLER is a large village and township, 1 mile W. by N. of Tithby, and near the Bingham canal. It was anciently called *Crophill Botiller*, from the circular hill, which rises betwixt it and Cropwell Bishop, and from its early possessors, the Botillers or Butlers, of Warrington, in Lancashire, from whom part of it passed to the Hutchinsons, who sold the farms to divers freeholders, and the demesne to the Earl of Kingston, to whose descendant, Earl Manvers, it still belongs; but the "Grange" and a large portion of the township is the property of John Musters, and the families of Parr and Marriott reside here on their own farms. After the Conquest, it was of the fee of Roger Pictavensis, who gave the *chapel*, of which no traces now remain, " to the monastery of St. Martin's, at Sais, in France," and from whom the manorial rights of Cropwell Butler, have descended to the Duke of Newcastle. A Methodist chapel was built here about 5 years ago. The *feast* is on the Sunday after Old St. Luke's-day. There are three *benefactions* belonging to the poor of the township, viz:—£50 left in 1777 by Mary Fillingham; £50 left in 1779, by Wm. Fillingham, and £100 left in 1813, by John Marriott. The latter is now vested in £108, new 4 per cents., and the others are in Smith and Co.'s bank, at Nottingham.

TITHBY,—(FARMERS, &c.)
Bates Wm.
Beecroft Thos.
Beecroft Wm.
Braithwaite Chs.
Crane Jas.
Derry Thos.
Dowell Thos.
Harwood Benj.
Hallam John
Paling John
Pollard John
parish clerk
Rayner William,
shopkeeper
Roberts George
gamekeeper
Walker John
blacksmith

CROPWELL BUTLER.
Allroyd William, shopkeeper
Baguley Mr. Samuel
Barratt John, beer-house
Barratt Matthew, baker and shopkeeper
Carver Thomas, blacksmith
Carver William, blacksmith
Clark Charles, castrator
Clark Jackson, gardener
Clark William, gardener
Crampton Thomas, tailor and shopkeeper
Davis William, shoemaker

Doncaster John, brickmaker
Huskisson William, tailor
Innocent Francis, victualler and maltster
Innocent William, butcher
Kemp George, shoemaker
Kemp Randall, shoemaker
Marriott John, victualler, Leather Bottle
Newton George, joiner
Parr Mrs. Catherine
Raynor Mrs. Martha
Smith Rev. Henry
Taylor Thomas, wheelwright
Tinsley Joseph, brickmaker
Widdowson John, shoemaker
Widdowson William, blacksmith
Wright Thomas, joiner

FARMERS.
Baldock Jph.   Fisher Thomas,
Barratt Henry,   and overseer
Barratt John   Hopewell John
Clark Mary   Innocent John
Dixon Wm.   Marriott Jph.

Marriott Wm. Raynor Martha
Newton Wm. Saxton Wm.
Parr Geo. & Jno. Smith Thos.
Parr John Smith Wm.

Willoughby J. Willoughby W.

CARRIERS, John Barratt and Richard Marriott, to Notting-ham, Sat. 6 mg.

TOLLERTON PARISH.

TOLLERTON is a small picturesque village and parish, upon a pleasant declivity, 4½ miles S. by E. of Nottingham, containing 149 inhabitants, and 1200 acres of land, which was enclosed many years ago, and an allotment made in lieu of the tithes.— In Domesday Book this manor is called *Roclaveston*, and afterwards *Torlaston*, and was of the fees of Roger de Busli and Roger Pictavensis. As early as the reign of Edward II. it was possessed by the Barry family, whose heiress, about 1560, carried it in marriage to Richard Pendock, from whom is descended its present lord and owner, Pendoc Neale Barry, Esq. who resides in TOLLERTON HALL, which was rebuilt about 20 years ago, in imitation of the gothic, with towers, turrets, &c. and with a cloister that communicates with the church. The grounds are very extensive, and have a fine piece of water with a small woody island. The new gateway, and the lodge near it, together with the bridge, assimilate well with the surrounding scenery. The *church* is a small ancient structure, dedicated to St. Peter. The living is a rectory, valued in the King's books at £15. 9s. 4d. P. N. Barry, Esq. is the patron, and the Rev. Edward Smith the incumbent. The *poor* have 50s. yearly from the bequest of Agnes Crosse, in 1722.

Barry Pindoc Neale, Esq., Tollerton Hall
Smith Rev. Edward, rector
Thurman John, blacksmith
Thurman W. joiner & wheelwgt

Farmers.
Baldock Wm. Russell —
Brice Thos. Thurman — -
Holmes Rd. Wild John

WHATTON PARISH

Includes the two townships of Whatton and Aslacton, which keep their poor separately, and contain together 677 inhabitants, and about 3400 acres of land, in the vale of the Smite, where that river is augmented by the Wipling.

WHATTON village and township is on the south side of the Smite, and on the Grantham road, 3 miles E. by S. of Bingham. It was anciently called *Watone*, from its watery situation, the flood water lying longer here than in many other places. It contains 1800 acres, and was enclosed in the year 1790, when 36A. 1R. 18P. were allotted to the vicar, and 120A. 3R. 5P. to

2 Y

the impropriator, G. S. Foljambe, Esq., in lieu of tithes. The latter sold his allotment to Thos. Hall, Esq., of Nottingham, who now owns 800 acres here, having purchased several farms of the lord of the manor, the Earl of Chesterfield, who still holds 320 acres, and the remainder belongs to several smaller freeholders. After the Conquest, this manor was of the fee of Gilbert de Gand. It was long held by the Whattons, Newmarches, and Gascoignes, the latter of whom sold it to the father of the first Earl of Chesterfield; but some of the lands were successively held by the Whalleys, Gelsthorps, and others. The *church*, which Adelina de Whatton gave to Welbeck abbey, is dedicated to St. John of Beverley, has a handsome tower and spire with five bells, and contains many ancient monuments of the Whatton, Newmarch, Cranmer, and other families. The whole was repaired and new pewed in 1807, at the cost of £1700, except the chancel, which is in a very decayed state, and the duty of repairing which belongs to the owner of the impropriate lands. The *vicarage* is valued in the King's books at £5. 6s. 8d., and has now 92 acres of glebe, including its allotments at the enclosure of Whatton and Aslacton. G. S. Foljambe, Esq. is the patron, and the Rev. H. N. Bousfield, B. A. is the incumbent. A Methodist chapel was built here in 1825. The charities consist of the *Poor's close*, (one acre,) the tenant of which distributes three tons of coals yearly; and £12 left by John Clayter, in 1738, and now in the bank at 2½ per cent.

ASLACTON is a pleasant village and township on the N. side of the Smite, one mile N. by W. of Whatton, and 2½ miles E. of Bingham. It contains 289 inhabitants, and 1600 acres of land, most of which is occupied by the owners, except the Abbey farm, (200 acres,) which belongs to King's-Cliffe school, in Northamptonshire, and the following allotments made at the enclosure in 1780, viz. 65 acres to Alex. Heaton and William Bilbie, Esq. in lieu of the impropriated tithes, and 44 acres to the vicar of Whatton, in lieu of the vicarial tithes. It consists of as many manors as it has owners, and was formerly a chapelry, but its *chapel* was in ruins many years ago, and a writer in the 62d vol. of the Gentleman's Magazine, says, "part of the walls still remain; these are visible under a modern built house of brick and tile, and the chapel itself is now a common alehouse." The inhabitants now use Whatton church, and pay one-third of the church rate. After the Conquest, Aslacton was of the fees of Walter D'Agincourt, Ilbert de Lacy, and Gilbert de Gand, and a portion of it was long held by a family of its own name, and from them passed to the Cranmers, of whom was ARCHBISHOP CRANMER, the great church reformer and martyr, who was born here in 1489, and became in 1532, the first Protestant archbishop of Canterbury. The life of this eminent prelate is the subject of a volume, therefore a brief notice of his last sufferings, under the persecution of Queen Mary, must here suffice. "After condemnation, he was induced to sign a recantation; but having nobly denied his error, and withdrawn that confession, he was condemned to the stake, at which he suffered on the 21st of March, 1556. To this he was brought without any official notice, though he had reason to expect it; and when tied to it was obliged to listen to all the charges and aspersions of Dr. Cole; but Cranmer boldly replied, 'I believe every word and sentence taught by our Saviour Christ, his apostles, and the prophets of the Old and New Testament; but as to the pope, I refuse him as Christ's enemy, or Antichrist, with all his false doctrines.' So great was his sorrow for his recantation, and so determined was his spirit at the last hour, that he calmly held his right hand in the flames till it dropt off, saying, 'this hand has offended;' and this he was enabled to, as his executioners had taken care to keep up a slow fire, in order that he should suffer the utmost pain of his punishment, as a proof of their regard for *Christian mercies.*—It has been stated that after his whole body had been reduced to ashes, his heart was found entire, and untouched by the fire, which by some of the bystanders was considered as an argument in favour of his hearty love of the truth; whilst others looked upon it as a proof of the heretical obduracy of that vital part, which would not yield even to the warm argument of a blazing Catholic fire!"

The site of the *manor house*, which was the seat of Archbishop Cranmer and many of his ancestors, is now occupied by the farm-house of Mr. Wm. Green. Near it may still be distinctly traced several moats, islands, and other remains of the pleasure grounds, and at a short distance is a raised walk which leads to Orston, and is yet called *Cranmer's walk.* At the west end, on crossing a moat, the visitor may ascend a square mount of considerable elevation, and from thence have an extensive prospect. Here are also two other mounts, said to have been raised by the archbishop, but they have been greatly reduced by some of the former owners of the estate. On one of them, tradition says the archbishop "was wont to sit and survey the surrounding country, and listen to the tunable bells of Whatton." In 1816, *John Marriott* left 20s. yearly out of his farm at Aslacton, to be distributed in bread at Christmas.

WHATTON.

Blyton James, shoemaker
Bousfield Rev. H. Newham, B.A.
Caunt William, saddler
Dove Alice, vict. & shopkpr
Greaseley John, gardener
Heathcote Mrs. Ann
Hooper William, butcher
Mason William, blacksmith

Oliver Thomas, gardener
Parnham Thomas, victualler and gamekeeper
Parnham William, tailor
Pell William, joiner, and beerhouse
Riddish John, baker and flour dealer
Sharrack Robert, shoemaker

Talbott Fras. veterinary surgeon
Tyler William, joiner
Upton John, corn miller

Farmers and Yeomen.

Bower Wm.
Carpendale G.
Clay Eliz.
Foster Richard
Gelsthorpe J.
Hooper Wm.
Innocent Geo.

Mann Thos.
Mason Wm.
Morley Joseph
Smith John
Walker Henry
Watson Robert
Wheatley Thos.

CARRIERS, George Moss, carrier to Nottingham, Wed. & Sat.; William Tutbury, to Newark, Wed., and to Nottingham, Sat., 5 morn.

ASLACTON.

Bates James, bricklayer & shopkeeper
Dawn John, tailor
Franks Thomas, shoemaker
Freeman Thomas, land and bldg. surveyor

Freeman William, painter and shopkeeper
Hand John, blacksmith
Keyworth, Robert, maltster
Marriott John, schoolmaster
Morley George, tailor
Morley William, baker
Oliver William, corn miller
Payling Robert, butcher
Pepper John, shoemaker and beerhouse
Porter Mr. William
Smith Richard, shoemaker
Thornton Thomas, vict. Grey Hound
Wilson Richard, wheelwright.

Farmers and Yeomen.

Chettle J.
Edge
Clifton Edward,
Lane Ends
Grant Richard
Green William

Grim Keyworth John
Marriott Mary
Oliver John
Porter Henry
Upton Thomas
Walker ——

WIVERTON (EXTRA PAROCHIAL.)

WIVERTON HALL, with a demesne of 1002 acres of fine grazing and arable land, forms an extra parochial liberty, bounded on the E. by the river Smite, and on the W. by Tithby parish, and distant 2½ miles S. of Bingham. After the Conquest, Wiverton, or as it is commonly called, *Werton,* was of several fees, and gave name to a resident family who became its principal owners, and gave part of it to Welbeck and Thurgarton monasteries. The whole manor subsequently passed to the Bassets, Brets, and Caltofts. The heiress of the latter carried it in marriage to *Sir Wm. Chaworth,* in the reign of Edward III., previous to which, Thoroton says it had become utterly depopulated, though, under the date 1257, he found "many mentions in the ledger book of Thurgarton priory, of the church of Wiverton;" but he never could discover any other document to show that there ever was a church here, except what referred to the domestic chapel in the house, which was then in ruins. In the reign of Henry VI., *Sir Thomas Chaworth,* by his marriage, became possessed of the estates of the ancient and wealthy families of Aylesbury, Pabenham, Engaine, Basset, and Kayne, "and he made a park here, in which he built a large and beautiful mansion, sufficiently in the castellated style to be a garrison for the King in the civil wars which occasioned its ruin;" since then, Thoroton says, (1677,) "most of it has been pulled down and removed, except the old uncovered *gatehouse*, which yet remains a solitary memorial of departed grandeur and ancient hospitality." But since our author's time, the remains of the old castellated mansion have, with some modern additions, been converted into a comfortable gothic dwelling, which is now occupied by *John George Chaworth Musters, Esq.*, the son of the present owner, John Musters, Esq. of Colwick Hall, who obtained all the extensive possessions of the Chaworths by marrying *Mary Chaworth*, the sole heiress of that ancient family, who died Feb. 12, 1832.— She was the lady to whom the late Lord Byron was so passionately attached, and to whom his early poems are addressed; she, however, preferred Mr. Musters to the "lame bashful boy lord," and perhaps one cause which swayed her in this choice was his Lordship's notorious impetuosity, and her knowledge that her paternal grandfather had been killed in a duel with William, the fifth Lord Byron. After her marriage, her husband assumed the name of *Chaworth*, which he continued till the death of the late *Mr. Musters*, when he re-assumed that name, and the name of Chaworth ceased in the county.

BROXTOW HUNDRED

Is the most populous division of the county, though it contains some of the wildest tracts of Sherwood Forest, (see p. 35,) and does not form more than one-seventh part of the whole extent of the shire. It is bounded on the south by Nottingham and the Trent, on the west and north by Derbyshire, and on the east by the Hundreds of Bassetlaw and Thurgarton. It averages about seven miles in breadth from east to west, and 17 miles in length from north to south, stretching southward from Pleasley and Mansfield to the vicinity of Nottingham, and including the populous market town of Mansfield, and many large villages busily employed in the *lace and hosiery manufactures*. It is noted for its *lime and freestone quarries*, and on its western side are a few *coal mines*. Its clay is of an excellent quality either for *bricks* or *tiles*, and some of it near Mansfield is used in making coarse earthenware. It has generally a deep sandy *soil*, especially on its eastern side, where there are yet several large tracts of open forest land, though many extensive enclosures and plantations have been made during the last forty years. (Vide p. 39.) The *rivers Maun and Erwash* rise within its limits, and the latter forms its western boundary for about fourteen miles. It is also intersected by the Trent navigation, by the canal from Cromford to Nottingham, by the *railway* from Pinxton to Mansfield, (see p. 51 to 55,) and by the turnpike from Sheffield to Nottingham and London. In

Domesday Book it is called *Broculston Wapentac*, and most o it is in the *Honour of Peverel*. (Vide p. 22 & 138.) From an early period it has been partitioned into two *divisions*, under two chief constables or *Bailiffs*, who gave for their offices or *Bailiwicks* in the reign of John, half a mark (6s. 8d.) and in that of Edward I. nine marks! which was then considered a very extravagant sum, and was much complained of. The POPULATION of Broxtow Hundred has nearly doubled itself during the last thirty years, in which it has encreased from 35,274 to 66,187 souls, living in 28 parishes, of which the following is an enumeration, shewing the number of persons in each in 1801, 1821, and 1831, and the ANNUAL VALUE of the lands and buildings, as assessed for the property tax in 1815. Marked thus * are in the North Division.

ANN. VAL. £.	PARISHES.	POPULATION IN			ANN. VAL. £.	PARISHES.	POPULATION IN		
		1801.	1821.	1831.			1801.	1821.	1831.
*2104	Annesley with Felley	359	326	335	*1364	Linby	515	439	352
356		33	71	67	*13,326	Mansfield	5,988	7,861	9,426
*5276	Arnold	2768	3572	4054	*4527	Mansfield Woodhouse	1,112	1,598	1,859
3523	Attenborough P. Chilwell and	638	623	892	*1883	Nuthall	378	485	509
2328	Toton	175	208	202	*1019	Papplewick	709	593	359
*5239	Basford	2,124	3,599	6,325	1532	Newstead	143	174	159
4139	Beeston	948	1,534	2,530	5208	Radford	2,269	4,806	9,806
3157	Bilborough	307	291	330	*1556	Skegby	416	584	656
2444	Bramcote	354	441	562	*2513	Selston	833	1,321	1,580
*2116	Bulwell	1,585	2,105	2,611	2392	Stapleford	748	1,104	1,533
1322	Cossal	353	317	341	1600	Strelley	259	350	426
1707	Eastwood	735	1,206	1,395		Sutton-in-Ashfield,			
8350	Greasley	2,968	3,673	4,583	*6976	Hucknall-under-Huthwaite	2801	3,943	4,805
*—†	Fulwood Extra P.		..	12			519	712	929
*3119	Hucknall Torkard	1,407	1,940	2,200	*2354	Teversall	333	416	400
					1952	Trowell	235	464	402
*3708	Kirkby in Ashfield	1,002	1,420	2,032	2929	Wollaton	838	571	537
8997	Lenton*	893	1,240	3,077					
					112,501	Total	35,274	48,823	66,187

*, Exclusive of 10 debtors in the *Peverel Prison* at Lenton, in 1831.

† The valuation of Fulwood (*Extra Parochial*) is included with the parish of Sutton-in-Ashfield. Brewhouse-yard, Standard-hill, and Nottingham Castle, are extra-parochial, and in the North Division of Broxtow. (See pages 76 and 123.)

MANSFIELD PARISH,

AT the north end of this Hundred, is about five miles in length and three in breadth, and comprises 4287A. 3R. 36P. of enclosed land, and nearly 2,000 acres of the open forest. Its surface is generally a fertile sand, and is picturesquely broken into hill and dale, and watered by the Maun, the Meden, the Flood Dike, (see page 415,) and several smaller streams. It possesses inexhaustible beds of *red and white freestone*, of which there have long been many extensive quarries ; and amongst its botanical productions may be found that rare plant, the *Deadly-night-Shade*. Its *population*, by the influence of the *lace and hosiery manufactures*, has been encreased since the year 1801, from 5,988 to 9,426 souls, living in 1889 houses, and consisting of 1,998 families, of whom 1,400 are employed in trade, manufacture, or handicraft, and 144 in agriculture, and the remaining 454 are either engaged in professional pursuits or unemployed. According to the census taken in 1831, the number of males is 4,462, and females 4,964, and there were then 19 houses building, and 109 uninhabited, swelling the total number of dwellings to 2,017 ; most of which form the populous town of Mansfield, and the remainder are dispersed in the HAMLETS of *Dalestorth, Pleasley-Hill, Radmanthwaite, Moorhaigh, Penniment Houses, Bleakhills, Oakham, Bury Hill*, and *Littleworth*.

MANSFIELD, the capital of this parish and of the Hundred of Broxtow, is a very ancient, large, but straggling market town, distant 14 miles N. by W. of Nottingham, 13 miles W.N.W. of Southwell, 12 miles S. by W. of Worksop, 9 miles E.N.E. of Alfreton, 24 miles S.E. of Sheffield, and 139 miles N. by W. of London. It stands principally on the north-west bank of the river *Maun*, from which it has its name, and has diverging from its market-place four *streets* of considerable length, which communicate with several shorter streets, and with many courts, lanes, and alleys. From the great age of many of its houses, and the gloomy colour of the stone of which most of them are built, the town has generally a sombre aspect ; and until a few years ago, was proverbially "dirty and badly paved," and disgraced by several obstructions in its most public thoroughfares,—the word *police* being then unknown in the lexicography of its inhabitants ; but in 1823, two *Acts of Parliament* were obtained, under which it has been well paved and lighted with gas, its principal avenues widened, and such other improvements effected as have raised it to the rank of a clean and commodious town, though it is not very compact, but stretches its long arms on the four roads that converge in the market-place, which has also been considerably improved and enlarged by the removal of the *Spittaller's gates*, a pile of ancient building, that caused a dangerous contraction in the entrance from the Nottingham road. These improvements have, however, been such a heavy tax upon the inhabitants, that many of the best houses are now unoccupied, but we trust that the Commissioners will in a short time make a considerable

reduction in the *rate*, as the projected alterations have nearly
all been made, and the work of cleansing and paving extended
to every part of the town. As at Nottingham, the lace and
hosiery manufactures (see p. 193) have here been greatly extended during the last thirty years, and the population has in
consequence nearly doubled itself. About 400 *new houses*
have been erected here during the last ten years, most of them
of stone, from the prolific quarries in the vicinity, and many of
them forming large and handsome villas, occupied generally by
their owners. The exterior of the *Moot-Hall* (built in 1752, by
Lady Oxford) was re-chiselled in 1831, and the whole so
cleansed and beautified as to give it the appearance of a new
edifice. The great room (48 feet by 17) is used for Assemblies,
and also for County Meetings; but balls and assemblies are
occasionally held at the *Bowling Green Inn*. The neighbouring Magistrates hold a *Petty Session* on every alternate
Thursday, at the Swan Inn, where there is a subscription *News
Room*, well supplied with London and country papers, &c.
The other sources of amusement are the *Theatre*, a small
building in Mr. McLellan's yard, in Church-street; the *Harmonic Society*, which was established about 50 years ago, at the
Nag's Head, where it meets every Thursday evening, has an
annual concert, and is supported by about seventy subscribers;
and the four *Circulating Libraries*, one of which, at Mr. Collinson's, is the property of a number of subscribers, and was
established about four years ago. Those who wish for the
salubrious exercise of immersion, may be accommodated at the
Cold Bath, which occupies a picturesque situation, and is approached by a short and pleasant walk from Leeming-street,
above the Rock Valley; indeed, the walks on every side of the
town afford a pleasing variety of scenery, in which may be
seen the wild forest heath, bordering upon the highly cultivated
inclosures, the winding streams of the Maun and the Flood
Dike; the stupendous *Railway Bridge*, (vide p. 54); numerous
stone quarries; and several extensive *cotton mills*, with their
capacious dams of crystal water, reflecting the buildings and
the adjacent hills. At the top of Ratcliffegate the tourist will
find many of those domestic excavations in the rocks, where
the modern *Troglodytes* have their huts, and even their gardens
formed in the bosom of the steril stone; and in some parts
the incautious visitor may run the risk of stepping down a
chimney.

The MARKET is held on Thursday, and is well supplied with
corn and provisions, the former of which is sold by sample.
FAIRS are held on July 10th, and on the 2nd Thursday in October, for horses, cattle, and sheep, and the latter is also a considerable mart for cheese. A *cattle and sheep market* is now
held on the 2nd Thursday in every month, and a *hiring for
servants* on the 1st or 2nd Thursday in November, as fixed by

the chief constable. The RACES, held on the 11th and 12th of July, are rising into considerable repute, being now supported by the liberal contributions of the Duke of Portland, the neighbouring gentry, and the representatives of the county. The COURSE is on the forest, near SHERWOOD HALL, a large sequestered mansion, with extensive and tasteful pleasure grounds, now belonging to that veteran of the turf, Thomas Holdsworth, Esq. the great cotton spinner of Manchester, who occupies it as his racing establishment, under the superintendence of Mr. Wm. Beresford.

TRADE.—The seven large *cotton mills* in the vicinity of the town, give employment to upwards of 700 of the inhabitants; indeed, one of them alone employs about 160 individuals, and has no fewer than 2,400 spindles, with the necessary carding and roving machinery. Here are also upwards of 700 *stocking frames* employed in making silk and cotton hosiery, and several hundred *bobbin net machines*, each employing one or two hands. The town likewise derives much of its wealth from the *malting* and *stone* trades; and William Brodhurst, Esq. of *Gilcroft House*, within the boundaries of the town, is said to be the largest maltster in England. Here are also several corn mills, three iron foundries, two tan yards, a coarse pottery, a brush manufactory, a mustard mill, and several fellmongers, wood turners, machine makers, millwrights, nail makers, hat manufacturers, dyers, bleachers, &c. &c. Two late ingenious mechanics of this town deserve a notice in its history, viz.— John Rogers, who made great improvements in the *double point net machine*, and James Murray who invented the *circular saw*, for which his employer, Mr. Brown, obtained a patent.

ANCIENT HISTORY.—There is no doubt that Mansfield is justified in boasting a very early antiquity; but the story that the *Counts of Mansfield*, in Germany, came here to attend at the tournament of King Arthur's Round Table, and gave their name to it, is considered as a mere fable. It was anciently called *Maunsfield*, and no doubt had that name from the river *Maun*, which rises near Annessley, and flows round the south and east side of the town. That it was a *British*, and afterwards a *Roman Station*, is generally believed; indeed its latter occupancy is proved by the discovery of many *Roman coins* of Vespasian, Constantine, Marcus Aurelius, and others of the lower empire; by the exploratory camps, which are numerous in its vicinity; and particularly by the discovery of a *Roman villa*, near Mansfield Woodhouse. (See p. 18.) During the Saxon Heptarchy, Mansfield appears to have been a favourite, though only temporary, residence of the Mercian Kings, in consequence of its central situation in Sherwood forest, then well supplied with beasts of chase. In the time of Edward the Confessor, it was royal demesne, and was continued as such by William the Conqueror, and by his son, William Rufus, whose

fondness for forests hastened his death, being accidentally shot by
an arrow, in the New Forest, near London. The latter
monarch gave the *church of Mansfield* and all its possessions to
Lincoln Cathedral. The *manor* was granted by King Stephen
to Ranulph de Gernon, Earl of Chester; but that line ending
in co-heiresses, it was regranted by Henry III. to the Hastings,
and to John Comyn, Earl of Buchan, previous to which it had
been a favourite resort of the Norman Sovereigns. The well-
known story of Henry II. and the Miller of Mansfield, (see p.
36) it is unnecessary to repeat, though we suspect the event (if
it ever did happen) to have taken place at a much later period,
at least the rhyming tale preserved by Percy in his Reliques is
of much latter composition, and so replete with uncouth in-
decency, that we are surprised even a fondness for antiquity
could have induced the learned bishop to insert it in his interesting miscellany. The inhabitants, however, still consider
the honour of the town connected with the antiquity of the story;
and tradition says, that the *King's mill* and the house, which
are situated nearly a mile and a half from the town, in the deep
glen that is crossed by the Railway bridge or viaduct, were
built on the site of the house and mill where the King was entertained. The miller's house stood partly in the parish of
Sutton, but has just been rebuilt, and is now wholly in the
parish of Mansfield. In the reign of John, the inhabitants paid
15 marks to the crown for the right of common in Clipston
Park, as they were wont to do before its enclosure; and by
paying five marks to Henry VIII. they obtained a charter for a
weekly market on Monday, and the privilege of having *House-
boat* and *Hayboat*, in the forest of Sherwood. In the time of
Edward III. they had common pasturage in a place called
Woodhouse Wood. Richard II., in 1377, granted them a *fair*
on the feast of St. Peter. Henry VIII. granted this manor to
the Earl of Surrey, for his gallant conduct at Floddenfield; but
the King afterwards gave him some other lands in exchange
for it; after which it went to the then Dukes of Newcastle, who
from hence took the title of *Viscount Mansfield*.[*] From them
it passed by descent to the Portland family, and its present lord,
the Duke of Portland, (see p. 451) generously allows the resident
gentry to kill and preserve the game, for which purpose they
employ two keepers.

The MANOR CASTOMS of Mansfield are curious in many
instances; and it is recorded in an old forest book that the

[*] The title of VISCOUNT MANSFIELD became extinct on the death of the last
Duke of Newcastle, of the Cavendish family, in 1691. (Vide p. 457.) William
Murray, 4th son of Viscount Stormont, in Scotland, was created EARL OF MANS-
FIELD, in 1776, and that title is now borne by his descendant, Wm. Murray, the
present Earl of Mansfield, Viscount Stormont, in Scotland, and Lord Lieutenant
of Clacmannanshire.

" Tenaunts be fre of blode and lefully may marye them after ther willes as well men as women. That the eyres (heirs) as sone as they bene borne byn of full age. That lands are departabil, betwex sonnes; or doughters if ther be no sonne ;"— this seems a remnant of the old Saxon custom of *Gavelkind.* A *Court, Baron* is held once in three weeks, and a *Court Leet,* or great court, twice a year, within a few days after Michaelmas and Lady-Day. At these courts all the copyholders owe suit and service, and they each pay 6d. yearly for their respective copyholds, be they small or large. The jury of the half-yearly courts meet at the Moot-Hall, and dine at the Swan Inn. The *Swainmote* Court, for the forest of Sherwood, used to be held here, but all that now remains of the custom is an annual feast, on *Holyrood Day.* (See p. 41.) The jury for that part of the forest within the manor, is appointed at the Court Leet. The *boundaries of the parish* are perambulated yearly on Rogation Monday, by the vicar and other parishioners. According to a memorandum, dated 1642, " they begin at Ransdale nook, take in the Straight-hill, pass along Packman's-gate, and by the side of Lyndhurst to Lincolndale; cross the Nottingham road, going by the side of Sutton field, and encompassing the New field, whence they return through the Westfield lane." Thos. Walkden, Esq., of Ratcliffegate, is STEWARD of the Duke of Portland's manors of Mansfield, Bolsover, Clipstone, and Sutton-cum-Lound, and also BURROGATE for proving wills, and granting administrations within the dean of Lincoln's *Rectorial Court,* of Mansfield, which extends its jurisdiction over the whole manor and parish. At the Domesday Survey, the King's great manor of *Mansfield* included Woodhouse and the *Berues,* or hamlets of Sutton and Skegby, and had *soc* in many of the manors in the Hundred of Bassetlaw. The lascivious Queen Isabella, in the reign of her son, Edward III., (see p. 84) claimed in this royal manor, " view of frank pledge, and emendation of the assize of bread, and ale broken, pillory, tumbrell, gallows, wick, weyf, and a market every Thursday." Many large patches of the FOREST LAND have been taken into cultivation by persons who pay a trifling annual rent per acre to the lord of the manor; but by a recent regulation, no person is now allowed to enclose more than one acre. Several poor families have built themselves houses upon their little plots, and now produce an abundance of potatoes and vegetables, both for their own tables and for the market; the soil being a deep sand, well suited for the growth of roots, &c.

The parish CHURCH, dedicated to St. Peter, stands near the Maun, at the foot of the street to which it gives name. Though but a low edifice, it is large and commodious, having a middle and two side aisles, and being 93 feet in length, and 63 feet in breadth. It is in the later gothic style, and was partly burnt down in 1304,* along with many of the adjacent houses, but was soon afterwards re-edified, and is now in good preservation. Its body is supported by handsome pillars; over each side aisle there is a spacious gallery; and at the west end a fine-toned organ of 14 stops, which was erected in 1795, at the expence of 200 guineas. In the preceding year, the inhabitants, by paying £15. 16s. 3d., obtained the archbishop's license not only to erect this organ, but also to build the new gallery over the south aisle, to remove the pulpit to its present situation, and to convert a private pew into a churching one, &c. Several other faculties have been obtained for the erection of other lofts, and copies of them, as well as a copious abstract of the numerous charities belonging to the parish, have recently been written upon the 27 pannels in the fronts of the galleries. The whole was thoroughly cleansed and beautified in 1831, when a new gallery for the Sunday scholars was raised on the site of the ancient and decayed oak pews under the north aisle. The tower is surmounted by a small spire, 44 yards in height, and contains eight tuneable bells, cast betwixt the years 1610 and 1726. A set of musical *chimes*, purchased in 1762, play upon the bells at the hours of four, nine, and twelve. In the windows are some remains of painted glass, and in the aisles are many mural monuments of stone, and some brass plates, both inscribed and armorial. In a list of the church property, dated 1634, we find " a desk to which was chained the book of martyrs." The *living* is a *vicarage*, valued in the King's books at £7. 7s. 6d., and is now enjoyed by the Rev. Thomas Leeson Cursham, D. C. L. The Dean of Lincoln is the patron and appropriator, and receives in lieu of the *rectorial* tithes a composition of 8s. per acre from all the enclosed land in the parish. There were anciently in the church ten *chantries*. Hid behind a pew lies the effigy of *Lady Cecily Flogan*, who lived in an ancient house in Church-street, now the White Hart Inn, and bequeathed in 1521, that house and many other tenements, &c. to the church, for a priest to sing mass for her soul, and those of her family. Philip and Mary granted all the possessions of these chantries, and the property left by Lady Flogan, to the vicar and church-wardens, in trust that they should find a *chaplain* to celebrate divine service for ever. This property has long been intermixed with other lands and tenements left for the support of the *grammar school*, and the whole now produces upwards of £300 a-year, of which ⅔rds are paid to the vicar; and the master has ⅔rds of the remainder, and the usher ⅓rd. Two small portions of land, left by Lady Flogan, were, pursuant to

* FIRES.—Mansfield appears to have been visited by two other conflagrations, for Harrod says, in 1546, " Coll. Davy wilfully set the town on fire, whereby was burned 131 bays of buildings, and she was hanged at the next assizes, at Nottingham for it." And in 1581, " there was a casual fire in Stockwellgate, whereby was burned 150 bays of houses and old Dunstan's wife."

her will, held by tenants, who in stead of paying rent kept a *bull and boar*, for the use of the parish: The Rev. Geo. Heaton is the *curate*, John Mark Sellors, the *parish clerk*; Joseph Webster, the *organist*; and George Revill, the *sexton*.

CHAPELS.—There are in the town six dissenting places of worship, which are generally neat and commodious, and numerously attended. The *Unitarian chapel* is an ancient stone building, approached by a long narrow passage from Stockwellgate: It is now under the ministry of the Rev. John Williams, and has a library of 200 volumes. The *Independent chapel*, built in 1795, and enlarged in 1829, has a burial ground, and a Sunday school with 200 scholars. The Rev. Robert Weaver is the pastor. The *Quaker's meeting house* is a plain stone fabric, erected about forty years ago, in a retired situation, at the head of Chapel-alley. Its burial ground is partly cultivated as a flower garden, and its congregation is numerous and respectable. The *Baptist chapel*, in Stockwellgate, was purchased some years ago, of Mr. Brodhurst, and the Rev. Joseph Austin is now its minister. The *Wesleyan Methodist chapel* occupies an elevated site, at the foot of Ratcliffegate, and was originally a large family mansion, in which it is said the accomplished Earl of Chesterfield was born; but which was purchased in 1812, by the Methodists, who pulled down the centre part of the building, and built upon its site the present spacious chapel, leaving the wings standing for the residence of the two ministers. The *Primitive Methodists* have a small chapel in Union-street, which they have occupied about 8 years.

The GAS WORKS are situated at Limetree-place, close to the river Maun, and were built under the powers of an act of Parliament, passed in 1823. The whole is judiciously planned. The condensing pipes are laid in the bed of the river, and the gas engendered here is as pure as that of any town in the kingdom. The total cost of the works was about £5000, raised in shares of £27. 10s. each. The gasometer will hold 18,000 cubic feet. Considering the price of coal at Mansfield, the charge to the consumers of gas is very moderate, being only at the rate of 10s. per 1000 cubic feet, subject to a discount of 5 per cent. on all sums from £5 to £10; of 20 per cent. on those from £10 to £20, and of 20 per cent. on those above £20. Mr. Stephen Simpson is the manager and engineer. The works were finished in 1824, and the town was first lit with their lucid vapour on the 10th of July, in that year. The town has no public *water-works*, but is well supplied with springs and pumps. Four *fire engines* for the use of the inhabitants, are stationed in a building in Toothill-lane, erected in 1815. The RAILWAY from Pinxton to Portland wharf, at Mansfield, is already noticed in the general history of the county, at pages 54 and 55.

CHARITIES.—Ample provision is made here for the education

2 z

and relief of the poor, there being in the town three endowed
schools, several Sunday-schools conducted by gratuitous teachers, many benefactions left for the periodical relief of the indigent, and several benevolent societies, to which the principal inhabitants subscribe liberally. The commissioners
appointed by Parliament to enquire into the state of public
charities in England, (see p. 60,) have not yet published their
report of those at Mansfield, where it is believed there have
been several abuses of public trust, and where the property,
the accounts, and the distributions of some posthumous charities,
have been for years so blended together, as to render them now
undistinguishable; and though the pannels around the church
galleries have been covered with what is called "a correct abstract of the charities belonging to the parish of Mansfield," nothing is said about the present annual value of the land, and
some other trust property.

The FREE GRAMMAR SCHOOL, founded in 1561, by Queen
Elizabeth, stands in the church yard. The original endowment is unknown, no specification of property appearing in the
letters patent, incorporating the vicar and churchwardens of
Mansfield governors of its possessions. This probably arises
from the same persons being previously incorporated by Philip
and Mary, in 1556, as governors of the chantry lands and
buildings, which, after the dissolution of the monasteries, were
given for the support of a chaplain in the church, as has already
been noticed. After much litigation betwixt the two masters
and the governors, it was determined in the Court of Equity, in
1682, that in future the rents of the church and school property
should be divided as already specified. This property includes
97 acres of assart land, called the "Eight Men's Intake," and
several other lands, tenements, and quarries, together with
£581. 17s. 11d., three per cent. Consols, arising from fines
taken upon leases. Carlisle, who wrote in 1818, says "the
master and usher have received as their proportion of fines for
the last 20 years, a sum of not less than from £1500 to £2000."
The school is now of no benefit to the poor, being only free for
the classics, and five guineas per annum being charged by the
usher for teaching each scholar the other branches of education. Amongst the eminent men who have been pupils here,
we may enumerate the late Dr. Halifax, Bishop of Gloucester;
Dr. Wylde, a prebendary of Southwell; Dr. Stanhope, Bishop
of Sodar and Man; and the 4th Earl of Chesterfield, whose
epistolary writings are universally admired. The Rev. Wm.
Bowerbank has many years held the office of *head master*, and
Mr. Hodgson Brailsford has lately been appointed usher. Archbishop Sterne, in 1673, founded two *scholarships* of £10 per
annum each for two poor Nottinghamshire scholars, in Jesus
College, Cambridge, and directed that one of them should be a
native of Mansfield.

CLERKSON'S CHARITY SCHOOL is a large and lofty house, near Portland Wharf, built in 1731, pursuant to the will of Mrs. Faith Clerkson, who in 1725, bequeathed £2000 for the foundation of two schools, and for other charitable uses, in Mansfield and Mansfield Woodhouse. After purchasing about two acres of land, and erecting the school and two houses thereon, the surplus was expended in the purchase of 233A. 3R. of land at Everton, near Bawtry, now let for upwards of £200 a-year, half of which is appropriated to Mansfield Woodhouse. The master and mistress who reside in the schoolhouse here, have only £40 per annum, for teaching 35 boys and 27 girls, who have each a suit of clothes allowed yearly by the trustees. The teachers have also a small garden, and £2 yearly for coals, but the large croft of nearly 2 acres, which belonged to them and which adjoined the school, has been sold to the Railway Company, and is now included in their store yard, called Portland Wharf. A Mr. Toplis, one of the trustees, died in 1831, after which it was discovered that he was owing to this charity no less than £600, which has not, and never will be paid! There should be three trustees, but they are all dead, and no fresh ones have yet been appointed, though the nomination rests with the vicar and the assistants of the Grammar School.

THOMPSON'S and BRUNT'S SCHOOL, in Toothill-lane, is a large and handsome building, erected in 1786, agreeable to the will of Mr. Charles Thompson, who endowed it with £600, three per cent consols, to be vested with the trustees of Mr. Samuel Brunt, who had previously left £4 a-year, out of his charity estate, for the education of poor boys born in Mansfield. The master now receives from the trustees £32, and the mistress £12 per annum, for which they teach 40 boys and 40 girls.

An INFANT SCHOOL has lately been established at the Independent chapel, and is supported partly by annual subscriptions, amounting to about £40. It has 150 scholars, who each pay 2d. per week.

BRUNT'S CHARITY is the richest of all the Mansfield benefactions, consisting of lands and buildings in the town, in Nottingham Market place, at East Bridgeford, and at Claypool, in Lincolnshire, worth about £1000 per annum, and bequeathed in 1709, by Mr. Samuel Brunt, for the following yearly distributions,—viz: 20s. to the minister of the Unitarian chapel, and 40s. in bread to the poor of his congregation; £4 for educating poor children; £4 for apprenticing one poor boy; and £4 each to as many poor parishioners, who do not receive any other alms, as the surplus income of the estate will extend to, and the whole to be paid in equal moieties at Lady-day and Michaelmas. Upwards of 220 poor persons now receive £4 yearly from this charity. The trustees are William Brodhurst, Wm. Paulson, Henry Hollins, James Heygate, and Abraham Booth, Esqrs.

and we understand both them and their predecessors have
faithfully discharged their duty.

MR. CHARLES THOMPSON, who left in 1784, £600 to the
above-named school, also bequeathed £600 in the three
per Cent. Consolidated Bank Annuities, in augmentation
of Brunt's charity; and £400 in the same Stocks, for providing yearly ten poor men and ten poor women with coats and
petticoats. He also left £100 to the "Society's Mill, in Mansfield," but the Society failed many years ago, and the windmill, which stands near the Rock Houses, is now private property. This charitable individual lived to the age of 70. He
was long resident in Persia, as agent to the Russian Company,
and afterwards settled at Lisbon, where he had the good fortune
to save his life in 1755, when that city was destroyed by an
earthquake. Having experienced various changes of fortune,
he at length realised a competency, and settled in his native
place. Being often shocked at the sight of the neglected,
mutilated, and too often dishonoured remnants of mortality in
churchyards, he directed, in a most whimsical will, that he
should be buried on Sherwood Forest, about one mile east of
the town, where his remains were accordingly deposited, and
the spot afterwards planted with trees, and encompassed with a
circular wall. It occupies an elevated situation, and is known
to every frequenter of the forest by the name of Thompson's
Grave.

HEATH'S ALMSHOUSES, on the south side of the town, consists of twelve comfortable dwellings for as many poor people,
half of whom are to be members of the Society of Friends,
and the remainder of the Established Church. Each inmate receives £1 monthly, and two tons of coals and a
gown yearly. Elizabeth Heath, the foundress, died in 1693,
and lies buried under a tomb in the hospital yard, where many
of the former alms-people have also been interred. The endowment consists of land near Chesterfield, Duffield, Ripley,
and North Wingfield, all in Derbyshire. William Ellis and
others are the trustees.

JOSEPH SALES, by will, dated 1795, left after the death of
his wife, which happened in 1815, £1000, three per Cent.
Consols, to the vicar, in trust, for him to distribute the dividends half-yearly amongst six poor honest housekeepers of the
age of 50 or upwards, who have never received parochial relief.
JOHN BOLD, in 1726, gave £10 a-year out of Brownlow Close,
in Mansfield, to be distributed on January 1st, amongst 40 poor
housekeepers, who have never received parochial alms. Ro-
LAND DAND, in 1670, left Bowser's Land in the Westfield,
containing 2A. 1R. 27P, and 3 roods in Knavesgreave Close, to
the vicar and churchwardens, in trust, that they give yearly
8 Grey Cloth Coats to six poor men of Mansfield, and two
poor men of Mansfield Woodhouse. RICHARD GIRDLER, in

1665, left 20s. yearly, out of Bury-lane Close, to provide six coats for the poor. JOHN LITCHFIELD, gent., in 1693, left 40s. out of his house in Mansfield, to be distributed in bread on " St. John's Day in Christmas, and St. John's in Midsummer." Dr. LAYCOCK, at some date unknown, left £5 yearly out of Bath Closes, to provide ten petticoats for as many poor women on All Saints' Day. Two yearly sums of 20s. are paid out of the Ruffs and out of a Close in Bishop's Piece Lane, and are also distributed in petticoats. Eight small *Rent Charges*, amounting to £3. 1s. 8d. yearly, and bequeathed by as many individuals out of different tenements in the town, are distributed in *bread* on Good Friday, and St. Thomas' Day, by the Churchwardens. The WORKHOUSE is on the Nottingham road, and its number of inmates is generally about 60. The overseers meet in the vestry-room, in the Market-place, but we understand they intend to build a new parochial office, with a magistrates' meeting room, and a lock-up house attached. The amount of the *poor-rates* in the year ending March 1829, was £3950; in 1830, £3915, and in 1831, £3550, collected in six rates, at 1s. 3d. in the pound, on an estimated annual rental of £12,812. The sum paid to the *county rates*, in 1831, was £186. 15s. 7d. Mr. Joseph Johnson is the *governor*, and John Paulson the *assistant* overseer.

The CONSTABLES are John Freeman, (lessee of market tolls,) and William Winter, for the parish; and John Mcham, for the manor of Mansfield. William Powell is the *pinder*. Thos. Lees and James Daws are the *gamekeepers*, and Sebastian Sales is the *town crier*. Mr. Joseph Platts is the *sheriff's officer*, and William Cooke the *chief constable* for the North Division of Broxtow Hundred, and the former collects the Mansfield Improvement Rate.

SAVINGS' BANK, &c.—Though the poor rates here are higher than at many other places, there are in the town several provident institutions, at the head of which we may place the Savings' Bank, established in 1818, and now containing deposits amounting to upwards of £32,000, belonging to about 800 individuals and 44 *Friendly Societies*. The Bank is in the Swan Inn yard, and is open every Monday, from twelve to one o'clock. Mr. H. F. Shacklock is the secretary.—Besides many Sick Clubs or Friendly Societies, here is a *Lodge of Odd Fellows*, (Minerva, No. 10,) held at the Crown and Anchor. Here are likewise two *Co-operative Societies*, both established in 1830, and each having about 30 members, a retail store, and a sick fund.

EMINENT MEN.—Mansfield presents several instances of Biography worthy of a brief notice. Here was born *William Mansfield*, a Dominician friar, highly esteemed for " his great proficiency in logics, ethics, physics, and metaphysics." *Henry Ridley, M.D.*, born here in 1653, wrote " the Anatomy and

2 z 2

Physiology of the Brain," also a particular "Account of Animal Functions, and Muscular Motion." *Dr. William Chappel*, another native, and partly educated here, was Provost of Dublin College, and Bishop of Cork and Ross. He was a close reasoner and very subtle disputant. During the reign of James the First, and in the presence of that Monarch, there was a public commencement solemnized at Cambridge, when Dr. Roberts, of Trinity, being *Respondent* in St. Mary's, Mr. Chappel opposed him so closely, and with such ingenuity, that the Doctor finding himself unable to solve or to answer his arguments, actually fell into a swoon; so that the king, in order to hold up the commencement, undertook to maintain the thesis himself; but Chappel pushed him so home, that the pedantic Monarch, thanked God the opponent was his subject, and not anothers, lest he should lose the *throne* as well as the *chair*. When the rebellion broke out in Ireland in 1641, he returned to England; died at Derby; and was buried at Bilsthorpe, in this county. *Colonel Lichfield*, after distinguishing himself in the Duke of Kingston's Light Horse, during the rebellion of 1745, returned afterwards to reside at Mansfield, where he built in 1762, a large house called Ratcliffegate. The father of *Archbishop Sterne*, from whom descended the celebrated *Lawrence Sterne*, lived in Mansfield, as has been seen at page 30. The well-known and amiable *Dodsley*, the friend of Shenstone, and the protégé of Pope, was a native of Anston, but was bound apprentice to a stocking weaver, in Mansfield, from which employment, however, he decamped, and entered the service of a lady in London, where he soon rose to fame, and wrote the dramatic entertainment of the "*King and Miller of Mansfield*," which first brought him into notice, though it is but a flimsy production, full of anachronisms, for he makes guns and gunpowder in common use in the reign of Henry II., at which time the story is supposed to have happened, though some have brought it down as low as Edward IV. It met; however, with unbounded applause, and out of the profits of its exhibition, he was enabled to set up a shop, which, with his own prudence and integrity through life, laid the foundation of his subsequent good fortune.

HAMLETS IN MANSFIELD PARISH.

BLEAKHILLS, or Blackhills, 1 mile S. of Mansfield, where there are two cotton mills, one of which is called *Little Matlock*, from the picturesque beauties of this part of the vale of the Maun.

BURY-HILL, or *Berry-hill*, is 1½ mile S. by E. of Mansfield. Here is the seat of Mrs. Walker, and near it a few farm houses and cottages. A little below, and upon the Nottingham road, is a large iron foundry, with a long pile of dwellings, called FOUNDRY ROW; at a short distance west of which is HIGH

OAKHAM, where Mr. John Boaler, Mrs. Healey, and Solomon Foster, Esq., have each a pleasant mansion. Nearly half a mile W. of Bleakhills, is the HERMITAGE, the large cotton mill, and residence of James Heygate, Esq.; near which is the *Railway bridge* and the *King's mill,* already noticed. On the Nottingham road, near the south end of the town, is the extensive cotton mill and mansion of Francis Wakefield, Esq., from which there is a romantic walk to the STONE QUARRIES, where there are a number of dwellings for the workmen.

LITTLEWORTH is an ancient hamlet, forming the south-western suburb of the town, near the Bleach works.

DALESTORTH, PENNIMENT HOUSES, and MOORHAIGH, extend from 1 to 3 miles W.N.W. of Mansfield, and are approached by Bancroft lane. *Dalestorth House* is a good mansion near the Sutton road, occupied by Mr. and Mrs. Miller, as a Ladies' Boarding Academy.

PLEASELEY HILL is a pleasant hamlet on the Chesterfield road, 3 miles N.W. of Mansfield, upon the small stream called the Medin, which divides it from the village of Pleasley, in Derbyshire, where there are two extensive mills employed in spinning yarn for the hosiers. The rivulet runs through a deep and narrow glen, richly clothed with wood, through which in many places may be seen the limestone rock, broken into a thousand romantic shapes. A *Methodist Chapel* was built here in 1831.

RADMANTHWAITE, 1½ mile N. of Mansfield, is an estate con-sisting of two farms and a few cottages, belonging to William Taylor, of Radcliffe-on-Trent. A mile to the N.E. is *Nettle-worth* and *Park Hall,*—(See p. 448,)—and a little to the south-east is the large and ancient village of *Mansfield Woodhouse,* three miles E. of which, is *Clipstone Park,* and near it the ruins of *King John's Palace,*—(Vide p. 417,)—all of which are worthy the attention of the antiquary and the lover of the pic-turesque; as also is *Newstead Abbey,* distant five miles south of Mansfield.

RIOTS, STORMS, &c.—On September 5th, 1757, there was a great riot in Mansfield, in opposition to the *Militia Act.* When the magistrates of the county were assembled to prepare the lists of such as were liable to serve, a mob of 500 persons assailed them and took their papers away by force, and after-wards illtreated many gentlemen in the streets, among whom was that great patriot, Sir George Savile, of Rufford. On August 21st, 1794, the town was visited by a dreadful *thunder storm*; and on October 20th a remarkable *Aurora Borealis* was seen. On March 19th, 1795, an alarming *meteor* appeared over the town, having the appearance of a ball of fire, which suddenly burst into two, and strongly illuminated the atmosphere in its course from N. W. to S. E. On the 18th of November following, a smart shock of an *earthquake* was felt in the neigh-

bourhood. On December 25th, 1796, about ten o'clock in the
morning; there appeared floating in the atmosphere small par-
ticles of *ice*, which in an hour afterwards fell in sleet to the
ground,—a phenomenon never before seen, except in very high
latitudes. In 1798, the town displayed its loyalty by forming a
respectable corps of *Volunteers*, under the command of Captain
Greaves, and Lieutenants Wragg and Bagshaw. In the sultry
summer of 1831, Mansfield and some other places in the county
were visited by several awful storms of *thunder* and *lightning*,
and on one occasion two persons were killed, and several others
seriously injured near the west end of Stockwellgate. In the
succeeding autumn, Mansfield did not escape the storms of popular frenzy which were excited by the loss of Lord John Russell's *Reform Bill*, (in October 1831) but the mischief here
consisted principally of broken windows, and amounted only to
about £137. (See page 109 to 115.)

MANSFIELD DIRECTORY.

POST OFFICE, *Market-place*, *William Holt*, *Postmaster*.

The London and South bags are made up at 10 night; and the Sheffield, Leeds,
and North bags at ¼ past 11 morning.—(See list of mails and coaches.)

The Newark and Southwell mail gig, (Joseph Robinson,) is despatched daily
at ¼ past 4 morning; returns ¼ past 2 afternoon.

A foot postman to and from SUTTON-IN-ASHFIELD, (Dennis Whatton,) daily;
arrives 11 morning, departs 3 afternoon.

MANSFIELD WOODHOUSE foot post, (Nancy Sissons,) departs at ½ past 12 noon,
daily.

☞ Mary Barnes, of Old Post Office yard, Stockwell-gate, is *letter carrier* for
the town, and letters are conveyed to the neighbouring villages by the common
carriers.

Allcroft Jno. cowkpr. Red Lion court
Alsop Chas. cabinet mkr. Leeming street
Andrews Eliz. gent. The Hill
Ashmore Mr. Geo. Bridge st
Atkin Miss Eliz. Westgate
Austin Rev. Jph. Bap. minister & smallware dlr. Westgate
Bacon Nathl. bookpr. Cockpit
Bakewell Jph. trunk & blacking mkr. Leeming st
Ball Wm. sawyer, Brunt st
Barber Mr. John, Union st
Barks John, turner, Leeming st
Barlow Mr. John, Catlow st
Barnard Bartw. supervisor, Ratcliffe street
Battye Mrs. Martha, Belvidere st
Beardall Jas. hay, &c. dlr. Baptist hill
Bell Mrs. Sarah, Westgate
Bell Mr. Wm. Leeming st
Beresford Wm. race horse trainer to T. Holdsworth, Esq. Sherwood hall
Bickley Edw. Leeming st
Bingham Thos. carrier, Cockpit
Bingley Mrs. Ann, Cockpit
Bingley Mr. J. Belvidere st
Blackwell Hy. carrier, Leeming street
Blackwell Ralph, mattress mkr. Church street
Bland John, coachman, Catlow st
Booth Abm. gent. Westgate
Bowerbank Rev. Wm. Grammar school

Bradder Luke, mason, Belvidere street
Bradley John, wire worker, Back lane, W.
Bradshaw Abbot, founder, Foundry row
Bradley Elias, cowkpr. Westgt
Brodhurst Wm. Esq. Gilcroft house
Brodhurst John, Esq. Portland house
Brodhurst Hy. Esq. barrister, High Oakham
Bromley John, atty's. clk. Belvidere street
Brown Saml. stenciller, Bancroft lane
Bullard Miss Eliza, Church st
Burton Wm. carter, Stockwell gt
Butterworth Mr. Jph. Belvidere street
Carrington Jph. brewer, Leeming street
Clay Wm. bailiff, Clerkson's alley
Clayton Rt. ostler, Leeming st
Cooke Wm. chief constable of Broxtow N div. Nottingham rd
Cook Mr. Wm. Union st
Cursham Rev. Thos. Leeson, D.C.L. vicar, Bridge st
Cutts Saml. cowkpr. Westgt
Davy John, huckster, Leeming st
Daws Jas. gamekpr. Chesterfield road
Dawson Geo. gent. Westgt
Dodd Wm. exciseman, Stockgt
Dodsley Miss Mary, Terrace
Downs Wm. gigs & horses to hire, 1, Bridge st
Drury Chas. medicine vender & herbalist, Listergate
Earp Mrs. Mary, Belvidere st
Ellis Mrs. Cath. Westgt
Fletcher Wm. shopman, Dragon court
Flower Mrs. Jane, Westgt
Foster Sol. mert. High Oakham
Foster Thos. mert. Crow hill
Freeman John, constable, Limetree place
Frisby Mr. Jph. Belvidere st
Frost Mr. John, Queen st
George Wm. groom, Queen st

Goulding Rd. clerk to the magistrates, to the comssrs. of taxes, and to the deputy lieutenancy, Leeming street
Green Miss Susanna, Leeming st
Greenhalgh Rd. cotton spinner, Westgate
Gresham John, gent. Westgt
Greenwood Mr. Wm. Ratcliff gt
Healey Mrs. gent. High Oakham
Heaton Rev. Geo. B.A. curate
Heywood Isaac, gent. Limetree place
Higginbottom G. carriers' agent, Westgate
Hodgson Rev. John, (Methodist) Bridge street
Holden Rev. J. Pleasley rectory
Holehouse Mrs. Ann, Church side
Hurst Chas. banker's clk. Westgt
Hutchinson John, Stockwell gt
Inglis Mrs. Mary Jane, Limetree place
Jackson Miss Mary, Westgt
Jackson Wm. carrier, Toothill ln
Jalland Mrs. Sarah, Leeming st
James Jph. basket mkr. Leeming street
Jefford Mrs. Mary, Bridge st
Johnson Mrs. Dorothy, Queen st
Johnson Geo. mert. Leeming st
Johnson Wm. gent. Church st
Johnson Jph. carter, Ratcliff gt
Johnson Jph. gov. Poor house
Kent Mrs. Mary, Westfield
Kershaw Saml. Westgate mill
Kirkland Saml. Thompson's alley
Kitching John, banker's clerk, Clerkson's alley
Knight Rt. cowpr. Duck lane
Lee Thos. keeper, Bleakhills
Lindley Mrs. Ann, Ratcliff gt
Maltby Jas. Esq. banker, Chesterfield road
Maltby Rev. Wm. Terrace
Marshall Sarah, Leeming st
Mellors Paul, overlooker, Bull's head lane
Metham John, constable, Portland bldgs
Miller John, gent. Dalestorth hs
Miller Saml. coachman, Queen st

Milner Rev. J. T. (meth.) Bridge street
Milner Mrs. gent. Chesterfield rd
Moore Gamaliel, coal and lime agent, Portland wharf
Nicholson Wm. bookpr. Blind ln
Oldfield John, carrier, Brunt st
Osborne John, cowkpr. Church side
Padley Geo. mfr. Nottingham rd
Parsons Mrs. Ann, Westgate
Paulson John, assistant overseer, Alfred court
Peck Thos. ostler, Rose ct
Peet Mr. John, Bancroft ln
Pickering Isaac, Leeming st
Pickering Jas. carriers' agent, Portland wharf
Pigot Mrs. Emma, Belvidere st
Pigot John, setter-up, Ratcliff gt
Poole John, joiner, Sutton rd
Poulton Ts. waiter, Belvidere st
Poynton Mrs. Sarah, Belvidere st
Powell Wm. pinder, Dun yard
Preston John, carrier, Cockpit
Radcliffe John, Swan coach office
Rawlins Rev. Js. M.A. West hill
Raworth John, cutler, Black's Head yard
Reddish Mrs. Mary, Duck ln
Revell Geo. sexton, Church side
Revell Jas. warper, Clerkson's alley
Richards Mrs. Cath. Stone ct
Richardson Mr. Wm. Ratcliff gt
Roberts G. carrier, Back ln. W.
Robinson Mrs. Ann, Leeming st
Robinson Jas. Esq. banker, Chesterfield road
Robinson Geo. Esq. Crow hill
Robinson Jno. exciseman, Stockwell gate
Robinson Jph. Newark postman, Cockpit
Rodgers Mr. John, Leeming st
Rycroft Eliz. upholsterer, Lg. st
Sales Sebastian, town crier, Currier's alley
Scott Eliz. cowkpr. Leeming st
Sellars John Mark, parish clerk, Toothill lane
Sellars Saml. setter-up, Bridge st
Senior Miss Eliz. Westgate

Shaw Thos. earthenware mfr. Nottm. rd. h. Union st
Shaw Wm. glazier, Leeming st
Shepherd Wm. Cross Keys yd
Siddon Saml. Esq. Pleaseley hill
Simes Mrs. Eliz. Church side
Simpson Stephen, Gas works
Smith Fanny, Belvidere st
Smith Mr. John, Queen st
Smith Wm. Anson, gent. Woodhouse grove
Sneath Jas. jun. White Bear ln
Stanton Mrs. Dorothy, gent. Car bank
Stenton Mrs. Eliz. Wass lane
Stirrup Mrs. High Oakham
Stirrup Saml. coach proprietor, Leeming street
Swymmer Lieut. Thos. Holworthy, Belvidere st
Taylor Geo. carter, Union st
Tomlinson Jph. carter, George ct
Topham Mrs. Mount Pleasant
Toplis Miss Dorothy, Westgt
Turner Sampson, (Prim. Meth. min.) Windmill lane
Tweltridge John, joiner, Cockpit
Unwin Miss Louisa, Westgate
Vickers Geo. gent. Leeming st
Wakefield Fras. Esq. Nottm. rd
Walker Mrs. gent. Berry hill
Ward Wm. fishmonger, Church st
Watson Geo. coachman
Watson Rt. mert. Chesterfield rd
Weaver Rev. Rt. (Ind.) West hill
Webster Isaac, organist & music teacher, Belvidere st
Whipp Wm. coachman, Queen st
White Mrs. Hannah, Stockgt
Wigley John, coal agent, &c. Belvidere street
Wild John, shopman, Rock valley
Wilson Thos. gardener, Stockgt
Wingfield Saml. keeper, Berry hill
Winter Wm. constable, Back lane, E.
Wood Ptr. bleacher, h. Stockgt
Wolstencroft Job, cowkpr. Duck lane
Woodcock Miss Eliz. Westgate
Wragg Miss Ann, Queen st.

ACADEMIES.

*Those marked * are Bourding Schools.*

Armisson Robt. Stanhope street
Armisson Walter, 8, Bells court
Chapman Jonas, Westgate
*Cresswell Eliz. Church side
*Charity School, (Clerkson's,) Cockpit, John & Mrs. Fowler
*Charity School, (Thompson's & Brunt's) Toothill ln, Hy. Fras. Shacklock, h. Leeming st
Free Grammar School, Church yd. Rev. Wm. Bowerbank, master, Hodgson Brailsford,* usher, Grove house
Hardy Wm. (music) Leeming st
Infant School, Independent Chapel, John Curtis, h. Belvidere street
Knowles John Bowmar, Cockpit
*Long Geo. Ratcliffegate
*Miller Mrs. Dalestorth house
Parsons Eliz. & Jane, Westgate
Ramsbotham Sarah, Leeming st
Radcliffe Jas. (dancing) Pleasley hill
Williams Rev. J., Chesterfield rd

ATTORNIES.

Flower Geo. Westgate
Parsons Rd. New road
Walkden Geo. (steward, and registrar of Wills for the manor of Mansfield, and steward of the manors of Clipstone, Sutton-cum-Lound and Bolsover) Bridge street
Woodcock Wm. (& clerk to Commissioners of the Improvement Act, and to the Gas Company) Stockwellgate

AUCTIONEERS.

Dobb Matthew, Bridge st
Marsh ——, Leeming street
Platts Joseph, (Sheriff's officer,) Leeming street
Randall Richd. Westgate
Winter Wm. Back lane

BAKERS & FLOUR DEALRS.

Marked † are also Corn Millers.

Ashmore David, Cockpit
Atkinson John, Westgate
†Bingley John, New road

Brocksop Samuel, Pleasley hill
Case Peter Smith, Stockwellgate
Clark John, Wass lane
Coupe John, Leeming street
Frearson Wm. Ratcliffgate
Garratt Thos. Church side
Marsh Wm. Cockpit
Mee Samuel, Union street
†Millns Wm. Westgate
Pike John, Clerkson's alley
†Wallis Hphy, Church street
White Saml. Stockwellgate
†Widdowson Wm. Thompson's alley

BANKERS.

Maltby & Robinson, Market pl. (drawn on Glynn & Co.)
Wylde & Bolger,Southwell bank ; Rt. Collinson, agent, Westgate, (drawn on Lubbock & Co.)
Savings' Bank, Swann Inn, open every Mon. from 12 till 1, H. F. Shacklock, clerk

BESOM MAKERS.

Briggs Wm. Rockhouses
Clark Geo. Sandy lane
Clark John, Rockhouses
Freeman Geo. Rockhouses
Freeman Joseph, Rockhouses
Holloway Saml. Westgate
Stocks Benj. Lady brook

BLACKSMITHS.

Ball John, Stockwellgate
Clay Richard, New road
Clay Saml. Ratcliffgate
Draycott John, Leeming st
Haywood Isaac, Stockwellgate
Haywood Thos. King's Head yd
Stevenson Jas. Church st
Vallance Chas. Pleasley hill

BOBBIN NET MAKERS.

Banner Thos. Stanhope street
Bullivant John, Union street
Burrow Ralph, Westgate
Cadman Wm. Union street
Cash Wm. Portland square
Chew John Union street
Chew Walter, Westgate
Clay J. L., Stockwellgate
Comery Geo. Ratcliffgate
Cutts Richard, Westgate
Dutton Thos. Ratcliffgate
Elliott Thos. Westgate

Fiddler Jph. Stockwellgate
Harvey Wm. Newgate lane
Hudson Jas. Westgate
Hutchinson Thos. Portland sqr
Humphreys Fras. White Bear ln
Maltby John, Club row
Marsh Rd. Nag's Head yard
Mossmann Thos. Church st
Parnham Wm. Back ln. E.
Poe Thos. Sutton road
Sadler Jas. Rock court
Scott Jph. Ratcliffgate
Simpson John, Union street
Sneath Jas. & Son, Stockwellgt
Spencer Hy. Ratcliffgate
Watson Wm. Chapel court
Wightman Wm. Littleworth
Wilkey Saml. Union street
Worthington Isaac, Market place

BOOKSELLERS, PRINTERS,
PAPERHANGERS, &c.
See also Libraries.
Collinson Rt. (and sub. dis. of
stamps) Westgate
Langley Geo. Market place

BOOKSLRS. (PERIODICAL.)
Hogarth Thos. Portland square
Udall John, Leeming street

BOOT & SHOE MAKERS.
Backas Joseph, Church st
Benton John, Market place
Birks John, Westgate
Botham Jas. Cockpit
Bowering Nichs. Bancroft lane
Brailsforth John, Leeming st
Bramwell Saml. Westfield lane
Brown Geo. Stockwellgate
Butler Jas. Stockwellgate
Clay Thos. Cockpit
Clayton Wm. Pleasley hill
Davis Wm. Toothill lane
Frost Geo. Stockwellgate
Furniss John, Westgate
Godley Joph. Ratcliffgate
Hancock Geo. Rosemary lane
Hibbard Matthw. Baptist hill
Hibbard Thos. Church side
Hibbard Wm. Sutton road
Hill Geo. Wass lane
Hobson John, Bridge street
Holmes Ezechias. Stanhope st
Jones Robert, Westgate
Liller Asher, Stockwellgate

Lindley Thos. Club row
Mason Thos. Belvidere st
Mellors Wm. Pleasley hill
Pogmore Saml. Plumber's court
Porter Thos. Ratcliffgate
Robotham Matthew, Stockwellgt
Sadler Thos. Cockpit
Scott Isaac, Church street
Slaney John, Pleasley hill
Towlson Hy. Currier's alley
Unwin Geo. Leeming street
Ward Stephen, Leeming street
Woolhouse Daniel, Market place
Wightman Mttw. Leeming st
Wood Samuel, Westgate

BRAZIERS & TINNERS.
Bousfield Chas. Westgate
Midworth Samuel, Leeming st
Nuttall John. Clerkson's alley

BRICK & TILE MAKERS.
Bromhead Richard, Westgate
Lindley Charles, Westgate

BRUSH MAKER.
Ellis John, Leeming street

BUILDERS.
See Stonemasons & Joiners.

BUTCHERS.
*Thus marked † have shops in the
Shambles.*
Allwood Wm. Cockpit
Ancliffe Fras. Stockwellgate
Beardall Wm. Littleworth
Bucklow Wm. Church street
†Cook Thos. Westgate
†Curtis Sarah, Leeming street
†Curtis Samuel, Leeming st
Dean Jonas, Church street
†Downs Fras. Leeming street
Fletcher Hy. Stockwellgate
Fletcher John, Belvidere st
Goodman John, Bridge street
Greenwood Thos. Ratcliffgate
†Harrison John, Black's head yd
Herret Richard, Church st
Jepson Daniel, Westgate
Mettham Wm. Church street
Moor James, sen. Church street
†Moor Jas. jun. Belvidere st
Moor John, Leeming street
†Parsons Hy. Leeming street
†Ratcliffe Jph. Back lane W
Roper Hy. Stockwellgate
Raynor John, Woodhouse road

†Storey John, Thompson's alley
Walker Edward, Stockwellgate
†Wightman Wm. Littleworth
CABINET MAKERS.
See Joiners.
CHAIR MAKERS.
Lester John, Leeming street
Sansom Rd. Stockwellgate
Sansom Thos. Rose court
CHIMNEY SWEEPERS, &c.
Watson Robert, Rockhouses
Wheat Geo. King's Head court
CHYMISTS & DRUGGISTS.
Bunting Edward, (and soda water
mfr.) Market place
Gething Wm. Church street
Harrop John, Market place
Heald John, Stockwellgate
Wilson Wm. Stockwellgate
COACH MAKERS, &c.
Stones & Hervey, Westgate and
Nottingham, (Saml. Johnson,
agent)
COAL & LIME MERCHNTS.
(Pinxton Coal & Chrich Lime.)
Butterley Company, John Wig-
ley, agent, Portland Wharf
Coke John, Esq.; Gamal. Moore,
agent, Portland Wharf
COLLECTORS.
Elliott Thos. (rents) Westgate
Hurst John, (debts) Listergate
Paulson John, (poor rates) Alfred
court
Platts Jph. (Imp. rate) Leeming
street
Winter Wm. (land tax) Bk. ln. E
COLOUR MANUFACTURER.
Ellis John (& vinegar) Rock val
CONFECTIONERS.
Edge Wm. Leeming street
Hett John Leo, Leeming street
COOPERS.
Hickson Thos. Stockwellgate
Jefferies John, Plumber's court
Moss John, Stockwellgate
CORN MERCHANTS.
Buss Thos. Currier's alley
Shippam Chas. Stockwellgate
CORN MILLERS & FLOUR
DEALERS.
See also Bakers.
Adlington Wm. King's mill

Carding Wm. Pleasley, (Derbs.)
Cupid Edw. Woodhouse lane
Paulson John, Stockwellgate
Pike Wm. Clerkson's alley
Reason Thos. Moorhaigh
Withers John, Ratcliffgate
Speed David, Ratcliffgate
COTTON SPINNERS & LACE
THREAD MANUFACTRS.
Chambers John, Little Matlock
Hardwick Richard, Bath mill
Heygate James, Hermitage
Hodson Wm. & Co. Westgate &
Eddingley
Hollins, Siddons & Co. (hosiery
yarn) Pleasley Works
Sneath Jas. & Son, Bleakhills
Stanton Chas. (& angola) Bath ln
Unwin Saml. & Co. Sutton Works
Wakefield Fras. & Thomas, Not-
tingham road & Bridge st mills
CURRIERS, &c.
Field Wm. Church street
Littlewood Robert, Church st
Parker Robert, Stockwellgate
Wooding Geo. Leeming street
DYERS.
Beard Jas. Rock valley
Brown John & Co. (& bleachers)
Lister lane & Basford
Cooper Jph. White Hart yd
EATING-HOUSES.
Poe Catherine, Cockpit
Fisher Chas. Church street
Hurt Samuel, Stockwellgate
Wright Mary, Leeming st
FARMERS.
Atkin John, Derby road
Bagshaw Geo. Dalestorth
Boaler John, High Oakham
Barratt Geo. Nottingham road
Dickons Wm. Nottingham rd
Duckmanton William, Radmanth-
waite
Eyre John, Dalestorth
Featherstone Wm. Bull farm
Fletcher Wm. Radmanthwaite
Hill Chas. Dalestorth
Hardwick Thos. Hill top
Hodgkinson Wm. Moorhaigh
Hodgkinson Thos. Nottingham rd
Hurst Joseph, Ratcliffgate
Jackson Wm. Penniment hs

3 A

Lindley Geo. Radmanthwaite
Lindley Jas. Pleasley hill
Marsh Mttw. Penniment houses
Millns Wm. Nottingham road
Neal Wm. Berry hill
Neape John, Dalestorth
Parsons John, Pleasley hill
Pearce Sampson, Dalestorth
Reason Wm. Pleasley hill

FELLMONGERS.
Bamford David, Bridge street
Ellis Dickinson, (& mustard mfr.) Rock valley

FIRE & LIFE OFFICES.
Clerical & Medical Life, George Walkden, Bridge street
Guardian, William McLellan, Church street
Norwich Union, Robt. Collinson, Westgate
Royal Exchange, John Ellis, Stockwellgate

FRAMESMITHS.
See also Machine Makers and Whitesmiths.
Hucknall Jas. Stockwellgate
Maltby Wm. Church side
Orton Thos. (& valuer) Belv. st
Parker Hy. Ratcliffgate
Salmon Thos. Ratcliffgate
Soar Joseph, Portland square

FRAMEWORK KNITTERS.
Binch James, Westgate
Brodley Wm. Club row
Bullivant Wm. Bridge street
Butler Hephzibah, Ratcliffgate
Carr George, Bancroft lane
Clay Isaac Lovatt, Stockwellgt
Corbitt Wm Stockwellgt
Crampton Benj. Littleworth
Crenidge John, Leeming st
Cullumbine Jas. Ratcliffgate
Dabley James, Baxter hill
Goldsby Wm. Stanhope st
Green John, Plumber's court
Grosvenor Thomas, Rookery
Haines Edw. Mount pleasant
Haines Maria, Stockwellgate
Harvey Wm. Newgate lane
Heath John, Toothill lane
Horwood John, Bancroft ln
Hucknall Jas. Stockwellgate
Hurst Jas. Bancroft lane

Jackson Thomas, Cockpit
Kirkwood John, Belvidere st
Limb Job, Belvidere st
Limb Jph. Queen street
Lowe Wm. Bancroft lane
Marriott John, Cross Key's yard
Marshall Jph. Bancroft lane
Newsham John, Union street
Orton Thos. Belvidere st
Poole John, Pleasley hill
Radford Wm. Leeming street
Raines Fras. Club-square
Richards Thos. White Bear ln
Richardson Thos. Ratcliffgate
Sansom John, Cockpit
Sansom John, Back lane E.
Simpson Thos. Plumber's court
Simpson John, Union street
Simpson Wm. Baptist hill
Slack Gilbert, Bancroft lane
Slack Geo. Rookery
Slaney Zach. Belvidere street
Spencer Hy. Ratcliffgate
Ward Samuel, Ratcliffgate
Wells Thos. Belvidere st
White Thos. Cockpit
Wilson Wm. Bancroft lane
Wragg John, Newgate lane

FURNITURE BROKERS.
Cursham Geo. Church street
Drury John, Church street
Shipston Eliz. New road

GARDENERS, &c.
Backas Rd. Stockwellgate
Booth Geo. Market place
Brailsford John, Stockwellgate
Gadsby Thos. Woodhouse rd
Green Thos. Westgate
Hunter Jeremiah, Stockwellgate
Jones Robert, Westgate
Neale Kelham, Market place
Shippam Geo. Church street
White Clay, Cockpit
White Samuel, Leeming street

GLOVE & BREECHES MKR.
Blackmore Geo. Church street

GROCERS & TEA DLRS.
See also Shopkeepers.
Bagshaw Benj. Stockwellgate
Butterworth Wm. Stockwellgt
Ellis John, Leeming street
Ellis William, (and tobacco mfr.) Church street

Nicholson Thos. Westgate
Savage Thos. Westgate
Shipman Thos. Market place
White Thos. Ratcliffgate
Wood Joseph, Church street
Wragg John, Church st

GUN MAKER.
Marsh John, Church street

HAIR DRESSERS.
Bingham Jas. Cockpit
Drury John, Church street
Greenwood Jph. (and toy dealer) Church street
Hinde Thos. Leeming street
Hinde Wm. Stockwellgate
Jeffries Abhm. Church street
Lockwood John, Clerkson's alley
Randall John, Westgate
Randall Rd. (& toy & fancy whs.) Westgate

HAT MANUFACTURERS.
Dobb Wm. Market place
Holt Wm. Market place
Watson John, Church street

HOP & SEED MERCHANTS.
Bagshaw Benj. Stockwell court
Ellis Wm. Church street
Shipman Thos. Market place

HOSIERY MANUFACTRS.
See also Framework Knitters.
Foster, Watson, & Co. Crow hill
Richardson Thos. Ratcliffgate
Siddon & Johnson, Dragon ct

INNS & TAVERNS.
Admiral Nelson, Wm. Hemsall, Stockwellgate
Angel, John Stanley, Westgate
Black Boy, George Needham, Stockwellgate
Black Bull, Thomas Andrews, Westgate
Black Horse, Thos. Eyre, Stockwellgate
Black's Head, Sarah Parker, Market place
Black Swan, John Hill, Cockpit
Blue Bell, John Gascoine, Church street
Blue Boar, Daniel Heald, Stockwellgate
Bowl-in-Hand, Sarah Harvey, Leeming street

Brown Cow, John Hurst, Ratcliffgate
Cock, Geo. Dobb, Cockpit
Cross Keys, Jph. Smith, Westgt
Crown and Anchor, Thos. Warren, Market place
Durham Ox, Jas. Butler, Stockwellgate
Eclipse, Sarah Cadman, Market place
Elm Tree, John Francis, Ratclgt
George and Dragon Inn, Sarah White, Leeming street
Grey Hound, John Reed, Stockwellgate
King & Miller, Saml. Slack, Sutton road
King's Arms, Thos. Woodhouse, Ratcliffgate
King's Head, Edw. Smith Dawson, Stockwellgate
Masons Arms, Joseph Fenton, Leeming street
Nags Head, Geo. Page, Westgate
New Inn, Jph. Beresford, Westgt
Old Dial, Geo. Bowman, Stockwellgate
Old Eclipse, Wm. Blagg, Westgt
Old Horse & Jockey, Sarah Leach, Leeming street
Peacock, Joseph Chapman, Belvidere street
Pheasant, John Pearson, Chesterfield road
Portland Arms, Mary Reed, Cockpit
Queen's Head, John Pratts, Queen street
Ram Inn, Wm. Shooter, Church street
Ram Tavern, John Mellors, Littleworth
Rein Deer, Rd. Parker, Hill top
Royal Oak, Ntn. Newton, Stockwellgate
Swan Inn, Thos. Morton, Mktpl
Three Horse Shoes, John Ball, Stockwellgate
Wheat Sheaf, Rt. Bonsall, Stgt
Waggon and Coals, Jas. Lindley, Bridge street
White Hart, Rd. Fowler, Church street

White Lion, Joseph Brailsford, Church street
White Swan, Thos. Booth, Pleasley hill

NEW BEER HOUSES.

Bee Hive, Wm. Wragg, Lister ln
Cross Keys, Rd. Banes, Union st
Eight Bells, Rd. Herret, Church street
New Inn, J. Naylor, Pleasley hl
Nursery House, Rt. Jones, Woodhouse road
Old Yew Tree, Wm. Worsley, Leeming street
Queen Adelaide, Jph. Betts, Stockwellgate
Red Lion, Jas. Hucknall, Stgt
Robin Hood, John Sansom, Ratcliffgate
Rock Houses, John Greenwood
Stag & Pheasant, Geo. Peacock, Toothill lane
Sherwood Inn, Thos. Watkinson, Newgate lane
Wm. IV. Wm. Harrington, Sutton road

IRON & BRASS FOUNDERS.

Butterley Iron Works Co. John Wigley, agent, Portland Wharf
Hind John, (mfr. of agricultural implements) Portland Foundry
Midworth Saml. (& brass cock mfr.) Leeming street
Wakefield and Padley, Sherwood Foundry

IRONMONGERS.

Bousfield Charles, (silversmith, &c.) Westgate
Green John, Stockwellgate
Simes John, Church st

JOINERS & CABINET MKRS.
Thus § are also Upholsterers.
§Alsop Peter & Co. Westgate
Ashby Rd. Newgate ln
Cash Wm. Portland sqr
Day Wm. Church st
§M'Lellan Wm. Church st. h. Toothill lane
M'Lellan John, Dragon ct
Peet John, Bancroft ln
Pegg Jas. New Rookery
Taylor Wm. Westgate
Woodhead Jph. Brunt st

§White Saml. Stockwellgt
Wright Jph. Leeming st

LIBRARIES (CIRCULATG.)
Drury John, Church st
Collinson Robt. (subs.) Westgt
Langley Geo. Market pl.
Unwin Ann, Bridge st

LACE MFRS. & MERTS.
See Bobbin Net Mkrs.
Foster, Watson, & Co. Crow-hill

LAND SURVEYORS, &c.
Marsh John, Belvidere st
Sanderson George (valuer, &c.) Bridge street

LIME BURNERS.
See Mansfield Woodhouse.
Tideswell Saml. Stockwellgt.

LINEN & WLN. DRAPERS.
Andrew John, Market place
Brothwell Thomas (& hosier) Moot-hall
Ellis John, Stockwellgt
Hudson Jas. Westgate
Ince Thomas, Market pl
Maltby Wm. Market place
Worthington Isaac, Market-pl

MACHINE MAKERS.
Green John (patent roving) Stockwellgate
Marsh Rd. (twist) Nag's head yard
Simpson Thos. (spinning) Westgt

MALTSTERS.
Adlington Wm. King's Mill
Beresford Joseph, Westgt
Brailsford Job, Bridge st
Brodhurst Wm. Esq. Gilcroft hs
Buss Thos. Currier's Alley
Davy Thos. Stockwellgate
Dixon Wm. Stanhope street
Featherstone Wm. Back lane W
Flower Dd. Thompson's Alley
Foster Wm. Stockwellgate
Freeman John, Lime Tree place
Howett John, Back lane, W
Saml. Jackson, Rose court
Jepson Daniel, Westgate
Jepson Wm. Westg. & Rowthorn
Lindley Jas. & Wm. Stone-hill
Newton Danl. Stockwellgate
Booth Joseph, Westgate
Walliss Hphy. Church street
Watson Jas. West-hill

MILLINERS & DRESS MKRS.
Allcroft Hanh. Bridge street
Berridge Ann. Belvidere street
Binch Ann, Westgate
Clark Eliz. Bridge street
Dickon Ann, Leeming street
Hardstaff Ann, Belvidere street
Jackson Caroline, Church street
Lester Eliz. (& tea dlr.) Back
  lane W
Locke Eliz. Stockwellgate
Mosley Eliz. Lister lane
Pierrepoint Sarah, Church st
Robinson Sar. Leeming street
Taylor A. & M. Westgate
Unwin M. & A. Leeming street
Unwin Ann, Belvidere street

MILLWRIGHTS.
Jamison John, Stanhope street
Kirkland Thos. (engineer, &c.)
  Westgate

NAIL MAKERS.
Bousfield Chas. Westgate
Evans Moses, Ratcliffgate
Green John, Stockwellgate
Snape Chas. Wass lane
Walker John, Cockpit

NEEDLE, PUSHR. &c. MKRS.
Bartram, Wm. Sutton road
Booth John, Stockwellgate
Jackson James, Stanhope st
Neal Wm. Toothill lane
Taylor Wm. Bridge street
Vickers John, Union street
Wass Geo. Bancroft lane
Wass, Wm. Stockwellgate

PAINTERS, STAINERS, AND
  GILDERS.
Frost Reynolds, Leeming st
Heane Wm. Leeming street
Moss Jph. Rock court
Sheppard Thos. Stockwellgate
Wright John, Leeming street

PATTEN MAKERS.
Snape Chas. Wass lane
Walker John, Cockpit

PAWNBROKER.
Gresham Robt. (silversmith and
  clothes broker.) Stockwellgate

PLASTERERS & STAINERS.
Hollis John, Thompson's alley
Linfoot Robt. Cockpit
Lockwood Wm. Portland bldgs

Vallance Geo. Westgate

PLUMBERS & GLAZIERS.
Elsam Rd. Back lane W
Mason Wm. Leeming street
Midworth Saml. jun. Leeming st
Place Rd. Stockwellgate

PORTER DEALERS.
Ellis Wm. Church street
Shipman Thos. Market place
Yates John, Stockwellgate

RAG DEALERS.
Shipman Robt. Stockwellgate
Shipston Wm. Meeting hs. ln

ROPE & TWINE MAKERS.
Wilkinson Jas. Church street
Wood John, Leeming street

SADDLERS, &c.
Fowler Rd. Church street
Jackson John, Leeming street
Merriman Thos. Stockwellgate
Palmer John, Church street

SHOPKEEPERS.
(Dealers in Grocery, Flour, &c.)
Allen Timothy, Leeming street
Ashby Rd. Newgate lane
Backas Rd. Stockwellgate
Beardsell John, Stockwellgate
Bishop John, Newgate lane
Blythe Richard, Westgate
Chappel Thos. White Bear ln
Boyle Hannah, Baker's court
Clifton Henry, Westgate
Co-operative Stores, Wm. Tay-
  lor, Westgate, and Wm. Bust,
  Ratcliffgate
Cooke Wm. Leeming street
Cutts John, Leeming street
Ellers Eliz. Ratcliffgate
Goose Ann, Thompson's alley
Green Thos. Westgate
Herrett Jph. Back lane W
Hodgkinson Saml. Sutton road
Jeffries Job, Westgate
Jepson Saml. Cockpit
Pearson Thos. Pleasley hill
Radford Wm. Leeming street
Reed John, Union street
Sansom Hy. Back lane E
Sansom John, Cockpit
Shipman Robt. Stockwellgate
Simpson Thos. Westgate
Thacker Wm. Church street
Ward John, Westgate

White Ann, Westgate
Wilson Thos. Chesterfield road
Winter Martha, Cockpit
Witham Jph. Belvidere street
Yates John, Stockwellgate

SINKER MAKERS.
Hickman Wm. (& bobbin & carriages) Stockwellgate
Holland Saml. Bridge street
Holmes Geo. Stanhope street
Jackson Wm. Keirs' bldgs

STONE MASONS & QUARRY OWNERS.
*Marked thus * only Masons.*
Bingham Wm. jun. Cockpit
Bromhead Rd. Westgate
Buckles Anthony, Cockpit
Hallam John, Pleasley hill
Hopewell John, Quarry lane
Lindley Chas. Westgate
*Lindley Jas. & Jph. Bridge st
*Millott Jas. Stockwellgate
*Sharp Fras. Windmill lane
Thrall Chas. Bridge street
Thrall Benj. Ratcliffgate

STRAW HAT MAKERS.
Clark Sus. Leemington street
Jackson Mary, Church street
Jeffries Rebecca, Leeming st
Carnell Clem. Westgate
Locke Eliz. Stockwellgate
Hardisty Mary, Lister lane
Mossman Thos. Church street
Raynor Frances, Ratcliffgate
Taylor A. & M. Westgate
Unwin Ann, Bridge street
Webster Mary, Church street

SURGEONS.
Barker Robt. Leeming street
Cooper Nathan, Westgate
Furniss and Paulson, Westgate
Furniss Martin, Westgate
Hulme John, M. D. Westgate
Hurt Saml. Westgate
Paulson Wm. Heywood, Westg

TAILORS.
Allen Thos. Windmill lane
Aslin Wm. Stockwellgate
Baggaley Wm. Stockwellgt
Baker John, Westgate
Banes Rd. Union street
Farnsworth Wm. Black's Hd. yd
Hobson Wm. Leeming street

Hopewell James, Westgate
Hopewell Jas. jun. Churchside
Leaver Saml. Mount pleasant
Lee Wm. (& cleaner) Cockpit
Marriott Geo. (furrier & rabbit mert.) Ratcliffgate
Merrill Saml. Pleasley hill
Stanhope John, Bancroft lane
Watson John, Queen street
West Jph. Leeming street
White Geo. Stockwellgate
Witham Geo. Ratcliffgate
Woolley John, Black's Head yd
Woolley Thos. Back lane W

TALLOW CHANDLERS.
Ellis Wm. Church st
Shipman Thos. Market place

TANNERS.
Girdler Rd. Littleworth
Lowe Wm. Church st

TURNERS IN WOOD.
Birks Bingley, (brush head & handles, bobbins, &c.) Littleworth
Lester John, Leeming st
Simpson Thos. Westgate
Wightman Jas. (bobbins, &c.) Rock valley

VETERINARY SURGEONS.
Reynolds Rd. Leeming st
Stanley John, (and cow leech,) Westgate

WATCH & CLOCK MKRS.
Chew Walter, Westgate
Platts John, Leeming st
Simpkins Wm. Church st

WHEELWRIGHTS.
Fox John, Pleasley hill
Gabbitass Jph. New road
May Thos. Cockpit
Robinson Jph. Cockpit
Smith John, Back lane, E
Woodhead Geo. Stockwellgt
Woodhouse Thos. Ratcliffgt

WHITESMITHS, &c.
Baxter Geo. Westgate mill, h. Union st
Bousfield Chas. Westgate
Green John. Stockwellgate
Marsh Rd. Nag's Head yd
Simes John, Church st
Vickers Saml. Wass lane

WINE & SPIRIT MERTS.
Bagshaw Benj. Stockwellgt

Ellis Wm. Church st
Nicholson Thos. Westgt
Rolfe Jph. Queen street
Savage Thos. Westgate

WOOL STAPLER.
Corbitt Wm. (& worsted dlr.) Stockwellgate

COACHES.
From Saml. Stirrup's Coach Office, Swan Inn Yard.
The *Royal Mail* to London, at 4 mg. and to Sheffield, Leeds, &c. at 12 noon, daily.
The *Hope* to London, &c. at 1 aft. and to Sheffield, Halifax, and Huddersfield, at 12 noon, daily.
The *Express* to London, at 5 aft. and to Leeds, &c. at half-past 10 mg. daily.
The *Champion* to Manchester at 9 mg. daily; through Chesterfield, &c. and to Newark and Lincoln, at 4 aft.
The *Volunteer* to Liverpool, at half-past 8 mg. daily.
The *Royal Hope* to Derby at 1 afternoon, daily.
The *Royal Union* to York, Worksop, and Doncaster, at 8 mg. daily, except Sunday.
Coaches to Nottingham five times a day, viz. at 4 mg.; ¼ past 12 noon; and at 4, 5, & 6, aft.
A *Coach* to Gainsbro' every mg. except Sunday, at ¼ past 8; through Worksop, Tickhill, &c.
From the Old Eclipse Inn.
The *Courier* to London, at 9 night, and to Sheffield and Leeds, at 8 morning, daily.
From the Eclipse Inn.
The *Robin Hood* to Nottingham, daily, except Sunday, at 8 mg. Wm. Whipp & Saml. Miller, owners.
From Portland Wharf.
To Pinxton, on the Railway, Wm. Epperstone's Van, every Thurs. at 3 aft.

CARRIERS.
From Deacon, Harrison, & Co's Waggon Warehouse, Westgt.

To London, Nottingham, &c. daily, 12 noon. To Chesterfield, Sheffield, Wakefield, Leeds, Chapel-en-le-Frith, Manchester, Liverpool, &c. every evening, at 6. G. Higginbottom, agent.
From Pickford & Co's Van & Waggon Office, Westgate.
Van to London, every morning, except Sunday, at ¼ past 2, and to Sheffield, &c. 10 night.
A *Waggon* to Nottingham, London, &c. at 8 morning, and to Manchester, Sheffield, &c. at ¼ past 10 night. Samuel Walsh, agent.
From Wheatcroft & Co's. Railway Waggon Warehouse, Portland Wharf.
Two or three Waggons, every morning, at 6 or 7 o'clock, on the Railway to Pinxton, whence goods are forwarded to all parts of the kingdom by land & water. James Pickering, agent.
CARRIERS FROM THE INNS, &c.
To Alfreton, from the *Royal Oak*, John Bond and Francis Wheatley, from the Black Horse, Thu. 3 aft.; and John Scatchard, from Blue Boar, Mon. Thu. & Sat. 3 aft.
Bilsthorpe, *Black's Head*, John Bucklow, Thu. 3 aft.
Blidworth, *Old Dial*, Wm. Wright, Thu. 3 aft.
Bolsover, Angel, John Mellors, Thu. 4 aft.
Chesterfield, Thos. Bingham, from the Cockpit, Tu. Thu. and Sat. 5 mg.; and Thos. Andrews, from Chesterfield road, Saturday, 5 morning.
Clown, Black Bull, Mr. Mallinder, Thu. 3 aft.
Eakring, White Hart, Saml. Wibberley and Geo. Tomlinson, M. & Thu. 3 aft.
Epperston and Nottingham, *Black's Head*, John Taylor, Thu. 3 aft.
Farnsfield, White Hart, Hy. Smith, daily, at 2 aft.

Kirkby-in-Ashfield, *Blk. Horse,* Reuben Hayes; & Angel, Hodg-kinson Lowe, Thu. 3 aft.

Langworth, Black Bull, John Brown, Thu. 4.

Laxton, Black Bull, John Newbold, Thu. 3 aft.

Newark and Southwell, Thos. Andrew, from Chesterfield road, W. & S. 4 mg.; also, the *Mail Gig,* Jph. Robinson, from the Cockpit, every morn. ½ past 4.

Newark & Ketlington, Nag's Head, Thos. Wood, Tu. & Thu. 3 aft.

Normanton (South) *Blk. Horse,* Geo. Slater, Mon. Wed. & Thu. 3 aft.

Nottingham, Henry Blackwell, of Leeming-street; Wm. Jackson, of Toothill-lane; and John

Oldfield, of Brunt-street; every Wed. & Sat. at 4 mg.

Ollerton. See Eakring.

Pinxton, Black Horse, Wm. Epperstone, (on the Railroad,) Thu. 3 aft.

Rufford, Angel, Jph. Morley, Thu. 4 aft.

Southwell, White Hart, Hy. Ferne, Mon. & Thurs. 2 aft.; and Angel, W. Revill, Thurs. 4 aft. See also Newark.

Sutton-in-Ashfield, *Blue Boar,* John Massey, and *Black Horse,* Dennis Whatton, daily, 2 aft.

Tibshelf, Black Horse, Jas. Newton, daily 12 noon.

Worksop, John Preston, from the Cockpit, and Geo. Roberts, from Back-lane-West, every M. W. F. & Sat. at 6 morn.

ANNESLEY PARISH

Contains the two townships of *Annesley and Felley,* and forms a romantic district of 3356 acres, of which 289 acres belong to the Duke of Portland, and the remainder to John Musters, Esq. except one farm at Felley, belonging to Mr. Charles Antill. The soil rests on a substratum of red sandstone, and in many places rises into mountainous ridges.

ANNESLEY is a small irregularly built village, in a pictur-esque situation, 6¼ miles S. S. W. of Mansfield. At the Conquest it was of the fee of Ralph Fitz-Hubert, whose tenant took the name of *Annesley,* and the manor was held by his de scendants till the reign of Henry VI., when their heiress carried it in marriage to the *Chaworth's* of Wiverton, with whose late heiress it passed to its present lord, John Musters, Esq., who assumed the name of Chaworth, and resided here till the death of the late Mr. Musters, when he re-assumed that name and removed to his paternal seat of Colwick Hall. (See Wiverton, p. 517.) ANNESLEY HALL is a large ancient mansion, sur-rounded by a fine park, with about 580 acres of woods, planta-tions, and water. It has been many years unoccupied and neglected, but is now undergoing a complete restoration, for the occasional residence of its owner. The *church,* dedicated to All Saints, stands on an eminence near the hall, and has a tower with two bells. The living is a perpetual curacy, certified at £20. J. Musters, Esq. is the impropriator and patron, and the Rev. J. L. Cursham, D. C. L. is the incumbent. The *feast* is on the Sunday after Old Michaelmas day.

ANNESLEY WOODHOUSE is a hamlet and grange, of 289 acres, belonging to the Duke of Portland, and distant 1 mile N. of Annesley. *Coal* lies under the surface, but it has never been worked.

FELLEY is a hamlet and small township, of 300 acres, partly upon a lofty eminence, 1½ mile W. by S. of Annesley, where are the ruins of a PRIORY, which was founded soon after the Conquest by Radulph Britto, aided by his son Reginald de Annesley. It was dedicated to the Blessed Virgin Mary, and was subordinate to the priory of Worksop. At is dissolution it was valued at £41. 19s. 1d. Nothing now remains of the monastic building except what is incorporated in the large house which is partly occupied by a farmer, whose garden occupies the site of the chapel. The priory farm was purchased by Mr. Musters of a Mr. Hodgkinson, who had bought it of the Holdens, of Nuthall.

CHARITY.—*Mr. William Booth*, of Annesley Woodhouse, bequeathed in 1825, his house and garden, for the use of a chapel, and the interest of £928, (at 5 per cent.) to be distrbuted as follows, viz.—£20 to his trustees; £5 to the poor of Annesley Woodhouse; £2. 10s. for a preaching room; £5 to the Particular Baptist Minister of Sutton-in-Ashfield, and £12. 17s. to the Independent Minister of Kirkby Woodhouse. About 40 years ago, this donor was surprised by the return of two of his *sheep*, which had been buried on the forest upwards of a month, under 13 feet of *snow !*

Marked thus † live at Annesley Woodhouse.

Musters John, Esq. Annesley hall
†Amatt Wm. shoemkr. Woodhse
Beck Mr. Wm
†Burrows Ralph, vict
Davies John, shoemaker
Deakin Paul, corn miller, Felley
  mill
†Gelsthorp Jas. smith & maltster
Gibson Jph. beerhouse, Forest
†Hardstaff Geo. butcher & shopr
Hardstaff Rd. joiner
Harvey Timothy, blacksmith
Hollingsworth Wm. weaver and
  parish clerk
Horabin Richard, shopkeeper
Horabin Wm. shopkeeper
†Robinson Geo. corn miller
Robinson Hy. corn miller
†Shipley John, warp lace manfr

Stanley Fras. veterinary surgeon,
  &c. Annesley lodge
Turner John, gamekeeper
Turner Richard, shoemaker
Whitman Wm. shoemaker

FARMERS.
†Allin George   Robinson Wm.
Goodall Chpr.   Smith Thomas
Hardy Wm.   Turner Samuel
Hibbert Eliz.   Turner Wm.
Hickton Rt.   Webster Jph.
Hodgkinson C.   Wilkinson John,
Lindley Wm.   Closes
Lindley Thos.   Winterbottom
Line Geo.   William

FELLEY TOWNSHIP.
Hollingsworth Ralph, beerhouse
Hunt John, farmer
Saunders Thos. farmer, Abbey

ARNOLD PARISH

Extends from 3 to 5 miles N of Nottingham, and formerly comprised 2280 acres of the open forest of Sherwood; but it was enclosed in 1789, when 700 acres were allotted to the impropriator, and 23A. 3R. 37P. to the Crown. Mrs. Sherbrooke, of Oxton, is the principal owner, and lady of the manor; and her heir, Colonel Samuel Coape, resides here at *Sherwood Lodge*, a pleasant modern mansion, with handsome plantations on the verge of the forest. The Duke of Devonshire was the impropriator, but he has sold his allotment to Thomas Holdsworth, Esq., of Manchester; besides whom here are several smaller proprietors; viz. Thomas Panton, Esq., of *Arnot Hill*; Mark Denison, Esq., of *Daybrook House*; and Mr. Benjamin Chambers, of the village. The population of the parish has encreased since 1801, from 2768 to 4054 souls.

ARNOLD is a long and populous village, half a mile E. of the Mansfield road, and 4 miles N. of Nottingham. Its inhabitants are mostly employed in the lace and hosiery trades, and on two streams which form the Daybrook rivulet, are two Bleach-works. There was formerly a large Worsted mill here, but after being several years unoccupied, it was taken down. The village stands upon a sand rock, is clean and comfortable, and has several neat mansions, one of which, called *Arnold Grove*, is occupied by William Turbutt, Esq., Barrister.

The CHURCH is dedicated to St. Mary, and has a tower and five bells. It is well pewed and all in good repair, except the chancel, the cost of repairing which belongs to T. Holdsworth, Esq., as owner of the rectorial land. The *vicarage*, valued in the King's books at £7. 17s. 8d., is in the patronage of the Duke of Devonshire. The Rev. George Francis Holcome is the incumbent, and the Rev. William Howard the curate. Besides 90A. 2R. 3P. of glebe, the vicar has a yearly modus in lieu of the small tithes. The Wesleyan, Kilhamite, and Primitive Methodists, and the Particular and General Baptists, have each a *chapel* in the village. The annual *feast* is on the last Sunday in September. There are nine *Sick Clubs* in the parish, and the Nelson Lodge of *Odd Fellows*, (No. 26,) held at the Horse and Jockey. A *fire engine* is stationed in the village.

DAYBROOK is a considerable hamlet on the Mansfield road, at the southern verge of the parish, 3 miles N. of Nottingham. Near it is *Cockcliff* farm, the property of Colonel Need; and a little to the S.E. is *Swinnows*, where there are two farms and a brick yard.

RED-HILL is a large modern village with seven public-houses, on the Mansfield road, half a mile W. of Arnold. To the north are five Forest farms within the limits of the parish, whence a road diverges to Oxton and Southwell.

CHARITIES.—The *Free School*, at Arnold, was rebuilt, and the master's house repaired, in 1814, at the cost of £135, since which a room has been built over it for a Sunday school. It is endowed with about £22 per annum, for the education of 32 poor children. Its founder was Daniel Chadwick, who endowed it with £50 laid out in the purchase of *Roecroft Houses*, for which £12. 10s. is paid yearly, out of the poor rates to the master, and 30s. to the poor in respect of £30 left by Bartholomew Fillingham, and expended in the same purchase. Henry Sherbrooke, Esq., left a yearly rent charge of £3 to the school, and it is now paid by Mrs. Sherbrooke, together with £2 yearly, left by Margaret Birch. In 1785, Rebecca Elley, bequeathed to it the interest of £6, and the master receives £5 yearly as one moiety of the rent of *Denison Land*, which was purchased with poor's money, of which there still remains £34, and the interest thereof is distributed in bread. *Henry Sherbrooke*, Esq., left £3 per annum to be distributed amongst the poor on the 5th of November. Of the latter, 22s. is paid by Mrs. Sherbrooke, and £1. 18s. by Jeremiah Rhodes, out of his house, near the Red-hill mill.

Marked 1 reside at Daybrook, 2 at Red-Hill, and the rest at Arnold, or where specified.

Allen Wright, surgeon
Atherley John, sinker maker
Barrows Timothy, horse dealer
Barton Luke, watchmaker
Bartrum Mrs. Elizabeth
Bigsby Mrs. Eliz. Arnot vale
Butler Mr. Wm. Harvey hill
Chamberlain Thos. schoolmaster
Chambers Benjamin, gent
Coape Col. Saml. Sherwood Ldge
Denby Stephen, butcher
Denison Mark, Esq. Daybrook hs
Denison Rt. cart owner
Diggle Jas. bleacher & trimmer
Empson Sarah, straw hat maker
Fearfield Jph. brickmaker, Swin-nows
1 Frignall Mrs. Elizabeth
Frost Thos. lace manufacturer
Gelthorpe John, surgeon & drugt
George Wm. butcher
1 Harding Mrs. Lydia
Hickling Geo. gardener, Harvey hill
Hill Thos. bleacher, King's well

Howard Rev. Wm. curate and boarding academy
Hutchinson Mr. Wm.
Johnson John, blacksmith
Kent John, bricklayer
2 Kirk John, thread agent, Lodge
Kirk Wm. sinker maker
Knight Mr. Samuel
Knott John, whitesmith, &c.
Lang Wm. brazier, &c.
Lee Matthw. needlemkr. & drapr
Leeson John, gentleman
Leverton Wm. butcher
Maddock Mrs. Mary
Marshall Gervase, sinkermaker
Marsland Wm. confectioner
1 Mattack Thos. worsted mfr
Mew Wm. gent. Derry Mount
Moore Wm. plumber & glazier
Nix Samuel, bricklayer
Panton Thos. Esq. Arnot hill
Parr Gervase, butcher
2 Pearce Geo. gardener
Peck Wm. well sinker
Phipps Geo. woolstapler

Rastall Mrs. Ann, Harvey hill
Revington Wm. butcher
2 Rhodes Jerh. corn miller
Rhodes Geo. butcher
Richardson Mrs. Elizabeth
Rimmer Mrs. Elizabeth
Rimmer Robert, butcher
Robinson Thos. maltster
2 Rose John, setter-up
Rushton Rt. schoolmaster
Simpson John, gentleman
Stamp John, plumber & glazier
Stirtevant Mrs. Sarah
Taylor John, painter & glazier
1 Thomas Wm. gent
Tinsley John, blacksmith
Tinsley Sarah, straw hat maker
Tinsley Wm. blacksmith
Tomlinson Mrs. Elizabeth
Turbutt Wm. Esq. barrister, Arnold grove
Turner Maria, dressmaker
2 Vickers Wm, gent
2 Walker Mr. William
Ward Hannah, straw hat maker
White John, gent
Wolstenholm Thos. maltster
Wood Uriah, maltster

INNS & TAVERNS.
1 Black Swan, Thomas Bostock
Cross Keys, W. Dickinson
Druid's Tavern, W. Spreckley
2 Fox and Hound, L. Richmond
Horse and Jockey, G. Phipps
2 Old Spot Inn, Peter Bramley
2 Ram Inn, Philip Ariss
Robin Hood, Mary Daft
Seven Stars, John Robinson, and brickmaker
2 Three Crowns, John Wood
2 White Hart, Sarah Hickling

BEER HOUSES.
Board, Giles Hudson
1 Board, William Preston
Friendly Tavern, Jesse Towle
1 Griffin's Head, Thos. Jackson
2 New Inn, Ann Broffitt
2 Ram, Thomas Bradley
Royal Oak, Richard Housley
Bakers & Flour 1 Jeffrey John, dealers.   (& miller)
2 Farnsworth I. 1 Jeffrey W.
(& miller)   Lamin Rd

Redgate Jph
Shaw David
Walters, John
Bobbin Net manufacturers.
Barton Luke
Darker John
Dodson Wm.
Flint Thos.
Gadsby John
Hudson Giles
Hulse Jph
1 Jacklin Thos.
Jeffery, Saml.
Jeffery Wm.
Kelk Wm.
Redgate Jph.
Rhodes —
Smith Chas.
Smith Thos.
Watts Wm.
Willis Robt.
Boot & Shoemkrs
Baguley Mark
Barradell Rd.
Fish George
Fish William
Fisher Samuel
Germen Jph
Hemsley John
Holmes Wm.
Housley Rd.
Mann Robert
Turner Thos
Farmers.
Bates James
Bramley Wm.
2 Brown Jph
Broyan Wm.
Cook Jph.
Denison John
Edwards John
Edwards Thos.
Fowler Richd.
Hallam John
Holmes Samuel
Leivers Chas.
Newham Jonth.
Pilkerton —
Rhodes Thos.
Robinson John
Robinson John
Robinson Thos.

Savile —
Simpson John
& Thos.
Smith John
Taylor Saml.
Tomlinson S.
1 Walker Wm.
Wells Geo.
Whitaker Jph.
Williamson L.
Williamson W.
Framesmiths.
Atherley John
Kelk Wm.
2 Piggen Stirt.
Settle Robert
Webster Wm.
Grocers, &c.
Atkin Samuel
Bottemore Jas.
Bradley Geo.
1 Brewster Sar.
Bullivant Robt.
Foulds Thos.
Humphreys J.
Humphreys —
Jackson Jas.
Jones Richard
Mayfield Geo.
Parr Ann
Powley William
Shelburn Wm.
Showell John
Smith Samuel
Stones Samuel
Wilkinson Ann
1 Wood Anthy.
Hosiery Agents.
2 Beresford John
1 Birtte Edward
Bradley George
2 Breffitt Ann
Eddishaw John
Garratt John
Jackson Matw.
Jew William
Oscroft William
Sharland Wm.
1 Smith Samuel
Willis Robert

Joiners, &c. Foster Wm	§ Rogers Jas.	Fish Wm.
Marked ‡ *are* 2 Hardstaff Jph	‡ Skellington	Hufton Samuel
Cab. Mkrs. & Hardstaff Wm.	William	Mann Jph.
§ *Whtwrights* Jacklin Wm.	*Tailors.*	Shirtcliff Saml.
2 § Bradley T § Lucas Math.	Blasdall Geo.	Taylor Geo.
2 ‡ Challand W Rhodes Thos.	Blasdall John	

ATTENBOROUGH PARISH

Consists of the two manors and *townships of Chilwell and Toton*, which contain 1094 inhabitants, and upwards of 2600 acres of land, at the south western corner of Broxtow Hundred, where the Erwash divides it from Derbyshire, and falls into the Trent, which forms its southern boundary. The whole is enclosed and tithable. Thomas Charlton, Esq. is principal owner, and lord of the manor of Chilwell; and Lady Warren owns most of the land, and is lady of the manor of Toton. But the rectorial tithes of the parish belong to Chesterfield free school, being granted to that institution by the Foljambe family, who obtained the impropriation and advowson from Edward VI. after the dissolution of Felley priory, to which they had previously belonged.

ATTENBOROUGH is a very small and poor village, standing in the two townships of Chilwell and Toton, on the north side of the Trent, 5 miles S. W. by W. of Nottingham. The church is a large fabric dedicated to St. Mary, and has a tower with five bells, surmounted by a handsome spire. It has some armorial glass, as well as rude figures on the capitals of the pillars. The *vicarage* has the church of Bramcote annexed to it, and is valued in the King's books at £4. 15s. Francis Ferrand Foljambe, Esq. is the patron, and the Rev. Samuel Turner the incumbent, for whom the Rev. Thomas Wilkinson officiates. The village is remarkable as being the birth-place of HENRY IRETON, the regicide, and son-in-law of Cromwell, who, after being very active both in the army and the councils of the commonwealth, died at Limeric in 1650, when a pension of £2000 per annum was settled upon his widow and children. His body was brought in state to London, and buried under a costly tomb in Henry the Seventh's chapel, where, however, he was not long permitted to remain, his tomb being destroyed at the Restoration, and his body, as well as Judge Bradshaw's and Cromwell's, disinterred, and buried it is supposed under the gallows at Tyburn.

CHILWELL is a considerable village, on the high road to Ashby-de-la-Zouch, 5 miles W. S. W. of Nottingham. Its township comprises 1450 acres, and 892 inhabitants, many of whom are employed as framework knitters and bobbin net makers. The manor was of the fee of Roger Fitz Huberts, and

3 B

was successively held by the Strelleys, Martells, Babyngtons, Sheffields, Pymmes, Hunlakes, and others ; but it is now possesed by Thomas Charlton, Esq., except several small freeholds and some extensive nurseries belonging to Mr. John Pearson. The *hall*, a handsome modern mansion, is occupied by Owen Davies, M. D. In 1831, after the *reform rioters* had destroyed the large silk mill in the neighbouring village of Beeston, they threatened to " fire Chilwell Hall," but the late Mr. Charlton being then dead in the house, they were dissuaded from their nefarious intention—(see p. 112)—the corpse, however, was removed to a barn at some distance, and was not brought back till next morning, when the incendiaries had dispersed. The *feast* is on the first Sunday in October.

Toton, or *Toueton*, is a pleasant village of scattered houses, on the east bank of the Erwash, nearly 6 miles W.S.W. of Nottingham. Its township extends to the Trent, opposite Barton Ferry, and contains about 1200 acres, mostly belonging to Lady Warren, who has provided a *school-house* and garden; and pays 12s. per week to the master and mistress for teaching 20 boys and 20 girls, whom she also furnishes with a yearly supply of clothing.

CHARITIES.—In consideration of several benefactions to the poor of Attenborough parish, left since 1689 by several of the Charlton family; a rent charge of £5. 6s. is paid out of Ashfield Close, in Bramcote. Out of this, the vicar has £1 for preaching a sermon on the 5th of November. In 1697 Wm. Drury gave two *alms-houses*, in Chilwell, and endowed them with 16s. yearly for two poor inmates, out of the Town-end Close. *Henry Handley*, of Nottingham, left £2, and *Mr. Jefferies* 12s. 6d. per annum, to the poor of the parish. In 1716, *Thomas Newton* left to the poor of Chilwell, Hoegate close and two cottages, and directed the rents to be distributed on Plough Monday. In 1747, *Samuel Garton* left to the same poor, the Hall croft, at Beeston. Several other small legacies swell the *yearly amount* of the Chilwell benefactions to £5. 7s. 6d., exclusive of the two cottages occupied by paupers, and 13s. belonging to the poor of Toton.

CHILWELL.

Marked † reside at Attenborough.

Burdett Thos. bricklayer & mkr
Cartwright John, wheelwright
Cheetham John, maltster
Clark John, yeoman
Davies Owen, M.D. Chilwell hall
† Day Hy. vict. Blue Bell
Felton John, gentleman
Flewitt Benj. vict. Chequers
Garton John, brickmaker
Godber Edw. shopkeeper
Hallam Jarvis, shopkeeper
Holmes Geo. butcher
Hopwell John, vict. Cadland Inn
Jackson John, farmer
Keetley Thos. blacksmith
Keetley Thos. jun. tailor
King John, tailor
Meades Jas. Jph. & Saml. cattle dealers
† Merrill Jph. yeoman
Morris Thos. cattle dealer
Oldfield John, shopkeeper

Pearson John, nursery & seeds-
man
Pearson John, warper
Porter Rebecca, vict. Red Lion
Plackett John, schoolmaster
Posnett Rt. overseer
Rowland Saml. tailor
Rowland Wm. shopkeeper
Salmon Math. shopkeeper
Savage John, joiner
Thompson John, ropemaker
Tipping Mrs. Mary
Tipping Wm. butcher
Townsend Leaf, farmer
† Widdowson Mr. John
Wilson Jarvis, gardener
Wright John, chief constable for
South Division of Broxtow

Bobbin Net Makers.
Baxter Chas.   King John
Brown Saml.   Morris Jph.

Hickling Saml.   Wilmott John
Kirkland John

Boot and Shoe Makers.
Burton Jph.   Shilcock Rt.
Eaton Thos.   Stephenson W.
Flewitt Wm.   Truswell Thos.
King John   Willerts Jph.
Carrier.—S. Lee, to Nottingham,
Wed. and Sat. 7 mg.

TOTON (FARMERS, &c.).
Attenborough Lee Wm.
W. cattle dlr. Moulds John
Earp John   Shaw Rt. school-
Eaton Benj.   master
Glover John   Smalley Francis,
Holbrook John   maltster
Howard Thos.   Toulson Wm.
Hubbard John,   Wragg Geo.
corn miller
Jowitt William,
wheelwright

BASFORD PARISH

Lies principally in the vale of the *Leen*, where that river is
augmented by two small streams called the *Day-Brook* and
White-moor Spring, but its eastern extremity rises to the lofty
hills of Mapperley. It extends from 1¼ to 3 miles north of
Nottingham, and comprises about 2650 acres, of which 1158
were enclosed in 1792, and several large tracts have since been
covered with thriving plantations. It has generally a rich
sandy soil, which lets for about 30s per acre, but some small
allotments are let for more than double that amount. The
Duke of Newcastle is lord of the manor, and owner of a large
portion of the land, which was anciently divided into several
manors, held of the fee of *William Peverel*, whose *Honour
Court* was formerly held here.—(See p. 22 and 138.) At *Scottom*, near the Leen, are three covered springs and a large reservoir, formed in 1827, for the purpose of supplying the Nottingham Old Waterworks, as has already been seen at page 187.
It is to the *lace and hosiery manufactures*, and to its contiguity
with Nottingham, that Basford parish owes its present wealth
and consequence, and from which causes its *population* has been
tripled during the last thirty years, having encreased since the
year 1801, from 2124 to 6305 souls. For the accommodation
of this great augmentation in the number of its inhabitants, several *new villages* have been built in the parish, which now contains
seven *bleaching* establishments, five corn mills, and several
hundred stocking frames, and bobbin net machines. Here is

also a large WORKHOUSE, which has been built by "*forty associated parishes.*"

BASFORD old village is very extensive, and lies in the vale of the Leen, 2¼ miles N.N.W. of Nottingham. The scenery around it is rich in the extreme, being well clothed with wood and thickly studded with modern mansions, and populous new villages in this and the adjacent parish of Radford, mostly built of brick and covered with blue slate. The stone bridge which here crosses the Leen, was built in 1831. The *church,* dedicated to St. Leodigarius, has a handsome tower, and a spacious nave and side aisles in good preservation; but the ancient armorial bearings that formerly decorated its windows are gone. The living is a *vicarage,* valued in the King's books at £8. 17s. 7d., and is in the patronage of the King. The Rev. Thomas Hoskins is now the incumbent, and the Rev. William Herbert the curate. The Wesleyan and Kilhamite *Methodists* have each a chapel here, and the former have another in New Basford, built in 1825. There are also in the parish two *General Baptist Chapels,* one in Old Basford, built in 1819, and another in New Basford, erected in 1827, at the cost of £300, on land given by Mr. James Smith; and at Carrington, there is a small Primitive Methodist Chapel, built in 1828.

NEW BASFORD is a large village, which has been raised during the last ten years, near the southern extremity of Old Basford, within 2 miles N.W. of Nottingham, and consists of several good streets which cross each other at right angles, and are occupied principally by bobbin net makers. *Algarthorpe,* afterwards called *Eland Hall,* from its former owners, stands on a fine eminence half a mile E. of the old village, and is now commonly called *Bagthorpe.* It belongs, with the demesne, to the Duke of Newcastle, and is occupied by Lieut. John Wright, Esq. The *Tinker House* estate, on the north side of Basford, has been bequeathed by its late proprietor to a number of legatees.

CARRINGTON, upon the Mansfield road, on the east side of the parish, 1¾ mile N. of Nottingham, is another new village, and consists partly of handsome villas, occupied by merchants and lace manufacturers, who have their warehouses in Nottingham. It has its name from Lord Carrington, who some years ago sold the estate to Ichabod Wright, Esq., who has since re-sold it in building lots.

MAPPERLEY PLACE, 2 miles N. of Nottingham, is another range of modern villas, partly upon the same road, and extending eastward from the vicinity of Carrington, to the summit of Mapperley Hills, below which, but upon a commanding eminence, is *Mapperley House,* the handsome seat of Ichabod Wright, Esq., banker, who has beautified the estate with many thriving plantations, and brought the land into a fine state of cultivation, though much of it is high and cold, rising to the bleak and clayey hills which form part of the Burgess Grounds of Nottingham.—(See p. 135.)

SHERWOOD, at the north-east corner of the parish, is another populous district of newly built houses, on the Mansfield road, 2¼ miles N. of Nottingham. Near it is *Daybrook Lodge*, the seat of Captain George Phillips, Esq., and *Woodthorpe House*, the property of Mr. Richard Hooton, but occupied by Martin Roe, Esq.

TWO-MILE-HOUSE is a scattered village, at the west end of the parish, on the Alfreton road, 2 miles N.W. of Nottingham, where Samuel Hall and Co. have a large establishment for singing lace by gas, for which process Mr. Hall is the patentee.

WHITEMOOR PLACE is a hamlet of modern houses, on the same road, a quarter of a mile S. of the above. Here is an extensive warp lace manufactory, belonging to George Morrison and Co.

The only CHARITY possessed by this parish is, £40 bequeathed by John Smith and others, and now vested in Messrs. Wright's bank in Nottingham. The yearly interest (24s.) is distributed at Christmas among 12 poor widows.

In the following Directory of Basford Parish, those marked 1 reside at Basford Old Village, 2 at Carrington, 3 Mapperley Place, 4 New Basford, 5 Sherwood, and 6 at Two-Mile-House.

1 Allcock John, farmer
1 Alton Elias, tanner
Ashton Wm. governor of the Associated Workhouse
4 Bailey Philip, gentleman
1 Bailey Thos. wine merchant
2 Berresford Rd. draper
6 Biggs Mr. Joseph
1 Birch Mrs. Eliz
4 Birkin Rd. lace manufacturer
4 Birkin Wm. turner & winding machine maker, George st
1 Blakely Henry, cowkeeper
4 Booth James, Scotland place
1 Bramley John, farmer
4 Brandreth John, cow leech, Chapel st
1 Brewitt Bellamy, gent
2 Brown Bratt, cowkeeper
1 Brown John, jun. bleacher
4 Brown John, cowkeeper
1 Caddick Wm. jun. brazier and tin plate worker
1 Caddick Mr. Wm
1 Carnell Jas. lace mfr
6 Carr Jas. bookkeeper
4 Carrington Lieut. Wm
5 Cato Mr. Thomas
1 Chamberlain John, farmer
1 Cliff John gent
5 Clower Wm. cowkeeper
1 Cockerham Mrs. Hannah
1 Cooke John, bookkeeper
Cooper Mr. John, Sherwood hill
1 Dexter Geo. carter
4 Elliott Rd. cowkeeper
1 Farrand Mr. John
3 Fidler Mr. George
1 Firth Mr. George
1 Fowler John, saddler
1 Fox John, bleacher
6 Goodson Jph. gentleman
2 Grew Mr. Jph
3 Hall John, gentleman
1 Hall Rt. traveller
4 Harrison Geo. carter
1 Hemingway Wm. hair dresser
4 Hewes John, gentleman
2 Hopkins John, lace mfr
1 Jackson Thos. farmer
1 King Stephen, carter
1 Kirkland Wm. farmer

3 B 2

3 Linford Thos. gent
3 Maltby Thos. gent
1 Mellows Mr. John
4 Miller Mr. Marmaduke
6 Mitchell James, fkr
1 Monkman Thos. excise officer
3 Morley Wm. agent to the Norwich Union Fire Office
4 Newton Geo. gent
Parker Wm. farmer, Little Farm
4 Pepper Mr. Thos. Pepper st
Phillips Capt. George, Daybrook Lodge
3 Rawson Rd. gent
4 Raynor Mr. John
4 Rean John, warper
Richards John, Basford cottage
Roe Martin, Esq. Woodthorpe house
1 Robinson Samuel, lace mfr
1 Robinson Wm. maltster
2 Rogers John, hosier
1 Rogers Moses, cowkeeper
1 Rose Mr. Thos.
2 Russell Wm. lace thread dlr
4 Sanders Mr. John
1 Sanders Saml. solicitor
3 Shelton Geo. hosier
4 Smith Mr. John
4 Southam Abm. carter
4 Spray Geo. warper
1 Strover Thos. R. N.
4 Strover Mrs. Mary
2 Swinscow Geo. warper
1 Swinton Jph. parish clerk
2 Taylor Wm. bobbin & carriage maker
2 Telfer Wm. hawker
5 Tilley Rd. gent
3 Tibbetts John, lace mfr
2 Tomlin Abm. maltster
2 Tomlin Wm. bookkeeper
1 Torr Mrs. Jane
5 Tull Wm. cowkeeper
6 Twiger John, carter
2 Wagstaff, Mrs. Eliz
Watson Wm. wine mert. Daybrook

6 Wayte Wm. bookr
6 Webster John, carter
1 Williams Wm. solicitor
2 Wilson Mr. Jas
4 Winrow Mrs. Ruth
2 Woolley Mrs. Ann
Wright Ichabod, Esq. banker, Mapperley
Wright Lieut. John, Adjutant to the Nottingham Yeomanry Cavalry, Bagthorpe

BLEACHERS.
Brown Geo. White Moor Spring
1 Brown John, (& lace dresser)
Diggle John, (& finisher) White moor place
Farrand Geo. Day brook works
1 Hall Saml. & Co. patent gasers Two-mile-house
1 Milnes John, Hall mill
1 Pearson Jph

INNS & TAVERNS.
1 Barley Mow, Wm. Pidgeon
1 Fox and Crown, John Stanyon
1 Fox & Hounds, Jph. Swinton
4 Horse & Groom, Jas. Taylor
1 Horse & Jockey, W. Bagdale
2 King Wm. IV. Thos. Pepper
1 Old Pear Tree, Rd. Charlton
4 Plough & Harrow, Fs. Ward
1 Queen's Head, Thos. Stoddart
6 Red Lion, John Hartshorn
1 Rose, John Kirkby
1 Shoulder of Mutton, J. Abbott
1 White Swan, Thos. Briggs

BEER HOUSES.
2 Board, Matthew Walker
4 Board, Wm. Sander
4 Board, John Hodgkinson
1 Bull & Butcher, John Cooper
2 Carrington, Wm. Corbett
5 Generous Briton, Jas. Shaw
4 Jolly Farmer, Wm. Bromley
1 King Wm. IV. Jas. Sturgess
5 Robin Hood, John Cockayne
2 Royal Oak, Chas. Fulforth
6 Sir John Barley Corn, John Webster

Academies.
2 Marshall Eliz
2 Morris Thos
4 Thurman Sal. Meed

1 Perrin John
4 Strover Jane Maria
4 Tookey Sarah
1 Wroughton Thos

Agents (Comss.).
4 Millnes Mark
4 Pearson Andrew
5 Simms Richard

Bakers, &c.
1 Bird Wm
2 Daykin John
1 Hancock Matthew
4 Reddish Mary
1 Thorpe Thos
Blacksmiths.
6 Attenborrough John
1 Grocock John
1 Horsman John
1 Keyworth Thos
1 Lees Geo
1 Shepherd Samuel
1 Shipstone Geo
4 Shipston Wm
2 Wall John
Bobbin Net Makers.
4 Allen Jph. Northgt
2 Astill Wm. (mfr)
4 Atkin Isaac
4 Atkin Wm
4 Bailey William
1 Bancroft William
1 Bertie John
4 Barton John
4 Biddle & Birkin
4 Bingham Wm
4 Bingley Wm
4 Birch Noah
4 Birch Thomas
5 Bradbury Thomas
5 Briggs Amos
5 Brocklehurst Rd
1 Brown Charles
4 Butters Edward
1 Charlton Richard
2 Churchard Jph
5 Clarkson Paul
5 Cooper Henry
2 Corbett William
2 Cox John
5 Crawford Jph
5 Dealtry John
2 Dickinson John
1 Donald John
2 Drage William
4 Eakins Francis
4 Falkner William
2 Fido John
1 Flewitt George
1 Flewitt Samuel
5 Flower William
1 Ford William

5 Foster Samuel
1 Fox Edward
4 Gamble John
2 Glover Thomas
5 Green Walter
4 Green William
4 Grimley John
2 Grundy Joshua
4 Hallam John
4 Hammond Rd
4 Hankin Jonth
2 Hardy Edw
2 Hardy Thos.
4 Haslam John
2 Hayes Philip
2 Hazeldine Jas
4 Hewes Jas
1 Higgate John
2 Hill Robt
2 Hirst Wm.
4 Hind & Sneath
4 Hodgkinson Jph
5 Hollowell John
5 Holmes John
2 Hurt Wm
2 Key Wm
4 Illig John
2 Kirk Jas
2 Luke Thos
4 Leatherland Wm
2 Lee Stephen
2 Leeman —
2 Lord Thos
5 Lovegrove John
1 Lowe John
5 Maidens John
2 Maltby Chas
2 Mansfield John
4 Marriott Jph
4 Massey Wm
5 May Thos
2 Mee Wm
4 Miller Asa
4 Miller Ire
4 Miller Mdk
4 Millnes Mark
Morrison Geo. & Co.
    Whitemoor
5 Myott Thos
4 Oliver Thos
4 Owen Harriet
4 Pearson Fdk
4 Palmer Edwin

5 Penn Wm
1 Rhodes Thos
4 Robinson Mary
4 Robinson Thomas
5 Rogers William
4 Ryle George
4 Sander Noah
4 Saxton William
2 Shaw John
5 Shipman John
5 Shepperson Wm
4 Simms Francis
5 Simms Richard
4 Skelston Samuel
4 Slack Thomas
3 Smith Chas. Lostcar
    cottage
2 Smith Mr. Wm
2 Spencer John
4 Spray William
1 Starr John
4 Summers William
4 Taw Charles
2 Taylor Thomas
4 Thompson Robert
2 Tollington Thomas
2 Tomlinson Wm
2 Fritchley John
2 Walker David
5 Walker John
2 Walker Saul
4 Walker William
4 Webb Francis
5 Willott Jonathan
1 Wingfield Thomas
4 Withers Charles
1 Wright Robert
Boot & Shoe Makers.
1 Henson John
2 Howett John
4 Maskery Wm
6 Pettener Wm
4 Robinson Giles
1 Rowland Thos
5 Saunders Jph
4 Sisling Wm
1 Stenson Thos
2 Walker Matthew
2 Wash Fras
1 Watson Wm
Bricklayers.
1 Hooton John
4 Kirk Jas

1 Oscroft Jph
1 Stretton Thos
4 Walker Benj
  Brick Makers.
3 Bean Samuel
3 James Thomas
3 North Thomas
  Butchers.
Ayre Thos, Shewood-
  hill
1 Bellairs Wm
4 Bostock Geo
1 Cartledge George
5 Cockayne John
4 Dawes John
4 Mason John
4 Mellows Thos
1 Mellows Thos
1 Pilkinton Thos
4 Toon James
2 Toon Thos
2 Whelvand John
1 Woodward Mark
  Corn Millers.
1 Champion John
1 Hancock Joseph
5 Oliver William
5 Reddish William
1 Thorpe John and
  Thomas
  Druggists.
4 Atkin William
1 Bramley James
Framesmiths & Ma-
* chine Mkrs.*
1 Bertie John
2 Fletcher Joseph
4 Hammond Rd
4 Riley Joseph
Shipstone Wm
4 Soar John, South st
1 Soar William
2 Wall John

  Gardeners.
1 Brown Francis
Mason Wm. Tinker hs
  Hosiery Mfrs.
1 Bamford Samuel
1 Bickerstaff Rd
1 Binks Joseph
1 Constable William
1 Ellis George
1 Flinders John
1 Jebbett William
1 Lowe John
1 Mellors J. Buckwd
1 Wroughton Jph
  Joiners.
4 Cargill Samuel
1 Cooke John
2 Gale George
1 Gwynn Wm
4 Oldham John
4 Radford Garvis
1 Robinson Samuel
1 Watson William
  Maltsters.
1 Holmes & Robinson
  Milliners.
5 Cooper Ann
5 Garton Sarah
1 Oakley Elizabeth
4 Palmer Elizabeth
4 Rose Elizabeth
1 Stretton Jane
2 Taylor Sophia
4 Webster Ann
  Needle, &c. Makers.
1 Marriott Samuel
Stephenson John
Painters & Glaziers.
1 Abbott John
1 Lee Joseph
  Shopkeepers.
2 Baker George
2 Bradley Losto

5 Briggs Amos
1 Carlile Robert
1 Cartledge George
5 Crawford Joseph
4 Davenport Edw
1 Derby James
4 Fidler John
4 Fish Samuel
1 Flewitt George
1 Freeman John
2 Fulforth Charles
1 Grocock Rd
4 Holders Edw
4 Hollis John
1 Hufton Joseph
1 Jebbutt William
4 Kirkman Sarah
1 Lowe Ann
1 Mather Ann
1 Mee William
1 Mozeley William
1 Raven John
6 Shaw William
5 Shepperson Wm
  Sinker Maker.
1 Scott William
  Surgeons.
1 Fitzpatrick Rd. Jas
1 Morley William
1 Walker Frederick
  Tailors.
1 Bramley James
2 Brown Alexander
6 Byard Alexander
1 Cooper John
2 Hilton John
1 Jefferson Isaac
2 Leeman —
1 Towle John
  Wheelwrights.
1 Hanson John
6 Hill Thomas
1 Massey Samuel

BEESTON PARISH.

BEESTON, 4 miles W.S.W. of Nottingham, is a populous village and parish upon the road to Ashby-de-la-Zouch, and near the Trent canal. During the last ten years, its inhabitants have encreased from 1534 to 2530, and many new houses have been erected. Here are now upwards of 100 bobbin net machines, a number of stocking frames, and a wholesale brewery; but the large *silk mill* which employed 200 workmen, was burnt down in the Reform riots of 1831,—(See p. 112,)—and is not likely to be rebuilt, as the proprietor has removed to another mill near Derby. The parish comprises about 1500 acres of rich land, enclosed in 1809, when the tithes were commuted for an allotment of 75A. 2R. 23P. to the vicar; 97A. 2R. 1P. to Lord Cavendish, as impropriator of the corn tithe, and 54A. 2R. 17P. to P. B. Strey, Esq., in lieu of the hay tithe. The corn tithe land was afterwards sold to Lord Middleton, besides whom here are several other freeholders; but P. B. Strey, Esq., is the principal owner and lord of the manor.

The *church* is dedicated to St. John the Baptist, and was anciently appropriated to Lenton Priory. The *vicarage* is valued in the King's books at £4. 15s. The Duke of Devonshire is the patron, and the Rev. John Woolley, M.A., the incumbent, and has 32A. 3R. 23P. of ancient glebe, besides the allotment just named. Here is both a Methodist and a General Baptist Chapel; the former erected in 1830. A *school* is supported by Miss Evans, of Lenton Grove, for the education of 60 poor girls. The parish *feast* is on the Sunday before July the 12th. *Hassock Close*, and two allotments received at the enclosure, belong to the poor, being purchased, in 1727, with £70 left by Mary Charlton and others. This land (7A. 1R. 34P.) is now let for £19. 18s. per annum, which, with £1, the interest of timber money; £1 from Handley's Charity, and £2. 10s. out of the Horse-Dole Meadow, is distributed amongst the poor parishioners.

Postman.—Joseph Oldham, to Nottingham, at 10 in the morning; returns 6 in the evening.

Abbott Rev. Rt. (Bap.) schoolr
Aislabie William, schoolmaster
Aram John, bricklayer
Attenborough Mrs. Mary
Baguley Edward, staymaker
Bailey Samuel small ware dlr.
Barker Edward, parish clerk
Barker Thomas, earthenware dlr
Barker William, Beeston Lock
Barnard Thos. tea and coal dlr
Barnes John, plumber & glazier
Bond Edward, gent.
Boot Fras. mfr. Beeston Cottage
Bramley John, butcher
Broadburst Louisa, schoolmrs
Burrows Robert, gent
Burton John, auctioneer
Cheetham Misses Sarah & Mary
Chouler Thos. & Wm. maltsters
Chouler Tmy. and W. maltsters
Colson James, painter
Cooling Wm. needlemaker
Cross James, blacksmith
Cross Thomas, gardener
Dix William, blacksmith
Fellows Elihu Samuel, gent
Fellows Alfred, Esq. banker
Flamstead Mrs. Dorothy
Frettingham G. nurseryman, &c.
George John, cart owner
Gollin John, plumber & glazier
Greasley John, gardener
Hammond Mr. Wm. jun.
Heath James Tatlock, solicitor
Hollingworth Chas. hosier agent
Hurst William, solicitor, & Not.
Hutchinson Jas. hosier agent
Latham Wm. bricklayer
Lidgett John, nailmaker
Lomas Joseph, gent

Morrill George, saddler
Moult John, bricklayer
Muxlow John, stonemason
Needham John Manning, brewer,
and dealer in London porter
Nixon James, gent.
Nutt Robert, butcher
Orton Henry, surgeon
Orton Richard, gent
Pearson Mr. John
Reed Miss Eliz.
Roberts Wm. sen. overseer
Roebuck Hy. earthenware dlr
Roebuck John, cart owner
Salthouse Mrs. Ann
Shardlow Geo. hair dresser
Swann Saml. Hy. hop and seed
merchant, and Nottingham
Taylor, Robert, gardener
Tipping Francis, butcher
Toplis Charles, gentleman
Treece John, overlooker
Vose William, boat owner
Wainman, Mr. —
Wakefield Saml. mr. & Nottm
Ward, Edw. carver, gilder, and
bookseller
Wilkinson John, rope mkr., Lock
Wilson George, gentleman
Woolley Rev. John, M.A. vicar
Wootton William, painter
Wright Mrs. Mary

Bakers & Flour
Dealers.
Arnell Simeon
Bramley John
Burton John
Cross Henry
Day William
Witham Wm

Bobbin Net Mkrs
Antcliffe Geo.
Attenboorugh R
Attenborough Sl
AttenboroughW
Ball William
Booth Jerh
Booth Wm
Brightmore Jas
Cox John
Crichlow W& T
Cross Henry
Foster Robert

Frettingham W
George John
Gibson Daniel
Goodliffe Wm
Hood James
Hood Thomas
Horsley & Faw-
kes

Hough James
Humphrey J
Hutchinson —
Jackson John
Lee Joseph
Maltby William
Mayfield Henry
Pearson Wm
Powdrill Thos.
Roberts Wm
Sibbert Thomas
Smith Jas
Smith Edw

Soar Francis
Spencer Isaac
Thornell Rt
Towle Thomas
Turner Jph
Walker Thos
Walker Wm
Wood William
Wootton Jph
Wright Wm
Boot and Shoe
Makers.
Facer Thomas
Grose Samuel
Harwood Wm.
Hudson John
Shaw John
ShrewsberyThos
Towlson Thos
Webster Thos
Farmers.
Barker Robert
Cheetham Chas
Hammond Wm
Hardy Henry

Harris Thomas
Hurt Wm
Surplice Wm
Walker Jph
Walker Wm
Frame and Ma-
chine Smiths.
Mather James
Oldknow Rd
Turner Jph
Wilkins John
Winrow John
Grocers & Shks.
Chambers Saml
Fletcher Benj.
Fawkes &. Cow-
ling
Goodall F & S
Henson John
Hough Jas
Penneston Wm
Surplice Ann
Walker Thos
Witham Wm
Wyld Wm

INNS AND TAVERNS.

Boat and Horses, Rd Harwood
Durham Ox, Edw. Smith
Greyhound, Wm. Martin

BEER HOUSES.

Board, William Asher
Board, William Heard
Board, John Bramley
Commercial Inn, John Burton
Cottage Inn, William Birkin
Cricket Players, Robert Taylor
Jolly Anglers, John Wilkinson
Royal Oak, Edw. Bradshaw
Three Horse Shoes, Wm. Flewitt
White Lion, Cath. Wilson

Joiners, &c.
Barker Thos
Burnham John
Foster Robert
Henson Thos
Stead Wm.
Walker John
Tailors.
Bland Wm

Bradshaw Edw
Bradshaw Thos
Brown John
Pollard John
Roberts William
and draper
Shardlow Geo
Swann Saml
Thornley Wm

Wm Martin's Van to Nottingham every Sat. mg. at 10.

Coach to Birmingham at ¼ past
past 8 mg. ; Notm. at ½ past 3 aft.

BILBOROUGH PARISH.

BILBOROUGH is a small but pleasant village and parish, 3½ miles W.N.W. of Nottingham, where, in Thoresby's time, *coal* was got at the depth of 100 yards, but the mines have long been exhausted. The church is dedicated to St. Martin, and is a rectory valued in the King's books at £3. 12s. 6d. Both it and the neighbouring rectory of Strelley, are in the patronage of Thomas Webb Edge, Esq. and incumbency of the Rev. J. W. Edge, who, at the enclosure of the two parishes, received an allotment of 220 acres in lieu of tithes. Mr. Edge is also principal owner and lord of the manor.

BROXTOW, at the east end of the parish, three miles N.W. of Nottingham, is an ancient house and manor of 300 acres, which gives name to this Hundred, and was of great consequence in Saxon times, when it had a chapel, of which no traces now remain. It belongs to Lord Middleton, and is occupied by Mr. Shepperson. The house is prettily embowered in trees, but much of its picturesque effect is destroyed by some uncouth modern additions.

Bilborough School was endowed by Richard Smedley, in 1744, with £5 per annum, now paid by the Earl of Stamford, for the education of four children of this parish and four of Strelley.

Briggs John, schoolr. & clerk
Chambers Samuel, shoemaker.
Oldershaw, Wm. land bailiff
Sabin Thomas, wheelwright
Shepperson Joseph and Thomas, Broxtow

Smith Matthew. blacksmith
Ward Richard, blacksmith
Farmers.
Blunston Jno. Towle Henry
Calam W. Chil- Underwood W.
   well-dam   Wagstaff Oliver

BRAMCOTE PARISH.

BRAMCOTE, 5 miles W. by S. of Nottingham, is a highly picturesque village and parish, occupying several lofty hills, and having some large and handsome mansions occupied by their owners. It contains 562 inhabitants, and about 980 acres of rich land, which was enclosed in 1771, when 32A. 2R. 35P. were allotted to Chesterfield School for the corn tithe; 23A. 3P. to Mr. H. Hudson for the hay tithe; 4A. 2R. 2P. to the vicar, and 5A. to the churchwardens. The CHURCH stands upon an abrupt eminence, and is annexed to to the vicarage of Attenborough. (See p. 549.) Here is interred *Henry Handley, Esq.* whose charities to this and other parishes are noticed at page 165. The poor here have also 17s. yearly from *Pilkington Close*, left in 1675 by Thomas Hollingworth to the poor of Bramcote, Long-Eaton, and Sawley. Bramcote Moor close was purchased for the poor with £10 left in 1786 by Mary

Charlton, and now lets for 25s. yearly. *Bramcote Hills* is the beautiful seat of John Sherwin Sherwin, Esq., the principal owner and lord of the manor. He is the eldest son of Mrs. Longden, and assumed his present name pursuant to the will of the late owner of the estate. *Bramcote Grove*, is the seat of H. Mundy, Esq. who purchased it in 1829. The parish *feast* is on the Sunday after Old Michaelmas day.

Sherwin John Sherwin, Esq.
Aislabie Samuel, gent
Allcock George, gent
Allcock Wm. butcher
Atkin William, joiner
Bagshaw Samuel, victualler and maltster
Cliff Daniel, beerhouse
Ellis George, excise officer
Felkin Mr. William
Fox Mrs. Ann
Gibbins Jph. nursery and seedsman
Gibbins Thomas, gardener
Hall Lawrence, starch mfr
Hall Thomas, manager Starch works
Harker John, gent
Jackson Thomas, gent
Lindley Miss Mary, boarding academy
Longden Mrs. Charlotte, gentlewoman
Munday Henry, Esq. Bramcote grove

Renshaw George, hosier
Scatterwood Peter, gamekpr
Snow William, butcher
Spray William, sen. & jun. blacksmiths
Surplis Samuel, land surveyor
Wallis Mrs. Elizabeth
Wilkinson Rev. Thomas, curate.
Wright Charles, Esq. banker

Bobbin net Makers.
Booth J. tatting　Horsley W. and
Briggs Edw　　　tatting
Hewitt Jsha　　Horsley Wm
Hewitt Rd　　　Soar Saml
　　　　　　　Wheatley Jph

Boot and Shoe Makers.
Beighton John　Hobson John
Farnsworth G　Inger Wm
Farnsworth Jas　Spray John
Freeman Jph　Walker Wm

Farmers.
Briggs Wm　　Morley John
Clawer John　Radford Wm
Henson Sarah　Tebbutt Wm.
Husband Fras　Manor house

BULWELL PARISH.

BULWELL, in the vale of the Leen, 4 miles N.N.W. of Nottingham, is a populous village and parish, where there are three bleach works, a lace thread mill, three corn mills, several extensive limestone quarries and kilns, and a number of stocking frames and bobbin net machines. It contains 2,611 inhabitants; and upwards of 1600 acres of land, all enclosed except 120 acres in the open forest. Lord Melbourne, Sir Charles Colville, Mr. Faulkenbridge, and the Rev. Alfred Padley, are owners of nearly all the land, and the latter is lord of the manor and patron of the rectory, having purchased his estate here in in 1827 of the assignees of Godfrey Wentworth, Esq. The *church,* dedicated to St. Mary, stands upon a steep declivity. The rectory is valued in the King's books at £5. 5s. 10d.; and is now enjoyed by by the Rev. J. W. Armytage, M.A. The Wesleyan and Primitive Methodists and the Baptists have each a chapel here. The *Free School* was erected in 1668, by George Strelley, Esq. who endowed it with land and buildings, now worth £18 per annum, for which the master teaches eight free scholars. *John Dams*, in 1786, left 7 acres, now worth 10 guineas per annum, for the preaching of nine lectures yearly in the church, viz. on the last Tuesday in every month, except July, August, and November. The interest of £50, vested in the Nottingham Flood road, and left by George Robinson, in 1798, is distributed amongst the poor at Christmas. *Bulwell House*, a handsome mansion with thriving plantations, is the seat of the Rev. A. Padley.

Those marked 1 *reside at Blenheim,* 2 *New Bulwell,* 3 *Hempshill.*

Adams John, joiner
Allcock Chas. miller & bleacher
Ash Henry, grocer & chandler
Ashmore Wm. shoemaker
Banks Rev. Saml. B.A. curate
Barber Richard, butcher
Barlow John, shoemaker
Best Peter, surgeon
Brocleburst Edward, shoemaker
Brown John, tailor
Brummitt Dowager, Red Lion
Calladine Joseph, schoolmaster
Cartledge Samuel and Son, lace thread manufacturers
Chambers J. plumber & glazier
Cook Joseph, shopkeeper
Dore Richard, joiner
Faulconbridge Alfred, maltster and brickmaker
Fisher James, vict. Star
Foulkes Wm. baker, &c.
Gent John, shopkeeper
Gent John, butcher & shopkpr
1 Granger John, maltster
Hackitt Samuel, stonemason
Heaton Robert, schoolmaster
Hind Sl. vict. Horse & Groom
Holmes George, stonemason
Horsley John, basket maker
Howley John, shoemaker
Jennison & Robinson, bleachers
Jennison Rd. jun. blacksmith
Jerrom William, baker, &c.
2 Key John, shopkeeper
Knight John, bricklayer
Leivers Geo. shoemaker & vict.
Leivers Geo. Hetches, butcher
Leivers Jno. shoemaker & vict.
2 Levers W. vict. and shopkpr

Lormer Jas. farrier & shopkpr
Manley Wm. mason & shopkpr
Marshall Mrs. Catherine
Marshall Hy. Limekiln Inn
Marshall Misses Eliz. and Mary
Monks ——, tailor
Moore Henry, shoemaker
Ogle John, butcher & shopkpr
Oldham Samuel, joiner
Oldham William, joiner
Padley Rev. Alf. Bulwell House
Parker William, shoemaker
2 Pearson James, grocer
Pickard Thomas, farrier
Pickering Edwin Geo. boarding academy
Porter William, tailor
Raworth William, butcher
Read Fras. butcher and vict
Reed Thos. vict. Limekilns
Robinson Ann, vict. White Lion
Robinson John, grocer
Sansom, Rd. gardener & seedsman
Savage Thos. plumber & glazier
Shelton John, bobbin & carriage maker and shopkeeper
Shipstone George, joiner
Sills Goodacre, blacksmith
2 Sims George, hosiery agent
Smedley James, shopkeeper
Smith Chas. vict. Scotch Grey
Stafford Martha, vict. Ball
Stanford and Co. bleachers
Taylor John, vict. Masons' Arms
Thompson Chas. blacksmith
Tilley Joseph & Wm. tailors
Walker Geo. blacksmith
Walker Joseph, corn miller
Walker T. vict. Three Crowns

3 c

Walton John, corn miller
Wesson John, vict. White Hart
West Joseph, shoemaker
White Latimer, bookkeeper
Wilkinson John, wheelwright
Wood John, shopkeeper
Wright Jph. grocer and miller

Bobbin Net Makers.
Marriott John   Walker Thos.
Marshall, Josh   Wood John
Mitchell Josiah   Wright Jph
Tye William   Wright Wm

Farmers.
Adin Wm.   1Botham John

1Fewster Thos   Oldham Geo
3Houghton Hy   Stout Samuel
Houghton Jph   Turner Jph
3Houghton Luke   Wilkinson Rd
Hutchinson W

Limeburners.
Ball Geo   Marshall ——
Bartram Sam   Oldham Geo
Chamberlain J   Reed Thos
Hollingsworth J   Stout Saml
Lane Thos   Walker & Hird
Marshall Hy   Wilkinson J & R
Marshall Jos

COSSAL PAR. CHAP.

COSSAL is a small village and parochial chapelry, annexed to the rectory of Trowell, and situated on an eminence near the Derbyshire border, 6 miles W.N.W. of Nottingham. It contains 341 inhabitants, and about 900 acres of land, all belonging to Lord Middleton, except 40 acres of glebe. The church or chapel is a small ancient edifice with a short spire, and under it is an old vault belonging to the Willoughby family; near it is an *Hospital*, endowed by George Willoughby, Esq. with property that now produces £132 yearly, for four men and four women, the former of whom have each 5s. and the latter 4s. weekly, besides a yearly allowance of coals, and each a suit of clothes every two years. The *feast* is on the nearest Sunday to Martinmas-day.

COSSAL MARSH is a hamlet half a mile N. of Cossal, where the Awsworth, Babbington, and Strelley collieries have each a wharf on the Nottingham and Cromford Canal. There was formerly a colliery at Cossal, but it was exhausted many years ago.

Haseldine Joseph, bricklayer
Hooley Esau, shoemaker
Johnson Henry, shopkeeper
Lowe Rd. weaver & parish clerk
Riley Ann, vict. Royal Oak
Tarlton David, butcher

Farmers.
Hasledine Wm   Shorley Fras
Fritchley Rd   White Jph
Johnson Thos   Wilson Isaac
Sills Thos

EASTWOOD PARISH.

EASTWOOD is a well built village, pleasantly situated on an eminence on the Derby road and the Cromford canal, 8¼ miles N.W. of Nottingham. The parish contains 1395 inhabitants, and, 900A. 2R. 4P. of land, under which there were excellent beds of coal at various depths, from 5 to 50 yards, but they have all been got. A wonderful story is told here of a farmer being *swallowed up alive*, in the parlour of the village alehouse, whilst he was swallowing a cup of ale, to the great surprise of the host, who by this means discovered that his mansion was built on an exhausted coal mine. George Walker, Esq. is the principal owner and lord of the manor, which was of the fee of Wm. Peverel. At the enclosure in 1791, the tithes were commuted for an allotment of 138A. 0R. 21P. in addition to 7A. 0R. 6P. of old glebe. The *church*, dedicated to St. Mary, was rebuilt in 1764, and greatly enlarged in 1826, so that it has now 234 free sittings. The rectory is valued in the King's books at £4. 13s. 1d. John Plumptre, Esq. is the patron, and the Rev. John Western Plumptre, the incumbent. The overseers distribute 20s. yearly, as the interest of 20 guineas left to the poor by Benjamin Drawater. Through the exertions of the curate an *Infant School*, has been established, and it has now 80 scholars.

LANGLEY BRIDGE, half a mile W. of Eastwood, gives name to a large village which is partly in Derbyshire. The present bridge was built in 1830, and crosses the Erwash, which is navigable from hence to the Trent, and here forms a junction with the Cromford, Derby, and Nottingham canals. Here are several large coal wharfs, a steam corn mill, and extensive lime kilns.

NETHER-GREEN is a hamlet, half a mile N. of Eastwood, and one mile to the S. are two corn mills, and a few houses called NEW MANLEY MILLS.

Marked * *riside at Nether Green,* † *at New Manley Mills.*

Walker George, Esq. colliery owner, Nether green	Davenport Rev. Samuel, curate
Askew George, framesmith	†Day Misses Ann & Millicent
Askew John, shoemaker	†Day Mrs. Sarah
Bailey John, blacksmith	Eaton William, shoemaker
Barber, Walker, & Co. colliery owners	Eley Luke, tailor
	Farnsworth Wm. shoemaker
	Fletcher William, joiner
Barber Robert, joiner & builder	Godber John & Son, spirit mer.
Barton James, butcher	Godber Thos. & Robt. drapers
Barton Adcock, baker and vict	Godber Wm. vict. Sun Inn
Bentley Wm. vict. Moon & Stars	Goodman Wm. beerhouse
Birch James, tailor	*Goodwell Thos. colliery agent
Bircumshire Aaron, sinkermkr	*Goodwell T. Holland, bookpr
Brown Wm. framework knitter	Handford John, hosier agent
Bullock Robert, blacksmith	Halford Robert, gent
Carlin Mr. Benjamin	Harpham Ann, ladies school
Chambers Mrs. Sarah	*Harrison John, colliery agent
*Chambers John, shoemaker	Harrison Rt. coal and land agent
Chambers Wm. pawnbroker	Harrison Thomas, gent
Coope John, hosiery agent	Haslam Thos. schoolr. & drug.
† Cooke Mr. William	Hickling Mary, schoolmistress

Hirst John, ropemaker
Jackson John Halford, grocer, chandler, and miller
Jackson, Wm. corn miller
Lees Jane, dress maker
Lees Robert, baker
Morris Mrs. Maria
Pickering Geo. coal agent
Pollard Rt. & Wm. needlemaker
Pollard Wm. jun. shoemaker
Shepherd Joseph, wheelwright
Slater Caleb, Ropemaker
Smith Benjamin, surgeon
Smith Henry, shopkeeper
Smith William, surgeon
Spencer Eliz. & Sarah, shopkpr
Twigher Thomas, shopkeeper
†Walters James, corn miller
Weston John, millwright
White John, blacksmith
White John Bullock, do.
Widdowson David, framesmith
Wild Vincent, net maker
Wilkinson William, joiner
Wood Goodman, maltster

Farmers.

Bartle ——
Barton Solomon
Brentall ——
Buxton John
*Farnsworth J
Frearson Stepn

Shepherd Sarah
Stephens ——
*Turner John

CARRIER. — William Bentley, to Nottingham, Wed. & Sat. mg.

LANGLEY-BRIDGE.

*Marked * are in Derbyshire.*

Alfred Joel, carrier & shopkpr
Aldred Rt. vict. Jaw Bone
Barber Walker, and Co. colliery owners
*Bowes Mrs. Betty
*Bowes Jph. miller & vict
Briley James, coal agent
*Brough Wm. joiner
Butterley Comp. colliery owners
Fletcher Wm. limeburner
Flintoff Wm. canal agent
Haslam Wm. canal agent
Heafield George, chainmaker
Ingram Eliz. draper, &c.
Kimberlin Nathaniel, cooper
Lovatt Joseph, blacksmith
Ludlam Thomas, canal agent
Lygo Thomas, vict. New Inn
Paterson Samuel, canal agent
Shaw Samuel, joiner
Shaw Samuel, jun. plumber, &c.
Wharton Geo. limeburner

GREASLEY PARISH

Is very extensive, consisting of the six hamlets and constable-wicks of Brinsley, Kimberley, Moor-Green, Newthorpe, Watnall-Cantelupe, and Watnall-Chaworth, which maintain their poor conjointly, but their roads separately. They contain 4,583 inhabitants, and upwards of 6,000 acres of enclosed land, with about 260 acres of High-Park and Willey woods.

GREASLEY, seven miles N.W. by N. of Nottingham, is a pleasant village, commonly called MOOR-GREEN, from its being included in that constablewick. The CHURCH is a spacious edifice, with a handsome lofty tower, and four good bells. The Rev. John Hides now enjoys the vicarage, which is valued in the King's books at £8. 5s., and has had several augmentations from Queen Anne's bounty. Lord Melbourne is the patron, impropriator, and lord of the manor, which was of the fee of William Peverel. The Calvinists have a large *Chapel* here. A little to the south are the ruins of GREASLEY-CASTLE, which was the mansion of Nicholas de Cantelupe, who obtained a license to fortify it, from Edward III. About a mile N. of the church are the ruins of BEAUVALE PRIORY, which was founded in the same reign by the Lord Cantelupe, for a prior and 12 Carthusian monks, whose yearly revenue was valued at the dissolution at £196. 6s. The parish *school* was built in 1751, by the widow of Lancelot Rolleston, who left £300 for its foundation, to which his said widow, in 1757, added £100 more. The master now teaches 22 free scholars, and has besides a house and garden, 3A. 1R. of land in Little-field, and £6 yearly from land occupied by the Derby canal. In 1797, *Mrs. Mary Mansell* left £500, and John Mansell £20 to the poor of this parish. These sums are vested in £1,000 three per cent. consols. Out of the yearly dividends (£30) £5 is paid for teaching 8 poor girls; 1s. per week to four poor widows, and the remainder is distributed at Candlemas and Christmas. The hamlet of Newthorpe is entitled to send one poor person to Ilkeston Almshouse, in Derbyshire, and to receive £5 yearly for teaching 18 poor children, from the bequest of Mr. Smedley, the founder of that almshouse.

BRINSLEY is a good village, 2½ miles N.N.W. of Greasley church; and near it is NEW BRINSLEY, where there is a large coal wharf on the Nottingham and Cromford canal, belonging to William Fenton, Esq., and Messrs. Barber, Walker, & Co., who have extensive *collieries* in this constablewick, which contains about 888 acres of land, mostly belonging to the Duke of Newcastle and the Earl of Mexborough. A Wesleyan chapel was built here in 1829.

KIMBERLEY is a considerable village, upon elevated and broken ground at the southern extremity of the parish, 5½ miles N.W. of Nottingham, on the Derby road, near BABBINGTON COLLIERY, which has its name from an estate of 90 acres belonging to the executors of the late Gervase Bourne, Esq. This constablewick contains 635 acres, a great part of which belongs to Lord Melbourne, the lord of the manor of the whole parish. The Old and New Methodists have each a chapel here. The ancient *chapel of ease*, which was in ruins in Thoresby's time, has entirely disappeared.

NEWTHORPE hamlet and constablewick includes the small village of its own name, and the scattered dwellings of BAGGA-LEE and HILL TOP, one mile W. of Greasley church, and 7 miles N.W. of Nottingham. It comprises 975 acres, mostly belonging to Lord Melbourne; but *Baggalee Colliery* is worked by Barber, Walker, & Co. The Kilhamite *Methodist chapel* here was enlarged in 1830.

WATNALL CANTELUPE and WATNALL CHAWORTH form one village upon an eminence 6 miles N.W. of Nottingham, and derived the distinctive parts of their names from the ancient owners of the two estates. Cantelupe contains 490 acres, and Chaworth 1681 acres. Lord Melborne is the principal owner; but Lancelot Rolleston, Esq. has an estate here, and resides in

Watnall Hall. Beauvale Priory, and a colliery belonging Barber, Walker, & Co., are in Watnall Chaworth. The *feast* here is on the Sunday after the 2nd of October, but the feast at Kimberley is held on the Sunday fortnight afterwards.

HEMPSHILL, an estate of 50 acres, belongs to Greasley parish, though it is separated from it by Nuthall and Bulwell, and belongs to the Rev. A. Padley, of the latter place.

BRINSLEY.

Marked † are at New Brinsley.

†Amatt Jph. ground bailiff
†Barber, Walker, & Co. colliery owner
Booth Wm. colliery agent
Calvert John, tailor
Cresswell Robert, butcher
†Fenton Wm. Esq. colliery owner
Gething Jph. cooper, vict., and butcher
Haley Eliz. schoolmistress
†Holridge John & Jph. colliery owners
†Holridge Joseph, draper
†Hopkinson John, butcher & vict
Hopkinson John, shoemaker
Macklacer John, shopkeeper
Meakin Jesse, schoolmaster
Moss Saml. vict. Robin Hood
Millington Rev. John, (Ind.)
Nix Samuel, butcher
†Parkin Mr. Samuel
Paulson Wm. baker
Riley John, shoemaker & vict
†Saxton Vincent, butcher
†Sedgwick Wm. shopkeeper
Shelton James, butcher
Shelton Stephen, hosiery manfr
†Shepley John, schoolmaster
Smelton Jas. vict. Horse & Grm
†Smith Wm. wharfinger
Smithurst Robert, hosiery mfr
Trueman Thos. shopr. & vict
Vickers Wm. shopkeeper
†Wardle Jacob, shopkeeper
Wharton George, lime burner
Wilcock Geo. shopkeeper

FARMERS.

Buxton Robert   Moss Myra
Elliott Mary   Parker Eliz.
Flint Thomas   Sarson Samuel
Maltby Wm

CARRIERS, Thos. Truman and

Geo. Moss, to Nottingham, Wed. and Saturday, 6 morning.

KIMBERLEY.

Barton Moses, engr. Babbington
Bell John, tailor
Birkin Thomas, shopkeeper
Bradley Ellen, vict. Greyhound
Farnsworth John, shoemaker
Goulder Hy. bricklayer & vict
Greensmith John, blacksmith
Hanson Gilbert, shoemaker
Hanson Wm. draper & schoolmr
Leivers James, tailor
Longden Jacob, vict. Ld Nelson
Morley James, beerhouse
Needham Jph. shopr. and vict
North Thomas, colliery owner, Babbington cottage
Sabin Martha, vict. Stag
Shaw John, shopkeeper
Shaw Wm. shopkeeper
Shaw Thomas, butcher
Sills Joseph, corn miller
Slack Chas. vict. King William
Slater Geo. vict. Horse & Groom
Smith Jas. agent, Babbington
Walker William, net maker
Whittock James, brickmaker

Farmers.   Green Jph
Attenborough J Robinson John
Clay Joseph   Slight Henry
Dennis Rd

CARRIERS.

Chas. & Michael Leivers to Nottingham, Wed. & Sat. 8 mg.

GREASLEY MOOR GREEN.

Allcock George, joiner
Barber Thos. Fras. Php. Hutchinson, Esq., Lamb Close Hs.
Brassington, Wm. gardener
Clifton John, shoemaker
Gelstharp Geo. shopkeeper
Gelstharp Jph. parish clerk
Gugler Jph. shopkeeper

Hides Rev. John, Vicar, and boarding academy
Jackson Rt. gent. land agent to Lord Melbourne
Jackson Thomas, blacksmith
Ogden John, blacksmith
Preston John, butcher
Roberts George, tailor
Rolling Chas. warp lace mfr
Sharley Mary, shopkeeper
Shaw John, shopkeeper
Smedley John, vict. Horse & Grm
Turner Thomas, shoemaker
Wilcockson Rt. vict. Royal Oak
Yeomen Rd. ploughmaker

Farmers.
Anthony Saml   Leivers Eliz
Barlow Jph   Leivers Benj
Clifton Gervas   Reed J Felly
Flint Mary   Renshaw Mary
Grammer Thos   Sharley George

NEWTHORPE.
Those marked 1 reside at Baglee, 2 at Hill Top, 3 at Newthorpe.
3 Ball John, butcher
1 Barber, Halton, and Co. colliery owners
3 Flint Mrs. Ann
3 Goodall Edw. vict. Old Bull
1 Hays John, vict. Ram
2 Hodgkinson Edmd. butcher
3 Hogdell John, blacksmith
3 Hooley John, baker, &c.
Hopewell John, gardener, &c.
1 Hopkin Jph. hat manfr
1 Jackson John, butcher
1 Jackson Rd. framesmith, & vic
1 Jackson Wm. baker
1 Leivers Emanuel, joiner
3 Leivers, Wm. vict. Bk. Bull
1 Lindley Edw. shopkeeper
2 Meakin George, farrier
3 Morley Mary, corn miller
3 Newton John, net maker
3 Newton William, shopkpr
1 Paxton Rt. & Wm. grocers and drapers
3 Riley Abm. shoemaker

1 Riley Thomas, shoemaker
2 Robinson Edwd. shoemaker
1 Rowbotham, Geo. shopkpr
2 Severn Sampson, victualler
3 Toplis John, tanner, Gilt brk
3 Twells Matt. colliery agent
3 Walker Flint, vict. New Bull
3 Wood Goodman, net maker and maltster
1 Wood John, corn miller
3 Wood Mrs. Mary
1 Woolley John, draper
3 Woolley Wm. shopkeeper
Farmers.   3 Hall Edward
2 Annable Jph 3 Leivers Jph
3 Ball John   2 Nix Samuel
3 Barton Thos 1 Paxton Saml
3 Bentley Geo 3 Robinson J
3 Cooke John   3 Shaw John
1 Cooper John 3 Shaw Adcock
3 Daws Geo   3 Toplis Wm
3 Grammer My 1 Wilcockson S
3 Grundy Geo   1 Woolley Edw

WATNALL.
Attenborough John, schoolmaster
Barber, Walker, & Co. coal owns
Bolton Saml. gent. Hempshill
Clark Thomas, wheelwright
Jackson Jph. colliery agent
Marlow Eliz. shopkeeper
Raven Eliz. vict. Royal Oak
Rolleston Chpr. Esq. Watnall cot
Rolleston Lancelot Esq, Hall
Shaw Wm. blacksmith
Smith William tailor
Smith Rt. tailor and shopkeeper
Towers Thomas, Queen's Head
Twells John, Wheat Sheaf
Twells William, joiner
Winfield Thomas, shoemaker
Winfield Thos. jun. shoemaker
Farmers.   Sleight Henry
Annable Rt   Tatum Jph
Birks Chas   Toule David
Clark Wm   Walton Jph
Flint Rd   Watkinson Rt
Giniver John Watkinson Wm
Paling Thos   Watson Stpn
Rippen Theods

HUCKNALL TORKARD.

HUCKNALL TORKARD is a large but indifferently built vil-

lage, consisting principally of one long street, 7 miles N. by W.
of Nottingham, and 8 miles S. of Mansfield. Its parish contains about 3,000 acres, and 2,200 inhabitants, many of whom
are framework knitters, occupying small farms. The open
land was enclosed in 1769, when allotments were made in exchange for the tithes. The Duke of Portland is the principal
owner and lord of the manor, which formerly belonged to the
Byron family, one of whom, Richard Lord Byron, lies buried
in the church, under a mural monument, dated 1679. The
church is a neat fabric, with a tower and three bells. The
vicarage is valued in the King's books at £4. 18s. 1d., and was
anciently in the patronage of Newstead Priory; but the Duke
of Devonshire is now the patron, and the Rev. Charles Nixon
the incumbent. The Baptists and the Kilhamite and Primitive Methodists have each a *chapel* here, and in the parish is a
Club Mill belonging to several Friendly Societies. The Rev.
Luke Jackson and Mr. John Godber have each estates here,
and a part of the parish was held for more than five centuries
by the family of Curtis, the last of whom died in 1777. *Forge
Mill*, upon the river Leen, now employed in grinding corn, is
said to have been first an iron forge, and afterwards a cotton
mill. *Bulwood Hall*, an ancient farm-house, was once an occasional seat of the Byrons, of Newstead.

CHARITIES.—*John Byron, Esq.,* in 1571, left Broom-hill
closes, consisting of 23A. 3R. 24P., let for £20, and directed
the rents to be divided as follows, viz.:—One-third to the poor,
one-third to the church, and one-third to be employed for the
benefit of the parish in such way as his trustees should think
fit. About 40 years ago, the timber cut down on this land was
sold for £440. 10s. 6d., now vested in £778. 11s. 11d. three
per cent. consols. In 1813, more timber was cut down and
sold for £71, which was laid out in £121. 8s. 1d. of the same
stock, making the total yearly income of the charity £47.
The Rev. Charles Nixon, and Thomas Hurt, and Luke Jackson, Esqrs. are the trustees. In 1596, *Edward Mearinge* left
26s. yearly out of lands in Fenton and Sturton to one poor
man of this parish. At the enclosure, 24A. 2R. 16P. were
allotted to the poorhouse-keepers, and now let for £22. 10s.
per annum. The ancient *Poor's land* was at the same time
exchanged for 3 roods, now let for 15s. yearly, which is given
to poor widows.

*Those marked 1 reside at Bulwood Hall, 2 Farleys, 3 Forge Mill,
4 Groves, 5 Misk, 6 Nabbs, 7 Poor's Farm, 8 Rough Common,
9 Short Wood, 10 Whyburn, and 11 in Shepherd's Lane.*

HUCKNALL TORKARD.
Allcock & Hewes, framesmiths
Allcock John, victualler
Anson Thomas, lime burner
Beeson John, needle maker

Beardall Jph. vict. Yew Tree
Brown Thomas, tailor
Buck Jph. needle maker
Butler Eliz. vict. Coach & Six
Chadburn Jph. framesmith

Clark Wm. wheelwright
Co-opv. Store. Wm. Callandine
Cumberworth Mark, joiner
Daws Jph. corn miller
Daykin John, blacksmith
Daykin John, jun. blacksmith
Flint Wm. grocer and draper
3 Gee Thos. corn miller
10 Godber John, spirit mercht
Green Geo. parish clerk
Hall Wm shoemaker
4 Hardy Mr. John
Haslam Geo. shopkeeper
Heath Saml. drug. & shopkpr
Jackson Rev. Luke
Jackson Rd. blacksmith
Kirkby Saml. net maker
Mellows John, beerhouse
Mellows Paul, shopkeeper
Mellows Samuel, shoemaker
Mellows Wm. corn miller
Mettham John, stone-mason
Oldham Thos. baker & vict
Parkins Robert, joiner
Piggin John, butcher
Porter Thomas, saddler
Price John, vict. Chequers
Revill John, wheelwright
Smith, Joseph, beerhouse
Sneath Samuel, shoe maker
Sneath Sylvester, framemith
Taylor John, beerhouse
Thompson Jas. sinker maker
Thorpe Thomas, tailor
Tomlinson George, tailor
Tomlinson Mark, shoemaker
Trueman John, beerhouse
Truman & Taylor, framesmiths
Wain John, shoemaker
Walker Thomas, shoemaker
Walker Wm. vict. Seven Stars
Ward Fred. boarding academy
Widdowson Rt. vict. Half Moon,

miller, baker, butcher, malt-
ster, and lime burner
Widdowson Thos. beerhouse
Wilkinson Rt. wheelwright
Willmott Thos. watchmaker
Willmott Thos. jun. grocer
Woollatt John, bobbin net maker

FARMERS.

Allcock John	Hardstaff Thos.
4 Allcock Saml.	Hatfield Mary
Allcock Wm.	2 Hewes Wm.
5 Allcock Wm.	Kirk Wm.
Appleton Edw.	Mellows Wm.
Ball Wm.	8 Needham Ann
Beardall James	Palmer John
5 Beastall John	Severn Joseph
Betts Charles	Shaw Jonathan
Bonnington J.	Smith Henry
Buck Fras.	2 Stanford Rt.
7 Burton Jane	6 Starr Eliz.
Coupe Thomas	Taylor Wm.
Daws Mary	1 Trueman Mar.
Daws Henry, &	11 Turner Sml.
maltster	Wagstaff John
Daws Wm.	Walker Benj.
9 Foster Sarah	Watson Joseph
Hankin Jph. &	Widdowson Rd.
overseer	4 Woodhead O.
8 Hardstaff Corl.	Woollat John

HOSIERY AGENTS.

Allcock John	Mellows Wm.
Ball Anthony	Smith Thomas
Cocker George	Storr Thomas
Green Richard	2 Thorpe Chas.
Heath Samuel	& netmaker
Kirkby William	Widdowson Rt.
Limb Matthew	Wilkinson Geo.

CARRIERS, Thomas Wilmott &
Wm. Thumbs to Nottingham,
Wed. & Sat. 8 mg.; and Thomas
Hanson, to Mansfield, Thur. and
Nottingham, Sat. 8 morning.

KIRKBY-IN-ASHFIELD PARISH.

KIRKBY-IN-ASHFIELD, 5 miles S.W. of Mansfield, is a considerable village, where there are many framework knitter
and bobbin net makers, and some of the former are also small
farmers. The parish, which includes several small hamlets
and in which the rivers Maun and Erwash have their sources,
contains 2,032 inhabitants, and 5,724 acres of land, of which
2,023 acres were not enclosed till 1795, when 1,050 acres were

allotted to the rector in lieu of tithes, and in addition to 200 acres of ancient glebe. The Duke of Portland is the principal owner and lord of the manor, which passed from the Stutevilles to the Cavendishes, but the Rev. D'Ewes Coke, and Thomas Clarke and George Hodgkinson, Esqrs. have estates in the parish. "Sir Charles Cavendish began to build a great house in this lordship, on a hill by the forest side, near Annesley Woodhouse, where, being assaulted by Sir John Stanhope and his man, as he was viewing the work, he resolved to leave off his building, because some blood had been spilt in the quarrel, which was then very hot between these two families." The *church* is spacious and handsome, with a fine spire, and a beautiful stained glass window; it is dedicated to St. Wilford. The rectory is in the gift of the Duke of Portland, and is valued in the King's books at £18. 1s. 8d. The Hon. and Rev. John Venables Vernon is the rector. The General Baptists have a small *chapel* in the village. The parish SCHOOL, with a house for the master, was built in 1826, at the cost of £300, raised by subscription, except £60, which was the amount of several benefactions to the poor, and the interest of which is yearly distributed out of the annual contributions to the school. The master teaches 40 free scholars. KIRKBY HARD-WICK, one mile N.E. of the village, was given to Felley Priory, but is now the estate of the Duke of Portland. The hamlet of KIRKBY WOODHOUSE, distant 1 mile S. is partly the property of Mr. Wm. Booth, and half a mile S.W. of it is *Portland Colliery*, which is worked by the Butterley Company.

BROOK-HILL HALL, the picturesque seat of the Rev. D'Ewes Coke, stands near PINXTON, which village is in Derbyshire, but has a suburb in this parish, near the termination of the Mansfield Railway.

Marked 1 reside at Flander-ground. 2 Grives, 3 Kirby Cliff, 4. Kirby Woodhouse, 5 Lane End, 6 Nuncargate, 7 Parks, 8 Portland Colliery, 9 Pinxton, 10 Todd's-row, and the others in Kirkby.

Vernon, The Hon. & Rev. John Venables, M.A., rector
Coke Rev. D'Ewes, *Brook Hill*
Bateman Wm. grocer & draper
8 Bean Wm. colliery agent
4 Booth Wm. gentleman
Bowmar Wm. butcher
Bradley Fras. grcr. & hosiery agt.
10 Bradley Elias, beerhouse
Brittain John, fwk. knitter
Brunt John, shoemaker
Brunt Wm. blacksmith
8 Butterley Company, colliery owners
Clarke Thos. Esq. Kirkby Hardwick
Cooke Wm. frame work knitter

8 Cope Stead. shopr. & beerhs
Davenport Henry, grocer
Davenport Thos. hosiery agent
Ellis George, joiner
2 Fisher John, lime burner
5 Fletcher Leonard, beerhouse
Frith Wm. blacksmith
Hardstaff Jeremiah, wheelwright
Hardstaff John, warp lace manfr
Hayes John, hosiery agent
Hodgkinson George, Esq.
Hodgkinson Miss Catharine
Jarratt Wm. vict. & net manfr
Kennington Jas. shoemkr. & vict
Kinder Fras. vict. & limeburner
5 Kirk Wm. shoemaker & vict.
Lees Wm. warp lace manufactr

4 Lamb John, warp lace mfr.
5 Lowe Wm. beerhouse
4 Morris John, beerhouse
Nixon Rev. Thos. M.A. curate
Robinson Mrs. —
Robinson Hy. corn miller
Sansom Joseph, free school
Shacklock John, tailor & shopkr
Shacklock John, jun. tailor
Shacklock Thos. parish clerk
9 Short Wm. blacksmith
8 Skevington Thos. victualler
4 Smith Joseph, hosiery agent
Stanley Jph. vict. Green Man
4 Stanley Mrs. Mary
Sterland Thomas, net maker
Tallents Thos. grocer
Turner Samuel, butcher
Turner Samuel, baker
4 Walker Joseph, beerhouse

White Saml. maltster & beerhs
10 Whiteman Jas. shoemkr. & shr
Wilkinson Jas. shoemaker
1 Wright Wm. shoemaker

FARMERS.

3 Beardmore J. Hogg Samuel,
9 Beardmore J. 6 Holmes John
4 Bird John   1 Ingleby –
6 Bowmar Thos. Kinder Rd.
Bradley John   3 Lee John
Chadwick. Thos.6 Lee John
3 Clark Benj.   Lee Rueben
7 Dodson John 10 Massey Peter.
1 England Wm. Oscroft Dennis
Farnsworth T. Salmon Fras.
2 Fisher John 7 Saunders Jas.
Hardwick Rd. Stanley Wm.
Hardwick Thos. Thompson Jph.
7 Heath Thos. 7 Whiteman G.
4 Hodgkinson C.

LENTON PARISH

Has its name from the river Leen, and lies in the vale of that river, near its confluence with the Trent, on the west side of the park and meadows of Nottingham, betwixt them and the parishes of Beeston, Wollaton, and Radford, except its detached member called Beskwood Park, which is distant 5 miles N. from any other part of the parish. *Lenton* contains 2,300 acres of rich sandy land, of which Gregory Gregory, Esq. of Rempston, is the principal owner, and lord of the manor, which is held on a lease by Lord Middleton, who is working a 5 feet seam of *coal* here, and whose beautiful park contains 112A. 0R. 15P. belonging to this parish, within which stands the handsome park gate, on the Derby road. *Beskwood Park* comprises 3409A. 1R. 1P. of mountainous forest land, and forms a manor of which the Duke of St. Albans is lord and owner, but it has only 19 scattered houses. Lenton has, however, felt them anufacturing impulse of its neighbour, Nottingham, having increased its *population* more than three fold during the last thirty years; for we find that in 1801 it amounted only to 893, and in 1821 to 1,240, but in 1831, it had swelled to 3,077 souls, living in 631 houses, of which 400 were built after the year 1821, and most of them form the new villages of *Middleton Place*, *Spring Close*, and *Hyson Green*, which latter is principally in Radford parish, being situated upon the *common land* (261 acres,) which was enclosed in 1796, and divided betwixt the two parishes, though that portion allotted to Lenton is completely surrounded by the land and buildings of Radford.

Lenton is a large and beautiful village, 1½ mile W. of Nottingham, consisting principally of handsome villas and neat cottages, with gardens and shrubberies, and some of them stuccoed in the gothic style. Here is situated the *Peverel Prison*, noticed at page 139, and a pleasant bowling green and tea gardens, which are visited by numerous parties from Nottingham, especially on Sunday evenings. Two annual FAIRS, granted by Henry I. and Charles II. are held here on the Wednesday in Whit-week, and on November 11th, for horses, horned cattle, and hogs. It was anciently noted for its richly endowed PRIORY of Cluniac monks, which was founded by William Peverel, the illegitimate son of William the Conqueror, and was subject to the great foreign abbey of Clugny, till it was enfranchised by Richard II. At its dissolution in the reign of Henry VIII. its yearly revenue was valued at £329. 15s. 10d. and its last prior was convicted of high treason. Its possessions were subsequently granted to various persons. The manor was sold for £2,500 in the 6th of Charles I. to William Gregory, of Nottingham, whose son afterwards gave £1,460 for the fee farm rent (£94. 5s.) which had been granted by the crown to the Duke of Richmond. The site of the priory was granted to Sir Wm. Hicks, and now belongs to Colonel Sempronius Stretton, whose father erected the present handsome house, which bears the name of *Lenton Priory*, and is now occupied by Thomas Jerram, Esq. This mansion is in the ancient monastic style, and there are in the garden several stone coffins, and a curious Saxon font, found when digging the foundation, together with several bases of the pillars of the conventual church, and a curious brass plate of the crucifixion, supposed to have been left there by Cardinal Wolsey, on his way to Leicester abbey, where he closed his ambitious and disquiet life. Thoroton, in 1677, says "there was only one square steeple left of the monastery, which not long since fell down, and the stones of it were employed to make a causeway through the town." In and near the village are several other handsome and spacious mansions, viz. *Lenton Hall, Lenton Abbey, Lenton Firs, Lenton Fields, Lenton Grove*, and *High Field House*, all picturesquely situated, commanding fine views of the vale of the Trent, and occupied by their owners as named in the subjoined directory. Within the precincts of the priory there was a small establishment of White Carmelite Friars, and also an hospital for the reception of those afflicted with St. Anthony's fire. The parish *church* is a small fabric, supposed to have been built on the site of the ancient hospital, after the destruction of the priory, before the foundation of which, Lenton belonged to the parish of Arnold. The *vicarage* is valued in the King's books at £9. 2s. 5d., and is in the patronage of the King. The Rev. Edward Creswell is the incumbent. Within the last five years, the Methodists and the Baptists have built two *chapels* on Church-hill close, and in digging the foundations several stone coffins were found, the place having been used as the priory burial ground. The Wesleyan Chapel, at Middleton-place, and the Kilhamite and Independent chapels, at HYSON GREEN are in this parish.—(See Radford.) In 1781, *Rebecca Garland* left £10 to the poor of Lenton, for which James Nutt now distributes 10s yearly in bread.

MIDDLETON PLACE is a new village, containing upwards of 200 houses, all built during the last ten years, and mostly occupied by bobbin net makers. It is commonly called *New Lenton*, and is only a quarter of a mile N.E. of the old village; at the same distance S. of which is SPRING CLOSE, another modern village, but of a much smaller population.

BESKWOOD PARK, forms a detached portion of this parish, and occupies several wild and broken ridges of the forest on the west side of the Mansfield road, 5 miles N. of Nottingham. It comprises upwards of 3400 acres, and was once a royal demesne with plenty of deer, but is now the property of the Duke of St. Albans. Henry I. granted to the priory of Lenton, the privilege of having two carts to fetch dead wood and heath out of his park at Beskwood. The hall which has been rebuilt, and is now unoccupied, was for some time the residence of the celebrated *Nell Gwynne*, the mistress of Charles II., from whose illegitimate issue the Duke of St. Albans is descended. The estate is divided into 13 farms, and was not all brought into cultivation till 55 years ago, when a Mr. Barton, from Norfolk, brought over a whole colony of his county labourers, who broke it up according to their mode of husbandry

Those marked 1 in the following Directory of Lenton parish reside at Beskwood Park, 2 at Hyson Green, 3 at Lenton, 4 at Middleton Place, and 5 at Spring Close.— The CONTRACTIONS *used are* Lr. *for Lenton-row;* Pst. *Priory-street;* Cts. *Cloisters;* Ctp. *Castle-place;* Bvp. *Belvedere-place;* Ur. *Union-row; and* Wst. *Willoughby-street.*

2 Anderson Mrs. Grace, Lr.
3 Bardsley Edwin, gentleman
4 Bleesdale Saml. & Wm. agents
3 Bayley Isaac, fellmonger & leather dresser, h. Middleton pl
Blount Geo. coal agt. Lenton lk
4 Boot Isaac, bookkeeper
2 Brandreth Mrs. Hanh. 9, Lr
3 Brothwell Wm. Hopkin, mfr
3 Brownlow Thos. parish clerk
4 Burr Geo. bookbinder
2 Burton Rev. Thomas Blount, (Ind.) 22. Lr
3 Burton Wm. fwk. knitter
4 Cartwright Geo. clerk
3 Christie Lorenzo, lace mfr
4 Creswell Rev. Edw. vicar of Lenton and Radford

4 Dodsley Henry, overlooker
Evans Mrs. Dorothy, Lenton gv.
4 Eyre Miles
Fisher Isaac, Esq. Lenton Abbey
4 Galloway John, fwk. knitter
4 Gee John, toy dealer
4 Gray Mr. Peter
4 Goff Isaac, lace manufacturer
3 Goodacre Mrs. Mary
4 Goodman Eliz. midwife
4 Gregory Saml. shopkeeper
3 Hanmer Wm. Esq. barrack mtr.
3 Harrop Saml. painter, Cloisters
Haviland Mrs. Maria, Lenton ter
4 Hill Richard, bookkeeper
2 Holmes Benj. f. knitter, 18, Lr
4 James Mr. Robert
Jeffs Miss Ann, Lenton terrace

3 D

Jerram Thos. Esq. Lenton Pry
3 Johnson Saml. constable
3 Jowett John, gentleman
Killingley Mrs. Eliz. Lenton ter
Lowe Alfred, Esq. Highfield hs
4 Maples John, overseer, Wst
Needham Mattw. Esq. merchant, Lenton fields
4 Nelson Misses Eliz. and Jane, Willoughby street
4 Panton Thos. gentleman
2 Platts Robt. warper, 23, Lr
4 Pyke Mrs. Jane, Willoughby st
3 Read Matthew, f. knitter
Renshaw Miss Eliz. Priory cott
Renshaw Rupert, lace mfr. Middleton cottage
3 Reynolds Geo. f. knitter
Roberts Benj. boat bldr. Grove bridge

3 Roberts Elias, warper
4 Roe Thos. lace manufacturer.
3 Roughton Mr. Thomas
4 Shephard Samuel, warper
2 Sheraton Ninian John, builder, Bedford square
2 Stones Mr. Geo. 14, Union row
Smedley John, agent to coal proprietors, Lenton lock
Storer John, M.D. Lenton firs
Surplice Thos. gent. Lenton cott
Thornell Wm. miller, Priory mill
3 Wade Thos. bricklayer
4 White Frederick, printer
4 Wilkinson Thos. hair dresser
Willoughby Rd. canal agent
3 Wilmot John, coach propr
Wright John, Esq. Lenton hall
3 Wright Thos. capital bailiff & gaoler of the Honour of Peverel

Academies.
4 Bailey Ann
2 Blackwell Eliz. (bdg) Poplar cottage
4 Creswell Edw. (bdg)
4 Downs Ann, Wst.
3 Naylor Ann
3 Roughton John
2 Smith John, Lr
4 Stones Lucy & Ann, (boarding)

Bakers, &c.
4 Knight John, Wst
2 Newball Alfred
3 Wells Thomas
3 Weston William

Bleachers.
5 Daws John
3 Milnes Thos. Brown, (& lace thread mfr.)

Bobbin net makers.
2 Analt Dothy, 35, Lr
2 Arnold John, 13, Lr
2 Atkinson Rt. 5, Ur
2 Austin John, 8, Lr
4 Bailey W. (lace mfr.)
5 Ball Geo. (& hosy.)
4 Bartle Geo. Park Rd
2 Bass Saml. 26, Lr
4 Bates Mary, Wst
4 Bell Joseph
4 Bentley Thomas
4 Beresford Wm

2 Birks John, 29, Lr
2 Birks Wm. 15, Ur
4 Blasdale Matthew
2 Brown John, 9, Ur
2 Burton Isaac, 4, Ur
2 Burton Thos. B. 22, Lenton row
2 Butler Wm. 20, Lr
2 Coleman Wm, 38, Lr
2 Comery Wm. Ctp
2 Cooper John, 38, Lr
4 Crofts Wm
Day Chpr. 15, Lr
4 Downs Benj. Wst
4 Dring John, Park rd
4 Farmer John, Wst
2 Gadsby Jas. 25, Lr
4 Grayson Wm
4 Grayson Wm
2 Hall Geo. 16, Ur
4 Hall S. & T. E. (by power)
2 Harvey Wm. 19, Ur
2 Harvey Wm. 36, Lr
2 Hefford Geo. 32, Lr
4 Herbert John, Wst
4 Jacklin Thos. (& lace dresser) Wst
2 Johnson Thos. 1, Lr
2 Johnson Wm. 2, Lr
4 Kendall John
4 Kendell Wm. Wst
4 Kirk Wm. Wst

2 Lake Jas. 20, Ur
2 Lamb Wm. 3, Ur
4 Langford Geo
2 Lees John, 12, Ur
4 Martin Benj
4 Mason Gervas
2 Matthews Gervas, 22, Union row
2 Merriman John, 6, Union row
2 Merriman Wm. 13, Union row
4 Peet Joseph
4 Peet William
4 Pegg Thomas
2 Perkins Thos. 18, Ur
2 Porter George. Ctp
2 Reavill Wm. 31, Lr
2 Revell Jas. Bvp
4 Revell Matthew
2 Roberts John, 28 Lr
4 Roe John
4 Roe Samuel
4 Roe William
2 Rogers Wm. 21, Lr
4 Sands Richard, Wst
2 Saxton Wm. Ctp
4 Selby John, Wst
3 Selby Wm. Priory st
2 Shaw Robert, Wst
5 Shephard Samuel
5 Shephard Thos

2 Smith Jas. 11, Ur
4 Smith Jas. Wst
2 Sneath Wm. Lr
5 Stanton George
5 Stanton Wm
5 Swain Joseph
2 Thornton Fras. 24, Lenton row
2 Thurman Sml. Meed, Castle place
2 Tomlinson Jas. 33, Lenton row
2 Toone Jph. 17, Ur
2 Toone Wm. 34, Lr
3 Turner Wm. Pst
4 Vincent John, Wst
2 Wulwin John, 3, Lr
2 Weston Saml. 7, Ur
2 White Wm. 21, Ur
2 Wincles John, Lst
2 Wood Thos. 37, Lr
2 Wood Wm. 17, Lr
4 Wright Thomas

Shoemakers.

3 Barnes John. Pst
3 Beaumont John
3 Deeton John, 12, Lr
2 Haskard Thos. Ctp
3 Hudson Samuel
4 Jackson James
3 Pearson Thos
2 Rowell Robert
3 Sharp John
5 Towle Thomas
3 Turney Wm. Pst
3 Widdison John

Butchers.

2 Beeson William
4 Brewell Wm. Wst
4 Eite Edw. Wst
2 Kirk Thos. Ctp
3 Nutt James

Corn Millers.

3 Goodacre Rd. Pst
3 Goodacre Saml. Old Mill

Gardeners, &c.

Cheshire John
3 Cope Thomas
4 Crinage Wm. (job)
1 Daft Rd. (nursery)
3 Lee Wm. (florist)
3 Moody William

3 Noble William
2 Robey John, Bvp
3 Wallis Martha

Druggists.

4 Bestwick Robert
4 Boot John, Wst
2 Thornton Fras. 24, Lenton row
2 Thornton John, Bvp

Inns & Taverns.

Grove Tavern & Tea Gardens, Jon. Ward
2 Lumley Castle, Thomas Haskard
4 New Inn, John Clayton, Willoughby st
3 Rose & Crown, Wm. Hickling
3 Three Wht. Sheaves, Hphy. Hopkins
3 White Hart, Thos. Wright

Beerhouses.

3 Boat, Rd. Widdison
2 Carpenters' Arms, Wm. Collingburn, 2, Union row
4 Dove and Rainbow, John Barton
4 Keen's Head, Henry Cox, Park road
5 Peacock, Thomas Towle

Farmers.

Those marked † are Cowkeepers.

1 Beerdall Thomas
1 Bennett Wm. & Thos
3 Boot Thomas
1 Challand George
1 Challand John
1 Challand Joseph
3 Chamberlain Rd
†Cheetham Fras
1 Cliff Wm
4 †Etherington Thos
†Gibbens Wm. Lenton fields
1 Houghton William, Goosedale
†Holmes Wm
3 Humphrey Wm
†Kirk Thomas

†Langsdale Thomas
1 Lamin John
3 Lovett Edward
1 Needham John
3 Pearson Thomas
1 Potter Thomas
3 Shephard Thomas
1 Stout Fras
†Swain John
3 Townsend Samuel
1 Wilson Edward
3 Wilkinson John
1 Wilkinson Wm
†Wood Alice
†Wood Thomas

Joiners.

4 Clay Joseph
2 Collingburn Wm. 2, Union row
3 Elvidge Thos. (wght)
4 Hopewell Wm. Wst
3 Naylor Richard
3 Wade Thomas, jun.
3 Wallis Humphrey
3 Windle Jas. Canal
3 Yeomans Wm

Machine Makers and Framesmiths.

4 Bombroff Edward
2 Barr Saml. 10, Ur
4 Crofts Wm. Wst
4 Hill John, Wst
3 Keelley Samuel
4 Martin Benjamin

Maltsters.

3 Hall and Harrison
4 Pidcock Joseph

Shopkeepers.

3 Brown Joseph
3 Brown Joseph
4 Coope Edward
2 Co-operative society Wm. Bronson, agt. 1, Union row
2 Dabell John, 16, Lr
3 Emery Ann
3 Johnson Samuel
2 Leonard Rt. 8, Ur
4 Martin Thomas
4 Nutter Elijah, Wst
4 Peet Wm. Wst
3 Poyser Saml. Pst
2 Revell James, Bvp

	Tailors.	Turners:
2 Shaw Wm. Lst	3 Burton Richard	4 Birks Samuel, Wst
4 Simpson Wm.	2 Roberts Thos. Bvp	4 Trueman Wm
3 Wells Isabella, Pst	4 Smith Thomas	
4 Wells Thos. Wst		

LINBY PARISH.

LINBY is a small ancient village and parish 7¼ miles S. of Mansfield, containing 352 inhabitants and 1479 acres of land. Andrew Montagu, Esq., (the son of Fountayne Wilson, Esq., and now a minor,) is lord of the manor, and owner of all the land except 125 acres belonging to Colonel Wildman; about 40 acres belonging to Mr. Dalby, and 18 acres of *Whighay Common*, which are the property of the two latter and the rector. The Linby and Papplewick estates were of the fee of William Peverel, and were bequeathed by their late proprietor the *Right Hon. Frederick Montagu*, in 1800, to Fountayne Wilson, Esq., and his heirs, on condition that they use the sirname of Montagu, which he himself has refused to comply with, but has conferred it upon his son, together with the said estates; though he still retains the authority of landlord, and has discharged all the stocking frames from the parish, so that its population has been decreased from 515 to 352 souls. Two ancient *crosses* stand at the north and south ends of the village. The *church* is a small fabric, dedicated to St. Michael. The rectory, valued in the King's books, at £4. 9s. 9½d. is in the gift of Andrew Montagu, Esq., and incumbency of the Rev Thomas Hurt. The *feast* is on the Sunday after Old Michaelmas Day, or on that day when it falls on a Sunday.

Allcock John, limeburner
Allcock William, butcher
Chadburn Jph. jun. butcher
Clarke John, wheelwright
Daykin Luke, shopkeeper
Farnsworth William, joiner
Glover John, gent
Hopper Richard, Esq.
Hurt Rev. Thomas, rector
Newton Robert, stonemason
Sneath John, vict. & shoemkr
Stafford James, wheelwright
Swinton James, stonemason
Swinton Richard, blacksmith
Voce John, beerhouse

FARMERS.
Chadburn Jph. Shipley Chas.
Hardstaff, Jno. Swinton Geo.
Potter W. Wig- Swinton Fras
hay   Watson Robert
Shaw Thomas Wright Thos.

MANSFIELD WOODHOUSE PARISH.

MANSFIELD WOODHOUSE is a very large and ancient village nearly 1¼ mile N. of Mansfield, inhabited partly by framework knitters, but having several good houses which have long been the residence of respectable families. Its parish contains 1859 inhabitants, 3206 acres of enclosed land, and about 1500 acres of the open forest of Sherwood. The Duke of Portland is the principal owner, lord of the manor, and impropriator. Near the village are several prolific quarries of excellent *limestone*. In the reign of Henry VI., Sir Robert Plumpton died possessed of one bovate in this manor, called *Wolfhuntland*, held by the service of winding a horn and driving or frightening the wolves in Sherwood forest. The dwelling upon this land was called *Wolf-house*, and is now occupied by Mr. Housley. In a forest book written on parchment in 1520, it is recorded, that the " town of Mansfield Woodhouse was *burned* in the year of our Lord MCCCIIII, and the Kirk stepull with the belles of the same; for the stepull was afore of tymbre worke." Before this accident, the CHURCH had three aisles, but it has now only two. It is 98 feet long and 32 broad. The spire steeple is 108 feet high and contains four bells, and a small *saint's bell*, which in Catholic times was rung when the priest came to that part of the Latin service which is translated " holy! holy! Lord God of Sabaoth!" in order that those who staid at home might join with the congregation in the most solemn part of the ceremony. The church is dedicated to St Edmund, and contains a few ancient monuments. The living is a perpetual curacy, and has annexed to it that of Skegby. The Duke of Portland is the patron, and the Rev. William Goodacre the incumbent. The Independents and Methodists have each a chapel here, and in the village are three Sick Societies, and a Lodge of Odd Fellows. The *feast* is on the Sunday after the 10th of July. A sheep fair was formerly held here on the Monday after Mansfield cheese fair, but it was discontinued some years ago, though the ancient cross round which it was held, has recently been repaired. At the east end of the village, is *Winnyhill*, on which there are some remains of a Roman exploratory camp.

The late *Major Rooke*, F.R. and A.S.S., lived in a pleasant mansion about midway between Mansfield and Woodhouse, and died there in 1806, " after a long period of useful services to his country as a soldier, antiquary and meteorologist. His communications in the Archæologia are very extensive in Vols. 8, 9, 10, and 11." The Major's researches in this parish were very productive. In the *Northfield*, he found the site of an extensive ROMAN VILLA, which had consisted of seven elegant rooms with richly painted walls, and a beautiful *mosaic pavement*, composed of red, yellow, white, and grey *tesseræ*, about the size of a die. John Knight, Esq., on whose estate this discovery was made, erected a building over the tessellated pavement for its better preservation, but Laird on visiting it in 1811, " found the doors broken open, the pavement ruined, and the floor strewed with the cubic pieces, the walls written over with ribaldry, and its only tenants a mare and her foal, who had taken shelter from the noon tide heat." About 100 yards south-east of the villa, the Major discovered some remains of two *sepulchres*, in which were found many fragments of pa-

teræ, and pots of Roman ware, with several articles of household convenience.

DEBDALE HOUSE, a handsome mansion, half a mile W. of Mansfield Woodhouse, is the seat of John Coke, Esq. WOODHOUSE GROVE, 1½ mile S. by W. of the village is the mansion of William Anson Smith, Esq. *Grassfield Cottage, Northfield House,* and *North Lodge,* are within the parish, and are occupied by their owners, but the *Warren* and *Old Club Mill Farms,* belong to the Duke of Portland, and the *Park Farm* to Francis Hall, Esq., of Park Hall.—(See Nettleworth p. 448.) Col. Need, E. Sykes, Esq., and some other gentlemen, have neat houses in the village.

The CHARITIES belonging to Mansfield Woodhouse are as follows:—The *Blue Coat School* where 50 boys are clothed and educated gratuitously, was founded and endowed by Mrs. Faith Clarkson, whose charity is already noticed at page 527. Another *Charity School,* were 32 poor boys and girls are educated, was founded in 1827, by Richard Radford, grocer, who endowed it with £800. The trustees are, Samuel Housely and Thomas Kirkland. Seven closes called the *Clay Pits,* and containing 26A. 2R. 23P., are let for £74 per annum, and belong to the church for its repairs, &c. *Rosamond Watson* left £100 for apprenticing poor children, but it was expended in building the present *Workhouse,* and £5 is now paid yearly as the interest of it, by the trustees of the church land. *Mrs. Fisher* left £100 to the poor, and it is now vested in the Chesterfield Turnpike. The indigent parishioners are also relieved by the yearly distribution of the following small annuities, viz. 10s. left by *Roland Dand,* (See p. 528;) 10s. by *Mr. Price,* out lands in Mansfield; 10s. by *John Bingham,* out of his two Old Mill Closes; 5s. by *Richard Eyre,* out of lands in Mansfield Woodhouse, now belonging to George Eyre, of Sookholme; 2s. by *William Whelpdale,* out of the estate of John Coke, Esq.; 6s. by *Paul Wilson,* out of Little Rough Close; and £2. 10s. by *Mrs. Cross,* out of Brackenhurst Closes.

Letters arrive from Mansfield at 1 noon.

Blankley Rd. governer of workhs	Potter Wm. gentleman
Brightmore Hy. turner & rakemkr	Robinson Rt. needlemaker
Clark Rd. brazier & tinman	Scott Thos. gardener, Debdale
Clark Wm. gent. North lodge	Smith Wm. Anson, Esq. Grove
Clark Wm. glover	Stanley Abner Clarke, teacher
Coke John, Esq. Debdale house	Sykes Edmand, Esq.
McDonald Wm. tax collector	Tatley Wm. mason
Lambert Edw. excise-officer	Toplis Mrs. Ellen
Milner Edmund, R.N.	Walker Mrs. Hannah
Neale Chas. Esq. land valuer &	Wilkinson John, architect
agent to the Duke of Portland	Willey John, turner
Need Colonel John	INNS AND TAVERNS.
Oakes John, plumber & glazier	Angel, Joseph Marsh
Pearse John, gentleman	Bulls Head, William Heath

Greyhound, John Brooke
Half-way-house, Ann Whelpdale
Parliament Oak, Philip Oakes
Ram, Daniel Slater
Red Lion, Mary Shippam
Star, John Pogmore
White Swan, Thomas Mason

BEERHOUSES.

Fox and Crown, John Duckman-
ton
Jug and Glass, Samuel Short
Masons' Arms, Barnet Lucas
Board, Thomas Warner

Academies.
Stanley Joseph
Unwin Lybby
    Bakers, &c..
Shippam Thomas
Yates William
    Blacksmiths.
Butler John
Timmons James
Womersley John
    Shoemakers.
Bennett William
Denby John
Swallow Richard
Tebbutt John
    Butchers.
Booth William
Brightmore Isaac
Harrison Henry
Harvey George
Harvey Thomas
Housley Samuel
Kinder Thomas
Shippam Thomas
    Corn Millers.
Cupid Edward
Lucas Barnet
Harker John
    Farmers.
Beardall John

Booth John
Burgoine Samuel
Bell Jthn. Warren hs
Cowpe John
Cox Jph. Grassfield
    cottage
Eadison J. Park farm
Fletcher William
Hazard Robert
Hollaway Jas. Sunny-
    dale
Holland William
Lucas Ts. Northfield
Huntington Thomas
M'Donald John
Newton William
Slater Daniel
Tebbutt Robert
    Fwk. Knitters.
Butler Thomas
Dole John
Elliott Isaac
Hett John
Taylor John
Warner William
Whittaker John
    Gardener, &c.
Bowman George
    Grocers, &c.
Booth Mary

Darby William
Dole John
Heath William
Housley Richard
Morriss Abel
Simpson George
Taylor George
Wright James
    Joiners, &c.
Chambers John
Pashley John
Pashley Samuel
    Lime Burners.
Brooke John
Houseley William
Wilkinson John
    Maltsters.
Fletcher Robert
Fletcher William
Frith Thomas
    Tailors.
Betterney William
Darby John
Darby William
Warner Thomas
    Wheelwrights.
Hufton Joseph
Marsh Joseph
Pogmore John

NEWSTEAD ABBEY

Stands in a delightful situation, six miles S. of Mansfield, and
with an estate of 3226A. 3R. 33P. forms a parochial chapelry,
which, till 1830, was considered to be *extra parochial*, but in
that year the present owner, Colonel Wildman, was defeated
in an assize trial, instituted for the purpose of compelling him
and his tenants here, to support their own poor. The estate
has about 290 acres of woods and plantations, and several spacious lakes, which cover upwards of 67 acres, and give rise to
the river Leen. It has 159 inhabitants, and 25 scattered dwellings, one of which is the noted Inn called the *Hutt*, situated
upon the Nottingham and Mansfield road, on the margin of an

open tract of Sherwood Forest, 1 mile E. of the *abbey*, which
has been greatly improved by its present owner and occupant,
who purchased the estate for £100,000, in 1818, of T. Clawton,
Esq., to whom it had been sold by the late Lord Byron, in
1815, for £140,000. Newstead Abbey was founded as a priory
of black canons, about 1170, by Henry II. At the dissolution,
its revenues were estimated at £229; and it was granted to Sir
John Byron, at that time Lieutenant of Sherwood Forest. Sir
John immediately fitted up part of the edifice; but the church
was suffered to go to decay, though the south aisle was actually
incorporated into the dwelling-house, at one end of which
the front of the abbey church is still a majestic ruin, being
in the form of the west end of a cathedral, adorned with
rich carvings. The house is quite in the antique style, with
towers and battlements, and has just undergone a thorough reparation, having suffered much by the neglect of the two last
Lords Byron. It has numerous apartments, and two spacious
galleries, one of which passes over the ancient *cloisters*, which
resemble those of Westminster abbey. An extensive crypt
under the ruined conventual church has been long used as
cellars, and the singing room is fitted up as a bath. The ancient *chapel*, of which the Rev. Luke Jackson is pastor, has
been used as a cemetery, and its light clustered pillars and ancient carved widows add much to the melancholy expression of
the scene. An ancient gothic greenhouse opens into the garden, which was once the abbey burial ground; and in which
the late Lord Byron erected a handsome pedestal of white
marble, with an inscription to the memory of a *Newfoundland
dog*, to whom his lordship once owed his life. This garden also
includes the dilapidated part of the church, and is altogether a
very interesting spot. The extensive park is now divided into
farms, except in the vicinity of the house, where the landscape
is extremely beautiful, having two spacious *lakes*, and several
fine plantations and ornamental buildings, all of which harmo-
nize with the monastic ruins and the gothic mansion.

The *Byron family* is more ancient than the Conquest, and
had large possessions near Rochdale, in Lancashire, where they
had their principal seat till after the reformation, when they
obtained a grant of Newstead. Being active partisans in the
cause of Charles I. several of their estates were sequestered by
parliament, but were afterwards restored to them by Charles
II., whose father had raised *Sir John Byron* to the peerage, in
1643. William, the fifth Lord Byron, killed Wm. Chaworth,
Esq. in a duel, in 1765, under circumstances which led to his
impeachment, on a charge of murder, before the house of
peers, who found him guilty of manslaughter, upon which he
claimed the benefit of the statute of Edward VI., and was discharged. He died without issue, in 1798, and was succeeded
by his grand-nephew, George Gordon, the late LORD BYRON,

the illustrious poet, who died of a fever, at Missolonghi, on the 19th of April, 1824, lamented by the whole Greek nation, to whose glorious cause he had devoted his fortune, his talents, and his life. His lordship having left an only daughter (without male issue) by his lady, Anne Isabella, daughter of Sir Ralph Noel, (late Milbank) Bart., was succeeded in his title by his cousin, George Anson, the present "Baron Byron, of Rochdale." The late Lord Byron succeeded to the title at the early age of ten years, and received the rudiments of his education at the grammar school, in Aberdeen, to which place his mother had retired soon after his birth, when the licentious conduct of his father had compelled him to become an exile from England. After completing his residence at Cambridge, his lordship took up his abode at Newstead abbey, where he wrote his "Hours of Idleness," a miscellaneous volume, on which the Edinburgh Review passed such a severe criticism as awakened the sleeping energies of the youthful poet's mind, and called forth his "English Bards and Scotch Reviewers," in which he took vengeance, we may almost say on friends as well as foes. Previous to this he had become attached to Miss Chaworth, but his passion was unreturned. (See p. 517.) From this time he became prodigal of his time, thoughts and feelings. After a two years' tour on the continent he returned to England, in 1811, and published "*Childe Harold*," and several other works which gained him an unlimited popularity. He subsequently married Miss Milbank Noel, but the union was not productive of happiness, and he soon afterwards bad adieu to the shores of Britain, and continued to change his residence from one part of Italy to another, till he formed the noble determination of proceeding to Greece, in order to assist the suffering inhabitants in their efforts for freedom, and for that purpose he sold his large estate at Rochdale, but he died in the following year. As a poet, Lord Byron was as great as a poet can be, whose universe is in himself; and as a man there was more in him to be loved than to be despised, but more deserving of reprobation than of pity; though the peculiar circumstances of his situation go far to excuse many of his errors, and contributed much to form his poetical character.

Wildman Thos., Esq. colonel of the 9th Lancers and the Sherwood Rangers, Newstead abbey
Beardsall Mrs. Phœbe
Beardsall Jas. lime burner
Johnson Wm. gardener
Hodgkinson Thos. corn miller
Pickard Wm. brickmaker

Palin Wm. vict. Hutt, Nottigham road

FARMERS.
Beardsall Wm. Slaney
Cocks Chas
Heath John
Howes John
Smith Wm
Taylor Saml
Voce Susanna

NUTHALL PARISH includes the township and chapelry

of Awsworth, and contains 509 inhabitants, and about 1200 acres of land.

NUTHALL is a small rural village on the Alfreton road, 4¼ miles N.W. by N. of Nottingham. Near it, in an extensive park with a beautiful lawn, lake, gardens, and plantations, is NUTHALL TEMPLE, the elegant seat of Robert Holden, Esq. who purchased it in 1820, of the Hon. George Vernon, whose father had obtained it in marriage with the daughter of the late Charles Sedley, Esq. The house is square, with two very low wings, and a handsome portico in front, approached by a light ballustraded range of steps. The roof rises rapidly to a large and lofty dome in the centre, which hides all the chimneys, and is surrounded with an airy ballustrade, commanding an extensive view of the adjacent country. The dome within displays a profusion of ornamental plaster work, and has a light gallery supported by the pillars of the magnificent hall, which is lighted from the dome, and is of an octagon figure, 36 feet in diameter; decorated with the richest exhibition of the plastic art in the county. The original rotunda of *Palladio*, of which this house is a copy, is the Villa Capra, near Vicenza, in Italy, of which there are two other copies, viz. Mereworth Castle and Footscray Place, in Kent, both of which, as well as this, are much inferior to the original, which stands pre-eminent for simplicity, commodiousness, and elegance, though its style of architecture is altogether incongruous in our climate. The CHURCH stands on the north side of the park, and is dedicated to St. Patrick. The living is a rectory, with about 50 acres of glebe, and valued in the King's books at £3. 14s. 9d. The Rev. Charles Nixon is the incumbent, and Robert Holden, Esq. the patron, besides whom here are several smaller land-owners, viz. Peter Fearnhead, Thos. Nixon, Wm. Faulconbridge, and Chas. Antill.

CINDER-HILL is a small hamlet in the township of, and one mile S. E. of Nuthall.

AWSWORTH township and chapelry borders upon Derbyshire, and has a small village on the Nottingham canal, 2¼ W. of Nuthall. The manor, which has an extensive *colliery*, was anciently called *Aldesworth*, and was given to the priories of Burton and Lenton, but the Earl of Stamford is now its lord, and also owner of all the land, except 300 acres belonging to Lord Middleton. The *chapel* was consecrated about 1760, and is a curacy endowed with about £50 a-year. The Rev. Gervase Browne is the incumbent, and the rector of Nuthall the patron. The chapelry is entitled to send one poor person to *Ilkeston almshouses*, and to receive £5 yearly from the funds of *Smedley's charity*, for teaching 18 poor children; the Earl of Stamford is trustee.

NUTHALL.	
Holden Rt. Esq. Nuthall temple	Faulconbridge Wm. gent
Daykin Saml. colliery owner	Hurd Geo. shoemaker
	Kirkland Edw. overseer

Knighton Solomon, bricklayer and vict
Lilley Wm. vict. Goat's Head
Nixon Rev. Chas. rector
Plant Moses, gardener, &c.
Richardson Wm. engineer
Robinson Edw. shoemaker
Sharp Saml. saddler, Cinderhill
Stapleton Edw. gardener, Cinderhill
White Wm. shopkeeper

Farmers.

Dennis Rd   Houghton Hy

Jarvis W. Sark   Wigley Hy
Sands ——   Wigley Thos

AWSWORTH.

Chambers John, chapel clerk
Chambers Wm. bricklayer
Jackson Rev. Luke, colliery owner, Hucknall Torkard
Millward Thos. shopkeeper
Reeve Edw. farmer
Richards Mat. vict. Jolly Colliers
Sharpe Rd. colliery agent
Spray Martha, farmer
Taylor John, farm bailiff

PAPPLEWICK PARISH.

PAPPLEWICK, 6 miles S. of Mansfield, is a small village and parish on the east bank of the Leen, opposite to Linby, and belongs to the lord of that manor, (see p. 576,) who has here also interdicted stocking frames, and we suppose cotton mills likewise, as the extensive mills here have been unoccupied ever since he came into possession. *Papplewick Hall,* built in 1787, by the late Hon. Frederick Montagu, and now occupied by Thomas Nixon, Esq. is an elegant stone edifice, in a small but beautiful park, commanding extensive prospects. Near it is the *church,* which was rebuilt in 1795, and is dedicated to St. James. It has a handsome stained glass window, and is completely embowered in trees. The living is a curacy, certified at £17. 8s. 6d. Andrew Montagu, Esq. is the patron, and the Rev. Thomas Hurt the incumbent, as at Linby.—Population, 359.

Bowman John, farmer
Bradley Wm. farmer
Brown John, shopr. & p. clerk
Burton Wm. butler
Carter Rt. farmer
Dawn John, schoolmaster
Goodall Fras. shoemaker
Gee Thos. miller & bone crusher
Heath Thos. wheelwright
Howett Wm. farmer

Johnson John, shoemaker
Mellows Wm. farmer
Machin Rd. butcher
Nixon Ts. Esq. Papplewick hall
Riley John, land agent
Thorp James, tailor
Widdison J. vict. Griffin's Head
Wilkinson Mark, joiner
Wood Edw. blacksmith

RADFORD PARISH

Is bounded on the south by Lenton and Nottingham, and has drank so deeply of the manufacturing spirit of the latter town, that it now ranks as the second most populous parish in the county, though it does not comprise more than 600 acres of land, belonging to numerous freeholders, and forming a parcel of the manor of Lenton, being given by Wm. Peverel to the

priory which he founded in that parish. As has been seen at
pages 76 and 77, the population of Radford has increased more
than four-fold during the last thirty years; but the greater part
of this augmentation has taken place during the last *ten* years,
in which the number of *houses* has has been swelled from 973
to 2073, and the population from 4806 to 9806 souls! The
1100 new houses built betwixt 1821 and 1831, form several
handsome villages, occupied chiefly by *bobbin net makers*, and
forming a number of parallel and cross streets, bearing different
names, and regularly built of brick and roofed with blue slate.
There are also in the parish three bleach works, two corn mills,
an extensive cotton and worsted mill, and two immense bobbin
net manufactories, in one of which the machines are worked
by the agency of steam, and in the other, by hand, like those
domestic machines which are to be found in the upper rooms
of most of the houses in this and the adjacent parishes.—See
page 193 to 204.

RADFORD old village is situated on the river Leen, 4½ N. W.
by W. of Nottingham. The *church*, dedicated to St. Peter,
was rebuilt in 1812, at the cost of £2000. It is a neat gothic
edifice, with a gallery and tower at the west end, and near it
is that delightful place of public resort called *Radford grove,*
(see p. 183.) The benefice is a vicarage, valued in the King's
books at £3. 9s. 4½d. The King is the patron, and the Rev.
Edward Creswell the incumbent. The Wesleyan chapel here
was built in 1825, and enlarged in 1828, and there are twelve
other *Dissenting chapels* in the other villages of the parish.—
The *school* here was built by the late Wm. Elliott, Esq., and
has been given up to the parishioners by his executors, in lieu
of £60 which he had bequeathed to the poor, and the interest
of which is now paid out of the poor rates.

NEW RADFORD forms a large modern suburb, extending to the western limits of Nottingham on the Derby and
Alfreton roads. It contains 4032 inhabitants, several spacious streets extending nearly to Bloomsgrove, and having, on a
plot of building ground, a large square set apart for the purpose of forming a central market place for the parish. Here
are four *chapels* belonging to the Wesleyan, Kilhamite, Independent, and Primitive Methodists. The principal streets are
De Ligne-street; Denman-street; Pelican-street; Chapel-street;
Montford-street; Heath-street; Hayhurst-street; George-street;
Earl-street; Elliott-street; Sion-hill; and Gregory-street; in
the latter of which are the *waterworks*, established in 1824, by
Mr. Joshua Beardmore. The water is raised by a steam engine from a well 60 yards deep, into a reservoir at the top of
the engine house, and is thence sent in pipes to the houses in
this part of the parish, and also to many of those in Nottingham park; this district being higher than the level of any of the
town reservoirs.—(See p. 187.) There are also two small

waterworks at Messrs. Walkers', on the Derby road, and at Messrs. Fishers and Levers, in George-street, so that this newly created neighbourhood is now well supplied by pipes and carts with excellent water for every culinary purpose.

ASPLEY, nearly one mile N.W. of Radford, is a small hamlet which gives name to a large estate belonging to Lord Middleton, and extending into the parishes of Wollaton and Bilborough. It was anciently one of the woods of Sherwood forest. The hall is a neat mansion, occupied by William Stamford Burnside, Esq.

BLOOMSGROVE, another new village, lies betwixt Old and New Radford, within 1 mile W. by N. of Nottingham, and contains 1307 inhabitants, and two *chapels*, built in 1824-5, for the Independent Methodists, and the Unitarians.

BOBBERS MILL, an ancient corn mill upon the Leen, half a mile N. of Old Radford, gives name to a new village where there are two bleach works, and a Kilhamite and Wesleyan Methodist Chapel, upon the Alfreton road, nearly 1½ mile N.W. of Nottingham.

HYSON GREEN, 1 mile N.W. of Nottingham, is another well built village, which has been erected during the last ten years, and is said to have had its name from the *tea gardens*, to which parties frequently resorted after a summer's walk, to quench their thirst with hyson and other nectareous draughts, for which purpose one of these establishments is still in existence here. Part of the village is in the parish of Lenton, as has been seen at page 573. Its population amounts to upwards of 2000 souls, and its principal streets, &c., are Lenton-street; Forest-street; Holland-street; Sheridan's-row; Saville-row; Castle-row; Pleasant-row; Forest-terrace, &c. &c. The Wesleyan and Kilhamite Methodists, and the Independent Calvinists, and the General Baptists, have each a chapel here.

KENSINGTON, about a quarter of a mile E. of Old Radford, has upwards of 500 inhabitants occupying newly built houses, and having a Primitive Methodist chapel.

LOVETT MILLS is a hamlet with a corn mill and bleach works on the Leen, three quarters of a mile N. of Old Radford, near to which latter, is the new village of PROSPECT PLACE.

SHERWOOD HILL, 1 mile N. of Nottingham, and near the race course, is a small modern village, pleasantly situated, and containing several very handsome mansions, occupied by wealthy families.

RADFORD PARISH DIRECTORY.

☞ *Those marked* 1 *reside at Bloomsgrove ;* 2. *Bobbers Mill;* 3 *Hyson Green ;* 4 *Kensington ;* 5 *New Radford ;* 6 *Prospect place ; and* 7 *Old Radford.*

3 E

The CONTRACTIONS *used for the names of* STREETS, &c.—are Afd. for Alfreton road; Adp. Adam's place; Atr. Aspley terrace; Brw. Birch row; Crw. Castle row; Cht. Chapel street; Dgt. De Ligne street; Dnt. Denman street; Drd. Derby road; Elt. Elliot street; Fst. Forest street; Ftr. Forest terrace; Ggt. George street; Gst. Gregory street; Gkt. Greek street; Hst. Holland street; Hgt. High street; Hcl. Holland's close; Hth. Heath street; Ird. Ilkeston road; Kgt. King street; Lst. Lenton street; Lnt. Lion street; Mst. Montford street; Nst. Newton street; Pst. Pelican street; Ptr. Pleasant row; Ppl. Prospect place; Pkl. Park hill; Pbs. Parker's buildings; Svr. Saville row; Shr. Sheridan's row; Shl. Sion hill; Sst. South street; Sdl. Sherwood hill; Wst. Wood street; and Tyd. Terrace yard.

3 Adams Wm. gent. Adp
4 Akers Hy. medicine vender Gst
5 Allen Mr. Cornls. Brw
5 Allen Mr. Wm. Aspley, ter
5 Allen Wm. stenciller, Gst
5 Alton Mrs. Eliz. Sion hill
3 Anderson Mrs. Grace, Lst
8 Aston Saml. ironfounder
5 Atherstone Mr. T. Aspley ter
3 Abeson Stockdale, lace manufacturer. Ftr
5 Basford Wm. manager, Atr
5 Bason Hy. spirit mert. Atr
4 Beck Mrs. Martha, Geoge st
5 Birch Mr. Rd, Alfreton rd
2 Blenston John, farmer, Aspley
5 Bloomer Miss, Sion hill
3 Booth Abm. Warper, 38, Ptr
5 Bramman John, hawker, Pkl
5 Branson Thos. warper, Ard
5 Branson Wm. piano fort tuner,
  Dnt
5 Breedon Mr. Saml. George st
5 Bromhead Mrs. Ann, Montford st
3 Bryan Mr. Jonath. Adam's pl
Burnside Wm. Stamford. Esq.
  Aspley hall
1 Bywater Mr. James, sen
7 Caunt Thos. gov. of the poor-
  house, overseer, & constable
5 Claringburn Mr. Jph. Augts.
  Birch row
5 Constable Wm. millwrgt. Pbs
5 Coope Jesse, solr. Sion hill
3 Cox Jas. whsman, 4, Saville rw
1 Creswell Rev. Sl. B.A. curate
3 Daft Rt. gent. Forest ter
5 Dale Rd. gent. Aspley ter
5 Daykin Wm. bookpr. Pkl

3 Deacock Mr. Wm. Adam's pl
5 Deakin John, hosier, Aspley tr
3 Dewrose Saml. overlkr. Adp
5 Duffin Mrs. Rachel, Derby rd
5 Dutton John, Cowkpr. Atr
7 Edson Eliz. farmer
5 Fairfield Wm. plasterer, Mst
5 Fairholm Jph. Heath st
3 Foote Rt. Esq. Scottom lodge
5 Forman Capt. Geo. Shl
Frearson John, lace thread dlr.
  Denman st
7 Freer John, farmer
5 Gass Mrs. Mary, Derby road
Gibson Mrs. Lucy, Sherwood hill
1 Gibson Thos, warper
5 Gibson Wm. bookkeeper, Drd
5 Glaskin Mrs. Sarah, Ird
3 Goodacre Lieut. Rd. Ftr
5 Hall John, mfr. Derby rd
5 Hall Liskum, wbsman. Lnt
5 Hannay Wm. mfr. 11, Park hill
5 Harrison Wm. cowkpr. Pst
5 Hickling Wm. pawnbroker, Shl
5 Hill Mr. Chas. Shl
7 Hill Mrs. Jane
5 Hillock Revd. John, Atr
7 Hooke Jph. parish clerk
5 Hovey Mrs. Eliz. Sion hill
5 Hudson John, saddle tree mkr.
  Sion hill
3 Hughes Mrs. Mary, Fst
5 Hydes Hphy. gent. Aspley ter
2 James Rd. cowkeeper
2 Jobson Henry, farmer
Johns Mrs. Mary Ann, 13, Ppl
3 Johnson Wm. portrait painter,
  Hst
5 Kain Danl. contractor, Shl
3 Kidney Mrs. Mary, 35, Ptr

5 Langworth Saml. schoolr. Sbl
Locke Wm. cabtmkr. Forest pl
Mc Donald John, mfr. Shl
5 Malbon Mr. John, Derby rd
5 Marriott Mrs. Rebecca, Drd
5 Marsh Mrs. Mary, Sion hill
3 Martin Geo. tanner, 29, Ptr
7 Miller Samuel, manager
7 Mitchell Wm. cowkeeper
5 Mullen Mrs. Mary, Wood st
4 Murray Saml. tea dealer
Newball Thos. mfr. Shl
3 Newman Benj. gent. Hcl
5 Owencroft John, Professor of
  Dancing, Derby road
5 Page Jas. mfr. Park hill
5 Parker Mr. John, Pbs
Pawlett Daniel, grocer, Pkl
7 Peet Thos. mfr. Vicarage
5 Peverel Thos. canvasser. Tyd
3 Pepper Thos. farmer, Adp
5 Potts Rt. warehouseman, Atr
3 Prew Mrs. Ann, Fst
Price Mrs. Mary, Radford farm
5 Riley Thos. cir. library, Gst
3 Royle Shord, 2, Svr

Academies.
5 Barrett Eliz. Ggt
Birks Mgt. 29, Ppl.
3 Blackwell Eliz. Bdg
Bradley Ann, 17, Ppl
3 Cheetham Eliz. Fst.
5 Goodman John, Gst
7 Hampson Frances
Harvey John, 31, Ppl
3 Haslam Rd. Shr
5 Higton Job, Dnt
2 Hill Joseph
5 Humber Sarah, Gst
5 Lockwood Ann, Gst
3 Smith Wm. Lst
4 Taylor Saml
5 Thorpe Sarah, Cht
7 Widdowson John
1 Woolley Saml
Agents (Bobbin Net.)
Ashwell John, H
5 Booth Thos. Wst
5 Carver John, Ggt
5 Gibson Thos. Dgt
3 Gough John, Adp
5 Gutridge Hy. Dgt
5 Hall Wm. Dnt

Hulse Saml. Sdl
5 Kettleband Wm. Ggt
5 Maples Rd. Atr.
5 Wheatley Wm. Pst
Bakers, &c.
1 Bywater Chas
3 Bywater Wm. Hst
5 Cope Geo. Afd
1 Hebb Daniel
5 Johnson Ann, Sbl
5 Lees Wm. Ggt
7 Moore Elizabeth
5 Newball Hanh. Afd
5 Palethorpe Thos. Pkl
5 Percy Wm. Grove
5 Toyne Thos. Hth
Twigg Benj. Ppl
5 Wells Sydney, Est
7 Weston Saml. (Conf)
5 Woodroffe Wm. Dnt
Bleachers.
Bostock Edward, sen.
  Lovett Mills
2 Bostock Edwd. jun
2 Mitchell William
Bobbin & Carriage
  Makers.

3 Rudd John, warper, Hst
5 Sanderson Wm. Surgeon, Elt
5 Saywell Thos. warper, Sst
3 Schofield Mr. John, Hcl
3 Shepherd Jph. cowkeeper
Sheperson John, farmer, Aspley
5 Shelton Mrs. Jane, Derby rd
5 Smith Thos. gent. Ashley ter
5 Smith Wm. gent. Derby rd
5 Soar Mr. Saml. Ilkeston rd
5 Stanley Mr. Jph. George st
5 Starr Thos. cotton preparer, Gst
5 Stevens Edw. warper, Est
3 Sykes John, trimmer, Ptr
Thackeray John. mfr. Forest hs
Trueman Dd. mfr. Sherwood hs
3 Walker Wm. Fryer, bookr. Hcl
5 Ward Jph. Sep. solr. Aspley tr
Wells John, draper, 11, Forest hs
5 Wigley Saml. trunk & paper
  box maker, Sion hill
Whitlark John, bookr. Sdl
7 Wilson Wm. cotton spinner
1 Wood John, coal agent
4 Yates Mr. Thos. Geo. st
Young Wm. traveller, Pkl

3 Bird Jas. 16, Svr
5 Bostock Jph. Gst
5 Boyes Rt. Pkl
5 Garrett Paul
15 Hobson Thomas.
  (Springer, &c.)Lion
  street
Bobbin Net Makers.
3 Adams, Isc. 19, Svr
1 Allen John
5 Alton, Wm. Shl
Amos Alex. 2, Ppl
7 Amos Joseph
5 Archer Saml. Mst
3 Ashton Wm. 7, Svr.
5 Atkin Matth. Afd
3 Atkin Wm. Shr
7 Atkinson Edmd
3 Attenborough Ths.
  Pleasant row
1 Bacon Elizabeth
1 Bacon Samuel
5 Bailey Thos. Mst
Bamford Jas. Ppl
5 Barker John, Ird
4 Bateman John
5 Bates Wm. Dgt

5 Bates Saml. Ird
3 Beardsley Geo. Ptr
1 Beardsley Samuel
4 Beck Adam
5 Berrington Th. Ird
5 Bills Geo. Wst
Bird John, Ppl
3 Birks Wm. Crw
5 Bloore John, Shl
7 Bodell John
5 Bosworth Geo. Atr
3 Boyer Edw. 36, Ptr
1 Brazier John
5 Briley Geo. Ird
3 Brookes Sam. 19. Pr
3 Brookes Thos. Ptr
3 Brown Wm. Hst
Burdett Wm. 30, Ppl
5 Burgin John, Pkl
4 Burton John, Nst
7 Burton Php. & Jph
5 Butler Saml. Wst
5 Calvert Wm. Ird
3 Cartledge Wm. Ptr
4 Chambers Wm
3 Cheetham Wm Ptr
5 Chettle Saml. Pst
3 Chettle Wm. 24, Ptr
Clarkson Wm. Ppl
Cleaver Jph. 3, Ppl
5 Clifford John, Ggt
3 Clifton Rd. 5, Ptr
3 Clifton Thos. 40 Ptr
5 Coggan Geo. Tyd
5 Cooley Wm. Ird
3 Cooper Saml.12, Shr
5 Couldwell Saml. Aft
3 Crofts Enoch Fst
1 Cross Israel
5 Cullen Benj. Wst
3 Day Hy. Hst
3 Day Wm. 5, Svr
3 Dexter Thos.14, Svr
7 Draper Samuel
5 Dufty John, Ggt
5 Dufty Thos. Gkt
5 Dunk John, Afd
Eagles Wm. Fdk. 37,
    Prospect place
5 Ellison Wm. Ird.
5 Elson Wm. Ird
1 Farmer Joseph
3 Fidler Geo. Svr

5 Fisher Jas. Afd
5 Fishers & Levers,
    George street
5 Foot Rt. Dnt
3 Foster Wm. 2, Ptr.
3 Fox Jha. Ptr
5 Gadsby Ann, Dnt
5 Garratt Paul, Ggt
3 Garton Thos. Shr
5 Gibson Jph. Brw
5 Gibson John, Ird
1 Gibson Robert
5 Gill Danl. 27, Ptr
5 Gill Jas. Mnt
3 Godby Edwd. Crw
5 Goddard John, Ird
5 Goodall James
5 Goodall Chas. Pkl
5 Green Wm. Ggt
1 Gregory Robert
5 Gregory Rd. Ggt
5 Gripper Wm. Brw
3 Gunn John, Ptr
5 Guttridge Thos. Mst
3 Hackforth Hy. Ptr
7 Hall Thomas
1 Hallam George
5 Hancock, Heb. Ird
3 Hancock Saml. Fst
3 Harold Wm. Ptr
5 Harper John, Pkl
5 Harrington Reb.Atr
1 Harris John
3 Haslam John, Hst
1 Haughton ——
5 Haynes John, Brw
5 Hazeldine John, Shl
5 Hazeldine, Sar. Ggt
Hemsley Jas. S. (warp
    net) 27, Prospect pl
1 Henshaw George
5 Hewitt John, Ird
3 Hickling Thos. Hst
1 Higton John
5 Hill Benj. Pst
5 Hill Jph. Chapel st
3 Hill Mattw. Ptr
5 Hill Wm. Ggt
7 Hind John
5 Holland Saml. Ird
Holmes Jtn. Ppl
5 Holt Wm. Dgt
Hooke Danl. 15, Ppl

7 Hooke Joseph
1 Hooton James
3 Hooton John, Svr
5 Hooton Saml. Pkl
3 Hopewell John. Ptr
5 Hopkin John Wst
Hopkin Wm. 20, Shr
1 Hubbard John, Ird
1 Husbands Saml
5 Huskinson Hy. Ggt
Jackson Wm. 36, Ppl
5 James Cornls. Ggt
Jarvis Fras. Ppl
Jeffs Crescent, Ppl
5 Johnson John, Afd
5 Johnson Wm. Wst
5 Keary John, Dgt
5 KettlebandWm. Ggt
Kirk Joseph, Ppl
1 Knight Joseph
5 Knight Wm. Sst
5 Knight Wm. Hth
3 Lamb Rt. Hst
3 LeatherlandW. Crw
4 Ledger Thos. Ggt
5 Ledlie James Ggt
5 Lever John, Gst
3 Lees John, Svr
5 Levers Jph. Shl
5 Locke William
5 Longmire Wm. Atr
3 Lymbery John, Ptr
3 Maltby Jph. Ptr
Maltby Thos. Sdh
3 Marriott H & Wm
3 Marriott Thos. Shr
3 Martin Geo. Ptr
Martin John, Ppl
3 Mather Eml. Shr
5 Merchant Rt. Pst
Middleton John, Sdh
5 Middleton Saml. Shl
5 Moore Stph. Ird
1 Morrell William
5 Morris John, Shl
5 Morris Wm. Brw
4 Murray Samuel
3 Needham Jn. Svr
3 Needham Saml. Ptr
3 Nelson John, Svr
5 Newham Hy. Dgt
1 Newton Thomas
5 Oliver John, Cht

3 Owen Jph. Ptr
Palmer John, Ppl
3 Parker John, Ptr
5 Parker Saml. Gst
3 Pedder Wm. Shr
3 Peet Geo. Shr
5 Piercy John, Sst
4 Pilkington, Joseph
Plowright John, Ppl
Poltney John, Shr
5 Poole Wm. Atr
3 Potter Thos. Ftr
Proctor Benj. Ppl
1 Ragg Joseph
5 Ratcliffe Saml. Shl
5 Redfern Thos. Ird
3 Renew Michl. Ptr
5 Rigby David, Ggt
3 Richardson, Jas. Ptr
3 Robinson John, Ftr
1 Robinson Wm. & J
5 Robinson William
5 Roe Eliz. Ird
3 Sampson Hy. Ptr
3 Savage Jph. Ptr
5 Saywell Wm. Sst
3 Scott Abm. Shr
5 Scottorn Thos. Pkl
5 Seal Frs. Pkl
4 Seives Benjamin
Selby Thomas, Shr
5 Sewell Wm. Nst
Shipman Thos. Ppl
5 Simpson Jas. Ird
Skevington Samuel, 8.
  Prospect place
3 Slack Geo. 8, Shr
5 Slack Saml. Brw
5 Smith James
5 Smith James
5 Smith John, Ird
5 Smith Saml. Afd
1 Smith Samuel
5 Smith Thomas, Dgt
5 Smith Thomas, Ggt
3 Sneath Wm. Lst
5 Soar Wm. Gst
4 Stanton Abm. Kst
4 Stanton John
3 Storer Benj. Ptr
3 Street John, Ptr
5 Street Saml. Atr
Street Wm. Ppl

7 Streeton William
5 Summer Wm. Wst
1 Sutton George
5 Synyer Hy. Dgt
5 Taylor John, Gst
7 Taylor John
1 Taylor Thomas
5 Tetley Wm. Ird
3 Thurman Samuel
  Meed, Castle place
3 Tinkler Rt. Crw
5 Tingley Thos. Gst
1 Tomlinson George
5 Tomlinson Thomas
5 Trueman Saml. Pkl
5 Upton Geo. Islingn
4 Vann Walter, Kgt
5 Walker Geo. Fdk.
  (bdg. surveyor) Est
5 Walker Thos. Atr
5 Walker Wm. Pst
3 Ward Edwin Hst
5 Warner Thos. Dgt
Warwick John, Sdl
5 Watton Saml. Ggt
West Eb. 21, Ppl
West Fras. 24, Ppl
3 White Saml. Shr
3 Whittle Wm. Ptr
7 Wild Wm. & Geo
5 Willbond Wm. Ggt
Willey Saml. Sdl
3 Wilson Wm. Shr
5 Woodroffe W. Dnt
Woodward Jas. Ppl
5 Wright Thos. Ird
Wright Thos. Ppl
5 Wrighton John, Ird
  Boot & Shoe Mkrs.
5 Baguley Jph. Dnt
Benton Wm. Ppl
2 Birkinshaw Thos
3 Blatherwick Jn. Fst
3 Brown Chs. Sst
4 Burton John
5 Cartwright Th. Afd
1 Chesterfield John
5 Cresswell Thos
5 Dunk Benj. Ard
Dring James, Ppl
5 Fisher Edm. Ard
3 Gibson Jas. Crw
3 Gibson Wm. Hst
3 E 2.

3 Hallam John, Hst
5 Hannah Benj. Ggt
5 Hedderley Geo. Shl
1 Herring Benjamin
1 Higginson Samuel
3 Idwell John, Shr
4 Pilkington Richard
5 Riley Jonth. Gst
5 Shaw Thos. Ard
5 Smith William
1 Swift James
5 Taylor William
7 Turpin John
2 Walker John
3 Warren Edwd. Fst
7 Walker William
4 Whitehurst Jacob
5 Wood Thomas Wil-
  son, Gst
5 Wright Jph. Brw
  Bricklayers.
3 Attenborough Geo.
  8, Pleasant row
5 Butler Michl. Mnt
2 Chambers Thomas
1 Harlow John
1 Knight Jn. (mason)
4 Knight Wm. (ma-
  son) Hague street
5 Parker Thos. Atr
5 Wright Thos. Ird
  Butchers.
3 Addicott Dd. Ftr
5 Alkin Rd. Afd
7 Dickens Edward
5 Gould James, Afd
5 Hayles Thos. Dnt
3 Kirk Thos. Svr
5 Mason Mat. Ird
5 Parker Levi, Shl
5 Richards Saml. Afd
3 Stokes Mat. Hst
4 Tandy Rt. Abbeyr
1 White William
5 Wright John, Gst
  Cart Owners.
3 Abbot Rd. Hcl
7 Anthony Samuel
7 Braithwaite Thos
5 Burton John, Sst
5 Lowen John
5 Maples Thos
5 Southern Thos. Afd.

7 Taylor John
5 Watson Wm. Sst
Cotton Spinners.
Wilson Wm. & Saml.
  (and Angola, and
  fancy yarns)
Corn Millers.
Bostock Edw. sen.
  Lovett mills
Burton John, Bur-
  ton's mill——John
  Bonner, manager
7 Harrison George
2 Simpson Joseph
7 Smith Edward
Druggists.
5 Houldgate Rt. Pbs
5 Need & Coltman,
  Saville row
5 Saunders Sarah Ggt
*Framesmiths & Ma-
chine Makers.*
4 Brookhouse Thos.
  Prince street
3 Chater & Kinder,
  8, Saville row
1 Bunting & Ragg,
  Bloomsgrove st
5 Cheswell John, Atr
5 Evans David, Dgt
5 Gregory Rd. Ggt
3 Hancock Saml. Fst
INNS & TAVERNS.
5 Cannon, Saml. Gunn, Derby rd
3 Cricket Players & Tea Gardens, John Pepper
1 Peacock Inn, Saml. Elliott, Ird
5 Pelican, Mary Cooper, Pel. st
7 Plough, James Wood
Radford Grove and Tea Gardens,
  William Parr
7 Rose, Joseph Wild
5 Sir J. B. Warren, Ann Webster, Sion hill
7 Three Tons, Wm. Streeton
2 Wheat Sheaf, Samuel Scott
7 White Horse, Wm. Whitworth
5 White Lion, Wm. Fletcher, Gst
5 Wind Mill, John Godfrey, Afd
BEERHOUSES.
1 Black Horse, Wm. Mason
5 Samuel Ingram, High street

3 Kenrick Wm. Fst
5 Kerry Rd. & Co.
  Denman street
5 Levers Thos. Shl
7 Littlewood Thomas
5 Mottershaw Ts. Ird
1 Ragg Reuben
5 Simpson Thos. Shl
3 Smith James, Gkt
Smith Thomas Ppl
5 Tomlinson Ts. Gkt
5 Twigg James, Dgt
7 Wild Wm. & Geo
Framework Knitters.
3 Collins John
3 Diggle Nathaniel
5 Fawcett Wm. Atr
5 Floyd William
3 Gunn Thomas, Ptr
5 Horner Hy. Gst
1 Kingsley William
5 Lockwood Wm. Gst
5 Preston John, Pst
5 Shipman Luke, Pkl
3 Storey Chas. Hst
3 Watson John, Svr
1 Wells James
Wells Thomas, Ppl
Gardeners.
4 Cresswell Patrick
5 Culley John, Sst
5 Down Jas. (job) Gst
5 James Gould, Alfreton road
5 Thomas Marlow, Ilkeston rd
3 Joshua Overend, Forest st
4 William Smith, Abbey row
7 John Winfrey
7 Isaac Mosley
3 Coffee-house, Wm. Leatherland
1 Dog & Pheasant, John Higton
5 Generous Briton, Wm. Wilson,
  Heath street
4 Jolly Higler, Eliz. Copestick
5 Jolly Miller, Ann Johnson, Shl
3 Jolly Sailor, Thos. Brown, Hst
5 King Wm. IV. Wm. Page, Cht
3 New Inn, Hy. Warren, Hst
3 Odd Fellows, Hy. Ward, Hst
5 Old Oak, Rd. Wheatcroft, Dnt
Pheasant, William Street, Ppl
5 Polish Lancer, Geo. Barton, Atr
5 Wheat Sheaf, Jn. Harrison, Ird

1 Goodman Jph. (job)
5 Heath Thos. (job)
5 Hind Hy. Ird
5 Hind Wm. Ggt
2 Johnson Richard
Kerry John, Aspley
2 Milton George
7 Richards Edward
5 Tomlins John, Hgt
5 Turner Wm. Hgt
7 Wilkins Thomas
Hair Dressers.
5 Allen Thos. Shl
7 Kidman Henry
5 Need Jph. Brw
3 Shephard Jon. Crw
3 Taylor William
Hosiery Manuftrs.
5 Collyer Saml. (silk)
  Islington road
3 Helson John, Fst
5 Jenkins Chas. Wat-
  son, & Co. Park
  hill, & Milk street,
  London
3 Ratcliffe John, Sst
3 Richardson Jas. Ptr
7 Saxton John
Thorne Wm. Byfpl
3 Ward John, Hst
3 Whittle Wm. Ptr

Joiners & Cabinet
Makers.
1 Brutnell Wm
3 Pinner Geo. Adp
5 Simons Wm. Elt
5 Smith John & Wm.
De Ligne Street
5 Taylor John, Hst
7 Wild William
5 Wilson Saml. Cht
Maltsters.
4 Burton & Pidcock,
King street
1 Underwood Wm. Bst
7 Winfred John
Nail Makers.
1 Jackson John, Bst
5 Taylor John, Sst
Needle Makers.
3 Cherry Saml. Hst
5 Litchfield Jn. Gst
5 Noble Saml. Gst
5 Redwood Hy. Brw
5 Shipman John, Pst
3 Wylde Rd. Ptr
Painters.
3 Biddulph John, Ptr
5 Malbon Geo. Drd
3 Stainforth Jn. Crw
Plumbers & Glaziers.
5 Gunn Saml. Drd
1 Shelton George
3 Stephenson George
Sadler.
5 Bradwell John Gst
Shopkeepers.
5 Atkin Matt. Afd
5 Bailey Thos. Mst
5 Bainbridge Jn. Gst
3 Ball Wm. Hst

4 Beck Adam, Ggt
5 Bostock Jph. Gst
5 Brown Eliza, Shl
5 Cartwright Jn. Sst
5 Cheadle John, Dnt
5 Chimley Thos. Est
1 Crooks John
4 Dickisson Henry
5 Ellis John, Shl
5 Fallowell Geo. Sst
4 Greaves John, Ird
5 Hall Wm. Dnt
3 Hextall Ann, Adp
5 Hollingworth F. Pst
1 Hubbard John, Ird
5 Humber Saml. Ggt
5 Husbands Jph Brw.
5 Lees Fras. Dnt
4 Johnson John
3 Manners My. Svr
5 Marlow Thos. Ird
5 Maycock Wm. Dgt
7 Morley George
5 Nelson Adam, Ggt
2 Page William
5 Peach Samuel
3 Pilkington Jn. Ptr
Redgate George
5 Redgate Wm. Gst
1 Scotton Jas. (& dpr)
Shipman Th. 11, Ppl
7 Smith Edward
5 Smith John, Brw
7 Taylor William
4 Tookey Sarah
7 Turpin John
5 Unwin Wm. Est
1 Walker John
5 Wells John, Dnt
4 White William

5 White John Ber-
ridge (bacon dealer)
Brw
5 Williamson Rd. (&
broker) Afd
5 Wilson Wm. Hth
7 Wilson Ann
Sinker Makers.
5 Millward Geo. Dgt
5 Millward Jn. Mst
5 Wells Saml. Gst
Tallow Chandler.
5 Beardmore J. Shl
Tailors.
1 Bywater James
5 Fox John, Ird
3 Gibbons John, Hst
7 Goulding John
3 Hasty Geo. Svr
5 Hill Jph. Cht
1 Hitchcock Saml
5 Kettleband Jn. Brw
5 Kingsley Zep. Gst
7 Newton Isaac
2 Parker William
3 Redwood, Wm. Hst
1 Rigg Jph. Ird
5 Tait James, Brw
4 Taylor Robert
Tetley Geo. Ppl
5 Wall John, Gst
Turners.
5 Bennet John Afd
5 Halfpenny John (&
fancy chair) Earl st
Wood Benjamin
5 Wood Wm. Brw
Wheelwrights.
7 Buck Wm. & Son
4 Ledger William

SELSTON PARISH lies near the source of the Erwash, which divides it from Derbyshire within three miles of Alfreton. It abounds in *coal* and *ironstone,* and comprises 2050 acres of enclosed land, and 900 acres of open common, of which Viscount Melbourne, Lord Mexborough, and Sir Willoughby Dixie are the principal owners, and joint lords of the manor. The latter gentleman is also impropriator, and patron of the *vicarage* which is valued in the King's books at £5, and is now enjoyed by the Rev. Joseph Churchill Dixie. The population amounts to 1321 souls, living in 256 houses, which are scattered through the hamlets of SELSTON, BAGTHORP, and UNDERWOOD, the two latter of which are distant from one to two miles south of the former, and 10 miles N.N.W. of Nottingham. The *church*, dedicated to St. Helen, has a tower and two bells. In the parish are three *chapels*, viz. one at Selston belonging to the Calvinists, one at Hand-Stubbing occupied by the Wesleyans, and one at Bagthorpe tenanted by the Primitive Methodists. The *feast* is on the nearest Sunday to Old Michaelmas.

BAGTHORPE is the centre division of the parish, and in it is the ancient hall of WANSLEY, or *Wandesley*, near which, in 1830, a urn full of silver coins was found.

UNDERWOOD, where a colliery has lately been opened, is at the south end of the parish, adjoining to Brinsley. The Selston colliery has been established several years, and a railway is laid from it to Pinxton.

CHARITIES.—Three cottages in Selston were built with £32. 10s. belonging to the poor, for which the overseers distribute 22s. 6d. yearly, together with 10s. as the interest of £10 arising from several benefactions. Lady Dixie left 6s. per annum to be distributed in bread in this parish, "on Nottingham goose fair eve."

Those marked 1 reside at Bagthorpe, 2 at Hand-Stubbing hill, 3 Jack's Dale, 4 Selston, 5 Toadhole, 6 Underwood, 7 Westwood, and 8 at Woodnook.

2 Ball John, beerhouse
6 Barber Walker and Co. colliery owners
6 Beardsall John, beerhouse
4 Bland John, victualler Bull & Butcher
4 Bland Robert, baker
4 Brabley John, wheelwright
8 Carlin Thomas and Son, hosiery manufacturers
2 Clark William, yeoman
3 Clark J. vict. Portland Arms
6 Coates Eli, maltster
2 Cook Chpr. cooper
1 Farnsworth John, beerhouse
6 Granger Samuel, maltster
4 Hardstaff Rev. Geo. (Baptist)
1 Holmes John, smith, and beerhouse
4 Howitt Rebecca, Horse and Jockey
Jones Thomas, draper and beerhouse
3 Jowitt Peter, mason
4 Lee Matthew, butcher
2 Lilley Henry, shopkeeper

4 Littlewood Samuel, joiner
4 Oakes James and Co. colliery owners
8 Robinson Mary, victualler
4 Salmon Matthew, blacksmith
4 Saunders Samuel, joiner
2 Smith Mr. Benjamin
4 Waterhall John, farrier
4 Waters Henry, shopkeeper
4 Webster James, blacksmith
6 Wharmby William, beerhouse
6 Wilcockson, Samuel, engineer
6 Williamson Edward, miller
4 Wilson James, tailor & p. clerk
1 Wilson John, vict. Dixie Arms
1 Wilson Thomas, gent
6 Wilson Thomas, butcher, brickmaker and horse dealer
4 Wilson Samuel, tailor

FARMERS.

4 Allsebrook J	4 Clark John
7 Bett Geo	4 Clark Joseph
4 Birkinshaw J	4 Clark Robert
4 Bland Mary	4 Clark Samuel
1 Booth Martha	4 Day Richard
4 Clark John	4 Dodson Thos

6Fisher Wm   7Hill George | 4Salmon Sarah 3Sterland John
4Fletcher Jph 4Hunt Samuel | 4Sant John   4Waterhall Sam
  Selston Hall 1Jackson Rd | 1Saunders Thos 6Wharmby Jno
4Flint James   1Maltby E.Wan-| 4Saxton Sarah 4Whithers Thos
4Gill Joseph   sley Hall |
7Heald George 3Maltby Geo | CARRIER.—John Lee. to Not-
6Hewitt Henry 4Renshaw Ben | tingham, Wed. & Sat. 4 mg.

SKEGBY village is built on the two declivities of a deep and narrow valley, near the source of the river Meden, 3 miles W. of Mansfield. The *parish* contains 656 inhabitants and 1424 acres of land, and has a coal mine, a coarse pottery, and several limestone quarries and kilns, the latter of which are in Stoney-ford-lane. John Dodsley, Esq. of Skegby Hall, is the principal owner and lord of the manor, which was a parcel of the King's manor of Mansfield, until James I. granted it to an ancestor of its present lord. The church is a small ancient structure, and was formerly a chapel to Mansfield. It is a curacy, certified at £13. 16s. 8d. and is now enjoyed by the Rev. Wm. Goodacre. The dean of Lincoln is the patron and appropriator, but the Duke of Portland is his lessee, and holds a peculiar court for proving the wills, &c. of this parish and Teversal. The *feast* is on the Sunday after July 10th. In 1613, *Matthew Clark* left 10s. yearly to the poor, out of land now belonging to Mr. Wm. Ward. In 1741, Simon Smith bequeathed his real and personal estate to found an *hospital* here, but his devise was void by the mortmain act.

Dodsley John, Esq. Skegby Hall
Adlington Wm. miller & brick mr
Allen Thomas, blacksmith
Alvey Wm. hosiery agent
Booth John, lime burner
Bower Samuel, gardener
Chadwick Thomas, wheelwright
Chambers Saml. red ware and
  brick manufacturer
Coope George & Wm. coopers
Duffin Thomas, weaver
Dobb William, beerhouse
Hardstaff William, parish clerk
Herriott Samuel, mason & vict
Hibberd James, shoemaker
Hibberd William, shopkeeper
Judson Benjamin, tailor
Judson Wm. bobbin net maker

Milner Joseph, beerhouse
Ovendale William, lime-burner
Parsons Saml. vict. White Swan
Radford Wm. blacksmith
Rawson Saml. vict. Anchor
Robinson Henry, shoemaker
Rowe Saml. shopr. & hosiery agt
Ward Thos. S. hosiery agent
Ward William, gentleman
  FARMERS. Slack Thos.
Anthony Jph   Townroe Rt (&
Caladine Jph   maltster)
Caladine Wm. Townroe Roby
Dobb Matt   Wass John
Hall John   Wilson Saml
Parsons Cath Wilson Saml
Parsons Rd

STAPLEFORD is a large village, pleasantly situated on the Erwash, near the Derby road, 6 miles W. by S. of Nottingham. Here are upwards of 100 machines employed in making *tatting and warp lace.* The parish contains about 1100 acres, and its population has increased since the year 1801, from 748 to 1533 souls. The principal owners are Lady Warren, Mrs. Fisher, Mr. Charles Antill, Mr. John Dodsley, and John Jackson, Esq., the latter of whom is lord of the manor, and patron of the perpetual curacy; though the Lord Chancellor presented the two last incumbents. The *church* is a neat edifice with a tower and spire, and was repaired in 1785 and 1819. The living, which is now enjoyed by the Rev. Richard Hoggarth, has been twice augmented with Queen Anne's Bounty, and received at the enclosure in 1771, an allotment of 3A. 1R. 10P. In the village is an ancient *cross*, with a very curiously wrought shaft. The *feast* is on the Sunday before Old St. Luke's, or on that day when it falls on a Sunday. Here are two Methodist chapels, one built 40 years ago, and the other in 1831. Several sick societies, and a numerous lodge of Odd Fellows, meet in the village.

STAPLEFORD HALL is the seat of Lady Warren, relict of the late *Rt. Hon. Admiral Sir John Borlase Warren, Bart. and K. B.*, who rebuilt the house in 1797, and sheltered the lawn with beautiful plantations. It would far exceed our limits to enter on the biography of this gallant admiral, who died in 1825, but it is a fact worthy of recording here, that at the commencement of the American war, he went to the Fleet and King's Bench prisons, and released with his own purse all the naval officers confined there for debt. Lady Warren pays for the education of 40 girls, and a National school room has just been built by subscription. The poor parishioners receive 20s. yearly from Handley's charity, (see p. 165,) and 20s. yearly from the funds of Willoughby's hospital at Cossal.

NEW STAPLEFORD is a hamlet one mile N.E. of Old Stapleford, and near it is the "*Hemlock stone*," a ponderous fragment of a Druid's Temple.

Warren Lady Car. Stapleford hl
Antill Chas. tanner, Brockhill
Armston Samuel, painter
Atkin James, guide & needle mkr
Barton John, vict. & joiner
Barton Vincent, beerhouse
Bosquet Yelverton, surgeon
Bramley Thos. hosiery agent and manufacturer
Brentall Elijah, vict. & bricklr
Bramley Jn. vict. New Stapleford
Bramley Matthew, beerhouse
Cheetham James, machine mkr
Daykin John, parish clerk
Dodsley John, gentleman
Eaton William, blacksmith
Eyley Joseph, schoolmaster
Garrett John, painter
Godby John, guide & needle mkr
Gollin John, plumber & glazier
Greasley Eliz. victualler
Greasley James, tailor
Jackson John, Esq. brick maker
Jones Edward, joiner
Jones William, schoolmaster
Kent Peter, corn miller
Lambert William, blacksmith
Newell Wm. lace singer & vict
Palmer John, machine maker, and lace thread manufacturer
Salthouse Thomas Hill, gent
Scattergood Peter, machine mkr
Shepherd William, joiner
Sleigh Capt. Wm. Niagara Cot

Smalley Mrs. Ann & Sarah
Smith John, machine maker
Smith Joseph, tailor
Watkin William, baker, &c.
Wood Rev. Hugh, curate
Wood Robert, wheelwright
Wright Thomas, corn miller

Boot and Shoe Makers.
Barton V. & W Howard Thos
Butler Joseph   Oldershaw Wm
Foster Joseph   Watson John

Farmers.
Birch William Toft Wm. and
Hallam William   brick mkr
Hickinbotham Townsend Alex
   Wm. & brick Wallis John
   maker

Grocers and Shopkeepers.
Bramley Thos Daykin Saml
Chester Rd. (& Doar John
   draper)   Smedley John
Tatting and Warp Lace Mfrs.
*Those marked * purchase and*
finish the Tatting ; and † are
Bobbin Net makers.
Atkin Eliz   Smedley Thos
Atkin Isaac   † Smedley Gerv
Dalley Wm   Smedley John
Dann Saml   *Streets John &
†Greasley Dd   Son
Johnson Thos   *Taylor James
Kirkby John   Whiteley Thos
†Palmer Geo   †Wright Thos

STRELLEY PARISH is a district of scattered dwellings, 5 miles W.N.W. of Nottingham, and contains 426 inhabitants and 1800 acres of land, all of which belongs to T. W. Edge, Esq. of *Strelley Hall,* a plain but neat modern mansion, surrounded by tasteful pleasure grounds, commanding fine views of the romantic scenery in the vicinity. It anciently gave name to "one of the oldest and most famous knightly families in the county." The *church* is dedicated to All Saints, and has been much improved by Mr. Edge, who has ornamented it with an elegant stained glass window. The living is a rectory, in the same patronage and incumbency as that of Bilborough, (see p. 559.) The *feast* is on the same day as that at Stapleford. About one mile N.W. of the hall is *Strelley Park colliery,* whence coals are conveyed on a railway to the Nottingam canal.

Edge T. Webb, Esq. Strelley hl
Edge Rev. J. Webb, M.A. rector
Barber, Walker, & Co. coal owns
Blunston William, farmer
Cartwright Rd. corn miller
Day John, farmer
Dodsley John, vict. Broad Oak
Flewitt William, blacksmith
Hardstaff Thomas, gamekeeper

Martin John, shoemaker
Needham Jph. shopkr. & vict
Nixon Mr. Charles
Scavern Job, farmer
Shepperson John. farmer
Stevenson Emanuel, shopkpr
Watkinson Charles, bricklayer
White Mrs. ——
Woodhouse Mrs. Mary

SUTTON-IN-ASHFIELD PARISH extends from 3 to 5 miles west of Mansfield, and contains 5734 inhabitants and 5861A. 0R. 12P. of land, divided into the two townships of *Sutton-in-Ashfield* and *Hucknall-under-Huthwaite,* and of which 3155A. 2R. 14P. belong to the Duke of Portland, including 1100 acres allotted to him, at the inclosure in 1798, in lieu of the rectorial tithes ;—his grace being the impropriator, and lord of the manor, which is partly copyhold, and was a *Berue* of the Soke of Mansfield. Amongst the old tenures we find that Jordan de Sutton held land here of the crown by paying 14s. yearly, besides rendering homage, suit and service at the Mansfield court, and attending the king's army in Wales, " with one man, and horse and habergeon, cap of iron, lance and sword."

SUTTON-IN-ASHFIELD, 3½ miles W. S. W. of Mansfield, is a very large village and township, comprising more than four-fifths of the parish, and 4805 inhabitants, mostly employed in the cotton, hosiery, and lace manufactures, there being here no fewer than 1700 *stocking frames*, 20 *bobbin net machines*, and an extensive *factory* for spinning cotton, and making checks and nankeens. Here are likewise two *potteries* of coarse red ware. The ancient FAIRS which had long been obsolete were revived in 1832, with every prospect of success. They are held on the second Tuesday in April, and the last Tuesday in September, for the sale of horses, neat cattle, sheep, swine, cheese, &c. A *hiring for servants* is held Nov. 25th, or on the following day, if that date should be Sunday. The *feast* is on the 2d Sunday after July 10th. Near the village is *Mapple Wells*, the water of which is of a petrifying quality, and has been successfully used in rheumatic cases. The CHURCH stands on an eminence, and has a handsome octagonal spire. It is dedicated to St. Mary, and the benefice is a curacy, endowed with land at Edderley, purchased with Queen Anne's Bounty, and now let for £37 a-year. The Duke of Devonshire is the patron, and the Rev. Wm. Goodacre the incumbent. The *organ*, which was built in 1826, and cost £300, was the gift of the late John Shooter, an eccentric blacksmith, who died in 1829, aged 97. Here are five dissenting CHAPELS belonging to the Independents, (built in 1743) the Calvinistic and General Baptists, and the Wesleyan and Primitive Methodists, and they have each a Sunday school. There are here several friendly societies, a book club, an harmonic society, and a Dorcas society. The *National school* was established by subscription, in 1819, and the master now receives £9 yearly from the ancient school land, viz.—Fenny-bark close left in 1669, by Anne Mason, and Pothouse close, left by Eliz. Boot, about 40 years ago. In 1681, *John Newton* charged Wheldon's farm with the giving of two cloth coats to two of the most needy parishioners yearly. A horrid *murder* was committed in the village about 2 o'clock in the morning of Sep. 7th, 1830, by *Henry Shooter*, on the body of his father, after killing whom, he stabbed his mother, but before he could inflict on her a fatal blow, the pratricide heard some of the neighbours entering the house, and as he could not escape he cut his own throat and expired soon afterwards. This misguided youth was apprenticed to a surgeon, at Bakewell, and his impatience to possess his father's property, and that of an aunt at Nottingham, led him to invite the latter to visit his parents, with whom it was his intention to have sacrificed her to his diabolical concupiscence, but she happily did not obey his invitation. *Joseph Whitehead*, a framework knitter, who died here in 1811, aged 27, distinguished himself in the study of astronomy, constructed an orrory, and was an excellent musician.

EASTFIELD is a considerable village ¾ miles E. of the church, consisting principally of new houses and two potteries.

FULWOOD is a hamlet, 1 mile W. by S. of Sutton, and 1 mile further, in the same direction, is an *extra parochial* farm called FULWOOD CROW TREES, belonging to the Duke of Portland, and occupied by John Clark.

HUCKNALL-UNDER-HUTHWAITE is a village and township, containing 929 inhabitants, and about 1000 acres of land, bordering upon Derbyshire, and 1¼ miles W. N. W. of Sutton-in-Ashfield. It is situated upon a lofty declivity, and has an extensive colliery, many framework knitters, and two chapels belonging to the Methodists and Independents. The poor here have £3 yearly, from the bequest of Abraham Haslam, in 1831, and 8s. yearly, pursuant to the wills of William Day and another donor.

The CONTRACTIONS used in the following DIRECTORY of SUTTON-IN-ASHFIELD, are Bln. for Blind lane ; Bkn. Back lane ; Cht. Church street ; Clr. Club row ; Dkt. Duke street ; Efd. Eastfield ; Fst. Forest st. ; Fln. Forest lane ; Fld. Fulwood ; Hst. High st. ; Hpt. High Pavement ; Hsl. Haslam's hill ; Kgt. King st. ; Lst. Low st. ; Mkp. Market place ; Mst. Middle st. ; Nrw. New row ; Nrd. New road ; Ohl. Oates' hill ; Sbs. Smedley's buildings ; Sgn. Swine's green ; Upt. Upper st. ; and Wln. Water lane.

LETTERS *are conveyed daily to and from Mansfield, by Dennis Whetton.*

Barns T. gardener, Sgn
Berry John, setter-up, & toy dlr. Church street
Bilson William, cotton spinner, Sutton works
Brandreth John, par. clerk, Church st
Burrows Rev. Jph. New row
Cheetham Saml. nail maker, Ohl
Coope Wm. leather cutter, King st
Crofts Hy. pawnbkr. Low street
Cursham, Mrs. Ann

England Wm. saddler, Smedley's bdgs
Foxton Jas. watch maker, King st
Goodacre Rev. Wm. Blackmires
Hambleton Jph. hat maker, Low st
Jepson Mr. Rd. Hst
Knighton G. chairmk
Mayfield Mary, Lst
Oscroft Geo. bricklr
Oscroft Geo. painter
Sills Ephraim, constable, Church st
Swift Geo. wood agent to the Duke of Portland, Rushley

Stanhope Wm. maltster, King street
Waters Mr. G. Cht
Watson John, bookkeeper, Nrw
Woolley Saml. Esq. Sutton Hall
Academies.
Jennings Jas. Sbs
Litchfield John, Nrd
Nott Rev. Clement, Upper street
Rhodes Wm. Kgt
Roome Rev. T. Hpt
Bakers, &c.
Daubney John, Hst
Godley Wm. Cht
Gregory Chas. Kgt

3 F

Lindley John, Bln

Blacksmiths.
Clark John, Cht
Wright Wm. Lst

Bobbin Net Mkrs.
Bestall Chas. Cht
Bower Saml. Hsl
Boot John, Sbs
Burrows Jph. Nrw
Kirk Wm. Fst
Penisland Geo. Fln
Sheppard Saml. Wln

Boot & Shoe Mkrs.
Allen Cath. Hsl
Buckland Geo. Ohl
Coope Wm. Cht
Curtis John, Clr
Else Wm. Mst
Else Wm. Cht
Holbrooke Danl. Kgt
Jackson Thos. Clr
Jackson Wm. Sgn
Oscroft John, Kgt
Oscroft Matt. Mkp
Robinson Saml. Efd
Sells Stph. Clr
Sleighton John, Efd

Braziers, &c.
Gibson Rd. Mkp
Stanhope Jas. & iron-
 monger, Kgt
Wass Geo. Butcher's
 yard

Brick & Tile Mkrs.
Bains John, Efd
Heath John, Efd

Butchers.
Burton Thos. Lst
Clarke Saml. Hst
Clarke Wm. Bln
Elliott Peter, Cht
Oldham John, Wln
Rhodes John, Kgt
Wass John, Lst
Wass Wm. Fln
Witham Fras. Kgt

Chymists & Drugts.
Jackson Saml. Mkp
Littlewood Rd. Mkp

Confectioners.
Daubney John, Hst
Morrell Fred. Cht
Wilson John, Cht

Corn Millers.
Crofts Jas. Sbs
Hawkins John, Efd

Cotton Spinners and Manufacturers.
Unwin Samuel & Co.
 Sutton works

Earthenware Mfrs.
Heath John, Efd
Mee Pr. Redhouse

Farmers.
Allwood Hy. Kgt
Bacon Thos. Cht
Bailey Saml. Bkn
Beecroft Wm. Cht
Barns Saml. Fld
Burton John, Mkp
Chambers Sarah, Cht
Clark John, Cht
Clark Geo. Cht
Clay Rt. Fln
Clay Saml. Fld
Else Isaac, Ohl
Fisher Clay, Sgn
Fisher Saml. Sutton
 grange
Hall Hannah, Kgt
Hall Timothy, Forest
Handley Jph. Bkn
Hayes Isaac, Fln
Heathcote Saml. Bkn
Hill John, Fld
Hughes Wm. Bikmires
Jephson Jph. Sbs
Houseley Saml Mplt
Kitchen Wm. Redhs
Lee Benjamin, Cht
Lindley Jas. Stonehill
Nowell Wm. Fld
Marriott Saml. Fld
Morris Eliz. Fln
Outram Thos. Lst
Radford Wm. Fln
Shore Thos. Fld
Smith Jph. Fln
Straw Abm. Cht
Straw Rebecca, Sbs
White John
Wragg Wm.
Wright Wm. Cht

Frame Smiths.
Cawton James, Nrd
Daubney John, Clr

Dove Hy. Dkt
Jephson Wm. Hst
Marshall John, Kgt
Pitt Benj. jun. Clr
Salmon Thos. Fst
Sheppard Saml. Wall-
 stone street
Taylor Wm. Dkt
Turner James, Rus-
 sell square
Ward Wm. Hsl

Grocers.
Butterworth Hy. Mkp
Dodson Matt. Lst
Gadsby Thos. Lst
Glasby Eliz. Kgt
Hickton Saml. Lst
Jephson Wm. Hst
Sampson Wm. Kgt
Tudsbury Rd. Efd
Wright Chte. Mkp

Hair Dressers.
Barlow Geo. Clr
Burton Wm. Lst
Cooke Wm. Mst

Hosiery Agents and Manufacturers.
Alvey Jph. Clr
Betts Saml. Lst
Brooks Edw. Bkn
Butterworth H. Mkp
Hickton Ebenr. Kgt
Hickton Saml. Lst
Jackson Geo. Clr
Naylor Rd. Kgt
Oscroft Geo. Lst
Pitt Benj. Clr
Radford Benj. Clr
Radford John, Nrd
Shaw Thos. Kgt
Smith Joshua, Bln
Turner Thos. Hsl
Whiteman Jas. Lst

Inns and Taverns.
Black Bull, Francis
 Witham, Kgt
BlueBell, E. Evans, Ct
Brick and Tile, Wm.
 Bennett, Lst
Cart and Horse, Geo.
 Penistant. Fln
Crown and Woolpack,
 Eliz. Kirk, Ohl

Denman's Head, Jn. Cooper, Mkp
Dog and Duck, Wm. Wass, Fln
Duke of Sussex, Jph. Fletcher, Fld
Durham Ox, Samuel Wiley, Mkp.
George and Dragon, Sam. Chappell, Nrw
Nag's Head, Fras. Shacklock, Lst
New Inn, William Allcock, Swine's green
Old Blue Bell, John Heath, Efd
Old Trooper, Jph. Webster, Clr
Robin Hood, Thos. Dixon, Scott's hole
Unicorn, George Lawson, Low street
White Lion, James Hage, Portland st
White Swan, Eliz. Crofts, Church st

Beerhouses.
Beardsall John, Kgt
Bower Saml. Hsl
Chadburn Wm. Nrd
Crofts Jas. Sbs
England Wm. Sbs
Straw Wm. Efd
Tompkin Val. Efd
Turner Jas. Rsq
Wyeld Jph. Bkn

Joiners.
Adlington John, Clr

Adlington Saml. Bln
Brooks J. Duke st
Brooks Jph. Bkn
Fisher John, Sgn
Foxton Saml. Kgt
Haslam Wm. Hsl
Lee Jph. Cht
Ward Jph. Cht

Limeburners.
Barratt John, Hst
Lindley John, Bkn
Millwood Wm. Cht

Linen & Wln Drps.
Hawkins & Allin, Efd
Judd Robt. Mkp
Miller Benj. Mkp

Needle Makers.
Blasdale John, Clr
Butterworth Jn. Bkn

Plumbers & Glaziers.
Wass Saml. & Son, Church street
Wilson Thos. Clr

Shopkeepers.
Adin Wm. Cht
Allen Benj. Lst
Bower Saml. Hsl
Burton Hanh. Sbs
Clark Wm. Wst
Croft Hy. Lst
Elliot Peter, Cht
Fisher John, Sgn
Gadsby Matt. Ohl
Hawkins John, Efd
Hollingworth W. Hpt
Marriott Geo. Cht
Marshall Benj. Bln
Oates Wm. Ohl

Spencer Thos. Hsl
Straw Rt. Hsl
Turner Thos. Hsl

Sinker Makers.
Allen Saml. Kgt
Burgain Saml. Efd
Chasador John, Dkt
Tomlinson John Clr

Surgeons.
Sales Jph. & medicated baths, Hpt
Valentine Jas. Wm. Portland street

Tailors.
Bulline Thos. Ohl
Henstock John, and preserver of birds and beasts, Efd
Mitchell Moses, Hst
Shacklock, Fras. Bkn
West Jph. Cht
Wright Geo. Sgn
Wyeld Jph. Bkn

Tallow Chandlers.
Barratt Jph. Bkn
Dodson Matt. Lst

Wheelwrights.
Brown Thos. Sbs
Fox Jph. Cht
Leeson John, Hpt

Carriers.
Thos. Wilson, from Low street, and Thos. Bullock, from Back lane to Mansfield, W. & Sat. 5 mg.

HUCKNALL-UNDER-HUTHWAITE.
Allsop George, joiner
Barns John, shoemaker
Beardsmore George, grocer
Bower Saml. vict. Portland Arms
Brooks John, joiner
Burrows Jerb. vict. " Col. Wildman"
Burrows Jerb. jun. schoolmaster
Burton John, shopkpr & beerhs
Burton Benj. grocer and agent
Butterworth John, hosiery agent
Chambers Jane, vict. Swan
Clark George, shopkeeper

Columbine Mr. Jonth.
Ellis Eliz. shopkeeper
Heath William, corn miller
Hufton John, beerhouse
Machon Joseph, land agent
Mellors John, colliery owner
Pearce John, shoemaker
Smith Rd. grocer & hosiery agt
Stendall John, baker & flour dlr
Ward Richard, grocer and agent
Woodhead Tim. vict. & butcher

Farmers.
Addlington Rt   Allsop G. jun
Allsop Geo   Allsop Hy

Allsop Jno. Ful-	Herod John	Marshall Matt	Smith Samuel
wood	Herod Samuel	Mycroft Geo	Stendall Wm
Bacon John	Hill John	Shepherd Matt	Turner George
Bacon Mary	Hill Sarah	Short John	Ward Mary
Barns Rd	Johnson Rd	Smedley G. Ful-	Ward Wm
Bower Wm	Lowe Benj	wood	Wilson Wm
Chambers Thos	Lowe Wm	Smith Benj	Wright Jas
Haslam Abm	Marshall Thos	Smith Edward	

TEVERSAL is a small village seated on a lofty eminence near the source of the river Meden, 4 miles W. by N. of Mansfield. Its *parish*, which has a number of scattered dwellings, abounds in coal and lime, and contains 400 inhabitants, and 2450 acres of land, bounded on the north and west by Derbyshire, and including a small part (60A.) of the park of Hardwick Hall, in that county. The whole, except 40 acres of glebe, belongs to Viscount Porchester, who obtained the manor by marrying the heiress of the late Sir F. Molyneux. The *church*, dedicated to St. Catherine, was enlarged in 1617, by J. Molyneux, Esq. who made under the south aisle a large vault, in which all his family are now gathered. The rectory valued in the King's books at £9. 19s. 2d. is in the gift of Viscount Porchester, and incumbency of the Rev. Charles J. Simpson, M.A. The *benefactions* are £70, left in 1753 and 1764, by Diana, and Sir Charles Molyneux; and £20 left in 1728 by Timothy Wylde.

DUNSELL, 1¼ m. N.; FACKLEY LANE ¾ m. S. W.; STANLEY 1 m. W., and WHITEBOROUGH 2 m. S. W. are four hamlets, in this parish, which forms a junction with the parishes of Halt Hucknall, Pleasley, Skegby, and Mansfield, near *Newbound Mill*.

Marked 1, *reside at Dunsel*; 2, *Fackley-lane*; 3, *Moor-end*; 4 *Norwood*; 5, *Stanley*; 6, *Teversal*; and 7, *Whiteborough*.

3 Bagshaw Francis, miller, Newbound mill
6 Bramley William, wheelwright
2 Leverton Henry, blacksmith
2 Roper Hannh. vict. Cross Keys
6 Sympson Rev. Charles I. M.A.
  rector

Farmers.

2 Ashmore Jno
5 Bakewell Mary
5 Bingham W
7 Bowman Jph
Caladine Jno

1 Coope Wm
6 Cordwell Jph
5 Cordwell John
1 Cupit Jane
4 Hawksley Geo

2 Hickton Thos
7 Hill John
6 Hill Thos
6 Leverton Jas
2 Marsden Rt
6 Marshall Jph
6 Marshall Wm.
2 Mokes Thos
4 Poole Mary
3 Reynolds Geo
3 Reynolds Han
5 Roper Reb

1 Sanders Wm
1 Smith Matt
6 Taylor Wm
6 Webster Jno
2 Webster Rt
5 Woodhead W
2 Wragg Fras

Shoemakers.
7 Burnham T
7 Reeves Thos
6 Taylor Hy
5 Webster Peter

TROWELL is a pleasant village, at the foot of a steep declivity, near the river Erwash, 5¾ miles West of Nottingham.

The parish has 402 inhabitants, and 1600 acres of land, all belonging to Lord Middleton, except 200 acres allotted to the rector, at the enclosure, in 1788. His lordship has an extensive *colliery* on Trowell Moor, where there is a *workhouse*, supported by this parish and those of Cossal and Wollaton; and his lordship pays the governor for educating 30 poor boys belonging to the three parishes. He is also patron of the rectory which was in two medieties, valued in the King's books at £4. 14s. 4½d. each, and is now enjoyed by the Rev. George Sanders. The *church* is dedicated to St. Helen, and has a noble tower, with six bells, cast about 1790. The *feast* is on Whitsunday. The poor have 20s. yearly from Lord Middleton, pursuant to the will of Elizabeth Hacker, in 1780; and also 20s. from Handley's Charity. (See p. 165.)

Eaton John, limeburner
Farnsworth Wm. shoemaker
Goodacre Richard, corn miller
Hall Jno. governor, Workhouse
Hewitt Joshua, parish clerk
Hopewell James, butcher
Martin John, butcher
Smedley Mr. John
Walker Richard, colliery agent
Whitehead Ann, shopkeeper
Whitehead Mr. Humphrey
Whitehead Hphy. jun. & Chas.
  vety. surgeons & blacksmiths
Whitehead James, shoemaker
Whitehead John, vict
Wright John, wheelwright

Farmers.

Allcock Jno
Hopewell Geo
Hopkinson J
Palin John
Potter Thomas,
  Swansar
Shaw Mary
Smedley Wm

WOLLATON is a well built, but a straggling village, three miles W. of Nottingham, containing within its parish 537 inhabitants, and 2000 acres of land, nearly all belonging to Lord Middleton, who is lord of the manor, and patron of the *rectory* which has annexed to it the curacy of Cossal, and is valued in the King's books at £14. 2s. 6d. The Rev. George Saunders is the incumbent, and has 7 acres of glebe. The *church*, dedicated to St. Leonard, has a handsome spire and six bells, and under it is the family vault of the *Willoughby family*, who obtained this lordship in the reign of Edward III. by marrying the heiress of the *Morteins*, to whom it had descended from *Warner*, the tenant of *William Peverel*, whose fee it was. Sir Francis Willoughby built Wollaton hall, in the reign of Elizabeth. In 1711, Sir Thomas Willoughby, Bart. (a descendant of the Barons Willoughby of Eresby) was created *Baron Middleton, of Middleton, in Warwickshire*, of which title the present Right Hon. Henry Willoughby is the sixth possessor. The parish feast is on the Sunday after that at Stapleford. The poor have 20s. yearly from Handley's charity, (see p. 165) and 20s. from Willoughby's hospital, at Cossal.

WOLLATON HALL, the elegant seat of Lord Middleton, occupies a delightful situation in a beautiful park of 700 acres,

2¼ miles W. of Nottingham. It is built entirely of freestone, which came from Ancaster, in Lincolnshire, in exchange for coal, got on this estate. It is square, with four large towers, adorned with pinnacles; and in the centre the body of the house rises higher, with projecting coped turrets at the corners. The front and sides are adorned with square projecting ionic pilasters; the square stone windows are without tracery, and the too great uniformity of the whole is broken by oblong niches, circular ones filled with busts of philosophers, emperors, &c. and by some very rich mouldings. The interior is superbly furnished, has many stately apartments, and a very extensive and valuable collection of paintings, by the best masters. Near the house is a very handsome and extensive pile of stables and other exterior offices, erected in 1774. Close to the mansion is the ancient pleasure ground, in which the antique style is preserved, though with some modern alterations and additions: here are a number of statues and the other usual ornaments of such places. The modern flower and kitchen gardens are at some distance from this, and completely hid in wood, so as only to be visible from the upper part of the house, which commands enchanting views of the park and its various ornamental buildings and water, backed by fine groves, in which are seen shady walks, and all the beauties of garden scenery. The *summer house* is in the grotto style, pannelled and ceiled with looking glasses, and ornamented with paintings and shell work. Under it is a *water house*, formed completely in the grotesque, with shell and rock work. The *park gate*, on the south east side of the park, upon the Derby and Nottingham road, is a handsome modern erection of stone, with a neat lodge and light iron railing, and the approach to the hall is through a noble winding avenue of lime trees; nearly a mile in length. The park is well stocked with deer, hares, &c. and has a spacious sheet of water well supplied with a variety of fish, and enlivened by swans and other aquatic birds; and is broken into gentle swells well wooded with oak and elm, and at intervals admitting some very picturesque and extensive views of the surrounding landscape.

Middleton Lord, Wollaton Hall
Burton Jno. vict
Burton Wm. wheelgt
Chouler Ch. land agt
Chouler Mr. Charles
Chouler Wm. farmer
Clay John, clerk
Glew Saml. farmer
Hancock Col. Skinner, Wollaton house
Hewson J Bothamley, cabinetmaker

Higget John, shoemkr
Hook Joseph, tailor
Hubbard W. nurseryman, &c.
Jordan Thos. mason
Kirkland Ed. farmer
Kirkland Jph. netmkr
Middleton W. bsmith
Rollinson Saml. Colliery bailiff
Sanders Rev. G, M.A.
Skelston J. wheelgt

Slack Sam. shoemkr
Smith Hy. p. clerk
Smith Jph. butcher
Strike Peter, butler
Syson Lucy, shopkr
Taylor H. wharf agent
Warner John, joiner
Watkinson, J. bricklr
Wibberley Isc. gamekeeper
Woodward Thos. vict

NEWARK HUNDRED

Is that long, narrow, and irregularly formed district, which is bounded on the west by the Trent and Fleet rivers, on the north and east by Lincolnshire, and on the south by the hundred of Bingham. Its length in the vale of the Trent, from East Stoke northward to North Clifton, is about 17 miles, but its average breadth is not more than 4 miles. It is divided into two *divisions*, under two chief constables, and forms ecclesiastically the *deanery of Newark*. Its population has been considerably increased during the last thirty years, though it is chiefly dependent on agriculture, and its extensive trade in *malt*, *flour*, and *smock frocks*. The following is an enumeration of its 23 *parishes*, showing the number of inhabitants in each in 1801, 1821, and 1831, and the annual value of the lands and buildings, as assessed for the property tax in 1815 :

ANN. VAL. £.	PARISHES.	POPULATION IN			ANN. VAL. £.	PARISHES.	POPULATION IN		
		1801.	1821.	1831.			1801.	1821.	1831
26418	Newark ····	6730	8084	9557	923	Scarle South ⎱	119	151	157
6226	Balderton ····	636	773	830	1518	& Besthorp ⎰	216	217	322
1980	Barnby ······	195	247	237	1361	Shelton ······	73	105	113
3900	Clifton N.* ··	740	990	949	874	Sibthorpe ····	85	142	141
2595	Coddington ·	326	374	435	1397	Staunton & ⎱	128	142	93
4015	Collingham N.	500	805	881	1370	Flawbro' ·· ⎰	71	85	80
3440	Collingham S.	539	686	727	3171	Stoke (East) ··	293	424	330
1154	Cotham ·····	77	74	74	1423	Syerston······	109	129	138
1006	Elston···· · ·	394	446	552	2004	Thorney‡ ····	243	264	308
3929	Farndon······	387	499	570	1173	Thorpe ······	44	96	105
1473	Girton† ·····	125	182	183	1905	Winthorpe ··	196	235	228
2564	Hawton ······	107	216	258					
1292	Kilvington ··	40	43	45					
2069	Langford ····	124	147	125	79202	Total······	12505	15556	17426

* *Clifton (North)* includes South Clifton, Harby, and Spalford *twps.*
† *Mering*, which claims to be extra-parochial, is said to be in Girton parish.
‡ *Thorney* includes Broadholme and Wiggersley hamlets.

BOROUGH OF NEWARK.

NEWARK-UPON-TRENT is an ancient but well-built market town, borough, and parish; pleasantly situated in the centre of a fertile district, at the junction of the great north road with the turnpikes from Lincoln to Nottingham, Sheffield, &c., 124 miles N. by W. of London, 8 miles E. of Southwell, 21 miles N. E. by E. of Nottingham, 20 miles S.S.E. of Retford, and 16 miles S.W. of Lincoln. It is the capital of the hundred and deanery to which it gives name. As has been seen in the foregoing table, its population has swelled since the year 1801, from 6730 to 9557 souls, consisting of 4499 males, and 5058 females. There has also been a corresponding increase in the number of houses, and in the *trade* of the town, which consists principally in making *malt, ale, flour, linen,* and *smock frocks,* to a considerable extent, there being in the town and its neighbourhood a large brewery, 20 corn mills, a considerable number of malt kilns, and an extensive linen manufactory, (Hawton mills,) where fine linen is bleached after the Irish manner. Upwards of 480,000 bushels of malt were made here in 1830, for we find by the excise books, that in that year the duty paid (at the rate of 2s. 7d. per bushel) amounted to the sum of £66,990. 18s. 1d. But Newark derives much of its cheerfulness and wealth from its being a great public thoroughfare, from its well supplied markets, and from its participation in the traffic on the Trent navigation. The number of boats which passed the lock in 1818, was 6650, and the weight of the goods delivered and loaded here was 50,173 tons. The *market* is held on Wednesday, and is well supplied with corn, meat, &c.; and once a fortnight with cattle. Six FAIRS are held here annually, on the Friday before Careing Sunday;* May 14; Whit Tuesday; August 2nd; Nov. 1st; and Monday before Dec. 11, for horses, cattle, sheep, swine, &c. &c. A great *cheese market* was established in 1804, and continues to be held yearly on the Wednesday before Oct. 2nd. The MARKET PLACE is a spacious area lined with good buildings, which, on the south side, have a long piazza under the second floors. On the western side stands the elegant Town Hall, under which is an open space occupied on market days by those butchers who have no stalls in the adjacent *shambles.* The principal entrances into the Market place are Stodman street, Bridge street, and Church street, the latter of which has three houses that project into the area, and ought to be removed. The other *principal streets* are Appletongate, Baldertongate, Barnbygate, Cartergate, Castlegate, Lombard street, Middlegate, Millgate, Northgate, and Wilson street, in which there still remain many ancient houses, except in the last, which was built on an uniform plan in 1766, by the Rev. Dr. Wilson. The streets of a more modern date are Pelham street, Portland street, Guildhall street, and some others. An Act of Parliament for *paving* the town was passed so early as 1585, but it seems almost to have been a dead letter, till 1798, when it was strengthened by another Act, under which the work of paving, lighting, cleansing, &c. has been extended to every street and thoroughfare. There was anciently a cross in the Market place, but the only one now in the town is *Beaumond cross,* at the junction of Cartergate and Lombard street, which, as an inscription says, was erected in the reign of Edward IV., repaired by Charles Mellish, Esq. recorder, in 1778, and

* *Careing Sunday* is the Sunday before Palm Sunday.

again repaired and beautified by the corporation in 1801. In 1806, an Act was obtained for more effectually repairing the ROADS from Newark to Mansfield and Southwell, and to Leadenham Hill, in Lincolnshire.

Newark is not upon the TRENT, but upon the river DEVON, which, after receiving the Smite and the Car-dike, communicates with a short cut from the Trent, and passing under the majestic ruins of the castle, pursues a north easterly course to that river at Crankleys, near Winthorpe, so that the two streams form on the north west side of the town a large elliptical *island* of low but fertile pasture land, which they so frequently inundate, that about the year 1770, it was found necessary to connect the two bridges by a FLOOD ROAD, which cost £12,000, and now bids defiance to the highest floods. The BRIDGE at the Newark end of this elevated road, is a substantial brick fabric of seven arches, faced with stone, and erected in 1775, by the Duke of Newcastle, who, as lord of the manor under the crown, is empowered to take tolls on horses, cattle, swine, and loaded carts and waggons, for which he has to keep the bridge in repair. The bridge which crosses the Trent is supported by the owner of the *Kelham* estate, and is about 1¼ mile from Newark. The *haling path bridge*, which crosses the Devon near the large water mill, consists of five segmental arches, each 14 feet span, and was built in 1819, by the *Newark Navigation Company*, who, in 1772, obtained an Act of Parliament for widening and improving the stream, which, by a circuitous course of four miles, now brings the Trent navigation past the walls of Newark. Anciently three narrow and inconvenient *wooden bridges* occupied the sites of these durable structures of brick and stone.

ANCIENT HISTORY. Various antiquarian conjectures have been hazarded respecting the origin of Newark; the most plausible of which is, that it occupies the site of the Roman station *Eltavona*, which was subsequently enlarged by the Saxons from the ruins of several Roman cities in the neighbourhood, on or near the Roman *Fossway*, which passes through the town from Leicester to Lincoln, (Vide, p. 18.) After this re-edification, it is supposed to have been the Saxon *Sidnaceaster*, which in the early days of Christianity was a *bishopric*, having had a succession of nine bishops after the year A.D. 678; but some historians have placed that city at Stowe, in Lincolnshire. It is, however, certain, that Newark, during the Saxon heptarchy, was an important town, defended by a strong wall and fortress, and constructed partly of Roman materials. After being destroyed by the Danes, (See p. 17 to 20,) it was rebuilt; and hence *New-work*, (now corrupted to Newark,) was justly applied to it in the reign of Edward the Confessor. The domesday survey shews that the *Countess Godiva* had paid the Dane-geld for her manor of *Newarke* and its two

berues, *Baldertune* and *Farendune*, as 7 carucats and 2 bovats
of land, which in the Confessor's time had been returned as 26
carucates. In 1086, Remigius, bishop of Lincoln, had in
demesne here 7 carucates, 56 burgesses, 42 villains, and 4
bordars, having 21½ carucates. The manor had *soc* in nearly all
the parishes which now form the hundred and deanery of
Newark. It was given by Leofric Earl of Mercia, and his
Countess Godiva to the monastery of Stow, and was afterwards
claimed by the Bishops of Lincoln, one of whom, Alexander de
Blois, built the present castle, in the reign of Stephen. Military
erections were, however, even at that time deemed rather improper for an ecclesiastic to engage in, and to satisfy his troubled
conscience, the bishop, after finishing the castle, founded two
monasteries, but Stephen was not to be thus appeased, for he
seized both the bishop and his uncle, and kept them in durance
until they surrendered to him all their fortresses. In the reign
of John, and in the baronial wars, Newark several times
changed hands, and it was the scene of that monarch's death,
but whether by poison or otherwise has not been clearly
ascertained. Henry III. restored the castle to the Bishop of
Lincoln. In 1530, Cardinal Wolsey lodged in it with a great
retinue, in his way to Southwell, where he was accustomed to
spend part of the summer. James I. was at Newark in 1602,
and was addressed by the senior alderman, (there being then no
mayor) *Mr. John Twentyman*, in a long latin speech, with
which his majesty was so well pleased that he ordered him to
repeat it, then asked his name, and on being told, replied
sharply, " then by my saul man thou art a traytor, the
Twentymans pulled down Redkirk, in Scotland." This
however, was merely in jest; as he conferred on him many
favours, and was often accompanied by him in his hunting ex-
cursions in the forest. During the civil wars of Charles I, (See
page 88 to 91,) Newark was an important garrison in the cause
of royalty, in which the courageous inhabitants sustained three
violent *sieges*, at the first of which Sir John Henderson, the
governor, caused all Northgate and the Spital to be burned, " yet
the remains formed a receptacle for the enemy at the second
siege until they were routed by Prince Rupert on *Beacon Hill.*
Much gallantry was displayed during the third siege in 1645,
and much blood was spilt on both sides, but the town was at
length given up to the Scotch army, by the King's order. After
the surrender, the country people were ordered to come with
pick axes, shovels, &c. to demolish all the works, and circum-
vallation; but one of the sconces has been left entire.

The BOROUGH was first incorporated by Edward VI., under
whose charter it was governed by an alderman and 12 assistants.
It sent only one Member to Parliament until it received a new
charter from Charles I. instituting a body corporate, by the
name of the Mayor and Aldermen of Newark-upon-Trent, with

a learned man, to be Recorder. The same monarch also honoured the town by creating Robt. Pierrepont, Baron Pierrepont and Viscount Newark (See p. 421.) Though James II. imposed a charter upon the corporation, the town is now governed by that of his predecessor, Charles II. who confirmed all its former privileges, and modelled the corporation as it still continues, with power to hold a *Court of Record* every Thursday; the mayor and four senior aldermen to be justices of the peace, &c. &c. All the inhabitants who pay scot and lot have a right to vote for the borough representatives, but in the exercise of their elective franchise, it is said that some of them are controlled by their landlords, for disobeying whom, we have heard of several poor families being *ejected* from their humble dwellings. In consequence of such large sums of public money being at the disposal of the corporation and the four churchwardens, there have been of late years the most violent contests for several of the municipal offices, and Laird in 1811, says, "it is whispered that instances have taken place of three guineas being paid for a vote, in a contest for the office of churchwarden."— The number of freeholders in the borough, which is co-extensive with the parish and contains only about 800 acres, has during the last 30 years, been much increased by the division and sale of property, but the Duke of Newcastle is *Lord of the Manor*, and principal owner, and next to him, as individual proprietors, are Lord Middleton and the Earl of Winchelsea, the latter of whom succeeded to the property of the late Sir Jennison Gordon. There were anciently here six incorporated companies of tradesmen, called *Guilds*, and dedicated to different saints, one of whom was "Holy Richard de Newark." The present *Members of Parliament* for Newark are W. F. Handley, Esq. banker, and Thomas Wilde, King's Sergeant.

CORPORATION, (1831-2.)

Recorder.—Clinton Jas. Fynes Clinton, Esq.

Mayor.—Wm. Parker, Esq.

Senior Aldermen.—Wm. Parker, Rd. Fisher, Jas. Dyson, and Wm. Fillingham, Esqrs.

Aldermen.—Geo. Hodgkinson, Jas. Priory Lacy, Jas. Thorpe, jun., John Jeremiah Bigsby, M. D., Henry Rastall, Rd. Norton and Philip Rd. Walker, Esqrs.

Town-Clerk and Coroner.—Wm. Edward Tallents, Esq.

Chamberlain.—Mr. Isaac Palethorpe.

Coadjutors.—Jas. Wilson, Jas. Thorpe, sen., Samuel Ridge, Thos. Wilson, Thos. Becket, Anthony Killingley, Thos. Caparn, Geo. Harvey, John Sadler Sheppard, Robert Killingley, Jas. Betts, and Jas. Watson.

Commoners.—Jph. Branston and Jph. Gilstrap.

Serjeants-at-Mace.—John Etches and John Uffindale.

Chief Constable and Sheriff's Officer.—Mr. Rd. Bell.

Gaoler.—Mr. Joseph Cropper.

The CASTLE, though now in ruins, still presents an august appearance. The north front, overlooking the river, is the most perfect, having a large square tower at the north-east angle, and another in the centre. The general outline of the building is square, and its dimensions very great. The number of stories appears to have been five, but within the exterior walls very little now remains; and the plot has long been used as a *bowling-green*, for the use of which two rooms are neatly fitted up in the western tower. The vestiges of the great hall shew evidently that it was built in later times; indeed, its handsome projecting window must have been inserted after all the ancient modes of defence had gone out of use. Under this hall is a most curious arched vault or *crypt*, supported by a row of pillars in the middle, and having loops and embrasures towards the river, in which were planted cannon in the civil wars. At one end are some remains of the entrance to a subterraneous passage, said to have gone a great way under ground. The other parts of the ruins exhibit a curious specimen of the odd mixture of old Norman architecture, and of that which Bishop Gundulph first introduced at Rochester Castle. The *Castle* and its *Liberty*, (1,138 acres,) are in the parish of East Stoke, which is distant more than 4 miles from Newark, but their inhabitants vote at elections for Members of Parliament, as belonging to the borough, though they have no voice in the choice of church-wardens or other parochial officers. The WALL AND GATES which formerly enclosed the town have entirely disappeared, though two of the archways, viz. *North Gate* and *East Gate* were standing in the latter part of last century, the former being removed in 1762, and the latter in 1784. The *vicinity* of Newark was much cut up by military works in the civil wars, many traces of which still remain. Since the reign of the Charleses, Newark has displayed its loyalty and patriotism by the formation of a troop of *Yeomanry Cavalry* in 1794, under the command of Captain Chaplin, and a regiment of *Volunteers* in 1804, under the command of Lieut.-Col. Thoroton.

The TOWN HALL, built in 1773, at the cost of £17,000, is an elegant stone fabric, upon a rustic basement, with four handsome pillars in the centre, supporting a pediment ornamented with the corporation arms, above which is a statue of Justice and the Lion and Unicorn. The apartments are commodious, and handsomely finished, especially the ASSEMBLY ROOM, which has beautiful corinthian pilasters, and a rich coped ceiling. The *Borough Sessions* are held half yearly, at one end of it, and at the other the corporation meet to transact public business.

The CHURCH, dedicated to Mary Magdalen, is considered one of the finest parish churches in the kingdom. It is of the age of Henry VI., and Thoroton says it is better than "all the ten mentioned in Domesday Book," of which he supposes nine were not in the *town*, but in the parishes within the *soke*. It is indeed a noble edifice, its exterior most superb; mullions and tracery of excellent designs fill the windows; in different parts of the building are niches with statues, and other decorations; and there is perhaps no ecclesiastical structure which contains such a number of short ludicrous busts, forming spout heads, &c. except Magdalen College in Oxford. The tower possesses much symmetry and beauty, has a peal of 8 bells, and supports a lofty stone spire, adorned with the 12 Apostles in niches. The interior has much of a cathedral appearance, except the nave which is narrow and gloomy. The choir is inclosed by a rich screen of wooden carved work. The aisles are lofty, and the pavement is covered with sepulchral memorials; besides which, the numerous monuments and brasses are in good preservation. In the south transept is a large brass plate, on which is carved a numerous group of saints and angels surrounding the figure of *Alan Flemyng*, to whom tradition attributes the foundation of the church. The organ was built in 1804, and removed to its present situation in 1814. The *library* over the south porch, contains a great collection of Theological works, bequeathed by Dr. White, Bishop of Peterborough, and other donors. The *vicarage*, valued in the King's books at £21 5s. 2d. is in the gift of the Crown; and the Rev. Wm. Bartlell, M.A. is the incumbent. The curate is the Rev. T. Wild, M.A. In 1827, a Sunday evening *lecture* was established, and is now supported partly by Magnus' charity, and partly by the rent of several pews erected for that purpose. Of the other ancient religious foundations here, was *St. Leonard's Hospital* (which now exists as a charity), and two houses of *Austin and Observant friars*; besides which, here was an hospital for sick persons, belonging to the *Knights templars*, and "a great house in Northgate called the *Spital*, which was burnt down in the civil wars."

The CHAPELS of dissenters here are six in number, and they are generally clean and commodious, viz—the *Wesleyan*, built on the site of the old Guildhall in 1787, and enlarged in 1815; the *Protestant Methodist*, erected 1828; the *Independent*, founded in 1822; two *Particular Baptist chapels*, in Hawton lane and Lombard street; and the *Jehovah Jireh*. In 1827, the Rev. Jas. Yver, fitted up a large room in West hall, Millgate, as a *Catholic chapel*.

The Subscription LIBRARY AND NEWS ROOM occupy a handsome building, which was given to the members by Lord Middleton, in 1828, but the institution was commenced in 1825, and now possesses 2,500 volumes, and is well supplied with newspapers, magazines, &c. It belongs to 220 shareholders who subscribe one guinea yearly. The other places of amusement are the *assembly room*, at the Town hall; the *theatre* in Middlegate, built in 1774; and the *new bowling green*, formed

3 G

in 1809, behind the Castle and Falcon Inn: the old green within the castle ruins is now disused. Several of the numerous INNS here are of great antiquity; the *Saracen's Head* has existed as an inn ever since the days of Edward III.; the *White Hart*, since the time of Henry IV.; and the *Swan and Salmon*, since the reign of Henry VIII.

As has been seen at page 60, the CHARITY ESTATES bequeathed by various donors for the weal of Newark, produce upwards of £3,600 per annum, which is, or should be, expended in educating the poor children, in relieving the sick and indigent, in improving the town, &c. &c. as specified in the following notice of each bequest, abridged from the late " Parliamentary Enquiry."

MAGNUS' CHARITY :—Thomas Magnus, archdeacon of the East Riding of Yorkshire, bequeathed in the 28th of Henry VIII. for various charitable and public uses in the borough of Newark, 1,851 acres of land, 28 messuages, 11 cottages, 2 gardens, 1 fishery, and 2 rent charges, situated at Sandwath, in Yorkshire, and at Everton, Harewell, Mattersey, and some other places in Nottinghamshire. This property in 1828, produced no less than £2,380 per annum, and from a statement of its appropriation in that year, we find the following payments ; viz.—£220 to the master of the *grammar school*, £50 to his usher; £105 to the master of the *song school*, £4. 4s. to each of the six singing boys, and £2. 2s. to the six low boys.; £150 to the *national schools*; £50 towards building ditto; £150 to the *dispensary* ; £290 for *lighting and paving* the town ; £50 towards purchasing a house at Dry Bridge for widening the street ; £750 for the reparation and other uses of the *church* ; £450, as the balance of a debt incurred in draining the estate at Everton ; and £171, for assessments, salaries, &c. As the debts of this charity are all discharged, a larger appropriation of money is now made yearly to the above-named charitable institutions. The mayor, senior aldermen, vicar, and churchwardens, are the trustees. An act passed in 1798, requires the following annual payments to the commissioners for *lighting and paving the town* : viz.—£290 from this charity, £120 from Phillipott's, and £90 from Brown's.

The GRAMMAR SCHOOL is free for classical education to all the boys of Newark and its neighbourhood, but for the other branches of an English education the master charges 5 guineas for each boy, including books, as well classical as others, with which he furnishes the scholars ; but the funds are sufficient for making every department of this school free to the poor, agreeably to the will of the *Rev. Thos. Magnus*, the munificent founder, who is said to have been the son of a poor publican, and to have been educated at the joint expense of a party of Yorkshire othiers, who humourously used to call him *Thomas Amang-*, because he was maintained among them. Besides the two ms paid from his charity to the master and usher, as above stated, the latter receives £40 a-year from Phillipott's charity. The *song school* stands in the church-yard near the grammar school, and is now called the *organist school*, the master being the organist of the church. The six singing boys sing in the choir in surplices, and the six low boys supply their places as they become vacant. The *national schools* are also supported by Magnus's charity, for the education of 130 boys and 70 girls, in Dr. Bell's system. There are in the town two *infant schools*, and several *Sunday schools*, supported by subscription.

BROWN'S CHARITY:—*Robert Brown, Esq.*, in 1532, bequeathed in trust to the mayor and vicar, "for the commonwealth of Newark, "lands and tenements at Bilderton, Coddington, Barnby-in-the-Willows, Eiskerton, and Newark. This property produces £232 a-year, which is expended in lighting, paving, and improving the town, in repairing the church, in paying salaries to police officers, &c. &c.

PHILLIFOTT'S CHARITY:—*Wm. Phillipot, merchant,* bequeathed to the aldermen and 12 assistants, in 1556, lands and buildings at Newark, North Muskham, Bathley, and Farndon, now let for £557 per annum, for the endowment of an *almshouse,* and for "the common good of the town." Out of the rents, the corporation now pay yearly £280 to the 24 almspeople; £40 to the usher of the grammar school; £120 for lighting and paving; and other sums for repairing the church, improving the town, &c. The ALMSHOUSE was enlarged in 1738, 1783, and 1822, and has now apartments for 10 men and 14 women, who each receive 3s. per week in summer, and 4s. per week in the winter half year, except five of the oldest men, and the man that reads prayers in the chapel, who have each 1s. extra every week. They have *all* a ton of coals, and a supply of clothing yearly. Part of their stipends is derived from the dividend of £1,839 1s. 7d. three per cent. consols, purchased with £1,000 left in 1797, by Geo. Lawrence.

SUMMERS' AND OTHER CHARITIES:—In 1705, *Thos. Summers* left £500, to provide weekly 1s. each for five of the oldest "beadsmen" in Phillipot's almshouse. This sum, with £460 bequeathed by other donors, was laid out by the corporation in the purchase of a farm of 96A. 1R. 4P. land, at Laughton, in Lincolnshire, now tithe and tax free, and let for £117 per annum. The two other principal benefactions used in this purchase were £200, left in 1694, by *Hercules Clay;* and £100 left in 1690, by *Lady Frances Leake,* the latter of whom also left £200 for communion plate. Till 1828, the corporation only paid 4 per cent. interest for the £960, but in that year they promised the parliamentary commissioners, that in future they would distribute the whole rent of the farm.

STONE'S AND WHITE'S CHARITY:—In 1688, Henry Stone left £700, to be invested in land, for the foundation of a *Jersey school,* and for the employment of poor people. In 1690, *Thos.*

White, Bishop of Peterborough, left £240, to be laid out in land, out of the rents of which, he directed £10 to be given yearly to the poor, and the rest to the vicar. In 1699, the corporation laid out these sums in the purchase of an estate at Besthorpe and Girton (161 acres), now let for £238 per annum, of which, £188 belongs to Stone's, and £55 to White's charity, though till 1829, the corporation considered the estate as their *own* property, and only paid about £24 yearly as the interest of the two benefactions; but, in that year, the Commissioners made them " *sensible* that the whole of the rents belonged to these charities," and they consequently agreed, in future, to appropriate them agreeable to the wills of the donors; so that the poor receive £10, and the vicar £40 yearly, and the remainder (£188) is employed " in providing wheels, wool, jersey, and other materials and means for employing the poor in spinning, and in manufacturing stockings and other articles, and in paying salaries to the master and mistress of the Jersey school, and such *wages* as may render such employment a profitable source of relief to the poor and their children."

JOHN LILLEY in 1623, bequeathed the Bathley Grange estate (63 acres) to the corporation, in trust that they distribute the rents among the poor children of the Jersey school, or in default of such school, amongst the poor of Newark, except a rent charge of 7 guineas, which had been previously left out of the said estate by John Smith, to the poor of Bathley. Until 1828, the corporation only distributed £34 per annum in Newark, but they then promised in future to apply the net rent, (after paying the before named rent charge), " in maintaining any poor children who shall work in the *Jersey school*, and in default thereof, to distribute the same in coals, corn, flour, or clothing, amongst the most needy poor of Newark, at Candlemas in every year."

ANTHONY COLLINGWOOD, in 1678, left his lands at Allington and Farndon for the *vicar* to read *prayers* twice every day in the church. The land at Allington was sold for a rent-charge of £10, besides which the vicar has £20 yearly as the rent of the land at Farndon. The same donor also bequeathed a house in *Cartergate* for the repairs of the church, (since sold for £250, three per cent. consols,) and the *Packhorse* public-house in Stodman-street, for the use of the poor. The latter is now let for £50 a year, out of which the corporation only distributed £8. 9s. 9d. up to 1829, in which year the *Parliamentary Commissioners* declared in their report that the civic body here had improperly appropriated to their " *own use*" the following yearly sums, amounting to £422. 6s. 3d., viz. of *Stone's charity*, £167. 3s.; of *Summer's and Others*, £85. 16s.; of *Bishop White's* £48. 4s.; of *Lilly's* £79. 13s.; and of *Collingwood's* £41. 10s. 3d. They, however, promised to act more justly *in future*, but gave the Commissioners to under-

stand " that they have *no corporate funds* wherewith to answer
any call that might be made on them by a *Court of Equity*, to
re-imburse the monies they have misapplied."

ALMSHOUSES.—*John Johnson*, in 1651, left a rent-charge of
£5 out of a house in Wilson-street, for 50 poor aged widows
and widowers, and four *cottages* in Guildhall-street for the residence of four old widows, who are now placed there by the
parish officers. In 1619, a *Mr. Chapman* left a house in Appletongate for the residence and maintenance of four poor
widows; but it has been sold, and the corporation have provided rooms for the widows in Guildhall-street, and pay to each 6d.
per week. In 1704, *Timothy Ellis* left three chambers over
the shambles for three poor widows, and directed they should
have the rents of the shops under them, and of three houses in
Northgate, Churchgate, and Castlegate. In 1775, the chambers and shops were pulled down, and the alms-women removed to a building in Guildhall-street, where they now receive 8d.
a-week each from the corporation.

VARIOUS BENEFACTIONS.—In 1675, *Rd. Lamb* left to the
poor 25s. yearly out of a house in Cartergate, now belonging
to Dr. Staunton. In 1679, Nicholas Earl of *Scarsdale*, left
£10 per annum to the *vicar* for sermons on Good Friday and
St. Thomas' day. In 1657, *Wm. and Emma Watson* left 20s.
yearly out of the Rutland Arms public-house to the vicar for a
sermon on Dec. 25th. *Sir John Londe*, in the 6th of Edward
VI, gave two tenements in Millgate, and £20 in gold, to the
corporation for the benefit of the town, but the tenements are
now unknown. In 1729, *Mr. Hobman*, town-clerk, left £50
to the poor, now sunk in other charity funds. In 1739, *Eleanor
Douglas* left £100 to be employed with Summers' charity. The
Duke of Newcastle pays £5 yearly to 20 poor widows, pursuant to the will of *John Smith*. In 1768, *Mary Sturtevant* bequeathed £200, and directed the interest to be given yearly to
as many poor families as it would extend to at 10s. each. It
has been vested in £230. 4s. 3d three per cent. consols, by the
churchwardens and overseers, who distribute the dividends. In
1737, *Jane Heron* left land, which, in 1771, was exchanged for
other land and buildings at Claypole, let for £20 a-year, and
directed the rent to be distributed to as many poor persons as it
will extend to at 5s. each. Sir Robert Heron is the present
trustee. In 1769, the *Rev. Bernard Wilson, D. D.* left £40
a-year out of his estates, to be distributed on August 21st, and
January 11th, amongst such poor as the vicar should direct.
He also left £10 a-year to the vicar for two sermons on the
days of distribution. *Anthony Foster* in 1558 devised all his
lands in *Meryn close*, in Newark, to the corporation, upon trust,
to apply the rents for the assistance of those afflicted with the
plague, but this disease has long been unknown, therefore the
rents ought to be given to the Dispensary.

3 G 2

St. Leonard's Hospital, which was founded by Alexander Bishop of Lincoln, betwixt the years 1123 and 1147, still exists, though the original building has long since disappeared. In 1642, the hospital lands and buildings, were granted in exchange for others of more value, to the Countess of Exeter, who erected the present hospital at the foot of Northgate. There are three poor men on the foundation, one of whom is nominally a *chaplain;* but the *master,* who is appointed by the Bishop of Lincoln, does not reside in the house, nor in the town, as was the intention of the founder, though he draws a large yearly revenue from the charity estate which comprises upwards of 360 acres of land at Balderton, Newark, Girton, Claypole, Elston, and Stoke, and about 40 houses in the town. Out of the ample funds the master can only afford to each of the three alms people, the following yearly allowances:—viz. £13. 8s, a coat, waistcoat, and gown, and a supply of coals.

The Dispensary at the Town-hall is open daily for the gratuitous administration of medical and surgical aid to the afflicted poor. It was established in 1813, by subscription, but it is now aided by the yearly grant of £150 from the funds of Magnus' charity. Several thousand lame and sick parishioners, and poor married lying-in women have partaken of the healing benefits of this excellent charity.

The Workhouse on the Hawton road was built in 1786, from the funds of Magnus, Brown, and Phillipot's charities. It is a good built brick building, well adapted for its purpose. The sum collected for *poor rates,* in 1830, was £3,498. 8s. 11d½, of which £446, was paid to the county rates. Adjoining the workhouse is the Borough Goal, a small edifice with only two rooms for debtors and offenders.

The Savings' Bank was established in 1817, and the building which it now occupies in Lombard street, was built out of its profits, 1832. Its deposits in 1830, amounted to £43,430, belonging to 1,160 individuals, 7 *friendly societies,* and 2 *charitable institutions.* W. F. Handley, Esq. is the treasurer, John Wilson, the secretary, and W. H. Caparn, the actuary.

The POST-OFFICE is in Castlegate, and Mr. Thos. Burgin, is the Post-master. Letters for London and all parts of the south are despatched daily, at 3 afternoon; and for Edinburgh and all parts of the north, at 10 morning. *Mail gigs* depart to Lincoln, Nottingham, Southwell, and Mansfield, at 11 morning.

The Contractions used for the names of Streets, &c. in the following *Directory of Newark,* are Ast. for Albion street; Agt. Appletongate; Blg. Baldertongate; Brg. Bargate; Bng. Barnbygate; Bnd. Barnby road; Bhn. Beadhouse lane; Bdc Beaumond cross; Bst. Beaumond street; Bln. Boar lane; Bgt. Bridge street; Bdr. Brodhurst row; Crg. Cartergate; Csg. Castlegate; Chn. Chain lane; Cmt. Chatham street; Cht. Church street; Clt. Clin-

ton street; Clr. Collingham row; Csq. Colton square; Cyd.
Cawkwell's yard; Est. Eldon-street; Frd. Farndon road; Frw.
Farndon row; Gst. Guildhall street; Hrd. Hawton road; Hld.
Hill end; Jyd. Jalland's yard; Kgt. Kirkgate; Kst. King street;
Lrd. Lincoln road; Lst. Lombard street; Lvn. Lover's lane; Mkp.
Market place; Mdg. Middlegate; Mlg. Millgate; Mln Mill-
lane; Mlr. Millington's row; Mtn. Mount lane; Ngt. Northgate;
Plt. Parliament st; Prt. Portland st; Pmt. Pelham st.; Ppl. Pepper
hill; Qst. Queen st.; Smr. Smithy row; Spr. Spittal row; Rst.
Regent st.; Stn. Saint Mark's lane; Sst. Stodman st.; Ur. Union
terrace; Wln. Water lane; Wsd. Waterside; Wst. Wilson st; and
Yst. York st.

Adams Jph. chief constable of
  S. Div. of Newark Hund. and
  Surveyor of sewers, Ngt
Armstrong J. town cr. Town Hall
Atkinson Miss Margt. Pmt
Bailey Neal, excise officer, Ast
Bacon Rev. Hy. Bowman, Crg
Banks Mrs. Sarah, Bng
Barber Mrs. Eliz. Castlegate
Barker Mrs. Sarah, Appletongt
Barry Rev. Wm. mert. Cartergt
Barnsdall Saml. gent. Millgate
Bardsley Capt. Jas. Balderton rd
Bartlell Rev. Wm. vicar, Agt
Baxter Jph. coachman, Mlg
Beaumont Wm. bookpr. Mlg
Beevor Rev. Thos. B. D. Wst
Bell Rd. constable, &c. Cyd
Bills John, waiter, Plt
Birkett Mr. Wm. Farndon rd
Bland Mrs. Jane, Appletongate
Bonner Matthias, bookpr. Lst
Booth John, boat master, Mlg
Bristow Saml. gent. Pelham st
Brodhurst W. jun. maltster, Cgt
Brooks Mrs. Ann, Millgate
Brooks Wm. coachman, Prt
Brown Saml. organ bldr, Lst
Bucklow Saml. coachman, Mkp
Bulson John Gates, colliery agt
Burnaby Thos. Fowke Andrew,
  solicitor, h. Appletongate
Caparn W. Horner, p. clerk Wst
Cartledge Mrs. Jane, Albion st
Cartledge Jas. malster, Lvn
Cawkwell Rd. Doubleday, gent.
  Stodman st
Chambers Geo. bookpr. Bst
Childs Martin, maltster, Ngt
Clark Jas. mert. Pelham st
Clark John, mert. Millgate

Clark Thos. pump mkr. Blg
Clark Wm. sailmaker, Mlg
Clark Mr. Wm. St. Mark's ln
Clark Wm. cheese dlr. Agt
Claypole J. banker's clerk, Mkp
Cooper Mr. John, Cartergate
Corby John, sexton, Clumber ln
Corden Wm. shopman, Bgt
Crampern Mrs. Ann, Farndon rd.
Cox Mr. Geo. Northgate
Crisp Saml. bookpr. Ast
Cropper Mrs. Ann, Portland st
Cropper Jph. gaoler, Hawton rd
Cropper Wm. gent. Millgate
Crosby Benj. gent. Pelham st
Curtis Langley, shopman, Agt
Dale Mr. Robert, Regent street
Dale Mrs. Lombard street
Deeping Wm. wine mert. Lst
Denby Mrs. Mary, Hawton road
Derry Mr. John, Wilson street
Dickinson John, cowkpr. Lst
Edmunds Mrs. Sarah, Albion st
Elson Wm. collector of naviga-
  tion dues, Lockhouse
Emerson Mr. John, Eldon street
Esam Wm. bookpr. Union st
Etches J. mayor's officer, Wst
Falkner Philip Rd. coroner, Csg
Farmer Mrs. Han. Guildhall st
Fearn John, bookpr. Albion st
Fearnihaugh Jno. boat owner, Ngt.
Fermerie Miss Philippa, Agt
Fisher Mr. John, Plt
Flower Geo. fishing net mkr. Mlg
Fotherby Wm. brewer, Wilson st.
Fox Jas. Chas. gardener, Hrd
Franke Rd. gent. Chatham st
Gilby John, gent. Pelham st
Gilby Philip, gent. Portland st
Gladwin John, excise officer, Ngt

Godfrey Ed. Smith, Esq. banker and clerk of the peace, Ngte
Goodill Mrs. Eliz. Barnbygate
Green Mrs. Ann, Barnbygate
Guthrie, Mrs. Mary, Castlegate
Hage Mrs. Lombard street
Hall Mrs. Catharine, Wst
Hall Mrs. Mary, Fardon road
Handley Wm. Farnsworth, Esq. M.P. Northgate
Hardy John, gov. workhouse
Haslam Mrs. Rebecca, Pelham st
Harvey Mrs. Ann, Barnbygate
Hebb Jph. model mkr. Lrd
Hives John, gent. Northgate
Holliday Mrs. Lombard street
Holmes Miss, Portland street
Huddlestone. T. Creswick, Esq
Hunt Chas. gent. Bng
Hurst Geo. boat owner, Ngt
Hutchings Rev. Wm. (Bap.) Utr
Hutchinson W. gent. Appletongt
Ingham Mr. John, Portland st
Jebb Mrs. Ann, Regent street
Job Mrs. Mary, Cartergate
Johnson Benj. stenceller, Lst
Kelk Mrs. Sarah. Portland st
Key Rev. Wm. Castlegate
Kirk Geo. bobbin net mkr. Crg
Kirk Thos. excise officer, Bng
Lambe Mrs. Sarah, Castlegate
Lammin Mrs. Ellen, Millgate
Laughton Geo. clerk, Northgate
Lawton Jph. maltster, Lvn.
Laxton Mrs. Sarah, Gst.
Linney Geo. gent. Appletongate
Lloyd Rev. Jph. (Meth.) Gst
Lyne Jas. clerk, Wst
Mc Kitrick, Rev. W. (Meth.) Gst
Mallet Job, boat owner, Pmt
Meginley J. baker, Rst
Midworth J. iron founder, Ngt
Milhouse R. mus. inst. mkr. Mdg
Moore Miss, Appletongate
Morton Misses Eliz. & Mary, Agt
Moscroft John, coachman, Prt
Moth Robert, supervisor, Ast.
Naylor Mr. Samuel, Eldon st
Neale Robert, gent. Barnbygate
Nicholson Saml. rush mrt. Mlg.
Nix Mr. Jph. Winthorpe Cottage
Norledge Francis, bookr. Ngt
Norton Rd. wine mer. Kirkgate

Owen Wm. & Son, fishing tackle and net mkrs. Sst
Pacey Wm. bookpr. Blg
Parker Rt. cheese dlr. Cartergate
Parnell Miss Eliz. Church-yard
Patrick Miss Hannah, Pst
Patterson Mrs. Hanh. Wilson st
Penell Mrs. Mary, Lombard st
Pettefor Rt. upholsterer, Wst
Pilsworth Mr. John, Northgate
Pocklington T. coachman, Stn
Poole Mrs. Jeffrey, Stn
Proctor Jph. boat master, King st
Readett Mrs. Ann, Lombard st
Ridge Mrs. Mary, Middlegate
Robinson Mrs. Castlegate
Rogers Mrs. Eliz. Balderton rd
Rose Wm. gent. Kirkgate
Rouse Miss Sarah, Northgate
Rous Wm. Sparrow, Esq.
Rowbottom J. carrier's agent, Lst
Scott Mrs. Eliz. Millgate
Selby Peter, gent. Bowbridge
Sewell Mrs. Eliz. Lombard st
Sikes Rev. Jph. L.L.B. Chantry House
Singleton Mrs. Eliz. Northgate
Sketchley S. surv. of taxes, Cgt
Smith Chas. gent. Lincoln road
Smith, Mrs. Jane, Wilson street
Smith Wm. grocer, Pelham st
Stephenson, Rev. J. (Unit.) Chyd
Stephenson Rev. H. J. M.A. Mgt
Sudbury Mr. John, Hawton road
Sutton Hy. shopman, Hawton rd
Tallents Wm. Ed. solicitor. Crg
Thompson Mrs. Dorothy, Agt
Thoroton Miss Isabella, My. Mlg
Tinsley Rt. gent. Barnbygate
Toder Mrs. Mary, Cartergate
Tomlinson Miss Susanna, Prt
Trueman Isaac, bookpr. Pmt
Turner Saml. boat master, Plt
Turpin Rd. gent. Bargate
Turpin Wm. gent. Appletonga te
Uffindall Geo. gent. Prt
Uffindall Wm. bookpr. Mlg
Wagstaff Mrs Arabella. Agt
Wakefield Lieut. Edw. (Notts Militia) Wilson st
Warwick W. banker's clerk, Ngt
Watson Wm. boat owner, Wgt
Weldon Thos. writer, Castle

Whillock Mrs Judeth Agt
Wild Rev. Wm. Taylor, Agt
Williams Rev. Chas. (Ind.) Mlg
Wilmot Miss Ann, Bdc
Wilson Mrs. Mary, Millgate
Wilson John, bookpr. Bng

Wing Wm. clerk, Wilson st
Winrow James, gent. Lombard st
Withers Jph. gent. Stodman st
Wright George, gent. Millgate
Yver Rev. Jas. Gabriel, (Catholic) West hall, Millgate

Academies.
*Marked * take brds.*
Brown Ann, Lst
Colton Thos. (and appraiser) Millgt
*Carmans Mary and Reb. Prt
*Collins James, Crg
Fletcher Geo. Hrd
Grammar School,
Appletongate. — Rev.
Jph. Cooke, M. A.
master ; Rev. Richd.
Latham, M.A. *usher ;*
Chs. Wm. Bewsher,
mathematician
Infant Schools.—J.
Jones, Lst. ; and Jn.
Kingdom, Lvn
Harris Francis, Est
Lane John, Lvn
National Schools.—
John Sheppard, Stn. &
Cht. Davison, Church
yard
Newton Paul, Rat
Pawson Ann, Bng
Ridley Betsy Mosley,
Bdr
Shephard Jph. Plt
Spilsbury & Newzam,
(ladies') Lst
Thompson Aml. Agt
Turvey Hy. Lst
Weaver Edw. Costall, Crg
Wilkinson, Wm. Mlg
Attornies.
Caparn Robt. Kgt
Fox & Falkner, Lst
Hodgkinson Geo. Ngt
Lee John Would. Csg
Rastall Henry, Lst
Stephenson Jno. Mlg
Tallents and Burnaby,
Cartergate

Auctioneers.
Hage John, Sst
Harrison Geo. Mdg
Orson John. (& corn inspector) Cgt
Ridge Sl. & Chs. Mkp
Rippendale Fras. Lvn
Bakers & Flour Dlrs.
Atkinson Wm. Brg
Baker Wm. Geo st
Beighton Wm. Plt
Bettison Michael, Csg
Burden Jph. Mlg
Cartledge Thos. Crg
Craven Geo. Kgt
Darcy John, Blg
Dickenson, Jph. jun.
Csg
Else Jas. sen. Mkp
Else Jas. jun. Prt
Elson Geo. Stn
Fletcher Rd. Mlg
Hardy Anthy. Ast
Hollinsworth Jn. Ngt
Lawton John, Bst
Lilly Dennis, Ngt
Neale Thos. Mlg
Parnham John, Plt
Pearce John, Ngt
Peet Geo. Lilly's rw
Young Wm. Wst
Bankers.
Godfrey, Hutton. and
Co. Market pl. (draw
on Barclay & Co.)
Handley, Peacock, &
Handley, Castlegt.
(draw on Barnetts,
Hoars, and Co.)
Savings' Bank, Lombard st. open every
Monday from 10 to
11.
Basket Makers.
Bates Ann, Wst
Bates John, Wst
Clarke Jas. Lst

North John, Csg
Blacking Mfr.
Proctor John, Csg
Blacksmiths.
Barnsdall Jane, Csg
Burton Joshua, Bnd
Foster Rd. Csg
Johnson, Geo. Bst
Pacey Saml. Kst
Spencer Thos. Hrd
Woodward Jn. Mkp
Boat Builders.
Flint Wm. Ngt
Hurton Wm. Mlg
Bone Dust Mfr.
Curtis J. Bigsby, Csg
*Booksellers, Printers,
Stationers, &c.*
*Thus * are not printers*
Bridges Jas. Cht
Hage Henry, Sst
*Lincham Anw. Csg
Ridge Saml. & Chas.
Market place
*Sharp W. Elsey, Frd
Boot & Shoe Mkrs.
Andrew Wm. Blg
Atkinson Wm. Mln
Burgh Jph. Brg
Brailsford Job, Cow l
Bycroft Jas. Mkp
Cutts Jph. Lrd
Flower Geo. Mkp
Harding Thos. Blg
Hardy Hezikiah, Mlg
Hawkins, Geo. Mkp
Heaton John, Bln
Henfrey Geo. Crg
Henfrey Rd. Lst
Higgat Thos. Csg
Hoyland Wm. Ngt
Lunn Geo. Prt
Lumley Fras. Mtn
Mayfield John, Ngt
Miller Jas. Sst
Moore Reuben, Bgt
Reilly Patrick, Kgt

Robinson Thos. Mkp
Robinson Wm. Crg
Saunders Jas. Ngt
Sharpe Jas. Bln
Smith Sml. Mlg
Soar Thos. Ast
Stapleford, Saml. Kgt
Summers John, Agt
Surgey Geo. Kgt
Taylor Jas. Kgt
Thornhill Wm. Csg
Turnbull Walter, Kgt
White John, Lst
Withers John, Blg
Wood Hy. Rst
Wright John, Plt

Braziers & Tinmen.
Bousfield Wm. Kgt
Cudworth Abm. Hrd
Edmondson Jn. Mlg
Lang Jas. Sst
Odlin Wm. Prt
Wilson Thos. Bng

Brewers.
Handley Wm. F. and
  John, Northgate

Bricklayers.
Chambers John, Gst
Chambers J. jun. Lvn
Cutts Chas. Mlg
Duke Wm. Mlg
Duke Thos. Lst
Sheppard John S. Blg
Sutton Edw. Mlg
Ward Wm. Bng

Brick Makers.
Norton J. Orme, Blg
Robinson & Wilson,
  Blg
Sheppard H. Ngt
Sheppard John, Blg
Brush Mkrs. & Dlrs.
Hibbert John, Sst
Sedwell Han. Mlg
Shaw Fras. Frw

Butchers.
Abraham James, Mlg
Abraham John, Lst
Bell Hy. Kgt
Bell James, Ngt
Bell Wm. Millgt
Bennett John, Ngt
Blow John, Mkp

Branston John, Kgt
Curman Wm. Agt
Collins Rd. Mlg
Cutts Wm. Plt
Foottit Saml. Prt
Goodbarne Ths. Mdg.
Hall Rd. Cht
Harvey Jph. Kgt
Harvey Paul, Mlg
Heaton, Jph. Csg
Hutchinson Ed. Mdg
Johnson Robt. *Beck-*
  ingham
Killingley Rt. Bng
Lilly Wm. Blg
Lamb John, Sst
Lumley Hy. Ngt
Lilly Robt. Ngt
Mansford Jph. Sst
Morris Robt. Bln
Morris Thos. Stn
Pocklington Jph. Hrd
Radford Wm. Csg
Shephard Jph. Mdg
Staveley Wm. Blg
Taylor Geo. Kgt
Taylor Geo. Brg
Taylor Rd. Mkp
Taylor Wm. Blg
Wand Geo. Ngt
Wand Reuben, Agt
Wand Stephen, Cgt
Williamson Barzillac
  Lst
Wood Hy. Hrd

Cabinet Makers.
Those marked ‡ are
Upholsterers also.
‡Barber J. Foster. Brg
‡Barber Peter, Crg
‡Harston Wm. Agt
‡Jameson Danl. Bgt
Thompson J. jun. Gst
Wells Wm. Brg

Carver & Gilders.
Barber J. Foster, Brg
Bellatti G. & Son, Sst
Chair Makers.
Miles Wm. Blg
Thompson John, Kgt
China, Glass, &c. Dls.
Armstone Thos. Ngt
Clay Dalton P. (glass)

  Market place
Locking Thos. Kgt
Lowe Ann, Wst
Siddons Jph. Prt
Winterbottom, T. Blg
Chymists & Druggists
Betts Jas. Mkp
Caparn Thos. Mkp
Heaton Jph. Sst
Jackson Wm. Sst
Snow Jas. (& British
  wine dlr.) Sst
Weightman W. Kgt
  Coach Builder
Hall Wm. Lst
  Coa. Dealers.
Babbington Collery
  Wharf, J. G. Bulson
  agent, Mlg
Clarke J. & Son, Mlg
Foster J. & W. & Rt.
  Bishop, Ngt
Holloway Rt. Kst
Huddleston J. and S.
  Csg
Jackson John Arm-
  strong, Ngt
Massey Thos. Hacket,
  Ngt
Morley John, Ngt
Thorpe J. & Sons, Mlg
Turner Thos. Mlg
Walster Wm. Mdg
Widdison Rt. Ngt
Withers G. & T. Mlg
  Confectioners.
Dunn Benj. Bst
Eggleston Fred. Mkp
Howlenn Sarah, Sst
Kirby Nicholas, Blg
Thorpe Jas. (and Bri-
  tish wine dlr) Mkp
Walker. Wm. Sst
  Coopers.
Austin Samuel, Sst
Houghton John, Bng
Kay Joseph, Brg
May William, Bln
  Corn Merchants.
Clark James and Son,
  (and lineseed and
  rape cake) Mlg
Boler William, Mlg

Craven George, Kgt
Dixon George, Ngt
Fisher George, Mlg
Gabbitas William, Ast
Hewes Wm. Bng
Hilton Rt. and Geo.
(& hop & seed) Mdg
Thornton John, Gst
Thorpe Jas. & Sons,
Millgate
Withers Geo. & Thos.
Millgate

Corn Millers, &c.
Marked * are Millers,
and the rest are flour
and corn dealers
*Abbott Edw. Mdg
*Bullen Tho. Kgt
Curtis J. Bigsby, Csg
Dickenson Jph. Bng
Flear Rd. Mdg
*Flear Thos. Csg
Gamble Richd. Blg
*Greaves Wm. Agt
Grokes John, Blg
*Harvey James, Brg
†Harvey Tim. Crg
Lightfoot Wm. Sst
Oldham Jas. Bst
Pacey John, Crg
Pearce John, Ngt
Reddish Thos. Mlg
Rowbotham Wm. Mlg
*Thorpe Jas. & Sons,
Watermill & Mlg
Townrow Benj. Chn
Waddington T. Mlg

Curriers and Leather
Cutters.
Brown Rd. (attends
Wd.) Blg and *Gran-*
tham
Doubleday Geo. Kgt
Miller Wm. Crg
Selby Peter, Sst

Dyers.
Brown Geo. Wet
Jackson Jas. Brg
Mangan John, Crg

Eating Houses.
Morris Same. Kgt
Taylor Eliz. Stn

Engraver.
Harston John, Kgt

Farmers.
Marked † are Cowkprs
†Abraham Cuth. Est
Allin John, Bng
†Cobb John, Rst
Cooper Wm. Crg
Crich Wm. *Winthorp*
hill
Fillingham Rd. Bst
†Green Wm. Bmkt
Hall Rt. (carts) Agt
Heffield Ann, Ngt
†Hind Wm. Stn
†Jackson John, Ngt
Lacy Danl. Blg
Lilly John, Svn
†Predgeon Wm. Blg
Proctor Wm. Bhrd
Sheppard Thos. Bng
†Southeron Wm. Gpl
†Shereston Sarah, Prt
†Wilkinson Wm. Plt
†Wray Thos. Bhn

Fire and Life Offices.
Atlas Wm. Harston.
Appletongate
British S. & C. Ridge,
Market place
County Fire and Pro-
vident Life, Jph.
Smith, Mkp
Globe W. Brown, Mgt
Guardian, Rt. Caparn,
Kirkgate
Leeds and Yorkshire.
Rd. Clark. Csg
Phœnix Isaac Pale-
thorpe, Bng
Royal Exchange Wm.
Fillingham, Sst
Sun Jas. Betts, Mkp
Yorkshire John Would
Lee, Csg

Felmongers.
Renshaw Thos. Spr
Wells Anty. Mlg

Fishmongers.
Neaves Thos. Kgt
Uffindall John, Mdg
Ward Jonas, Agt
Woolfit Jph. Sst

Flour Dealers
Darbyshire Wm. Sst
Reddish Thos. Mlg
Rowhotham Thos. Mlg
Wood Timothy, Bln
Woodall Cath. Sst

Furniture and Clothes
Brokers.
Those marked † are
Clothes Dealers only.
†Heath Saml. Blg
†Hoben Thos. B. Blg
†Hughes Even. Blg
†Haywood Mary, Sst
Hind Thos. Prt
Roberts G. sen. Brg
Roberts G. jun. Sst
Shields Hy. Mlg
Watson James, (and
pawnbroker,) Cht

Gardeners and Seeds-
men.
Cawkwell John, Mkp
Cawkwell Richd. Crg
Cuckson John, Sst
Dalman Thos. Bgt
Eggleston Wm. Agt
Fletcher F. Hawton rd
Franks Rt. Kgt
Grimley Thos. Bng
Hague John, Lrs
Hudson Mattw. Ngt
King Wm. Mlg
Palethorpe Jph. Chn
Sharp Edw. Lst
Williamson, Wm. Bkt

Glovers and Breeches
makers.
Colbie John, Cht
Portwood John, Mlg

Grocers & Tea Dlrs.
Branston Jph. Cht
Bush John, Csg
Chew Jas. Mlg
Drury John, Mkp
Gibson Robert, Sst
Gillson Joseph, Sst
Jackson Sarah, Csg
Marshall Wm. Mdg
Mills Geo. Mkp
Morley Daniel, Ngt
Moss Sophia Ch. Csg
Oldham Henry, Mlg

Popplewell John, Mkp
Ridge James, Mdg
Robinson J. & Son, Agt
Robinson Robert, Agt
Simpson Jph. Lst

Gun Makers.

Boaler Joseph, Mkp
Boaler & Welch, Mkp
Doubleday Thos. Bln
Nixon David, Sst

Hair Dressers.
Marked ‡ are Perfrs

Allin John Mkp
Bradley Wm. Chn
Cain Jesse, Csg
Chambers James, Brg
‡Chapman Jas. Mdg
Curtis John, Mlg
‡Harrison Thos. Sst
Key John, Crg
Marshall George (and
grinder) Cow ln
‡Pinder Thomas, Crg
‡Silverton Geo. Kgt
Simnitt Jph, Mlg
‡Smith Samuel, Bgt
Wand Thomas, Kgt

Hardware Dealers.

Brown S. T. Sst
Tipper Benjamin, Kgt

Hat Manufacturers.

Collin Thomas, Sst
Hage John, Sst
Higton William, Sst
Seymour Hanh. Kgt

Hosiers.

Carter John, Bgt
Hardy Jn (& worsted
manufacturers) Mlg
Sharp Eli, Hrd
Wand Stph. Crg

Inns and Taverns.

Angel, Rd. Hemstock,
Mdg
Bell, T. Savage, Mkp
Black Bull, Jn. Watkin, Crg
Black Swan, Samuel
Tharratt, Stn
Blue Lion, Thos Taplin, Middlegate
Boars Head, Richard
Gadd, Middlegate

Castle & Falcon Inn,
Wm. Moore, Bst
Clinton Arms Inn, Ann
Lawton, Mkp
Cross Keys, William
Hunt, Beaumond st
Dolphin, Wm. Hague,
Barnbygate
Duke of Cumberlmd,
S. Spreekley, Mdg
Duke of Wellington,
Saml. Ulyet, Millgt
Fox and Crown, Chas.
Gadd, Appletongate
Generous Briton, S.
Outram, Lst
George and Dragon,
Sarah Ringrose, Cgt
Golden Fleece, Marth.
Ringrose, Lst
Horse and Gears, T.
Jackson, Prt
Horse and Jockey, W.
Cooper, Blg
Hotel, Jph. Gilstrap,
Kirkgate
King's Arms, John
Lacy, Kirkgate
King's Head, Francis
Jackson, Chain ln
Lion and Adder, John
Drake, Northgate
Lord Nelson, John
Pogson, Blg
Marquis of Granby,
John Hunt, Blg
Newark Arms, Henry
Nall, Agt.
Old Castle, J. White,
Millgate
Old King's Arms, S.
Horspool, Kgt
Old King's Head, W.
Gregory, Blg
Pack Horse, William
Weaver, Hrd
Queen's Head, John
Allin, Mkp
Ram Hotel, Mary
Hancock, Csg
Rein Deer, Jas. Cook,
Northgate

Robin Hood, John Allen, Lst
Royal Oak, John Wilson, Castlegate
Royal Oak, W. Taylor, Stodman street
Rutland Arms, John
Welby, Bng
Saracen's Head, Sam
Shaw, Mkp
Ship, Jonas Smith,
Water lane
Spread Eagle, George
Harrison, Mdg
Swan and Salmon, W.
Nall, Castlegate
Spring House, Wm.
Cambridge, Frd
Talbot, (excise office)
Jas. Carver, Crg
Waggon and Horses,
Wm. Briggs, Csg
Water Mill, Rt. Ironmonger, Mlg
Wheat Sheaf, John
Groves, Kgt
White Hart, R. Crampern, Mkp
White Hind, A. Sharp,
Cartergate
White Horse, J. Harvey, Millgate
White Horse, Thomas
Walton, Barnbygt
White Lion, Thomas
Gardner, Sst
White Swan, Rd. Gee,
Northgate
Wing Tavern, Rich.
Parlby, Market pl
Woolpack, Thos. Nevett, Stodman st

Beerhouses.

Barely Mow, Abm.
Cudworth, Hrd
Black's Head, Wm.
Reynolds, Crg
Blue Goat, William
Porter, Ngt
Blue Man, Rt. Widdison, Ngt
Blue Sergeant, George
Stevenson, Ast

Board, J. Ward, Blg
Bricklayer's Arm, T. Duke, Lst
Carpenter's Arm, Jas. North, Albion st
Crown & Anchor, Rd. Starr, Parliament st
Free Mason's Arms. Wm. Duke, Mlg
Gardener's Arms, Ed. Marshall, Mdg
King's Arms, George Rickett, King st
King W. IV. Samuel Morris, Kirkgate
Nag's Head, John Wright, Kgt
Pack Horse, William Palin, Middlegate
Plough, W. Jackson, Guildhall street
Rose and Crown, Hy. Shaw, Pelham st
Salmon, Jonas Ward, Appletongate
Sun, John Hollingsworth, Northgate
Union Flag, Stanley Leedle, Barnby rd
Wilde's Arms, Wm. Cutts, Plt
K. William IV. Isaac Willock, Plt
Wind Mill, William Beighton, Plt

Iron & Brass Founders
Ingledew, Geo. Millgt
Wilson and Midworth Wellington Fndry, Northgate

Ironmongers.
Chambers Rt. Mkp
Gillson Thomas, (iron mercht. & printing press maker) Bng
Nicholson Benj. Mkp
Touge Edw. Sst

Joiners.
Alliss Wm. Hrd
Barrett Jas. Lst
Bettison & Hart, Prt
Branston Saml. Brg

Brown W. & Son, Kst
Clark Thomas, (pump mkr) Baldertongt
Copestake Chs. Sheppard's row
Elson Wm. Plt
Hutchinson T. Mlg
Hutchinson Wm. Ngt
Johnson William, Frw
Mackenzie G. (pump mkr.) Baldertongt
Nall John, Gst
North Jas. Ast
Parr John, Bng
Pinknay John, Gsg
Skinner John, Mlg
Sumners Wm. Wst

Lacemen.
Carter John, Bgt
Smith Hy. Bgt

Land & Bldg. Srvrs.
Adams Jph.(& valuer) Ngt
Harrison Geo. Mdg

Linen & Wln. Draps.
Angrave Edw. Ngt
Becket Thomas, (and stamp distr.) Mkp
Bonifant Henry, Mkp
Butler Henry, Sst
Chambers Wm. Mkp
Clark Richard, Mkp
Dodd Caleb, Mkp
Fillingham Wm. Sst
Fisher & Fillingham, Market place
Hall Henry, Mkp
Johnson Thos. Sst
Mc Myn Thos. Ngt
Oliver John & John, Market place

Linen Manufacturers.
Hardy Jph. (Damask) Mlg
Scales Geo. & Son, (& bleachers) Hawton Mills
Simnit W. (& weaver) Csg
Thompson J. (sacking &c.) Castle
Unday J. (& weaver) Bng

Livery Stables.
Shaw Saml. Mkp
Spencer Rt. Stn
Wilson James, Sst

Maltsters.
Adams Jph. Ngt
Betts Jas. Blg
Boler W. & Co. Mlg
Branston Jph. Wln
Brodhurst W. & Sons, Ngt. & Mansfield
Caparn R. & Brothers, Lst. h. Cartergate
Carver Jas. Crg
Chappeli Simon, Ngt
Clark Jas. & Son, Mlg
Dixon George, Ngt
Fisher Geo. Mlg
Foster J. & Co. Ngt
Hancock Walter, Mlg
Handley W. P. & J. Northgate
Harvey Geo. Crg
Hilton Rt. & Geo. L. Middlegate
Hole Samuel, Csg.
Jackson Hy. Ngt
Marfleet Hy. & Fdk. Millgt.& Winthorpe
Massey Thos. Hacket, Castlegate
Middleton Wm. Lockyer, Lovers' In
Readett Wm. Hy. Lst
Smith Wm. Bst
Thorpe J. & Sons, Mlg
Wilson John, Gst
Wright Saml. Lst

Milliners & Dress Makers.
Berriff Sarah, Bng
Brooks Ann, Blg
Carter Henrietta, Bgt
Collin Ameris, Sst
Crampern Ann, Crg
Dalman Ann & Eliz. Bgt
Dalman Matilda, Blg
Elson Eliz. Plt
Farmer Mary, Agt
Franks Rebecca, Wst
Grubb Alice, Sst
Hardy Ann, Rst

3 H

Hardy Mary, Millgt
Henfrey Eliz. Csg
Hoggan Jane, Mdg
Holmes Sarah, (& tea dlr,) Mdg
Johnson My. Ann, Lst
Lineham Eliz. Kst
Naylor Eliz. Plt
Pilgrim Mary, Brg
Rawding Frances, Ast
Pybus My. & Ann, Agt
Rose Mary, Ast
Watkin Mary, Crg
Watson Charlotte, Wst
WhittinghamCath.Prt
Williamson My. Ngt
Wilson Frances, Blg

Millwrights, &c.
Marked † are Machine Makers.
†Chambers Rt. Mkp
English Wm. Pmt
Ingledew Geo. (& millstone mkr.) Mlg
†Spencer Thos. Stn

Nail Makers.
Burgess Wm. Blg
Gillson Thos. Bng
Gregory Rd. Lst

Nurserymen, &c.
See also Gardeners.
Clark Geo. (& florist) Strawberry hall, Lrd
Flower Mary, Lrd
Girton John, Blg
Girton Jph. Sst
Withers Geo. & Thos. Mkp. & Millgt

Painters.
Harston John, (and gravestone cutter,) Kgt
Harston Robt. (& engraver) Lst
Kirkham Ann, Mlg
Slater Jas. R. Wst
Summers Jph. Ast
Watkin John, Crg
Winter Wm. Mdg

Patten & Clog Mkrs.
Bradley Rose, Stn
Bradley Jph. Pmt
Tipper Benj. Kgt

Turnbull Walter, Kgt

Physicians.
Bigsby John Jerh.
Friary, Agt
Chawnor Darwin, Cgt
Morton Hugh, Bgt

Plaster Mrchts. &c.
Norton Jno. Orme, Blg
Robinson & Wilson, Blg
Shaw Hy. (plasterer) Pelham st
Sheppard John Sadler, Balderton gt
Ward Wm. Bng

Plumbers & Glaziers.
Brown Geo. Bng
Brown John, Csg
Lang Wm. Sst
Pawson Sarah & Sons. Kirkgate
Rayner John B. Sst
Thompson Wm. Kgt

Professors.
Brydges Wm. (organist) Church yd
Crow Wm. (music) Lst
Curtis Jph. Bigsby, (landscape and portrait) Csg
Dyer Thos. (dancing) Osbornethorpe hs
Hardy Wm. (music) Stodman st
Hurst Rt. (music) Sst

Register Office.
Robinson Ann, Crg

Rope & Twine Mkrs.
Lee Saml. Brg
Marshall Edw. Mkp
Peart Rt. Sst
Pollard Wm. (sack) Ngt

Saddlers, &c.
Clark John, Lst
Cooper Wm. Csg
Edlin Chas. Spr
Hardy Jas. Sst
Loversidge Jph. & Son, Castlegate
Moss Wm. Bridge st
Pinder John, Kgt

Shopkeepers.
Asher Benj. Ngt

Adams Hy. Wln
Barker Ann, Agt
Birkitt Eliz. Crg
Bousfield Alice, Sst
Brown John, Plt
Cartledge Amelia, Csg
Driver Thos. Kgt
Goodacre Wm. Blg
Gregory Rd. Lst
Heppenstall Fdk. Blg
Hibbert Sarah, Lock
Hunt Thos. Stn
Johnson Eliz. Kst
Johnson John, Frd
King Wm. Mlg
Marriott Rd. York st
Mason Wm. Tenter bds
Mattlock Rebecca, Lst
Miller & Joycey, Hrd
Morley Jph. Wln
Osborne Jas. Prt
Outram Geo. Csg
Pacey John, Mlg
Parkinson Eliz. Kgt
Pocklington Saml. Ast
Robinson Mary, Mlg
Rushton Barton, Csg
Simpson Eliz. Kgt
Spring Geo. Lst
Taylor Thos. Ngt
Wakefield Rd. Sst
Wand Thos. Kgt
White Geo. Ngt
Worrall Hy. Hrd

Silversmiths & Jwlrs.
Clay Dalton Parr, Mkp
Smith Hy. Bgt

Smallware Dealers.
Barrows Jas. Blg
Cole Wm. Pepper hill
Lilley Rt. Ngt
Newey Jas. Agt
Saunders Jas. Ngt
Taylor John, Sst

Smock Frock Mfrs. & Slop Sellers.
Clark Rd. Csg
Gelsthorp Thos. Kgt
Little H. C. & Co. Mgt
Moore Reuben, Bgt
Rippingale W. (frocks only) Castlegate

Stay Makers.
Brown Charlotte, Kgt
Grantham Thos. Bgt
Knight Charlotte, Wst
Mather Thos. Kgt
Matthews Eliz. Gst
Parkinson Thos. Crg
Stanhope Thos. Bng
Taylor John, Mkp
Thompson Eliz. Kgt
Stone Masons, &c.
Chamberlain Rt. Blg
Marshall Rd. Csg
Nicholson John, Ngt
Sheppard Chp.Haneer,
  Blg
Sheppard Geo. Lst
Straw Hat Makers.
Aram E. & J. Sst
Bilson David, Sst
Colbre Sarah, Cht
Harston Maria, Kgt
Lampin Mary, Cht
Makenzie Reb. Stn
Marshall Harriet, Csg
Sheppard Maria, Blg
Snell Ann, Sst
Worley Mary, Lst
Surgeons.
Anders James, Kgt
Deeping William, Lst
Dobbs William, Agt
Lacy Jas. Prior, Csg
Parker Wm. Mdg
Pearson Samuel, Ngt
Thompson W. jun Agt
Waring Samuel, Bng
Welby William, Csg
Tailors.
marked ‡ are Drapers.
‡Barker Rt. Chn
Brooks Andrew & up-
  holsterer
Brown William, Wst
Buttery and Cawthan,
  Mdg
Calcraft John, Bng
‡Carpendale Ths. Mg
Chatterton Wm. Mkp
Coleam Francis & up-
  holsterer
Emerson Wm. Ast
Franks John W. Crg

Gelsthorp Thos. Chn
Holmes Samuel, Blg
‡Little H. C. & Co Mg
Lyne William, Chn
Mather Thomas, Cyd
Neaves William, Frd
Moore Reuben, Bgt
Morley John, Ngt
Parlby William, Wst
‡Pettefar Rd. Kgt
Rogers Nathan, Blg
Simmons Joseph, Jyd
Spurrett Wm A. Hrd
Turner John, Plt
‡Wells Jsph. Sst
Wood John, Mdg
‡Wright John, Sst
Tallow Chandlers.
Drury John, Mkp
Gibson Rt. Sst
Gillson Jph. Sst
Jackson Sarah, Csg
Morley Daniel, Ngt
Moss F. Evelyn, Csg
Oldham Henry, Mlg
Poplewell John, Mkp
Ridge James, Mdg
Robinson J. & Son Agt
Tanner.
Killingley A. Mlg
Timber Merchants.
Clark J. & Son, Mlg
Handley W. F. & J.
  Northgate
Huddlestone J. & Son
  Castlegate
Nall John, (English)
  Guildhall-street
Tobacco Manfrs.
Hardstaff John, Bng
Hodgkinson John, &
  J. Froggatt, Bng
Tobacco Pipe Manfrs.
Edmunds Wm. Ast
Simnit J. Lyne, Est
*Trunk and Box
  Makers.*
Stapleford S. Kgt
Hobin T. Barnes, Blg
Pate George, Bng
Turners in Wood, &c
Ellis John, Bln
Hibbert, John, Sst

WilsonKirby, Csg
Veterinary Surgeons.
Cotchefer John, Kgt
Foster Richard, Csg
Goodacre Thos. Blg
Johnson George, Rst
Watch & Clock Makers
Goodwin Henry, Sst
Hardy Richard, Mkp
Holt Richard, Kgt
Priest J. & J. Mdg
Priest William, Bln
Wharfingers.
Clark J. & Son Mlg
Fisher W. & G. Mlg
Huddlestone J. & Son
  Castlegate
Hurst & Carver, Ngt
Jackson J. Armstrong
  Northgate
Withers G. & T. Mlg
Wheelwrights.
Bedford Edw. Brg
Selby Joseph, Blg
Weightman Wm. Mlg
Wilson Wm. Blg
Whitesmiths.
Buck Wm. Bng
Ingledew Geo. Mlg
Geary Joseph, Bln
Palethorpe Arthur, (&
  Iron mrt.) Tonges
  Yard.
Revill John, Sst
Revill T. (machine,)
  Balderton-gate
Spencer Rt. Stn
Wallis Gude, Lst
Walton Wm. Mlg
Wine & Spirit Mrts.
Dyson Js. Market-pl
Gardner Thomas, Sst
Gilstrap Joseph, Kgt
Norton, Deeping, &
  Co. Kirkgate
Taplen Thomas, Mdg
Thompson Wm. Kgt
Wire Workers.
Norton Rd. Ngt
Petchell Thomas, Crg
Wool Merchants.
Hardy John, Mlg
Young Edward, Utr

COACHES, &c.

From Gilstrap's Hotel.

To *London*, Royal Mail, 3 aft. ; Express, 6 evg. ; Highflyer, ¼ before 2 mg. ; Wellington, ½ past 4 mg. ; Rockingham, 3 afternoon

To *York*, *Newcastle*, & *Edinbro'*, Royal Mail, 10 mg. ; Express, ½ past 10 night. ; Highflyer, 12 night ; Wellington, 8 mg

To *Leeds*, Rockingham, ½ past 6 morning

To *Norwich*, Union, 6 morning, through Sleaford, Boston, Lynn, &c.

To *Manchester*, Champion, half-past 6 morning

To *Nottingham*, Imperial, every aft. at 4 (except Sund.) and to *Lincoln*, &c. ½ past 11 mg

To *Nottingham* & *Derby*, The Wonder, every mg. at 8

To *Lincoln*, Queen Adelaide, every evg. at 7, except Sund. ; and to *Cambridge* at 7 mg

From the Castle & Falcon.

To *Gainsbro'*, Regulator, ¼ before 5 morning

To *Southwell* & *Nottingham*, Accommodation, 8 mg. ; and the Pilot, ½ past 3 afternoon

☞ The Rockingham, Champion, and Queen Adelaide, call at this Inn as well as the Hotel

From the Swan & Salmon.

To *Worksop* & *Doncaster*, the Amity, at 2 afternoon

To *Lincoln*, the Perseverance, ¼ before 8 mg. ; and to *Nottingham* & *Southwell*, at ½ past 3 aft. The Hope, to *Nottingham* at 8 morning

To *Southwell* & *Mansfield*, the Mail Gig, 11 morning

From the Clinton Arms.

The Royal Mail to *Glasgow*, at 10 mg. ; and to *London* at ¼ before 4 afternoon

The Union to *London*, at 10 ngt., and to *Leeds*, at 6 mg. The Norwich Union, at 6 mg

CARRIERS.

Deacon, Harrison, & Co., Castle-gate ; Vans to London, Cambridge, &c. every Wed. Fri. & Sat. mgs. at 6 ; and waggons every mg. at 6. To Doncaster, Wakefield, & Leeds, at 6 evg

Rt. Hunt & Son, Lombard street, to London, every Tues. Wed. Fri. & Sat. evgs. at 7 ; and to Sheffield and all parts of the North, every Sun. Mon. Wed. & Friday morning at 7

Jackson & Co. Lombard street, to London, 1 morning

To *Grantham*, Joseph Woolfit, Stodman st. ; & Sl. Hewland, Clark's yard, daily, 5 mg

To *Lincoln*, W. & J. Pettifer, from the Robin Hood, Sunday, Tues. & Thurs. mg. ; Joseph Woolfit, Stodman st. Tues. 10 mg. & Fri. 4 mg. ; and John Uffindale, Middlegate, Tues. & Thurs. 12 noon

To *Nottingham*, W. & J. Pettifor from the Robin Hood, Mon. Wed. & Friday

CARRIERS BY WATER.

☞ *See Warfingers, page 623*

MARKET CARRIERS.

They arrive on Wednesday about 10 morng. and depart 3 aft. from their respective INNS

Those marked 1 put up at the Angel ; 2, Duke of Cumberland ; 3, King's Head ; 4, Robin Hood ; 5, Rein Deer ; 6, Royal Oak ; 7, Spread Eagle 8, White Hart ; 9, White Horse ; and 10, Waggon and Horses.

Aslockton, Hy. Sanders, 8

Barnby, Fox & Crown, Rt. Mills, and Hy. Taylor

Bassingham, Jph. Newbutt, 5 ; and Thos. Knapp, 8

Bennington, Generous Britain, Rd. Lynn ; & Bell, Wm. Luty

Besthorp, Wm. Spouton, 5

Bingham, Wm. Jackson, 1 ; and Ann Moult, Bell Inn

Bottesford, John Wilson, 3 ; Wm.

Jackson, 8; & Rd. Hucknall, Packhorse

Broughton & Sleford, Rt. Whitaker, 8; Rd. Hucknall, 9

Carcolston, John Baker, 4; and Thos. Cragg, 10

Carlton-on-Trent, Mr. Price, 6

Caunton, Wm. Barnes, 7

Caythorpe, Wm. Wetherill, 8

Claypole, Bell, {William Daws; Lord Nelson, Mr. Hubbard

Clifton, Geo. Dovener, 1; and Wm. Turner, 2

Collingham, John Bailey, 3; and Jph. Groves, 1, Wed. & Sat

Cropwell, S. Swinscoe, 7

Eagle, Jph. Moorby, 1

Eakring, Mr. Weatherby, 7

Elston, John Long, 8

Farndon, W. Allwood, 10, Wed. & Saturday

Fiskerton, Mr. Foster, 6

Flintham, Tho. Cupit, 4

Foston, W. Ellis & M. Bell, 8

Fulbeck, John King, 9

Grantham, Rd. Pyband, 2

Hawkesworth, J. Padget, 4

Hoveringham, Cphr. Armstrong, Bell

Leadenham, &c. John Duty, 9

Mansfield, Thos. Wood, Wed. & Sat. Swan & Salmon

Marnham, Rd. Smith, Blue Lion

Muskham (South) Geo. Butterworth, King's Arms

Normanton, Thos. Waller, 6; & Jarvis Newbold, 1

Norwell, Thos. Radford, 2; Wm. Warsop, 1; and J. Hallam, Ram Hotel

Nottingham, Jph. Wilcocks, 3; & Geo. Skidmore, 1; Wed. & Saturday

Ollerton, J. Scatchard, 2

Orston, John Fryer, 4; and Wm. Greaves. 8

Radcliffe, Saml. Wood, 8

Redmill, Wm. Patchell, 7

Rolleston, Thos. Brailsford, 6

Scarle, (N. & S.) Wm. Linney, 1; Wm. Saxby & Wm. Brown, 5

Screveton, Jph. Hallam, 1

Sedgbrook, Wm. Scoffins, 10

Sibthorpe, J. Fisher, 4

Southwell, J. Fearn, & W. Cooling, 1: Jph. Pilgrim, 2; and J. Fryer, 7

Stapleford Moor, J. Priestly, 1

Sutton-on-Trent, S. Whitworth, and Wm. Atkinson, 1; Wm. Shephard, 7

Swinderby, R. Collingham, 1

Syerston, Wm. Bramley, 4

Tuxford, Mr. Todd, 1; Wm. Godfrey, 7

Wellow, Jph. Moorby, 1

Westborough, John Miles, Old King's Head

Whatton, Wm. Tutbury, White Hind

BALDERTON is a pleasant village and parish, 1¼ mile S.E. of Newark, containing 830 inhabitants, and about 360 acres of land, belonging to several proprietors, of whom the Duke of Newcastle is the principal, and also lord of the manor, which was *soc* to Newark. The *church* is a neat but ancient structure, dedicated to St. Giles. The benefice is annexed to the vicarage of Farndon. The prebendary of Farndon, in Lincoln cathedral, is the appropriator, but he and the incumbent received allotments at the inclosure in 1768, in lieu of all the tithes, except those which are still paid on about 125 acres of crown land.— A *Methodist chapel* was erected here in 1825. An annual *feast* is held on September 12th, and *hirings for servants* at Mayday and Martinmas. The vicar receives £2 yearly, and the schoolmaster £18 for teaching 18 free scholars, from an estate at Fishtoft, in Lincolnshire, bequeathed to this parish and that of

3 H 2

Sleaford, by *Wm. Alvey*, in 1726. The following rent charges are received yearly for the poor of this parish, viz 40s. left in 1724, by Gabriel Alvey; 6s. 8d. by Alice Newcombe; 20s. out of land at Caythorpe; 10s. out of land in Balderton; 8s. out of E. S. Godfrey's estate; 1s. 2d. out of Steadfold's close; 10d. out of Hunt's close; and 3s. 4d. out of 2¾ acres belonging to Mr. Harvey. Three closes in Scarsdale parish, now let for £12. 12s., were bequeathed to them by a *Mr. Wigglesworth*; also two cottages and gardens (let for £12) by *Benjamin Gibson*, in 1727; and the poor's close, (3 acres, let for £8,) left by Francis Leek.

Bell William, Gentlemen
Birkett Mr. John,
Birkett Wm. miller and baker,
Greasley Mr. Benjamin,
Daybell John, butcher
Dickenson John, bricklayer
Esam Mrs. Ann
Fisher James, tailor
Hancer Christopher, gentlemen
Hand John, butcher
Harvey Mr. John
Kerchevall Mrs Ann
Lineker Robert, brickmaker
Marriott Geo. Esq. Round House
Newstead Francis, gentlemen
Oldham John, Surveyor of the turnpike from Foston to Musham Bridge.
Oldham Thomas, tailor
Padgett William, beer-house
Read Matthew, joiner
Rose Edward, gentlemen
Selby John, wheelwright
Selby Samuel, parish clerk,
Smith B. victualler, Turk's Head

Smith William, schoolmaster.
Smithson John, victualler, Cock
Stevenson Wm. joiner & cabinet maker
Tyerman Wm. tailor & beerhouse
Upsall Richard, gentlemen
Welby Miss Elizabeth & sisters Balderton Hall

Farmers.   Wilson C & W.
Bramley Wm.   *Maltsters.*
Calvert John   Clark James
Caunt Thomas   Harvey Rt.
Fillingham Rd.   Oldham Geo.
Hand John   *Shoemakers.*
Harrison Rd.   Cawthan Jph.
Oldham William, Crow Richard
Padgett John   Hunt Joseph
Page Thomas   Tinley Thos.
Rawding Thos.   *Shopkeepers.*
Stevens George Antcliff Edm.
Thompson Jno. Glover Wm.
Withers Wm.   Harvey Edw.
   Blacksmiths.   Smith Thomas
Bramley Ts.

BARNBY-IN-THE-WILLOWS is a small village and parish, on the river Witham, which divides it from Lincolnshire, 4 miles E.S.E. of Newark. It has 237 inhabitants, and about 1400 acres of land, belonging to Colonel Noel, Rd. Fisher, Esq. and several other freeholders. An ancient moated house, which had belonged to the Nevilles and Brownes, (*Barons Montagu*,) was taken down about 15 years ago. The *church* is dedicated to All Saints. The vicarage, valued in the King's books at £5. 9s. 9½d., is in the patronage of Southwell collegiate church, and incumbency of the Rev. Jas. Footit; but Mr. John Brown and Col. Noel are the impropriators, the former having 11 and the latter 4 shares of the rectorial tithes. *Flawford* a farm of 250 acres, anciently belonged to the

Knights. Templar, but is now the property of W. F. and J. Handley, Esqrs.

Newstead John, parish clerk
Rose Benj. joiner
Taylor Hy. shopkeeper
Vessey Gevas, jun. beer hs
Vessey John, beer house

FARMERS.
Bark Michl   Birkett Rd
Birkett John   Brown Thos
Birkett Mary   Doughty John

Featherstone Js   Salmon Michl.
Kinning Thos   Flawford
Mason Rt   Squires T. & G.
Peet John, Fo-   Taylor Hy. & G.
   rest   Vessey Gervas
             Wilson Rd

CARRIERS TO NEWARK.—Hy. Taylor & Rt. Mills, Wed. 8 mg.

NORTH CLIFTON parish comprises the four villages and *townships* of North Clifton, South Clifton, Harby, and Spalford, which maintain their poor separately, and contain together 949 inhabitants, and 4337 acres of land, which was all exonerated from tithes at the enclosure, and anciently formed four manors of the Bishop of Lincoln's fee, and one of Roger de Busli's. NORTH CLIFTON is a small village on the east bank of the Trent, 12¼ miles N. by E. of Newark, near a long red cliff, in which numerous fragments of *urns, bones,* and *scalps* have been found, near the spot which is supposed to have been anciently occupied by a castle. 'The inhabitants have each a free passage across the ferry at South Clifton, for which privilege they give the *ferryman* a "prime loaf" on Christmas-day; when he and his dog have by *custom* each a good dinner at the vicarage, "and the parson's dog is always turned out whilst the ferryman's eats his share of the entertainment." The *church*, dedicated to St. George, stands on an eminence between North and South Clifton. It had formerly a collegiate chantry for secular priests. The vicarage, valued in the King's books at £7. 6s. is now enjoyed by the Rev. Fdk. Parry Hodges. The prebendary of North Clifton, in Lincoln cathedral, is the patron and appropriator. The Duke of Newcastle is lord of the manors of N. and S. Clifton, each of which contains about 1100 acres, belonging to a number of freeholders and a few copyholders. Colonel Sibthorpe is lessee of the prebendal lands. At the enclosure, 11 acres were allotted to the church, and two acres of the Sandhills for repairing the roads. In 1669, *Simon Nicholson* left to the poor £100, which was laid out in the purchase of 16A. 3R. 9P. of land, let for £17 a year, of which ten guineas are given to the master of the school, which was built in 1799, for the use of the two townships. The poor have £3. 10s. yearly, as half the rent of a house in South Clifton, left in 1737, by Susannah Hall. The parish *feast* is on September 12th.

SOUTH CLIFTON, 1 mile S. of North Clifton, is the largest village in this parish, having 340 inhabitants. Here is the vicarage house, a Methodist chapel, and the ferry already noticed. Much damage was done here by the overflowing of the Trent in the *floods* of 1736, 1770, 1795, 1824, and 1828.

HARBY, at the east end of the parish, bordering upon Lincolnshire, and 13 miles N.N.E. of Newark, is a village and chapelry with 304 inhabitants. It is remarkable as the place where *Queen Eleanor* lay ill and died, in the 19th of Edward I. who founded a chantry here, which he afterwards removed to Lincoln. The *chapel of ease* was repaired about twelve years ago. The Duke of Portland is principal owner and lord of the manor, which contains 1187 acres, and was enclosed in 1803, but Col. Sibthorpe and some others have estates here.

SPALFORD, 10 miles N. by E. of Newark, has only 80 inhabitants, and 900 acres of land, enclosed in 1814. Two of its farms are in Girton parish. Sir Wm. Welby, Bart. is the principal owner and lord of the manor.

NORTH CLIFTON.
Banes John, blacksmith
Briggs Richard, tailor
Glew Hannah, corn miller
Hammond George, gent
Harvey Matthew, corn miller
Hills Wm. shoemaker and vict
Squier Jacob, schoolmaster
Starr William, shoemaker
Turner Wm. shopkr. & carrier
Tustin William, tailor
Wheatcroft Edward, gent
Wilson Timothy, joiner

Farmers.
Chapman Rd   Minnett John
Cooling John   Shepherd Thos
Lownd John   Wells Henry
Milns Wm   Wells John

SOUTH CLIFTON.
Buffham Ann, vict. Red Lion
Clark John, butcher and draper
Cooper Joseph, corn miller
Cooper William, grocer & draper
Curtis John, shoemaker
Dinsdale William, parish clerk
Freeborough, Robert, tailor
Freeth Miss
Gambles Thomas, blacksmith, & axe and bill manufacturer
Gordon Rev. Geo. Cyrus, curate
Kirk George, vict
Maltby John, butcher
Pennington Edward, gent
Lamb John, wheelwright
Smith William, joiner
Truelove Robert, joiner

Turner Henry, butcher
Walker John, coal merchant
Watson Hy. tanner, saddler, &c
Wells William, shoemaker

Farmers.
Bonifant Thos   Derry John
Cooper Wm   Higgat Geo
Derry James   Kirk Geo
Derry Wm. and   Tuxford Sarah
  maltster   Woolfit John

Carrier.—George Daubner to Gainsborough, Tuesday, and to Newark, Wednesday, 5 morn.

HARBY.
Ashlin Joseph, blacksmith
Brown George, joiner
Cobb John, wheelwright
Conlon Pat. weaver & beer house
Dixon Benjamin, tailor
Gourley Jno. & W. brickmkrs
Harrison James, joiner
Higgat Anthony, shopkeeper
Higgat Edward, shoemaker
Hodson William, wheelwright
Lobley Thomas, corn miller
Lund William, bricklayer
Lyon John, shopkeeper
Ormond Joseph, shoemaker
Parr George, joiner and vict
Peck Samuel, blacksmith
Simpson William, bricklayer
Smalley Joseph, shoemaker
Smith William, tailor
Wilkinson Robert, butcher
Withers Wm. schoolr. & grocer

Farmers.		SPALFORD—*Farmers.*	
Bolton John	Howitt Thos	Brown Robert	Gibson Jha
Curtis Wm	Simpson Cphr	Cooling John	Hill John
Curtis Thomas	Skinner Wm	Gibson Wm. &	Parkin Wm
Dixon Benj	Wilkinson Geo	miller	Tongue Rd
Doncaster Wm	Withers Thos		

COLLINGHAM, seated on a gentle eminence above the Trent marsh, 6 miles N. by E. of Newark, is one of the largest and handsomest villages in the county, and is all comprised in the two parishes of *North and South Collingham*, which contain together 1608 inhabitants and upwards of 4000 acres of land. A *feast* is held on the last Sunday in October, and *hirings* for servants twice a year.

NORTH COLLINGHAM parish includes more than half of the village, and *Potter Hill* on the borders of Lincolnshire, where tradition says, there has been a Roman Pottery, but it is more likely to have been a military station. The *church* stands near the centre of the village, and is dedicated to All Saints. The vicarage is valued in the King's books at £8. 14s. 2d., and has been augmented with Queen's Anne's Bounty. The Rev. Charles Lesiter, A.B., is the incumbent, and the Dean and Chapter of Peterborough are the patrons and appropriators, but they received land at the enclosure, in lieu of tithes. The *Baptist chapel* here has been several times enlarged, and near it is a *school* endowed (for the education of the poor children of both parishes,) by William and Mary Hart, in 1699 and 1718, with land now let for £39 per annum. The *benefactions* to the poor of North Collingham are £2 yearly, left by William Storr, and the interest of £30 left by Thomas Fisher and William Lonsdale. They have also £6. 6s. yearly from the Poor's close, the rest of which £2. 14s. is paid to the surveyors of the highways. The poor of South Collingham have £2 yearly left by William Storr; £12. 10s. yearly from land bequeathed by William Hart; and the interest of £70 left by Thomas Fisher, and Elizabeth Bradford.

SOUTH COLLINGHAM parish includes the southern part of the village of Collingham, and the hamlets BROUGH and DERNE-THORPE distant 2½ miles to the S.E. It has 727 inhabitants, and nearly 3000 acres of land, of which the Earl of Stamford is principal owner and lord of the manor, which he holds on a lease under the Dean and Chapter of Peterborough, whose bishop has the advowson of the rectory, which is valued in the King's books at £14. 1s. 10½d, and is now enjoyed by the Rev. Joseph Mayor. In the parish are two *Wesleyan chapels*, one at Collingham, and the other at BROUGH, which latter is supposed to be the *Crocolana* of Antoninus, from the number of Roman coins, pots, urns, bricks, &c., that have been dug up there at various periods. *Dernethorp*, which occupies an eminence a little to the south of Brough, had anciently a *chapel* annexed to Thurgarton priory, and human bones are still frequently discovered in a garden which was the burial ground. At Collingham, was born the late *John Blow*, the celebrated organist of Westminster Abbey, who died in 1708. *John Armstrong*, now living in the village, is 27 years of age, and only 3 feet 5 inches in height.

NORTH COLLINGHAM.

Addinsell John, schoolmaster
Bentley Mrs. Sarah
Boot Mrs. Mary
Broadberry John, sen. coal mert
Broadberry John, jun. bookpr
Burbank Baraak, gardener, &c
Burrell Thomas, watchmaker
Chambers Joseph, tailor
Clark John, gent
Cleaver John, gent
Coles John, coal merchant
Cooling Mrs. Sarah
Cooper Robert, surgeon
Crossland George, cooper
Dominichitte Captain Wm
Fish Thomas, butcher
Fletcher Geo. Harwood, surgeon
Glasier Mrs. Mary
Groose Arthur & Jas. saddlers
Hage John, joiner
Hewes George, hair dresser
Hickling Wm. glazier, &c.
Lonsdale, Mrs. Elizabeth
Lesiter Rev. Charles
Millns William, bricklayer
Mosley Henry, wheelwright
Newton Thos. veterinary surgeon
Nichols Rev. Wm. Baptist min.
Pickering Thomas, joiner
Pope Rev. Geo. (Bapt.) & schoolmaster
Shelburn Thomas, joiner
Sherlock George, gov. workhouse
Skerritt Samuel, mason
Smith William, tailor
South Joseph, miller
Turner Jonathan, gent
Turner Louisa, ladies' school
Vickers William, painter
White John, gunsmith & p. clerk
White George, boat owner
Widnall George, glazier, &c.

Willis Edward, bricklayer
Wilson, Mr. James
Wright, Mrs. Mary

Farmers.
Bestall Wm
Edlington J
Fish Thos
Grimes Henry
Jackson Dd
Pate John
Skelton Wm
Tasker Geo
Taylor Abm
Taylor Wm
Temporal John
West Wm

Blacksmiths.
Hall Wm.
Ragg John
Watson Wm

Maltsters.
Beedham Bk
Cooling Thos
Wright John

Shoemakers.
Bagley Jph
Brown Samuel
Curtis Thomas
Johnson David
Kirkus Thomas

Shopkeepers.
Cadman Wm
Good Wm
Harston Rd
Hewes Wm
Newton Thos
Woodcock Jas
Woolley H. and chandler

Publicans.
Arnold Mtw
Battle Wm
Bradberry W
Fearnehough T
Marriot Wm.

SOUTH COLLINGHAM.

Anderson John, gent
Bailey William, grocer
Brown Thomas, tailor
Chappell Sandy, gent. Lodge
Clayworth John, vict
Gray John, tailor
Greenberry Rt. miller & beerhs
Guilford Miss Ann and Sisters
Hall Samuel, blacksmith
Hall Willoughby, schoolmaster
Harrison William, gardener
Lee Lewis, ropemaker
Lewis John, shoemaker
Long Rt. Furniss, grazier
Mayor Rev. Joseph, rector
Milnes Robert, grazier
Norris William, tailor
Pilgrim John, shoemaker

Priestley William, joiner
Proctor Michael, grocer
Ragg John, blacksmith
Stepnall John, blacksmith
Stocks John, blacksmith, Brough
Tinley Daniel, miller and baker
Wells Joseph, shoemaker
Whittall John, excise officer
Woolley Thos. Smith, land agent
  and valuer

Farmers.
Marked † live at Brough, and ‡
  at Dernethorpe.
Chaster Chtte   Hardy Hosea
Coles Thos   Hatfield John
†Colton John   Hewson Wm
‡Eastgate Mary ‡Holmes Thos

Hopkinson W. Oldham Wm
  and brickmkr ‡Paling Geo
†Horner Edw   ‡Paling Wm
‡Horner Edm   Priestley Wm
†Horner Martha†Quibell Jph
Hunt Jph   Skellett Thos
Hutchinson J   Taylor Jas
Johnson Chpr   ‡White Benj
Lilley Matth
  A *coach* to Gainsborough and
Newark, daily. *Letters* are re-
ceived by a horse post.
  Carriers.—Joseph Grosse to
Gainsborough, Mon. and to New-
ark, Wed. and Sat. John Bailey,
to Newark, Wed. and Sat. and to
Lincoln, Fri.

COTHAM, is a small village and parish on the east bank of
the Devon, 4 miles S. of Newark. It contains only 74 inhabitants and 1200 acres of land, all belonging to the Duke of Portland, who is also patron of the *church*, which is dedicated to
St. Michael, and was partly rebuilt, and new pewed in 1831,
The living is a curacy valued in the King's books at £7. 18s.
and is now enjoyed by the Rev. E. Otter, for whom the Rev.
J. E. S. Hutchinson officiates. This place was long the seat of
the knightly families of Leek and Markham, but it is now
divided into three *farms*, occupied by John Booth, Thos. Rose,
and the executors of the late John Fisher.

ELSTON, 5 miles S. S. W. of Newark, is a straggling village
and parish, containing 552 inhabitants and 1500 acres of land,
forming two MANORS, distinguished by the names of *Church-
parish* and *Chapel-parish*, from the latter having a small ancient
chapel of ease annexed to the vicarage of East Stoke. Sir R.
H. Bromley is lord and principal owner of the latter; and Wm
Brown Darwin, Esq. of the former manor, in which he has just
rebuilt, upon a handsome and commodious scale, his ancient
family residence, called Elston Hall. The *church* is a neat
edifice dedicated to All Saints. The rectory, valued in the
King's books, at £9. 8s. 9d, is in the gift of W. B. Darwin,
Esq., and incumbency, of the Rev. J. Holt, M.A. The tithes
were all commuted for allotments of land in 1798. An *hospital*
here, in which 4 poor widows have each 1s. per week, is about
to be rebuilt, and was founded in 1722 by Ann Darwin. *The
school*, which is endowed with land, &c. worth £12. per annum,
was rebuilt by the late Mr. Darwin, in 1812. It was founded
by Lawrence Pendleton, in 1650, and endowed with £100. by
Eliz. Darwin, in 1784. The poor have 6s. yearly out of a public house from the bequest of Mary Piper, in 1788, and the

interest of £200. left in 1798, and 1820, by Eliz. and John Summer. They have also the *Poor's Close*, which in 1801, was given in Exchange for several small parcels of land, left in 1715, and 1764, by the Bristow and Darwin families. It contains 3A. 2R. 25P. and lets for £12 a-year. In the village is a *Methodist Chapel*, erected in 1815, and a *Sick Club*, which holds its feast on the Monday after June 21st. Those marked † in the following directory reside in the Chapel-parish.

Darwin Wm. Brown, Esq. Elston Hall
†Bell Thos. vict
Brown Jph. shoemkr
Elston Jn. vict
Fisher Jn. bsmith
Fryer Mk. butcher
†Greasley Rd. vict
Green Sar. shopr
Hardstaff J shopr
Harrison Rev. Henry M.A. curate
Hickman S. shoemkr
†Key Hy. shopr
Long John, schoolr
†Mills G. bricklr
†Moss Wm. saddler
Parkinson J. surgeon
†Pickering Wm. blksmith & p. clerk
†Rose Nat. baker
†Rowbotham T. miller
Rowbotham W. vict
†Spowage W. shoemr
Turner J. joiner
†Walker Rd. tailor
†Ward J. wheelgt
Watson J. chair mkr
†Whitworth R. buchr
Whitworth W. joiner
Farmers.
Fryer John
†Gretton Wm
†Harrap Rd
†Harvey Edw
Hickerby Jph
Long J. Lodge
Read Jas
†Read Wm.
Smith John
†Spafford Wm
Spafford John
†Taylor John
†Ward Anthy
Carrier.
J. Hardstaff to Newark.

FARNDON parish has a well-built village on the Trent, 2 miles W. S. W. of Newark, and contains 570 inhabitants, and about 1800 acres of land. It was a Berue of Newark and of the Bishop of Lincoln's fee. The Duke of Newcastle is lord of the manor, but owns only a small portion of the land. The church is dedicated to St. Peter, and is in the appropriation and patronage of its own *prebendary* in Lincoln Cathedral. The vicarage has the church of Balderton annexed to it, and is valued in the King's books at £6. 13s. 4d. The Rev. Fdk. Apthorpe is the incumbent. Both the great and small tithes were commuted for allotments of land at the enclosure in 1768. The *feast* is on the Sunday after St. Peter's day. Ten poor children are educated from the rents of two cottages left by Mrs. Draper. The poor have three benefactions: viz. a house and close let for £9. 3s. and left by *Mrs. Moore.* 1A. 3R. of land left by the Rev. M. Alt; and £100. left in 1771, by Mr. Hempsall, and now vested in the North Turnpike at 5 per cent.

Apthorpe Rev. W. H.
Atheis Geo. wharfinger & coal mert
Barnes Wm. bricklr
Barth Capt. Jacob
Beckett G. shoemkr
Beighton J. glazier
Birkett John, vict
Birkett Wm. tailor
Brockton Wm. gent
Brooksby Fras. gent
Buck Edw. gent
Cartledge Geo. beer hs. Markham bdg
Chettle J. butcher
Chettle Mrs. Mary
Chettle Wm. gent
Coddington Geo. blk.-smith & shopr
Faulkes B. shoemkr
Faulkes Rd. p. clerk

Fisher John, tailor
Franke Chas. miller
Hayes J. blacking mfr
Hilton Jas. gent
Johnson Eliz. shopr
Kirk Wm. miller
Lamb Mrs. Cath
Lee John, wheelgt
Lee Rd. smith
Manchester G. shoemr
Marriott J. boatnr
Mettam Capt. Thos
Newton John, joiner

Pearson J. shoemr
Pearson W. boatnr
Pettinor J. shoemr
Radford J. shoemr
Sampey Miss Mary
Sharpe Mrs. Ann
Sharpe W. schoolr
Spiek Thos. wheelgt
Stansall T. joiner
Stevens T. shoemr
Swann Wm. knitting
   worsted manfr
Welburn Mrs. Eliz

Farmers.
Butler Dinah
Chettle William
Horner Edmund
Kirk William
Parker Thomas
Pattinson William
Sharpe Thomas
Walker Matthew
Walstow Thomas
Ward Ann

GIRTON is a small village and parish on the east bank of the Trent, 9 miles N. by E. of Newark. It has 183 inhabitants, and 1000 acres of land, belonging to several proprietors. The *church* is a humble edifice, and is annexed to the vicarage of South Scarle, being in the same patronage and appropriation. See also Spalford p. 628.

Gee John, fisherman
Gee Wm. fisherman
Holland Edw. vict. & shopr
Howard Isaac, gentleman
Minnitt Wm. gentleman
Selby Wm. gentleman

Farmers.
Checkley Thos
Harrison Wm
Hunt John
Minnitt Thos
Proctor Geo
Thompson Jas

Thompson Jph
Turner Saml
Carrier.
Jph. Checkley
  to Newark,
  Wed. 6 mg.

HAWTON, on the river Devon, 2 miles S. S. W. of Newark, is a small but pleasant village and parish, comprising 258 inhabitants, and about 2000 acres of land, mostly belonging to Rt. Holden, Esq., of Nuthall Temple, but the Dukes of Newcastle and Portland have small estates here, and the latter is lord of the *manor*, which was *soc* to Newark, to which this parish adjoins near the extensive linen manufactory called *Hawton Mills*. The *church* is an handsome structure dedicated to All Saints, and has some ancient monuments of the Molyneaux family. Its stalls are rich in decorations of carving. The rectory, valued in the King's books at £17. 13s. 4d, is in the gift of Roger Newdigate, Esq., and has a neat parsonage house, and 60 acres of glebe.

Helps Rev. Wm. rector
Porter Thos. farmer
Rimington Rd. farmer

Sampey John, farmer, Grange
Sampey Wm. farmer
Seales Geo. & Sons, linen mfrs

LANGFORD, is a straggling but picturesque village, upon an eminence above the Trent marsh, 4 miles N. N. E. of Newark, comprehending within its parish, 125 inhabitants, and

3 a

nearly 2000 acres of land. *Langford House* a handsome modern mansion near the village, is the residence of Slingsby Duncombe, Esq., who in 1832 sold the extensive estates of Langford and Winthorpe, to Lord Middleton. The church is a perpetual curacy in the appropriation and patronage of Trinity College, Cambridge. The Rev. Thos. Blades is the incumbent, and has about 30 acres of glebe purchased with Queen Anne's Bounty. The following are the resident FARMERS :—John Arnold, Wm. Birkett, Thos. Bonifant, Rt. Bradbury, Jph. Branston, Saml. Brown, Wm. Else, John Kirkham, Thomas Ringrose, Thomas Roberts, Sarah Turner, Thomas & Wm. Weightman.

MERING, on the Trent bank, near Girton, 8 miles N. of Newark, is an extra-parochial farm of 460 acres of low marshy grazing land, occupied by Elizabeth Catliffe, and belonging to Chas. Chaplin, Esq,, Capt. C. Neville, and some others. It anciently gave name to a resident family, who gave part of it to the priories of Lenton and Radford.

SOUTH SCARLE, is a pleasant village, including within its parish the township of Beesthorp, and distant 7 miles N. N. E. of Newark. Each township contains about 1100 acres, and belongs to a number of freeholders and copyholders, but the Duke of Newcastle is lord of the *Manor of Morland*, which compromises this parish and Girton, and is held by his Grace, of the Crown, for the annual rent of £23. 4s. 5¾d. The *church*, dedicated to St. Helen, is a vicarage, valued in the King's books at £5. 2s. 6d, and is in the patronage and appropriation of its own *prebendary* in Lincoln Cathedral. The Rev. Henry Gordon is the present vicar, and has 22 acres of glebe purchased with Queen Anne's Bounty. A Methodist chapel was built here in 1829. The poor have an annuity of 26s. 8d. out of Griffin-bridge Close, and the interest of £20. left in 1754, by Edward Ward.

BESTHORP is a good village near the Fleet river, 2 miles W. N. W. of South Scarle. It contains the vicarage house, and had formerly a Quakers' Meeting-house and a Chapel of Ease. The latter, in 1734, was converted into a *school*, with a dwelling for the master, who teaches 8 free scholars, in consideration of £5. a-year, left by Geo. Carver, in 1709, and the interest of £91. 7s. left in 1824, by Wm. Wilson. The Methodists built a chapel here in 1832. The Corporation of Newark, John Milnes, W. E. Tallents, Esq., and some others have estates in the township. The *feast* is on the Sunday after Old Michaelmas.

SCARLE (SOUTH).
Barnsdall Geo. wheelwright
Dakin Fredk. corn miller
Dakin John, butcher
Hunt Mrs. Sarah
Pennington Samuel, butcher
Spooner Rev. Rt. Denny Rix
Tenney Mrs. Mary
Woodroffe Jph. shoemaker

Farmers.
Banks John
Brown Wm.
Clayworth Edw. Pate John
Cook John
Dakin Robert, Saunders Wm.
Doncaster C.
BESTHORP.
Bell John, butcher
Booth William, shopkeeper
Cook John, joiner
Crumpton Geo. cattle dealer
Elliott George, cow leech
Gorden Rev. Hy. vicar
Hammond Wm. corn miller
Hitchin John, joiner
Hunt Philip, gent
Naylor Mrs. Stella

Holmes George
Jackson Edw.

Pratt Thomas

Walton Carter

Pawson Rd. vict. & grocer
Shipley Jph. schoolmaster
Smalley Aukland, blacksmith
Spittlehouse Thos. bricklayer
Talbot Rd. tailor
Wells John, shoemaker
Williamson Chas. tailor
Withers Wm. beerhouse
Woodroffe Wm. shomaker
Farmers:
Hanson Wm.   Palian Martin
Hopkinson W.   Vessey John
Howitt Wm.   Vessey Jph.
Hunt John   Walker Thos.
Lee Richard   Wilson John
Carrier, Wm. Spawton, to New-
   ark, Wed. 6 mg. A *Coach* to
   Newark & Gainsbro' daily

SHELTON village and parish on the west bank of the Smite, 7 miles S. by W. of Newark, has only 113 inhabitants, and 840 acres of land, mostly belonging to Major Robert Hall, the lord of the manor, who resides in the *hall,* a neat modern mansion. The *church* is a small edifice dedicated to St. Mary, and was partly rebuilt and new pewed in 1831, at the cost of £400. The *rectory,* valued in the King's books at £6. 14s. 4¼d, is in the gift of the Rev. Robt. Ffarmerie, and incumbency, of the Rev. John Ince Maltby, who has forty acres of glebe. The principal residents are George Brett, *blacksmith,* and Edward Warren, *wheelwright.* The poor have £9. per annum, from 4 acres of land at Aslacton, purchased with £90. left 1744, by Geo. Burghope.

SIBTHORPE village and parish lies on the Cardike, 7 miles S. S. W. of Newark, and was once a place of importance, having a *College* founded by Geffrey le Scroop in the reign of Edward II. The lordship contains of 900 acres, and 141 inhabitants, and is all the property of the Duke of Portland, who has also the patronage of the perpetual curacy which is now enjoyed by the rector of Shelton. The church is dedicated to St. Peter, and has some ancient tombs of the Burnell family, who had a large mansion here, of which nothing now remains. The father of *Secker,* Archbishop of Canterbury, was born here. The feast is on the Sunday after Old Michaelmas. The principal *residents* are Mrs. Lee, Eliz. Faulkes, Thos. Faulkes, Rd. Hall, Jn. Kenyon, and Rn. Lee, farmers; Wm. Bradley, shoe-mkr; Jn. Fisher and M. Richmond, shoprs; Wm. Hollingwith baker.

STAUNTON is a small village picturesquely situated *in the vale of Belvoir,* near the point where the three counties of Nottingham, Leicester, and Lincoln unite, 7 miles S. by E. of Newark, and near the source of the river Devon. Its parish

includes part of the hamlet of Alverton, and the chapelry of
Flawborough, and has now united with it the parish of Kilvington. The *lordship* of *Staunton* has 93 inhabitants, and
1300 acres of land, which was enclosed in 1760. It has been
the sole property of a family of its own name from the time of
the Saxons, and one of them, *Sir Mauger Staunton*, successfully defended Belvoir Castle against William the Conqueror,
"and there made his composition and contract for his lands,
and had the strongest fortress therein, ever since called by his
name 'Staunton's Tower.'" Job. Staunton Charlton, Esq., the
last male heir of this ancient family died in 1777, after which,
this lordship was possessed by his two maiden daughters, the
survivor of whom died in 1807, and left her estates here and in
Yorkshire, to her second cousin, Elizabeth, wife of the Rev.
John Apinshaw, L.L.D., on condition that they should take
the name and bear the arms of Staunton only, so that this gentleman is now the Rev. Dr. Staunton, and is not only owner
and lord of the manor, but also patron and incumbent of the
rectory, which is valued in the King's books at £16. 13s. 11½d.
He resides in the HALL, a large and commodious mansion with
beautiful gardens and pleasure grounds, situated near the
CHURCH, which is dedicated to St. Mary, and has many antique
monuments of the Stauntons. The poor have 26s. yearly, from
the bequest of Elizabeth Sherwin, in 1725. The FEAST at
Staunton, Alverton, and Kilvington, is on the Sunday after
Sep. 19th, and at Flawborough, on the Sunday after St. Peter's
day. The residents of Staunton are Dr. Staunton, Miss Jane
Mounsey, Hy. Barker, smith and victualler; Wm. Rose,
joiner; Wm. Woolfit, tailor; and Rd. Bradley, Geo. Brewster, John Gurnell, Thos. Martin, Hy. Shepherd, Wm. Stevenson, and John White, *farmers*.

ALVERTON township is mostly in Kilvington parish, and contains only 16 inhabitants, and about 400 acres of land, 8 miles
S. by E. of Newark. It was enclosed in 1806, when 60 acres
were allotted in lieu of tithes. The rest belongs to the Duke
of Portland, but Dr. Staunton is lord of the manor. Its two
farmers are Robert Cross and Charles Neale.

FLAWBOROUGH, township and chapelry has 80 inhabitants, and
900 acres of land, 8 miles S. of Newark; and is the property of
the Duke of Newcastle. It is partly in the parish of Orston,
and formerly paid a small modus in lieu of tithes to that parish,
and another to Shelton, but the rector of Staunton now claims
and retains the whole of the tithes, though his portion by an ancient agreement was limited to £60 a year. He occasionally
performs divine service in the ancient chapel. At the foot of
the eminence on which the village stands, is the small hamlet
of DALINGTON. The principal occupants of the chapelry are
Robt. Fukes, *shoemaker*, Wm. Fukes, *joiner*, and Cath. Birkett, Jno. Bland, Thos. Faulkes, Rd. Jackson, Livi Smith,
and Samuel Wilson, *farmers*.

KILVINGTON, 7¼ miles S. of Newark, is a hamlet and parish, with only 45 inhabitants and 650 acres of land, of which 142 were allotted for the tithes at the enclosure in 1750. The Rev. Dr. Staunton is the principal owner, lord of the manor, and patron and incumbent of the *rectory*, which is valued in the King's books at £6. 12s. 1d., and was consolidated with the rectory of Staunton, in 1826, when the church here was reduced to a roofless ruin, and seat-room provided for the inhabitants in the neighbouring church of Staunton. The principal residents are, Thos. Allin, *corn miller;* Wm. Marshall and Wm. Wilson, *farmers*, and Thomas Allin, *carrier* to Newark,

EAST STOKE is a very pleasant village on the south bank of the Trent, and upon the Roman fosseway, 4 miles S.W. by W. of Newark. It contains 320 inhabitants and 1200 acres of land, exclusive of Newark Castle Liberty, which forms a part of its township.—(See p. 608.) Its parochial jurisdiction includes Elston chapel,—(See p. 631,) and the parochial chapelries of Coddington and Syerston. Sir Robt. Howe Bromley, Bart., is principal owner, and lord of the manor of East Stoke, and resides in the HALL, a handsome mansion with picturesque pleasure grounds which overlook the vale of the Trent. Upon a rising ground in front of the hall, stands the *church*, which is dedicated to St. Oswald, and has a prebendal stall in Lincoln cathedral, occupied by the Chancellor of that church, who has the appropriation of the rectorial tithes, and also the patronage of the vicarage, which is valued in the King's books at £8. 13s., and is now enjoyed by the Rev. William Bartlett. The tithes here were commuted at the enclosure, for about 250 acres. There was anciently an *hospital* here dedicated to St. Leonard, for a master, chaplain, brethren, and sick persons. *John Lightfoot, D.D.*, a celebrated Hebrician was born here in 1602, and died in 1675. STOKEFIELD, as it is called, was the scene of the BATTLE between Henry VII., and the army under the Earl of Lincoln, who had espoused the cause of the impostor Lambeth Simnel, the pretended Earl of Warwick, and claimant of the crown. This bloody conflict occurred in June, 1487, and after three hours hard fighting, the whole rebel line was broken, and all the chieftains slain. The total slaughter of both armies amounted to 7000 men. Several historians say, that *Lord Lovel*, one of the insurgents, was drowned in attempting to cross the Trent, but Bacon says "another report leaves him not there, but that he lived long after in a cave or vault." Gough in his additions to Camden says, that in pulling down the house of Minster Lovel, in Oxfordshire, which belonged to Lord Lovel, there was found in a vault, the body of a man, in rich clothes, seated in a chair, with a table and mass book before him. The body was entire when found, but upon admission of the air, it soon fell into dust. From this, Mr. Gough concludes, that after the battle of Stoke field, Lord Lovel retired to this vault, where he perished, either through treachery or some accident which befel his servant, or at least those intrusted with the secret of his retreat. It is extremely probable, from the coincidence of name and other circumstances, that this event formed the ground work of Miss Clara Reeve's elegant romance of the "Old English Baron." Stoke *feast* is on the first Monday in June. The poor have £2. 10s. yearly, out of land belonging to the Hall family, left by an unknown donor.

CODDINGTON is a small village and parochial chapelry, distant 6½ miles N.E. of East Stoke, and 2½ E. of Newark, on the Sleaford road. It contains 434 inhabitants, and 1500 acres of land, of which 213 acres were allotted at the enclosure in lieu of tithes to the vicar and prebendary of East Stoke, to which parish the church, dedicated to all Saints, is annexed. The Duke of Newcastle is lord of the manor, but the land belongs to a number of proprietors. A Methodist chapel was built here in 1827. *Joseph Birch*, in 1738, left to the poor a farm of 98A. 2R. 8P., now let for £140 per annum, out of which the schoolmaster has 4s. per week for teaching 12 free scholars, and the rest is distributed amongst the poor inhabitants. They have also £2 yearly out of Beacon field, left by Mr. Bell, and the interest of £20 left in 1809, by Jacob Ordoyno.

SYERSTON, another parochial chapelry annexed to the vicarage of East Stoke, has a small village 6 miles S.W. of Newark, and contains 138 inhabitants and 800 acres of land, enclosed in 1794, when allotments were made for the tithes, to the vicar and prebendary of Stoke. George Fillingham, Esq., of *Syerston Hall*, a neat modern brick mansion, is lord of the manor, and owner of a great part of the soil. The *church* is a small fabric, 1½ mile S. of Stoke. The *feast* is on the Sunday after Lammas.

STOKE (EAST).
Bromley Sir R. Howe, Bart. Stoke-hall
Bonsor W. shoemaker
Bramley Wm. smith
Chester Wm. ground bailiff
Cowlishaw Wm. basket maker
Cuckson J. tailor
Cupit Wm. tailor
Gee F. basket maker
Gilbert Rd. miller
Hall Mrs. Eliz.
Hutchinson Rev. J. Entwistle Scholes, M.A. curate
Lee Fras. butcher
Lee Wm. miller
Pacey John, wheelgt
Pacey Sarah, vict
Rawson J. basket mkr
Shephard J. shoemkr
Wakefield Geo. gent

Farmers.
Bennett Hannah
Brockton John
Padgett Thomas
Spafford Dorothy
Taylor Thos.
Weightman James

CODDINGTON.
Asling Dd. tailor
Atter John, shoemkr
Barfoot Oliver, vict
Beaumont Edward, wheelwright
Birkett Mr. John
Blackburn Wm. vict
Carby Wm. shopkr
Ellis John, shoemker
Godfrey T. Spraggon, Esq. Baconfield-hse,
Grocock S. bricklayer & shopkeeper
Hall John, joiner
Hough W. blacksmith
Hudson Ji W. limeburner
Jalland Charles, gent.
Johnson E. miller
Lee William, miller
Marshall Jas. vict.
Pilgrim J. blacksmith
Robinson Mr. George
Taylor John. tailor
Weightman W butcher

Farmers.	Ordoyno Garratt	Challand H. victualler
Ashwell Michael	Seargill James	Cawley Rev. Edward
Booth W. & W.	Seagrave John	Fillingham Miss Ann
Clayton John	Stokes William	Gilby Edmund Gent.
Daybell William	Young John	Jackson Rd. farmer
Fearfield Thomas	SYERSTON.	Johnson S. gardener
Hilton William	Fillingham Geo. Esq.	Savage T. shoemaker
Jalland John	Syerstone Hall.	Silkston M. shopkr
Kirkland John	Bramley, W. blcksth	Wade Ths. joiner

THORNEY is a small village 8 miles E. of Tuxford, and 14 miles N. by E. of Newark. Its parish forms part of that tongue of land which stretches into Lincolnshire. It comprises the three townships of Thorney, Broadholme, and Wigsley, in which are 308 inhabitants and nearly 4000 acres of land, of which 300 acres are in woods, and a great part of the rest was formerly low and swampy moors, but it is now drained and in high cultivation. The manor of Thorney has long been possessed by the Nevill family, and now belongs to Captain Christopher Nevill, who resides in the Hall, a neat modern mansion, near the church, which is dedicated to St. Helen, and contains some ancient monuments of his family. He is also the impropriator, and patron of the vicarage, which is valued in the King's books at £4. 7s. 6d., and is now enjoyed by the Rev. Christopher Nevill, jun. The benefice has 18 acres of land purchased with Queen Anne's Bounty. At DINSEY NOOK, on the Lincoln and Dunham road, 1 mile N. of Thorney, is a public-house, occupied by John Clark, where a *hiring of servants* is held yearly about May-Day. Near it is the post on which Thomas Otter was hung in chains, for murdering his wife in 1806. The farmers of Thorney are, Dd. Balflour, John Ray Beckitt, Edw. Cammack, Wm. Drakard, Rd. Hill, Thos. Howitt, Wm. Hudson, Wm. Radley, Saml. Roberts, and Wm. Thompson.

BROADHOLME, 3 miles E. of Thorney, is a scattered hamlet with 67 inhabitants, and had formerly a Præmonstratensian *Nunnery*, which was founded in the reign of Stephen, by Agnes de Camville, wife of Peter Gousla, and possessed at its dissolution, a yearly revenue of £16. 5s. 2d. The township contains 410 acres, more than half of which belongs to Thomas Redgate, Esq., the lord of the manor, which at the enclosure, had allotted to it 71 acres of Saxelby Common, the rest of which is in Lincolnshire. The residents are Charles Stacey, gent ; and Matthew Cartman, William Cartwright, John Culley, Nathan Giles, and John Rogers, farmers.

WIGSLEY, or *Wiggesley*, is a hamlet and township, 1½ mile S. of Thorney, containing 86 inhabitants and about 1000 acres of land, which was enclosed in 1814, and allotments made in lieu of the tithes. It was *soc* to Newark, and part of it was given to St. Katherine's priory at Lincoln. The poor have 20s.

yearly, out of land left by Thomas Unwin, in 1719. The principal residents are Mrs. Ann Howard; William Harrison, *beerseller;* George Peck, *blacksmith;* and Thomas Bottomley; John Gibson, Joseph Heald, Edward Howard; Sampson Howard, and William Welch, *farmers.*

THORPE-by-NEWARK is a village and parish with only 105 inhabitants and 697 acres of land; 3¼ miles S.W. of Newark. About 180 acres of common land was enclosed 40 years ago, and exonerated from tithes, but all the rest still remains titha- ble. Sir Robert Howe Bromley is the principal owner and lord of the manor. The *church* dedicated to St. Lawrence, is a small fabric upon an eminence, and has 40 acres of glebe. The *rectory* valued in the King's books at £8, is in the patron- age of the Lord Chancellor, and the Rev. John Guthrie is the incumbent, for whom the Rev. William Barry officiates. The occupants are John Dixon, parish clerk; Edward Hart, shoemaker; and George Atheis, Thomas Fryer, John James, William Smith, and John Tomlin, *farmers.*

WINTHORPE is a picturesque and well-built village, upon a richly wooded eminence above the Trent, 3 miles N. E. by N. of Newark. Its parish includes 228 inhabitants, and 635 acres of land, which was exonerated from tithe at the inclosure in 1757, by an allotment of 82 acres. Slingsby Duncombe, Esq., was the principal owner, but he has lately sold his exten- sive estates here and at Langford, to Lord Middleton. The Duke of Newcastle is lord of the manor, which was mostly *soc* to Newark. WINTHORPE HALL which was the seat of the late Roger Pocklington, Esq., and owes all its present beauties to that gentleman, is now *unoccupied.* It is an elegant mansion of two stories on a rustic basement. The plantations and grounds are very extensive, and on a gentle rise, which com- mands a charming prospect, particularly over the vale of Bel- voir, there is an octagonal *temple* with a table made out of part of the wrecks of the Spanish floating batteries destroyed in the memorable attack on Gibratar. The *church* stands in the highest part of the village, and is dedicated to All Saints. It was rebuilt of brick in 1778 and 1779, except the south wall. The *rectory* is valued in the King's books at £7. 11s. 0¼d, and the Rev. Robert Rastall is both incumbent and patron. In 1616, *Thos. Brewer* left to the poor of Winthorpe, £20, "and his new white house in the village, with two oxgangs of land." This house and land were exchanged at the enclosure in 1778, for five tenements and gardens occupied by poor families, and 21 acres of land (including the great Poor's Close), let for £48. per annum, of which £10. is paid to the schoolmaster for 12 free scholars, and the residue is distributed in coals and money to the poor parishioners. In the school garden is a fine elm tree, the trunk of which is 10 yards in circumference. The parish feast is on the last Sunday in June.

Astill John. victualler
Beale Mr. Richard
Beastall John, farmer
Beaumont G. L. land
  agent & valuer
Bellamy W. shoemkr
Camamile, J whlwrght

Cawthan T. tailor
Fox Mrs,
Gamble Geo. miller
Hampson Job, vict.
Holt Mrs. Mary,
Hyde Mrs. Sarah,

Marfleet J. maltster,
  Grove House
Milton John, Gent.
North W schoolmaster
Rastall Rev. Rt.
Smith James, farmer
Wright J. wheelwright

RUSHCLIFFE HUNDRED

Is divided into two divisions, (North and South,) and contains 26 parishes, belonging ecclesiastically to the *deanery of Bingham*, and of which the following is an enumeration, showing the number of inhabitants in each in 1801, 1821, and 1831, and the annual value of the lands and buildings as assessed for the property tax in 1815.

POPULATION OF RUSHCLIFFE HUNDRED.

Those marked * are in the *North*, and the rest in the *South* division.

ANN. VAL. £	PARISHES	POPULATION IN 1801	1821	1831	ANN. VAL. £	PARISHES	POPULATION IN 1801	1821	1831
2047	*Barton-in-Fabis	232	403	379	1677	*Ratcliffe-on-Soar	156	168	177
1924	*Bradmore	325	410	369	2072	*Rempston	324	368	398
5452	*Bridgeford (West)†	332	312	338	4195	Ruddington	868	1133	1438
2604	*Bunney	359	395	371	2081	Stanford-on-Soar	110	160	129
2723	Clifton	381	470	405	976	*Stanton-on-Wolds	98	119	125
1710	Costock	294	341	412	4034	Sutton Bonnington	790	903	1136
1044	*Edwalton	126	119	130	947	Thorpe-in-Glebis	20	33	39
2525	Gotham	475	625	748	1493	*Thrumpton	121	109	132
1453	*Keyworth	325	464	552	2123	Widmerpool	206	229	180
2011	Kingston-on-Soar	152	166	175	3005	*Wilford	478	569	602
2865	Leake (East)	608	783	975	2691	Willoughby	355	450	465
1787	Leake (West)	171	911	203	1626	Wysall	260	287	271
2196	Normanton-on-Soar	265	326	365					
4902	*Plumptre‡	373	579	605	64433	Total	8163	10207	12009

† West Bridgeford includes *Gamston* hamlet.

‡ Plumptre includes *Clipston* and *Normanton-on-the-Wolds*.

It is the extreme south-western division of the county, bounded on the north by the Trent, on the east by Bingham hundred, and on the south and west by Leicestershire. It is about ten miles in length and breadth, and is intersected by the turnpikes from Nottingham to Leicester and Melton Mowbray, and watered by the Trent and the Soar, and several of their tributary streams. Its surface is in many places broken into bold swells and mountainous ridges called the *Wolds*, but it is generally a fertile district, having been much improved by the modern systems of cultivation, (see p. 43.) Its name is perhaps derived from some rushy hill or bank, on which the wapentake or hundred court was anciently held, but it now comprehends that district which in Domesday Book is called *Plumptre hundred.*

BARTON-IN-FABIS, or *Barton-in the-Beans*, is a well built village on the south side of the Trent, at the point where that river first enters Nottinghamshire, after receiving the Erwash, 5 miles S. W. of Nottingham. Its parish comprises 1540 acres, and was exonerated from tithes at the enclosure in 1759, by an allotment of 150 acres, in addition to 65 acres of old glebe, and three acres of church land. Sir Robert Clifton is lord of the manor, which was of the fee of Ralph Fitzhubert, except that portion which is called *Gerhodthorp*, and was of the Peverel fee, of which it was held by Gerbod de Eschaud, who annexed it to Clifton rectory, which now receives a yearly modus of £25 from this parish. On the south side of the village is that lofty eminence called *Brents hill*, on which are the remains of a *Roman camp*, (see p. 18,) and in the vicarage farm yard there is now a Roman pavement. The *church* is dedicated to St. George, and has several monuments of the Sacheverel family. The rectory, valued in the King's books at £19. 13s. 9d. is in the patronage of the Archbishop of York, and incumbency of the Rev. F. Wintour, who pays for the education of 8 poor children. The interest of £20 poor's money is distributed every 3 or 4 years. The residents are the Rev. Fitzgerald Wintour, rector; Charlotte Bamford, vict.; John Barrow, schoolmaster; Saml. Cross, shopkeeper; John Gunn, joiner; Thos. Oliver, blacksmith; Thos. Witby, tailor; Thos. Wright, shoemaker; and Thos. Redfern, sen. and jun., Rd. Stephenson, (& maltster,) Gervase Thorpe, Dorothy and Thos. Wilson, John Woodward, and John Wright, *farmers.*

BRIDGEFORD (WEST) is a pleasant and well built little village and parish, on the south side of the Trent, 1¼ mile S. by E. of Nottingham. The lordship contains 1078A. 1R. 15F. of land, all belonging to John Musters, Esq. except one estate, which is the property of Mr. Clifford Caunt. In Saxon times, the "famous Lady of Mercia built a fortification here, to repress the violence of the Danes who possessed Nottingham, and to obstruct their passage over the noble bridge which here crosses the Trent, (see p. 189 and 190.) The commodious *Bridge inn* stands partly in the parish of St. Mary's. The *church*, dedicated to St. Giles, is a fine ancient edifice, which appears to great advantage peeping above the trees that surround it. The benifice is a rectory, valued in the King's books at £16. 14s. 2d. J. Musters, Esq. is the patron, and the Rev. Edward Levitt Thoroton, the incumbent. The *school* here was built in 1802, by the Rev. Wm. Thompson, who endowed it with £912 stock, for the education of ten poor children of this parish and that of Colwick. West Bridgeford also partakes of Dame Frances Pierrepont's charity.

GAMSTON is a small village and township, in the Bingham hundred, and partly in Holme Pierrepont parish, 1 mile E.S.E. of West Bridgeford; and it contains the rectory house of this parish. The rectors of the two parishes having had many disputes in the division of the tithes of Gamston, obtained an Act of Parliament in 1809 for apportioning to each his share, (see page 499, where a further notice of this place will be found.)— Its farmers are John Lowe, Thos. Morris, Ann Parr, John Shipman, and Samuel Young. The inhabitants of WEST BRIDGEFORD are as follow : —

Billings Ralph, gent	Smith Mrs. Mgt. Bridgeford hs
Chapman Mary Ann, Bridge inn	*Farmers.*
Caunt Clifford, gent	Barnett John Julian Thos
Clark Mrs. Ann	Barwick John Morley Wm
Daykin John, brickmaker, &c.	Birch Wm Selby John
Franks Joseph, joiner	Clark Jph Singlehurst Wm
Parker Alex. schoolmaster	Ellis Geo Williamson Luke
Peatfield Rev. John, curate	Hearson Wm Willis ——
Singlehurst Edw. blacksmith	

BUNNEY or *Bunny*, is a straggling village under the wolds 7 miles S. of Nottingham, upon the Leicester road. Its parish has united with it the adjacent parish of Bradmore, and they together contain 2900 acres of land, of which Lord Rancliffe is lord, owner, and impropriator, but the rectorial tithes are included in the rent of the farms, and the vicarial tithes were exchanged for allotments of land at the enclosure in 1798. Bunney *church* is dedicated to St. Mary, and contains several monuments of the Parkyns family, who purchased these lordships in the reign of Elizabeth. In the chancel is a tomb to the memory of *Sir Thomas Parkyns, Bart.*, the famous wrestler, who died in 1741, aged 78. By the inscription we are informed that he new roofed the chancel, built the vault below, and erected this monument wrought out of a fine piece of marble by his chaplain ; that he studied physic for the benefit of his neighbours, and wrote the "Cornish Hug Wrestler." He is represented on one part of the monument in a posture ready for wrestling, and on another, he appears thrown by time, accompanied with a suitable stanza. The *vicarage* is valued in the King's books at £6. 14s, and has annexed to it the curacy of Bradmore, the

church at the latter place being long since destroyed by fire,
except the tower and spire, which still remain. The Rev. John
Tidy Beetham is the incumbent, and the Rt. Hon. George
Augustus Henry Anne Parkyns, Lord Rancliffe* is the patron,
and resides in his ancient family mansion of Bunney Park Hall,
a strong and heavy looking building close to the road side, with
a very heavy gateway in front, built in the ancient style of two
centuries ago. The park has a fine sheet of water and a long
avenue of lofty trees, with a profusion of bramble and other
cover for game. The *school* with four rooms for poor widows,
and apartments for the master, was built in 1700, by the before named Sir Thomas Parkyns. His mother, Lady Anne
Parkyns, endowed the building in 1709, with 23A. 3R. 3P. of
land at Thorpe-in-the-Clods, now let for £30. a-year, of which
£26. is paid to the master, and £2. is spent in two gowns and
petticoats for two poor women of Bunney and Bradmore alternately. The master has also 2A. 3R. 26P. of land which
was allotted to the school at the enclosure. The four alms
women have also from Lord Rancliffe a weekly allowance
of 6s. among them, out of the Newton estate, which consists of 24A. 0R. 20P. let for £37. a-year, and purchased
with £200. left in 1711, by Miss Anne Parkyns, for apprenticing poor boys of Bradmore, Bunney, and Costock, and
for other uses. Sir Thomas Parkyns also left two rent charges
of £5. 4s. each, for weekly distributions of bread amongst the
poor of Bunney and Bradmore, and those of the former parish
have 2A. 1R. 3P. of land, in that part of the Nottingham meadows
called the Rye Hills.

BRADMORE village stands on an eminence, 1 mile north
of Bunney, with which its parish is united, as has just been
seen. It has a Wesleyan chapel, erected in 1830.

BUNNEY.		
Lord Rancliffe, Bun-	Smith G. blacksmith	Harwood T. shoemkr
ney Park	Staton J. shoemaker	Henson Mary, vict.
Beetham. Rev. John	Stephens Wm. vict.	James Ed. smith
Bennet J. shoemaker	Wright T. land agent	Marriott W. shopkpr
Buxton J. tailor	*Farmers.*	Price C. butcher
Cross Wm. shoemaker	Attenborough George	Rowbotham T. joiner
Dexter Wm. shopkpr	Cocks John,	Walker G. shopkeeper
Harrison J. tailor	Marshall Joseph,	*Farmers.*
Hart Wm. shopkeeper	Peet John,	Attenborough Wm.
Henson Wm. joiner	Savidge John,	Glover John
Holmes C. butler	Wootton William,	Goodacre James
Parker J. gardener	BRADMORE.	Harwood John
Pickard W. brickmkr	Cheetham R. butcher	Lane John
Robinson J. schoolmtr	Dalby, H. shopkpr	Nixon John,
Rowbotham R. joiner	Dalby S. tailor	Peet J. (& malster)
Sharp J. wheelwright	Dalby Wm. miller	Voce Isaac; & Samuel
	Dutton J. shopkeeper	Walker Richard

* Lord Rancliffe is an Irish non-representative title, which was conferred on
the late Sir Thomas B. Parkyns in 1795.

CLIFTON village lies on a flat upon the south bank of the Trent, 4 miles S. W. of Nottingham, and contains a number of neat rural cottages finely shaded with trees, and also a few pretty villa looking residences. Near it is CLIFTON HALL, the beautiful seat of *Sir Robert Clifton, Bart.*, deeply embowered in groves of oak, fir, and elm, and commanding most extensive prospects over the Trent, the town of Nottingham, and the adjacent counties of Derbyshire and Leicestershire. At the end of a gravelled walk which leads along the river's bank is a handsome park gate that opens to the grounds and leads to *Clifton Grove*, a long avenue forming the approach to the house, about a mile in length, and broad enough for a dozen carriages to drive a breast. It is entirely covered with the green sward, and thickly sheltered with trees. Near the upper end of this avenue, the cliff nearly overhangs the Trent, whose silver stream meanders most pleasingly round it. "Here," we are told by Throsby, "tradition says, the *Clifton beauty*, who was debauched and murdered by her sweetheart, was hurled down the precipice into her watery grave;"—the place has long been held in great veneration by lovers, and the story is the subject of one of the earliest and longest poems of the late Henry Kirk White, who often visited the spot. (See page 179.) The *hall* which has been the seat of the Clifton family for many centuries, stands upon a rock of gypsum, curiously interspersed in many places with beautiful spar. It was formerly very antique but it is now much modernized, indeed in some parts almost rebuilt. The centre of the principal front is ornamented with ten handsome columns of the Doric order. The apartments are many of them superb, and contain some good family paintings. The gardens and pleasure grounds are extensive and tastefully laid out. The CHURCH, dedicated to St. Mary, stands close to the mansion, and though ancient, is yet in good preservation. Under it is the family vault, in which are deposited several generations, its entrance bearing the date of 1632.— Some of the table monuments with ancient knights, &c. are worth inspection, as well as the brasses, and the fragments of stained glass in the windows. The *rectory* is valued in the King's books at £21. 6s. 10½d., but it has now about 150 acres of glebe. The Rev. Henry Spencer Markham is the incumbent. Sir Robert Clifton is the patron, and likewise lord and owner of the whole parish, which contains 1500 acres of land, including the ancient hamlet of GLAPTON, that forms part of the village and is now almost lost in the general name of Clifton, its own name being seldom used except in the parish documents, in which the parish is sometimes called "Clifton-cum-Glapton." The common was enclosed in 1756. The *feast* is on the Sunday before Oct. 2nd. The ALMSHOUSE here for 6 poor women was founded in 1712, by George Wells, with an endowment of 2s. per week for each inmate, and an allowance of coals yearly, charged on the estate of Sir R. Clifton, who in 1828 was found to be indebted to the charity £193. 16s. which he has since invested in £226 three per cent. consols, in the name of himself and Wm. Lindley and Thomas Thorpe, in trust for the benefit of the almspeople. The interest of several small benefactions, amounting to £60, is distributed amongst the poor at Easter.

Clifton Sir R. Bart.	Stevenson J blacksmih	Deverill Benjamin
Bradley J. joiner	Vose John, tailor	Gray James
Brookes J. shoemaker	Woodcock Rt. clerk	Hopewell John
Hallam T. shoemaker	Wootton A. schmrs	Kirk ———
Langford Rd. baker	Wootton J shoemkr	Lambert Thomas
Markham Rev. Henry	Wootton J. joiner	Morris John
Morris Rd. shopkpr	*Farmer.*	Moss William
Smith Geo. shopkpr	Butler Thomas	Thorpe Thomas
Spencer W. schoolmtr		

COSTOCK, or *Cortlingstock*, is a village and parish on the Leicester road, 9¼ miles S. of Nottingham. It has 412 inhabitants, and nearly 2000 acres of land, of which 202 acres were allotted at the inclosure in 1761, in lieu of all the tithes except those paid on the Highfield estate, which contains 500 acres, and belongs to Lady Jane Parkyns. Lord Rancliffe owns nearly all the rest of the parish, and is lord of the manor, but S. B. Wild, Esq. has a neat mansion in the village. The *church* is a small edifice dedicated to St. Giles. The rectory, valued in the King's books at £7. 18s. 4d., is in the patronage and incumbency of the Rev. Wm. Beetham. A Wesleyan chapel was built here in 1828.

Attenborrow C..surgn	Woodroffe G. c. miller	*Bobbin Net Makers.*
Peetham Rev. Wm. Rector	Woodroffe Wm. Gent.	Bentley William
Crabtree John, Road Surveyor	*Farmers.*	Dring John
	Asher William	Litchfield Matthew
Hallam Wm. vict. & maltster	Cripwell Richard	*Blacksmiths.*
	Eggleston William	Blackett William
Harrison J. beerhouse	Hallam William	Tunnicliffe Robert
Hopkin G. parish clrk	Millington ———	*Shoemakers.*
King Thomas, joiner	Norman Ann	Fellows Thomas
Marshall J. hosiery agent	Oldershaw Thomas	Hall Thomas
	Oldershaw William	Sorby John
Milner T. butcher	Taylor Stephen	*Tailors.*
Tunnicliffe J. shopkpr	Woodroffe John, lime-burner	Daycock Joseph
Wild S. Bagnall, Esq.		Helmsley William

EDWALTON is a small secluded village and parish, near the Melton Mowbray road, 3¼ miles S.S.E. of Nottingham, containing 130 inhabitants, and about 800 acres of land, all belonging o John Musters, Esq. the lord of the manor and patron of the perpetual curacy, which has been augmented with Queen Anne's. Bounty. The church, dedicated to the Holyrood, is a humble edifice of brick, and in its burial ground is a stone to the me-mory of *Rebecca Freeland*, which says, " she drank good ale, good punch, and wine, and lived to the age of ninety-nine."— The Rev. Leonard Chapman is the incumbent. The *feast* is on the Sunday after Old St. Luke's. The inhabitants are George Smith, Esq., Wm. Hickling, shoemaker, Hy. Hancock, parish-clerk, Mrs. Mary Holmes; and Hannibal Day, John Holmes, Thos. Holmes, Benj. Howard, Matthew Martin, Edward Peet, and Wm. Sanders, *farmers.*

GOTHAM, 7 miles S.S.W. of Nottingham, is a considerable village bounded on the west by the lofty hills of the Wolds, and on the east by an extensive tract of low marshy land, which is often flooded by the numerous streams that roll from the heights after heavy rains. Its parish contains 748 inhabitants, and 2200 acres of land, enclosed in 1804, when 427a. 3r. 11p. was allotted to the rector in lieu of tithe, in addition to 43a. of Key-worth Common, allotted to him in the 38th of Geo. III. Earl Howe is the principal owner and lord of the manor. All the water near the village is strongly tainted with decomposed ve-getable matter, and with the gypsum that lies under the surface, so that the villagers are obliged to fetch their water for drinking and other purposes, from the summit of a hill distant half a mile to the north; but is said that the Earl intends to form a reservoir in the village, and to supply it with pure water from the same hill, by means of pipes. In 1829, his lordship erected a large *school* here, and supports the master, who has under tuition 130 free scholars. The indigent parishioners have the interest of £57, left by John Barrow and three other benefac-tors. The church, dedicated to St. Lawrence, was partly re-built about 50 years ago, but its tower and spire are now in a dangerous state of decay. The *rectory*, valued in the King's books at £19. 8s. 6½d., is now enjoyed by the Rev. John Kirkby, and is in the alternate patronage of the Duke of Portland, Earl Howe, and Lord St. John, the latter having the next turn.— The Wesleyan and Primitive Methodists have each a chapel here. Upon a hill about a mile south of the village is the CUCKOO BUSH, said to have been planted to commemorate a trick which the inhabitants put upon King John, and which no doubt gave rise to the fabulous and ridiculous stories "that were so much valued and cried up in Henry 8th's time," under the name of " the merry tales of the mad men of Gotham." Fuller says a custom prevailed, even among the earliest nations, of stigmatising some particular spot as remarkable for stupidity.— Amongst the Asiatics, Phrygia was considered as the Gotham of that day; Abdera, amongst the Thracians; and Bœotia among the Greeks. The book containing the merry tales of the " wise" Gothamites, is said to have been written by one

Andrew Borde, a facetious travelling quack of the 16th century, whose professional fooleries are supposed to have given rise to the name and occupation of a "Merry Andrew." The tales of this whimsical charlatan we shall leave for the grave chroniclers of the neighbouring parishes, who are very careful to remember what the good people of Gotham seem rather anxious should be forgotten, believing that the folly of their ancestors was like Edgar's madness, put on for the occasion, and that the cuckoo bush story originated from the following circumstance:—The inhabitants having prevented King John from crossing their meadows, he afterwards sent messengers to enquire into the cause of their rudeness; and to prevent any punishment from falling upon their heads, they thought of an expedient to turn away the royal displeasure. When the messengers arrived, they found some of the inhabitants endeavouring to drown an eel in a pond; some employed in dragging carts upon a large barn, in order to shade a wood from the sun; others were tumbling their cheeses down a hill, that they might find their way to Nottingham market; and some employed in hedging in a cuckoo, which had perched upon an old bush that stood on the site of the present one; in short they were all occupied in some ridiculous employment, which convinced the King's officers that they were a village of fools, and consequently unworthy of the King's notice. Fuller says, after alluding to these stories, "Gotham doth breed as *wise* people as any which causelessly laugh at their simplicity. Sure I am *Mr. Wm. de Gotham*, fifth master of Michael House, Cambridge, anno 1339, and twice chancellor of the University, was as grave a governor as that age did afford; and Gotham is a goodly lordship, where the ancient and right well respected family of *St. Andrew* have flourished some hundreds of years, till of late the name is extinct, and the lands divided betwixt female coheirs, matched unto very worshipful persons." From one of these coheiresses is descended the present Rt. Hon. St. Andrew St. John, BARON ST. JOHN, of Bletshoe, in Bedfordshire.

Archer Thomas. schoolmaster	*Bobbin Net* Cliff William
Bampton Joseph. corn miller	*Makers.* Coleman Wm.
Burton Mr. Philip	Barts J. & W. Cox William
Carver Thomas, blacksmith	Bush William Draper George
Helps Rev. Wm. curate	Harrison Geo. Helmsley Henry
Hemsley John, wheelwright	Holland T. J. & & malster
Hickland William, joiner	W. Julian Richard.
Maltby J. & Pepper T. tailors.	Maltby Samuel Parr William
Oliver John, baker	Redfern Wm. Redfern Jas.
Redfern Francis, maltster	Woolley Thos. Spencer Wm.
Redfern John, butcher	*Farmers.* Talbot John
Sharp William, joiner	Bampton John *Publicans.*
Smith Sarah, shopkeeper	Burton Eliz. Hives George
Smith Ths. parish clerk	Butt Jeremiah Hives Hannah
Staton William, butcher	Cliff John.

Sharp John   Flavell George | CARRIERS, John Hemsley, to
Woolley Thos. Hallam James | Nottingham, Saturday; and Thos.
Shoemakers. Truswell John | Maltby, Wednesday.
Ellis Joseph   Walker John |

KEYWORTH village and parish, 7 miles S. by E. of Nottingham, contains 552 inhabitants, and 1373 acres of land, on the north-eastern side of the wolds. It was enclosed in 1798, when 214 acres were allotted in lieu of tithes, and 6A. 3R. 12P. to the church. Lord Rancliffe is the principal proprietor, lord of the manor, and patron of the *rectory*, which is valued in the King's books at £7. 5s. and is now enjoyed by the Rev. Wm. Beetham. The *church*, dedicated to St. Mary Magdalen, has a curious tower surmounted by an octagan spire. The Independents have a chapel here, built in 1768, and the Primitive Methodists another, erected in 1828. An annual *feast* is held on Whitmonday. The ancient *poor's land* was exchanged at the enclosure for 4A. 1R. 12P. in the Mill Field. The poor have also the interest of £10 left by an unknown donor.

KEYWORTH PARISH.
Alsop Richard, corn miller
Archer Thomas, butcher
Brex William, schoolmaster
Eggleston Francis, sen. gent
Fosbrook John Edw. surgeon
Hallam Luke, tailor
Harvey Samuel Greaves, gent
Hemson Wm. framework knitter
Hodgett Matths. blacksmith and beerhouse
Hopkin Thos. vety. surgeon
Price Hy. & Crofts J. bricklyrs
Richmond & Prichett, shoemkrs
Simpson Hanh. vict. Gate
Smith Rev. John. (Indpt)

Farmers.
Attenborough Mary
Barnett Jph
Belshaw Geo
Burrows Thos
Cook Wm.
Disney Thos
Eggleston Eliz
Eggleston Fras.
Eggleston Jno
Hebb Henry
Hemsley Thos

Hornbuckle G
Shepperson W
Webster Mary
Joiners.
Gunn Wm.
White J. & vict
White Wm.
Shopkeepers.
Attewell Wm
Eggleston Thos
Hallam Sar
Millington W
Towle Jno

CARRIERS.—John Walker and Thomas Eggleston, to Nottingham, Sat.

KINGSTON-UPON-SOAR is a small village and parish 10 miles S.W. by S. of Nottingham, betwixt the Wolds and the Leicestershire border. It has only 157 inhabitants and 1300 acres of land, all belonging to Edward Strutt, Esq., the lord of the manor and patron of the *curacy*, which is now enjoyed by the Rev. Thomas Barton. The *church* was rebuilt in 1832, except the south transept which is very ancient, and contains some curious ornamental screen work, and a richly sculptured monument of the *Babyngtons*, who had a large mansion here till the reign of Elizabeth, when one of them was attainted and executed for favouring the cause of Mary Queen of Scots. The poor have the interest of £10 left by Gervase Redfern. The *feast* is on the first Sunday after St. Luke's Day. The

3 x 2

principal inhabitants are John Berson, parish clerk; Elizabeth Clerk, shopkeeper; William Hardy, blacksmith; John Hudson, gardener; William Shardlow, tailor; and John Bowley, Sarah Bramley, Charles Stokes, and William Tebbutt, *farmers.*

LEAKE (EAST,) 10 miles S. by W. of Nottingham, is a well built village on the south bank of a small rivulet that flows westward through the Wolds to the Soar, near Kingston. Its parish contains 2431 acres of land, and 975 inhabitants, many of whom are bobbin net makers and framework knitters. At the enclosure in 1798, 466 acres were allotted in lieu of tithes. The rest belongs to several proprietors, but Lord Rancliffe is the principal owner, and lord of the manor. The *church* has a fine lofty spire and is dedicated to St. Mary. The *rectory* is united with West Leake, and valued in the King's books at £25. 4s. 7d. The Marquis of Hastings is the patron, and the George Holcombe, D.D., the incumbent. The Methodists and Baptists have each a chapel here, and a PETTY SESSION is held on every alternate Monday, at the Three Horse Shoes; and a *hiring for servants* four times a-year. The *free school* was built in 1724, by *John Bley,* who endowed it with £450, which was laid out in the purchase of 25 acres of land, at Barton and Wimeswold, let for £48. 10s. per annum, for which the master teaches all the poor boys and girls of the parish. The town lands consist of 21 acres, let for £30 a-year, which is carried to the poor rates. The interest of £11, left in 1681, and 1686, by John Wright and Thomas Spencer, is distributed in bread. Here is both a male and a female *sick club;* the former has its feast on Whit-Monday, and the latter on Whit-Wednesday.

LEAKE (WEST) is a small village and parish 1 mile W. of East Leake, to which its small church dedicated to St. Helen, is united. It has 203 inhabitants and 1500 acres of land, all belonging to Lord Middleton, except one farm, and the rectory house with 10 acres of glebe. The *feast* is on the Sunday after Martinmas.

LEAKE EAST.

Burrows Mrs. Dorothy
Burrows W. butcher & maltster
Burton Joseph, shoemaker and parish clerk
Cooke Thomas, governor of the workhouse
Cross John, gentleman
Fosbrooke Wm. Blunt, solicitor
Guttridge Wm. wheelwright
Hardy Thomas, corn miller
Hardy John, vict. three horse shoes
Hawley Rd. schoolmaster
Heath Thomas, joiner
Jacques John, bricklayer
Kirk William, corn miller
Marcer John, gentlemen
Marshall G. needle maker
Mason Henry, butcher
Mills John & Wm. basket makers
Riste James, bricklayer
Smedley James, joiner
Tunnadine Rd. brickmaker and victualler
Tunnicliff George, tailor
Woodroffe John, chief constable of North division of Rushcliffe.
Woodroffe John, butcher

Farmers.
Angrave Thos.
Angrave Wm.
Burrows Edw.
Cook John
Follows Henry
Kirk William
Marshall John
Marshall John
Neale John
Nixon William
Oldershaw Joh
Wilde, Mattw.
Wootton, John
Blacksmiths.
Carver Edward

Follows Henry
Hardy William
Bobbin Net
Makers.
Bently Thomas
Flowers Rd.
Gadd Sampson
Hallam John
Hallam Thomas
James Isaac
Neale William
Smith Samuel
Voce John
Shoemakers.
Hall Charles
Tuckwood J.

Shopkeepers. Tait J. & A.
Bosworth Thos. *Hosiery Agents.*
Cook William Reed William
Marcer Wm. Savadge Edward
Maltby Hugh
LEAKE WEST.
Holcombe Rev. Geo. D D rector
Hardstaff William, parish clerk
Platts T. joiner, & W. net maker
Wilde Mrs. Cath. & E. shopkpr
Farmers. Place John
Hardy Thomas Platts John
Henson Matt. Shepperson Wm
Marshall Bryan Wilde Mathew
Marshall Joseph

NORMANTON-ON-SOAR, 13 miles S. by W. of Nottingham, is a village and parish in the vale of the Soar, bounded on the south by Leicestershire, and on the north by the Wolds. It has 365 inhabitants and 1200 acres of land, of which 240 acres were allotted in 1770 in lieu of tithes. The church is very ancient, and the living is a rectory, valued in the King's books at £7. 11s. 0½d., and now enjoyed by the Rev. Joseph Powell. The manor and the advowson belong to John Buckley, Esq., and others, who are the successors of the late *Thomas Buckley and James Richards, Esqrs.,* two eminent breeders and graziers, to the former of whom the late Duke of Bedford gave 700 guineas for the use of one of his rams, for one season. This parish receives on every fifth year, £8. 6s. 8d. from *William Willoughby's charity.*—See p. 168.

Barlow Jsph. & Cox J. butchers
Buckley John, Esq. Normanton Hills.
Dennis George, coal merchant
Gaze Jas. shoemkr, & Jsph joiner
Hayfield John, gardener
Kirk Joseph, tailor
Marshall Samuel, gentlemen
Marston Andrew, bobbin net maker

Marston Thomas, parish clerk
Mason Samuel, maltster
Powell Rev. Joseph, rector
Stenson Wm. victualler & coal merchant
Stubbs Joseph, brickmaker
Farmers, Pepper Richard
Bosworth Thos. Woodroffe Wm.
Hands J J & W & maltster
Kiddey John

PLUMPTRE is a small but pleasant village on the Melton-Mowbray road, 5½ miles S.S.E. of Nottingham, and was once the capital of a wapentake of its own name. Its parish, which contains 605 inhabitants and about 3500 acres of land, is divided into the three *townships* of Plumptre, Normanton-on-the-Wolds, and Clipston. The *manor of Plumptre* has 1800 acres, and William Elliott Elliott, Esq., is its lord and principal owner; and also patron of the rectory, which is valued in the King's books at £19. 19s. 7d., and is now enjoyed by the Rev. John Burnside. At the enclosure in 1805, land was allotted for the tithes. The church dedicated to St. Mary, was re-pewed in 1818. The poor have the interest of £34, left in 1755, by Richard Pritchett, and an unknown donor. The *feast* is on the second Sunday after Trinity.

CLIPSTON township is in Bingham Hundred.—See p. 489.

NORMANTON-ON-THE-WOLDS has 185 inhabitants and 1000 acres of land, and lies on the same road half a mile E. of Plumptre. It is owned chiefly by Samuel Smith, Esq., and Messrs. Cole and Goodall. A Wesleyan chapel was built here in 1827. The poor have the interest of £20 left by Messrs. Kirkby, Row, and Seawell.

PLUMPTRE.		
Allcock Wm. sadler	Burnside Rev. J. B A	Hickling Jno. miller
Astill Wm. clerk	Chapman Wm. smith	Parr S. schoolmaster
Bexon T. shoemkr	Crafts Thomas, vict.	Turner Jno. shopkpr
Btett Robert, vict.	Glover Thos. butcher	Wilson Tho. joiner

Farmers.

Alsop John	Bradley Thos.	Butler Thomas Holmes Wm.
Bestall Thomas	Brewster John	Gibson John Stephenson A.

NORMANTON.		
Bamford F. wheelgt	Flewitt S. shoe maker	Harby Thos. joiner
Cole Richard, gent.	Goodall C. E. gent.	Marshall Wm. farmer
Dodson Thos. farmer	Gunn John, vict.	Smedley Edw. tailor

RATCLIFFE-ON-SOAR is a village and parish near the junction of the Trent and Soar navigation, 9 miles S.W. of Nottingham. It has 177 inhabitants and 1200 acres of land, belonging to Earl Howe, who is lord of the manor, impropriator, and patron of the vicarage, which is valued in the King's books at £10. 11s. 3d., and is now in the incumbency of the Rev. William Helps. It has been augmented with land at Misson, purchased with Queen Anne's Bounty. The church dedicated to St. Mary, contains nothing remarkable but an epitaph to the memory of *Robert Smith,* who held the office of parish clerk upwards of fifty years. The *Sacheverells* had a large manor house here, but it was pulled down in 1719, except the dining room, which is now used as a barn by Mr. Hickingbotham. The residents are William Allen, navigation agent; John Ankers, shoemaker; Israel Chamberlain, Esq., Red Hill; John Hickingbotham, maltster; Thomas Moor, parish clerk; John Palmer, shopkeeper; William John Boot Withers, basket maker; William Woolley, joiner; Charles Bosworth, Lydia Sadler, and John Withers, *farmers;* and William Moor, *carrier.*

REMPSTON is a pleasant village and parish 4 miles N. of Loughborough, and 10¾ miles S. of Nottingham, containing 398 inhabitants and 1365 acres of land, a large portion of which belongs to the lord of the manor, Gregory Gregory, Esq., who built the present Hall, which is now occupied by John Smith Wright, Esq., whose lady pays for the education of 30 poor girls. The present church is dedicated to All Saint's, and was built in 1771, out of the ruins of the ancient church of St. Peter's-in-the-Rushes, and an old chapel which had been long in disuse; the latter stood in the village and the former was distant half a mile to the N.E., where its burial ground is now an open field, though a corpse was interred in it so lately as two years ago. The rectory is valued in the King's books at £13. 2s. 6d. and received at the enclosure in 1768, an allotment of 259 acres in lieu of tithes. The master of Sidney College, Cambridge, is the patron, and the Rev. Thomas Hosking, the incumbent. In 1748, Robert Marsden, archdeacon of Nottingham, who lies buried in the old church-yard, left to the successive rectors, Little Grange close, on condition that they distribute 50s. amongst the poor, every Christmas. The poor have also the interest of £10 left in 1716 by Thomas Woodroffe. The *Particular Baptists* have a burial ground here but no chapel.

Alsop John, butcher
Austin L. butcher
Bonser Thos. vict.
Bradwell J. saddler
Bramley J. shoe mkr
Bramley W. shoemkr
Cresswell Stn. schoolmaster
Cross Edw. net maker
Dodson Edw. yeoman
Hallam J. shoemaker
Hopkin G. brickmkr
Hosking Rev. T. B D
Hunter John, Esq.
James Charles, joiner
Newton Nat. yeoman
Orson Thos. smith
Pagett Lydia, school
Stubbs Thos. framesmith & net maker
Wadkin John, miller
Walkington W. joiner & beerhouse
Werner Geo. tailor
Wilson Wm. baker
Wright John Smith, Esq. Rempston Hall

Farmers.
Blount W.
Blount G. & J.
Burrows John
Chapman John
Morris Geo.
Morris John
Woodroffe J & T.

RUDDINGTON 5 miles south of Nottingham, is a large and well built village, which has encreased its population since 1801, from 868 to 1428 souls, many of whom are employed in the lace and hosiery manufactures. Its parish comprises 2781 acres of land, of which Lady Jane Parkyns is the principal owner and lady of the manor, and has a handsome cottage in the village, where there are several other neat and pleasant mansions. At the enclosure in 1768, the vicar received 52 acres, and Sir Charles Cavendish (the impropriator) 466 acres in lieu of tithes. Of the latter 340 acres have been sold to Charles Paget, Esq. The church was repaired in 1718, and was rebuilt upon a larger scale in 1824, at the cost of £1100, except the chancel and steeple, which are the only remaining parts of the ancient fabric. It was, however, a chapel of ease till 1773, when its burial ground was consecrated, and enclosed with part of the materials of the original mother church, that stood in an open field one mile east of Ruddington, where there had formerly been a village called Flawford. This church of *Flawford* was a Saxon edifice dedicated to St. Peter, and had a lofty spire steeple, and many curious monuments with cross-legged figures, but having been deserted by the parishioners it became ruinous, and a license was obtained from the archbishop in 1773, to take it down. Its ancient tombs and other ornaments were all destroyed or mutilated by the "colliers" employed in the work of demolition, and Throsby says, many of them were taken to build bridges and pigsties, and to mend the roads. The vicarage is valued in the King's books at £6. 13s. 4d., and is in the gift of the Rev. C. Simeon, and the Society for purchasing small livings. The Rev. Edward Selwyn is the incumbent. The General Baptists and Wesleyan and Primitive Methodists have each a chapel in the village, where there is a large workhouse built in 1805, and now belonging to 13 associated parishes and townships. Ruddington school was founded in 1641, by James Peacock, who endowed it with 40A. 2R. 14P. of land, now let for £70, for which (and a house and garden) the master teaches all the poor children of the parish. The school house was rebuilt in 1827, at the cost of £400, to be liquidated by a yearly payment of £10 from the rent of the land. Ten acres of land at Bulwell was purchased with several benefactions, and are now let for £20 a-year, which, with a yearly rent charge of £3. 18s., left by the founder of the school, is distributed in weekly doles of bread every Sunday, at the church.

Berkins Misses Mary and Ann
Betton John, bricklayer
Breedon Henry, gentleman
Briggs John, framesmith
Cave Wm. surgeon
Cocker Mrs. C. & Cole Mrs Ann
Cripwell Rd. maltster
Gilbert Mrs Ann
Grey Lieut. General John
Handley Jas. brickmaker
Hardmett Mary, maltster & miller
Harrison John, needlemaker
Hodgkin John, gentleman
Hodgkin John, jun. butcher
Jakeman Caroline, schoolrs
Moore Thos. Esq. banker
Newman George
Oliver John & Wm. bricklayers
Page Wm. butcher
Paget Chas. Esq.
Parkyns Lady Jane

Radford Misses
Richards Saml. butcher
Rogers Clement, schoolmaster
Selwyn Rev. Edw. vicar
Shaw Mr. William
Simpson Isaac, wheelwright
Smellie John, surgeon
Sutton Rt. maltster
Tyers John, vict. Three Crowns
Widdinson Wm. vict. Red Hart
Wilkinson Israel, butcher
Winfield Geo. gov. workhouse

Farmers.
Barker Edw
Barker Rd
Burrows John
Burrows Rd
Cripwell John
Cripwell Thos
Gunn Thos
Hardmett —

Harwood John
Holmes John
Kempson Thos
Peet John
Shaw Jn. & Wm
Slater Rd

Bobbin Net Mkrs
Beeston. Thos.
Breedon Frs

Cripwell Rd	Sergent Geo.	Lee Saml	Pigott Geo
Fletcher Saml	Smith Geo	Stephenson Wm	*Joiners.*
Harrison Jno	Smith John	Wright Wm	Hardy Rd
Henson Eliz	*Hosiery Agts.*	*Shopkeeprs.*	Parker John
Henson J. G.	Baxter Hy	Chapman Wm.	Sandy Wm
and J	Hickling Thos	and druggist	Whitworth G
Marshall W & P	James Mtw	Cripwell Hy	Widdison Sl
Saxby J. & W	Savage Chas	Henson Jas	*Carriers* to
Wilson S. & G	Underwood Dl	James Geo	Nottingham, W.
Blacksmiths.	*Shoemakers.*	Stubbs Wm	Marshall, daily,
Gunn Thos	Buttery Js	*Tailors.*	and J. Dennis
Smith Rd. & Rt	Dutton John	Cross John	and Ed. Smith.
Beerhouses.	Ellis John	Henson & Pike	Saturday.
Handley John	Hardy John		

STANFORD-on-Soar is a small picturesque village and parish, 1¼ mile N. of Loughborough, at the point were the river Soar enters Leicestershire. It has 129 inhabitants, and 1500 acres of land, all belonging to the Rev. Samuel Dashwood, who is both patron and incumbent of the rectory, and resides in the *hall*, a modern mansion with pleasing grounds and plantations. The *church* is a handsome fabric embowered in thick foliage. The rectory is valued in the King's books at £9. 7s. 8d. A rent charge of £5 was left to the poor in 1765, by Sophia Phillips, out of the Stanford estate. The parishioners are Mrs. Lydia Dashwood; Edw. Birch, shoemaker, and John Birch, John Coates, John Rowland, and Samuel Walker, *farmers.*

STANTON-ON-THE-WOLDS is a small parish of scattered dwellings, near the Melton Mowbray road, 8 miles S. S. E. of Nottingham. It has 125 inhabitants, and 1300 acres of land. The Rev. — Bingham, of Kettleby, is lord of the manor, but the land belongs to Ichabod Wright, Esq. the Rev. Thomas Randolph, and George, John, Joseph, and Elizabeth Page, who each occupy their own farms. The other occupants are Wm. Shaw and John Ward, *farmers,* and the Rev. Thomas Smith, the *curate.* The *church* is a small mean looking edifice which Throsby says "is the most despicable he ever beheld." It is a rectory valued in the King's books at £2. 13s. 4d. The Rev. Thos. Randolph is the patron, and the Rev. George Randolph the incumbent. The poor have a house and 3 acres of land bequeathed in 1718, by the Rev. Thomas Ouseley, and now let for £6 a-year.

SUTTON-BONNINGTON is an extensive village under the Wolds, on the eastern bank of the Soar, 11 miles S. S. W. of Nottingham. It is in the two parishes of *Sutton St. Ann,* and *Sutton St. Michael,* which support their poor conjointly, and contain 1136 inhabitants, and upwards of 2000 acres. Lord Tamworth is principal owner, and lord of the manor of St. Ann's, and George Paget, Esq. of St. Michael's. At the enclosure, in 1775 and 7, the tithes of both parishes were commuted for allotments of land. There were anciently two distinct villages, the more southerly one being Sutton *juxta* Bonnington, and the other Bonnington, but they have long been connected by modern buildings, and borne the common name of Sutton-Bonnington. *St. Ann's Church* is the smallest of the two, and stands in the southern part of the village. It is a rectory valued in the King's books at £4. 17s. 6d. The Lord Chancellor is the patron, and the Rev. John Lafont the rector. *St. Michael's* is a large handsome fabric, with a lofty tower and spire. It is also a rectory, and is valued in the King's books at £15. 2s. 1d. The dean and chapter of Bristol are the patrons, and the Rev. Richard Foster is the rector. The Wesleyan and Primitive Methodists, and the General Baptists have each a chapel in the village, where a *feast* is held on the Sunday after St. Michael's day, or on that day if it falls on a Sunday or Monday. The *Free School* was built by subscription 1718, and is endowed with upwards of 26 acres of land at Barrow-upon-Soar, purchased with £100, left by Charles Liversey, and £111 raised by subscription. This land is let for £50 a-year. Several *benefactions*, amounting to £110, were laid out in 1734, in the purchase of 6 acres of land at Hose, now let for £10. 10s. The poor have also several small rent charges, amounting to £1. 10s. This parish and those of Rempston and Normanton, each receive a *bible* yearly from Hickling's charity, at Loughbro'.

ZOUCH BRIDGE which crosses the Soar, 1 mile S. of Sutton-Bonnington, gives name to a small village which is partly in the parishes of Sutton, Normanton, and Hathorn. Near it is *Kirk Hill*, on which a number of Roman urns and coins were found in 1825.

Bacon Edwd. gentleman
Barton Thos. curate
Berridge John, chief constable of Rushcliffe, South Division
Cross Mrs. Ann
Darker Eliz. bdg. academy
Domleo John, overseer
Doughty John, joiner
Dutton Thos. gardener
Frankland Bartw. schoolr
Hayfield Wm. gardener
Marshall Saml. and Son, coal merchts. Zouch Wharf
Orme Jas. gentleman
Paget Geo. Esq. Sutton Manor
Paget and White, worsted spinners and corn millers, Zouch Mills and Loughbro
Pepper Wm. brickmaker, Kegworth Bridge

Rice John & Wm. bricklayers
Smith Thos. jun. butcher
Stapleton Rev. John, (Indpt).
Tunnicliff Wm. saddler
Whitaker Mr. Saml
Wilkinson John, wheelwright

Farmers.
Bates Eliz
Bramley John
Burley John
Doughty Saml
Doughty Wm
Lacey Ann
Rouse John
Sarson Wm
Wild Wm
Wilkinson John

Blacksmiths.
Dalby John
Kinsley Hy

Bobbin Net Mkrs
Burton John
Cripwell Wm
Hardy Thos
Henson Thos
Hardy Jas
Leicester Hy
Simpkin Geo
Smith John
Smith Thos
Whitby John

Hosiers.
Berridge John
Clark John

Smith Wm ~ ·Beswick John
Shoemakers. Cooper John
Doughty Geo Darnell Geo
Hemsley John Paulucci Ptr
Keightly Sam Pepper Rd
Pepper John Simpkin Jas
Shopkeepers. Smith Thos
Bainbridge Chs Smith Wm

Publicans. Wildboy John
Bolland John Tailors.
Domelo Geo Dennis Geo
Marshall Geo. Newham John
Newham John Priestly Wm
Simpkin John
Carriers. T. Dutton & Wm
Marshall, to Nottingham, Sat.

THORPE-IN-GLEBIS, or *Thorpe-in-the-Clods*, is a small churchless parish, 11 miles S. by E. of Nottingham, containing only 39 inhabitants, and 800 acres of land. Lord Rancliffe is the principal owner, lord of the manor, and patron of the rectory, which is valued at £2. 9s. 4d. The church has been in ruins more than a century, and very little of it now remains. The present rector, the Rev. T. Graham, preached his induction sermon upon its ruins about 15 years ago, and has never since officiated in the parish. The four resident *farmers* are Richard and William Cross, Thomas Miller, and Wm. Scottorn.

THRUMPTON is a picturesque village and parish near the confluence of the Trent and Soar, 8 miles S. W. of Nottingham. It has 132 inhabitants, and 1000 acres of land, all belonging to John Emmerton Wescomb, Esq. of *Thrumpton Hall*, a handsome mansion, which was built by the Pigot family in 1630, but has been greatly improved by its present possessor, who is also impropriator and patron of the perpetual curacy which is now enjoyed by the Rev. Wm. Cantrell. The church is a small fabric dedicated to All Saints. The principal villagers are Richard Barrow, gamekeeper; Wm. Daft, gardener; Thomas Elliot, gent.; John Holmes, shopkeeper; Mrs. Catherine Kirkland; Daniel Ward, parish clerk; Mary and Elizabeth Wilkinson, boarding academy; George Golder, Wm. Hemsley, Edward Massey, and Richard Wilkinson, *farmers*; and John Clark, *carrier*, to Nottingham, Wednesday and Saturday.

WIDMERPOOL is a small neat village, on the sides of two opposite declivities of the Wolds, 9 miles S. S. E. of Nottingham. Its parish contains 180 inhabitants, and about 2000 acres of land, enclosed in 1803, when 460 acres were allotted to the rector in lieu of tithes. Frederick Robinson, Esq. is the proprietor, lord of the manor, and patron of the rectory, which is valued in the King's books at £4. 16s. 0½d. and is now enjoyed by the Rev. John Robinson, M.A. who has just rebuilt the rectory house in the gothic style, and is about to re-edify the *church*, which is dedicated to St. Peter, and has long been in a state of decay, having undergone but few repairs since 1594, when the chancel was renewed. The General Baptists have a chapel in the village; and about 1¾ miles to the E., is Widmerpool *New Inn*, on the Nottingham and Melton Mowbray road. The residents are the Rev. J. Robinson, rector; Rev. George

3 L

Heaton, B.A. curate; Jph. Hallam, parish clerk; Jph. Flewitt, gamekeeper, Wm. Hear, *New Inn;* Ann Hull, blacksmith; Thomas Morris, butcher; John Shepherd, schoolmaster; John Stafford, shoemaker; and Thomas Allwood, James Bonsor, Job Cowlisher, Eliz. Morris, John Mousley, John Payne, John Seagreave, George Thirlby, and John White, *farmers.*

WILFORD is a delightful village on the south bank of the Trent, 1½ mile S. of Nottingham, by the ferry, and 3 miles by the turnpike. It has several neat villas belonging to opulent families, engaged in the trade and commerce of Nottingham. It is altogether neatly built and extremely rural. The *church* stands close to the Trent, and is not only a handsome object in itself, but also commands a most pleasing view of Nottingham and its vicinity, and of the river which is here lined by a long row of lofty elms. It is dedicated to St. Wilfrid, and the name of the village is evidently a contraction of *Wilfrid's ford*, as there is both a ford and a ferry close by; the tower is low, but the nave and two side aisles are spacious, and the chancel has a neat altarpiece. The living is a rectory valued in the King's books at £18. 17s. 6d., and received at the enclosure in 1766, an allotment of 227 acres in lieu of tithes. The Rev. Thos. Thorpe is the incumbent, and Sir Robert Clifton Bart., the patron. The latter is also lord of the manor, and owner of a great part of the parish, which contains 602 inhabitants, and 1800 acres of land. Wilford seems to have been anciently a *Roman station,* as many Roman coins were dug up here about 30 years ago, most of which were of the latter emperors. The *Free school* was built in 1736, pursuant to the will of Mr. Benjamin Carter, who, in 1732, left £200 for that purpose, and bequeathed for its support and for other charitable uses property which now produces £210 per annum, of which £60 is paid to the master, £5 for school books, £10 to the poor of Wilford, and £20 to St. Giles' and St. George's charity school, in London. The residue is expended in apprenticing poor boys, in repairing the buildings, &c. &c. Sir Robert Clifton is one of the trustees. The same donor rebuilt the rectory house, and repaired and beautified the church. In 1828, Lady Lucy Smith erected an *Infant school* in the village, and continues to pay a salary to the teacher. The poor of Wilford have £5 yearly from Henry Handley's charity. (See p. 165.) Gervas Handley endowed two *Bede Houses*, with property, which has partly been changed for £260. 1s. 9d. three per cent. consols: the yearly proceeds (£8. 2s.) are given to two poor widows, but the alms-houses are improperly let to two labourers for the annual rent of 13s. each. In 1810, *Joseph Felton* left a yearly rent charge of £2. 10s. out of four houses in Spaniel-row, Nottingham, to Wilford. The *feast* is on the Sunday before St. Luke's, or on that day if it falls on a Sunday. Numerous parties from Nottingham resort here in summer to the *Public Garden*, at the

Ferry Coffee house, and often extend their walk to the sylvan scenes of Clifton Grove. (Vide p. 645.)

Abbott Mr. Thomas	Cox John, silk mert	Ollis Ann, schoolmrs
Abbott Rd. butcher	Cox Thomas, gent	Pilkington R. tailor
Buckland J. shoemkr	Day John, tailor	Potter Eliz. miller
Burnham Wm. joiner	Facon Wm. shopkpr	Pyatt Geo. smith
Carter B. shoemaker	Fox Thos. gardener	Quinton H. wheelwht
Carter J. shoemaker	Harker Wm. tailor	Robinson C. schoolr.
Carver W. victualler	Harpham G. butcher	Smith Henry, Esq.
coffee-house	Henson T. net maker	Stafford Wm. shopkpr
Cheetham Mr. John	Leeson Rt. Esq, solr.	Thorpe Rev. T. rectr.
Cox Chs. lace maker	Merren J basket mkr	Witham J. wheelgt
Cox James, gent.		

Farmers.

	Hankin Eliz.	Hazard S.	Oakley John
Carver John	Harpham Wm.	Holbrooke J.	Pyatt William
Daft William	Harwood Edw.	Jameson Wm.	Richardson Wm.
Hall Henry			

WILLOUGHBY-on-the-WOLDS, 11 miles S. by E. of Nottingham, and near the Leicestershire border, is a long rural village, sheltered by the embowering foliage of a double row of trees, and seated upon a declivity near the ancient fosse-way. Though so retired in its situation, it did not escape the baneful effects of the civil wars, in the reign of Charles I., when a bloody contest was fought in *Willoughby field*, in which Col. Stanhope was numbered among the slain. The lofty *cross* in the village was doomed for destruction, by the *pious* soldiers of Cromwell, who tied ropes round it in order to pull it down; but their *religious* enthusiasm was so much damped by some strong beer given them by the vicar, after he had made a long speech in defence of its innocence, that it was permitted to remain unmolested. Willoughby is considered by Horsley as the *Vernomentum*, so often mistaken for *Margidunum*. Stukely tells us that the old Roman town (of which the ditch and mound still exist) was in a field called "Henings," where tradition says there was an old city called Long Billington, but the site is now designated the Black field, from the colour and richness of the soil. Near the source of Willoughby brook is *Crosshill*, an ancient *tumulus* on which an annual revel is held in allusion to some traditionary festival of the Roman mythology. Some coins and other antiquities have been found near the present village. The *church*, dedicated to St. Mary, has many ancient and splendid monuments of the Willoughby's, ancestors of Lord Middleton, whose predecessors sold this lordship many years ago to various proprietors, whose estates have since undergone a further subdivision. Frederick Robinson, Esq. is lord of the manor, and Wm. Melville, Esq. is patron of the vicarage, which is valued in the King's books at £6. 18s. 6¼d., and is now enjoyed by the Rev. John Clifton. The church was repewed, and a gallery erected at the west end, in 1829, so that it has now

100 free sittings. In removing the old pews a tessellated pavement was found, and it now forms part of the floor of the north aisle. The *parish* contains 465 inhabitants, and 2000 acres of land, which was enclosed in 1794, when 367 acres were allotted to the impropriator, (the Duke of Portland,) and 86 to the vicar in lieu of all the tithes; and 1A. 3R. to the church. The overseers distribute 16s. yearly, as the interest of £16. left to the poor. Samuel Wells left £50 for the education of six poor children, and £20 for the poor; the interest is now paid out of the highway rates.

WEST THORPE is a hamlet ¼ mile S.W. of Willoughby, and those marked * in the following Directory, reside in it.

Barnett Saml. miller
Cooper Jph. cooper
Cross R. & T. gardnrs
Dalby John, smith
* Dawson W. wheelgt
Day Wm. bobbin net maker
Garton Thos. butcher

Gee Josh. butcher & beerhouse
Hickling Geo wheelgt
Howell T mole catchr
Johnson Jno. bobbin net maker
Kettleband M. miller
Newby John, tailor

Peet Wm. shopkpr
Screaton R schoolmtr.
Screaton Rt. bricklyr.
Smith Jph. beerhouse
Turner Wm. joiner & shopkeeper
Wakerly W. shopkpr
Whyman J. yeoman

Farmers.
Atkin Isaac
* Baker Charles
* Baker Charles
Barnett Wm.
Bryans Samuel
Buss George
Charles Thos.
* Tuckwood Jph*
Turner Henry

Clark Robert
Garton Eliz.
Gilbert Henry
Harding Samuel,
Hardy Samuel
* Holmes Wm.
Hubbard Wm.
Marsh Mary
Wells Samuel
Widdowson J.

Turner John
Wakerly Jph
* Walker Thos.
Walker Wm.
Wells Joseph

Shoemakers.
Bailey John
Marsh Daniel
Skinner John
Woollerton J.

CARRIERS to Nottingham, J. Goodacre, Saturday; & William Wakerly, Wednesday, and to Loughbro', Thursday.

WYSALL is an indifferently built village upon the Wolds, 9¼ miles S. by E. of Nottingham. Its parish contains 271 inhabitants and 1500 acres of land, enclosed in 1800, when 321 acres were awarded to the impropriator (Earl Gosford) and 80 acres to the vicar in lieu of tithes. Lord Rancliffe is lord of the manor, but the three coheiresses of the late James Kersley, Esq., are the principal owners of the soil. The church is dedicated to the Holy Trinity, and has some ancient monuments of the Armstrong family. The vicarage has been augmented with Queen Anne's Bounty, and is valued in the King's books at £4. 11s. 0¼d. Earl Gosford, of Ireland, is the patron, and the Rev. Leonard Chapman, the incumbent. A Methodist chapel was built here in 1825. The *feast* is on Trinity Sunday. The poor have two fields at Barton, in Leicestershire, let for £5 a-year. The *church land* let for £9. 5s., consists of 3¼A. at Wysall, 3A. 2P. at Keyworth, and 10P. at Widmerpool.

Bramley J blacksmith
Bryans W. joiner
Deakin G. schoolmtr
Derrick W parish clk

Goodacre J. gent.
Hogg C. bobbin net maker

Lovett Thos. tailor
Mather Benj. gent.
Morris J. bricklayer

Farmers.			Shoemakers.
Annabel Thos.	Bowley T. jun.	Eggleston Jph	Derrick John
Baldock J & W.	Brown John	Harrison John	Garner Joseph
Bowley Geo.	Burrows Robert	Hogg Thomas	Shepperd John
Bowley Thomas	Cox John	Shaw Thomas	Wright Edward
	Derrick W. jun.		

THURGARTON HUNDRED,

In its civil jurisdiction, is separated into three *Divisions*, which together contain 42 parishes, of which the following is an enumeration, showing the number of inhabitants in 1801, 1821, and 1831, and the estimated *annual value* of the lands and buildings, as assessed for the property tax in 1815. Those marked * are in the *North Division*, and ‡ in the Liberty of Southwell and Scrooby; the others are in the *South Division*. In *ecclesiastical* matters, those marked † are in the *Deanery of Newark*, § in the *Deanery of Nottingham*, and the rest in the *peculiar jurisdiction* of Southwell and Scrooby.

ANN. VAL. £	PARISHES	POPULATION IN 1801.	1821.	1831.
4634	*†Averham	230	280	243
2116	‡Bleasby	215	290	324
3167	‡†Bidworth	407	744	061
3152	§Burton Joyce	695	650	675
2690	‡Calverton	696	1064	1196
483	*Caunton	366	467	542
4360	§Colwick	116	120	145
2105	‡†Cromwell	203	184	184
1840	§Edingley	296	344	308
2815	§Epperstone	422	513	518
3079	†Farnsfield	564	911	1010
144	†Fiskerton	230	343	314
5384	†Fledborough	71	75	86
9628	§Gedling	1630	2017	2343
1772	§Gonalston	146	96	107
1803	§Halam	294	310	371
1006	‡Halloughton	50	101	103
3698	*Hockerton	211	220	289
1708	§Hoveringham	324	305	347
4891	*Kelham	327	199	189
2363	‡Kirklington	140	240	243
3349	‡Kneesall	418	496	403
814	§Lambley	457	690	884
5171	§Lowdham	959	1334	1463
1238	**Mapplebeck	163	198	181
4873	*†Marnham	365	361	373
608	‡Morton	101	150	166
3694	*Muskham N.	361	617	681
4063	*Muskham S.	234	278	961
1075	‡†Normanton	108	297	940
4043	*Norwell	776	974	039
2606	*Osington	217	301	857
5311	Oxton	607	798	778
3397	†Rolleston	265	306	872
4185	§Sneinton	558	1912	3005
10462	§Southwell	2305	3061	3384
3000	‡‡Sutton-on-Trent	860	884	890
3406	§Thurgarton	334	330	329
2256	‡Upton	329	432	533
2271	**Weston	246	300	385
1863	*†Winkburn	153	169	134
3218	‡Woodborough	597	717	774
130671	Total	18029	23161	27542

☞ Southwell return includes the prisoners in the House of Correction.
‡The rest of Southwell and Scrooby Liberty is in the Hundred of Bassetlaw. See p. 301.
†‡Haywood, Oakes, and Lyndhurst, in the S. Div. and Parkleys in the N. Div. are Extra-parochial.

It is encompassed by the other five great divisions of the county, and is larger than any of them except Bassetlaw, which bounds it on the north, as the Trent does on the south and east, and Broxtow Hundred on the west. It has its name from a village within its limits, but its most important place and only market town is Southwell, though Nottingham, Mansfield, Tuxford, Newark, and Bingham, are all within a short distance of its boundary lines. Its soil is mostly a stiff but fertile clay, except in the vale of the Trent, which has a rich vegetable mould, and is here nearly 30 miles in length. (See p. 42.)

AVERHAM is a small rural village near the Trent, 3 miles W. by N. of Newark. Its parish includes the township of Staythorpe, and contains 2063 acres, and 243 inhabitants. The large *island* formed by the two branches of the Trent navigation, opposite Newark, is in the manor of Averham or Aram, which has long been possessed by the Suttons of Kelham; who had anciently a park and seat here. Many of their sepulchral memorials may be seen in the *church,* which is dedicated to St. Michael. The rectory is valued in the King's books at £20. and has the rectory of Kelham annexed to it. John Manners Sutton, Esq. is the patron, and the Rev. Robert Chaplin, the incumbent. The other residents are Rt. Lee, wheelwright; Thos. Marsh, blacksmith; Thos. Parker, shopr; and Rt. Clark, Wm. Esam, Jas. Gordon, Geo. Maltby, Saml. Stevens, and William Weightman, *farmers.*

STAYTHORPE, or *Starthorpe,* 1 mile W. of Averham, is a hamlet and township, with only 61 inhabitants and 568 acres of land, all belonging to Trinity College, Cambridge, to which it was granted after the dissolution of Newstead Abbey. —Barlow, Esq. is the lessee. The *farmers* are John Adwick, John Arnold, (beerseller), Edw. Driver, John Hall, and Thos. Upton.

BLEASBY is a straggling village, on the north bank of the Trent, 4 miles S. of Southwell. Its parish, which is all in the Liberty of Southwell and Scrooby, comprises the neighbouring hamlets of *Gourton, Gibsmere,* and *Notown,* and contains 324 inhabitants, and 1461 acres of land, which was enclosed in 1777, when the tithes were exonerated by an allotment of 122 acres. The principal land owners are Sir Robt. Sutton, Bart. (lord of Gourton manor), and Robt. Kelham Kelham, Esq. of Bleasby Hall, which was built by the Grundys. The small church is dedicated to St. Mary, and its vicarage is valued in the King's books at £4. The chapter of Southwell are the patrons, and the Rev. J. D. Becher the incumbent. The poor have 20s. out of the Town-end close, left in 1720, by Eliz. Crosland. Near the *ferry* here, the Trent takes two channels, and encompasses an island of about 20 acres of land called the *Knabs.*

Those marked 1 reside at Bleasby; 2 Gibsmere; 3 Gourton; and 4 at Notown.

1 Cording John, bsmith & p. clk
1 Dixon Rd. jun. wheelwright and beerhouse
1 Dixon Rd. overseer & constable
1 Foster John, shopkeeper
3 Hind Thos. gent. chief constable for South Division of the Thurgarton Hundred
1 Horspool Mary, vict. Haselford Ferry
1 Kelham Rt. Kelham, Esquire, Bleasby Hall
3 Lee Jph. corn miller
4 Mountaney Wm. tailor & shopr
3 Parker Thos. butcher
2 Richards Wm. butter dealer
1 Sharp Wm. vict. Waggon and Horses
2 Wilson Wm. shopkeeper

Farmers.
3 Aldridge Wm
1 Booth Saml
1 Dring Jas
2 Fish Saml.
2 Foster Hy
4 Harvey Hanh
3 Harvey Matw
3 Harvey Wm
3 Heather John
1 Holmes John
1 Lambley Wm
2 Marriott John
1 Parker John
4 Reynolds John
1 Sharp Eliz
2 Simon Wm
1 Wilson Wm

Shoemakers.
3 Catliff John
4 Challand Stpn
2 Dixon Jph
1 Saxton John

BLIDWORTH, 5 miles S.S.E. of Mansfield, is a large village pleasantly situated upon an eminence surrounded by some of the finest sylvan scenery of Sherwood Forest. Its parish is in the Liberty of Southwell and Scrooby, and contains 901 inhabitants and 5302A. 3R. 20P. of land, including Blidworth, Dale, and Rainworth, which latter gives name to the forest rivulet that rises near Robin Hood's Hills,—(See p. 19,)—and a conical rock supposed to have been used as a Druid's altar. All the tithes were commuted for allotments at the enclosure in 1809. The Archbishop of York is lord of the manor, and the two prebendaries of Oxton are the appropriators. The principal copyholders are General and Colonel Need, and Henry Walker, Esq. The vicarage, valued in the King's books at £3. 17s, 6d. is annexed to the vicarage of Oxton. The church was partly rebuilt in the early part of last century, but the ancient tower and chancel still remain. Amongst the monuments is one to Thomas Leake, a noted outlaw who was slain in 1608. *Fountain Dale*, the handsome mansion of General Need, is distant 1½ mile N. of Blidworth, near the romantic scenery of Thieves Wood and Harlow Wood.

Allen Jas. nail mkr. & beerhs
Bailey Jas. land surveyor, Pythorn Hill
Berridge Jas. wheelwright
Blatherwick John, shopr
Brelsford Jas. butcher & beerhs
Calladine Thos. vict. White Lion
Clark Thomas vict. & butcher, Black Bull
Crampton Thos. joiner
Dixon Paul, shopkeeper
Downall Rev. John, curate
Hardstaff Wm. schoolmaster
Hawkins John, corn miller
Hearson Wm. blacksmith
Heath Thos. gardener, &c.
Hill John, hedge carpenter
Jerrom Chas. blacksmith
Jerrom Mr. John
Lowe Wm. tailor
Marlowe John, wheelwright
Need Genl. Saml. Fountain Dale
Ramsden Fras. vict. & wheelgt Robin Hood

Robinson Rt. hosiery agent
Ward Rowland, cotton manfr.
Warren Wm. tailor
Winfield Jph. p. clerk & beerhs
   Farmers.   Heath John
Blagden Thos Heaton John
Blatherwick T Hodgkinson Jas
Bowler Wm Hodgkinson Job

Johnson Ann Wilson Jas
Johnson Wm   *Shoemakers.*
Lucas John Ashley John
Mellows Chas. Flint Rd
Mellows Wm Frost Sl
Renshaw Wm Kirk Wm
Temporal Wm Pogson Thos
Wheeldon Jas

BURTON JOYCE, or *Burton Jorz,* is a good village on the Southwell road, 6 miles N.E. by E. of Nottingham, sheltered on the north by a range of lofty hills, which bound the vale of the Trent. Its parish includes the small chapelry of *Bulcote,* and contains 675 inhabitants, and 2200 acres of land, enclosed in 1770, when allotments were made in lieu of the tithes. Burton Joyce (1500A.) is mostly the property of the Earl of Chesterfield, Robert Padley, Esq. and Misses Jamson. The Earl is also lord of the manor, impropriator, and patron of the *vicarage,* which is valued in the King's books at £4. 19s. 2d. and has now 70 acres of glebe, exclusive of land at Lowdham, purchased with Queen Anne's Bounty. The Rev. John Rolleston is the incumbent. The *church,* dedicated to St. Helen, contains several tombs of the ancient families of Frescheville, Jorz, Roose, Stapleton, &c. A *Methodist chapel* was built here in 1824. A legacy of £24, left to the poor by Wm. Martin, in 1786, was expended in the erection of a *poor-house* for the united parishes of Gedling, Burton Joyce, and Shelford.

BULCOTE is a small village and chapelry, 1 mile W. of Burton Joyce, to which its humble church or chapel is annexed. It has only 142 inhabitants, and 700 acres of land. Smith Wright, Esq. is the principal owner and lord of the manor. It keeps its poor separately, and they have 7s. yearly left by an unknown donor. The *feast* is on Trinity Sunday. The principal residents are Robert Wilkinson Padley, gent. *Bulcote Lodge;* Wm. Alcock, yeoman; Wm. Blatherwick; joiner; John Culham, shopkeeper; John Slater, victualler and bricklayer; and Godfry Fothergill, Samuel Taylor, and Gill Wilson, farmers. Those of BURTON JOYCE are as follows.

Alvey Jph. bsmith
Ashwell John, vict
Bage Miss Mary
Blackwell Wm. auctioneer (& Nottgm)
Bllatherwick Joseph, parish clerk
Blatherwick William, joiner
Butler John, shopkr
Clark Rd. vict
Dixon Mich. shoemkr
Hardy John, shopkr
Heaford J. shoemkr

Jamson Misses M & E
Padley Robert, Esq.
Peck Geo. tailor
Porter John, tailor
Rolleston Rev. John, vicar
Saxton Hy. shoemkr
Scothearn J. shoemkr
Siston T. & W. wheelwrights
Smith Wm. net mkr
Stokes Sl. butcher
Stones Wm. butcher
Swinscoe J. cattle dlr

Taylor J. butcher
   Farmers.
Brett John
Brett Wm
Cooper John
Dams John
Marshall John
Mertin Jas
Martin Wm
Tomlinson John
Wood John
  John Swinscoe *carrier* to Nottingham, Wed. & Sat. 7 mg.

CALVERTON is a considerable village in a narrow and picturesque valley, 7 miles N.N.E. of Nottingham. Its parish contains 1196 inhabitants and 3500 acres of land, enclosed in 1780, when upwards of 400 acres were allotted to the appropriators, and 203 acres to the vicar in lieu of tithes. The Duke of Newcastle, as lord of the manor, also received an allotment. Lady Catherine Sherbrooke, and Thomas Redgate, Esq.; have large estates here, and the former has a handsome mansion in the village. *Sansom Wood* and *Watch Wood*, on the western side of the parish, now constitute a farm of 700 acres, belonging to the Duke of Portland, all the timber having been felled, except about 20 acres. Near it are three other forest farms of considerable extent. The *Rev. William Lee,* the inventor of the *Stocking frame,*—(See p. 196,)—was born here, and there are now in the village nearly 300 of these complicated pieces of machinery. The church, dedicated to St. Wilfrid, is a vicarage, valued in the King's books at £4. The prebendaries of Oxton are the patrons, and the Rev. Samuel Oliver the incumbent. The Methodists and Baptists have each a chapel here. For some years after 1790, a meeting house in the village was occupied by *John Roe,* a dissenting preacher, who bid defiance to the discipline of the Established church, respecting matrimony, and for some time persisted in marrying his flock in " his own way," in opposition to the threats of the clergy, the magistracy, and the parish officers. The consequence was, that several of his female followers suffered a long imprisonment in Nottingham gaol, for refusing to swear to the fathers of their children, and for declaring that they were as firmly united in wedlock as it was possible for the mother church to make them. The school, at Calverton, was endowed with £12 per annum, by Jonathan Labray, in 1718.—(See p. 164.) The poor have the rents of three closes, which let for £11. 16s. per annum, and were bequeathed by Jane Pepper, and two unknown donors.

Abbott Rt. tanner
Baines Wm. wheelwright
Chamberlain Wm. gent
Colyer Wm. joiner
Colton Capt. Edw. Antonius
Fletcher Saml. vict. & maltster
Hind Cornelius. tailor
Moore Hy. butcher & maltster
Moss Fras, currier, &c.
Munks Wm. tailor
Oliver Rev. Saml. vicar
Palin Wm. brickmaker
Patching Hy. Chart, bricklayer
Roworth Wm. blacksmith
Shepherd Matt. schoolmaster
Sherbrooke Lady Catherine.

Shipley Jas. framesmith
Smith Lot, beer house
Taylor Saml. joiner & beer hs
Turton Geo. butcher
Ward Wm. saddler
Ward Wm. vict. Admiral Rodney
Watson Thos. & Wm. bricklayers
Watts Ann, beer house
Wesson John, framesmith
Wibberley Jas. butcher
Wood John, blacksmith
Wright Wm. hawker

Farmers.
Beckett Chpr.
Forest

Beckett John,
Sansom Wood
Blatherwick
Charlotte

		Hosiery Mfrs.	Greaves Sl
Brooks Wm	Hodgkinson Geo	Filer Saml	Hind Jas
Chappell Wm.	Hodgkinson Jph.	Flower Thos	Pearson John
Lodge	Forest	Smith Thos	Shopkeepers.
Farnsworth Rd	Moore John	Sulley Rd	Baguley Jph
Fox John	Moss Rt	Shoemakers.	Brunt Jph
Hardy John	Potts Jph	Bell Wm	Clark Wm
Hardy Thos	Theadle Wm	Culley Fras	Cundy Simon
Harwood Thos.	Wibberley Wm		
Broom house			

CAUNTON is a large but indifferently built village upon a small rivulet, 6 miles N. W. of Newark. Its parish has 542 inhabitants, and 2900 acres of land, of which 1600a. are in *Caunton*, 800a. in *Beesthorpe*, and 500a. in *Knapthorpe*, which form three separate manors, and contain 176 acres of woods. The tithes were commuted at the enclosure in 1793, for an allotment of 171a. to the appropriator, and 124a. to the vicar. Lord Middleton and Samuel Hole, Esq. are the principal owners of Caunton, and the latter is lord of the manor, and resides in the hall, a handsome modern mansion. The ancient farm house, called *Dean Hall*, belongs to Lord Scarborough, as also does *Worney Wood*. The *church* dedicated to St. Andrew is a vicarage, valued in the King's books at £4. 2s. 1d., and is annexed to the vicarage of North Muskham. The prebendary of North Muskham is the patron and appropriator, and the Rev. J. A. Wright the curate. A *sick club* holds its annual festival in the village on Whit-Monday.

BEESTHORPE hamlet and manor, 1 mile W. of Caunton, is the sole property of Samuel Ellis Bristowe, Esq. The *Hall*, a spacious mansion in the old style, of the reign of James I. is occupied by Wm. Miles, Esq. Near it is *Earlshaw*, an ancient mansion now occupied by a farmer.

KNAPTHORPE hamlet, 1 mile S. W. of Caunton, belongs to Richard Parkinson, Esq. It was anciently called *Chenapethorpe* and was partly *soc* to Laxton.

Bark Jph. grocer
Chappell Chas. joiner
Chappell Wm. shoemaker
Cocking Wm. timber dealer
Cutts Wm. miller, Mount Sorrell
Elvidge Geo. shoemaker
Elvidge Geo. wheelwright
Fox Rd. vict. & maltstr. Common
Hodson Geo. tailor
Hole Jas. maltster & farmer
Hole Saml. Esq. Caunton moor
Manners John, brklyr. Mt. Plsnt
Mellers Thos. school master
Miles Wm. Esq. Beesthorpe hall
Morris Wm. joiner

Parkinson Rd. Esq. Knapthorpe and Wellow
Shaw Jph. beerhouse
Talbot Geo. vict. Harrow
Taylor John, butcher
Trafford John, vict. & farrier
Ward Wm. corn miller
West Rd. gardener
Willis Mr. John Pearse
Woodhead John, blacksmith

Farmers.
Marked ‡ are in Beesthorpe.

Atkin Jph	Elvidge Hy
‡Bettinson Ts	Elvidge Wm
‡Chappell Thos	‡Farrands Wm

‡Herrington Ts Martin Wm   ‡Powell Abm.   Theaker Thos
Martin George, Palmer Wm.   Taylor Jph   Wood Wm
  Dean Hall   Holme hall

COLWICK is a small but pleasant village, under a long range of hills, on the north bank of the Trent, nearly 3 miles E. of Nottingham, containing 145 inhabitants, and 1235a. 3r. 15p. of land, belonging to John Musters, Esq. of Colwick Hall, whose ancestor obtained the manor from the Byron family, in the early part of the 17th century, either by purchase or at the card table. The HALL stands about half a mile west of the village, and forms the termination of a most agreeable evening's walk from Nottingham. The steep rock at its rear, rising in abrupt precipices, and finely tufted with overhanging woods, has a very picturesque appearance, and throws a sombre shade over the rest of the park, which is stocked with the antlered natives of the forest. The pleasure grounds and ornamental plantations exhibit a good specimen of modern improvement engrafted on the ancient model. The house consists of an elegant centre, crowned with a pediment, resting on four well proportioned ionic pillars, and joined by two wings of one lofty story, with an entablature supported by square pilasters with plain capitals, and lightened much in its effect by a handsome ballustraded parapet. It was built in 1776, by Mr. Stretton, of Nottingham, from an architectural design by Mr. Carr, of York. Mr. Thorosby complains of the dog kennels as being more elegant than many of the parsonage houses which he had seen in the county. As has been seen at page 111, Colwick Hall suffered considerably from a daring attack of the Nottingham *reform rioters*, in 1831, and the fear and dismay which this assault brought upon the family is supposed to have hastened the death of the late Mrs. Musters, who was the sole heiress of the ancient and wealthy family of *Chaworth*. (Vide p. 517 and 544.) The *church*, dedicated to St. John the Baptist, stands close to the hall, embosomed in foliage, and contains some ancient monuments of the Byrons and the Musters. The chancel was rebuilt by Sir John Musters Knt, in 1684. The *rectory*, valued in the King's books at £6. 1s. 0¼d., is in the gift of Mr. Musters, and incumbency of the Rev. L. E. Thoroton. This parish participates in the benefits of the *free school*, at West Bridgeford. The village has given its name to a thin soft kind of *cheese*, which is often seen amongst the refreshments set before parties at the tea gardens, and other places of public resort around Nottingham. The principal residents are John Musters, Esq.; Charles George Balguy, Esq.; Wm. Lacy, gent.; Rev. Levett Edward Thoroton, rector; and John Blackner, Rd. Clarkson, Thomas Housley, George Neale, Thomas Newham, Daniel Parker, Samuel Parr, and Samuel Waldram, *farmers*.

CROMWELL village and parish, on the great north road, 5 miles N. of Newark, contains 184 inhabitants, and 1400 acres of land, which was exonerated from tithes at the enclosure, in 1772, when 240 acres were allotted to the rector. It was anciently the seat of the Cromwell family, of whom was the Lord Treasurer Cromwell, who lived in great splendour at Tattershall castle, in Lincolnshire, in the reign of Henry VI. The Duke of Newcastle is the principal owner, lord of the manor, and patron of the rectory, which is valued in the King's books at £13. 2s. 3½d., and is now enjoyed by the Rev. Charles John Fiennes Clinton. The other principal residents are Wm. Bellamy, shoemaker; Joseph Blonk, vict.; John Mitchell, shopkeeper; John Richmond, basket maker; Thomas Summers, joiner; Wm. Swallow, blacksmith; and Samuel Banks, William Bradley, Thomas Footitt, John and Thomas Goodman, Edward Howson, Benjamin Smith, and Thomas Taylor, farmers.

EDINGLEY, 3 miles W. N. W. of Southwell, is a village and parish with 398 inhabitants, and about 2000 acres of land, which was enclosed in 1767, when allotments were made in lieu of the tithes. It is in the liberty of Southwell and Scrooby; the Archbishop of York is lord of manor, and the Chapter of Southwell are the appropriators and patrons of the vicarage, which is valued in the King's books at £4. A great part of the soil is copyhold or leasehold under them, and the rest belongs to a number of freeholders; the principal of whom, are Thomas Houldsworth, Henry Machon, and P. P. Burnell, Esqrs. The church is an ancient edifice, and the Rev. R. H. Fowler is the vicar. The *feast* is on the Sunday after Old St. Giles's Day. The *school* was endowed by John Lamb and Samuel Wright, in 1731, with a house and 5½ acres of land, to which 3A. 1R. 22P. was added at the enclosure. The poor have £14. 11s. yearly, arising from several benefactions.

OSMONDTHORPE, 1 mile N.E., and GREAVES LANE, 1 mile S.W. of the village, are two hamlets within the parish. Those marked * live at the latter.

Alvey Wm. schoolmaster
*Blagg Thos. joiner
Brown Wm. & Crich Wm. shoe-
  makers
Hurst Chas. butcher
Hutchinson Thos. tailor
Robinson Geo. corn miller
Robinson John, blacksmith
Taylor Thos. vict. & joiner

Whitelee Jas. & Linney Thos.
  shopkeepers

Farmers.
Allcock Saml   *Pursey Geo
Barrett Hy   Robinson Geo
*Beckett Wm   Smith Wm.
Bilbie Mary   Tagg Fras
*Blyton Geo   Wagstaff Thos
*Carver John   *Walstow Thos
*Elvidge Chas

EPPERSTONE, 7 miles S. W. of Southwell, is a village and parish in the deep vale of the Dover Beck, containing 518 inhabitants, and 2000 acres of land, of which nearly 350 acres are in woods. The common was enclosed in 1768, when 254 acres were allotted in lieu of tithes. Thos. Houldsworth, Esq. is principal owner and lord of the manor, which he purchased of the late Earl Howe. The *church* is dedicated to the Holy Cross, and has a tiled roof, a spire, and some curious old monumental stones. It is a rectory, valued in the King's books at £13. 1s. 8d., and the patronage has lately been purchased by the College at Manchester. The Rev. Thos. White, M.A. is the incumbent. The Wesleyan and Primitive Methodists have each a chapel in the village. The *feast* is on the first Sunday after All Saints' Day. The *poor* have £10. 10s. a-year, from four tenements purchased in 1765, with £50. left by Mary Leake. They have also the interest of £30, left by the Walker family.

Allwood Ts. butcher
Barnard John, tanner
Barnard W. & T. gent
Blagg Chpr. butcher
Clarke Lieut. Wm
Dufty Lieut. W. R.N.
Eperson Wm. vict
Foster Rd. paper mfr
Foster Wm. beer hs
Hall Edw. surgeon
Hodson Thos. saddler
Hopkinson Rt. vict
Knowles Jph. shoemkr
Lealand Miss Ann
Millward John, miller
Osborne J. surgeon
Pacey Wm. shopr
Parker Ts. wheelgt
Rose Thos. shoemkr
Sampson A. joiner
Sansom Wm. shoemkr
Sumner Peter, shopkr
White Rev. Ths. M.A.
Willis Saml. blksmith
Worthington & Pearson, shopkrs
Farmers.
Barrett Mr. ——
Greaves Richard
Heathcote John
Hurt Mr. Park
May John
Milward Thomas
Neep William
Parr Richard
Pacey Wm. Norwood
Wallis Samuel
Ward Edward
Geo. Addison, Jas. Taylor, & Jph. Smith, *carriers* to Nottingham, Sat.

FARNSFIELD is a large village, seated upon an eminence, 4 miles W. N. W. of Southwell. Its parish is within the liberty of Southwell and Scrooby, and contains 1010 inhabitants, and 3689A. 1R. 32P. of land, which was enclosed in 1780, when 350 acres were allotted to the three prebendaries of Normanton, Norwell Overhall, and Pallishall; 157A. 3B. 15P. to the vicar, and 5A. 1R. 21P. to the Chapter of Southwell, in lieu of tithes. The Archbishop of York is lord of the manor, in which E. Howitt, Esq., Wm. Houldsworth, Esq., and some others have estates, and also neat houses in the village. The *church* has one aisle and a square tower; is valued in the King's books at £4., and has 19A. 3B. 5P. of glebe, besides the allotment made at the enclosure. The Chapter of Southwell are the patrons, and Archdeacon Wilkins, D.D. is the incumbent. The Wesleyan and Primitive Methodists have each a chapel here. The *school*, with a house and 2 acres of land, was purchased in 1790 with £400 arising from the benefactions of Messrs. Watson and Hornby, and the sale of the Bull land. The master teaches 11 free scholars. The poor have the interest of £73. 15. from

3 M

the poor rates, left by several donors, and £45 bequeathed in 1820, by Samuel Higgs, and now in the Southwell Savings' Bank. They have also £6 yearly from *Temple Croft Close*, left by an unknown donor, and the interest of £20 left in 1827, by Mary Awdes.

Bonnigton Mrs. Mary
Brockelsby Thos. surgeon
Buckels John, painter
Bull John, vict. Plough
Butler Hy. blacksmith
Camm John, vict. White Post
Challand Hy. brickmaker
Cobb Geo. horsebreaker
Cottingham John, butcher
Dalby John, joiner
Denman John, gent
Denman W. miller, & W. butcher
Dixon John & Wm. bricklayers
Hage John, & Hall Rd. gent
Higgs Mrs. Eliz.
Hodgson Geo. saddler
Holliday Rt. maltster
Holliday Thos. vict. Wheat Sheaf
Holliday Wm. corn miller
Houldsworth William, Esq
Howitt Emanuel, Esq
Hurt John & Wm. gent
Kemble Geo. schoolmaster
Kemp Wm. Stay maker
Moises Miss Mary
Moody Cornelius, mole catcher
Moore Wm. rope maker
Pesson Mr. Charles
Rumford Rd. butcher
Shacklock Jph. hat manufacturer
Smedley Wm. beerhouse
Smith Hy. cart owner

Swift Thos. & Wm. wheelwrights
Tipping Fras. vict. & butcher
Todd Stephen, vict. Red Lion
Towne Leonard, druggist
Unwin Wm. joiner
Wright Grace, vict. Stag Inn
Wright Thos. blacksmith

Farmers.
Blyton Mary
Butler Wm
Cording John
Challand Geo.
Deaman Eliz.
Franks Rd.
Habbijam Hy.
Hall Rd.
Holliday Rt.
Howitt Ralph
Jackson Hy.
Jenkins Chas.
Mosley Geo.
Munks John
Palfreman Mr.
Paulson John
Shacklock Abm.
Stendell Edw.
Tipping Fras.
Todd Wm.
Truswell John
Truswell Rd.

Shoemakers.
Dixon Hy.

Doughty John
Glazebrook W.
Hind Richard
Knutton Geo.
Pettinger John
Pettinger James
Sumner Rd.
Tongue Thos.

Shopkeepers.
Burton Ann
Burton Eliz.
Cooley Job
Cooper Dl.
Smith Wm.
Stephenson Jno.
Tomlinson Wm.

Tailors.
Bartles Wm.
Gilbert Thos.
Hind John
Mycroft Geo.

Carrier.
Edm. Hodgson, to Nottm. Sat.

FLEDBOROUGH is a scattered village on the Trent bank, 6 miles E. by N. of Tuxford, at the northern extremity of Thurgarton Hundred. Its parish includes the hamlet of *Wood-cotes*, and comprises 1500 acres, and 314 inhabitants. Earl Manvers is the owner, lord of the manor, and patron of the rectory, which is valued in the King's books at £9. 7s. 6d., and is now enjoyed by the Rev. Thomas Trevenon Penrose. The church is an ancient fabric, dedicated to St. Gregory. In the early part of the last century, this place obtained the name of the *Gretna Green of Nottinghamshire*, from the then rector (a Mr. Sweetapple,) who, like the blacksmith of the Scottish border, immediately fettered with the chains of wedlock, all who applied to him for that happy purpose. The residents are the Rev. John Galland, curate; and Edward Bellyard, John Cooling, John Hague, John Charles Picking, William Billyard, Wm. Jackson, and George Pinder, farmers. The three last live at Woodcotes, 1½ mile W. of Fledborough.

GEDLING village, 4 miles E.N.E. of Nottingham, stands pleasantly in a small but picturesque valley which opens into the vale of the Trent. Its parish comprises the three townships of Gedling, Carlton, and Stoke Bardolph. Gedling contains 458 inhabitants and about 1000 acres of land. The Earl of Chesterfield is the principal owner, lord of the manor, and patron of the rectory, which is valued in the King's books (in two medieties) at £21. 2s. 8½d., and received at the enclosure three large allotments in lieu of tithes. The Rev. Charles Williams is the present incumbent. The church, dedicated to All Saints, has a handsome lofty spire and four bells. The large workhouse was built in 1787, and now belongs to thirty associated parishes. The poor's land consists of 7A. 0R. 17P. in Arnold, let for £14. 15s. per annum, and was purchased in 1735, with £122. 10s., which had been bequeathed to the poor of the whole parish; who have also the dividends of £550. 9s. 2d. consolidated 3 per cents., left in 1779 by Bishop Chenevix. Those of Carlton have 20s. yearly, out of the estate of the late John Aslin, who died in 1803. The *feast* is on the Sunday after All Saints', or on that day when it falls on a Sunday. Gedling House, on a steep declivity overlooking the Trent, is the handsome modern mansion of William Elliott Elliott, Esq.

CARLTON, 3 miles E. by N. of Nottingham, is the largest village and township in the parish, having 1370 acres, and 1704 inhabitants, many of whom are employed in the hosiery and lace manufactures. The hills above the village command extensive views of Nottingham and the vale of the Trent, and on one of them a new village has been built. A Methodist chapel was built in 1801, and another for the Baptists in 1823. Earl Manvers is lord of the Manor, but the Earl of Chesterfield is the greatest landowner.

STOKE BARDOLPH is a secluded village and township upon the Trent bank, two miles E. by S. of Gedling, and five miles E. of Nottingham. It has 181 inhabitants, and 1050 acres of land, which was enclosed in 1793. It had anciently a small chapel, and holds a *feast* on the Sunday after St. Luke's, and has a *ferry* across the Trent to Shelford. Earl Manvers and the Earl of Chesterfield are proprietors and joint lords of the manor.

GEDLING.

Bridger John, vict. Chesterfield Arms
Deabill John, shoemaker
Devill James, tailor
Elliott Wm. Elliott, Esq. Gedling House
Hemsley Rd. overseer
Neale Thos. yeoman
Palethorpe T. Oldknow, beerhs
Parr Thos. bobbin net maker
Pogson Alfred, bobbin net mkr
Shelton Wm. bsmith. & bnet. mkr
Shepherd John, gov. workhouse

Skellington Thos. blacksmith
Walker Geo. Esq. Gedling Lodge
  and Eastwood
Williams Rev. Chas. rector

Farmers.

Aslin John   Greenfield T.
Barnes Thos   Hardey Wm.
Bird Jas.   Higgat James
Bird John   Mitchelson T.
Brierley Wm.   Pogson Fras.
Butler Samuel   Savage John
Greenfield Jph. Tomlinson J.

CARLTON.

Those maked † reside at New
       Carlton.

Alvey John, blacksmith
Baker Wm. butcher
Barker John, vict. Volunteer
Blatherwick John, joiner
Brentnall Samuel, painter
Burton Thos. basket maker
Cave Ellz. vict. & maltster, Royal
  Oak
Cave Thos. vict. Windsor Castle
† Crampton Jas. Corn Miller
Davies John, gardener & beerhs
Davison Sandford Tatham, sur-
  geon
Deavill Jas. & John, tailors
Fearfield John & Sl. tailors
Holmes Wm. gent
Horsley Jas. beerhouse
Horsley Edw. basket maker
†Houlton John, corn miller
Jagger John, butcher
JaggerPamela, vict Black's Head
Kirk Hy. gardener
Mann Geo. butcher
Morris Thos. beerhouse
Pickels Mrs. Hannah
Porter Wm. gent
Richards Rd. wheelwright
Richmond W. butcher & beerhs
Savidge Geo. schoolmaster
Savidge John, corn miller
† Screeton John, Gen. Washing-
  ton beerhouse
Shelton Rt. maltster
Shelton Mrs. Sarah

Shipley Geo. frame smith
Smith Rt. King Wm. IV. beerhs
Smith John, blacksmith
Thornton Wm. butcher
Turner Saml. joiner
Twells Mrs. Hannah
Wilson Thos. gent

Bobbin Net Mkrs. Birch Wm
†Boyer Wm   Bradshaw Wm
Bush Caleb   Brammer Saml
†Chambers Wm Butler Rt
†Dawson Saml   Holmes John
Green Wm   Lee John
†Hummel Edw. Lee Saml
Lomas Saml   Mackley Rt
†Screeton John Mackley Rt
Tomlinson Rd   Martin Jas
†WheatcroftWmMartin Gvs
Shoemakers.   Newham Saml
†Blackner Ls   Newham Wm
Glew Wm   Richards John
Kaye Thos   Roulson Thos
Kaye Ts. jun.   *Hosiers.*
Marshall John   Brotherwood W
Rose Alfred   Dring Hy. (agt)
White Wm   Seagrave Thos
Whitworth Ts   Ward Rd
Brickmakers.   *Shopkeepers.*
†James Saml   Barker John
North Thos   Bell Rd
Smith John   Brittle Thos
Taylor John   Lock Martha
Wyler Chpr   †Lynam Jas
  Farmers.   Shard John
Alvin Saml   †Stubbs Saml
Aslin Rt   Turner Saml
Aslin Wm   †Waters & Clark
Baggaley John

STOKE BARDOLPH.

Cupit Wm. vict. Ferry Boat
Kirkham Fras. bobbin net mkr
Musson Geo. joiner
Salvin John, bobbin net mkr
  Farmers.   Kitchen John
Bage Susanna   Marshall John
Dring Eliz   Salvin Rd
Gill Wm   Shelton G & J
Jerram Rt

GONALSTON is a small rural village and parish, near the
Dover Beck, 5 miles S. S. W. of Southwell, containing 107 inhabitants, and 1200 acres of land, enclosed in 1768, when 155

acres were allotted for the tithes. R. D. Franklin, Esq. owns the whole lordship, and is patron of the rectory, which is valued in the King's books at £7. 19. 2d., and is now enjoyed by the Rev. Samuel Oldacre, M. A. The *church* is dedicated to St. Lawrence, and in Thoroton's time had some ancient effigies of crusaders, but they are now destroyed, as also are the remains of *Gonalston Spital*, which gives name to a small hamlet, and was founded by " Wm. Heriz, temp. of Henry III., to the honour of St. Mary Magdalen." The successive rectors being masters of this hospital, formerly preached their induction sermon upon its ruins. Its site was anciently called *Bradebusk*, from a remarkably broad thorn tree which grew near it. The poor have the interest of £17, left by an unknown donor. The principal residents are the Rev. S. Oldacre, John Barnes, shopkeeper; John Grocock, blacksmith; Wm. Walker, shoemaker; and Wm. Darby, Wm. Palethorpe, and Jas. Thos. and Wm. Hind, *farmers*. The *feast* is on the second Sunday after Sept. 19th.

HALAM is a pleasant village at the foot of a lofty range of hills, 1½ miles W. by N. of Southwell. Its parish, which is in the Liberty of Southwell and Scrooby, contains 370 inhabitants and 1600 acres of land, enclosed about 50 years ago, when allotments were made for the tithes. The Archbishop of York is lord of the manor, and the soil is held by a number of copyholders and leaseholders, except a few small freeholds, which are generally occupied by their owners. In the church windows are some rude paintings, one of which represents Adam digging, and Eve spinning. The living is a curacy in the'patronage of the Chapter of Southwell, and incumbency of the Rev. T. Still Basnett, M.A. The *feast* is on the Sunday after Old Michaelmas Day. Mary Sturtevant bequeathed to this parish in 1771, £230. 4s. 3d. three per cent. consols, and directed half the yearly dividends to be applied in repairing the church, and the remainder to be given to the poor, in 10s. shares. *Sower's close* was purchased with £14 poor's money, in 1686, and now lets for 25s. per annum.

Bailey Wm. land valuer	Wright John, wheelwright
Blighton Saml. joiner	*Farmers.*
Bull Wm. blacksmith	Bennett Saml Moore Jas
Chantry J. & Paulson J. shoprs	Bennett Wm Morley Thos
Glazebrook John, shoemaker	Craven Rt Rich John
Green Sl. & Smith Sl. joiners	Flint Wm Rogers Geo
Hallam Hy. vict. Waggon&Horses	Fountain Mr Smith Jas
Parks Wm. corn miller	Hallam Geo Thorpe Wm
Story Matthew, vict. & butcher	Hurt Saml Weightman Jno.
Taylor Wm. & Watts J. tailors	Leeson J. & W & Wm
Wilson Mr. James	Milward John

HALLOUGHTON is a small village upon an eminence 1¼ mile S. W. of Southwell, and its parish, which has 103 inhabitants, and 900 acres of land, is within the liberty of Southwell and Scrooby. Sir Robert Sutton, Bart. is the principal owner and lord of the manor. An ancient house here is supposed to have been the dwelling of some religious fraternity. In taking up its kitchen floor some years ago, the entrance to a subterraneous passage was discovered, and at the same time many human skeletons, principally of *children*, were found in a recess in the middle of a large stack of chimneys. The church is a small structure dedicated to St. James, and is in the appropriation and patronage of its own *Prebendary* in Southwell collegiate church. The perpetual curacy has been augmented with Queen Anne's Bounty, and is now enjoyed by the Rev. Richard Barrow. The *farmers* are Pp. Green, Thos. Kemp, John Marriott, Geo. Moore, Wm. Pogson, and John Tongue.

HAYWOOD OAKES, near Blidworth, 6 miles S.E. of Mansfield, is an extra-parochial liberty of 700 acres, belonging to Wm. Brodhurst, Esq., of Mansfield, and occupied by Mr. Samuel White.

HOCKERTON parish has a small village 2 miles N. by E. of Southwell, and contains 108 inhabitants and about 1600 acres of land. It anciently belonged to the families of Botiler and Cryche, but Admiral Southeron is now the sole lord and owner, and also patron of the rectory, which is valued in the King's books at £9. 9s. 4½d., and is now enjoyed by the Rev. Benjamin Clay, who has 50 acres of glebe. The small church is dedicated to St. Nicholas.—Rev. Hy. Good, curate; James May, shoemaker; James May, jun., beerseller; Geo. Wheatcroft, parish clerk; and John Holloway, John Rumford, and John and Richard Millwood, *farmers.*

HOVERINGHAM is a pleasant village near the Trent, 5 miles S. by W. of Southwell, comprising within its parish 347 inhabitants and 850 acres of land, a great part of which was given by the Goushill family to Thurgarton priory, from which it passed to Trinity College, Cambridge, which has since received other lands in lieu of the tithes. Sir Robert Sutton is lessee of the manorial rights, and of about 500 acres of the college land. The church, dedicated to St. Michael, is in the patronage of the same college, and is a curacy annexed to that of Thurgarton. The two livings only yield about £45 per annum. Near the village is a ferry across the Trent to Knighton, and a few scattered houses called *New Hoveringham.* The *feast* is on the Sunday after Old Michaelmas Day.

Allen Jph. fwk. knitter
Allwood W. vict. Dk. Wellington
Alvey Jph. bricklayer
Baines Jas. vict. & lime & coal mert. Ferry house
Beeston Mrs. Hannah
Cugson Jph. tailor
Flinders Mrs. Eliz
Hall Thos. joiner
Horsley Thos. blacksmith
Huthwaite Col. Hy. Hovgm. hall
Kirk John, beerhouse
Lown John, corn miller
Maltby Gilbert, gent.

Maltby Rd. gent, Lodge field
Oxley Wm. parish clerk
Saxton H. & Taylor W. shoemkrs
Smith John, fwk. knitter

Farmers.
Bradley John
Dalby Thos
Hall John

Isaacs Benj
Keyworth Thos
& maltster)
Morris Abm

Savage John
Wilson Thos
Wright Thos
Butchers.
Bainbridge Levi
Foster John

Hall Thos
Shopkeepers.
Davison Saml
Lee Ann
Thornton Thos

KELHAM is a small but pleasant village upon the Worksop road, and on the west bank of the Trent, 2 miles N.W. of Newark. Its parish contains 189 inhabitants and 1251 acres of land, of which 484 acres are on the island formed by the two rivers betwixt it and Newark.—(See p. 605.) It has long been the seat and property of the Suttons, who once held the title of Lord Lexington.—(See p. 377.) It is now the property of John Manners Sutton, a minor, who resides with his mother, Mrs. Harriet Henriette Manners Sutton, at KELHAM HALL, a plain but elegant building of brick, with stone corners and window frames, standing in a handsome lawn near the Trent, and consisting of a centre and two wings. A curious wooden bridge crosses the river close to the lawn and pleasure grounds, which, though not very extensive, are extremely pleasing and kept in good order. The *church*, dedicated to St. Winifred, has a handsome tower, and a richly wrought monument of the last Lord Lexington and his lady, of fine statuary marble, but the figures are strangely placed *back* to *back*. The living is a rectory valued in the King's books at £19. 8s. 4d., and is annexed to that of Averham, being in the same patronage and incumbency. The poor have the interest of £25 left by an unknown donor. The villagers are John Beetham, shoemaker; John Clark and Richard Hall, farmers; Rd. Fox, vict.; Jph. Hill, cattle dealer; Geo. Oldham, blacksmith, Jno. Robinson, wheelwright; John Shepherd, gardener; Mr. Pp. Spencer, Grove Cottage; James Taylor, tailor; and Mrs. Sarah Thompson.

KIRKLINGTON, in the Liberty of Southwell and Scrooby, 2½ miles N.W. by W. of Southwell, is a village and parish with 243 inhabitants and about 3000 acres of land, all belonging to Vice-Admiral Frank Southeron, except 400 ares owned by Earl Manvers. The admiral resides in the hall, and is lord of the manor, and lessee of the great tithes under the Chapter of Southwell Collegiate Church, the youngest vicar of which (now the Rev. R. H. Fowler,) alway enjoys the vicarage of this parish, which is valued in the King's books at £6. 13s. 4d. The *church* is dedicated to St. Swithen, and has a large chancel with some relics of old monumental stones and crosses. The poor have £30 left by Winifrid Arthur, in 1780.

otheron Vice-Admiral, Frank
Butler Edw. blacksmith

Ellis Thos. wheelwright
Freeman Wm. shopkr

Knight John, shoemaker
Smith Jas. gardener
Weightman Agar, tailor
Weightman H. joiner & p. clerk
White Jas. vict. White Hart
Winfield Jas. shoemaker

Farmers,
Bilbie John   Little Wm
Brocksop Rt   Oldham John
Foulds Rd   Robinson John
Harvey Edw   Winter John
Keyworth Geo

KNEESALL parish contains the three townships of *Kneesall, Kersall,* and *Ompton,* the latter of which is in the Bassetlaw Hundred, and is already described at page 384. Kneesall is a considerable village on the Newark turnpike, 4 miles E.S.E. of Ollerton, comprising within its township 399 inhabitants and 2000 acres of land, most of which belongs to Earl Manvers, who is lord of the manor, and built a lofty *cross* in the village in 1798. The *feast* is on the Sunday nearest to St. Bartholomew's Day, to which saint the church is dedicated. The vicarage, valued in the King's books at £10, is in the patronage and appropriation of the Chapter of Southwell. It has the curacy of Boughton annexed to it, and is now in the incumbency of the Rev. John Ison.

KERSALL, 1¼ mile S.E. of Kneesall, is a hamlet and township with only 94 inhabitants and 640 acres of land, belonging to S. E. Bristowe, Esq. and others ; but Earl Manvers is lord of the manor under the Crown. At the enclosure in 1778, the tithes were commuted for an allotment of 92 acres, of which the Earl is lessee.

KNEESALL.
Blank Wm. blksmith
Bradley J. blksmith
Broomhead Ts. shpr
Cook John, wheelgt
Cougill Rd. butcher
Duckmanton J. whlgt
Hurt Edmd. shoemkr
Ison Rev. John, vicar
Gee Jph. tailor
Grasby Thos. vict
Lee Wm. wheelgt
Marriott John, bsmith
Raynor Wm. tailor
Rose Benj. shoemkr

Rose John, joiner
Tongue Thos. vict
Trueman Wm. brick-
  layer & beer hs
Turton John shoemkr
Turtle Wm. miller
Farmers.
Bills Rt.
Birkett Saml
Furness G. Mainwood
Lee Geo
Moseley Jph. Park
Pearce W. Bucksher
Pinder Mrs. Lodge

Rose Jno. (& hop gwr.)
  Lound
Sampson John
Townrow Wm
Whittington Wm
Whitworth Arthur
KERSALL.
Hawksley J. yeoman
Haywood Wm. beerhs
Lightfoot Rd. miller
Moseley John, gent
  Kersall Lodge
Moseley Wm. gent
White Geo. sawyer
Wright Abm. joiner

LAMBLEY, 8 miles N.E. of Nottingham, is a large village at the head of a deep valley, sheltered by an amphitheatre of hills rising range above range. The parish has 824 inhabitants and 2092 acres of land, enclosed in 1793. Upon an eminence, 1 mile N.W. of the village, is *Lambley House,* the handsome seat of the rector, but the property of Lewin Cholmley, Esq., the lord and principal owner of the manor, in which there are, however, a number of other freeholders, and also an estate belonging to an hospital at Nottingham.—(See p. 164.) The church, dedicated to the Holy Trinity, is a small structure with a low tower. The rectory is valued in the King's books at £10. 16s. 3d., and has 90A. 2R. 11P. of glebe. The Rev. Alvery Dodsley Flamstead, is both patron and incumbent. The Methodists have a chapel here built in 1807. The *feast* is on Whit-Sunday. The poor receive 6s. yearly from the Nottingham Corporation, pursuant to the bequest of Samuel Martin.

Asling Edw. hosier	Renshaw Sl. miller	Dore John
Asling Jno. schoolr	Seston Jph. wheelgt	Fisher Edw
Cooper Wm. beer hs	Smith Sl. miller	Godby Rt. & Thos
Cowlishaw Wm. baker	Tomlinson Mr. Thos.	Hoffen Edw
Dearnley T. bricklr	& Ths. jun. butcher	Lane Wm
Dickman Rt. tailor	Walker Thos. butcher	Martin Rt
Flamstead Rev. A. D.	*Farmers.*	Robinson Wm
Kirk Saml. vict	Bennett Jph	
Marriott Jph. shoemr	Bridges John	Jno. Selby &Wm.Watson, carriers to Nottgm. Wed. & Sat
Parr Wm. bsmith	Brownlow Mordecai	
Plumb Dd. vict	Dearnley Henry	

LINDHURST, on the forest, 2½ miles S. E. of Mansfield, is an *extra-parochial* liberty of 700 acres, bounded on the north and south by two small streams, which unite at its eastern extremity, and form the Rainforth-water, near two extensive *fox covers*. It was anciently part of *Harlow wood*, but has been cleared and cultivated by its owner, the Duke of Portland. Mr. Rd. Godson Millns is the farmer.

LOWDHAM parish includes the three townships of Lowdham, Caythorpe, and Gunthorpe, which contain 1463 inhabitants and 2040 acres of land, which was enclosed in 1765, when 268 acres were allotted to the Duke of Kingston, and 93 to the vicar, in lieu of the tithes. *Lowdham* is a large village near the Dover Beck, 6 miles S. S. W. of Southwell. Its township contains 791 inhabitants, and 1800 acres. Peter Broughton Strey, Esq., is the principal owner and lord of the manor. S. and F. Wright, Esqrs., and Earl Manvers have estates here, and the latter is the impropriator, and patron of the vicarage, which is valued in the King's books at £4. 18s. 4d. and is now enjoyed by Archdeacon Wilkins. The church stands at the foot of a declivity, and has some antique monuments of the Lowdhams and Broughtons. The poor have 50s. yearly, from Agnes Cross's charity, and the interest of several benefactions amounting to £21. 10s.

CAYTHORPE is a small village and township, ¾ mile S. E. of Lowdham, containing 289 inhabitants, and 420 acres, belonging mostly to P. B. Strey, Esq., and Mr. Rd. Faulkes, the former of whom is lord of the manor. The poor have an *annuity* of 12s. left by John Smith, and another of 6s. left by Richard Whitehead.

GUNTHORPE village and township has 383 inhabitants, 820 acres of land, and a ferry across the Trent, opposite East Bridgeford, 9 miles E. N. E. of Nottingham. P. B. Strey, Esq., is lord of the manor, but most of the land belongs to Samuel and J. S. Wright, Esqrs. It had an ancient *chapel*, which in Thorosby's time was converted into a blacksmith's shop. The feast is on the second Sunday in October.

LOWDHAM.

Billings Wm Lockton, surgeon
Bradley & Hervey, lace thread manufacturers, Lowdham Mills.
Burton Jph. beerhs
Cooper Jph. shopkpr
Dennison B. schoolr
Foster Sml. paper mkr

Freeman John, vict. & joiner
Green Matt. joiner
Grocock Thos. vict. & blacksmith
Harvey Jph, manuftr
Laming W. shoemkr
Martin Wm. blacksth
Oldham John, miller
Paling Joseph, vict
Paling Jph. shopkpr

Paling Thos. shoemkr
Parr Geo. shoemaker
Porter Robert, tanner
Raisin Samuel, joiner
Reynolds J. wheelwbt
Savidge Jas. tailor
Savidge J. wheelwright
Stokes Wm. tailor
White Geo. net maker
Wignall Wm. shoemkr

Farmers.
Abbott Samuel,
Abbott Thos.
Brett Henry
Foster Wm.

Foster Wm. jun. & brickmaker
Franks Ambr.
Harding Fras.
Hill Henry
Jarratt John

Lown John
Palin William
Savadge James

Stanley Thos.
Talbot Gilbert
Webster John

Joseph Reddish, *carrier* to Newark, Wed. & Nottingham, Sat.

CAUNTHORPE.
Thus * *are yeomen.*
Bailey Wm. shopkpr
Bosworth Mrs. Eliz.
* Faulkes Rt. miller
Fitchett Jph. baker
Giles Mr. Henry
Hucknall Mrs. Eliz.
* Hucknall Mr. Thos
Jerram Wm. beerhs
* Keyworth, Rt
Maltby Geo. miller
Paling Henry, vict

* Pearce James
* Ragstall William
Stapleton M. shoemkr
Tomlinson J. beerhs
GUNTHORPE.
Attwood Rd. vict.
Bullan J. gardener
Burrows Stn. tailor
Dansey Danl. R. Esq. Gunthorpe Lodge.
Fisher Edw. shoemkr
Heald John, wheelgt
Huskisson William

Knight R. & W. net
Leek John, wheelgt
Marriott Jno. shopkr
Marriott Thomas vict. miller & maltster,
Ferry House
Pilkington W. butcher
Scraton Wm. grocer
Stokes Robert vict
Towers Thos. net mkr
Walker John, smith
Ward John, agent
Williams T. net mkr

Farmers.
Beecroft Thos
Brittle Thomas
* Hall Jas

Jamson Samuel
Johnston Edw.
Lealand John

Palethorpe Jno. Peck W. & Edw. John Bullan, & Gervas Mayfield, carriers to Nottingham, Wednesday and Saturday.

MAPLEBECK is a village and parish, 5 miles S. E. by S. of Ollerton. It contains 181 inhabitants, and about 1200 acres of land, of which the Duke of Newcastle is lord and principal owner. His grace is also patron of the curacy, which was certified at £19. 10s. and is now in the incumbency of the Rev. Joseph Blandford. The church is a small edifice with a tower and short spire. The Markhams had a large hall here, which cost more than the lordship sold for in 1666, when it was pulled down. The poor have £3 a-year from *Sudbury's charity.* (See Egmanton.)

Blyton Geo. shoe mkr	Henfry John, wheelgt	Knight J. shoe maker
& parish clerk	Henfry John, vict. &	Whitton Fras. tailor &
Hall Ann, schoolmrs	shopkeeper	shopkpr
Haywood Rd. wheelgt	Key Mrs. Catherine	

Farmers.	Key James	Turner Thomas	Wood Samuel
Doncaster Matt.	Key John	Wainwright Jno.	Wright Charles
Doncaster Wm.	Law Henry	Wood James	Wright Job
Johnson Wm.	Moore George		

MARNHAM parish, on the west bank of the Trent, comprises the two townships of Marnham and Grassthorpe. The former contains 1767 acres of land, (besides the Holme, which is divided into cow-gates,) and 258 inhabitants, resident in the neighbouring hamlets of *Ferry Marnham* and *Church Marnham,* distant 5 miles E. by S. of Tuxford. Earl Brownlowe is the principal owner and lord of the manor of Marnham, which was of the fee of Roger de Busli. The hall, which stood betwixt the two villages, was the property of the Cartwrights, but was sold and taken down about 40 years ago, before the death of the late patriotic Major Cartwright, who was born in it, and had several extensive estates in the neighbourhood. (See page 310.) A large *fair* is held here on Sept. 12th, for horses, horned cattle, and merchandise. The *church* is a small fabric dedicated to St. Wilfrid, and is a *vicarage,* valued in the King's books at £8. 19s. Earl Brownlowe is the impropriator and patron, and the Rev. John Alexander Lawrence the incumbent. One of the *De Chaurces* or *Chaworth* family gave this church to the Knights Templar; and another, in the reign of John, granted to the monks of Radford, " free passage for themselves, their servants, and their carriages, in his *ferry boat* here." The Ferry is at the northern village, and crosses the Trent to South Clifton. In 1677, *Henry Nicholson* left to the poor of Marnham township, land at Normanton, Grassthorpe, and East Markham, which now lets for £40. 10s. per annum, out of which £10 is paid to the master of the school, which was built by Earl Brownlowe in 1827. The poor of Grassthorpe have £4. 5s. yearly out of a field, left in 1677, by the said Henry Nicholson.

GRASSTHORPE or *Greisthorpe,* 1 mile S. W. of Marnham, is a village and township with 118 inhabitants, and 820 acres of land, enclosed in 1799, when allotments were made in lieu of all the tithes. About one-third of it is in the parishes of Normanton and Sutton. It is a member of the *manor of Normanton,* for which J. E. Denison, Esq., holds a copyhold court and a court baron, for the transfer of property, &c.

SKEGBY, 3½ miles E. of Tuxford, is a hamlet and three farms in the township of Marnham.

MARNHAM.	Broom Rd. joiner	Merchant Hy. shopkr
*Those marked * are in*	Lawrence Rev. J. A.	* Taylor W. shoemkr
North Marnham, † *in*	Machin Hy. pig jobber	* Walsham W. shoemr
Skegby, and the rest	* Marshall Cphr. vict.	* Walters Jph. beerhs
in South Marnham.	Ferry House	

Farmers.	Eyre Robert	Marshall Thos.	† Wilkinson W.
Burton Nathan	* Fletcher Saml	* Porter John	—
† Clarke Bryan	Forest Mary	Whitworth Fras.	Richard Smith,
Clarke Mary	* Fox William	Wilkinson Jph.	*Carrier* to New-
Curtis Samuel	Marshall Chpr	Wilkinson J.	ark, Wednesday.
Davison Wm	† Marshall John	jun.	

GRASSTHORPE.	Rhodes Rd. yeoman	Ward Wm. farmer
Jackson Geo. beerhs	Seels Wm. & Ward	Wilkinson Thos. vict.
Kirkland Wm. farmer	Ann, millers	Plough

MORTON, in the Liberty of Southwell and Scrooby, and 3 miles S. E. of Southwell, is a village and parish, with only 156 inhabitants, and about 500 acres of land, exclusive of the open fields, (1600 acres) in which the lands of this parish and Fiskerton, are so intermixed as to be almost undistinguishable. The *church* is a small brick building, and is a curacy with 30 acres of glebe. The prebendary of Dunham is the patron, and the Rev. Chas. Fowler the incumbent. John Pemberton Plumptre is lord of the manor, impropriator, and principal owner of the soil. In 1695, Richard Daybell left 50s. yearly for the education of four poor children of Morton and Fiskerton, and it is now paid by Thos. Bolger, Esq.

Ainsworth T. shoolr	Jowett Mrs. Elizabeth	Wilson Jas. cow leach
shopkpr & carrier	Scrimshaw Ben. joiner	Wilson R. blacksmith
Blyton Jas. shoemkr		

Farmers.	Hutchinson T	Marriott Wm.	Rawson George
Allcock Wm	Jenkinson John	Moore James	Wilson Joseph
Daybell Thos	Jowett Chpr	Neale Edward	

MUSKHAM (NORTH) parish contains the three townships of *North Muskham, Bathley,* and *Holme,* in which are 802 inhabitants, and 2900 acres of land, enclosed in 1771, when 91 acres were allotted to the vicar, and 300 to Earl Fauconberg, in lieu of the tithes. The Earl has since sold the impropriate lands to various persons.

NORTH MUSKHAM is a pleasant village on the great north road, 3 miles N. of Newark. Its township comprises 484 inhabitants, and 1200 acres of rich land, on the west bank of the Trent. Joseph Pocklington, Esq., is lord of the manor, and the soil belongs to him and several other freeholders. *Muskham House,* a superb mansion, built by the Pocklingtons in 1793, is now unoccupied. The *Grange,* an ancient mansion, now occupied by John Handley, Esq., was the seat of the late *Wm. Dickenson Rastall, Esq.,* who distinguished himself as a topographer of some of the most interesting parts of his native county. A *Mr. Wass*, who died here in 1805, had not been out of his own house for nearly 30 years, in consequence of a vow which he had taken, and which he religiously kept; notwithstanding the entreaties of his friends. The *church* is a neat Gothic fabric of the 14th century, dedicated to St. Wilfrid.— The *vicarage* is valued in the King's books at £5. 6s. 8d. and has 22 acres at Skegby, purchased with Queen Anne's bounty besides the 91 acres mentioned above. It is in the patronage of the *Prebendary* of North Muskham, and incumbency of the Rev. J. M. Parry, M.A. The *school* was endowed in 1727 and 1745, by Mary Woolhouse and Mary Disney, with a house and 3 acres of land, which received at the enclosure an allotment of 11A. 34P. For this endowment the master and mistress teach 10 boys and 10 girls. Ten poor parishioners receive 20s. and a black gown each every year, from the *Bathley Grange Estate*, pursuant to the bequest of John Smith, in 1581. In 1663, John Kemp, left two cottages, a house, and 15 acres of land, to the poor of North Muskham township. They are now let for £25. a-year. The parish *feast* is on the Sunday after September 12th.

BATHLEY is a straggling village and township, with 197 inhabitants, and 800 acres of land, 1 mile W. of North Muskham. Joseph Pocklington, Esq. is lord of the manor, but the soil belongs to several freeholders.

HOLME, 3½ miles N. of Newark, is a village and parochial chapelry, annexed to the vicarage of North Muskham, its small church being in the same patronage and incumbency. About the year 1600, the Trent changed its course, so that this township is now on the east side of its present channel. The church has many monuments of the Barton family, and over the south porch is a chamber called "*Nan Scott's*," from a woman who is said to have lived in it for several weeks when the plague was so fatal in the village that only one person escaped its ravages. The lordship contains 121 inhabitants, and 900 acres, belonging to the Duke of Newcastle, Thos. Adwick, and others.

NORTH MUSKHAM.		
Atkin George, joiner	Handley John, Esq.	Thompson J. ferryman
Atkin John, schoolmr	Muskham Grange	& overseer
Bennett John, cooper	Harrison Rd. baker	Tinker G. starch mfr
Brown Edw. shopkpr	Harrod Wm. vict	Weightman S. butcher
Brown Wm. miller	Hewes Edw. miller	Weightman Thos vict.
Chatwen S. parish clrk	Hewing Wm. excise	Welby Mrs. Mary
Cragg Wm. shoe mkr	officer	Whitworth J. wheelgt
Doubleday W. butcher	Howson D. horse dr	Worsley Capt. Thos
& beerhouse	Hutchinson Hy. tailor	Taylor
Fogg Jph. shoemaker	Lawson John, tailor	*Farmers.*
Foster John, maltster	Nicholson J. shoemkr	Bourne John
Foster John, smith	Parry Rev. Joseph	Howsin Wm
	Robinson Mrs. Mary	Key Edward
	Taylor John, wheelgt	Levers Wm

3 N

Robinson Jno	Capps John	*Farmers.*
Shepherd Wm	Cartwright Bryan	Blundy William
Smith Dd. Foxholes	Dixon Joseph	Crapper Eliz.
Smith Chas	Goodman Rd	Dickenson Saml
Weightman Saml	Goodman Thos	Dixon William
BATHLEY.	Holmes Samuel	Doncaster Thos
Capps Rich. vict	Roberts John	Hindley Thomas
Holmes Saml shoemkr	HOLME.	Knight George
Hough Thomas smith	Adwick Thos. gent	Pacey Frances
Farmers.	Holt John, joiner	Wells William

MUSKHAM (SOUTH) is a village and pariah, on the north road, close to the clumsy and dangerous wooden bridge, which crosses the broad stream of the Trent, two miles N. by W. of Newark. It has 261 inhabitants, and belongs to Lord Middleton, who is also the impropriator. The church is dedicated to St. Wilfrid, and is in the patronage of its own Prebendary in Southwell Collegiate church. The vicarge is valued in the King's books at £4, and is now enjoyed by the Rev. Richard Barrow. The *feast* is on the second Sunday after Old Michaelmas day. The inhabitants are Jph. Bean, shopkeeper, John Fletcher, parish clerk; Charles Foster, smith; Gervis Foster, victualler; George Radford, shoemaker; George Whitworth, joiner; Eliz. Mackley, Chas. Neale, Robert Parlby, Richard Tallington, John Toder, Jph. Brown, Henry Gilbert, Cath. Hole, Henry Hole, and Richard Simson, farmers; and Wm. Tidybridge, shoemaker. The last six live in LITTLE CARLTON, a hamlet 1 mile W. of the village, but within the parish.

NORMANTON-ON-TRENT, 4 miles S. E. by E. of Tuxford, is a pleasant village upon a declivity, 1½ mile W. of the river, to which its parish extends, including within its limits 349 inhabitants, and 1270 acres of land. The open fields were enclosed in 1804, when 124A. 3R. 30P. were alloted to the impropriator, and 56A. 2R. 12P. to the vicar in lieu of the tithes. The church is a small edifice dedicated to St. Matthew, and is in the patronage of the Duke of Devonshire, who has lately sold the impropriate land to the Rev. Wm. Doncaster, who now enjoys the *vicarage*, which is valued in the King's books at £4. 5s. J. E. Denison, Esq. is lord of the manor, which is held by a number of copyholders. The *school* was built in 1776, by Henry Jackson, and was endowed in 1781, by Mrs. Hall, with land that now lets for £9 a-year, for which, and a house and garden, the master teaches 10 free scholars. In 1781, *Eliz. Gaches* built two houses for poor women. In 1790, Eliz. Hall erected four *almshouses* for four poor women, and endowed them with land at Little Hale, in Lincolnshire, which now lets for £45 per annum. The indigent parishioners have £12. 15s. yearly, arising from the *poor's land*, left by Walter Mellor and several other benefactors.

Doncaster Rev. Wm. Normanton Hall
Brown Wm. joiner & beerhouse
Cooper John, maltster
Fowe R. shopkeeper & beerhouse
Newton Henry, joiner
Parkin & Newbert, smiths
Saxby Henry, tailor
Shaw Mr. Joseph
Sims John, shoemaker
Stevens William, schoolmaster
Templeman John, wheelwright

Townrow Eliz. miller & shopk'pr
Townrow John, victualler
Farmers.
Adcock John
Atkin Joseph
Brownlow Wm.
Buttery John
Derry Samuel
Eyre William
Ingham William
Johnson John
Johnson Wm.
Johnson Jph
Mills George
Newbert Francis
Selby Benjamin
Skelton George
Wallace Thos.
Wright Hannah

NORWELL parish comprises the three townships of Norwell, Norwell-Woodhouse, and Carlton-on-Trent, in which are 939 inhabitants, and about 4,000 acres of land, which was exonerated from tithes at the enclosure in 1826. *Norwell* is a large village upon a declivity, 7 miles N. N. W. of Newark. It has within its lordship 533 inhabitants, and 2700 acres, of which its three *prebendaries* in Southwell Collegiate church are lords and principal owners, but have let their lands to several lessees. Their prebends are distinguished by the names of *Norwell Overhall, Norwell Pallishall,* and *Norwell Tertia;* and the first is said to be richer than any other possessed by the chapter of Southwell. The *church* is a large edifice, dedicated to St. Lawrence, and was formerly in two vicarages, each valued at £4. 12s. 11d., but they are now consolidated in the patronage of the two prebendaries of Norwell Overhall and Tertia. The Rev. Edward Chaplins is the present vicar. *Preston chapel,* on the site of an ancient mansion called Preston Hall, was built for the Methodists in 1827. The *school* was endowed in 1727, by Thomas Sturtevant, with three acres of land at Holme, which has since been exchanged for 6 acres at Bathley. Several benefactions left to the school and poor, amounting to £164. 4s., were laid out in 1733, in the purchase of *Wellfen closes,* (11 acres) which are now let for £30 a-year. In 1782, Samuel Wood left £80, and directed 40s. of the yearly interest to be given for the education of four poor boys, and the rest to the poor. The master's salary is now about £40, for which he teaches 28 poor boys and girls. He has also a small garden, which was given to the school in 1827, by J. E. Denison, Esq. one of the trustees. The poor parishioners have the interest of £105, left by Mrs. Margaret Sturtevant and Leonard Esam, and the dividends of £230. 4s. 3d. three per cent. consols, purchased with the bequest of Mary Sturtevant, in 1768, partly for clothing the free scholars.

MIDDLETHORPE, 2¼ miles S. W. of Norwell, and in that township, is an estate of 160 acres completely encompassed by the parish of Caunton. It is the property of Mr. G. Doncaster.

NORWELL WOODHOUSE is a scattered village, 1¼ mile

W. N. W. of Norwell. Its township contains 141 inhabitants, and 444 acres of land, most of which is leasehold, under the prebendaries of Norwell. The poor have the interest of £10.

WILLOUGHBY is a hamlet, in the township of, and 1 mile N. E. of Norwell. It forms a separate manor, of which S. E. Bristowe, Esq. is lord, but R. Pocklington, Esq. and other free-holders have estates in it. The ancient manor house, which had long been in ruins, was taken down in 1785.

CARLTON-ON-TRENT is a pleasant village and chapelry, 7 miles N. of Newark, containing 265 inhabitants, and 1000 acres of land, mostly belonging to Roger Pocklington, Esq. the lord of the manor, who resides at *Carlton House,* a hand-some mansion which was built in the last century, and was long the seat of Sir William Earle Welby, Bart. The ancient chapel has a brick tower, and is annexed to the vicarage of Norwell. Here is a commodious inn upon the great north road, and a ferry across the Trent to Besthorpe and South Scarle. Carlton Steam Mill was burnt down in 1831, and has just been rebuilt, but it stands within the adjacent parish of Sutton.

NORWELL.

Blonk Joseph, blacksmith
Bradley James, gent. Willoughby
Brownlow T. shopkpr & beerhs
Cooper W. & Wright W. wheelgts
Cox William, tailor
Curtis John, victualler & butcher
Herring Rev. Edmund, curate
Houghton George, shopkeeper
JacksonG. & ScatchardJ. bsmiths
Knight Wm. grocer & chandler
Templeman Jph. miller & beerhs
Weightman Thos. vict. & shopkpr
Wheatcroft Samuel, corn miller
Wheatcroft John, farrier &c.
Wilson William, schoolmaster

Farmers. Templeman Jno.
Bomford Thos. Templeman T.
Bomford Thos. Whitley John
Clarke George Wilson Thomas
Clarke William, *Shoemakers.*
Lodge Chappell Joseph
Cobb William Davison James
Curtis Samuel Hallam George
Doncaster Chas. North Thomas
Esam Leonard Stacy William
Jackson George *Carriers,* Tho.
Nettleship Tho. Radford & Wm.
Radford Thos. Wass to Newark,
Scatchard Saml. Wednesday.

CARLTON-ON-TRENT.

Pocklington Roger Esq. Carlton

Hutton Geo. Wm. Esq. solicitor
Brown J. & Buttery W. joiners
Bulley Fras. coal mercht. wharf
Buttery Joseph, vict. Bell Inn
Hole Saml. Esq. maltster & miller
Mayfield Edward, shoemaker
Moore John, saddler
Price Samuel, tailor
Price Wm. & Starkey W. shoemks
Revill W. blacksmith, farrier, &c.
Smith Thos. attorney & maltster
Taylor William & Co. millers &c.

Farmers. Smith William
Dewick John Taylor Richard
Gibson Daniel Weightman Hgh
Pinder William

Wm. Morriss, *postman,* to Newark, departs 9 morning, arrives 12 noon.

NORWELL WOODHOUSE.

Broomhead George, bricklayer & beerhouse
Broomhead Thomas, bricklayer
Caudwell John, beerhouse
Gilby T. & Pearce H. shoemakrs
Taylor William, blacksmith

Farmers. Marshall George
Atkin John Pearce John
Baines Ann White Hugh
Chappell John Wilmot Thomas
Clay John Wood John
Drury Thomas

OSSINGTON is a pleasant village and parish, 4 miles S. S. E. of Tuxford, on the Carlton and Kneesall turnpike, which was formed in 1812. It has 257 inhabitants, and 2355A. 1R. 3P. of good clay land, of which John Evelyn Denison, Esq. M.P. is sole lord and owner, and resides in the hall, a handsome modern mansion, with an extensive park and pleasure grounds, built on the site of the ancient house which was partly destroyed in the civil wars, and was for many generations the seat of a branch of the Cartwright family, that ended in four coheiresses, who sold the estate to the late Wm. Denison, a rich woollen merchant of Leeds, who died in 1782, after realizing a fortune of £700,000, a large portion of which he gained, it is said, by one ship's cargoe which arrived at Lisbon immediately after that city had been nearly destroyed by an earthquake. On his monument in the church he is represented standing upon a pedestal with his ship unloading in the haven of Lisbon. The *church*, which is a neat structure, dedicated to the Holy Rood, has several other beautiful monuments, particularly two belonging to the families of Cartwright and Peckham. The living is a perpetual curacy, and the Rev. John Galland is the incumbent. J. E. Denison, Esq. is the patron and impropriator. The Rev. — Snowden left to the poor of this parish a rent charge of 18s., which was exchanged in 1799, for an allotment of 1R. 26P. at Grassthorpe. The schools were built in 1828, by Mr. Denison, who pays for the education of all the poor boys and girls of the parish.

Denison John Evelyn, Esq. M.P. Ossington Hall
Cook John, parish clerk
Garrad Wm. butler
Hallam John, shoemaker
Herod Joseph, gardener
Holmes George, gamekeeper
Pearson Thos. wheelgt. & smith
Taylor Wm. blacksmith
Tustin J. & Crooks E. shopkrs.
Tustin Wm. vict. Star
Weightman Hugh, schoolmaster
Farmers.
Lees Geo
Palmer John
Pawson Hy
Pawson Rt
Pawson Thos
Smith Wm
Taylor John
Wilson Thos.

OXTON, 5 miles W. by S. of Southwell, is a large village in an open vale, under the hills, on the eastern side of the Dover Beck. It has within its parish 778 inhabitants, and 4000 acres of land, of which upwards of 1500 acres are in the open forest of Sherwood, where there is an extensive *rabbit warren*. The late Wm. Sherbrooke, Esq. who died in 1831, was principal owner and lord of the copyhold manor of Oxton, and his widow, Mrs. Ann Sherbrook, now resides in the *hall*, a neat mansion with a projecting centre, and a handsome pediment. Thos. Redgate, Esq.; John Richardson, Jas. Harvey, Thos. Lamb, and several others have estates here. Near the village are three large *tumuli*. (See p. 19.) The church is an ancient fabric, with a low tower and four bells, and is in the
3 N 2

patronage and appropriation of its two *Prebendaries*, who form part of the chapter of Southwell. The vicarage is valued in the King's books at £24. 10s. and has the vicarge of Blidworth annexed to it. The joint livings are now enjoyed by the Rev. Collingwood Fenwick, for whom the Rev. John Downall officiates. The Wesleyan and Primitive Methodists have each a chapel here. The *school*, which was rebuilt in 1831, was endowed by Margaret Sherbrooke, in 1783, with land at Austerfield, now let for £20 per annum, for which, and £6 given by the present Mrs. Sherbrooke, the master teaches 30 free scholars. The poor have the following yearly sums, viz. £5 from a field left in 1690 by a Mr. Godfrey; £3 left in 1714 by Henry Sherbrooke; 4s. left by Rd. Chapman, in 1725, and 5s. bequeathed by John Little, in 1756.

Alvey Thos. bricklayer
Ashmore John, tailor
Bean Rd. joiner
Birch Rd. smith
Brett Saml. Fox beerhouse
Coape Miss Eliz
Cooke John, maltster
Cottingham William, butcher
Handley Wm. baker & flour dlr
Lamb Rt. hosiery mafr. & shopr
Marshall John, nurseryman, &c.
Miller John vict. Green Dragon
Moore Hy. vict. Royal Oak
Mountenay Thos. net maker
Naylor Jph. hosier & shopr
Oates John Coupe Sherbrooke, Esq. & Mrs. Sarah
Palethorpe John, baker, &c.
Paulson John, wheelwright
Pettison Jas. joiner
Richardson Sl. and Rt. net mfrs
Sherbrooke, Mrs. A. Oxton Hall
Stansall Thos. joiner

Thurman Burgess, tailor
Thurman Jph. shopkpr
Wood Saml. painter, &c.
  Corn Millers. Rowland Wm
Harvey Paul Shooter John
Howitt Ann Simpson Saml
Palethorpe Rd Smedley John
  Farmers. Spurr Esther
Adams John Summer Thos
Bell Jonth Wain Saml
Bird Thos Wood Rd
Butler D. & Sl *Shoemakers.*
Chapman Edw Berridge Thos
Dodson Jas Gibson Rt
Gibson John Greaves Thos
Harvey J. & W Parker Ntl
Hopkinson John Parnell Wm
Lamb T. & G Revill Fras
May Wm Strutt Jno
Needham Jb *Carriers.*
Palethorpe John Eliz. Thorpe
Parker Wm and T. Dalton,
Richardson Jn to Nottm. Sat

PARK LEYS, 5 miles N.W. by W. of Newark, is an extra-parochial farm of 300 acres, occupied by James Clark, and belonging to J. Manners Sutton, Esq., of Kelham.

ROLLESTON is a pleasant village 3 miles E. by S. of Southwell, including within its parish the two townships of Rolleston and Fiskerton, in which are 586 inhabitants and 2600 acres of land, intersected by the river Greet, and bounded on the south and east by the Trent. *Rolleston* has 272 inhabitants, and 1500 acres, nearly all belonging to John Manners Sutton, Esq., who is also lessee of the great tithes under the Chapter of Southwell, with whom the patronage of the vicarage, valued in the King's books at £10. 1s. 3d., is vested. The Rev.

Charles Fowler is the incumbent, and has about 27 acres of glebe. The church is an ancient structure dedicated to St. Wilfrid. The poor have the interest of £130 bequeathed by Sir Thomas Lodge, Diana Gibson, Luke Williamson, and Nicholas Kirkby.

FISKERTON, 3 miles S.E. of Southwell, is a village on the north bank of the Trent, opposite Stoke. It has a ferry, several coal wharfs and warehouses, a cotton mill employed in doubling lace thread, and a large blacking manufactory. Here was anciently an *Austin cell*, founded by Ralph de Ayncourts, and supplied with black canons from Thurgarton priory. It had a chapel dedicated to the Blessed virgin. The Methodists have a small chapel here. The township contains 314 inhabitants, and 1100 acres of rich loamy land. John P. Plumptre, Esq., is the principal owner, lord of manor, and impropriator, but here are several other freeholders.

ROLLESTON.		
Aulsbrook Rd. miller	Fryer John	Preston Sus. shopr
Chamberlain &Whit-	Galland Geo	Taylor Benjamin, coal
ton F. tailors	Knutton Thos	mercht. & wharfgr
Chappell J. shoemkr	Lloyd John	Taylor Benj. & Sons,
Cocking Wm. butcher	Pluckwell Wm	boat owners
Crossland Mrs. Mary	Peck Thos	Wright Wm. & Ger-
Fowler Rev. Chas	Wise Sarah	vase, blacking, ink,
Haywood J. shoemkr	FISKERTON.	and stove polish
Ollive Rd. vict	Bolger Thos. Esq.	mfrs. and wharfgrs
Pepper Sl. shoemkr	Bennett J. shoemkr	*Farmers.*
Revill Sl. smith	Daybell J. shoemkr	Bailey S. & W
Smith Wm. willow gr	Eaton Jn. lace thread	Butt Wm
Wise Rt. ferryman	manufacturer	Handley Geo
Woodward J. joiner	Foster Saml. shopr	Pattinson John
Farmers.	Gent John, shoemkr	Preston Geo
Aldridge John	Hunt J. boat owner	Richards John
Cullen John	Mason Geo. joiner	Searcy Thos
	Pacey T. boat owner	Theobald Chas

SNEINTON parish forms a populous eastern suburb of Nottingham, and has partaken so largely of the prosperity of that town, that, since the year 1801, its population has encreased more than sixfold, so that it now amounts to 3567 souls, living in the hamlets of *Old Sneinton*, *New Sneinton*, *Middle Sneinton*, *Element Hill*, and the *Hermitage*, as has been seen at pages 76 and 77. Most of this augmentation has taken place during the last ten years, in which upwards of 400 new houses have been erected, forming several handsome streets extending on the Southwell road to the eastern limits of Nottingham, though the old village is more than a mile E. of the market-place. The parish contains about 800 acres of land, and Earl Manvers is the principal owner and lord of the manor, which was originally crown land; but King John granted it to *Wm. de Briwere*; from whom it went in the

reign of Edward I., to *Tibetot*, and was held of him at the same
time by *Robert Pierrepont*, by the service of a pair of gloves,
or one penny. It has continued ever since in the Pierrepont
family, who gave the common near St. Anne's Well to the
parishioners. Its ancient name was *Snottington* or *Nottington*,
(see page 81,) and its first inhabitants dwelt in the *rocks and
caves* which are already described at page 122. The old village is very romantic, and has a number of pleasant villas and
cottages. Its small and ancient *church*, dedicated to St. Stephen,
is covered with rough plaster, and has nothing to recommend it
particularly to notice, except the views from the burial ground,
which occupies the summit of a bold excavated rock, and commands extensive prospects over the vales of Trent and Belvoir,
as far as the "Leicestershire forest rock," at a distance of 20
miles. From this elevated spot, the spectator looks down upon
the beautiful seat of Colwick Hall, and upon the wharfs and
warehouses near the Trent-bridge, some of which are in this
parish. The benefice is a *perpetual curacy*, certified at £12.,
and was annexed to the vicarage of St. Mary's, in Nottingham,
until 1831, when Dr. Wilkins, being, we suppose, overladen
with more valuable church preferment, gave up this poor living
to the Rev. Wm. Whyatt. Earl Manvers is the patron both
here and at St. Mary's. The poor have £3. 12. yearly, from
£120. 2s. 6d. three per cent. consols, purchased with £100,
bequeathed in 1771, by Elizabeth Teage.

Those marked 1 in the following *Directory of Sneinton Parish*,
live in Bond st.; 2 Byron st.; 3 Carlton rd.; 4 Colwick st.; 5
Dale st.; 6 Elment hill; 7 Eyre st.; 9 Hermitage; 10 Harold st.;
11 Haywood st.; 12 Manvers st.; 13 Middle st.; 14 North st.; 15
Nottington place; 16 Pierrepont st.; 17 Sneinton rd.; 18 Sneinton hill; 19 South st.; 20 West st.; 21 Windmill hill; and 22 at
Trent Bridge. Those marked ‡ are bookkeepers or warehouse-
men.

18 Acton Capt. Geo
11 Arnold Mrs
3 Bails J. sinker mkr
11 Baker Geo. gent
11 Barber Mr. gent
17 Barlow Mr. John
15 Barlow Rt. gent
22 Barnsdall Sl. boat
  builder & coal dlr.
1 Barton Chas. auc-
  tioneer & land agent
17 Beardsley C. & Co.
  druggists
1 Bond Abijah & Son
  hosiery manufrs
21 Bond Hy. organist
11 Booth John, mason

15 Booth Saml. gent
17 Bowler Solm. gent
5 Bramley Mrs. Eliz.
17 Brewster James,
  glazier, &c
15 Britland T. painter
22 Brummit Saml. na-
  vigation agent
17 Caldicott Car. li-
  brary
17 Cave Tho. gent
15 Chamberlain W. gt
11 Clarkson Rev. W.
20 Cocking Mrs. Eliz
15 Cole John. gent
17 Cowen Rt. ironfdr
2 Dalby J. millwrgt

17 Dean Geo. whsmn
1 Dennis Mrs. Maria
19 Dodds J. coachman
15 Dawson Rphh. dpr
14 Elliott Wm. excise
  officer
12 Elliot W. setterup
19 Fletcher George,
  excise officer
2 Flewker W. Snein-
  ton Place
15 Fothergill Mrs. J
15 Fothergill J. slater
21 Goodhead Richard
  Hooton
15 Goodwin T. gent
5 Green Geo. gent

11 Gregg Edw. Wm. attorney's clerk
13 Hall Mrs
17 Hardy Luke, gent
17 Harpham Mr
5 Harrison Mrs. My
17 Hawkins W. timber merchant
11‡ Hearnshaw, Thos
14‡ Hinton J. whsmn
17 Hollingsworth Edw. warper
11 Holmes, T. & Sam. machine makers
14 Homer Mr. James
22 Hopkin J. surveyor to the Trent navigation company
1 Howe Dixon, permit writer
17 Hunter Rev. Hugh
17‡ Hutchinson Jas
13 Inger John, gent
15 Jennings, Mrs. J
6 Jones Edw. artist
4 Lane Mr. Richard
19 Leech Thomas excise officer
12 Limb Mrs. Mary
19 Lomas Mrs. Eliz
12 Loverseed Jno. excavator
15 Moore Saml. attorney's clerk

18 Morley Rd. hosier
4 Morris Thos. director, Lunatic Asylum
1 Nelson Wm. George post office clerk
11 Newman B. gent
15 Nichols Mrs. L
17 Norris T. solicitor
3 Orange Rev. James. (Ind.)
17 Palmer Miss Emma
11 Pickering Rev. W. (Bap.)
22 Pycock J. overlkr
5 Renshaw J. stamper
17 Robinson John coal merchant
16 Rogers Jonth. silk throwster
15 Shilton C. D. solr
21 Shoults Mr. Wm
15 Skipwith Mrs. M
20 Smeeton Mrs. R
14 Smith Abm. gent
17 Smith Rev. Adam (Bpt.)
12 Smith John, thong mkr
15 Smith John, solr
13 Smith Mrs. Ruth. Middle st
1 Smith Mr. Wm
12 Smith Wm. matting & mat basket mkr

22 Stanton J. collector of Trent Navigation dues
15 Sterland Oct. gent
4 Tansley John
13 Taylor Mr. Wm
14 Thurman Wm. law stationer
17 Twible Mrs. Eliz
5 Walker Geo. bsmith
Ward John, draper, West house, & Nottingham
13 Ward Mrs. Eliz
13 Ward Mr. Wm
19 Warlow W. supervisor
15 Webster Miss Ann
14 ‡ Wells Edw
16 White James, sen. combmaker
19 ‡ White Thomas
21 Wilkinson Mr. Sl
17 Wilson Rev. Jas (meth)
11 Wood Mrs. Eliz
16 Woodford Mr. W.
22 Woodward Wm. collector of the canal dues
15 Woolley Jon. coal merchant
2 Young J. cart owner

Academies.
19 Anderson S
17 Blasdall M
17 Norris Eliz
Potchett John, Eyre st
20 Thurman E
16 White Mary

Agents.
19 Butler Alfrd
12 Green James
1 Kelk John
14 Riley James
17 Start Wm
17 Steere Wm

Bakers, &c.
12 Allcock Sml
17 Barradell W

17 Hutchinson Wm
20 Pick Edw
20 Webster Rt

Bobbin & Carriage Makers.
17 Hose Chas
12 Potter Thos
15 Taylor Dd

Bobbin Net Mks.
17 Allen John
21 Banwell Thos
21 Barlow Wm
5 Barrs Benj
1 Barton Jph
14 Bellnay Jph
17 Black Hor
3 Chambers Jas
17 Cooper Wm

1 Curtis John
19 Davis Alph
14 Daws Jonth
12 Dewey Saml
Doubleday W West street
3 Doucher Wm
21 Dodson Wm
14 Dowse Wm
3 Dutton Wm
2 Ferguson Saml
21 Flinders Edw
1 Frost John
14, Frost Saml North street
21 Giles Jph
19 Gell John
21 Hall Frdk
19 Holbrook Ed

12 Holloway Jn
1 Hooton Walter
17 Hose Chas
1 Houghton G
20 Hunnell Edw
5 Jelley Henry
18 Johnson Thos
21 Johnson Wm
19 Large John
21 Litchfield Jph
14 Ludlam Wm
11 Moore Olive
4 Morgan Geo
16 Morley John
21 Morris Geo
19 North Wm
17 Page Jas. (& small ware dlr)
20 Parker Wm

21 Price Geo
21 Price Wm
3 Pole John
10 Radford John
16 Rhodes John
17 Seacroft Jas
1 Skeavington B
14 Stapleton Jas
17 Start Wm
17 Steer Wm
6 Sterland Thos
19 Summers Rt
16 Thornton W
19 Tollinton J
16 Turner Wm
18 Ward Rd
10 Warsop Hy
18 Watson Wm
3 Waudby Wm
3 Webster Rd
14 West Geo
5 Wilford John
19 Wilson Jph
11 Wood Thos
16 Wright John

Boot & Shoemkrs
16 Brown Geo.
5 Clements Ts
12 Cooke Hy
19 Cooke Saml
4 Corbridge C
17 Fellows Wm
16 Sawyer Saml
16 Walker Geo.
6 Windall T.

Brazier.
17 Knight John

Brickmakers.
6 Bradshaw John
6 Daykin John
6 Hooton Richard
6 Wood & Burgess

Bricklayers.
10 Baker Chas
6 Huddlestone J
17 Kirk Mark
6 Scattergood J

Butchers.
17 Brailsford A

20 Farrands T
16 Fisher Mich
17 Scottorn Ty
17 Severn Wm
17 Wingfield J

Corn Millers.
15 Dickinson S
5 Innocent Fras
Morley William
West Mill
5 Wagstaff Geo

Earthenware Dealers.
17 Batty Zach
17 Watson Wm

Farmers.
13 Bywater Ann
13 Cooper John
5 Hornbuckle J
Lacy Wm Sneinton Cottage
5 Lockton John
13 Morley Jas
Riley John
9 Robson Edw. & asst. oversr.
Sheppard John & mlstr. L st.

Framesmiths.
5 Hopcroft Wm. & John
12 Young Wm

Framework Knitters.
14 Earl William
14 Hanston Geo
3 Kirkman Jph
3 Leavers John
17 Margison Jon
4 Martin Saml.
4 Peach Wm.

Gardeners.
17 Hockerby W.
12 Nall Joseph
Straw W. L st

Hair Dressers.
6 Barnes Rbt.
12 Birkinshaw C
16 White J. jun.

Inns & Taverns.
9 Manver's Arms Jno. Seymour
5 Fox. W. Boxall
13 Lord Nelson, I. Hornbuckle
17 New Inn, Geo. Trickett
17 Wheat Sheaf Saml Welsh
9 White Swan, Saml. Eyre
7 William Jas. Cordley
13 Wrestlers, T. Morley & parish clerk.

Beerhouses.
6 Brickmakers' Arms, James Hodson
14. Carpenters, Arms, S.
2 Heartygood Fellow, S. Brown
17 Paul Pry, J. Wingfield

Joiners.
9 Blundell John
12 Dabill Geo
19 Dickinson R.
14 Hodson Thos
17 Hopewell W.
12 Mitchell Jas.
14, Nall Richard
17 Scattergood T
3 Stead Samuel
2 Watson Geo.

Lace Manufrs.
15 Atherstone S
14 Clayton Chs.
19 Frost Josph
15 Johnston Jh
13 Kerry Wm. n
15 Morley Jo
15 Morrison Jbn

Linen & Woollen Drapers. (Travelling)
11 Blake Wm.

14 Coulthard J.
19 Davidson W,
14 Henderson T
19 Hill Robert
11 Smith Mungo
14 Smith Thos.

Maltsters.
1 Allcock John
19 Carver Thos. and Son
5 Harrison John
17 Harvey Geo.
1 V.5 Hutchinson W.

Milliners, &c.
17 Booth Stella
19 Dickinson S
16 Elston S. & J
14 Fletcher Hen
3 Hodgkinson M
19 Holbrook Sar
1 Lockton A
3 Mason Sarah
8. Cooper

Shopkeepers.
17 Armstrong J
11 Beardshall F
3 Bristow Wm
17 Gould Eliz
2 Groves Wm
17 Hallam Thos
7 Heaford Mary
6 Huddleston J
1 Hutchinson J
4 Lane R. junior
6 Mimmack Ger
Morley T. grocer
14 Whitfield Jno
14 Whitworth T
13 Wood John

Straw Hat Mkrs
17 Chatwin Ann.
17 Mabbott Soph
3 Mason Eliza

Tailors.
17 Armstrong J
4 Corbridge Rt
12 May James
16 Skinner John
10 Whittle Jas

SOUTHWELL.

SOUTHWELL, which is the head both of an *ecclesiastical* and a *civil* jurisdiction, and was once the occasional seat of the arch-bishops of York, is an ancient market town, pleasantly situated upon a gentle eminence, embosomed in trees, and in the centre of an amphitheatre of swelling hills, on the western bank of the little river Greet, 14 miles N.E. of Nottingham, 8 miles W. of Newark, 12 miles E.S.E. of Mansfield, and 129 miles N. by W. of London. Its *market* is on Saturday; its annual *fair* for horses, cattle, and sheep, on Whit-Monday; and its *hirings for servants* at Old and New Candlemas and Martinmas. The town has been much larger than it is at present, and it is said that the foundations of a whole street have been at times dis-covered running in an east and west direction, in a part of the immediate vicinity where now there are no traces of inhabitants; but with its adjacent hamlets of East Thorpe and West Thorpe, it has still the appearance of a pretty large though much scattered country town. It is properly divided into two parts or consta-blewicks; viz.: the *Burgage* and the *Prebendage*, the former of which comprehends all that space between the market-place and the river Greet, whilst the other, which is commonly called the *High Town*, is the Collegiate church and its property. Its *parish* is very extensive, comprising about 4500 acres of land, di-vided into the five *constablewicks*, of High Town, Burgage, East Thorpe, West Thorpe, and Normanton, in which are the four *parks* of Hexgrave, Hockerwood, Norwood, and Southwell, and many scattered farm-houses bearing different names. The five districts maintain their poor conjointly, and their roads separately Its population has encreased since 1801, from 2305, to 3384 souls, living in 643 houses. The soil is generally a rich clay; one-third is arable, about 200 acres in hop grounds, and the rest in pasturage. Normanton, on the east side of the river Greet, is enlosed, and has land allotted in lieu of the tithes, but the other hamlets have large open fields both in tillage and pasturage. Part of the soil is freehold, and the rest is either leasehold under the Chapter of Southwell, or copyhold, under the Archbishop of York, who is lord of the manor.

That Southwell was a *Roman station*, there can be no doubt; though antiquaries have quarrelled about its name. On the *Burridge* or *Burgage hill*, are the remains of a Roman fosse, evidently the *Burgus*, or camp; and many old Roman bricks have been found in the ruins of the prebendal houses; and the discovery of the foundation of the Roman bridge in the Trent, near to Winthorpe, from which to Southwell the road was traced by Mr. Dickinson Rastall, has tended very much to confirm the belief that Southwell was the true AD PONTEM of the Romans. Horsley indeed, in his Britannia Romana, whilst commenting on the sixth Iter, thinks that if the distance of Ad Pontem from Margidunum is set off from the station near East Bridgeford, it will bring us to Farndon over against Southwell; but he adds, that though Newark has by some been supposed to be the place which Bede calls "Tiovulfingaceaster," yet that termination seeming to imply a Roman station somewhere in its neighbourhood, (which he did not believe Newark to have been,) might apply to Southwell, "an ancient place, but on the wrong side of the river." He still, however, considers Ad Pontem to have been in this neighbourhood. The modern name of the town is supposed to have arisen from a spring or well on the south side of the church. Leland, in his Itinerary, says, "Southwell town is metely well builded, but there is no market public. The minster of our lady is large but of no pleasant building, but rather strong."

The MINSTER or Collegiate Church has now, however, an appearance that even Leland might have admired, (though more a man of industry than of taste,) as much has of late years been done to give it a thorough repair. For this purpose, a subscription was opened as far back as 1804, the whole of the venerable pile having been long in a decayed and ruinous state. Towards accomplishing this praiseworthy design, Colonel Eyre set a munificent example by subscribing £100; and many others contributed liberally in conjunction with the prebendaries, so that the fabric has been completely repaired and beautified. Its extreme length is 306 feet, and its breadth in the nave and chancel 59 feet, and in the transept 121 feet. All historians have agreed in attributing its first foundation to Paulinus, the first Archbishop of York, (see p. 19,) about the year 628. During a succession of ages, until the dissolution, this church had been encouraged and endowed by the liberality of both monarchs and nobles, and protected by the decrees of popes, and the regulations of various prelates; and it is said by Mr. Rastall, that scarce a person was advanced to the see of York, that did not render it more independent on his promotion, whilst its own members always manifested their attention by some augmentation of its revenues, whenever they had been long in the enjoyment of their benefices. In the early part of Hen. VIII.'s reign, its chantries were dissolved, and that order of its priests expelled; and soon after, it shared in the general wreck of collegiate foundations. It was, notwithstanding, declared by act of Parliament in Henry's 34th year (1542,) to be the mother church of Nottinghamshire; a favour which it owed, partly to Cranmer, and partly to the intercessions of the gentry of the county. In Edward's reign, the chapter was dissolved and granted to the Duke of Northumberland, but restored by Mary to the archbishop and chapter, in whose hands the property still remains; and queen Elizabeth, in her 27th year, ordained a new code of laws, which, with some occasional decrees of different archbishops, form its present municipal law. It suffered much in the civil wars, being sequestrated, but afterwards restored; but it has not even yet recovered the damages done by Cromwell's troops, who converted it into a stable for their horses, broke down the monuments, and ransacked the graves of the dead for lead and other valuables. Even as late as 1793, some of the iron rings, driven into the walls to fasten the horses to, were still in existence. On Nov. 11, 1711, it was struck by lightening, which set fire to the south spire, melted the lead and bells of the great middle tower, and destroyed the organ. The damage was £4000. This massive pile has however lost but little of its pristine appearance, except in some of the windows, whose Saxon arches have given way to the gothic pointed ones of the 14th century; and in the western towers and chapter house, which were formerly surmounted by wooden *spires* covered with lead, but taken down about 30 years ago. It is supposed to be the oldest building in the kingdom, except St. Augustine's, at Canterbury, which was founded in 605. The approach to this venerable fabric from the north, is through a large gothic gateway with reducing parapets, commanding a view of the west front, with the chapter house on the left, and the ruins of the archbishop's palace on the right. The *west front* consists of two lofty square towers, divided into seven stories, and decorated with ornamented windows and arched recesses; whilst between the towers are the western entrance, and the great window which are insertions of a latter date than the original edifice, having pointed heads and much tracery. The north side is most strictly Saxon; having five stories, with breaks or pilasters between the windows, and a plain parapet above them. On entering the western door, the visitor soon leaves the plainness of Saxon architecture, for all the richness and elegance of the meridian pride of the gothic of the 14th century, displayed in the *screen* at the entrance to the choir, which has large arched openings with recesses, and in the interior a kind of cloister full of the richest tracery. The choir is elegantly pewed and has a richly carved stall for each of the 16 prebendaries. The *chapter house*, at the north-east corner, is an octagonal building, approached by one of the richest archways in the kingdom, and having its stalls ranged in niches round the room, and separated by small cylindrical columns. The variety in the devices which ornament these niches is extreme; as no two of them are alike. The roof has rich light groins, and the windows pleasing tracery; and below the latter are recesses with columns and arches enriched with a variety of heads in ancient costume. Within the rails near to the altar, is the large alabaster *tomb of Archbishop Sandys*, with his effigy reclining upon it, and having on the front his widow and nine children kneeling. This magnificent church is both parochial and collegiate. The *vicarage* is valued in the King's

3 o

books at £7. 13s. 4d., and is in the patronage of the Prebendary of Normanton, and incumbency of the Rev. Morgan Watkins, B.A. Its collegiate establishment consist of 16 *prebendaries* (see p. 63,) 6 *vicars choral,* 6 *choristers,* 6 *singing
boys,* an *organist,* a *parish clerk,* a registrar, a treasurer, an audi-
tor, a verger, &c. Two *synods,* at which all the Nottinghamshire
clergy attend, are held here yearly; and a certain number of the
prebendaries and other clergymen are nominated by the Archbishop of York, to preside over them.

The ARCHBISHOP'S PALACE, on the south side of the Minster yard, has long been in ruins, but still there is enough
standing to shew its ancient magnificence and extent. In the
ruined walls are still many pointed gables, gothic windows, and
circular chimneys, of the age of Henry VIII.; and being
deeply overshadowed with ivy, they add much to the beauty of
Southwell. The north wing, which contained the chapel and
great hall, has been fitted up as a *Sessions House* for the liberty,
and has consequently been preserved from the ravages of time,
though much modernized in its appearance. The quadrangle,
once surrounded by the offices, is now a garden encompassed
by the crumbling walls of this once proud archiepiscopal seat,
which appears to have been first neglected in the reign of Elizabeth, for that at Scrooby. (Vide p. 442.) There were attached
to it the four parks described at page 696, but they have long
been divided and enclosed. The palace is supposed to have
been founded either by Cardinal Wolsey or Archbishop Bothes.
During the civil wars, it was completely gutted of every thing
that was valuable or useful. In those unhappy times, Charles I,
was often here, and lodged sometimes at the palace and sometimes at the inn now called the Saracen's Head, but formerly
the King's Arms. Here it was that he surrendered himself to
the Scotch commissioners, on May 6, 1646. (Vide p. 88 to 91.)
A story is current in the town, that the King when walking
about the town, and being unknown, entered the shop of one
Lee, a fanatic shoemaker, whom he desired to take his measure
for a pair of shoes; but Lee, after some little hesitation, refused,
saying that *he* was the customer whom he had seen in a dream
the preceding night, and of whom he had been warned as a man
devoted to destruction, being told at the same time that those
who worked for him would never thrive! Throsby gives a Mr.
Savage as the narrator of the tale, but we imagine there is as
little truth in it as in many others which are told of the same
unfortunate monarch.

The RESIDENTIARY, which is occupied by one of the prebendaries for three months in rotation, is a handsome modern
building, near the east end of the Minster, and has on each side
of it the houses of the vicars choral, built on the site of the
ancient vicarage, which was taken down in 1780.

The *civil government* of Southwell is divided between the

clergy and laity; the prebendage being under the jurisdiction
of the one, and the burgage subject to the other. Twenty
parishes are within its civil limits, called the "liberty of Southwell and Scrooby," for which a sessions of the peace is held
independent of the county. The ecclesiastical jurisdiction of
the chapter extends over the whole of this liberty, and also to
eight other parishes, as has been seen at pages 301 and 661.—
The civil administration is held by magistrates nominated by
the archbishop, but acting under a commission from the crown;
and the *chapter*, in the person of their *vicar-general*, exercise
all episcopal functions within the *peculiar*, except ordination
and confirmation. The only *Dissenting places of worship* in
the town are a Baptist and a Wesleyan chapel, both in Westgate.

The *Grammar School* is a handsome building, with a house
for the master, adjoining the Minster yard, and is under the
care of the chapter. The date of its foundation is unknown,
for though Robert Batemanson, in 1512, left land at Egmanton
for that purpose, his will does not appear to have been carried
into effect, as the chapter were never put in possession of the
said land. The master, who is one of the vicars choral, has
now a yearly salary of £24, arising as follows, viz. £10 from
the exchequer, pursuant to a grant of Edward VI.; £12 from
the chapter revenues, and £2 from the prebendary of Normanton. For this annuity the master teaches Latin and Greek
gratuitously to all those boys born in Southwell, who are prepared and wish for such instruction. There are two *fellowships*
and two *scholarships* in St. John's college, Cambridge, to be
presented by the masters and fellows of that college to any of
those persons who have been choristers of Southwell. These
were founded by Dr. Keton, canon of Salisbury, in the reign
of Henry VIII.

The House of Correction, in the burgage part of the
town, is used as a prison both for the liberty of Southwell and
the county at large. The original bridewell was erected 1656,
and enlarged in 1787, but the whole was rebuilt in 1808, and
has since been considerably enlarged, so that it is now very
spacious and commodious. The parish *workhouse*, in Moor-
lane, was also erected in 1808.

The Charities bequeathed for the benefit of Southwell parish, are as follows:—In 1677, *Henry Nicholson* left to the
poor of Southwell and Gainsbro' an estate at Elston, which now
lets for £100 per annum, half of which is distributed here. An
annuity of ten guineas is distributed out of the poor rates, as
the interest of £210 left in 1696, 1717, and 1725, by Bartholomew Fillingham, Jeremiah Brailsford, and Bartholomew
Burton. In 1744, *Thomas Brailsford, Esq.* left a house, two
cowgates, and three feet of Easthorpe pasture, to the family of
Conde, in trust that each successive possessor should teach ten

poor children to read, knit, and sew. In 1771, *Rd. Stenton* bequeathed the interest of £150 to the vicar and churchwardens, to be employed in teaching ten poor boys and girls; and it is now paid to a schoolmistress. The *Rev. John Laverack*, in 1775, left Stone Croft close, (2 acres, let for £6,) to educate and clothe poor children, but it is now applied solely in clothing. In 1826, *Thos. Spofforth* bequeathed £360 (now on mortgage) for the same purpose, and six poor boys are now educated and clothed with the interest. *Wm. Thornton*, in 1714, left £3, 12s. yearly out of a house and draper's shop in the Market-place, to provide six coats, for as many poor men of High Town, Easthorpe, and Normanton. The *common lands of Easthorpe* have been held in trust from time immemorial, for the support of the highways of that constablewick, but since the inclosure, and the improvement of the roads, part of the rents have been appropriated for the foundation of a school, at which the master teaches 30 free boys and girls, for which he has a house, garden, and £25 a-year. The trust land now consists of 32A. 1R. 23P., let for £69. 13s. per annum. The poor of Westhorpe have £5 yearly from the bequest of Charles Northage, in 1807.

There are in the town several *friendly societies*, and two lodges of Druids and Odd Fellows. The *savings' bank* was established in 1818, and its deposits now amount to upwards of £11,000, belonging to 369 individuals, and three societies.

EASTHORPE and WESTHORPE hamlets, form, as has already been seen, two handsome suburbs of Southwell. NORMANTON is a hamlet upon a declivity, one mile N. of the town, on the opposite side of the river Greet. *Brackenhurst*, 1¼ mile S. W. is the modern seat of the Rev. Thos. C. Cane. In the town and in other parts of the parish, are several other handsome villas, besides the following:—

HEXGRAVE PARK is distant 5 miles N. W. of Southwell, and separated from the rest of this parish, by Kirklington, Hockerton, and Edingley. It contains 500 acres, and is held of the the Chapter, by Edwd. Werg and Rd. Milward, Esqrs., who have mansions here. Upon a hill are evident vestiges of a *Roman encampment;* the ditch and vallum may in some places be traced, but the intermediate lines are completely destroyed by the plough.

HOCKERWOOD PARK lies between Normanton and Hockerton, 1¼ mile N. E. of Southwell, and is now a farm of 180 acres, held on a leasehold tenure, by Mr. Thos. Holloway. *Southwell Park* adjoins the town and is partly in Easthorpe, but it has long been divided.

NORWOOD PARK, 1 mile N. W. of Southwell, contains 190 acres, and is now the beautiful seat of Sir Richard Sutton, Bart., to whose family it was granted in fee by the Archbishop, in exchange for other land of equal value. When the lands of the see in this neighbourhood, were sold by Cromwell, for £5000, this park was purchased by Edward Cludd, Esq., who, as a civil magistrate, and according to the custom of the commonwealth often, performed the marriage ceremony here under the branches of a tree, which is still standing and known by the name of "*Cludd's Oak*."

Those marked 1 in the following DIRECTORY of SOUTHWELL PARISH live in Church-street; 2, Easthorpe; 3, King-street; 4, Moor-lane; 5, Market-place; 6, Westgate; 7, Westhorpe; 8, Burgage green; 9, Burgage hill; 10, Bar lane; 11, Back lane; 12 Vicarage; 13, Mansfield road, and 14 in Normanton.

Post Office, Market place, William Lawton, Post Master.—Letters for London, Newark, and Nottingham, are despatched at ½ past 6 morning, and received at 12 noon. The Post from Mansfield arrives at 6 morning and departs 12 noon.

6 Abbott Geo., livery stable keeper and farrier
6 Ames Wm. clerk
Barrow John, Esq., the Palace
1 Barrow Rev. R. B.D.
6 Barrow Rd. B. solr
6 Barrow Rev. Wm. D. C. L.
12 Basnett Rev. Thos. Still, M. A.
10 Bausor Paul, land surveyor, overseer, and secretary to the savings bank
Bean and Johnson, silk throwsters, and lace thread mfrs, Maythorn mill
1 Becher Carnsfd. Esq
4 Becher Henry Esq
9 Becher Rev. John Drake
9 Becher Rev. John Thos. M. A., vicar-general
7 Bennett Miss Mat
7 Birkett Mrs. Mary
1 Bradwell John, agent to the county fire office, and sub-disb of stamps
8 Bristowe Miss M. A.
Cane Rev. T. Coats Brackenhurst
3 Clark Mrs. Ann
6 Clarke W. castrator

6 Clay Mrs. E. and J.
9 Clay Wm. Waldegrave Pelham Esq.
7 Claye Rev. Wm
6 Collinson Mr. John
3 Cooling Wm. fishmr
6 Cooper Mrs. Eliz
11 Dallaway B. basket
13 Ellis J. timber dlr
1 Falkner Miss Cath.
3 Fern Hy. fishmr
12 Foottit Rev. J. B. A
12 Foottit Rev. J. jun
8 Fowler Miss Carl
12 Fowler Rev. Chas
12 Fowler Rev. Rt. H
6 Fowler Mrs. Margt
3 Geeson Eliz. flax dsr
6 Hawksley Mrs Ann
1 Hawley Col. Hy.
6 Heathcote Rev. Gfy
8 Heathcote E. organist
6 Hodgkinson Miss E
2 Hodson Miss Eliz
2 Holmes W. p clerk
2 Holles Miss Eliz
8 Howson Mrs. Ann
6 Huish Mark Esq
6 Hurt Mrs. Mary
1 Hutchinson Mrs. J
2 Ince Mrs. Eliz
1 Ingleman R architect
8 Jenkinson Mrs. Sar
Johnson John mfr Maythorn mill
6 Johnson Mr. Thos
1 Keeton Miss Sus
6 Kirkland Mr. Jph

6 Leacroft W. S. gent
6 Lowe Mrs. Bridget
3 Machin My. currier
3 Maltby Chas. gent
2 Maltby Mrs. Mary
2 May Wm. Jas. Esq Milward Rd. Esq. Hexgrave Park
Mole Matthews, gov house of correction
1 Nicholson Mrs. Jane
6 Pearsall B. nail mkr
8 Pigot Capt. Rd. Hy
1 Pool Mrs. Frances
6 Porter John Esq
2 Rawson T. basket m
1 Richmond Mrs. Eliz
6 Shaw Wm. gent
2 Shepherd Tuffin, Esq
6 Sherlock Col. Fras
5 Shilton Rd. P. gent
6 Simpson Wm. gent
6 Smith Mrs. B. E. A
6 Spencer Mr. John
6 Standley Jph chorister, Westgate
6 Stenton Capt. Hy
Sutton Sir Rd. Bart. Norwood Park
1 Taylor Jph. livery stable keeper
1 Tinley Mr. Fras. D
2 Trebeck Capt. Thos
6 Thompson Richard, chorister
3 Turner John, watch and clock maker

4 Wass Wm. governor of the workhouse
1 Watkins Rev. Morgan, B. A
2 Watson Misses F.

and M
Werg Edwards, Esq.
Hexgrave Park
3 Wilkinson V. roper
6 Williamson Lodge

11 Windle George contractor
6 Wright Rev. Adps
1 Wylde Wm. Esq.

Academics.
3 Bucklaw Edw
5 Cargill James
2 Cockayne John
1 Fletcher Rev
6 Foottit Rev. J
Gram-school
8 Heathcote Mrs
4 Hill Misses
1 Woodward A.

10 Jones Thos
1 Keetley Hny
6 Shumack Geo.
3 Smedley Matt
C2 Snowden John
3 Swift William
7 Taylor John
5 Walker Wm
6 Widdeson Geo
7 Withers John

Walker John,
Water Mill :
Farmers.
7 Adamson Rd
7 Attenborough
John & Rd
2 Bausor Thomas
Easthorpe
Bennett Geo
Holbeck
4 Booth John
7 Bradley Gvs
Clark John
Sunny Dale
14 Couzin Jas
2 Brindley John
14 Elston Jph
2 Fryer Saml
14 Furness Jph
Holloway Ths
Hockerwood
14 Holmes John,
Howit Thomas
Brackenhurst
Hutchinson R
Norwood
Kemp John New
Radley
Maids' Joseph,
Weldon
6 Maltby John,
7 Marsh Thos
Picker William,
Dardham
Nall Edward,
Brinckley
10 Revill Clem
Saxby: Leonard,
Thorney Abbey
Saxby S. & W.
Radley O.
7 Vincent John
Welsh F. Weldon
7 Yates Richard
Gardeners, &c.
7 Hibbitt Saml
3 Sandaver John
Sandaver Saml

Grocers.
1 Aldridge Thos
5 Bailey James
6 Bush Richard
1 Hatfield John
5 Hatfield J. jun
5 Keeton Jph. &
wine dealer
10 Little Edward
3 Marriott T. &
cheese & bacon
3 Preston Wm.
3 Tinley G. & E.
3 Wright James
Hair Dressers.
3 Mallison Matt
10 Marriott Wm
3 Simpson James
Hat Manufactrs.
10 Ratcliffe Hy
1 Shacklock W.
sen & jun
Hop Growers.
3 Elsam Thos
5 Hawksley Rd
Hilton Wm. Rt
& Co. Upton
3 Horsley Saml
Jenkinson John,
Morton
3 Maltby John,
Milward John,
Goldhill
3 Nicholson Jas.
2 Nicholson Jer.
10 Revill Clem
1 Revill George
10 Revill Saml
1 Shacklock Wm
8 Walker Chas
Inns & Taverns.
3 Adm. Rodney,
W. Bettinson
3 Black Bull, R.
Rawson
Crown Hotel,
Wm. Smith

Attornies.
6 Barrow G. H.
& Son.
Barrow Wm.
5 Shilton C. D.
(& Nottm.)
Bakers, &c.
6 Adamson Wm
3 Bacon John,
3 Dunston Jas
7 Heather Thos
6 Mason Wm
3 Preston Wm
5 Tinley G & E
1 Tinley Saml,
Bankers.
1 Wylde &Bolger
draw on Lubbock & Co
Blacksmiths.
10 Butler Wm.
7 Foster John
7 Leighton Jas
2 Revill John
Bobbin Net Mks,
2 Duckmanton J
3 Duckmanton W
7 Stubbs Joseph
Booksellers.
5 Ridge S. & C.
10 Whittingham Js
Boot and Shoe Makers.
4 Bolton Thos.
5 Bowmer Wm
3 Buckland Wm
2 Catliffe Rt.
8 Fletcher Jas

Braziers.
3 Bousfield Edw
3 Denman Geo.
10 Medley Wm
Bricklayers.
7 Adamson John
6 Ingleman John
6 Parker Geo.
6 Parker Wm
4 Ward John
Brickmakers.
2 Nicholson J
6 Singleton Jane
Butchers.
2 Bramley John
6 Foster George
6 Foster John
3 Geeson Geo.
1 Hatfield John
5 Hatfield J. jun
5 Hill Edward
3 Jallings Wm
3 Thompson J&W
6 Tongue Thos
China, &c. Dlr.
1 Birch Wm
Druggists,
3 Gibson George
3 Jones Wm
Coopers.
6 Dixon John
10 Marriott Thos
10 Ulyatt Rd
Corn Millers.
7 Heather Thos
3 Horsley & Son
6 Pinder Wm

1 Geo. & Dragon 3 Parr Jonth
_ H. Woodward 1 Reville Geo
1 Harty-good-   *Drapers.*
  Fellow, Saml, 1 Aldridge Thos
  Revill   5 Bailey Jas
6 Lord Nelson, 3 Gelsthorpe W
  T. Woodward 1 Hatfield John
3 Portland Arms 3 Little H. C. &
  Saml. Horsley   Co
5 Saracens Head 3 Wright Jas
  Inn, Rt. East   *Maltsters.*
6 Shoulder of 3 Aldridge John
  Mutton, John 6 Lamb Thos
  Smith   3 Maltby John
3 Wheat Sheaf, 3 Rawson Rd
  Jno. Hardisty 1 Smith Wm
2 White Lion, M.8 Walker Chas
  Bramley   6 Woodward T's
3 White Swan,   *Painters.*
  Thos. Elsam 2 Cobb Joshua
  Beerhouses. 3 Dodd John
6 Abbott Geo 6 Mason John
10 Cooke Adw 3 Richardson Hy
7 Fairholme W *Plumbers, &c.*
7 Glazebrook J 3 Butler Wm
7 Hibbert Sml 6 Lee Edward
3 Jallings Wm 3 Lee Frances
11 Stanfield Jph 2 Leeson John
  Ironmongers. 3 Rayner Wm
5 Hawksley Rd   *Saddlers.*
5 Maltby Wm- 1 Blancher Thos
Joiners & Cabinet 5 Hawksley Rd
  makers.   3 Hodgkinson G
1 Breckels Thos *Shopkeepers.*
1 Brown Joshua 2 Holland Jane
3 Nicholson Jas 7 Hopkinson Jno

1 Maltby Edw 6 Pyzer Thos
6 Parker Geo 10 Revill Saml
11 Smith Wm   2 Skellington J
Stone Masons. 3 Townrow Frs
1 Ingleman Rd 6 Townrow Jno
2 Nicholson Jer *Tallow Chandlrs.*
1 Parkin Ntl   3 Adams Rt
  Surgeons. 1 Birch Wm
5 Batchelor Jno 3 Maltby John
6 Cooke Fras   *Tanners.*
6 Foster Rt. Ts.7 Calvert E. W.
3 Warrick J. B, 6 Neep John
  Tailors.   *Wheelwriyhts.*
10 Aram John 2 Butler James,
3 Baker Wm   Easthorpe
3 Chapman Wm 6 Fairholme W
3 Gelsthorpe W.2 Newbound W
6 Mason Robert *Whitesmiths.*
3 Pigott John 10 Adams Jas
6 Pyzer Gabl 3 Carlile Jas

COACHES.

To Mansfield, &c. ½ p. 7 mg.;
  Newark ¼ past 6 evg., and to
  Nottingham 9 mg & ½ p. 4 aft

CARRIERS.

To Mansfield, Hy. Fearn & Wm.
  Cooling, from King st. every
  Monday and Thursday
To Newark, H. Fearn, J. Pilgrim,
  & J. Fryer, Mon. Wed. & Fri
To Nottingham, J. Pilgrim. W.
  & B. Revill, & J. Fryer, Tues
  and Saturday

SUTTON-UPON-TRENT is a large and well built village, pleasantly situated on the great north road, and on the west bank of the Trent, 8 miles N. of Newark. It has within its parish 890 inhabitants, and about 2500 acres of land, enclosed in 1803, when allotments were made in lieu of the tithes, to the vicar and Sir Edward Hulse. J. E. Denison, Esq. is now the principal owner and lord of the manor, which anciently belonged to the Suttons, one of whose co-heiresses married Bertram Monboucher, who, in the reign of Edward III., claimed a market here every Monday, and a fair for two days, on the eve and feast of St. James the apostle, but they have long been disused. The *church* is a handsome structure, dedicated to All Saints, and has a tower surmounted by a slender spire. It is a vicarage, valued in the King's books at £5. 6s. 8d. Sir

Charles Hulse, Bart. is the patron, the Rev. Thomas Hulse the incumbent, and the Rev. Edmund Herring the curate.— The Methodists and Baptists have each a chapel here. The *school* is endowed with the interest of £120, left in 1816, by Mary Sprigg. *Hobb close*, purchased with poor's money in 1745, is now let for £5. 5s. yearly, which is given to poor widows. The indigent parishioners have 5 tons of coals yearly, from the owner of *Ling-wong* and *Cold-moor closes*, pursuant to the will of John Smith, dated 1581.

Ashling Wm. vet. surgeon
Baker Eliz. & Bassett G, gent
Clay Jph. schoolmaster
Crossley John, vict. Nags Head
Downing Miss Jane & Sisters
Garrett John, corn miller
Godson Thomas, beerhouse
Hooton Wm. vict. Lord Nelson
Hutchinson John, beerhouse
Hutchinson Wm. wine & spirit merchant
Measey John, gent
Milnes Jas. glazier & beerhouse
Milnes Mrs. Mary
Palmer Wm. & Son, maltsters
Pettinger Geo. surgeon
Richmond Saml. tailor & vict
Robb Wm. gent
Shaw John, saddler
Smith Jph. attorney
Smith Rd. machine maker
Smith Mr. Thos
Spry Mrs. Mary
Stocks Thos. blacksmith
Talbot Mrs. Esther
Turner Hy. vict. Maltshovel
Wall Eliz. boarding academy
Walster Thos. blacksmith
Warner Mrs. & Whildon Ann

West Jabez, land agent
Whitworth Launcelot, beerhs
Wild Wm. maltster
Winterbottom Wm. smlware dlr

Farmers.
Buttery Wm
Dodson Wm
Esam John
Leverton J. & R.
Maples Rt
Palmer Wm
Pinnington Saml
Plummer Wm
Spittlehouse J
Taylor Jas
Wilmot John

Butchers.
Empsall Jno
Lee Henry
Marsden Rt
Newbold Jno
Sykes Jph
Vessey Gerv

Boat Owners.
Gandy John
Greenwood Wm
Hooton Wm
Skinner Wm
Snell Jph

Joiners & Whgts
Ashling Edw
Ashling Jno
Foster Wm
Hutchinson W
Mosley Wm

Shoemakers.
Ancliffe Jno
Harrison Jph
Hunt Wm
Turtle John

Shopkeepers.
Atkinson Rd
Atterbery G. J.
Collingham W.
Curtis Jno
Harrison Wm
Sykes Caleb

Tailors.
Ancliffe Thos
Brown Wm
Corbett Wm
Foster Thos
Stanfield Wm
Turtle John

THURGARTON, which gives name to this hundred, is a village and parish at the foot of a declivity overlooking the vale of the Trent, 3 miles S. of Southwell. It contains 329 inhabitants, and 2500 acres of land, enclosed about 60 years ago, when land was allotted for the tithes to Trinity College, Cambridge, which has the patronage of the curacy, and about one-third of the lordship. The rest belongs to Rd. Milward, Esq. but Col. John Gilbert Cooper Gardiner is lord of the manor, which was granted to the Cooper family after the dissolution of the priory, that was founded here in 1130, by Ralph de Ayncourt, for canons of the order of St. Austin. This ancient priory possessed a yearly revenue of £259. 15s. 10d., and was pulled down about 70 years ago, by J. G. Cooper, Esq., who built upon its site the present mansion, which is occupied by W. B. Martin, Esq. Near this seat is the church, which is dedicated to St. Peter, and has been a large magnificent structure, though it now consists only of one dark aisle. The curacy has been augmented with two lots of Queen Anne's Bounty, and is now enjoyed by the Rev. J. T. Becher, M. A. The *school* has a rent charge of £10, for the education of 20 boys of this parish and Hoveringham. The poor of Thurgarton have the interest of £110, left by the families of Baker and Matthews, and now in the hands of Col. Gardiner.

Branston Page, shoemaker
Branston William, shopkeeper
Brettle Mrs. Mary
Hinde Rt. joiner, & Wm. schoolr
Horspool Richard, vict
Kemp Thomas, tailor
Martin W. Bennet, Esq. Priory
Palfreyman Richard, gent.
Richardson Crispin, shoemaker

Richardson William, joiner
Thornton John, vict. Red Lion
Wetton John, shopkeeper
Woodward John, blacksmith
Farmers.
Cooper John
Farrands Thos
Hart Elizabeth
Leake William

Mellows, Edward
Milward Thos
Newham John
Paulson Thos

UPTON is a handsome village, pleasantly situated on a declivity, 2½ miles E. of Southwell. Its parish is in the liberty of Southwell and Scrooby, and contains 533 inhabitants, and 1384 acres of land, enclosed in 1795, and exonerated from tithes by allotments to the vicar and the appropriators. There are a few freeholders in the manor, but it is mostly copyhold under the Archbishop, or leasehold under the Chapter of Southwell.— The latter are the appropriators and patrons of the vicarage, which is valued in the King's books at £4. 11s. 5d¼, and is now enjoyed by the Rev. James Foottit, B. A. The *church* is a small Gothic fabric dedicated to St. Peter. Here is a small *Methodist chapel;* and a large *workhouse* built in 1824 at the cost of £6596, (including furniture, land, &c.) for the use of 49 associated parishes and townships. The *Parish Land* consists of 20A. 2R. 17P. bequeathed in 1578, by John Collie, for the repairs of the church, highways, &c. It is now let for £50 a-year, out of which £5 is paid for 8 free scholars, at the *school* which was built by subscription in 1827. The *"charity land,"* 5A. 0R. 17P. was purchased with the bequests of Mr. Cooper and others, in 1717, and now lets for £15, which is distributed yearly among the poor, who have also £2 9s. yearly from the bequests of John Trueman, Eliz. Kirk, and Jph. Tinlay. A cottage and garden at the east end of the village were left by Ralph Babthorpe, for the residence of the oldest poor widow or widower of the parish.

Clark Geo. vict. Cross Keys
Doubleday J. tailor & beeths

Fogg John, gov. workhouse
Foottit John, butcher

Foster Thos. vety. surgeon
Fryer John & Wm. corn millers
Kitchen. Eliz. vict. French Horn
Kitchen John, gent
Longstaff David, gent
Miles Fras. brickmaker
Peart Edward, gent
Rycroft Henry, corn miller
Shepherd Wm. blacksmith
Shore Sml. schoolmaster
Spick Mr. Robert
Turner Dd. & White J. tailors
Williamson John, blacksmith
Wright Thos. Esq. Upton hall

Farmers.
Broadbent Jas
Collingham Geo
Foster Thos
Foster Wm
Kitchen Thos
Machin Saml
Marshall Wm
Smith Jph
Smith Wm
Whitaker John
Shoemakers.
Gratton Wm

Parlby Jph
Taylor Mary
Shopkeepers.
Doubleday Es
Foster Jno
Launders Jno
Rawson Jno
Joiners & Whts.
Gill Jph
Keyworth Jno
Thompson Wm
Whitworth Abm

WESTON, near the north road, 3 miles S. E. of Tuxford, consists of the two hamlets of *North* and *South Weston*, situated on the opposite declivities of a narrow vale, where the waters from Laxton and Egmanton unite, and roll in one small stream to the Trent. The parish has 395 inhabitants, and 1700 acres of land, and was enclosed in 1814, when 315 acres were allotted to the rector in lieu of tithes. Earl Manvers is the principal owner, patron of the rectory, and lord of the manor, but here are a number of small freeholders. The *church* is at South Weston, and is dedicated to All Saints. The rectory is valued in the King's books at £19. 2s. 11d. and is now in the incumbency of the Rev. John Cleaver, for whom the Rev. Wm. Doncaster officiates. In 1736, Richard Hawksworth, gave £50 to build a *school* here, and endowed it with 5 acres of land at South Scarle, now let for £7 a-year, for which the master teaches ten free scholars. The parish *feast* is on Nov. 12th.

SCARTHING MOOR, 2 miles S. E. of Tuxford, is in Weston parish, but is now enclosed, and noted for its commodious inn, on the great north road.

*In the following list those marked * live at North Weston; † at Scarthing Moor; and the rest at South Weston.*

Burton John & William, tailors
*Chambers Mary, vict. Blue Bell
Chappell J & Hunt W. shoe mkrs
Chappell William, blacksmith
* Cougill George, tailor
Heath William, grocer
Hodson Joseph, beerhouse
Johnson John, beerhouse
Johnson Benj. miller & maltster
† Martin Elizabeth, corn miller
Moss James, wheelwright
Ramshaw William, blacksmith
† Sharp Wm. Scarthingmoor Inn
Taylor Joseph, vict. boot & shoe
Sheppard Sml. schoolmr & grocer

* Volckers Mrs. Elizabeth
*Volckers Peter, auctioneer &
　spirit merchant
Watmore George, butcher
Farmers.
* Atkin John　　Hunt J. & Mry
* Bee John　　Hunt William
Brandreth Hy　Hutchinson Edm
Cox Sarah　　Marshall George
Doncaster Wm * Pinder William
* Flear William Skelton John
Harpham S & W* Skinner Fras
Hodson Wm　　Tomlimson W.
Howsen Edward *Webster Jph

WINKBOURNE, 3 miles N. of Southwell, is a village and parish with 134 inhabitants and 1800 acres of land, exclusive of 420 acres of woods. Peter Pegge Burnell, Esq., is the proprietor and lord of the manor, and resides in the hall, a handsome brick mansion with a park of 40 acres. It was anciently the property of the priory of St. John of Jerusalem. The church stands near the hall, and its tower is completely covered with ivy. In the chancel are several monuments of the ancestors of Mr. Burnell, who has the patronage of the curacy, of which the Rev. Thomas Coats Cane is incumbent. The other residents are Edw. Valentine Steade, Esq.; Thos. Booth, schoolmaster; Jno. Norton, parish clerk; Wm. Raworth, smith and beerseller; and Jph. and Saml. Addlington, Hy. Barker, Geo. Machin, Thos. Radford, John Rawson, Edward Sampson, and John Smith, farmers. The school was built in 1738 by the Burnell family, who endowed it with 20 acres of land at Upton, now let for £30 per annum, for which the master teaches 14 free scholars.

WOODBOROUGH is a large straggling village, in a narrow dale near the Dover Beck, 8 miles N.E. by N. of Nottingham. Its parish contains 774 inhabitants and about 1800 acres of land. The common was enclosed in 1798, when 252 acres were allotted to the three prebendaries of Oxton and Woodborough, 66a. 1r. 1p. to John Taylor, Esq., and 53a. 3r. 11p to the late John Bainbridge Story, Esq., in lieu of the great tithes and their manorial claims; they being both impropriators and lords of the manor, which is now in three divisions called the *Prebendal,* the *Copyhold,* and the *Freehold* estates. The latter now belongs to Wm. Taylor, Esq. The hall, occupied by Wm. Worth, Esq., was the seat of the Strelleys and Bainbridges, and now belongs, with the Copyhold estate, to the three coheiresses of the late J. B. Story, Esq. The church is a large fabric dedicated to St. Swithen, and has some fragments of ancient armorial glass in its windows. It is a curacy, and has been augmented with Queen Anne's Bounty. The Prebendaries of Oxton are the patrons, and the Rev. Charles Fowler the incumbent. The Baptists and Methodists have each a chapel here. The *feast* is on the Sunday after the 2d of July. The FREE SCHOOL, founded by the Rev. Montague Wood, in 1736, now possesses a yearly income of £95, arising from a farm of 58a. 2r. 1p. at Blidworth, and a cottage and 7a. 4r. 31p. at Stapleford. The poor have 20s. and the singers 20s. yearly, from the bequest of Wm. Edge, in 1796, and the former have 50s. yearly, as the rent of Nether Close in Calverton parish, which was awarded to them at the enclosure.

Alvey Samuel, bricklayer
Blyton Stephen, blacksmith
Gadsby John, vict. 8 Bells
Greaves Benjamin, butcher
Hewes Rev. Jas. curate, & master of the free school
Hogg Wm. vict. Cock & Falcon
Hucknall Mr. Joseph

Lee Thomas, butcher
Moore W. game dlr. Grimes moor
Orm John, blacksmith
Rose Benj. & John, wheelwrights
Sardinson Dd. miller, Dover beck
Toplis John, brickmaker
Toplis John, jun. beerhs
Wood Thos. vict. Punch Bowl
Worth Wm. Esq. Woodborough
  Hall

Farmers.
Allen Wm
Branston J. T.
Brett Mr.
Butler Samuel,
  Moor field
Clay Richard
Cumberland Ann
Donnelly Wm
Duke William,
  Brockwell
Flinders Saml.
Miers Copy
Glover Mordecai
Howett Sarah
Hucknall W. C.
Lee John

Matthews Saml.
  Stoup hill
Pocklington Jn
Robinson Edw.
  Riddings
Stephenson Jn
B. Net mkrs.
Middleton Jph
Hogg Wm
Stephenson Sl
Williamson Fs
Shoemakers.
Baguley Jph
Foster Thos

Glover John
Shopkeepers.
Brown Geo
Crafts Rd
Maids Moses
Richardson Pl
Wild Wm
Tailors.
Clay Wm.
Hind Js. & Jph
Publicans.
Gadsby John
Hogg Wm

CARRIERS.—John Bish. Jas.
Caunt, and Wm. Pool, Grimes
moor, to Nottngm. Wed and Sat.
and John Bish, to Tuxford, Mon.

TABLE SHEWING THE DISTANCES

OF

THE MARKET TOWNS IN NOTTINGHAMSHIRE,

FROM EACH OTHER AND FROM THE METROPOLIS.

	BAWTRY									
									Distance from London 152	
Bingham, ····	37	Bingham								123
Blyth, ········	4	35	Blyth							149
Mansfield, ····	22	22	18	Mansfield						138
Newark, ·······	28	11	25	20	Newark					124
Nottingham, ··	36	10	32	14	20	Nottingham				124
Ollerton, ·····￼	21	19	16	9	14	20	Ollerton			137
Retford, ······	9	28	6	18	19	32	11	Retford		144
Southwell, ···	30	9	26	12	3	13	10	21	Southwell	132
Tuxford, ····	16	21	13	15	12	26	6	7	14 Tuxford	137
Worksop. ····	11	27	6	12	22	26	9	9	19	13 Worksop 146

SHEFFIELD:
PRINTED BY R. LEADER, ANGEL-STREET.

LB N 29

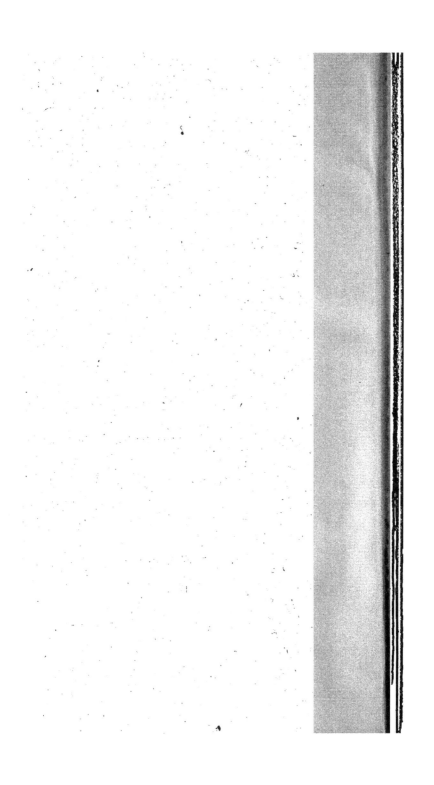

Lightning Source UK Ltd.
Milton Keynes UK
UKOW05f1911020317
295772UK00009B/592/P

9 781363 294411